AMERICA ON WHEELS

South Central States & Texas

ARKANSAS, KANSAS, LOUISIANA, MISSOURI, OKLAHOMA, AND TEXAS

D1567750

MACMILLAN • USA

Frommer's America on Wheels: South Central States & Texas

Regional Editor: Bob Sehlinger, Menasha Ridge Press
Associate Regional Editor: Holly Brown
Assistant Regional Editor: Robert Clay White
Inspections Coordinator: Laura Van Zee

Contributors: Scott Baradell, Carol Barrington, Tommy Brown, Craig Fisher, Stephen Ingram, Edie Jarolim, Sarah Mazer, Jeff McGinnes, Marc Molina, Honey Naylor, Beth Reiber, Bernadette Steele, Monte Turner, and Tina Ward

Frommer's America on Wheels Staff
Project Director: Gretchen Henderson
Senior Editor: Christopher Hollander
Database Editor: Melissa Klurman
Assistant Editor: Marian Cole
Editorial Assistant: Tracy McNamara

Macmillan Travel
A Simon & Schuster Macmillan Company
1633 Broadway
New York, NY 10019-6785

Find us online at **http://www.mgr.com/travel** or on America Online at keyword **Frommer's**.

MACMILLAN is a registered trademark of Macmillan, Inc.

Manufactured in the United States of America

ISSN: 1082-0876
ISBN: 0-02-860934-4

SPECIAL SALES
Bulk purchases (10+ copies) of Frommer's and selected Macmillan travel guides are available to corporations, organizations, mail-order catalogs, institutions, and charities at special discounts, can be customized to suit individual needs. For more information write to Special Sales, Macmillan General Reference, 1633 Broadway, New York, NY 10019.

Contents

Introduction   5

Abbreviations   9
Toll-Free Numbers and World Wide Web Addresses   10
The Top-Rated Lodgings   14

Arkansas

STATE INTRODUCTION   **15**
Back to Basics   15
A Brief History   16
A Closer Look   17
Best of the State   19

DRIVING THE STATE   **23**
Scenic 7 Byway   23

THE LISTINGS: LODGINGS, DINING, AND ATTRACTIONS   **28**

Kansas

STATE INTRODUCTION   **55**
Land of the Far Horizon   55
A Brief History   55
A Closer Look   57
Best of the State   59

DRIVING THE STATE   **63**
Kansas Interstate 70   63

THE LISTINGS: LODGINGS, DINING, AND ATTRACTIONS   **68**

Louisiana

STATE INTRODUCTION   **96**
Let the Good Times Roll   96
A Brief History   97
A Closer Look   98
Best of the State   100

DRIVING THE STATE   **107**
Cajun Country   107
Plantation Country   111

THE LISTINGS: LODGINGS, DINING, AND ATTRACTIONS   **115**

Missouri

STATE INTRODUCTION   **154**
    A Study in Contrasts   154
    A Brief History   154
    A Closer Look   156
    Best of the State   158

DRIVING THE STATE   **163**
    Mississippi River Valley   163

THE LISTINGS: LODGINGS, DINING, AND ATTRACTIONS   **167**

Oklahoma

STATE INTRODUCTION   **215**
    Native America   215
    A Brief History   216
    A Closer Look   218
    Best of the State   220

DRIVING THE STATE   **227**
    Northeast Oklahoma and Route 66   227

THE LISTINGS: LODGINGS, DINING, AND ATTRACTIONS   **232**

Texas

STATE INTRODUCTION   **262**
    An American Epic   262
    A Brief History   263
    A Closer Look   265
    Best of the State   267

DRIVING THE STATE   **273**
    The Hill Country   273
    South Padre Island and the Southern Tip of Texas   277

THE LISTINGS: LODGINGS, DINING, AND ATTRACTIONS   **281**

INDEX   **397**
MAPS   **M-1**

Introduction

America on Wheels introduces a brand-new lodgings rating system—one that factors in the latest trends in travel preferences, technologies, and amenities and is based on thorough inspections by experienced travel professionals. We rate establishments from one to five flags, plus a unique rating we call Ultra, a special award reserved for only a handful of outstanding properties in each category. Our restaurant selections represent the ethnic diversity of today's dining scene and are categorized with symbols according to their special features, ambience, and services available. In addition, the series provides in-depth sightseeing information, including driving tours and best-of-the-state highlights.

State Introductions

Coverage of each state in the *America on Wheels* series begins with background information that will help familiarize you with your destination. Included is a summary of the state's history and an overview of its geography, followed by practical tips that we hope you will find useful in planning your trip—what kind of weather to expect, what to pack, sources of information within the state, driving rules and regulations, and other essentials.

The "Best of the State" section provides you with a rundown of the top sights and attractions and the most popular festivals and special events around the state. It also includes information on spectator sports and an A-to-Z list of recreational activities available to you.

Driving Tours

The scenic driving tours included guide you along some of the most popular sightseeing routes. Every tour is keyed to a map and includes mileage information and precise directions, refreshment stops, and, for longer tours, recommended places to stay.

The Listings

The city-by-city listings of lodgings, dining establishments, and attractions together make up the bulk of the book. Cities are organized alphabetically within each state. You will find a brief description or "profile" for most cities, including a source to contact for additional information. Any listings will follow.

TYPES OF LODGINGS

Here's how we define the lodging categories used in *America on Wheels.*

Hotel
A hotel usually has three or more floors with elevators. It may or may not have parking, but if it does, entry to the guest rooms is likely to be through the lobby rather than directly from the parking lot. A range of lodgings is available (such as standard rooms, deluxe rooms, and suites), and a range of services is available (such as bellhops, room service, and a concierge). Many hotels have a restaurant or coffee shop open for breakfast, lunch, and dinner; they may have a cocktail lounge/bar. Recreational facilities may be available (such as a swimming pool, fitness center, and tennis courts).

Motel
A motel usually has one to three floors, and many of the guest rooms have doors facing the parking lot or outdoor corridors. A motel may only have a small, serviceable lobby and usually offers only limited services; the nearest restaurant may be down the street. A motel is most likely to be located alongside a highway or in a resort area.

Inn
An inn is a small-scale hotel or lodge, usually in an older building that may or may not have been designed for lodgings, and it is often located in scenic surroundings. An inn should have a warm,

welcoming atmosphere, with a more homelike quality to its furnishings and facilities. The guest rooms may be individually decorated in a style appropriate to the inn's age and location, and the rooms may or may not have telephones, televisions, or private bathrooms. An inn usually has a lounge or sitting room for guests (with parlor games and perhaps a television) and a small dining room that may or may not be open to the public. Breakfast, however, is almost always served.

Lodge
A lodge is essentially a small hotel in a rural, remote, or mountainous location. The atmosphere, service, and furniture may be more casual than you'd find in a regular hotel, and there may not be televisions or telephones in every guest room. The facilities usually include a coffee shop or restaurant, bar or cocktail lounge, games room, and indoor or outdoor swimming pool or hot tub. In ski areas, the lounge usually has a fireplace and facilities for storing ski gear.

Resort
A resort usually has more extensive facilities and recreational activities than a hotel, and offers three meals a day. The atmosphere is generally more informal than at comparable hotels.

HOW THE LODGINGS ARE RATED
Every hotel, motel, resort, inn, and lodge rated in this series has been subjected to a thorough hands-on inspection by our team of accomplished travel professionals. We ask the kinds of questions that readers would ask if they could inspect the rooms in advance for themselves (How good is the soundproofing? How firm is the bed? What condition are the room furnishings in?). Then all of the inspection reports are reviewed by regional editors who are experts on their territories. The top-rated properties are then rechecked by a special consultant who has been reviewing and critiquing luxury hotels around the world for almost 25 years. *Establishments are not charged to be included in our series.*

Our ratings are based on *average* guest rooms—not lavish suites or concierge floors—so they're not artificially high. Therefore, in some cases a hotel rated four flags may indeed have individual rooms or suites that might fall into the five-flag category; conversely, a four-flag hotel may have a few rooms in its lowest price range that might otherwise warrant three flags.

The detailed ratings vary by category of lodgings

—for example, the criteria imposed on a hotel are more rigorous than those for a motel—and some features that are considered essential in, for example, a four-flag city hotel are relaxed for a resort that offers alternative attractions, sporting facilities, and/or beautiful and spacious grounds. Likewise, amenities such as telephones and televisions—essential in hotels and motels—are not required in inns, whose guests are often seeking peace and quiet. Instead, the criteria take into account such features as individually decorated rooms and complimentary afternoon tea.

There are, of course, several basic attributes that apply to all lodgings across the board: the cleanliness and maintenance of the building as a whole; the housekeeping in individual rooms; safety, both indoors and out; the quality and practicality of the furnishings; the quality and availability of the amenities; the caliber of the facilities; the extent and/or condition of the grounds; the ambience and cleanliness in the dining rooms; and the caliber and professionalism of the service in relation to the rates and types of lodging. Since the *America on Wheels* rating system is highly rigorous, just because a property has garnered only one flag does not mean it is inadequate or substandard.

WHAT THE INDIVIDUAL RATINGS MEAN

One Flag
These properties have met or surpassed the minimum requirements of cleanliness, safety, convenience, and amenities. The staff may be limited, but guests can generally expect a friendly, hospitable greeting. Rooms will have basic amenities, such as air conditioning or heating where appropriate, telephones, and televisions. The bathrooms may have only showers rather than tubs, and just one towel for each guest, but showers and towels must be clean. The one-flag properties are by no means places to avoid, since they can represent exceptional value.

Two Flags
In addition to having all of the basic attributes of one-flag lodgings, these properties will have some extra amenities, such as bellhops to help with the luggage, ice buckets in each room, and better-quality furnishings. Some extra services may include availability of cribs and irons, and wake-up service.

Three Flags
These properties have all the basics noted above but also offer a more generous complement of ameni-

ties, such as firmer beds, larger desks, more drawer space, extra blankets and pillows, cable or satellite TV, alarm clock/radios, room service (although hours may be limited), and dry cleaning and/or laundry services.

≣≣≣ Four Flags
This is the realm of luxury, with refinements in amenities, furnishings, and service—such as larger rooms, more dependable soundproofing, two telephones per room, in-room movies, in-room safes, thick towels, hair dryers, twice-daily maid service, turndown service, concierge service, and 24-hour room service.

≣≣≣≣ Five Flags
These properties have everything the four-flag properties have, plus a more personal level of service and more sumptuous amenities, among them bathrobes, superior linens, and blackout drapes for lightproofing. Facilities normally include a business center and fitness center. Generally speaking, guests pay handsomely to stay in these properties.

◐ Ultra
This crème-de-la-crème rating is reserved for those rare hotels and resorts, possibly also motels and inns, that are truly outstanding in every or almost every department—places with a "grand hotel" presence, an almost flawless level of service, and a standard of dining equal to that of the finest restaurants.

UNRATED
In the few cases where an inspector was not able to make a detailed inspection, the property is listed as unrated. Also, in some cases where a property was in the process of changing owners or managers, or if the property was undergoing the kind of major renovations that made formal evaluation impossible, then, again, it is listed as unrated.

TYPES OF DINING

Restaurant
A restaurant serves complete meals and almost always offers seating.

Refreshment Stop
A refreshment stop serves drinks and/or snacks only (such as an ice cream parlor, bakery, or coffee bar) and may or may not have seating available.

HOW THE RESTAURANTS WERE EVALUATED

All of the restaurants reviewed in this series have been through the kind of thorough inspection described above for lodgings. Our inspectors have evaluated everything from freshness of ingredients to noise level and spacing of tables.

Unique to the *America on Wheels* series are the easy-to-read symbols that identify a restaurant's special features, its ambience, and special services. (See the inside front cover for the key to all symbols.) With them you can determine at a glance whether a place is a local favorite, offers exceptional value, or is "worth a splurge."

HOW TO READ THE LISTINGS

LODGINGS

Introductory Information
The rating is followed by the establishment's name, address, neighborhood (if applicable), telephone number(s), and fax number (if there is one). Where appropriate, location information is provided. In the resort listings, the acreage of the property is indicated. Also included are our inspector's comments, which provide some description and discuss any outstanding features or special information about the establishment. You can also find out whether an inn is unsuitable for children, and if so, up to what age.

Rooms
Specifies the number and type of accommodations available. If a hotel has an "executive level," this will be noted here. (This level, sometimes called a "concierge floor," is a special area of a hotel. Usually priced higher than standard rooms, accommodations at this level are often larger and have additional amenities and services such as daily newspaper delivery and nightly turndown service. Guests staying in these rooms often have access to a private lounge where complimentary breakfasts or snacks may be served.) Check-in/check-out times will also appear in this section, followed by information on the establishment's smoking policy ("No smoking" for properties that are entirely nonsmoking, and "Nonsmoking rms avail" for those that permit smoking in some areas but have rooms available for nonsmokers). This information may be followed by comments, if the inspector noted anything in particular about the guest rooms, such as their size, decor, furnishings, or window views.

Amenities
If the following amenities are available in the majority of the guest rooms, they are indicated by symbols

(see inside front cover for key) or included in a list: telephone, alarm clock, coffeemaker, hair dryer, air conditioning, TV (including cable or satellite hook-up, free or pay movies), refrigerator, dataport (for fax/modem communication), VCR, CD/tape player, voice mail, in-room safe, and bathrobes. If some or all rooms have minibars, terraces, fireplaces, or whirlpools, that will be indicated here. Because travelers usually expect air conditioning, telephones, and televisions in their guest rooms, we specifically note when those amenities are not available. If any additional amenities are available in the majority of the guest rooms, or if amenities are outstanding in any way, the inspector's comments will provide some elaboration at the end of this section.

Services

If the following services are available, they are indicated by symbols (see inside front cover for key) or included in a list: room service (24-hour or limited), concierge, valet parking, airport transportation, dry cleaning/laundry, cribs available, pets allowed (call ahead before bringing your pet; an establishment that accepts pets may nevertheless place restrictions on the types or size of pets allowed, or may require a deposit and/or charge a fee), twice-daily maid service, car-rental desk, social director, masseur, children's program, babysitting (that is, the establishment can put you in touch with local babysitters and/or agencies), and afternoon tea and/or wine or sherry served. If the establishment offers any special services, or if the inspector has commented on the quality of services offered, that information will appear at the end of this section. Please note that there may be a fee for some services.

Facilities

If the following facilities are on the premises, they are indicated by symbols (see inside front cover for key) or included in a list: pool(s), bike rentals, boat rentals (may include canoes, kayaks, sailboats, powerboats, jet-skis, paddleboats), fishing, golf course (with number of holes), horseback riding, jogging path/parcourse (fitness trail), unlighted tennis courts (number available), lighted tennis courts (number available), waterskiing, windsurfing, fitness center, meeting facilities (and number of people this space can accommodate), business center, restaurant(s), bar(s), beach(es), lifeguard (for beach, not pool), basketball, volleyball, board surfing, games room, lawn games, racquetball, snorkeling, squash, spa, sauna, steam room, whirlpool, beauty salon, day-care center, playground, washer/dryer, and guest lounge (for inns only). If cross-country and downhill skiing facilities are located within 10 miles of the property, then that is indicated by symbols here as well. Our "Accessible for People With Disabilities" symbol appears where establishments claim to have guest rooms with such accessibility. If an establishment has additional facilities that are worth noting, or if the inspector has commented about the facilities, that information appears at the end of this section.

Rates

If the establishment's rates vary throughout the year, then the rates given are for the peak season. The rates listed are EP (no meals included), unless otherwise noted. We'll tell you if there is a charge for an extra person to stay in a room; if children stay free, and if so, up to what age; if there are minimum stay requirements; and if AP (three meals) and/or MAP (breakfast and dinner) rates are also available. The parking rates (if the establishment has parking) are followed by any comments the inspector has provided about rates.

If the establishment has a seasonal closing, this information will be stated. A list of credit cards accepted ends the listing.

DINING

Introductory Information

If a restaurant is a local favorite, an exceptional value (one with a high quality-to-price ratio for the area), or "worth a splurge" (more expensive by area standards, but well worth it), the appropriate symbol will appear at the beginning of the listing (see inside front cover for key to symbols). Then the establishment's name, address, neighborhood (if applicable), and telephone number are listed, followed by location information when appropriate. The type of cuisine appears in boldface type and is followed by our inspectors' comments on everything from decor and ambience to menu highlights.

The "FYI" Heading

"For your information," this section tells you the reservations policy ("recommended," "accepted," or "not accepted"), and whether there is live entertainment, a children's menu, or a dress code (jacket required or other policy). If the restaurant does not have a full bar, you can find out what the liquor policy is ("beer and wine only," "beer only," "wine only," "BYO," or "no liquor license"). This is also where you can check to see if there's a no-smoking policy for the entire restaurant (please note that smoking policies are in flux throughout the country; if smoking—or avoiding smokers—is important to you, it's a good idea to call ahead to verify the policy). If the restaurant is part of a group or chain, address and phone information will be provided for additional locations in the area. This section does not appear in Refreshment Stop listings.

Hours of Operation

Under the "Open" heading, "Peak" indicates that the hours listed are for high season only (dates in parentheses); otherwise, the hours listed apply year-round. If an establishment has a seasonal closing, that information will follow. It's a good idea to call ahead to confirm the hours of operation, especially in the off-season.

Prices

Prices given are for dinner main courses (unless otherwise noted). If a prix-fixe dinner is offered throughout dinner hours, that price is listed here, too. This section ends with a list of credit cards accepted. Refreshment Stop listings do not include prices.

Symbols

The symbols that fall at the end of many restaurant listings can help you find restaurants with the features that are important to you. If a restaurant has romantic ambience, historic ambience, outdoor dining, a fireplace, a view, delivery service, early-bird specials, valet parking, or is family-oriented, open 24 hours, or accessible to people with disabilities (meaning it has a level entrance or an access ramp, a doorway at least 36 inches wide, and restrooms that are on the same floor as the dining room, with doorways at least 36 inches wide and properly outfitted stalls), then these symbols will appear (see inside front cover for key to symbols).

ATTRACTIONS

Introductory Information

The name, street address, neighborhood (if located in a major city), and telephone number are followed by a brief rundown of the attraction's high points and key attributes so you can quickly determine if it's worth a full day of exploration or just a brief detour.

Hours of Operation & Admission

Service information includes hours of operation ("Peak" indicates that the hours listed are for high season only) and the cost of admission. The cost is

ABBREVIATIONS

A/C	air conditioning
AE	American Express (charge card)
AP	American Plan (rates include breakfast, lunch, and dinner)
avail	available
BB	Bed-and-Breakfast Plan (rates include full breakfast)
bkfst	breakfast
BYO	bring your own (beer or wine)
CC	credit cards
CI	check-in time
CO	check-out time
CP	Continental Plan (rates include continental breakfast)
ctr	center
D	double (indicates room rate for two people in one room (one or two beds))
DC	Diners Club (credit card)
DISC	Discover (credit card)
EC	EuroCard (credit card)
effic	efficiency (unit with cooking facilities)
ER	En Route (credit card)
info	information
int'l	international
JCB	Japanese Credit Bureau (credit card)
ltd	limited
MAP	Modified American Plan (rates include breakfast and dinner)
MC	MasterCard (credit card)
Mem Day	Memorial Day
mi	mile(s)
min	minimum
MM	mile marker
refrig	refrigerator
rms	rooms
S	single (indicates room rate for one person)
satel	satellite
stes	suites (rooms with separate living and sleeping areas)
svce	service
tel	telephone
V	Visa (credit card)
w/	with
wknds	weekends

indicated by one to four dollar signs (see inside front cover for key to symbols). It's a good idea to call ahead to confirm the hours.

Special Information

Disabled Traveler Information

The Americans with Disabilities Act (ADA) of 1990 required that all public facilities and commercial establishments be made accessible to disabled persons by January 26, 1992. Any property opened after that date must be built in accordance with the ADA Accessible Guidelines. Note, however, that not all establishments have completed their renovations to conform with the law; be sure to call ahead to determine if your specific needs can be met.

Taxes

State and city taxes vary widely and are not included in the prices in this book. Always ask about the taxes when you are making your reservations. State sales tax is given under "Essentials" in the introduction to each state.

A Disclaimer

Readers are advised that prices fluctuate in the course of time, and travel information changes under the impact of the varied and volatile factors that affect the travel industry. The publisher cannot be held responsible for the experiences of readers while traveling. Readers are invited to send ideas, comments, and suggestions for future editions to: *America on Wheels,* Macmillan Travel, 1633 Broadway, New York, NY 10019-6785.

TOLL-FREE NUMBERS/WORLD WIDE WEB SITES

The following toll-free telephone numbers and URLs for World Wide Web sites were accurate at press time; *America on Wheels* cannot be held responsible for any number or address that has changed. The "TDD" numbers are answered by a telecommunications service for the deaf and hard-of-hearing. Be sure to dial "1" before each number.

Lodgings

Best Western International, Inc
800/528-1234 North America
800/528-2222 TDD

Budgetel Inns
800/4-BUDGET Continental USA and Canada

Budget Host
800/BUD-HOST Continental USA

Clarion Hotels
800/CLARION Continental USA and Canada
800/228-3323 TDD
http://www.hotelchoice.com/cgi-bin/res/webres?clarion.html

Comfort Inns
800/228-5150 Continental USA and Canada
800/228-3323 TDD
http://www.hotelchoice.com/cgi-bin/res/webres?comfort.html

Courtyard by Marriott
800/321-2211 Continental USA and Canada
800/228-7014 TDD
http://www.marriott.com/lodging/courtyar.html

Days Inn
800/325-2525 Continental USA and Canada
800/325-3297 TDD
http://www.daysinn.com/daysinn.html

DoubleTree Hotels
800/222-TREE Continental USA and Canada
800/528-9898 TDD

Drury Inn
800/325-8300 Continental USA and Canada
800/325-0583 TDD

Econo Lodges
800/55-ECONO Continental USA and Canada
800/228-3323 TDD
http://www.hotelchoice.com/cgi-bin/res/webres?econo.html

Embassy Suites
800/362-2779 Continental USA and Canada
800/458-4708 TDD
http://www.embassy-suites.com

Exel Inns of America
800/356-8013 Continental USA and Canada

Fairfield Inn by Marriott
800/228-2800 Continental USA and Canada
800/228-7014 TDD
http://www.marriott.com/lodging/fairf.html

Fairmont Hotels
800/527-4727 Continental USA

Forte Hotels
800/225-5843 Continental USA and Canada

Four Seasons Hotels
800/332-3442 Continental USA
800/268-6282 Canada

Friendship Inns
800/453-4511 Continental USA
800/228-3323 TDD
http://www.hotelchoice.com/cgi-bin/res/
webres?friendship.html

Guest Quarters Suites
800/424-2900 Continental USA

Hampton Inn
800/HAMPTON Continental USA and Canada
800/451-HTDD TDD
http://www.hampton-inn.com

Hilton Hotels Corporation
800/HILTONS Continental USA and Canada
800/368-1133 TDD
http://www.hilton.com

Holiday Inn
800/HOLIDAY Continental USA and Canada
800/238-5544 TDD
http://www.holiday-inn.com

Howard Johnson
800/654-2000 Continental USA and Canada
800/654-8442 TDD
http://www.hojo.com/hojo.html

Hyatt Hotels and Resorts
800/228-9000 Continental USA and Canada
800/228-9548 TDD
http://www.hyatt.com

Inns of America
800/826-0778 Continental USA and Canada

Intercontinental Hotels
800/327-0200 Continental USA and Canada

ITT Sheraton
800/325-3535 Continental USA and Canada
800/325-1717 TDD

La Quinta Motor Inns, Inc
800/531-5900 Continental USA and Canada
800/426-3101 TDD

Loews Hotels
800/223-0888 Continental USA and Canada
http://www.loewshotels.com

Marriott Hotels
800/228-9290 Continental USA and Canada
800/228-7014 TDD
http://www.marriott.com/MainPage.html

Master Hosts Inns
800/251-1962 Continental USA and Canada

Meridien
800/543-4300 Continental USA and Canada

Omni Hotels
800/843-6664 Continental USA and Canada

Park Inns International
800/437-PARK Continental USA and Canada
http://www.p-inns.com/parkinn.html

Quality Inns
800/228-5151 Continental USA and Canada
800/228-3323 TDD
http://www.hotelchoice.com/cgi-bin/res/
webres?quality.html

Radisson Hotels International
800/333-3333 Continental USA and Canada

Ramada
800/2-RAMADA Continental USA and Canada
http://www.ramada.com/ramada.html

Red Carpet Inns
800/251-1962 Continental USA and Canada

Red Lion Hotels and Inns
800/547-8010 Continental USA and Canada

Red Roof Inns
800/843-7663 Continental USA and Canada
800/843-9999 TDD
http://www.redroof.com

Renaissance Hotels International
800/HOTELS-1 Continental USA and Canada
800/833-4747 TDD

Residence Inn by Marriott
800/331-3131 Continental USA and Canada
800/228-7014 TDD
http://www.marriott.com/lodging/resinn.html

Resinter
800/221-4542 Continental USA and Canada

Ritz-Carlton
800/241-3333 Continental USA and Canada

Rodeway Inns
800/228-2000 Continental USA and Canada
800/228-3323 TDD
http://www.hotelchoice.com/cgi-bin/res/
webres?rodeway.html

Scottish Inns
800/251-1962 Continental USA and Canada

Shilo Inns
800/222-2244 Continental USA and Canada

Signature Inns
800/822-5252 Continental USA and Canada

Super 8 Motels
800/800-8000 Continental USA and Canada
800/533-6634 TDD
http://www.super8motels.com/super8.html

Susse Chalet Motor Lodges & Inns
800/258-1980 Continental USA and Canada

Travelodge
800/255-3050 Continental USA and Canada

Vagabond Hotels Inc
800/522-1555 Continental USA and Canada

Westin Hotels and Resorts
800/228-3000 Continental USA and Canada
800/254-5440 TDD
http://www.westin.com

Wyndham Hotels and Resorts
800/822-4200 Continental USA and Canada

CAR RENTAL AGENCIES

Advantage Rent-A-Car
800/777-5500 Continental USA and Canada

Airways Rent A Car
800/952-9200 Continental USA

Alamo Rent A Car
800/327-9633 Continental USA and Canada
http://www.goalamo.com

Allstate Car Rental
800/634-6186 Continental USA and Canada

Avis
800/331-1212 Continental USA
800/TRY-AVIS Canada
800/331-2323 TDD
http://www.avis.com

Budget Rent A Car
800/527-0700 Continental USA and Canada
800/826-5510 TDD

Dollar Rent A Car
800/800-4000 Continental USA and Canada

Enterprise Rent-A-Car
800/325-8007 Continental USA and Canada

Hertz
800/654-3131 Continental USA and Canada
800/654-2280 TDD

National Car Rental
800/CAR-RENT Continental USA and Canada
800/328-6323 TDD
http://www.nationalcar.com

Payless Car Rental
800/PAYLESS Continental USA and Canada

Rent-A-Wreck
800/535-1391 Continental USA

Sears Rent A Car
800/527-0770 Continental USA and Canada

Thrifty Rent-A-Car
800/367-2277 Continental USA and Canada
800/358-5856 TDD

U-Save Auto Rental of America
800/272-USAV Continental USA and Canada

Value Rent-A Car
800/327-2501 Continental USA and Canada
http://www.go-value.com

AIRLINES

American Airlines
800/433-7300 Continental USA and Western Canada
800/543-1586 TDD
http://www.americanair.com/aahome/aahome.html

Canadian Airlines International
800/426-7000 Continental USA and Canada
http://www.cdair.ca

Continental Airlines
800/525-0280 Continental USA
800/343-9195 TDD
http://www.flycontinental.com

Delta Air Lines
800/221-1212 Continental USA
800/831-4488 TDD
http://www.delta-air.com

Northwest Airlines
800/225-2525 Continental USA and Canada
http://www.nwa.com

Southwest Airlines
800/435-9792 Continental USA and Canada
http://iflyswa.com

Trans World Airlines
800/221-2000 Continental USA
http://www2.twa.com/TWA/Airlines/home/
home.html

United Airlines
800/241-6522 Continental USA and Canada
http://www.ual.com

USAir
800/428-4322 Continental USA and Canada
http://www.usair.com

TRAIN

Amtrak
800/USA-RAIL Continental USA
http://amtrak.com

BUS

Greyhound
800/231-2222 Continental USA
http://greyhound.com

The Top-Rated Lodgings

FIVE FLAGS

Four Seasons Hotel Houston Center, Houston, TX
The Mansion on Turtle Creek, Dallas, TX
Windsor Court Hotel, New Orleans, LA

FOUR FLAGS

Adam's Mark Hotel, St Louis, MO
Adam's Mark Tulsa at Williams Center,
Tulsa, OK
The Adolphus, Dallas, TX
Arkansas Excelsior, Little Rock, AR
Barton Creek Conference Resort, Austin, TX
Big Cedar Lodge, Ridgedale, MO
The Crescent Court Hotel, Dallas, TX
Crowne Plaza, Kansas City, MO
Fairmont Hotel, New Orleans, LA
Fairmount Hotel, San Antonio, TX
Four Seasons Hotel Austin, Austin, TX
Four Seasons Resort and Club
Dallas at Las Colinas, Irving, TX
Heritage House, Topeka, KS
Hotel Inter-Continental, New Orleans, LA
Hotel St Germain, Dallas, TX

Hyatt Regency Crown Center, Kansas City, MO
Hyatt Regency Hill Country Resort,
San Antonio, TX
Lancaster Hotel, Houston, TX
Omni Austin Hotel, Austin, TX
Omni Houston Hotel, Houston, TX
Omni Royal Orleans, New Orleans, LA
Overland Park Marriott Hotel,
Overland Park, KS
Plaza San Antonio, San Antonio, TX
The Ritz-Carlton, Clayton, MO
The Ritz-Carlton, Kansas City, MO
The Ritz-Carlton Houston, Houston, TX
The Tremont House, Galveston, TX
The Waterford Hotel, Oklahoma City, OK
Worthington, Fort Worth, TX
Wyndham Anatole Hotel, Dallas, TX

Back to Basics

Riding the national wave of nostalgia for tradition-al values and simple living, Arkansas has steadily come into its own. Arkansas's natural gifts and down-home pleasures have easily withstood the scrutiny the state has undergone since it proved to be the spawning ground for a US president.

The state's rolling ridges, sheltering forests, and sparkling lakes have made it a popular spot for all manner of outdoor enthusiasts—campers, hikers, boaters, and fishers, to name a few. And as increasing numbers of curious visitors arrive to enjoy a landscape unspoiled by runaway develop-ment or industrial pollution, what was once a source of economic backwardness—the state's isolation—has become a virtue. Homespun is not only in vogue, it has become a marketable commodity. Visitors enamored of bygone days enjoy sampling mountain culture at museums in the Ozark highlands and, especially, at country fairs featuring fiddlers and cloggers. Pioneer crafts like white oak baskets, quilts, and "cobweb getters" fly off the shelves of local shops and festival booths.

Thanks to the big push towards industrialization in the 1960s and '70s, most Arkansans now earn their living from electronics, aviation, and manufacturing. But the state still honors its connection to the earth. Local festivals celebrate everything from pink tomatoes, watermelons, and pickles to pine trees, crawfish, and, yes, even mosquitoes. The park services protect pristine natural springs, where millions of gallons of pure mineral water bubble to the surface daily. And long caravans of cars wind through the Ozark and Ouchita mountains in annual homage to the stunning palette of autumn colors.

Fishing also remains an Arkansan passion, whether done from a wooden skiff on the slow waters of a mangrove swamp or in a sleek fiberglass bass boat with a 200-horse-power engine and hydraulic pedestal seat. During the annual ritual of the hunt, one in eight residents can still be found slogging through wetlands to stalk migrating ducks,

STATE STATS

CAPITAL
Little Rock

AREA
53,187 square miles

BORDERS
Mississippi, Tennessee,
Missouri, Oklahoma,
Texas, Louisiana

POPULATION
2,350,725 (1990)

ENTERED UNION
June 15, 1836 (25th state)

NICKNAMES
Land of Opportunity,
The Natural State

STATE FLOWER
Apple blossom

STATE BIRD
Mockingbird

FAMOUS NATIVES
Maya Angelou, Johnny Cash,
Eldridge Cleaver,
Bill Clinton, Alan Ladd,
Douglas MacArthur,
Brooks Robinson

or tramping through the woods at dawn to wait out white-tailed deer.

Even for those Americans enthusiastically high-tailing it down the information superhighway, the scenic byways and backroads are beckoning anew. And as the concept of the good life undergoes yet another transformation, expatriate Arkansans and outlanders alike are streaming to the state with the notion that this just may be the place after all.

A Brief History

A Humble Beginning Spanish conquistadors led by Hernando De Soto were the first Europeans to arrive in what is now Arkansas. They crossed the Mississippi River amid a hail of Indian arrows to the land south of Helena in 1541. Aside from the old-world diseases they visited upon the Native Americans in return, the Spaniards' only other legacy was the introduction of pigs, stragglers from De Soto's commissary-on-the-hoof. Legend has it they were progenitors of the razorback hogs (a popular state icon after which the University of Arkansas football and basketball teams were named).

The French stayed a bit longer, but had little more impact. Arkansas Post, a fort and fur trading post established in 1686 near the mouth of the Arkansas River by Henri de Tonti, claimed fewer than 50 soldiers and settlers some 100 years later. Between 1762 and 1800, control of Arkansas and the rest of the Mississippi Valley bounced from the French to the Spanish before finally landing in the court of French Emperor Napoleon Bonaparte, who sold off the entire territory to the United States in the Louisiana Purchase of 1803.

Planting the Seeds of Division During this period, the first great tide of settlers poured in from Tennessee and the Appalachian Valley, rugged highlanders with a distinctive mountain culture. The population swelled rapidly, and Arkansas was designated a separate territory in 1819. Two years later, Arkansas Post in the eastern swamps was abandoned as a territorial capital in favor of the more centrally located—and comparatively mosquito-free—Little Rock.

The federal government cleared more land for settlement through its relocation of Native Americans from treaty lands to the newly created Indian Territory in present-day Oklahoma. In the delta area, increasingly powerful plantation owners led Arkansas into the Union as a slave state in June 15, 1835. This move was opposed by northern hill farmers, who had no stake in slavery and feared higher taxes.

The Civil War brought the rift between highland farmers and lowland planters to a head. Fifty thousand Arkansans fought with Confederate troops, while another 15,000, mostly uplanders, joined the Union Army. After several battles on Arkansas soil, Union troops captured Little Rock in 1863. The Confederates relocated their capital south to Washington, and Arkansas found itself with two governors and legislatures until the war's end in 1865.

From Feast to Famine After the bankruptcy and bitterness of the war and Reconstruction, prosperity returned with the arrival of the railroad. A new wave of settlers drained the eastern swamplands to create rich farmland in the delta, and by the late 1890s, the unruly frontier along the western Arkansas border succumbed to civilization, thanks to the efforts of an army of federal marshals and the busy Fort Smith gallows of Judge Isaac Parker.

Agriculture, the bulwark of the state's economy, was crippled in the wake of World War I by a precipitous drop in cotton prices, followed by the disastrous Great Plains drought and the onset of the Great Depression. The post–World War II emergence of large-scale agribusiness delivered the final blow to the family farm, decimating two-thirds of Arkansas's small farms. People left in droves to look for work. Further damage to the state's psyche and image was inflicted in September 1957, when Governor Orval Faubus called up National Guard troops to block the integration of Little Rock's Central High School.

Rebirth During the 1960s and 1970s Arkansas shared in the sunbelt industrial boom, due largely to efforts led by Winthrop Rockefeller, scion of the

Fun Facts

- The only diamond mine in North America can be found in Arkansas. In fact, visitors can dig for their own jewels—one tourist excavated a 16-carat diamond here.
- Arkansas was the first Southern state to integrate public colleges and universities after World War II.
- In 1932, Arkansas elected the first woman to the US Senate: Hattie Caraway.
- The bubbling spring waters at Hot Springs National Park can reach 147°F.

wealthy Eastern family. As the economy expanded and diversified, jobs and people began flowing back into the state. Little Rock blossomed into a modern urban center, refurbishing its image in 1981 with the election of its first African-American mayor.

In recent years, Arkansas has become a leading retirement haven, and the once remote Ozark region is now the country's fastest-growing rural area. Although poverty remains a problem in some parts of the state, the position of Arkansas in the national landscape has been irrevocably altered with the election in 1992 of native son William Jefferson Clinton as 42nd president of the United States.

A Closer Look
GEOGRAPHY

The lowlands of the **Delta** cover the eastern third of Arkansas, where cotton, soybean, and wheat sprout from former swamplands. Here, the nation's most prodigious rice paddies cover the once-barren Grand Prairie between the Arkansas and White Rivers. The narrow spine of hills known as Crowley's Ridge bisects the Delta like a bony finger pointing north from **Helena** to the Missouri border. The city's restored antebellum mansions overlooking the Mississippi River serve as graceful reminders of the days when Helena was a major shipping center for cotton.

The flat expanse of the Gulf Coastal Plain sweeps northward from Louisiana into south Arkansas. Much of this lowland area is blanketed with stands of pine and white oak, grist for the area's lumber mills and furniture factories. Rows of pumpjacks tap the rich oil deposits that underlay the region. In the southwest corner of the state, **Texarkana,** a busy railroad center after the Civil War, straddles the Arkansas-Texas border.

At the junction of lowlands and highlands is central Arkansas. **Little Rock,** the locus of the state's political, financial, and cultural affairs, and its companion city, **North Little Rock,** perch on opposite banks of the Arkansas River and together comprise the only metropolitan area in the state with a population over 100,000.

West-central Arkansas swells up from the lowlands into the crests and wide valleys of the **Ouachita Mountains.** These heavily forested hills are sprinkled with clear lakes and webbed with hiking trails. A rolling expanse of pastures, farmland, orchards, and small towns, the upper Arkansas River Valley winds along the northern edge of the Ouachitas. The town of **Hot Springs,** on the range's eastern slopes, has recaptured some of its former glory as a mecca for those who seek healing from thermal springs. **Fort Smith,** now one of the state's largest manufacturing centers, still evokes its early days as a frontier outpost and riverboat town.

The Ozark Plateau is the predominant feature of northern Arkansas; extending north from the Arkansas River into Missouri, it has been eroded over time into sinuous valleys and ridges with craggy limestone outcroppings. The area was all but isolated until the middle of this century, and still retains its rural flavor. As the nation's leading poultry producer, this is a place where chickens outnumber people. **Eureka Springs,** a mountainside arts colony and natural springs spa, hosts a collection of prettily restored Victorian homes and shops, but the cultural hub of the Ozarks is **Fayetteville,** where the main campus of the University of Arkansas resides.

CLIMATE

Arkansas serves up four distinct seasons, none of them overly harsh. Spring and autumn are the mildest, with shirtsleeve daytime temperatures and crisp evenings. The fall is a particular favorite with visitors, especially in late October and early November, when the foliage is at its most glorious.

Be prepared for some sticky days in summer, when temperatures in the 90s—and even, occasion-

---

DRIVING DISTANCES

Little Rock

53 miles NW of Hot Springs
119 miles E of Helena
133 miles SW of Jonesboro
138 miles E of Memphis, TN
143 miles NE of Texarkana
153 miles S of Mountain Home
159 miles SE of Fort Smith
176 miles SE of Branson, MO

Fort Smith

63 miles S of Fayetteville
84 miles S of Rogers
108 miles SW of Eureka Springs
111 miles SE of Tulsa, OK
128 miles NW of Hot Springs
159 miles NW of Little Rock
181 miles N of Texarkana

Texarkana

34 miles SW of Hope
71 miles N of Shreveport, LA
78 miles SW of Arkadelphia
87 miles W of El Dorado
112 miles SW of Hot Springs
143 miles SW of Little Rock
181 miles S of Fort Smith

ally, in the triple digits—are accompanied by high humidity. Daytime temperatures in the 50s make winter a reasonable time to visit, but the mercury often dips below freezing after nightfall, so pack accordingly. In general, daytime temperatures in the highlands are from 4° to 8°F lower than in the lowlands.

April and May are the rainiest months; October is the driest. Winter snowfall is light: January, the snowiest month, gets an average of only 2.3 inches.

WHAT TO PACK

Casual dress is the norm in mostly rural and unassuming Arkansas. Clothing made of cool, porous material like cotton is the best way to deal with summer's high temperatures and high humidity, but bring along a sweater if you're heading for the hills at this time of year. For chilly winter nights, warm garments are a must. Pack a light jacket for a visit in autumn or spring.

If you plan to spend much time in or around the water, be sure to bring along sunscreen and sunglasses. Insect repellent is a worthwhile precaution whether you're heading lakeside or into the woods (the mosquitoes, especially, are nighttime diners). Whether you're going to take advantage of the many great hiking trails or just peruse block after block of shops and historic sights, it's essential to pack suitable footwear.

TOURIST INFORMATION

For a free state highway map, *Arkansas Tour Guide*, and calendar of state events, write or call the **Arkansas Department of Parks & Tourism,** One Capitol Mall, Little Rock 72201 (tel 800/628-8725). The State of Arkansas maintains a Web page (http://state.ar.us) with general information about the state. If you have a particular area in mind to visit, include a request for the regional tour guide that covers it. For information on Little Rock's attractions, dining, and lodging, contact the Little Rock Convention & Visitors Bureau, PO Box 3232, Little Rock 72203 (tel 800/844-4781). Other local chambers of commerce or convention and visitors bureaus, listed in

the regional tour guides, can also help acquaint you with their areas.

DRIVING RULES AND REGULATIONS

The minimum driving age in Arkansas is 16. Drivers and front-seat passengers have to buckle up, and children age 4 and under must be secured in an approved child safety seat. Motorcyclists are required to wear a helmet. Auto insurance is mandatory, and you must carry proof of both insurance and registration in the car at all times.

Aircraft, radar, and laser are used to enforce speed limits. Radar detection devices are legal except on commercial vehicles. Don't drive with an open container of alcohol. Under the state's zero tolerance law, any driver under 21 caught with a blood alcohol level of .02% or more will have his or her license revoked for one year.

To find out about road conditions, call the state police at 501/569-2374.

AVG TEMPS (°F) & INCHES OF RAINFALL		
	Little Rock	Fayetteville
Jan	40/4.66	37/2.28
Feb	43/3.90	41/3.28
Mar	50/4.67	47/3.52
Apr	62/5.07	59/4.84
May	70/4.91	67/6.96
June	78/3.69	74/4.59
July	81/3.43	79/5.36
Aug	80/3.32	78/3.18
Sept	73/3.39	71/3.45
Oct	62/2.67	61/3.03
Nov	50/4.16	48/2.89
Dec	42/4.19	40/2.16

RENTING A CAR

All the major car rental firms have at least one office in the state (Little Rock or Harrison are the most likely locations) and the largest have multiple locations. The minimum age to rent varies from 21 to 25; some firms impose an additional charge for drivers between 21 and 24. Most companies have no restrictions on driving a rented car outside the state, but it's always best to check.
- **Alamo** (tel 800/327-9633)
- **Avis** (tel 800/331-1212)
- **Budget** (tel 800/527-0700)
- **Dollar** (tel 800/421-6868)
- **General** (tel 800/327-7607)
- **Hertz** (tel 800/654-3131)
- **National** (tel 800/227-7368)
- **Thrifty** (tel 800/367-2277)

ESSENTIALS

Area Code: The area code for all of Arkansas is **501.**

Emergencies: Dial 911 for police, fire department,

or ambulance service; dial *55 on cellular phones.

Liquor Laws: You must be 21 years of age with proper identification to purchase or consume alcoholic beverages. Sunday liquor sales are permitted only in restaurants serving food. Some Arkansas counties are dry.

Taxes: The state sales tax is 4½%; you'll also see additional city and county sales taxes on your bill in many locations. A hefty 10% supplemental sales tax on alcoholic beverages sold for on-premises consumption, plus another 4½% tax on mixed drinks, will inflate your bar tab. A 2% tourism tax is levied on hotel rooms, admissions to tourist attractions, and watercraft and marine equipment rentals. The state car-rental tax is 4½%.

Time Zone: Arkansas is in the central time zone.

Best of the State
WHAT TO SEE AND DO

Below is a general overview of some of the top sights and attractions in Arkansas. To find out more detailed information, look under "Attractions" for individual cities in the listings portion of this book.

National & State Parks Arkansas's two largest outdoor playgrounds are in the highlands, a combined 2.6 million acres of rolling hills, hardwood thickets, and spring-fed mountain streams. For a leisurely backpacking journey through the **Ozark National Forest** in the northwest, try the Ozark Highland Trail. You can also see the forest by car via National Scenic Byway 7. In the **Ouachita National Forest,** the Talimena Scenic Drive reveals breathtaking ridgeline views of the Ouachita Mountains, while Lake Ouachita, the state's largest, provides wonderful water sports opportunities.

Pristine and wild **Buffalo National River,** threading its way around 500-foot bluffs, caves, and waterfalls for more than a hundred scenic miles in the northwest part of the state, is a favorite for tranquil float trips and heart-stopping white-water adventures alike. A different way to get wet is to visit **Hot Springs National Park,** the city of Hot Spring's version of an old-fashioned European-style spa. You can immerse yourself in mineral waters along the restored Bath House Row or at a number of nearby hotels.

A system of 48 state parks provides access to some of the prettiest spots in Arkansas. **Petit Jean State Park** charms visitors with its rustic mountaintop lodge, 95-foot waterfall, and magnificent views of the Arkansas River Valley; the park's Museum of Automobiles is a treat for vintage car buffs. **DeGray Lake Resort State Park,** in the foothills of the Ouachitas, has something for everyone, from an island lodge to a golf course, tennis courts, and marina. The Ozark's **Bull Shoals Lake State Park** is a boater's and angler's paradise, offering trophy trout and canoeing on the White River, and monster bass upstream in the huge lake.

Natural Wonders Time and water have sculpted several spectacular underground caverns deep in the limestone of the Ozark Mountains. **Blanchard Springs Caverns** near Mountain View is a must-see, with massive underground chambers and nearly every type of calcite formation known. You can view beautiful "organ pipe" and "popcorn" formations in the twin caves at **Mystic Caverns** near Dogpatch, and Arkansas's largest underground lake in **War Eagle Cavern** at Rogers. The entrance to **Hurricane River Cave** near Harrison is veiled by a 45-foot waterfall.

Historic Sites **Old Washington Historic State Park,** a restored 19th-century community, is home to the Arkansas Confederate Capitol; the tavern where the heroes of the Alamo are said to have planned the Texas revolution; and a 19th-century blacksmith shop that's purported to have produced the Bowie knife. **Pea Ridge National Military Park** and **Prairie Grove State Park** commemorate the two most significant Civil War battles waged on Arkansas soil through a variety of exhibits, museums, and battlefield tours. At **Fort Smith National Historic Site,** you can stroll past the mid-19th-century fort and a reproduction of Judge Parker's famous gallows. The **Old State House** at Little Rock, seat of government from 1836 to 1911, is one of the loveliest Greek Revival structures west of the Mississippi. You can tour Little Rock's **Quapaw Quarter** to see restored buildings from frontier days to the early 20th century; the **Arkansas Territorial Restoration** hosts a collection of 14 pre–Civil War buildings. Delve into Arkansas's earliest history at **Toltec Mounds Archeological State Park,** site of the state's tallest Native American burial mounds, which date from between AD 650 and 950.

Museums The **Ozark Folk Center** in Mountain View, a living museum devoted to preserving Arkansas's mountain culture, stages craft demonstrations, musical performances, workshops, and fairs. The hands-on exhibits at **Mid-America Museum** in Hot Springs explore science, nature, and art. The **Arkansas Oil and Brine Museum** in Smackover chronicles the 1920s oil boom in south Arkansas and the beginnings of the brine industry, oil's watery by-product. Prairie life comes alive in a replica of an 1890s farming village at the **Stuttgart Agricultural Museum** in Scott. Little Rock's **Arkansas Museum of Science and History** is housed in the 1838 Old Arsenal Building, also the birthplace of General Douglas MacArthur.

Family Favorites Travel through time on the vintage 1900 passenger trains of the **Arkansas & Missouri Railroad,** originating at Van Buren, which offers scenic excursions through the Ozarks; or take a shorter steam locomotive ride in restored, turn-of-the-century elegance on the **Eureka Springs & North Arkansas Railway** in Eureka Springs. Ports along the Mississippi and Arkansas Rivers, including Helena, Van Buren, and North Little Rock, offer excursions and dining cruises on authentic paddle wheel riverboats. For a one-of-a-kind experience, take the kids diamond prospecting in **Crater of Diamonds State Park,** an ancient 35-acre volcanic crater that has yielded more than 70,000 diamonds since 1906 (you can keep what you find).

EVENTS AND FESTIVALS

- **Professional Championship Rodeo,** Texarkana at Four States Fairgrounds. Early March. Call 501/773-2941.
- **Arkansas Folk Festival,** Mountain View at Ozark Folk Center State Park. Mid-April. Call 501/269-8068.
- **Arts and Crafts Fairs** throughout the Ozarks. First weekend in May and second weekend in October. Top fairs include War Eagle Fair in Hindsville (tel 501/789-5398), Old Applegate and Sugar Creek Festivals in Bentonville (tel 501/273-7478 or 273-2841), War Eagle Mill Fair in Rogers (tel 501/789-5343), the Festival in Bella Vista (tel 501/855-2064), and the Arkansas Craft Guild Show in Eureka Springs (tel 501/269-3897).

- **Magnolia Blossom Festival** and **World Championship Steak Cook-Off,** Magnolia. Air show, bass and archery tournaments, antique car show, steak dinners under the magnolia trees. Third weekend in May. Call 501/234-6122.
- **Riverfest,** Little Rock at Riverfront Park. Entertainment, food, crafts, and fireworks. Memorial Day weekend. Call 501/376-4781.
- **Annual Rodeo of the Ozarks,** Springdale at Parsons Arena. First week in July. Call 501/751-4694.
- **Greers Ferry Lake Water Festival,** Fairfield Bay and Heber Springs. First weekend in August. Call 501/362-2444.
- **Hope Watermelon Festival,** Hope. Third weekend in August. Call 501/777-6164.
- **Autumnfest,** Fayetteville. Arts and crafts, food booths, street dancing, chicken cook-off. First weekend in October. Call 501/582-5000.
- **King Biscuit Blues Festival,** Helena in the downtown historic district. Second weekend in October. Call 501/338-9144.
- **Arkansas State Fair & Livestock Show,** Little Rock at the State Fairgrounds. Mid-October. Call 501/372-8341.
- **National Bluegrass Fiddle Championships,** Mountain View at Ozark Folk Center State Park. First weekend in November. Call 501/269-3851.

SPECTATOR SPORTS

Basketball You can watch the **University of Arkansas Razorbacks,** 1994 NCAA National Champions, at the Bud Walton Arena in Fayetteville (tel 501/575-5151).

Football The **University of Arkansas Razorbacks** play three home games of Southeast Conference football at Razorback Stadium, Fayetteville, and three home games at War Memorial Stadium in Little Rock (tel 501/575-5151).

Greyhound Racing Watch the greyhounds run at **Southland Greyhound Park** in West Memphis (tel 800/467-6182), one of the largest tracks in the country.

Horse Racing Catch world-class thoroughbreds January to April at **Oaklawn Park** in Hot Springs (tel 800/625-5296), with satellite broadcasts and simulcast wagering in summer and fall.

ACTIVITIES A TO Z

Bicycling Mild weather and glorious scenery along lightly traveled byways make bicycling popular year-round. For information on routes and excursions around the state contact the Arkansas Department of Parks & Tourism, One Capitol Mall, Little Rock 72201 (tel 800/628-8725) for their *Bike Arkansas* pamphlet.

Bird Watching Arkansas sits along the Mississippi Flyway, and its lakes and wetlands host many migrating species in late fall and winter. Spotting American bald eagles and golden eagles is especially thrilling; there are organized watches at Bull Shoals Lake, DeGray Lake, and other sites around the state. Millwood Lake near Texarkana is a favorite birding spot, as is Felsenthal National Wildlife Refuge in south-central Arkansas near Crossett.

Boating & Watersports In a state that has 600,000 acres of lake surface, you needn't travel far for fun on or in the water. Many of Arkansas's natural and manmade lakes offer marinas, boat launches, and marine equipment rental. Swimming is popular at beaches along lake shores, and some of the deeper mountain lakes are clear enough for scuba diving.

Camping Year-round camping is possible in Arkansas's mild climate, and many campsites are available in the national forests, wilderness areas, state parks, and private campgrounds around the state. For the *Arkansas Camper's Guide,* contact the Arkansas Department of Parks & Tourism, One Capitol Mall, Little Rock 72201 (tel 800/628-8725).

Canoeing, Kayaking & White-Water Rafting The Buffalo National River in North Arkansas ranks among the nation's finest waterways for floating or white-water rafting; there are guides and outfitters at several points along the shore. Other favorites for float trips are the nearby White River and the Ouachita River in the west. Experts might try the Cossatot River near Mena, with its Class III, IV, and V rapids; the Mulberry River in western Arkansas and the Illinois Bayou in the Ozarks offer slightly less challenging fun.

Fishing Arkansas's lakes and streams are jumping with world-class specimens. Bass fishing is especially popular—Bull Shoals, DeGray, Ouachita, and Norfork Lakes are among the top spots. The Little Red, White, and Norfork Rivers are well-known for brown, rainbow, and other trout, but walleye, crap-

---

SELECTED PARKS & RECREATION AREAS

- **Hot Springs National Park,** Park Superintendent, PO Box 1860, Hot Springs 71902 (tel 501/624-3383)
- **Buffalo National River,** Park Superintendent, PO Box 1173, Harrison 72602 (tel 501/741-5443)
- **Ouachita National Forest,** Forest Supervisor, USFS Box 1270, Hot Springs 71902 (tel 501/321-5202)
- **Ozark National Forest,** Forest Supervisor, PO Box 1008, Russellville 72801 (tel 501/968-2354)
- **St. Francis National Forest,** Rte 4, Box 14A, Marianna 72360 (tel 501/295-5278)
- **Bull Shoals,** PO Box 205, Bull Shoals 72619 (tel 501/431-5521)
- **Crater of Diamonds,** Rte 1, Box 364, Murfreesboro 71958 (tel 501/285-3113)
- **Crowley's Ridge,** PO Box 97, Walcott 72474 (tel 501/573-6751)
- **DeGray Lake Resort,** Rte 3, Box 490, Bismarck 71929 (tel 501/865-2801)
- **Devil's Den,** 11333 W Arkansas Hwy 74, West Fork 72774 (tel 501/761-3325)
- **Lake Catherine,** 1200 Catherine Park Rd, Hot Springs 71913 (tel 501/844-4176)
- **Lake Chicot,** Rte 1, Box 1555, Lake Village 71653 (tel 501/265-5480)
- **Lake Fort Smith,** PO Box 4, Mountainburg 72946 (tel 501/369-2469)
- **Lake Ouachita,** 5451 Mountain Pine Rd, Mountain Pine 71956 (tel 501/767-9366)
- **Millwood,** Rte 1, Box 37AB, Ashdown 71822 (tel 501/898-2800)
- **Moro Bay,** 6071 Hwy 15 S, Jersey 71651 (tel 501/463-8555)
- **Old Washington,** PO Box 98, Washington 71862 (tel 501/983-2684)
- **Petit Jean,** Rte 3, Box 340, Morrilton 72110 (tel 501/727-5441)
- **Village Creek,** Rte 3, Box 49B, Wynne 72396 (tel 501/238-9406)
- **White Oak Lake,** Rte 2, Box 28, Bluff City 71722 (tel 501/685-2748)

---

pie, catfish, and other game species are plentiful, too. Contact the Arkansas Game and Fish Commission, 2 Natural Resources Dr, Little Rock 72205 (tel 501/223-6378) for more information.

Hiking The state has more than 250 designated hiking trails, most of them in the scenic Ozarks, Ouachita Mountains, and upper Arkansas River

Valley, but you can find a few scattered through the southern timberlands and the eastern delta, and along Crowley's Ridge in the far east. You can also blaze your own trail through a dozen wilderness areas around the state, or backpack on specially designated trails in the national forests. Contact the Arkansas Department of Parks & Tourism, One Capitol Mall, Little Rock 72201 (tel 800/628-8725) for the *Hiker's Guide to State and Federal Trails.*

Hunting Seasonal migrations make the rice fields of the Grand Prairie excellent duck-hunting grounds. Hunters also like to take their best shot at white-tailed deer and wild turkey, which abound throughout the state. For information, get in touch with the Arkansas Game and Fish Commission, 2 Natural Resources Dr, Little Rock 72205 (tel 501/223-6378). Nonresident licenses can be obtained by mail (tel 800/364-4263).

SCENIC 7 BYWAY

Start	Eureka Springs
Finish	Hot Springs
Distance	Approximately 200 miles
Time	3 days
Highlights	Historic towns; mineral springs; a drive through national forest; arts and crafts galleries; a trip aboard a 1920s steam-powered train; one of the Ozarks' best caverns; interesting and unusual museums

You've got to love it—a state with towns named Flippin, Yellville, Gassville, and Grubbs, and probably the most yard art this side of the Mississippi. But Arkansas, which found itself thrust into the international limelight when its most famous resident, Bill Clinton, moved into the White House, is also largely undiscovered. Here you'll find pristine national forests, stunning vistas, clear-running streams, and uncontrived sophistication—along with a healthy dose of hillbilly goofiness.

This driving tour begins in the Victorian hillside resort of Eureka Springs and winds through several small towns until reaching the National Scenic 7 Byway. One of the Ozarks' most beautiful highways, the byway passes through forests, over mountains and clear-running rivers, and around lakes. After stopping at a couple of natural wonders along the way—including one of the region's best caverns—you'll be rewarded with a visit to charming Hot Springs, where a soak in one of the resort's therapeutic baths, perhaps followed by a massage, constitutes the grand finale of the tour.

For additional information on lodgings, restaurants, and attractions, refer to specific cities in the listings portion of this book.

Less than 50 miles southwest of Branson, MO, reachable via US 62, is:

1. **Eureka Springs.** The approach to Eureka (as the town is more simply called) on US 62 is an unsightly strip of motels, tacky souvenir shops, and fast-food joints. But turn off onto the Historic Loop—an oddly configured street that hugs steep slopes as it zigs and zags around a mountain—and you're instantly transported back to the Victorian era, with turn-of-the-century structures housing hotels, bed-and-breakfasts, craft shops, restaurants, and ornately decorated homes.

Following the discovery of the area's abundant

streams (42 to be exact), Eureka Springs grew to become one of the country's most popular resorts, as the afflicted and the stressed flocked here to take their cures in the therapeutic waters. At its peak, Eureka had more than 20,000 residents, but while the population today has dwindled to 1,900 and bathing is now offered only in one small hotel, it remains one of Arkansas' top tourist destinations. For a lesson in the town's history, stop off at the **Eureka Springs Historical Museum,** 95 S Main St. The **Queen Anne Mansion,** on US 62 near the tourist office, is a three-story Victorian home open for self-guided tours. The **Arkansas Craft Gallery,** 33 Spring St, showcases Arkansas talent with beautifully crafted woodwork, jewelry, glass, pottery, and more.

Most of Eureka's attractions lie outside the historic district and are best reached by car. Just north, on AR 23, is the **Eureka Springs and North Arkansas Railway,** (tel 501/253-9623) a restored early-1900s steam passenger train offering 40-minute trips down memory lane. A few minutes farther north on AR 23 brings you to the **Abundant Memories Heritage Village,** a great family attraction offering valuable lessons in American history. Owned, built, and operated by the Harold Drayer family, the a 60-acre village features 26 reconstructed buildings representing America from 1776 to 1900 and is packed with an incredible wealth of historic artifacts and antiques collected over the past 40 years. Of special note is Harold Drayer's one-man "historama" show (presented three times daily), a personalized and entertaining account of American history; it's a truly memorable experience.

West of town on US 62, the remarkable **Miles Musical Museum,** another unusual family-run attraction, features more than a 100 different musical instruments from around the world, including player pianos, nickelodeons, roller organs, and gramophones. Just a couple minutes farther west on US 62 is **Thorncrown Chapel,** a nondenominational glass-and-wood chapel that blends in agreeably with the mountainside landscape surrounding it and provides a peaceful retreat for motorists to rest and meditate. Still farther west on US 62, about 5 miles from Eureka, is the **Eureka Springs Gardens,** 33 acres of botanical gardens set around Blue Spring that comprise a woodland area, a garden of wild flowers, a rock garden, and more. For those with a lot of time on their hands, two of the regions

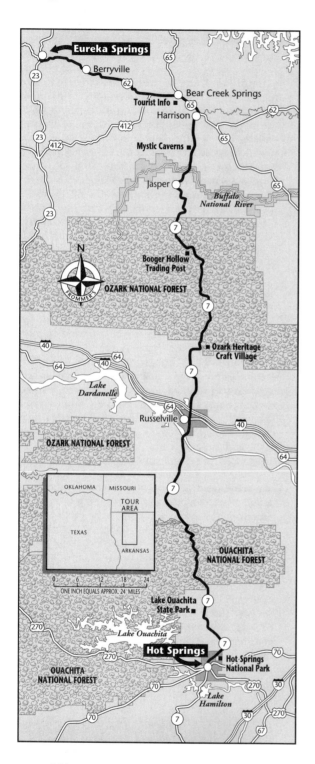

walls and trees sprouting from an earthen floor; and **Dinosaur World,** located west of town off US 62 on AR 187, a kitschy tribute to prehistoric life that features several dozen painted concrete statues of dinosaurs, prehistoric men, a pregnant-looking saber-tooth tiger, King Kong, and other oddities. Resembling products from a sixth-grade science project, they can be viewed by car along a two-mile rutted gravel road.

But for many visitors, the most compelling reason for spending the night in Eureka is the **Great Passion Play.** Located a few miles east of town, it claims to be "America's number one attended outdoor drama," and features a 500-by-400-foot stage and a cast of more than 200 actors and actresses (mostly locals), 12 horses, 30 sheep, 20 dogs, and 3 camels in a re-creation of Jesus' life, death, resurrection, and ascension (achieved by lifting Jesus 55 feet into the air with a flying harness). Most folks arrive a few hours before the show to see the grounds' other attractions, like the 67-foot Christ of the Ozarks statue, a section of the Berlin Wall, and a Bible museum with an original 1611 King James Bible. The **Sacred Arts Center** houses a small but invaluable collection of Christian art, including a few works by Rubens, Rembrandt, Michelangelo, Titian, Tintoretto, Murillo, and El Greco, and ranging from sculptured marble and porcelains to paintings. The **New Holy Land** offers close to 40 "archeologically correct" reproductions of structures referred to in the Bible, such as Jacob's well, Gordon's Tomb, the Tabernacle in the Wilderness, and the cave stable where Christ was born. Other possible evening diversions include several **country music shows,** such as those presented at the Ozark Mountain Hoe-Down Music Theater, Gem of the Ozarks Music Theater, Pine Mountain Jamboree, and Country Legends Theatre.

Eureka Springs offers numerous lodging possibilities. The most famous of them is the **Crescent Hotel,** 75 Prospect St (tel 501/253-9766 or 800/342-9766), a sprawling, 68-room, 110-year-old complex offering commanding views and old-fashioned ambience. Rooms are moderately priced from May through October, and a bargain the rest of the year. The **Basin Park Hotel,** in the center of the historic district at 12 Spring St (tel 501/253-7837 or 800/643-4972), was built in 1905 and features 60 moderately priced rooms that are a bit worn around the edges but full of character. The **Palace Hotel and Bath House,** 135 Spring St (tel 501/253-7474), occupies a 1901 limestone building offering eight expensive suites complete with whirlpool baths, refrigerator stocked with complimentary snacks and drinks, and cable TV, and is the only place remaining in where you can still find

quirkiest attractions are **Quigley's Castle,** 4½ miles south of Eureka on AR 23, a castle hand-built by the Quigley family and featuring unusual stone mineral baths and massages. If you wish to spend the night between Eureka and Hot Springs, the **Cliff House Inn,** on Scenic 7 Byway south of Jasper (tel 501/446-2292), offers four inexpensive doubles and one two-room suite, all modestly furnished but offering breathtaking views of the "Arkansas Grand Canyon."

Take a Break

For a meal in the heart of the historic district, one of the most popular eateries is the chef-owned **Plaza,** S Main St (tel 501/253-8866), consisting of a casual second floor that becomes open air in summer months, and a more formal ground-floor dining room. Both serve basically the same French/American menu of soups, salads, and sandwiches for lunch, and dinner entrees ranging from filet mignon and broiled lobster tail to linguine and chicken breast. Main dishes cost $10 to $20. Also centrally located is the Italian restaurant **DeVito's,** 5 Center St (tel 501/253-6807), popular for its toasted ravioli, fettuccine, lasagna, and trout (raised on the chef's own trout farm). Dinner entrees range from about $11 to $17.

Farther out on the Historic Loop and easily reached by trolley or car is **Victorian Sampler,** 33 Prospect St (tel 501/253-8374), located in a home dating back before the turn of the century. Soups, salads, and sandwiches are available for lunch, while dinner entrees range from strip steak and pork medallions to shrimp scampi. Dinner entrees start at $11.

Depart Eureka Springs by heading east on US 62. After about 12 miles, 62 will bring you straight to the small town square of:

2. **Berryville.** On the west side of Berryville Square is the **Carroll County Historical Museum and Heritage Center,** a pioneer museum with furniture, tools, clocks, barbed wire, and household items, as well as a restored school room, kitchen, funeral parlor, law office, and other shops. Off the other side of the square is the **Saunders Museum,** 115 E Madison, featuring a collection of rare firearms and artifacts, including guns used by Jesse James, Cole Younger, Billy the Kid, Wild Bill Hickock, and Buffalo Bill Cody. Berryville, incidentally, is the last "wet" county before Hot Springs.

Continue east on US 62 another 27 miles to:

3. **Harrison,** founded in the 1860s and the seat of Boone County. Several historic buildings in town dating from the first few decades of this century can

be experienced in a self-guided walking tour, available at the Arkansas tourist information center.

Harrison is at the northern end of:

4. **Scenic 7 Byway,** which became the state's first official scenic byway in 1994. Free of the excess of billboards, tourist shops, and heavy traffic that plagues US 62, Scenic 7 Byway climbs, plunges, winds, and twists through some of Arkansas' most breathtaking scenery, including two national forests. It's particularly beautiful at the height of autumn's color changes, from about mid-October into early November.

After traveling approximately 9 miles south on Scenic 7 Byway, you'll come to:

5. **Mystic Caverns,** on your right. One of the Ozarks' many caverns, it was discovered in the 1850s and has been open to the public for more than 70 years. It is said there are more formations per square foot here than in any other cave in Arkansas. Highlights include the 8-story Crystal Dome and the 28-foot-high, 20-foot-wide Pipe Organ.

After Mystic Caverns, Scenic 7 turns into a zigzag of curves, and scattered billboards advertising canoe rentals will begin appearing. After 5 miles you'll reach the:

6. **Buffalo National River,** which had the honor of being the first stream in America designated a national river by Congress. This free-flowing 150-mile river is great for canoeing, camping, and fishing. After crossing the bridge, you'll find the Pruitt access area to the right, where a gravel bar,

Take a Break

If you want to rub elbows with the locals in Jasper, head to the **Ozark Cafe** (tel 501/446-2976) on Scenic 7, which serves burgers, sandwiches, and salads for lunch, all priced less than $4.50. The dinner menu adds chicken-fried steak(a favorite in these parts), catfish, chicken livers, pork chops, steak, and a few other dishes. If you'd rather have a view, however, there's no better place anywhere on Scenic 7 than the **Cliff House Inn** (tel 501/446-2292), approximately 5 miles south of Jasper. A combination gift shop, five-unit motel, and restaurant, it provides a spectacular view of the so-called Arkansas Grand Canyon—especially from its balcony, which seems suspended in air. Offerings include breakfast items, more than a dozen varieties of burgers and sandwiches (all priced at less than $3), entrees ranging from trout and catfish to chicken-fried steak, and homemade desserts.

river, hiking trail, and picnic site are set against a backdrop of towering limestone cliffs.

Another 4 miles farther south is **Jasper,** population 330, and not much more than a bend in the highway. It is, however, home of the Ozark National Forest Visitor Center, where you can stop for brochures and information on Scenic 7's upcoming attraction.

From Jasper you'll soon find yourself in the heart of the:

7. **Ozark National Forest,** a million acres of rugged landscape. The Ozarks, a gently mountainous region that stretches through northwest Arkansas and southern Missouri, has been eroded and carved by weather and time into a series of high plateaus, stream-lined valleys blanketed with oaks and hickory, limestone bluffs, caves, and springs. Surrounded by nothing but nature (and providing a convincing argument for Arkansas' claim as the ''Natural State''), this stretch of Scenic 7 is one of the best.

Among the several craft and gift shops astride Scenic 7 you might try:

8. **Nellie's Craft Shop,** approximately 19 miles south of Jasper on the right. Located on the front yard of Nellie Dotson's yard, this shop is distinguished by its approximately 150 quilts, all locally made. Those done by hand start at about $200; the machine-quilted ones are cheaper. There are also baskets, jams, jellies, relishes, the ubiquitous sun bonnet, dolls, clocks, wood crafts, and other souvenirs.

Approximately 20 miles farther down Scenic 7 is another gift shop:

9. **Booger Hollow Trading Post,** which heavily advertises itself in billboards dotting the long stretch of highway that leads to it. The billboards claim Booger Hollow has a population of 7 (''countin' one coon dog''). There's no dog in sight, but plenty of the usual Ozark kitsch, along with cured hams and a small hamburger joint that also sells ice cream, shakes, and soda pop.

From here Scenic 7 flattens out, passing farms, horses, and cows. Just before Russellville at the Scenic 7 and I-40 junction, there's one more craft shop, the:

10. **Ozark Heritage Craft Village,** a large store carrying handmade items of more than 200 crafters, including pecan sculptures, handmade quilts, white oak baskets, walnut crafts, toys, hams, jellies, wind chimes, T-shirts, and more.

Upon leaving Russellville Scenic 7 twists and turns through Ouachita National Forest, and after approximately 70 miles you will be entering the historic heart of:

11. **Hot Springs** (population 32,000), the boyhood home of Bill Clinton. With its historic Bathhouse Row, Hot Springs National Park, art galleries, lakes, and many attractions, Hot Springs is a great family destination. In fact, the area's 47 thermal springs have made it a popular destination for centuries, first among Native Americans; then for its first European visitor, Hernando de Soto, who arrived in 1541; and then for crowds of health seekers following the construction of the first crude bathhouse in 1830. By 1922 the springs and their surroundings were designated a national park, with a complement of grand bathhouses strung along Central Avenue. Modeled after the old European style, with marble and tile decorations, fountains, and even gymnasiums, they attracted various movie stars and presidents.

For a look at Hot Springs' history, stop by the **Museum of Hot Springs,** 201 Central Ave, which traces the town's development from 1850 to 1950. From the museum it's just a short walk up Central Avenue to **Bathhouse Row,** a wonderful promenade lined on one side with eight stately bathhouses and magnolia trees, and on the other with shops, art galleries, and restaurants. Although the popularity of therapeutic bathing declined after World War II, forcing the closure of most of the bathhouses, the exteriors of the historic buildings (most dating from 1892 to 1936) and their gardens have been meticulously preserved. The **Fordyce Bathhouse Visitor Center** operated as a public bathhouse from 1915 to 1962 and now serves as a bathhouse museum and

Take a Break

Fine dining in Hot Springs can be found at the **Hamilton House,** located off Scenic 7 at 130 Van Lyell Terrace (tel 501/525-2727). Set in a 1930s estate surrounded by gardens and terrace dining, it specializes in seafood and steaks, with entrees priced at $13 to $23. For dining in the historic district, try **Cafe New Orleans,** 210 Central Ave (tel 501/624-3200), located in one of downtown's oldest buildings. Po-Boys, red beans and rice, jambalaya, catfish, and sandwiches cost $4.50 to $8, while the dinner menu has shrimp Creole, scallops, oysters, blackened redfish, steak, and other dishes for $7 to $12. **Magee's,** 362 Central Ave (tel 501/624-2148), another restaurant located in an historic downtown building (this one dating from 1871), is a good choice for families; it offers a children's menu. Available are breakfasts, hamburgers, sandwiches, Cajun shrimp, Arkansas red beans, chicken fried steak, and more, with most items priced between $4.50 to $10.

visitor center for Hot Springs National Park. Restored to its early 1920s grandeur, it displays bath halls, tubs, therapy and message rooms, dressing rooms, and gym. Only one historic Bathhouse Row facility is still open for bathing—the **Buckstaff Bathhouse,** built in 1912. It operates on a first-come, first-served basis, and no suits or towels are necessary; an attendant guides visitors each step of the way. A few hotels also offer therapeutic bathing, including the Arlington and Majestic hotels. At the end of Bathhouse Row is a fountain offering free spring water; visitors are welcome to fill their own jugs to take home.

Other diversions on Central Avenue include the **Tussaud Wax Museum,** 250 Central Ave, with the recent additions of Bill and Hillary Clinton; the one-room **National Park Aquarium,** 209 Central Ave; **the Arkansas House of Reptiles,** 420 Central Ave, boasting more than 200 reptiles; and the **Arkansas Craft Galleries,** 231-A Central Ave, a cooperative with some of the best handmade crafts in the state. There are also a surprising number of **art galleries** for a town this size, most in restored Victorian and early 20th-century buildings that also serve as living spaces for gallery owners and artists. A gallery walk the first Thursday and Friday evenings of the month has become a Hot Springs tradition, drawing more than 1,500 people from Little Rock and beyond.

And of course there's **Hot Springs National Park,** which practically surrounds part of the city. The grounds just behind Bathhouse Row, where a few springs gush forth at their natural 143°F temperature (after percolating underneath the earth for about 4,000 years), are the most accessible by foot. There are hiking trails here, but for those with less time on their hand, a 4½-mile loop driving trail beginning from Fountain Street near Arlington Hotel takes visitors to the Hot Springs Mountain Tower, a 216-foot-tall structure offering an unobstructed view of the town and park.

The place to stay in Hot Springs has long been the centrally located **Arlington Resort Hotel and Spa,** Central Ave and Fountain St (tel 501/623-7771 or 800/643-1502), with 486 moderately to expensively priced rooms, outdoor pools, and a public bathhouse with therapeutic treatments. Inexpensive lodging can be found at **Happy Hollow,** 231 Fountain St (tel 501/321-2230), a two-story motel offering comfortable rooms with kitchenettes. It's conveniently located across from Hot Springs National Park just off Bathhouse Row.

Arkansas Listings

Altus

ATTRACTIONS 🏛

St Mary's Catholic Church
Exit 41 off I-40, AR 186; tel 501/468-2585. Located atop Mount Bethel, this Roman Basilica–style church (circa 1902) is listed on the National Register of Historic Places. The church is built of native sandstone and is decorated with ornate goldleaf work; local people were used as models for the murals of the Passion of Christ located inside. **Open:** Daily 7am–7pm. **Free**

Wiederkehr Wine Cellars, Inc
Exit 41 off I-40, AR 186 S; tel 800/622-WINE. Since Johann Andreas Wiederkehr hand-dug the first wine cellar in 1880, the family business has grown to include a restaurant featuring old-world cuisine, vineyards, and a gift shop. Visitors may tour the Swiss alpine-style winery and partake in free wine tasting. Annual Weinfest held at the end of September. **Open:** Daily 8:30am–9pm. **Free**

Post Family Vineyards & Winery
Exit 41 off I-40; tel 501/468-2741. Founded in 1880, this winery produces a large selection of wine and grape products, such as Chardonnay and muscadine juice and jam. Tours take visitors through all stages of the winemaking process, from the vineyards to the tasting room. **Open:** Mon–Sat 8am–7pm, Sun noon–5pm. **Free**

Arkadelphia

Located along the scenic Caddo River, Arkadelphia was incorporated in 1842. The area offers a variety of water sports along with the annual Festival of Two Rivers held in the spring. This town is home to Henderson State University and Ouachita Baptist University. **Information:** Arkadelphia Area Chamber of Commerce, 6th and Caddo Sts, PO Box 38, Arkadelphia, 71923 (tel 501/246-5542 or toll free 800/874-4289).

HOTEL 🏨
≣≣≣ Holiday Inn
Jct I-30/US 67, PO Box 450, 71923; tel 501/246-5831 or toll free 800/HOLIDAY; fax 501/246-5831. Exit 78 off I-30. Attractive and adequately maintained. Near many shopping and dining opportunities, downtown, and the airport. **Rooms:** 100 rms and stes. Executive level. CI 3pm/CO 11am. Nonsmoking rms avail. **Amenities:** 🛏 ♨ A/C, cable TV w/movies. Microwaves and refrigerators in some rooms. **Services:** � 🛅 🕬 **Facilities:** 🔂 350 ♿ 1 restaurant. All-you-can-eat buffets. Children 18 and under eat free. **Rates:** $45–$52 S; $48–$57 D; $52 ste. Extra person $5. Children under age 18 stay free. Parking: Outdoor, free. AE, CB, DISC, JCB, MC, V.

MOTELS
≣≣ Best Western Continental Inn
Jct AR 7/I-30, PO Box 296, 71923; tel 501/246-5592 or toll free 800/528-1234; fax 501/246-3583. Exit 78 off I-30. This property is in need of some minor repairs, but is fine for an overnight or budget stay. Caddo River is a few blocks away. **Rooms:** 59 rms. CI 3pm/CO 11am. Nonsmoking rms avail. **Amenities:** 🛏 🕿 A/C, cable TV w/movies. In-room coffee available. **Services:** 🛅 🕬 Roll-away beds $9. **Facilities:** 🔂 1 restaurant (see "Restaurants" below), washer/dryer. Truck and bus parking. **Rates:** $39–$49 S; $45–$55 D. Extra person $5. Children under age 12 stay free. Parking: Outdoor, free. Government and corporate rates avail. AE, CB, DC, DISC, JCB, MC, V.

≣≣≣ Quality Inn
Jct AR 7/I-30, PO Box 420, 71923; tel 501/246-5855 or toll free 800/221-2222. Exit 78 off I-30. Pleasant and dependable, near downtown and airport. **Rooms:** 63 rms and stes. CI 3pm/CO noon. Nonsmoking rms avail. King leisure rooms available. **Amenities:** 🛏 ♨ A/C, cable TV w/movies. Some units w/whirlpools. **Services:** 🛅 🕬 🍽 **Facilities:** 🔂 ♿ **Rates:** Peak (Mar–Aug) $40–$65 S or D; $40–$65 ste. Extra person $4. Children under age 16 stay free. Lower rates off-season. Parking: Outdoor, free. AE, MC, V.

RESTAURANTS

★ Bowen's

In the Best Western Continental Inn, Jct AR 7/I-30; tel 501/246-8661. Exit 78 off I-30. **American.** Cozy, comfortable family restaurant with friendly service. Traditional Southern fare includes chicken, flounder, shrimp, steak, soup, and sandwiches. The buffet is sure to have something for any appetite. **FYI:** Reservations accepted. No liquor license. **Open:** Daily 7am–9pm. **Prices:** Main courses $5–$8. AE, DISC, MC, V.

★ Fish Net Family Restaurant

5000 Valley; tel 501/246-7885. Off I-30. **Seafood/Steak.** Cheerful colors decorate this relaxed, homey, family-style restaurant. **FYI:** Reservations accepted. Children's menu. No liquor license. **Open:** Daily 11am–9pm. **Prices:** Main courses $6–$13. AE, DISC, MC, V.

ATTRACTIONS

Crater of Diamonds State Park

Murfreesboro; tel 501-285-3113. 25 mi SW of Arkadelphia. Park visitors can search for genuine diamonds (with tools available for rent or to buy) and keep what they find. Camping, interpretive programs, hiking trails, and picnicking facilities, also available. **Open:** Mem Day–Labor Day, daily 8am–8pm. Reduced hours off-season. **$$**

DeGray Lake Resort State Park

AR 7, Bismarck; tel 501/865-2851 or toll free 800/737-8355. 13 mi N of Arkadelphia. Located on the north shore of 13,000-acre DeGray Lake and surrounded by the Ouachita Mountains. Gulf fishing, hiking, boating, camping, and tennis available. Programs and special events include guided nature hikes and lake cruises, evening movies, square dances, spring wildflower walks, and fall color hayrides and cruises. **Open:** Daily 24 hours. **Free**

Daisy State Park

US 70, Kirby; tel 501/398-4487. 30 mi NW of Arkadelphia. Situated in the foothills of the Ouachita Mountains, this park is anchored by manmade Lake Greeson. The lake is stocked for fishing with stripers, black bass, crappie, bream, northern pike, walleye, and (in winter and spring) rainbow trout. The park also features camping and picnicking facilities, guided nature hikes, games, and crafts. **Open:** Daily 24 hours. **Free**

Arkansas Post National Memorial

For lodgings and dining, see Pine Bluff

Located 7 mi S of Gillett. The site of a decisive Union victory in 1863, today the park is a wildlife sanctuary offering picnic facilities and fishing. Visitors center with audiovisual exhibits explain the area's history; Civil War rifle pits also open to the public. For more information, contact Superintendent, Arkansas Post National Memorial, Rte 1, Box 16, Gille H, 72055 (tel 501/548-2432).

Ashdown

See Texarkana

Batesville

Continuously occupied since 1804 and considered the oldest surviving settlement in Arkansas, this town lies along the beautiful White River in the foothills of the Ozark Mountains. The town is an active antiques center and boasts numerous historic structures. It is also rich in festivals, carnivals, and outdoor sports venues, and is home to Arkansas College, the oldest independent college in the state. **Information:** Batesville Area Chamber of Commerce, 409 Vine St, Batesville, 72501 (tel 501/793-2378).

HOTEL

≡≡≡ Ramada Inn of Batesville

1325 N St Louis, PO Box 2555, 72501; tel 501/698-1800 or toll free 800/RAMADA; fax 501/698-1800. On US 69, 1 mi off US 167. A reliable Ramada with an affable and efficient staff. Near the historic district and downtown. **Rooms:** 123 rms and stes. CI 3pm/CO 11am. Nonsmoking rms avail. **Amenities:** A/C, cable TV w/movies. Some rooms have hot tubs, refrigerators, and/or microwaves. **Services:** VP Facilities: 1 restaurant, 1 bar (w/entertainment), washer/dryer. **Rates:** Peak (Mar–Aug) $40–$53 S; $45–$59 D; $90 ste. Extra person $6. Children under age 12 stay free. Lower rates off-season. Parking: Outdoor, free. AE, CB, DC, DISC, EC, JCB, MC, V.

MOTEL

≡≡ Best Western Scenic Motor Inn

773 Batesville Blvd, 72501; tel 501/698-1855 or toll free 800/528-1234; fax 501/698-1855. US 167 and AR 25. Standard motel with good maintenance; convenient to Lyon College, restaurants, and a local golf course. **Rooms:** 40 rms and stes. CI 4pm/CO 11am. Nonsmoking rms avail. Some rooms have recliners; all have views of Ozark Mountains. King rooms available. **Amenities:** A/C, cable TV w/movies. Some rooms have refrigerators. **Services:** Facilities: 1 restaurant. **Rates:** $37–$44 S; $42–$51 D; $42–$51 ste. Extra person $4. Children under age 12 stay free. Parking: Outdoor, free. AE, DC, DISC, MC, V.

Benton

Named for Thomas Hart Benton, the noted Missouri senator who helped Arkansas gain admission to the Union in 1836. The small community is a short drive southwest from Little Rock and is surrounded by outdoor recreation sites. The county courthouse's unique architecture makes it a popular area landmark. **Information:** Benton Chamber of Commerce, 607 N Market St, Benton, 72015 (tel 501/778-8272).

MOTELS 🏨

≣≣≣ **Best Western Inn**

17036 I-30, 72015; tel 501/778-9695 or toll free 800/528-1234; fax 501/776-1699. Exit 117 off I-30. Pleasant, well-maintained property with a cozy lobby. Near many shops and restaurants. **Rooms:** 65 rms and stes. CI 3pm/CO 11am. Nonsmoking rms avail. King-size beds available. **Amenities:** 🛁 ⚿ A/C, satel TV w/movies. **Services:** 🍴 🕭 Roll-away beds $5. Friendly, helpful staff. **Facilities:** 👥 ⅙ 1 restaurant, games rm, playground, washer/dryer. Truck parking. **Rates:** $34–$40 S; $38–$44 D; $40 ste. Extra person $4. Children under age 12 stay free. Parking: Outdoor, free. Senior discounts avail. AE, DISC, MC, V.

≣≣ **Days Inn**

1501 I-30, 72015; tel 501/776-3200; fax 501/776-0906. Exit 118 off I-30. Clean, comfortable accommodations. **Rooms:** 117 rms and stes. CI open/CO noon. Nonsmoking rms avail. **Amenities:** 🛁 ⚿ A/C, cable TV w/movies. **Services:** 🍴 **Facilities:** 👥 🏊 ⅙ **Rates:** $35–$40 S; $40–$45 D; $42–$47 ste. Extra person $5. Children under age 12 stay free. Parking: Outdoor, free. AE, DISC, MC, V.

≣≣ **Econo Lodge**

1221 Hot Springs Rd, 72015; tel 501/776-1515 or toll free 800/424-4777; fax 501/776-1515. Exit 117 off I-30. Tastefully decorated budget motel with neatly kept grounds. Good for short stays. **Rooms:** 60 rms. CI 2pm/CO 11am. Nonsmoking rms avail. **Amenities:** 🛁 ⌗ A/C, cable TV w/movies. Some units w/terraces. **Services:** 🍴 🕭 Babysitting. **Facilities:** 🏊 ⅙ **Rates:** $40–$46 S; $50–$56 D. Extra person $4. Children under age 15 stay free. Parking: Outdoor, free. AE, DISC, MC, V.

Blytheville

Located along the Great River Road of the Mississippi River, this agricultural community functions as the northeastern gateway to Arkansas. The area is world-famous for its Mississippi Flyway duck hunting, and the town hosts several major festivals annually. **Information:** Blytheville Area Chamber of Commerce, 124 W Walnut, PO Box 485, Blytheville, 72316-0485 (tel 501/762-2012).

HOTEL 🏨

≣≣≣ **Holiday Inn**

Jct AR 18/I-55, 72315; tel 501/763-5800 or toll free 800/HOLIDAY; fax 501/763-1326. Exit 67 off I-55. Average accommodations about a mile from the airport. Fairly new fitness center. Convenient to restaurants, shopping, and downtown. **Rooms:** 150 rms and stes. CI 3pm/CO 11am. Nonsmoking rms avail. **Amenities:** 🛁 ⚿ A/C, cable TV w/movies. **Services:** 🚐 🏊 🍴 **Facilities:** 👥 🏋 🚗 ⅙ 1 restaurant, 1 bar (w/entertainment), sauna. **Rates:** $49–$59 S; $59–$69 D; $79 ste. Extra person $5. Children under age 12 stay free. Parking: Outdoor, free. AE, DC, DISC, JCB, MC, V.

MOTELS

≣≣≣ **Best Western Cotton Inn**

Jct AR 18/I-55, PO Box 1229, 72315; tel 501/763-5220 or toll free 800/528-1234; fax 501/763-5220. Exit 67 off I-55. Recently renovated and very well cared for. A few miles from the Mississippi River; near shopping, dining, tennis courts, and a theater. **Rooms:** 87 rms. CI 3pm/CO 11am. Nonsmoking rms avail. **Amenities:** 🛁 A/C, cable TV w/movies. Some units w/terraces. **Services:** 🏊 🍴 🕭 Small pets only. **Facilities:** ⅙ 1 restaurant. **Rates:** Peak (May–Sept) $37–$43 S; $39–$45 D. Extra person $4. Children under age 12 stay free. Lower rates off-season. Parking: Outdoor, free. AE, CB, DC, DISC, JCB, MC, V.

≣≣≣ **Comfort Inn of Blytheville**

Jct I-55/AR 18, PO Box 1408, 72316; tel 501/763-7081 or toll free 800/228-5150; fax 501/763-7081. Convenient for visitors to Eaker Air Force Base; one block from downtown. Nicely decorated, pleasant staff. **Rooms:** 105 rms. CI 3pm/CO noon. Nonsmoking rms avail. **Amenities:** 🛁 📠 ⌗ A/C, cable TV w/movies. **Services:** 🍴 🕭 **Facilities:** 👥 🚗 ⅙ 1 restaurant, 1 bar. **Rates (CP):** $40–$45 S; $44–$50 D. Extra person $6. Children under age 17 stay free. Parking: Outdoor, free. Business, government, and military rates avail. AE, DISC, MC, V.

≣≣ **Days Inn**

I-55, PO Box 1342, 72315; tel 501/763-1241 or toll free 800/DAYS-INN; fax 501/763-6696. Exit 67 off I-55. Standard lodging that's clean and comfortable. Golf, tennis, hunting, fishing, and shopping are within 20 miles. **Rooms:** 122 rms and stes. CI 3pm/CO 11am. Nonsmoking rms avail. **Amenities:** 🛁 A/C, cable TV w/movies. **Services:** 🍴 🕭 **Facilities:** 👥 🏋 ⅙ 1 restaurant, spa, playground. Truck parking available. Guests have access to coin laundry. **Rates (CP):** Peak (Apr–Sept) $33–$38 S; $39–$47 D; $41 ste. Extra person $5. Lower rates off-season. Parking: Outdoor, free. Children under 18 are charged $1. AE, DISC, MC, V.

ATTRACTION

Hampson Museum State Park

2 Lake Dr, Wilson; tel 501/655-8622. 20 mi S of Blytheville. Exhibits feature archeological artifacts, such as arrowheads and backswamp clay pottery, excavated from the Nodena Indian site. Picnicking available on museum grounds. **Open:** Tues–Sat 8am–5pm, Sun 1–5pm. **$**

Bull Shoals

See also Mountain Home

Located in north central Arkansas on one of the state's largest lakes, this town marks the entrance to Bull Shoals State Park. Camping, fishing, and boating are available on Bull Shoals Lake and the White River below the dam. **Information:** Bull Shoals Lake–White River Chamber of Commerce, PO Box 354, Bull Shoals, 72619 (tel 501/445-4443 or toll free 800/447-1290).

LODGE

≣≣ Dogwood Lodge

505 Shorecrest Dr, 72619; tel 501/445-4311. 2 blocks N of US 178. A special place to stay, this very small lodge on the outskirts of town offers a beautiful view and homey atmosphere. Shopping and restaurants about five miles away. **Rooms:** 20 rms. CI 3pm/CO 11am. Nonsmoking rms avail. **Amenities:** 🛏 ⚬ A/C, cable TV w/movies. **Services:** ⌇ **Facilities:** 🎱25 **Rates:** $35–$45 S; $45–$55 D. Children under age 12 stay free. Parking: Outdoor, free. AE, DISC, MC, V.

RESORT

≣≣≣ Chastains Bull Shoals Resort

2 Crestline Dr, PO Box 290, 72619; tel 501/445-4242 or toll free 800/423-5253. On US 178. 7 acres. The exterior of this well-maintained resort is old, but elegant and interesting. It's located off Bull Shoals Lake and White River, near fishing and other entertainment opportunities; shopping and most restaurants are about 20 minutes away. **Rooms:** 60 rms and stes. CI 3pm/CO noon. Nonsmoking rms avail. Economy, guest, and deluxe units; executive suites; guest houses; and condominiums available. **Amenities:** 🛏 ⚬ A/C, cable TV w/movies. **Services:** ⌇ Resort can recommend nearby kennels for pets. Amiable staff. **Facilities:** 🎱 ⛳2 🛶 🎱250 ⚬ 1 restaurant, 1 bar, lawn games, sauna, playground. **Rates:** $45–$150 S or D; $125–$150 ste. Extra person $10. Children under age 12 stay free. Parking: Outdoor, free. Three-night minimum stay may apply. AE, DISC, MC, V.

ATTRACTIONS

Mountain Village 1890 and Bull Shoals Cavern

1011 CS Woods Blvd; tel 501/445-7177 or toll free 800/445-7177. Two attractions at the same location. Guests tour a restored 1890 mountain community, which includes a general store, a one-room schoolhouse, a blacksmith and coffin shop, a doctor's office, and a hitching post. The Caverns, also open to the public, create an underground trout stream, miniature lake, cathedral room, and a rotunda with evidence of prehistoric peoples. **Open:** Peak (June–Aug) daily 9am–6pm. Reduced hours off-season. **$$$**

Bull Shoals State Park

AR 178; tel 501/431-5521. Located on the White River and Bull Shoals Lake, this 680-acre park is a favorite of fishing enthusiasts. The White River is famous for record rainbow and brown trout, and the 45,440-acre lake is filled with lunker bass, trout, catfish, crappie, and bream. Hiking trails, picnic areas, playgrounds, boat rentals. **Open:** Daily sunrise–sunset. **$**

Conway

Situated 31 miles north of Little Rock on US 65, Conway is both the county seat and the gateway to Lake Conway. Noted for its catches of bass, bream, catfish, and crappie, the lake covers 6,700 acres and is thought to be the largest in the United States ever constructed by a state game and fish commission. **Information:** Conway Area Chamber of Commerce, 1234 Main St, PO Box 1492, Conway, 72032 (tel 501/327-7788).

MOTELS

≣≣≣ Best Western Kings Inn of Conway

Jct US 64 E/I-40, PO Box 1619, 72032; tel 501/329-9855 or toll free 800/528-1234; fax 501/327-6110. Exit 127 off I-40. Convenient for sightseeing and shopping in Conway. Very attractive and accommodating. **Rooms:** 70 rms and stes. CI 2pm/CO noon. Nonsmoking rms avail. **Amenities:** 🛏 A/C, cable TV w/movies. Some units w/terraces. **Services:** 🛎 ⌇ Roll-away beds $7. **Facilities:** 🎱 ⚬ **Rates:** $39–$52 S; $46–$56 D; $65 ste. Extra person $5. Children under age 12 stay free. Parking: Outdoor, free. AE, CB, DC, DISC, JCB, MC, V.

≣≣≣ Comfort Inn

150 US 65 N, PO Box 88, 72033; tel 501/329-0300 or toll free 800/228-5150; fax 501/329-0300. Exit 125 off I-40. Very clean and comfortable. Near the University of Arkansas, and within 10 miles of the Arkansas River and Toadsuck Park. **Rooms:** 60 rms. CI 2pm/CO noon. Nonsmoking rms avail. **Amenities:** 🛏 A/C, cable TV w/movies. Some units w/terraces. **Services:** 🛎 ⌇ 🐾 **Facilities:** 🎱 ⚬ Whirlpool. Truck parking. **Rates (CP):** Peak (May–Oct) $37–$52 S; $46–$62 D.

Extra person $5. Children under age 14 stay free. Lower rates off-season. Parking: Outdoor, free. Business, government, and military discounts avail. AE, DISC, MC, V.

≣≣≣ Holiday Inn

I-40, PO Box 998, 72033; tel 501/329-2961 or toll free 800/HOLIDAY; fax 501/329-2961. Exit 125 off I-40. Very well maintained, within miles of Hendrix College and the University of Central Arkansas. Lake Conway also nearby. **Rooms:** 108 rms and stes. CI 3pm/CO noon. Nonsmoking rms avail. **Amenities:** 🛉 A/C, cable TV w/movies. Some units w/terraces. **Services:** ✗ △ 🖵 **Facilities:** 🔓 ⟦340⟧ ⚿ 1 restaurant, sauna, steam rm, whirlpool. **Rates:** $50–$55 S; $54–$59 D; $65 ste. Extra person $4. Children under age 13 stay free. Parking: Outdoor, free. AE, DC, DISC, JCB, MC, V.

RESTAURANT 🍴

★ China Town

In Conway Shopping Mall, 201 US 65 N; tel 501/450-9090. **Chinese.** Tastefully decorated restaurant that's a favorite among locals and out-of-towners alike. Bright colors are offset by soft music. Expect all the traditional favorites, as well as spicy Mongolian beef and several Hunan specialties. **FYI:** Reservations accepted. Children's menu. No liquor license. **Open:** Mon–Thurs 11am–9pm, Fri–Sat 11am–10pm, Sun 11am–9pm. **Prices:** Main courses $5–$17. MC, V. 👥

El Dorado

El Dorado's main street is lined with beautifully restored business buildings and homes from the 1920s and '30s. A large antiques mall, housed in a rustic 1926 former dry goods store, helps draw visitors to the downtown historic district. Area lakes and rivers offer a wide variety of outdoor recreational activities. **Information:** El Dorado Chamber of Commerce, 201 N Jackson, PO Box 1271, El Dorado, 71731-1271 (tel 501/863-6113).

MOTEL 🏨

≣≣≣ Comfort Inn

2303 Junction City Rd, 71730; tel 501/863-6677 or toll free 800/221-2222; fax 501/863-6677. US 82 at US 167 bypass. Undergoing remodeling—but the lobby and rooms are already nicely decorated. It's a few miles from the business district, and parks and playgrounds also nearby. Very friendly and helpful staff. **Rooms:** 70 rms. CI 3pm/CO 11am. Nonsmoking rms avail. **Amenities:** 🛉 A/C, cable TV w/movies. **Services:** △ 🖵 ⟸ **Facilities:** 🔓 ⟦25⟧ ⚿ Sauna. **Rates:** $45–$55 S; $51–$61 D. Extra person $6. Children under age 12 stay free. Parking: Outdoor, free. AE, DISC, MC, V.

ATTRACTION 🏛

Arkansas Oil and Brine Museum

3853 Smackover Hwy, Smackover; tel 501/725-2877. 10 mi N of El Dorado. The museum's 25,000-square-foot exhibit center displays oil-drilling rigs from the boom years of the 1920s and '30s. Two films—*The Arkansas Boom* and *Oil Blowing Wild*—are shown each day. Lectures, workshops, and educational programs also available. **Open:** Mon–Sat 8am–5pm, Sun 1–5pm. **Free**

Eureka Springs

Settled as a spa in the mid-1800s to take advantage of the numerous mineral springs in the area, this charming and very Victorian city now thrives as an antiques and crafts center. Country music and comedy performances, art galleries, and beautiful public and private gardens serve as additional attractions. Approximately 10 miles southeast is Berryville, a historic pioneer town filled with shops and museums, and the site of the Pioneer Days festival in the fall. **Information:** Eureka Springs Chamber of Commerce, 81 Kingshighway, PO Box 551, Eureka Springs, 72632 (tel 501/253-8737).

MOTELS 🏨

≣≣≣ Bavarian Inn

US 62, 72632; tel 501/253-8128; fax 501/253-8128. 1¼ mi W of town. Downtown shopping and restaurants nearby. Nicely maintained and decorated. **Rooms:** 21 rms and stes. CI 2pm/CO 11am. Nonsmoking rms avail. **Amenities:** 🛉 ⚷ A/C, cable TV w/movies. Some units w/terraces, some w/fireplaces, some w/whirlpools. **Services:** △ 🖵 **Facilities:** 🔓 ⟦20⟧ 1 restaurant (*see* "Restaurants" below), sauna, whirlpool. Picnic area. **Rates:** $38–$45 S; $45–$52 D; $65–$85 ste. Children under age 12 stay free. Parking: Outdoor, free. Closed winter. MC, V.

≣≣ Best Western Eureka Inn

1 Van Buren, PO Box 329, 72632; tel 501/253-9551 or toll free 800/528-1234; fax 501/253-9692. Jct US 62/AR 23. Near downtown, the historic district, and numerous shopping and dining opportunities, this Best Western is great for a weekend stay. **Rooms:** 85 rms. CI 2pm/CO 11am. Nonsmoking rms avail. Honeymoon suites available. **Amenities:** 🛉 ⧉ A/C, cable TV w/movies. Some units w/terraces, some w/whirlpools. **Services:** △ 🖵 Roll-away beds $11. **Facilities:** 🔓 ⟦150⟧ ⚿ 1 restaurant, spa, sauna. **Rates:** Peak (June–Aug) $35–$89 S; $39–$89 D. Extra person $5. Children under age 16 stay free. Lower rates off-season. Parking: Outdoor, free. Closed Dec 3–Feb 23. AE, CB, DC, DISC, JCB, MC, V.

≣≣≣ Best Western Inn of the Ozarks

US 62, PO Box 431, 72632; tel 501/253-9768 or toll free 800/528-1234; fax 501/253-9768. ½ mi W of jct US 62/AR 23. A beautiful property located near the historic district;

suitable for extended stays. **Rooms:** 122 rms. CI 2pm/CO 11am. Nonsmoking rms avail. **Amenities:** 🛎 A/C, cable TV w/movies. All units w/terraces. **Services:** ✗ 🖼 🍴 🍽 Rollaway beds $10. Trolleys available to transport visitors and locals to/from most attractions. **Facilities:** 🍴 ⅃ 1 restaurant, games rm. Miniature golf. **Rates:** Peak (June 9–Aug 12) $35–$76 S; $39–$83 D. Extra person $5. Children under age 18 stay free. Lower rates off-season. Parking: Outdoor, free. AE, CB, DC, DISC, JCB, MC, V.

≣≣≣ Carolyn's Ozark Swiss Inn
US 62, 72632; tel 501/253-6688 or toll free 800/833-8450; fax 501/253-6688. Well-maintained grounds surround this quaint, lovely property. The local trolleys stop on the property to take guests to the entertainment and dining locations in town. **Rooms:** 50 rms. CI 3pm/CO 11am. Nonsmoking rms avail. Honeymoon suites available with whirlpool baths. King, double, and mini-suites also available. **Amenities:** 🛎 🌢 A/C, cable TV w/movies. **Services:** 🍴 Complimentary morning coffee. **Facilities:** 🍴 🔲 ⅃ Sauna, whirlpool. Picnic area near pool. **Rates:** $45–$68 S or D. Extra person $5. Children under age 18 stay free. Min stay wknds. Parking: Outdoor, free. Group rates avail. AE, MC, V.

≣≣≣ Colonial Mansion Inn
AR 23, PO Box 527, 72632; tel 501/253-7300 or toll free 800/638-2622; fax 501/253-7149. This picturesque, estatelike property is distinguished by meticulous landscaping and interior decorating. Located near the historic district and downtown. **Rooms:** 30 rms and stes. CI 2pm/CO 11am. Nonsmoking rms avail. One luxury suite. **Amenities:** 🛎 🌢 A/C, cable TV. Some units w/terraces, some w/fireplaces. **Services:** 🍴 Free coffee. **Facilities:** 🍴 🔲 **Rates:** Peak (Mar–Aug) $49 S; $59 D; $69 ste. Extra person $5. Children under age 18 stay free. Lower rates off-season. Parking: Outdoor, free. Group rates avail. AE, DISC, MC, V.

≣≣ Comfort Inn
Jct US 62/AR 23 S, 72632; tel 501/253-5241 or toll free 800/228-5150; fax 501/253-5241. Typical chain hotel located near historic downtown. Botanical gardens and Beaver Lake within 10 miles. **Rooms:** 51 rms. CI 2pm/CO 11am. Nonsmoking rms avail. **Amenities:** 🛎 🌢 🍽 A/C, cable TV w/movies. Some units w/terraces. **Services:** 🖼 🍴 **Facilities:** 🍴 & **Rates (CP):** Peak (May 25–Oct) $34–$64 S; $39–$125 D. Extra person $5. Children under age 14 stay free. Lower rates off-season. Parking: Outdoor, free. AE, DISC, MC, V.

≣≣≣ Dogwood Inn
AR 23, 72632; tel 501/253-7200 or toll free 800/544-1884. A nice, quaint, little property with a gazebo and picnic area near the pool. Near a trolley stop. **Rooms:** 30 rms. CI 3pm/CO noon. Nonsmoking rms avail. **Amenities:** 🛎 🌢 A/C, cable TV w/movies. Some units w/terraces. **Services:** 🍴 🍽 **Facilities:** 🍴 🔟 Playground. **Rates:** $45–$51 S; $50–$56 D. Extra person $5. Children under age 18 stay free. Parking: Outdoor, free. AE, DISC, MC, V.

≣≣≣ East Mountain Lodge
US 62, PO Box 87, 72632; tel 501/253-9521 or toll free 800/533-9521. A small, quaint, lodge-style property that's a unique place to stay near the historic downtown area. Good value. **Rooms:** 25 rms and stes. CI 3pm/CO noon. Nonsmoking rms avail. **Amenities:** 🛎 🌢 A/C, cable TV. Some units w/terraces, some w/whirlpools. **Services:** 🍴 Friendly staff. **Facilities:** 🍴 🔟 **Rates:** $42–$50 S; $45–$57 D; $50–$75 ste. Extra person $5. Children under age 16 stay free. Parking: Outdoor, free. AE, DISC, MC, V.

UNRATED Eureka Matterhorn Towers
98 Kingshighway, 72632; tel 501/253-9602 or toll free 800/426-0838; fax 501/253-9602. On US 62. Unique landscaping, featuring a mini-waterfall, several fountains, and lots of verdurous plants and trees, makes a nice first impression. Excellent service and attractive accommodations make this a great place for a special stay. **Rooms:** 35 rms and stes. CI 3pm/CO 11am. Nonsmoking rms avail. **Amenities:** 🛎 🌢 A/C, cable TV. Some units w/terraces, some w/whirlpools. **Services:** 🍴 In-room breakfast. **Facilities:** 🍴 🔲 **Rates (CP):** $43–$53 S; $46–$56 D; $56–$70 ste. Extra person $5. Children under age 18 stay free. Parking: Outdoor, free. AE, MC, V.

≣≣≣ The Hartland Coach House Inn
140 S Main St, 72632; tel 501/253-7171 or toll free 800/451-1511. The grounds here are very attractive and meticulously maintained. Located near shopping and restaurants. **Rooms:** 51 rms and stes. CI 3pm/CO noon. Nonsmoking rms avail. **Amenities:** 🛎 🌢 🖥 A/C, cable TV w/movies. **Services:** 🖼 🍴 Babysitting. Continental breakfast served on weekends. Pleasant staff. **Facilities:** 🍴 & Whirlpool. Picnic area. **Rates:** $51–$55 S; $56–$62 D; $68 ste. Extra person $6. Children under age 18 stay free. Parking: Outdoor, free. AE, DISC, MC, V.

≣≣≣ Hartland Victorian Village Inn
US 62, 72632; tel 501/253-7171; fax 501/253-7171. This gray and white, Victorian-style property sits next to the Pine Mountain Jamboree. Rooms are pleasant and comfortable and staff is friendly and helpful. **Rooms:** 30 rms. CI 3pm/CO 11am. Nonsmoking rms avail. **Amenities:** 🛎 🌢 A/C, cable TV w/movies. **Services:** 🍴 **Facilities:** 🍴 **Rates:** $40 S; $50 D. Extra person $6. Children under age 18 stay free. Parking: Outdoor, free. AE, MC, V.

≣≣≣ Holiday Inn Express
US 62 E, PO Box 111, 72632; tel 501/253-5040 or toll free 800/HOLIDAY; fax 501/253-5040. ½ mi E of jct US 62/US 62B. Near Beaver Lake, this standard property is especially suitable for business travelers. Golf nearby. **Rooms:** 81 rms. CI 3pm/CO 11am. Nonsmoking rms avail. **Amenities:** 🛎 🌢 A/C, cable TV w/movies. Some units w/terraces, some w/whirlpools. Sun decks in some rooms. **Services:** 🖼 🍴 **Facilities:** 🍴 🔳 & Games rm. **Rates (CP):** $49–$54 S; $55–$60 D. Extra person $4. Children under age 14 stay free. Parking: Outdoor, free. AE, CB, DC, DISC, JCB, MC, V.

≣≣ Joy Motel

US 62 W, PO Box 270, 72632; tel 501/253-9568; fax 501/253-9568. ½ mi W of jct US 62B/AR 23. Not painted in the most pleasant of color schemes, it's nonetheless a festive and friendly place. Near downtown. **Rooms:** 45 rms and stes. CI 3pm/CO 11am. Nonsmoking rms avail. **Amenities:** 🛗 ⚱ A/C, cable TV w/movies. Some units w/terraces. **Services:** ⊲ **Facilities:** 🔲 Picnic area. **Rates:** $34–$44 S; $45–$55 D; $49–$59 ste. Children under age 16 stay free. Parking: Outdoor, free. AE, DISC, MC, V.

≣≣≣ Land-O-Nod Victorian Inn

US 62, 72632; tel 501/253-6262 or toll free 800/LAND-263. This attractive, comfortable motel has a slide and picnic area near the pool, plus a restaurant next door. The city trolley stops here to pick up/drop off guests. **Rooms:** 40 rms and stes. CI 3pm/CO 11am. Nonsmoking rms avail. **Amenities:** 🛗 ⚱ A/C, cable TV w/movies. Some units w/terraces. **Services:** ◩ ⊲ Accommodating staff. **Facilities:** 🔲 Playground. **Rates:** $45–$65 S or D; $65 ste. Extra person $5. Children under age 18 stay free. Parking: Outdoor, free. AE, DISC, MC, V.

≣≣ 1876 Inn

US 62, 72632; tel 501/253-7183; fax 501/253-7183. Average, simple motel. **Rooms:** 50 rms. CI 2pm/CO 11am. Nonsmoking rms avail. **Amenities:** 🛗 A/C, cable TV. **Services:** ◩ ⊲ Babysitting. **Facilities:** 🔲 ♿ **Rates:** $45–$55 S; $55–$65 D. Extra person $4. Children under age 15 stay free. Parking: Outdoor, free. AE, DISC, MC, V.

≣≣≣ Ozarka Lodge

Jct AR 23 S/US 62, 72632; tel 501/253-8992 or toll free 800/321-8992; fax 501/253-8992. Welcoming lodgelike appearance. City trolley stops here to pick up/drop off guests. **Rooms:** 45 rms. CI 2pm/CO 11am. Nonsmoking rms avail. **Amenities:** 🛗 ⚱ A/C, cable TV w/movies. Some units w/terraces. **Services:** ⊲ **Facilities:** 🔲 Bus parking. Picnic area near pool. **Rates:** $40–$65 S or D. Extra person $5. Children under age 18 stay free. Parking: Outdoor, free. Group rates for parties larger than 20. AE, DISC, MC, V.

≣≣≣ Swiss Village Inn

US 62 E, 72632; tel 501/253-9541 or toll free 800/447-6525. ½ mi E of jct US 62/US 62 B. Attractive lodging providing luxury suites and hideaway rooms among its accommodations. **Rooms:** 55 rms and stes. CI 3pm/CO 11am. Nonsmoking rms avail. **Amenities:** 🛗 ⚱ A/C, cable TV w/movies. Some units w/whirlpools. Some rooms have ceiling fans and refrigerators. **Services:** ⊲ ⊲ Friendly, helpful staff. **Facilities:** 🔲 **Rates:** $45–$65 S or D; $65 ste. Extra person $6. Children under age 18 stay free. Parking: Outdoor, free. AE, MC, V.

≣≣≣ Tall Pines Motor Inn

Jct US 62/Pivot Rock Rd, 72632; tel 501/253-8096. This motel is well maintained and offers a nice, secluded atmosphere, yet it is only about a mile from historic downtown.

Better than most motels in the area. **Rooms:** 19 rms; 15 cottages/villas. CI 3pm/CO noon. Nonsmoking rms avail. Suites, family unit, and special Knotty Pine suite available. **Amenities:** 🛗 ⚱ 🖭 A/C, cable TV w/movies, refrig. Some units w/fireplaces, some w/whirlpools. Some cabins have fireplaces and kitchens. **Services:** ⊲ Complimentary coffee and tea in lobby. **Facilities:** 🔲 **Rates:** $49–$65 S or D; $65 cottage/villa. Extra person $5. Children under age 18 stay free. Parking: Outdoor, free. AE, MC, V.

≣≣ Travelers Inn

US 62 E, 72632; tel 501/253-8386 or toll free 800/643-5566. Exterior is slightly dated, but motel as a whole is adequate. Located on local trolley route to shops and restaurants. **Rooms:** 60 rms and stes. CI 2pm/CO 11am. Nonsmoking rms avail. **Amenities:** 🛗 ⚱ 🖭 A/C, cable TV w/movies. **Services:** ⊲ ◁ Babysitting. Free morning coffee. Catering available on request. Courteous staff. **Facilities:** 🔲 🔲100 ♿ Picnic area. **Rates:** $48–$54 S; $53–$59 D; $62 ste. Extra person $5. Children under age 16 stay free. Parking: Outdoor, free. Group rates avail. AE, DC, DISC, MC, V.

INN

≣≣≣ Heartstone Inn & Cottages

35 Kings Highway, 72632; tel 501/253-8916. 5 acres. Located in the historic downtown district, this beautiful hotel is tastefully decorated with fine furniture and lovely artwork. Gazebo and many decks/porches are shaded by beautiful trees. Unsuitable for children under 12. **Rooms:** 12 rms and stes; 2 cottages/villas. CI 3pm/CO 11am. Nonsmoking rms avail. Each room features country or Victorian design and antique furniture, plus fresh flowers, lovely green plants, and gorgeous linens and draperies. Chocolate mint on pillow is a nice touch. **Amenities:** 🛗 ⚱ A/C, cable TV. Some units w/terraces, some w/whirlpools. **Services:** ⊲ **Facilities:** Guest lounge w/TV. **Rates:** $45–$65 S or D; $65–$100 ste; $100–$120 cottage/villa. Extra person $5. Children under age 18 stay free. Parking: Outdoor, free. AE, DISC, MC, V.

LODGE

≣≣≣ Pine Top Lodge

US 62, 72632; tel 501/253-7331 or toll free 800/643-2233; fax 501/253-7331. Located near the historic district, this well-maintained property is walking distance from shops and restaurants—great for travelers who like to be in the middle of the action. The lodge is beautiful and accommodating. **Rooms:** 35 rms and stes. CI 4pm/CO noon. Nonsmoking rms avail. Some rooms have king-size beds. **Amenities:** 🛗 ⚱ A/C, cable TV w/movies. Some rooms have whirlpools for two. **Services:** ◩ ⊲ ◁ Complimentary morning coffee. Staff will make reservations for guests at local attractions. **Facilities:** 🔲 🔲15 **Rates:** Peak (Mar–Aug) $49–$65 S or D; $60 ste. Extra person $5. Children under age 16 stay free. Lower rates off-season. Parking: Outdoor, free. AE, DISC, MC, V.

RESORT

≣≣≣ Red Bud Valley Resort

Rock House Rd, 72632; tel 501/253-9028. 180 acres. Beautiful and secluded, this resort offers elegant resort-style accommodations. A few miles from shopping and dining. **Rooms:** 17 cottages/villas. CI 3pm/CO 11am. Nonsmoking rms avail. Each of the unique log cabins features large porch with swing. Tastefully decorated in country decor. Honeymoon cabins have lovely stained-glass windows. Fine bed linens. **Amenities:** 🛏 🕐 📺 🍴 A/C, cable TV, refrig. Some units w/terraces, some w/fireplaces, some w/whirlpools. Stereos available. **Services:** 🍽 **Facilities:** 🏊 🏕 Whirlpool. Picnic area. **Rates:** $70 cottage/villa. Extra person $5. Children under age 18 stay free. Parking: Outdoor, free. AE, MC, V.

RESTAURANTS 🍴

★ Devitos

5 Center St; tel 501/253-6807. **Italian/Seafood.** A handsome restaurant located in the historic district. Expect to see a lot of locals. The dishes range from simple salads and sandwiches to Italian entrees and seafood platters; the signature special is trout, grilled or broiled. The Italian family that runs the operation prepares authentic sausage and meatballs, as well as the best alfredo sauce in the area. **FYI:** Reservations accepted. Children's menu. **Open:** Lunch Wed–Mon 11:30am–2:30pm; dinner Wed–Mon 5:30–9pm. **Prices:** Main courses $5–$22. AE, DISC, MC, V. 💟

Hylander Steak and Ribs

US 62 W; tel 501/253-7360. 1 mi from town. **Barbecue/Steak.** The menu is in the name. Equally good for casual family dinners or for special occasions. The ribs are especially good. **FYI:** Reservations accepted. Children's menu. **Open:** Mon–Thurs 11am–9pm, Fri–Sat 11am–11pm. **Prices:** Main courses $6–$17. AE, CB, DC, DISC, MC, V. 👥

Restaurant

In Bavarian Inn, US 62 (Historic District); tel 501/253-7741. **Eclectic/International.** Lovely flowerboxes adorn the outer walls of the inn and family-friendly restaurant, and the Bavarian theme continues inside. Sauerbraten and knockwurst top the list of German specialties; also available are smoked salmon appetizers, roast duck, and cappuccino cake for dessert. **FYI:** Reservations recommended. Children's menu. **Open:** Mon–Thurs 4–10pm, Fri–Sat 4pm–midnight. **Prices:** Main courses $6–$14. AE, DISC, MC, V. 👥

★ Victorian Sampler Restaurant

33 Prospect (Downtown); tel 501/253-8374. **Eclectic.** This old Victorian home has been tastefully remodeled, providing a special setting for home-cooked meals and desserts. Quiche, crepes, soups, and sandwiches are specialties. **FYI:** Reservations recommended. Children's menu. **Open:** Lunch daily 11am–3pm; dinner daily 5–8pm. **Prices:** Main courses $6–$17. AE, CB, DC, DISC, MC, V.

ATTRACTIONS 📷

Rosalie House

282 Spring St; tel 501/253-7377. Renovated 1883 Victorian house built in the Queen Anne and Gothic architecture styles. Highlights include gold leaf moldings, hand-hewn woodwork, and period furnishings. Guided tours available. **Open:** Mar–Nov, daily 10am–5pm. **$$**

Queene Anne Mansion

US 62 W; tel 501/253-8825. This Victorian house (circa 1891) was originally built in Carthage and later moved to Eureka Springs. The interior features hand-carved oak and cherry woodwork, seven fireplaces, stained glass windows, and period furnishings. **Open:** Peak (Mar–Nov) daily 10am–5pm. Reduced hours off-season. **$$**

Eureka Springs and North Arkansas Railway

299 N Main St; tel 501/253-9623. Restored vintage steam locomotives (circa 1906) and passenger cars take visitors on a scenic route through the Ozark Hills. Displays of handcars, coaches, and railway motorcars. Dinner and lunch excursions. **Open:** May–Nov, Mon–Sat 10am–4pm. **$$$**

Saunders Memorial Museum

113-115 E Madison St, Berryville; tel 501/423-2563. 10 mi E of Eureka Springs. C Burton "Buck" Saunders's collection of turn-of-the-century artifacts and antiques from around the world includes guns used by Jesse and Frank James, Billy the Kid, and Wild Bill Hickok; Sitting Bull's war bonnet; and an Arab sheik's tent. **Open:** Mon–Sat 10:30am–5pm. Closed Nov 6–Apr 15. **$**

Miles Musical Museum

US 62 W; tel 501/253-8961. Houses an extensive collection of musical instruments including nickelodeons, player pianos, calliopes, and reed and band organs. Special displays include a chapel, Christmas and toy animations, and a miniature animated circus. **Open:** May–Oct, daily 9am–5pm. **$$$**

Thorncrown Chapel

US 62 W; tel 501/253-7401. Located 1 mi W of Eureka Springs. The 48-foot-tall chapel has won worldwide recognition for its design, which includes 6,324 square feet of glass. Daily 15-minute tours available; call for church music performance times. **Open:** Apr–Nov, daily 9am–5pm. Reduced hours off-season. **Free**

The Great Passion Play

US 62; tel 501/253-8559 or toll free 800/882-7529. Religious extravaganza portraying the last week of Jesus' life in an outdoor theater with a cast of 250 people, 40 sheep, 12 horses, 5 donkeys, and 3 camels. Other exhibits include the seven-story Christ of the Ozarks, the second-largest statue of Jesus in the world. **Open:** Apr 26–Oct 26, Tues–Wed and Fri–Sun 8:30pm, 7:30pm after Labor Day. **$$$**

Pine Mountain Jamboree

US 62 E; tel 501/253-9156. Tourists can enjoy bluegrass, gospel, pop, rock, big band, Cajun, and country music performed by national entertainers. Activities before the show include shopping, dining, carriage rides, and crafts. Special Christmas performance begins in November. **Open:** Mar–Dec, Mon–Sat. **$$$$**

Eureka Springs Gardens

US 62; tel 501/253-9244. Located 5 mi W of downtown Eureka Springs. Botanical gardens in woodland, meadow, hillside, and rock settings. **Open:** Apr–Oct, daily 9am–6pm. **$$$**

Fayetteville

See also Rogers, Springdale

A resort area as well as the home of the University of Arkansas, this energetic town hosts the annual Music Festival of Arkansas every June. Nearby, the upper stretches of the White River offer some of the best trout fishing in the state. **Information:** Fayetteville Chamber of Commerce, 123 W Mountain St, PO Box 4216, Fayetteville, 72702-4216 (tel 501/521-1710).

HOTELS

Fayetteville Hilton

70 N East St, 72701 (Downtown); tel 501/442-5555 or toll free 800/445-8667; fax 501/442-2105. On Business OK 71. Offering the quality one might expect from a Hilton, this elegant and immaculate property located near shopping and restaurants is suitable for all types of travelers. Great for a special stay in Fayetteville. **Rooms:** 236 rms and stes. Executive level. CI 3pm/CO 11am. Nonsmoking rms avail. **Amenities:** A/C, cable TV w/movies, dataport. Some rooms have coffeemakers. **Services:** X VP 1 restaurant, 1 bar (w/entertainment). **Rates:** $74 S; $82 D; $175–$300 ste. Children under age 21 stay free. Min stay special events. Parking: Indoor, free. AE, DC, DISC, MC, V.

Holiday Inn Express

1251 N Shiloh Dr, 72704; tel 501/444-6006 or toll free 800/HOLIDAY; fax 501/442-9857. Exit 45 off US 71. Basic rooms in excellent condition. It's a few miles from the University of Arkansas campus. **Rooms:** 110 rms and stes. CI 3pm/CO 11am. Nonsmoking rms avail. Bunk beds available. **Amenities:** A/C, cable TV w/movies, refrig. Most rooms have microwaves. Kitchenettes available. **Services:** Facilities: **Rates (CP):** $49–$65 S; $59–$75 D; $85 ste. Extra person $5. Children under age 12 stay free. Parking: Outdoor, free. AE, CB, DC, DISC, ER, JCB, MC, V.

Ramada Inn

3901 N College Ave, 72703; tel 501/443-3431 or toll free 800/2-RAMADA; fax 501/443-1927. Two-story motel located one block from the mall and a few miles from the University of Arkansas campus. Well maintained, clean, and

comfortable. **Rooms:** 120 rms and stes. CI 3pm/CO noon. Nonsmoking rms avail. **Amenities:** A/C, cable TV w/movies. **Services:** Facilities: **Rates:** Peak (Mar–Aug) $53–$75 S; $60–$75 D; $55 ste. Extra person $6. Children under age 12 stay free. Min stay special events. Lower rates off-season. Parking: Outdoor, free. Many special events require minimum stays, higher rates, and deposits; call ahead. AE, DC, DISC, MC, V.

MOTELS

Clarion Inn

1255 S Shiloh Dr, 72701; tel 501/521-1166 or toll free 800/252-7466. US 62 exit off US 71. Clean and comfortable. Within five miles of airport and bus station. **Rooms:** 197 rms. CI 3pm/CO 11am. Nonsmoking rms avail. **Amenities:** A/C, cable TV w/movies. **Services:** Facilities: 1 restaurant, 1 bar, sauna, whirlpool. **Rates:** $66–$95 S; $70–$99 D. Extra person $4. Children under age 13 stay free. Parking: Outdoor, free. AE, DISC, MC, V.

Days Inn

2402 N College Ave, 72703; tel 501/443-4323 or toll free 800/DAYS-INN; fax 501/443-4323. Two-story property with courtyard and lovely gazebo. Close to airport, University of Arkansas, downtown, and mall. **Rooms:** 150 rms and stes. CI 3pm/CO 11am. Nonsmoking rms avail. Two-bedroom suites available. **Amenities:** A/C, cable TV w/movies. **Services:** Facilities: Washer/dryer. **Rates:** $40–$69 S; $45–$69 D; $80–$120 ste. Extra person $5. Children under age 12 stay free. Parking: Outdoor, free. AE, DISC, MC, V.

RESTAURANTS

★ AQ Chicken House

1925 N College Ave; tel 501/443-7555. **Eclectic/Steak.** Near the University of Arkansas campus, this youthful, cheery, and casual restaurant draws a large student crowd as well as downtown business types. **FYI:** Reservations accepted. Children's menu. **Open:** Sun–Thurs 11am–9pm, Fri–Sat 11am–9:30pm. **Prices:** Main courses $5–$10. AE, MC, V.

Coy's Place

2908 N College Ave; tel 501/521-6265. **Seafood/Steak.** Not your typical student hangout. With its well-maintained lawn and parking lot and cheerfully decorated interior, Coy's is more attuned to the tastes of professors and deans. Excellent steak is the main draw, but you may want to ask about the prime rib and other special cuts, too, as well as the delicious desserts. Features the most complete beer and wine selection in the state. **FYI:** Reservations accepted. Children's menu. **Open:** Mon–Sat 5–10pm. **Prices:** Main courses $7–$21. AE, CB, DC, DISC, MC, V.

★ The Old Post Office Restaurant

1 Center Sq (Downtown); tel 501/443-5588. **Eclectic.** Yes, it's actually an old post office, converted into an attractive, atmospheric restaurant. The dining room, which affords a

terrific view of downtown, exudes 1930s ambience and features chandeliers and wood and brass all around. Recommended dishes include chicken tortilla soup, blackened catfish or tuna, Italian vegetable plate, and fried artichoke hearts. **FYI:** Reservations accepted. Children's menu. **Open:** Daily 11am–10pm. **Prices:** Main courses $7–$10. AE, CB, DC, DISC, MC, V. ♥ ▮ ▦ ⅙

ATTRACTIONS 🖼

Arkansas Air Museum
Drake Field; tel 501/521-4947. Patrons may look at exhibits detailing the history of manned flight, or tour a hangar featuring historic aircraft such as open-cockpit and closed-cabin monoplanes. In the museum's restoration shop, guests may observe airplane restorers at work. **Open:** Daily 9:30am–4:30pm. **$**

Devil's Den State Park
11333 AR 74 W, West Fork; tel 501/761-3325. 20 mi S of Fayetteville. Located in a steep valley at the bottom of the Boston Mountains. Visitors can hike the 14-mile Butterfield Trail, wet-water hike down shallow Lee Creek, camp, boat, and swim. Annual special events include the Arkansas Mountain Bike Championships and Bat-O-Rama. **Open:** Daily sunrise–10pm. **Free**

Fort Smith

Originally a frontier fort built in 1817 on the banks of the Arkansas River, Fort Smith played an important part in America's westward expansion. Tours of the fort show how rugged and demanding life was during the 1800s. The Belle Grove Historic District contains restored homes and buildings dating from the 1860s. **Information:** Fort Smith Chamber of Commerce, 612 Garrison Ave, PO Box 1668, Fort Smith, 72902 (tel 501/783-6110).

HOTEL 🏨

▤▤▤ Fifth Season
2219 S Waldron Rd, 72903; tel 501/452-4880 or toll free 800/643-4567; fax 501/452-8653. At Rogers Rd. Luxurious and posh, this extra-special place located one block from downtown offers a beautiful atrium/lobby, peaceful waterfalls, an abundance of plants and trees, and lots of seating along the hallways and common areas. **Rooms:** 138 rms and stes. CI 3pm/CO 11am. Nonsmoking rms avail. **Amenities:** 🗄 ⚷ ▤ A/C, cable TV w/movies. Some units w/whirlpools. **Services:** ✕ 🆅🅿 ⊸ Complimentary coffee in lobby. **Facilities:** 🛌 ⬜30 ⅙ 1 restaurant, 1 bar (w/entertainment), sauna, whirlpool. **Rates (BB):** $45–$54 S; $55–$64 D; $75 ste. Extra person $5. Children under age 16 stay free. Parking: Outdoor, free. AE, DISC, MC, V.

MOTELS

▤▤▤ Best Western Kings Row Inn
5801 Rogers Ave, 72903; tel 501/452-4200 or toll free 800/528-1234; fax 501/452-0201. Off I-540. About a mile from the airport and near the historic district, this Best Western is much nicer than most. **Rooms:** 111 rms. CI 3pm/CO 11am. Nonsmoking rms avail. **Amenities:** 🗄 ⚷ A/C, cable TV w/movies, refrig. **Services:** ✕ 🆅🅿 🚗 ⬜ ⊸ Roll-away beds $10. **Facilities:** 🛌 ⬜100 ⅙ 1 restaurant, 1 bar. **Rates (CP):** $49–$54 S; $53–$58 D. Extra person $5. Children under age 12 stay free. Parking: Outdoor, free. AE, CB, DC, DISC, JCB, MC, V.

▤ Budgetel Inn
2123 Burnham Rd, 72903; tel 501/484-5770 or toll free 800/4-BUDGET; fax 501/484-0579. Acceptable budget accommodations. Close to shopping and restaurants. **Rooms:** 70 rms. CI 3pm/CO 11am. Nonsmoking rms avail. **Amenities:** 🗄 ⚷ A/C, cable TV w/movies. **Services:** ⊸ **Facilities:** 🛌 ⬜15 ⅙ **Rates:** $35 S; $45 D. Extra person $5. Children under age 12 stay free. Parking: Outdoor, free. AE, DISC, MC, V.

▤▤▤ Holiday Inn Fort Smith Civic Center
700 Rogers Ave, 72901; tel 501/783-1000 or toll free 800/HOLIDAY; fax 501/783-0312. Exit 8A off I-540. Adjacent to the civic center, this nine-story facility featuring an indoor pool and an efficient, friendly staff is good for business travelers or conventioneers. It's also two blocks from the national park and near the historic downtown district. A beautiful waterfall splashes near the lobby. **Rooms:** 120 rms and stes. CI 2pm/CO 11am. Nonsmoking rms avail. **Amenities:** 🗄 ▤ 🍴 A/C, cable TV w/movies. Some units w/terraces, some w/whirlpools. Suites with refrigerators available. **Services:** 🆅🅿 🚗 ⬜ ⊸ **Facilities:** 🛌 ⬜1600 ⅙ 1 restaurant, 1 bar (w/entertainment), spa, sauna, whirlpool. **Rates:** $40–$45 S; $43–$48 D; $60 ste. Extra person $6. Children under age 14 stay free. Parking: Outdoor, free. AE, CB, DC, DISC, JCB, MC, V.

▤▤▤ Sheraton Inn Fort Smith
5711 Rogers Ave, 72903; tel 501/452-4110 or toll free 800/325-3535; fax 501/452-4891. Exit 8A off I-540. Immaculate hotel with well-manicured grounds and an attractive lobby. About five miles from the airport, near shops and restaurants. **Rooms:** 245 rms. CI 2pm/CO 11am. Nonsmoking rms avail. **Amenities:** 🗄 ⚷ ▤ A/C, cable TV w/movies. Some units w/terraces. **Services:** 🚗 ⬜ ⊸ ⬢ Car-rental desk. **Facilities:** 🛌 ⬜500 ⅙ 1 restaurant, 1 bar (w/entertainment). **Rates:** $49–$54 S; $55–$60 D. Extra person $5. Children under age 18 stay free. Parking: Outdoor, free. AE, DISC, MC, V.

RESTAURANTS 🍴

⑤ Calico County Restaurant

2401 S 56th St; tel 501/452-3299. 56th St exit off I-40. **Eclectic.** A casual, quiet setting distinguished by rich colors, paintings, and antiques is a place to enjoy typical American favorites. The Philly Swiss is the best sandwich; for a real treat try the smothered steak. **FYI:** Reservations accepted. Children's menu. Beer and wine only. **Open:** Mon–Sat 11am–10pm. **Prices:** Main courses $5–$10. AE, MC, V. 🖼️ &

Catfish Cove

1615 Phoenix; tel 501/646-8835. 1 mi off I-540. **Seafood.** Conveniently located in a nice neighborhood near downtown, this eatery serves some of the best seafood in the area. Great for families. **FYI:** Reservations accepted. Children's menu. No liquor license. **Open:** Lunch Tues–Sat 11am–2pm; dinner Tues–Thurs 4:30–9pm, Fri–Sat 4:30–9:30pm; brunch Sun 11:30am–8:30pm. **Prices:** Main courses $8–$17. AE, DISC, MC, V. ●

★ John Q's

700 Rogers Ave; tel 501/783-1000. At 7th St. **American.** Vacationing families will find tasty steak and chicken dinners here. Strip steak is the standout. **FYI:** Reservations recommended. Piano/singer. **Open:** Lunch daily 11am–2pm; dinner daily 5–9:30pm. **Prices:** Main courses $11–$22. AE, CB, DC, DISC, MC, V. ● 🖼️ &

Jumper's Fiesta

In Fort Smith Business Park, 3105 S 70th; tel 501/484-5205. Just S of I-540. **Tex-Mex.** Bright colors and festive music attempt to turn even the most sedate guest into a Mexican jumping bean. Quesadillas and burritos head the menu. **FYI:** Reservations accepted. Children's menu. **Open:** Daily 11am–9pm. **Prices:** Main courses $6–$7. AE, DISC, MC, V. 🖼️

★ Taliano's Restaurant

201 N 14th St; tel 501/785-2292. At B St. **Regional American/Italian.** A tastefully decorated old home, this pastaria offers everything from angel-hair to ziti. Chicken-stuffed ravioli in particular is worth a try. **FYI:** Reservations accepted. Children's menu. **Open:** Mon–Sat 5–10pm. **Prices:** Main courses $7–$13. AE, MC, V. 🖼️ &

Weidman's Old Fort Brew Pub

422 N 3rd (Downtown); tel 501/782-9898. At E St. **Pizza/Pub.** Traditional English pub in an old stone building. A wide selection of imported beers go well with bar food and gourmet pizzas. **FYI:** Reservations accepted. Children's menu. **Open:** Daily 5pm–midnight. **Prices:** Main courses $4–$12. AE, CB, DC, DISC, MC, V. ■ &

ATTRACTIONS 📷

Fort Smith National Historic Site

3rd and Rogers; tel 501/783-3961. Preserves and interprets the history of Fort Smith—the military occupation of its two forts; the Federal Indian Removal Policy; and the court period of Judge Isaac C Parker, a promoter of Native rights, from 1875 to 1896. Located at the site are reproductions of 19th-century buildings, including a barracks, courthouse, and gallows. Guided tours, living history programs, and museum exhibits. **Open:** Daily 9am–5pm. $

Fort Smith National Cemetery

522 Garland St; tel 501/783-5345. Established in 1867 as a burial site for veterans of the US Armed Forces and their family members. Gen William O Darby, of WW II's Darby's Rangers, is buried here, as are Judge Isaac C Parker and many of his deputy marshals. **Open:** Daily 24 hours. **Free**

Old Fort Museum

320 Rogers Ave; tel 501/783-7841. Founded by area women in 1910, the museum relates the history of this American frontier town. Native American origins, early European settlers, the Civil War, and an 1820s weaving loom are among the exhibits. **Open:** Peak (June–Aug) Tues–Sat 9am–5pm, Sun 1–5pm. Reduced hours off-season. $

Fort Smith Trolley Museum

100 S 4th St; tel 501/783-0205. From the first mule-drawn horse cars of 1883 to the scrapping of electric trolley cars in 1933, patrons learn about the history of the Fort Smith trolley system. On display are restored trolley cars, cabooses, railroad passenger cars, and antique city buses. Trolley rides available year-round. **Open:** Peak (May–Oct) Mon–Sat 10am–5pm, Sun 1–5pm. Reduced hours off-season. $

Harrison

Harrison's location on the popular Little Rock-to-Branson route (US 65) and its proximity to the Ozarks has earned it the title "Crossroads of the Ozarks," and has encouraged its growth. The town is central to exploring the north central region of Arkansas; the Buffalo National River, America's first national scenic river, is nearby and offers extensive camping, canoeing, and hiking. The theme park Dogpatch, USA (inspired by Al Capp's Li'l Abner comic strip) is eight miles south of town, and is a popular stop on scenic AR 7.

MOTELS 🏨

🏨🏨🏨 Best Western of Harrison

401 S Main, 72601; tel 501/743-1000 or toll free 800/528-1234. On US 65B. Located near Buffalo River and Eureka Springs, it's convenient while still being far from the hubbub of urban life. Caters primarily to vacationing families. Shops and restaurants nearby. **Rooms:** 54 rms. CI 3pm/CO noon. Nonsmoking rms avail. Extra-large rooms available for families. **Amenities:** 🛁 🍽️ A/C, cable TV w/movies. All units w/terraces. **Services:** 🧺 🛎️ **Facilities:** 🏊 & Playground. **Rates:** Peak (July) $39–$56 S; $40–$65 D. Extra person $5. Children under age 12 stay free. Lower rates off-season. Parking: Outdoor, free. Senior discounts avail. AE, CB, DC, DISC, JCB, MC, V.

☰☰☰ Holiday Inn

816 N Main, 72601; tel 501/741-2391 or toll free 800/HOLIDAY; fax 501/741-1181. Off US 65. Standard, two-story motel suitable for business travelers and families. **Rooms:** 61 rms. CI 3pm/CO noon. Nonsmoking rms avail. **Amenities:** 🛏 A/C, cable TV w/movies. Some units w/terraces. **Services:** ⛷ ⛺ 🌊 Small pets only. **Facilities:** 🏪 🎳 🍴 ♿ 1 restaurant, games rm, sauna, whirlpool. Wet/dry saunas. **Rates:** $45–$50 S; $50–$55 D. Extra person $6. Children under age 12 stay free. Parking: Outdoor, free. AE, DC, DISC, JCB, MC, V.

☰ Super 8 Motel

1330 US 62/US 65 N, 72601; tel 501/741-1741 or toll free 800/800-8000; fax 501/741-1741. Minimally maintained, but okay for a brief, low-cost stay. **Rooms:** 48 rms. CI 3pm/CO 11am. Nonsmoking rms avail. **Amenities:** 🛏 🐾 A/C, cable TV w/movies. **Services:** ⛺ **Facilities:** 🏪 🏊 ♿ **Rates (CP):** $45–$44 S; $45–$54 D. Extra person $5. Children under age 18 stay free. Parking: Outdoor, free. AE, DISC, MC, V.

LODGE

☰☰☰ Lost Spur Guest Ranch

Rte 3, PO Box 93, 72602; tel 501/743-SPUR or toll free 800/207-6116. Near Crooked Creek. Located on an authentic dude ranch only a few miles from downtown, this place is fun for couples or the whole family. Horseback riding, hay rides, fishing, canoeing, hiking, sand volleyball, and trail rides are included in the price of the room. **Rooms:** 25 rms and stes. CI 3pm/CO 11am. Nonsmoking rms avail. **Amenities:** 🛏 🐾 🍴 A/C, cable TV w/movies, refrig. **Services:** ⛺ **Facilities:** 🏪 Playground. **Rates:** $60–$80 S or D; $70 ste. Extra person $5. Children under age 18 stay free. Parking: Outdoor, free. AE, MC, V.

ATTRACTION 📷

Buffalo National River

402 N Walnut; tel 501/741-5443. Originating high in the Boston Mountains, the Buffalo drops steadily into its confluence with the White River, crossing the Arkansas Ozarks from west to east. A favorite activity is "floating the Buffalo," as visitors glide down-river past 440-foot bluffs, wooded hillsides, and seasonal wildflowers. Fishing, canoeing, guided walks and hikes, and Ozark crafts and folk music are among the park's other activities. **Open:** Visitor center open daily 8am–4:30pm. **Free**

Heber Springs

Because of its location on the shores of Greers Ferry Lake in north-central Arkansas, near one of the state's largest concrete dams, Heber Springs offers a large number of outdoor recreational attractions. A world-record brown trout was taken from the Little Red River east of town. **Information:** Heber Springs Area Chamber of Commerce, 1001 W Main, Heber Springs, 72543 (tel 501/362-2444 or 362-9953).

MOTEL

☰☰☰ Holiday Inn Express

3450 AR 25B, 72543; tel 501/362-1000 or toll free 800/HOLIDAY; fax 501/362-8833. Near Dam Site State Park, numerous hiking trails, and Medicinal Spring Park, this nicely maintained property with helpful staff is convenient for the vacationing family. **Rooms:** 64 rms and stes. CI 2pm/CO 11am. Nonsmoking rms avail. Large king rooms with sofa beds available. **Amenities:** 🛏 A/C, cable TV w/movies. Some units w/terraces. **Services:** ⛷ ⛺ **Facilities:** 🏊 ♿ Boat parking available. **Rates (CP):** $49–$54 S; $54–$59 D; $66 ste. Extra person $5. Children under age 16 stay free. Parking: Outdoor, free. Corporate discounts avail. AE, DC, DISC, JCB, MC, V.

INNS

☰☰☰ The Anderson House Inn

201 E Main, 72543; tel 501/362-5266. 6 acres. Pretty, homelike inn located near the historic district of Heber Springs. Unsuitable for children under 18. **Rooms:** 11 rms. CI 3pm/CO 11am. Nonsmoking rms avail. **Amenities:** 🛏 🐾 A/C, cable TV w/movies. **Facilities:** Guest lounge w/TV. **Rates (BB):** $50–$70 S or D. Extra person $10. Children under age 18 stay free. Parking: Outdoor, free. AE, MC, V.

☰☰☰ Oak Tree Inn

1802 W Main, 72543; tel 501/362-7731. At Ely. 7 acres. This pretty little inn furnished with antiques sits on tree-shaded grounds not far from shops and restaurants. A special place. Unsuitable for children under 12. **Rooms:** 10 rms. CI 3pm/CO 11am. Nonsmoking rms avail. **Amenities:** 🛏 🐾 A/C, cable TV w/movies. **Services:** ⛺ Friendly and pleasant service. **Facilities:** Guest lounge w/TV. **Rates:** $50–$65 S or D. Extra person $5. Children under age 18 stay free. Parking: Outdoor, free. AE, MC, V.

Helena

The site of a major Civil War battle in 1863 as well as the birthplace of the Blues, this scenic Mississippi River town entertains with the largest blues festival in the state. The downtown historic district is listed on the National Register of Historic Places, and riverboats still visit this town as they did during the 1800s. **Information:** Phillips County Chamber of Commerce, PO Box 447, Helena, 72342 (tel 501/338-8327).

INN 🏨

≣≣≣ Edwardian Inn
317 Biscoe, 72342; tel 501/338-9155 or toll free 800/598-4749. 2 mi S of US 49. Built in 1904, this quaint little home near the Mississippi River has been meticulously maintained over the years. Charming and lovely, and filled with antiques, it is suitable for couples, honeymooners, single travelers, and history enthusiasts. **Rooms:** 12 rms and stes. CI 2pm/CO 11am. No smoking. Lighted walk-in closets. **Amenities:** 🛋 📞 A/C, cable TV w/movies. VCRs available. **Services:** ✕ 🖨 🛎 Stocked, open bar operates on honor system. **Facilities:** 🛏50 🔥 1 bar, washer/dryer, guest lounge. Communal refrigerator. **Rates (CP):** $50–$59 S; $50–$79 D; $56–$69 ste. Extra person $16. Children under age 16 stay free. Higher rates for special events/hols. Parking: Outdoor, free. AE, MC, V.

Hope

Birthplace of Bill Clinton, the 42nd president of the United States, Hope is also known for growing some of the world's largest watermelons. Nearby Millwood State Park contains a popular bass lake, and Old Washington State Park offers a 19th-century museum village. **Information:** Hope–Hempstead County Chamber of Commerce, 108 W 3rd, Hope, 71801 (tel 501/777-3640).

MOTELS 🏨

≣≣≣ Best Western Inn of Hope
I-30 and AR 4, 71801; tel 501/777-9222 or toll free 800/528-1234; fax 501/777-9077. Very attractive, well-maintained, two-story motel. Shopping, dining, fishing, and hunting are all nearby, and Washington State Park is six miles away. **Rooms:** 75 rms. CI 3pm/CO 11am. Nonsmoking rms avail. **Amenities:** 🛋 📞 🍴 A/C, cable TV w/movies. Some units w/terraces. **Services:** 🖨 🛎 ⚑ Babysitting. Roll-away beds $10. **Facilities:** 🔥 🛏100 🔥 1 restaurant. **Rates:** $40–$65 S; $40–$70 D. Extra person $5. Children under age 12 stay free. Parking: Outdoor, free. AE, CB, DC, DISC, JCB, MC, V.

≣ Days Inn
1500 N Hervey, 71801; tel 501/722-1904 or toll free 800/DAYS-INN; fax 501/777-1911. Exit 30 off I-30. Only minimally maintained; acceptable for an overnight stay. **Rooms:** 56 rms and stes. CI 2pm/CO noon. Nonsmoking rms avail. **Amenities:** 🛋 📞 A/C, cable TV w/movies. **Services:** 🛎 **Facilities:** 🔥 🔥 **Rates:** Peak (Apr–Sept) $35–$50 S; $40–$60 D; $60–$80 ste. Extra person $5. Children under age 12 stay free. Lower rates off-season. Parking: Outdoor, free. AE, DC, DISC, MC, V.

≣≣≣ Holiday Inn
I-30 and AR 4, 71801; tel 501/777-8601 or toll free 800/HOLIDAY; fax 501/777-3142. Well maintained, tastefully decorated. Near golf course and tennis courts. **Rooms:** 130 rms. CI 3pm/CO noon. Nonsmoking rms avail. **Amenities:** 🛋 📞 🍴 A/C, cable TV w/movies. Some units w/terraces. **Services:** 🛎 **Facilities:** 🛏180 🔥 1 restaurant. Truck parking. **Rates:** $39–$46 S; $43–$49 D. Extra person $5. Children under age 14 stay free. Parking: Outdoor, free. AE, CB, DC, DISC, JCB, MC, V.

≣≣ Quality Inn
Jct I-30/US 29 N, 71801; tel 501/777-0777 or toll free 800/228-5151; fax 501/777-3777. Exit 31 off I-30. Budget property near bus and train stations. **Rooms:** 54 rms. CI 3pm/CO 11am. Nonsmoking rms avail. **Amenities:** 🛋 📞 A/C, cable TV w/movies. Some units w/terraces, some w/whirlpools. **Services:** 🖨 🛎 Fax and copy services available. **Facilities:** 🔥 🛏150 🔥 1 restaurant. **Rates:** Peak (Mar–Aug) $30–$44 S; $35–$54 D. Extra person $5. Children under age 14 stay free. Lower rates off-season. Parking: Outdoor, free. AE, DC, DISC, MC, V.

Hot Springs

See Hot Springs National Park

Hot Springs National Park

Hernando de Soto "discovered" the springs in 1541, but Native Americans had long recognized the healing powers of the hot flowing water and revered the place as holy. Proclaimed a federal reservation in 1832 by the US Congress and promoted to the status of a national park in 1921, the springs and the picturesque charm of their locale annually attract hundreds of thousands of visitors seeking treatment for rheumatic and nervous conditions. Every day about a million gallons of water gush forth at a temperature of 143°F, from the 47 separate hot springs within the park. Visitors can still get the traditional full spa treatment at Buckstaff Bathhouse, on Bathhouse Row. The park also offers 24 miles of hiking trails that traverse woodland and wildflowers. Visitors center located in the elaborate Fordyce Bathhouse. **Information:** Hot Springs Convention & Visitors Bureau, 134 Convention Blvd, PO Box K, Hot Springs, 71902 (tel 501/321-2277 or toll free 800/772-2489).

HOTELS 🏨

≣≣≣ Hot Springs Park Hilton
305 Malvern Ave, 71901; tel 501/623-6600 or toll free 800/445-8667; fax 501/623-6600. 1 block N of Grand. An elegant, exceptional Hilton offering a gorgeous view of the Quachita Mountains. Located near Bathhouse Row and many shops and restaurants. **Rooms:** 200 rms and stes. Executive level. CI 3pm/CO noon. Nonsmoking rms avail. **Amenities:**

🛏 🛁 🗄 ⌐ A/C, cable TV w/movies, dataport. Some units w/minibars. **Services:** ✗ ☞ VP 🚐 🖾 ⌐ ⌐ Twice-daily maid svce, masseur. **Facilities:** ⌐ 3700 ⌐ ⌐ 1 restaurant, 1 bar (w/entertainment), spa. **Rates:** $45–$65 S; $65–$90 D; $90–$300 ste. Extra person $6. Children under age 12 stay free. Parking: Outdoor, free. AE, DISC, MC, V.

≡≡≡ Ramada Inn Towers

218 Park Ave, 71901; tel 501/623-3311 or toll free 800/2-RAMADA; fax 501/623-8871. N of US 70. Well maintained and tastefully decorated. One block from Hot Springs National Park and Bathhouse Row. Golf and tennis available nearby. **Rooms:** 191 rms and stes. CI 3pm/CO noon. Nonsmoking rms avail. **Amenities:** 🛏 🖾 A/C, cable TV w/movies. **Services:** 🚐 🖾 ⌐ **Facilities:** ⌐ 500 ⌐ 1 restaurant, 1 bar (w/entertainment). Large parking garage. **Rates:** Peak (Mar–Aug) $58–$65 S; $68–$75 D; $110 ste. Extra person $10. Children under age 12 stay free. Lower rates off-season. Parking: Outdoor, free. AE, DC, DISC, ER, MC, V.

MOTELS

≡≡ Avanelle Motor Lodge

1204 Central Ave, 71902; tel 501/321-1332 or toll free 800/225-1360. At Grand Ave. Though the exterior is slightly dated and worn, this is conveniently located and affordable—suitable for families on short vacations who want a place to leave their gear while they tour the area. Three blocks from Bathhouse Row, near Oaklawn Jockey Club. **Rooms:** 40 rms and stes. CI open/CO 11am. Nonsmoking rms avail. **Amenities:** 🛏 🖾 A/C, cable TV w/movies. **Services:** ⌐ **Facilities:** ⌐ 10 1 restaurant. **Rates:** $35–$45 S; $42–$52 D; $45–$55 ste. Extra person $5. Children under age 18 stay free. Parking: Outdoor, free. AE, DISC, MC, V.

≡≡ Econo Lodge

4319 Central Ave, Hot Springs, 71913; tel 501/525-1660 or toll free 800/424-4777; fax 501/525-1660. Off AR 7. Solid budget motel. **Rooms:** 55 rms and stes. Executive level. CI 3pm/CO 11am. Nonsmoking rms avail. **Amenities:** 🛏 🖾 A/C, cable TV w/movies. **Services:** ⌐ **Facilities:** ⌐ 50 ⌐ **Rates:** Peak (Mar–Sept) $49–$69 S or D; $65–$80 ste. Extra person $5. Children under age 18 stay free. Lower rates off-season. Parking: Outdoor, free. AE, DISC, MC, V.

≡≡≡ Hamilton Inn Resort

106 Lookout Point, 71913; tel 501/525-5666 or toll free 800/945-9559. Just off US 7. 10 acres. A pretty property just off Lake Hamilton offering adequate seclusion while remaining convenient to local shopping and dining. **Rooms:** 50 rms. CI 4pm/CO 11am. Nonsmoking rms avail. **Amenities:** 🛏 🖾 A/C, cable TV w/movies. **Services:** ⌐ Masseur. **Facilities:** ⌐ 15 Whirlpool, playground. Whirlpool overlooks lake; the Hamilton Inn Trolley entertains children and children-at-heart. **Rates:** $50 S; $60 D. Extra person $5. Children under age 12 stay free. Parking: Outdoor, free. AE, DISC, MC, V.

≡≡ Happy Hollow Motel

231 Fountain St, 71901; tel 501/321-2230. 1 block off Central. Quite small but adequately maintained. Located one block from shops and restaurants. Fine for a short stay. **Rooms:** 15 rms. CI open/CO 11am. Nonsmoking rms avail. **Amenities:** 🛏 🖾 🗄 A/C, cable TV w/movies. **Services:** ⌐ **Rates:** $35 S; $45 D. Extra person $5. Children under age 18 stay free. Parking: Outdoor, free. AE, MC, V.

≡≡≡ Lakeside Inn

4813 Central Ave, 71913; tel 501/525-1391 or toll free 800/HOLIDAY; fax 501/525-0813. AR 7 S to Lake Hamilton. Attractive chain property, adequately maintained. Less than five miles from the airport. **Rooms:** 151 rms and stes. CI 2pm/CO 11am. Nonsmoking rms avail. **Amenities:** 🛏 🗄 ⌐ A/C, cable TV w/movies. Some units w/terraces. **Services:** 🖾 ⌐ **Facilities:** 500 ⌐ 1 restaurant, 1 bar (w/entertainment), racquetball. Boat ramp 200 yards from property. **Rates:** $42–$48 S; $50–$56 D; $65 ste. Extra person $6. Children under age 14 stay free. Parking: Outdoor, free. AE, CB, DC, DISC, JCB, MC, V.

≡≡ Margarete Motel

217 Fountain St, 71901; tel 501/623-1192. 1 block off Central. Small, attractive motel in decent condition. **Rooms:** 20 rms. CI 3pm/CO 11am. Nonsmoking rms avail. **Amenities:** 🛏 🖾 A/C, cable TV w/movies. **Services:** ⌐ **Rates:** $40–$60 S or D. Extra person $5. Children under age 18 stay free. Parking: Outdoor, free. AE, MC, V.

≡≡≡ Quality Inn

1125 E Grand Ave, 71901; tel 501/624-3321 or toll free 800/228-5151; fax 501/624-3321. Off US 70. A standard chain property, adequately maintained and nicely decorated. Near fishing, golf, and tennis. **Rooms:** 132 rms. CI 2pm/CO 11am. Nonsmoking rms avail. **Amenities:** 🛏 A/C, cable TV. **Services:** 🖾 ⌐ ⌐ **Facilities:** ⌐ ⌐ 125 ⌐ 1 restaurant, whirlpool. Food court on premises. **Rates:** $45–$60 S; $50–$70 D. Extra person $5. Children under age 18 stay free. Parking: Outdoor, free. AE, DISC, MC, V.

RESORTS

≡≡≡ Arlington Resort Hotel & Spa

239 Central Ave, PO Box 5652, 71902; tel 501/623-7771 or toll free 800/643-1502; fax 501/623-2243. 5 acres. Renovated several times and meticulously maintained, this luxurious resort dating back to 1875 offers old-time elegance and sophistication, plus terrific service. Beautiful chandeliers and antique furniture decorate the lobby. Located near Bathhouse Row and downtown dining and shopping, this little slice of heaven is great for honeymoons or other special occasions. **Rooms:** 485 rms and stes. CI 3pm/CO 11am. Nonsmoking rms avail. Parlor suites available. **Amenities:** 🛏 🖾 A/C, cable TV. Some units w/terraces. **Services:** ✗ VP 🖾 ⌐ Twice-daily maid svce, social director, masseur, children's program, babysitting. Massage therapy available. **Facilities:** ⌐ ⌐ ⌐ 1000 ⌐ 3 restaurants, 2 bars (1 w/entertainment),

games rm, spa, sauna, steam rm, whirlpool, beauty salon, washer/dryer. Bathhouse. **Rates (BB):** $44–$60 S; $54–$74 D; $74–$350 ste. Extra person $18. Children under age 18 stay free. Parking: Indoor/outdoor, $6/day. AE, DC, DISC, MC, V.

≡≡≡ **Summit Lake Resort**
350 Lakeland Dr, 71913; tel 501/525-1162. 10 acres. Average property, consisting of brick cabins set on Lake Hamilton. **Rooms:** 25 rms. CI 3pm/CO 11am. Nonsmoking rms avail. **Amenities:** 🛏 📞 A/C, cable TV w/movies. **Services:** 🍽 **Facilities:** 🌊 Whirlpool. Picnic area, sun deck, and row boats avail. **Rates:** $50–$75 S or D. Extra person $5. Children under age 12 stay free. Parking: Outdoor, free. AE, DISC, MC, V.

RESTAURANTS ¶¶

★ **Coy's**
300 Coy St; tel 501/321-1414. Off E Grand Ave. **American/Steak.** The place for a hearty dinner after a day at the nearby national park, this casual steakhouse serves cuts of meat usually found only in fancier restaurants. The most popular steaks are the small prime rib or fillet. Veal, pork, and chicken dishes are also available. **FYI:** Reservations accepted. Country music/rock/singer. Children's menu. **Open:** Sun–Thurs 5–10pm, Fri–Sat 5–11pm. **Prices:** Main courses $6–$17. MC, V.

♟ **Hamilton House**
130 Van Lyell Terrace (Lake Hamilton); tel 501/525-2727. Just off US 7. **Seafood/Steak.** Ask anybody in town and they'll tell you this is the best restaurant in the area for a romantic splurge. It offers a quiet secluded atmosphere with a view of Lake Hamilton. Order any of the steaks or seafood entrees like red snapper amandine or salmon steak. **FYI:** Reservations recommended. **Open:** Peak (Feb–Apr) Mon–Thurs 5:30–9pm, Fri–Sat 5:30–9:30pm. Closed 1st 2 weeks of Jan. **Prices:** Main courses $7–$23. AE, DC, DISC, MC, V. ♥ 🆅🅿

Mrs Miller's Chicken & Steak House
6013 Central Ave; tel 501/525-8861. **American/Steak.** For the past six decades, Mrs Miller's has been feeding locals and visitors family style at large tables in a casual atmosphere. The specialty is—what else—chicken and steak, especially the pan-fried variety. Whichever you choose, don't pass up the homemade biscuits, regarded as the best around. **FYI:** Reservations accepted. Children's menu. No liquor license. **Open:** Lunch Mon–Sat 11am–1pm; dinner Mon–Sat 5–9pm. **Prices:** Main courses $6–$17. AE, DISC, MC, V. 🖼 🚻

ATTRACTIONS 🎦

Belle of Hot Springs Riverboat
5200 Central Ave; tel 501/525-4438. Dinner dance, luncheon, and narrated sightseeing cruises offered daily on Lake Hamilton. Children may "guest pilot." The Ice Cream Social Cruise disembarks daily at 3pm during summer months. **Open:** Daily 9am–7pm. $$$

Music Mountain Jamboree
2720 Albert Pike Rd; tel 501/767-3841. Three generations of the Mullinix family and supporting cast perform music and comedy numbers nightly. Miniature golf, go-cart racing, dining, and shopping are available before and after the show. **Open:** Feb–Dec, hours vary. $$$$

Lake Catherine State Park
1200 Catherine Park Rd; tel 501/844-4176. The 2,000-acre park includes 10 miles of hiking trails, campsites, cottages, gift shop, boat rentals, and a visitors center. Family-oriented programs include summer recreational and nature activities. **Open:** Daily 24 hours. **Free**

Josephine Tussaud Wax Museum
250 Central Ave; tel 501/623-5836. More than 100 lifelike wax figures are on display here, including President Bill Clinton and his family, and 16th-century explorer Hernando de Soto, who "discovered" Hot Springs. **Open:** Peak (Mem Day–Labor Day) daily 9am–10pm. $

National Park Aquarium
209 Central Ave; tel 501/624-FISH. Displays fish native to Arkansas as well as saltwater species. Reptile exhibit includes alligators and a 90-pound snapping turtle. **Open:** Peak (Mem Day–Labor Day) Mon–Sat 9am–9pm, Sun 9am–5pm. Reduced hours off-season. $$

Jonesboro

Situated in the foothills of a 150-mile-long stretch of rolling hills in the middle of the eastern Arkansas delta, Jonesboro is the largest city in the region. Home to Arkansas State University, it offers visitors excellent shopping and a downtown historic district with numerous antique stores and galleries. City-owned Craighead Forest Park provides recreation on the southern outskirts of town. **Information:** Greater Jonesboro Chamber of Commerce, 593 S Madison, PO Box 789, Jonesboro, 72403-0789 (tel 501/932-6691).

MOTELS 🏨

≡≡≡ **Jonesboro Best Western**
2901 Phillips Dr, 72401; tel 501/932-6600 or toll free 800/528-1234; fax 501/935-1677. ½ mi S of jct US 49/AR 18. Standard chain property. **Rooms:** 60 rms and stes. CI 3pm/CO noon. Nonsmoking rms avail. **Amenities:** 🛏 A/C, cable TV w/movies. Suites with kitchens and whirlpools are available. **Services:** ✉ 🍽 🐾 Small pets only. Roll-away beds $9. **Facilities:** 🌊 🚻 1 restaurant. **Rates (CP):** $43–$49 S; $51–$54 D; $65–$81 ste. Extra person $7. Children under age 12 stay free. Parking: Outdoor, free. AE, CB, DC, DISC, JCB, MC, V.

☰☰ Park Inn of Jonesboro

1421 S Caraway Rd, 72401; tel 501/935-8400 or toll free 800/437-PARK; fax 501/935-7644. Fine for short stays. Less than a mile from the airport and near shops, restaurants, and Arkansas State University. **Rooms:** 145 rms and stes. CI 2pm/CO 11am. Nonsmoking rms avail. **Amenities:** ☎ A/C, cable TV w/movies. Some units w/terraces. **Services:** 🚐 ⊠ ⊲ **Facilities:** ⬚ 🔲 ⟨250⟩ ⧑ 1 bar, washer/dryer. **Rates (CP):** $42–$49 S; $49–$54 D; $65–$95 ste. Extra person $5. Children under age 17 stay free. Parking: Outdoor, free. AE, DISC, MC, V.

☰☰ Scottish Inn's Colonial Motel

3116 Mead Dr, 72401; tel 501/972-8300; fax 501/972-8300. Exit 1B off US 63. Attractive, small, single-proprietor motel with neatly kept grounds. **Rooms:** 125 rms. CI 3pm/CO 11am. Nonsmoking rms avail. **Amenities:** ☎ 🕾 A/C, cable TV. **Services:** ⊠ ⊲ ⟨100⟩ Roll-away beds $7. **Facilities:** 🛋 ⟨100⟩ ⧑ 1 restaurant. **Rates (CP):** $43–$49 S; $50–$55 D. Extra person $5. Children under age 17 stay free. Parking: Outdoor, free. AE, DC, DISC, MC, V.

☰☰ Super 8 Motel

2500 S Caraway Rd, 72401; tel 501/972-0849 or toll free 800/800-8000; fax 501/972-0849. Off I-63 B. Standard budget motel located near shops, restaurants, and Arkansas State University. **Rooms:** 107 rms. CI 3pm/CO 11am. Non-smoking rms avail. **Amenities:** ☎ 🕾 📺 A/C, cable TV w/movies. **Services:** ⊠ ⊲ **Facilities:** 🛋 ⧑ **Rates:** $45–$49 S; $50–$54 D. Extra person $4. Children under age 17 stay free. Parking: Outdoor, free. AE, DISC, MC, V.

☰☰☰ Wilson Inn

2911 Gilmore Dr, 72401; tel 501/972-9000; fax 501/972-9000. Off US 63B. Small, quaint motel with a lovely lawn and neatly kept landscaping. **Rooms:** 150 rms and stes. CI 3pm/CO 11am. Nonsmoking rms avail. **Amenities:** ☎ 📺 A/C, cable TV w/movies. **Services:** ⊲ **Facilities:** 🛋 ⧑ 1 restaurant. **Rates (CP):** $45–$49 S; $50–$54 D; $63–$68 ste. Extra person $5. Children under age 14 stay free. Parking: Outdoor, free. AE, DISC, MC, V.

RESTAURANT 🍴

★ The Front Page Cafe

1101 S Caraway Rd; tel 501/932-6343. **Cafe/Deli.** The theme at this quaint, cozy cafe is "where the memories fly by, and the rolls do too," because one employee spends the entire evening bringing freshly baked hot rolls and fried okra to each table. In fact, some people come just for the rolls, baked with butter and served with honey. Bigger appetites can sample from the range of sandwiches and hot lunches. **FYI:** Reservations recommended. Children's menu. **Open:** Mon–Sat 11am–2pm. **Prices:** Main courses $7–$10. AE, CB, DC, DISC, MC, V. ❤

ATTRACTIONS

Crowley's Ridge State Park

AR 168, Walcott; tel 501/573-6751 or toll free 800/264-2405. 10 mi N of Jonesboro. An erosional remnant from rivers of long ago, the park stands 100 to 200 feet above the Delta plains. Catfish and large-mouth bass fishing, camping, swimming, and baseball are among the park's attractions. Guided hikes, nature talks, and movies are available during the summer. **Open:** Daily sunrise–sunset. **Free**

Lake Frierson State Park

7904 AR 141; tel 501/932-2615. Located 10 mi N of Jonesboro. On the eastern shores of Lake Frieson, this 135-acre park's main attraction is fishing. Annual stocking assures abundant bass, bream, channel catfish, and crappie. Hiking trails, picnicking, boat rentals also available. **Open:** Daily sunrise–sunset; visitors center, daily 8am–5pm. **Free**

Little Rock

See also North Little Rock

The state capital of Arkansas, Little Rock and the area surrounding it are known as the "Heart of Arkansas." Located along the banks of the Arkansas River, the city offers a wide variety of cultural activities ranging from a symphony orchestra and theatrical groups to numerous museums and art galleries. Several in-town historic districts present restored structures from the 1820s to the 1900s. Pinnacle Mountain and Toltec Mounds State Parks provide outdoor adventures at the city's doorstep. Little Rock is home to the Arkansas State Fair and a branch of the University of Arkansas. **Information:** Little Rock Convention & Visitors Bureau, PO Box 3232, Little Rock, 72203 (tel 501/376-4781 or toll free 800/844-4781.

PUBLIC TRANSPORTATION

The **Central Arkansas Transit (CAT)** operates citywide bus service. The standard fare is 80¢, 40¢ for seniors and children 4–11; children under 4 ride free. For information call 501/375-1163.

HOTELS 🏨

☰☰☰☰ Arkansas Excelsior

3 Statehouse Plaza, 72201 (Downtown); tel 501/375-5000 or toll free 800/527-1745; fax 501/375-4721. 1 block from Main St. A very attractive, special hotel in the center of downtown. Its 18-story glass atrium affords incredible views of Little Rock. Beautiful plants and potted trees, intricate chandeliers, plush carpeting, lovely furniture, and all-glass elevators are features of the elegant lobby. **Rooms:** 419 rms and stes. Executive level. CI 3pm/CO 11am. Nonsmoking rms avail. Everything—from basic rooms to the Presidential Suite—is luxurious and immaculate. **Amenities:** ☎ 🕾 A/C, cable TV w/movies, dataport. Some units w/whirlpools.

Bathrobes available on concierge floor. **Services:** ⦿ ⌁ VP ☎ ⛱ ↵ Twice-daily maid svce, car-rental desk, babysitting. Sharply dressed staff is eager and helpful. **Facilities:** ⛾ ⏚ ⓵ 3 restaurants (see "Restaurants" below), 2 bars. Shopping arcade. **Rates:** $75–$129 S; $109–$139 D; $75–$584 ste. Extra person $10. Children under age 18 stay free. Parking: Outdoor, free. AE, CB, DC, DISC, MC, V.

⊨⊨⊨ Camelot Hotel

424 W Markham St, 72201 (Downtown); tel 501/372-4371; fax 501/372-4371. Attractive, with well-manicured grounds and tasteful decor. **Rooms:** 50 rms and stes. CI 3pm/CO 11am. Nonsmoking rms avail. **Amenities:** ☎ ⏚ A/C, cable TV w/movies. **Services:** ↵ **Facilities:** ⛾ ⏚ **Rates:** $48–$68 S or D; $65–$85 ste. Extra person $5. Children under age 18 stay free. Parking: Outdoor, free. AE, MC, V.

⊨⊨⊨ Courtyard by Marriott

10900 Financial Center Pkwy, 72211; tel 501/227-6000 or toll free 800/321-2211; fax 501/227-6000. Near downtown. Ideal for extended stays—even for a couple of months. Though marketed for business travelers, it's suitable for all types of guests. **Rooms:** 200 rms and stes. Executive level. CI 3pm/CO 11am. Nonsmoking rms avail. **Amenities:** ☎ ⏚ A/C, cable TV w/movies, dataport. Some units w/whirlpools. **Services:** ↵ **Facilities:** ⛾ ⏚ 🖥 ⓵ 1 restaurant, 1 bar (w/entertainment), washer/dryer. **Rates:** $49–$65 S; $59–$75 D; $69 ste. Extra person $5. Children under age 18 stay free. Parking: Outdoor, free. AE, MC, V.

⊨⊨⊨ Guesthouse Inn

301 S University Ave, 72205; tel 501/664-6800; fax 501/664-6800. Near University of Arkansas campus. This homey little property is housed in a lovely brick building on the busiest street in Little Rock. Close to St Vincent's and the University hospitals, the hotel primarily caters to visitors in town for medical reasons. Near two major malls and only blocks from zoo and city golf course. **Rooms:** 103 rms and stes. CI 3pm/CO 11am. Nonsmoking rms avail. **Amenities:** ☎ ⏚ A/C, cable TV w/movies, dataport. **Services:** ↵ **Facilities:** ⛾ **Rates:** Peak (Mar–Aug) $45–$55 S; $56–$65 D; $70 ste. Extra person $5. Children under age 18 stay free. Lower rates off-season. Parking: Outdoor, free. AE, MC, V.

MOTELS

⊨⊨ Amerisuites

10920 Financial Pkwy, 72211; tel 501/225-1075. Small chain property located about 10 minutes from downtown. **Rooms:** 117 rms. CI 4pm/CO noon. Nonsmoking rms avail. **Amenities:** ☎ ⏚ 🖳 A/C, cable TV w/movies. **Services:** ↵ ⟳ Babysitting. **Facilities:** ⛾ ⏚ ⓶ ⓵ Games rm. **Rates (CP):** $43–$45 S; $47–$50 D. Extra person $4. Children under age 13 stay free. Parking: Outdoor, free. Group rates avail. AE, DC, DISC, MC, V.

⊨⊨⊨ Best Western Governor's Inn

1501 Merrill Dr, 72211; tel 501/224-8051 or toll free 800/528-1234; fax 501/224-8051. Rodney-Parham exit off I-430. An attractive, three-story, all-suite motel with a lovely atrium. **Rooms:** 49 stes. CI 2pm/CO noon. Nonsmoking rms avail. Honeymoon suites available. **Amenities:** ☎ ⏚ 🖳 A/C, satel TV w/movies. Some units w/terraces, some w/whirlpools. **Services:** ⛱ ↵ **Facilities:** ⛾ ⏚ ⓷ ⓵ 1 restaurant (lunch and dinner only), 1 bar. Guests have access to nearby fitness center. **Rates (CP):** $64–$89 ste. Extra person $10. Children under age 12 stay free. Parking: Outdoor, free. AE, CB, DC, DISC, JCB, MC, V.

⊨⊨ Days Inn South

2600 W 65th St, 72209; tel 501/562-1122 or toll free 800/DAYS-INN. Exit 135 off I-30. Pleasant chain property located near the mall and downtown. **Rooms:** 83 rms. CI 3pm/CO 11am. Nonsmoking rms avail. **Amenities:** ☎ ⏚ 🖳 A/C, cable TV w/movies. **Services:** 🚌 ⛱ ↵ ⟳ Roll-away beds $5. **Facilities:** ⛾ ⏚ ⓵ 1 restaurant, 1 bar. **Rates:** $32–$39 S; $37–$44 D. Extra person $5. Children under age 16 stay free. Parking: Outdoor, free. AE, DISC, MC, V.

⊨⊨⊨ Hampton Inn Little Rock I-30

6100 Mitchell Dr, 72209; tel 501/562-6667 or toll free 800/HAMPTON; fax 501/568-6832. Exit 133 off I-30. Four-story motel, clean and comfortable. Near downtown, airport. **Rooms:** 122 rms. CI 3pm/CO noon. Nonsmoking rms avail. Recliners available in king rooms. **Amenities:** ☎ ⏚ A/C, cable TV w/movies. **Services:** ⌁ ⛱ ↵ ⟳ Board games available at front desk. Closed caption/TDD services offered. **Facilities:** ⛾ ⓸ ⓵ **Rates:** $51–$52 S; $59–$60 D. Extra person $4. Children under age 17 stay free. Parking: Outdoor, free. Corporate rates avail. AE, DISC, MC, V.

⊨⊨⊨ Holiday Inn Airport

3201 Bankhead Dr, PO Box 95040, 72295; tel 501/490-1000 or toll free 800/HOLIDAY; fax 501/490-2029. Exit 3 off I-440 E. Well-maintained property about one mile from the airport and four miles from the Children's Hospital and downtown. **Rooms:** 201 rms. CI 2pm/CO 11am. Nonsmoking rms avail. **Amenities:** ☎ ⏚ 🍴 A/C, satel TV w/movies. Some units w/terraces. **Services:** ⛱ ↵ **Facilities:** ⛾ ⓺ ⓵ 1 bar, spa, whirlpool. Well-known Bobbisox Lounge provides lots of entertainment. **Rates:** $52–$58 S; $55–$60 D. Extra person $6. Children under age 14 stay free. Parking: Outdoor, free. AE, CB, DC, DISC, JCB, MC, V.

⊨⊨ Holiday Inn Express

3121 Bankhead Dr, 72206; tel 501/490-4000 or toll free 800/HOLIDAY; fax 501/490-0423. Exit 3 off I-440 E. Clean, comfortable, and accommodating, this is a great little place for a visit to Little Rock. Downtown, University of Arkansas, and War Memorial Stadium are less than five miles away. **Rooms:** 190 rms. CI 2pm/CO 11am. Nonsmoking rms avail. **Amenities:** ☎ ⏚ A/C, cable TV w/movies. **Services:** ⛱ ↵ **Facilities:** ⛾ ⏚ ⓸ ⓵ Whirlpool. **Rates (CP):** $50–$55

S; $55–$59 D. Extra person $5. Children under age 12 stay free. Parking: Outdoor, free. Senior discounts avail. AE, CB, DC, DISC, JCB, MC, V.

⭐⭐ La Quinta Inn Fair Park

901 Fair Park Blvd, 72204; tel 501/664-7000; fax 501/664-7000. Exit 4 off I-630. Dependable, Southwestern-styled downtown motel within walking distance of shops and restaurants, good for business travelers or visitors to the University of Arkansas. **Rooms:** 152 rms and stes. CI 3pm/CO 11am. Nonsmoking rms avail. **Amenities:** 🛏 📺 A/C, cable TV w/movies. Some units w/terraces. **Services:** ✗ 🚗 🖼 🧺 🐕 **Facilities:** 🏊 🍽 85 👤 **Rates (CP):** $45–$50 S; $50–$55 D; $65–$75 ste. Extra person $4. Children under age 15 stay free. Parking: Outdoor, free. Group rates avail. AE, DC, DISC, JCB, MC, V.

⭐⭐⭐ Little Rock Hilton Inn

925 S University Ave, 72204 (Downtown); tel 501/664-5020; fax 501/664-5020. Nicely decorated, well-kept three-story hotel with a comfortable lobby. Located minutes from downtown. **Rooms:** 80 rms and stes. CI 3pm/CO 11am. Nonsmoking rms avail. **Amenities:** 🛏 📺 🍽 A/C, cable TV w/movies. Some units w/terraces. **Services:** ✗ 🖼 🧺 Roll-away beds $5/night. **Facilities:** 🏊 🍽 100 👤 **Rates (CP):** $52–$58 S; $57–$64 D; $68 ste. Extra person $6. Children under age 14 stay free. Parking: Outdoor, free. Group and corporate rates avail. AE, DC, DISC, JCB, MC, V.

⭐⭐ Motel 6

7501 I-30, 72209; tel 501/568-8888 or toll free 800/800-8000; fax 501/568-8888. Adequately maintained, no-frills motel with surprisingly well-groomed grounds. Near many shops and restaurants. **Rooms:** 150 rms. CI 3pm/CO 11am. Nonsmoking rms avail. **Amenities:** 🛏 📺 A/C, cable TV w/movies. Some units w/terraces. **Services:** ✗ 🖼 🧺 **Facilities:** 📱 🏊 100 👤 **Rates (CP):** $49–$54 S; $55–$60 D. Extra person $5. Children under age 17 stay free. Parking: Outdoor, free. AE, DC, DISC, JCB, MC, V.

⭐⭐ Red Roof Inn

7900 Scott Hamilton Dr, 72209; tel 501/562-2694; fax 501/562-2694. Budget motel with a pleasant, comfortable atmosphere. Several restaurants are a few blocks away. **Rooms:** 90 rms and stes. CI 3pm/CO 11am. Nonsmoking rms avail. **Amenities:** 🛏 🍽 A/C, cable TV w/movies, dataport. **Services:** 🧺 **Facilities:** 50 **Rates:** $50–$68 S or D; $68 ste. Extra person $5. Children under age 18 stay free. Parking: Outdoor, free. AE, MC, V.

RESTAURANTS 🍴

Alouette's

11401 N Rodney Parham; tel 501/225-4152. **French.** French decor both inside and out, attentive service, and a classic, wide-ranging French menu make this a spot for a special occasion or a romantic dinner. **FYI:** Reservations recommended. Children's menu. **Open:** Daily 5–10pm. **Prices:** Main courses $7–$14. AE, DC, DISC, MC, V. ♥ 👤

Bruno's Little Italy

315 N Bowman Rd (Downtown); tel 501/224-4700. 1 block S of Main. **Italian.** A fixture in town since 1949. It really is little, and if you can forget you're in Arkansas, it really does feel like Italy. Handmade pastas and sauces are the specialty here, but heartier meals like veal parmigiana, saltimbocca, and pizzas are also available. The antipasto trays are also notable. **FYI:** Reservations accepted. Children's menu. **Open:** Daily 5–10pm. **Prices:** Main courses $7–$13. AE, DISC, MC, V. ♥ 👤

Cafe Saint Moritz

225 E Markham (Downtown); tel 501/372-0411. At Cumberland. **Cafe.** The service is warm, familiar, and inviting, just like the French country decor and the bistro food. Soufflés, salads, seafood, and sandwiches are some of the offerings. **FYI:** Reservations accepted. Children's menu. **Open:** Daily 11am–3pm. **Prices:** Main courses $6–$11. AE, DISC, MC, V. ♥

Graffiti's

7811 Cantrell Rd; tel 501/224-9079. At US 430. **Eclectic.** Casual and comfortable with a wide-ranging menu, this is a perfect spot for a quiet lunch or a casual conversation over dinner. Seafood fettucine and fresh wild mushroom dishes are specialties. **FYI:** Reservations accepted. Children's menu. **Open:** Daily 11am–11pm. **Prices:** Main courses $7–$13. AE, DISC, MC, V. ♥ 👤

🏆 ⭐ Josephine's

In Arkansas Excelsior, 3 Statehouse Plaza (Downtown); tel 501/375-5000. **Eclectic.** One of the poshest places in town, where diners can enjoy creative, gourmet dining in a room overlooking the river. Helpful, friendly service. **FYI:** Reservations recommended. Children's menu. Jacket required. **Open:** Daily 5–11pm. **Prices:** Main courses $9–$26. AE, CB, DC, DISC, MC, V. ♥ VP 👤

Juanita's Mexican Cafe & Cantina

1300 Main St (Downtown); tel 501/372-1228. **Mexican.** Sombreros, paintings, and colorful Mexican flags hang from the walls and ceilings of this festive restaurant with a basic Mexican menu. **FYI:** Reservations accepted. Children's menu. **Open:** Daily 11am–9pm. **Prices:** Main courses $6–$10. AE, DISC, MC, V. 👥 👤

1620 Restaurant

1620 Market St (Downtown); tel 501/221-1620. **Eclectic.** Dim lights and a casual romantic atmosphere make this the place for couples. Try the daily seafood specials like grilled cod or halibut. Extensive wine list. **FYI:** Reservations accepted. Children's menu. **Open:** Daily 11am–9pm. Closed 1 week in Dec. **Prices:** Main courses $6–$13. AE, CB, DISC, MC, V. ♥

★ Purple Cow

8026 Cantrell Rd; tel 501/221-3555. **Eclectic.** Pink and purple dominate the breezy 1950s decor in this diner/soda fountain, where vintage rock 'n' roll plays on the jukebox. Caesar salad, burgers, and fries top the offerings. Milkshakes are particularly good. **FYI:** Reservations accepted. Children's menu. **Open:** Daily 5–10pm. **Prices:** Main courses $6–$14. AE, DISC, MC, V. ●

Regas Grill

317 Shackleford (Downtown); tel 501/227-0009. 1 block S of Main. **Diner/Eclectic.** Little Rock's people "on the go" eat here. The slightly formal dining room has a nonetheless casual atmosphere. Most days, it's busy, lively, and upbeat. **FYI:** Reservations accepted. Children's menu. **Open:** Mon–Sat 11am–9pm. **Prices:** Main courses $5–$9. AE, MC, V. ●

Star of India

301 N Shackleford (Downtown); tel 501/227-9900. **Indian/International.** Original art, including some authentic pieces from India, dominates the decor at this family restaurant. Cuisine includes traditional favorites as well as some unique Indian delights. Curry dishes are a specialty. **FYI:** Reservations accepted. Children's menu. Beer and wine only. **Open:** Sun–Thurs 11am–9pm, Fri–Sat 11am–10pm. **Prices:** Main courses $5–$10. MC, V. ●

★ Tapas

10301 N Rodney Parham; tel 501/224-7707. **Eclectic.** Tapas (the appetizers) lead off an affordable menu of Spanish foods, including paella, at this favorite among students and families alike. Beware, though: the bill can quickly add up when ordering tapas as well as entrees. **FYI:** Reservations accepted. Children's menu. **Open:** Daily 5–10pm. **Prices:** Main courses $10–$24. AE, CB, DC, DISC, MC, V. ● &

The Terrace

10700 N Rodney Parham; tel 501/224-1677. **Deli/Eclectic.** Housed in a red brick building with a neatly manicured lawn, it's quaint and cozy with a warm, comfortable atmosphere. Chicken Terrace, pasta, gourmet pizza. **FYI:** Reservations accepted. Piano. Children's menu. **Open:** Daily 11am–9pm. **Prices:** Main courses $7–$14. AE, MC, V. &

★ The Villa

1510 S University; tel 501/663-4412. **Eclectic.** Frequented by a young, student crowd, this eatery has a lively and youthful attitude. The menu ranges from sandwiches to Italian dinners. **FYI:** Reservations accepted. Children's menu. **Open:** Daily 11am–9pm. **Prices:** Main courses $6–$16. AE, DISC, MC, V. ▮

ATTRACTIONS 🏛

State Capitol

W Capitol Ave; tel 501/682-5080. A scaled-down replica of the US Capitol constructed of Arkansas white marble. The building was first used for the Arkansas legislature of 1911. Highlights of the interior include a two-ton brass chandelier, Tiffany doors, stained-glass domes, and barrel-vaulted ceilings. **Open:** Mon–Fri 7am–4:30pm, Sat–Sun 10am–4pm. **Free**

Old State House

300 W Markham St; tel 501/324-9685. A museum of Arkansas history housed in the state's original Greek Revival capitol building (circa 1836). Permanent exhibits include Arkansas's First Ladies' Gowns, and the restored legislative chambers and governor's office. **Open:** Mon–Sat 9am–5pm, Sun 1–5pm. **Free**

Arkansas Territorial Restoration

200 E 3rd St; tel 501/324-9351. The state's oldest neighborhood contains eight renovated 19th-century buildings, including Hindeliter Grog Shop (circa 1820), the oldest house in Little Rock. During the summer, actors portraying the first residents of the homes conduct tours and re-create local historic events. **Open:** Mon–Sat 9am–5pm, Sun 1–5pm. **$**

Villa Marre

1321 Scott St; tel 501/371-0075. Victorian house built in 1881 in an Italianate style. Features ornate parquet floors, indoor plumbing, and 19th-century furnishings. The exterior of the home, with its distinctive arched windows and French mansard roof, was featured in the opening credits of the TV show *Designing Women*. **Open:** Mon–Fri 9am–1pm, Sun 1–5pm. **$$**

Arkansas Museum of Science and History

MacArthur Park (Downtown); tel 501/396-7050 or toll free 800/880-6475. Founded in 1927, the museum houses more than 15,000 scientific and anthropological objects. In addition to several Arkansas history exhibits, there are many interactive, hands-on displays for guests of all ages. **Open:** Mon–Sat 9am–4:30pm, Sun 1–4:30pm. **$**

Arkansas Arts Center

9th and Commerce Sts; tel 501/372-4000. Located in MacArthur Park, the center houses six exhibition galleries that display paintings, drawings, sculptures, and ceramics from the 16th century to the present. Also located here is the Children's Theatre. Museum shop, restaurant. **Open:** Mon–Sat 10am–5pm, Sun noon–5pm. **Free**

Little Rock Zoo

1 Jonesboro Dr; tel 501/666-2406. The 40-acre park is home to more than 600 animals, including primates, lions, and tigers. Tropical rain forest exhibit. **Open:** Daily 9am–5pm. **$**

Magnolia

The seat of Columbia County in southwestern Arkansas and home to Southern Arkansas State University, this town lives up to its name with large magnolia trees everywhere. Logoly State Park as well as an artificial marsh boasting wildlife and more than 80,000 aquatic plants are located nearby.

Information: Magnolia–Columbia County Chamber of Commerce, 202 N Pine, PO Box 866, Magnolia, 71753 (tel 501/234-4352).

MOTEL

≣≣≣ Best Western Coachman's Inn
420 E Main St, 71753; tel 501/234-6122 or toll free 800/528-1234; fax 501/234-1254. On US 82B. Attractive and well-managed; two blocks from downtown. **Rooms:** 84 rms and stes. CI 4pm/CO 1pm. Nonsmoking rms avail. VIP suites available. **Amenities:** A/C, cable TV, refrig. Some units w/terraces. **Services:** Free coffee in lobby. Tour packages for historic district available. **Facilities:** 1 restaurant. **Rates:** $40–$50 S; $45–$58 D; $43–$58 ste. Extra person $5. Children under age 14 stay free. Parking: Outdoor, free. AE, CB, DC, DISC, JCB, MC, V.

Mena

Surrounded by the natural beauty of the Ouachita National Forest, Mena is the supply point for visitors to Queen Wilhelmina State Park. Canoeists, photographers, and fishermen enjoy the Ouachita River east of town. **Information:** Mena/Polk County Chamber of Commerce, 524 Sherwood Ave, Mena, 71953 (tel 501/394-2912).

MOTEL

≣≣≣ Best Western Limetree Inn
US 71 N, 71953; tel 501/394-6350 or toll free 800/528-1234; fax 501/394-6350. Newly remodeled, this motel is special compared to most. Attactively decorated, efficiently managed. Golf and fishing nearby. **Rooms:** 78 rms. CI 3pm/CO noon. Nonsmoking rms avail. **Amenities:** A/C, cable TV w/movies. Some units w/terraces. Two suites with kitchens available. **Services:** Small, trained pets only. Roll-away beds $9. **Facilities:** & **Rates:** $36–$52 S; $41–$52 D. Extra person $5. Children under age 12 stay free. Parking: Outdoor, free. Senior discounts avail. AE, CB, DC, DISC, JCB, MC, V.

ATTRACTIONS

Queen Wilhelmina State Park
AR 88 W; tel 501/394-2863. Located 13 mi W of downtown Mena on Rich Mountain, Arkansas's second-highest peak, the 640-acre park features picnic areas, a miniature railroad, hiking trails, and miniature golf. In the late 1800s, an inn was built here to honor the queen of the Netherlands. The current lodge is a reconstruction of the original. **Open:** Daily sunrise–sunset. $

Cossatot River State Park
AR 246 or AR 4, Wickes; tel 501/385-2201. 20 mi S of Mena. The 5,233-acre park extends 11 miles along the Cossatot River, which forms Cossatot Falls, a rugged and rocky canyon offering Class IV rapids to experienced canoeists and kayakers. Facilities include picnic sites, nature trails, and a river access point for floating. **Open:** Daily sunrise–sunset. **Free**

Morrilton

ATTRACTIONS

The Museum of Automobiles
AR 154 (Petit Jean Mountain); tel 501/727-5427. Founded by Gov Winthrop Rockefeller, the permanent collection of antique and classic automobiles includes Bill Clinton's 1967 aqua Mustang convertible. Also on display is an antique gun collection and automobile-related memorabilia. Lower-level 1902 drugstore serves as a gift shop in summer. **Open:** Daily 10am–5pm. Closed Dec 25. $$

Petit Jean State Park
Exit 108 off I-40; tel 501/727-5441. Located between the Ouachitas and the Ozarks, Petit Jean Mountain stands 1,100 feet above sea level, offering panoramic views of the Arkansas River Valley. The natural beauty of Petit Jean inspired the creation of Arkansas's state park system in 1923.

The 3,471-acre park contains pine and hardwood forests, more than 20 miles of interconnected hiking trails, and two lakes, Lake Bailey and Lake Roosevelt, which are stocked annually with bass, crappie, bream, and catfish. Cedar Creek, which runs through the park, cascades into a spectacular 95-foot waterfall. The park also offers picnic areas, playgrounds, tennis courts, a swimming pool, and a boathouse with boat rentals. **Open:** Daily sunrise–sunset. $

Mountain Home

See also Bull Shoals

Surrounded by a number of picturesque lakes and rivers, Mountain Home is an outdoors paradise in the Ozarks of north central Arkansas. Fishing, boating, canoeing, and other water sports are year-round options on Lake Norfork and Bull Shoals Lake. **Information:** Mountain Home Area Chamber of Commerce, 1023 US 62 E, PO Box 488, Mountain Home, 72653 (tel 501/425-5111 or toll free 800/822-3536).

MOTELS

≣≣≣ Best Western Carriage Inn
963 US 62 E, 72653; tel 501/425-6001 or toll free 800/528-1234; fax 501/425-6001. 1 mi E of town center. Unique because of its superb maintenance and unusual gardens. A shopping center is across the street; White River and Norfolk Lake are close by. **Rooms:** 82 rms. CI 2pm/CO 2pm. Nonsmoking rms avail. **Amenities:** A/C, cable TV w/movies. Some units w/terraces. **Services:** Small pets only. Roll-away beds $8. **Facilities:** & 1 restaurant (dinner only). Elegant dinner club on premises. **Rates:** Peak

(May–Oct) $36–$57 S; $40–$67 D. Extra person $6. Children under age 12 stay free. Lower rates off-season. Parking: Outdoor, free. AE, CB, DC, DISC, JCB, MC, V.

≡≡≡ Holiday Inn
1350 US 62 SW, 72653; tel 501/425-5101 or toll free 800/HOLIDAY; fax 501/425-5101. Attractive two-story property located less than a mile from downtown and about 10 miles from the airport. Bull Shoals and Norfolk Lakes are nearby. **Rooms:** 107 rms. CI 2pm/CO 11am. Nonsmoking rms avail. **Amenities:** 🔒 A/C, cable TV w/movies. **Services:** 🛆 🖵 Float fishing trips can be arranged. **Facilities:** 🔟 ⓖ 1 restaurant, 1 bar (w/entertainment). **Rates:** $50–$55 S; $54–$59 D. Extra person $4. Children under age 14 stay free. Parking: Outdoor, free. AE, CB, DC, DISC, JCB, MC, V.

≡≡≡ Ramada Inn
1127 US 62 NE, 72653; tel 501/425-9191 or toll free 800/2-RAMADA; fax 501/424-5192. A pleasant, well-managed property minutes from downtown. Also near Norfolk and Bull Shoals Lakes and Buffalo River. **Rooms:** 80 rms. CI 2pm/CO 11am. Nonsmoking rms avail. **Amenities:** 🔒ⓐ A/C, cable TV w/movies. Some units w/terraces. **Services:** 🛆🖵 **Facilities:** 🔟 ⓖ 1 restaurant. **Rates:** Peak (Mar–Aug) $38–$42 S; $45–$49 D. Extra person $7. Children under age 14 stay free. Lower rates off-season. Parking: Outdoor, free. AE, CB, DC, DISC, EC, JCB, MC, V.

≡≡ Super 8
865 US 62 E, 72653; tel 501/424-5600 or toll free 800/800-8000; fax 501/424-5600. Suprisingly nice budget motel. Located about 5 miles from downtown. **Rooms:** 150 rms and stes. CI 3pm/CO 11am. Nonsmoking rms avail. **Amenities:** 🔒 ⓐ 🖵 A/C, cable TV w/movies. Some units w/terraces. **Services:** ✗🖵🖵 **Facilities:** ⓖ **Rates (CP):** $50–$54 S; $55–$59 D; $60–$64 ste. Extra person $4. Children under age 15 stay free. Parking: Outdoor, free. AE, DISC, MC, V.

LODGE

≡≡≡ Silver Leaf Lodge
Buzzard Roost Rd, 72653; tel 501/492-5187. Off US 62. Located on Lake Norfolk, this lodge offers large rooms and many entertainment opportunities. Beautiful landscaping and some of the best scenery around. Golf and miniature golf are nearby. **Rooms:** 12 rms; 2 cottages/villas. CI 3pm/CO 11am. Nonsmoking rms avail. Cottages and mini-lodges are ideal for families. **Amenities:** 🔒 ⓐ 🖵 A/C, cable TV w/movies. Some units w/terraces, some w/fireplaces. **Services:** 🖵 🖵 **Facilities:** ⓖ Guests can bring own boat or use the complimentary fishing boat. Motors rent for $25/day or $125/week. Pontoon boats rent at $100/day. Free docking. **Rates:** $39 S; $70 cottage/villa. Extra person $5. Children under age 15 stay free. Parking: Outdoor, free. 5% discount for cash payment. Call for rates on cottages and mini-lodges. AE, DISC, MC, V.

RESORTS

≡≡≡ Scott Valley Resort & Guest Ranch
Rte 2, PO Box 1447, 72653; tel 501/425-5136; fax 501/424-5800. 625 acres. Offers many resort-type amenities and opportunities for recreation and relaxation. Well maintained and tastefully decorated. Good for families. **Rooms:** 30 rms. CI 3pm/CO 11am. Nonsmoking rms avail. **Amenities:** 🔒 ⓐ A/C, cable TV w/movies. **Services:** 🖵 Social director. **Facilities:** 🔟 ⚠ 🔲 ⚓ Snorkeling, washer/dryer. **Rates (CP):** $85–$98 S. Children under age 2 stay free. Min stay. AP and MAP rates avail. Parking: Outdoor, free. Rates based on occupancy and age. AE, MC, V.

≡≡≡ Teal Point Resort
US 62, 72653; tel 501/492-5145. Located on Lake Norfolk, this cottage colony offers a nice little getaway that's still convenient to local shopping and dining. **Rooms:** 9 stes; 8 cottages/villas. CI 3pm/CO 9am. Nonsmoking rms avail. **Amenities:** 🔒 ⓐ 🖵 A/C, cable TV w/movies. Some units w/terraces, some w/fireplaces. **Services:** 🖵 🖵 Babysitting. **Facilities:** 🔟 ⓖ Games rm. Docking available for free. Bass, ski, and pontoon boats available. Barbecue grills and picnic tables. **Rates:** Peak (May–Sept 4) $98–$101 ste; $54–$114 cottage/villa. Extra person $5. Children under age 17 stay free. Lower rates off-season. Parking: Outdoor, free. Rates vary with each unit. AE, DISC, MC, V.

RESTAURANTS 🍴

★ Fred's Fish House
US 62 E; tel 501/492-5958. Near jct AR 101. **Seafood.** A relaxed, family-oriented restaurant based on the Arkansas pastime of fishing. Great for authentic Arkansas catfish, shellfish, and hush puppies. A "catch of the day" is featured. **FYI:** Reservations accepted. Children's menu. **Open:** Daily 5–10pm. **Prices:** Main courses $6–$12. AE, DISC, MC, V. 👥ⓖ

Raintree Restaurant
207 N College; tel 501/425-9988. **Seafood/Steak.** Subtly and attractively decorated, the Raintree caters to a large clientele of couples and business lunchers. Basic steak and seafood menu with daily specials. **FYI:** Reservations accepted. Children's menu. **Open:** Daily 5–10pm. **Prices:** Main courses $7–$10. AE, DISC, MC, V.

Mountain View

Mountain View is the self-proclaimed "Folk Music Capital of the World," and when weather permits, its village square is the site of informal music gatherings. The nearby Ozark Folk Center and Blanchard Springs Caverns are also major tourist draws. **Information:** Mountain View Area Chamber of Commerce, PO Box 133, Mountain View, 72560 (tel 501/269-8068).

MOTELS

≝≝ Dogwood Motel
AR 14, 72560; tel 501/269-3847; fax 501/269-3847. ½ mi E of jct AR 5/AR 9. Basic motel in good condition. **Rooms:** 87 rms. CI 3pm/CO 11am. Nonsmoking rms avail. **Amenities:** ☎ ▯ A/C, cable TV w/movies. Some units w/terraces. **Services:** ✕ ▨ ⌂ ⟲ **Facilities:** ⅙ 1 restaurant. **Rates:** $45–$50 S; $50–$55 D. Extra person $5. Children under age 14 stay free. Parking: Outdoor, free. AE, DC, DISC, MC, V.

≝≝≝ The Inn at Mountain View
307 W Washington St, 72560; tel 501/269-4200. Small, attractive inn dating to 1886 and tastefully decorated with antiques. Neatly kept grounds. **Rooms:** 65 rms and stes. CI 3pm/CO 11am. Nonsmoking rms avail. **Amenities:** ☎ ▯ A/C, cable TV w/movies. Some units w/terraces. **Services:** ▨ ⌂ ⟲ **Facilities:** ⌗ ⅙ 1 restaurant. **Rates:** $48–$52 S; $50–$55 D; $60 ste. Extra person $5. Children under age 14 stay free. Parking: Outdoor, free. AE, DISC, MC, V.

≝≝≝ Ozark Folk Center Lodge
AR 382, PO Box 500, 72560; tel 501/269-3871. A pretty, small lodge-style property that is well managed and well maintained. Located 10 miles from shops and restaurants, it retains a sense of seclusion and privacy. Grounds are well manicured. **Rooms:** 45 rms. CI open/CO 11am. Nonsmoking rms avail. **Amenities:** ☎ A/C, cable TV w/movies. Some units w/terraces. **Services:** ▨ ⌂ ⟲ **Facilities:** ⌗ ⅙ 1 restaurant (*see* "Restaurants" below). **Rates:** $43–$48 S; $50–$55 D. Extra person $4. Children under age 16 stay free. Parking: Outdoor, free. AE, DISC, MC, V.

RESTAURANT

★ Restaurant
In Ozark Folk Center Lodge; tel 501/269-3139. **Eclectic.** Rock walls, rustic decor, and waiters in traditional mountain dress lend this restaurant an air of authenticity and regional pride, but the linens, silver, and food are strictly big city. A good place for fresh trout and catfish. Salad bar. **FYI:** Reservations accepted. Children's menu. No liquor license. **Open:** Daily 11am–9pm. **Prices:** Main courses $5–$10. AE, DISC, MC, V. ♥ ⅙

ATTRACTION

Ozark Folk Center
AR 382; tel 501/269-3851. The only facility in the country dedicated to preserving the heritage of the Ozark mountain people. Guests can listen to mountain music; watch blacksmithing, pottery making, and cooking demonstrations; or try their hand at weaving, spinning, or 18 other pioneer crafts. **Open:** Daily 10am–5pm. $$$

Newport
Headquarters of the Arkansas pearling industry on the White River, Newport gained world attention when one of the fresh-water pearls collected there was selected to be mounted in the Crown Jewels of England. Historic buildings and museums as well as sites for hunting, fishing, and other recreational opportunities dot the surrounding area. **Information:** Newport Area Chamber of Commerce, 210 Elm St, PO Box 518, Newport, 72112 (tel 501/523-3618).

MOTEL

≝≝ Days Inn
101 Olivia Dr, 72112; tel 501/523-6411 or toll free 800/DAYS-INN. On US 67 N. Dependable accommodations for a short stay. **Rooms:** 40 rms. CI 3pm/CO noon. Nonsmoking rms avail. **Amenities:** ☎ A/C, cable TV w/movies. **Services:** ☛ ▨ ⌂ ⟲ **Facilities:** ⅙ Truck parking. **Rates:** $36–$38 S; $40–$46 D. Extra person $3. Children under age 14 stay free. Parking: Outdoor, free. AE, DISC, MC, V.

ATTRACTION

Jacksonport State Park
AR 69; tel 501/523-2143. Highlights Jackson County's thriving 19th-century river port history. The restored 1869 courthouse contains historical exhibits, and there are walking tours of the *Mary Woods II*, a reconstructed White River paddlewheeler. Swimming beach, pavilion, campsites, and picnic grounds. **Open:** Daily sunrise–sunset. $

North Little Rock
Situated on a plateau, this railroad center and residential/shopping city sits at the intersection of I-30 and I-40, across the Arkansas River from Little Rock. Visitors enjoy its Old Mill landmark, the centerpiece of a pretty garden park in the Lakewood area. Burns Park is one of the largest metro parks in the country, and the new Riverfront Park, which will include a multi-purpose sports/entertainment arena, is under development. **Information:** North Little Rock Chamber of Commerce, 3807 McCain Park Dr, #113, PO Box 16482, North Little Rock, 72231-6482 (tel 501/753-5600 or 753-8433).

HOTELS

≝≝≝ Holiday Inn
111 W Pershing Blvd, 72114; tel 501/758-1440 or toll free 800/HOLIDAY; fax 501/758-2094. Exit 153A off I-40. Quite nice and comfortable. **Rooms:** 206 rms. CI 3pm/CO 11am. Nonsmoking rms avail. **Amenities:** ☎ ⅙ ▯ A/C, cable TV w/movies. Some units w/terraces. Nintendo hook-up in some rooms. **Services:** ✕ ⓋⓅ ⛟ ▨ ⌂ ⟲ **Facilities:** ⌗ ⟦ ⌗ ⟦200⟧ ⅙ 1 restaurant, racquetball, spa, sauna, steam rm,

whirlpool. **Rates:** $49–$59 S; $55–$65 D. Extra person $4. Children under age 12 stay free. Parking: Outdoor, free. Government and weekend rates avail. AE, DC, DISC, JCB, MC, V.

≡≡≡ Ramada Inn

120 W Pershing Blvd, 72114 (Downtown); tel 501/758-1851 or toll free 800/2-RAMADA; fax 501/758-5616. At Main. Very attractive chain motel located in the heart of downtown. **Rooms:** 146 rms and stes. CI 3pm/CO 11am. Nonsmoking rms avail. **Amenities:** �ⓐ A/C, cable TV w/movies. **Services:** ✕ 🚐 ⊠ ⊷ **Facilities:** 🔥 🔲 ⅄ 1 restaurant, 1 bar (w/entertainment). **Rates:** Peak (Mar–Aug) $51–$62 S; $59–$70 D; $86–$105 ste. Extra person $8. Children under age 12 stay free. Lower rates off-season. Parking: Outdoor, free. AE, DC, DISC, MC, V.

MOTELS

≡≡ Hampton Inn

500 W 29th St, 72114; tel 501/771-2090 or toll free 800/HAMPTON; fax 501/771-0410. Off I-40. Basic motel in good condition. **Rooms:** 123 rms. CI 2pm/CO 11am. Nonsmoking rms avail. **Amenities:** 📺 🔳 A/C, cable TV w/movies. Some units w/terraces. **Services:** ⊠ ⊷ **Facilities:** 🔲 ⅄ **Rates:** $45–$53 S; $51–$59 D. Extra person $4. Children under age 16 stay free. Parking: Outdoor, free. AE, CB, DISC, MC, V.

≡≡≡ Riverfront Hilton Inn

2 Riverfront Place, 72114; tel 501/371-9000; fax 501/371-9000. 6 blocks off I-30. On well-manicured grounds, this beautiful little motel featuring a greenhouse atrium is located near shops and restaurants. **Rooms:** 88 rms and stes. CI 3pm/CO 11am. Nonsmoking rms avail. **Amenities:** 📺 🔳 A/C, cable TV w/movies. Some units w/terraces. **Services:** ✕ ⊠ ⊷ **Facilities:** 🔲 ⅄ 1 restaurant, 1 bar. **Rates:** $53–$55 S; $55–$58 D; $62 ste. Extra person $4. Children under age 18 stay free. Parking: Outdoor, free. Group and corporate rates avail. AE, DISC, MC, V.

≡ Super 8

1 Gray Rd, 72114; tel 501/945-0141 or toll free 800/800-8000; fax 501/945-0141. Gray Rd exit off I-55. No-frills budget motel fine for short stays. Near downtown. **Rooms:** 48 rms. CI 3pm/CO 11am. Nonsmoking rms avail. **Amenities:** 📺 ⓐ A/C, cable TV w/movies. **Services:** ⊷ **Facilities:** 🔥 🔲 ⅄ **Rates:** $38 S; $48 D. Extra person $5. Children under age 18 stay free. Parking: Outdoor, free. AE, DISC, MC, V.

RESTAURANTS 🍴

♦ ✻ Cassinelli 1700

1700 Main St (Downtown); tel 501/753-9399. **Italian.** Located right in the heart of the city, this beautifully decorated dining room offers great Italian dishes and elegant, traditional meals. Choose from among several parmigiana dishes,

freshly prepared pasta, brook trout in blackened butter sauce, quail, and veal chops. **FYI:** Reservations accepted. **Open:** Daily 11am–10pm. **Prices:** Main courses $12–$30. AE, DC, DISC, ER, MC, V. ♥

Sir Loin's Inn

801 W 29th St; tel 501/753-1361. **Seafood/Steak.** Nouvelle cuisine is out, sirloin's in at this steak and seafood house decorated colonial-style. Provides a pleasant dining atmosphere for families with older children. Prime rib is available. Salad bar. **FYI:** Reservations recommended. Children's menu. **Open:** Daily 5–10pm. **Prices:** Main courses $12–$26. AE, MC, V. ♥ ⅄

Pine Bluff

Surrounded by thick forests of southern pine in southern Arkansas, Pine Bluff offers visitors historic homes and good fishing for largemouth bass in the nearby Arkansas River. **Information:** Greater Pine Bluff Chamber of Commerce, 121 W 6th Ave, PO Box 5069, Pine Bluff, 71611 (tel 501/535-0110).

HOTELS 🏨

≡≡≡ Best Western Pines

2700 E Harding, 71601; tel 501/535-8640 or toll free 800/528-1234; fax 501/535-2648. Commerce Rd exit off US 65. Comfortable lodging offering a friendly atmosphere and lots of charm. **Rooms:** 117 rms and stes. CI 3pm/CO 11am. Nonsmoking rms avail. **Amenities:** 📺 ⓐ A/C, cable TV w/movies. Some units w/whirlpools. **Services:** ⊷ ⊷ Babysitting. **Facilities:** 🔥 🔲 ⅄ 1 restaurant. **Rates:** $44–$50 S; $46–$52 D; $48–$54 ste. Extra person $6. Children under age 12 stay free. Parking: Outdoor, free. AE, CB, DISC, MC, V.

≡≡ Holiday Inn Pine Bluff Convention Center

2 Convention Center Plaza, 71601; tel 501/535-3111 or toll free 800/HOLIDAY; fax 501/534-5083. Nothing extravagant, but solid, standardized accommodations. Large lobby contains a central pool and lots of tables and chairs. Popular with business groups. **Rooms:** 200 rms and stes. CI 2pm/CO 11am. Nonsmoking rms avail. **Amenities:** 📺 ⓐ A/C, satel TV w/movies. Some units w/terraces. **Services:** ⊠ ⊷ ⊷ **Facilities:** 🔥 🎳 🔲 ⅄ 1 restaurant, 1 bar, games rm, sauna, steam rm, whirlpool, beauty salon, washer/dryer. **Rates:** $69 S or D; $79 ste. Extra person $5. Children under age 18 stay free. Parking: Outdoor, free. AE, CB, DC, DISC, JCB, MC, V.

MOTEL

≡≡ The Inn of Pine Bluff

210 N Blake St, 71601; tel 501/534-7222 or toll free 800/890-7222; fax 501/534-5705. Jct US 79. Generally well kept, but the parking lot is rather dilapidated. There is a small

lobby. Located near many local restaurants. **Rooms:** 88 rms. CI 11am/CO noon. Nonsmoking rms avail. **Amenities:** 🔟 🅰 🖭 A/C, cable TV w/movies, CD/tape player. Some units w/whirlpools. **Services:** ← ↔ **Facilities:** 🔄 🖭 🔲25 🔲 ♿ Picnic tables and grills. **Rates (CP):** $39–$45 S; $42–$47 D. Extra person $5. Children under age 15 stay free. Parking: Outdoor, free. AE, CB, DC, DISC, MC, V.

ATTRACTION 📷

Cane Creek State Park
AR 293, Star City; tel 501/628-4714. 25 mi S of Pine Bluff. The 2,053-acre park is situated on Cane Creek Lake, where the Mississippi Delta and the Gulf Coastal Plain come together. This warm-water lake is filled with bass, crappie, sunfish, bream, and bass. In addition to fishing, park activities include picnicking, camping, nature trail, and guided walks. **Open:** Daily 8am–5pm. **Free**

Pocahontas

Centered in an area settled by French traders and mountain men, this small town on the Current River is home to the first post office for the Arkansas Territory (1817). Camping, hiking, and fishing at nearby Old Davidsonville State Park are popular during the summer months. **Information:** Randolph County Chamber of Commerce, 121 E Everett, PO Box 466, Pocahontas, 72455 (tel 501/892-3956).

ATTRACTION 📷

Old Davidsonville State Park
7953 AR 166 S; tel 501/892-4708. Located at the foothills of the Ozark Mountains and near the confluence of the Black River and the Eleven Point and Spring Rivers. Permanent exhibit in the visitors center displays area archeological artifacts. Camping, nature trail, fishing, boating, and picnicking facilities. **Open:** Daily 24 hours. **Free**

Rogers

Nestled in the northwestern Ozarks along US 62, Rogers marks the western entrance to the Beaver Lake State Park area. Nearby caverns, lakes, and rivers are popular attractions for outdoor enthusiasts. **Information:** Rogers Chamber of Commerce, 113 N 4th St, PO Box 428, Rogers, 72757-0428 (tel 501/636-1240).

HOTELS 📷

☰ Days Inn
2102 S 8th St, 72756 (Downtown); tel 501/636-3820 or toll free 800/DAYS-INN; fax 501/631-8952. On US 71B. Located near the Wal-Mart headquarters, this property caters primarily to business travelers and visitors to the Wal-Mart complex. Minimally maintained, but adequate. **Rooms:** 55

rms and stes. CI 3pm/CO 11am. Nonsmoking rms avail. **Amenities:** 🔟 🅰 🖭 A/C, cable TV w/movies. **Services:** ← **Facilities:** 🔄 ♿ 1 restaurant, washer/dryer. **Rates:** Peak (Apr–Sept) $35–$38 S; $38–$47 D; $42–$50 ste. Extra person $5. Children under age 12 stay free. Lower rates off-season. Parking: Outdoor, free. AE, DISC, MC, V.

☰☰☰ Ramada Inn of Rogers
1919 US 71B S, 72756; tel 501/636-5850 or toll free 800/2-RAMADA; fax 501/636-5850. Dependable, standard two-story Ramada. A few miles from downtown, Beaver Lake, and Ozark Mountain Music. **Rooms:** 127 rms and stes. CI 2pm/CO 11am. Nonsmoking rms avail. **Amenities:** 🔟 A/C, cable TV w/movies. **Services:** ✕ 🖂 ← Roll-away beds $6. **Facilities:** 🔄 🔲100 ♿ 1 restaurant, 1 bar (w/entertainment). **Rates:** Peak (Mar–Aug) $41–$49 S; $41–$55 D; $65 ste. Extra person $6. Children under age 13 stay free. Min stay special events. Lower rates off-season. Parking: Outdoor, free. Higher rates, deposits, and minimum stays required for football weekends. AE, CB, DC, DISC, EC, JCB, MC, V.

RESTAURANTS 🍴

Crumpet Tea Room
In Vinson Square, 107 W Elm; tel 501/636-7498. **International.** Located in a blue-and-white-trimmed building, this casual and cozy second-floor restaurant decorated with wreaths specializes in bridal showers, birthday parties (for adults, not children), and other big-group events. The unique menu ranges from simple salads and quiche to crumpets and the signature hot orange rolls with orange frosting. **FYI:** Reservations accepted. No liquor license. **Open:** Mon–Sat 11am–2pm. **Prices:** Lunch main courses $2–$7. AE, DISC, MC, V. ♥ ♿

★ Tale of the Trout
4611 New Hope; tel 501/636-0508. **Seafood.** Located in an old elevated house with large windows and a rustic elegance overlooking a gorgeous lake and stream. The menu is limited to fresh fish (primarily trout) raised in the lake below, plus a few sandwiches. In warmer months, seating is available outside. **FYI:** Reservations accepted. Dress code. BYO. **Open:** Mon–Thurs 5–9:30pm, Fri–Sat 5–10pm. **Prices:** Main courses $7–$10. No CC. 🅿

ATTRACTIONS 📷

War Eagle Mill
11045 War Eagle Rd; tel 501/789-5343. This reproduction of an 1873 water-powered grist mill is the only working mill in Arkansas. Stone-ground cornmeal, whole-wheat flour, rye flour, and corn grits are available at the general store. Guided tours. **Open:** Daily 8:30am–5pm. **Free**

War Eagle Cavern
AR 12 E; tel 501/789-2909. Visitors are taken on a 40-minute guided tour of the underground natural cavern which

features an underground stream, fossils, rimestones, domes, and onyx. Gift shop with Ozark crafts. **Open:** May 1–Oct 26, Mon–Sat 9am–5pm, Sun 1–5pm. **$$$**

Beaver Lake State Park
AR 12; tel 501/789-2380. 10 mi E of Rogers. The 11,644-acre park is part of the Hobbs State Management Area and provides access to 28,000-acre Beaver Lake. The park contains a public firing range and regulated seasonal hunting. Two trails offer 10 miles of hiking. **Open:** Daily sunrise–sunset. **Free**

Russellville

Just south of I-40 on Scenic Highway 7, this thriving community borders both Lake Dardanelle and the Arkansas River. Russellville is home to Arkansas Tech University and hosts major festivals and craft shows. Several state parks and wildlife preserves are easily reached from town. **Information:** Russellville Chamber of Commerce, 708 W Main, Russellville, 72801-3617 (tel 501/968-2530 or 968-6509).

HOTELS

≡≡≡ Comfort Inn
3019 E D St, 72801; tel 501/967-7500 or toll free 800/221-2222; fax 501/967-7500. Exit 84 off I-40. Well-maintained, attractive hotel with a large lobby and lots of comfortable seating. Close to Lake Dardenelle, Mount Nebo, and the Ozarks. **Rooms:** 61 rms. CI 3pm/CO 11am. Nonsmoking rms avail. **Amenities:** A/C, cable TV w/movies. **Services:** **Facilities:** 1 restaurant, 1 bar. **Rates:** $40–$50 S; $43–$55 D. Extra person $5. Children under age 12 stay free. Parking: Outdoor, free. AE, DISC, MC, V.

≡≡≡ Holiday Inn
2407 N Arkansas, PO Box 460, 72801; tel 501/968-4300 or toll free 800/HOLIDAY; fax 501/968-4300. Exit 81 off I-40. Typical Holiday Inn near shopping, dining, Arkansas Tech. **Rooms:** 149 rms. CI 3pm/CO 11am. Nonsmoking rms avail. Town house suites available. **Amenities:** A/C, cable TV w/movies. Some units w/terraces. Refrigerators and microwaves on request. **Services:** **Facilities:** 1 restaurant. **Rates:** $45–$53 S; $50–$58 D. Extra person $4. Children under age 12 stay free. Parking: Outdoor, free. AE, DC, DISC, MC, V.

MOTEL

≡≡ Best Western Inn
AR 7, PO Box 2006, 72801; tel 501/967-1000 or toll free 800/528-1234; fax 501/967-1000. Jct I-40 at exit 81. Standard lodgings. Fishing is less than a mile away. Jogging path nearby. **Rooms:** 100 rms and stes. CI 2pm/CO noon. Nonsmoking rms avail. **Amenities:** A/C, cable TV w/movies. Some units w/terraces. Some rooms have refrigerators. **Services:** One small dog (under 12 lbs) allowed per

room. **Facilities:** Spa. **Rates:** $40–$48 S or D; $59 ste. Extra person $3. Children under age 12 stay free. Parking: Outdoor, free. AE, CB, DC, DISC, JCB, MC, V.

RESTAURANT

Madame Wu's Hunan Chinese Restaurant
914 Arkansas; tel 501/968-4569. Off I-40. **Chinese.** Oriental lamps, tapestries, and colorful paintings fill the room, and traditional Chinese entrees fill plates and stomachs. Attentive service. **FYI:** Reservations accepted. Children's menu. No liquor license. **Open:** Daily 11am–10pm. **Prices:** Main courses $4–$8. AE, MC, V.

Searcy

Adjacent to US 64, Searcy is the commercial hub and county seat for White County and acts as the eastern gateway to the Little Red River and Greers Ferry Lake region. Home to Harding University. **Information:** Searcy Chamber of Commerce, 200 S Spring St, Searcy, 72143 (tel 501/268-2458).

HOTEL

UNRATED Comfort Inn
107 S Rand St, 72143; tel 501/279-9100 or toll free 800/221-2222; fax 501/279-9100. Inexpensive, well-cared-for lodgings a few miles from Harding University. **Rooms:** 59 rms. CI 3pm/CO 11am. Nonsmoking rms avail. **Amenities:** A/C, cable TV w/movies. **Services:** **Facilities:** **Rates:** $40–$60 S; $45–$60 D. Extra person $5. Children under age 12 stay free. Parking: Outdoor, free. AE, DISC, MC, V.

MOTEL

≡≡ Hampton Inn
3204 E Race Ave, 72143; tel 501/268-0654 or toll free 800/222-2222; fax 501/268-0654. Exit 46 off I-67. Fairly attractive motel in good condition. **Rooms:** 60 rms. CI 3pm/CO 11am. Nonsmoking rms avail. **Amenities:** A/C, cable TV w/movies. **Services:** **Facilities:** **Rates:** $50–$60 S; $55–$65 D. Extra person $5. Children under age 18 stay free. Parking: Outdoor, free. AE, DISC, MC, V.

Springdale

A thriving city in the northwest Ozarks, Springdale hosts one of the state's largest events, Rodeo of the Ozarks, every Fourth of July. Bracketed by Fayetteville to the south and Rogers to the north, the Springdale area boasts a wide variety of outdoor recreational activities. **Information:** Springdale Chamber of Commerce, 700 W Emma St, PO Box 166, Springdale, 72765-0166 (tel 501/751-4694 or toll free 800/972-7261).

HOTELS 🏨

≣≣≣ Comfort Inn

4540 W Sunset Ave, 72762; tel 501/751-6700 or toll free 800/221-2222. Exit 412 E off US 71. The management here takes special care of their centrally located property, a good choice for business travelers visiting Tyson Foods or Wal-Mart headquarters. About 10 miles from the airport, 5 miles from the business district and University of Arkansas. **Rooms:** 60 rms and stes. CI open/CO 11am. Nonsmoking rms avail. **Amenities:** 🕾 ⌀ A/C, cable TV w/movies. Some units w/whirlpools. **Services:** 🖼 ⌐ **Facilities:** 🛗 🛏 12 ⅗ **Rates:** $42–$125 S; $50–$150 D; $50–$150 ste. Extra person $5. Children under age 12 stay free. Parking: Outdoor, free. AE, DC, DISC, MC, V.

≣≣≣ Holiday Inn Northwest Arkansas

1500 S 48th St, 72762; tel 501/751-8300 or toll free 800/HOLIDAY; fax 501/751-4640. An attractive, classy hotel boasting a five-story waterfall in view from the glass elevator. Well-suited for business travelers and convenient for Razorback fans and vacationers to Beaver Lake and Springdale. **Rooms:** 206 rms and stes. Executive level. CI 3pm/CO 11am. Nonsmoking rms avail. **Amenities:** 🕾 🖭 A/C, cable TV w/movies. Some units w/terraces. **Services:** 🚐 🖼 ⌐ 🖘 **Facilities:** 🛗 🛏 1100 ⅗ 1 restaurant, racquetball, spa, sauna, whirlpool. **Rates:** $59–$69 S; $64–$74 D; $89 ste. Extra person $5. Children under age 12 stay free. Parking: Indoor, free. AE, DC, DISC, JCB, MC, V.

MOTEL

≣≣ Executive Inn

2005 US 71B S, 72764; tel 501/756-6101; fax 501/756-6101. Two-story budget motel that's adequate but nothing special. **Rooms:** 78 rms. CI 2pm/CO 11am. Nonsmoking rms avail. **Amenities:** 🕾 ⌀ 🖭 A/C, cable TV w/movies. **Services:** ✗ 🖼 ⌐ **Facilities:** 🛗 🛏 ⅗ 1 restaurant, whirlpool. **Rates (CP):** $50–$54 S; $53–$57 D. Extra person $4. Children under age 17 stay free. Parking: Outdoor, free. AE, DISC, MC, V.

RESTAURANT 🍴

★ AQ Chicken House

US 71B; tel 501/751-4633. **American/Deli.** One of a small but popular chain of family restaurants featuring a homey, comfortable atmosphere. Southern pan-fried chicken and hickory-smoked ribs are the mainstays. **FYI:** Reservations accepted. Children's menu. Beer and wine only. **Open:** Daily 11am–10pm. **Prices:** Main courses $5–$12. AE, DISC, MC, V. 🍷 👪 ⅗

Texarkana

Named after three states (Texas, Arkansas, and Louisiana), this city straddles the state line between Texas and Arkansas,

making it a popular site for photographs among those wishing to have a foot in each state. Having four states within a 30-mile radius makes Texarkana the crossroads for the south-central region of the United States. (Oklahoma is the fourth state.) One of the most noteworthy annual events is the Four States Fair and Rodeo which attracts contestants from the neighboring states. Millwood Lake State Park and the Red River offer numerous outdoor activities. **Information:** Texarkana Chamber of Commerce, 819 State Line Ave, PO Box 1468, Texarkana, TX, 75504-1468 (tel 903/792-7191).

HOTEL 🏨

≣≣≣ Holiday Inn

5100 N State Line Ave, 75502; tel 501/774-3521 or toll free 800/HOLIDAY; fax 501/772-3068. I-30 and US 59/71 on TX/AR border. Four-story, Holidome property located near many shops and restaurants in both Texas and Arkansas. **Rooms:** 210 rms and stes. CI 3pm/CO 11am. Nonsmoking rms avail. **Amenities:** 🕾 A/C, cable TV w/movies. Some units w/terraces. **Services:** VP 🖼 ⌐ 🖘 Fax and copy services available. **Facilities:** 🛗 🛏 240 ⅗ 1 restaurant (lunch and dinner only), spa, sauna, whirlpool. **Rates:** $44–$49 S; $54–$64 D; $75 ste. Extra person $4. Children under age 12 stay free. Parking: Outdoor, free. AE, DC, DISC, JCB, MC, V.

MOTELS

≣≣≣ Best Western Kings Row Inn

4200 N State Line Ave, 75502; tel 501/774-3851 or toll free 800/643-5464; fax 501/772-8440. On US 59/71, off I-30. This lovely property has a nice lobby with a rustic, old, chandelier and plenty of seating. Located near fishing and horse racing. **Rooms:** 116 rms and stes. CI 3pm/CO 11am. Nonsmoking rms avail. **Amenities:** 🕾 ⅌ A/C, cable TV w/movies. Some units w/terraces. Refrigerators in some rooms. **Services:** ✗ 🚐 🖼 ⌐ 🖘 Limited airport transportation. Small pets only. **Facilities:** 🛗 110 ⅗ 1 restaurant. **Rates:** $32–$43 S; $38–$47 D; $39–$47 ste. Extra person $5. Children under age 12 stay free. Parking: Outdoor, free. AE, CB, DC, DISC, JCB, MC, V.

≣≣ Shoney's Inn

5210 State Line Ave, 75502; tel 501/772-0070 or toll free 800/222-2222; fax 501/773-1408. Exit 223B off I-30. Average motel located near Red River Arsenal, Lake Texarkana, a theater, shopping, and dining. **Rooms:** 72 rms. CI 2pm/CO noon. Nonsmoking rms avail. Whirlpool suites available. **Amenities:** 🕾 A/C, cable TV w/movies. **Services:** 🖼 ⌐ 🖘 Complimentary coffee in lobby. **Facilities:** 🛗 🛏 100 ⅗ 1 restaurant. **Rates:** $42–$47 S; $50–$55 D. Extra person $5. Children under age 13 stay free. Parking: Outdoor, free. AE, CB, DC, DISC, MC, V.

RESTAURANT 🍽

★ **Cattleman's Steakhouse**
4018 State Line Ave; tel 501/774-4481. ½ mi S of I-30.
Steak. Round up the kids and take the whole family for steak
and ribs. Those who don't delight in red meat will find
chicken and seafood alternatives. **FYI:** Reservations accepted.
Children's menu. No liquor license. **Open:** Mon–Sat 5:30–
10pm. **Prices:** Main courses $4–$23. AE, DISC, MC, V. 🅿️

ATTRACTION 🏛

Millwood State Park
AR 32, Ashdown; tel 501/898-2800. Located 15 mi NE of
Texarkana. A popular fishing area, the 29,500-acre lake is
home to largemouth, white, and hybrid bass, as well as
crappie, catfish, and bream. The park also hosts bird-watching enthusiasts who come to see wintering bald eagles and
flocks of migrating pelicans and ducks. Hiking trails, picnic
sites, marina, pedal boats. **Open:** Daily sunrise–sunset. **$$**

KANSAS

Land of the Far Horizon

For many of us, the horizon extends all the way to our neighbor's roofline, in which case Kansas may come as something of a shock. Here, your field of vision encompasses more sky than land, and the land, with its forest of grasses and fields of wheat, ebbs and swells and ripples like the sea.

This is a spiritual place, this marriage of heaven and earth at the far horizon, and strong moral beliefs are woven deeply into the fabric of the Kansan character. Many people of conscience were among its original settlers. Some came to minister to the displaced Native Americans, whose own deep bonds to the land had been brutally, irrevocably severed. Others came to preserve the land from the appalling institution of slavery, and the blood spilled on the prairie for this cause foreshadowed the national blood-letting a few years later. The life of the homesteaders, confronted with blizzards, prairie fires, locusts, and crushing loneliness, seems itself an act of faith, whether in a higher power or one's own tenacity.

It is ironic, but not surprising, that most visitors are drawn to the old frontier forts and Wild West cowtowns, those relics of the aggression and debauchery of the most romanticized chapter in American mythology. Yet as fun as they are to explore, they reveal little about the true nature of Kansas. To experience that, stop along the road, talk to the people who work the land, and wander the incredible expanses of land. Breathe in all that space—there's not much of it left anymore—and let it tell you something you'll never hear back in the urban canyons or suburban sprawl.

A Brief History

No Home on the Range Spaniard Francisco Coronado's gold-hunting sojourn through southwest Kansas in 1541 went relatively unnoticed by the native Wichita, Osage, Kansa, Pawnee, and Apache peoples. The amicable French fur trade in northeast Kansas in the early 1700s also had little

STATE STATS

CAPITAL
Topeka

AREA
82,277 square miles

BORDERS
Missouri, Nebraska, Colorado, Oklahoma

POPULATION
2,478,099 (1990)

ENTERED UNION
January 29, 1861 (34th state)

NICKNAMES
The Sunflower State, The Jayhawker State

STATE FLOWER
Sunflower

STATE BIRD
Meadowlark

FAMOUS NATIVES
Robert Dole, Amelia Earhart, Walter Chrysler

impact on them. But the United States's acquisition of the region, part of the 1803 Louisiana Purchase, was to alter their lives forever.

Under the terms of an 1825 treaty, the Osage and the Kansa, for whom the state was eventually named, relinquished a portion of their eastern Kansas lands to the US government. Between 1830 and 1842, nearly 30 Indian tribes from east of the Mississippi were forcibly resettled on these lands, and many of them perished within a few years from exposure, lack of food, and hardship.

In the meantime, the Santa Fe and Oregon Trails were funneling an increasing volume of settlers and trade across Kansas Indian Territory and fueling illegal white settlements around trail way stations. Indian attacks on travelers and settlers escalated, particularly in the west, where High Plains Comanches were enraged at the growing encroachment on their hunting grounds, and a string of Army outposts was built to provide protection along the trails. Under increasing pressure from settlers and the railroads, the United States reclaimed 13 million acres of eastern treaty lands in 1853, eventually relocating most of the indigenous and emmigrant Native American groups into present-day Oklahoma.

> ## Fun Facts
>
> • Ninety-six percent of the land area in Kansas is devoted to farming.
>
> • Wyatt Earp, James Butler (Wild Bill) Hickok and William B (Bat) Masterson were three of the legendary lawmen who kept the peace in rowdy Kansas frontier towns.
>
> • The east–west span of Kansas is so great that the sun rises and sets on the state's western border 30 minutes later than it does on the eastern end.
>
> • Dr James A Naismith, who invented the game of basketball in 1891, was the first basketball coach at the University of Kansas in Lawrence.
>
> • In 1887, the residents of Argonia elected the nation's first female mayor, Susanne Medora Salter.

Bleeding Kansas Kansas was organized as a territory in 1854 under the controversial Kansas-Nebraska Act, which allowed residents rather than Congress to determine if slavery would be permitted. New England abolitionist groups quickly sponsored "free-state" settlements such as Lawrence and Topeka, while pro-slavery Missourians poured in to settle—or merely to vote—in elections. Large-scale violence erupted, beginning with the 1856 sacking of Lawrence by "Border Ruffians" and the retaliatory slayings of five pro-slavers near Osawatomie by fanatical abolitionist John Brown and his followers. The territory was deemed "Bleeding Kansas" in its wake.

Slavery never established a stronghold, and Kansas entered the Union as a free state on January 29, 1861. After the Civil War erupted later that year, Kansas provided, and lost, a proportionally higher number of soldiers than any other Union state. The only formal battle fought on Kansas soil occurred at Mine Creek; nonetheless, the populace suffered murderous Confederate guerrilla attacks, the worst one costing 150 citizens their lives in the 1863 raid on Lawrence by William Clarke Quantrill and his 300 "bushwhackers."

Where Buffalo Roamed Under the Homestead Act of 1862, 160 acres of land awaited anyone with $10 and the wherewithal to get to Kansas. The railroads, having also received generous federal land grants, laid track further westward, and towns sprouted like Kansas sunflowers along the new routes. Between 1850 and 1874, nearly 20 million buffalo were wantonly slaughtered for their meat, their hides, or simply the sport of it. The Comanche, Apache, Arapaho, and Cheyenne did not sit by peaceably while their hunting territory and primary source of food disappeared, and the military waged full-scale warfare against them, with atrocities committed by both sides. By 1880, Native Americans and their buffalo had disappeared from the High Plains of western Kansas.

The next assault on the prairie began in 1867 as Longhorn cattle drives from Texas moved up the Chisolm Trail to railroad shipping points in Kansas. First Abilene, then Newton, Wichita, and finally the quintessential Wild West town of Dodge City catered to rowdy cowboys fresh off the cattle drives, with mythic lawmen like Wyatt Earp and Bat Masterson barely keeping the peace.

Swedes, Mennonites, Amish, and other immigrants of the late 1800s brought a more positive influence to Kansas. Irrigation projects and the hardy winter wheat introduced by Mennonites rendered cultivation of the western plains possible. Freed slaves from the South started new lives in Nicodemus and Dunlap. In the late 1880s, however, droughts, blizzards, and plummeting wheat prices drove many Kansans off their homesteads to the refrain "In God we trusted, in Kansas we busted."

The Nation's Breadbasket Between 1900 and 1912, Kansas spearheaded sweeping political change, giving women the vote, creating election primaries, and, to less acclaim, ushering in Prohibition. Discoveries of coal, petroleum, and natural gas spawned a prosperous mining industry. World War I increased the demand for wheat, and with improved farming techniques Kansas eventually became a world leader in grain production. Kansas was dealt crushing blows, however, first by the Great Depression, then by devastating droughts and blinding dust storms that swept across the Great Plains in the mid-1930s.

World War II pulled Kansas out of a slow and difficult recovery, giving a tremendous boost to agriculture and the infant aircraft industry. Native son Dwight D Eisenhower served as supreme commander of Allied forces in Europe and, from 1953 to 1961, as the 34th president of the United States. Today most Kansans earn their livelihood in manufacturing and service jobs, but croplands and pastures still constitute most of the face, and heart, of Kansas.

A Closer Look

GEOGRAPHY

The plains of **eastern Kansas,** contrary to popular misconception, have been eroded into river bluffs and wide, undulating valleys, much of it stitched into quadrangles of cropland and dotted with pockets of trees. Though dwarfed by its fraternal twin across the Missouri border, **Kansas City** is an important manufacturing, rail, and financial center. **Lawrence,** with its historic downtown and picturesque university campuses, manages small-town charm and cultural sophistication. Industrialized **Topeka,** the state capital, is still a thriving railroad town.

The rolling limestone ridges of the **Flint Hills** abut the west edge of the eastern plains. These treeless hills, the largest remaining segment of true prairie in the country, are carpeted with tall bluestem prairie grasses and embroidered with wildflowers in the spring and fall. They provide high-quality grazing land for Kansas cattle and a large population

---

DRIVING DISTANCES

Wichita

54 miles SE of Hutchinson
94 miles S of Abilene
136 miles SW of Topeka
154 miles E of Dodge City
156 miles N of Oklahoma City, OK

Topeka

61 miles SW of Leavenworth
62 miles W of Kansas City
65 miles E of Junction City
136 miles NE of Wichita
272 miles NE of Dodge City

Dodge City

62 miles SW of Larned
89 miles SE of Scott City
105 miles SW of Hays
154 miles W of Wichita
272 miles SW of Topeka

---

of wild prairie chickens.

The gentle sandstone and limestone folds of the Smoky Hills region of **north-central Kansas** are punctuated by rocky outcroppings and occasional oddities, like Mushroom Rock State Park's huge sandstone boulders balanced on slender pedestals. No less surprising are hundreds of miles of stone fenceposts marching across Lincoln County, demonstrating the versatility of limestone in a land with no timber. A small monument near **Lebanon** marks the geographic center of the contiguous 48 states.

The prairie sinks into the flat Arkansas River lowlands of **south-central Kansas,** where the Cheyenne Bottoms and Quivira marshes host small nations of migrating waterfowl. In the Red Hills region near the southern border, stretches of flat farmland are interrupted by red buttes and mesas of the Gypsum Hills and rugged river-carved gorges of the Cimmaron Break. **Wichita,** world leader in the production of executive aircraft, is graced with parks, museums, and a lively arts scene. **Hutchinson's** massive grain elevator testifies to the continuing importance of wheat in the region.

On the High Plains of **western Kansas,** the prairie stretches out its wrinkles in a smooth, shallow tilt upward toward the foothills of the Rockies. Where rapidly diminishing groundwater is tapped for irrigation, fields of wheat ripple in the ever-present breeze. Elsewhere, the smooth expanses of buffalo grass and tumbleweeds conform to the celluloid image of the Old West. The tall, wind-sculpted forms of the Chalk Pyramids in west-central Kansas make a stunning statement about vertical nonconformity. The wagon ruts of the Santa Fe Trail are still visible on the prairie floor near **Dodge City,** which trades heavily on its raucous cowtown beginnings.

CLIMATE

For an average of 275 days a year, that huge sky topping the Kansas prairie is filled with sun. Summer days are hot, with average highs in the low 90s, although northern Kansas stays a few degrees cooler than southern Kansas. Expect to encounter high humidity with the heat in eastern Kansas. Winters are cold, sometimes harsh, with the mercury dipping well below freezing at night.

Eastern Kansas receives an average of 34 to 37 inches of precipitation a year, while only 18 to 20 inches falls in the arid west. But nothing is certain in Kansas, and a year of drought can be followed by floods. About half of the annual precipitation falls from May through August.

Ever since Dorothy and Toto's little adventure, Kansas has been closely associated with tornadoes; half the annual allotment of twisters blows through during May and June. But the weather can hold other suprises, too, such as hailstorms, thunderstorms, and blizzards that counter the pleasant monotony of all those sunny days.

WHAT TO PACK

If you plan to visit in summer —the height of the touring season despite the hot temperatures—bring lightweight, comfortable clothing. Casual dress is the norm. Autumn is shirtsleeve weather, warm and pleasant, although you'd be wise to pack a jacket for the evenings.

Whatever the season, bring along high-quality sunglasses, a hat with a brim or visor, and good suntan lotion. A pair of sturdy, comfortable walking shoes is also a necessity, whether you're exploring museums or trail-hopping.

AVG HIGH/LOW TEMPS (°F)

	Wichita	Topeka
Jan	39/19	42/20
Feb	44/23	47/23
Mar	54/31	54/29
Apr	66/43	66/41
May	75/53	76/52
June	85/63	87/62
July	91/68	93/67
Aug	89/66	92/67
Sept	81/57	83/58
Oct	71/45	71/46
Nov	54/31	55/30
Dec	43/22	46/24

TOURIST INFORMATION

For helpful vacation planning information, see the *Kansas Travel Guide,* calendar of events, and state transportation map, all free from the **Travel & Tourism Development Division,** Kansas Department of Commerce & Housing, 700 SW Harrison St., Suite 1300, Topeka 66603 (tel 800/252-6727). Many local visitors bureaus and chambers of commerce will send more detailed information about their area; you'll find them listed throughout the *Kansas Travel Guide.* The Infomation Network of Kansas maintains a Web page (http://www.state.ks.us) with general information about the state.

DRIVING RULES AND REGULATIONS

You must be at least 16 years old to drive in Kansas. Driver and front-seat passengers must buckle up, and you must secure children under 4 years of age in an approved child safety seat. Motorcyclists under 18 must wear a helmet. Auto insurance is mandatory; have proof of insurance and auto registration in the car at all times.

You can make a right turn on red after stopping unless posted otherwise. The highway patrol enforces speed limits with radar and aircraft, and radar detection devices are permitted in all vehicles. Open containers of alcohol are prohibited in the car. For statewide road conditions, call 800/585-7623.

RENTING A CAR

Most major car rental firms have at least one rental location in Kansas. The minimum age to rent ranges from 21 to 25; you may find some companies imposing an additional charge for drivers between 21 to 24.

* **Avis** (tel toll free 800/331-1212)
* **Budget** (tel 800/527-0700)
* **Dollar** (tel 800/421-6868)
* **General** (tel 800/327-7607)
* **Hertz** (tel 800/654-3131)
* **National** (tel 800/227-7368)
* **Thrifty** (tel 800/367-2277)

ESSENTIALS

Area Code: Kansas has two area codes. For northern Kansas, including Kansas City, Lawrence, Topeka and Abiliene, use **913**. Southern Kansas, including Dodge City, Wichita, and Hutchinson, uses **316.**

Emergencies: Call 911 for police, fire department, or ambulance services throughout Kansas. For highway emergencies call 913/296-3102, or *47 on cellular phones.

Liquor Laws: The minimum age for purchasing or consuming alcoholic beverages is 21, and you may be required to produce proper identification. Licensed food-serving establishments can sell liquor on Sunday. Some counties are dry, and alcohol is served only in "private clubs," most of which offer courtesy memberships for the duration of your stay.

Taxes: A 4.9% state sales tax, plus 1% to 2% local tax in most counties and cities, will be added to your purchases. An additional lodging tax, typically 4% to 6%, is levied on hotel rooms, and car rentals may be subject to an additional tax up to 3½%.

Time Zone: Most of Kansas is in the central time zone; Sherman, Wallace, Greeley, and Hamilton Counties on the western border are in the mountain time zone.

Best of the State

WHAT TO SEE AND DO

Below is a general overview of some of the top sights and attractions in Kansas. To find out more detailed information, look under "Attractions" for individual cities in the listings portion of this book.

State Parks Kansas boasts 24 state parks, most of which are located in the central and eastern parts of the state and developed around manmade lakes. They provide a multitude of recreational opportunities in a diversity of settings, from tree-dotted **Clinton** to rocky and rugged **Wilson,** or a smattering of everything at huge **El Dorado.** In the far west, **Lake Scott State Park,** with its spring-fed fishing lake, also houses the El Cuartelejo Pueblo ruins, a 1600s Taos Indian dwelling.

Natural Wonders Monument Rocks National Landmark, also called the Chalk Pyramids, is the Stonehenge of western Kansas. White ridges and monoliths, first deposited under a cretaceous sea then later carved into surreal shapes by wind and rain, tower above the High Plains. Thanks to their aqueous beginnings, even the casual hiker may be fortunate enough to stumble across a shark's tooth or other fossilized remains of ancient sea creatures.

The Wild West Kansas's famed frontier forts are far more appealing than the rickety wooden stock-ades depicted in Hollywood westerns. At fully restored **Fort Scott National Historic Site,** home to the famed dragoons, a combined cavalry and infantry from the Mexican War period, costumed troops and guides re-create mid-1800s military life. **Fort Larned National Historic Site,** an important Santa Fe Trail outpost, has 10 handsome sandstone buildings originally used from 1860 to 1878 as barracks, officers' quarters, storehouse, blockhouse, shop and commissaries. Four original structures still stand at **Fort Hays State Historic Site,** including the late 1860s stone blockhouse. **Fort Leavenworth National Historic Site,** oldest military post in continuous operation west of the Mississippi, and **Fort Riley,** former home of the US Cavalry and the African-American Buffalo Soldiers, are both active military reservations with top-notch military museums and several original structures that will appeal to history buffs.

The rough-and-tumble Kansas cowtowns of western lore have been restored or re-created, complete with stagecoach rides and staged shootouts. The two-block reproduction of **Historic Front Street,** lifted from the pages of Dodge City's 1870s heydays, includes celebrated landmarks Boot Hill Cemetery, Long Branch Saloon, and Miss Kitty. **Old Abilene,** the granddaddy of the cowtowns, and Wichita's **Old Cowtown Museum,** an open-air living history museum, include several original structures from their rambunctious Chisolm Trail days.

Historic Buildings Several historic buildings in Kansas are constructed in handsome native limestone, including the **State Capitol Building** in Topeka, completed in 1903 and awash in murals and statuary depicting famous Kansans; Victoria's "Cathedral of the Plains," **St Fidelis Church,** a striking example of Romanesque architecture and exquisite stained glass; and **Chase County Courthouse** in Cottonwood Falls, an ornate 1873 French renaissance creation and the oldest operating courthouse west of the Mississippi. Fairway's **Shawnee Methodist Mission,** founded in 1830 as a Native American school and mission, became a jumping-on point for the Oregon and Santa Fe Trails and, later, housed the first territorial legislature. The **Dwight D Eisenhower Boyhood Home** is preserved in Abilene near the **Meditation Chapel,** where the late president is buried.

Museums Topeka's excellent **Kansas Museum of History** traces the state's history through thousands of exhibits, including a replica of a Wichita Indian grass lodge and an authentic, restored Cyrus K Holliday steam locomotive and railcars. Several high-quality, intimate museums offer unique perspectives on Kansas or local history, including **Kaufman Museum** in Newton, which focuses on the Mennonites in Kansas, Fort Leavenworth's **Frontier Army Museum,** and the **Wichita-Sedgwick County Historical Museum** in Wichita. The **Eisenhower Presidential Library** and the **Eisenhower Museum** in Abilene house papers, memorabilia, and other materials related to Dwight D Eisenhower's life and presidency.

Dyche Museum of Natural History at the University of Kansas in Lawrence features a notable fossil collection and a panorama of North American plants and wildlife. The not-to-be-missed **Kansas Cosmosphere & Space Center** in Hutchinson, housing the largest collection of space artifacts outside the Smithsonian, displays the Mercury, Gemini, and Apollo space capsules, astronaut spacesuits, and a full-scale lunar module and rover.

The University of Kansas's **Spencer Art Museum** in Lawrence is noted for its fine collections of European art ranging from the renaissance through the baroque period, and 19th-century American paintings. The **Wichita Art Museum** features an impressive collection of American paintings and sculpture, including many works by famed "cowboy artist" Charles Marion Russell. Wichita's **Mid-America All-Indian Center Museum** exhibits traditional and contemporary artifacts and artworks from many native American cultures.

Family Favorites   Along with the **Kansas Cosmosphere & Space Center** in Hutchinson, the hands-on exhibits at Wichita's **Omnisphere & Science Center,** including the hair-raising Van de Graaff generator, will appeal to kids with enquiring minds. Other kinetic experiences await at the Discovery Place in Topeka's **Kansas Museum of History,** where children can dress in clothing from different historical periods and cultures and explore other touchable artifacts, and Wichita's **Children's Museum,** featuring a crawl-though maze, prairie house, and other fun interactive exhibits. **Sedgwick County Zoo** in Wichita is an all-family treat with a full-sensory jungle including the exotic flora and fauna of the African veldt and Australian Pampas-outback. Step into the glass enclosure at **Topeka Zoo's** "Gorilla Encounter" and suddenly you're on display for the curious gorillas. Youngsters can pet the barnyard critters at **Deanne Rose Children's Farmstead** in Overland Park, a replica of an 1850s homestead complete with working windmill, Texas longhorn cattle, and buffalo, or see authentic farm life at **High View Ranch** in Alta Vista and **Philip Ranch** in Hays.

EVENTS AND FESTIVALS

- **River Festival,** Wichita downtown along Kansas River. Mid-May. Call 800/288-9424.
- **Good Ole' Days,** Fort Scott downtown. Street fair celebrating area's 19th-century history. First weekend in June. Call 800/245-3678.
- **Beef Empire Days,** Garden City, at Finney County Fairgrounds. Beef judging and tasting, rodeo, western art show, cowboy poets. First weekend through second weekend in June. Call 316/275-6807.
- **Wah-Shun-Gah Days,** Council Grove. Indian powwow, parade, carnival, crafts, and historical demonstrations. Second weekend in June. Call 316/767-5413.
- **Midsummer's Day Festival,** Lindsborg, at Swensson Park. Traditional Swedish folk celebration. Third Saturday in June. Call 913/227-3706.
- **Sundown Salute,** Junction City. Kansas's largest Independence Day celebration. July 4th weekend. Call 800/528-2489.
- **Dodge City Days and Roundup Rodeo,** Dodge City. Parades, street dancing, concerts, cowboy poets, barbecue contest, and rodeo. Last weekend in July and first week in August. Call 316/225-8186 or 316/225-2244 (rodeo information only).
- **Railroad Days Festival,** Topeka, at Forbes Field. Labor Day weekend. Call 913/232-5533.
- **Kansas State Fair,** Hutchinson, at State Fairgrounds. Mid-September. Call 316/669-3600.
- **Walnut Valley Festival,** Winfield, at Cowley County Fairgrounds. Top acoustic music festival, national guitar picking championships. Third weekend in September. Call 316/221-3250.
- **Indian Art Show,** Market and Pow Wow, Lawrence. Second weekend in September through third weekend in October. Call 913/864-4245.
- **Apple Days,** Topeka, at Ward-Meade Park. Apple harvest festival on grounds of Victorian mansion. First Sunday in October. Call 913/295-3888.

SPECTATOR SPORTS

Auto Racing   **Lakeside Speedway** (tel 913/299-2048) in Kansas City hosts NASCAR, late model and stock car racing. Watch professional and amateur drag racing at Topeka's **Heartland Park** (tel 800/437-2237) or **Wichita International Raceway** (tel 316/722-9965).

Baseball   You can watch the **Wichita Wranglers** (tel 316/267-3372), a farm team of the Kansas City Royals, play Class AA baseball at Lawrence-Dumont Stadium in Wichita.

Basketball   Catch the **University of Kansas Jayhawks,** 1988 NCAA Champions and consistently one of the country's top collegiate basketball teams, at Allen Fieldhouse in Lawrence (tel 913/864-3141).

Hockey   See the **Wichita Thunder** for Central Hockey League action at the Kansas Coliseum (tel 316/264-GOAL) in Wichita, November through March.

Horse & Dog Racing   The **Woodlands** (tel 913/299-9797) in Kansas City, with its unique two-track layout, offers year-round greyhound racing and summer-season horse racing. **Wichita Greyhound Park** (tel 316/755-4000) at Kansas Coliseum in Wichita features year-round dog racing and pari-mutuel wagering.

Soccer   The **Wichita Wings** (tel 316/262-3545) bring professional indoor soccer to the Kansas Coliseum in Wichita from late October through March.

ACTIVITIES A TO Z

Ballooning   For a truly uplifting experience, get a bird's-eye view of the Kansas countryside in a colorful hot air balloon. One-hour flights for two to six passengers are capped with the traditional landing ceremony and champagne toast. Vendors include Sail Away Adventures (tel 800/733-7627) in Topeka, Sky's the Limit (tel 913/681-6666) in Kansas City, and Wichita's Freeflight, Inc (tel 316/684-5264).

Bird Watching   Over 250 bird species, including egrets, pelicans, herons, and the endangered whooping crane, await the bird watcher and photographer at Quivira National Wildlife Refuge (tel 316/486-2393) or Cheyenne Bottoms Wildlife Refuge (tel 316/793-7730) near Great Bend, where almost half of all migrating North American shorebirds touch down during summer and autumn.

Boating & Watersports   Kansas has nearly 200 state reservoirs, fishing lakes, and community lakes where you can boat or splash to your heart's content. Add the steady breezes that sweep across western and central Kansas and you'll find perfect sailing and windsurfing conditions, like those at much celebrated Cheney Lake in Wichita. Most state parks have swimming beaches and boat ramps; you'll find marinas and boat rentals at several of them.

Camping   Kansas's Rent-a-Tent program takes the hard work out of camping. Arrive to a fully outfitted campsite—you bring only bedding, cookware, tableware, and food. The program is available at Cheny, Clinton, El Dorado, Pomona, Tuttle Creek and Wilson State Parks. Contact Kansas Department of Wildlife & Parks, Rte 2, Box 54A, Pratt 67124 (tel 316/672-5911). Conventional and primitive campsites are also in plentiful supply, the largest number being in eastern Kansas. Get a free *Kansas Campgrounds and RV Parks* guide from **Kansas Travel & Tourism,** KDOC & H, 700 SW Harrison, Suite 1300, Topeka 66603 (tel 800/252-6727).

Fishing   Numerous well-stocked reservoirs and fishing lakes entice anglers with catfish, walleye, bass, and crappie. Trophy flathead catfish have been taken at Pomona Reservoir, near Vassar; reservoirs in Milford, Clinton, and Perry State Parks are other popular spots. Contact the **Kansas Department of Wildlife & Parks,** 512 SE 25 Ave, Pratt 67124 (tel 316/672-5911) for regulations and license information.

Recreational Ranching   A number of working ranches cater to greenhorns questing for the authentic cowboy experience, including horse-mounted cattle herding, barnyard chores, and bunkhouse living. Contact Prairie Star Guest Ranch in Cassoday (tel 316/735-4295) or Prairie Women Adventures and Retreat (cowgirls only) near Matfield Green (tel 316/753-3465).

Trails   Trails played a central role in Kansas's early history; not surprisingly, trails also figure prominently in the state's recreational choices. A few long trails, such as 30-mile Perry Lake National Recreational Trail, offer hiking and backpacking. The Konza Prairie Nature Trail in Riley County, Dillon Nature Center Trail in Hutchinson, and other shorter trails provide glimpses of distinctive Kansan topography and ecology. Many trails are accessible for

SELECTED STATE PARKS

- **Cedar Bluff,** 36 mi SW of Hays, Box 76A, Ellis 67637 (tel 913/726-3212)
- **Cheney,** 30 mi NW of Wichita, RR 1, Box 167A, Cheney 67025 (tel 316/542-3664)
- **Clinton,** 4 mi W of Clinton, 798 N 1415 Rd, Lawrence 66049 (tel 913/842-8562)
- **Crawford,** 22 mi NE of Pittsburg, Farlington 66734 (tel 316/362-3671)
- **Eisenhower,** 8 mi SW of Lyndon, RR 2, Box 306, Osage City 66523 (tel 913/528-4102)
- **El Dorado,** 5 mi NE of El Dorado, RR 3, Box 29A, El Dorado 67042 (tel 316/321-7180)
- **Elk City,** 7 mi NW of Independence, PO Box 945, Independence 67301 (tel 316/331-6295)
- **Fall River,** 17 mi SE of Eureka, RR 1, Box 44, Toronto 66777 (tel 316/637-2213)
- **Glen Elder,** 12 mi W of Beloit, Box 162A, Glen Elder 67446 (tel 913/545-3345)
- **Kanopolis (including Mushroom Rock),** 25 mi SW of Salina, RR 1, Box 26D, Marquette 67464 (tel 913/546-2565)
- **Lovewell,** 15 mi NE of Mankato, RR 1, Box 66A, Webber 66970 (tel 913/753-4971)
- **Meade,** 12 mi SW of Meade, Box K, Meade 67864 (tel 316/873-2572)
- **Milford,** 6 mi NW of Junction City, 8811 State Park Rd, Milford 66514 (tel 913/238-3014)
- **Perry,** 15 mi NE of Topeka, RR 1, Box 464A, Ozawkie 66070 (tel 913/246-3449)
- **Pomona,** 8 mi NE of Lyndon, RR 1, Box 118, Vassar 66543 (tel 913/828-4933)
- **Prairie Dog,** 6 mi SW of Norton, Box 431, Norton 67654 (tel 913/877-2953)
- **Scott,** 8 mi N of Scott City, RR 1, Box 50, Scott City 67871 (tel 316/872-2061)
- **Toronto,** 15 mi SW of Yates Center, RR 1, Box 44, Toronto 66777 (tel 316/637-2213)
- **Tuttle Creek,** 5 mi N of Manhattan, 5020-B Tuttle Creek Blvd, Manhattan 66502 (tel 913/539-7941)
- **Webster,** 8 mi W of Stockton, RR 2, Box 153, Stockton 67669 (tel 913/425-6775)
- **Wilson,** 5 mi N of Wilson exit off I-70, RR 1, Box 181, Sylvan Grove 67481 (tel 913/658-2465)

those with disabilities, and some double as bridal or mountain bike trails. Contact Kansas Travel & Tourism, KDOC & H, 700 SW Harrison, Suite 1300, Topeka 66603 (tel 800/2-KANSAS) and ask for the brochure *Hitting the Trails in Kansas.*

Wagon Train Trips   For an authentic pioneer experience, pack the family into a covered wagon for an overnight weekend junket across the rolling Flint Hills, complete with hearty meals around the campfire. The excursion, offered by Flint Hills Overland Wagon Train (tel 316/321-6300), departs from Cassody near El Dorado.

KANSAS INTERSTATE 70

Start	Lawrence
Finish	Hays
Distance	325 miles
Time	3–4 days
Highlights	Rolling farmland, prairie, and cattle grasslands; traces of the Santa Fe, Oregon, and Chisolm Trails; frontier military forts; the boyhood home and museum of Dwight D Eisenhower; a myriad of unique museums; farming communities, ethnic settlements, and small college towns

Interstate 70, a major US east–west highway, runs straight like an arrow through the heart of Kansas for approximately 400 miles. Unfortunately, the interstate is all many travelers ever see as they race through on their way to someplace else. But there's a treasure trove of small towns and attractions just off the highway—and, contrary to popular opinion, Kansas is not flat. It does, however, boast wide-open spaces, and a lot of it is downright beautiful. This tour takes in some of the best scenery, attractions, and towns the state has to offer, beginning with the tree-covered rolling hills of eastern Kansas and traveling westward along I-70 to small towns near the interstate that offer glimpses of the Wild West and pioneer life on the plains, and simple, old-fashioned pleasures.

For additional information on lodgings, restaurants, and attractions covered in this tour, refer to specific cities in the listings portion of this book.

Approximately 37 miles east of Kansas City, take the east exit (exit 204) off the I-70 turnpike to:

1. **Lawrence,** a college town that is probably the hippest community in the state. Its downtown, which spreads along four, tree-shaded blocks on Massachusetts St, is among the liveliest in the Midwest, with 19th-century brick storefronts and specialty shops ranging from art galleries and gift boutiques to clothing stores and antiques shops. A changing outdoor sculpture exhibition along the main street features the works of national artists, while several outdoor cafes and beer gardens add to the town's laid-back atmosphere. Attracting shoppers from throughout the region, Lawrence is especially popular for its two factory outlet centers, the Lawrence Riverfront Plaza, located just off Massachusetts St overlooking the Kansas River, and

Tanger Factory Outlet Center, just off the 104 east turnpike exit. Two downtown antiques malls house more than 100 dealers—the Antique Mall, 830 Massachusetts St, and Quantrill's Flea Market, around the corner at 811 New Hampshire St.

Founded in the mid 1850s by abolitionists, Lawrence is situated on the historic Oregon Trail. In 1863 the city endured the terrible raid of William Quantrill and his band of pro-slavery supporters, who killed 150 men and sacked and burned most of the businesses and homes—an incident that looms large in Lawrence's history. Today Lawrence is home to both Haskell Indian Nations University, founded more than a century ago and now serving students from more than 160 tribes from 35 states, and the University of Kansas, prettily situated atop a hill in the center of town. The history of Lawrence, including Quantrill's raid and Dr James Naismith's 40 years in Lawrence (Naismith, inventor of basketball, served as KU's first coach), is the focus of the **Watkins Community Museum of History,** 1047 Massachusetts St. Another fascinating museum, especially for children, is the **KU Natural History Museum** in Dyche Hall, located on Jayhawk Blvd on the KU campus. It features a huge panorama of North American plants and animals as well as the stuffed hide of Comanche, sole survivor of the Seventh Cavalry in the Battle of Little Bighorn. Nearby on Mississippi St is the **Spencer Museum of Art,** which houses one of the most comprehensive university art collections in the United States; especially noteworthy are its 17th- and 18th-century European art and 19th-century American paintings, with works by Rossetti, Fragonard, Homer, and Benton.

The historic **Eldridge Hotel** (tel 913/749-5011 or 800/527-0909), first built in 1855 and burned to the ground twice by pro-slavery forces, is a fine choice for an overnight stay in the heart of downtown Lawrence. The impressive brick hotel at 7th and Massachusetts Sts offers 48 two-room suites at moderate to expensive prices, a restaurant, and a bar, all decorated in turn-of-the century elegance.

From Lawrence, it's a 22-mile drive farther west on I-70 to:

2. **Topeka,** the state capital. Take I-70 through town to Wannamaker Rd at exit 356, where you'll find the **Kansas Museum of History,** 6425 SW 6th St, which does an excellent job in telling the story of Kansas from prehistoric times through the 1980s.

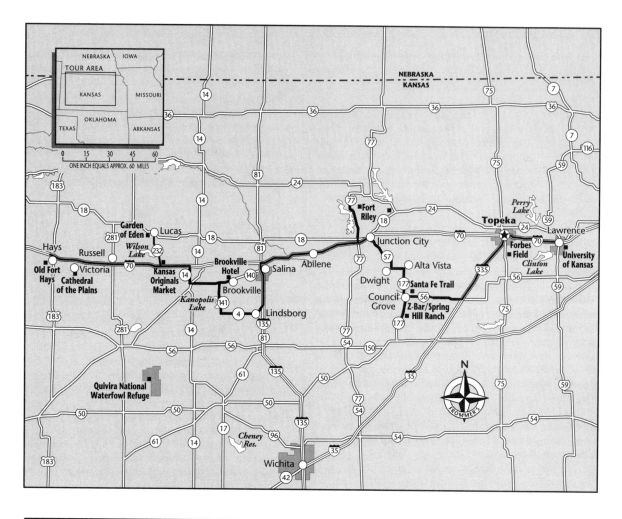

Take a Break

A local favorite, especially with KU students, is the **Free State Brewing Company,** a micro-brewery located in the city's former bus depot at 636 Massachusetts St (tel 913/843-4555). Available are thirst-quenching wheat beer, sandwiches, and hearty main fare ranging from seafood to pasta, with most prices between $4.50 and $8. **Paradise Cafe,** 728 Massachusetts St (tel 913/842-5199), is Lawrence's most popular breakfast spot and is also great for sandwiches, enchiladas, and seafood; most dinners average $10 to $15. For more upscale dining, **Teller's,** 746 Massachusetts (tel 913/843-4111), is a smartly decorated American/Italian restaurant occupying a one-time bank building dating from 1877. It offers pasta and pizza for less than $12 and entrees of veal and chicken for less than $17.

From the museum, take US 75 south about 20 minutes to Forbes Field, which closed as a military airport in 1976 but continues to house the unique **Combat Air Museum** in hangars 602 and 604. It displays more than 30 military aircraft dating from 1918.

Backtrack north on US 75 to reach Kansas Turnpike 335 (a toll road), take it 30 miles south, and then exit onto US 56 W, a scenic two-lane blacktop that roughly parallels—and at times even covers—the tracks of the old Santa Fe Trail. Farms gradually give way to the Flint Hills, one of the country's largest tall-grass prairies and premier pasture land. With its 500 million acres and wide-open spaces, this region probably best fits most people's image of Kansas.

After 24 miles, US 56 leads directly to the heart of:

3. Council Grove, which once served as a major stop

on the Santa Fe Trail, the commercial trading route that linked Independence, Missouri with Santa Fe. As you drive into town on Main St you'll pass Council Oak on the right. There, on August 10, 1825, a treaty was signed between US commissioners and Osage Indians granting Americans and Mexicans free passage through the parts of the Santa Fe Trail that ran through Indian territory in return for $800. Council Grove derives its name from this historic meeting. Other historic sites include the **Last Chance Store** on Main St, the last opportunity for traders on their way to Santa Fe to stock up on supplies, and the **Kaw Mission State Historic Site/Museum** on Mission St, built in the 1850s to serve as a boarding school for Kaw boys. Council Grove's two-block downtown is dominated by the handsome **Farmers and Drovers Bank,** built in 1892 and still in operation.

Take a Break

One of the most historic restaurants in Kansas is the **Hays House,** 112 W Main St (tel 316/767-5911). Opened in 1857, it claims to be the oldest continuously operating restaurant west of the Mississippi; the eatery's founder was Seth Hays, Daniel Boone's great-grandson and Council Grove's first official resident. Vacuum-packed steaks aged 28 days are the specialty, but diners can also enjoy ham, catfish, fried chicken, brisket, and pork chops, all served with side dishes and all priced at less than $14. For lunch, the brisket sandwich is a treat.

A good place for an overnight stay in town is the **Cottage House,** 25 N Neosho St (tel 316/767-6828 or 800/727-7903), a preserved Victorian hotel complete with antiques, gazebo-style porches, and clawfoot tubs. Rates are moderate.

If you're interested in exploring the surrounding Flint Hills, head 15 miles south of Council Grove on KS 177 to:

4. **Z-Bar/Spring Hill Ranch,** a 114-year-old working cattle ranch open free to the public daily from sunrise to sunset. A 1½-mile-loop hiking trail, an old schoolhouse in use until 1930, an enormous barn, a limestone mansion, and more than 10,000 acres of tall-grass prairie are among the highlights here.

Back in Council Grove, head north on KS 177 13 miles to KS 57 and continue north on this scenic two-lane road, which curves through more farmland and cattle ranches, until you reach I-70. Go west to the next exit (exit 301) and then follow the signs north for:

5. **Fort Riley,** founded in the early 1850s to protect settlers from Native American attack and, by virtue of its strategic location between the Santa Fe and Oregon Trails, to protect travelers on the overland trails. Once the home of the US Cavalry for nearly a century, it is now the base for the Army's First Infantry Division. General Custer and his 7th Cavalry were based here, and the 9th and 10th regiments, all-black troops popularly known as the Buffalo Soldiers, formed here in 1866. The **US Cavalry Museum,** Building 205 on Custer Ave, provides a fascinating overview of the many wars both soldier and horse participated in since 1776.

Just down the street is the **Custer House,** the only surviving officers' quarters from the fort's early history (though the General himself didn't live in them). Guided tours (summer only) provide insight into fort life during the frontier period.

Continue west on I-70 another 27 miles to:

6. **Abilene,** taking exit 275 and heading south on Buckeye Ave (KS 15), Abilene's main thoroughfare and gateway to its major attractions. The visitors bureau is located just off Buckeye, at 201 NW 2nd St, and occupies the town's former depot. More than 100 years ago, Abilene was the epitome of the Wild West: home to cowboys, the largest stockyards west of Kansas City, and lawmen like Wild Bill Hickok. Between 1867 and 1872 more than three million head of cattle were driven up the Chisolm Trail from Texas to Abilene, where they were then shipped out by rail to stockyards in Kansas City and beyond. Although the end of the cattle drives meant the end of an era, Abilene has a more recent claim to fame as the hometown of Dwight D Eisenhower, the 34th president. The **Eisenhower Center,** S Buckeye Ave and SE 4th St, is a five-building complex comprising the Dwight D Eisenhower Library, the Eisenhower Museum, a visitor's center showing films of Eisenhower's life, the Place of Meditation (the gravesite of Dwight and Mamie Eisenhower), and Eisenhower's boyhood home.

You may never have given much thought to the world's fastest dogs, but a walk through the **Greyhound Hall of Fame,** across from the Eisenhower Center at 207 S Buckeye Ave, may change that. It depicts the history of the breed from its Greek origins to the present, and a resident greyhound is always on hand to greet visitors.

Two other Abilene attractions worth considering are **Seelye Mansion,** 1105 N Buckeye, a 25-room Georgian mansion built in 1905 by an entrepreneur who made a fortune selling patent medicines, and open to the public for two daily tours at 10am and 2pm (on Sunday at 2pm only); and the **Abilene & Smoky Valley Railroad,,** just south of the Greyhound Hall of Fame, which offers a 10-mile journey aboard a 100-year-old wooden coach or open-air coach, pulled by a 1945 engine.

For an overnight stay with a personal touch, you might try **Victorian Reflections,** 820 NW 3rd St in Abilene (tel 913/263-7774), a bed-and-breakfast in a turn-of-the-century home owned by a friendly couple.

Take a Break

The **Kirby House,** 205 NE 3rd St (tel 913/263-7336), is a large Victorian home built in 1885 now offering 10 rooms for public and private dining. Probably Abilene's most well-known restaurant, it specializes in steaks for dinner but also serves seafood, breaded pork tenderloin, and fried chicken, with dinner entrees ranging from $9 to $17.

From Abilene, continue west on I-70 approximately 24 miles to Salina, where you should then take I-135 south in the direction of Wichita. After another 20 miles or so you'll see KS 4 going west to:

7. **Lindsborg,** one of Kansas's most unique ethnic towns and certainly one of its most charming. Founded in 1869 by a group of Swedish immigrants who were pioneers of cooperative farming, Lindsborg is a small and peaceful village of some 3,200 residents, with brick streets, white clapboard homes (most of which have a painted Dala horse of welcome outside the door), and a two-block downtown filled with shops selling Swedish imports, Christmas decorations, and original arts and crafts. The **Birger Sandzén Memorial Gallery,** located on the Bethany College campus at 401 N 1st St, features amazing works by Birger Sandzén, a graphic artist and painter who came to Lindsborg from Sweden at the age of 23 to teach at Bethany College and ended up staying the rest of his life. He is best known for his impressionist landscapes of Kansas, Colorado, and the Southwest.

The **McPherson County Old Mill Museum & Park,** 120 Mill St, is a museum complex of 11 buildings housing more than 22,000 items, most of them relating to the history of the area. The most important building is the **1898 Smoky Valley Roller Mill,** one of the few fully operational roller mills left on the prairie. More historic buildings are across the street, including the Swedish Pavilion,

constructed in Sweden for its exhibit in the 1904 World's Fair in St Louis and then donated to Bethany College. And last but not least, there's the **REO Auto Museum,** located on the east end of Lincoln Street in a 1930s gas station complete with antique hand-operated gas pumps. There are probably more REOs on display here than anywhere else in the country.

For a touch of Swedish hospitality in Lindsborg, the inexpensive **Swedish Country Inn,** 112 W Lincoln (tel 913/227-2985), features authentic Swedish pine furniture, imported lace curtains, handmade quilts, tandem bicycles, a sauna, and great Scandinavian buffet breakfasts.

Take a Break

The **Swedish Crown,** located downtown at 121 N Main (tel 913/227-2076) is a family restaurant offering American and Swedish cuisine, including Swedish meatballs, Swedish hamloaves, baked cod, and steaks, with dinner entrees costing less than $13. For lunch there are open-face Scandinavian sandwiches and Swedish specialties, as well as burgers and American-style sandwiches. (Lindsborg, by the way, is "dry," which means there are no liquor stores, public bars, or restaurants that serve alcoholic drinks.) Approximately 35 miles outside Lindsborg on KS 140 (see below for information on getting there) in the tiny community of Brookville is the **Brookville Hotel** (tel 913/225-666), one of the best family restaurants in all of Kansas. Originating as a hotel in the 1870s, it began serving chicken dinners in 1915, and today that's all it serves, together with an astounding array of side dishes. Meals are $10.75 per adult and $5.95 per child. You can ask for second helpings, and dining rooms have been kept pretty much like they were a century ago.

Depart Lindsborg by driving south on Main St to KS 4 W, which you should follow for 16 miles to KS 141. Head north on KS 141, passing Kanapolis Lake, bare, windswept hills, and tree-filled ravines along the way. After 14 miles you'll come to KS 140 (another 6 miles to the right is the Brookville Hotel (see above)). Turn left and go west 14 miles and then north 7 miles on KS 14, which brings you back to I-70. Head west, driving through what is known as "Post Rock Country," a reference to the many limestone rocks once used as fence posts on the treeless grasslands and still visible on some of the fences along this stretch of the highway. After approximately 15 minutes, take exit 206 to KS 232 north. Immediately to your right you'll see:

8. **Kansas Originals Market,** a large store offering crafts, folk art, and Kansas products from more than 500 artists around the state, including wheat weavings, corn-husk dolls, pottery, wood carvings, T-shirts, quilts, foodstuffs, and of course, lots of items imprinted with sunflowers, Kansas's official flower.

   Continue north on KS 232, which passes by eroded limestone bluffs and hills, a landscape completely different than one you've encountered so far. The road skirts Lake Wilson, and after 16 miles will deliver you to KS 18 and Lucas, where you'll find one of Kansas's most bizarre attractions, the:

9. **Garden of Eden,** Kansas and 2nd Sts, the ultimate in folk-art kitsch. The year was 1907 when S P Dinsmoor, a 64-year-old retired farmer and school teacher, began fashioning concrete and limestone into sculptures. He eventually filled his small yard with a wild and tangled display of animals and figures. Dinsmoor died in 1932 at the age of 89 but hasn't yet left the premises—at his request, he was interred in a mausoleum that he had built in the back yard, and he's now visible behind glass. Winter hours are irregular so call beforehand (tel 913/525-6395).

   Return to I-70 the way you came and continue west, passing Russell, home of politician Bob Dole and the **Oil Patch Museum,** which is followed by fields of oil drills. After 38 miles on I-70, take exit 168 for Victoria, where you'll find the unexpectedly grand:

10. **St Fidelis Church,** popularly known as the Cathedral of the Plains. Completed in 1911 and constructed of native limestone by German-Volga settlers, it looms large on the Kansas prairie, looking slightly out of place with its Romanesque facade and 141-foot twin towers. The colorful interior is even more impressive, boasting a Gothic ceiling, stained-glass windows, a magnificent altar, and carved reliefs of the crucifixion.

    From here it's just another 10 miles west on I-70 to:

11. **Hays,** where you should take the first exit. Visible from I-70 is one of its star attractions, the dome-shaped **Sternberg Museum of Natural History,** just off 27th and Canterbury Sts, which does an imaginative job displaying fossils, animal and plant life, and exhibits on the history of the Great Plains region. Some of the most exciting exhibits for kids are the life-size dinosaur models hooked to motion sensors, which allow them to react to both the humans in their midst and each other.

    Old Fort Hays, located on the southwest edge of town on Bypass 183, was established in 1867 to provide protection to Union Pacific railway workers, as well as stage coaches, wagon trains, and settlers. At its peak, it boasted 565 men, among them such notables as George Custer, Phil Sheridan, Buffalo Bill Cody, and Wild Bill Hickok. It was abandoned in 1889 when the relocation of Native Americans to reservations was completed. Today, there are four buildings on the site—two officer's quarters, a stone blockhouse, and guardhouse. Weirdly enough, the fort is now surrounded by a golf course, while across the street resides a small buffalo herd.

Kansas Listings

Abilene

Abilene was established in 1857 and, with the arrival of the railroad, became a thriving cattle town at the end of the Chisholm Trail. This "City of the Plains" is home to many antiques shops, craft stores, and quaint bed-and-breakfast establishments. **Information:** Abilene Convention & Visitors Bureau, 201 NW 2nd, PO Box 146, Abilene, 67410 (tel 913/263-2231 or toll free 800/569-5915).

MOTELS

Best Western Inn
2210 N Buckeye, 67410; tel 913/263-2800 or toll free 800/701-1000; fax 913/263-3285. ½ mi S of exit 275 off I-70. Standard motel with a newly painted light blue exterior. Extremely spacious guest rooms are great for families. **Rooms:** 80 rms and stes. CI open/CO noon. Nonsmoking rms avail. **Amenities:** A/C, cable TV w/movies. Some rooms have dataports. **Services:** Facilities: 40 1 restaurant. **Rates:** $38–$42 S; $42–$46 D; $62 ste. Extra person $4. Children under age 12 stay free. Parking: Outdoor, free. AE, CB, DC, DISC, MC, V.

Diamond Motel
1407 NW 3rd, 67410; tel 913/263-2360. This doesn't look very appealing from the outside (it's a little tacky), but it has a rather attractive, new Victorian decor on the inside. Previously an apartment building, it could use some renovation, but it's suitable for budget travelers. **Rooms:** 30 rms. CI open/CO noon. Nonsmoking rms avail. **Amenities:** A/C, cable TV, refrig. **Services:** Facilities: Rates: $20–$28 S. Extra person $4. Children under age 6 stay free. Parking: Outdoor, free. Prices depend on how recently rooms were redecorated. MC, V.

RESTAURANTS

Green Acres Restaurant & Lounge
I-70 and KS 15; tel 913/263-1001. Exit 275 off I-70. **Burgers/Cafe.** Standard diner housed in a you-can't-miss-it pink brick building. **FYI:** Reservations not accepted. Children's menu. **Open:** Daily 6am–10pm. **Prices:** Main courses $4–$8. AE, MC, V.

Kirby House
205 NE 3rd; tel 913/263-7336. **Seafood/Steak.** Built in 1885 by an Abilene statesman and banker, this two-story house is the place to go for fine dining in an elegant setting. Notable features include beautiful wood floors and unique historical artifacts. Peppercorn steak and chicken Marco Polo are specialties. **FYI:** Reservations accepted. Beer and wine only. No smoking. **Open:** Lunch Mon–Sat 11am–2pm, Sun 11am–3pm; dinner daily 5–9pm. **Prices:** Main courses $9–$17. AE, DISC, MC, V.

ATTRACTIONS

Eisenhower Presidential Library
SE 4th St at Buckeye; tel 913/263-4751. Ike's boyhood home and final resting place. The 1887 house is shown with many of the original furnishings used by the President and his family. On display are changing exhibits of presidential papers and mementos of Eisenhower's military and civilian careers. Visitors center shows movie depicting the life of Eisenhower. **Open:** Daily 9am–5pm. $

Old Abilene Town and Western Museum
SE 6th and Buckeye; tel 913/263-4194. Contains original and replicated buildings from the cattle boom era. A re-created street features a restored 1874 red schoolhouse; a 100-year-old log church with antique pump organ; homesteader's cabin; Merchants' Hotel; and Wild Bill's unofficial headquarters, the Alamo Saloon. Special events include performances by can-can girls, gunfights, and stagecoach rides. **Open:** Peak (Mar–Sept) daily 8am–8pm. Reduced hours off-season. **Free**

Arkansas City

This city of parks is located at the confluence of the Arkansas and Walnut rivers in south central Kansas, just north of the Oklahoma border. Arkansas City was the starting point for the Cherokee Strip Land Rush, and a wide assortment of historic memorabilia from that era can be viewed at a local museum. **Information:** Arkansas City Convention & Visitors Bureau, 126 E Washington Ave, PO Box 795, Arkansas City, 67005-0795 (tel 316/442-0230).

HOTEL

UNRATED Best Western Hallmark Motor Inn
1617 N Summit, 67005; tel 316/442-1400 or toll free 800/ 343-7234; fax 316/442-4729. 1 mi E of US 166 on US 77. Modern-looking chain motel. **Rooms:** 47 rms. CI noon/CO 11am. Nonsmoking rms avail. **Amenities:** A/C, cable TV w/movies. **Services:** **Facilities:** **Rates (CP):** Peak (May–Sept) $41 S; $47 D. Extra person $5. Children under age 12 stay free. Lower rates off-season. Parking: Outdoor, free. AE, CB, DC, DISC, MC, V.

RESTAURANT

Daisy Mae's Cafe
511 W Madison; tel 316/442-9877. W on US 166 off US 77. **American/Cafe.** A small-town cafe offering simple country fare. **FYI:** Reservations accepted. Children's menu. No liquor license. **Open:** Tues–Sat 5am–10pm, Sun 7am–3pm. **Prices:** Main courses $4–$8. No CC.

ATTRACTIONS

Arkansas Strip Land Rush Museum
S Summit St Rd; tel 316/442-6750. On September 16, 1893, thousands of pioneers staked their claim in the area. The museum commemorates the event by displaying more than 15,000 artifacts, pictures, documents, and research materials relating to the land rush. Also on display are exhibits relating the plight of the American Indians who were displaced. **Open:** Peak (Apr–Aug) Tues–Sat 10am–5pm, Sun 1–5pm. Reduced hours off-season. **$$**

Chaplin Nature Center
Off US 166; tel 316/442-4133. 5 mi NW of downtown Arkansas City. More than 200 acres of woodlands, prairies, and streams near the Arkansas River are traversed with a series of walking trails. Facilities include a visitors center, nature library, and bookstore and gift shop. A variety of nature programs are offered. **Open:** Daily sunrise–sunset. **Free**

Atchison

Situated on bluffs overlooking the Missouri River, Atchison is the birthplace of famed aviator Amelia Earhart as well as the seat of Atchison County. Atchison State Lake to the west provides visitors a chance to enjoy camping and water activities. **Information:** Atchison Area Tourism Bureau, 200 S 10th, PO Box 126, Atchison, 66002 (tel 913/367-2427).

HOTEL

Comfort Inn
10th and Skyway, 66002; tel 913/367-7666 or toll free 800/ 221-2222; fax 913/367-7566. Beautifully landscaped, this nice hotel sits on a hill overlooking Atchison. If you're looking for that something extra, this could be it. **Rooms:** 36

rms. CI 2pm/CO 11am. Nonsmoking rms avail. **Amenities:** A/C, cable TV w/movies. **Services:** **Facilities:** 1 bar. **Rates (CP):** $47 S; $60 D. Extra person $4. Children under age 18 stay free. Parking: Outdoor, free. AE, DC, DISC, MC, V.

MOTEL

Atchison Motor Inn
Jct US 73/US 59, 66002; tel 913/367-7000. For a nice place at a good price, this budget motel with rooms slightly better than average is the best choice in town. Popular with families. **Rooms:** 42 rms. CI 2pm/CO 11am. No smoking. **Amenities:** A/C, cable TV. **Services:** **Rates:** $34–$36 S; $38 D. Extra person $4. Children under age 17 stay free. Parking: Outdoor, free. AE, CB, DC, DISC, MC, V.

RESTAURANT

★ Drury Pennel House
519 N 5th St; tel 913/367-4996. 1 mi E of US 59. **American.** Located in a two-story 1876 house included in the National Register of Historic Places. A romantic spot for good American cuisine. **FYI:** Reservations recommended. **Open:** Lunch Wed–Fri 11:30am–1pm; dinner Fri–Sat 5:30–7:30pm. **Prices:** Main courses $7–$16. MC, V.

ATTRACTIONS

Amelia Earhart Birthplace
223 N Terrace; tel 913/367-4217. Built in 1852, this house overlooking the Missouri River was the scene of Amelia Earhart's birth on July 24, 1897. The nine rooms on view feature the famous pilot's childhood and family belongings. **Open:** Apr–Oct, Mon–Fri 9am–4pm, Sat–Sun 1–4pm. **$**

Atchison Rail Museum
200 S 10th; tel toll free 800/234-1854. Visitors tour tracks lined with historical train cars. Leading the display is the #811, a 1902 steam engine; also featured are one of the first all-stainless-steel 40-foot box cars, baggage cars, tack car, merchandise car, and passenger cars. Museum car contains artifacts. **Open:** May–Oct, Sat 10am–4pm, Sun noon–4pm. **Free**

Beloit

This community in north-central Kansas on the banks of the Solomon River still boasts original brick streets from its early years. Beloit is the Mitchell County seat, and the nearby Waconda Lake area offers excellent fishing and hunting opportunities. **Information:** Beloit Area Chamber of Commerce, 123 N Mill, PO Box 582, Beloit, 67420-0582 (tel 913/ 738-2717).

MOTEL 🛏

≣≣ Mainliner Inn

US 24 E, 67420; tel 913/738-3531 or toll free 800/
749-8514. Jct KS 9/KS 14. This family-oriented, highway
motel sits across the street from a Dairy Queen. The inexpensive suite is a great value. **Rooms:** 26 rms and stes. CI 11/CO
2pm. Nonsmoking rms avail. Two newer buildings have the
better rooms with more amenities. **Amenities:** 🛏 ☖ A/C,
cable TV w/movies. 1 unit w/whirlpool. Older rooms lack
fans, heating lamps, and radios. **Services:** ⤵ ◁⫷ **Facilities:** 1
restaurant (lunch and dinner only). **Rates:** $40 S; $45 D; $55
ste. Extra person $5. Children under age 11 stay free.
Parking: Outdoor, free. CB, MC, V.

Chanute

See also Iola

Bounded on the north and east sides by the Neosho River,
Chanute is the agricultural trade center for the area. Santa Fe
Park on the south edge of town provides shoreline fishing
and recreation. **Information:** Chanute Area Chamber of
Commerce, 21 N Lincoln Ave, PO Box 747, Chanute,
66720-0747 (tel 316/431-3350).

MOTEL 🛏

≣≣ Holiday Park

3030 S Santa Fe, 66720; tel 316/431-0850 or toll free 800/
842-9910; fax 316/431-6639. 35th St exit off US 169. Basic
motel with typical rooms. **Rooms:** 60 rms and stes. CI 3pm/
CO 11am. Nonsmoking rms avail. **Amenities:** 🛏 A/C, cable
TV. **Services:** ⤵ ◁⫷ **Facilities:** 🛱 ⛾100⛿ ☖ 1 restaurant, 1 bar,
playground. **Rates:** $41 S or D; $60 ste. Extra person $5.
Children under age 12 stay free. Parking: Outdoor, free. AE,
CB, DC, DISC, MC, V.

Coffeyville

Site of an 1892 raid by the dreaded Dalton Gang, the city
celebrates its heritage and this famous event with the annual
Dalton Defender Days in early October. Coffeyville also hosts
the Interstate Fair and Rodeo—the largest in southeast
Kansas—in mid-August. **Information:** Coffeyville Convention & Visitors Bureau, 807 Walnut, PO Box 457, Coffeyville,
67337-0457 (tel 316/251-1194 or toll free 800/626-3357).

HOTEL 🛏

≣≣≣ Appletree Inn

820 E 11th St, 67337; tel 316/251-0002. W end of town on
US 169. Catering to business travelers, this is the most
complete full-service hotel in town. The contemporary decor
includes dark gold colors and many mirrors on the walls and
ceiling. **Rooms:** 43 rms and stes. CI 4pm/CO 11am. Non-

smoking rms avail. Rooms have a mixture of modern and
Southwest decor. **Amenities:** 🛏 A/C, cable TV w/movies. 1
unit w/minibar, 1 w/whirlpool. **Services:** ⤵ ◁⫷ **Facilities:** 🛱
☖ Sauna, steam rm, whirlpool. **Rates (CP):** $46 S; $52 D; $65
ste. Extra person $5. Parking: Outdoor, free. AE, DISC, MC,
V.

MOTEL

UNRATED **Super 8**

104 W 11th St, 67337; tel 316/251-2250 or toll free 800/
343-7234. Guests will find personal service at this motel
featuring a contemporary decor with bright purple wall
coverings. **Rooms:** 90 rms. CI open/CO 11am. Nonsmoking
rms avail. **Amenities:** 🛏 A/C, cable TV w/movies. **Services:**
⤵ ◁⫷ **Facilities:** 🛱 ☖ **Rates:** $44 S; $48 D. Extra person $6.
Children under age 13 stay free. Parking: Outdoor, free. AE,
DISC, MC, V.

RESTAURANT 🍴

Sirloin Stockade

US 166 and US 169; tel 316/251-8156. **Burgers/Steak.**
You'll find large portions at affordable prices at this chain
steak house. Full food bar. **FYI:** Reservations not accepted.
Children's menu. No liquor license. **Open:** Mon–Sat 6am–
10pm, Sun 6am–9pm. **Prices:** Main courses $3–$12. AE, DC,
DISC, MC, V. 🖼 ☖

ATTRACTIONS 🖼

The Brown Mansion

Eldridge and Walnut; tel 316/251-0431 or toll free 800/
626-3357. Completed in 1906, the mansion features 16
fireplaces—one for each room and each with a different
design. Visitors see gas- and electric-powered chandeliers,
hand-painted canvas and wall coverings, and many of the
original furnishings of the Brown family. The main doorway
features leaded Tiffany-glass accents, and the dining room
contains a Tiffany chandelier believed to be personally hung
by the designer, Thomas Wight. **Open:** Peak (mid-May–mid-
Sept) daily 9am–5pm. Reduced hours off-season. Closed
Jan–Feb. $$

Dalton Defenders Museum

113 E 8th St; tel 316/251-1194 or toll free 800/626-3357.
The outlaw Dalton Brothers and three confederates nearly
made off with $25,000 of the town's bank money in 1892,
except for the heroism of "the Dalton Defenders." This
museum gives background on the raid and its aftermath
(including eight deaths), via memorabilia and court records.
Open: Peak (June–Aug) daily 9am–7pm. Reduced hours off-
season. $

Colby

Colby sits just north of I-70 on State Highway 25 and is the seat of Thomas County and the service center of northwest Kansas. The county courthouse, built in 1906, is a fine example of period woodwork and architecture. **Information:** Colby Convention & Visitors Bureau, 265 E 5th St, PO Box 572, Colby, 67701-9912 (tel 913/462-7643).

HOTEL 🏨

≡≡≡ Ramada Inn
1950 S Range, 67701; tel 913/462-3933 or toll free 800/272-6232. 1 block N of I-70. Recently renovated, this quality facility is relatively quiet and has very attractive grounds. A good value. **Rooms:** 117 rms. CI 2pm/CO noon. Nonsmoking rms avail. **Amenities:** 🛁 A/C, cable TV w/movies. **Services:** ✗ 🚗 🏊 ⤴ 🐾 **Facilities:** 🏋 🎱 ⛹ 1 restaurant, 1 bar. **Rates:** Peak (June–Aug) $39–$54 S; $44–$59 D. Extra person $5. Children under age 12 stay free. Lower rates off-season. Parking: Outdoor, free. AE, CB, DC, DISC, EC, ER, JCB, MC, V.

MOTELS

≡≡ Best Western Crown Motel
2320 S Range, 67701; tel 913/462-3943 or toll free 800/528-1234; fax 913/462-6127. S of exit 53 off I-70. Very nice chain motel with basic rooms and an exceptionally friendly staff. Located next to outlet mall. **Rooms:** 29 rms. CI 1pm/CO 11am. **Amenities:** 🛁 📺 A/C, satel TV w/movies. **Services:** ⤴ 🐾 **Facilities:** 🏋 **Rates:** Peak (May 15–Aug) $38–$49 S; $43–$56 D. Extra person $10. Children under age 12 stay free. Lower rates off-season. Parking: Outdoor, free. AE, CB, DC, DISC, EC, ER, JCB, MC, V.

≡≡ Super 8
1040 Zelfer Ave, 67701; tel 913/462-8248 or toll free 800/800-8000. 2 blocks N of exit 53 off I-70. Basic motel with friendly staff offering dining opportunities and economy lodgings at reasonable prices. Good for families. **Rooms:** 63 rms and stes. CI 2pm/CO noon. Nonsmoking rms avail. **Amenities:** 🛁 A/C, cable TV w/movies. Some units w/whirlpools. **Services:** ⤴ 🐾 **Facilities:** ⛹ Whirlpool, washer/dryer. **Rates (CP):** Peak (June–Sept) $37–$41 S; $43–$59 D; $52 ste. Extra person $3. Children under age 12 stay free. Lower rates off-season. Parking: Outdoor, free. AE, CB, DC, DISC, MC, V.

ATTRACTION 🏛

Prairie Museum of Art and History
1905 S Franklin; tel 913/462-6294. Encompassing a 24-acre complex. The museum houses a collection of more than 28,000 artifacts including rare bisque and china dolls; glass and crystal; Chinese and Japanese artifacts; textiles; and furniture from around the world. On the museum premises are a sod house, a restored 1930s farmstead, a one-room schoolhouse, and one of the largest barns in Kansas. **Open:** Tues–Fri 9am–5pm, Sat–Sun 1–5pm. $$

Concordia

Located in north-central Kansas, this city is the educational and commercial hub of the region. Migrating birds are attracted to the Jamestown State Waterfowl Management Area, to the city's northwest. **Information:** Concordia Area Chamber of Commerce, 606 Washington, Concordia, 66901 (tel 913/243-4290).

MOTEL 🏨

UNRATED Super 8
1320 Lincoln, 66901; tel 913/243-4200 or toll free 800/800-8000; fax 913/243-1246. On W side of US 81. A rectangular, brick building with a tiny blue lobby. Located on the south end of town, not far from downtown. A great value. **Rooms:** 44 rms. CI 3pm/CO 11am. Nonsmoking rms avail. **Amenities:** 🛁 A/C, cable TV w/movies. **Services:** ⤴ 🐾 **Facilities:** 🎱 ⛹ Sauna, whirlpool. **Rates:** $39 S; $43 D. Extra person $4. Children under age 12 stay free. Parking: Outdoor, free. AE, CB, DC, DISC, MC, V.

Dodge City

Established as a trade center for buffalo hunters and travelers heading west on the Santa Fe Trail, Dodge City was once the wildest town on the western frontier. Today's visitors can ride a trolley to historic sites, the cattle stockyards, and old Fort Dodge. Old times come alive during Dodge City Days in mid-summer. **Information:** Dodge City Convention & Visitors Bureau, 4th and Spruce, PO Box 1474, Dodge City, 67801 (tel 316/225-8186).

MOTELS 🏨

UNRATED Astro Motel
2200 W Wyatt Earp Blvd, 67801; tel 316/227-8146. On US 56. Budget property with a white brick exterior and blue metal doors. **Rooms:** 39 rms. CI 2pm/CO 11am. Nonsmoking rms avail. **Amenities:** 🛁 A/C, cable TV. **Services:** ⤴ 🐾 **Facilities:** 🏋 Pool area is unattractive and very small. **Rates:** $36 S; $40 D. Parking: Outdoor, free. AE, DISC, MC, V.

UNRATED Super 8
1708 W Wyatt Earp Blvd, 67801; tel 316/225-3924 or toll free 800/800-8000; fax 316/225-5793. On US 50. Within walking distance of Boot Hill Historic Museum and Park, this basic, budget motel has the standard Super 8 stucco and wood decor. Parking is really inconvenient. **Rooms:** 64 rms. CI open/CO 11am. Nonsmoking rms avail. **Amenities:** 🛁 ⛄ 📺 A/C, cable TV w/movies. **Services:** 🏊 ⤴ 🐾 **Facilities:** 🏋

Rates (CP): $38 S; $42 D. Extra person $5. Children under age 12 stay free. Parking: Outdoor, free. AE, CB, DC, DISC, MC, V.

ATTRACTIONS

Boot Hill Museum
Front St; tel 316/227-8188. In 1872, two cowboys had a gunfight while camping at the site, and the loser was wrapped in his blanket and buried right where he fell, boots and all, creating the legendary Boot Hill Cemetery. The bodies of many other cowboys and buffalo hunters followed soon after. Today—the old graves have been moved—the site contains a museum with audiovisual exhibits and a reconstructed Dodge City with an 1865 jail, blacksmith shop, and two blocks of historic Front Street running parallel to the Santa Fe Depot and tracks. Summer events include gunfights, medicine shows, and stagecoach rides. Open: Peak (June–Aug) daily 8am–8pm. Reduced hours off-season. $$

Dodge City, Ford & Bucklin Railroad Company
Watersports Campgrounds; tel 316/225-3232. The one-and-a-half hour railroad tour takes passengers through 16 miles of area history: buffalo; Kiowa and Camanche tribal lands; the Santa Fe Trail; cattle drives and cowboys; and the famous lawmen of Dodge City. Entertainment and dining available on board. Open: Daily 10am. $$$

Carnegie Center for the Arts
701 2nd St; tel 316/225-6388. Listed on the National Register of Historic Sites, the restored Carnegie Library building was built in the classical architectural design, an unusual style for the area. The center features varied art exhibits. Open: Feb–Dec, Tues–Fri noon–5pm, Sat 11am–3pm. Free

El Dorado

Gateway to the largest state park in Kansas, El Dorado Lake and State Park, this farm town specializes in outdoor recreation. Rides through the nearby Flint Hills aboard a prairie schooner or stagecoach are also popular. Information: El Dorado Chamber of Commerce, 383 E Central, PO Box 509, El Dorado, 67042 (tel 316/321-3150).

MOTEL

≡≡≡ Best Western Red Coach Inn
2525 W Central Ave, 67042; tel 316/321-6900 or toll free 800/362-2034; fax 316/321-6900. At jct I-35/US 54. Located close to the turnpike, this features a recently remodeled decor. Rooms: 73 rms. CI open/CO noon. Nonsmoking rms avail. Amenities: A/C, cable TV w/movies. Services: X Facilities: Games rm, washer/dryer. Rates (CP): $38–$58 S; $42–$58 D. Children under age 12 stay free. Parking: Outdoor, free. AE, DISC, MC, V.

Emporia

Founded in 1857, Emporia serves as the Lyon County seat and home to Emporia State University. Located six miles above the confluence of the Neosho and Cottonwood rivers, the city offers proximity to the Kansas Flint Hills and outdoor recreation opportunities. Information: Emporia/Lyon County Convention & Visitors Bureau, 427 Commercial, PO Box 417, Emporia, 66801-0417 (tel 316/342-1600 or toll free 800/279-3730).

HOTEL

UNRATED Holiday Inn/Holidome
2700 W 18th, 66801; tel 316/343-2200 or toll free 800/465-4329; fax 316/343-2200. Extensive renovations were expected for this standard chain property. Located across the street from a mall. Rooms: 269 rms and stes. CI 3pm/CO noon. Nonsmoking rms avail. Amenities: A/C, satel TV. 1 unit w/whirlpool. Services: X Facilities: 1 restaurant, games rm, sauna, steam rm, whirlpool, washer/dryer. Rates: $55 S or D; $73 ste. Children under age 18 stay free. Parking: Outdoor, free. AE, DISC, MC, V.

RESTAURANT

★ Lujan's Waterworks
402 Merchant St; tel 316/343-9981. Steak. This high-quality, Western-themed steak house charges by the ounce for its steaks (top sirloin is $2.25 per oz). Dinner specials include fillets stuffed with crabmeat and shrimp. FYI: Reservations recommended. Children's menu. Open: Lunch Tues–Fri 11am–2pm; dinner Tues–Sat 5–10pm. Prices: Main courses $12–$30. AE, DC, DISC, MC, V.

ATTRACTIONS

Emporia Zoo
Soden's Grove Park; tel 316/343-4265. Founded in 1934, this zoo houses 88 species of mammals, birds, and reptiles from all over the world. Whitetail deer, black swans, and bobcats are among the exhibits. Picnic facilities available. Open: Peak (June–Aug) Mon–Tues and Thurs–Sat 8am–4:30pm, Wed and Sun 8am–8pm. Reduced hours off-season. Free

Schmidt Natural History Museum
ESU Campus, Basement of Science Hall; tel 316/3443-5611. Mounted specimens of Kansas vertebrates prepared by master taxidermist Richard Schmidt. Exhibits include whooping crane, flamingos, bald and golden eagles, porcupines, and armadillos. Open: Sept–May, Mon–Sat 8am–5pm. Free

Kaw Mission Museum
500 N Mission, Council Grove; tel 316/767-5410. 20 mi NW of Emporia. An 1851 stone building where Methodist missionaries once taught Native Americans relocated from their reservation near Topeka in 1847; also one of the first area

schools for pioneer children. On display are thousands of artifacts from the early pioneer days. On premises are other government-funded stone houses of the Indian mission. **Open:** Tues–Sun 10am–5pm. **Free**

Fort Scott

This military fort just west of the Missouri border was established in 1842 and is now fully restored as a national historic site. Victorian architecture lines the town's shaded streets. **Information:** Fort Scott Area Chamber of Commerce, 231 E Wall St, PO Box 205, Fort Scott, 66701 (tel 316/223-3566).

MOTEL 🏨

≣≣≣ Best Western Fort Scott Inn

101 State St, 66701; tel 316/223-0100 or toll free 800/528-1234; fax 316/223-1746. Convenient to downtown Fort Scott, features colonial decor and better-than-average public areas and facilities. **Rooms:** 77 rms. CI 2pm/CO noon. Nonsmoking rms avail. **Amenities:** 🏨 ⚴ A/C, cable TV w/movies. **Services:** ⭐ ⌂ ⇔ **Facilities:** ⚐ 🎱 250 1 restaurant, 1 bar, whirlpool, washer/dryer. **Rates (CP):** $43 S; $47 D. Extra person $4. Children under age 12 stay free. Parking: Outdoor, free. AE, CB, DC, DISC, MC, V.

ATTRACTIONS 📷

Fort Scott National Historic Site

Old Fort Blvd; tel 316/223-0310. Commemorates Fort Scott's role in the opening of the West and the Civil War. The fort has been restored to its 1840s appearance. There are 20 historic structures, 33 historically furnished rooms, displays and exhibits, and an audiovisual program. **Open:** Daily 8am–5pm. **$**

Historic Trolley Tours

231 E Wall; tel 316/223-3566 or toll free 800/245-FORT (3678). Visitors tour historic Fort Smith on "Dolly the Trolley." The narrated tour includes Victorian mansions; a one-room schoolhouse; the Old Congregational Church, an 1873 landmark; and the Fort Scott National Historic Site, a restored 1840s military fort. Tours leave on the hour. **Open:** Apr–Dec, Mon–Fri 11am–3pm, Sat–Sun 11am–4pm. **$**

Garden City

Garden City stretches along the Arkansas River and is a popular jumping-off point to the Finney Game Refuge and the High Plains region of eastern Kansas. A unique drive-through zoo and one of the largest municipal swimming pools in the world are top attractions. **Information:** Finney County Convention & Tourism Bureau, 1511 E Fulton Terrace, Garden City, 67846-6165 (tel 316/276-3264).

HOTEL 🏨

UNRATED **Budget Host**

123 Honey Bee Court, 67846; tel 316/451-6133 or toll free 800/333-4164. Family-owned franchise motel with a brick facade, located near the community college. Good for budget travelers. **Rooms:** 68 rms. CI 2pm/CO noon. Nonsmoking rms avail. **Amenities:** 🏨 ⚴ A/C, cable TV. **Services:** ✕ ⌂ ⇔ **Facilities:** ⚐ ⚿ 1 restaurant, washer/dryer. Lounge in restaurant is dark and a bit run down. **Rates (CP):** $36–$48 S; $48–$52 D. Extra person $5. Children under age 13 stay free. Parking: Outdoor, free. AE, DISC, MC, V.

MOTEL

≣≣ Best Western Wheat Lands Motor Inn

1311 E Fulton, 67846; tel 316/276-2387 or toll free 800/333-2387; fax 316/276-4252. Standard motor inn with a tan and red exterior and a modern interior decor. Near the zoo and downtown. **Rooms:** 86 rms and stes. CI 3pm/CO 11am. Nonsmoking rms avail. Some maintenance problems (torn chair upholstery, carpet stains). **Amenities:** 🏨 ⚴ 🍴 A/C, cable TV. Some units w/whirlpools. **Services:** ✕ 🚗 ⛄ ⌂ ⇔ **Facilities:** ⚐ 200 ⚿ 2 restaurants, 1 bar, beauty salon, washer/dryer. Restaurant turns into a nightclub after hours. **Rates:** $38–$48 S; $46–$56 D. Extra person $4. Children under age 12 stay free. Parking: Outdoor, free. AE, CB, DC, DISC, MC, V.

ATTRACTION 📷

Finnup Park/Lee Richardson Zoo

Finnup Park; tel 316/275-6664. On 110 acres, park grounds feature one of the world's largest swimming pools. The zoo displays more than 450 mammals and birds. Facilities include picnic areas, tennis courts, horseshoe pits, and a historical museum with memorabilia of early settlers. **Open:** Zoo: Peak (Mar–Nov) 8am–9pm. Park: daily sunrise–11pm. Reduced hours off-season. **Free**

Goodland

This agricultural community in the heart of America's farmland, accessible via I-70, is near streams and plentiful wildlife areas that offer excellent fishing and hunting opportunities. **Information:** Sherman County Convention & Visitors Bureau, 104 W 11th, PO Box 628, Goodland, 67735-0628 (tel 913/899-3515).

HOTEL 🏨

≣≣ Holiday Inn

2218 Commerce Rd, 67735; tel 913/899-3644 or toll free 800/272-9273; fax 913/899-3646. 1 mi N of I-70. Standard Holiday Inn with a contemporary pastel decor. Amenities and services geared toward business travelers. **Rooms:** 79 rms. CI 2pm/CO 11am. Nonsmoking rms avail. **Amenities:** 🏨 A/C, cable TV w/movies. **Services:** ✗ ⛟ ➥ ⬭ **Facilities:** ⬛ ▭₁₂₀ ⬩ **Rates:** $55 S; $60 D. Extra person $5. Children under age 18 stay free. Parking: Outdoor, free. AE, CB, DC, DISC, MC, V.

MOTEL

▤▤ Goodland Super 8

2520 Commerce Rd, 67735; tel 913/899-7566 or toll free 800/800-8000; fax 913/899-7566. N side of I-70. Located along the interstate, this standard motel is appropriate for budget travelers. **Rooms:** 48 rms and stes. CI 11am/CO 11am. Nonsmoking rms avail. **Amenities:** ⬛ A/C, cable TV w/movies. **Services:** ➥ ⬭ **Facilities:** ⬩ **Rates (CP):** Peak (June–Sept) $36–$40 S; $49 D; $66 ste. Extra person $6. Children under age 12 stay free. Lower rates off-season. Parking: Outdoor, free. AE, CB, DC, DISC, MC, V.

ATTRACTION

High Plains Pioneer Museum

1717 Cherry St; tel 913/899-4595. The history of the area is related via a restored sod house, and farming and transportation exhibits (from horse-and-buggy days to the arrival of the railroad). The highlight is the first patented helicopter, invented in Goodland in 1910. **Open:** Mon–Fri 9am–8pm, Sat 9am–5pm, Sun 1–4pm. **Free**

Great Bend

Situated geographically in the heart of Kansas and incorporated in 1872, the city was named for a grand curve of the Arkansas River south of town. The nearby Cheyenne Bottoms Wildlife Area and Quivira National Wildlife Refuge attract migratory waterfowl and shorebirds. Southwest of Great Bend is Larned, the major agricultural and transportation hub for Pawnee County, and a community known for its many historical museums and antiques stores. **Information:** Great Bend Chamber of Commerce, 1307 Williams, PO Box 400, Great Bend, 67530-0400 (tel 316/792-2401).

MOTELS

UNRATED Best Western Angus Inn

2920 10th St, 67530; tel 316/792-3541 or toll free 800/862-6487; fax 316/792-8621. A large red brick facility with a pool housed in a spacious, airy atrium. **Rooms:** 90 rms. CI open/CO noon. Nonsmoking rms avail. **Amenities:** ⬛ A/C, cable TV w/movies. **Services:** ✗ ⛟ ➥ ⬭ Courtesy car available during the day. **Facilities:** ⬛ ⬩ 1 restaurant (see "Restaurants" below), sauna, whirlpool. **Rates (CP):** $44–$61 S; $48–$65 D. Extra person $7. Children under age 18 stay free. Parking: Outdoor, free. AE, CB, DC, DISC, MC, V.

UNRATED Holiday Inn

3017 10th St, 67530; tel 316/792-2431 or toll free 800/465-4329; fax 316/792-5561. On US 56. Standard brick and siding property with a colonial-style pillared porch. A Pizza Hut is across the street. **Rooms:** 174 rms and stes. CI open/CO noon. Nonsmoking rms avail. **Amenities:** ⬛ A/C, satel TV w/movies. 1 unit w/whirlpool. **Services:** ✗ ⛟ ➥ ⬭ **Facilities:** ⬛ ▭₅₀₀ ⬩ 1 restaurant, 1 bar, sauna, whirlpool. Table tennis available. **Rates:** $52 S; $55 D; $85 ste. Extra person $6. Children under age 19 stay free. Parking: Outdoor, free. AE, CB, DC, DISC, MC, V.

RESTAURANT

Black Angus Steak Ranch

In the Best Western Angus Inn, 2920 10th St; tel 316/792-4386. Off US 56. **Burgers/Steak.** Conveniently located on the main road in town, this steak house has a rustic decor with prominent dark wood accents throughout. It offers a full salad/food bar to go with the hearty steaks. The friendly staff aims to please. **FYI:** Reservations not accepted. Children's menu. No liquor license. **Open:** Mon–Sat 6am–11pm, Sun 6am–10pm. **Prices:** Main courses $6–$20. AE, DISC, MC, V.

ATTRACTIONS

Barton County Historical Museum and Village

85 US 281 S; tel 316/792-2204. In 1976 local Boy Scouts disassembled, rock by rock, an 1873 sandstone house located five miles northeast of town and reassembled it here. (Other village structures include an 1898 Lutheran church, the turn-of-the-century Santa Fe Depot, and a schoolhouse constructed in 1899 for $655.) The museum itself houses, among other exhibits, a Victorian parlor, dining room, and bedroom; a collection of 300 antique dolls dating from 1850; and a 1910 general store, barbershop, beauty shop, and doctor's office. **Open:** Mid-Apr–mid-Nov, Tues–Sun 1–5pm. **Free**

Brit Spaugh Park and Zoo

N Main St; tel 316/793-4160. The 46-acre park features a 12-acre zoo, picnic areas, horseshoe pits, tennis courts, swimming pool, basketball courts, softball diamonds. A variety of playground equipment is available. **Open:** Park: daily 6am–midnight. Zoo: daily 8am–5pm. **Free**

Greensburg

Popular attractions in this south-central Kansas town are the largest Pallasite meteorite yet discovered and the world's largest hand-dug well. Kiowa County State Lake lies north of town. **Information:** Greensburg Chamber of Commerce, 315 S Sycamore, Greensburg, 67054 (tel 316/723-2261).

MOTEL

▤ Best Western J-Hawk Motel

515 W Kansas Ave, 67054; tel 316/723-2121 or toll free 800/528-1234; fax 316/723-2650. On US 54. This single-story, overnight budget motel lies on the edge of town near a lake. The somewhat dilapidated exterior could use some

renovation, but the lobby and rooms are in relatively good condition. **Rooms:** 90 rms. CI open/CO noon. Nonsmoking rms avail. **Amenities:** A/C, cable TV w/movies. **Services:** Facilities: Sauna. **Rates (CP):** $44–$48 S or D. Extra person $4. Children under age 4 stay free. Parking: Outdoor, free. AE, DISC, MC, V.

Hays

Originally a frontier military post on the Smoky Hill Trail, Hays is a good base for enjoying area lakes and streams. The city is the seat of Ellis County and home to Fort Hays State University, which is located at the site of the original fort. **Information:** Hays Convention & Visitors Bureau, 1301 Pine, #B, Hays, 67601 (tel 913/628-8202).

HOTEL

Comfort Inn
2810 Vine St, 67601; tel 913/628-8008 or toll free 800/221-2222; fax 913/628-8168. 1 block S of I-70. Standard chain accommodations located on the main road into Hays, near lots of restaurants. Not recommended for travelers with disabilities, since rooms are accessed from stairs from lobby. **Rooms:** 32 rms. CI 3pm/CO 11am. Nonsmoking rms avail. **Amenities:** A/C, cable TV. **Services:** Facilities: 1 restaurant, whirlpool. **Rates (CP):** $55 S; $59 D. Extra person $4. Children under age 12 stay free. Parking: Outdoor, free. AE, DC, DISC, MC, V.

MOTELS

UNRATED Days Inn
3205 N Vine St, 67601; tel 913/628-8261 or toll free 800/329-7466. 1 mi S of I-70 on US 183. Reasonably priced standard chain motel fine for overnight. **Rooms:** 104 rms and stes. CI 3pm/CO noon. Nonsmoking rms avail. **Amenities:** A/C, cable TV w/movies. **Services:** Facilities: 1 restaurant, games rm, playground, washer/dryer. **Rates (CP):** Peak (May–Sept) $44–$52 S or D; $58–$80 ste. Extra person $5. Children under age 16 stay free. Lower rates off-season. Parking: Outdoor, free. AE, CB, DC, DISC, JCB, MC, V.

Hampton Inn
3801 Vine St, 67601; tel 913/625-8103 or toll free 800/426-7866; fax 913/625-3006. Family-style hotel with a friendly staff. Decorated with lots of browns and tans. **Rooms:** 117 rms and stes. CI 3pm/CO noon. Nonsmoking rms avail. **Amenities:** A/C, TV w/movies. Room for guests with disabilities is quite small. **Services:** Facilities: Guests may use facilities of Holiday Inn next door: pool, whirlpool, sauna, steam room, miniature golf, and table tennis. **Rates (CP):** $46 S or D; $90 ste. Extra person $5. Children under age 18 stay free. Parking: Outdoor, free. AE, CB, DC, DISC, MC, V.

RESTAURANT

Vagabond Family Restaurant
2524 Vine St; tel 913/625-5914. 2 mi S of I-70. **American/Italian.** Country-style fare served in an all-you-can-eat buffet. Family dining is available on one side of the restaurant, while a lounge with a full bar awaits on the other side. **FYI:** Reservations not accepted. Piano. Children's menu. **Open:** Daily 6am–9pm. **Prices:** Main courses $5–$13. AE, DISC, MC, V.

ATTRACTIONS

Fort Hays State Historic Site
1472 US 183 Alt; tel 913/625-6812. A public park that contains four of the remaining structures of Fort Hays, a military post built to protect railroad workers from Indian attacks in 1865. The stone blockhouse, guardhouse, and two officers' quarters are open for viewing; there's also a visitors center. Special events include the Wild West Festival (July 4th), Pioneer Days (mid-September), and Christmas Past (early December). **Open:** Tues–Sat 9am–5pm, Sun–Mon 1–5pm. **Free**

Frontier City
4800 US 183 Alt; tel 913/625-8650. A complex of re-created and restored buildings from late 19th century frontier life. The historical city includes the Missouri-Pacific Depot; Calamity Jane's wildest house in the West, Baby Barnyard, an 1870s log cabin, Munjor House, Crystal Palace Saloon, and an 1800s church. **Open:** Peak (June–Aug) Mon–Sat 9am–8pm. Reduced hours off-season. **$**

Hiawatha

Situated at the junction of US 36 and US 159 in northeast Kansas, Hiawatha marks the southern entrance to the Sac and Fox Tribe Indian Reservation. To the east, a state park and fishing lake provide outdoor recreation. **Information:** Hiawatha Convention & Visitors Bureau, 413 Oregon St, Hiawatha, 66434 (tel 913/742-7136).

RESTAURANT

Danny's Restaurant
606 Oregon; tel 913/742-2900. On town square across from courthouse. **American.** A small-town grill and diner with a wide variety of menu selections. Good, hearty food served quickly. **FYI:** Reservations not accepted. Children's menu. No liquor license. **Open:** Mon–Sat 11am–8am. **Prices:** Main courses $4–$9. No CC.

Hutchinson

A short drive northwest from Wichita, this city is host in September to the largest event in the state, the Kansas State

Fair. Sand Hills State Park to the northeast is a prize meld of dunes, prairie, woodlands, and wetlands. **Information:** Greater Hutchinson Convention & Visitors Bureau, 117 N Walnut, PO Box 519, Hutchinson, 67504-0519 (tel 316/662-3391).

HOTEL

≡≡≡ Ramada Inn
1400 N Lorraine St, 67501; tel 316/669-9311 or toll free 800/362-5018. Recently remodeled, this attractive hotel has an exceptional decor and a small indoor garden/atrium. Located across from a mall and next to fast food restaurants. **Rooms:** 225 rms and stes. CI 3pm/CO noon. Nonsmoking rms avail. **Amenities:** 🛎 🍴 A/C, satel TV w/movies, voice mail. Some units w/whirlpools. **Services:** ✕ 🛄 🖨 🐾 Social director. Courtesy van for transportation within Hutchinson. After dark, guests can be escorted to and from room or car. **Facilities:** 🏋 🏊 [100] ♿ 1 restaurant, sauna, steam rm, whirlpool, washer/dryer. **Rates:** $69 S; $73 D; $150 ste. Extra person $4. Children under age 18 stay free. Parking: Outdoor, free. AE, DC, DISC, MC, V.

MOTEL

UNRATED Comfort Inn
1621 Super Plaza, 67501; tel 316/663-7822 or toll free 800/221-2222; fax 316/663-1055. A standard motel with a warm decor of wood and brown hues. Near the mall, a laundry, and downtown. **Rooms:** 45 rms. CI 2pm/CO noon. Nonsmoking rms avail. **Amenities:** 🛎 🍴 A/C, cable TV. **Services:** 🛄 🖨 🐾 **Facilities:** 🏋 🏊 ♿ Games rm. **Rates (CP):** $51 S; $53 D. Extra person $6. Children under age 18 stay free. Parking: Outdoor, free. AE, DC, DISC, MC, V.

RESTAURANTS

★ Prime Thyme
2803 N Main; tel 316/663-8037. Near downtown and US 56. **Seafood/Steak.** The natural-style decor is done in green hues with prominent wood accents. The full salad bar complements the variety of baked and grilled seafood, steak, and chicken dishes. Banquet facilities available. **FYI:** Reservations not accepted. **Open:** Sun–Thurs 11am–9pm, Fri–Sat 11am–10pm. **Prices:** Main courses $8–$10. AE, DISC, MC, V. ♥ 👥

Sirloin Stockade
925 E 30th; tel 316/663-5951. **Steak.** This standard buffet steak house, part of a chain, features wooden booths and a full food bar. Large portions at affordable prices. **FYI:** Reservations not accepted. Children's menu. No liquor license. **Open:** Sun–Thurs 11am–9pm, Fri–Sat 11am–10pm. **Prices:** Main courses $5–$11. MC, V. 👥 ♿

Tommassi Restaurant
In Plaza Towers Building, 17 E 2nd St; tel 316/663-9633. **Italian/Steak.** Conveniently located downtown, this romantic establishment features a decor of deep rich colors and lots of wood. Prime rib, seafood, pasta. **FYI:** Reservations recom-

mended. Children's menu. Dress code. **Open:** Mon–Thurs 4:30–10pm, Fri–Sun 5–11pm. **Prices:** Main courses $9–$19. MC, V. ♥ ♿

ATTRACTIONS

Kansas Cosmosphere and Space Center
1100 N Plum; tel 316/662-2305. One of the major space science centers in the Midwest. Museum exhibits NASA memorabilia, computerized interactive exhibits, and one of the largest collection of space suits in the country. Omnimax theater features wrap-around 44-foot tilted dome. Planetarium offers a simulated view of the nighttime sky, complete with special audio and video effects. Summer camp sessions for children. **Open:** Mon–Wed 9am–4pm, Thurs–Fri 9am–9pm, Sat 10am–9pm. **$**

Dillon Nature Center
3002 E 30th St; tel 316/663-7411. This urban wildlife sanctuary features gardens (in bloom from spring to fall), hiking trails, and an arboretum. Evening and weekend programs include canoeing, owl prowls, wildflower hikes, and gardening seminars. The visitors center houses displays of Great Plains ecology and exhibits on area wildlife. **Open:** Mon–Fri 8am–sunset, Sun 10am–sunset. **Free**

Independence

During the last full week of October this town holds the largest celebration in southeast Kansas, Neewollah (Halloween spelled backwards). Fishing, camping, and boating at nearby Elk City Lake create a recreational paradise for summer visitors. **Information:** Independence Area Chamber of Commerce, 322 N Penn, PO Box 386, Independence, 67301 (tel 316/331-1890).

HOTELS

≡≡≡ Appletree Inn
201 N 8th, 67301; tel 316/331-5500; fax 316/331-0641. 2 blocks N of jct US 75 and US 160. An above-average establishment for the price and area, with modern decor. **Rooms:** 67 rms and stes. CI 2pm/CO noon. Nonsmoking rms avail. **Amenities:** 🛎 A/C, cable TV w/movies. 1 unit w/minibar, 1 w/whirlpool. **Services:** 🖨 🐾 **Facilities:** 🏋 ♿ Sauna, steam rm, whirlpool. **Rates (CP):** $45 S; $52 D; $68 ste. Extra person $5. Parking: Outdoor, free. AE, CB, DC, DISC, MC, V.

UNRATED Best Western Prairie Inn
US 75 and US 160 W, 67301; tel 316/331-7300 or toll free 800/343-7234. Typical Best Western with a muted white and tan decor. Good for budget travelers. **Rooms:** 40 rms. CI 3pm/CO 11am. Nonsmoking rms avail. **Amenities:** 🛎 A/C, cable TV w/movies. **Services:** 🛄 🖨 🐾 **Facilities:** 🏋 **Rates (CP):** $36 S; $41 D. Extra person $5. Children under age 12 stay free. Parking: Outdoor, free. AE, DISC, MC, V.

ATTRACTIONS

Independence Museum
123 N 8th St; tel 316/331-3515. A former post office listed on the National Historic Register, the museum houses local artifacts, antiques, and paintings. Guided tours available. **Open:** Thurs–Sat 10am–2pm. **$**

Little House on the Prairie
US 75; tel 316/331-6247. 13 mi SW of Independence. The Ingalls family lived on this site in a one-room cabin from 1869 to 1870. A cabin was reconstructed in 1977 following the description of the famous children's author Laura Ingalls Wilder. Relocated to the grounds are the Sunny Side School, built in 1872, and the Wayside post office. **Open:** May–Sept, Mon–Sat 10am–5pm, Sun 1–5pm. **Free**

Riverside Park and Zoo
Oak St and Park Ave; tel 316/331-4820. The 124-acre park includes Kiddy Land, miniature train rides, a merry-go-round, miniature golf, swimming pool, picnic area, tennis courts, and playground. The zoo exhibits bears, buffalo, monkeys, a cougar, an elephant, and an aviary with a flock of tame peacocks. **Open:** Daily 6am–midnight. **Free**

Iola

See also Chanute

Located on the banks of the Neosho River at the junction of US 54 and US 169, Iola is the Woodson County seat and an economic center for the region. **Information:** Iola Area Chamber of Commerce, 208 W Madison, PO Box 722, Iola, 66749-0722 (tel 316/365-5252 or 365-3129).

MOTELS

Best Western Motel
N State St (US 169), 66749; tel 316/365-5161 or toll free 800/769-0007; fax 316/365-6808. Secluded and quiet, with a better-than-average decor for most chain properties. **Rooms:** 53 rms. CI 2pm/CO noon. Nonsmoking rms avail. **Amenities:** A/C, cable TV w/movies, refrig. **Services:** **Facilities:** 1 restaurant (*see* "Restaurants" below), 1 bar. **Rates (CP):** $41 S; $45 D. Extra person $4. Children under age 12 stay free. Parking: Outdoor, free. AE, CB, DC, DISC, MC, V.

Crossroads Motel
N State St (US 169), 66749; tel 316/365-2183; fax 316/365-2183. Budget motel with dark wood exterior and rustic interior decor. Clean, comfortable rooms. **Rooms:** 54 rms and stes. CI open/CO 11am. Nonsmoking rms avail. **Amenities:** A/C, TV. **Services:** **Facilities:** **Rates:** $36–$39 S; $42–$47 D; $43–$47 ste. Extra person $4. Children under age 11 stay free. Parking: Outdoor, free. AE, DISC, MC, V.

RESTAURANT

Greenery Family Restaurant
In Best Western Motel, 1315 N State St; tel 316/365-7743. On US 169. **American.** This family-oriented restaurant has a gold decor and a small dining room; private rooms are available for large groups at no charge. An all-you-can-eat salad bar and well-prepared, moderately priced American dishes make this a solid choice for families or groups. **FYI:** Reservations not accepted. Children's menu. **Open:** Mon–Sat 6am–9pm, Sun 7am–2pm. **Prices:** Main courses $3–$4. AE, DISC, MC, V.

Junction City

Located at the union of the Smoky and Republican rivers, Junction City is the southern entrance to the Fort Riley Military Reservation. It also borders Milford Lake, the largest body of water in Kansas. The site of the first territorial capital lies northwest of the city. **Information:** Junction City Area Chamber of Commerce, 814 N Washington, PO Box 26, Junction City, 66441 (tel 913/762-2632).

HOTEL

Econo Lodge
211 Flinthills Blvd, 66441; tel 913/238-8181 or toll free 800/762-0270; fax 913/238-5092. Exit 299 off I-70. Standard chain hotel with a tan, barnlike exterior. **Rooms:** 58 rms. CI open/CO 11am. Nonsmoking rms avail. Rooms are comfortable and have nice wicker furniture, but the color schemes are poorly coordinated. **Amenities:** A/C, cable TV w/movies. **Services:** **Facilities:** **Rates (CP):** $38 S; $45 D. Extra person $3. Children under age 12 stay free. Parking: Outdoor, free. AE, DC, DISC, ER, MC, V.

MOTEL

Harvest Inn
KS 57 and Reynolds, 66441; tel 913/238-8101 or toll free 800/762-0270. 3 mi N of exit 299 off I-70. This two-story tan and green motel has a spacious lobby and a lovely picnic area near the pool. **Rooms:** 101 rms and stes. CI open/CO noon. Nonsmoking rms avail. **Amenities:** A/C, cable TV w/movies. **Services:** **Facilities:** 1 restaurant, 1 bar (w/entertainment). **Rates:** $37–$40 S; $45–$47 D; $65–$67 ste. Extra person $5. Children under age 13 stay free. Parking: Outdoor, free. AE, DC, DISC, MC, V.

RESTAURANTS

★ Chubby's Bar-B-Q
203 S Washington; tel 913/762-2773. At Chestnut. **Barbecue.** You can buy barbecue in bulk here, or just order a plate or sandwich in the restaurant. Classic decor features red carpet and a wood beam ceiling in a wide-open dining area. Orders are taken at the counter, and most business is carry-

out/drive-through. **FYI:** Reservations not accepted. Beer and wine only. **Open:** Mon–Sat 11am–9pm, Sun 11am–7pm. **Prices:** Main courses $4–$8. AE, MC, V. 🖼 �

Country Kitchen
416 Goldenbelt Blvd; tel 913/762-4477. Exit 296 off I-70. **Eclectic.** Enjoy down-home cooking in a relaxing country dining room done in white and blue. A great place for families. **FYI:** Reservations accepted. Children's menu. No liquor license. **Open:** Sun–Thurs 6am–11pm, Fri–Sat noon–midnight. **Prices:** Main courses $5–$10. AE, MC, V. 🖼 ⅛

ATTRACTIONS 🏛

Custer House
Building 24, Sheridan Ave, Fort Riley; tel 913/239-6727. 10 mi N of Junction City. Constructed in 1855 of native limestone, the building is the only surviving set of quarters from the fort's earliest era. Fully restored, the house relates military life on the western frontier during the Indian Wars period. **Open:** Mem Day–Labor Day, Mon–Sat 10am–4pm, Sun 1–4pm. **Free**

US Cavalry Museum
Building 205, Sheridan Ave, Fort Riley; tel 913/239-2743. 10 mi N of Junction City. Originally a post hospital built in 1854, the building later became post headquarters. Today the museum houses artifacts depicting the role the US Cavalry has played in the expansion of the West. Among the exhibits are murals, dioramas, picture and sculpture galleries, cavalry and military history books, and limited-edition fine art prints. **Open:** Mon–Sat 9am–4:30pm, Sun 12:30–4:30pm. **Free**

Milford Lake
Jct US 77/KS 57; tel 913/238-2885. One of the largest bodies of water in Kansas, the 15,700-acre reservoir features a 163-mile shoreline, an arboretum, a fish hatchery, and nature center. Recreational activities include fishing, camping, picnicking, waterskiing, and swimming. Annual events are the Sundown Salute July 4th Celebration and the Crappiethon, USA fishing tournament. **Open:** Daily 24 hours. **Free**

Kansas City

See also Independence (MO), Kansas City (MO), Leavenworth, Overland Park

The sister city to Kansas City, Missouri, it anchors a metropolitan area that is the largest in the state. A major economic and cultural center for the northeast portion of Kansas, it offers activities ranging from a symphony orchestra and ballet company to art museums and professional sports teams. Historic sites throughout the city illustrate its rich frontier past. **Information:** Kansas City Kansas Area Chamber of Commerce, 727 Minnesota Ave, PO Box 171337, Kansas City, 66117-0337 (tel 913/371-3070).

HOTEL 🏨

🏨🏨🏨 Riverview Inn
424 Minnesota Ave, 66101; tel 913/342-6919; fax 913/371-4660. Near I-35. White, modern decor; convenient to downtown Kansas City. **Rooms:** 202 rms and stes. CI 2pm/CO 11am. Nonsmoking rms avail. **Amenities:** 🛏 ⓠ A/C, cable TV w/movies. **Services:** ✕ ⌑ **Facilities:** 🔲 1 restaurant, whirlpool. **Rates (CP):** $51 S or D; $110 ste. Parking: Outdoor, free. AE, CB, DC, DISC, MC, V.

MOTEL

UNRATED Best Western Inn
501 Southwest Blvd, 66103; tel 913/677-3060 or toll free 800/528-1234; fax 913/677-7065. Standard Best Western with a colonial facade. Restaurants nearby. **Rooms:** 113 rms and stes. CI 2pm/CO noon. Nonsmoking rms avail. **Amenities:** 🛏 🖳 A/C, refrig. **Services:** 🐾 ⌑ ⌕ **Facilities:** 🔲 **Rates:** Peak (first 3 weeks of Nov) $62–$69 S; $73–$94 D. Extra person $7. Children under age 13 stay free. Lower rates off-season. Parking: Outdoor, free. AE, CB, DC, DISC, EC, ER, JCB, MC, V.

RESTAURANTS 🍽

Applebee's Neighborhood Grill & Bar
3434 Rainbow Blvd; tel 913/236-4224. **American.** The atmosphere is casual, with eclectic decorations ranging from sports memorabilia to street signs hanging on the walls. Standard grill food includes burgers, sandwiches, specialty chicken salads, and fajitas. **FYI:** Reservations not accepted. Children's menu. **Open:** Mon–Thurs 11am–11pm, Fri–Sat 11am–1am, Sun 10am–11pm. **Prices:** Main courses $8–$10. AE, MC, V. 🖼 ⅛

★ Gates BBQ
1026 State Ave; tel 913/621-1134. State Ave exit off I-35. **Barbecue.** This barbecue joint offers an inviting atmosphere with casual, rustic decor and a great staff. There are no set dinner prices—everything is à la carte. **FYI:** Reservations not accepted. Children's menu. Beer and wine only. **Open:** Mon–Thurs 11am–midnight, Fri–Sat 11am–2am, Sun 11am–11pm. **Prices:** Main courses $9–$15. No CC. 🖼 ⅛

ATTRACTIONS 🏛

National Agricultural Center & Hall of Fame
630 N 126th St, Bonner Springs; tel 913/721-1075. Located 18 mi W of downtown Kansas City. Patrons tour exhibits featuring early farm trucks, steam engines, and threshing machines; re-creations of a county store and a veterinarian's office; a plow used by Harry Truman; and collections of barbed wire and rural art. Seasonal activities include making lye soap, dipping candles, shelling and grinding corn, planting and cultivating crops, and flailing and winnowing corn. **Open:** Mid-Mar–Nov, Mon–Sat 9am–5pm, Sun 1–5pm. **$$**

Children's Museum of Kansas City

46th and State Ave; tel 913/287-8888. Located in the Indian Spring Mall. Aimed at children 4–12, all of the exhibits are hands-on and deal with science, art, and technology. Children may try on costumes in the dress-up closet, crawl through the bottom of the "ocean" in a marine-life aquarium, and shop the isles of a miniature grocery store. Changing exhibits mean the museum is different for every visit. **Open:** Tues–Fri 9:30am–4:30pm, Sat–Sun 1–4:30pm. **$$**

Grinter House Museum

1420 S 78th St; tel 913/299-0373. The two-story home was built in 1856 by Moses Grinter, the first European settler in the area. Later it would become the site of the first civilian post office/trading post in Kansas. It was modeled after an 1800s Kentucky farmhouse and made with local walnut and white pine hauled from Leavenworth by ox team. Today it houses a state-owned museum with period furnishings. **Open:** Tues–Sun 10am–5pm. **Free**

Huron Indian Burial Ground

6th and Minnesota Aves; tel 913/321-5800. Tribal burial grounds of the Wyandots in the heart of the city's business district. An estimated 400 burials took place here from 1844 to 1855. **Open:** Daily sunrise–sunset. **Free**

River City USA

1 River City Dr; tel toll free 800/373-0027. The *Missouri River Queen*, a turn-of-the-century paddle-wheel steamer, and the *America*, a multilevel yacht, tour the Missouri River. Passengers can enjoy live entertainment, listen to one-hour narrations, and sightsee. Call for schedule. **$$$$**

Lakeside Speedway

5615 Wolcott Dr; tel 913/299-2040. This half-mile paved asphalt track features a full season of auto racing. The NASCAR Winston Series Event is held on Friday night with five classes of cars: late models, modifieds, chargers, street stocks, and pony stocks. Several national events are held here, including NASCAR Super Trucks and the World Cup 300. **Open:** May–Sept. Call for schedule. **$$$**

Larned

ATTRACTIONS 📷

Fort Larned National Historic Site

KS 156; tel 316/285-6911. Fort Larned was built in the 1860s to protect the Santa Fe Trail. Nine original buildings and a reconstructed blockhouse surround the restored parade ground with a 100-foot flag pole in the center. More than 40 rooms are furnished in keeping with the period. Guided tours and living history programs are presented throughout the summer. **Open:** Peak (Mem Day–Labor Day) daily 8am–6pm. Reduced hours off-season. **$**

Santa Fe Trail Center

KS 156; tel 316/285-2054. A 25-acre complex dedicated to the historic trade route between Mexico and the United States. Museum exhibits show how the trail blended Native American, Spanish, and American cultures through displays including tribal artifacts, a Wichita grass lodge, a full-size mounted buffalo, and a commercial freight wagon. Outdoor exhibits include a sod house, dugout home, limestone cooling house, one-room schoolhouse, and a railroad depot. **Open:** Peak (Mem Day–Labor Day) daily 9am–5pm. Reduced hours off-season. **$**

Lawrence

Perhaps best known as the site of William Quantrill's infamous raid in 1863, Lawrence now is home to Kansas University and Haskell Indian Nations University. Bordered by the Kansas River, the city is near a number of lakes and state parks. **Information:** Lawrence Chamber of Commerce, 734 Vermont St, #101, PO Box 586, Lawrence, 66044-0586 (tel 913/865-4411).

HOTELS 🏨

🔳🔳🔳 Eldridge Hotel

701 Massachusetts, 66044; tel 913/749-5011 or toll free 800/527-0909; fax 913/749-4512. Located in the heart of downtown, this quaint, charming hotel is listed in the local directory of historical places. **Rooms:** 48 rms and stes. CI 3pm/CO noon. Each suite is dedicated to a historical figure from Lawrence, with biographies of each person in rooms. Great views overlooking downtown. **Amenities:** 📦 🛁 📺 A/C, cable TV, refrig, VCR. 1 unit w/terrace, 1 w/fireplace, 1 w/whirlpool. **Services:** ✗ 🚗 🛄 🛎 Babysitting. **Facilities:** 🍽 🏊 💻 ⚿ 1 restaurant, 1 bar, spa, beauty salon. **Rates:** $64 S; $98 D; $74–$82 ste. Extra person $8. Children under age 12 stay free. AE, DISC, MC, V.

🔳🔳🔳 Holiday Inn

200 McDonald Dr, 66044; tel 913/841-7077 or toll free 800/465-4329; fax 913/841-2799. W Lawrence exit off I-70. This two-story, brick hotel was recently purchased by new owners, who plan to upgrade the decor. **Rooms:** 192 rms and stes. CI 3pm/CO 11am. Nonsmoking rms avail. **Amenities:** 📦 🛁 A/C, cable TV. 1 unit w/minibar, 1 w/terrace, 1 w/whirlpool. **Services:** ✗ 🚗 🛄 🛎 🐾 **Facilities:** 🏊 🅿 ⚿ 1 restaurant, games rm, whirlpool, washer/dryer. **Rates (CP):** $75 S; $89 D; $125 ste. Children under age 18 stay free. Parking: Outdoor, free. AE, DC, DISC, MC, V.

MOTELS

🔳🔳 Best Western Hallmark Inn

730 Iowa, 66044; tel 913/841-6500 or toll free 800/528-1234; fax 913/841-6612. 1 block N of 6th St. Chain hotel with an unusually appealing gold and white decor and a very small lobby. Near KU campus and tollway. Call ahead—

it's always booked on weekends. **Rooms:** 59 rms. CI 2pm/CO noon. Nonsmoking rms avail. **Amenities:** 🛅 🛆 🖭 🍷 A/C, cable TV. **Services:** 🛏 🐧 Great service. **Facilities:** 🕭 Small sitting area with TV. **Rates (CP):** $43–$47 S; $50 D. Extra person $4. Children under age 12 stay free. Parking: Outdoor, free. AE, CB, DC, DISC, MC, V.

≣≣ Days Inn Lawrence
2309 Iowa, 66046; tel 913/843-9100 or toll free 800/329-7466; fax 913/843-0486. 2 mi S of West Lawrence exit off I-70. Two single-floor buildings and two two-story buildings. Lots of wood in the decor. Grocery store and pizza nearby. **Rooms:** 112 rms. CI 2pm/CO noon. Nonsmoking rms avail. **Amenities:** 🛅 🖭 A/C, cable TV w/movies. King rooms have refrigerators. **Services:** 🖂 🛏 🐧 **Facilities:** 🖪 🕭 **Rates (CP):** $43–$47 S; $51 D. Extra person $5. Children under age 18 stay free. Parking: Outdoor, free. AE, CB, DC, DISC, JCB, MC, V.

UNRATED Super 8
515 McDonald Dr, 66044; tel 913/842-5721 or toll free 800/800-8000; fax 913/842-8243. 1 mi S of I-70. Large, above-average facility with a barn-style exterior and wood and stucco frame. Contemporary, pastel interior. **Rooms:** 48 rms. CI 3pm/CO 11am. Nonsmoking rms avail. **Amenities:** 🛅 A/C, cable TV. **Services:** 🚐 🖂 🛏 **Facilities:** 🕭 Washer/dryer. **Rates (CP):** Peak (Apr–Sept) $41 S; $46 D. Extra person $8. Children under age 8 stay free. Lower rates off-season. Parking: Outdoor, free. AE, DISC, MC, V.

RESTAURANTS 🍴

⑤ Amigos
1819 W 23rd St; tel 913/842-1620. At Ousdahl. **Mexican.** Traditional Mexican fare in a colorful Southwestern setting. The food is very fresh—right down to the tortilla chips. Family oriented, the restaurant offers a playground for children and kids meals starting at 79¢. **FYI:** Reservations not accepted. Children's menu. No liquor license. **Open:** Sun–Tues 10:30am–2am, Wed 10:30am–3am, Thurs 10:30am–4am. **Prices:** Main courses $4–$6. No CC. 👪 🕭

♣ Castle Tea Room
1307 Massachusetts; tel 913/843-1151. 2 blocks S of Courthouse. **American.** This historic setting recalls a medieval castle, but it masks a cozy dining room inside. It's always crowded—reservations are a must. Traditional American fare. **FYI:** Reservations recommended. BYO. **Open:** Daily 6–8pm. **Prices:** Prix fixe $12–$14. No CC. ♥ 🍽

ATTRACTIONS 📷

Dyche Museum of Natural History
Jayhawk Blvd; tel 913/864-4540. Located on the University of Kansas campus. The stuffed body of Comanche, General Custer's horse (of Custer's Last Stand), is on display. The sole survivor of that famous battle between the Seventh Cavalry and the Sioux Indians, the severely wounded horse was found standing over his master's body, nursed back to health, and handed over to a taxidermist upon his death. Other exhibits include fossils, live snakes, and other mounted animals. **Open:** Mon–Sat 8am–5pm, Sun 1–5pm. **Free**

Museum of Anthropology
Jayhawk Blvd; tel 913/864-4245. Located in the oldest building on the University of Kansas campus. The museum features ethnic artifacts from around the world. Plains Indian beadwork, African masks, a totem pole, and an exhibit describing Homo sapiens' life cycle are among the permanent collection. **Open:** Mon–Sat 9am–5pm, Sun 1–5pm. **Free**

Spencer Museum of Art
1301 Mississippi St; tel 913/864-4710. Among the Spencer's more than 20,000 works of art are a Spanish *reja*, an iron grille from a 17th-century chapel, and a 400-year-old gold Amida Buddha from Japan. Other exhibits highlight medieval art; European and American painting, sculpture, and prints; photography; Japanese Edo-period painting; and Chinese painting. **Open:** Tues–Wed and Fri–Sat 10am–5pm, Thurs 10am–9pm, Sun noon–5pm. **Free**

Clinton State Park
798 N 1415 Rd; tel 913/842-8562. Heavily-wooded park on Clinton Lake—a 12,800-acre body of water with 85 miles of shoreline, noted for its walleye fishing. Archeological sites indicate prehistoric peoples lived here as early as 8000 BC. The park has a full-service marina with boat rentals, a beach, three campgrounds, public hunting grounds, and hiking trails. **Open:** Daily 24 hours. **Free**

Leavenworth

The first settlement incorporated in the state (1854), this town began as Fort Leavenworth, which was established in 1827 and is the oldest continuously operating fort west of the Mississippi. Also the county seat, Leavenworth is home to Saint Mary College and numerous historical points of interest. **Information:** Leavenworth-Lansing Convention & Visitors Bureau, 518 Shawnee, PO Box 44, Leavenworth, 66048 (tel 913/682-4113 or toll free 800/844-4114).

HOTEL 🏨

UNRATED Ramada Inn
3rd and Delaware, 66048; tel 913/651-4649 or toll free 800/272-6232. A very nice hotel with a skilled staff equipped to serve business travelers. **Rooms:** 97 rms and stes. CI 1pm/CO 1pm. Nonsmoking rms avail. **Amenities:** 🛅 A/C, cable TV w/movies, refrig. **Services:** ✗ 🚐 🖂 🛏 **Facilities:** 🖪 🛒 🕭 1 restaurant, 1 bar. **Rates:** $43–$70 S; $49–$70 D; $50–$150 ste. Extra person $6. Children under age 18 stay free. Parking: Outdoor, free. AE, CB, DC, DISC, EC, JCB, MC, V.

MOTEL

≣ Super 8

303 Montana Court, 66048; tel 913/682-0744 or toll free 800/800-8000; fax 913/682-0744. On US 73. Difficult to see from the main road, this budget motel is located behind a Taco Bell and is not much to look at: a basic, brick rectangle on a large, barren parking lot. **Rooms:** 60 rms. CI 2pm/CO 11am. Nonsmoking rms avail. **Amenities:** 🛎 A/C, cable TV, refrig. **Services:** 🚐 ⤴ ⤶ **Facilities:** ᷓ **Rates:** $38 S; $48 D. Extra person $6. Children under age 12 stay free. Parking: Outdoor, free. AE, CB, DC, DISC, MC, V.

RESTAURANT 🍴

★ The Skyview Restaurant

504 Grand Ave; tel 913/682-2653. **American.** An 1892 Victorian house with antique tile fireplaces and a gazebo. Seatings in the rather formal dining room are held every half-hour. Steak, seafood, chicken. **FYI:** Reservations accepted. Children's menu. Dress code. Wine only. **Open:** Tues–Sat 5:30–8:30pm. **Prices:** Main courses $8–$16. No CC. ♥ ▇

ATTRACTION 🖼

Frontier Army Museum

100 Reynolds Ave, Bldg 801; tel 913/684-3767. The history of the Frontier Army (1817–1917) and of Fort Leavenworth (1827–present) are presented in over 20,000 square feet of exhibit space. Patrons can view an army contractor's freight wagon; Mexican War, Civil War, and Indian War military uniforms, weapons, and equipment; and a carriage used by Abraham Lincoln in 1859. A "Frontier Fort" story hour is given for children. **Open:** Mon–Fri 9am–4pm, Sat 10am–4pm, Sun noon–4pm. **Free**

Liberal

Calling itself the "Gateway to the Land of Oz," this agricultural and commercial hub claims to be the location of the fictional house that transported Dorothy to that mythical land. Nearby Arkalon Wildlife Area provides outdoor recreation. **Information:** Liberal Area Chamber of Commerce, 505 N Kansas, PO Box 676, Liberal, 67905 (tel 316/624-3855).

HOTELS 🖼

UNRATED Best Western

229 W Pancake Blvd, 67901; tel 316/624-5601 or toll free 800/950-3111; fax 316/624-7524. Located on the Oklahoma border, this standard hotel features a pastel modern decor. Located adjacent to a family restaurant. **Rooms:** 46 rms. CI open/CO noon. Nonsmoking rms avail. **Amenities:** 🛎 🕭 A/C, cable TV. **Services:** ⤴ ⤶ **Facilities:** ᷓ ▣⁴⁰ ᷓ **Rates:** $38 S; $44 D. Extra person $4. Children under age 12 stay free. Parking: Outdoor, free. AE, CB, DC, DISC, MC, V.

UNRATED Liberal Inn

603 E Pancake Blvd, 67901; tel 316/624-7254; fax 316/624-7254. A modern hotel designed with rich brilliant colors; near the downtown area. **Rooms:** 123 rms and stes. CI open/CO 11am. Nonsmoking rms avail. **Amenities:** 🛎 🕭 ▣ A/C, cable TV, refrig. **Services:** ✗ ⊠ ⤴ ⤶ **Facilities:** ᷓ ▣³⁰ ᷓ 1 restaurant (see "Restaurants" below), 1 bar, sauna, whirlpool, washer/dryer. **Rates:** $43 S; $48 D; $65 ste. Extra person $4. Children under age 12 stay free. Parking: Outdoor, free. AE, CB, DC, DISC, MC, V.

RESTAURANT 🍴

Branding Iron

In Liberal Inn, 603 E Pancake Blvd; tel 316/624-7254. **American/Steak.** Solid fare, including steaks, served in a rustic setting. Note that patrons must be guests at the hotel to be served alcohol. **FYI:** Reservations accepted. Children's menu. BYO. **Open:** Mon–Sat 6am–10pm, Sun 7am–10pm. **Prices:** Main courses $7–$13. AE, DC, DISC, MC, V. ᷓ

ATTRACTIONS 🖼

Dorothy's House

567 E Cedar; tel 316/624-7624. Built in 1907, Dorothy's House has been restored and furnished with period pieces reproducing the farmhouse where the *Wizard of Oz* character lived. Visitors wander down a yellow brick road leading to 5,000 square feet of animated entertainment—good and bad witches, Munchkins, talking trees, winged monkeys, and Dorothy, the Scarecrow, Tin Man, and Cowardly Lion. Also on display are Oz memorabilia, including the original model of Dorothy's house used in the 1939 film. **Open:** Peak (Mem Day–Labor Day) Mon–Sat 9am–6pm, Sun 1–5pm. Reduced hours off-season. **$$**

Dalton Gang Hideout

502 S Pearlette, Meade; tel 316/873-2731. 30 mi NE of Liberal. The home of the outlaws' sister, Eva Dalton, preserved and restored as it was in the 19th century. It features an escape tunnel leading from the house down the hill to the barn. At the end of the passageway is the museum, which displays a collection of pioneer items, including the WS Dingess antique gun collection. **Open:** Mon–Sat 9am–5pm, Sun 1–5pm. **Free**

Lindsborg

Settled by Swedish immigrants in 1869, this town calls itself "Little Sweden, USA." The Maxwell Wildlife Refuge east of town offers limited public access for viewing buffalo and prairie elk. **Information:** Lindsborg Chamber of Commerce, 104 E Lincoln, PO Box 191, Lindsborg, 67456 (tel 913/227-3706 or 227-4120).

MOTEL

▤▤ Viking Motel

446 Harrison, 67456; tel 913/227-3336. 1 block S of KS 4. Scandinavian-style exterior, comfortable rooms with standard chain motel decor. A Pizza Hut is adjacent to the property. **Rooms:** 24 rms. CI open/CO noon. Nonsmoking rms avail. **Amenities:** ▤ A/C, cable TV w/movies. **Services:** ⤸ **Facilities:** ▤ ⊛ Lawn games. **Rates:** $35 S; $39 D. Extra person $4. Parking: Outdoor, free. AE, CB, DC, DISC, MC, V.

INN

▤▤▤ Swedish Country Inn

112 W Lincoln, 67456; tel 913/227-2985 or toll free 800/231-0266. In town center. This romantic bed-and-breakfast will overwhelm you with old-world charm the minute you set foot in the quaint Swedish pine lobby. **Rooms:** 19 rms and stes. CI 1pm/CO 11am. No smoking. Individually decorated rooms have handcrafted quilts and Swedish furniture. **Amenities:** ▤ ⊛ A/C, cable TV. **Services:** ⤸ Afternoon tea served. **Facilities:** Guest lounge w/TV. Two tandem bicycles available for guest use. **Rates (BB):** $50 S; $61 D; $61–$91 ste. Extra person $5. Parking: Outdoor, free. AE, MC, V.

RESTAURANTS ▥

Brunswick Hotel Restaurant

202 S Main; tel 913/227-2903. In town center. **Swedish.** Located only two blocks from downtown's main square, this restaurant features beautiful wood beam ceiling, hardwood floors, and wood tables—much of it Swedish pine. Prime rib and seafood are the main offerings, along with a salad bar. **FYI:** Reservations accepted. Children's menu. Beer and wine only. **Open:** Lunch Tues–Fri 11am–1:30pm, Sun 11am–1:30pm; dinner Tues–Fri 5–9pm, Sat 5–9pm. **Prices:** Main courses $8–$17. AE, DISC, MC, V. ▪ ▥ ⅙

The Swedish Crown Restaurant

121 N Main; tel 913/227-2076. In town center. **Regional American/Swedish.** Located in the downtown plaza, this restaurant makes guests feel cozy with a country decor done in a cream and blue color scheme and big, comfortable booths. Renowned for their Swedish specialties: ham loaf, curried pork, Swedish meatballs, and smorgasbords. The Swedish sampler platter offers a good introduction to the cuisine. **FYI:** Reservations accepted. Children's menu. Dress code. Wine only. No smoking. **Open:** Mon–Sat 11am–9pm, Sun 10:30am–8pm. **Prices:** Main courses $8–$13. AE, DISC, MC, V. ❤ ⅙

ATTRACTIONS ▥

McPherson County Old Mill Museum

120 Mill St; tel 913/227-3595. Complex consisting of 12 buildings housing more than 22,000 items including Native American artifacts, natural history and Swedish heritage displays, pioneer history and collections, crafts, and farm machinery. The featured roller mill, built in 1898, is in full operating condition. Picnic area and campground on premises. **Open:** Peak (Mem Day–Labor Day) Mon–Sat 9am–5pm, Sun 1–5pm. Reduced hours off-season. $

Bethany Lutheran Church

320 N Main; tel 913/227-2167. Located in a valley of the Smoky Hill River, the community founded by Swedish settlers in 1868 calls itself "Little Sweden, USA." The church and the town's early history are very much entwined. The interior of the church features a hand-crafted altar and large oil paintings, reminiscent of rural Swedish churches. **Open:** Mon–Sat 10am–6pm. Call to confirm schedule. **Free**

Konstverk Gallery

131 Harison; tel 913/227-2998. The Swedish word *konstverk* means "masterpiece." The gallery features paintings, prints, ceramics, and sculptures by local and regional artists. **Open:** Tues–Sat 10am–5pm, Sun 1–5pm. **Free**

Manhattan

See also Junction City

This picturesque city in the northern Flint Hills provides access to Spillway State Park and Tuttle Creek Lake to the north. Manhattan is home to Kansas State University and the Konza Prairie Research Natural Area; the latter is a 916-acre tallgrass laboratory for the university. **Information:** Manhattan Convention & Visitors Bureau, 555 Poyntz, PO Box 988, Manhattan, 66502 (tel 913/776-8829).

HOTELS ▥

UNRATED Holiday Inn/Holidome

530 Richards Dr, 66502; tel 913/539-5311 or toll free 800/465-4329; fax 913/539-8368. Great for families because of its extensive recreational facilities. Handsome decor of dark paisley designs done in brown and greens. **Rooms:** 197 rms and stes. CI 2pm/CO noon. Nonsmoking rms avail. **Amenities:** ▤ ⊛ A/C, cable TV, dataport. 1 unit w/minibar. **Services:** ✕ ▤ ⤸ ⧉ **Facilities:** ▤ ▥ ▥ ⅙ 1 restaurant, games rm, sauna, whirlpool, washer/dryer. **Rates:** $73 S; $89 D; $165 ste. Extra person $5. Children under age 18 stay free. Parking: Outdoor, free. AE, DC, DISC, MC, V.

UNRATED Ramada Inn

17th and Anderson, 66502; tel 913/539-7531 or toll free 800/272-6232. Comfortable accommodations with hunter green and burgundy decor. **Rooms:** 116 rms and stes. CI 4pm/CO noon. Nonsmoking rms avail. **Amenities:** ▤ ⊛ ▥ A/C, cable TV w/movies, voice mail. **Services:** ✕ ▤ ⧉ ▤ ⤸ ⧉ Social director. **Facilities:** ▤ ▥ ⅙ 1 restaurant. **Rates (CP):** $58 S; $63 D; $89 ste. Extra person $8. Children under age 18 stay free. Min stay special events. Parking: Outdoor, free. AE, CB, DC, DISC, EC, MC, V.

MOTELS

≣≣ Best Western Continental Inn

100 Bluemont, 66502; tel 913/776-4771 or toll free 800/452-5111; fax 913/776-0990. E end of Bluemont. Budget motel with green and white 1970s-style exterior. **Rooms:** 92 rms and stes. CI 2pm/CO noon. Nonsmoking rms avail. Clean, dependable rooms have wardrobes for closets. **Amenities:** 🛁 ⚲ 📻 A/C, cable TV w/movies. 1 unit w/whirlpool. **Services:** 🛏 🗘 🍴 **Facilities:** 🛋 ⚻ 1 restaurant (lunch and dinner only; *see* "Restaurants" below), 1 bar, whirlpool, beauty salon. **Rates (CP):** $52–$58 S or D. Children under age 12 stay free. Parking: Outdoor, free. AE, CB, DC, DISC, MC, V.

≣≣≣ Days Inn

1501 Tuttle Creek Blvd, 66502; tel 913/539-5391 or toll free 800/329-7466; fax 913/539-0847. Located on the outskirts of town. **Rooms:** 119 rms. CI open/CO 11am. Nonsmoking rms avail. **Amenities:** 🛁 ⚲ 📻 A/C, cable TV. **Services:** 🛏 🗘 **Facilities:** 🛋 ⚻ Playground, washer/dryer. **Rates (CP):** $50 S; $54 D. Extra person $4. Children under age 18 stay free. Parking: Outdoor, free. AE, CB, DC, DISC, MC, V.

≣≣≣ Super 8 Motel

200 Tuttle Creek Blvd, 66502; tel 913/537-8468 or toll free 800/800-8000; fax 913/537-8468. Typical budget property. **Rooms:** 80 rms. CI 2pm/CO 11am. Nonsmoking rms avail. Basic, clean rooms have brown and tan color scheme. **Amenities:** 🛁 A/C, cable TV. **Services:** 🛏 🗘 **Facilities:** ⚻ **Rates (CP):** $45 S; $55 D. Children under age 12 stay free. Parking: Outdoor, free. AE, CB, DC, DISC, MC, V.

RESTAURANTS 🍴

★ Giorgio's

In Best Western Continental Inn, 100 Bluemont; tel 913/537-0444. At Tuttle Creek Rd. **Italian.** A bit of old-world Italy, with kegs in the entrance and Leonardo da Vinci prints on the walls. Traditional Italian fare is served by a very courteous staff. Nice wine selection. Sunday buffet. **FYI:** Reservations accepted. Children's menu. Dress code. **Open:** Mon–Thurs 11am–9pm, Fri–Sat 11am–10pm, Sun 11am–8pm. **Prices:** Main courses $7–$16. AE, DISC, MC, V. 💗

Kearby's Restaurant

8385 US 24; tel 913/539-1332. 2 mi E of town on US 24. **Burgers/Steak.** A basic steak house, with tile floors and light wood accents. Full food bar. (Good news for nonsmokers—the smoking area is located in the opposite corner of the building.) **FYI:** Reservations not accepted. Children's menu. No liquor license. **Open:** Tues–Sat 11am–9pm, Sun 10am–2pm. **Prices:** Main courses $6–$8. MC, V. 👥 ⚻

ATTRACTIONS 🏛

Goodnow House State Historic Site

2301 Claflin Rd; tel 913/539-3731. Owned and renovated by pioneer educator Isaac Goodnow in 1861, the house contains many quirky details traced back to Goodnow and his wife. A window centered on the south wall has a chimney built to curve around it, and a downstairs ventilating system (designed by the educator) includes six holes bored into the brick wall. The home also contains period furnishings. **Open:** Wed–Sat 10am–5pm, Sun 1–5pm. **Free**

Wolf House Museum

630 Fremont; tel 913/565-6490. This 1868 stone house, with 1880s and 1938 additions, was used as a family home and boarding house. Period furniture and special exhibits are featured. **Open:** Sat 1–5pm, Sun 2–5pm. **Free**

Pioneer Log Cabin

City Park; tel 913/565-6490. This 1916 cabin has been transformed into a museum operated by the Riley County Historical Society. Exhibits include a re-created pioneer home and a collection of mid-19th-century agricultural tools. **Open:** Apr–Oct, Sun 2–5pm. **Free**

Manhattan's Sunset Zoo

2333 Oak St; tel 913/587-APES. Featuring more than 200 animals from around the world, including cheetahs, red pandas, and snow leopards. Children's petting zoo features a turtle pond and monkey island. Programs include tours, live animal demonstrations, lectures, and summer classes. **Open:** Peak (Mar–Nov) daily 10am–6pm. Reduced hours off-season. $

Mankato

RESTAURANT 🍴

Buffalo Roam Steak House

US 36; tel 913/378-3971. **American/Burgers.** The only restaurant in Mankato—don't blink as you go through town or you'll miss it. Good food at great prices, this is convenient for a quick lunch or dinner. **FYI:** Reservations not accepted. Children's menu. Beer and wine only. **Open:** Lunch Mon–Fri 11am–1:30pm; dinner Mon–Sat 5–9pm. **Prices:** Main courses $5–$7. DISC, MC, V. 👥 ⚻

Marysville

Situated on the Big Blue River, Marysville is surrounded by rounded hills and broad valleys carved by glaciers. An important stop along the Pony Express route, this Marshall County seat draws visitors with its historical attractions and events. A state park to the north of town offers recreational opportunities. **Information:** Marysville Chamber of Commerce, 1016 Center St, PO Box 16, Marysville, 66508 (tel 913/562-3101).

MOTELS 🏨

≣≣≣ Best Western Surf Motel

2005 Center St, 66508; tel 913/562-2354 or toll free 800/528-1234. 2 mi W of town on US 36. Conveniently located in business district with restaurants nearby. Large lobby with open, comfortable atmosphere and nicely decorated sitting area. **Rooms:** 52 rms. CI 11am/CO 11am. Nonsmoking rms avail. Rooms have dark colors and wood furniture. **Amenities:** 🛏 🕹 🍴 A/C, cable TV w/movies. **Services:** ⤺ **Facilities:** 🏋 📓 ⅙ Games rm, sauna, whirlpool, washer/ dryer. **Rates (CP):** $34–$47 S; $43–$49 D. Extra person $5. Children under age 18 stay free. Parking: Outdoor, free. AE, CB, DC, DISC, MC, V.

≣≣ Super 8

1155 Pony Express, 66508; tel 913/562-5588 or toll free 800/800-8000; fax 913/562-5588 ext 402. On US 36. Larger-than-average rooms. **Rooms:** 42 rms and stes. CI open/ CO 11am. Nonsmoking rms avail. **Amenities:** 🛏 🕹 A/C, cable TV w/movies. **Services:** ⤺ ⬦ Friendly staff. **Facilities:** 🏋 📓 ⅙ Washer/dryer. **Rates (CP):** $38–$42 S; $46–$49 D; $78 ste. Extra person $5. Children under age 12 stay free. Parking: Outdoor, free. AE, CB, DC, DISC, MC, V.

ATTRACTIONS 🏛

Koester House Museum
919 Broadway; tel 913/562-3101. A white clapboard 1876 home of German immigrant Charles F Koester and his family. The restored Victorian house was donated to the city by fourth-generation heirs in 1972. Visitors tour an interior featuring original furnishings and 19th century costumes. **Open:** May–Oct, Tues–Sun, call for hours. **$$**

Pony Express Barn-Museum
106 S 8th; tel 913/562-3101. Built in 1859 by Joseph Cattrell, the barn is the sole remaining Pony Express station still located at its original site along the Pony Express route. The museum displays Native American artifacts, Pony Express memorabilia, a doll collection, and antique tools and harness equipment. **Open:** May–Sept, Mon–Sat 9am–5pm, Sun 1–5pm. **$**

McPherson

Located in the center of the state, McPherson was founded in 1872 by farmers leaving the Santa Fe Trail just south of town. Visitors are drawn to the McPherson County courthouse and the McPherson opera house, both listed on the National Register of Historic Places. **Information:** McPherson Chamber of Commerce, 306 N Main, PO Box 616, McPherson, 67460 (tel 316/241-3303).

MOTEL 🏨

≣≣ Red Coach Inn

2111 E Kansas, 67460; tel 316/241-6960 or toll free 800/ 362-0072. At jct I-135/US 56. Conveniently located near the convention center. **Rooms:** 87 rms, stes, and effic. CI 3pm/ CO 11am. Nonsmoking rms avail. Rooms have dark paneling and an orange color scheme. **Amenities:** 🛏 A/C, cable TV

w/movies, VCR. Some units w/whirlpools. **Services:** ⤺ ⬦ **Facilities:** 🏋 📓 ⅙ Games rm, sauna, whirlpool, playground. **Rates:** $35 S; $45 D; $83 ste. Extra person $4. Children under age 12 stay free. Parking: Outdoor, free. AE, DISC, MC, V.

ATTRACTION 🏛

Maxwell Wildlife Refuge
US 56, Canton; tel 316/628-4592. 14 mi E of McPherson. Bison, elk, and coyote roam this 2,000-acre refuge, where guests may take guided excursions aboard covered trams or view wildlife from the county road or an observation tower. Special tours on wildflowers, bird life, and other topics are available by reservation. **Open:** Daily 24 hours. **Free**

Medicine Lodge

Named for lodges built by the Kiowa Indians, this small town enjoys easy access to the scenic Gypsum Hills to the east. The Medicine River and Barber County State Fishing Lake provide fishing and boating. **Information:** Medicine Lodge Area Chamber of Commerce, 209 W Fowler, PO Box 274, Medicine Lodge, 67104 (tel 316/886-3417).

MOTEL 🏨

UNRATED **Best Western Copa Motel**
401 W Fowler, 67104; tel 316/886-5673 or toll free 800/ 528-1234; fax 316/886-5241. At jct US 160/281. Located outside town; offers rooms with a pleasant decor of gold and blue. **Rooms:** 53 rms. CI 3pm/CO noon. Nonsmoking rms avail. **Amenities:** 🛏 A/C, cable TV w/movies. **Services:** ✗ ⤺ ⬦ **Facilities:** 🏋 ⅙ 1 restaurant. **Rates (CP):** $32 S; $36–$40 D. Extra person $3. Children under age 12 stay free. Parking: Outdoor, free. AE, DISC, MC, V.

ATTRACTIONS 🏛

Carry Nation Home
211 W Fowler Ave; tel 316/886-3553. Famed temperance leader Carry Nation began her crusade in 1899, outside one of the town's seven saloons. She attacked the saloon door with a black umbrella, and in later protests, would switch to an ax. Her home is a typical, small Kansas house, now restored with her personal belongings and period furnishings. **Open:** Wed–Sun 1–5pm. **$**

Medicine Lodge Stockade Museum
209 W Fowler Ave; tel 316/886-3417. Replica of the 1874 stockade that surrounded the town. The complex includes a two-story log cabin furnished with 1800s pieces, a house built of gypsum, and a museum with pioneer memorabilia. **Open:** Mon–Sat 10am–5pm, Sun noon–5pm. **$**

Newton

Located just north of Wichita, this frontier cattletown was the 1872 railhead of the famed Chisholm Trail. Newton's pioneer spirit is expressed through festivals, historic buildings, and antique shops. The Mennonite influence in this area is visible in the architecture and culture of the community. **Information:** Newton Area Chamber of Commerce, 500 N Main, #101, Newton, 67114 (tel 316/283-2560).

MOTELS

≡≡ Best Western Red Coach Inn

1301 E 1st St, 67114; tel 316/283-9120 or toll free 800/777-9120; fax 316/283-4105. At jct I-35. Family-oriented motel with a vibrant red decor. **Rooms:** 81 rms. CI 1pm/CO 11am. Nonsmoking rms avail. Some stains on furniture and carpet. **Amenities:** A/C, cable TV w/movies. **Services:** X Facilities: 1 restaurant, games rm. Pool table available. **Rates:** $36–$48 S; $40–$60 D. Extra person $6. Children under age 12 stay free. Parking: Outdoor, free. AE, DISC, MC, V.

UNRATED Days Inn Newton

105 Manchester, 67114; tel 316/283-3330 or toll free 800/329-7466. Exit 31 off I-135. Basic property offering an airy ambience with white embossed wallpaper and mauve carpeting. Tennis courts and golf are a few miles away. Sidewalks are in need of maintenance. **Rooms:** 82 rms. CI 2pm/CO 11am. Nonsmoking rms avail. **Amenities:** A/C, satel TV. **Services:** Pet fee $10. **Facilities:** **Rates (CP):** $39 S; $43 D. Extra person $4. Children under age 12 stay free. Parking: Outdoor, free. AE, CB, DC, DISC, MC, V.

Norton

Originally a stagecoach and wagon train depot on Prairie Dog Creek, Norton has grown into an economic and recreational center for northwest Kansas. The Sebelius Reservoir provides swimming, camping, and boating enjoyment, and the nearby Almena Wildlife Area offers visitors a close look at regional wildlife. **Information:** Norton Convention & Visitors Bureau, #3 Washington Square, PO Box 97, Norton, 67654 (tel 913/877-2501).

MOTEL

≡≡ Brooks Motel

US 36 and US 283, 67654; tel 913/877-3381 or toll free 800/528-1234; fax 913/877-2188. Budget property catering to families, located in the center of town. **Rooms:** 35 rms. CI 7am/CO noon. **Amenities:** A/C, cable TV w/movies. **Services:** **Facilities:** **Rates:** Peak (May–Sept) $35–$44 S; $36–$46 D. Extra person $5. Children under age 12 stay free. Lower rates off-season. Parking: Outdoor, free. AE, CB, DC, DISC, MC, V.

RESTAURANT

★ Town & Country Kitchen

US 36 E; tel 913/877-6960. **American.** This small-town cafe has tile floors, plastic tables, and a soda shop counter. Perfect for families with children, the menu offers burgers, sandwiches, and chicken-fried steak. **FYI:** Reservations not accepted. Children's menu. No liquor license. **Open:** Mon–Sat 6am–8pm, Sun 7am–7pm. **Prices:** Main courses $3–$9. No CC.

ATTRACTIONS

Also Ran Gallery

105 W Main; tel 913/877-3341. A unique gallery highlighting those who ran for President—and lost. Exhibited are 52 framed portraits of failed Presidential contenders accompanied by a brief biography. Also on display is a collection of more than 1,000 elephants, including elephants of gold, silver, brass, coal, pewter, ceramic, glass, and fabric. **Open:** Mon–Fri 9am–3pm. **Free**

Old Fort Bissell Museum

City Park, US 36, Phillipsburg; tel 913/543-6212. 30 mi E of Norton. Built in 1872 to protect settlers from attack by Native Americans, the fort is now a museum. The grounds also contain many buildings moved to the site: an 1885 store, an 1887 schoolhouse with its original desks, a walnut log cabin built in 1872, a sod house of the type constructed by homesteaders in the 1870s, and a section car used by the Rock Island Railroad. **Open:** Mid-May–mid-Sept, Tues–Sun 1–6pm. **Free**

Oakley

Oakley, located off I-70 on US 40, lies just north of the Monument Rocks area, the first (1969) National Natural Landmark in Kansas. The area south of town has produced numerous fossils. **Information:** Oakley Area Chamber of Commerce, 313 Center Ave, Oakley, 67748-1715 (tel 913/672-4862).

RESTAURANT

★ Colonial Steakhouse

Jct I-70 and US 83; tel 913/672-4720. **American.** The front dining room features a rustic decor; in the back an elegant dining area is set off by chandeliers. Lots of beef items on the menu with specialties in brisket and prime rib. **FYI:** Reservations not accepted. Children's menu. No liquor license. **Open:** Daily 6am–10pm. **Prices:** Main courses $3–$13. AE, DISC, MC, V.

Ottawa

Named after the Ottawa tribe, this Franklin County seat is home to Ottawa University. The downtown business district boasts the only complete block of businesses in Kansas to be listed on the National Registry of Historical Places. Outdoor activities provided at five federal reservoirs located near town. **Information:** Franklin County Convention & Tourism Bureau, 109 E 2nd, PO Box 580, Ottawa, 66067-0580 (tel 913/242-1000).

HOTEL 🏨

≣≣ Econo Lodge
2331 S Cedar Rd, 66067; tel 913/242-3400 or toll free 800/424-4777; fax 913/242-1796. At jct I-35 and US 59. Budget hotel with plain yet clean accommodations. Many restaurants nearby. **Rooms:** 57 rms. CI open/CO noon. Nonsmoking rms avail. **Amenities:** 🛏 🍸 A/C, cable TV w/movies. **Services:** ⌐〉 🔊 **Facilities:** 🛗 🏊 ᵭ **Rates (CP):** $57 S; $61 D. Extra person $4. Children under age 12 stay free. Parking: Outdoor, free. AE, JCB, MC, V.

MOTEL

≣≣ Best Western Hallmark Inn
2209 S Princeton, 66067; tel 913/242-7000 or toll free 800/343-7234. Exit 183B off I-35. A standard, budget, family-oriented lodging with a colonial exterior; inside are paneling and floral designs. **Rooms:** 60 rms. CI 2pm/CO noon. Nonsmoking rms avail. **Amenities:** 🛏 🔊 🍸 A/C, cable TV w/movies. **Services:** ⌐〉 🔊 **Facilities:** 🛗ᵭ **Rates (CP):** $48 S; $56 D. Extra person $4. Children under age 12 stay free. Parking: Outdoor, free. AE, CB, DC, DISC, MC, V.

Overland Park

One of several major suburbs south of Kansas City, Overland Park is home to the NCAA Visitors Center, the nation's only tribute to all 80 NCAA-sponsored championships. **Information:** Overland Park Convention & Visitors Bureau, 10975 Benson Dr, #360, Bldg 12, Overland Park, 66210 (tel 913/491-0123 or toll free 800/262-PARK).

HOTELS 🏨

≣≣≣ Courtyard by Marriott
11301 Metcalf Ave, 66212; tel 913/339-9900 or toll free 800/321-2211; fax 913/339-6091. ½ mi S of I-435. A standard Courtyard with a contemporary, bright white decor and wooden ceiling beams. **Rooms:**. CI 3pm/CO 11am. Nonsmoking rms avail. Rooms have a simple, beige decor. Some have a loveseat. **Amenities:** 🛏 🍸 🔊 A/C, satel TV, dataport. 1 unit w/minibar, some w/terraces. **Services:** ✕ 🚐 🔊 ⌐〉 Complimentary coffee and tea in rooms. **Facilities:** 🛗 🏊 ᵭ 1 restaurant (bkfst only). **Rates (BB):** $59 S or D; $107 ste. Children under age 12 stay free. Parking: Outdoor, free. AE, DC, DISC, MC, V.

≣≣≣ Embassy Suites Hotel
10601 Metcalf Ave, 66212; tel 913/649-7060 or toll free 800/362-2779; fax 913/649-9382. Upscale hotel with a tropical atrium lobby filled with lush plants and trees and beautiful fountains. A few miles from two major malls. **Rooms:** 199 rms and stes. CI 3pm/CO 11am. Nonsmoking rms avail. Mix-and-match furniture with beige color scheme. **Amenities:** 🛏 🍸 🔊 🍸 A/C, cable TV, refrig, dataport, voice mail. **Services:** ✕ 🚐 🔊 ⌐〉 🔊 Social director. **Facilities:** 🛗 🏊 ᵭ 1 restaurant, 1 bar, games rm, sauna, steam rm, whirlpool. **Rates (BB):** $99 S or D; $179 ste. Children under age 12 stay free. Parking: Outdoor, free. AE, CB, DC, DISC, MC, V.

≣≣ Hampton Inn
10591 Metcalf Frontage Rd, 66212; tel 913/341-1551 or toll free 800/426-7866; fax 913/341-8668. 2 blocks N of I-435. This standard Hampton has a sunken lobby with a relaxing seating area and a microwave. **Rooms:** 72 rms. CI 3pm/CO noon. Nonsmoking rms avail. Comfortable rooms in dark green and orange. **Amenities:** 🛏 🍸 🔊 A/C, cable TV w/movies. **Services:** ⌐〉 **Facilities:** 🛗 🏊 ᵭ **Rates (CP):** $66–$74 S or D. Extra person $4. Children under age 12 stay free. Parking: Outdoor, free. AE, DISC, MC, V.

≣≣≣ Holiday Inn Express
7200 W 107th St, 66212; tel 913/648-7858 or toll free 800/465-4329; fax 913/648-1867. 1 block W of Metcalf. Colonial-style exterior, comfortable accommodations, and excellent housekeeping standards. **Rooms:** 100 rms. CI 3pm/CO noon. Nonsmoking rms avail. Well thought out individual room decor. **Amenities:** 🛏 🔊 A/C, cable TV, voice mail. Excellent amenities for travelers with disabilities. **Services:** 🚐 🔊 ⌐〉 🔊 Car-rental desk. **Facilities:** 🛗 🏊 ᵭ **Rates (CP):** $69 S; $76 D. Children under age 18 stay free. Parking: Outdoor, free. AE, CB, DC, DISC, MC, V.

≣≣≣≣ Overland Park Marriott Hotel
10800 Metcalf Ave, 66210; tel 913/451-8000 or toll free 800/451-8000; fax 913/451-5914. At jct I-435. A ritzy, full-service hotel with newly remodeled rooms and an elegant marble lobby with many chandeliers. **Rooms:** 400 rms and stes. Executive level. CI 2pm/CO noon. Nonsmoking rms avail. Rooms with modern decor and dark blue and red color scheme. **Amenities:** 🛏 🍸 🔊 🍸 A/C, cable TV w/movies, voice mail. Some units w/whirlpools. **Services:** ✕ 🚐 🔊 ⌐〉 🔊 Social director. **Facilities:** 🛗 🏊 🏊 ᵭ 2 restaurants, 1 bar, sauna, steam rm, washer/dryer. One restaurant offers steak and seafood; the other is a Japanese grill. **Rates (BB):** $69–$104 S; $275–$475 ste. Children under age 18 stay free. Parking: Outdoor, free. AE, CB, DC, DISC, JCB, MC, V.

≣≣≣ Radisson
8787 Reeder, 66214; tel 913/888-8440 or toll free 800/333-3333; fax 913/888-3438. Near I-35. Located near the center of Overland Park, this elegant hotel with high-quality facilities caters mainly to business travelers. Luxurious gold and white modern decor. **Rooms:** 190 rms and stes. CI 3pm/

CO noon. Nonsmoking rms avail. **Amenities:** 🛅 🔌 📺 A/C, cable TV w/movies. 1 unit w/whirlpool. **Services:** ✕ 🔑 🚐 🖼 🛏 🕭 **Facilities:** 🏋 💆 📞 ⚓ 1 restaurant, 1 bar. **Rates (BB):** $60–$90 S; $60–$97 D. Children under age 18 stay free. Parking: Outdoor, free. AE, CB, DC, DISC, MC, V.

MOTELS

🏨🏨🏨 Best Western Hallmark Inn

7000 W 108th St, 66211; tel 913/383-2550 or toll free 800/444-4191; fax 913/383-2099. At jct I-435. Located near the stadiums, this is a great choice for traveling sports fans, but its primary concern is its business clientele. Comfortable, with a lovely courtyard and an elegant gold decor. Excellent service. **Rooms:** 181 rms. CI 3pm/CO 11am. Nonsmoking rms avail. **Amenities:** 🛅 🔌 📺 🖥 A/C, cable TV w/movies, refrig. **Services:** ✕ 🚐 🖼 🕭 **Facilities:** 🏋 💆 ⚓ 1 restaurant, whirlpool, washer/dryer. **Rates:** $59–$67 S; $64–$72 D. Extra person $5. Parking: Outdoor, free. AE, CB, DC, DISC, MC, V.

🏨🏨 Fairfield Inn

4401 W 107th St, 66207; tel 913/381-5700 or toll free 800/228-2800; fax 913/381-5700. This budget Marriott property offers simple, clean accommodations. Located near but not on the main road. **Rooms:** 125 rms. CI 2pm/CO noon. Nonsmoking rms avail. **Amenities:** 🛅 A/C, cable TV, dataport. **Services:** 🖼 **Facilities:** 🏋 📞 ⚓ **Rates (CP):** $50–$66 S or D. Children under age 18 stay free. Parking: Outdoor, free. AE, CB, DC, DISC, MC, V.

🏨🏨🏨 White Haven Motor Lodge

8039 Metcalf Ave, 66204; tel 913/649-8200. 3 mi N of I-435. The mediocre exterior is misleading—look inside and you'll find a quaint decor with exquisite Victorian period furniture. A hidden gem. **Rooms:** 80 rms, stes, and effic. CI open/CO noon. Nonsmoking rms avail. **Amenities:** 🛅 🔌 A/C, cable TV. **Services:** 🚐 🖼 🕭 **Facilities:** 🏋 ⚓ **Rates (CP):** $35 S; $42 D; $60 ste; $46–$60 effic. Extra person $2. Children under age 12 stay free. Parking: Outdoor, free. AE, DC, DISC, MC, V.

RESTAURANTS 🍽

♣ La Mediterranée

In Glenwood Plaza, 9058B Metcalf Ave; tel 913/341-9595. At 91st. **French.** Superior cuisine and smooth service are hallmarks of this classic French restaurant. Comfortable booths, French oil paintings, and crystal light fixtures combine for an elegant, relaxing setting. Many dishes are prepared tableside. Specialties include bouillabaisse (which must be ordered in advance), lobster with vanilla sauce, sole belle meunière, and salmon en mille-feuille. Venison and elk are sometimes available. **FYI:** Reservations recommended. **Open:** Lunch Mon–Fri 11:30am–2pm; dinner Mon–Sat 6–10pm. **Prices:** Main courses $14–$24. AE, MC, V. ♥ ⚓

Ⓢ South Dragon

In Metcalf 103 Center, 6820 W 105th St; tel 913/649-2345. 103rd St exit off I-159 S. **Chinese.** Traditional Chinese dishes served in a subdued setting distinguished by pastel colors and stylish ivory artwork. **FYI:** Reservations accepted. Children's menu. No liquor license. **Open:** Mon–Fri 11am–10pm, Sat 11:30am–10pm. **Prices:** Main courses $7–$12. DISC, MC, V. 👪 ⚓

ATTRACTIONS 🖼

NCAA Hall of Champions

6201 College Blvd; tel 913/339-0000 or toll free 800/735-6222. This $3 million, 12,000-square-foot facility contains photographs and videos covering all 21 sports and 80 championships administered by the National Collegiate Athletic Association. A 96-foot mural in the building entrance depicts the history of the NCAA and the achievements of college athletes. **Open:** Peak (June–Aug) Mon–Sat 9:30am–6pm, Sun noon–4pm. Reduced hours off-season. **$**

Old Shawnee Town

W 57 and Cody Sts; tel 913/268-8772. 10 mi NW of Overland Park, N on I-35 then W on Johnson Dr. A pioneer town museum and gift shop. The buildings are both re-created and restored, depicting the town's frontier life in the late 1800s. Visitors view one of the first jailhouses in Kansas, dating from 1843, an 1878 Hart House, Amos Undertakers, All Faiths Chapel, and the Shawnee Fire Barn. **Open:** Apr–Oct, Tues–Fri 10am–5pm, Sat–Sun noon–5pm. **$$**

Pittsburg

Established in 1876, Pittsburg prospered as a coal mining center and was once the fourth-largest town in Kansas. Still the largest city and cultural center of Crawford County, it is home to Pittsburg State University. **Information:** Crawford County Convention & Visitors Bureau, 117 W 4th St, PO Box 1115, Pittsburg, 66762 (tel 316/231-1212).

MOTEL 🏨

🏨🏨 Holiday Inn Express

4020 Parkview Dr, 66762; tel 316/231-8700 or toll free 800/HOLIDAY; fax 316/231-8700. 2 mi from Camptown Races Greyhound Track. This Holiday Inn offers a 1970s color scheme of green, orange, and yellow in its comfortable, standard rooms. Some minor exterior maintenance problems. **Rooms:** 100 rms and stes. CI 3pm/CO 11am. Nonsmoking rms avail. **Amenities:** 🛅 A/C, cable TV w/movies. 1 unit w/whirlpool. **Services:** 🖼 **Facilities:** 🏋 💆 📞 ⚓ Games rm, whirlpool, washer/dryer. **Rates (CP):** $52 S; $58 D; $131 ste. Extra person $6. Children under age 18 stay free. Parking: Outdoor, free. AE, CB, DC, DISC, JCB, MC, V.

Pratt

The Pratt County seat sits on the banks of the south fork of the Ninnescah River, at the junction of US 54 and US 281 in south-central Kansas. A nearby fish hatchery keeps both the river and a state fishing lake well stocked for the angler. **Information:** Pratt Area Chamber of Commerce, 114 N Main St, PO Box 469, Pratt, 67124 (tel 316/672-5501).

MOTEL

≣≣≣ Pratt Super 8
1906 E 1st St, 67124; tel 316/672-5945 or toll free 800/800-8000; fax 316/672-2969. An exceptionally nice Super 8 located within walking distance of restaurants. **Rooms:** 45 rms. CI open/CO 11am. Nonsmoking rms avail. Linens and bedspreads in great condition; decor is tasteful. **Amenities:** A/C, cable TV. **Services:** **Facilities:** Whirlpool. **Rates (CP):** $30 S; $34 D. Extra person $5. Children under age 12 stay free. Parking: Outdoor, free. AE, MC, V.

ATTRACTION

Pratt County Historical Museum
208 S Ninnescah St; tel 316/672-7874. Three galleries depicting the area's history. Gallery one includes pre-Columbian artifacts; a covered wagon dating from 1878; and collections of pioneer quilts, fashions, and toys. Gallery two features period rooms—an old courtroom, schoolhouse, parlor, and dining room—and "Old Time Main Street," with general store, post office, and bank. Gallery three includes an old soda fountain, a photography studio, and the town's first TV. **Open:** Tues–Sun 2–4pm. **Free**

Russell

ATTRACTIONS

Fossil Station Museum
331 Kansas St; tel 913/483-3637. A former county jail, the 1907 building was built from greenhorn limestone, or "post rock." Displays portray the early history of Russell County, spanning 100 years of clothing, heartland politics, Native American life, and the roles of the buffalo and the Kansas Pacific Railroad. **Open:** Mem Day–Labor Day, Tues–Sun 1–4pm. **Free**

Oil Patch Museum
Jct I-70/US 281; tel 913/482-6640. Exhibits on the importance of oil include an oil storage tank, cable tool drilling rigs, rotary drilling rigs, pulling units, pump jacks, and steam engines. **Open:** Mem Day–Labor Day, Mon 9am–2pm, Tues–Sat 9am–6pm, Sun 1–5pm. **Free**

Salina

See also Abilene, Lindsborg

Located near the junction of the Smoky Hill and Chisholm trails, Salina is the cultural, educational, and economic engine for this central Kansas region. The Saline County seat and home to Kansas Wesleyan University, Salina offers visitors outdoor activities on the Smoky Hill and Saline rivers. **Information:** Salina Area Chamber of Commerce, 120 W Ash St, PO Box 586, Salina, 67401 (tel 913/827-9301).

HOTEL

≣≣≣ Salina Holiday Inn Holidome
1616 W Crawford, 67401; tel 913/823-1739 or toll free 800/465-4329; fax 913/823-1791. Exit 92 off I-135. Quite nice; caters to both business travelers and families. Outstanding restaurants nearby. **Rooms:** 195 rms and stes. CI 2pm/CO noon. Nonsmoking rms avail. **Amenities:** A/C, cable TV w/movies, dataport, in-rm safe. Some units w/whirlpools. **Services:** **Facilities:** 1 restaurant, 1 bar, games rm, whirlpool, washer/dryer. **Rates:** $61 S; $64 D; $115–$120 ste. Children under age 18 stay free. Parking: Outdoor, free. AE, CB, DC, DISC, EC, JCB, MC, V.

MOTELS

≣ Budget Host Vagabond II
217 S Broadway, 67401; tel 913/825-7265 or toll free 800/283-4678; fax 913/825-7003. 1 block S of State St. No-frills, budget motel for those just needing a night's rest. **Rooms:** 45 rms. CI open/CO 11am. **Amenities:** A/C, cable TV w/movies. **Services:** **Facilities:** **Rates:** Peak (May–Oct) $34 S; $50 D. Extra person $4. Children under age 10 stay free. Lower rates off-season. Parking: Outdoor, free. AE, CB, DC, DISC, MC, V.

UNRATED Mid America Inn
1846 N 9th St, 67401; tel 913/827-0356 or toll free 800/528-1234. S of I-70. Multiple brick buildings with blue and gold interior. Family oriented; friendly staff. Restaurants nearby. **Rooms:** 108 rms. CI noon/CO noon. Nonsmoking rms avail. **Amenities:** A/C, cable TV w/movies. **Services:** **Facilities:** Sauna, whirlpool. **Rates:** Peak (May 15–Sept 15) $36–$40 S; $48–$60 D. Extra person $3. Children under age 18 stay free. Lower rates off-season. Parking: Outdoor, free. AE, CB, DC, DISC, JCB, MC, V.

RESTAURANTS

Beijing Restaurant
1601 W Crawford; tel 913/823-1685. 2 mi W of KS 143. **Chinese.** This small, family-owned operation has a white tile floor and lots of wood. It offers an extensive array of traditional Chinese entrees, providing large portions at low prices. **FYI:** Reservations not accepted. No liquor license. No

smoking. **Open:** Lunch Tues–Fri 11am–2:30pm, Sat–Sun 11am–10pm; dinner Tues–Thurs 4:30–9:30pm, Fri 4:30–10pm. **Prices:** Main courses $5–$10. AE, DISC, MC, V. 👥

⑤ Giorgio's Italian Restaurant
1200 E Crawford; tel 913/825-0200. **Italian.** Pleasant and relaxed atmosphere, with accommodating wooden booths and tables and good service. The kitchen turns out all types of appealing Italian food but the specialty is lasagna. **FYI:** Reservations not accepted. **Open:** Mon–Thurs 11am–9pm, Fri–Sun 11am–10pm. **Prices:** Main courses $7–$15. AE, DISC, MC, V. 👥

La Hacienda
641 S Broadway; tel 913/825-9600. **Mexican.** This standard Mexican restaurant, sporting a dark blue and tan decor, is owned and operated by a local family. Authentic cuisine includes tacos, burritos, enchiladas, and fine chips and salsa. Great for family dining. **FYI:** Reservations not accepted. Beer and wine only. **Open:** Mon–Thurs 11am–9:30pm, Fri–Sat 11am–10pm, Sun 11am–9pm. **Prices:** Main courses $4–$14. No CC. 👥

ATTRACTIONS 🏛

Smoky Hill Museum
211 W Iron Ave; tel 913/827-3958. Exhibits relating to the history of the area, including an old country store, period rooms, and local artifacts. Wheat weavings by local artist Donna Morgenstern are available for purchase. Changing exhibits last two to six months. **Free**

Salina Art Center
242 S Santa Fe; tel 913/827-1431. Located in a 1920s Spanish-revival building, the museum offers visitors changing exhibitions ranging from photographs to sculpture to folk art. The focus is on contemporary artists of regional and national stature. The Discovery Area includes hands-on exhibits in which children are encouraged to touch, weave, draw, design, and participate in scavenger hunts. **Open:** Tues–Wed and Fri–Sat noon–5pm, Thurs noon–7pm, Sun 1–5pm. **Free**

Smith Center

The geographic center of the lower 48 contiguous states is a few miles northeast of this Smith County seat. Nestled in the northern Smoky Hills region, Smith Center is primarily an agricultural community, and is near several recreational and historical sites. **Information:** Smith Center Chamber of Commerce, 113 S Main, Smith Center, 66967-0334 (tel 913/282-3895).

MOTEL 🏨

🔳 US Center Motel
116 US 36 E, 66967; tel 913/282-6611 or toll free 800/875-6613. Decor is nothing special, but motel is relatively clean and comfortable. Fine for families traveling the road

who need overnight lodging. **Rooms:** 21 rms. CI noon/CO 11am. **Amenities:** 🔌 🛁 A/C, cable TV. **Facilities:** 🛗 **Rates:** $36 S; $44 D. Extra person $4. Parking: Outdoor, free. AE, DC, DISC, MC, V.

Stafford

ATTRACTION 🏛

Quivira National Wildlife Refuge
KS 19; tel 316/486-2393. Big and Little Salt Marshes have attracted untold numbers of migrating waterfowl over the centuries. Spring and fall—when migrating ducks and geese, sandhill cranes, and bald eagles are in abundance—are the best times to enjoy the refuge, but hunting, fishing, hiking, and boating are available year-round. **Open:** Visitor Center and Refuge Headquarters: Mon–Fri 7:30am–4pm. **Free**

Topeka

See also Lawrence

Rich with history, this state capital of Kansas gives visitors a detailed glimpse of what life was like on the Oregon Trail and the Kansas prairie. Topeka supports a variety of activities ranging from a symphony orchestra and theatrical groups to living museums and drag racing events. The Kansas River and several state parks provide outdoor adventures at the city's doorstep. Topeka is home to Washburn University. **Information:** Topeka Convention & Visitors Bureau, 1275 SW Topeka Blvd, Topeka, 66603 (tel 913/234-1030 or toll free 800/235-1030).

HOTELS 🏨

🔳🔳🔳 Holiday Inn City Centre
914 Madison, 66607; tel 913/232-7721 or toll free 800/465-4329; fax 913/232-7721. A family-oriented, contemporary hotel in downtown Topeka featuring standard chain accommodations. **Rooms:** 196 rms and stes. Executive level. CI 3pm/CO noon. Nonsmoking rms avail. **Amenities:** 🔌 🛁 A/C, satel TV w/movies. 1 unit w/minibar, 1 w/whirlpool. **Services:** ✕ 🚗 🖨 🧺 🐕 **Facilities:** 🛗 ♿ 1 restaurant, 1 bar, washer/dryer. Pool area is a little claustrophobic. **Rates (BB):** Peak (July 4–last weekend of Sept) $55 S; $61 D; $95 ste. Extra person $6. Children under age 19 stay free. Lower rates off-season. AP and MAP rates avail. Parking: Outdoor, free. AE, CB, DC, DISC, EC, JCB, MC, V.

🔳🔳🔳 Holiday Inn Topeka West
605 Fairlawn Rd, 66606; tel 913/272-8040 or toll free 800/822-0216. At 6th St. This Holiday Inn is relatively small for a Holidome property, but it has a unique wrought-iron interior decor that is very attractive. Recreational facilities make it popular with families. **Rooms:** 198 rms and stes. CI 3pm/CO noon. Nonsmoking rms avail. **Amenities:** 🔌 🛁 📺 A/C, satel

TV w/movies. Some units w/whirlpools. **Services:** ✗ 🍽 ⊠ 📞 **Facilities:** 🏋 🚗450 ♿ 1 restaurant, spa, sauna, whirlpool. Some of the recreational equipment needs repair. **Rates:** $59–$79 S or D; $145–$225 ste. Extra person $6. Children under age 19 stay free. Parking: Outdoor, free. AE, DC, DISC, MC, V.

🏬🏬🏬 Ramada Inn & Tower

420 E 6th St, 66601; tel 913/234-5400 or toll free 800/272-6232. At jct I-70. Originally built in 1887, this used to be the governor's house and still possesses historic ambience and style. The exterior is weathered and beaten, but the interior is luxurious and beautiful, making it a great place for wedding receptions or other celebrations. Guest rooms, however, are not as nice as public areas. **Rooms:** 419 rms, stes, and effic. CI 2pm/CO noon. Nonsmoking rms avail. **Amenities:** 🎛 A/C, cable TV w/movies. 1 unit w/fireplace. **Services:** ✗ 🚗 ⊠ 📞 **Facilities:** 🏋 🚗4500 ♿ 3 restaurants (see "Restaurants" below), 2 bars, games rm, spa, sauna, whirlpool, playground, washer/dryer. **Rates:** $41–$70 S or D; $85–$175 ste; $85 effic. Extra person $7. Children under age 18 stay free. Parking: Outdoor, free. AE, CB, DC, DISC, EC, MC, V.

MOTELS

🏬🏬 Motel 6 West

709 Fairlawn Rd, 66605; tel 913/272-8283 or toll free 800/440-6000. Budget motel with very few services and amenities. Fine for short stays. **Rooms:** 91 rms. CI 2pm/CO noon. Nonsmoking rms avail. **Amenities:** 🎛 A/C, cable TV. **Rates:** $33 S; $39 D. Extra person $6. Children under age 17 stay free. Parking: Indoor/outdoor, free. AE, CB, DC, DISC, MC, V.

UNRATED Topeka Plaza Inn

3802 S Topeka, 66609; tel 913/266-8880 or toll free 800/833-8033; fax 913/266-4591. 3 mi S of Forbes Field. Stucco-style exterior and pleasant interior design. Was undergoing some major remodeling. **Rooms:** 166 rms and stes. CI open/CO noon. Nonsmoking rms avail. **Amenities:** 🎛 ⌀ A/C, cable TV w/movies, voice mail. **Services:** 🚗 ⊠ 📞 **Facilities:** 🏋 🚗250 ♿ 1 restaurant (lunch and dinner only), 1 bar (w/entertainment), washer/dryer. Nice spiral-shaped dining and entertainment area. **Rates:** $45 S; $54 D; $95 ste. Extra person $6. Children under age 16 stay free. Parking: Outdoor, free. AE, CB, DC, DISC, MC, V.

INN ·

🏬🏬🏬🏬 Heritage House

3535 SW 6th, 66606; tel 913/233-3800 or toll free 800/582-1937; fax 913/233-9793. Between Gage and McVicker Sts. 1 acre. This pleasant, high-quality bed-and-breakfast with beautiful, elegant rooms individually designed by award-winning architects specializes in romantic weekends and extended stays for couples. Unsuitable for children under 12. **Rooms:** 11 rms and stes. CI 2pm/CO noon. **Amenities:** 🎛 ⌀ A/C, cable TV. 1 unit w/whirlpool. **Services:** ✗ 🚗 **Facilities:**

🚗20 1 restaurant (see "Restaurants" below). **Rates (BB):** $79–$159 S or D. Parking: Outdoor, free. AE, CB, DC, DISC, MC, V.

RESTAURANTS 🍴

Annie's Santa Fe

In Westridge Shopping Mall, 1801 SW Wanamaker; tel 913/271-1060. Wanamaker exit off I-70. **American/Tex-Mex.** The Southwestern decor suits the traditional Tex-Mex specialties such as sizzling beef and chicken fajitas, shredded beef tamales, spicy burritos, empanadas, quesadillas, and more. **FYI:** Reservations accepted. Children's menu. Beer and wine only. **Open:** Daily 11am–10pm. **Prices:** Main courses $6–$16. AE, DISC, MC, V. 💺 ♿

♥ Heritage House

3535 SW 6th; tel 913/233-3800. Between Gage and McVicker. **Eclectic.** An entire wall of glass makes the small dining room bright and airy. Patrons can watch the chef cook their meals in the open kitchen. Each night's menu is based on what fresh produce is bought that morning; seafood is especially good. **FYI:** Reservations recommended. No smoking. **Open:** Breakfast daily 7–9am; lunch daily 11am–1:30pm; dinner daily 5:30–9pm. **Prices:** Main courses $15–$25. AE, CB, DC, DISC, MC, V. ♥ 🍴

La Flambeau

In Ramada Inn & Tower, 420 E 6th St (Downtown); tel 913/234-5400. 8th St exit off I-70 bypass. **American.** The small but tasteful dining area features blue pastel walls and a lot of woodwork. The limited menu offers steaks, chicken, and seafood dishes. Two banquet rooms on opposite sides of the dining area are available for large functions. **FYI:** Reservations accepted. **Open:** Daily 5–10pm. **Prices:** Main courses $5–$14. AE, DC, DISC, MC, V. ♥

Lane's Bar-B-Q

1306 S Kansas (Downtown); tel 913/232-3610. **Barbecue.** A boisterous atmosphere and Western decor are set off by rusted irons on the walls. Down-home barbecue sandwiches and plates are served by a friendly and efficient staff. **FYI:** Reservations accepted. Children's menu. No liquor license. **Open:** Lunch Mon–Fri 11am–2pm; dinner Mon–Fri 5–8pm. **Prices:** Main courses $6–$14. AE, MC, V. 💺 ♿

Steak and Ale

3225 SW Topeka Blvd; tel 913/267-1600. **Seafood/Steak.** Quite nice for a chain restaurant, with rustic decor and a quiet atmosphere. Specializes in seafood and steak. Great for casual dining or a special occasion. **FYI:** Reservations accepted. Children's menu. Dress code. **Open:** Sun–Thurs 11am–9pm, Fri–Sat 11am–10pm. **Prices:** Main courses $7–$20. AE, DISC, MC, V. ♥ ♿

Valentino's Ristorante

4011 W 29th; tel 913/273-3780. At Gage. **Italian.** A traditional pizzeria with a full salad bar, this is a fun and lively spot for a casual lunch or dinner. **FYI:** Reservations accepted.

Children's menu. **Open:** Mon–Thurs 11am–9pm, Fri–Sun 11am–10pm. **Prices:** Main courses $3–$8. AE, MC, V.

ATTRACTIONS

Kansas State Capitol
10th and Jackson Sts; tel 913/296-3966. The capitol building is situated on a 20-acre square and is modeled after the nation's capitol. On the grounds are statues of Lincoln and the Pioneer Woman, both by local artist Marrell Gage. The Capitol houses other works by native-born artists such as John Steuart Curry, Lumen Martin Winter, and David Overmeyer. Guided tours available. **Open:** Mon–Fri 8am–4pm, Sat–Sun 9am–3pm. **Free**

Cedar Crest–Residence of the Governor of Kansas
1 SW Cedar Crest Rd; tel 913/296-3966. Built in 1928, Cedar Crest has been the official residence of the Governor since 1962. The French Norman–style, 12-room home is surrounded by 244 acres of hiking trails, fishing ponds, and nature areas open to the public. Public tours of the home are conducted Friday afternoons. **Open:** Fri 1–3pm. **Free**

Kansas Museum of History
6425 SW 6th St; tel 913/272-8681. Presents the story of Kansas from prehistory to the present through galleries, tours, workshops, and folklife demonstrations. Interactive Discovery Place for children. **Open:** Mon–Sat 9am–4:30pm, Sun 12:30–4:30pm. **Free**

Historic Ward-Meade Park
124 NW Fillmore; tel 913/235-0806. The park's highlights include a tour through the restored Victorian mansion, rock barn, log cabin, turn-of-the-century depot, general store, caboose, and one-room schoolhouse. The botanical garden features more than 500 varieties of trees and shrubs, 9,000 annuals, and 5,000 tulips. **Open:** Peak (Apr–Oct) Tues–Fri 10am–4pm, Sat–Sun 1–4pm. Reduced hours off-season. **$$**

Mulvane Art Museum
17th St and Jewell Ave; tel 913/231-1010 ext 1324. More than 2,000 works offer a wide range of exhibits, including works by Dürer, Goya, and Kollwitz, a Japanese print collection, and many works by artists from Kansas and the Mountain Plains region. Gallery talks, docent-led tours, and video screenings also offered. **Open:** Peak (Sept–May) Tues–Wed 10am–7pm, Thurs–Fri 10am–4pm, Sat–Sun 1–4pm. Reduced hours off-season. **Free**

Combat Air Museum
Hangar 602, Forbes Field; tel 913/862-3303. Military aircraft and memorabilia ranging from World War I to the space shuttle program. The cockpit, galley, sleeping, navigation, and radar areas of the EC-121 Super Constellation, a huge radar plane, are all open for inspection. Also on display are a rare B-24 Liberator bomber from World War II, the AC-47, and several open-cockpit Jenny biplanes. Guided tours available by advance request. **Open:** Mon–Sat 9am–4:30pm, Sun 10am–4:30pm. **$$**

Gage Park
Gage Blvd between 6th and 10th Sts; tel 913/271-5468. The 160-acre park features a ride on the restored 1908 Hershell-Spillman carousel. Visitors may also walk the three-acre rose garden and conservatory, play tennis, swim, picnic, and ride the miniature train. **Open:** Daily 6am–11pm. **Free**

Topeka Zoological Park
Gage Park; tel 913/272-5821. Features almost 400 animals from around the world. Exhibits include a tropical rain forest habitat, a pride of lions, and several gorillas, orangutans, elephants, hippos, and giraffes. Petting zoo. **Open:** Daily 9am–4:30pm. **$$**

Heartland Park Topeka
7103 SW Montara Pkwy; tel 913/862-7223. Motor sports complex features professional and amateur racing. The state-of-the-art facilities include a quarter-mile drag strip and 2½-mile road course, offering six different configurations of race courses. Call ahead for scheduled events.

Wichita

See also El Dorado, Hutchinson, Newton

Named for the Wichita Indians, this city is the largest in the state and home to Wichita State University and McConnell Air Force Base. Originally a cattle town on the Chisholm Trail, Wichita serves as the cultural heart of the region and maintains a metropolitan ballet, symphony orchestra, several theatrical companies, and numerous museums. Eldorado State Park and Wildlife Area, Lake Afton, and Cheney Reservoir provide seasonal recreation. **Information:** Wichita Convention & Visitors Bureau, 100 S Main St, #100, Wichita, 67202 (tel 316/265-2800 or toll free 800/288-9424).

PUBLIC TRANSPORTATION
The **Wichita Metropolitan Transit Authority (WMTA)** runs citywide bus service on 23 routes. Standard fare is 85¢, and a transfer is 20¢. Exact change required. For seniors, the fare is 40¢, 10¢ for a transfer. Children under 5 ride free. For schedule and route information call 316/265-7221.

HOTELS

≣≣≣ Airport Hilton & Conference Center
2098 Airport Rd, 67277; tel 316/945-5272 or toll free 800/445-8667; fax 316/947-7620. A full-service hotel with modern decor and luxury accommodations located right next to the airport. Strong business orientation. **Rooms:** 302 rms and stes. Executive level. CI 3pm/CO 11am. Nonsmoking rms avail. **Amenities:** A/C, cable TV w/movies. Some units w/whirlpools. **Services:** X **Facilities:**

[1000] 🔒 1 restaurant, 2 bars, whirlpool. **Rates:** $112 S; $127 D; $200 ste. Extra person $15. Children under age 18 stay free. Parking: Outdoor, free. AE, CB, DC, DISC, MC, V.

Best Western Hallmark Inn

I-35 and 53rd St N, 67219; tel 316/832-9387 or toll free 800/362-0095; fax 316/832-9443. 2 mi S of I-70. Very nice hotel offering convenience, nice accommodations, and pleasant red and white decor. A great value. **Rooms:** 152 rms and stes. CI 2pm/CO 11am. Nonsmoking rms avail. **Amenities:** 🔒 ⊘ A/C, cable TV w/movies, VCR. **Services:** ✕ 🛏 🖐 **Facilities:** 🔥 [500] 🔒 1 restaurant, steam rm, whirlpool. **Rates (CP):** $48 S; $57 D; $119 ste. Extra person $4. Children under age 12 stay free. Parking: Outdoor, free. AE, DC, DISC, MC, V.

Clubhouse Inn

515 S Webb Rd, 67207; tel 316/684-1111 or toll free 800/258-2466; fax 316/684-0538. E Kellogg exit off I-35. In a lovely white building with green trim, rooms here are clean and inviting. Staff is friendly and helpful. **Rooms:** 120 rms and stes. CI 3pm/CO noon. Nonsmoking rms avail. **Amenities:** 🔒 A/C, cable TV w/movies, voice mail. Some units w/terraces, some w/whirlpools. Refrigerator in suites. **Services:** 🛏 🖐 **Facilities:** 🔥 [35] 🔒 Whirlpool. A gazebo and several grills around the pool provide a place for relaxing and family fun. **Rates (BB):** $69 S; $79 D; $99 ste. Extra person $5. Children under age 16 stay free. Parking: Outdoor, free. AE, DC, DISC, MC, V.

Comfort Inn

4849 S Laura, 67216; tel 316/522-1800 or toll free 800/221-2222. 3 mi S of Kellogg Rd off I-135. Standard chain accommodations distinguished by a glass bridge overlooking the beautiful courtyard pool. **Rooms:** 114 rms and stes. CI 2pm/CO noon. Nonsmoking rms avail. **Amenities:** 🔒 ⊘ A/C, cable TV w/movies. **Services:** 🛏 🖐 Free popcorn in lobby. Very small continental breakfast. Dependable, friendly service. **Facilities:** 🔥 🔒 **Rates (CP):** $52 S; $59 D; $75 ste. Extra person $8. Children under age 18 stay free. Parking: Outdoor, free. AE, CB, DC, DISC, ER, JCB, MC, V.

Comfort Suites

658 Westdale, 67209; tel 316/945-2600 or toll free 800/318-2607. 1 mi E of I-235 on US 54. Accessed by a small road, north of US 54, this property is slightly difficult to find, but its superior accommodations are worth the trouble. Rooms for guests with disabilities and adjoining rooms must be booked well in advance. **Rooms:** 50 stes. CI 3pm/CO noon. Nonsmoking rms avail. **Amenities:** 🔒 ⊘ 🖥 A/C, cable TV w/movies, refrig. Some units w/whirlpools. **Services:** 🚐 🖐 Extended continental breakfast. Friendly staff. **Facilities:** 🔥 🛁 [30] 🔒 1 bar, basketball. **Rates (CP):** $59–$80 ste. Extra person $5. Children under age 18 stay free. Parking: Outdoor, free. AE, DISC, MC, V.

Harvey Hotel

549 S Rock Rd, 67207; tel 316/686-7131 or toll free 800/922-9222; fax 316/686-0018. 1 mi W of Kellogg exit off I-35. Family oriented, yet elegant, with a mauve and rust decor and a beautiful atrium/lobby with relaxing sitting area. Located on main business road across from Town East Shopping Mall. **Rooms:** 259 rms and stes. CI 3pm/CO 1pm. Nonsmoking rms avail. **Amenities:** 🔒 ⊘ 🖥 A/C, cable TV w/movies. Some units w/terraces, some w/whirlpools. Refrigerators and microwaves for $10 fee. **Services:** ✕ 🔑 🚐 🖐 🖐 Social director. **Facilities:** 🔥 🛁 [750] 🔒 1 restaurant. **Rates:** $89 S; $99 D; $400 ste. Extra person $10. Children under age 12 stay free. Parking: Outdoor, free. AE, CB, DC, DISC, MC, V.

Holiday Inn Wichita Airport

5500 W Kellogg Dr, 67209; tel 316/943-2181 or toll free 800/255-6484; fax 316/943-6587. Kellogg exit off I-235. Full-service hotel with peach and green decor located west of town on major business road. **Rooms:** 152 rms. CI 3pm/CO noon. Nonsmoking rms avail. **Amenities:** 🔒 ⊘ 🖥 A/C, satel TV w/movies. **Services:** ✕ 🚐 🖐 🖐 🖐 Free transportation within 10-mile radius. **Facilities:** 🔥 [300] 1 restaurant (see "Restaurants" below), 1 bar, sauna, steam rm, whirlpool, washer/dryer. Pleasant courtyard near beautiful pool. Guests receive 25% discount on lunch and dinner at hotel's restaurant. **Rates (BB):** $87 S or D. Extra person $9. Children under age 18 stay free. Parking: Outdoor, free. AE, CB, DC, DISC, JCB, MC, V.

UNRATED The Inn at Tallgrass

2280 N Tara, 67226; tel 316/684-3466. A small, quaint, all-suite hotel with a fireplace in the lobby area and bright, white modern decor. Shopping mall nearby. **Rooms:** 88 stes. CI open/CO noon. Nonsmoking rms avail. **Amenities:** 🔒 ⊘ 🖥 A/C, cable TV w/movies. **Services:** 🖐 **Facilities:** 🔥 Whirlpool, washer/dryer. **Rates (BB):** $99–$132 ste. Parking: Outdoor, free. AE, DISC, MC, V.

La Quinta Motor Inn

7700 E Kellogg Dr, 67207; tel 316/681-2881 or toll free 800/531-5900; fax 316/681-0568. On US 54 at Rock Rd. Next to a large mall, with great shopping, dining, and entertainment opportunities. Best suited for families traveling on a budget. **Rooms:** 64 rms and stes. CI 3pm/CO noon. Nonsmoking rms avail. **Amenities:** 🔒 ⊘ A/C, cable TV w/movies. Microwave and refrigerator cost $5/day. **Services:** 🚐 🖐 🖐 Neighboring restaurant gives hotel guests 10% discount. **Facilities:** 🔥 [40] 🔒 **Rates (CP):** Peak (Mar–Dec) $67 S or D; $85 ste. Children under age 12 stay free. Lower rates off-season. Parking: Outdoor, free. AE, CB, DISC, MC, V.

Ramada Airport Inn

5805 W US 54, 67277; tel 316/942-7911 or toll free 800/272-6232; fax 316/942-0854. ½ mi W of I-235. Family-oriented hotel with a tasteful, blue and white decor and a beautiful courtyard. Professional, efficient staff. **Rooms:** 206

rms and stes. CI noon/CO noon. Nonsmoking rms avail. **Amenities:** 📺 ⚿ A/C, cable TV w/movies. 1 unit w/whirlpool. **Services:** ✗ 🛏 🖨 ⌁ ⟳ **Facilities:** 🏊 🏋 🅿 250 ♿ 1 restaurant, 1 bar (w/entertainment). **Rates:** $65 S; $69 D; $125 ste. Extra person $4. Children under age 18 stay free. Parking: Outdoor, free. AE, CB, DC, DISC, ER, JCB, MC, V.

☰☰☰ Residence Inn by Marriott

411 S Webb Rd, 67207; tel 316/686-7331 or toll free 800/331-3131; fax 316/263-3817. At Kellogg. Attractive facility catering to long-term guests. **Rooms:** 64 effic. CI 4pm/CO 1pm. Nonsmoking rms avail. Studios and penthouses also available. **Amenities:** 📺 ⚿ 🖨 A/C, cable TV w/movies, refrig. All units w/terraces, all w/fireplaces. Each room has full kitchen and microwave. **Services:** 🖨 ⌁ ⟳ Grocery shopping service. **Facilities:** 🏊 ♣ ♿ Basketball, whirlpool. Free access to local health club. **Rates (CP):** $99–$129 effic. Children under age 18 stay free. Parking: Outdoor, free. AE, CB, DC, DISC, JCB, MC, V.

☰☰☰ Wichita Marriott Hotel

9100 Corporate Hills Pkwy, 67207; tel 316/651-0333 or toll free 800/228-9290; fax 316/651-0333. High-quality, business-oriented hotel with an attractive pastel decor. Lobby has a piano. Convenient to many Wichita facilities and services; however, it's difficult to find. **Rooms:** 294 rms and stes. Executive level. CI 4pm/CO noon. Nonsmoking rms avail. Rooms have peach and green decor with relatively new furniture and large windows. **Amenities:** 📺 ⚿ 🖨 A/C, cable TV w/movies. Some units w/minibars, some w/terraces, some w/whirlpools. **Services:** ✗ 🗝 🛏 🖨 ⌁ Twice-daily maid svce, social director. **Facilities:** 🏊 🏋 1150 ♿ 1 restaurant, spa, sauna, steam rm, whirlpool. Restaurant has lovely outdoor sitting area where drinks are served. **Rates:** $115 S; $125 D; $125 ste. Extra person $10. Children under age 10 stay free. Parking: Outdoor, free. AE, CB, DC, DISC, JCB, MC, V.

☰☰☰ Wichita Suites

5211 E Kellogg Dr, 67218; tel 316/685-2233 or toll free 800/243-5953; fax 316/685-4152. Very nice all-suite facility. A good choice for an extended business trip. **Rooms:** 90 stes. Executive level. CI 2pm/CO noon. No smoking. Suites are exceptionally spacious, the size of an apartment, with mauve and white decor, pine night stands, and kitchens with white cabinets and wood trim. Furniture is new and fashionable. **Amenities:** 📺 ⚿ 🖨 A/C, satel TV w/movies, refrig, dataport, voice mail. **Services:** ✗ VP 🖨 ⌁ ⟳ Twice-daily maid svce. Friendly, efficient staff. **Facilities:** 🏊 40 ♿ 1 restaurant (bkfst only), sauna, whirlpool. **Rates (BB):** $53–$73 ste. Extra person $7. Children under age 6 stay free. Parking: Outdoor, free. AE, CB, DC, DISC, EC, ER, JCB, MC, V.

MOTELS

☰☰☰ Days Inn Country Inn

550 S Florence, 67209; tel 316/942-1717 or toll free 800/325-2525; fax 316/942-1717. On US 54. An exceptionally

quiet hotel for Wichita, this has a lobby with a high ceiling, lots of white and dark wood. **Rooms:** 42 rms. CI open/CO 2pm. Nonsmoking rms avail. Spacious rooms. **Amenities:** 📺 A/C, cable TV w/movies, refrig. **Services:** ⌁ **Facilities:** ♿ **Rates (CP):** Peak (May–Dec) $45 S; $50 D. Extra person $5. Children under age 12 stay free. Lower rates off-season. Parking: Outdoor, free. AE, DC, DISC, MC, V.

☰☰☰ Days Inn Tudor Wichita

9100 E Kellogg Dr, 67207; tel 316/685-0371. Kellogg exit off I-35. Located along the I-35 turnpike. Nicely decorated and very friendly; good for families. Pleasant, comfortable lobby. **Rooms:.** CI 3pm/CO 11am. Nonsmoking rms avail. **Amenities:** 📺 ⚿ A/C, satel TV w/movies. **Services:** 🖨 **Facilities:** 🏊 ♿ **Rates (CP):** $41 S; $43 D; $75 ste. Extra person $2. Children under age 14 stay free. Parking: Outdoor, free.

☰☰ Super 8 Motel

527 S Webb Rd, 67207; tel 316/686-3888 or toll free 800/800-8000. Just E of Kellogg exit off turnpike. A budget motel that charges higher than budget prices for its nice but standard rooms. Convenient to business district. **Rooms:** 120 rms. CI noon/CO 11am. Nonsmoking rms avail. **Amenities:** 📺 ⚿ A/C, cable TV w/movies. **Services:** ⌁ **Facilities:** ♿ Access to YMCA facilities. **Rates (CP):** $41 S; $48 D. Extra person $3. Children under age 12 stay free. Parking: Outdoor, free. AE, CB, DC, DISC, MC, V.

RESTAURANTS 🍴

Abigail's Restaurant

In Holiday Inn Wichita Airport, 5500 W Kellogg Dr; tel 316/943-2181. 2 mi W of town. **American.** Great for dining near the airport or the Holiday Inn, this restaurant has a lovely decor accented with wood and brass. The menu includes sandwiches, breakfast items, steaks, salads, and more. **FYI:** Reservations not accepted. Children's menu. Beer and wine only. **Open:** Breakfast daily 6–11am; lunch daily 11am–2pm; dinner daily 5–10pm. **Prices:** Main courses $8–$16. AE, CB, DC, DISC, MC, V. ♿

Anthony Miller's Chateau Briand Restaurant

In Days Inn Tudor Wichita, 9100 E Kellogg Dr; tel 316/682-4212. Kellogg exit off I-35. **American/Seafood.** A pink and red color scheme runs unchecked—through the art, tablecloths, napkins, and everything else. Limited service and an unfriendly relationship with the hotel make this an awkward and unpredictable place to dine. But the food is good and reasonably priced. The specialties are the beef entrees. **FYI:** Reservations recommended. **Open:** Mon–Sat 5–10pm. **Prices:** Main courses $8–$30. AE, DISC, MC, V. ♥

Bombay Bicycle Club Restaurant & Bar

7700 E Kellogg Dr; tel 316/686-3394. **Burgers/Italian.** Lots of live plants and a light-filled atrium give this dining room a sunny atmosphere. Although decorated in a Pacific Island theme, the best bet is the delicious burgers. The friendly bar area offers pool tables and backgammon sets. **FYI:** Reservations accepted. Children's menu. **Open:** Sun–Mon 11:30am–10pm, Tues–Wed 11:30am–midnight, Thurs–Sat 11:30am–2am. **Prices:** Main courses $4–$8. AE, DISC, MC, V. 👥 ♿

Cafe Chicago Sports Bar and Grill

5207 E Kellogg Dr; tel 316/684-5561. **American.** A typical sports bar, with limited seating. TVs are within range from just about every corner of the bar. Reliable for burgers, chicken wings, and beer. **FYI:** Reservations not accepted. **Open:** Daily 11am–2am. **Prices:** Main courses $4–$6. AE, DC, DISC, MC, V.

★ Chelsea Bar and Grill

2949 N Rock Rd; tel 316/636-1103. **American.** A massive bar dominates this room with great pub atmosphere. Piano entertainment is featured seven days, while a four-piece jazz combo jams four days a week. Reliable grill fare. **FYI:** Reservations accepted. Jazz/piano/rock. **Open:** Mon–Thurs 11am–10pm, Fri–Sat 11am–11pm, Sun 5–9pm. **Prices:** Main courses $5–$20. AE, DC, DISC, MC, V. ♥ ▾

Jimmie's Diner

3111 N Rock Rd; tel 316/636-1818. 1 block N of 29th St. **Burgers.** A 1950s soda shop where all the waitresses wear poodle skirts and pink ankle socks, and classic oldies can always be heard in the background. The light and fun atmosphere is great for families and dates. Typical diner menu includes burgers, fries, malts, and sodas. **FYI:** Reservations not accepted. Children's menu. No liquor license. **Open:** Daily 6am–midnight. **Prices:** Main courses $5–$13. CB, DC, MC, V. 👥 ♿

★ The Olive Tree

2949 N Rock Rd; tel 316/636-1100. **Italian.** An adjunct to the Chelsea Bar and Grill (see above). Open and airy dining rooms are separated by partitions of delicate etched glass. Fresh salmon and duck are featured. Highly professional service. **FYI:** Reservations accepted. **Open:** Mon–Thurs 11am–10pm, Fri–Sat 11am–11pm, Sun 5–9pm. **Prices:** Main courses $7–$20. AE, DC, DISC, MC, V. ♥

Potbelly's Restaurant

1211 E 47th St S; tel 316/524-0804. Off I-135. **American/Burgers.** A family-style restaurant right next to the Comfort Inn, this eatery specializes in breakfast and serves it all day long. A nice place for a quick meal before traveling on. **FYI:** Reservations not accepted. No liquor license. **Open:** Daily 6am–10pm. **Prices:** Main courses $6–$14. AE, DISC, MC, V. 👥 ♿

⑤ Ryan's Steak Buffet & Bakery

6633 W Kellogg Dr; tel 316/946-5533. ½ mi E of I-235 on US 54. **Eclectic.** A basic, family-style steak house with a full buffet. Located in the center of a very large, well-lighted dining area, the buffet has six separate bars of salads, Tex-Mex items, desserts, casseroles, and meats. A great place for family dining, the food is good and the prices are moderate.

FYI: Reservations not accepted. Children's menu. No liquor license. **Open:** Sun–Thurs 10:45–9, Fri–Sat 10:45–10. **Prices:** Main courses $4–$8. AE, DISC, MC, V. 👥 ♿

Scotch and Sirloin

3941 E Kellogg Dr; tel 316/685-8701. **American.** A dark wood and red decor gives this restaurant an English pub–style atmosphere. A proficient staff serves all types of beef, but the prime rib is probably the best dish. **FYI:** Reservations accepted. **Open:** Mon–Sat 11am–midnight, Sun 5–11pm. **Prices:** Main courses $9–$17. AE, DC, DISC, MC, V. ♥

ATTRACTIONS 🏛

Old Cowtown Museum

1871 Sim Park Ave; tel 316/264-0671. A historic village depicting Wichita in the early years, 1865–1880. Among the 35 exhibit buildings are Wichita's first jail, grain elevator, general store, one-room schoolhouse, and working blacksmith shop. During summer, living history demonstrations given; on the first full weekend of October, a re-created 1870s fair includes crafts, livestock, demonstrations, music, games, and a steam-operated carousel. **Open:** Mon–Sat 10am–5pm, Sun noon–5pm. **$$**

First National Black Historical Museum

601 N Water; tel 316/262-7651. The old Calvary Church (built circa 1917) now houses exhibits celebrating African American achievements in Wichita history, especially the role of the "Buffalo Soldiers" in the settling of the Plains. Visitors can also view collections of African wood carvings, jewelry, and other artifacts. **Open:** Aug–June, Mon, Wed, Fri 10am–2pm, Sun 2–6pm. **Free**

Wichita Art Museum

619 Stackman Dr; tel 316/268-4921. The largest art museum in Kansas showcases American painting, graphics, sculpture, and decorative arts. Major artists represented are Copley, Predergast, Hopper, and Charles M Russell. There's also an interactive children's gallery for the kids. **Open:** Tues–Sat 10am–5pm, Sun noon–5pm. **Free**

Kansas Aviation Museum

3350 S George Washington Blvd; tel 316/683-9242. Housed in the original Wichita airport terminal, the museum tells the story of local aviation. Wichita aviation pioneers such as Beech, Stearman, and Cessna are honored. On display are modern-day production models of Boeing and Lear Jets. **Open:** Tues–Fri 9am–4pm, Sat 1–5pm. **$**

Fellow-Reeve Museum of History and Science

2100 University; tel 316/292-5594. A general museum specializing in the history of the Midwest and Quaker missionaries in Africa. The collection includes North American big-game animals, Native American and pioneer relics, and African art. **Open:** Sept–May, Mon–Fri 1–4pm. **$**

Omnisphere and Science Center

220 S Main St; tel 316/264-3174. Planetarium, science demonstrations, and hands-on science center. **Open:** Tues–Fri 8am–5pm, Sat–Sun 1–5pm. **$$**

Botanica, The Wichita Gardens

701 N Amidon; tel 316/264-0448. Visitors walk the winding paths, photograph and identify plants, and enjoy the flowered walkways and small waterfalls. The gardens feature flowers and stone native to the area. Included are the Butterfly Garden, Shakespearean Garden, Aquatic Collection, and Xeriscape Demonstration Garden. **Open:** Apr–Dec, Mon–Sat 10am–5pm, Sun 1–5pm. **$$**

Sedgwick County Zoo

5555 Zoo Blvd; tel 316/942-2212. Featuring 1,331 animals covering 367 species. Exhibits include a petting farm; African and Asian animals such as hippos, giraffes, lions, tigers, and baboons; a herpetarium featuring Australasian turtles, boas, and giant tortoises; an Australian Outback with kangaroos, parrots, and wallaroos. Visitors can also view baby chimpanzees and orangutans in the zoo's breeding program. Special events scheduled year-round. **Open:** Peak (Mem Day–Labor Day) daily 9am–5pm. Reduced hours off-season. **$$$**

LOUISIANA

Let the Good Times Roll

STATE STATS

CAPITAL
Baton Rouge

AREA
43,566 square miles

BORDERS
Texas, Arkansas,
Mississippi, Gulf of Mexico

POPULATION
4,419,723 (1990)

ENTERED UNION
April 30, 1812 (18th state)

NICKNAMES
Bayou State, Pelican State

STATE FLOWER
Magnolia

STATE BIRD
Eastern brown pelican

FAMOUS NATIVES
Louis Armstrong,
Truman Capote, Fats Domino,
Lillian Hellman,
Jerry Lee Lewis, Huey P Long

For many visitors, Louisiana offers an experience that cannot be found elsewhere. They are intoxicated by the relaxed atmosphere and warm hospitality that have earned the state a reputation as a wonderful place to go for good times and celebrations. Festivals crowd the calendar year-round, from Mardi Gras madness to the month-long Christmas celebration of enchanting lights, madrigals, and bonfires along the Mississippi River.

Louisiana has not been homogenized by the forces of modern life. It retains the charm of an earlier time, with strong bonds of community and family and a lifestyle built around the enjoyment of all the pleasures life has to offer. It is the cradle of so much of America's music —jazz, blues, zydeco—as well as the home of Creole and Cajun cooking, the country's only truly native cuisine. Sometimes called the Bayou State, Louisiana boasts of more than 5,000 miles of navigable rivers, lakes, and bayous, all of which has also earned Louisiana the sobriquet "Sportsman's Paradise." Boating, fishing, and hunting are immensely popular, and the climate is conducive to other outdoor pursuits such as golf, tennis, and watersports virtually all year long.

Many people unfamiliar with Louisiana think of it as having predominantly French-Creole roots—no doubt because of New Orleans's famous French Quarter and the celebrated Cajun Country. But southern and northern Louisiana (referred to by the state's residents as North Louisiana and South Louisiana) are in fact quite distinct, not only in terms of terrain—the north is marked by rolling hills and piney woods, while the south is mostly flat marshlands—but in their ethnic and cultural makeup as well. The north resembles other Southern states in its Protestant, Irish-English-Scottish heritage, while the south is overwhelmingly Catholic and Cajun (except for the Feliciana parishes in the "instep" of boot-shaped Louisiana, which were settled by the English). And below New Orleans, the area around Des

Allemands has been known as the German Coast for the past 150 years. Many in the state thought they'd never live to see the day a north–south interstate connected Louisiana's two halves. But I-49 between Lafayette and Shreveport is near completion, and the two regions will be connected physically, if not quite in spirit.

A Brief History

Questionable Beginnings Louisiana history is characterized by a certain restlessness and the presence of colorful figures. One could even say that the term "crooked politicians" is practically one word in this state. For those Louisianians familiar with the state's history, none of this comes as much of a surprise. The state, after all, was founded by a crook. Not, to be sure, French explorer René Robert Cavelier, sieur de La Salle, who in 1682 followed the Mississippi River from Canada to the Gulf of Mexico and claimed for Louis XIV all of the territory drained by the river. And not the estimable Pierre Le Moyne, sieur d'Iberville, the French-Creole who in 1699 led expeditions into the lower Mississippi Valley. Nor his brother, the equally estimable Jean-Baptiste Le Moyne, who is credited with founding New Orleans in 1718. And certainly not the swashbuckling Frenchman Louis Juchereau de St Denis, who founded Natchitoches, the oldest permanent European settlement in the Louisiana Purchase (four years before the founding of New Orleans).

No, the gentleman in question was a certain John Law, an 18th-century Scotsman who departed England after killing a man and went to France, where he finessed his way into the French court. Law managed to become the confidante of Philippe II, duc d'Orleans, regent to the child-king, Louis XV. The savvy Law obtained from the French crown a 25-year franchise to exploit the Louisiana Territory. It was he who instructed Bienville to found a settlement, and to name it after the French regent.

Law advertised news of the vast riches and splendid Edens to be found in the new world throughout Europe, and his proclamations persuaded thousands

of Europeans to leave home and hearth and head for the Louisiana Territory. Yet instead of Eden, the new settlers found a hostile environment of hurricanes, yellow fever, scatterings of crude palmetto huts, and vast acres of thick canebrakes that had to be cut through and cleared. The French government set free various convicts, prostitutes, and miscreants from French jails, and sent them to settle in the new territory. The colonists had little choice but to dig in and make the best of things. It is possible that the statewide zest for festivals, food, and celebrations is rooted in the ways of those early Louisianians, who were determined to eat, drink, and be merry—come what may.

Change of Owners John Law's various schemes—known collectively as the Mississippi Bubble—eventually bankrupted France, and he himself fled the country. But the colony continued to develop. In 1762 the territory was transferred from France to Spain, and it remained under Spanish control until 1800. (Louisiana's unique system of parishes date from the Spanish period). That year, by secret treaty, it was ceded back to France, and in 1803, President Thomas Jefferson purchased the entire Louisiana Territory from Napoleon Bonaparte for $15 million. Following the Louisiana Purchase, Americans began pouring downriver on the Mississippi. In 1804, the US congress divided the vast tract into two sections —the Territory of Louisiana and the Territory of Orleans. The boundaries of the Territory of Orleans matched those of the present state—except for a vast area west of the Mississippi in the instep of the boot-shaped state. That region was in the hands of Spain (the parishes of the region are still often called the "Florida parishes"), though it had been settled by Americans of English ancestry. After a brief revolt by a small group of settlers in 1810, governor William C C Claiborne took possession of the area and formed the four parishes north of New Orleans. Louisiana became a state in 1812, and three years later, the final conflagration of the last war between England and the United States—the Battle of New Orleans, fought downriver on the green fields of Chalmette—saw Andrew Jackson's ragtag army defeat a far superior British army.

Fun Facts

• The nation's first movie theater, Vitascope Hall, opened in New Orleans on June 26, 1896.
• Rayne, Louisiana, claims that it is the "Frog Capital of the World." Most of the suppliers of frogs for gourmet dining and scientific experimentation are located here, and every September the town stages a frog festival that features frog races, frog beauty contests, and frog fireworks.
• At 181,157 feet, the concrete trestle along I-55/I-10 in Manchae is the longest bridge in the United States.

Prosperity & Peril The 1830s ushered in the Steamboat Era, with packets and floating palaces bringing goods and people down the Mississippi. In 1840, New Orleans, with a population of 100,000, was the fourth-largest city in the nation and one of the wealthiest.

Louisiana, along with 10 other southern states, seceded from the Union in 1861, and in 1862, New Orleans became one of the first southern cities to fall into Union hands. Bloody battles were fought all over the state, notably at Port Hudson—the site of the longest sustained siege in American military history, where a small army of Confederates finally fell to superior Union forces—and in Mansfield, where the battle ended with one of the South's last major victories. Following the war, Louisiana suffered under Reconstruction longer than any other southern state except South Carolina. Union forces finally departed in 1877, and the state began a long and difficult recovery.

The Kingfish Cometh Louisiana, along with the other southern states, was barely recovering from the devastation of war and reconstruction when the entire nation was sunk into the Great Depression. The poverty-stricken state was fertile soil for a demagogue like Huey Pierce Long, Louisiana's most cunning, colorful, and controversial politician, who rose to political prominence in the state in the 1920s and was elected governor in 1928. He came to power with campaign slogans such as "Share the Wealth" and "Every Man a King," and tens of thousands of Louisianians worshipped him as a veritable savior. The "Kingfish" continued to control the state even after his election to the US Senate. President Franklin Roosevelt was said to have feared him, and there is little doubt that Long aspired to the presidency of the United States. He may have given Roosevelt a run for his money had he not been assassinated in 1935. Though he served only one term as governor, Long's shadow still seems to hover over the political landscape

DRIVING DISTANCES
New Orleans
78 miles SE of Baton Rouge
118 miles SE of St Francisville
129 miles SE of Lafayette
188 miles SE of Alexandria
200 miles SE of Lake Charles
241 miles SE of Natchitoches
361 miles E of Houston, TX
Baton Rouge
40 miles SE of St Francisville
52 miles E of Lafayette
123 miles NE of Lake Charles
182 miles SE of Monroe
235 miles SE of Shreveport
274 miles E of Houston, TX
Shreveport
98 miles W of Monroe
181 miles N of Lake Charles
191 miles E of Dallas, TX
199 miles NW of Opelousas
214 miles NW of Lafayette
312 miles NW of New Orleans

of the state.

Boom, Bust & Beyond Prosperity came to Louisiana in a big way after the discovery of oil offshore of Louisiana in the Gulf of Mexico. The "Black Gold Rush" began on November 14, 1947, when Kerr-McGee struck oil in the gulf, about 45 miles south of Morgan City. Two years later, three major fields were discovered offshore of Louisiana. The oil and gas industry, and the state, flourished until the 1980s, when the oil boom finally went bust. Morgan City and other towns that had become wealthy with oil money have been hard hit by the resultant depression.

Louisiana now looks to the tourist industry to lead the way to economic recovery, and the state is pulling out all the stops in efforts to attract visitors. The north, in particular, has made some interesting cultural shifts for this purpose. Aware that most visitors to the state head to New Orleans and Cajun Country, cities such as Shreveport and Monroe have begun to get on the South Louisiana bandwagon. Both of those cities now celebrate Mardi Gras—something that was unheard of in the Protestant north 10 years ago—and have restaurants that serve traditional Cajun dishes. Tourism officials readily confess that it's all in the interest of attracting tourists—and their money. Clearly, many Louisianans feel that if it's South Louisiana that all those visitors come to see, then South Louisiana they will see—even in the north.

A Closer Look

GEOGRAPHY

At 535 feet above sea level, **Driskill Mountain,** near the little town of Arcadia in Florida parishes, is the highest point in the state. The foothills of the Ozarks extend south across the Arkansas border into **Florida parishes,** which is characterized by rolling hills, red-clay bluffs, tall pine trees, and plenty of lakes for boating and fishing. But at Alexandria, the state's mid-section, the landscape makes an abrupt switch to flat marshlands, gray earth, giant centuries-old live oak trees draped in Spanish moss, and bald cypresses jutting starkly out of the swamps. **Southwest Louisiana** is laced with meandering bayous, whose sluggish bottle-green waters are dotted with Cajun pirogues (canoes) and shaded by subtropical greenery. Along the gulf coast, salt domes—locally called "islands"—gently rise over the flat marshlands and savannas overlaid with luxuriant trees and subtropical greenery, and the coastal marshes are filled with lush vegetation and wildlife. **New Orleans** itself is an island—as recently as 1957 it was accessible only by water or air. Much of the city is reclaimed swamplands, and much of it lies five to eight feet below sea level. Above New Orleans, the piney hills lying within the instep of this boot-shaped state are similar to those of Florida parishes.

CLIMATE

Louisiana sits just 30° north of the Equator, not far from the Tropic of Cancer, which explains its sultry climate and oppressive humidity. The state's great weathermaker is the temperamental, unpredictable Gulf of Mexico. Hurricane season officially begins June 1 and ends November 1. Since hurricanes lose force as they travel overland, Florida parishes experiences only high winds and heavy rains, but some coastal towns have literally been decimated by big blows. The statewide annual rainfall is about 56 inches, with the northern region averaging 46 inches and some of the southern coastal parishes averaging as much as 66 inches of rainfall a year. In the north of the state, highs in July average 83°F, but the average number of days each year with temperatures 90° and above is 102. In southern regions, the highest July average is 81°. In January, lows in the northern regions average 49°, and in the southeast, 57°. Snow is rare, though not unheard of, even in New Orleans; icestorms, however, are not uncommon, especially in the northern regions.

AVERAGE TEMPERATURES & RAINFALL

	Temp °F	Inches of Rainfall
Jan	47.5	5.0
Feb	51.2	4.9
Mar	58.9	5.0
Apr	66.7	4.3
May	73.4	5.3
June	79.4	4.6
July	81.8	5.3
Aug	81.4	4.6
Sept	76.9	4.6
Oct	67.1	3.7
Nov	58.5	4.6
Dec	50.7	5.7

WHAT TO PACK

Whatever time of year you come, pack an umbrella, sunglasses, and sunscreen. Louisiana's unpredictable weather is such that you may need all three in a given hour. From late March until mid-October, pack loose-fitting cottons, and in the winter months, plan to layer with lightweight wools or cottons. An all-weather coat with a zip-out lining is ideal for winter. Men should bring a jacket and tie for upscale restaurants. Shreveport, on the whole, is much more formal than New Orleans, where streetwear—especially in the French Quarter—runs toward the least the law and the weather will allow; shorts, cut-offs, tee-shirts, and halters seem almost de rigueur. Bring comfortable walking shoes, and appropriate footwear if boating is planned. And don't forget the insect repellent.

TOURIST INFORMATION

Contact the **Louisiana Office of Tourism**, PO Box 94291, Baton Rouge 70804 (tel 504/342-7317 or 800/33-GUMBO) about a month before you plan to visit and they'll send you a copy of the *Louisiana Tour Guide* and a state highway map. The Louisiana Office of Tourism also maintains a Web page (http://sunset.hob.com/louisiana) with general information about the state. In addition, almost every town of any size at all has a chamber of commerce or visitors bureau that provides specific local and regional information; these are listed in the Louisiana Tour Guide. Other excellent sources are the New Orleans Metropolitan Convention & Visitors Bureau, 1520 Sugar Bowl Dr, New Orleans 70112 (tel 504/566-5005); the Lafayette Convention & Visitors Bureau, 1400 NW Evangeline Thruway, Lafayette 70501 (tel 318/232-3808 or 800/346-1958); the Southwest Louisiana Convention & Visitors Bureau, 1211 N Lakeshore Dr, Lake Charles 70601 (tel 800/456-SWLA), and the Shreveport-Bossier Convention & Visitors Bureau, 629 Spring St, Shreveport 71101 (tel 318/222-9391 or 800/551-8682).

DRIVING RULES AND REGULATIONS

State law requires use of seat belts by drivers and front-seat passengers. Child restraints are required for children age 4 or younger, or who weigh 40 pounds or less. Unless otherwise indicated, a right turn on red is legal after you've come to a complete stop.

RENTING A CAR

All major rental agencies are represented in Louisiana. Because New Orleans is the prime tourist destination, rates there tend to be more competitive than in other parts of the state. Most agencies have locations in downtown New Orleans as well as at the airport, but rates at downtown locations are higher than at the airport. (If you plan to rent a car during Mardi Gras, reserve it well in advance and get a confirmation number. Keep in mind that the entire French Quarter is closed to vehicular traffic during Mardi Gras, and that a car that blocks a parade route will be towed away and the owner fined $100.) If you pick up a car in one city and return it in another, there is usually a drop-off charge or one-way service fee.

- **Alamo** (tel 800/327-9683)
- **Avis** (tel 800/331-1212)
- **Budget** (tel 800/527-0700)
- **Dollar** (tel 800/800-4000)
- **Hertz** (tel 800/654-3131)
- **National** (tel 800/227-7368)
- **Sears** (tel 800/527-0770)
- **Thrifty** (tel 800/367-2277)

ESSENTIALS

Area Codes: The area code for the New Orleans and Baton Rouge metropolitan areas is **504.** For all other parts of the state, the area code is **318.**

Emergencies: Call 911 for ambulance, police, and fire department assistance.

Liquor Laws: You must be 21 years old and have proper identification to purchase or consume alcoholic beverages.

Road Conditions: Call the 24-hour Highway Safety Hotline at 800/259-4929 or 504/379-1541.

Smoking Laws: Smoking is prohibited in public buildings, elevators, airports, movie theaters and theater lobbies, hospitals, doctors' offices, and all public transportation. A few small restaurants have banned smoking, but most restaurants have separate smokers' and nonsmokers' sections. Smoking is permitted in bars. All major hotels have separate rooms or, in some cases, entire floors reserved for nonsmokers.

Taxes: The Louisiana state sales tax is 4%. However, local taxes—parish and city—can jack the sales tax up to 8%; in New Orleans, the combined total is 9%. The lodging tax ranges from about 3% (for bed-and-breakfasts) to 11% (New Orleans hotels). The bottom line on your New Orleans hotel bill will also include a surtax of $1 to $3 per room per night, depending upon the size of the hotel. In New Orleans, the tax on car rentals is 13½%.

Time Zone: Louisiana is in the central time zone, two hours ahead of the West Coast and one hour behind the East.

Best of the State

WHAT TO SEE AND DO

Below is a general overview of some of the top sights and attractions in Louisiana. To find out more detailed information, look under "Attractions" for individual cities in the listings portion of this book.

French Quarter   The state's best-known and busiest tourist destination is the French Quarter in New Orleans, a 96-square block living museum with music clubs, fine restaurants, hotels and guest houses, museums, bookstores and shops, and world-famous Bourbon Street. Jazz originated in New Orleans a century ago, and it flourishes all over town. The city's fine French Creole cuisine is no less legendary, and certainly no less abundant.

Mardi Gras   New Orleans is home to Mardi Gras, the biggest "block party" in all of North America, and there is nothing else like it in the country. Carnival season begins annually on January 6 and culminates with the famous parades and parties of Fat Tuesday.

Cajun Country Acadiana (also called French Louisiana and Cajun Country), west of New Orleans, is the state's second most popular visitors' destination, promising—and delivering—"big fun on the bayou." Lafayette, the unofficial capital of French Louisiana, is located in the center of Acadiana and makes a good starting point for touring the backroads, bayous, and villages of the region. Cajun fare is as well-known as New Orleans cuisine, and the fiddles and accordions in Cajun dancehalls encourage two-stepping, or, at the very least, toe-tapping. The motto of Acadiana is *Laissez les bons temps rouler*: "Let the good times roll." And roll they do.

National Historical Parks The **Jean Lafitte National Historical Park Service** is unique in that it is the only one in the National Park system that focuses on culture. There are seven outposts, or units, administered by the Jean Lafitte National Historical Park Service, including the French Quarter in New Orleans, where park rangers conduct daily free walking tours. Each unit has a museum and interpretative center—and in most cases a film presentation —with extensive displays pertaining to the many cultures that have contributed to the state's history and heritage. The **Barataria Unit,** south of New Orleans, is a 6,800-acre preserve with hiking and nature trails and canoeing on murky bayous. There is a **Wetlands Acadian Cultural Center** in Thibodaux; an **Acadian Cultural Center** in Lafayette; a **Prairie Acadian Culture Center** in Eunice; a **Chalmette** unit, on the site of the 1815 Battle of New Orleans; and an **Islenos** unit, downriver of New Orleans, where a group of Canary Islanders settled in the 1800s. For more information about the units contact the Jean Lafitte National Historical Park, 423 Canal St, New Orleans 70112 (tel 504/589-3882).

State Parks Louisiana state parks take full advantage of the many lakes, bayous, and rivers spread throughout the state. Fourteen state parks offer boating, picnicking, fishing, and, in some cases, camping, swimming, hiking or nature trails, and waterskiing; seven of them have rustic cabins for overnighting, two have lodges outfitted with cookware, cooking utensils, dinnerware, cutlery, and bed linens, and all have public restrooms. For more information about the state parks and commemorative areas, contact the **Louisiana Office of State Parks,** PO Box 44426, Baton Rouge 70804 (tel 504/342-8111).

Natural Wonders The **Mississippi River,** the world's third-longest river, ambles southward from its source in Lake Itasca, Minnesota, traveling 2,350 miles before emptying into the Gulf of Mexico. The river washes along the eastern border of Louisiana, separating the state from Mississippi. It was the Mississippi that carved out the crescent-shaped land mass upon which New Orleans sits, thus giving that city its "Crescent City" moniker. The state is laced with vast acres of swamplands and bayous (from a Choctaw word meaning "creek"), the largest of which is **Bayou Teche** in southwest Louisiana. Near Lafayette the **Atchafalaya Basin** is an 800,000-acre wilderness of hardwood forests, cypress swamps, marshes, and bayous. The state is also home to the **Alexander State Forest** and six ranger districts of the **Kisatchie National Forest** (tel 318/473-7160), where there are hiking, biking, and backpacking trails through magnificent hardwood forests. The Nature Conservancy maintains lush **Little Pecan Island,** south of Kaplan (and accessible only by water), preserving some of the world's last remaining chenieres (ancient isolated beaches).

Historic Sites & Areas Louisiana's State Commemorative Areas commemorate an historic event, person, or people. In most cases, there is a museum and interpretative center. The **Audubon State Commemorative Area** in St Francisville surrounds **Oakley Plantation,** where John James Audubon lived, tutored, and painted in the 1820s. **Fort Jesup SCA** in Many is on the site of a fort established by Zachary Taylor in 1822; **Fort Pike SCA,** on US 90 near New Orleans, is a masonry fort built in 1827 to defend the city. On the outskirts of St Martinville, the **Longfellow-Evangeline SCA** is a pretty, tree-shaded park in which Acadian structures depict life in the early 1800s. At the **Mansfield SCA,** museum exhibits interpret a significant Civil War battle that was fought on this site, and the **Port Hudson SCA,** north of Baton Rouge, commemorates a bloody Civil War battle which was also the longest sustained siege in American military history. Native American mounds and artifacts at the **Marksville SCA** reflect a culture that dates from AD 400, and **Poverty Point SCA,** one of the nation's most important archeological digs, interprets the mounds, artifacts, and earthworks of a culture more than 3,700 years old.

Museums The **Louisiana State Museum** in New Orleans is one of the nation's largest; among its several properties is the restored Cabildo, where transfer papers were signed for the historic Louisiana Purchase. In Baton Rouge the **Rural Life Museum,** an extensive indoor/outdoor facility, traces plantation culture, and the restored **Old State Capitol** houses the **Center for Political and Governmental History.** In Jackson, the **Republic of West Florida Historical Museum,** also a vast indoor/outdoor museum, traces the colorful history of the Florida parishes. The **New Orleans Museum of Art** has among its permanent collection works by masters of the 17th through 19th centuries, African and Asian artworks, and a fabulous collection of Fabergé eggs; galleries in **New Orleans's Contemporary Arts Center** exhibit avant-garde and alternative artists. Shreveport's **R W Norton Museum** has a vast collection of sculptures by Frederic Remington.

Gardens & Zoos   Louisiana's fertile soil is home to a number of lovely gardens. **Hodges Gardens** near Many offers 4,700 acres of woodlands, waterfalls, and botanical gardens. The **American Rose Center** in Shreveport, the nation's largest park devoted to roses and headquarters for the American Rose Society, has 118 acres of blooming beauties. **Avery Island,** where Tabasco sauce was invented and is still produced (you can tour the factory), has exotic jungle gardens and a bird sanctuary. Near New Iberia, **Live Oak Gardens** is a 20-acre showplace of year-round blooms. Every species of plants, trees, and flowers indigenous to the state is displayed and labeled in the **Louisiana State Arboretum** near Ville Platte. In New Orleans, 1,500-acre **City Park**—one of the nation's largest urban parks—has the world's largest mature stand of live oak trees, and **Audubon Park** has a world-class zoo in which more than 1,800 animals roam in natural habitats.

Plantations   A number of fine, old antebellum mansions are spread throughout the state, but the greatest concentration is along the **Great River Road** between New Orleans and St Francisville. Among those not to be missed are Rosedown in St Francisville, Nottoway near Baton Rouge, and Houmas House near Burnside. Madewood Plantation, a handsome home on Bayou Lafourche, and Shadows-on- the-Teche, a National Trust property in New Iberia, are other stand outs. Laura Plantation in Vacherie is unique in that it predates the antebellum era and is a restoration-in-progress. All are open for tours; Madewood, Rosedown, and Nottoway are bed-and-breakfasts.

Casinos   The state is awash with casinos, on land and on the water-ways. In New Orleans, Harrah's is constructing "the world's largest casino," scheduled for completion by the end of 1996, and presently operates a temporary facility. There are thriving casinos on tribal reservations of the Chitimacha (Cypress Bayou, in Charenton), the Coushatta (Grand Casino Coushatta, near Kinder), and the Tunica-Biloxi (Grand Casino Avoyelles, in Marksville), as well as **riverboat casinos** in New Orleans, Lake Charles, Baton Rouge, and Shreveport/Bossier City.

Family Favorites   Although New Orleans is perhaps best known for more-grown-up Bourbon Street, the city has a number of first-class family-oriented attractions. Among them are the excellent **Aquarium of the Americas,** with its several exhibition areas and new IMAX theater; the **Audubon Zoo;** the **Louisiana Children's Museum,** which has numerous hands-on exhibits; and the **Louisiana Nature & Science Center,** with planetarium, nature trails, and "discovery loft" for children. There is also an excellent hands-on children's museum in Lake Charles; a fun and educational science museum in Shreveport; and the **Natural History Museum & Planetarium** in Lafayette. Lafayette is home as well to the **Acadian Village,** a replica of an early Cajun settlement, and the **Vermilionville Living History Museum & Village,** where the early history of the region is traced in several authentic 19th-century structures.

Swamps & Bayous   Among the state's most intriguing features are the exotic swamps and bayous that flow sluggishly beneath canopies of moss-hung trees. The state's largest bayou is the **Teche,** which winds through the southeastern part of the state. Half- and full-day swamp tours are conducted throughout South Louisiana, often by colorful Cajun guides who spin tales of gators and swamp monsters.

Cuisine   South Louisiana is the only part of the United States that has two distinctive regional cuisines. New Orleans's world-famous Creole cuisine and the Cajun cooking of southwest Louisiana both have strong French roots. Though the two styles have merged in recent years into what is called "South Louisiana cuisine," the two are different. Creole cuisine, a highly sophisticated style developed over a couple of centuries in the city's kitchens, combines many local influences—French, Spanish, African American, and Native American—and is characterized by rich sauces. Cajun cooking, sometimes called the "country cousin" of Creole cuisine, is simpler, if not spicier, fare that employs French methods and rural southern ingredients; it relies heavily on seafood, game, and herbs. (Celebrity chef Paul Prudhomme, a native of Opelousas in Acadiana, popularized Cajun cooking, although his style is a flamboyant embellishment of traditional Cajun dishes. He made "blackening" a nationwide craze, but blackening was Prudhomme's innovation, not a traditional Cajun cooking technique.) In recent years, the Cajun craze has swept through the region, and Cajun dishes such as red beans and rice, gumbo, jambalaya, and crawfish étouffée appear on many menus.

EVENTS AND FESTIVALS

- **Sugar Bowl College Football Classic,** New Orleans. The annual New Year's Day collegiate "shoot-out" in the Louisiana Superdome. January. Call 504/525-8573 for information.
- **Mardi Gras,** New Orleans. The culmination of Carnival season, celebrated by parades and partying. February or March. Call 504/566-5005.
- **Cajun Mardi Gras,** Lafayette. Street festivals, music, and parades. February or March. Call 318/232-3737.
- **Mardi Gras of Imperial Calcasieu,** Lake Charles. Southwest Louisiana's Cajun Mardi Gras celebration. February or March. Call 318/436-7006.
- **French Quarter Festival,** New Orleans. A huge weekend block party featuring food, music, and crafts. April. Call 504/522-5730.
- **Festival International de Louisiane,** Lafayette. Four hundred artists from Africa, Canada, the Caribbean, Europe, and the Americas participate in a celebration of Louisiana's cultural heritage. April. Call 318/232-8086.
- **Holiday in Dixie,** Shreveport. A treasure hunt, air shows, parades, and tournaments during a 10-day festival. April. Call 318/865-5555.
- **New Orleans Jazz & Heritage Festival,** New Orleans. Musicians from all over the world participate in a 10-day festival of music and food. Last weekend in April through the first weekend in May. Call 504/522-4786.
- **Great Louisiana Gumbo Cook-off,** Oakdale. Professional and amateur chefs participate in gumbo

demonstrations and tastings. May. Call 318/335-9000.
- **Crawfish Festival,** Breaux Bridge. One of the state's largest festivals with Cajun food, music, dancers, various crawfish contests. May. Call 318/332-6655.
- **Seafood Festival,** Mandeville. Food, fireworks, arts and crafts, music, children's entertainment tent. July. Call 504/624-9762.
- **Red River Rally, A Hot Air Balloon Uprising,** Shreveport. Hot air balloonists from around the country gather for competitions. Tethered rides, antique car show. July. Call 318/862-9562.
- **Festival Acadiens,** Lafayette. Cajun music and food. September. Call 318/232-3808.
- **Southwest Louisiana Zydeco Festival,** Plaisance. Zydeco music, Creole cuisine, arts and crafts. September. Call 318/942-2392.
- **Louisiana Shrimp & Petroleum Festival,** Morgan City. One of the state's oldest festivals, with Blessing of the Fleet, live Cajun music, a children's village, shrimp cookoff. September. Call 504/385-0703.
- **Balloons & Barbecue festival,** Baton Rouge. Hot-air balloon contests and a barbecue cookout. Late September or early October. Call 504/383-1825.
- **Louisiana State Fair,** Shreveport. Top-name performers, midway rides, music, food. October. Call 318/635-1361.
- **Gumbo Festival,** Bridge City. Cajun food, music, games, a 5K run. October. Call 504/436-4712.
- **Louisiana Cattle Festival,** Abbeville. Livestock show, cooking contest, pageants, food booths, rodeo, parade, and carnival. October. Call 318/893-6328.
- **Festival of the Bonfires,** Lutcher. A weekend of nightly bonfires on the Mississippi River levee, arts and crafts, Cajun music and food. December. Call 504/562-2418.
- **A New Orleans Christmas,** New Orleans. Month-long events include Papa Nöel parade, bonfires, tours of homes, caroling. December. Call 504/522-5730.

SPECTATOR SPORTS

Baseball During the summer, the **New Orleans Zephyrs** (tel 504/282-6777), a AAA team affiliated with the Milwaukee Brewers, play at Privateer Park on the campus of the University of New Orleans.

The **Shreveport Captains,** (tel 318/636-5555) a AA club of the San Francisco Giants in the Texas League, play from April through August at Fair Grounds Field.

Auto Racing **Boothill Speedway** (tel 318/938-5373) in Shreveport is the South's fastest quarter-mile oval dirt track. The season runs from March through November, with races on Saturday nights.

Basketball The state's only professional basketball team is the **Shreveport Storm** (tel 318/424-SLAM) of the Continental Basketball Association. They play at Hirsch Memorial Coliseum from November through March.

Football Both North and South Louisiana have professional football clubs. The **New Orleans Saints** (504/522-2600) of the National Football League play their home schedule at the Louisiana Superdome, while the **Shreveport Pirates** (tel 318/222-3000) of the Canadian Football League take to the gridiron at Independence Stadium from July through November. The **Tulane University Green Wave** (tel 504/861-3661) entertain their fans in the Superdome. And college football's **Sugar Bowl Classic** (tel 504/525-8573) is played annually on New Year's Day, also in the Superdome.

Horse Racing The **New Orleans Fair Grounds** (tel 504/944-5515) is the country's third-oldest race-track, having been established in 1872. Thanksgiving Day is the traditional beginning of the live thorough-bred races, with the season continuing until mid-April. (The infield of the Fair Grounds is also the main turf for the New Orleans Jazz & Heritage Festival.) In Bossier City, **Louisiana Downs** (tel 318/742-5555 or 800/551-RACE), one of the South's largest tracks, offers thoroughbred racing from April through November. In Lafayette, **Evangeline Downs** (tel 318/896-7223) is home to thoroughbred racing from April until Labor Day. At Vinton's **Delta Downs Race Track** (tel 318/589-7441 or 800/737-3358), the thoroughbred racing season runs from September through March, and the quarterhorse season is April through Labor Day. For racing with a real Cajun flair, head for **Cajun Downs** (tel 318/893-8160 or 318/893-0421), a century-old bush track cut through country cane-fields where Sunday races year-round can feature horses, as well as mules, ponies, and even cows pounding down the red-dirt track.

ACTIVITIES A TO Z

Ballooning The Hot Air Balloon Place (tel 504/387-1259), based in Baton Rouge, offers rides state-wide; trips travel about 10 to 12 miles and average around 90 minutes (depending on wind conditions). Shreveport's Red River Rally and Baton Rouge's Ballons & Barbeque festival are popular annual ballooning events.

Bicycling The high humidity can put a damper on strenuous outdoor exertions, but the state's flat-lands and gently rolling hills make for easy riding. There are upwards of 100 marked bike trails in the state, and bicycle rental shops abound. Several bicycle clubs organize tours and provide information, among them Cajun Cyclists in Lafayette (tel 504/232-5854), the Baton Rouge Bicycle Club (tel 504/275-0595), Crescent City Cyclists in Metairie (tel 504/282-0307), Lake City Cyclists in Lake Charles (tel 318/433-7019), and the Shreveport Bicycle Club (tel 318/329-2335).

Bird Watching Amateur ornithologists flock to Louisiana each year (this is the state in which John James Audubon painted many of the specimens in his *Birds of America*). More than half of the birds in North America make a Louisiana layover during their trip along the Great Mississippi Flyway, and Louisiana is the southern terminus of the Central and Mississippi Flyways. Along the gulf coast, masses of migrating birds feed in the marshes and rice fields. Top spots for bird watching are the Sabine National Wildlife Refuge southwest of Sulphur; the Rockefeller Wildlife Refuge and Game Preserve on LA 82 (the "Hug the Coast Highway") south of Lake Charles; the Wisner Wildlife Management Area off LA 1 west of Grand Isle; Little Pecan Island south of Kaplan; and Longleaf Vista in the Kisatchie National Forest south of Natchitoches. In the summer, thousands and thousands of purple martins swarm to nest beneath the Lake Pontchartrain Causeway in New Orleans, while humans flock to the observation area to watch them.

Camping All of Louisiana's 14 state parks have camping facilities; all but two—Grand Isle State Park and Fontainebleau State Park—have hookups for water and electricity. For information about campsites, contact the Louisiana Office of State Parks, PO Box 44426, Baton Rouge 70804 (tel 504/342-8111).

Canoeing Louisiana's many waterways lure boaters and canoeists, with the exotic swamplands among the top attractions. Canoes can be rented, and guides hired, at Bayou Barn in Lafitte, south of New Pack & Paddle in Lafayette (tel 318/232-5854), Kistachie Cajun Expedition (tel 318/239-0119) in the Kisatchie National Forest, and Norris Outfitters in Shreveport (tel 318/949-9522). Pedal-boats and canoes can be rented for paddling out among the swans on manmade lagoons in New Orleans's City Park (tel 504/483-9371).

Fishing The state has the proverbial embarrassment of riches in sea creatures. The inland waterways are filled with bass, crappie, and speckled trout, while the Gulf of Mexico and the brackish waters of its coastal marshes harbor tarpon, cobia, snapper, yellowfin tuna, Spanish and king mackerel, sailfish, blue marlin, and wahoo—not to mention blue crabs, shrimp, and oysters. For information on fishing licenses and lake maps, contact the Louisiana Department of Wildlife & Fisheries, PO Box 98000, Baton Rouge 70898 (tel 504/765-2800).

Golfing Golfing is a year-round sport in Louisiana. The state's most challenging course is The Bluffs at Thompson Creek, near St Francisville, an 18-hole Arnold Palmer course which nonmembers are welcome to play. There are numerous public courses in the state, including 18-hole links in New Orleans and environs, Baton Rouge, Lake Charles, Shreveport, and Lafayette.

Hiking Louisiana's lush countryside forms a handsome backdrop for numerous scenic trails. There are miles and miles of hiking and backpacking trails through the hardwood forests of the Kisatchie National Forest. Along the river's route, the Mississippi River levee is great for hiking, running, and jogging. And the Barataria Unit of the Jean Lafitte National Park Service near Lafitte has miles of hiking, biking, and nature trails through wetlands.

Horseback Riding Horseback riding, rodeos, and horseshows are popular year-round, but there are few stables in the state where horses can be rented for solo rides. One of them is Broken Arrow Stables in New Iberia, which also provides hayrides. Guided trails are available through Audubon Park in New Orleans and at the 900-acre Global Wildlife Center in Folsom, where ostriches, zebras, gazelles, and other wildlife run free. You can also do a tour of the facility in a covered wagon.

SELECTED PARKS AND RECREATION AREAS

- **Bayou Segnette State Park,** US 90, New Orleans 70140 (tel 504/736-7140)
- **Chemin-A-Haut State Park,** US 425, Bastrop 71220 (tel 318/283-0812)
- **Chicot State Park,** US 167, Opelousas 70570 (tel 318/363-2503)
- **Cypremort Point State Park,** LA 87, Franklin 70538 (tel 318/867-4510)
- **Fairview-Riverside State Park,** I-12, Madisonville 70447 (tel 504/845-3318)
- **Fontainebleau State Park,** US 90, Covington 70433 (tel 504/624-4443)
- **Lake Bistineau State Park,** US 79, Minden 71055 (tel 318/745-3503)
- **Lake Bruin State Park,** I-20, St Josephs 71366 (tel 318/766-3530)
- **Lake Claiborne State Park,** I-20, Homer 71040 (tel 318/927-2976)
- **Lake Fausse Pointe State Park,** US 90, St Martinville 70582 (tel 318/228-4764)
- **North Toledo Bend State Park,** US 171, Zwole 71486 (tel 318/645-4715)
- **St Bernard State Park,** LA 39, New Orleans 70140 (tel 504/682-2101)
- **Sam Houston Jones State Park,** US 171, Lake Charles 70611 (tel 318/855-2665)

Hunting Louisiana has an eight-month hunting season. Beaver, nutria, bobcat, coyote, muskrat, red fox, and raccoon are among the fur-bearing creatures that can be hunted or trapped. White-tail deer, woodcock, quail, dove, turkey, geese, and duck are also plentiful. For information about hunting in the state contact the Louisiana Department of Wildlife & Fisheries, PO Box 98000, Baton Rouge 70890 (tel 504/765-2800).

Swimming Long, hot summers create a natural urge to plunge in cool waters. There are water parks scattered throughout the state, all with a plethora of flumes and slides. Among them are Water Town USA in Shreveport (tel 318/938-5473); Blue Bayou Water Park in Baton Rouge (tel 504/753-3333); and Waterland USA in Houma (tel 504/872-6143). There are pools at several of the state parks, notably Chicot State Park near Ville Platte, Fontainebleau State Park near Mandeville, Lake Bistineau State Park near Doyline, North Toledo Bend State Park near Zwolle, and Bayou Segnette State Park south of

New Orleans, (which has the state's largest wave pool).

Tennis The state's largest tennis facility is the 39-court center in New Orleans's City Park. Resort hotels throughout the state have tennis courts, and many of the state's public parks have tennis courts, notably in New Orleans, Baton Rouge, Lake Charles, Shreveport, and Lafayette.

Watersports Louisiana's more than 150 lakes, along with its bayous and rivers provide ample opportunities for boating, waterskiing, sailing, and other waterbound activities. Many of the state parks have boat rentals and launches.

Driving the State

CAJUN COUNTRY

Start	Houma
Finish	Lafayette
Distance	150 miles
Time	2 days
Highlights	Bayous, riverbanks, and swamps; fishing villages; an aviation museum; historic towns; the home of Tabasco hot sauce; the "Crawfish Capital of the World"; Cajun dancehalls, theme parks, and museums

This tour explores the colorful, fascinating Cajun culture that thrives in the bayous and along the riverbanks of "Acadiana," the official designation for the 22 southwestern Louisiana parishes otherwise collectively known as Cajun Country. Cajun music and food were a nationwide fad in the 1980s, but in southwestern Louisiana, the Cajun culture endures. Deeply religious and hard-working, Cajuns are also warm and friendly folk and welcome strangers to "pass a good time" on the bayous. Many of the inhabitants of this most unique region are descendants of the French colonists expelled by the British in the mid-19th century from *l'Acadie*—the old French name for Nova Scotia and the other maritime provinces ("Cajun" is a corruption of "Acadian"). The majority of residents speak a 17th-century form of French, which they learned from ancestors who had long been isolated from Mother France. Yet language poses no barriers to the excitement that pulses throughout the region (almost everyone speaks English, and most can speak or understand standard French as well). Here, the fiddles and accordions of Cajun bands raise the rafters in dancehalls for fais-do-dos (dances), and restaurants serve piles of étouffées, jambalaya, red beans and rice, and bread pudding. Food and fun are plentiful in the place where the motto is "Laissez les bons temps rouler"—let the good times roll. And roll they do.

For additional information on lodgings, dining, and attractions in the region covered by the tour, refer to specific cities in the listings portion of this chapter.

The gateway to Cajun Country lies 57 miles south of New Orleans on US 90, in:

1. **Houma,** the seat of Terrebonne Parish and a major shrimping and boating area. Several swamp tours take off from here. One of the state's prettiest drives is the circular loop along LA 56 and LA 57, which dips all the way down from Houma to the Gulf of Mexico and passes through the fishing villages of Dulac and Chauvin en route to Cocodrie on the Gulf. At Cocodrie ("crocodile" in French), **Coco Marina**, abutting the Gulf, is loaded with fishing guides and charter services. The **Houma-Terrebonne Parish Tourist Commission** at 1702 S St Charles St (tel 504/868-2732 or 800/668-2732) has maps, brochures, and free advice about the region.

From Houma, continue 16 miles northwest on US 90 to:

2. **Gibson** home to **Wildlife Gardens** (at the intersection of LA 311 and US 90), which offers guided tours of a 20-acre preserved swamp luxuriant with subtropical flowers, trees, and plants. Visitors can lure the resident alligators in for a closer look with dog food, which is tossed over the fence from big buckets passed out by park personnel. There is also an authentic trapper's cabin for overnight stays.

From Gibson, continue west on US 90 for 13 miles to:

3. **Morgan City,** which became a boom town on November 14, 1947, when the Kerr-McGee No 16 rig struck oil and ushered in the "black gold rush" offshore. The original 1917 film *Tarzan of the Apes*, starring Elmo Lincoln, was filmed in and around Morgan City, which sits on the Atchafalaya River, close to the Gulf of Mexico. Visitors can watch the video of the film at the **Morgan City Tourist Commission,** 725 Myrtle St (tel 504/384-3343). Adjacent to the office is the 22-foot-high floodwall of the **Atchafalaya River,** which is accessible and provides a good view of the river.

Cross the Atchafalaya River bridge west of Morgan City to Patterson. Just before the Calumet Bridge, turn right on Zenor Rd and drive less than a mile to the **Wedell-Williams Memorial Aviation Museum,** 394 Airport Circle (tel 504/395-7067). In the early 1930s, James Wedell, a nationally-known pioneer aviation ace, teamed with Harry Williams, the mayor of Patterson, to form a commercial air-mail service and build speed planes. This museum pays tribute to the two flyers, displaying airplane parts, trophies, newspaper clippings, and other memorabilia pertaining to their careers.

Go a mile west of Patterson to Calumet before veering right on Rte 182, which closely follows the winding Bayou Teche, 19 miles to:

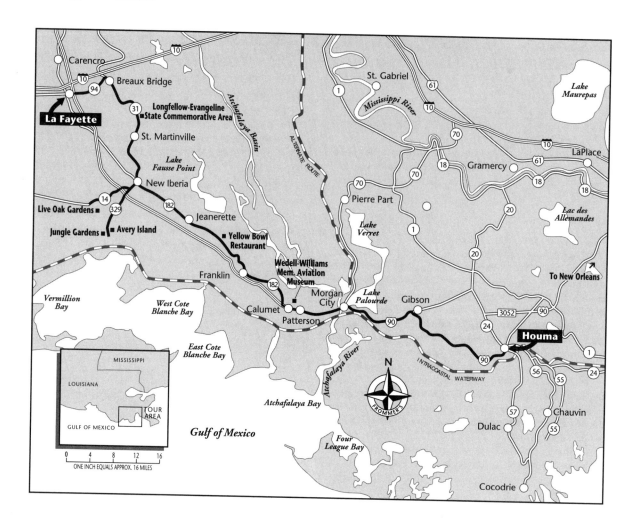

4. Franklin. This beautiful little town, an official Main Street USA town, boasts more than 400 historic houses and buildings. In fact, the entire town is listed on the National Register of Historic Places. The pretty Main Street is lined with Greek Revival mansions, leafy oak trees, and antique street lanterns. Franklin was settled not by Cajuns, but by Northerners (its residents sided with the Union during the Civil War). Stop at the **City of Franklin Tourist Commission,** 300 Iberia St (tel 318/828-6323 or 800/962-6889) to pick up walking and driving tour maps of the historic area. Among the mansions open to the public for tours are Arlington Plantation and the Grevemberg House.

Continue northwest on LA 182 for 23 miles to:

5. New Iberia, the "Queen City of the Teche." This small town offers several worthwhile attractions. Stop in the **Iberia Tourist Center** at 2704 LA 14, (tel 318/365-1540), for information about the town and the region. (Note that in downtown New Iberia, LA 182 splits into two one-way streets, Main St (westbound) and St Peter St (eastbound).) The town's most famous site is stately **Shadows-on-the-Teche,** 317 E Main St (tel 318/369-6446). Shaded by giant moss-draped oak trees on the banks of Bayou Teche, this lovely historic home was built by sugar planter David Weeks in 1834. The bricks used

---

Take a Break

The **Yellow Bowl Restaurant** (tel 318/276-5512), located 7 miles west of Franklin and 3 miles east of Jeanerette, on LA 182. Housed in a small, sunny cottage and open since the 1960s, this eatery is famed in these parts for its crawfish étouffée and other Cajun specialties (priced at $8 to $10).

in its construction were made of clay taken from the banks of the Teche. Period antiques are among the house's beautiful furnishings. Nearby, tours are conducted of the **Conrad Rice Mill,** one of the nation's oldest rice mills (it produces Wild Pecan Rice). New Iberia is also home to **Trappey's Fine Foods,** 900 Main St (tel 318/365-8281), which manufacturers spices and condiments.

Take a Break

Lagniappe, Too, 204 E Main St (tel 318/365-9419), located a block from the Shadows, is a cozy little restaurant decorated with paintings and handmade dolls created by chefs/owners Al and Elaine Landry. As small as it is, the restaurant offers a surprisingly extensive menu; the lunchtime fare is mostly soups, salads, and sandwiches, but the changing dinner menu might feature grilled quail, crab-and-corn bisque, steaks, or panéed catfish. Entrees cost $8 to $10.

If you are looking for a place to stay in New Iberia, you might consider the **Inn at le Rosier,** 314 E Main St (tel 318/367-5306), a small white cottage directly across the street from the Shadows. The inn offers four tiny, moderately priced, antique-filled rooms with private baths, plus a restaurant serving breakfast, lunch, and dinner.

New Iberia is the jumping-off point for trips to Avery Island and Live Oak Gardens. Seven miles southwest of New Iberia on LA 329 is:

6. **Avery Island.** This is not an island in the usual sense, but rather a salt dome covered with luxuriant subtropical vegetation, rising gently out of the surrounding marshlands. The 2,500-acre island is the property of descendants of Edmund McIlhenny, who developed the first Tabasco here in the 1880s. The world-famous hot sauce is still manufactured on Avery Island, and free tours of the factory are conducted every day except Sunday. Avery Island is also home to **Jungle Gardens,** with its bird sanctuary and profusion of exotic year-round blooms.

Six miles southwest of New Iberia on LA 14 is:

7. **Live Oak Gardens.** Also called Jefferson Island, this is, like Avery Island, a salt dome covered with splendid gardens. In the late 19th century American actor Joseph Jefferson, who toured the country portraying Rip Van Winkle, built his country estate here. An oil company drilling in nearby Lake Peigneur in 1980 pierced the salt dome; miraculously, workers in the salt mine managed to reach the surface before the cavity filled with the lake's

water. Parts of the landscaped gardens were destroyed, but Jefferson's Moorish-Gothic mansion was not damaged. Today the house and 20 acres of stunningly beautiful theme gardens are open for tours.

From New Iberia, LA 31 heads north along Bayou Teche for 10 miles to:

8. **St Martinville.** This is the town that most cherishes and perpetuates the legend of Evangeline, based on the real-life love affair betwen Emmeline Labiche and Louis Arceneaux and immortalized by Henry Wadsworth Longfellow. According to the legend, the couple was separated after the British forced the Acadians out of Nova Scotia (the period known as *Le Grand Derangement*); they were reunited briefly in St Martinville, but by that time Louis was betrothed to another. The town is dotted with icons of the legend. The **Evangeline Oak** is said to be the site where Emmeline/Evangeline came ashore and met Louis. On the town square, located behind the St Martin de Tours church, a bronze statue of Evangeline looks out over the small cemetery. The statue was donated to the town by the cast and crew of the film *The Romance of Evangeline,* which was shot on location here in 1929.

Two miles north of downtown St Martinville on LA 31 is the **Longfellow-Evangeline State Commemorative Area,** a luxuriant 160-acre park with picnic grounds, a boat launch on the bayou, and several Acadian structures in which Acadian culture is interpreted. Eleven miles north of the park, on LA 31, the sleepy little hamlet of **Breaux Bridge** rouses itself each May for one of the state's major festivals. Breaux Bridge is the "Crawfish Capital of the World," and its annual crustacean festival draws upwards of 200,000 to the town and its environs. The town is also home to La Poussiere, one of the oldest and best Cajun dancehalls in the state (or for that matter, the world). Live Cajun bands play every Saturday night for lively two-stepping, jigs, and Cajun waltzes.

In St Martinville, bed-and-breakfast accommodations and a full-service restaurant are offered at **Place d'Evangeline/Old Castillo Hotel,** 220

Take a Break

Mulate's, 325 Mills Ave (tel 318/332-4648) in Breaux Bridge, is known nationally as a down-home Cajun restaurant and dancehall. A simple roadhouse, it serves up prodigious portions of seafood—broiled, fried, baked, and "étouffeed"—while Cajun bands jam daily during lunch and dinner. Meals cost around $12.

Evangeline Blvd (tel 318/394-4010), a historic building adjacent to the Evangeline Oak and Bayou Teche. The five moderately priced rooms feature high-ceilings and period antiques; all have private baths. The restaurant specializes in seafood, including crawfish dishes, catfish, and alligator boulettes. Entrees are $8 to $10.

Traveling 8 miles west of Breaux Bridge via LA 94 will lead you to the last stop on the tour:

9. **Lafayette,** the unofficial capital of Cajun Country. This laid-back city of about 150,000 brings Cajun culture to life through theme parks like **Vermilionville** and **Acadian Village,** and such museums as the **Lafayette Museum,** downtown and the **Acadian Cultural Center,** operated by the Jean Lafitte National Historical Park Service. Nowhere, however, is the Cajun culture livelier and more evident than in the city's several dancehalls, such as **Grant Street** and **Antler's,** both longtime rustic bastions of live music and dancing. Zydeco is fea-

tured at **El Sido** and **Hamilton's** dancehalls. And you can enjoy both food and live music at **Randol's** and **Prejean's.** Lafayette's two biggest festivals are the **Festival International de Louisiane** in April, and **Festivals Acadiens** in September, both of which also feature plenty of food and live music. If you want to take a break from the Cajun deluge, the **Natural History Museum,** with its planetarium and many exhibits and activities, is a popular place for family outings.

Overnight lodgings in Lafayette range from chain motels to quaint bed-and-breakfasts. The **Best Western Hotel Acadiana,** 1801 W Pinhook Rd (tel 318/233-8120 or, out-of-state, 800/826-8386), is a sleek, modern, moderately priced hotel with a restaurant and lounge. Bed-and-breakfast accommodations (not for budget travelers) at **Á la Bonne Viellee,** off LA 339 west of Lafayette (tel 318/937-5495), are in a charming Acadian cottage; they offer two bedrooms, a kitchen, a fireplace, and TVs upstairs and down.

Driving the State

Start	Destrehan
Finish	White Castle
Distance	100 miles
Time	2–3 days
Highlights	Scenic drives along the Great River Road; classic antebellum plantations; an old Creole plantation; plantation B&Bs

Louisiana is sprinkled with antebellum mansions, but the greatest concentration of restored plantation homes adorn the banks of the Mississippi River from New Orleans to Baton Rouge. This tour follows what is locally called the Great River Road, but you should know that the term is a collective one. There are river roads on both sides of the Mississippi River, and they travel under several aliases, among them LA 48, LA 44, and LA 942 on the river's west bank, and LA 18 and LA 1 on the east bank. You can reach "Plantation Country" by taking either US 61 or I-10 west (upriver) from downtown New Orleans and following the clearly marked exit signs to the plantations. A plantation ramble can take a few hours or two or three days, depending upon how many interiors you want to see and how many yarns about Yankee gunboats and buried silver you want to hear. Visiting all of the plantations on this tour requires a fair amount of traveling back and forth across the river; you may want to split the tour into two or more parts. As a general rule the plantations are open daily from 10am to 5pm; admission charges for adults range from $5 to $8. Several of the plantations are bed-and-breakfasts, and in two of them —Madewood and Nottoway—are luxurious rooms with private baths in the main mansion.

The nearest plantation to downtown New Orleans is Destrehan, 23 miles west (upriver). After leaving Destrehan, you can return to US 61 or I-10 to continue touring, or you can opt to follow the two-lane paved roads—the actual river roads—that follow the winding of the river from plantation to plantation. Unfortunately, neither option offers splendid natural beauty, apart from the views of the Mississippi from atop the levees. The Great River Road is marred all along the way by sprawling petrochemical plants. The mansions themselves, the lush grounds that surround them, and the Mississippi provide the scenic beauty.

To reach Destrehan, take the I-310 exit south, just west of New Orleans International Airport, and follow the signs toward the river to LA 48 and:

1. **Destrehan Plantation,** the oldest intact plantation in the lower Mississippi Valley. Built in 1787, it is a simple West Indies–style house with a steep, hipped roof and dormer windows. Hand-hewn hearts-of-cypress timber and bousillage (a mixture of mud and moss used for insulation) were used in its construction, and Greek Revival flourishes were added as the house was expanded over the next several years. The Destrehan Plantation Fall Festival, held each November, features crafts, antiques, food, and music.

   From Destrehan turn right (west) on LA 48, passing the Norco industrial complex and the Bonnet Carre Spillway. In the town of La Place, the road becomes LA 44. Continue on LA 44 alongside the river until you reach:

2. **San Francisco Plantation,** 5 miles west of LA 53 (21 miles west of I-310). Though small in comparison to the other River Road plantations, this ornate Steamboat Gothic house is noted for its elaborate ceiling frescoes, handsome carved millwork, and unusual louvered roof topped by a widow's walk, which afforded residents a sweeping view of the Mississippi. The exterior staircases draped across the front gallery resemble gangplanks of a frilly riverboat. (In fact, the house was the model for Frances Parkinson Keyes's novel *Steamboat Gothic*.) The house was completed in 1856—at enormous cost—by Edmond Bozonier Marmillion, a Creole whose descendant, Norman Marmillion, now manages Laura Plantation on the west bank. The period antiques inside match the descriptions found in Edmond Marmillion's extensive documentation.

   From San Francisco, drive 5 miles west (upriver) of San Francisco and cross the Mississippi on Veterans Memorial Bridge. On the east bank, turn right (west) on LA 18 and proceed 4 miles to:

3. **Laura Plantation.** Newly opened in 1994, the mansion is particularly interesting in that it is a restoration-in-progress. Like San Francisco, Laura is a Creole plantation; the small yellow raised cottage contrasts with the big white plantations built by the Americans. The oldest and largest of the River Road plantations, Laura predates the antebellum period. It was built in 1805 by Spanish commandant Guillaume DuParc, who named it for his great-granddaughter, and was managed by women for 84 years. Laura Locoul, born on the

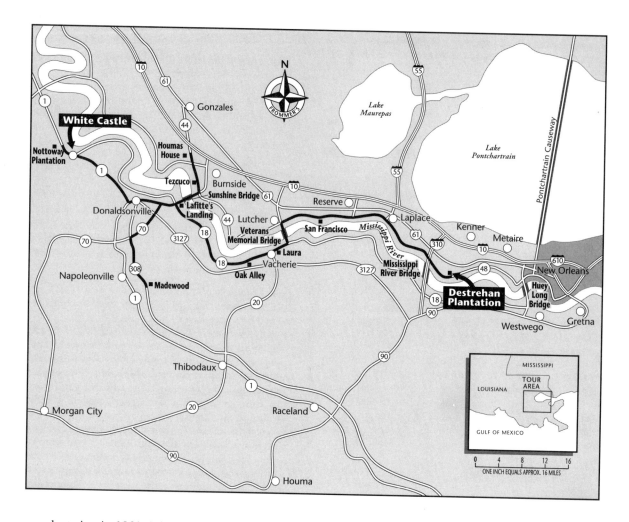

plantation in 1861, left a detailed 100-page diary that served as the foundation for the present restoration. According to plantation records, author Joel Chandler Harris adapted his famous stories of Br'er Rabbit from the folk tales he heard as a child told by Senegalese slaves on this plantation. Tour guides tell the secrets of the families who lived here, and also point out the Yankee cannonball embedded in the wall, the 19th-century false teeth, and the ancient family pictures. The plantation is neither opulent nor lavishly furnished; its appeal lies in the restoration process and in the fascinating history of its past occupants.

Three miles west of Laura Plantation on LA 18 is:

4. Oak Alley Plantation, the grounds of which are the most beautiful in this neck of the woods. The quarter-mile oak alley that gives the plantation its name is formed by 28 gnarled oaks—14 on each

side—whose branches form a stunning natural arch. The trees were planted sometime in the 1700s by an unknown Frenchman who had a small house on the site. This Greek Revival house was built between 1837 and 1839 by wealthy French sugar planter Jacques Telesphore Roman for his bride. The plantation was originally named Bon Sejour, but early steamboat passengers, viewing the grounds from the river, referred to it as Oak Alley, and the name was eventually changed. The exterior of the mansion, with its huge white columns and double galleries, is more impressive than the interior. The furnishings, comfortable but not opulent, are those of the Stewart family, who bought the house in 1925 and restored it. The view of the oaks from the second-floor gallery is breathtaking. Scenes from many films have been shot on the lavish grounds, including some for *Interview With the Vampire* and the TV version of *The Long, Hot Summer.*

Oak Alley's moderately priced bed-and-breakfast rooms are not in the mansion but in little white frame cottages with screened porches. All have private baths; some have kitchens. The light breakfast included in the rate is served in a small restaurant that is also open for lunch; lunch fare consists of jambalaya and other regional specialties. Call 504/265-2151 for more information.

Take a Break

Lafitte's Landing (tel 504/473-1232), 16 miles upriver from Oak Alley on LA 18, is one of Louisiana's finest restaurants. Located in a charming raised Acadian cottage on the access road of the Sunshine Bridge, it is owned and operated by internationally known chef John Folse, whose menu of Cajun, Creole, and classic French dishes changes daily. Look for such Folse specialties as oysters Rockefeller soup, Cajun caviar, and pecan-smoked shrimp. Desserts are spectacular. A three-course meal without wine will set you back approximately $30. Reservations are strongly recommended.

Head south on LA 70 and follow the signs to "Bayou Plantations." Seven miles south of the sign turn left on Spur 70 and drive 2 miles to the junction of LA 308. Turn left on LA 308 and follow the road 6 miles to:

5. **Madewood,** a grand Greek Revival mansion replete with white columns, galleries, sky-high ceilings, and lovely antiques. The 21-room house was built in 1846 for Thomas Pugh, whose family cemetery lies to the rear of the main house. So-named because it was "made of wood," the mansion was bought and restored in the 1960s by the Harold Marshall family of New Orleans. The polished hardwood floors are covered with oriental rugs, oil paintings adorn the walls, white Corinthian columns grace the central hallway, and beds are either canopy or half-tester. Unlike other plantations, Madewood is a family home as well as a showplace and bed-and-breakfast.

Madewood's overnight accommodations are in five rooms in the main house and three suites in Charlet House, a raised cottage on the mansion's grounds. All have private baths. Preprandial wine and cheese is served in the drawing room; dinner is by candlelight in the formal dining room, followed by brandy and coffee in the parlor. Continental breakfast is served in the morning. Accommodations ($165) are at once luxurious and homey. To reserve call 800/369-7151.

Return to the Sunshine Bridge and cross the

Mississippi River. One mile upriver of the bridge on LA 44 is:

6. **Tezcuco** (purportedly an Aztec word meaning "Resting Place"), a complex of buildings comprising the main house and several outbuildings, among them a chapel, dollhouse, carriage house, and commissary. The commissary is now an antiques shop. The main house—an 1855 Greek Revival raised cottage with broad galleries and dormer windows—was built of cypress from the plantation's trees, as well as brick from its kilns, and is furnished with period antiques. However, the cabins and the lush live oaks of the grounds are more interesting than the interior of the main house. Centrally located in the heart of plantation country, Tezcuco is a good base for exploring this area.

Should you decide to stay overnight at Tezcuco (tel 504/562-3929), you can find moderately priced lodgings in a third-floor suite in the main house or in one of the several cabins on the grounds. All have private baths, and are generally more cozy than elegant.

Take a Break

A restaurant on the grounds of Tezcuco (tel 504/562-3929) is open daily for lunch and serves regional specialties (crawfish étouffée, po-boys, and gumbo) in a high-ceilinged room with cloth-clad tables and a big open fireplace. Entrees cost $6 to $8.

Follow LA 44, which becomes LA 942, west for a little over 2 miles to:

7. **Houmas House,** which is actually two houses joined by a covered carriageway. The first house built on this site was a simple four-room, two-story cottage from the late 1700s. The splendid Greek Revival house to which it is attached was built in 1840 and is famous in these parts for its three-story spiral staircase and beautifully landscaped grounds. This house was the setting for the Grand Guignol film thriller *Hush . . . Hush, Sweet Charlotte,* which starred Bette Davis and Olivia de Havilland. Tours are conducted by docents dressed in antebellum gowns. The levee affords a lovely view of the Mississippi River.

Seventeen miles upriver of the Sunshine Bridge on LA 1, 2 miles past the village of White Castle lies:

8. **Nottoway.** This is far and away the most magnificent plantation of the tour. The South's largest extant plantation mansion boasts 64 rooms, 22 columns, and 200 windows. The nearby town of

White Castle was named for the castlelike Italianate/Greek Revival mansion. The house is filled with museum-quality antiques, and statuary graces the landscaped lawns. John Randolph of Virginia had Nottoway built in 1859 in accordance with the designs of noted architect Henry Howard. According to an oft-told tale, Yankee gunboats spared the house after one of the soldiers, a former guest in the house, recognized it and ordered a cease-fire.

An overnight stay at Nottoway (13 rooms are available) does not come cheap. Rooms, however, are luxurious, with canopy or tester beds, antiques, and TVs; there's a swimming pool as well. Some rooms and suites are in the main house, while others are in the attached garçonniere (the young bachelors' quarters of plantation days) and in a caretaker's cottage. Morning begins with a "first breakfast" of coffee, juice, and croissants served in-room, followed by a full breakfast in the dining room.

Louisiana Listings

Alexandria

This city located in the center of Louisiana was originally a fort established to protect Red River merchants from area bandits. Plantation home tours illustrate life in the 1800s, and numerous lakes and rivers nearby provide outdoor recreation. **Information:** Rapides Parish Convention & Visitors Bureau, 1470 MacArthur Dr, PO Box 8110, Alexandria, 71306 (tel 318/443-7049 or toll free 800/742-7049).

HOTEL 🏨

▆▆▆ Best Western of Alexandria

2720 W MacArthur Dr, 71303; tel 318/445-5530 or toll free 800/528-1234. Located near the center of town with plenty of shopping and dining nearby. The entertainment opportunities make this a great choice for families. **Rooms:** 154 rms and stes. CI 3pm/CO noon. Nonsmoking rms avail. **Amenities:** 🛊 ⚱ A/C, cable TV, refrig. **Services:** ✗ ⚃ ⌿ ⚓ Complimentary coffee and newspaper available. **Facilities:** ⚐ ⚑ 200 ⚲ 1 restaurant, 1 bar, washer/dryer. **Rates (CP):** $52 S; $58 D; $66 ste. Extra person $6. Children under age 18 stay free. Parking: Outdoor, free. AE, CB, DC, DISC, MC, V.

MOTELS

▆▆▆ Holiday Inn

2716 N MacArthur Dr, 71303; tel 318/487-4261 or toll free 800/HOLIDAY; fax 318/845-0891. Off I-49. A popular site for conventions, this Holiday Inn caters primarily to business travelers and corporations, but the great accommodations are suitable for anyone. **Rooms:** 127 rms. CI 2pm/CO noon. Nonsmoking rms avail. **Amenities:** 🛊 ⚱ A/C, cable TV w/movies. **Services:** ✗ 🚗 ⚃ ⌿ ⚓ Car-rental desk. **Facilities:** ⚐ 500 ⚲ 1 restaurant, 1 bar (w/entertainment). **Rates:** $55 S; $60 D. Extra person $5. Children under age 17 stay free. Parking: Outdoor, free. AE, CB, DC, DISC, MC, V.

▆▆ Ramada Inn

2211 N MacArthur Dr, 71301; tel 318/443-2561 or toll free 800/2-RAMADA. MacArthur exit off I-49. Next door to a huge convention center, this motel offers satisfactory accommodations for business travelers and others. Serene courtyard next to lovely pool. **Rooms:** 170 rms. CI 3pm/CO noon.

Nonsmoking rms avail. **Amenities:** 🛊 A/C, cable TV. **Services:** ✗ ⚃ ⌿ **Facilities:** ⚐ ⚑ ⚓ 2000 ⚲ 1 restaurant, 2 bars (1 w/entertainment), games rm, washer/dryer. **Rates:** $46 S; $51 D. Extra person $8. Children under age 18 stay free. Parking: Outdoor, free. AE, CB, DC, DISC, MC, V.

▆▆ Rodeway Inn

742 MacArthur Dr, 71301; tel 318/448-1611; fax 318/473-2984. Off I-49. Well-maintained economy motel near the interstate. **Rooms:** 121 rms and stes. CI 1pm/CO noon. Nonsmoking rms avail. **Amenities:** 🛊 A/C, cable TV w/movies. **Services:** ⚃ ⌿ ⚓ **Facilities:** ⚐ ⚲ Washer/dryer. **Rates:** Peak (June–July) $45 S; $50 D; $55–$64 ste. Extra person $5. Children under age 18 stay free. Lower rates off-season. Parking: Outdoor, free. AE, CB, DC, DISC, MC, V.

RESTAURANT 🍽

Tunk's Cypress Inn

LA 28 W at Kincaid Lake; tel 318/487-4014. 5 mi off MacArthur Blvd. **Regional American.** Although it offers a wide variety of foods, alligator is this restaurant's specialty. It's so popular that a local Air Force Unit had it shipped to Saudi Arabia during the Gulf War. (Be sure to try the alligator Parmesan.) Large picture windows recessed in the exposed rough wooden walls give great views of Kincaid Lake. **FYI:** Reservations not accepted. Children's menu. **Open:** Mon–Sat 5–10pm. **Prices:** Main courses $13–$15. AE, CB, DC, DISC, MC, V. ⛰ ⚲

ATTRACTION 🏛

Kent Plantation House

3601 Bayou Rapides Rd (Cenla); tel 318/487-5998. Completed in 1800, this French Colonial mansion is the oldest standing structure in central Louisiana. The main house features a collection of furniture from the Federal, Sheraton, and Empire periods, as well as pieces built by native Creole cabinetmakers. The four-acre grounds include gardens and outbuildings necessary for plantation life—kitchen, milk house, slave cabins, carriage house, barn, and blacksmith shop. Open-hearth cooking demonstrations are given Wednesdays, October through April; Herb Day held in early spring; Tradition Day presented in early summer. Guided tours; candlelight and special tours available upon request. **Open:** Mon–Sat 8:45am–4:45pm, Sun 12:45–4:45pm. **$$**

Baton Rouge

French explorer Iberville named this Mississippi River site "Red Stick" in 1699 upon sighting a large tree reddened with the blood of animals sacrificed by Indians. Now the capital of Louisiana, Baton Rouge invites travelers to tour its two distinctive capitol buildings, numerous restored plantations and antebellum mansions, and unique museums. The beautiful grounds of Louisiana State University also make for a worthwhile visit. **Information:** Baton Rouge Area Convention & Visitors Bureau, 730 North Blvd, PO Drawer 4149, Baton Rouge, 70821 (tel 504/383-1825 or toll free 800/LA-ROUGE).

HOTELS 🏨

≡≡≡ Best Western Château Louisianne

710 N Lobdell Ave, 70806; tel 504/927-6700 or toll free 800/256-6263; fax 504/527-6700. Exit 4 off I-12. An outstanding Best Western offering European charm and a full range of services for international visitors and tourist groups. **Rooms:** 50 rms and stes. Executive level. CI 2pm/CO noon. Nonsmoking rms avail. **Amenities:** 📺❓❓❓ A/C, cable TV w/movies, refrig, dataport, bathrobes. Some units w/whirlpools. **Services:** X ❓❓ Car-rental desk, babysitting. **Facilities:** ❓❓❓❓ 1 restaurant (lunch and dinner only), 1 bar, sauna, whirlpool, washer/dryer. **Rates (CP):** Peak (Feb–June/Sept–Nov) $69–$150 S; $69–$150 ste. Extra person $10. Children under age 12 stay free. Lower rates off-season. Parking: Outdoor, free. AE, CB, DC, DISC, MC, V.

≡≡ Budgetel Inn

10555 Rieger Rd, 70809; tel 504/291-6600 or toll free 800/4-BUDGET; fax 504/296-0474. Exit 163 off I-10. Standard budget motel with average rooms, located on the south side of the city, rather isolated from the goings-on of Baton Rouge. **Rooms:** 102 rms and stes. CI 3pm/CO noon. Nonsmoking rms avail. **Amenities:** 📺❓ A/C, satel TV w/movies. **Services:** X ❓❓❓ One pet under 10 lbs permitted. **Facilities:** ❓❓ Rates (CP): $40 S; $50 D; $51–$61 ste. Children under age 18 stay free. Parking: Outdoor, free. AE, CB, DC, DISC, EC, MC, V.

≡ Comfort Inn

2445 Acadian, 70808; tel 504/927-5790 or toll free 800/228-5150; fax 504/925-0084. Exit 157B off I-10. Below-average property near downtown and LSU. **Rooms:** 130 rms and stes. CI 2pm/CO noon. Nonsmoking rms avail. **Amenities:** 📺❓ A/C, cable TV w/movies. **Services:** X ❓❓ Car-rental desk, babysitting. **Facilities:** ❓❓❓❓ Washer/dryer. **Rates (CP):** $59–$65 S or D; $69–$89 ste.

Extra person $5. Children under age 18 stay free. Min stay special events. Parking: Outdoor, free. AE, CB, DC, DISC, EC, ER, JCB, MC, V.

≡≡≡ Crown Sterling Suites

4914 Constitution Ave, 70808; tel 504/924-6566 or toll free 800/336-7571; fax 504/923-3712. Exit 158 off I-10. This luxury hotel greets its guests with a tropical atrium lobby featuring a waterfall and fountains with torpedo-size goldfish and live ducks. **Rooms:** 224 stes. CI 3pm/CO 1pm. Nonsmoking rms avail. **Amenities:** 📺❓❓❓ A/C, cable TV w/movies, refrig, dataport, voice mail. All suites have two TVs. Microwave. **Services:** X ❓❓❓ Babysitting. **Facilities:** ❓❓❓ 1 restaurant (lunch and dinner only; see "Restaurants" below), 1 bar (w/entertainment), sauna, whirlpool, washer/dryer. **Rates (BB):** Peak (Mar–Apr/Sept–Nov) $106–$116 ste. Extra person $10. Children under age 12 stay free. Lower rates off-season. Parking: Outdoor, free. AE, CB, DC, DISC, ER, JCB, MC, V.

≡≡ Hampton Inn College

4646 Constitution Ave, 70808; tel 504/926-9990 or toll free 800/426-7866; fax 504/923-3007. Exit 158 off I-10. Tasteful appointments in an otherwise standard chain offering. **Rooms:** 141 rms and stes. CI 2pm/CO noon. Nonsmoking rms avail. **Amenities:** 📺❓❓ A/C, cable TV w/movies. **Services:** ❓❓ **Facilities:** ❓❓❓ Rates (CP): Peak (Sept–Dec) $75 S; $85 D; $140 ste. Extra person $10. Children under age 18 stay free. Min stay special events. Lower rates off-season. Parking: Outdoor, free. AE, CB, DC, DISC, MC, V.

≡≡≡ Holiday Inn South

9940 Airline Rd, 70816; tel 504/924-7021 or toll free 800/HOLIDAY; fax 504/924-7021. Airline Hwy exit off I-12, ½ mi N. Features excellent family recreational facilities in its Holidome, including miniature golf. Minutes from the airport. **Rooms:** 339 rms. Executive level. CI 3pm/CO noon. Nonsmoking rms avail. **Amenities:** 📺❓ A/C, cable TV w/movies. **Services:** X ❓❓❓ Babysitting. **Facilities:** ❓❓❓❓ 1 restaurant, 1 bar, games rm, whirlpool. **Rates:** $65–$72 S or D. Extra person $6. Children under age 12 stay free. Parking: Outdoor, free. AE, DISC, JCB, MC, V.

≡≡≡ Marriott's Residence Inn

5522 Corporate Blvd, 70808; tel 504/927-5630 or toll free 800/331-3131; fax 504/926-2317. Exit 158 off I-10, N on College, right on Corporate Blvd. Apartmentlike accommodations with contemporary decor. **Rooms:** 80 effic. Executive level. CI 3pm/CO noon. Nonsmoking rms avail. Bilevel, two-room suites on the second floor. **Amenities:** 📺❓❓ A/C, cable TV w/movies, refrig, dataport, voice mail. All units w/terraces, all w/fireplaces, some w/whirlpools. **Services:** X ❓❓ Babysitting. **Facilities:** ❓❓❓❓ Basketball, whirlpool, washer/dryer. **Rates (CP):** $73–$128 effic. Children under age 18 stay free. Parking: Outdoor, free. AE, CB, DC, DISC, JCB, MC, V.

MOTELS

≣≣≣ Courtyard by Marriott
2421 S Acadian Thruway, 70808; tel 504/924-6400 or toll free 800/321-2211; fax 504/923-3041. Acadian Thruway exit off I-10. Located near the university and close to the interstate, this standard Courtyard works for all types of travelers. **Rooms:** 149 rms and stes. CI 4pm/CO noon. Nonsmoking rms avail. **Amenities:** 🛏 ☎ 🖥 A/C, cable TV w/movies, dataport. All units w/terraces. **Services:** 🖿 🛁 Babysitting. **Facilities:** 🏊 ⛳ 🏊 100 🛁 1 restaurant (bkfst only), 1 bar, whirlpool, washer/dryer. **Rates:** Peak (Feb–July) $76 S; $86 D; $94–$100 ste. Extra person $10. Children under age 12 stay free. Lower rates off-season. Parking: Outdoor, free. AE, CB, DC, DISC, MC, V.

≣≣ Howard Johnson Plaza Suite Hotel
2045 N 3rd St, 70802; tel 504/344-6000 or toll free 800/487-8157; fax 504/387-2878. Exit 1A off I-110. Offers spacious suites with dated furniture. **Rooms:** 138 effic. CI 2pm/CO noon. Nonsmoking rms avail. **Amenities:** 🛏 🖥 A/C, cable TV w/movies. All units w/terraces. **Services:** ✗ 🖿 🛁 🛁 Car-rental desk. **Facilities:** 🏊 ⛳ 30 🛁 1 restaurant, washer/dryer. **Rates (CP):** $69–$79 effic. Extra person $5. Children under age 17 stay free. Parking: Outdoor, free. AE, CB, DC, DISC, EC, JCB, MC, V.

≣≣≣ La Quinta Inn
2333 S Acadian Thruway, 70808; tel 504/924-9600 or toll free 800/531-5900; fax 504/924-2609. Exit 157B off I-10. Recently renovated, well maintained. **Rooms:** 142 rms. CI 1pm/CO noon. Nonsmoking rms avail. **Amenities:** 🛏 ☎ A/C, cable TV w/movies, dataport. **Services:** 🚐 🛁 🛁 Car-rental desk. **Facilities:** 🏊 25 🛁 Washer/dryer. **Rates (CP):** $58 S; $65 D. Extra person $7. Children under age 18 stay free. Min stay special events. Parking: Outdoor, free. AE, CB, DC, DISC, MC, V.

≣≣ Quality Inn Sherwood Forest
10920 Mead Rd, 70816; tel 504/293-9370 or toll free 800/395-8847; fax 504/293-8889. Exit 4 off I-12, S on Sherwood Forest, right on Mead. Although right off the interstate and near the riverboat casinos, this property is surprisingly quiet. **Rooms:** 150 rms. CI 3pm/CO noon. Nonsmoking rms avail. Comfortable, spacious rooms. **Amenities:** 🛏 🖥 A/C, cable TV w/movies, dataport, in-rm safe. **Services:** ✗ 🛁 🛁 🛁 **Facilities:** 🏊 240 🛁 1 restaurant, 2 bars (1 w/entertainment), washer/dryer. Video poker games, billiards. Jamaica Jack's poolside cafe. **Rates:** $57–$68 S or D. Extra person $10. Children under age 18 stay free. Parking: Outdoor, free. AE, DC, DISC, MC, V.

≣≣ Red Roof Inn
11314 Boardwalk Dr, 70816; tel 504/275-6600 or toll free 800/THE-ROOF; fax 504/275-6792. Exit 4 off I-12, N on Sherwood Forest to Boardwalk. Clean, slightly larger than average rooms. A good choice for the budget traveler. **Rooms:** 109 rms. CI 2pm/CO noon. Nonsmoking rms avail.

Amenities: 🛏 A/C, cable TV. **Services:** 🛁 🛁 🛁 **Facilities:** 🛁 **Rates:** $35 S; $43 D. Extra person $7. Children under age 18 stay free. Parking: Outdoor, free. AE, CB, DC, DISC, EC, MC, V.

≣≣ Shoney's Inn of Baton Rouge
9919 Gwen Adele Dr, 70816; tel 504/925-8399 or toll free 800/222-2222; fax 504/927-1731. Exit 2B off I-12. Basic, clean accommodations. **Rooms:** 196 rms. CI 2pm/CO noon. Nonsmoking rms avail. **Amenities:** 🛏 A/C, cable TV. **Services:** 🛁 🛁 🛁 Coupons are available for Shoney's Restaurant next door. **Facilities:** 🏊 75 🛁 Washer/dryer. **Rates (CP):** $60 S; $66 D. Extra person $6. Children under age 18 stay free. Parking: Outdoor, free. AE, CB, DC, DISC, MC, V.

RESTAURANTS 🍴

Branberry's
In Crown Sterling Suites, 4914 Constitution Ave; tel 504/924-6566. Exit 158 off I-10, S on College 1/10 mi, left on Constitution 1/2 mi. **Continental.** A casual gardenlike setting complete with padded wrought-iron chairs. The main focus is on producing exquisite sauces. The fillet Madagascar offers twin medallions of beef garnished with green peppercorns, cream, and demiglacé. **FYI:** Reservations recommended. Dress code. **Open:** Lunch Mon–Sat 11am–2pm; dinner daily 5–10pm; brunch Sun 11:30am–2pm. **Prices:** Main courses $10–$15. AE, CB, DC, DISC, MC, V. 🛁

Dajonel's
7327 Jefferson Hwy; tel 504/924-7537. Exit 158 off I-10, right on Corporate, left on Jefferson, 1/4 mi on right. **Continental.** Intimate atmosphere with low lighting. Steak dauphin, a filet with marchand de vin, béarnaise, and lump crabmeat is excellent, as is rack of lamb. Seafood dishes add variety to a very good menu. **FYI:** Reservations accepted. Dress code. No smoking. **Open:** Lunch Mon–Fri 11:30am–2:30pm; dinner Mon–Sat 5–10pm; brunch Sun 11am–2pm. **Prices:** Main courses $15–$27. AE, DISC, MC, V. 🛁

Drusilla's
3482 Drusilla Lane; tel 504/923-0896. Exit 1B off I-12. **Seafood.** A Baton Rouge favorite that offers a comfortable atmosphere in which to enjoy a wide range of seafood dishes. The best bets are the fish caught in the Gulf of Mexico, like red snapper or orange roughy. **FYI:** Reservations accepted. Children's menu. Dress code. **Open:** Mon–Sat 11am–10pm. **Prices:** Main courses $10–$17. AE, CB, DC, DISC, MC, V. 🛁

★ Juban's
3739 Perkins Rd; tel 504/346-8422. Exit 157B off I-10, S on Acadian Thruway, left 1/10 mi. **Continental/Creole.** Locals love this restaurant, and with dishes like Hallelujah crab (a stuffed softshell crab with mustard-hollandaise sauce) it's not hard to see why. Also featured is an outstanding semi-boneless half duck with a seasonal berry sauce. Traditional southeast Louisiana dishes are also available. **FYI:** Reserva-

tions recommended. Children's menu. Dress code. **Open:** Lunch Mon–Fri 11:30am–2pm; dinner Mon–Sat 5:30–10pm. **Prices:** Main courses $12–$22. AE, MC, V. ♿

Maggio's
320 St Charles St; tel 504/272-0325. **Regional American.** A small diner that serves up po' boys and gumbo for downtown locals at lunch. The atmosphere is pure diner with no pretenses. The gumbo is the best option. Good breakfasts are also available. **FYI:** Reservations not accepted. No liquor license. **Open:** Daily 6am–3pm. **Prices:** Lunch main courses $4–$10. MC, V.

Magnolia Cafe
3535 Sherwood Forest Blvd; tel 504/291-2233. 4 mi S of exit 4 off I-12. **Cajun/Seafood.** Casual restaurant with a New Orleans–style townhouse exterior graced with wrought-iron balconies; popular with local businesspeople for lunch. The seafood platter offers a good sampling of standard Louisiana fare. **FYI:** Reservations not accepted. Children's menu. Dress code. **Open:** Mon–Thurs 11am–10pm, Fri–Sat 11am–11pm, Sun 11am–8:30pm. **Prices:** Main courses $7–$13. AE, DISC, MC, V. ♿

Maison Lacour
11025 N Harrells Ferry Rd; tel 504/275-3755. Exit 4 off I-12. **French.** Look carefully or you might miss this cottage set among the oaks and crape myrtles. Classic French cuisine is presented in a country home ambience. Dishes include veal chop, chateaubriand, shrimp with garlic butter, and lump crabmeat in puff pastry. "The Clam," a fresh puff pastry filled with vanilla ice cream and raspberries, is an excellent dessert item. **FYI:** Reservations accepted. Dress code. **Open:** Lunch Mon–Fri 11:30am–2pm; dinner Mon–Sat 5:30–10pm. **Prices:** Main courses $16–$33. AE, CB, DC, DISC, MC, V. ♥♿

Mamacita's
7524 Bluebonnet Blvd; tel 504/769-3850. 1½ mi S of exit 164 off I-10. **Tex-Mex.** Offers a fine array of mesquite-grilled items (fajitas, chicken, shrimp, and Spanish kabobs) in a typical Mexican eatery setting. **FYI:** Reservations not accepted. Children's menu. **Open:** Mon–Thurs 11am–10pm, Fri 11am–10:30pm, Sat 11:30am–10:30pm. **Prices:** Main courses $7–$16. AE, DISC, MC, V.

Mike Anderson's Seafood
1031 W Lee Dr; tel 504/766-7823. 5 mi S of exit 158 off I-10. **Seafood.** Part of a popular southern Louisiana seafood chain offering well-prepared, modestly priced fish and shellfish of all kinds. The fried and broiled seafood platters are most popular. **FYI:** Reservations not accepted. Children's menu. **Open:** Mon–Thurs 10am–10pm, Fri–Sat 10am–11pm. **Prices:** Main courses $6–$16. AE, DISC, MC, V. ♿

Mulate's
8322 Bluebonnet Rd; tel 504/767-4794. 3 mi S of exit 164 off I-10. **Cajun.** This famed Cajun restaurant with faux Cajun swamp cabin decor offers live Cajun music as well as zydeco dancing lessons (held nightly after 7pm). The good classic Cajun menu has fried seafood, alligator, frogs' legs, and many different blackened options. **FYI:** Reservations recommended. Zydeco. Children's menu. Dress code. **Open:** Sun–Thurs 11am–10pm, Fri–Sat 11am–11pm. **Prices:** Main courses $11–$17. AE, DC, DISC, MC, V. ♿

The Place
5255 Florida Blvd; tel 504/924-5069. Exit 2B off I-12. **Seafood/Steak.** With its exposed brick walls and patio with fountain, The Place offers sophisticated yet comfortable ambience. Well known for their steaks (the fillet of tenderloin is among the best) and outstanding seafood. Coconut-crusted shrimp with orange sauce is a standout. **FYI:** Reservations accepted. Children's menu. Dress code. **Open:** Lunch Mon–Fri 11am–2:30pm; dinner Tues–Sat 5:30–10pm; brunch Sun 11am–2:30pm. **Prices:** Main courses $14–$27. AE, DC, DISC, MC, V. ♿

ATTRACTIONS

Louisiana State Capitol
State Capitol Dr; tel 504/342-7317. The tallest statehouse in the nation (34 stories) was built in 1932 with 27 varieties of marble from every marble-producing country in the world. Memorial Hall features floors laid with polished lava from Mount Vesuvius, a gold-leafed ceiling, murals, and two-ton solid bronze doors leading to the Senate and House chambers. A 27th-floor observation tower offers views of the Mississippi River and capitol grounds, and the breezeway houses an exhibit of Louisiana folklife. Guided tours available. **Open:** Daily 8am–4:30pm. **Free**

Louisiana's Old State Capitol, Center for Political and Governmental History
100 North Blvd; tel 504/342-0500. Located in an 1847 Gothic Revival castle that was abandoned as the state capitol in 1932. The highly ornate interior features stained-glass windows, a cathedral dome, and a cast-iron staircase. As the state's official repository of film and video archives, the Center houses interactive exhibits and multimedia presentations on Louisiana history. Self-guided tour brochures available. **Open:** Tues–Sat 10am–4pm, Sun noon–4pm. **$$**

Louisiana State University
Highland Rd, SW; tel 504/388-3202. On the campus are two Indian burial mounds believed to be 1,600 years old, an outdoor Greek theater, Union Art Gallery, and a cage holding LSU's Bengal tiger mascot, Mike VI. The Memorial Tower houses the LSU Museum of Art, which features original 17th- through mid–19th-century rooms from England and America. The LSU Museum of Geoscience features the Indian Room, a prehistoric garden, and exhibits in the earth sciences and anthropology. The LSU Museum of Natural Science displays life-size dioramas, mastodon bones, and identification panels of Louisiana birds, mammals, reptiles, and amphibians. **Open:** Daily, call for schedule. **Free**

LSU Rural Life Museum
4600 Essen Lane; tel 504/765-2437. Re-creates an 1800s plantation in three main museum areas: The barn area contains exhibits of folk life from prehistory through the early 20th century. The architecture area displays seven buildings with diverse architectural techniques reflecting the cultures of Louisiana settlers. The plantation area includes relocated or re-created buildings, including a blacksmith shop, open-kettle sugar mill, commissary, and church. Guided tours available. **Open:** Mon–Fri 9am–4pm, Sat–Sun noon–4pm. Call to confirm hours. **Free**

Houmas House Plantation and Gardens
LA 942 at LA 44, Darrow; tel 504/473-7841. 25 mi S of Baton Rouge. The Houmas sugar plantation, built in 1800, produced 20 million pounds of sugar yearly in the late 1800s for Col William Porcher Miles. The restored Greek Revival mansion is furnished with pieces dating from the 1840s. The rear house is a late–18th-century structure combining Spanish and rural French architecture. Guided tours available. **Open:** Peak (Feb–Oct) daily 10am–5pm. Reduced hours off-season. **$$$**

Magnolia Mound Plantation
2161 Nicholson Dr; tel 504/343-4955 or fax 504/343-6739. This 16-acre estate from the early 19th century offers a good representation of French Creole architecture and plantation life. The house museum, which is surrounded by 200-year-old oak trees, has been restored to its original Federal decor. Visitors may cook in the open-hearth kitchen, spin, weave, and work with antique tools. Tours given by costumed guides. Annual special events are the Market Days Festival in March, History Day Camp for children in June and July, and Twelfth Night in December. **Open:** Tues–Sat 10am–4pm, Sun 1–4pm. **$$**

Greater Baton Rouge Zoo
Thomas Rd, Baker; tel 504/775-3877. Located 6 mi N of Baton Rouge on more than 140 acres, the zoo is home to 944 animals from all continents, presented in their natural settings. Children's petting zoo, sidewalk trams, and a miniature-train tour on grounds. **Open:** Peak (June–Aug) daily 10am–7pm. Reduced hours off-season. **$**

USS *Kidd* and Nautical Center
305 S River Rd; tel 504/342-1942. Fully restored after a Japanese kamikaze pilot crashed directly into her, the USS *Kidd* continued on to earn a total of 12 battle stars during World War II and the Korean conflict. Visitors are free to walk the decks and tour the more than 50 inner compartments. The Nautical Center features a full-scale model of the USS *Constitution* ("Old Ironsides") gundeck, a restored P-40 "Flying Tiger" fighter plane, and the largest model ship collection in the South. Veterans' memorial, visitors center, observation tower, cafe, gift shop. **Open:** Daily 9am–5pm. **$$**

Bossier City

See also Shreveport

Started in the 1840s as Cane's Landing, a small trading post, Bossier City was incorporated in 1907. Its sister city, Shreveport, is on the opposite bank of the Red River, and the two population centers join forces to host a large number of festivals and attractions throughout the year. **Information:** Bossier Chamber of Commerce, 710 Benton Rd, Bossier City, 71111-3797 (tel 318/746-0252).

HOTEL 🏨

≡≡≡ Isle of Capri Casino & Hotel
3033 Hilton Dr, 71111; tel 318/747-2400 or toll free 800/THE-ISLE; fax 318/425-7273. Exit 22 off I-20. This quite modern, large, luxurious hotel is fun for a casino weekend. **Rooms:** 245 rms and stes. CI 3pm/CO noon. Nonsmoking rms avail. **Amenities:** 🛢 🗐 A/C, cable TV w/movies. Some units w/minibars. **Services:** ✕ 🚙 🖾 Free shuttle to Isle of Capri Casino. **Facilities:** 🖪 500 ♿ 1 restaurant, 1 bar. **Rates:** $55–$65 S or D; $75–$85 ste. Parking: Outdoor, free. AE, MC, V.

MOTELS

≡≡ Best Western Airline Motor Inn
1984 Airline Dr, 71112; tel 318/742-6000 or toll free 800/635-7639; fax 318/742-4615. Exit 22 off I-20. Average budget accommodations easily accessible to Bossier City casinos. Plenty of on-site video poker machines. **Rooms:** 119 rms. CI 3pm/CO noon. Nonsmoking rms avail. **Amenities:** 🛢 A/C, cable TV. **Services:** ✕ 🚙 🖾 🗐 🛎 **Facilities:** 🖪 100 ♿ 1 restaurant, 4 bars. **Rates:** $33 S; $40 D. Extra person $7. Children under age 18 stay free. Parking: Outdoor, free. AE, CB, DC, DISC, MC, V.

≡≡ Days Inn
200 John Wesley Blvd, 71112; tel 318/742-9200 or toll free 800/673-2743; fax 318/747-5100. Exit 21 off I-20. Not too flashy, not too expensive, and not too far away, this is a great place for visitors to the casino scene in Bossier City who want dependable accommodations and services. **Rooms:** 177 rms. CI 3pm/CO 11am. Nonsmoking rms avail. **Amenities:** 🛢 A/C, cable TV. **Services:** 🚙 🗐 🛎 **Facilities:** 🖪 ♿ 1 restaurant (bkfst only). **Rates:** Peak (May–Sept) $47–$61 S; $53–$67 D. Extra person $6. Children under age 12 stay free. Lower rates off-season. Parking: Outdoor, free. AE, CB, DC, DISC, JCB, MC, V.

≡≡ La Quinta
309 Preston Blvd, 71111; tel 318/747-4400 or toll free 800/531-5900; fax 318/747-1516. Exit 22 off I-20. Sporting the trademark Southwestern look of the chain, this dependable motel offers clean, well-maintained accommodations. Near Bossier City casinos. **Rooms:** 130 rms and stes. CI 3pm/CO noon. Nonsmoking rms avail. **Amenities:** 🛢 ☖ A/C, cable TV.

Services: ▣ ◩ ⬠ ⬡ **Facilities:** ⬚ ▭ ♿ **Rates (CP):** $57–$65 S; $67–$75 D; $67–$77 ste. Extra person $10. Children under age 18 stay free. Min stay special events. Parking: Outdoor, free. AE, CB, DC, DISC, MC, V.

≣≣≣ Ramada Inn

150 Hamilton Rd, 71111; tel 318/746-8410 or toll free 800/931-3529; fax 318/742-4264. Exit 20 off I-20. Within a half-mile of a casino, this standard chain motel allows you to enjoy proximity, affordable prices, and nice accommodations without the flash and pomp of casino nightlife. **Rooms:** 40 rms. CI 2pm/CO noon. Nonsmoking rms avail. **Amenities:** ▣ ◩ A/C, cable TV. **Services:** ▣ ⬠ ⬡ **Facilities:** ⬚ ♿ **Rates:** $56 S; $60 D. Extra person $10. Children under age 16 stay free. Parking: Outdoor, free. AE, CB, DC, DISC, JCB, MC, V.

RESTAURANTS ⊪⊪

Monjuni's Italian Cafe

526 Benton Rd (LA 3); tel 318/747-3463. **Italian.** A small Italian restaurant with all the traditional features: red-and-white checkered tablecloths, garlic and cheeses hanging from columns, and good Italian fare in very large portions. The lasagna is good, but the shrimp fettuccine is the highlight of the menu. **FYI:** Reservations not accepted. Children's menu. Beer and wine only. **Open:** Mon–Thurs 10:30am–9pm, Fri–Sat 10:30am–10pm. **Prices:** Main courses $7–$9. AE, MC, V. ♿

Ralph & Kacoo's

1700 Old Minden Rd; tel 318/747-6660. **Cajun/Seafood.** A standard, chain restaurant offering a good reproduction of southeastern Louisiana cuisine. The decor is unique and interesting with a fishing and Cajun theme. The atmosphere is casual and oriented toward families. **FYI:** Reservations accepted. Children's menu. **Open:** Daily 11:30am–10:30pm. **Prices:** Main courses $9–$18. AE, DC, DISC, MC, V. ♿

Covington

Quiet 19th-century Victorian neighborhoods make up this bedroom community located 40 miles north of New Orleans. The area contains many antique shops, artist studios, and galleries. The Bogue Falaya and Tchefuncte rivers show off the area's natural beauty. **Information:** St Tammany Parish Tourist & Convention Commission, 600 N US 190, #15, Covington, 70433 (tel 504/892-0520 or toll free 800/634-9443).

HOTEL ▣

≣≣≣ Holiday Inn

501 N US 190, 70433; tel 504/893-3580 or toll free 800/HOLIDAY; fax 504/893-9969. Exit 63B off I-12. Located in a convenient, suburban location, this Holiday Inn has a beautiful atrium and good sports facilities. Great for a vacation in Covington or a weekend visit. **Rooms:** 156 rms and stes. CI 3pm/CO noon. Nonsmoking rms avail. **Amenities:** ▣ ◩ A/C, cable TV w/movies, dataport. **Services:** ✕ ◩ ⬠ **Facilities:** ⬚ ▧ ⬛ ▭ ♿ 1 restaurant, 1 bar, basketball, volleyball, games rm, whirlpool, washer/dryer. **Rates:** $73 S or D; $200 ste. Extra person $10. Children under age 18 stay free. Parking: Outdoor, free. AE, CB, DC, DISC, JCB, MC, V.

MOTEL ▣

≣≣ Best Western Northpark Inn

625 N US 190, 70433; tel 504/892-2681 or toll free 800/528-1234; fax 504/893-0115. Exit 63B off I-12. In a good suburban location, this motel has a restaurant and lounge next door and plenty of restaurants and shopping nearby. **Rooms:** 74 rms. Executive level. CI 3pm/CO 11am. Nonsmoking rms avail. **Amenities:** ▣ A/C, cable TV w/movies, dataport. **Services:** ✕ ◩ ⬠ **Facilities:** ⬚ ▭ Washer/dryer. **Rates (CP):** $53–$66 S; $59–$72 D. Extra person $6. Children under age 18 stay free. Min stay special events. Parking: Outdoor, free. AE, CB, DC, DISC, MC, V.

ATTRACTION ▣

Global Wildlife Center

26389 LA 40, Folsom; tel 504/796-3585. A refuge for hundreds of free-ranging animals representing 50 endangered, extinct, or rare species. Guided wagon tours roam the 900-acre grounds, with opportunities to feed the wild animals (giraffes, zebras, and buffalo, among others) that approach the wagon. Overnight safaris in the lodge require reservations, and a private guided tour for a personal photo session may be arranged. **Open:** Daily. Call for schedule. $$$

Epps

Situated in the northeast portion of the state, Epps is the gateway to the Poverty Point State Commemorative Area, notable for its Native American ceremonial mounds.

ATTRACTION ▣

Poverty Point State Commemorative Area

LA 577; tel 318/926-5492. A Native American settlement dating from 1800 BC to 400 BC. A vast array of artifacts unearthed from the Ohio and Tennessee River Valleys and the Appalachian foothills of Alabama and Georgia indicate the extensive trade activities and movement of the area's prehistoric inhabitants. Interpretive museum, video theater, viewing tower, outdoor displays, and self-guided marked hiking trails. Guided tram tours are held from Easter weekend through Labor Day, and during the summer visitors may watch excavations conducted by archeologists. **Open:** Daily 9am–5pm. $

Hammond

See also Baton Rouge, Covington

Hammond sits at the intersection of I-12 and I-55 and was once the heart of a great lumbering industry. Located 57 miles northwest of New Orleans, Hammond's quaint railroad junction–style downtown captures visitors' attention, as does nearby Global Wildlife Animal Park. **Information:** Hammond Chamber of Commerce, #2 Thomas St, PO Box 1458, Hammond, 70404 (tel 504/345-4457).

MOTEL

≣≣ Days Inn
42309 S Morrison Blvd, 70403; tel 504/542-1000 or toll free 800/325-2525. Exit 28 off I-55. Older property offering the easiest interstate access in Hammond. Rooms are clean and comfortable. Close to several restaurants. **Rooms:** 111 rms. CI 6pm/CO noon. Nonsmoking rms avail. **Amenities:** A/C, cable TV w/movies. **Services:** Babysitting. **Facilities:** 1 restaurant, 1 bar (w/entertainment), washer/dryer. **Rates:** $45 S; $56 D. Extra person $7. Children under age 18 stay free. Min stay special events. Parking: Outdoor, free. AE, CB, DC, DISC, MC, V.

RESTAURANT

Don's Seafood & Steak House
1915 S Morrison Blvd; tel 504/345-8550. Hammond exit off I-55. **Seafood/Steak.** Decor is nautical, in keeping with the emphasis on seafood. Try the fried seafood platter or the farm-raised catfish. **FYI:** Reservations accepted. Children's menu. **Open:** Sun–Thurs 11am–10pm, Fri–Sat 11am–11pm. **Prices:** Main courses $8–$16. AE, CB, DC, DISC, MC, V.

ATTRACTION

Kliebert's Turtle and Alligator Farm
1264 W Yellow Water Rd; tel 504/345-3617. This working turtle and alligator farm features a small lake with 250 alligators—some weighing more than 1,400 pounds—and compounds housing 15,000 turtles. Guided tours available. **Open:** Mar–Oct, daily noon–7pm. $

Houma

Named for the Houma Indians, the town was formed in 1834 in colorful Terrebonne Parish. Cajun music, cuisine, and festivals are a way of life here. Swamp tours and demonstrations of centuries-old traditions such as net making, woodcarving, and alligator skinning are memorable experiences. **Information:** Houma-Terrebonne Chamber of Commerce, 1700 St Charles St, PO Box 328, Houma, 70361-0328 (tel 504/876-5600).

MOTEL

≣≣ Quality Inn
1400 W Tunnel Blvd, 70360; tel 504/879-4871 or toll free 800/222-2121; fax 504/868-3607. Chain property with simple comfort. **Rooms:** 153 rms and stes. CI 2pm/CO noon. Nonsmoking rms avail. Some rooms have recliners. **Amenities:** A/C, cable TV. **Services:** Car-rental desk, babysitting. **Facilities:** 1 restaurant (bkfst only), 1 bar (w/entertainment). **Rates:** $55–$65 S; $49–$55 D; $95–$125 ste. Extra person $5. Children under age 18 stay free. Parking: Outdoor, free. AE, CB, DC, DISC, MC, V.

RESTAURANTS

Dave's Cajun Kitchen
2433 W Main St; tel 504/868-3870. LA 3040 exit off US 90. **Cajun.** A family-oriented restaurant offering a wide choice of meals. The sandwiches and po' boys are commendable, as are the shrimp and crab fettuccine and seafood salads. **FYI:** Reservations not accepted. Children's menu. **Open:** Mon 10:30am–2pm, Tues–Thurs 10:30am–9pm, Fri 10:30am–10pm, Sat 10:30am–9pm. **Prices:** Main courses $4–$12. AE, MC, V.

Miss Brandi's Restaurant
1023 W Tunnel Blvd; tel 504/872-9608. LA 3040 exit off US 90. **Cajun/Seafood.** The decor is nautical—complete with ships' wheels and nets on the walls—but the food is pure Cajun. The fried flounder is good, while the full range of étouffées will delight any fan. **FYI:** Reservations accepted. Cajun. Children's menu. **Open:** Peak (May/Dec) Mon 11am–1:30pm, Tues–Fri 11am–5pm, Sat 11am–7:30pm. **Prices:** Main courses $7–$12. AE, CB, DC, MC, V.

ATTRACTIONS

Southdown Plantation House, The Terrebonne Museum
LA 311 at St Charles St; tel 504/851-0154. Originally a Greek Revival home built in 1859, the owner's son added a second floor in the Victorian style in 1893. The collections displayed in the mansion's 21 rooms include 135 Boehm and Doughty porcelain birds; a re-creation of US Senator Allen J Ellender's private office in Washington, DC; original bedroom furniture of the Minor family; and Terrebonne Parish Oral History Room. Arts, crafts, and music at the Spring Market (Saturday before Easter weekend) and Fall Market (first Saturday in November). Southdown Victorian Christmas Dinner every December. **Open:** Tues–Sat 10am–4pm. $$

Oak Alley Plantation
3645 LA 18, Vacherie; tel 504/265-2151. Located 25 mi N of Houma, this is one of the most famous plantation houses in Louisiana. It was built in 1839 by Jacques Telesphore Roman, III, and named Bon Séjour, but any visitor who walks out to the levee and looks back at the ¼-mile avenue of 300-

year-old live oaks will see why steamboat passengers dubbed it "Oak Alley." The mansion's fluted Doric columns number the same as the oak trees—28 in all—and hold up a large second-story gallery. Costumed docents lead a tour of the Greek Revival structure and its traditional floor plan decorated with antique and modern furnishings. **Open:** Peak (Mar–Oct) daily 9am–5:30pm. Reduced hours off-season. **$$$**

Cajun Tours of Terrebonne
709 May Ave; tel 504/872-6157. Cultural tour of Louisiana bayou communities. Guided excursions take visitors to seafood factories, net makers, plantation homes, shipyards, mausoleums, pirogue builders, sugarcane fields, crawfish ponds, Native American fishing villages, fishing marinas, oil fields, alligator hunters, and fur trappers. **Open:** Daily 9am–5:30pm. **$$$$**

Cajun Tours Swamp Tour
709 May Ave; tel 504/872-6157. Offered by land or boat, visitors view waterfowl, alligators, marsh, bayous, and canals in a private swamp. The Terrebonne Swamp's shallow water guarantees alligators year-round, even in winter. **Open:** Daily 8am–5:30pm. **$$$$**

A Cajun Man's Swamp Cruise
US 90; tel 504/868-4625. Tours of bayou black country given on covered boats equipped with cellular phone and bathroom facilities. Tour guide Ron "Black" Guidry, the Cajun Man, plays the accordion and guitar and sings Cajun French tunes as the 49-passenger vessel explores the swampland's wildlife. He'll also teach you about the Cajun people and culture. Cajun meal available for groups of 20 or more. **Open:** Mon–Sat. Call for schedule. **$$$$**

Zam's Swamp Tours
135 Bayou Rd, Kraemer; tel 504/633-7881. 20 mi N of Houma. Narrated boat tours of Bayou Boeuf. Passengers tour the swamp under a canopy of oak and cypress trees. Wildlife such as nutria, alligators, turtles, snakes, and blue herons can be seen. Preserved local wildlife also exhibited. **Open:** Daily 10am–5pm. **$$$$**

Jennings

Originally a railroad town and supply center for area farmers, Jennings became known as the "Cradle of Louisiana Oil" with the discovery of black gold in 1901. Seat of Jefferson Davis Parish, the town's surrounding area is the Louisiana home of the Coushatta Indian tribe. Lake Arthur to the south is popular for water sports. **Information:** Greater Jennings Chamber of Commerce, 414 Cary Ave, PO Box 1209, Jennings, 70546 (tel 318/824-0933).

MOTELS

Days Inn
2502 Port Dr, 70546; tel 318/824-6550 or toll free 800/325-2525; fax 318/824-6550. Exit 65 off I-10. Older proper-

ty that has been adequately maintained. Located at the edge of town, it has easy access from the highway but is far from local commercial and business areas. **Rooms:** 69 rms. CI noon/CO noon. Nonsmoking rms avail. **Amenities:** A/C, cable TV w/movies. **Services:** **Facilities:** 1 restaurant (lunch and dinner only). **Rates (CP):** $45 S; $50 D. Extra person $5. Children under age 12 stay free. Parking: Outdoor, free. AE, DC, DISC, MC, V.

Holiday Inn
603 I-10 Service Rd, 70546; tel 318/824-5280 or toll free 800/HOLIDAY; fax 318/824-7941. Exit 64 off I-10. Standard, predictable accommodations. **Rooms:** 131 rms. CI 3pm/CO noon. Nonsmoking rms avail. **Amenities:** A/C, cable TV. **Services:** **Facilities:** 1 restaurant, 1 bar. **Rates:** $50 S; $55 D. Extra person $10. Children under age 18 stay free. Parking: Outdoor, free. AE, CB, DC, DISC, MC, V.

Kenner

The airport gateway to New Orleans, Kenner also attracts visitors with a variety of interesting museums, riverboat cruises on the Mississippi, and thoroughbred racing during spring and summer.

HOTELS

Holiday Inn Airport Holidome
2929 Williams Blvd, 70062; tel 504/467-5611 or toll free 800/HOLIDAY; fax 504/469-4915. ½ block S of I-10. Very clean and inviting hotel with easy access to the interstate. Lobby and lounge are decorated in a dark woods. **Rooms:** 304 rms and stes. Executive level. CI 3pm/CO noon. Nonsmoking rms avail. **Amenities:** A/C, cable TV w/movies, dataport, voice mail. **Services:** Car-rental desk, children's program, babysitting. **Facilities:** 1 restaurant, 1 bar, games rm, sauna, whirlpool, washer/dryer. **Rates:** $109 S or D; $215 ste. Extra person $10. Children under age 18 stay free. Min stay special events. AP and MAP rates avail. Parking: Outdoor, free. AE, DC, DISC, JCB, MC, V.

New Orleans Airport Hilton
901 Airline Hwy, 70062; tel 504/469-5000 or toll free 800/876-5514; fax 504/465-1101. Convenient to the airport, this hotel and conference center is perfect for business travelers and corporate meetings. **Rooms:** 317 rms and stes. Executive level. CI 3pm/CO 1pm. Nonsmoking rms avail. Beautiful muted decor. **Amenities:** A/C, cable TV w/movies, dataport, voice mail, bathrobes. All units w/minibars. **Services:** Car-rental desk, babysitting. **Facilities:** 1 restaurant, 1 bar, spa, whirlpool. **Rates:** Peak (Jan–May/Sept–Dec) $115–$155 S; $127–$167 D; $350–$460 ste. Extra person $12. Children

under age 18 stay free. Min stay special events. Lower rates off-season. Parking: Outdoor, free. AE, CB, DC, DISC, JCB, MC, V.

ATTRACTIONS

Destrehan Manor

LA 48, Destrehan; tel 504/764-9315. 5 mi W of Kenner. Built in 1787 by a free person of color, the plantation house is one of the oldest in the lower Mississippi Valley. Wings were added in 1805, and between 1830 and 1840 it was renovated from French Colonial to Greek Revival. During a recent restoration, some of the earliest methods of construction were uncovered and remain open for visitors to see. Craft fair held second full week of November. Costumed guides conduct tours daily. **Open:** Daily 9:30am–4pm. **$$$**

San Francisco Plantation

LA 44, Reserve; tel 504/535-2341. 15 mi NW of Kenner. The gothic three-story home features broad galleries that look like a ship's double decks. Twin stairs leading to a main portal appear much like one that leads to a steamboat's grand salon. Every room boasts carved woodwork and paintings with flowers, birds, nymphs, and cherubs on walls and ceilings. The restoration includes 18th-century French and English furniture and paintings. The house was the setting for Frances Parkinson Keyes's novel, *Steamboat Gothic*. Daily tours. **Open:** Daily 10am–4pm. **$$$**

Louisiana Toy and Train Museum

519 Williams Blvd; tel 504/468-7223. Museum displaying thousands of toy trains dating from the early 1800s. Exhibits include six operating train layouts, rare model trains, hands-on exhibits for children, and video presentations. **Open:** Tues–Sat 9am–5pm, Sun 1–5pm. **$**

Cytec Louisiana Wildlife and Fisheries Museum

303 Williams Blvd; tel 504/468-7232. More than 700 preserved specimens from butterflies to alligators are exhibited, many in displays portraying their natural habitat. A 15,000-gallon freshwater aquarium maintains a wide variety of Louisiana marine life including bass, perch, turtles, and eels. Part of Rivertown USA Museums, which also includes Saints Hall of Fame, Kenner Historical Museum, Science Center, Louisiana Toy and Train Museum, and Mardi Gras Museum. **Open:** Tues–Sat 9am–5pm. **$**

Lacombe

See Slidell

Lafayette

See also New Iberia, Opelousas, St Martinville

Both the heart of French Louisiana and the unofficial capital of Cajun Country, this modern city reveals its strong Cajun and Creole heritage in lively festivals throughout the year. Grand plantations, historical attractions, tropical gardens, horse racing, strong ethnic nightlife, water sports, and mysterious swamps also draw visitors. Home to the University of Southwestern Louisiana. **Information:** Lafayette Parish Convention & Visitors Bureau, PO Box 52066, 1400 NW Evangeline Thruway, Lafayette, 70505-2066 (tel 318/232-3737 or toll free 800/346-1958).

HOTELS

Best Western Hotel Acadiana

1801 W Pinhook Rd, 70508; tel 318/233-8120 or toll free 800/528-1234; fax 318/234-9667. Exit 103A off I-10. One of the best buys in Lafayette, this outstanding property offers better-than-average lodging without the added expense. **Rooms:** 300 rms and stes. Executive level. CI 3pm/CO noon. Nonsmoking rms avail. **Amenities:** A/C, cable TV w/movies, dataport. **Services:** Car-rental desk. Concierge-level guests receive complimentary cocktails, hors d'oeuvres, and continental breakfast. **Facilities:** 1 restaurant, 2 bars, whirlpool, washer/dryer. **Rates:** $60–$75 S; $70–$85 D; $150–$270 ste. Children under age 16 stay free. Min stay special events. Parking: Outdoor, free. AE, CB, DC, DISC, EC, ER, JCB, MC, V.

Comfort Inn

1421 SE Evangeline Thruway, 70501; tel 318/232-9000 or toll free 800/800-8752; fax 318/233-8629. Agreeable accommodations in a standard chain hotel with a very nice garden-style courtyard. **Rooms:** 200 rms and stes. CI 2pm/CO noon. Nonsmoking rms avail. **Amenities:** A/C, cable TV w/movies, dataport. All units w/terraces. **Services:** Car-rental desk. Deluxe continental breakfast. **Facilities:** 1 restaurant, 1 bar (w/entertainment), washer/dryer. **Rates (CP):** $49 S; $53 D; $99 ste. Extra person $5. Children under age 18 stay free. Min stay special events. Parking: Outdoor, free. AE, CB, DC, DISC, MC, V.

Holiday Inn Central Holidome

2032 NE Evangeline Thruway, 70509; tel 318/233-6815 or toll free 800/942-4868; fax 318/235-1954. Exit 103A off I-10. Lafayette's only indoor swimming pool and the recreational opportunities make this a good choice for families. Comfortable atrium. **Rooms:** 242 rms and stes. CI 2pm/CO noon. Nonsmoking rms avail. **Amenities:** A/C, cable TV w/movies, dataport. Some units w/terraces, 1 w/whirlpool. **Services:** Facilities: 1 restaurant, 1 bar (w/entertainment), games rm, steam rm, whirlpool. **Rates:** Peak (Jan–May/Sept–Nov) $69 S; $72 D; $150–$300 ste. Extra person $6. Children under age 18 stay free. Min stay special events. Lower rates off-season. Parking: Outdoor, free. AE, CB, DC, DISC, EC, JCB, MC, V.

🏨🏨🏨 Lafayette Hilton and Towers

1521 W Pinhook Rd (LA 182), 70503; tel 318/235-6111 or toll free 800/445-8667; fax 318/237-6313. Exit 103A off I-10, S on Evangeline. Luxurious rooms; very comfortable, large, open lobby. Great for travelers looking for a little extra. **Rooms:** 327 rms and stes. Executive level. CI 4pm/CO noon. Nonsmoking rms avail. **Amenities:** 🛁 🕎 A/C, cable TV w/movies, dataport. **Services:** ✕ 🚐 📧 ↪ **Facilities:** 🛗 3000 ♿ 1 restaurant, 1 bar (w/entertainment), sauna, washer/dryer. Excellent view of bayou from pool; boardwalk along bayou. **Rates:** $75–$85 S or D; $155–$375 ste. Extra person $10. Children under age 18 stay free. Min stay special events. Parking: Outdoor, free. AE, CB, DC, DISC, MC, V.

MOTEL

🏨🏨 Quality Inn

1605 N University (LA 182), 70501; tel 318/232-6131 or toll free 800/752-2682; fax 318/232-2682. Exit 102 off I-10. An older property with a less-than-attractive exterior, but the interior has a number of very modern touches. Good for budget travelers. **Rooms:** 153 rms. CI 2pm/CO noon. Nonsmoking rms avail. **Amenities:** 🛁 A/C, cable TV w/movies, dataport, in-rm safe. **Services:** 🚐 📧 ↪ 🐾 **Facilities:** 🛗 50 ♿ 1 bar, washer/dryer. **Rates:** $39–$49 S; $49–$59 D. Extra person $10. Children under age 18 stay free. Min stay special events. Parking: Outdoor, free. AE, CB, DC, DISC, MC, V.

RESTAURANTS 🍴

Angelle's

US 167 N, across from Evangeline Downs Racetrack; tel 318/896-8416. Exit 103B off I-10. **Seafood/Steak.** Located across from the Evangeline Downs Racetrack, this is a great spot to dine after a day at the track. The dining room has the look and feel of a country home with floral print wallpaper, exposed wooden beams, and pastoral art. The food is fine and moderately priced. **FYI:** Reservations recommended. Children's menu. **Open:** Daily 10am–10pm. **Prices:** Main courses $8–$15. AE, CB, DC, DISC, MC, V. ♿

Cafe Vermilionville

1304 W Pinhook Rd; tel 318/237-0100. **Regional American.** This small, quiet restaurant is housed in a National Historic Landmark columned building dating to 1799. Enjoy a view of the courtyard and herb garden from the glassed-in room while dining on the likes of shrimp Diane and snapper Anna, sautéed and topped with mushrooms and béarnaise. **FYI:** Reservations recommended. Children's menu. Dress code. **Open:** Lunch Mon–Fri 11am–2pm; dinner Mon–Sat 5:30–10pm; brunch Sun 11am–2pm. **Prices:** Main courses $15–$25. AE, DC, DISC, MC, V. 🍷 💳 ♿

Don's Seafood

301 E Vermilion St; tel 318/235-3551. Exit 103A off I-10. **Seafood/Steak.** A family-oriented restaurant with several locations in south Louisiana. This one is the original. Wheth-er ordering alligator or the complete shrimp dinner, you'll receive enormous portions. Good desserts. **FYI:** Reservations accepted. Children's menu. **Open:** Sun–Thurs 11am–10pm, Fri–Sat 11am–11pm. **Prices:** Main courses $8–$17. AE, CB, DC, DISC, MC, V. ♿

★ Enola Prudhomme's Cajun Cafe

4676 NE Evangeline Thruway; tel 318/896-7964. Exit 7 off I-49. **Cajun.** This comfortable little restaurant makes guests feel at home. Enola Prudhomme, the sister of chef Paul Prudhomme, claims to have taught her brother how to cook. Come and judge for yourself. The setting is unremarkable but the food is outstanding. The Cajun enchilada appetizer features shrimp in a Cajun cream sauce, and the catfish is great. The alligator sausage is also highly recommended. **FYI:** Reservations not accepted. **Open:** Tues–Sat 11am–10pm, Sun 11am–2:30pm. **Prices:** Main courses $9–$20. AE, MC, V. ♿

Poor Boy's Riverside Inn

240 Tubing Rd; tel 318/837-4011. Off US 90. **Cajun/Seafood.** An out-of-the-way location worth the drive for the relaxed family atmosphere and rural setting overlooking a pond. One of the popular Cajun items is the Riverside Extravaganza: local fish stuffed with crabmeat, grilled and topped with sautéed mushrooms and crawfish. The house salad with shrimp, lump crabmeat, crawfish, cheese, and bacon is exceptional. Great sandwiches. **FYI:** Reservations recommended. Children's menu. **Open:** Mon–Thurs 11am–10pm, Fri 11am–11pm, Sat 5–11pm. **Prices:** Main courses $6–$24. AE, CB, DC, DISC, MC, V. 👪 ♿

Prejean's

3480 US 167 N; tel 318/896-3247. **Cajun.** Authentic Cajun cuisine in a down-home setting. The restaurant is modeled after an old Cajun cabin with rough wood walls and exposed beams. Food is served on rough tables with red-and-white checkered tablecloths and wooden chairs, and Cajun music plays in the background. Flavorful and fun, the intriguing cuisine merits a little experimenting on the part of diners. **FYI:** Reservations accepted. Cajun. Children's menu. **Open:** Daily 11am–10pm. **Prices:** Main courses $13–$17. AE, DISC, MC, V. ♿

Randol's Seafood Restaurant and Cajun Dance Hall

2320 Kaliste Saloom Rd; tel 318/981-7080. Exit 103A off I-10, S to Kaliste Saloom, right 5 mi. **Cajun.** This good-times spot features dancing to live zydeco music on a large dance floor to go along with its traditional Cajun dishes and wide variety of fresh local seafood. **FYI:** Reservations not accepted. Zydeco. Children's menu. **Open:** Sun–Thurs 5–10pm, Fri–Sat 5–10:30pm. **Prices:** Main courses $10–$18. MC, V. ♿

Ruth's Chris Steak House

507 W Pinhook Rd (LA 182); tel 318/237-6123. Exit 103A off I-10 S. **Steak.** With its brick walls and dark woods this

classic steak house has a quiet and somber atmosphere but lively staff and food. The signature dish is the sizzling filet mignon. **FYI:** Reservations accepted. **Open:** Mon–Fri 11:30am–11:30pm, Sat 4–11:30pm, Sun 3–10pm. **Prices:** Main courses $20–$23. AE, DC, MC, V.

ATTRACTIONS 🏛

Lafayette Museum
1122 Lafayette St; tel 318/234-2208. Built circa 1800, the structure was once the home of Alexander Mouton, first Democratic governor of Louisiana. The museum depicts the history and culture of the area through period furnishings, historic memorabilia, and Mardi Gras costumes that were worn by Lafayette's krewe kings and queens. **Open:** Tues–Sat 9am–5pm, Sun 3–5pm. $

Acadian Village
200 Greenleaf Dr; tel 318/981-2364. This site preserves the heritage of southern Louisiana's Acadian people. The village offers visitors a view of 19th-century bayou community life through restored buildings—houses, a store, barns, and a chapel—that are furnished with authentic items. Cajun crafts and books on the culture are available at the gift shop. **Open:** Daily 10am–5pm. $$$

Chretien Point Plantation
Chretien Point Rd, Sunset; tel 318/233-7050. 15 mi N of Lafayette off LA 93. Rare 1831 Greek-Revival French plantation home that is famous for a number of reasons: The pirate Jean Lafitte supposedly buried treasure here (though it was never recovered); there have been tales of wandering ghosts on the site; a Civil War battle was fought in the front yard; the staircase in *Gone With the Wind* was modeled after the one in the house. Guided tours daily; ghost tours at night. **Open:** Daily 10am–5pm. $$$

Vermilionville
1600 Surry St; tel 318/233-4077 or toll free 800/99-BAY-OU. Reconstruction of a Cajun/Creole bayou village from the 1765–1890 era. Homes of every class in society are represented. Costumed staff provides vivid re-enactments of daily life; crafts demonstrations; authentic music, plays, and dancing in the performance center. **Open:** Daily 10am–5pm. $$$

Lake Charles

Inland water access makes this city a major Gulf coast port and the gateway to Cajun Country. Lake Charles swings during the Contraband Days every spring, the state's second-largest festival. Visitors also enjoy a white sand beach for swimming, a historic district filled with Victorian homes, and a growing number of riverboat casinos. **Information:** Southwest Louisiana Convention & Visitors Bureau, 1211 N Lakeshore Dr, Lake Charles, 70601 (tel 318/436-9588 or toll free 800/456-SWLA).

HOTEL 🏨

🗖🗖 Holiday Inn
505 N Lakeshore Dr, 70601; tel 318/433-7121 or toll free 800/367-1814; fax 318/436-8457. Exit 30 A off I-10. Standard lodging next to the casino boats. **Rooms:** 269 rms and stes. CI 3pm/CO noon. Nonsmoking rms avail. **Amenities:** 🗖 ⓐ A/C, cable TV w/movies, dataport. **Services:** ✗ 🖳 🖘 **Facilities:** 🖼 ⌷100⌷ ⓖ 2 restaurants, 2 bars. **Rates:** $88–$129 S; $98–$139 D; $350 ste. Extra person $10. Children under age 18 stay free. Parking: Outdoor, free. AE, CB, DC, DISC, MC, V.

MOTEL

🗖🗖 Château Charles Hotel & Conference Center
2900 US 90 W, at jct I-10, 70601; tel 318/882-6130 or toll free 800/324-2647; fax 318/882-6601. Exit 26. Set in a highly industrialized area, this motel is only four miles to Louisiana's only white sand beach. **Rooms:** 220 rms and stes. CI 12:30pm/CO noon. No smoking. Nonsmoking rms avail. **Amenities:** 🗖 A/C, cable TV w/movies. Some units w/whirlpools. Microwave. **Services:** ✗ 🖛 🖦 🖳 🖘 **Facilities:** 🖼 🖳 ⌷500⌷ ⓖ 1 restaurant, 2 bars, washer/dryer. Free shuttle to casino. **Rates (BB):** $59–$74 S; $69–$84 D; $125–$175 ste. Extra person $10. Children under age 12 stay free. Parking: Outdoor, free. AE, CB, DC, DISC, MC, V.

RESTAURANT 🍴

Cafe Margaux
765 Bayou Pines E; tel 318/433-2902. I-210 loop exit off I-10, N ½ mi on Lake St, right into Bayou Pines E subdivision. **Continental/French.** Sophisticated dining in a quiet and comfortable setting. Roast rack of lamb with fresh rosemary, honey peppers, and demiglacé is exceptional, as is the sautéed duck in raspberry-pepper sauce. The wine list is extensive and varied. **FYI:** Reservations recommended. Jacket required. **Open:** Lunch Mon–Fri 11am–2pm; dinner Mon–Sat 6–10pm. **Prices:** Main courses $17–$24. AE, DC, DISC, MC, V. ⓖ

ATTRACTION 🏛

Imperial Calcasieu Museum
204 W Sallier; tel 318/439-3797. Houses extensive collection relating to local history. Gibson-Barnham Gallery features fine arts exhibits. Re-created 19th-century pharmacy, Victorian bedroom, parlor, country store, and barbershop; toy collections; rare Audubon prints. On the grounds is the 300-year-old Sallier oak tree. **Open:** Tues–Fri 10am–5pm, Sat–Sun 1–5pm. $

Many

Nestled in the rolling hills east of Toledo Bend Reservoir, Many was founded in 1843 after 14 years of being in the middle of a treaty-created "neutral zone." Today, the once no-man's land is home to beautiful, 4,700-acre Hodges Gardens, the Fort Jesup State Commemorative Area, and many resorts and marinas on the 65-mile-long reservoir. **Information:** Sabine Parish Chamber of Commerce, 920 Fisher Rd, Many, 71449 (tel 318/256-3523).

ATTRACTIONS

Fort Jesup State Commemorative Area

32 Geoghagan Rd; tel 318/256-4117. The only frontier fort in Louisiana with original structures, the historic site interprets the frontier period of American history. The kitchen mess hall has been refurbished as it was in the 1840s, and the officer's quarters houses a museum where maps, documents, illustrations, and other military artifacts are displayed. With advanced notice, a costumed docent will greet and guide visitors through the compound. Special programs every month, sometimes with visitor participation; every spring a re-enactment of the encampment of the 7th infantry takes place. **Open:** Daily 9am–5pm. **$**

Hodges Gardens

US 171; tel 318/586-3523 or 424/9513. Multilevel formal gardens, set among 4,700 acres of pine forests and a 225-acre lake, where visitors see wild and cultivated flowers year-round. Greenhouses, wildlife pastures with deer, sheep, and buffalo, fishing boat rentals, and picnic areas. Special events include the Easter service, July 4th festival, and Christmas lights festival. Gift shop. **Open:** Daily 8am–5pm. **$$$**

Metairie

One of several major suburbs east of New Orleans, Metairie anchors the southern end of the Pontchartrain Causeway, the longest bridge in the world. This city offers easy access to New Orleans's attractions.

HOTELS

≣≣ Best Western Landmark Hotel

2601 Severn Ave, 70002; tel 504/888-9500 or toll free 800/277-7575. Exit 228 off I-10. Located near the business district, this oddly shaped hotel resembles a mushroom and features an open, airy atrium lobby with hanging plants. **Rooms:** 342 rms and stes. Executive level. CI 3pm/CO 11am. Nonsmoking rms avail. **Amenities:** A/C, cable TV w/movies, dataport. Some units w/terraces, some w/whirlpools. **Services:** ✗ Free shuttle to French Quarter. **Facilities:** 1 restaurant, 2 bars (1 w/entertainment), sauna, washer/dryer. Rooftop dining. **Rates:** Peak (Jan–May/Sept–Nov) $69–$109 S; $79–$119 D; $150–$275 ste. Extra person $10. Children under age 18 stay free. Min stay special events. Lower rates off-season. Parking: Indoor/outdoor, free. AE, CB, DC, DISC, EC, MC, V.

≣≣ Holiday Inn I-10

6401 Veterans Memorial Blvd, 70003; tel 504/885-5700 or toll free 800/HOLIDAY; fax 504/454-8294. Exit 225 off I-10. This standard chain property offers its guests the convenience of a complimentary shuttle to New Orleans' French Quarter. **Rooms:** 221 rms. Executive level. CI 3pm/CO noon. No smoking. **Amenities:** A/C, satel TV w/movies, dataport. All units w/terraces. **Services:** ✗ Babysitting. **Facilities:** 1 restaurant, 1 bar, whirlpool. Guests can use nearby fitness club. **Rates:** $70–$125 S or D. Extra person $10. Children under age 18 stay free. Min stay special events. Parking: Outdoor, free. AE, CB, DC, DISC, JCB, MC, V.

≣≣≣ Sheraton North

3838 N Causeway, 70002; tel 504/836-5253 or toll free 800/936-5253; fax 504/846-4562. Exit 228 off I-10, 1 mi on N Causeway to 6th St. Situated on magnificent Lake Pontchartrain, this hotel features mirrored walls that reflect off the water, plus jogging/walking trails that wind around the lake. In the heart of the Metairie Central Business District. **Rooms:** 210 rms and stes. Executive level. CI 3pm/CO noon. Non-smoking rms avail. Some rooms afford beautiful views of the lake. **Amenities:** A/C, cable TV w/movies, dataport, voice mail. **Services:** ✗ VP Masseur, babysitting. Complimentary shuttle to airport, downtown, and area attractions. **Facilities:** 1 restaurant, 1 bar, basketball, spa, sauna, whirlpool, beauty salon. **Rates:** Peak (Jan–May/Oct–Nov) $126–$156 S; $136–$156 D; $150–$210 ste. Extra person $10. Children under age 12 stay free. Min stay special events. Lower rates off-season. Parking: Indoor, free. AE, CB, DC, DISC, EC, JCB, MC, V.

RESTAURANTS

Andrea's

3100 19th St; tel 504/834-8583. **Continental/Italian.** This highly regarded Italian restaurant features cozy dining quarters hung with pretty chandeliers. A top entree is veal chop stuffed with cheese and prosciutto, then breaded and sautéed in a mushroom sauce. Also pasta and seafood dishes. Baking is done on premises. **FYI:** Reservations recommended. Children's menu. Dress code. **Open:** Mon–Thurs 11am–10pm, Fri–Sat 11am–11pm, Sun 11am–9pm. **Prices:** Main courses $14–$25. AE, CB, DC, DISC, ER, MC, V. ♥

Augie's Seafood Restaurant

3300 S I-10 Service Rd; tel 504/835-3300. **Creole/Seafood.** The charming gardenlike interior is distinguished by a huge skylight, fountains, and greenery. The veal Angie, sautéed with lump crabmeat and served with a hollandaise sauce, is a favorite. Bread pudding is a featured dessert. **FYI:** Reservations recommended. **Open:** Daily 11am–11pm. **Prices:** Main courses $8–$30; prix fixe $15. AE, CB, DC, DISC, MC, V. ♿

Bozo's

3117 21st St; tel 504/831-8666. Exit 228A off I-10, right on W Esplanade, right on Ridgelake, S 8 blocks. **Seafood.** The decor isn't much, but that's not what draws people here anyway: The abundant, fresh, inexpensive local shellfish does. Owner Bozo Voinovitch really knows his crawfish (his recipe has won international awards), and his delightful fried catfish, lightly breaded, is worth the trip. **FYI:** Reservations accepted. Children's menu. **Open:** Lunch Tues–Sat 11am–3pm; dinner Tues–Thurs 5–10pm, Fri–Sat 5–11pm. **Prices:** Main courses $6–$14. MC, V. &

Casa Garcia
8814 Veterans Memorial Blvd; tel 504/464-0354. Exit 226 off I-10, W on Veterans Memorial Blvd. **Mexican.** Tex-Mex may not be a New Orleans area specialty, but Casa Garcia does it well. A fountain graces the center of the tastefully decorated dining room. Chicken fajitas and pastas are some of the better options. **FYI:** Reservations accepted. Children's menu. Dress code. **Open:** Sun–Thurs 11am–10pm, Fri–Sat 11am–11pm. **Prices:** Main courses $8–$13. AE, DC, DISC, MC, V. &

Crazy Johnnie's Steak House
3520 18th St; tel 504/887-6641. Exit 228A off I-10. **Steak.** The menu used to be filet mignon only, but now includes tuna and shrimp. The real selling point however, is the steak: It rivals what you get at some New Orleans steakhouses and is at least half the price. This combination does, however, lead to lengthy waits on weekends. **FYI:** Reservations not accepted. Additional location: 1202 US 190, Covington (tel 893-5678). **Open:** Mon–Sat 11am–11pm, Sun 4–10pm. **Prices:** Main courses $7–$8. AE, MC, V. &

Crozier's Restaurant Francais
3216 W Esplanade; tel 504/833-8108. Exit 228A off I-10, N on Causeway, left on W Esplanade. **French.** Authentic, straightforward French food in a dining room tastefully decorated in red, white, and blue Louis XIV motif. Duck liver pâté, traditional onion soup, and trout Grenobloise with lemon butter and capers are some recommended dishes. **FYI:** Reservations recommended. Violin. Dress code. **Open:** Tues–Sat 5:30–10pm. **Prices:** Main courses $15–$17. AE, DC, DISC, MC, V. ♥ &

Impastato's Restaurant
3400 16th St; tel 504/455-1545. Exit 228A off I-10. **Italian/Seafood.** Owner Joe Impastato says everything on the menu is good, and he's just about right. Some dishes to try are the osso buco, the cannelloni, and trout with various toppings of mushrooms, crabmeat, and artichokes. The candle-lit dining room, done in rich maroon hues, boasts a stained-glass ceiling. **FYI:** Reservations recommended. Singer. Children's menu. Dress code. **Open:** Tues–Sat 5pm–midnight. **Prices:** Main courses $9–$19; prix fixe $20. AE, MC, V. ♥ &

La Riviera
4506 Shores Dr; tel 504/888-6238. Exit 227 off I-10, N on Clearview, left on W Esplanade, right on Shores. **Italian/Seafood.** This small and intimate dining room may be hard to find but it's a real gem. Chef Goffredo's crabmeat ravioli has

won a national award, while his osso buco is the best of six excellent veal dishes. The chef invites diners to visit the kitchen while meals are being prepared. **FYI:** Reservations recommended. Dress code. **Open:** Lunch Tues–Fri 11:30am–2pm; dinner Mon–Thurs 5:30–10pm, Fri–Sat 5:30–11pm. Closed week before Labor Day. **Prices:** Main courses $10–$17. AE, CB, DC, DISC, MC, V. ♥ &

⑤ Peking Duck House
4445 Veterans Blvd; tel 504/888-7888. **Chinese.** Some of the best Chinese food available in the New Orleans area, served in a quiet, relaxed atmosphere. The outstanding Peking duck is always ready upon demand. General Tso's chicken and Kung Pao dishes are also popular. Nightly dinner buffet. **FYI:** Reservations accepted. Jacket required. **Open:** Mon–Thurs 11am–10pm, Fri 11am–10:30pm, Sat–Sun noon–10:30pm. **Prices:** Main courses $6–$10. AE, DISC, MC, V. &

Ralph & Kacoo's
601 Veterans Memorial Blvd; tel 504/831-3177. Exit 228A off I-10. **Cajun/Seafood.** Part of a popular Louisiana seafood chain, the simple decor features the standard New Orleans nautical motif—nets, ropes, and various plastic shrimp and fish adorn the walls and ceiling. The casual, family-oriented atmosphere makes this a relaxing place to dine on southern Louisiana fare. **FYI:** Reservations accepted. Children's menu. Dress code. **Open:** Daily 11:30am–10:30pm. **Prices:** Main courses $9–$18. AE, DC, DISC, MC, V. &

Monroe

See also West Monroe

Initially a Spanish fort established in 1785, Monroe became a prosperous city located in the "Garden Spot of the Ouachita Valley." The economic and cultural center of northeast Louisiana, Monroe is the seat of Ouachita Parish and home to Northeast Louisiana State University. Nearby state and national wildlife areas offer seasonal recreation. **Information:** Monroe–West Monroe Convention & Visitors Bureau, 1333 State Farm Dr, PO Box 6054, Monroe, 71211 (tel 318/387-5691 or toll free 800/843-1872).

MOTELS 🏨

≡≡≡ Best Western Civic Center
Jct I-20 and Civic Center Expwy, 71203; tel 318/323-4451 or toll free 800/528-1234; fax 318/323-1728. Exit 118 off I-20. An older property that has been recently renovated and is very well maintained. Easy access to civic center and relatively close to many other Monroe facilities and attractions. Suitable for all travelers. **Rooms:** 92 rms. CI 3pm/CO 11am. Nonsmoking rms avail. **Amenities:** 📞 🍽 A/C, cable TV, refrig. **Services:** ✕ 🖼 🕽 **Facilities:** 🛗 💯 & 1 restaurant, 1

bar. **Rates:** $49 S; $55 D. Extra person $6. Children under age 18 stay free. Parking: Outdoor, free. AE, CB, DC, DISC, MC, V.

☰ Days Inn
2102 Louisville, 71201; or toll free 800/DAYS-INN; fax 318/323-3808. Exit 118 off I-20, N on US 165, left on Louisville. An older property, its rooms are a little outdated and could use some refurbishing but are nevertheless clean and comfortable. **Rooms:** 127 rms and stes. CI open/CO noon. Nonsmoking rms avail. **Amenities:** 🛏 A/C, cable TV. **Services:** 🛇 🍴 🍷 **Facilities:** 🔲 🏊 ⚿ 1 bar, playground, washer/dryer. **Rates (CP):** $37 S; $43 D; $51 ste. Children under age 18 stay free. Parking: Outdoor, free. AE, CB, DC, DISC, MC, V.

☰☰ Howard Johnson
5650 Frontage Rd, 71202; tel 318/345-2220 or toll free 800/446-4656; fax 318/343-4098. Exit 120 off I-20. The closest property to Monroe airport, this older building in top condition provides pleasant accommodations. **Rooms:** 58 rms. CI open/CO noon. Nonsmoking rms avail. **Amenities:** 🛏 🍷 A/C, cable TV, voice mail. **Services:** 🛇 🍴 🍷 **Facilities:** 🔲 ⚿ **Rates (CP):** $39–$42 S; $45–$49 D. Extra person $5. Children under age 18 stay free. Parking: Outdoor, free. AE, CB, DC, DISC, EC, ER, JCB, MC, V.

RESTAURANT 🍽

Warehouse No 1 Restaurant
1 Olive St; tel 318/322-1340. **Seafood/Steak.** Built in an old warehouse that sits over the river, this restaurant offers a great view from its lofty windows. The standout of the Cajun menu is the blackened platter, offering flavorful rib eye steak, shrimp, and red snapper. **FYI:** Reservations not accepted. Piano. Children's menu. Dress code. **Open:** Mon–Thurs 5–9pm, Fri–Sat 5–9:30pm. **Prices:** Main courses $8–$18. AE, CB, DC, DISC, MC, V. 📼 ⚿

ATTRACTIONS 📷

Emy-Lou Biedenharn Foundation
2006 Riverside Dr; tel 318/387-5281. The grounds include a museum, residence, and garden. The Bible Museum contains a collection of rare books (highlights include a 1560 Geneva Bible, 1568 Bishop's Bible, and a 1611 King James Bible), archeological artifacts, and antique musical instruments. The Biedenharn Home, built in 1914 by Joseph Biedenharn, first bottler of Coca-Cola, exhibits china, crystal, silver, and Coca-Cola memorabilia. ELsong Gardens, designed in 1946, features a porcelain fountain from the gardens of Catherine the Great and piped music triggered by lasers that greets visitors as they enter the separate gardens linked by winding paths. **Open:** Tues–Fri 10am–4pm, Sat–Sun 2–5pm. **Free**

Masur Museum
1400 S Grand; tel 318/329-2237. The former residence of the Masur family, this modified English Tudor-style structure

dating from 1929 was built of Indiana limestone blocks and roofed with Pennsylvania slate. It now houses a collection of paintings, prints, photographs, and sculptures, as well as changing exhibits. **Open:** Tues–Thurs 9am–5pm, Fri–Sun 2–5pm. **Free**

Northeast Louisiana University
University Ave; tel 318/342-1000. The campus is home to the Bry Hall Art Gallery, which features art exhibits and photographs by students, faculty, and American artists; the Museum of Natural History, which is home to Native American, African, and Latin American geological exhibits; and the Museum of Zoology, said to have one of the largest and most complete fish collections in the nation. **Open:** Mon–Fri 9am–5pm. **Free**

Louisiana Purchase Gardens and Zoo
Berstein Park Dr; tel 318/329-2400. Formal gardens, moss-covered trees, winding paths, and moats surround the naturalistic habitats of the many rare and exotic animals that live in the 80-acre zoo. Boat and miniature train rides; gift shop. **Open:** Apr–Oct, daily 10am–5pm. **$$**

Morgan City

Established in the early 1800s and incorporated in 1860, what was Brashear City renamed itself in 1870. Because of its location at the outpour of the Atchafalaya River into the Gulf of Mexico, this is a sailing and sportfishing center, and swamp tours are popular as well. **Information:** East St Mary Chamber of Commerce, 7332 US 90 E, PO Box 2606, Morgan City, 70381 (tel 504/384-3830).

ATTRACTIONS 📷

Brownell Memorial Park and Carillon Tower
LA 70 at Lake Palourde; tel 504/384-3191. The 9½-acre park set along a swamp is landscaped to display native fauna, including palmettos, elephant ears, iris, and moss-draped cypress trees. The 106-foot tower is one of the largest cast-bell carillons in the world, with 61 bronze bells that chime every 30 minutes from 9:15am to 5:15pm. **Open:** Daily 9am–5pm. **Free**

Swamp Gardens
725 Myrtle St; tel 504/384-3343. Guided tours through a 3½-acre park feature exhibits depicting swamp life over the years. Audio speakers at each exhibit provide information related to the displays, which include prehistoric Native Americans working next to their palmetto huts, lumberjacks harvesting cypress trees, moss pickers on specially designed boats for gathering moss, and the original mobile home—the houseboat. Visitors may watch alligators being fed in a small zoo containing animals indigenous to the area. **$**

Natchitoches

Founded in 1714, Natchitoches is the oldest permanent settlement in the Louisiana Purchase territory. Many historical attractions draw visitors, and a nearby national forest and area lakes provide outdoor activities and sports. Home to Northwestern State University. **Information:** Natchitoches Parish Tourist Commission, 781 Front St, PO Box 411, Natchitoches, 71458-0411 (tel 318/352-8072 or toll free 800/259-1714).

MOTEL

≡≡ Best Western
US 6W at I-45, 71457; tel 318/352-6655 or toll free 800/528-1234; fax 318/352-6655. Exit 138 off I-49. Newer Best Western with adequate rooms, very close to interstate. Fine for overnight. **Rooms:** 41 rms and stes. Executive level. CI 2pm/CO 11am. Nonsmoking rms avail. **Amenities:** A/C, cable TV, dataport. **Services:** **Facilities:** **Rates (CP):** $49–$54 S or D; $67 ste. Extra person $5. Children under age 12 stay free. Min stay special events. Parking: Outdoor, free. AE, CB, DC, DISC, JCB, MC, V.

RESTAURANTS

The Landing
530 Front St; tel 318/352-1579. Exit 138 off I-49. **Regional American/Continental.** Located right on the Natchitoches waterfront, this restaurant offers a very pleasant dining experience. A menu favorite is Piregue la Fouche—half an eggplant breaded and fried then filled with shrimp and crabmeat and topped with a creamy la Fouche sauce. Grilled fresh catfish is smothered in a crawfish étoufée sauce. **FYI:** Reservations accepted. Dress code. **Open:** Tues–Sun 11am–10pm. **Prices:** Main courses $10–$20. AE, MC, V. &

Merci Beaucoup
127 Church St; tel 318/352-6634. **Regional American/Cajun/Creole.** Ceiling fans waft cool breezes over the red-and-white checkered tablecloths in this comfortable little restaurant. There are at least three chalkboard specials each day, but the best meals may be the Diablo burger with Cajun seasonings and sautéed mushrooms or the 10-oz prime rib. The Louisiana "Su" Bon, a chocolate/strawberry dessert, is a tasty way to finish a meal. **FYI:** Reservations accepted. Children's menu. **Open:** Daily 10am–4pm. **Prices:** Lunch main courses $9–$15. AE, DISC, MC, V. &

ATTRACTIONS

Bayou Folk Museum/Kate Chopin Home
LA 1, Cloutierville; tel 318/379-2736 or 379-2233. The restored home of Kate Chopin, the 19th-century author of *The Awakening*, is now a museum featuring Cane River memorabilia. The focal point of the museum is an original of Chopin's collection of short stories, *Bayou Folk*. Behind the house are a blacksmith's shop, a country doctor's office, and antique farm implements. **Open:** Mon–Sat 9am–5pm, Sun 1–5pm. **$**

Melrose Plantation
LA 119, Melrose; tel 318/379-0055. 14 mi S of Natchitoches. A plantation of the colonial, ante- and post-bellum South. The complex includes eight buildings, three of which were built by freed slave Marie Therese Coincoin and her sons starting in 1796—the Big House, Yucca House, and "Africa" House. Also on the grounds is a cabin of primitive artist Clemetine Hunter. Guided tours. Melrose Arts and Crafts Show held here during the second week in June. **Open:** Daily noon–4pm. **$$**

Natchitoches National Fish Hatchery and Aquarium
130 Morrow St; tel 318/357-3101. Fish hatchery that raises fish for stocking in coastal river systems and estuarine waters. On display in 20 tanks are native fish and reptiles including striped and large-mouth bass, bluegill, redear sunfish, channel catfish, turtles, and alligators. **Open:** Daily 8am–4pm. **Free**

New Iberia

Settled by the Spanish in the 1770s, New Iberia lies 23 miles southwest of Lafayette in Acadiana territory. In addition to beautiful scenery and restored antebellum homes, the area is known for its abundant seafood and ethnic festivals. **Information:** Greater Iberia Chamber of Commerce, 111 W Main St, New Iberia, 70560 (tel 318/364-1836).

MOTELS

≡≡ Best Western
2714 LA 14, 70560; tel 318/364-3030 or toll free 800/328-1234; fax 318/367-5311. Exit 103A off US 90. Near the interstate, this frugal choice is near New Iberia–Avery Island attractions. **Rooms:** 103 rms and stes. CI 2pm/CO noon. Nonsmoking rms avail. **Amenities:** A/C, cable TV w/movies, dataport. Some units w/whirlpools. **Services:** **Facilities:** 1 restaurant, 1 bar (w/entertainment), washer/dryer. **Rates (CP):** $45 S; $51 D; $80–$86 ste. Extra person $6. Children under age 18 stay free. Parking: Outdoor, free. AE, CB, DC, DISC, MC, V.

≡≡≡ Holiday Inn New Iberia/Avery Island
2915 LA 14, 70560; tel 318/367-1201 or toll free 800/HOLIDAY; fax 318/367-7877. Exit 103A off US 90. Standard chain motel that's a popular site for conventions. Though it caters mostly to business travelers, it's suitable for any guest. **Rooms:** 174 rms and stes. CI 1pm/CO noon. Nonsmoking rms avail. **Amenities:** A/C, cable TV w/movies, dataport. 1 unit w/whirlpool. **Services:** Babysitting. **Facilities:** 1 restaurant (bkfst and

lunch only), 1 bar, washer/dryer. **Rates:** $38–$54 S or D; $125 ste. Extra person $10. Children under age 18 stay free. Parking: Outdoor, free. AE, MC, V.

RESTAURANT

★ Cafe Lagniappe Too

204 E Main St; tel 318/365-9419. **Cajun.** A great little cafe that features down-home decor and artwork by co-owner Al Landry. The food is simple too—gumbo and crab corn bisque are good ways to start off the meal. The Teche Queen club, a triple decker with grilled chicken breast, avocado, and veggies, is recommended. If the banana mango cake is available, order it in advance, because the locals, who know how good it is, will scarf it up quickly. **FYI:** Reservations not accepted. Beer and wine only. **Open:** Lunch Mon–Fri 10am–2pm; dinner Fri–Sat 6–9pm. **Prices:** Main courses $3–$6. AE, MC, V.

ATTRACTIONS

Oaklawn Manor

Irish Bend Rd, Franklin; tel 318/828-0434. 20 mi S of New Iberia. Greek revival mansion built in 1837, the 20-inch walls were constructed of brick made from surrounding soil. European antiques furnish the interior, and the outside grounds include the Old Butter House, landscaped gardens inspired by Versailles, and an aviary that houses a variety of domestic and tropical birds. With advance notice, tour guides will dress in antebellum costumes. **Open:** Daily 10am–4pm. $$$

Shadows-on-the-Teche Plantation

317 E Main St; tel 318/369-6446. Greek revival home built in 1834 for David Weeks, a wealthy planter. The two-story house is built of rose-colored brick and sits amid oak trees, camellias, and azaleas. One of the most authentically restored and furnished homes in the state. **Open:** Daily 9am–4:30pm. $$

Live Oak Gardens

5505 Rip Van Winkle Rd; tel 318/365-3332 or toll free 800/375-3332. This semitropical garden and nature preserve offers four main attractions: The Joe Jefferson House, built in 1870, contains a steamboat gothic dining room and Victorian furnishings; the Gardens cover 20 acres of live oaks and have literally thousands of blooming flowers year-round; the Gallery of the Gardens, an Acadian-style cottage, houses national and local exhibits; and the Decoy Museum, located in a 1925 schoolhouse, displays the largest collection of Louisiana-crafted waterfowl decoys in the state. Guided tours and specially tailored tours available. **Open:** Daily 9am–5pm. $$$

Konriko/Conrad Rice Mill

307 Ann St; tel 318/364-7242 or toll free 800/551-3245. The Konriko Company Store offers a slide presentation about Cajun culture, Cajun foods and crafts, and complimentary fresh Cajun coffee and rice mix. Tours of Conrad Rice Mill, the oldest in the United States, operating since 1912 using a rare, belt-drive power transmission, given Monday through Saturday. **Open:** Mon–Sat 9am–5pm. $

New Orleans

See also Kenner, Metairie, Slidell

Called the "Crescent City" because of the way its site has been shaped by the curving Mississippi River, New Orleans remains one of the world's most distinctive cities. Its famous French Quarter was the original colony, settled in 1718 and still rich with charm. Nearby, a freshly renovated riverfront pulses with promenades and activities, and the Garden District and museums should not be missed. Best known for its Mardi Gras celebrations, New Orleans also hosts professional sports teams and is the site of Loyola and Tulane Universities. **Information:** Greater New Orleans Convention & Visitors Bureau, 1520 Sugar Bowl Dr, New Orleans, 70112 (tel 504/566-5011).

PUBLIC TRANSPORTATION

The New Orleans bus system provides city-wide service. Call 569-2700 for more information, or pick up an excellent city map at the Visitor Information Center, 529 St Ann St. All fares are $1; express fares are $1.25. The **Vieux Carré Minibus** tours the French Quarter; it leaves Canal and Bourbon Sts at frequent intervals from 5am to 7:23pm and costs 60¢. Along the riverfront, vintage streetcars, known as the "Ladies in Red," run for close to two miles from the Old Mint to Riverview. Fare is $1.25. The streetcar line (designated a National Historic Landmark) runs 1½ hours down St Charles Avenue. The trolley run 24 hours a day at frequent intervals; fare is $1 each way (exact change required).

HOTELS

≡≡≡ Avenue Plaza Hotel

2111 St Charles Ave, 70130 (Garden District); tel 504/566-1212 or toll free 800/535-9575; fax 504/525-6899. A partial time-share condo property offering European-style efficiencies. Its mahogany-paneled drawing room features a large fireplace and sofas, and the window-lined dining room overlooks the avenue. On the St Charles street car line. **Rooms:** 250 effic. CI 3pm/CO 11am. Nonsmoking rms avail. Rooms are a mix of old world and modern convenience—antiques such as cherry four-poster beds are coupled with ornate floral window treatments and bright, white kitchens with contemporary touches. **Amenities:** 🛏 ⚲ A/C, cable TV w/movies. **Services:** ⊶ VP ⊠ ⤶ Masseur, babysitting. **Facilities:** 🖼 🛁 🗓 ⅖ 1 restaurant (bkfst and lunch only), 1 bar, spa, sauna, steam rm, whirlpool, beauty salon, washer/dryer. A full service health spa run by Mackie Shilstone, a consultant to Hollywood celebrities and various sports teams, is on the premises and available for $5 per day. The pool area is in a secluded courtyard with a beautiful brick deck and shade trees. **Rates:** Peak (Sept–Apr) $139 effic. Children under age 12 stay free. Min stay special events. Lower rates off-season. Parking: Indoor/outdoor, $8/day. AE, CB, DC, DISC, MC, V.

UNRATED Best Western Inn of Bourbon St

541 Bourbon St, 70130 (French Quarter); tel 504/524-7611 or toll free 800/535-7891; fax 504/568-9427. Located in the middle of Bourbon Street's colorful activity. **Rooms:** 186 rms and stes. CI 3pm/CO noon. Nonsmoking rms avail. **Amenities:** 🛏 A/C, cable TV w/movies, dataport, voice mail. Some units w/terraces. **Services:** ✗ ☎ VP ⬜ ↵ Car-rental desk, social director, babysitting. **Facilities:** ⬜ 🍴 125 & 1 restaurant, 1 bar (w/entertainment), spa. **Rates:** Peak (Jan–May/Sept–Nov) $155–$235 S or D; $470 ste. Extra person $15. Children under age 12 stay free. Min stay special events. Lower rates off-season. Parking: Outdoor, $9/day. AE, CB, DC, DISC, EC, JCB, MC, V.

☰☰☰ Château Motor Hotel

1001 Chartres St, 70116 (French Quarter); tel 504/524-9636; fax 504/525-2989. Located in a relatively quiet area of the French Quarter. The lobby is surrounded by elegant French windows and leads into a courtyard. **Rooms:** 45 rms. CI 1pm/CO 1pm. Nonsmoking rms avail. Each room has individualized furnishings and decor. Exterior rooms have balconies overlooking Chartres St and Philip St. **Amenities:** 🛏 ☕ 🍴 A/C, cable TV. Some units w/terraces. **Services:** ✗ ☎ VP ↵ Car-rental desk, babysitting. **Facilities:** ⬜ 1 restaurant (bkfst and lunch only), 1 bar. **Rates (CP):** $64–$145 S; $84–$104 D. Extra person $10. Children under age 18 stay free. Min stay special events. Parking: Outdoor, free. AE, CB, DC, EC, MC, V.

☰☰☰ Château Sonesta Hotel

800 Iberville St, 70112 (French Quarter); tel 524/586-0800 or toll free 800/SONESTA; fax 504/586-1987. Recently renovated, this hotel was restored from the historic 1842 D H Holmes department store; the exterior has been refurbished to its 1913 appearance. **Rooms:** 243 rms and stes. CI 3pm/CO noon. Nonsmoking rms avail. Many rooms have 12- or 14-foot ceilings. Rooms face Bourbon St, Iberville, and Dauphine St. **Amenities:** 🛏 ☕ 🍴 A/C, cable TV w/movies, dataport, voice mail. Some units w/minibars, some w/terraces, some w/whirlpools. **Services:** 🍴 ☎ VP ⬜ ↵ Twice-daily maid svce, car-rental desk, babysitting. **Facilities:** ⬜ 🍴 200 ⬜ & 1 restaurant (dinner only), 1 bar, beauty salon. The Clock Bar was named after the famous D H Holmes clock featured in the John Kennedy Toole novel *A Confederacy of Dunces* and will soon feature the actual clock. **Rates:** Peak (Jan–May/Sept–Nov) $125–$215 S; $155–$245 D; $275–$325 ste. Extra person $35. Children under age 17 stay free. Min stay special events. Lower rates off-season. Parking: Outdoor, $14/day. AE, CB, DC, DISC, JCB, MC, V.

☰☰☰ Dauphine Orleans Hotel

415 Dauphine St, 70112 (French Quarter); tel 504/586-1800 or toll free 800/521-7111; fax 504/586-1409. This elegant hotel has been under the care and hospitality of the same owners for over 25 years. A small, intimate lobby opens into several courtyards. **Rooms:** 109 rms and stes. CI 3pm/CO noon. The suites are located in the old slave quarters and open into a private courtyard. **Amenities:** 🛏 ☕ 🍴 A/C, cable TV w/movies, refrig, dataport, in-rm safe, bathrobes. All units w/minibars, some w/terraces. **Services:** ☎ VP ⬜ ↵ 🍸 Complimentary tea served every afternoon. **Facilities:** ⬜ 🍴 50 1 restaurant (bkfst and lunch only), 1 bar. **Rates (CP):** $129–$169 S; $149–$189 D; $179–$359 ste. Extra person $20. Min stay special events. Parking: Indoor, $10/day. AE, CB, DC, DISC, MC, V.

☰☰☰☰ Fairmont Hotel

123 Baronne St, 70140; tel 504/529-7111 or toll free 800/527-4707; fax 504/522-2303. An outstanding historic hotel with an impressive ornate canopy and intricately carved stone facade. This grand hotel is steeped in luxury, from the deep-red velvet chairs and sofas, splendid chandeliers, and wonderful oil paintings in the lobby to the spacious, high-ceilinged guestrooms. (The lobby at Christmas time is decorated with thousands of lights—a must-see even if you're not staying here.) **Rooms:** 77 rms and stes. CI 4pm/CO 1pm. Nonsmoking rms avail. Elegant rooms are individually decorated with antiques. Deluxe linens, cotton sheets, and goosedown pillows. **Amenities:** 🛏 ☕ 🍴 A/C, cable TV w/movies, dataport, voice mail, bathrobes. Handmilled soaps. Fax machines available. **Services:** 🍴 ☎ VP ⬜ ↵ Car-rental desk, babysitting. Multilingual staff. **Facilities:** ⬜ 🏊 2 🍴 2500 ⬜ & 3 restaurants (see "Restaurants" below), 3 bars (2 w/entertainment), spa, beauty salon. Rooftop health club. Fine dining in romantic Sazerac Restaurant. Sumptuous Sunday brunch offered in legendary Blue Room. **Rates:** Peak (Jan–May/Oct–Nov) $145–$245 S or D; $250–$500 ste. Extra person $25. Children under age 18 stay free. Min stay special events. Lower rates off-season. MAP rates avail. Parking: Outdoor, $10/day. AE, CB, DC, DISC, EC, JCB, MC, V.

☰☰☰ French Quarter Courtyard

1101 N Rampart St, 70116 (French Quarter); tel 504/522-7333 or toll free 800/290-4233; fax 504/522-3908. Located in a newly restored 1897 D'Hemecant building. A beautiful fountain-filled pool is the focus of the courtyard. **Rooms:** 33 rms. CI 3pm/CO noon. Nonsmoking rms avail. Rooms feature hardwood floors, four-poster beds, and 13-foot ceilings. **Amenities:** 🛏 ☕ A/C, cable TV. Some units w/terraces. **Services:** 🍴 VP ⬜ Social director. **Facilities:** ⬜ 20 1 bar. **Rates (CP):** Peak (Jan–May/Sept–Dec) $129–$149 S; $139–$159 D. Extra person $15. Children under age 17 stay free. Min stay peak and special events. Lower rates off-season. Parking: Outdoor, $10/day. AE, DC, DISC, MC, V.

☰☰☰ The Historic French Market Inn

501 Decatur St, 70130 (French Quarter); tel 504/561-5621 or toll free 800/827-5621; fax 504/566-0160. Features exposed beams and brass beds, providing more charm and character than most chain properties. Perfect for a cozy, authentic New Orleans vacation. **Rooms:** 83 rms and stes. CI 3pm/CO 11am. Nonsmoking rms avail. **Amenities:** ☎ & A/C, cable TV, dataport. **Services:** ☞ △ ⌐ **Facilities:** 1 bar, whirlpool. **Rates (CP):** $79–$300 S or D; $129–$400 ste. Children under age 16 stay free. Min stay special events. AE, CB, DC, DISC, EC, JCB, MC, V.

☰☰☰ Holiday Inn Château Lemoyne

301 Dauphine St, 70112 (French Quarter); tel 504/581-1303 or toll free 800/HOLIDAY; fax 504/523-5709. A blend of modern Holiday Inn and old New Orleans style, the Château Lemoyne was pieced together from four Gallier town houses. **Rooms:** 171 rms and stes. CI 3pm/CO 11am. Nonsmoking rms avail. Mainly standard motel rooms. The Creek Cottages, originally used as slave quarters, aim for a historic New Orleans feel, but some guests may consider them too musty, small, and dark. **Amenities:** ☎ & A/C, cable TV w/movies, dataport, voice mail. Some units w/terraces, 1 w/whirlpool. **Services:** ✗ ☞ VP △ ⌐ Twice-daily maid svce, social director, babysitting. **Facilities:** 🖼 ⌂100 & 1 restaurant, 1 bar (w/entertainment). Rear courtyard is especially charming in the evening. **Rates:** Peak (Feb–May/Sept–Nov) $115–$210 S or D; $275–$350 ste. Extra person $15. Children under age 17 stay free. Min stay special events. Lower rates off-season. AP rates avail. Parking: Outdoor, $10/day. AE, CB, DC, DISC, EC, JCB, MC, V.

☰☰☰ Holiday Inn Crowne Plaza

300 Poydras St, 70130 (Central Business District); tel 504/525-9444 or toll free 800/HOLIDAY; fax 504/581-7177. Better-than-average Holiday Inn; a good place to stay away from the bustle of Bourbon St. **Rooms:** 439 rms and stes. Executive level. CI 3pm/CO noon. Nonsmoking rms avail. Corner rooms offer best view. **Amenities:** ☎ & ▣ 🍴 A/C, cable TV w/movies, dataport, voice mail. Some units w/whirlpools. **Services:** ✗ ☞ VP △ ⌐ Car-rental desk, babysitting. **Facilities:** 🖼 ⛳ ⌂500 & 2 restaurants, 1 bar (w/entertainment). **Rates:** Peak (Sept–Nov/Mar–May) $165–$185 S; $180–$200 D; $350–$485 ste. Extra person $15. Children under age 12 stay free. Min stay special events. Lower rates off-season. MAP rates avail. Parking: Indoor, $8–$12/day. AE, CB, DC, DISC, EC, MC, V.

☰☰☰ Holiday Inn Downtown Superdome

330 Loyola Ave, 70112 (Central Business District); tel 504/581-1600 or toll free 800/HOLIDAY; fax 504/522-0073. Located two blocks from the Superdome, this large hotel is good for visitors in for a short visit who don't wish to stay in the French Quarter. **Rooms:** 297 rms and stes. Executive level. CI 3pm/CO noon. Nonsmoking rms avail. **Amenities:** ☎ & 🍴 A/C, cable TV w/movies, dataport, voice mail. Some units w/minibars, some w/terraces. **Services:** ✗ ☞ △ ⌐

Car-rental desk, babysitting. Nintendo available. Complimentary morning coffee and evening ice cream. **Facilities:** 🖼 ⌂400 & 1 restaurant, 1 bar, spa. Rooftop pool. **Rates:** Peak (Mar–May/Oct–Nov) $109–$189 S; $125–$205 D; $300–$450 ste. Extra person $15. Children under age 19 stay free. Min stay special events. Lower rates off-season. Parking: Indoor, $10/day. AE, CB, DC, DISC, MC, V.

☰☰☰ Hotel de la Poste

316 Chartres St, 70130 (French Quarter); tel 504/581-1200 or toll free 800/448-4927; fax 504/523-2910. A newcomer by French Quarter standards, this 27-year-old building is a replica of an older building. A very simple courtyard adjoins a pool. The unpretentious exterior is reflected in the modest interior. **Rooms:** 100 rms and stes. CI 3pm/CO noon. Nonsmoking rms avail. The size of each room varies from quite small to average. **Amenities:** ☎ & A/C, cable TV, dataport, voice mail. Some units w/terraces. **Services:** ✗ ☞ VP △ ⌐ Babysitting. **Facilities:** 🖼 ⌂50 & 1 restaurant, 1 bar. **Rates:** Peak (Jan–May/Sept–Nov) $125–$145 S; $150–$170 D; $155–$200 ste. Extra person $25. Children under age 16 stay free. Min stay special events. Lower rates off-season. AP and MAP rates avail. Parking: Indoor, $12/day. AE, CB, DC, DISC, EC, MC, V.

☰☰☰☰ Hotel Inter-Continental

444 St Charles Ave, 70130 (Central Business District); tel 504/525-5566 or toll free 800/445-6563; fax 504/585-4352. Located within two blocks of most major office buildings in central business district, near most major attractions. Great for those who don't want to be immersed in action of French Quarter. Contemporary lobby with arched ceilings, large windows, and many lush plants. **Rooms:** 482 rms and stes. Executive level. CI 4pm/CO 1pm. Nonsmoking rms avail. **Amenities:** ☎ & 🍴 A/C, cable TV w/movies, dataport, voice mail. All units w/minibars, some w/terraces, 1 w/whirlpool. Some rooms have mini-TV in vanity area. **Services:** ⦿ ☞ VP △ ⌐ Twice-daily maid svce, car-rental desk, babysitting. **Facilities:** 🖼 ⛳ ⌂600 ⬚ & 3 restaurants (see "Restaurants" below), 2 bars (1 w/entertainment), beauty salon. **Rates:** Peak (Jan–May/Sept–Nov) $180–$230 S; $200–$250 D; $250–$2,000 ste. Extra person $20. Children under age 12 stay free. Min stay special events. Lower rates off-season. Parking: Indoor/outdoor, $9–$12/day. AE, CB, DC, DISC, EC, JCB, MC, V.

☰☰☰ Hotel Maison de Ville

727 Toulouse St, 70130 (French Quarter); tel 504/528-9206; fax 504/528-9939. Ideal for guests who really want to relax and be pampered in an elegant and lush atmosphere. Feels more like a house than a hotel. **Rooms:** 23 rms and stes; 5 cottages/villas. CI 3pm/CO noon. Each room is individualized in terms of size and decor. All are comfortable and tastefully decorated. Rooms 3 and 4 face Toulouse St and have balcony access. **Amenities:** ☎ & 🍴 A/C, cable TV, bathrobes. Some units w/terraces. **Services:** ✗ ☞ △ Twice-daily maid svce. **Facilities:** 🖼 1 restaurant (see "Restaurants"

below). **Rates (CP):** Peak (Jan–May/Sept–Nov) $155–$205 D; $250–$270 ste; $375–$425 cottage/villa. Extra person $30. Min stay wknds and special events. Lower rates off-season. Parking: Indoor, $17/day. AE, CB, DC, DISC, EC, MC, V.

≣≣≣ Hotel Provincial

1024 Chartres St, 70116 (French Quarter); tel 504/581-4995 or toll free 800/535-7922; fax 504/581-1018. Owned by the same family for 60 years, the hotel comprises seven buildings, five patios, and several courtyards. Classical, wrought-iron balconies rest directly over the lobby entrance and give the place an authentic New Orleans air. **Rooms:** 107 rms and stes. CI 3pm/CO noon. Nonsmoking rms avail. **Amenities:** 🛁 A/C, cable TV. Some units w/terraces. **Services:** ✕ ☎ VP 🖨 🛎 Babysitting. **Facilities:** 📶 🛏 🔥 1 restaurant (bkfst and lunch only; *see* "Restaurants" below), 1 bar. **Rates:** Peak (Jan–May/Sept–Nov) $145–$160 S or D; $225–$325 ste. Extra person $15. Children under age 17 stay free. Min stay wknds and special events. Lower rates off-season. Parking: Outdoor, $7–$10/day. AE, CB, DC, DISC, JCB, MC, V.

≣≣≣ Hotel St Marie

827 Toulouse St, 70112 (French Quarter); tel 504/561-8951 or toll free 800/366-2743; fax 504/581-3802. One of the Valentino family's three French Quarter properties, this beautifully crafted hotel boasts wrought-iron railings and old-world ambience. Just a half-block from Bourbon St. **Rooms:** 100 rms and stes. CI 4pm/CO noon. Some rooms have period furnishings. **Amenities:** 🛁 A/C, cable TV, voice mail. Some units w/terraces. **Services:** VP 🚐 🛎 Car-rental desk, babysitting. **Facilities:** 📶 🛏 1 restaurant (bkfst and dinner only), 1 bar. **Rates:** Peak (Jan–May/Sept–Nov) $110–$140 S or D; $250–$385 ste. Extra person $20. Children under age 12 stay free. Min stay wknds and special events. Lower rates off-season. Parking: Indoor, $10/day. AE, CB, DC, DISC, MC, V.

≣≣≣ Hotel St Pierre

911 Burgundy St, 70116 (French Quarter); tel 504/524-4401 or toll free 800/225-4040; fax 504/524-6800. Three blocks from Bourbon St, the Hotel St Pierre sits in a quiet residential area. The hotel's European character is emphasized throughout, starting with the wall-to-wall mirroring and beautiful chandelier in the lobby. **Rooms:** 75 rms and stes. CI 3pm/CO 11am. **Amenities:** 🛁 A/C, TV, voice mail. Some units w/terraces, some w/whirlpools. **Services:** ☎ 🛎 🍴 Twice-daily maid svce, car-rental desk, children's program, babysitting. **Facilities:** 📶 1 restaurant (bkfst only). **Rates (CP):** Peak (Jan–May/Sept–Nov) $99–$109 S; $119–$129 D; $139–$159 ste. Extra person $10. Children under age 12 stay free. Min stay wknds and special events. Lower rates off-season. Parking: Outdoor, free. AE, CB, DC, DISC, MC, V.

≣≣≣ Hotel Ste Helene

508 Chartres St, 70130 (French Quarter); tel 504/522-5014 or toll free 800/348-3888; fax 504/523-7140. A charming

hotel, with elaborate wrought-iron railings and balconies, located in a quiet part of the Quarter. **Rooms:** 26 rms and stes. CI 3pm/CO 11am. Nonsmoking rms avail. Most rooms face the street or the courtyard. Some interior rooms available, but they are small and windowless. **Amenities:** 🛁 A/C, cable TV. Some units w/terraces, some w/fireplaces, some w/whirlpools. **Services:** 🛎 Babysitting. Complimentary champagne served upon arrival. **Facilities:** 📶 **Rates (CP):** Peak (Jan–May/Sept–Nov) $135–$185 S or D; $165–$225 ste. Extra person $20. Children under age 17 stay free. Min stay wknds and special events. Lower rates off-season. AE, CB, DC, DISC, JCB, MC, V.

≣≣ Hotel Villa Convento

616 Ursulines St, 70116 (French Quarter); tel 504/522-1793; fax 504/524-1902. A quaint hotel located in a converted family home. The lobby, like the rest of the property, has a European ambience but is unpretentious and neat. **Rooms:** 25 rms and stes. CI 3pm/CO noon. Each room is individually decorated. **Amenities:** 🛁 A/C, cable TV. Some units w/terraces. **Rates (CP):** $79–$89 S; $95–$125 ste. Extra person $10. Min stay special events. Parking: Outdoor, $10/day. AE, MC, V.

≣≣≣ Hyatt Regency New Orleans

500 Poydras Plaza, 70140; tel 504/561-1234 or toll free 800/233-1234; fax 504/523-0488. Overlooking the French Quarter, this striking high-rise offers a prime location for business travelers and others, as it's connected to the Superdome and the New Orleans Center. The 32-floor glass atrium is home to a fine restaurant and piano bar. Elegant accommodations. **Rooms:** 1,186 rms and stes. Executive level. CI 3pm/CO noon. No smoking. **Amenities:** 🛁 A/C, cable TV w/movies, dataport, voice mail. Some units w/minibars. **Services:** ✕ ☎ VP 🛎 🍴 Car-rental desk, babysitting. Complimentary shuttle to French Quarter and Mississippi riverfront. **Facilities:** 📶 🏋 🏊 🖥 🔥 2 restaurants (*see* "Restaurants" below), 2 bars (3 w/entertainment), spa, whirlpool, beauty salon, day-care ctr. **Rates:** Peak (Sept–May) $159–$175 S; $184–$200 D; $350–$525 ste. Min stay special events. Lower rates off-season. AP and MAP rates avail. Parking: Indoor, $12/day. AE, MC, V.

≣≣≣ Landmark Hotel French Quarter

920 N Rampart St, 70166 (French Quarter); tel 504/524-3333 or toll free 800/535-7862; fax 504/522-8044. A comfortable hotel on the very edge of the French Quarter. **Rooms:** 100 rms. CI 3pm/CO noon. Nonsmoking rms avail. Rooms are fairly standard. Each hallway is named after a street in the Quarter, so each guest room has an "address." **Amenities:** 🛁 A/C, cable TV w/movies, dataport, in-rm safe. Some units w/minibars, all w/terraces. **Services:** ✕ ☎ 🛎 🍴 Twice-daily maid svce, car-rental desk, social director, babysitting. **Facilities:** 📶 🛏 🔥 1 restaurant, 1 bar (w/entertainment), games rm, washer/dryer. **Rates:** Peak (Jan–May/Sept–Dec) $135 S; $145 D. Extra person $10. Children

under age 12 stay free. Min stay special events. Lower rates off-season. Parking: Indoor, $6/day. AE, CB, DC, DISC, EC, MC, V.

▦▦▦ Le Meridien Hotel

614 Canal St, 70130 (Central Business District); tel 504/525-6500 or toll free 800/543-4300; fax 504/525-8068. Looks out over French Quarter; soaring arches and ceiling provide elegant ambience. **Rooms:** 494 rms and stes. CI 3pm/CO noon. Nonsmoking rms avail. Beautiful, elegant, pastel decor in rooms. **Amenities:** 🛅 🐾 🍳 A/C, cable TV w/movies. All units w/minibars, some w/terraces, some w/whirlpools. **Services:** 🍽️ 🔑 VP 🛄 🐾 Twice-daily maid svce, car-rental desk, masseur, babysitting. **Facilities:** 🏋️ 🎾 ⟦500⟧ 🖥️ 🖐️ 1 restaurant, 2 bars (1 w/entertainment), sauna, steam rm, whirlpool, beauty salon. **Rates:** Peak (Sept–May) $159–$250 S; $170–$250 D; $500–$1,500 ste. Extra person $30. Children under age 17 stay free. Min stay special events. Lower rates off-season. MAP rates avail. Parking: Indoor, $12/day. AE, CB, DC, DISC, EC, JCB, MC, V.

▦▦▦ Le Pavillon Hotel

833 Poydras St, 70140 (Central Business District); tel 504/581-3111 or toll free 800/535-9095; fax 504/522-5543. Outstanding hotel with magnificent lobby featuring Italian marble floors and crystal chandeliers. **Rooms:** 233 rms and stes. CI 3pm/CO noon. Nonsmoking rms avail. Rooms are spacious, regal, and ornate with superb linens and above-average housekeeping. Many beds have canopies with shears. **Amenities:** 🛅 🐾 🍳 A/C, cable TV w/movies, dataport, in-rm safe. Some units w/minibars, some w/fireplaces. **Services:** 🍽️ 🔑 VP 🛄 🐾 Twice-daily maid svce, car-rental desk, children's program, babysitting. Late night snacks in lobby. **Facilities:** 🏋️ 🎾 ⟦200⟧ 🖐️ 1 restaurant, 1 bar, whirlpool. Pool on roof. Bar in lounge purchased from one of Al Capone's illustrious clubs. **Rates:** Peak (Jan–May/Sept–Dec) $210 S; $230 D; $395–$495 ste. Extra person $20. Children under age 12 stay free. Min stay special events. Lower rates off-season. Parking: Indoor, $11/day. AE, DC, DISC, ER, MC, V.

▦▦▦ Le Richelieu Motor Hotel

1234 Chartres St, 70116 (French Quarter); tel 504/529-2492 or toll free 800/535-9653; fax 504/535-9653. This elegant hotel has been under the same ownership for over 25 years. A favorite of numerous celebrities, including Paul McCartney (who happens to have the largest suite in the hotel named after him). There's a rather imposing portrait of Cardinal Richelieu in the lobby. **Rooms:** 86 rms and stes. CI 3pm/CO 1pm. Nonsmoking rms avail. Each room is individually decorated with antiques and oil paintings. The VIP suite has three bedrooms, a kitchen area, and a steam room. **Amenities:** 🛅 🐾 🍳 A/C, satel TV. Some units w/terraces. **Services:** ✗ 🔑 🛄 🐾 Car-rental desk, babysitting. **Facilities:** 🏋️ 1 restaurant, 1 bar. **Rates:** $85–$130 S; $160–$475 ste. Extra person $15. Min stay wknds and special events. Parking: Outdoor, free. AE, CB, DC, DISC, EC, JCB, MC, V.

▦▦▦ Maison Dupuy

1001 Toulouse St, 70112 (French Quarter); tel 504/586-8000 or toll free 800/535-9177; fax 504/525-5334. Located on the northern edge of the French Quarter, the Maison Dupuy is far away from the hustle and bustle of Bourbon St but still within walking distance of most attractions. The dark lobby opens into a courtyard/restaurant overlooking the pool. Easy access to the business district. **Rooms:** 198 rms and stes; 1 cottage/villa. CI 2pm/CO noon. Nonsmoking rms avail. **Amenities:** 🛅 🐾 🍳 A/C, cable TV w/movies, dataport, voice mail. Some units w/terraces. **Services:** ✗ VP 🛄 🐾 Twice-daily maid svce, car-rental desk, babysitting. **Facilities:** 🏋️ 🎾 ⟦150⟧ 🖥️ 🖐️ 1 restaurant, 2 bars (1 w/entertainment). **Rates:** Peak (Jan–May/Sept–Nov) $175–$205 S or D; $240–$675 ste; $800 cottage/villa. Extra person $20. Children under age 17 stay free. Min stay special events. Lower rates off-season. Parking: Indoor, $10/day. AE, CB, DC, DISC, JCB, MC, V.

▦▦▦ Marriott Hotel

555 Canal St, 70140 (French Quarter); tel 504/581-1000 or toll free 800/831-4004. Offers fine, clean rooms and easy access to local attractions. Has more modern feel than many of the other French Quarter hotels. Great for a "contemporary" visit to classic New Orleans. **Rooms:** 1,290 rms and stes. Executive level. CI 4pm/CO noon. Nonsmoking rms avail. **Amenities:** 🛅 🐾 🍳 A/C, cable TV w/movies, dataport, voice mail. **Services:** 🍽️ 🔑 VP 🛄 🐾 Car-rental desk, babysitting. **Facilities:** 🏋️ 🎾 ⟦3500⟧ 🖥️ 🖐️ 2 restaurants, 3 bars (1 w/entertainment), sauna, washer/dryer. **Rates:** Peak (Sept–May) $189–$219 S or D; $600–$1,000 ste. Children under age 12 stay free. Min stay special events. Lower rates off-season. Parking: Indoor, $12/day. AE, CB, DC, DISC, JCB, MC, V.

▦▦▦ Monteleone Hotel

214 Royal St, 70140 (French Quarter); tel 504/523-3341 or toll free 800/535-9595; fax 504/528-1019. The ornately sculpted facade of this old world–style hostelry leads into a huge lobby lighted by four chandeliers. Perfect for guests who want to enjoy historic New Orleans and the French Quarter. **Rooms:** 598 rms and stes. CI 3pm/CO noon. Nonsmoking rms avail. Rooms are large and comfortable; although they look old-fashioned, they are equipped with cutting-edge technology. **Amenities:** 🛅 🐾 A/C, cable TV. **Services:** ✗ 🔑 VP 🛄 🐾 Twice-daily maid svce, social director, babysitting. **Facilities:** 🏋️ 🎾 ⟦250⟧ 🖥️ 🖐️ 2 restaurants, 3 bars (1 w/entertainment). **Rates:** Peak (Jan–May/Sept–Nov) $130–$190 S; $140–$240 D; $300–$680 ste. Extra person $25. Children under age 18 stay free. Min stay special events. Lower rates off-season. Parking: Indoor, $10/day. AE, CB, DC, DISC, MC, V.

▦▦▦ New Orleans Hilton Riverside Hotel

2 Poydras St, 70140 (Central Business District); tel 504/561-0500 or toll free 800/HILTONS; fax 504/568-1721. This large, comtemporary property next door to the conven-

tion center features the on-site Flamingo casino. **Rooms:** 1,600 rms and stes. Executive level. CI 3pm/CO noon. No smoking. Nonsmoking rms avail. Rooms facing river offer impressive view. **Amenities:** 🛏 ⌂ A/C, cable TV w/movies, dataport, voice mail. Some units w/minibars, some w/whirlpools. **Services:** �|◎| ☎ VP ⊠ ⊐ ⊲ Twice-daily maid svce, car-rental desk, masseur, babysitting. **Facilities:** 🛏 🏊 ⊙12 🍴 ⟦3000⟧ ⓰ 4 restaurants (*see* "Restaurants" below), 7 bars, basketball, racquetball, squash, spa, sauna, whirlpool. **Rates:** $150–$285 S; $175–$310 D; $395–$1,410 ste. Extra person $25. Children under age 18 stay free. Min stay special events. Parking: Indoor, $11/day. AE, CB, DC, DISC, MC, V.

≣≣≣ Olivier House

828 Toulouse St, 70112 (French Quarter); tel 504/525-8456; fax 504/529-2000. A lesser known, yet very comfortable French Quarter establishment offering highly personalized service. **Rooms:** 40 rms and stes; 1 cottage/villa. CI 3pm/CO noon. Rooms are large with above-average housekeeping. The split-level garden room is as beautiful as any other hotel room in New Orleans. **Amenities:** 🛏 ⌂ A/C, cable TV. Some units w/minibars, some w/terraces. **Services:** ⊠ ⊐ ⊲ Babysitting. **Facilities:** 🛏 1 bar. **Rates:** Peak (Sept–May) $105–$175 S; $150–$245 D; $145–$285 ste; $245 cottage/ villa. Extra person $20. Children under age 12 stay free. Min stay special events. Lower rates off-season. Parking: Outdoor, free. AE, MC, V.

≣≣≣≣ Omni Royal Orleans

621 St Louis St, 70140 (French Quarter); tel 504/529-5333 or toll free 800/843-6664; fax 504/529-7016. This modern, first-class hotel was built in 1960 on the site of the 1836 St Louis Exchange Hotel. It has proved a worthy successor. Lobby impresses with marble and brass and crystal chandeliers. **Rooms:** 346 rms and stes. CI 3pm/CO noon. Nonsmoking rms avail. Rooms are uniquely furnished and are available in different sizes. **Amenities:** 🛏 ⌂ 🍷 A/C, cable TV w/movies, dataport, voice mail, bathrobes. All units w/minibars, some w/terraces, some w/whirlpools. **Services:** ⎮◎⎮ ☎ VP ⊠ ⊐ Twice-daily maid svce, social director, babysitting. **Facilities:** 🛏 🍴 ⟦500⟧ ⌨ ⓰ 2 restaurants (*see* "Restaurants" below), 3 bars (1 w/entertainment), spa, beauty salon. **Rates:** Peak (Feb–Apr/Oct–Nov) $159–$275 S; $179–$290 D; $350–$2,000 ste. Extra person $20. Children under age 17 stay free. Min stay special events. Lower rates off-season. Parking: Indoor, $12/day. AE, CB, DC, DISC, EC, JCB, MC, V.

≣≣ Parkview Guest House

7004 St Charles Ave, 70118; tel 504/861-7564; fax 504/ 861-1225. Attractive mansion with exceptionally clean rooms overlooking a beautiful park near Tulane University. **Rooms:** 22 rms. CI 2pm/CO noon. No smoking. **Amenities:** 🛏 A/C. No TV. Some units w/terraces. **Services:** ☎ ⊐ **Rates (CP):** $65–$75 S; $75–$85 D. Extra person $10. Children under age 12 stay free. AE, DISC, MC, V.

≣≣≣ Place D'Aremes Hotel

625 St Ann St, 70116 (French Quarter); tel 504/524-4531 or toll free 800/366-2743. A charming and appealing hotel owned by the Valentino family. Large repeat clientele. **Rooms:** 80 rms and stes. CI 4pm/CO noon. The rooms are unusually spacious (especially by French Quarter standards) and each has its own distinctive features. Some rooms surround an enclosed French-style courtyard, although the rooms surrounding the rear courtyard are more popular. **Amenities:** 🛏 ⌂ A/C, cable TV, voice mail. Some units w/terraces. **Services:** VP 🚐 ⊠ ⊐ Car-rental desk, babysitting. **Facilities:** 🛏 ⟦50⟧ **Rates (CP):** Peak (Jan–May/Sept– Nov) $110–$140 S or D; $165–$350 ste. Extra person $20. Children under age 12 stay free. Min stay wknds and special events. Lower rates off-season. Parking: Indoor, $10/day. AE, CB, DC, DISC, MC, V.

≣≣≣ Pontchartrain Hotel

2031 St Charles Ave, 70140 (Garden District); tel 504/ 524-0581 or toll free 800/777-6193; fax 504/529-1165. This old, charming hotel has plenty of modern touches. It's comfortable and convenient, offering the necessary amenities and located very close to the French Quarter. Situated on the St Charles Ave streetcar line. **Rooms:** 102 rms and stes. CI 3pm/CO 1pm. Nonsmoking rms avail. Rooms feature dark wood armoires, ornate window treatments, and small, simple chandeliers. **Amenities:** 🛏 ⌂ A/C, cable TV. Some units w/whirlpools. **Services:** ⎮◎⎮ ☎ VP ⊠ ⊐ Twice-daily maid svce, car-rental desk, babysitting. **Facilities:** ⟦300⟧ ⓰ 2 restaurants (*see* "Restaurants" below), 1 bar. The Caribbean Room features renowned Creole cuisine. **Rates:** Peak (Sept–May) $130–$165 S; $170–$185 D; $185–$360 ste. Extra person $15. Children under age 17 stay free. Min stay special events. Lower rates off-season. Parking: Outdoor, $10/day. AE, DC, DISC, MC, V.

≣≣≣ Prince Conti Hotel

830 Conti St, 70112 (French Quarter); tel 504/529-4172 or toll free 800/366-2743; fax 504/581-3802. Owned by the Valentino family (who also own the Place d'Aremes and Hotel St Marie) the Prince Conti is about tradition, not modernity. If you seek all the modern conveniences, look elsewhere. **Rooms:** 50 rms and stes. CI 4pm/CO noon. Rooms are individually decorated with antiques. The furnishings are not luxurious, but they are distinctive. **Amenities:** 🛏 ⌂ A/C, cable TV, voice mail. **Services:** VP 🚐 ⊠ ⊐ Car-rental desk, babysitting. Room service was scheduled to be added. **Facilities:** 1 restaurant (dinner only), 1 bar (w/entertainment). **Rates:** Peak (Jan–May/Sept–Nov) $100–$130 S or D; $145–$245 ste. Extra person $20. Children under age 12 stay free. Min stay wknds and special events. Lower rates off-season. Parking: Outdoor, $10/day. AE, CB, DC, DISC, MC, V.

≣≣≣ Radisson Hotel

1500 Canal St, 70112 (Downtown); tel 504/522-4500 or toll free 800/333-3333; fax 504/525-2644. Listed on the National Register of Historic Places, this 18-story hotel is five blocks from the French Quarter and four blocks from the Superdome. All guest rooms were renovated in 1994. **Rooms:** 759 rms and stes. CI 4pm/CO 11am. Nonsmoking rms avail. Spacious rooms feature a classic, muted decor and elegant window treatments. **Amenities:** 🛎 🍸 A/C, cable TV w/movies, dataport, voice mail. Some units w/minibars. **Services:** ✕ ☎ VP ⌲ Car-rental desk, babysitting. Complimentary shuttle to French Quarter, Riverwalk Marketplace, and Aquarium of the Americas. **Facilities:** 🏊 🏌 2500 💻 🏋 2 restaurants, 2 bars, whirlpool, washer/dryer. Praline's restaurant serves up excellent Cajun/Creole dishes. **Rates:** Peak (Jan–May/Sept–Nov) $119–$159 S; $134–$179 D; $150–$300 ste. Extra person $12. Children under age 17 stay free. Min stay special events. Lower rates off-season. Parking: Outdoor, $15/day. AE, CB, DISC, MC, V.

Ramada St Charles

2203 St Charles Ave, 70140 (Garden District); tel 504/566-1200 or toll free 800/2-RAMADA; fax 504/581-1352. Clean, dependable, well-run chain property. **Rooms:** 133 rms and stes. CI 3pm/CO noon. Nonsmoking rms avail. **Amenities:** 🛎 🍸 A/C, cable TV w/movies, dataport, voice mail. 1 unit w/whirlpool. **Services:** ✕ ☎ VP ⌲ Car-rental desk. **Facilities:** 100 🏋 1 restaurant, 1 bar. Access to European Spa next door. **Rates:** Peak (Nov–Apr) $99–$139 S; $109–$147 D; $149–$225 ste. Extra person $6. Children under age 18 stay free. Min stay special events. Lower rates off-season. Parking: Outdoor, $6/day. AE, CB, DC, DISC, EC, MC, V.

Royal Sonesta

300 Bourbon St, 70140 (French Quarter); tel 504/586-0300 or toll free 800/SONESTA; fax 504/586-0335. Distinguished by a heavily marbled lobby looking out onto a beautifully maintained, French-style courtyard. **Rooms:** 500 rms and stes. Executive level. CI 3pm/CO noon. Nonsmoking rms avail. Beware of rooms facing Bourbon St—they can be very noisy. **Amenities:** 🛎 🍸 A/C, cable TV w/movies, dataport, voice mail. Some units w/minibars, some w/terraces. **Services:** 🍴 ☎ VP ⌲ Twice-daily maid svce, car-rental desk, social director, children's program, babysitting. **Facilities:** 🏊 🏌 500 💻 🏋 2 restaurants, 4 bars (2 w/entertainment), beauty salon. **Rates:** Peak (Jan–May/Sept–Nov) $135–$225 S; $155–$260 D; $475–$950 ste. Children under age 17 stay free. Min stay special events. Lower rates off-season. Parking: Indoor, $12/day. AE, CB, DC, DISC, JCB, MC, V.

Rue Royal Inn

1006 Royal St, 70116 (French Quarter); tel 504/524-3900 or toll free 800/776-3901; fax 504/558-0566. Located in the middle of the antique district, away from the noise and activity of Bourbon St, this renovated 19th-century mansion is perfect for romantic couples. **Rooms:** 17 rms and stes. CI noon/CO noon. Rooms are dark and sparse, but have a historic feel about them. Each room is different, so be sure to ask about specifics. The old slave quarters are the smallest

rooms, while the larger rooms have balconies and views of the courtyard fountain. **Amenities:** 🛎 🍸 A/C, refrig. Some units w/terraces, some w/whirlpools. **Services:** ⌲ Free continental breakfast on Sundays. **Facilities:** 🏋 **Rates:** $60–$100 D; $125 ste. Children under age 12 stay free. Min stay wknds and special events. Parking: Outdoor, $7/day. Rates vary according to room. AE, CB, DC, DISC, EC, MC, V.

St Charles Inn

3630 St Charles Ave, 70115 (Garden District); tel 504/899-8888 or toll free 800/489-9908; fax 504/899-8892. Small, comfortable hotel close to streetcar line and within driving distance of most attractions. **Rooms:** 40 rms. CI 2pm/CO noon. Nonsmoking rms avail. **Amenities:** 🛎 🍸 A/C, TV. **Services:** ☎ ⌲ 🛎 Babysitting. **Facilities:** 20 2 restaurants, 1 bar. **Rates (CP):** Peak (Sept–May) $45–$55 S; $55–$65 D. Extra person $10. Children under age 11 stay free. Min stay special events. Lower rates off-season. Parking: Outdoor, $3/day. AE, CB, DC, DISC, MC, V.

St Louis

730 Bienville St, 70130 (French Quarter); tel 504/581-7300 or toll free 800/535-9111. Housed in a classic French *maison*, the St Louis surrounds a beautiful courtyard and fountain. It is close enough to Bourbon St and its attractions and nightlife, but far enough away to avoid the noise. **Rooms:** 72 rms and stes. Executive level. CI 3pm/CO 11am. **Amenities:** 🛎 🍸 A/C, cable TV, voice mail. Some units w/minibars, some w/terraces. Bidets in all rooms. **Services:** ✕ ☎ VP ⌲ 🛎 Twice-daily maid svce, car-rental desk, social director, babysitting. **Facilities:** 75 🏋 1 restaurant (bkfst and dinner only; *see* "Restaurants" below), 1 bar. The hotel shares a pool with the nearby St Ann, which is owned by the same company. **Rates:** Peak (Jan–May/Sept–Nov) $135–$195 S; $155–$225 D; $235–$645 ste. Extra person $15. Children under age 12 stay free. Min stay peak and special events. Lower rates off-season. Parking: Indoor, $10.50/day. AE, CB, DC, JCB, MC, V.

Soniat House

1133 Chartres St, 70116 (French Quarter); tel 504/522-0570 or toll free 800/544-8808; fax 504/522-7208. Guests enter this understated yet elegant hotel through a secured carriageway. Once inside, they may enjoy a collection of exquisite art on loan from the New Orleans Museum of Art. Attention to detail is the name of the game here. **Rooms:** 31 rms and stes. CI 3pm/CO 1pm. Nonsmoking rms avail. Rooms have hardwood floors, area rugs, antique furnishings, and *frete livres* bed linens. **Amenities:** 🛎 🍸 A/C, TV. Some units w/terraces, some w/whirlpools. **Services:** ✕ ☎ VP ⌲ Breakfast—featuring fresh biscuits and strawberry jam—is delivered to the room on silver trays and served on fine china. **Facilities:** 💻 **Rates:** $185–$215 S or D; $235–$550 ste. Extra person $25. Min stay wknds and special events. Parking: Indoor, $12/day. AE, MC, V.

≣≣≣ Westin Canal Place

100 Iberville St, 70130 (French Quarter); tel 504/566-7006 or toll free 800/228-3000; fax 504/553-5120. At Canal St. This sumptuous hotel overlooks both the Mississippi River and the French Quarter. The spectacular 11th-floor lobby features Carrera marble, fine paintings, antiques, and a breathtaking view. **Rooms:** 435 rms and stes. Executive level. CI 3pm/CO 1pm. Nonsmoking rms avail. Rooms are large and comfortable, and some have river views. **Amenities:** 🛎 🍷 A/C, cable TV w/movies, dataport. All units w/minibars, some w/whirlpools. In-room Nintendo video games and phone-based temperature control. **Services:** ⦿ 🔑 VP 🚐 🏖 🍴 Twice-daily maid svce, car-rental desk, social director, children's program, babysitting. English-style high tea served Monday–Saturday; champagne jazz brunch on Sunday. **Facilities:** 🏊 🎾 730 🖥 🚹 1 restaurant, 2 bars, beauty salon. Lounge and restaurant are nicely decorated with ancien régime–style furnishings and share the lobby's spectacular view. **Rates:** $175 S; $195 D; $300–$2,000 ste. Extra person $25. Children under age 18 stay free. Min stay special events. Parking: Indoor, $12/day. AE, CB, DC, DISC, MC, V.

≣≣≣≣≣ Windsor Court Hotel

300 Gravier St, 70130 (Downtown); tel 504/523-6000 or toll free 800/262-2662; fax 504/596-4513. Now owned by the swank Orient-Express hotels group, this striking 23-story hotel in rose-colored granite and tempered bronze glass rises from a brick driveway/courtyard with fountains and greenery. The outstanding, $6 million collection of art spanning four centuries turns public rooms into mini-museums (when were you last in a hotel with a Gainsborough, a Van Dyck, *and* a Joshua Reynolds?). **Rooms:** 322 rms, stes, and effic. CI 3pm/CO noon. Nonsmoking rms avail. Standard rooms are virtually junior suites. All units have bay windows and views of city or river (despite new casino rising across the street). Some units have pantries and wet bars; all have Italian marble bathrooms (some with separate shower stalls and bidets). Guests with physical disabilities were commissioned to restyle special handicapped rooms. **Amenities:** 🛎 🍷 A/C, cable TV w/movies, dataport, in-rm safe, bathrobes. All units w/minibars, some w/terraces. Caring details include laundry hampers in bathrooms, dulcet door chimes rather than loud knocks, eight glasses with each minibar (including three types of wine glasses). **Services:** ⦿ 🔑 VP 🚐 🏖 🍴 🐕 Twice-daily maid svce, car-rental desk, children's program, babysitting. 24-hour concierge. Town car for complimentary short drop-offs or pricey airport transfers. Room service meals from Grill Room served course by course by waiters in black-tie. Afternoon tea in main lounge is something of a New Orleans tradition (reservations advised). **Facilities:** 🏊 🎾 300 🚹 2 restaurants (*see* "Restaurants" below), 2 bars (1 w/entertainment), sauna, steam rm, whirlpool. Recreation terrace on fourth floor, with 75-foot, eye-level pool and poolside service. Elegant Grill Room features much-acclaimed chef. **Rates:** Peak (Sept–May) $235–$290 S or D;

$310–$525 ste. Extra person $20. Children under age 12 stay free. Min stay special events. Lower rates off-season. Parking: Indoor, $15/day. No reduced rates on weekends. AE, CB, DC, DISC, EC, MC, V.

INNS

≣≣≣ The Frenchmen

417 Frenchmen St, 70116 (Faubourg Marigny); tel 504/948-2166 or toll free 800/831-1781; fax 504/948-2258. Located in the quiet, low-key Faubourg Marigny district, this comfortable inn is housed in a renovated 19th-century building. Near the River Front Streetcar. **Rooms:** 27 rms and stes. CI 3pm/CO 11am. Some rooms have only showers. **Amenities:** 🛎 🍷 A/C, cable TV. Some units w/terraces. **Services:** ⦿ Babysitting. **Facilities:** 🏊 Whirlpool, washer/dryer. **Rates (CP):** Peak (Sept–May) Extra person $15. Children under age 12 stay free. Min stay wknds and special events. Lower rates off-season. Higher rates for special events/hols. Parking: Indoor/outdoor, free. AE, MC, V.

≣≣≣ Grenoble House

329 Dauphine St, 70112 (French Quarter); tel 504/522-1331 or toll free 800/722-1834; fax 504/524-4968. This 150-year-old building has been a home, business, "house of ill-repute," and finally a hotel. (Apparently the staff won't enter certain rooms alone because they might be haunted.) No children under 13 allowed. **Rooms:** 17 effic. CI 3pm/CO noon. Each apartmentlike room is unique in size and design. **Amenities:** 🛎 🍷 A/C, cable TV, refrig. All units w/terraces. Full-size kitchens feature stove, dishwasher, and refrigerator/freezer. **Facilities:** 🏊 Whirlpool. **Rates:** Peak (Sept–June) Extra person $30. Min stay wknds and special events. Lower rates off-season. Higher rates for special events/hols. Rates vary widely, so be sure to specify your price range when you make a reservation. AE, MC, V.

≣≣≣ Lafitte Guest House

1003 Bourbon St, 70116 (French Quarter); tel 504/581-2678 or toll free 800/331-7971; fax 504/581-2678. The first thing guests will see upon entering this classy Victorian-style guest house is the elegant parlor, which is decorated in deep red. The rooms are equally appealing. **Rooms:** 14 rms. CI 2pm/CO noon. No smoking. Each room is truly unique: most have chandeliers, and all are furnished with expensive antiques. Management discourages children. **Amenities:** 🛎 🍷 A/C, TV, refrig. Some units w/terraces. **Services:** ✕ ⦿ 🚐 🏖 🍴 Car-rental desk, social director, babysitting. Complimentary appetizers and champagne served each night in the parlor. **Facilities:** 30 **Rates (CP):** Peak (Sept–May) Extra person $20. Children under age 5 stay free. Min stay special events. Lower rates off-season. Higher rates for special events/hols. Parking: Outdoor, $8/day. AE, DISC, MC, V.

≣≣ Maison Esplanade Guest House

1244 Esplanade Ave, 70116; tel 504/523-8080 or toll free 800/892-5529; fax 504/527-0040. ½ mi N of Rampart St. Located two blocks from the French Quarter, this former guest house dating back to 1846 has been converted to a 10-room inn. Unlike most area accommodations because of its intimate size and stress on personal service. **Rooms:** 10 rms. CI 3pm/CO noon. Nonsmoking rms avail. **Amenities:** 🛁 🛎 A/C. No TV. Some units w/terraces. **Services:** 🖨 🎁 Babysitting. **Rates (CP):** Peak (Sept–May) Extra person $15. Min stay special events. Lower rates off-season. Higher rates for special events/hols. Parking: Outdoor, free. AE, CB, DC, DISC, EC, MC, V.

≣≣≣ New Orleans Guest House
1118 Ursulines St, 70116 (French Quarter); tel 504/566-1177 or toll free 800/562-1177. ½ block N of Rampart St. A small, intimate guest house that emphasizes personalized service. **Rooms:** 14 rms. CI 1pm/CO noon. All rooms are individually decorated, and some overlook the courtyard and gazebo. The management wishes to discourage children because of the rare and expensive antiques in every room. **Amenities:** 🛁 🛎 A/C, TV. Some units w/terraces. **Services:** 🖨 Check-in includes a guided tour of the property and a briefing on the neighborhood. **Rates (CP):** Extra person $25. Children under age 6 stay free. Min stay special events. Higher rates for special events/hols. Parking: Outdoor, free. AE, EC, MC, V.

≣≣≣ PJ Holbrook's Olde Victorian Inn
914 North Rampart St, 70116 (French Quarter); tel 504/522-2446 or toll free 800/725-2446. This quaint inn possesses plenty of charm and provides personal service but, lacking the modern amenities of most modern hotels, is not for everyone. **Rooms:** 6 rms. CI open/CO Open. No smoking. Rooms filled with Victorian antiques. **Amenities:** 🛁 A/C. No TV. Some units w/terraces. **Services:** ✗ 🚐 Breakfast is complete five-course meal. Cheese, fruit, and wine served in evenings. Reservations for restaurants and tours can be made in advance. **Facilities:** Washer/dryer. **Rates (BB):** Peak (Jan–May/Sept–Nov) Min stay special events. Lower rates off-season. Higher rates for special events/hols. Parking: Outdoor, free. AE, MC, V.

RESTAURANTS 🍽

Acme Oyster House
724 Iberville St (French Quarter); tel 504/522-5973. **Cajun/Creole.** In operation since 1910, this fun oyster bar now caters to a large tourist crowd. Enjoy oysters on the half-shell with a mug of beer, or try the oyster loaf or one of the sandwiches. **FYI:** Reservations not accepted. **Open:** Peak (Mardi Gras, Jazz Fest) Mon–Sat 11am–10pm, Sun noon–7pm. Closed July 4th week. **Prices:** Main courses $6–$10. AE, CB, DC, DISC, MC, V.

Anacapri
In Bienville House, 320 Decatur St (French Quarter); tel 504/522-9056. **Creole/Italian.** Pristine white tablecloths add to the atmosphere of this elegant restaurant, whose attractive dining areas overlook the patio and pool of the Bienville Hotel. Service is proper and efficient. One of the most

popular dishes is scaloppine Don Feder, veal dipped in egg and coated with bread crumbs and Parmesan cheese. Many pastas; daily grilled seafood specials. **FYI:** Reservations accepted. **Open:** Mon–Fri 7am–10pm, Sat–Sun 7am–11pm. **Prices:** Main courses $10–$22; prix fixe $20–$25. AE, CB, DC, DISC, ER, MC, V.

★ Antoine's
713 St Louis St (French Quarter); tel 504/581-4422. **Creole/French.** Over 150 years old, this New Orleans institution is a prime dining destination for many visiting the city. Dining rooms range from rather plain to grand; the restaurant includes, among other adornments, antique ceiling fans, white Corinthian columns, and walls lined with beautiful books. The wine cellar is one of richest in the country. Oysters Rockefeller, a house specialty, is a carefully guarded secret. Shrimp rémoulade, Antoine's fillet of beef, and escargot bordelaise are some other venerable choices. **FYI:** Reservations recommended. Jacket required. Beer and wine only. **Open:** Lunch Mon–Sat 11:30am–2pm; dinner Mon–Sat 5:30–9:30pm. **Prices:** Main courses $17–$25. AE, DC, MC, V.

Arnaud's
813 Bienville St (French Quarter); tel 504/523-5433. **Creole.** A longtime favorite, the restaurant, with its elegant crystal chandeliers, antique ceiling fans, mosaic tile floors, and potted plants, exudes traditional turn-of-the-century grace and pomp. The menu is uniquely New Orleans, and the house specialty is shrimp Arnaud's, a shrimp rémoulade made with a secret sauce. Stylish, formally attired waiters provide highly professional service. The fine Sunday brunch is accompanied by a jazz trio. **FYI:** Reservations recommended. Jazz. Jacket required. **Open:** Lunch Mon–Sat 11am–2:30pm; dinner daily 6–10pm; brunch Sun 10am–2:30pm. **Prices:** Main courses $18–$24. AE, CB, DC, DISC, MC, V. 🍷

Bacco
310 Chartres St (French Quarter); tel 504/522-2426. **Creole/Italian.** The dramatic interior features wall and ceiling murals, pink Italian marble floors, and Venetian chandeliers. Chef Haley Gabol offers numerous dishes combining Italian and Creole influences—the crawfish ravioli and red-bean ravioli are delicious examples of this intriguing fusion. For dessert, try the praline cinnamon ice cream sandwich. **FYI:** Reservations accepted. **Open:** Breakfast Mon–Fri 7–10am, Sat–Sun 8:30–10am; lunch daily 11:30am–2:30pm; dinner daily 6–10pm. **Prices:** Main courses $16–$21; prix fixe $20–$30. AE, CB, DC, MC, V.

Bailey's
In the Fairmont Hotel, 123 Baronne St (Central Business District); tel 504/529-7111. **New American.** Dark wood, antiques, and soft lighting help make this a cozy, elegant place. Fried calamari, blackened chicken, and caesar salad are recommended. A variety of omelettes, waffles, and pancakes are offered throughout the day. **FYI:** Reservations not ac-

cepted. Children's menu. **Open:** Sun–Thurs 6am–11pm, Fri–Sat 6am–midnight. **Prices:** Main courses $7–$13; prix fixe $10. AE, CB, DC, DISC, MC, V. 🔳 📋 ⚪

Bayona

430 Dauphine St (French Quarter); tel 504/525-4455. **French/Mediterranean.** Chef Susan Spicer's wonderful, innovative menu is studded with unique dishes. Patrons might want to start with grilled shrimp with black bean cakes in coriander sauce before moving on to dishes like grilled duck breast with orange-bourbon sauce or sweetbreads with lemon-caper butter. Like with so many New Orleans restaurants, the setting is formal but the attitude decidedly casual. Excellent wine list. **FYI:** Reservations recommended. Dress code. **Open:** Lunch Mon–Fri 11:30am–2pm; dinner Mon–Thurs 6–10pm, Fri–Sat 6–11pm. **Prices:** Main courses $13–$19; prix fixe $21. AE, DC, DISC, MC, V. 🔳

★ Bon Ton Cafe

401 Magazine St; tel 504/524-3386. **Regional American.** A quiet little restaurant at the edge of the Central Business District. The clientele is mostly business people, but if you like crabmeat, this is the place to be. A feature menu item is redfish Bon Ton, broiled with lemon butter and lump crabmeat. The crawfish soufflé is also popular. Spices are used lightly here. Save room for Bon Ton's bread pudding, considered by many the best in town. **FYI:** Reservations accepted. Children's menu. Dress code. **Open:** Lunch Mon–Fri 11am–2pm; dinner Mon–Fri 5–9:30pm. **Prices:** Main courses $18–$24. AE, CB, DC, MC, V.

★ Brennan's

417 Royal St (French Quarter); tel 504/525-9711. **Creole/French.** Breakfast here is a New Orleans institution, just like lunch at Galatoire's and dinner at Antoine's. A good start to a meal is a brandy milk punch or a Bloody Mary, followed by eggs hussarde (poached eggs on holland rusks with Canadian bacon, topped with hollandaise). Finish with bananas foster and coffee. Brennan's is much less frantic at dinner, when traditional Creole dishes are offered. **FYI:** Reservations recommended. Jacket required. **Open:** Breakfast daily 8am–2:30pm; dinner daily 6–10pm. **Prices:** Main courses $20–$35. AE, CB, DC, DISC, MC, V. ⚪

Brigtsen's

723 Dante St; tel 504/861-7610. **New American/Creole.** A small, intimate restaurant near Tulane University. The menu, which changes daily, offers an array of contemporary Creole dishes and New Orleans cooking. Dishes have included broiled Gulf fish with crabmeat Parmesan crust and lemon mousselline, and grilled beef tournedos with shallots and blue cheese in balsamic-garlic sauce. More moderately priced early dinner specials are offered Tues–Thurs 5:30–6:30pm. **FYI:** Reservations recommended. Dress code. No smoking. **Open:** Tues–Sat 5:30–10pm. **Prices:** Main courses $12–$24. AE, DC, MC, V. 🔳

Broussard's

819 Conti St (French Quarter); tel 504/581-3866. **Creole/French.** The entryway is covered with playful scenes painted on ceramic tiles, while the dining rooms display a comfortable formality. Chef Hoavey Loumiet III's menu focuses on rich, but generally not spicy, French-Creole dishes. Featuring one of the lushest, most attractive courtyards in the French Quarter, this is an excellent spot for fine summer dining. **FYI:** Reservations recommended. Piano. Dress code. **Open:** Daily 5:30–10:30pm. **Prices:** Main courses $20–$27; prix fixe $24–$30. AE, CB, DC, DISC, ER, MC, V.

Bruning's Seafood on the Lake

1924 West End Pkwy; tel 504/282-9395. **Regional American.** Dining at sunset in this simply decorated dining room overlooking Lake Pontchartrain can be quite lovely—the orange brilliance reflecting off the water highlights returning fishing boats. The seafood is excellent, with flounder—served whole and prepared fried, sautéed, or stuffed—one of the best offerings. **FYI:** Reservations not accepted. Children's menu. **Open:** Sun–Thurs 11am–9:30pm, Fri–Sat 11am–10:30pm. **Prices:** Main courses $9–$15. AE, DISC, MC, V. ⚪

Cafe Maspero

601 Decatur St (French Quarter); tel 504/523-6250. **New American/Cajun.** A lively spot offering good meals in informal surroundings, popular for after a concert, opera, or theater performance. Specializing in large deli sandwiches and burgers and other American favorites, this is a great place to lunch after several days of red beans and jambalaya. **FYI:** Reservations not accepted. **Open:** Sun–Thurs 11am–11pm, Fri–Sat 11am–midnight. **Prices:** Main courses $4–$8. AE, MC, V.

Cafe Pontalba

546 St Peter St (French Quarter); tel 504/522-1180. On Jackson Square. **Cajun/Creole.** Located in the Pontalba, the oldest apartment building in North America, this small, simple eatery has historic appeal. Diners can enjoy the street performers of Jackson Square while enjoying boiled shrimp, po' boys, and Cajun platters. **FYI:** Reservations not accepted. **Open:** Daily 10:30am–10:30pm. **Prices:** Main courses $9–$16. AE, DISC, MC, V. ⬛

Cafe Sbisa

1011 Decatur (French Quarter); tel 504/522-5565. **New American/Creole.** For its first 80 years, this was just a popular neighborhood Cajun and Creole restaurant. But starting in 1979, the owners began to dabble with fusion techniques from around the world—with great success. You will find such creative appetizers as grilled alligator with Creole sauce piquant and Tennessee trout with horseradish sour cream and caviar. The Sunday jazz brunch features a traditional New Orleans breakfast, live piano music, and a singer. **FYI:** Reservations accepted. **Open:** Dinner Sun–Thurs 5:30–10:30pm, Fri–Sat 5:30–11pm; brunch Sun 10am–3pm. **Prices:** Main courses $18–$24. AE, CB, DC, DISC, MC, V.

Caribbean Room

In Pontchartrain Hotel, 2031 St Charles Ave (Garden District); tel 504/524-0581. **New American/Creole.** Dine on some of the finest New Orleans cuisine in a setting of understated luxury. Crabmeat is a specialty here; crabmeat Remick, served on tortilla chips, is one of the many fine appetizers. Other expertly prepared dishes include trout Eugene and slow-roasted half-duckling. Though the menu has changed over the years, the service has not; Douglas Leman has been the maitre d' here for well over 40 years. **FYI:** Reservations recommended. Dress code. **Open:** Tues–Sat 6–10pm. **Prices:** Main courses $15–$22. AE, CB, DC, DISC, MC, V. **VP** &

Christian's

3835 Iberville St (Mid-city); tel 504/482-4924. **Creole/French.** You've probably never dined in a pink chapel before. You get your chance at this renovated church outfitted with cushioned pews lining the walls. Many of the seafood and other dishes served here are classically prepared with delicate French sauces. Menu items include veal Christian, served in a cream sauce with port wine and morels; sweetbreads with mushrooms, sherry, and demiglace; baked Alaska; and chocolate profiteroles. **FYI:** Reservations recommended. Children's menu. Dress code. **Open:** Lunch Tues–Fri 11:30am–2pm; dinner Tues–Sat 5:30–10pm. **Prices:** Main courses $13–$20; prix fixe $11–$17. AE, CB, DC, MC, V. ♥

The Coffee Pot Restaurant

714 St Peter St (French Quarter); tel 504/524-3500. **Cajun/Creole.** Black lacquered tables in the dining room are inlaid with red, orange, and yellow leaves. Traditional New Orleans favorites are served in large portions; the menu offers a wide range of seafood (including oyster, catfish, and shrimp platters) as well as unusual specials. Lunch specials change daily. **FYI:** Reservations accepted. **Open:** Mon–Thurs 8am–midnight, Fri–Sat 8am–1am. **Prices:** Main courses $14–$16. AE, DC, MC, V.

★ Commander's Palace

1403 Washington Ave (Garden District); tel 504/899-8221. **Creole.** This is the restaurant that brought fine service to New Orleans dining. The blue and white Victorian building features a patio, fountains, and lush tropical plantings. Staff is highly attentive, and the food is outstanding. Turtle soup wins raves, while tasso-stuffed shrimp is one of the better seafood dishes in New Orleans. The chateaubriand for two is prepared tableside and creates a nice spectacle. The famed bread pudding soufflé—a decadent dessert—should be ordered at the beginning of your meal. **FYI:** Reservations recommended. Jacket required. **Open:** Lunch Mon–Fri 11:30am–1:30pm; dinner daily 6–9:30pm; brunch Sat 11:30am–12:30pm, Sun 10:30am–1pm. **Prices:** Main courses $18–$25; prix fixe $29–$33. AE, CB, DC, DISC, MC, V. **VP** &

Copeland's

4338 St Charles Ave (Garden District); tel 504/897-2325. **Cajun/Creole.** Most of the vast menu here consists of good reproductions of dishes found elsewhere in the city. The best of Copeland's own creations include shrimp ducky (duck strips and sautéed shrimp in a burgundy-mushroom sauce) and the Dixie grilled chicken (chicken on a bed of fresh spinach, served with hot bacon dressing and topped with blue cheese). The attractive setting features a lot of dark wood, brass railings, stained glass, and red leather chairs. **FYI:** Reservations not accepted. Additional locations: 1001 S Clearview Pkwy, Jefferson (tel 733-7843); 701 Veteran's Memorial Blvd, Metairie (tel 831-3437). **Open:** Mon–Thurs 11am–11pm, Fri–Sat 11am–midnight, Sun 10am–11pm. **Prices:** Main courses $7–$16. AE, MC, V. **VP** &

Court of Two Sisters

613 Royal St (French Quarter); tel 504/522-7261. **Creole.** Two sisters originally operated this lovely, intensely atmospheric restaurant, always packed with patrons. The courtyard—filled with flowers, willows, and fountains—offers cool breezes (augmented by fans) during warm months and heaters when it's cool, making outdoor dining pleasant virtually year-round. The menu leans heavily toward fish and seafood, with crawfish étoufée the house favorite. Arrive early for the daily Jazz Brunch Buffet, featuring a strolling band and some 50 dishes. **FYI:** Reservations accepted. **Open:** Dinner daily 5:30–10pm; brunch Mon–Sun 9am–3pm. **Prices:** Main courses $18–$22. AE, CB, DC, DISC, MC, V. ⚓

Crescent City Brewhouse

527 Decatur St (French Quarter); tel 504/522-0571. **Eclectic/Pub.** New Orleans' only operating brewery offers four unique beers brewed on the premises. Large storage vats dominate the bar. Standard New Orleans fare. **FYI:** Reservations accepted. Blues/jazz. **Open:** Fri–Sat 11am–11pm, Sun–Thurs 11am–10pm. **Prices:** Main courses $12–$18. AE, CB, DC, DISC, MC, V.

Delmonico Restaurant

1300 St Charles Ave (Garden District); tel 504/525-4937. **Regional American/Creole.** Run by the same family since 1911. The dining room is elegant without being stuffy, and the food is steeped in New Orleans traditions. The turtle soup is a well-known house specialty. A particular favorite, the half-and-half catfish, offers an étoufée sauce on one side and a crawfish sauce on the other. **FYI:** Reservations accepted. Children's menu. Dress code. **Open:** Fri–Sat 11:30am–10:30pm, Sun–Thurs 11:30am–9pm. **Prices:** Main courses $13–$18; prix fixe $16–$22. AE, CB, DC, DISC, MC, V. ♥

Dipiazza's

337 Dauphine St (French Quarter); tel 504/525-3335. **Creole/Italian.** A small, cozy Italian eatery with plain wood tables and a casual atmosphere. Roast chicken with rosemary is the staple of a menu that also includes a wide variety of

pastas. **FYI:** Reservations recommended. **Open:** Mon–Thurs 6–10:30pm, Fri–Sat 6–11pm. **Prices:** Main courses $11–$20; prix fixe $25. AE, CB, DC, DISC, MC, V.

Dooky Chase

2301 Orleans Ave (Mid-city); tel 504/821-2294. **Creole/Soul/Southern.** A New Orleans tradition since 1941, Dooky Chase serves distinctive New Orleans–style soul food. The Creole gumbo is one of the best in a city with much competition; the fried chicken is superb. Great for a late night meal. Part of the owners' collection of African-American art hangs on the walls. **FYI:** Reservations recommended. Children's menu. Dress code. **Open:** Lunch daily 11:30am–3pm; dinner Sun–Thurs 5pm–midnight, Fri–Sat 3pm–1am. **Prices:** Main courses $8–$22; prix fixe $25. AE, DC, MC, V.

Emeril's

800 Tchoupitoulas St (Warehouse District); tel 504/528-9393. **Regional American.** One of New Orleans' favorite warehouse district restaurants. Dynamic chef Emeril Lagasse is highly regarded for his constant experimentation and innovative takes on traditional New Orleans dishes. Most everything in his dishes is made from scratch—including the Worcestershire sauce. Andouille-encrusted Texas redfish is a popular item, and the 16-oz grilled double pork chop with roasted sweet potatoes and green chile mole sauce is excellent. A real treat is Emeril's degustation dinner, a seven-course sampling of his latest creations. Outstanding desserts, extensive wine list. **FYI:** Reservations recommended. Dress code. **Open:** Lunch Mon–Fri 11:30am–2pm; dinner Mon–Thurs 6–10pm, Fri–Sat 6–10:30pm. **Prices:** Main courses $18–$30; prix fixe $65. AE, CB, DC, DISC, MC, V. **VP**

Ernst's Cafe

600 S Peters St (Warehouse District); tel 504/525-8544. **Regional American.** A no-nonsense New Orleans eatery that's been around since 1902, Ernst's caters to a lunchtime business clientele. The usual New Orleans cuisine is offered, but the sandwiches are the real highlight. The chicken subs are excellent, as are the classic po' boys. Plate lunches such as red beans and rice are also available. **FYI:** Reservations accepted. Dress code. **Open:** Mon–Fri 11am–3pm. **Prices:** Lunch main courses $5–$10. AE, DC, MC, V.

Felix's

739 Iberville St (French Quarter); tel 504/522-4440. **Cajun/Creole/Seafood.** A well-known location just on the edge of the French Quarter. The decor is unabashedly simple. All of Felix's shellfish specials are excellent and represent some of the best values in town. Stand at the oyster bar and slurp down some chilled oysters with the regulars. **FYI:** Reservations not accepted. **Open:** Mon–Thurs 10:30am–midnight, Fri 10:30am–1am, Sat 10:30am–1:30am. **Prices:** Main courses $10–$23. AE, DC, ER, MC, V.

Gabrielle

3201 Esplanade Ave (Mid-city); tel 504/948-6233. **Creole.** A small, lively restaurant featuring fine dishes with bold, robust flavors. Chef Greg Sonnier was named one of *Food & Wine*'s top 10 best new chefs in America in 1994. His menu changes weekly, but look for specialties like blackened lamb with orange-mint sauce, pan-roasted pork T-bone with a spicy orange mustard sauce and red cabbage, or sautéed veal with crabmeat sauce. **FYI:** Reservations accepted. Dress code. **Open:** Peak (Oct–May) lunch Fri 11:30am–2pm; dinner Tues–Thurs 5:30–10pm, Fri–Sat 5:30–11pm. **Prices:** Main courses $14–$24. AE, CB, DC, MC, V.

★ Galatoire's

209 Bourbon St (French Quarter); tel 504/525-2021. **Creole/French.** A New Orleans institution since 1905; at lunch time the line of people waiting to get in winds around the corner. With its mirrored walls, brass fixtures, and fine sense of tradition, this restaurant has an ambience like no other in the city. Classic local cuisine—especially seafood—is expertly prepared, and the kitchen produces some of the best Cajun dishes in town. Be sure to inquire about specials, because the best food is not always on the menu. Jackets required after 5pm and all day Sunday. **FYI:** Reservations not accepted. Jacket required. **Open:** Tues–Sat 11:30am–9pm, Sun noon–9pm. **Prices:** Main courses $10–$20. AE, MC, V.

G&E Courtyard Grill

1113 Decatur St (French Quarter); tel 504/528-9376. **Eclectic.** Columns and walls adorned with Italian-style frescoes make for a lovely dining room, but the best place to dine at this standout restaurant is the covered courtyard, where an open grill in back shows off chickens slowly turning on the rotisserie. Chef/owner Michael Uddo creates some incredible dishes, like soft shell crab rolls with caviar and wasabi, and rotisserie chicken in garlic, mint, tomato, and balsamic sauce. **FYI:** Reservations recommended. Children's menu. Dress code. **Open:** Lunch Tues–Sun 11:30am–2:30pm; dinner Tues–Sun 6–10pm, Fri–Sat 6–11pm. **Prices:** Main courses $12–$23. AE, CB, DC, DISC, MC, V. &

Gautreau's

1728 Soniat St; tel 504/899-7397. **Regional American/Creole.** Housed in what was originally a pharmacy built in 1911, this small, uptown restaurant offers an intimate setting for quality dining. Roasted chicken with garlic mashed potatoes is a hearty crowd-pleaser, while seared salmon with roasted beets, arugula, prosciutto, and French bean salad topped with summer melon sauce is one of the many creative seasonal specialties. **FYI:** Reservations recommended. Dress code. No smoking. **Open:** Tues–Sat 6–10pm. **Prices:** Main courses $11–$22. AE, CB, DC, DISC, ER, MC, V. **VP**

♛ The Grill Room

In Windsor Court Hotel, 300 Gravier St (Downtown); tel 504/523-6000. **Eclectic.** Refined, clublike aura, with fine china and crystal set off by bay windows, wood paneling, and impressive artwork. Chef Jeff Tunks, blending classic continental with Californian and Asian accents, reaches beyond the trendy to the adventurous: grilled melon to garnish pan-seared salmon; mango slaw served with barbecued wahoo; Texas goat cheese and chipotle peppers with venison quesadillas. Exceptional wine list with many Grands Cru de Bordeaux lording it over more modest bottles from California, Italy, and Germany. **FYI:** Reservations recommended. Jacket required. **Open:** Breakfast daily 7–10:30am; lunch Mon–Fri 11:30am–2pm; dinner daily 6–10pm; brunch Sat–Sun 11:30am–2:30pm. **Prices:** Main courses $22–$39; prix fixe $70. AE, CB, DC, DISC, MC, V. VP &

Gumbo Shop

630 St Peter St (French Quarter); tel 504/525-1486. **Cajun/Creole.** A tourist favorite, this dining room serves gumbo that's often been hailed as the best in town. Ceiling fans, a fireplace with an antique mirror, and wall murals of the old French Quarter provide much charm. It's best to go at odd times, because there is almost always a wait during peak hours, and the restaurant doesn't take reservations. The kitchen serves up a variety of gumbo in addition to jambalaya, red beans and rice, and other traditional items. Homemade desserts include pecan pie à la mode. **FYI:** Reservations not accepted. **Open:** Daily 11am–11pm. **Prices:** Main courses $5–$15; prix fixe $17. AE, DISC, MC, V. 🛥

Honfleur Restaurant

In the Hotel Provincial, 1024 Chartres St (French Quarter); tel 504/581-4995. **American/Creole.** Exposed beams and brick walls surround simple tables draped with spotless white tablecloths. Breakfasts are great, and sandwiches are an exceptional value for lunch. More substantial dishes include beef fillet with Creole bordelaise sauce. **FYI:** Reservations accepted. Children's menu. **Open:** Daily 7am–2pm. **Prices:** Lunch main courses $7–$15. AE, MC, V. VP

★ Irene's Cuisine

539 St Philip St (French Quarter); tel 504/529-8811. **Italian.** This Italian restaurant is a huge favorite with the locals. The rosemary chicken is good, but the chicken Irene with Parmesan, prosciutto, mozzarella, eggplant, and mushrooms is the real specialty. The interior is small and intimate—great for a romantic dinner. **FYI:** Reservations accepted. Dress code. **Open:** Tues–Sat 5:30–11pm, Sun–Mon 5:30–10pm. **Prices:** Main courses $10–$17. AE, DISC, MC, V. ●

Kabby's Sports Edition & Grille

In New Orleans Hilton Riverside Hotel, 2 Poydras St (Central Business District); tel 504/584-3880. **Eclectic.** Probably the best sports bar downtown, this offers a typical sports bar menu, with sandwiches the most abundant and popular items. The 20 TVs provide everyone with a great view of the action. Large windows offer more peaceful views of the Mississippi River. Beware of the spiced popcorn served at every table—it's got that authentic Cajun heat. **FYI:** Reservations not accepted. Dress code. **Open:** Daily 11am–11pm. **Prices:** Main courses $7–$12. AE, DC, DISC, MC, V. &

La Madeleine

547 St Ann St (French Quarter); tel 504/568-0073. On Jackson Square. **French.** With a view of historic Jackson Square and St Louis Cathedral, this spot—with a crowded dining room that makes it seem very much like a street-front cafe—is renowned among locals for its decadent French pastries. Devoted to breads and other baked goods, the menu features a fine selection that includes soups, salads, and soufflés as well. **FYI:** Reservations not accepted. No liquor license. Additional location: 601 S Carrolton Ave (tel 861-8661). **Open:** Daily 7am–9pm. **Prices:** Main courses $3–$7. AE, MC, V.

Le Bistro

In Hotel Maison de Ville, 727 Toulouse St (French Quarter); tel 504/528-9206. **New American/French/Mediterranean.** A small, intimate bistro offering fine, creative cooking. A banquette runs the length of the room. House specialties include a cassoulet with french white beans, duck, and merguez sausage; other dishes might include pan-seared tuna with black bean cakes and crawfish salsa. The crème brûlée is highly recommended. After dinner, you might want to sample one of the 32 single-malt scotches. **FYI:** Reservations recommended. Dress code. **Open:** Lunch Mon–Sat 11:30am–2pm; dinner Mon–Sat 6–10pm. **Prices:** Main courses $18–$24. AE, MC, V.

Louis XVI

In St Louis Hotel, 730 Bienville (French Quarter); tel 504/581-7000. **French.** One of the city's finest restaurants. A rich maroon carpet accents the very French decor of the main dining room, which looks out to a pretty courtyard with a fountain and lots of lush greenery. A wide array of French classics appear on the menu, with escargots and beef Wellington two of the noted specialties. **FYI:** Reservations accepted. Jacket required. **Open:** Breakfast Mon–Fri 7–11am, Sat–Sun 7am–noon; dinner daily 6–11pm. **Prices:** Main courses $6–$30. AE, CB, DC, MC, V.

Lucky Chang's

720 St Louis St (French Quarter); tel 504/529-2045. **Chinese/Creole/Eclectic.** All the "waitresses" are drag queens at this funky restaurant. Decor is described by the owner as "early Chinese bordello." Despite the gimmickry, the food is quite good: Asian barbecued shrimp is excellent, and wok dishes are also recommended. **FYI:** Reservations accepted. **Open:** Tues–Sun noon–11pm. **Prices:** Main courses $11–$16. AE, DC, DISC, MC, V.

Mama Rosa's

616 N Rampart St (French Quarter); tel 504/523-5546. **Pizza.** Red-and-white checked drapes shroud this small, very simple French Quarter restaurant. Traditional dishes like spaghetti and manicotti are available in addition to the main attraction—thick-crust pizzas, which are delivered throughout the French Quarter. **FYI:** Reservations not accepted.

Beer and wine only. **Open:** Tues–Thurs 10:30am–11pm, Fri–Sun 10:30am–midnight. **Prices:** Main courses $6–$7. MC, V.

Maximo's Italian Grill
1117 Decatur St (French Quarter); tel 504/586-8883. **Italian.** Located in a quiet section of the French Quarter, this very popular place offers an escape from the crowds of Bourbon St. Several innovative dishes share the menu with an extensive array of traditional Italian fare. The veal Cattouche—a pan-roasted 16-oz veal T-bone seasoned with garlic and herbs—is a house specialty. Two pasta dishes are recommended: penne Rosa, with shrimp, sun-dried tomatoes, arugula, and garlic; and penne Diablo, featuring crawfish tails, green onions, and a spicy cream sauce. **FYI:** Reservations recommended. **Open:** Daily 6pm–midnight. **Prices:** Main courses $9–$24. AE, DISC, MC, V. ▣

Mike Anderson's Seafood
215 Bourbon St (French Quarter); tel 504/524-3884. **Seafood.** Owned and operated by football hero Mike Anderson, this eatery offers good food in large portions. The steaks and salads are adequate, but the fried, baked, or broiled seafood dinners are what really bring in the locals. Carried from the kitchen on large, metal fish-shaped platters, the food hardly leaves room on the table. **FYI:** Reservations not accepted. Children's menu. **Open:** Sun–Thurs 11:30am–10pm, Fri–Sat 11:30am–11pm. **Prices:** Main courses $8–$12. AE, DISC, MC, V.

Mike's on the Avenue
In the Lafayette Hotel, 628 St Charles Ave (Central Business District); tel 504/523-1709. **Eclectic/Southwestern.** Chef Mike Fennelly has become one of the best new chefs in town in recent years with his inspired, bold cuisine—much of it reflecting an Asian or Southwestern influence. The honey-soy glazed duck and Mike's U-12 barbecue shrimp are a couple of featured favorites. The lively dining space is marked by high ceilings and original canvases on the walls. **FYI:** Reservations recommended. **Open:** Breakfast daily 7–10am; lunch Mon–Fri 11:30am–2pm; dinner daily 6–10pm. **Prices:** Main courses $16–$26. AE, CB, DC, MC, V. ▣ ▣ &

Molly's at the Market
1107 Decatur St (French Quarter); tel 504/525-5169. **American.** This Irish bar with a restaurant attached is a local favorite, offering cheap drinks and delicious half-pound burgers. Thursday nights are "celebrity bartender" nights, with luminaries ranging from the mayor or the governor to TV personalities. **FYI:** Reservations not accepted. **Open:** Daily 10am–6am. **Prices:** Main courses $4–$7. AE, CB, DC, DISC, MC, V.

Mother's
401 Poydras St (Central Business District); tel 504/523-9656. **Cajun/Creole.** Great home cooking. Decor is simple but the staff is fun and lively, and folks line up early for the renowned po' boys. The famous Ferdi Special—with delicious baked ham, roast beef, and thick gravy and served on fresh, crispy french bread—has long been a favorite. Also fine are the jambalaya and the gumbo, not to mention the breakfasts. Home-style desserts, too. **FYI:** Reservations not accepted. Dress code. **Open:** Mon–Sat 5am–10pm, Sun 7am–10pm. **Prices:** Main courses $6–$17. No CC. ⬤

Mr B's Bistro and Bar
201 Royal St (French Quarter); tel 504/523-2078. **Creole.** A quaint and very attractive bistro with polished oak floors, wood paneling, and bay windows. The New Orleans barbecue shrimp and the pasta jambalaya, featuring Gulf shrimp, andouille sausage, and smoked duck, are two of the house favorites. Jazz brunch on Sunday. **FYI:** Reservations accepted. **Open:** Lunch daily 11:30am–3pm; dinner daily 5:30–10pm. **Prices:** Main courses $9–$13. AE, CB, DC, MC, V.

Napoleon House
500 Chartres St (French Quarter); tel 504/524-9752. **Cajun/Creole.** This designated National Historic Landmark was intended to be Napoleon's home after his escape from exile in St Helena. As history shows, the plot failed, but the restaurant—owned by the same family for over 80 years—has been a success. Aside from its authentic exterior and no-nonsense decor, the place is renowned for its sandwiches, especially the Italian muffuletta and po-boys. Patrons can relax at the old bar or outside in the courtyard while soaking up a bit of old New Orleans. **FYI:** Reservations not accepted. **Open:** Daily 6am–midnight. **Prices:** Main courses $4–$6. AE, DC, MC, V. ■

Nola
534 St Louis St (French Quarter); tel 504/522-6652. **Regional American.** The swirling multihued tables tell you this hot spot is not an old-fashioned restaurant. Superchef Emeril Lagasse serves what he calls "New New Orleans" cuisine, in which old favorites are updated to reflect modern concerns and tastes with healthy and more exotic ingredients. Sample dishes include crabcake with jalapeño tartar sauce, cedar plank trout with citrus-horseradish crust, and roasted chicken stuffed with andouille and eggplant. Good wine selection. **FYI:** Reservations recommended. Dress code. **Open:** Lunch Mon–Sat 11:30am–2pm; dinner Sun–Thur 6–10pm, Fri–Sat 6pm–midnight. **Prices:** Main courses $12–$20. AE, CB, DC, DISC, ER, MC, V.

Olde N'Awlins Cookery
729 Conti St (French Quarter); tel 504/529-3663. **Cajun/Creole.** This traditional-style New Orleans restaurant's simple brick walls and undecorated tables show its emphasis on food, not fluff. The dinner menu is a bit pricey for what it offers; the best values are the good array of lunch specials and the tasty bread pudding with whiskey sauce. **FYI:** Reservations accepted. **Open:** Daily 8am–11pm. **Prices:** Main courses $14–$19; prix fixe $20. AE, MC, V.

Palace Cafe

605 Canal St (French Quarter); tel 504/523-1661. **Creole/Seafood.** A grand cafe featuring a spiral staircase in the center, booth seating, and an open, airy feel. The contemporary Creole cuisine, particularly the seafood, is excellent. You might start with the crabmeat cheesecake, then move on to the traditional seafood boil served on a raised platter. Also good are the rotisserie chicken and the rotisserie pork chop with candied yams. Save room for the white chocolate bread pudding. **FYI:** Reservations recommended. Children's menu. Dress code. **Open:** Lunch Mon–Sat 11:30am–2:30pm; dinner daily 5–10pm; brunch Sun 10:30am–2:30pm. **Prices:** Main courses $14–$20. AE, CB, DC, MC, V.

Pascal's Manale

1838 Napoleon Ave (Garden District); tel 504/895-4877. **Creole/Italian/Seafood.** The photographs in the bar area show off the dozens of celebrities who have dined at this uptown favorite. It's known for the food, not the plain decor, and easily the most popular dish is the misleadingly named barbecued shrimp—enormous shrimp that have been *baked* in a butter and pepper sauce. (Many other New Orleans restaurants have copied the dish, but Pascal's is still the best.) Other excellent entrees include veal Puccini in lemon-butter and mushroom sauce, and pasta with seafood. **FYI:** Reservations recommended. Dress code. **Open:** Mon–Fri 11:30am–10pm, Sat 4–10pm, Sun 4–9pm. **Prices:** Main courses $9–$17. AE, CB, DC, DISC, MC, V.

Père Antoine Restaurant

714 Royal St (French Quarter); tel 504/581-4478. **Cajun/Creole.** The corner entrance (at Royal and St Ann) of this attractive restaurant has two beautiful, full-length french doors, great for watching passersby as you dine. Crawfish pie is a signature dish, and the seafood platter is a good value. Lighter fare like sandwiches, burgers, and omelettes also available. **FYI:** Reservations accepted. Beer and wine only. **Open:** Daily 9am–midnight. **Prices:** Main courses $6–$15. MC, V.

Petunia's

817 St Louis St (French Quarter); tel 504/522-6440. **Cajun/Creole.** This local favorite resides in a 1830s Creole townhouse whose interior has gone pink. The bright and lively atmosphere contrasts with many of the dark French Quarter restaurants. There is an adequate Cajun-Creole menu, but the real show here is the world's largest crepes. Dinner crepes include everything from roast beef to crabmeat ratatouille, and the dessert crepes are not to be missed. **FYI:** Reservations recommended. Dress code. **Open:** Daily 8am–11pm. **Prices:** Main courses $13–$22. AE, CB, DC, DISC, ER, MC, V.

Port of Call

838 Esplanade Ave (French Quarter); tel 504/523-0120. **American.** This often packed, cozy restaurant with a wood interior, netting draped from the ceiling, and other nautical touches offers a variety of unique drinks and some of the best burgers in New Orleans. Good filet mignon, rib eye, and New York strip steaks, plus pizzas, are also served. **FYI:** Reservations not accepted. **Open:** Sun–Thurs 11am–midnight, Fri–Sat 11am–3am. **Prices:** Main courses $6–$17. AE, MC, V.

Praline Connection

542 Frenchmen St (Faubourg Manigny); tel 504/943-3934. **Soul/Southern.** The waiters, decked in white button-down shirts, ties, black pants, and black fedoras, match the black-and-white checkerboard of the floor at this fun and noisy place. The fare is traditional soul food with a unique Creole twist. Favorites include crispy fried chicken and crowder peas with okra or collard greens. For dessert try the sweet potato pie. The location on S Peters St provides jazz, gospel, and R&B almost every night. **FYI:** Reservations not accepted. Children's menu. Additional location: 901-07 S Peters (tel 523-3973). **Open:** Sun–Thurs 11am–10:30pm, Fri–Sat 11am–midnight. **Prices:** Main courses $10–$13. AE, CB, DC, DISC, MC, V.

The Quarter Scene

900 Dumaine St (French Quarter); tel 504/522-6533. **Cajun/Creole.** Diner-style eatery frequented mainly by locals. The otherwise simple decor is set off by a fountain and statuary in the main dining room. The brief menu offers familiar fare such as chicken-fried steak and fried seafood; for a lighter meal try the Camus, a salad of fresh spinach, tomato wedges, sliced egg, mushrooms, bacon, and cheese. Nightly specials are tailored to local tastes. **FYI:** Reservations not accepted. BYO. **Open:** Wed–Thurs 7am–midnight, Fri–Sat 24 hrs. **Prices:** Main courses $7–$13. AE, MC, V. 🕐

Ralph & Kacoo's

519 Toulouse St (French Quarter); tel 504/522-5226. **Cajun/Creole/Seafood.** This well-known local restaurant became famous in the 1960s for its crawfish, fried catfish, and well-prepared Creole dishes. The bar (set inside a ship) serves a wide variety of drinks and food. Neatly set tables and large dining spaces set the place apart from many of its jammed French Quarter companions. Families are welcome. **FYI:** Reservations accepted. Children's menu. Additional location: 601 Veterans Ave, Metairie (tel 831-3177). **Open:** Daily 11:30am–10:30pm. **Prices:** Main courses $9–$18. AE, DC, DISC, MC, V.

Red Lantern

1011 Gravier St (Central Business District); tel 504/523-0337. **Chinese.** Popular with the business crowd of the Central Business District, this restaurant offers an extensive buffet in an unpretentious setting. **FYI:** Reservations accepted. Children's menu. **Open:** Mon–Fri 11am–6pm. **Prices:** Lunch main courses $4–$6. AE, CB, DC, DISC, ER, MC, V.

Rib Room

In Omni Royal Orleans, 621 St Louis St (French Quarter); tel 504/529-7045. **Regional American.** The name notwithstanding, Raymond Toupes' restaurant is not famous for ribs but for great steaks and seafood. The elegant table settings and casual atmosphere make dining here pleasant and comfortable. Meat lovers can try anything from the rotisserie. Enjoy the piano bar in the lounge before or after dinner; there is also a cigar room. **FYI:** Reservations recommended. Piano. Children's menu. **Open:** Daily 6:30am–11pm. **Prices:** Main courses $23–$25. AE, CB, DC, DISC, ER, MC, V. VP &

Ristorante Carmelo
541 Decatur St (French Quarter); tel 504/586-1414. **Italian.** A very romantic setting, this restaurant is the perfect place for an intimate dinner. The menu offers fresh pasta and a strong list of classic Italian dishes, with a focus on fresh Louisiana seafood. For that New Orleans ambience, ask for seating near the windows. **FYI:** Reservations recommended. **Open:** Daily noon–11pm. **Prices:** Main courses $12–$34. AE, CB, DC, ER, MC, V. ♥

★ Rita's Olde French Quarter Restaurant
945 Chartres St (French Quarter); tel 504/525-7543. **Cajun/Creole.** This very casual and comfortable, not-at-all-fancy restaurant is held in high regard with locals for both lunch and dinner. Plaster walls with exposed brick and basic wooden chairs and tables make up the setting. The dinner menu features a heavy dose of seafood and fish in meunière sauces. Lunch specialty is veal Willy, a veal cutlet grilled with onions and bell peppers. **FYI:** Reservations not accepted. Children's menu. Beer and wine only. **Open:** Daily 11am–10pm. **Prices:** Main courses $11–$16. AE, CB, MC, V.

Royal Cafe
700 Royal St (French Quarter); tel 504/528-9086. **Creole.** Located in one of the most photographed buildings in the French Quarter, this cafe offers an excellent view from its famous second-floor balcony. Spicy shrimp Creole and po' boys for lunch; garlic-roasted duck and pan-seared salmon for dinner. Also New Orleans sampler platter. **FYI:** Reservations not accepted. Piano. **Open:** Lunch daily 11am–3pm; dinner daily 5:30–10pm; brunch Sat–Sun 10am–3pm. **Prices:** Main courses $10–$18. AE, MC, V.

Ruth's Chris Steak House
711 N Broad St; tel 504/486-0810. **Steak.** Part of a popular chain, this upscale steak house promises the very best steaks—and it delivers them, too. The filet mignon is served sizzling in a specially seasoned butter sauce. Menu is à la carte. **FYI:** Reservations accepted. Dress code. **Open:** Daily 11:30am–11:30pm. **Prices:** Main courses $19–$29. AE, DC, MC, V. VP &

St Ann's Cafe & Deli
800 Dauphine St (French Quarter); tel 504/529-4421. **Cajun/Creole.** Great for late-night eating, this very small restaurant/grocery combination offers meals to eat in or take out. Although the ambience isn't memorable, there are good versions of some New Orleans staples and a choice of pizzas. **FYI:** Reservations not accepted. Beer and wine only. **Open:** Daily 24 hrs. **Prices:** Main courses $5–$8. AE, DC, DISC, MC, V.

Santa Fe
801 Frenchmen St (Faubourg Marigny); tel 504/944-6854. **Tex-Mex.** A great little seafood place, even though the menu offers only a few items. The blue-green decor features very comfortable padded wicker chairs. The house recommends the chile rellenos and the seafood fajitas, featuring shrimp, mussels, crab, and monkfish. **FYI:** Reservations accepted. Guitar. Children's menu. **Open:** Tues–Sat 5–11pm. Closed last two weeks of Dec. **Prices:** Main courses $9–$17. AE, MC, V.

Sebastians
536 St Philip St (French Quarter); tel 504/524-2041. **Creole.** A wonderful restaurant that is not at all touristy. The interior is decorated with relatively good neo-impressionist artwork by the owner, and the inner covered courtyard is very romantic. Shrimp Sebastian—shrimp in a honey dijon mustard, shallot, and herb sauce—and veal marsala are favorites. **FYI:** Reservations accepted. Dress code. Beer and wine only. **Open:** Daily 5:30–10pm. **Prices:** Main courses $8–$15. AE, DISC, MC, V. ♥

Top of the Dome
In Hyatt Regency, 500 Poydras Plaza (Central Business District); tel 504/561-1234. **Cajun/Southwestern.** Located on the 32nd floor of the Hyatt Regency, this restaurant has a 360° view of the entire city—the river view shows why New Orleans is called the Crescent City. Chef Ed Esneault's limited menu features an outstanding mix of Cajun dishes with a Southwestern flair. Veal chops with chipotle demiglacé and pistachio-horseradish crusted salmon share the spotlight with unique soups and salads. **FYI:** Reservations recommended. Children's menu. Dress code. **Open:** Tues–Sat 5:30–10:30pm. **Prices:** Main courses $14–$22. AE, CB, DC, DISC, ER, MC, V.

Tujague's
823 Decatur St (French Quarter); tel 504/525-8676. **Creole.** The first restaurant to occupy this site opened in 1856. The second restaurant has become a New Orleans institution, offering a very limited menu that reflects the chef's inspiration for each day. Lunch offers three entrees—possibly including shrimp rémoulade or fresh fish—and a five-course meal. A seven-course meal is served at dinner. **FYI:** Reservations recommended. **Open:** Lunch daily 11am–3pm; dinner daily 5–10:30pm. **Prices:** Prix fixe $22–$28. AE, DC, DISC, MC, V.

Upperline
1413 Upperline (Garden District); tel 504/891-9822. **Regional American/Creole.** A fine, uptown restaurant with a bistro atmosphere and colorful artwork. Unique, Creole-inspired preparations are the draw. Roasted duck with port sauce has been a recent hit; other choices might include spicy rack of lamb, or a shrimp sampler including shrimp rémoulade, barbecue shrimp, and jalapeño cornbread. Special seasonal events (like the garlic festival) are held; call ahead. Nightly specials vary greatly. **FYI:** Reservations recom-

mended. Children's menu. Dress code. **Open:** Wed–Mon 5:30–9:30pm. **Prices:** Main courses $13–$19; prix fixe $21–$27. AE, CB, DC, ER, MC, V.

The Veranda Restaurant

In the Hotel Inter-Continental, 444 St Charles Ave (Central Business District); tel 504/525-5566. **Continental/Creole.** This memorable hotel restaurant features the highly respected talents of chef Willy Coln plus a comfortable, elegant private dining room and glass-enclosed courtyard. An excellent, varied menu includes a special rack of lamb glazed with herbs, Creole mustard, and honey; evidence of Coln's impressive command of seafood ranges from his marinated Norwegian salmon to the red snapper. **FYI:** Reservations recommended. Jazz. Dress code. **Open:** Breakfast daily 6:30–11am; lunch daily 11am–2pm; dinner daily 5:30–10pm; brunch Sun 11am–2:30pm. **Prices:** Main courses $11–$19. AE, DC, DISC, MC, V.

Versailles

2100 St Charles Ave (Garden District); tel 504/524-2535. **Creole/French.** From the red-walled Marie Antoinette Room to the St Charles Room with its lovely street view, this is dining in high style. Veal dishes here are outstanding, in particular veal Versailles, which is surrounded by crawfish (in season) or crabmeat. The crabmeat Monte Cristo appetizer is sautéed in dill and cream, served with a purée of spinach and artichokes, and topped with bread crumbs. Baking done on premises. Outstanding wine selection. **FYI:** Reservations recommended. Dress code. **Open:** Mon–Sat 6–10pm. Closed July. **Prices:** Main courses $20–$29. AE, CB, DC, MC, V.

REFRESHMENT STOPS

★ Cafe du Monde

In the French Market, 813 Decatur (French Quarter); tel 504/581-2914. **Desserts.** A great place to relax after a day in Jackson Square or the shops, this New Orleans landmark serves terrific beignets, stout coffee, and hot chocolate. Enjoy a café au lait and one of the classic square French donuts, doused in confectioner's sugar, on the patio and watch the crowd go by. The street performers outside the restaurant provide hours of entertainment. **Open:** Daily 24 hrs. No CC.

Molly's Irish Pub

732 Toulouse St (French Quarter); tel 504/568-1915. **Pub.** This classic, no-frills local bar has absolutely no tourist gimmicks—only a solitary pool table and a good jukebox. It can be loud, but the atmosphere is a relief from the more tourist-oriented places on Bourbon St. Standard pub fare. **Open:** Daily 24 hrs. No CC.

ATTRACTIONS
MUSEUMS

New Orleans Museum of Art

1 Collins Diboll Circle, City Park; tel 504/488-2631. Located in a neoclassical building, the museum houses pre-Columbian, Renaissance, and contemporary art. NOMA recently underwent a $23 million expansion project that created more gallery space for portions of the museum's collection (both Western and non-Western art from the pre-Christian era to the present) that had previously been relegated to storage. In addition, there is now an entire floor devoted to non-Western and ethnographic art, including Asian, African, pre-Columbian, Oceanic, and Native American art. **Open:** Tues–Sun 10am–5pm. **$$$**

Contemporary Arts Center

900 Camp St (Warehouse District); tel 504/523-1216. The CAC houses 10,000 square feet of gallery space dedicated to painting, photography, performance art, and sculpture created by Louisiana and international artists. Exhibits change every six to eight weeks. Local performers stage several dozen plays, dance events, and music concerts a year. Artists' Studio Days workshops held for children. **Open:** Mon–Sat 10am–5pm, Sun 11am–5pm. **$**

The Historic New Orleans Collection

533 Royal St (French Quarter); tel 504/523-4660. A museum and research center for state and local history located within a complex of historic buildings. Visitors may tour one of the "hidden houses" of the Vieux Carre—the Williams Residence, a 19th-century town house furnished with antiques, Chinese porcelains, and pieces of Louisiana origin. The history galleries house original maps, manuscripts, prints, photographs, and rare books related to the region. **Open:** Tues–Sat 10am–4:45pm. **Free**

Confederate Museum

929 Camp St; tel 504/523-4522. Established in 1899, the museum houses battle flags, weapons, personal items of Confederate President Jefferson Davis (including his evening clothes), part of Robert E Lee's silver camp service, and many portraits of Confederate military and civilian figures. A series of detailed pictures traces Louisiana's history from secession through Reconstruction. **Open:** Mon–Sat 10am–4pm. **$$**

New Orleans Historic Voodoo Museum

724 Dumaine St; tel 504/523-7685. A dark, musty interior is the setting for displayed artifacts of the occult from all over the globe. Visitors learn about the mixture of African and Catholic religions and rituals brought to New Orleans in the late 1700s by former Santo Domingo slaves. Authentic music; psychic readings; voodoo, swamp, and cemetery tours. Gift shop. **Open:** Daily 10am–dusk. **$$**

Blaine Kern's Mardi Gras World

223 Newton St; tel 504/361-7821. Located across the river at Algiers Point are these huge warehouses where Mardi Gras

floats are under construction. Guided tours take visitors to see sculptors at work—first making sketches and finally creating and painting the enormous sculptures that adorn the Mardi Gras floats every year. A film about Mardi Gras is presented. Visitors may get a souvenir picture taken with one of the colossal float figures. **Open:** Daily 9:30am–4:30pm. **$$$**

Musée Conti Wax Museum

917 Conti St (French Quarter); tel 504/525-2605 or toll free 800/233-5405. New Orleans history is depicted through life-size wax figures of Louisiana legends in authentic costumes and settings (Andrew Jackson, Jean Lafitte, Huey Long, Louis Armstrong, and Pete Fountain, among others). A "Haunted Dungeon" illustrates well-known horror tales. Self-guided tours; guided group tours available by reservation. **Open:** Daily 10am–5pm. **$$$**

New Orleans Pharmacy Museum

514 rue Chartres (French Quarter); tel 504/565-8027. In 1823, the first licensed pharmacist in the United States, Louis J Dufilho Jr, opened an apothecary shop. The Creole-style town house doubled as his home, and in the interior courtyard he cultivated the herbs he would need for creating his medicines. Inside the museum are old apothecary bottles, pill tile, and suppository molds; an old glass cosmetics counter (pharmacists of the 1800s also manufactured make-up and perfumes); and an 1855 black and rose Italian marble soda fountain. **Open:** Tues–Sun 10am–5pm. Closed some hols. **$**

Louisiana Children's Museum

420 Julia St; tel 504/523-1357. The museum features colorful hands-on exhibits for visitors of all ages. Visitors can build a dam at the Water Works exhibit; explore the powers of math and physics through 45 new exhibits in "The Lab"; and take in a performances in drama, dance, art, or puppetry at the museum theater. The Earth Balloon, a 22-foot diameter globe, provides an unusual look at geography and the environment; it accommodates 30 students. The "Challenges" is designed to give children greater sensitivity to mentally and physically challenged persons by simulating temporary loss of sight, hearing, and movement through the use of wheelchairs, goggles, and headsets. **Open:** Tues–Sat 9:30am–5:30pm, Sun noon–5:30pm.

LOUISIANA STATE MUSEUM COMPLEX

Cabildo

Jackson Sq (French Quarter); tel 504/568-6968. The museum is located at the site of the Louisiana Purchase signing. Exhibits include a Mississippi River collection of steamboat-era artifacts and paintings, Napoleon's death mask, and early Louisiana settlement items. The museum also holds interactive exhibits, china, basketry, wood-carvings, and 19th-century paintings. The Cabildo has been renovated and completely restored after a devastating fire. **Open:** Tues–Sun 9am–5pm. **$$**

Old US Mint

400 Esplanade Ave (French Quarter); tel 504/568-6968. The Old US Mint houses exhibits on New Orleans jazz and the city's Carnival celebrations. These displays contain a comprehensive collection of pictures, musical instruments, and other artifacts connected with jazz greats (Louis Armstrong's first trumpet is here), as well as a video theater. Across the hall there's an array of Carnival momentos—from ornate Mardi Gras costumes to a street scene complete with maskers and a parade float. **Open:** Tues–Sun 9am–5pm. **$$**

Presbytere

Jackson Sq (French Quarter); tel 504/568-6968. The Presbytere exhibits paintings by Louisiana artists as well as displays on local history and culture, maritime history, decorative arts, and costumes. **Open:** Tues–Sun 9am–5pm. **$$**

1850 House

523 St Ann, Lower Pontalba, Jackson Sq (French Quarter); tel 504/568-6968. These historic apartments are located in the Baroness Pontalba's famous antebellum building on Jackson Square. The museum depicts mid–19th-century family life through period artifacts and furniture. Guided tours available. **Open:** Tues–Sun 9am–5pm. **$$**

HISTORIC BUILDINGS

Tony Moran's Old Absinthe House

240 Bourbon St (French Quarter); tel 504/523-3181. The house was built in 1806 by two Spaniards and is still owned by their descendants. The drink for which it was named is outlawed in this country now, but with a little imagination visitors can sip a modern-day libation and visualize Andrew Jackson and the Lafitte brothers plotting the desperate defense of New Orleans in 1815. The building was a speakeasy during Prohibition, and when federal officers closed it in 1924, the interior was mysteriously stripped of its antique fixtures, including the long marble-topped bar and the old water dripper (used to drip water into absinthe), all of which just as mysteriously reappeared down the street at a corner establishment called, oddly enough, the Old Absinthe House Bar. **Open:** Daily 9:30am. **Free**

Beauregard-Keyes House

1113 Chartres St (French Quarter); tel 504/523-7257. A raised cottage with Doric columns and twin staircases built around 1826. Visitors can tour the main house, servant quarters, and side garden. The novelist Frances Parkinson Keyes wrote many of her books in the servant quarters, which is still furnished with her books, antiques, and family heirlooms. Guided tours by costumed docents. **Open:** Mon–Sat 10am–3pm. **$$**

Gallier House Museum

1132 Royal St (French Quarter); tel 504/523-6722. This 1857 townhouse was built by famous New Orleans architect James Gallier Jr as his residence. Period furnishings and interiors, a working bathroom, and a passive ventilation system are among the highlights. The adjoining building houses historical exhibits and films on decorative plaster work, ornamental ironwork, wood-graining, and marbling. Special seasonal programs offered. **Open:** Mon–Sat 10am–4:30pm, Sun noon–4:30pm. **$$**

Pitot House Museum

1440 Moss St (Faubourg St John); tel 504/482-0312. The Pitot House is a typical West Indies–style plantation home, restored and furnished with Louisianan and American antiques from the early 1800s. In 1810, it became the home of James Pitot, the first mayor of incorporated New Orleans, and it is now known by his name. It has wide galleries on the sides and large columns supporting the second floor. **Open:** Wed–Sat 10am–3pm. **$**

Old Ursuline Convent

1112 Chartres St (French Quarter); tel 504/529-3040. Across from the Beauregard-Keyes House is the Archbishop Antoine Blanc Memorial, which includes the Old Ursuline Convent. The Sisters of Ursula were for years the only teachers and nurses in New Orleans—they established the first schools for Catholic girls, for African Americans, and for Native Americans, and they set up the first orphanage in Louisiana. The nuns moved out of the convent in 1824 (they're in an uptown location these days), and in 1831 the state legislature met here. It now houses Catholic archives dating from 1718. Especially noteworthy is the fact that this is the oldest building of record not only in New Orleans but also in the entire Mississippi Valley, and it is the only surviving building from the French colonial effort in the United States. Included in the complex is the beautiful, restored old Chapel of the Archbishops, erected in 1845 and still used as a house of worship. Guided tours available. **Open:** Tues–Sun. **$$**

St Louis Cathedral

Jackson Square; tel 504/525-9585. One of the oldest (1794) and most photographed churches in the United States. The minor basilica was remodeled in 1851 (to the outrage of modern critics and historians) modifying the Spanish style of the church with steeples and a Greek Revival portico. Inside, there are six stained-glass windows depicting St Louis (French King Louis IX) at various stages of his life and canonization. There is also a portrait of the saint painted above and behind the main altar. The garden behind the cathedral was once a notorious dueling ground. **Open:** Mon–Sat 9am–5pm, Sun 1:30–5pm. **Free**

Longue Vue House and Gardens

7 Bamboo Road; tel 504/488-5488. The Greek Revival mansion and surrounding eight-acre gardens were the home of the late philanthropists Edgar Bloom Stern and his wife, Edith Rosenwald Stern. Both gardens and house interior were designed by the "Dean of American Women Landscape Architects," Ellen Biddle Shipman. Longue Vue House has changing exhibitions in the galleries, and wildflower watercolors and sculpture are on view at the playhouse. Year-

round activities include educational programs, symposia, workshops, and daily tours. **Open:** Mon–Sat 10am–4:30pm, Sun 1–5pm. **$$$**

Jackson Barracks

6400 St Claude Ave; tel 504/271-6262 ext 242 or 278-6242. A series of brick buildings with white columns built in 1834–35 for troops stationed at the river fronts. The barracks now serve as headquarters for the Louisiana National Guard. There is a museum in an 1837 powder magazine, which contains an extensive collection of military weapons, flags, and memorabilia of all American wars through Desert Storm. **Open:** Mon–Fri 7:30am–3:30pm. **Free**

PARKS AND GARDENS

Audubon Park

6500 Magazine St; tel 504/861-2538. In 1884–85, the area was the site of the World's Industrial and Cotton Exhibition, where man-made electric lightening startled visitors. Today, park-goers walk tree-shaded winding paths and enjoy 100-year-old oaks, lagoons, fountains, and gardens. Swimming pool, 18-hole golf course, 1.8-mile jogging track, tennis courts, horseback riding, and picnicking facilities are available. **Open:** Daily 6am–7pm. **Free**

Audubon Zoological Gardens

6500 Magazine St; tel 504/861-5101. Considered to be one of the top zoos in the country. Waterfalls, lagoons, tropical vegetation, and exotic flowers provide natural surroundings for the 1,500 animals on display. Exhibits include the African Savanna, Australian Outback, Asian Domain, Tropical Birdhouse, and World of Primates. **Open:** Mon–Fri 9am–4:30pm, Sat–Sun 9am–5:30pm. **$$$**

Washington Artillery Park

Between Jackson Sq and the Mississippi River; tel 504/529-5284. The riverside park has a raised walk that serves as New Orleans's "promenade." There are fountains, plantings, and benches from which to view the city's main industry—its busy port (second only to Amsterdam for tonnage handled each year). **Open:** Daily sunrise–sunset. **Free**

Jean Lafitte National Historical Park and Preserve

8606 W St Bernard Hwy, Chalmette; tel 504/589-4428. 10 mi E of New Orleans. The 141-acre park encompasses the site of the Battle of New Orleans and the National Cemetery. The last major land engagement between British and American troops, led by Andrew Jackson, took place on these grounds in 1815. Jackson became a national hero as a result of the victory and went on to become president. Visitors follow markers charting the course of the battle in detail. The National Cemetery dating from 1864 holds the remains of 14,000 Union soldiers killed in the Civil War. Also on the grounds is the Beauregard Home and a visitors center containing audiovisual exhibits on the battle. Rangers give interpretive talks, and two self-guided auto tours are available. **Open:** Daily 8:30am–5pm. **Free**

Woldenberg River Park

Along Mississippi River from Canal St to St Peter St (French Quarter); tel 504/861-2537. The city's first direct access to the river in 150 years. Covering 13 acres of river front, the large center lawn is the beginning point of a brick promenade leading to the Mississippi. The park features more than 600 trees—including oaks, magnolias, willows, and crape myrtles—and 1,400 shrubs. **Open:** Daily sunrise–sunset. **Free**

City Park

1 Dreyfous Ave; tel 504/482-4888. Encompassing 1,500 acres, the park is known for its ancient live oaks and lagoons. Visitors tour the botanical gardens, boat, fish, golf, play tennis, picnic, and ride horses and a miniature train. Also in the park is Storyland for children and the New Orleans Museum. Holiday light display from late November to early January. **Open:** Tues–Sat 10am–5pm, Thurs 5–9pm, Sun 12:15–6pm. Closed some hols. **Free**

TOURS

French Quarter Walking Tours

523 St Ann St (French Quarter); tel 504/523-3939. Offered by the nonprofit volunteer group, Friends of the Cabildo, which furnishes guides for a two-hour exploration that provides an overview of the history, folklore, and architecture of the area. Departing from the Museum Store, 523 Saint Ann St, your guide will take you to most of the Quarter's historic buildings' exteriors and the interiors of selected Louisiana State Museum buildings. Fee includes admission to two museums—Cabildo, Presbytere, 1850 House, or Old US Mint. No reservations necessary; tickets may be purchased in advance. **Open:** Daily. Call for schedule. **$$$**

Steamboat *Natchez*

1340 World Trade Center of New Orleans; tel 504/586-8777 or toll free 800/233-BOAT. Daily two-hour cruises on the Mississippi on a sternwheeler steamboat. Nightly dinner/jazz cruises from April to October. Narration is provided by professional tour guides, and there is a cocktail bar, optional creole buffet, and a gift shop on board. **Open:** Call for schedule. **$$$$**

John James Audubon

1340 World Trade Center of New Orleans; tel 504/586-8777. Passengers travel the Mississippi by sternwheeler, tour the busy port, and dock to visit both the Audubon Zoo and the Aquarium of the Americas. There are four trips daily. Call for prices, scheduling, and reservations. **$$$$**

Lil Cajun Swamp Tours

LA 301, Lafitte; tel 504/689-3213 or toll free 800/725-3213. 20 mi S of New Orleans. Narrated two-hour tours of a cypress swamp with Captain Cyrus Blanchard, or "Cyrus the Cajun," who is native to the area. Large vessels seat 49 passengers and float past scenes of bayou wildlife and fauna, including moss-covered cypress trees, nutria, alligators, and raccoons. **Open:** Daily 10am and 2pm. **$$$$**

Jean Lafitte Swamp Tour

LA 3134, Marrero; tel 504/689-4186 or toll free 800/445-4109. 20 mi S of New Orleans. Guided tours through the heart of Louisiana's swamplands in 40- to 60-passenger boats. Guides native to the region relate the legends and lore of Cajun wilderness while pointing out wildlife such as alligators, white nutria, cranes, and owls. Bus transportation provided from New Orleans; call for pick-up times and reservations. **Open:** Daily 8am–4pm. **$$$$**

OTHER ATTRACTIONS

Louisiana Superdome

1500 Poydras St; tel 504/587-3810. Approximately 27 stories high, with a seating capacity of 76,000, the windowless structure has a computerized climate control system that uses more than 9,000 tons of equipment. Inside, the 13-acre grounds have no posts that obstruct the view for spectators watching football, basketball, and baseball, and the moveable partitions and seats give it the flexibility to form the best seating arrangement for almost any event. The building also hosts conventions, trade shows, and large theatrical productions. **Open:** Call for schedule. **$$$$**

World Trade Center of New Orleans

2 Canal St; tel 504/522-9795. Houses the offices of many maritime companies and foreign consulates involved in international trade. Visitors may take an outside elevator to the 31st-floor observation deck that provides a view of the city and harbor. There is also a revolving cocktail lounge on the 33rd floor. **Open:** Daily 9am–5pm. **$**

Preservation Hall

726 St Peter St; tel 504/523-8939. At this local favorite, traditional jazz is presented without refinements such as air conditioning, refreshments, or seating for most audience members. The musicians are old-time greats who never left New Orleans. Arrive at least 45 minutes before doors open to get a seat on benches or pillows up front. **Open:** Daily 8–11pm. **$**

Aquarium of the Americas

1 Canal St; tel 504/861-2537. More than 7,500 specimens of marine life are on display in tanks that re-create their natural habitat. Major exhibits include a Caribbean reef, the Amazon River Basin, the Gulf of Mexico, and the Mississippi River. Penguins, sharks, stingrays, red-bellied piranhas, and endangered sea turtles are among the many creatures that can be seen. **Open:** Sun–Thurs 9:30am–6pm, Fri–Sat 9:30am–7pm. **$$$**

Storyland

New Orleans City Park; tel 504/483-9382. A playground where youngsters may slide down Jack and Jill's hill, climb Little Miss Muffet's spiderweb, or fish in the Little Mermaid's pond. Larger-than-life fairy-tale figures such as Puss-n-Boots, Rapunzel, and Jack and the Beanstalk will delight children from six months to six years. **Open:** Peak (Mar–Dec) Wed–Sun 10am–4:30pm. Reduced hours off-season. **$**

Opelousas

Founded by French settlers in 1720, Louisiana's third-oldest town briefly served as capital during the Civil War. Cajun and Creole French are still spoken by many of the residents, and the local dance halls specialize in Cajun and Zydeco music. Historic buildings and homes lend additional charm and interest to the city's "cultural gumbo." **Information:** Opelousas–St Landry Chamber of Commerce, 121 W Vine St, PO Box 109, Opelousas, 70570 (tel 318/942-2683).

RESTAURANT

Palace Cafe
167 W Landry St; tel 318/942-2142. **Cajun.** This down-home restaurant has plain wooden tables and green-cushioned chairs. The featured meal is the fried chicken salad, more filling than it sounds. The baked eggplant with crabmeat dressing topped with crawfish sauce is also very good. **FYI:** Reservations accepted. Beer and wine only. **Open:** Sun 7am–3pm, Mon–Sat 6am–9pm. **Prices:** Main courses $4–$14. MC, V.

Ruston

Pine-forested hills, serene lakes, and quiet campgrounds surround Ruston, home of Louisiana Tech University. Located on I-20, some 28 miles west of Monroe in northeast Louisiana, Ruston hosts the annual Peach Festival during the second week of June. **Information:** Ruston/Lincoln Chamber of Commerce, PO Box 150, Ruston, 71273-0150 (tel 318/255-2031).

MOTELS

Comfort Inn
1801 N Service Rd, 71270; tel 318/251-2360 or toll free 800/221-2222. Exit 85 off I-20. Standard chain property close to interstate, but set back in a quiet, peaceful setting. Most appealing to highway travelers. **Rooms:** 60 rms. CI 3pm/CO 11am. Nonsmoking rms avail. **Amenities:** A/C, cable TV, refrig, dataport. **Services:** **Facilities:** **Rates (CP):** $50 S; $55 D. Extra person $5. Children under age 18 stay free. Parking: Outdoor, free. AE, CB, DC, DISC, MC, V.

Days Inn
1300 N Trenton, 71270; tel 318/255-2911 or toll free 800/DAYS-INN. Exit 84 off I-20. In need of some renovations, this standard Days Inn offers fairly nice accommodations. Okay for traveler just passing through. **Rooms:** 34 rms. CI 3pm/CO 11am. Nonsmoking rms avail. **Amenities:** A/C, cable TV. **Services:** **Facilities:** **Rates:** $45 S; $50 D. Extra person $4. Children under age 18 stay free. Parking: Outdoor, free. AE, DISC, MC, V.

Holiday Inn
Frontage Rd, 71270; tel 318/255-5901 or toll free 800/HOLIDAY; fax 318/255-3729. Exit 85 off I-20. Located on access road to interstate, near shopping center. **Rooms:** 228 rms and stes. CI 3pm/CO 11am. Nonsmoking rms avail. **Amenities:** A/C, cable TV. **Services:** **Facilities:** 1 bar, washer/dryer. **Rates:** $59 S; $69 D; $129 ste. Extra person $10. Children under age 18 stay free. Parking: Outdoor, free. AE, CB, DC, DISC, MC, V.

St Martinville

Established as a military trading post in the Attakapas Indian Nation, this picturesque community is now the seat of St Martin Parish. Local musicians and storytellers congregate under the shade of the Evangeline Oak downtown and provide entertainment to both visitors and residents. **Information:** St Martinville Tourism, 201 S Main St, PO Box 436, St Martinville, 70582 (tel 318/394-7578).

RESTAURANT

La Place d'Evangeline
220 Evangeline Blvd; tel 318/394-4010. LA 96 exit off US 90. **Cajun/French.** The inn that houses this homey, comfortable, and relaxed restaurant is listed in the National Registry of Historic Places and sits under the branches of the famed Evangeline Oak. Best options include corn and crab bisque and the crawfish, crab, or shrimp dinners. Traditional Southern desserts include peach cobbler and fudge pecan pie. **FYI:** Reservations recommended. Children's menu. **Open:** Mon–Tues 8am–5pm, Wed–Sat 8am–9pm, Sun 8am–2pm. **Prices:** Main courses $5–$15. AE, MC, V.

Shreveport

See also Bossier City

Named for Capt Henry Miller Shreve, who made the Red River navigable by clearing a massive log jam in the 1830s. Visitor attractions range from horse racing to the performing arts, as well as the lakes, rivers, and forests that surround the city. **Information:** Shreveport-Bossier Convention & Visitors Bureau, 629 Spring, PO Box 1761, Shreveport, 71166 (tel 318/222-9391).

HOTELS

Best Western Chateau Suite Hotel of Shreveport
201 Lake St, 71101; tel 318/222-7620 or toll free 800/845-9334; fax 318/424-2014. This elegant downtown hotel providing excellent service is a perfect choice for business travelers, corporate relocation guests, or anyone willing to spend the extra money for a luxury stay. Large suites are a good value. **Rooms:** 103 rms and stes. Executive level. CI

1pm/CO noon. Nonsmoking rms avail. All are stylishly and individually appointed. **Amenities:** ⛉ ⛱ ▣ ⚑ A/C, cable TV, refrig. Some units w/minibars, some w/whirlpools. **Services:** ⬥ 🚗 ⛉ ⟲ Babysitting. **Facilities:** ⛉ ⛊ ⛏ 💻 ⛭ 1 restaurant (bkfst only), 1 bar, whirlpool, washer/dryer. **Rates (BB):** $69 S or D; $84–$99 ste. Extra person $10. Children under age 12 stay free. Parking: Outdoor, free. AE, CB, DC, DISC, MC, V.

≣≣≣ Holiday Inn Downtown Riverfront

102 Lake St, 71101; tel 318/222-7717 or toll free 800/HOLIDAY; fax 318/221-5951. Exit 19A off I-20. A newer property located near the riverfront and casinos, this Holiday Inn is a fine choice for a visit to Shreveport. **Rooms:** 186 rms. CI 3pm/CO noon. Nonsmoking rms avail. **Amenities:** ⛉ ⛱ ▣ ⚑ A/C, cable TV, refrig, VCR. Some units w/minibars. **Services:** ✕ 🚗 ⛉ ⟲ Transportation available to casinos. **Facilities:** ⛉ ⛭ ⚷ 1 restaurant, 1 bar. **Rates:** $74 S; $84 D. Extra person $10. Children under age 18 stay free. Parking: Outdoor, free. AE, CB, DC, DISC, MC, V.

≣≣ Super 8 Lodge

5204 Monkhouse Dr, 71109; tel 318/635-8888 or toll free 800/800-8000; fax 318/635-8888. Exit 13 off I-20. Large economy hotel offering average rooms. **Rooms:** 143 rms and stes. CI 2pm/CO noon. Nonsmoking rms avail. **Amenities:** ⛉ A/C, cable TV. **Services:** 🚗 ⟲ **Facilities:** ⛉ ⚷ **Rates:** $42 S; $54 D; $59 ste. Extra person $4. Children under age 12 stay free. Parking: Outdoor, free. AE, DISC, MC, V.

MOTELS

≣≣ Days Inn

4935 W Monkhouse Dr, 71109; tel 318/636-0080 or toll free 800/DAYS-INN. Exit 13 off I-20. Close to airport and interstate, this standard chain property offers dependable accommodations and services suitable for all travelers. **Rooms:** 148 rms. CI 3pm/CO 11am. Nonsmoking rms avail. **Amenities:** ⛉ A/C, cable TV. **Services:** ⟲ ⛳ Social director. **Facilities:** ⛉ ⚷ 1 restaurant (bkfst only). **Rates:** $30–$34 S; $35–$40 D. Extra person $10. Children under age 18 stay free. Parking: Outdoor, free. AE, DISC, MC, V.

≣≣ Red Roof Inn

7296 Greenwood Rd, 71101; tel 318/938-5342 or toll free 800/THE-ROOF. Exit 9 off I-20. Close to inner and outer loop of Shreveport, as well as interstate, this motel is perfect for budget travelers, including families. **Rooms:** 97 rms. CI open/CO noon. Nonsmoking rms avail. **Amenities:** ⛉ A/C, cable TV. **Services:** ⟲ **Facilities:** ⚷ **Rates:** $35–$46 S; $41–$49 D. Extra person $7. Children under age 18 stay free. Parking: Outdoor, free. AE, CB, DC, DISC, MC, V.

RESTAURANTS 🍴

Don's Seafood & Steak House

3100 Highland Ave; tel 318/865-4291. **Seafood.** A member of a family-owned and -operated chain of restaurants. If the decor isn't memorable the great seafood is. The fried and broiled seafood platters are the most popular. And be sure to try the homemade bread pudding. **FYI:** Reservations not accepted. Children's menu. **Open:** Sun–Thurs 11am–10pm, Fri–Sat 11am–11pm. **Prices:** Main courses $7–$13. AE, MC, V. 🚫 ⚷

Monsieur Patou

855 Pierremont Rd; tel 318/868-9822. **French.** A Louis XV decor with elegant furniture sets the ambience of this small, intimate restaurant. Excellent fine dining fare includes rack of lamb roasted with garlic, and a butter puff pastry with lobster and truffles. The swan chocolate mousse is a special dessert. **FYI:** Reservations recommended. Dress code. **Open:** Lunch Tues–Fri 11:30am–2pm; dinner Mon–Sat 6–11pm. **Prices:** Main courses $13–$48. AE, CB, DC, DISC, MC, V. ⚷

Randol's

101 Travis St; tel 318/424-4FUN. Exit 19A off I-20, N on Commerce. **Cajun.** This family-oriented restaurant serves exemplary traditional Cajun dishes, but the real highlight is the nightly Cajun dancing and entertainment. If you love to dance, you shouldn't miss this place; guests are encouraged to join the festivities. Great for a family night out. **FYI:** Reservations not accepted. Zydeco. Children's menu. **Open:** Lunch Mon–Fri 11am–2pm, Sat 11am–4pm, Sun noon–4pm; dinner Mon–Fri 5–10pm, Sat 4–10:30pm, Sun 4–9pm. **Prices:** Main courses $10–$18. MC, V. 🚫 ⚷

ATTRACTIONS 🏛

Louisiana State Exhibit Museum

3015 Greenwood Rd; tel 318/632-2020. Take fairgrounds exit off I-20. Exhibits depict the state's culture, history, industry, agriculture, natural resources, and wildlife. Miniature dioramas and murals, antiques, works of local artists, and Native American artifacts are displayed. **Open:** Mon–Sat 9am–4:30pm, Sun 1–5pm. **Free**

RW Norton Art Gallery

4747 Creswell Ave (Central); tel 318/865-4201. Opened to the public in 1966, the 20 exhibition rooms house vast collections of European and American art spanning four centuries. Among the artists featured are Frederic Remington and Charles M Russell; among the exhibits are a doll collection dating from 1720, an antique firearms gallery, Flemish tapestries, and Dutch landscapes. The 40-acre landscaped area features azalea gardens containing over 10,000 plants. **Open:** Tues–Fri 10am–5pm, Sat–Sun 1–5pm. **Free**

Barnwell Memorial Gardens and Art Center

601 Clyde Fant Pkwy; tel 318/673-7703. Dome-shaped botanical conservatory features seasonal and native plants, a walk-through bronze sculpture, and a fragrance garden for the visually impaired. The gallery is devoted to changing art and flower exhibits. The rear of the building offers a panoramic view of the Red River. **Open:** Mon–Fri 9am–4:30pm, Sat–Sun 1–5pm. **Free**

American Rose Center

Jefferson-Paige Rd; tel 318/938-5402. The 118-acre pine-woods park features more than 20,000 rose bushes, 500 azaleas, and other flowering plants in more than 60 individually designed gardens. Also a research center for the American Rose Society. During the annual Christmas in Roseland, the Center displays more than 100,000 lights every evening from the day after Thanksgiving through New Year's Eve. **Open:** Apr–Oct, daily 9am–6pm. **$**

Water Town

I-20 W; tel 318/938-5473. Twenty-acre water theme park with speed slides, adventure slides, wave pool, and separate areas for small children and adults. Showers, lockers, and picnicking facilities available. **Open:** Peak (June–Aug) Mon–Wed 10am–6pm, Thurs–Sat 10am–9pm, Sun noon–6pm. Reduced hours off-season. **$$$$**

Slidell

Settled in the 1850s, Slidell was the source of most of the bricks used in New Orleans homes. The downtown district contains many antique stores and historic buildings. Nearby Lake Pontchartrain and Pearl River Wildlife Management Area combine to create a sportsman's playground. **Information:** Greater Slidell Area Chamber of Commerce, 118 W Hall Ave, Slidell, 70468 (tel 504/643-5678).

MOTELS 🏨

≣≣ Budget Host

1662 Gause Blvd, 70458; tel 504/641-8800 or toll free 800/BUD-HOST. Exit 266 off I-10. Clean and comfortable—a pleasant surprise. **Rooms:** 100 rms. CI 2pm/CO noon. Nonsmoking rms avail. **Amenities:** 🛏 A/C, cable TV w/movies. **Services:** 🍽 ☐ **Facilities:** ☐ ☐ 1 bar. **Rates:** $34 S; $39–$44 D. Extra person $5. Children under age 18 stay free. Parking: Outdoor, free. AE, DC, DISC, EC, MC, V.

≣≣ Econo Lodge

58512 Tyler Dr, 70459; tel 504/641-2153 or toll free 800/424-4777; fax 504/646-2910. Exit 266 off I-10. Well maintained property with eager-to-please staff. **Rooms:** 57 rms. CI open/CO 11am. Nonsmoking rms avail. **Amenities:** 🛏 A/C, cable TV. **Services:** ☐ ☐ **Facilities:** ☐ Washer/dryer. **Rates:** Peak (Mar–May/Sept–Dec) $38–$75 S; $43–$75 D. Extra person $5. Children under age 18 stay free. Lower rates off-season. Parking: Outdoor, free. AE, CB, DC, DISC, EC, MC, V.

≣≣≣ Ramada Inn

798 E I-10 Service Rd, 70461; tel 504/643-9960 or toll free 800/RAMADAS; fax 504/643-3508. Exit 266 off I-10. Typical, well maintained accommodations. **Rooms:** 148 rms and stes. CI 2pm/CO noon. Nonsmoking rms avail. **Amenities:** 🛏 A/C, cable TV w/movies. **Services:** ✗ ☐ ☐ ☐ **Facilities:** ☐ 🚌 ☐ 1 restaurant, 2 bars (1 w/entertainment), washer/

dryer. **Rates:** Peak (June–July/Nov–Feb) $85 S; $90 D; $200 ste. Extra person $8. Children under age 18 stay free. Lower rates off-season. Parking: Outdoor, free. AE, CB, DC, DISC, JCB, MC, V.

RESTAURANT 🍴

La Provence

25020 US 190 E, Lacombe; tel 504/626-7662. Exit 228 off I-10. **French.** Featuring tile floors, provincial furniture, and huge stone fireplaces, the dining room has an old-world ambience that's enhanced by the excellent service. The kitchen turns out an outstanding rack of lamb, a delicious duck à l'orange, and numerous rabbit dishes. Try the quail gumbo for a twist on a local favorite. All meals come with fresh pâté and baguettes. **FYI:** Reservations recommended. Dress code. **Open:** Wed–Thurs 5–10pm, Fri–Sat 5–11pm, Sun 1–9pm. **Prices:** Main courses $18–$28. AE, MC, V. 🖼 ☐

ATTRACTIONS 🏛

Gator Swamp Tours

US 90; tel 504/649-1255 or toll free 800/875-4287. Tours given daily on small boats through the Honey Island Swamp, one of the wildest and least-altered swamps in the United States. Visitors may view moss-draped trees and abundant wildlife, including alligators, turtles, eagles, and wild pigs. Reservations required. **Open:** Daily. Call for schedule. **$$$$**

Honey Island Swamp Tours

Crawford Landing; tel 504/641-1769. Visitors explore the swamp in boats while native guides relate the history and ecology of the Louisiana swamp. The wildlife that may be encountered includes bald eagles, alligators, egrets, hogs, nutria, and beaver. Customized small group trips for birding, duck hunting, evening tours, and special occasions. **Open:** Daily. Call for schedule. **$$$$**

West Monroe

At one time this site competed with Monroe for commercial trade on the D'Arbonne River. West Monroe now hosts numerous festivals and special events and provides access to D'Arbonne National Wildlife Refuge. **Information:** West Monroe–West Ouachita Chamber of Commerce, 1613 N 7th St, PO Box 427, West Monroe, 71294 (tel 318/325-1961 or 322-1195).

MOTELS 🏨

≣≣≣ Holiday Inn Express

401 Constitution Dr, 71292; tel 318/388-3810 or toll free 800/HOLIDAY; fax 318/322-2088. Exit 114 off I-20. A good choice for extended stays. **Rooms:** 120 rms and stes. CI 3pm/CO 11am. Nonsmoking rms avail. **Amenities:** 🛏 ☐ A/C, cable TV, refrig. **Services:** ☐ ☐ ☐ **Facilities:** ☐ 🍴 🚌 ☐

Washer/dryer. **Rates (CP):** $44 S; $49 D; $55 ste. Extra person $5. Children under age 18 stay free. Parking: Outdoor, free. AE, CB, DC, DISC, MC, V.

Red Roof Inn

102 Constitution Dr, 71292; tel 318/388-2420 or toll free 800/THE-ROOF; fax 318/388-2499. Economy motel close to interstate, shopping, restaurants.. **Rooms:** 97 rms. CI 4pm/CO noon. Nonsmoking rms avail. **Amenities:** A/C, cable TV, dataport. **Services:** **Facilities:** **Rates:** $35–$46 S; $41–$49 D. Extra person $7. Children under age 18 stay free. Parking: Outdoor, free. AE, CB, DC, DISC, MC, V.

Super 8 Motel

1101 Glenwood Dr, 71292; tel 318/325-6361 or toll free 800/800-8000; fax 318/325-6361. Exit 114 off I-20. Offering standard economy lodgings, this is great for highway travelers but is located far enough from the interstate to be quiet and secluded. **Rooms:** 99 rms. CI 2pm/CO noon. Nonsmoking rms avail. **Amenities:** A/C, cable TV. **Services:** **Facilities:** **Rates:** $39 S; $44 D. Extra person $5. Children under age 12 stay free. AP and MAP rates avail. Parking: Outdoor, free. AE, DISC, MC, V.

MISSOURI

A Study in Contrasts

A drive through Missouri is a uniquely bipolar experience. The gentle undulation of corn and wheat fields on the prairies can lull you into deep meditation, while hairpin curves and 500-foot bluffs in the highlands can stand your hair on end.

At its heart, Missouri is still rural, a quilt of small family farms—the second-highest number of any state in the nation. But the pastoral vision dissolves at the eastern and western edges, where glass-eyed towers and steel monoliths crowd along the rivers like behemoths waiting to drink. St Louis and Kansas City offer the best, and worst, of the postmodern megalopolis. Where lines of Conestoga wagons bound for the western frontier once lumbered through these towns, now thousands of autos roll off huge assembly lines, and aviation and aerospace giants are busy conquering the next frontier.

Farther south in the green hills and "hollers" of the Ozarks, the values and traditions of the early pioneers still define the rhythm of daily life. If the woodsy Ozarks are Missouri's emerald, then Branson is its rhinestone, the brash and glittery Johnny-Cash-come-lately of the country music scene.

As the place in American history where East met West and North met South, Missouri's political, social, and cultural landscapes have been shaped by diverse, sometimes contrary, lifestyles and beliefs. Even Mother Nature is especially contrary here: having blessed Missouri with abundant natural resources and the two mightiest rivers in the land, she brings it to its knees with an occasional killer tornado or flood of near-biblical proportions. But like the well-tempered steel of its magnificent Gateway Arch, this state holds its shape and character with considerable grace.

A Brief History

At the Meeting of the Great Waters

Missouri's earliest settlers were the cave-dwelling "Bluff Shelter" people. By 2000 BC they had become part of a mound-building culture that reached its zenith with the Mississippians. The most advanced culture north of Mexico, the Mississippians endured until AD 1200, their achievements culminating in an enormous temple complex at the confluence of the Missouri and Mississippi rivers and extending into present-day St Louis.

Three groups of modern aboriginal peoples, the Osages, Missouri, and Iowa, were living in Missouri when French trappers and traders arrived in the mid-1600s. French prospectors soon opened lead mines near the St Francois Mountains, working them with African slaves, and the nearby Creole community of Ste Genevieve (established 1735) soon prospered as Missouri's earliest permanent European settlement. In 1764 Pierre Laclede Liguest, anticipating the commercial importance of the great river crossroads, began building his planned city of St Louis.

After France yielded its holdings west of the Mississippi to Spain in 1762, generous Spanish land grants attracted many Americans to increasingly cosmopolitan St Louis and other Missouri settlements. In 1800 the region, including Missouri, reverted back to France, whereupon the United States made the deal of the century, purchasing it in 1803 for $15 million.

To All Points West The following year, at President Thomas Jefferson's request, Missourians Meriwether Lewis and William Clark left St Louis on a most excellent adventure, exploring the newly acquired real estate and blazing a trail to the Pacific. As a result, St Louis and the Missouri River became the gateway to America's westward expansion and the fulfillment of its vision of Manifest Destiny. In 1812, Missouri was organized as a territory and settlers rushed to the new frontier. As part of the controversial Missouri Compromise, Missouri was admitted to the Union on August 10, 1821, as a slave state.

The rivers pulsed with steamboat commerce. St Louis blossomed into the heart of the burgeoning fur trade. Independence became the terminus for

the Santa Fe Trail and its wealth of Mexican trade. It and other Missouri towns funneled wagon trains onto the Oregon Trail as well as trails to the California and Colorado gold fields.

Native Americans were the main victims of the great land grab by white settlers that followed statehood. The US Congress went on a rampage of treaty-breaking and, by 1840, had cleared the state, sometimes forcibly, of its remaining indigenous peoples plus several tribes who had been pledged Missouri lands after being dislocated from homelands east of the Mississippi.

Fun Facts

• Missouri's nickname, the Show-Me State, originated when Congressman Willard Vandiver explained, ". . . frothy eloquence neither convinces nor satisfies me. I am from Missouri. You have got to show me."

• Of the 43 species of mammals in the Missouri Ozarks, 13 of them are from the bat family.

• St Joseph, Missouri was the starting point for the Pony Express, the short-lived yet legendary mail delivery system. Riders delivered letters 2,000 miles to the end of the line: Sacramento, California.

• There are some 45,000 caves in Missouri—more than in any other state.

The War Within By 1860 about 10% of Missourians were African-Americans in bondage. Missouri slaveholders and Kansan abolitionists had been waging a bloody border war for years, a situation further aggravated by the Supreme Court's infamous 1857 *Dred Scott* decision in St Louis, which negated the Missouri slave's claim to freedom. Longstanding pro-Southern sympathies of political leaders were outweighed by growing anti-slavery sentiment, and Missouri remained in the Union. After the start of the Civil War, a defiant Governor Claiborne Jackson led the state militia against Union Troops at Boonville and was subsequently removed from office. However, Confederate troops maintained a stronghold in southwest Missouri until their decisive defeat at Pea Ridge, Arkansas, in March 1862.

Missouri endured a thousand battles and skirmishes on its soil during the war, and guerrilla bands from both sides inflicted further devastation on its citizens. For years after the war, marauding gangs, many of them former Confederate Quantrill's Raiders like Jesse and Frank James, continued the mayhem.

Onto the World Stage Although Chicago replaced St Louis as the de facto capital of the Midwest, railroads crisscrossing the plains brought great commerce to St Louis and Kansas City, establishing the latter as the nation's beef capital. St Louis's 1904 Louisiana Purchase Centennial Exposition hosted 20 million visitors, who relished their first hot dog and ice cream cone while marvelling at such technological miracles as the motion picture and the automobile.

While the country soberly weathered Prohibition during the 1920s, the proliferation of speakeasies and bourbon along Kansas City's Vine and 18th Streets spawned world-class jazz and the dazzling careers of such greats as Duke Ellington and Count Basie.

With the onset of World War II, even Kansas City sobered up. Missouri provided nearly half a million troops, mountains of war supplies, and its native son General Omar Bradley, commander of the US 1st Army during the D-Day invasion of Europe. Thirty-third US President Harry S Truman, the man from Independence catapulted onto the world stage upon Franklin Roosevelt's 1945 death, led the nation out of World War II and through the Korean War.

Trains & Boats & Rains Today, Missouri, whose name means "town of the big canoe," is a leading transportation equipment manufacturer. St Louis and Kansas City are major hubs for air, rail, highway, and water transport, as well as important financial centers. Both have grappled with pollution, urban blight, and other big-city problems, undertaking successful, even model, cleanup and redevelopment efforts.

After weathering the mid-1980s farm crisis, agriculture remains a major part of Missouri's economy. The state's two great rivers showed their dark side in recent floods—the disastrous 1993 flood caused billions in damages to property and crops worth billions, and only through the tireless efforts of citizens and volunteers were the historical treasures of Ste Genevieve and Hannibal saved.

A Closer Look

GEOGRAPHY

Glacial ice once covered **northern Missouri,** extending south to the Missouri River and leaving in its retreat the fertile black soil that turned Missouri into an agricultural powerhouse. Streams have since softened the prairie's flat face into a gently rolling surface, and indigenous seven-foot tall grasses have given way to fields of soybeans, corn, and wheat and herds of livestock. **Kansas City,** the "Paris of the Prairie" with its juxtaposition of statue-lined boulevards, corporate headquarters, and stockyards, straddles the Kansas-Missouri border—the action is on the Missouri side. Just a few minutes east is Harry Truman's home town of **Independence.** Meat-packing center **St Joseph** was home to the pistol-packing James brothers and the Pony Express.

The undulating prairie with its ubiquitous corn and grain fields rolls on into **west-central Missouri,** where it becomes the Osage Plain. The rainfall here ends up mainly in gigantic Truman Lake or the region's two other large reservoirs and recreational sites. **Joplin** offers evidence of its past as a lead-mining boom town in the 1800s.

The ancient and picturesque Ozark Plateau, the state's largest and most prominent geographic feature, spreads across **southern Missouri.** Eroded into ragged ridges and deep valleys, the highlands are blanketed by most of Missouri's remaining forests and are marked by streams and caves, as well as shaded hollows that are home to an anachronistic mountain culture. The granite peaks of the St Francois Mountains punctuate the southeastern edge of the plateau. **Springfield,** heart of the region's dairy industry, is the stepping-off point to the region's recreational, historical, and scenic attractions. Little **Branson** has nearly outgrown its britches as millions flock to country music's "Second City." The diminutive state capital, **Jefferson City,** commands a position overlooking the Missouri River at the point where plateau meets prairie in the center of the state.

Along Missouri's eastern edge, the **Mississippi River Valley** and its towns have been indelibly imprint-

DRIVING DISTANCES
Kansas City
55 miles S of St Joseph
65 miles E of Topeka, KS
87 miles W of Sedalia
148 miles W of Jefferson City
167 miles NW of Springfield
252 miles W of St Louis
St Louis
54 miles N of Ste Genevieve
115 miles N of Cape Girardeau
117 miles SE of Hannibal
215 miles NE of Springfield
252 miles E of Kansas City
291 miles SW of Chicago, Il
Springfield
43 miles N of Branson
70 miles E of Joplin
87 miles SW of Lake of the Ozarks (Osage Beach)
167 miles SE of Kansas City
190 miles NE of Tulsa, OK
215 miles SW of St Louis

ed with the river's history and character. **St Louis,** the state's largest metropolitan area, is a mix of high culture, ethnic flavor, and rich history. **Hannibal** lives on as a monument to the Missouri immortalized in the writings of Mark Twain, while **Cape Girardeau,** perched on high bluffs above the Mississippi, retains some of the flavor of its Spanish beginnings.

The southeastern corner of the state, commonly known as the **Bootheel,** lies in the flat Gulf Coastal Plain. The bottomlands were drained to create a fertile delta, which is the source of prodigious amounts of cotton, soybeans, and rice.

CLIMATE

There is no confusing Missouri's four distinct seasons, but the weather can be fickle. Summertime highs, typically in the 90s and paired with high humidity, may occasionally top the century mark, creating very oppressive conditions; nonetheless, this is still the most popular time for touring. Spring brings pleasant daytime temperatures but a higher risk of windy, rainy weather. Temperate autumn days and crisp evenings are perfect for fall foliage treks to the Ozarks, while winters are nippy, with occasional sub-zero dips in the mercury and nightly freezes the norm. At the higher elevations in the Ozarks, the weather becomes a bit milder; summer nights are slightly cooler, and winter temperatures a few degrees warmer, than Kansas City, St Louis, and the lower-lying prairies.

Missouri's annual precipitation varies from 50 inches in the southeast to about 30 inches in the northwest, with the wettest months being April, May, and June. May and early June are also the peak of the tornado season—the state is situated in the notorious "Tornado Alley" and gets an average of 27 twisters annually. Heavy snows are possible during winter months, but snowfall tends to be light, ranging from 4 to 5½ inches in January.

WHAT TO PACK

The Ozarks and the prairie towns are quite laid-back; casual clothing is appropriate most anywhere. You may want to pack your better duds for Kansas City

AVG TEMPS (°F) & INCHES OF RAINFALL		
	St Louis	Springfield
Jan	41/1.8	43/1.8
Feb	45/2.1	47/2.1
Mar	54/3.6	55/3.9
Apr	66/3.5	66/4.1
May	75/3.9	75/4.4
June	85/3.7	85/5.0
July	90/3.8	90/2.9
Aug	88/2.8	90/3.5
Sept	80/3.1	83/4.6
Oct	70/2.6	72/3.6
Nov	54/3.2	56/3.7
Dec	44/3.0	46/3.1

and St Louis, however, especially if you're sampling the high culture and night life. Pack a light jacket or sweater to contend with the summer air-conditioning in most public places.

The summer sun is best confronted with a hat, sunglasses, and sunscreen. If you plan to camp, boat, or otherwise enjoy the great outdoors, pack an effective repellant to protect you against the usual rogue's gallery of entomological pests. Sturdy, comfortable walking shoes are a necessity for sightseeing or shopping.

TOURIST INFORMATION

You can obtain a free *Missouri Travel Guide,* calendar of events, and state road map by contacting the Missouri Division of Tourism, Truman State Office Bldg, Box 1055, Jefferson City 65102 (tel 573/751-4133). The Missouri Department of Economic Development maintains a Web page (http://www.ecodev.state.mo.us) with general information about the state. Detailed visitors guides to Missouri's two largest cities are also available from the St Louis Convention and Visitors Commission, 10 S Broadway, Suite 1000, St Louis 63102 (tel 800/916-0092), and the Kansas City Convention and Visitors Bureau, 1100 Main St, Suite 2550, Kansas City 64105 (tel 800/767-7700). Local visitors bureaus and chambers of commerce in many towns around the state provide detailed information for their area; see the *Missouri Travel Guide* for a list. Responses are generally prompt, but make your request at least a month before your planned departure.

DRIVING RULES AND REGULATIONS

Missouri's minimum driving age is 16. Driver and front-seat passengers are required to wear seat belts, and children under four years of age must be secured in an approved child safety seat. Helmets must be worn by motorcyclists.

You can make a right turn on red after stopping unless posted otherwise. Speed limits are enforced by radar and aircraft, and radar detection devices are legal in noncommercial vehicles. Don't carry an open container of alcohol in the car; periodic spot-checks for drunk drivers are conducted throughout the state, especially during holiday periods. For state-wide road conditions call 800/222-6400.

RENTING A CAR

You'll find all the major car rental firms have offices in Missouri. The minimum age ranges from 21 to 25; some companies may impose an additional charge for drivers between 21 to 24. A few locations limit where their cars may be driven outside Missouri; ask your rental office about restrictions.

- **Alamo** (tel 800/327-9633)
- **Avis** (tel 800/331-1212)
- **Budget** (tel 800/527-0700)
- **Dollar** (tel 800/421-6868)
- **General** (tel 800/327-7607)
- **Hertz** (tel 800/654-3131)
- **National** (tel 800/227-7368)
- **Thrifty** (tel 800/367-2277)

ESSENTIALS

Area Code: There are three area codes for Missouri. Eastern and central Missouri, which encompass St Louis, Hannibal, Cape Girardeau, Jefferson City, Columbia, and Osage Beach, use **314.** The code for northern and western Missouri, including Kansas City, St Joseph, and Sedalia, is **816.** Springfield, Branson, Joplin, and the rest of southwestern Missouri use **417.**

Emergencies: Calling 911 will link you to police, fire department, or ambulance services in the cities; small towns and rural areas may not be on the 911 system, so check a local directory. For highway emergencies call 800/525-5555.

Liquor Laws: You must be 21 years of age with proper identification to purchase or consume alcoholic beverages. Licensed food-serving establishments can sell liquor on Sunday.

Taxes: The state sales tax is 4.225%; city and county sales taxes could add another 2–3¾%. Expect total tax on hotel rooms to range from 6½% to as high as 14% in the big cities. Your tax bill on a rental car will vary between 6% and 7¼%, but airport locations may levy an additional access charge.

Time Zone: Missouri is in the central time zone, two hours ahead of the West Coast and one hour behind the East Coast.

Best of the State

WHAT TO SEE AND DO

Below is a general overview of some of the top sights and attractions in Missouri. To find out more detailed information, look under "Attractions" for individual cities in the listings portion of this book.

National Parks Eight units of southeastern Missouri's 1.5 million-acre **Mark Twain National Forest** provide a wide array of outdoor recreational opportunities. You can find unspoiled serenity in its seven wilderness areas or more action on miles of special trails set aside for ATVs and trail bikes. Camp or canoe in scenic splendor in the **Ozark National Scenic Riverways;** the protected area along the Current and Jacks Forks rivers has pristine forestland, abundant wildlife, and gushing natural springs.

State Parks Missouri's park system includes 79 state parks and unique historic sites. **Lake of the Ozarks State Park** is the centerpiece of the park system, with over 17,000 acres for camping, hiking, swimming, and boating on one of the largest man-made lakes in the world. Over 1,300 miles of shoreline and 200 resorts outside the park present a multitude of options for enjoying the lake. **Table Rock Lake State Park,** located in the scenic Ozarks, offers big-lake recreation and a great base camp for excursions into nearby Branson. The ice-age mastodon bones and human artifacts unearthed in the fossil beds of **Mastodon State Park** will appeal to the amateur paleontologist.

Natural Wonders The Ozark Highlands are home to over 5,000 caves, some of them works of natural art carved from limestone bedrock by underground streams and embellished with surreal calcite formations. Nearly two dozen caves are open to the public, the most spectacular including **Marvel Cave** near Branson, which sports a 500-foot waterfall; **Meramec Caverns** in Stanton, once a station on the Underground Railroad; **Fantastic Caverns** in Springfield, which can be toured in wheelchair-accessible motorized trams; and the beautiful "show" cavern at **Onondaga Cave State Park.**

Manmade Wonders   **Gateway Arch,** in **Jefferson National Expansion Memorial Park** along St Louis's refurbished riverfront, is the nation's tallest monument, breathtaking in the elegant simplicity of its 630-foot steel curve inscribed against the St Louis skyline. Interior passenger capsules will lift you to an enclosed observation platform at the arch's top for a unparalleled panorama of the city and its great rivers.

Parks & Zoos   **St Louis Zoological Park,** one of the country's best, houses its animals in naturalistic habitats, and offers a mini-train ride through the primate and big cat habitats that is the next best thing to being on safari. **Kansas City Zoo,** with a large collection of animals from around the world, is also worth a visit. The folks with the green thumbs at St Louis's **Missouri Botanical Gardens** display the impressive fruits of their labor, which includes the country's largest Japanese garden, a rainforest located under glass, and a unique scented garden for the visually impaired.

Historic Sites & Monuments   During its early history Missouri was the journey's end for some, and the start of the trail for others. Genteel **Ste Genevieve,** the first permanent French settlement in Missouri, retains its colonial flavor through quaint customs and beautifully preserved 18th and early 19th-century homes, including several excellent examples of French Creole architecture. **Arrow Rock State Historic District,** near Marshall, looks much as it did when wagon trains on the Santa Fe Trail stopped there to cross the Missouri River; 19th-century buildings on view include the courthouse, tavern, church, and home of pioneer artist George Caleb Bingham. The **Bethel German Colony** religious settlement in Bethel was short-lived, but nearly 30 original buildings from the mid-1800s have been preserved, including a working blacksmith shop.

Missouri's role in the Civil War may have begun at the Old Courthouse in St Louis, the setting for the historic *Dred Scott* case, which now houses a vintage photographic collection on early St Louis. **Wilson's Creek National Battlefield** near Springfield, one of many battle sites around the state, commemorates the first major battle west of the Mississippi.

Two of Missouri's most famous citizens are memorialized at the **George Washington Carver National Monument** near Joplin, which preserves the renowned African-American agronomist's home and chronicles his life and work, and the **Harry S Truman National Historic Site** in Independence, the former President's lovely Victorian home and summer White House. If the infamous also piques your interest, check out the **Jesse James Birthplace** in Kearney, the **James Home** in St Joseph, where the outlaw met his Maker, and the **Jesse James Bank Museum** in Liberty, site of the first bank robbery in US history.

Museums   It's only natural St Louis would be home to several good historical museums highlighting the region's role as the gateway to the West. The **History Museum at Missouri Historical Society** contains 15 galleries highlighting St Louis's history, including a section devoted to the 1904 World's Fair. The **Museum of Westward Expansion,** located beneath the Gateway Arch, screens an audiovisual history of western settlement. The **National Museum of Transport** illustrates Missouri's contribution to transportation and has the world's largest collection of locomotives, plus most other types of vehicular transport used in the last 200 years. On the other side of the state, **Kansas City Museum,** housed in a grand mansion with its own planetarium, spotlights that region's history. The short but glorious history of the Pony Express and its daredevil riders is explored in St Joseph at the **Pony Express National Memorial.**

For a look at memorable moments and important people from the 20th century, try the **Liberty Memorial** in Kansas City, both a monument and the only US museum dedicated to World War I. The **Harry S Truman Library and Museum** in Independence houses millions of documents and fascinating artifacts and memorabilia from the Truman presidency, including material on the development of the atomic bomb. The **Winston Churchill Memorial Library,** which displays many of Churchill's papers, paintings and memorabilia, is housed in a London church that was transported stone by stone and rebuilt on Westminster College campus in Fulton, the site of Churchill's famous 1946 "Iron Curtain" speech.

Missouri is blessed with two top-notch art museums. The **Nelson-Atkins Museum** in Kansas City is acclaimed for its Asian art collection, and the **St Louis Art Museum,** housed in the Fine Arts Palace from the 1904 World's Fair, features a world-class collections of pre-Columbian artworks and German expressionism.

Family Favorites Several amusement parks around the state are tailor-made for high-energy family fun. The huge theme park **Six Flags over Mid-America,** south of St Louis, has over 100 rides, including a giant Ferris wheel and roller coaster, plus other attractions and special events. In Kansas City, **World of Fun's** Timber Wolf ranks among the world's great wooden roller coasters. You can immerse yourself in Branson's wet and wild **White Water** park, or combine thrills with a little learning at nearby **Silver Dollar City,** a re-created 19th-century Ozark mountain village with rides, pioneer craft demonstrations, hoedowns, and festivals.

Mark Twain fans won't want to miss Hannibal, the sleepy town that has made a career of preserving the world of Tom Sawyer and Huckleberry Finn. Visit the **Mark Twain Boyhood Home & Museum, Mark Twain Cave, Becky Thatcher House,** and other places that inspired Samuel Clemens's writings about life along the Mississippi in the early 1800s. The enormous **St Louis Science Center** offers marvelous hands-on experiences in natural history, science and medicine, and also boasts a planetarium and IMAX theater. The **Toy and Miniature Museum** in Kansas City and **Magic House Children's Museum** in St Louis are other good bets.

Riverboat Excursions Several riverboats, including replicas of old-time paddle-wheelers, ply the Missouri and Mississippi Rivers. You might consider a sightseeing excursion, or perhaps a romantic dining and dancing cruise. Riverboats are docked in St Louis, Hannibal, St Charles, Lake Ozark, and other towns.

Music Shows Whether Nashville agrees or not, little Branson is now purported to be the "Country Music Capital of the World." Sporting more than three dozen glittering theaters and over 50,000 seats, live performance venues feature big names in country and a respectable smattering of pop, rock n' roll, bluegrass, gospel, and jazz.

Winery & Brewery Tours Missouri's thriving wine industry has its roots in the winemaking tradition of early German immigrants. Many wineries conduct tours and tastings, some in historic and lovely old buildings; you'll find several in the Hermann and Augusta areas and others sprinkled throughout the Ozarks and around Kansas City. Another German legacy as well as the world's largest brewery, St Louis's Anheuser-Busch offers tours of its brewhouse, packaging plant, and the stables of those famous Clydesdales.

Antique Shopping Thanks in part to its historic role as a commercial hub, Missouri has accumulated a treasure trove of vintage furniture, tools and implements, Civil War memorabilia, and other booty of interest to the serious or weekend collector. The Ozark region, St Louis, and Kansas City have the highest concentration of shops, but many antiques malls and stores throughout the state also promise happy hunting.

EVENTS AND FESTIVALS

St Louis and Eastern Missouri

- **Riverfest,** Cape Girardeau. Entertainment, craft demonstrations, river excursions, and more. Second weekend in June. Call 573/335-1388.
- **Fair St Louis,** St Louis at Jefferson National Expansion Memorial. Independence Day extravaganza. Fourth of July weekend. Call 314/434-3434.
- **National Tom Sawyer Days,** Hannibal in Historic District. National Fence Painting Championship, frog jumping competition, and more. First week in July. Call 573/221-2477.
- **Jour de Fete,** Ste Genevieve Historic District. Historic home tours, arts and crafts. Second weekend in August. Call 573/883-7097.
- **Great Forest Park Balloon Race,** St Louis at Forest Park. Third weekend in September. Call 314/821-6724.
- **Oktoberfest,** Hermann at various wineries. Every weekend in October. Call 573/486-2744.

Kansas City and Western Missouri

- **St Patrick's Day Parade,** Kansas City downtown. One of the largest in the state, with day-long festivities. March 17. Call 816/221-5242.
- **Scott Joplin Ragtime Festival,** Sedalia downtown. Concerts, grand ball, and other events. First week in June. Call 816/826-2271.
- **Missouri State Fair,** Sedalia at Missouri State Fairgrounds. Second half of August. Call 816/530-5600.
- **18th & Vine Heritage Festival,** Kansas City at 18th and Vine Sts. Blues and jazz music. Last weekend in August. Call 816/474-1080.
- **American Royal Livestock,** Horse Show and Rodeo, Kansas City at American Royal Center. First two weeks in November. Call 816/221-9800.

SPRINGFIELD AND SOUTHERN MISSOURI

- **Lake of the Ozarks Dogwood Music Festival,** Camdenton. Music, food, arts and crafts, and carnival amid dogwoods in bloom. Third weekend in April. Call 800/769-1004.
- **Ozark Empire Fair,** Springfield at Fairgrounds. Livestock competition, exhibits, carnival, music. First week in August. Call 417/833-2660.
- **National Crafts Festival,** Branson at Silver Dollar City. Throughout October. Call 417/338-2611.

SPECTATOR SPORTS

Baseball The American League **Kansas City Royals** (tel 816/921-8000) play at Ewing M Kauffman Stadium Truman Sports Complex. You can catch the National League **St Louis Cardinals** (tel 314/421-3060) at Busch Stadium in St Louis.

Basketball You can see exciting collegiate basketball played by the **St Louis University Billikens** (tel 314/622-5435) in St Louis, the **University of Missouri Tigers** (tel 573/882-2386) in Columbia, and the **Southwest Missouri State University Bears** (tel 417/836-7678) in Springfield.

Football Missouri now serves up two ways to catch NFL football action: the **Kansas City Chiefs** (tel 816/924-9400) play at Arrowhead Stadium in Kansas City's Truman Sports Complex, and the **St Louis Rams** (tel 800/847-7267) have moved from California to the Dome at America's Center in St Louis.

Hockey The **St Louis Blues** (tel 314/291-7600) play NHL ice hockey at Kiel Center in St Louis. The **Kansas City Blades** (tel 816/842-1063) of the International Hockey League are affiliated with the NHL San Jose Sharks and can be seen at Kemper Arena in Kansas City. The **St Louis Vipers** (tel 314/622-5435) offer up professional roller hockey at Kiel Center in St Louis.

Horse & Greyhound Racing Watch thoroughbred racing (March through October) and harness racing (January through March) just 10 minutes from St Louis at **Fairmount Park Race Track** (tel 618/345-4300) in Collinsville, Illinois. In the Kansas City area, catch thoroughbred and quarter horse racing from August to October and year-round greyhound racing at **The Woodlands** (913/299-9797) in Kansas City, Kansas.

Soccer You can watch professional indoor soccer with the **St Louis Ambush** (tel 314/622-5435) at Kiel Center in St Louis, and the **Kansas City Attack** (tel 816/474-2255) at Kemper Arena in Kansas City.

ACTIVITIES A TO Z

Boating & Watersports Flood control projects around the state have created 14 lakes that are popular playgrounds for boating, swimming, and a host of other watersports. Stockton Lake is a favorite for sailing, Table Rock Lake draws scuba enthusiasts, and giants Truman Lake and Lake of the Ozarks are dotted with resorts and facilities offering a full spectrum of water fun.

Camping Good campsites abound in Missouri, especially in the wooded Ozarks. The Mark Twain National Forest, numerous state parks, and other public areas, plus many private campgrounds, all offer possibilities. Call the Department of Natural Resources (tel 800/334-6946) about camping on state lands; other campgrounds are listed in the *Missouri Getaway Travel Guide,* available from the Missouri Division of Tourism, Truman State Office Bldg, Box 1055, Jefferson City 65102 (tel 800/877-1234).

Canoeing Southern Missouri is laced with dozens of navigable rivers and creeks, some among the finest in the country and operable year-round; the Current and Jacks Fork Rivers in the Ozark National Scenic Riverways are two of the top spots. Guides and outfitters are also plentiful; see the listings in the *Missouri Getaway Travel Guide.* Call or write the Missouri Division of Tourism, Truman State Office Bldg, Box 1055, Jefferson City 65102 (tel 800/877-1234).

Fishing With all those lakes and streams, it's no wonder fishing is a Missouri passion. Many lakes have great bass, catfish, and crappie fishing, including top-rated Truman Lake with its 9,000 acres of flooded standing timber. The cold waters of Lake Taneycomo serve up rainbow and brown trout, while the Current, Black, James, and other Ozark rivers also provide exciting game fishing. Call the Missouri Department of Conservation (tel 573/751-4115) for more details, season dates, and permit costs.

Hiking The state's premier trail is the Katy Trail, which threads its way along the former Missouri-Kansas-Texas Railroad right-of-way, blending exercise, nature, history, and beautiful Missouri River views. Two long segments totalling 130 miles are now open, with trailheads in St Charles and Jefferson City. Several sections of the Ozark Trail, which meanders from St Louis through the Ozarks into Arkansas, are now open for hiking and backpacking; some sections also permit equestrian and mountain bike traffic. Call the Missouri Department of Natural Resources (tel 800/334-6946) for maps and status of both trails.

Horseback Riding The pretty Ozarks have many miles of equestrian trails. Lope along with a guide for a leisurely day ride, or bunk down for a week at a ranch and play out your cowboy fantasies; several offer cattle drives, team penning, and roping, or overnight pack trips. For more information contact Coldwater Ranch (tel 573/226-3723) or Cross Country Trail Ride (tel 573/226-3492), both in Eminence, or Golden Hills Trail Rides (tel 800/874-1157) in Raymondville.

Hunting Over two million acres of Missouri public lands are open to hunters, ensuring lots of opportunities for bagging deer and small game. The three National Wildlife Refuges—Swan, Squaw Creek, and Mingo—are also open for waterfowl hunting on a controlled basis. Call the Missouri Department of Conservation (tel 573/751-4115) for information on season dates and licenses.

Riverboat Gaming Legalized riverboat gambling (no minors allowed) can be found along the Mississippi and Missouri Rivers. Dockside casinos and gaming cruises typically offer video and table games, slot machines, live entertainment and dining. Boarding times are regulated and entry is on a first-come, first-served basis. Casinos include the President Casino on the Admiral (tel 800/772-3647) in St Louis, Casino St Charles (tel 800/325-7777) in St Charles, and St Joe Frontier Casino (tel 800/888-2946) in St Joseph.

SELECTED PARKS & RECREATION AREAS

- **Mark Twain National Forest,** southern Missouri, 401 Fairgrounds Rd, Rolla 65401 (tel 573/364-4621)
- **Ozark National Scenic Riverways,** southeastern Missouri, PO Box 490, Van Buren 63965 (tel 573/323-4236)
- **Sam A. Baker,** 3 mi N of Patterson, RFD 1, Box 114, Patterson 63956 (tel 573/856-4411)
- **Bennett Spring,** 12 mi W of Lebanon, 26250 Hwy 64A, Lebanon 65536 (tel 417/532-4338)
- **Cuivre River,** 3 mi E of Troy, Rte 1, Box 25, Troy 63379 (tel 314/528-7247)
- **Hawn,** 14 mi SW of Ste Genevieve, 12096 Park Dr, Ste Genevieve 63670 (tel 573/883-3603)
- **Johnson's Shut-Ins,** 8 mi N of Lesterville, HC Rte 1, Box 126, Middlebrook 63656 (tel 573/546-2450)
- **Knob Noster,** 2 mi S of Knob Noster, 873 SE 10, Knob Noster 65336 (tel 816/563-2463)
- **Lake of the Ozarks,** off Hwy 42 near Osage Beach, PO Box 170, Kaiser 65047 (tel 573/348-2694)
- **Long Branch,** 2 mi W of Macon, 28615 Visitor Center Rd, Macon 63552 (tel 816/773-5229)
- **Mark Twain,** ½ mi S of Florida, RR 1, Box 53, Stoutsville 65283 (tel 573/565-3440)
- **Mastodon,** 20 mi S of St Louis off I-55, 1551 Seckman Rd, Imperial 63052 (tel 314/464-2976)
- **Meramec,** 4 mi E of Sullivan, 2800 S Hwy 185, Sullivan 63080 (tel 573/468-6072)
- **Onondaga Cave,** 7 mi SE of I-44 Leasburg exit, Rte 1, Box 115, Leasburg 65535 (tel 573/245-6576)
- **Pershing,** 2 mi SW of Laclede, PO Box 133, Laclede 64651 (tel 816/963-2299)
- **Roaring River,** 7 mi S of Cassville, Rte 2, Box 2530, Cassville 65625 (tel 417/847-2539)
- **St Joe,** 3 mi S of Flat River, 2800 Pimville Rd, Park Hills 63601 (tel 573/431-1069)
- **Stockton,** 8 mi SE of Stockton, Rte 1, Box 1715, Dadeville 65635 (tel 417/276-4259)
- **Table Rock,** 7 mi SW of Branson, 5272 Hwy 165, Branson 65616 (tel 417/334-4704)
- **Thousand Hills,** 4 mi W of Kirksville, Rte 3, Kirksville 63501 (tel 816/665-6995)
- **Trail of Tears,** 10 mi N of Cape Girardeau, 429 Moccasin Springs, Jackson 63755 (tel 573/334-1711)
- **Washington,** 9 mi S of Desoto, Rte 2, Box 450, DeSoto 63020 (tel 314/586-2995)
- **Watkins Mill,** 6 mi E of Kearney, 26600 Park Road N, Lawson 64062 (tel 816/296-3387)

Driving the State

MISSISSIPPI RIVER VALLEY

Start	Hannibal
Finish	Ste Genevieve
Distance	Approximately 188 miles
Time	3–4 days
Highlights	Scenic drives along the mighty Mississippi River; historic river towns; the Gateway Arch, Anheuser-Busch Brewery, Missouri Botanical Garden, and other major attractions of St Louis; antique and craft shops; restored homes

The Mississippi River, the most well-known and widely used river in the United States, is a constant and powerful backdrop to this driving tour, which begins fittingly enough in Hannibal, the boyhood hometown of Mark Twain immortalized in *The Adventures of Tom Sawyer* and *The Adventures of Huckleberry Finn*. Following the winding contours of the fertile river valley, you'll then head south, stopping off in the picture-perfect historic town of St Charles. Next is St Louis, the metropolitan heart of Missouri and a center for excellent family-oriented attractions. The tour ends south of St Louis in Ste Genevieve, the first white settlement on the west bank of the Mississippi.

For additional information on lodgings, restaurants, and attractions, refer to specific cities in the listings portion of this book.

US 36, US 61, and MO 79 all provide easy access to:

1. **Hannibal,** located about 120 miles north of St Louis on the banks of the mighty Mississippi. Had Mark Twain not grown up here, Hannibal would undoubtedly be just another sleepy river town, but as it is about a quarter of a million visitors arrive annually to pay tribute to one of America's greatest authors and humorists. Hannibal capitalizes on its favorite son by conjuring up storybook attractions and naming everything from motels to restaurants after Twain, who no doubt would have been amused. And yet Hannibal is not nearly the tourist trap it could be—it's simply not sophisticated enough for that. A great family destination, it remains remarkably and refreshingly small-town, friendly, charming, and unassuming, and probably not much different from the days when the young Samuel Clemens restlessly roamed its streets.

After stopping off at the **Hannibal Visitor's Bureau,** 505 N Broadway (tel 573/221-2477), it's just a minute's walk to Hannibal's foremost attrac-

tion, the **Mark Twain Boyhood Home and Museum,** 208 Hill St. Next door is the small white clapboard home occupied by the Clemens family from 1844 to 1853, while across the street is the law office of Twain's father. Both figure prominently in *Tom Sawyer*, which Twain patterned after his boyhood years. The museum contains memorabilia of the Clemens family (including one of Twain's trademark white jackets), as well as first editions of Twain's works.

Across the street are the **Becky Thatcher House and Bookshop,** home of Twain's childhood sweetheart Laura Hawkins and the role model for Becky Thatcher, and the **Haunted House on Hill Street,** a quirky mix of spook-house and wax museum, with 27 life-size figures representing the Clemens family and fictitious characters from Twain's books. From May through October, one-hour sightseeing cruises and two-hour dinner cruises narrated with legends, lore, and facts about the river are launched daily aboard —what else– the *Mark Twain*.

Hannibal also has a number of fine older homes, but none match the grandeur of **Rockcliff Mansion,** 1000 Bird St, the home of lumber magnate John Cruikshank, completed in 1900 and perched above the city. In a departure from the earlier Victorian style, this 30-room house was decorated in art nouveau and equipped with all the modern conveniences of the day.

Evening diversions include the **Mark Twain Outdoor Theatre,** a two-hour presentation of Hannibal in the 1840s with episodes taken from *Tom Sawyer* and other Twain books, and the **Molly Brown Dinner Theatre,** named after Hannibal's other famous personality and featuring a musical revue based on Hannibal's history and the Mississippi River.

For those who plan to stay overnight in Hannibal, the best place to experience its small-town atmosphere is at one of the following bed-and-breakfasts, all located in historic homes. **Garth Woodside Mansion** (tel 573/221-2789), situated on 39 rolling acres just south of Hannibal, is the most elegant, featuring Victorian furnishings, a wrap-around veranda, rooms with private bath, and even the Victorian bed where Mark Twain is reputed to have slept while visiting the original owners. (Note that this place accepts adults only.) The moderately priced **Queen Anne's Grace,** 313 N 5th St (tel 573/248-0756), is an attractive 1880s Queen

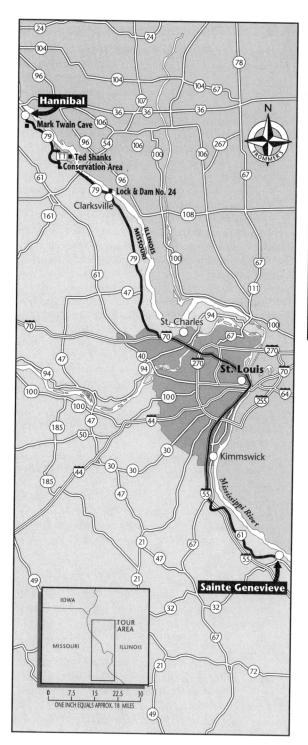

5th St (tel 573/221-0445 or 800/874-5661), built in 1858 in Italianate style by a former mayor and offering seven moderately priced rooms, all with private bath.

Take a Break

Just a stone's throw from Twain's boyhood home, the **Mark Twain Dinette and Family Restaurant,** 3rd and Hill Sts (tel 573/221-5511), has changed little since its 1942 opening. It is the epitome of a small-town restaurant, with informal and friendly service and even drive-in service out back. Specialties include tenderloins, burgers, fried chicken, catfish from the Mississippi, and onion rings. Most meals cost $4 to $7. For more sophisticated dining you might try the **Missouri Territory Steakhouse,** 600 Broadway (tel 573/248-1440), which occupies the first floor of an impressive limestone building dating from 1888. The steaks come in a variety of sizes and cuts, and are priced at $10 to $18.

Depart Hannibal by heading south on MO 79 (3rd St). After 1½ miles, to your right will be the:

2. **Mark Twain Cave,** discovered in 1819. Sam Clemens played here as a young boy and later used it in *Tom Sawyer* and *Huckleberry Finn* as the cave containing buried treasure where Tom and Becky were lost and where Injun Joe met his demise. One-hour guided tours covering less than a mile along smooth walkways are fun and informative. Across the highway is **Sawyer's Creek,** a family amusement center; its Riverview Cafe offers great views of the Mississippi, especially from a covered outdoor deck.

Continue south on MO 79, dubbed the Great River Road. It hugs the curves of the Mississippi and adjacent railroad tracks, winding past limestone bluffs and riots of wild flowers in summer and glorious changing leaves in autumn. If you're a birdwatcher, turn left after about 16 miles onto country road TT, which will bring you to the:

3. **Ted Shanks Conservation Area,** 6,600 acres of bottom wetlands, marsh, and lakes bordering six miles of the Mississippi. Although hunting, camping, fishing, and hiking are allowed, birding is the main activity, especially during spring and fall migrations. A room at the visitor's center is stocked with binoculars; if you're lucky you might see bald eagles, warblers, American bitterns, king rails, and various waterfowl.

After another 23 miles south on MO 79, which passes through the tiny town of Louisiana and its two-block Victorian downtown, you'll come to:

Anne–style home just a few blocks from Hannibal's main attractions; it boasts ornate woodwork inside and out. Not far away is the **5th St Mansion,** 213 S

4. Clarksville, home to a thriving population of 480. Established in 1815, Clarksville is an attractive village of 19th-century architecture that is home to several shops selling antiques, collectibles, custom Shaker furniture, primitives, and other local crafts. To your right as you enter town is the **Skylift,** which will take you to a bluff 670 feet above the river for an unparalleled view of the surrounding countryside—on clear days you can see 800 square miles. Next to the hilltop observation tower are empty frontier-style wooden buildings. Constructed during a wave of entrepreneurial optimism, they are now dusty and cobwebbed from neglect, giving the whole bluff an eerie, ghost town–like atmosphere. In January it's a premier spot for eagle watching.

The other prominent attraction here is the Mississippi's **lock and dam No 24,** managed by the US Army Corps of Engineers, which can be toured if enough personnel are on duty. (You can straddle two states at once along the dam in the middle of the river.)

From Clarksville, the river valley flattens into farmland and open pastures dotted by old farmhouses, silos, barns, churches, and cemeteries. After approximately 45 miles, you'll reach I-70, where you should head east about 9 miles to exit 229, where 5th St N will take you to the historic heart of:

5. St Charles, one of the prettiest small towns in Missouri. It was established in 1769 as a fur-trading post before becoming a French settlement on the banks of the Missouri River. Lewis and Clark spent five days here in 1804 preparing for their historic explorations of the Louisiana Territory. When Missouri became the 24th state in 1821, St Charles served as the temporary seat of government while the city of Jefferson was being built in the center of the state. The **First State Capitol of Missouri,** located at 200–216 S Main St, a federal-style brick building, looks pretty much as it did 170 years ago, with a general store, carpenter shop, and private residence on the ground floor, and senate and house chambers on the second. It is open for tours. More of St Charles's history is presented at the **Lewis & Clark Center,** 701 Riverside Dr, which describes the famous expedition with dioramas and displays.

One of the most enjoyable things to do in St Charles is to stroll several blocks along S Main St, a brick road lined with quaint two-story brick and stone buildings, most dating from about 1799 to 1860 and constructed in French colonial and federal styles. If you like antiques, be sure to drive to Frenchtown, the original French settlement, with about 20 antique shops spread along the 800–1700 blocks of N 2nd St. There's also a riverboat casino moored close to the historic district.

Take a Break

Lewis and Clark's, 217 S Main St (tel 314/947-3334), is a family restaurant located across the street from the First State Capitol. Upstairs, an atrium skylight bathes the dining area in a white glow, while the third-floor balcony overlooks Main St. Hamburgers, sandwiches, steaks, chicken, pasta, soups, salads, and Mexican fare are featured on the extensive menu, with entrees priced at $5 to $17. For casual dining, snacks, or drinks, there's no better place than **Winery of the Little Hills,** 501 S Main St (tel 314/946-9339), which specializes in Missouri wines, sausages, and cheeses and offers outdoor patio seating.

Back on I-70 heading east, you'll soon find yourself in:

6. St Louis, one of the Mississippi River's largest cities, with a population of almost 400,000. Founded by French fur traders in 1764 and named after King Louis IX of France, St Louis gained national prominence as a major river port following the Louisiana Purchase. Today, St Louis celebrates its river heritage and its role as a gateway to the west with its most famous landmark, the **Gateway Arch,** located downtown just off I-70 on the banks of the Mississippi. America's tallest monument, this graceful rainbow of shining steel soars 630 feet; two small trams transport visitors to an observation room at the top affording panoramic views to the east and west. Underneath the Arch is the **Museum of Westward Expansion,** which traces the westward journey of Lewis and Clark and of the pioneers, cowboys, and soldiers who followed. Just below the Gateway Arch on the banks of the Mississippi are three replica paddlewheelers, the *Huck Finn, Tom Sawyer,* and *Becky Thatcher,* which offer one-hour narrated cruises daily, as well as dinner cruises with live bands. There are also two casino boats moored on the riverfront.

There are enough attractions in St Louis to keep the whole family entertained for a week. Foremost among them is **Union Station,** located just west of downtown at 18th and Market Sts. First opened as a passenger rail terminal in 1894 and now a shopping and entertainment complex, it boasts more than 70 specialty shops, more than two dozen food and drink outlets, a comedy club, a hotel, and even a lake with paddleboats.

Forest Park, located about 10 minutes farther west on I-64, is a jewel of a park that is home to several fine attractions: the excellent St Louis Art Museum, which is situated in the Fine Arts Palace of the St Louis 1904 World's Fair and houses an art collection spanning the ages; the top-rated St Louis Science Center, offering more than 600 exhibits ranging from dinosaurs and aviation to medicine and the human body; and the St Louis Zoo.

The **Missouri Botanical Garden,** 4344 Shaw Blvd, is the nation's oldest botanical garden (1859). Highlights of this 79-acre site include rose, iris, and azalea/rhododendron gardens, a 14-acre Japanese garden, a scented garden, the world's first geodesic-domed greenhouse (which contains a rain forest), and sculpture by Henry Moore and Carl Milles. The **Anheuser-Busch Brewery,** located just a few minutes' drive south of downtown off I-50 at the Arsenal St exit, offers free 1¼-hour tours of the brewing process, as well as visits to the famed Clydesdale stables. Anheuser-Busch owns and operates another great St Louis attraction, **Grant's Farm,** 10501 Gravois Rd (tel 314/843-1700). Open free to the public, the 280-acre estate features a log cabin once inhabited by Ulysses S Grant; a game preserve where buffalo, antelope, zebra, and other exotic creatures roam free; a beer garden with complimentary samples of beer, a stable of Clydesdale horses, and a collection of horse-drawn carriages and coaches. Advance reservations required.

In St Louis, two historic, and expensive, downtown hotels include the **Hotel Majestic,** 1019 Pine St (tel 314/436-2355 or 800/451-2355), a small establishment with old-world European charm built in 1913 in Renaissance revival style, and popular with both businesspeople and celebrities; and **DoubleTree Suite Hotel,** 806 St Charles St (tel 314/421-2500 or toll free 800/222-8733), built in 1925

Take a Break

St Louis's finest and most famous restaurant is **Tony's,** downtown at 410 Market St (tel 314/231-7007), in operation since 1949 and arguably one of the best Italian restaurants in the country. The food is sublime, from the lobster Albanello and four-inch veal chops to fresh seafood flown in daily and pasta dishes cooked to order. Reservations for meals, which generally run more than $45 per person, are required, and men must wear jackets. For casual Italian dining there's the **Old Spaghetti Factory** at 727 N 1st St in Laclede's Landing (tel 314/621-0276). This family restaurant is filled with antiques and is housed in the basement of a beautiful six-story, cast-iron and brick warehouse. More than a dozen selections of spaghetti and other pasta are available, all of which come with salad, bread, a drink, and ice cream and cost $4.50 to $8.

but boasting updated and modern spacious rooms and suites. For those on a budget, the **Drury Inn Union Station,** just down the street from Union Station at 201 S 20th St (tel 314/231-3900 or toll free 800/325-8300), offers moderately priced, clean rooms in a lovingly restored 1907 hotel that was originally built to serve transient railroad workers. Depart St Louis via I-55 going south. Approximately 25 miles from downtown St Louis is exit 186 and County Rd K, which will take you to the riverside hamlet of:

7. **Kimmswick,** founded and settled by Germans in the mid-1800s. A dreamy, low-key, and increasingly popular destination for St Louis day-trippers, it consists of just a few streets dotted with homes and free-standing buildings, many dating from the 1880s and now housing antiques and craft shops. Well worth the stop, and a good place to get out of your car and stretch your legs.

Return to I-55 and continue south another 12 miles or so to exit 170, where you can then take the more scenic and enjoyable two-lane MO 61 south another 25 miles to:

8. **Ste Genevieve.** Founded in the 1730s, Ste Genevieve was the first settlement on the west bank of the Mississippi. It boasts more 18th-century French Creole buildings than any other city in North America. Market St will take you into the heart of its historic district. A good first stop is the **Great River Road Interpretive Center,** located on the corner of Market and S Main Sts, which offers information about Ste Genevieve as well as exhibits on the town's history.

Several of the historic buildings can be toured. The oldest of these is the **Bolduc House,** 125 S Main, built in 1770 as a one-room cabin and moved (due to floods) to its present site in 1784, when another room and the porch were added. It's one of the finest examples of French Creole architecture, constructed in a style known as *poteaux sur sole* (in which logs are placed vertically on a stone foundation and then packed together with a mixture of clay and chopped straw) and furnished with authentic 18th-century French colonial pieces. The next oldest building is the **Maison Guibourd-Valle,** 4th and Merchant Sts, built around 1784 by a pioneer French settler and best known architecturally for its attic with Norman truss and hand-hewn oak beams. Filled with French antiques, it's the most elaborately furnished house open to the public. Finally, there is the restored **Felix Valle House,** Merchant and 2nd Sts, built in 1818 in federal-style of native limestone—a marked departure from the wooden log structures of the French colonial period.

Missouri Listings

Blue Springs

Named for a spring that flows into a tributary of the Blue River, this small city just off I-70 acts as the eastern gateway to the Kansas City metro area's suburban attractions. A state park and nature center feature hiking trails and wildlife viewing areas. **Information:** Blue Springs Chamber of Commerce, 1000 SW Main, Blue Springs, 64015 (tel 816/229-8558).

MOTEL

≣≣ Ramada Inn
1110 N Seven Hwy, 64014; tel 816/229-6363 or toll free 800/2-RAMADA; fax 816/228-7299. Just off I-70. Recommended for short stay for any traveler. Small but comfortable lobby with sofas, chairs, TV. **Rooms:** 137 rms and stes. CI 3pm/CO noon. Nonsmoking rms avail. **Amenities:** A/C, satel TV w/movies. **Services:** Facilities: 1 bar (w/entertainment), games rm, washer/dryer. **Rates (CP):** Peak (June–Aug) $45–$60 S or D; $75–$115 ste. Extra person $5. Children under age 18 stay free. Lower rates off-season. Parking: Outdoor, free. Rates increase for sporting events. Weekend super saver rates avail. AE, CB, DC, DISC, MC, V.

Branson

The self-proclaimed "Live Entertainment Capital" of America, Branson boasts more than 30 music theaters that cater to local and world-famous country and pop music talent. Founded in 1882 by Reuben Branson, this small town now entertains some 6 million visitors annually, who are also drawn to the area's abundant outdoor recreational opportunities. **Information:** Branson/Lakes Area Chamber of Commerce, PO Box 1897, Branson, 65615-1897 (tel 417/334-4136).

HOTELS

≣≣ Best Western Music Capital Inn
3527 Shepherd of the Hills Expwy, 65616; tel 417/334-8378 or toll free 800/528-1234; fax 417/334-8855. Well-appointed rooms. Open and airy lobby visible from the first two floors is well decorated with a burgundy and blue color scheme and a large gold chandelier. **Rooms:** 93 rms and stes. CI open/CO 11am. Nonsmoking rms avail. **Amenities:** A/C, cable TV w/movies. Some units w/whirlpools. **Services:** Golf can be arranged. **Facilities:** Games rm, sauna, whirlpool, washer/dryer. **Rates (CP):** Peak (Sept–Oct) $73 S; $77 D; $89–$125 ste. Extra person $4. Children under age 13 stay free. Lower rates off-season. Parking: Outdoor, free. Closed Jan–Mar. AE, CB, DC, DISC, JCB, MC, V.

≣≣ Branson Towers Hotel
236 Shepherd of the Hills Expwy, 65616; tel 417/336-4500 or toll free 800/683-1122; fax 417/334-6838. MO 248 exit off US 65, 4 mi W to Shepherd of the Hills Expwy, left. Located near Anita Bryant's theater, this hotel has an antebellum exterior with large white pillars and a spacious lobby decorated in a simple country motif with a large wooden staircase as its focal point. **Rooms:** 210 rms and stes. CI 3pm/CO 11am. Nonsmoking rms avail. Very pink rooms resemble standard chain accommodations. **Amenities:** A/C, cable TV w/movies. Some units w/fireplaces. **Services:** Social director. **Facilities:** 1 restaurant, games rm, whirlpool, washer/dryer. **Rates (CP):** Peak (May/Sept–Nov) $55–$80 S or D; $88–$109 ste. Extra person $5. Children under age 13 stay free. Lower rates off-season. Parking: Outdoor, free. AE, CB, DC, DISC, EC, JCB, MC, V.

≣≣ Cascades Inn
3226 Shepherd of the Hills Expwy, 65616; tel 417/335-8424 or toll free 800/588-8424; fax 417/334-1927. Comfortable lobby has many plants and a fountain. Conveniently located near music theaters. **Rooms:** 159 rms and stes. CI 3pm/CO 11am. Nonsmoking rms avail. Pink and teal color scheme, light wood economy furniture. Floral design of bedspreads is a bit garish. **Amenities:** A/C, cable TV w/movies. Some units w/whirlpools. **Services:** **Facilities:** Games rm, sauna, steam rm, whirlpool, washer/dryer. Indoor pool area has exceptionally open and airy feel, with floor-to-ceiling arched windows. **Rates (CP):** Peak (Sept–Oct) $60–$80 S or D; $70–$90 ste. Extra person $5. Children under

age 19 stay free. Lower rates off-season. Parking: Outdoor, free. Packages include honeymoon, Valentine's Day, and three-day Christmas specials. AE, CB, DC, DISC, MC, V.

The Crowne Plaza

120 S Wildwood Dr, 65616; tel 417/335-5767 or toll free 800/428-3386; fax 417/335-7979. Brand-new nine-story hotel features spacious lobby with dark marble pillars, lush potted plants, and sofas and chairs. **Rooms:** 500 rms and stes. Executive level. CI 3pm/CO 11am. Nonsmoking rms avail. Contemporary rooms with navy decor. **Amenities:** 🛎 🗄 📺 🍴 A/C, dataport. Some units w/minibars, some w/terraces, some w/whirlpools. **Services:** ✕ 🔑 🛅 🔔 Masseur. More than 100 videos available for rent. Executive level offers complimentary continental breakfast, cocktails, hors d'oeuvres, and turndown service. **Facilities:** 🏊 🚣 500 🕭 1 restaurant, 2 bars, games rm, sauna, whirlpool, beauty salon. **Rates:** Peak (Sept–Oct) $65–$95 S or D; $150–$300 ste. Extra person $10. Children under age 20 stay free. Lower rates off-season. Parking: Outdoor, free. Special packages include bed-and-breakfast, honeymoon, golf, and music shows. AE, CB, DC, DISC, EC, JCB, MC, V.

Gazebo Inn

2424 MO 76 W, 65616; tel 417/335-3826 or toll free 800/873-7990; fax 417/335-3889. Attractive hotel has appearance of quaint Victorian cottage, with pink siding, white railing, and turret. Near many music theaters. **Rooms:** 73 rms, stes, and effic. CI 2pm/CO 11am. No smoking. Floral pink and green decor with wood armoires for TVs and carved wooden headboards. **Amenities:** 🛎 A/C, cable TV. Some units w/terraces, some w/whirlpools. **Services:** 🍽 🔔 Babysitting. **Facilities:** 🏊 🕭 **Rates (CP):** Peak (Apr–Dec) $63 S or D; $83–$103 ste; $133 effic. Children under age 18 stay free. Lower rates off-season. Parking: Outdoor, free. AE, DISC, MC, V.

Home Suite Home

3706 W MO 76, 65616; tel 417/335-3233; fax 417/335-3922. Offers well-appointed suites in a building featuring a unique geometrical design and surrounded by many shade trees. **Rooms:** 40 rms and stes. CI 1pm/CO 11am. Nonsmoking rms avail. **Amenities:** 🛎 A/C, cable TV. Some units w/fireplaces, some w/whirlpools. **Services:** 🔔 **Facilities:** 🏊 🚣 50 Whirlpool, washer/dryer. **Rates (CP):** $45–$55 S or D; $65–$115 ste. Children under age 17 stay free. Parking: Outdoor, free. Closed Jan–Feb. AE, DISC, MC, V.

Lighthouse Inn

2375 Green Mountain Dr, 65616; tel 417/336-6161 or toll free 800/237-5444; fax 417/336-2449. 1 block S of MO 76. Manicured lawn accented with flowers and lobby with high ceilings, fans, and potted plants. Patio off lobby. **Rooms:** 91 rms. CI 3pm/CO 11am. Nonsmoking rms avail. **Amenities:** 🛎 📺 A/C, cable TV. Some units w/whirlpools. **Services:** 🔔 🔔 **Facilities:** 🏊 🕭 Whirlpool. **Rates (CP):** Peak (Apr–Oct)

$67–$77 S or D. Extra person $2. Children under age 18 stay free. Lower rates off-season. Parking: Outdoor, free. 10% discount for first-time guests; guests who stay Fri–Sat may stay Sun for half-price. Closed Jan–Feb. AE, DC, DISC, MC, V.

Lodge of the Ozarks

3431 W MO 76, 65616; tel 417/334-7535; fax 417/334-6861. 3 mi W of jct US 65. Western lodge atmosphere, with spacious lobby accented by wooden ceiling beams, skylight, stone fireplace, copper chandelier, hanging plants, and potted trees. Next to Roy Clark Theater, Whitewater Theme Park, and a go-cart track. A great bargain. **Rooms:** 191 rms and stes. CI 3pm/CO 11am. Nonsmoking rms avail. **Amenities:** 🛎 A/C, cable TV. Some units w/terraces, some w/whirlpools. **Services:** 🛅 🔔 Masseur. **Facilities:** 🏊 500 🕭 3 restaurants, 2 bars (1 w/entertainment), games rm, whirlpool, beauty salon. Several gift shops. **Rates (CP):** Peak (May–Dec) $80 S or D; $95 ste. Children under age 18 stay free. Lower rates off-season. Parking: Outdoor, free. AE, DISC, MC, V.

Rosebud Inn

2400 Roark Valley Rd, 65616; tel 417/336-4000 or toll free 800/767-3522; fax 417/336-4919. Attractive new hotel offering many amenities. **Rooms:** 64 rms. CI 2pm/CO 10:30am. Nonsmoking rms avail. **Amenities:** 🛎 A/C, cable TV. **Services:** 🔔 **Facilities:** 🏊 48 🕭 Basketball. **Rates (CP):** Peak (May–June/Sept–Oct) $40–$59 S or D. Extra person $5. Children under age 12 stay free. Lower rates off-season. Parking: Outdoor, free. AE, DISC, MC, V.

Southern Oaks Inn

3295 Shepherd of the Hills Expwy, 65616; tel 417/335-8108 or toll free 800/324-8752; fax 417/335-8861. Near popular music theaters. Oversized lobby has TV. **Rooms:** 150 rms and stes. CI 3pm/CO 11am. Nonsmoking rms avail. **Amenities:** 🛎 A/C, cable TV. Some units w/terraces, some w/whirlpools. **Services:** 🔔 Complimentary coffee in lobby. **Facilities:** 🏊 85 🕭 Whirlpool. **Rates (CP):** Peak (May–June/Sept–Oct) $58 S or D; $68–$95 ste. Extra person $4. Children under age 18 stay free. Lower rates off-season. Parking: Outdoor, free. AE, DISC, MC, V.

MOTELS

Baldknobbers Motor Inn

2843 MO 76 W, 65616; tel 417/334-7948; fax 417/334-7232. Affordable, comfortable accommodations next door to the Baldknobbers theater. Very small, well decorated lobby. **Rooms:** 75 rms. CI 2pm/CO 11am. **Amenities:** 🛎 A/C, cable TV. Some units w/whirlpools. **Services:** 🔔 **Facilities:** 🏊 1 restaurant. **Rates:** Peak (May–Oct) $59–$70 S or D. Children under age 19 stay free. Lower rates off-season. Parking: Outdoor, free. Spring package includes tickets to Baldknobbers show and free meal. Closed Dec–Feb. AE, CB, DISC, MC, V.

Expressway Inn
691 Shepherd of the Hills Expwy, 65616; tel 417/334-1700 or toll free 800/688-3682; fax 417/334-2018. 248 exit off US 65, 2 mi W of Shepherd of the Hills Expwy. Basic motel accommodations, located near several theaters. **Rooms:** 106 rms. CI 2pm/CO 11am. Nonsmoking rms avail. **Amenities:** A/C, cable TV. **Services:** **Facilities:** Washer/dryer. **Rates (CP):** Peak (Apr–Nov) $52–$63 S or D. Extra person $5. Children under age 13 stay free. Lower rates off-season. Parking: Outdoor, free. Closed Dec–Mar. DISC, MC, V.

Good Shepherd Inn
1023 W Main St, 65616; tel 417/334-1695 or toll free 800/324-3457; fax 417/335-4295. 2 blocks from jct US 65 and MO 76. Basic economy motel in a convenient location. Car rental service next door. **Rooms:** 63 rms. CI 10am/CO 10am. Nonsmoking rms avail. **Amenities:** A/C, cable TV. Some rooms have VCRs. **Services:** **Facilities:** **Rates:** Peak (May–Aug) $36 S; $40 D. Extra person $5. Children under age 15 stay free. Lower rates off-season. Parking: Outdoor, free. Special rate for five-day stays. AE, DC, DISC, MC, V.

Honeysuckle Inn
3598 Shepherd of the Hills Expwy, 65616; tel 417/335-2030 or toll free 800/942-3553; fax 417/339-2039. At MO 76. Country ambience throughout. Located near major highways. **Rooms:** 213 rms. CI 2pm/CO 11am. Nonsmoking rms avail. **Amenities:** A/C, cable TV. **Services:** Babysitting. **Facilities:** Whirlpool. **Rates:** Peak (May–Dec) $60 S or D. Children under age 17 stay free. Lower rates off-season. Parking: Outdoor, free. Closed Jan–Feb. AE, DISC, MC, V.

Magnolia Inn
3311 Shepherd of the Hills Expwy, 65616; tel 417/334-2300 or toll free 800/222-7239; fax 417/336-4165. Quaint motel with plenty of country charm and well-decorated, comfortable rooms; near local theaters. **Rooms:** 152 rms and stes. CI open/CO 11am. Nonsmoking rms avail. **Amenities:** A/C, cable TV. Some units w/whirlpools. **Services:** Babysitting. **Facilities:** 1 restaurant, beauty salon, washer/dryer. Gift shop sells country crafts. **Rates:** Peak (May/Sept–Oct) $45–$62 S or D; $67–$77 ste. Extra person $4. Children under age 13 stay free. Lower rates off-season. Parking: Outdoor, free. AE, DISC, MC, V.

Ozark Regal Hotel
3010 Green Mountain Dr, 65616; tel 417/336-2200 or toll free 800/243-1903; fax 417/336-2210. Acceptable rooms. Small but attractive lobby is accented with potted plants and beautiful gold chandelier. **Rooms:** 96 rms, stes, and effic. CI 3pm/CO 11am. Nonsmoking rms avail. **Amenities:** A/C, cable TV. Some units w/whirlpools. **Services:** **Facilities:** 1 restaurant, 1 bar, games rm, whirlpool, washer/dryer. **Rates (CP):** Peak (May–June/Sept–Oct) $49–

$59 S or D; $59–$79 ste; $117–$135 effic. Children under age 15 stay free. Lower rates off-season. Parking: Outdoor, free. CB, DC, DISC, EC, JCB, MC, V.

Ozark Valley Inn
2693 Shepherd of the Hills Expwy, 65616; tel 417/336-4666 or toll free 800/947-4666; fax 417/336-4750. Modest yet still comfortable motel located on major local expressway, near Music Theater. **Rooms:** 66 rms. CI 2pm/CO 10am. Nonsmoking rms avail. **Amenities:** A/C, cable TV. **Services:** **Facilities:** Games rm, whirlpool, washer/dryer. **Rates (CP):** $40–$59 S or D. Extra person $5. Children under age 15 stay free. Parking: Outdoor, free. AE, DC, DISC, MC, V.

Peach Tree Inn
2450 Green Mountain Dr, 65616; tel 417/335-5900 or toll free 800/364-7322; fax 417/335-6606. Modestly decorated rooms, but comfortable and affordable. Located near music theaters. **Rooms:** 64 rms. CI 10am/CO 10am. Nonsmoking rms avail. **Amenities:** A/C, cable TV, voice mail. **Services:** **Facilities:** Whirlpool. **Rates (CP):** Peak (Sept–Oct) $49–$59 S or D. Extra person $5. Children under age 12 stay free. Lower rates off-season. Parking: Outdoor, free. Closed Jan–Feb. AE, DC, DISC, MC, V.

Settle Inn
3050 Green Mountain Dr, 65616; tel 417/335-4700 or toll free 800/677-6906; fax 417/335-3906. This lovely white siding motel with stone pillars is surrounded by many trees, walkways, and small pools stocked with fish. **Rooms:** 300 rms and stes. CI 2pm/CO 11am. Nonsmoking rms avail. Theme suites include jungle suite filled with lush plants, attractive wicker furniture, ceiling fan, and sheer netting over king-size bed with deluxe linens; and medieval suite featuring faux stone walls, knights of armor, wall sconces, and beautiful king-size wrought iron bed. **Amenities:** A/C, cable TV w/movies, dataport, voice mail. Some units w/terraces, some w/whirlpools. **Services:** **Facilities:** 1 restaurant (lunch and dinner only; see "Restaurants" below), 1 bar (w/entertainment), games rm, whirlpool, washer/dryer. "Murder mystery" dinner theater. **Rates (CP):** Peak (Apr–Dec) $35–$69 S or D; $49–$129 ste. Children under age 12 stay free. Lower rates off-season. Parking: Outdoor, free. AE, DISC, MC, V.

Stonewall West Motor Inn
1030 W Main (MO 76 W), 65616; tel 417/334-5173. Acceptable, affordable accommodations near all the popular attractions. Suitable for a brief stay. **Rooms:** 26 rms. CI noon/CO 11am. Nonsmoking rms avail. **Amenities:** A/C, cable TV w/movies. **Services:** **Facilities:** **Rates:** Peak (Sept–Oct) $22–$42 S or D. Extra person $4. Children under age 12 stay free. Lower rates off-season. Parking: Outdoor, free. Closed Dec–Feb. AE, CB, DISC, MC, V.

INN

⧉⧉⧉ Bradford Inn

US 265, 65616; tel 417/338-5555 or toll free 800/3571-INN. 2 mi S of US 76. 6½ acres. Bright white inn with well-manicured landscaping in a country setting. Offers beautiful view of Ozark hills from public areas and rooms. **Rooms:** 30 rms and stes. CI 3pm/CO 11am. Each room is beautifully decorated in warm colors with deluxe linens. Some rooms feature antiques and reproductions, such as four-poster beds and elegant mirrors. **Amenities:** 🛏 👤 🖵 A/C, cable TV, refrig. All units w/terraces, some w/fireplaces, some w/whirlpools. **Services:** ⌑ **Facilities:** ⊡ & Guest lounge w/TV. **Rates (CP):** Peak (Apr–Dec) $49–$69 D; $79–$89 ste. Extra person $5. Children under age 12 stay free. Lower rates off-season. Parking: Outdoor, free. Honeymoon packages avail. DISC, MC, V.

RESORTS

⧉ Allendale Resort and Sharp's Resort

411 N Commercial St, 65616; tel 417/334-3327. Downtown Branson near Lake Taneycomo. 3 acres. Situated by a large trout stream that flows into Lake Taneycomo and is covered with towering shade trees. **Rooms:** 42 cottages/villas. CI 2pm/CO 10am. Nonsmoking rms avail. **Amenities:** 🖵 A/C, cable TV, refrig. No phone. Some units w/terraces. Cottages have complete cooking facilities. **Services:** ⌑ Babysitting. **Facilities:** ⊡ 🖵 & Games rm, whirlpool, playground, washer/dryer. **Rates:** Peak (Mem Day–Labor Day) $30–$52 cottage/villa. Min stay. Lower rates off-season. Parking: Outdoor, free. DISC, MC, V.

⧉⧉⧉⧉ Big Cedar Lodge

612 Devil's Pool Rd, Ridgedale, 65739; tel 417/335-2777; fax 417/335-2340. 10 miles S of Branson on Table Rock Lake. 62 acres. Beautiful Northwest-style lodge in expansive rural setting surrounded by rolling hills, large shade trees, and panoramic view of Table Rock Lake. Both rustic and majestic, the lodge—made of natural materials such as rough stone and richly grained wood—is an attraction not to be missed, whether staying overnight or just visiting for the day. **Rooms:** 208 rms, stes, and effic; 61 cottages/villas. CI 3pm/CO 11am. Nonsmoking rms avail. Deluxe king rooms feature handcarved furniture, high ceilings, ceiling fans, mounted game, and furs. Bathrooms uniquely designed with large tree between bath and sink. Exquisite individual log cabins boast handcarved furniture and are available with special views. **Amenities:** 🛏 👤 🖵 🍽 A/C, cable TV w/movies, in-rm safe. Some units w/terraces, some w/fireplaces, some w/whirlpools. Log cabins have stone fireplaces and are available with grills. **Services:** ✕ 🖛 🖼 ⌑ Social director, masseur, children's program, babysitting. Shuttle service available to restaurants and activities. **Facilities:** ⊡ △ 🖵 ▷9 ⛴ 🏊 🖼 🛥 🚣 ⛳225 & 3 restaurants (*see* "Restaurants" below), 1 bar (w/entertainment), basketball, volleyball, lawn games,

sauna, steam rm, whirlpool, playground, washer/dryer. Restaurant offers delicious country cooking: Ozark trout, "hillbilly" meat loaf, and thick fried pork chops. **Rates:** Peak (June–Oct) $109 S; $125–$189 D; $229–$849 ste; $229–$849 effic; $139–$529 cottage/villa. Extra person $15. Children under age 12 stay free. Min stay wknds. Lower rates off-season. Parking: Outdoor, free. Special packages include golf, fishing, bed-and-breakfast, Christmas, and romance. AE, DISC, MC, V.

RESTAURANTS 🍴

★ Branson Cafe

120 W Main St; tel 417/334-3021. **Regional American/Diner.** This casual diner—a real regular's hangout—is the place to go for down-home cooking. After trying one of the sandwiches, burgers, or home-style blue plate specials, sample one of the famous pies (they have the highest meringue you'll likely ever see). **FYI:** Reservations accepted. Children's menu. No liquor license. **Open:** Mon–Sat 5:30am–8pm. **Prices:** Main courses $5–$9. AE, CB, DC, DISC, MC, V. 🍷 👥 &

BT Bones

Shepherd of the Hills Expwy at Gretna Rd; tel 417/335-2002. **American/Steak.** This dimly lit country bar specializes in steaks, though chicken and fish dishes are also available. Luckenbach Chicken, grilled with mushrooms, onions, cheese, bacon, and honey mustard is an especially hearty item. **FYI:** Reservations not accepted. Country music/dancing. Children's menu. **Open:** Mon–Sat 11am–1am, Sun 11am–midnight. Closed Jan. **Prices:** Main courses $10–$18. AE, CB, DC, DISC, MC, V. 👥 &

Buckingham's Restaurant and Oasis

In Palace Inn, MO 76 next to the Grand Village; tel 417/337-7777. **Regional American.** Decorated with animal skin prints, carved wooden totems, and date palms, with lighting that is dim but not dark. Small dining rooms can be closed off for privacy. Try simple specialties such as veal medallions, mesquite-smoked duck, grilled tuna, and braised rabbit. Save room for one of the rich desserts. **FYI:** Reservations recommended. Children's menu. Dress code. No smoking. **Open:** Peak (Mar–Dec) dinner daily 4:30–9pm; brunch Sun 10am–2pm. **Prices:** Main courses $14–$23. AE, DISC, MC, V. ♥ 👥 &

Cowboy Cafe

Shepherd of the Hills Expwy, between Gretna & 248; tel 417/335-4828. **American/Steak.** The style is thoroughly country, from the decor to the music to the food. Steaks and ribs are featured specialities, though the cafe serves an all-you-can-eat champagne buffet with salads, vegetables, chicken, meats, barbecue brisket, and a glass of champagne. **FYI:** Reservations not accepted. Children's menu. Beer and wine only. **Open:** Sun–Thurs 4–9pm, Fri–Sat 4–10pm. Closed Dec 22–Apr. **Prices:** Main courses $9–$17. AE, MC, V. 👥 &

Devil's Pool

In Big Cedar Lodge, 612 Devil's Pool Rd, Ridgedale; tel 417/335-5141. 10 mi S of Branson on Table Rock Lake. **Regional American.** The restaurant has the appearance of a large, log cabin and offers a spectacular view of Table Rock Lake, and the surrounding hills and beautiful forest. The decor is rustic, with large, stuffed mammals, fish, and fowl hanging about. A good bet is the grilled fresh salmon fillet basted with a teriyaki ginger glaze. **FYI:** Reservations not accepted. Children's menu. No smoking. **Open:** Peak (June–Oct) breakfast Mon–Sat 7–11am; lunch Mon–Sat 11am–2pm; dinner Mon–Sat 5–9:30pm; brunch Sun 9am–2pm. **Prices:** Main courses $10–$19. AE, DISC, MC, V.

Lone Star Steakhouse

201 Wildwood Dr; tel 417/336-5030. **Steak.** Decorated in a country-western style that features cowboys and cattle, this place possesses the ambience of a saloon. It's mostly steaks, but you can also order chili, burgers, and chicken kebab. **FYI:** Reservations not accepted. Children's menu. **Open:** Sun–Thurs 11am–11pm, Fri–Sat 11am–12am. **Prices:** Main courses $8–$18. AE, DISC, MC, V.

Paradise Grill

3250 Shepherd of the Hills Expwy; tel 417/337-7444. **American.** A brightly decorated eatery with neon and lots of skylights. The menu features a variety of appetizers, salads, and hot and cold sandwiches; entrees include chicken, lamb chops, fish, and pasta. Ozark Mountain Chicken, stuffed with ham and cheese, is a popular dish. **FYI:** Reservations accepted. Children's menu. **Open:** Peak (July–Dec) Mon–Thurs 11am–9pm, Fri–Sat 11am–12am, Sun 10:30am–9pm. **Prices:** Main courses $10–$12. AE, DC, DISC, MC, V.

Radio Cafe

In Settle Inn, 3050 Green Mountain Dr; tel 417/335-4700. **Deli.** The decor here is Music City, and once a week a lunchtime radio show is broadcast on site featuring local pickers plus a special guest. The menu is limited; sandwiches, soups, desserts. **FYI:** Reservations accepted. Blues/country music/folk/guitar. Children's menu. **Open:** Daily 11am–midnight. **Prices:** Main courses $4–$6. AE, DISC, MC, V.

ATTRACTIONS

THEATERS

The Grand Palace

2700 W MO 76; tel 417/33-GRAND or toll free 800/5-PALACE. The elaborate Grand Palace is the largest theater in town and hosts some of the biggest-name performers to come to Branson, such as Kenny Rogers (who is a part-owner), the Mandrell Sisters, and the *Radio City Christmas Spectacular* featuring the Rockettes. **Open:** Mar–mid-Dec, Sat–Tues 3 and 8pm, Wed–Fri 8pm. $$$$

Shoji Tabuchi

3260 Shepherd of the Hills Expwy; tel 417/334-7469. An art deco, purple and silver 2,000-seat theater with one of the most popular shows in Branson. Featuring elaborate production numbers, laser-light effects, an 18-piece orchestra, and the violin/fiddling talent of Tabuchi. **Open:** Mon–Fri 3 and 8pm. $$$$

Welk Resort Center and Champagne Theatre

1984 MO 165; tel 417/337-SHOW or toll free 800/505-WELK. The 2,300-seat theater stars many of the original cast members of *The Lawrence Welk Show* including the Lennon Sisters and Jo Ann Castle. After the show, audience members may meet and get autographs from performers in the lobby. The complex also includes a hotel, a gift shop, and a restaurant. **Open:** Apr 10–Dec 31. Call for schedule. $$$$

Mel Tillis Theater

2527 MO 248; tel 417/335-6635. This 2,700-seat theater is the home base of country singer Tillis, who has had a successful singing career despite his stutter. Tillis is joined by a 20-piece band (the Stutterettes), and is often accompanied by his two daughters. A huge concession and gift shop area is located just off the lobby. **Open:** Mid-Mar–Dec, daily. Call for schedule. $$$$

Mickey Gilley Theatre

3455 MO 76 W; tel 417/334-3210 or toll free 800/334-1936. Mickey Gilley performs his roadhouse hits with the Urban Cowboy Band. Also offered is a morning show with Jim Owen performing the songs of Hank Williams Sr. The comfortable theater features big-screen monitors for a closer look at the action onstage. **Open:** Mar–Dec, daily. $$$$

Glen Campbell Goodtime Theatre

MO 248 and US 65; tel 417/336-1220 or toll free 800/884-GLEN. One of the newest and flashiest showcases in the area, with a glass-and-wood entrance and two huge projection screens reflecting the on-stage action. The country superstar performs his nearly three dozen hits with a supporting cast of dancers, singers, comedians, and ventriloquists. Other local stars—such as Barbara Mandrell and John Davidson—have been known to stop in for a number or two. **Open:** Mar–Dec, Tues–Sun. $$$$

Pump Boys and Dinettes Dinner Theatre

625 MO 165 S; tel 417/336-4319 or toll free 800/743-2386. Branson's only Broadway musical dinner theater. Waitresses and gas-station jockeys sing, dance, and joke around while diners eat lunch or supper. A morning show features Buck Trent and other fiddlers and performers, as well as a breakfast buffet. $$$$

Bobby Vinton Blue Velvet Theatre

2701 MO 76 W; tel 417/334-2500 or toll free 800/US-BOBBY. A 1,600-seat European-style theater with hand-painted ceiling murals reminiscent of the Italian Renaissance, Spanish wrought-iron railings, and a custom-made blue velvet stage curtain edged with 14-carat gold thread. Bobby Vinton performs hits from his long career, with backing from the Glenn Miller Orchestra. **Open:** Apr–Dec, Tues–Sun. Call for schedule. $$$$

76 Music Hall

76 Country Music Blvd; tel 417/335-2484. Several shows offered daily, including a music-and-dance show by the Memory Makers spanning the decades from the 1950s to the present. Adjoining 76 Mall Complex features a 36-hole miniature-golf course, 3-D movies, shops, and a video arcade. **Open:** Daily. Call for schedule. **$$$$**

Cristy Lane Theatre

3600 MO 76 W; tel 417/335-5111. In a 500-seat, plain-stage theater, Ms Lane sings country and gospel tunes, including her big hit, "One Day at a Time." Opening acts include comedian Foster Brooks and other musical performers. **Open:** Daily. Call for schedule. **$$$$**

THEME PARKS

Mutton Hollow Entertainment Park and Village

MO 76 W; tel 417/334-4947 or toll free 800/531-7893. Attractions include shows featuring gospel, bluegrass, and country music; a old-time "county fair" with an antique Ferris wheel, carousel, and tilt-a-whirl; more than 30 specialty craft shops with demonstrations by craftsmen; and horseback rides on Ozark trails. Ethnic festivals with food and entertainment are scheduled periodically. **Open:** Peak (mid-May–Oct) daily 9am–5pm. Reduced hours off-season. Closed Nov–mid-Apr. **$$$**

Silver Dollar City

MO 265; tel 417/338-8100 or toll free 800/952-6626. The first and biggest of the area's theme parks, this one features rides, live entertainment, restaurants, and shops in an 1880s mountain town setting. Staff members dress in turn-of-the-century costumes, and glass blowers, jewelers, weavers, and other craftspeople demonstrate their trade throughout the park. This site was originally known as the location of Marvel Cave, which is still accessible today; visitors descend more than 200 feet below the earth's surface where they can explore 32 miles of passages and view the 20-story-high main room. The park also boasts a 1,000-seat Opera House, and a 3,000-seat outdoor amphitheater called Echo Hollow, where the nightly show *Top 100 Country Songs of All Time* is performed. **Open:** Peak (May–Aug) daily 9:30am–7pm. Reduced hours off-season. **$$$$**

Shepherd of the Hills

MO 76; tel 417/334-4191. 2 mi W of the strip. Part theme park and part entertainment venue, the highlight here is the nightly enactment of Harold Bell Wright's 1907 novel, *The Shepherd of the Hills,* in a 2,000-seat amphitheater. The play utilizes an entire herd of sheep, Clydesdale horses, a bonfire, and a cast of 70 people to perform this Ozarks morality play. Craftspeople, playground, Inspiration Point scenic tower, horseback and wagon rides. **Open:** Apr–Dec, daily, call for schedule. **$$$$**

White Water Park

MO 76; tel 417/334-7487 or 336-7100. Twelve acres of water rides, including water slides, wave pool, double tubing, and a rapids ride. **Open:** Peak (June–Aug) daily 9am–8pm. Reduced hours off-season. **$$$$**

OTHER ATTRACTIONS

Lake Queen

280 N Lake Dr; tel 417/334-3015. Narrated sightseeing, breakfast, and supper cruises aboard a sternwheel riverboat on Lake Tanyecomo. Passengers can enjoy views of downtown Branson, feed ducks and geese, and listen to live onboard entertainment. Call for information on the special July 4th Pizza and Fireworks Cruise. **Open:** Mar–Dec, daily 8am–7pm. **$$$$**

Showboat *Branson Belle*

MO 265; tel 417/336-7400 or toll free 800/417-7770. Tourists can dine, view Ozark scenery, and watch a music-and-comedy revue on this multilevel, climate-controlled floating theater. Children are invited to see the wheelhouse and meet the captain. **Open:** Mar 22–Dec 31, daily. **$$$$**

Polynesian Princess

Gage's Long Creek Marina, MO 86; tel 417/334-4191. Narrated boat tours of Table Rock Lake. Visitors can choose between breakfast, dinner, sightseeing, or sunset cruises. Dinner cruise features live Polynesian entertainment. **Open:** May–Oct, daily, call for schedule. **$$$$**

Ride The Ducks

MO 76 W; tel 417/334-3825. These clunky amphibious trucks take tourists on a 70-minute land-and-water sightseeing tour of Branson including Table Rock Dam and Lake, the fish hatchery, and mountain scenery. Tours depart daily, every 15 minutes. **Open:** Mid-Feb–mid-Dec, daily 8am–5pm. **$$$$**

Stone Hill Winery

601 MO 165; tel 417/334-1897. A family-run winery in the German Rhineland tradition. The hour-long tour begins with a movie on winemaking, proceeds to an informative lecture and demonstration, and ends with a tasting of various Stone Hill wines. **Open:** Mon–Sat 8:30am–sunset, Sun 11am–6pm. **Free**

Snow Bluff Ski and Fun Area

5659 MO 13, Brighton; tel 417/376-2201. During winter, visitors can ski the Ozarks on nine trails (ranging from beginner to advanced) or try the special areas set aside for tubing and snowboarding. During the warm-weather months, visitors are offered a wide array of outdoor activities including go-carts, bumper boats, miniature golf, driving and batting ranges, swimming, volleyball, trampoline, and basketball. **Open:** Dec 26–Oct 31, hours vary. **$$$$**

Bridgeton

See St Louis–Lambert Int'l Airport

Cameron

Situated at the junction of I-35 and US 36, this small town is near Kansas City's attractions to the south and St Joseph's historical sites to the west. Wallace State Park and Smithville Reservoir provide a variety of outdoor recreational activities. **Information:** Cameron Chamber of Commerce, PO Box 252, Cameron, 64429 (tel 816/632-2005).

MOTEL 🏨

▭▭ Super 8 Motel

US 69, 64229; tel 816/632-8888 or toll free 800/800-8000; fax 816/632-8888. At jct US 36. Rooms are better than average for an economy motel. Convenient for people on the road. **Rooms:** 41 rms and stes. CI 1pm/CO 11am. Nonsmoking rms avail. **Amenities:** 🕾 A/C, cable TV w/movies, dataport. 1 unit w/whirlpool. **Services:** 🛎 **Facilities:** 🛠 🏊 25 & Whirlpool. **Rates (CP):** Peak (Apr–Oct) $35–$45 S; $44–$55 D; $60–$80 ste. Lower rates off-season. Parking: Outdoor, free. Rates increase on weekends. AE, DC, DISC, MC, V.

Cape Girardeau

This historic southeastern Missouri city dates back to the 1730s; today it is home to Southeast Missouri State University.

HOTEL 🏨

▭▭▭ Holiday Inn

3257 Williams St, PO Box 1570, 63701 (West Park); tel 573/334-4491 or toll free 800/HOLIDAY; fax 573/334-7459. Exit 96 off I-55. This exceptional interstate motel was fully renovated in 1995. **Rooms:** 186 rms, stes, and effic. CI 3pm/CO 11am. Nonsmoking rms avail. Many of the well-appointed rooms open to the indoor pool area. **Amenities:** 🕾 A/C, cable TV w/movies, dataport. 1 unit w/whirlpool. **Services:** ✕ 🚐 🏊 🛎 Babysitting. **Facilities:** 🛠 🏋 800 & 1 restaurant, 1 bar, games rm, spa, sauna, whirlpool, washer/dryer. Large pool/lounge area nicely decorated with live plants. Access to adjacent fitness center $5. **Rates:** $68–$86 S; $86–$92 D; $160 ste; $68–$82 effic. Children under age 18 stay free. Parking: Outdoor, free. AE, CB, DC, DISC, JCB, MC, V.

MOTEL

▭▭▭ Victorian Inn

3265 William St, 63702 (West Park); tel 573/651-4486 or toll free 800/331-0445; fax 573/651-3970. Exit 96 off I-55.

Attractive, modern motel (renovated in 1995) in quiet, off-street location. Beautifully landscaped, well-manicured grounds. **Rooms:** 133 rms and stes. CI 3pm/CO 11am. Nonsmoking rms avail. **Amenities:** 🕾 🔥 🍷 A/C, cable TV w/movies, dataport. Some units w/whirlpools. **Services:** 🚐 🏊 🛎 🐕 **Facilities:** 🛠 50 & Games rm, whirlpool. Poolside deli open in evenings. Access to adjacent Holiday Inn outdoor pool and fitness center for $5. **Rates (CP):** $54 S; $69 D; $125 ste. Children under age 19 stay free. Parking: Outdoor, free. Family and tour group discounts avail. AE, CB, DC, DISC, JCB, MC, V.

RESTAURANT 🍴

★ Cedar Street

In Drury Lodge, 104 S Vantage; tel 573/334-7151. Exit 96 off I-55. **Southwestern/Tex-Mex.** Lariats, sombreros, and chili peppers adorn the walls of this sprawling restaurant. The menu offers a good selection of chicken, pork, and beef dishes prepared Southwestern style with peppers and onions. The bread is baked in flower pots and delivered to your table with whipped strawberry butter. The most popular menu items are the smoked pork ribs, sizzling steak, and chicken fajitas. **FYI:** Reservations not accepted. **Open:** Sun–Thurs 6am–9pm, Fri–Sat 6am–10pm. **Prices:** Main courses $7–$13. AE, CB, DC, DISC, MC, V. &

Carthage

See also Joplin

Site of a major Civil War land battle and the home of the outlaw queen Belle Starr, Carthage achieved widespread recognition with the discovery of its marble quarries in 1885. The city basks in its historic past by reenacting it during a variety of festivals and celebrations. **Information:** Carthage Chamber of Commerce, 107 E 3rd St, Carthage, 64836 (tel 417/358-2373).

MOTEL 🏨

▭▭ Econo Lodge

1441 W Central, 64836; tel 417/358-3900 or toll free 800/424-4777; fax 417/358-6839. US 71 and MO 96. Basic property. **Rooms:** 83 rms. CI 2pm/CO 11am. Nonsmoking rms avail. Comfortable accommodations are larger than average. **Amenities:** 🕾 A/C, cable TV w/movies. Senior rooms have alarm clocks with large digits and phones with oversized key pads. **Services:** 🛎 🐕 **Facilities:** 🛠 & Whirlpool. **Rates (CP):** $43–$50 S; $50–$60 D. Extra person $5. Children under age 18 stay free. Parking: Outdoor, free. AE, DC, DISC, MC, V.

Cassville

Cassville offers travelers a scenic approach to the Ozark Hills and the lakes that surround Branson, and is also a gateway to the Mark Twain National Forest to the east. Nearby Roaring River State Park provides trout fishing and hiking. **Information:** Cassville Area Chamber of Commerce, 504 Main St, Cassville, 65625 (tel 417/847-2814).

MOTEL 🏨

⬛ Super 8 Motel

MO 37, 65625; tel 417/847-4888 or toll free 800/800-8000; fax 417/847-4888 ext 403. At jct MO 76/MO 86. Clean, straightforward motel rooms. **Rooms:** 46 rms and stes. CI 2pm/CO 11am. Nonsmoking rms avail. **Amenities:** 🛏 A/C, cable TV w/movies, voice mail. 1 unit w/whirlpool. **Services:** 🛍 🖨 ⬤ **Facilities:** 🛗 30 🚭 **Rates:** $37 S; $42–$44 D; $63–$76 ste. Extra person $4. Children under age 13 stay free. Parking: Outdoor, free. AE, CB, DC, DISC, JCB, MC, V.

Clayton

A suburban community west of St Louis, Clayton is second to it as a business and financial center in the region. Forest Park, site of the 1904 World's Fair, is nearby, and offers a number of museums and other pleasures. **Information:** Clayton Chamber of Commerce, 7730 Bonhomme, #100, Clayton, 63105-1909 (tel 314/726-3033).

HOTELS 🏨

⬛⬛⬛ Hilton Hotel Daniele

216 N Meramec, 63105; tel 314/721-0101 or toll free 800/325-8302; fax 314/721-0609. I-170 S exit off I-70, Ladue exit off I-170 S. A friendly and efficient staff and intimate size make this tastefully decorated European-style hotel ideal for those looking for quality accommodations on a smaller scale. Cozy lobby is decorated with lovely, green plants, colorful floral arrangements, brass chandeliers, and leather sofas and chairs. **Rooms:** 82 rms and stes. CI open/CO noon. Nonsmoking rms avail. **Amenities:** 🛏 A/C, cable TV w/movies, dataport. **Services:** ✕ VP 🚗 🛍 🖨 ⬤ Car-rental desk, babysitting. **Facilities:** 🛗 100 🚭 1 restaurant, 1 bar. Free limo service provided to local fitness center, airport, and Clayton vicinity. **Rates (CP):** $99–$109 S or D; $150–$375 ste. Parking: Indoor, free. AE, DC, DISC, MC, V.

⬛⬛⬛ Holiday Inn

7730 Bonhomme, 63105; tel 314/863-0400 or toll free 800/HOLIDAY; fax 314/863-8513. Off Forest Park Pkwy. A solid Holiday Inn located two blocks from tennis courts, roller skating, and ice skating. Relaxing lobby features leather sofas and chairs, potted plants and floral arrangements, and brass chandeliers. **Rooms:** 253 rms and stes. CI 2pm/CO noon.

Nonsmoking rms avail. **Amenities:** 🛏 A/C, cable TV w/movies, dataport, voice mail. **Services:** ✕ 🖨 🚗 🛍 🖨 Car-rental desk. **Facilities:** 🛗 🏊 450 🚭 1 restaurant, 1 bar, games rm, spa, sauna, steam rm, whirlpool, beauty salon, washer/dryer. **Rates:** $79–$89 S; $86–$96 D; $99–$250 ste. Extra person $7. Children under age 18 stay free. Parking: Indoor/outdoor, free. Romance packages avail. AE, CB, DC, DISC, JCB, MC, V.

⬛⬛⬛ Radisson Hotel

7750 Carondelet Ave, 63105; tel 314/726-5400 or toll free 800/333-3333; fax 314/726-6105. Handley Rd N exit off I-40 W. Located near many restaurants and shops, this comfortable hotel offering a good range of facilities is suitable for all travelers. Small but attractive lobby with marble floors and lovely sofas and chairs. **Rooms:** 190 rms, stes, and effic. CI 3pm/CO noon. Nonsmoking rms avail. **Amenities:** 🛏 🧊 A/C, cable TV, refrig, dataport. Some units w/fireplaces, some w/whirlpools. **Services:** ✕ 🖨 VP 🚗 🛍 🖨 ⬤ Babysitting. **Facilities:** 🛗 🏊 250 🚭 1 restaurant, 1 bar (w/entertainment), games rm, spa, sauna, steam rm, whirlpool, washer/dryer. **Rates (CP):** Peak (spring/fall) $55–$105 S or D; $119–$150 ste; $119–$150 effic. Extra person $10. Children under age 18 stay free. Min stay special events. Lower rates off-season. Parking: Indoor, free. AE, DC, DISC, JCB, MC, V.

⬛⬛⬛⬛ The Ritz-Carlton

100 Carondelet Plaza, 63105; tel 314/863-6300 or toll free 800/241-3333; fax 314/863-7486. Near Ladue exit off I-70. Located in a quiet area on the edge of the business district, this elegant and beautiful 1990 property, filled with millions of dollars of 18th- and 19th-century antiques and fine art, is perfect for discriminating guests. The lobby is predictably spacious and elegant, with an antique china hutch, a marble fireplace, marble tile floors and check-in desk, and several brass and crystal chandeliers. **Rooms:** 301 rms, stes, and effic. Executive level. CI 3pm/CO noon. Nonsmoking rms avail. Handsomely decorated guest rooms feature mahogany furniture, plush chairs, marble bathroom, and vanity table with lighted mirror. **Amenities:** 🛏 🧊 A/C, cable TV w/movies, dataport, in-rm safe, bathrobes. All units w/minibars, some w/terraces, 1 w/fireplace, 1 w/whirlpool. **Services:** 🍴 🖨 VP 🛍 🖨 Twice-daily maid svce, car-rental desk, babysitting. Same-day laundry/dry cleaning. Elaborate afternoon tea (served on Rosenthal china) daily. **Facilities:** 🛗 🏊 1000 🚭 2 restaurants (see "Restaurants" below), 2 bars (1 w/entertainment), sauna, steam rm, whirlpool. **Rates:** $155–$195 S or D; $295–$1,500 ste; $1,500 effic. Parking: Indoor/outdoor, $10/day. B&B, weekend, and Grand Occasion packages avail. AE, CB, DC, DISC, ER, JCB, MC, V.

⬛⬛⬛ Seven Gables Inn

26 N Meramec, 63105; tel 314/863-8400 or toll free 800/433-6590; fax 314/863-8846. I-170 S exit off I-70, Ladue exit off I-170 S, right on Ladue, right on Merrimec. Built in the 1920s as an apartment complex, this small, quaint hotel

with a whitewashed timbered facade and the ambience of an elegant B&B is listed on the National Register of Historic Monuments. The small lobby is decorated in a rustic style with paintings and replica antique tables and desks. Rooms are on three floors; there is no elevator. **Rooms:** 32 rms and stes. CI 3pm/CO 1pm. Nonsmoking rms avail. Unique rooms feature sitting area with lovely chair and ottoman. **Amenities:** 🛏 ♨ A/C, cable TV w/movies, dataport, bathrobes. VCR available. **Services:** ✗ ⒱ᴾ 🖨 🛎 🦮 Babysitting. **Facilities:** 🏊 💻 2 restaurants (*see* "Restaurants" below), 1 bar (w/entertainment), day-care ctr. Guests have free access to nearby fitness center, health spa, and pool. **Rates:** $135 S; $145 D; $175 ste. Extra person $10. Children under age 10 stay free. Parking: Indoor, $8/day. Lower weekend rates include free continental breakfast. AE, CB, DC, DISC, JCB, MC, V.

RESTAURANTS 🍴

Bofinger
200 S Brentwood Blvd; tel 314/721-0100. Brentwood exit off I-170 S, left. **New American/French.** A casual but refined dining room decorated with oil paintings and brass chandeliers. The menu offers a good variety of appetizers, soups, salads, and hors d'oeuvres. A good bet is magret de canard, a sautéed breast of duckling served with an orange and pepper sauce. **FYI:** Reservations recommended. Piano. Dress code. **Open:** Peak (Sept–Dec) lunch Mon–Fri 11:30am–2:30pm; dinner Mon–Sat 5:30–10:30pm. **Prices:** Main courses $10–$15. AE, CB, DC, DISC, MC, V. ⒱ᴾ &

Cafe Napoli
7754 Forsyth; tel 314/863-5731. At Bemiston. **Italian.** Whether enjoying the breeze at an outdoor table or admiring the many paintings and murals inside, this is a fine place to enjoy well-prepared Italian specialties. One example: the modenese, breaded veal topped with imported cured prosciutto, cheeses, marsala sauce, sage, and rosemary. **FYI:** Reservations recommended. Reservations accepted. **Open:** Lunch Mon–Fri 11am–2pm; dinner Mon–Thurs 5–10pm, Fri–Sat 5–11pm, Sun 5–9pm. **Prices:** Main courses $10–$25. AE, MC, V. &

Candicci's
7910 Bonhomme; tel 314/725-3350. **Italian.** This cozy little place has a big menu, including a wide variety of pizzas, sandwiches, and burgers, as well as pasta, seafood, veal, and chicken entrees. A good bet is vitello Candicci, a lightly-breaded veal cutlet, grilled and served in a sauce with sun-dried tomatoes and fresh shiitake mushrooms and topped with melted Provolone. **FYI:** Reservations accepted. No smoking. Additional location: 12513 Olive St, in the Heritage Plaza, St Louis (tel 878-5858). **Open:** Mon–Thurs 11:30am–11pm, Fri–Sat 11:30am–midnight, Sun 4:30–9:30pm. **Prices:** Main courses $9–$19. AE, CB, DC, DISC, MC, V.

Cardwell's
8100 Maryland; tel 314/726-5055. At Brentwood. **Regional American.** Bill Cardwell's imaginative California-style cuisine

is a definite hit among the discriminating diners who frequent this Clayton standout. The frequently changing menu reflects the freshest seasonal ingredients available. Such delights as grilled farm-raised Atlantic salmon with a glaze of chardonnay, herbs, and three mustards have been offered. Outdoor dining on a street-side patio is available. Very popular for business lunches. **FYI:** Reservations recommended. **Open:** Lunch Mon–Sat 11:30am–3pm; dinner Mon–Thurs 5–10pm, Fri–Sat 5–11pm. **Prices:** Main courses $16–$23; prix fixe $16. AE, MC, V. ⛴ ⒱ᴾ &

The Fatted Calf
12 S Bemiston Ave; tel 314/726-1141. **Burgers.** Metal beer tankards and photographs decorate this dark and cozy place. Burgers are the specialty, but several sandwiches and salads are also available. **FYI:** Reservations not accepted. Children's menu. Beer and wine only. **Open:** Mon–Sat 11am–8pm. **Prices:** Main courses $4–$7. No CC. 👥 &

Gables Room
In Seven Gables Inn, 26 N Meramec; tel 314/863-8400. I-170 exit off I-70, Ladue exit off I-170, right and right onto Meramec. **Continental.** Cozy and comfortable. Gables' filet mignon, a house specialty, is prime beef tenderloin with grilled mushrooms, anchovies, chile demiglacé, and crispy leeks. Also assorted beef, seafood, chicken, lamb, and pasta dishes. **FYI:** Reservations accepted. Jazz. Children's menu. **Open:** Mon–Sat 6:30am–11:30pm, Sun 7am–9pm. **Prices:** Main courses $9–$20. AE, CB, DC, DISC, MC, V. ⒱ᴾ &

Nantucket Cove
101 S Hanley; tel 314/726-4900. At Carondelet. **Seafood.** Large canvas umbrellas, hanging brass light fixtures, a large aquarium, and various floral arrangements set the scene for a menu offering a wide variety of hot and cold appetizers, soups and salads, and many seafood, steak, and chicken entrees. One of the favorite house specialties is the trout and vine: fresh Missouri trout with a dijon crabmeat stuffing, wrapped in grape leaves and served with carrots gaufrette. **FYI:** Reservations recommended. Children's menu. **Open:** Lunch Mon–Fri 11am–2pm; dinner daily 5–10pm. **Prices:** Main courses $9–$20. AE, CB, DC, DISC, MC, V. 🔲 &

Restaurant
In the Ritz-Carlton, 100 Carondelet Plaza; tel 314/863-6300. Ladue exit off I-70, E to Handley, right on Carondelet Plaza. **American.** A formal dining room with crystal chandeliers and light fixtures, oil paintings, and a large window with ornate drapes. The kitchen offers up expertly prepared continental food, and table settings and service both achieve the Ritz-Carlton's high standards. **FYI:** Reservations recommended. Children's menu. Dress code. **Open:** Peak (Nov 15–Dec) daily 6:30am–2:30pm. **Prices:** Lunch main courses $8–$15. AE, CB, DC, DISC, MC, V. ♥ ⒱ᴾ &

Saint Louis Bread Company
10 S Central Ave; tel 314/725-9666. **Cafe/Bread.** Outdoor seating gives this cute little place a sidewalk cafe atmosphere.

The menu consists of sandwiches, soups, and salads, plus fresh baked breads, muffins, croissants, and specialty coffee drinks. **FYI:** Reservations not accepted. No liquor license. No smoking. Additional locations: 6701 Clayton Rd (tel 725-9922); 1445 Galleria Pkwy, Richmond Heights (tel 727-5300). **Open:** Peak (June–Aug) Mon–Fri 6:30am–7pm, Sat 6:30am–5pm, Sun 7:30am–5pm. **Prices:** Main courses $4–$5. No CC. 🍴 ♿

Columbia

See also Fulton

Founded in 1821, Columbia is currently the largest city in central Missouri. The midpoint along I-70 between St Louis and Kansas City, the city is home to Columbia and Stephens Colleges as well as the main campus of the University of Missouri, the first state university founded west of the Mississippi River. Columbia is a major center for both medical services and the insurance industry, and boasts numerous historic homes and more than 1,500 acres of parkland. **Information:** Columbia Convention & Visitors Bureau, 300 S Providence Rd, PO Box N, Columbia, 65205 (tel 573/875-1231).

HOTELS 🏨

🔳🔳🔳 Holiday Inn

1612 N Providence Rd, 65202; tel 573/449-2491 or toll free 800/HOLIDAY; fax 573/874-6720. Exit 126 off I-70. Distinguished by a large indoor atrium pool and sauna area. **Rooms:** 142 rms and stes. CI 4pm/CO noon. Nonsmoking rms avail. **Amenities:** 🔳 ♨ A/C, cable TV w/movies, dataport. Some units w/whirlpools. **Services:** ✕ 🚐 🖅 🍴 🛎 **Facilities:** 🛗 🎱 🛏 1 restaurant, 1 bar, games rm, sauna, whirlpool, washer/dryer. **Rates:** Peak (Mem Day–Labor Day) $69 S; $72 D; $175 ste. Extra person $8. Children under age 19 stay free. Min stay special events. Lower rates off-season. Parking: Outdoor, free. Special packages include Great Rates and Honeymoon. AE, CB, DC, DISC, MC, V.

🔳🔳🔳 Holiday Inn Executive Center

2200 I-70 Dr SW, 65203; tel 573/445-8531 or toll free 800/465-4329; fax 573/445-7607. I-70 and Stadium. Modestly decorated rooms. Spacious lobby has water fountain, skylights, and plenty of seating. **Rooms:** 311 rms and stes. Executive level. CI 4pm/CO 11am. Nonsmoking rms avail. **Amenities:** 🔳 ♨ 🍴 A/C, cable TV w/movies, dataport, voice mail. Some units w/minibars, some w/terraces, 1 w/whirlpool. **Services:** 🍽 🔑 🚐 🖅 🛎 🍴 **Facilities:** 🛗 🎱 🖥 ♿ 2 restaurants, 2 bars (1 w/entertainment), spa, sauna, whirlpool, beauty salon. **Rates:** $65–$75 S or D; $175–$250 ste. Extra person $10. Children under age 12 stay free. Parking: Outdoor, free. Rates increase for sporting events. New Year's package avail. AE, CB, DC, DISC, MC, V.

🔳🔳 Ramada Inn

1100 Vandiver Dr, 65202; or toll free 800/2-RAMADA; fax 573/874-8963. Exit 127 off I-70. Attractive lobby with beautifully upholstered seating, potted plants and trees, and brass chandelier. **Rooms:** 202 rms and stes. CI 4pm/CO noon. Nonsmoking rms avail. **Amenities:** 🔳 ♨ A/C, satel TV w/movies, dataport. **Services:** ✕ 🚐 🖅 🍴 🛎 **Facilities:** 🛗 🎱 🖥 ♿ 1 restaurant, 1 bar, games rm. Free access to Gold's Gym. **Rates:** $49–$54 S; $54–$71 D; $95–$150 ste. Extra person $8. Children under age 18 stay free. Parking: Outdoor, free. Bed-and-breakfast and football packages avail. AE, CB, DC, DISC, JCB, MC, V.

MOTELS

🔳🔳 Best Western Columbia Inn

3100 I-70 Dr SE, 65201; tel 573/474-6161 or toll free 800/321-3185; fax 573/474-9323. Attractive lobby decorated with beautiful fireplace, antique piano, potted plants, and lovely floral arrangements. Located near I-70. **Rooms:** 125 rms and stes. CI 3pm/CO 11am. Nonsmoking rms avail. **Amenities:** 🔳 A/C, satel TV w/movies, dataport. **Services:** ✕ 🛎 **Facilities:** 🛗 🎱 ♿ 1 restaurant, 1 bar, games rm. **Rates:** $65–$75 S or D; $90–$125 ste. Extra person $5. Children under age 18 stay free. Parking: Outdoor, free. AE, CB, DC, DISC, MC, V.

🔳 Budget Host

900 Vandiver Dr, 65202; tel 573/449-1065 or toll free 800/456-1065; fax 573/442-6266. Exit 127 off I-70. Acceptable economy motel. **Rooms:** 156 rms. CI 3pm/CO 11am. Nonsmoking rms avail. Some water beds, bunk beds. **Amenities:** 🔳 A/C, cable TV w/movies. Some rooms have dataports, microwaves, and refrigerators. **Services:** 🛎 🍴 VCRs and movies can be rented. Several restaurants deliver to motel and offer discounts to guests. **Facilities:** 🛗 ♿ Washer/dryer. **Rates (CP):** $27 S; $39 D. Extra person $6. Parking: Outdoor, free. Honeymoon package avail. AE, CB, DC, DISC, MC, V.

🔳 Comfort Inn

901 Conley Rd, 65203; tel 573/443-4141 or toll free 800/221-2222; fax 573/443-4049. Exit 128A off I-70. Clean, basic motel rooms. **Rooms:** 60 rms. CI noon/CO 11am. Nonsmoking rms avail. **Amenities:** 🔳 A/C, cable TV. **Services:** 🛎 Movies available for rent. **Facilities:** 🛗 **Rates (CP):** $41–$46 S; $46–$51 D. Extra person $5. Children under age 19 stay free. Parking: Outdoor, free. AE, CB, DC, DISC, JCB, V.

🔳 Days Inn

1900 I-70 Dr SW, 65203; tel 573/445-8511 or toll free 800/DAYS-INN; fax 573/445-7991. At Stadium Blvd. Standard Days Inn. Clean. **Rooms:** 156 rms and stes. CI 4pm/CO noon. Nonsmoking rms avail. **Amenities:** 🔳 A/C, cable TV w/movies, dataport. **Services:** 🚐 🖅 🛎 🍴 **Facilities:** 🛗 🎱 ♿ 1 restaurant, 1 bar, washer/dryer. **Rates (CP):** $40–$52 S;

$46–$58 D; $175 ste. Extra person $6. Children under age 12 stay free. Parking: Outdoor, free. AE, CB, DC, DISC, EC, ER, JCB, MC, V.

〓〓 Drury Inn

I-70 and Stadium Blvd, 65203; tel 573/445-1800 or toll free 800/325-8300; fax 573/445-1800. Attractive sunken lobby tastefully decorated with plenty of seating and potted plants and trees. **Rooms:** 123 rms and stes. CI 3pm/CO noon. Nonsmoking rms avail. **Amenities:** 📞 A/C, satel TV w/movies, dataport. **Services:** ⚐ 🍴 ⟲ **Facilities:** 🏊 🏋 45 ⬦ Whirlpool. **Rates (CP):** $65 S or D; $95 ste. Extra person $10. Children under age 18 stay free. Parking: Outdoor, free. AE, CB, DC, DISC, MC, V.

〓 Red Roof Inn

201 E Texas Ave, 65202; tel 573/442-0145 or toll free 800/THE-ROOF; fax 573/499-9588. I-70 and Providence Rd. Basic budget lodging with good housekeeping standards. **Rooms:** 109 rms. CI 3pm/CO noon. Nonsmoking rms avail. **Amenities:** 📞 A/C, cable TV w/movies, dataport. **Services:** 🍴 ⟲ **Facilities:** ⬦ **Rates:** $34 S; $53 D. Extra person $9. Children under age 18 stay free. Parking: Outdoor, free. AE, CB, DC, DISC, MC, V.

RESTAURANTS 🍴

Alexander's Steak House

In the Biscayne Mall, 301 N Stadium Blvd; tel 573/445-1282. **Steak.** This dark and cozy room is dominated by a large barbecue grill on which diners can personally cook their hand-selected steaks (or the house chef will be happy to prepare them himself). Besides steak there are kabobs and some seafood, chicken, and pork dishes available. **FYI:** Reservations recommended. Children's menu. **Open:** Mon–Thurs 5–10pm, Fri–Sat 5–11pm, Sun 4–9pm. **Prices:** Main courses $12–$16. AE, CB, DC, DISC, MC, V. 📇 ⬦

Boone Tavern

811 E Walnut; tel 573/442-5123. Next to courthouse. **American.** A dark, cozy, and attractive restaurant with stained-glass windows and lamps. Historic photographs of Boone County hang on the walls. Plenty of appetizers, including pasta and pizza. Entrees are primarily steaks and seafood. **FYI:** Reservations accepted. Children's menu. **Open:** Mon–Sat 11am–midnight, Sun 10am–midnight. **Prices:** Main courses $9–$17. AE, CB, DC, DISC, MC, V. ⬦

Everett's

1601 Rangeline; tel 573/443-6200. Off I-70. **American.** Dark, cozy restaurant decorated with plants, ceiling fans, and a large aquarium. The menu offers a large variety of appetizers, soups, salads, burgers, sandwiches, pastas, barbecue, and Mexican dishes. The Cajun catfish, two charbroiled fillets of catfish marinated in Cajun seasonings and served with rice pilaf, is a popular item. **FYI:** Reservations accepted. Chil-

dren's menu. **Open:** Sun–Thurs 11am–10pm, Fri–Sat 11am–11pm. **Prices:** Main courses $8–$17. AE, CB, DC, DISC, MC, V. ⬦

Glenn's Cafe

29 S 9th St; tel 573/443-3094. At Cherry. **New American.** This relaxed, neon-lit cafe boasts an oyster bar among its attractions. Along with more traditional fare are several unique Creole and Cajun dishes like honey-and-chile-glazed duck accented with sherry and served with plantains. **FYI:** Reservations not accepted. Children's menu. **Open:** Tues–Thurs 11:30am–9pm, Fri–Sat 11:30am–10pm. **Prices:** Main courses $9–$16. AE, CB, DC, DISC, MC, V.

Haden House

4515 MO 763 N; tel 573/874-6060. 2 mi N of I-70. **American.** The dining room is an addition to an 1831 house and is surrounded by trees and an outdoor garden and patio. The ambience is cozy, decorated with dark wood, ceiling fans, mirrors, and paintings. Entrees include hickory-smoked chicken and ribs, lamb, seafood, steaks, and prime rib. For a special treat try the tournedos Rossini: two petite steaks topped with artichokes, mushrooms, and béarnaise sauce. **FYI:** Reservations recommended. Children's menu. Dress code. **Open:** Tues–Sat 5–10pm, Sun 11:30am–9pm. **Prices:** Main courses $10–$22. AE, CB, DC, DISC, MC, V. ⬦

Jack's Gourmet Restaurant

1903 Business Loop 70 E; tel 573/449-3927. **American.** Dark and cozy, with oil paintings, mirrors, and crystal light fixtures on the walls. Along with a wide variety of appetizers there are entrees of seafood, chicken, steaks, lamb, and veal. The brandied pork chop, a boneless broiled chop topped with brandy-laced crabmeat and cheese, is a highlight. **FYI:** Reservations recommended. Guitar/piano. **Open:** Mon–Sat 5–10pm. **Prices:** Main courses $10–$25. AE, CB, DC, DISC, MC, V.

Katy Station

4th and Broadway; tel 573/449-0835. **American.** A series of renovated railroad cars, each decorated with hanging plants, ceiling fans, and photographs of the original railroad station. Large selection of appetizers, salads, sandwiches, and burgers. Entrees include steaks, chicken, seafood, and pastas. Brandy pepper steak is a 10-oz sirloin marinated in brandy, then flame-broiled and topped with bacon, green onions, and mushrooms. **FYI:** Reservations accepted. Children's menu. **Open:** Sun–Thurs 11am–10pm, Fri–Sat 11am–11pm. **Prices:** Main courses $8–$16. AE, CB, DC, DISC, MC, V. ⬦

Los Bandidos

220 S 8th St; tel 573/443-2419. **Mexican.** The dining area, decorated with pottery and other Mexican artwork, has the ambience of a colorful old Mexican cantina. Offered are a wide variety of appetizers, salads, sandwiches, and chicken, beef, and seafood entrees. A healthy appetite will likely be satisfied by the plato de la casa, a king-sized chicken burrito filled with guacamole, sour cream, lettuce, tomato, and

cheese and smothered with salsa verde and enchilada sauce. **FYI:** Reservations accepted. Children's menu. **Open:** Lunch Mon–Thurs 11:30am–2pm, Fri–Sun 11:30am–11pm; dinner Mon–Thurs 4–9:30pm. **Prices:** Main courses $6–$9. AE, DC, MC, V. ♿

Mandarin House

In the Columbia Mall, 2300 Bernadette Dr; tel 573/445-7660. **Chinese.** Attractive dining area decorated in Chinese prints, potted plants, and floral arrangements. In addition to familiar Chinese entrees are special Korean dishes. The house specialty is Jap Tung: sliced sea cucumber, jumbo shrimp, sliced steamed pork, and scallops, all sautéed in garlic sauce with Chinese vegetables. **FYI:** Reservations accepted. **Open:** Mon–Thurs 11am–9:30pm, Fri–Sat 11am–10:30pm, Sun noon–9:30pm. **Prices:** Main courses $4–$20. AE, DC, DISC, MC, V. ♿

The Pasta Factory

1020 E Broadway; tel 573/449-3948. Broadway and Hitt. **Italian.** Attractive dining area decorated with stained-glass windows and light fixtures, photographs, and slow ceiling fans. The menu features a wide variety of appetizers, salads, and sandwiches, as well as chicken, steak, pasta, and seafood entrees. The house specialty, seafood straw and hay, contains shrimp, whitefish, and crabmeat sautéed together and tossed with spinach fettuccine. **FYI:** Reservations not accepted. Children's menu. **Open:** Daily 11am–10pm. **Prices:** Main courses $6–$13. AE, DC, DISC, MC, V. ♿

Fulton

Fulton takes its name from the inventor of the steamboat, Robert Fulton, and is centered in the area known as "Little Dixie" because many of the original settlers came from Kentucky and Virginia. The city is the Callaway County seat and home to Westminister College. **Information:** Kingdom of Callaway Chamber of Commerce, 409 Court St, Fulton, 65251-1724 (tel 573/642-3055).

MOTELS 🏨

▤ Budget Host

422 Gaylord Dr, 65251; tel 573/642-5991 or toll free 800/BUD-HOST; fax 573/642-5991. Standard budget motel with acceptable lodgings. **Rooms:** 20 rms and stes. CI 1pm/CO 11am. Nonsmoking rms avail. **Amenities:** 🛁 🍴 A/C, cable TV w/movies, refrig, dataport. Some units w/whirlpools. **Services:** 🚗 🛎 **Facilities:** 🛗 🅿️ **Rates:** Peak (Apr 15–Oct) $40 S; $50 D; $75–$85 ste. Extra person $5. Children under age 10 stay free. Lower rates off-season. Parking: Outdoor, free. Special rates for extended stays. Honeymoon package avail. AE, DC, DISC, MC, V.

▤ Super 8 Motel

US 54, Kingdom City, 65262; tel 573/642-2888 or toll free 800/800-8000; fax 573/642-2888. Exit 148 off I-70. Basic budget hotel with access to I-70. **Rooms:** 62 rms. CI 2pm/CO 11am. Nonsmoking rms avail. **Amenities:** 🛁 🅰️ A/C, cable TV w/movies. **Services:** 🛎 **Facilities:** ♿ **Rates (CP):** $39–$50 S; $48–$54 D. Extra person $3. Children under age 13 stay free. Parking: Outdoor, free. Group and extended stay discounts avail. AE, DC, DISC, MC, V.

Hannibal

Founded in 1818 and still an important river and rail trade center, Hannibal is best known as the childhood home of Mark Twain. The town celebrates its heritage and the famous author every July with National Tom Sawyer Days. **Information:** Hannibal Chamber of Commerce, 623 Broadway, PO Box 230, Hannibal, 63401 (tel 573/221-1101).

HOTELS 🏨

▤▤ Best Western Hotel Clemens

401 N 3rd St, 63401 (Downtown); tel 573/248-1150 or toll free 800/528-1234; fax 573/248-1155. Conveniently located off US 36, this hotel greets guests with an attractive, spacious lobby decorated with water fountains, potted plants and trees, and floral arrangements. **Rooms:** 78 rms. CI 1pm/CO 11am. Nonsmoking rms avail. **Amenities:** 🛁 🅰️ A/C, cable TV w/movies, dataport. Some units w/whirlpools. **Services:** 🚐 🛎 **Facilities:** 🛗 🏊 ♿ Games rm, whirlpool, washer/dryer. **Rates (CP):** Peak (June 25–Sept 10) $55–$85 S; $65–$95 D. Extra person $7. Lower rates off-season. Parking: Outdoor, free. AE, CB, DC, DISC, EC, ER, JCB, MC, V.

▤▤ Holiday Inn

4141 Market St, 63401; tel 573/221-6610 or toll free 800/325-0777; fax 573/221-3840. At US 61. A large atrium lobby decorated with palm trees and other potted plants gives this property an airy, tropical ambience. **Rooms:** 241 rms and stes. CI 3pm/CO 11am. Nonsmoking rms avail. **Amenities:** 🛁 🅰️ A/C, cable TV w/movies, dataport. Some units w/terraces. **Services:** ✕ 🛏 🛎 🍽 Car-rental desk. **Facilities:** 🛗 🏊 🅿️ ♿ 2 restaurants, 2 bars, volleyball, games rm, lawn games, sauna, whirlpool, beauty salon, playground, washer/dryer. **Rates:** Peak (Mem Day–Labor Day) $47 S or D; $125 ste. Extra person $7. Children under age 19 stay free. Lower rates off-season. Parking: Outdoor, free. AE, CB, DC, DISC, JCB, MC, V.

MOTELS

▤ Econo Lodge

612 Mark Twain Ave, 63401; tel 573/221-1490 or toll free 800/424-4777. On US 36. Clean, economy lodging fine for a short stay. **Rooms:** 48 rms. CI 1pm/CO 11am. Nonsmoking rms avail. **Amenities:** 🛁 A/C, cable TV w/movies. **Services:** 🛎 🍽 **Facilities:** 🛗 ♿ **Rates:** Peak (May–Oct 10) $43 S; $65 D. Extra person $5. Lower rates off-season. Parking: Outdoor, free. AE, DISC, MC, V.

▤▤ Travelodge

502 Mark Twain Ave, 63401; tel 573/221-4100 or toll free 800/578-7878; fax 573/221-4190. US 36, 1 block W of Mississippi River. Standard chain accommodations suitable for all travelers. **Rooms:** 42 rms, stes, and effic. CI noon/CO noon. Nonsmoking rms avail. **Amenities:** 🛎 🍴 📺 A/C, cable TV w/movies. **Services:** 🚐 🗝 🚳 **Facilities:** 🖼 **Rates (CP):** Peak (Mem Day–Labor Day) $52 S or D; $68 ste; $42 effic. Extra person $4. Children under age 18 stay free. Lower rates off-season. Parking: Outdoor, free. AE, CB, DC, DISC, JCB, MC, V.

RESTAURANTS 🍽

Mark Twain Dinette and Family Restaurant

3rd and Hill Sts; tel 573/221-5511. In Hannibal's historic district adjacent to Mark Twain House. **American.** A comfortable, informal eatery with ceiling fans, mirrors, and pictures of Mark Twain all around. Breakfast features biscuits and gravy, pancakes, and eggs. Other items are sandwiches, burgers, soups, and salads, and entrees like catfish and other seafood, chicken, steaks, and barbecue. **FYI:** Reservations accepted. Children's menu. No liquor license. **Open:** Sun–Thurs 6am–10pm, Fri–Sat 6am–11pm. **Prices:** Main courses $6–$12. MC, V. ♿

Missouri Territory Restaurant & Lodge

600 Broadway; tel 573/248-1440. **American.** Housed in a one-time federal courthouse building, this attractive dining room is distinguished by high ceilings, pillars, and a large brass and crystal chandelier. The menu offers a modest array of appetizers and salads. Entrees consist mainly of steaks, although some chicken and seafood dishes are available. **FYI:** Reservations accepted. Children's menu. **Open:** Tues–Sat 4–10pm, Sun 11am–2pm. **Prices:** Main courses $8–$15. DISC, MC, V.

ATTRACTIONS 🏛

Mark Twain Boyhood Home and Museum

208 Hill St; tel 573/221-9010. At the age of four, Samuel Clemens (aka Mark Twain) moved into this modest white clapboard home. Twain would later use it as the basis for Tom Sawyer's home, and other nearby locales are recognized as the autobiographical setting in Twain's novels. An adjoining museum contains first editions of Mark Twain's books, one of Twain's famous white suits, and a collection of Norman Rockwell paintings. **Open:** Peak (June–Aug) daily 8am–6pm. Reduced hours off-season. **$$**

Rockcliffe Mansion

1000 Bird St; tel 573/221-4140. Famous for a 1902 visit by Mark Twain, the turn-of-the-century mansion of the Cruikshank family has been restored with its original art nouveau details and furnishings. Guided tours are given daily. **Open:** Daily 9:30am. **$$**

Mark Twain Riverboat

Center Street Landing; tel 573/221-3222 or toll free 800/621-2322. During the one-hour tour of the Mississippi River, a guide describes legends, lore, and facts about the river. Dinner cruises feature live music and dancing. **Open:** Peak (June–Aug) departures daily at 11am and at 1:30, 4, and 7pm. Reduced hours off-season. **$$$**

Mark Twain Cave and Village

MO 79 S; tel 573/221-1656. The cave is made up of miles of passageway carved out of limestone by an ages-old underground stream. The 55-minute guided tour brings visitors through formations such as the Alligator, Aladdin's Place, and the Large Parlor (with its "grand piano"). Above ground, there's a picnic area, hiking trails, a rock shop, a restaurant, and a visitors center. **Open:** Peak (Mem Day–Labor Day) daily 8am–8pm. Reduced hours off-season. **$$$$**

Harrisonville

Once home to one of the wild West's most notorious outlaw families, the Younger brothers, this town now serves as the economic capital of the vast farming region that lies south of Kansas City. The seat of Cass County, it is known for its parks and vintage homes. **Information:** Harrisonville Area Chamber of Commerce, 400 E Mechanic, Harrisonville, 64701 (tel 816/884-5352).

MOTEL 🏨

▤ Super 8 Motel

2400 Rockhaven Rd, 64701; tel 816/887-2999 or toll free 800/800-8000; fax 816/887-5761. Standard budget property. **Rooms:** 39 rms and stes. CI 2pm/CO 11am. Nonsmoking rms avail. **Amenities:** 🛎 A/C, cable TV w/movies. 1 unit w/minibar. **Services:** 🗝 **Facilities:** ♿ Washer/dryer. **Rates:** $36 S; $44 D; $44–$54 ste. Extra person $3. Children under age 7 stay free. Parking: Outdoor, free. Rates increase for FFA convention in Sept. AE, CB, DC, DISC, JCB, MC, V.

Hermann

MOTEL 🏨

▤ German Haus Motel and B&B

113 Market St, 65091; tel 573/486-2222. On US 19. Quaint little motel with rooms decorated in attractive country motif. **Rooms:** 12 rms and stes. CI 2pm/CO 11am. Nonsmoking rms avail. **Amenities:** 🛎 A/C, cable TV. **Services:** Deluxe continental breakfast offered daily with queen rooms and suites, and on weekends with every other room. **Rates:** $32–$36 S; $36–$42 D; $55–$65 ste. Extra person $3–$5. Parking: Outdoor, free. AE, DISC, MC, V.

INNS

UNRATED **Market Street Bed & Breakfast**
210 Market St, 65041 (Historic District); tel 573/486-5597; fax 573/486-5597. Built in 1906, this romantic late-Victorian bed-and-breakfast presents individually decorated rooms with beautiful antique furniture. A fine choice for couples. Unsuitable for children under 18. **Rooms:** 3 rms. CI 3pm/CO 11am. No smoking. **Amenities:** 🛁 A/C. No phone or TV. **Facilities:** Guest lounge w/TV. **Rates (BB):** $70 S or D. Parking: Outdoor, free. MC, V.

UNRATED **Patty Kerr Bed and Breakfast**
109 E 3rd St, 65041 (Historical District); tel 573/486-2510. A bed-and-breakfast with an attractive patio in back overlooking a large garden. Its pretty rooms have a quaint, country ambience. Great for couples. Unsuitable for children under 18. **Rooms:** 3 rms; 1 cottage/villa. CI open/CO 10am. No smoking. **Amenities:** 🛁 📺 A/C, cable TV w/movies, refrig. No phone. Cottage has VCR. **Facilities:** Whirlpool. **Rates (BB):** Peak (Oct, May) $65–$85 S or D; $50–$85 cottage/villa. Extra person $25. Min stay special events. Lower rates off-season. Higher rates for special events/hols. Parking: Outdoor, free. Honeymoon packages avail. MC, V.

RESTAURANTS 🍴

Buckler's Deli and Pizza
100 Schiller St; tel 573/486-1440. In town center. **Deli/Pizza.** A sit-down deli and pizzeria decorated more attentively than most, with ceiling fans, floral arrangements, and a large aquarium. In addition to deli sandwiches and pizzas, choose from spaghetti, shrimp, and other substantial lunch items. **FYI:** Reservations not accepted. Beer and wine only. **Open:** Peak (Mem Day–Labor Day) daily 10am–10pm. **Prices:** Main courses $3–$4. MC, V. 🛇

Vintage 1847 Restaurant
In the Stone Hill Winery, Stonehill Hwy; tel 573/486-3479. 15 mi S of I-70 on US 19. **American/German.** Once the stable of this 1847 winery, the predictably rustic dining room is beautified by numerous potted plants. German dishes, the specialty here, include schnitzel (lightly breaded and seasoned pork cutlet served with a zesty sour cream–dill sauce). Steaks and fresh seafood are available as well. **FYI:** Reservations accepted. Children's menu. Wine only. **Open:** Sun–Thurs 11am–8:30pm, Fri 11am–9pm, Sat 11am–10pm. **Prices:** Main courses $12–$18. AE, DISC, MC, V. 🍴 🛇

Independence

See also Blue Springs

Important in the 1800s as the trailhead for the Santa Fe, California, and Oregon Trails, this historic city now is best known as the enjoyable hometown of former US President Harry S Truman. Independence is an ideal base for exploring nearby Kansas City. **Information:** Independence Chamber of Commerce, Box 1077, Independence, 64051 (tel 816/252-4745).

MOTELS 🏨

🛏 Red Roof Inn
13712 E 42nd Terrace, 64055; tel 816/373-2800 or toll free 800/843-7663; fax 816/373-0067. I-70 and Noland Rd. No-frills property. **Rooms:** 108 rms. CI 2pm/CO noon. Non-smoking rms avail. **Amenities:** 📺 A/C, cable TV w/movies. **Services:** 🚗 🛎 Car-rental desk. **Facilities:** 🛗 Adult guests have access to Bally's Health Club nearby. **Rates:** Peak (Mem Day–Nov) $38–$46 S; $44–$52 D. Extra person $8–$10. Children under age 18 stay free. Lower rates off-season. Parking: Outdoor, free. AE, CB, DC, DISC, MC, V.

🛏🛏 Shoney's Inn
4048 S Lynn Court Dr, 64055; tel 816/254-0100 or toll free 800/222-2222; fax 816/254-6796. I-70 and Noland Rd. Better-than-average, economy hotel fine for overnight guests or weekend travelers on a budget. Laundromat, fitness center, beauty salon, and shopping center nearby. **Rooms:** 114 rms. CI 3pm/CO noon. Nonsmoking rms avail. **Amenities:** 📺 A/C, cable TV w/movies. **Services:** 🖨 🚗 **Facilities:** 🏊 🏊 🛗 1 restaurant. **Rates:** Peak (May–Sept) $38–$45 S; $44–$51 D. Extra person $6. Children under age 19 stay free. Lower rates off-season. Parking: Outdoor, free. Rates increase for Royals baseball games. AE, CB, DC, DISC, ER, MC, V.

🛏 Super 8 Motel
4032 S Lynn Court Dr, 64055; tel 816/833-1888 or toll free 800/800-8000; fax 816/833-1888. I-70 and Noland Rd. Modest accommodations with easy access to interstate. Fine for overnight travelers on budgets. **Rooms:** 81 rms and stes. CI 3pm/CO 11am. Nonsmoking rms avail. **Amenities:** 📺 A/C, cable TV w/movies. **Services:** 🚗 🛎 **Facilities:** 🛗 **Rates:** Peak (Apr–Sept) $35–$45 S; $40–$65 D; $40–$50 ste. Extra person $5. Children under age 12 stay free. Lower rates off-season. Parking: Outdoor, free. Special rates for full-week visit. AE, CB, DC, DISC, MC, V.

RESTAURANTS 🍴

★ The Courthouse Exchange
113 W Lexington; tel 816/252-0344. **American.** Historic photographs, mirrors, exposed wooden beams, large wooden pillars, and gorgeous brass chandeliers dress up this eatery offering basic fare—hot and cold sandwiches, homemade bread, soups, and pies. **FYI:** Reservations not accepted. Piano. Children's menu. **Open:** Mon–Sat 11am–9pm. **Prices:** Main courses $7–$15. DISC, MC, V. 🍴 🛋

The Rheinland Restaurant
208 N Main; tel 816/461-5383. **German.** The attractive dining room features stained-glass hanging lamps and hanging plants, antique hutches, and an antique piano. German

specialties include Jaeger schnitzel with mushroom sauce and fries, and spaetzle. **FYI:** Reservations accepted. Guitar. Children's menu. Beer and wine only. **Open:** Tues–Thurs 11am–9pm, Fri–Sat 11am–9:30pm, Sun noon–7:30pm. **Prices:** Main courses $10–$14. AE, DISC, MC, V.

REFRESHMENT STOP

Clinton's
100 W Maple; tel 816/833-2625. At Main St. **Ice cream.** Located in the building that housed JH Clinton's Pharmacy (hence the name)—where Harry Truman had his first job—this will bring back memories for some folks of the ice cream parlors of yesteryear. The ice cream sodas here are particularly good; souvenirs and candy are also sold. **Open:** Peak (June–Aug) Mon–Thurs 10:30am–8pm, Fri–Sat 10:30am–10pm, Sun 12:30–6pm. No CC.

ATTRACTIONS

Harry S Truman National Historic Site
223 N Main St; tel 816/254-7199. Best known as the "Summer White House" of Bess and Harry Truman. Completed in 1885 by Mrs Truman's grandparents, the 14-room Victorian house was home to four generations of the family. The house contains the Trumans' antiques and heirlooms and remains as it was when the couple retired here in 1957. Tickets for guided tours are sold at the Ticket Center, located four blocks away on Truman St. **Open:** Peak (Mem Day–Labor Day) daily 8:30am–5pm. Reduced hours off-season. **$**

Harry S Truman Library and Museum
US 24 and Delaware St; tel 816/833-1400. The library contains more than 14 million pages of manuscripts, books, and other historical materials relating to the former president. The museum focuses on Truman's life and career, and features an exact reproduction of the Oval Office as it appeared in the 1950s, complete with a recording of Truman describing the items in his office. Both Harry and Bess Truman are buried in the courtyard of the library. **Open:** Daily 9am–5pm. **$**

Bingham-Waggoner Estate
313 W Pacific Ave; tel 816/461-3491. Built in 1855 on a 20-acre site, the home was owned by Missouri artist George Caleb Bingham from 1864 to 1870, and then served as the home of the Waggoner family for nearly a century until 1976. The 26 rooms are furnished almost entirely with belongings of the Waggoner family. The interior features eight coal-burning fireplaces, marble washbasins, a walk-in ice box, and an intercom system. Guided tours last 45 minutes. **Open:** Mon–Sat 10am–4pm, Sun 1–4pm. **$**

1859 Jail, Marshal's Home and Museum
217 N Main St; tel 816/252-1892. Visitors learn about 19th-century frontier justice at this site administered by the Jackson County Historical Society. On view are the jail cells that held Frank James, brother of Jesse, and Southern sympathizers during the Civil War—crowding up to 20 men and women in the same 8-by-10-foot cell. The museum houses interactive exhibits; and the Federal-style marshal's home is furnished with period pieces. Also on the premises is a one-room schoolhouse and a courtyard complete with an iron tub for watering horses and mules. **Open:** Peak (Apr–Oct) Mon–Sat 10am–5pm, Sun 11am–4pm. Reduced hours off-season. Closed Jan–Feb. **$**

Vaile Mansion
1500 N Liberty; tel 816/325-7111. A fine example of Second Empire architecture built during the state's boom years, this 30-room mansion features colorful ceiling paintings, hand-grained woodwork, and Victorian period furniture. **Open:** Apr–Oct, Mon–Sat 10am–4pm, Sun 1–4pm. **$**

Latter-Day Saints Mormon Visitor Center
937 Walnut; tel 816/836-3466. Guided tours explain the origin, purpose, and function of the Church of Jesus Christ of Latter-Day Saints. Walking history tour of the Missouri area, with special emphasis on artifacts from the 1800s. Spiritual and historical videos available for viewing. **Open:** Daily 9am–9pm. **Free**

National Frontier Trails Center
318 W Pacific Ave; tel 816/254-0059. The museum commemorates Independence's historic role as the only location that served as the starting point for the three major westward trails—the Santa Fe, California, and Oregon. Items on display include letters and diary entries describing the pioneers' journeys. A short film describes the three trails. **Open:** Mon–Fri 9am–4:30pm, Sat–Sun 12:30–4:30pm. **$**

Jefferson City

Named after Thomas Jefferson, whose actions enabled the Missouri territory to join the United States via the Louisiana Purchase, Jefferson City became the state capital on land donated for this purpose by the federal government. Straddling the banks of the Missouri River and located in the central part of the state, the city is a major transportation hub for the region and is home to Lincoln University. **Information:** Jefferson City Area Chamber of Commerce, 213 Adams St, PO Box 776, Jefferson City, 65102 (tel 314/634-3616).

HOTELS

Capitol Plaza Hotel
415 W McCarty, 65101; tel 573/635-1234 or toll free 800/338-8088; fax 573/635-4565. 2 blocks from state capitol. Large atrium/lobby offers plenty of comfortable seating and is decorated with lovely floral arrangements, trees, and a waterfall. A great choice for a relaxing evening or weekend in Jefferson City. **Rooms:** 255 rms and stes. Executive level. CI 3pm/CO noon. Nonsmoking rms avail. **Amenities:** A/C, satel TV w/movies. Some units w/whirlpools. **Services:**

Full breakfast available with suites. Additional movies can be purchased. **Facilities:** ⓕ 🛁 🔲 ☐ ⅋ 2 restaurants (see "Restaurants" below), 2 bars (1 w/entertainment), games rm, spa, sauna, whirlpool. **Rates:** Peak (Jan–Apr/Sept–Oct) $74–$99 S or D; $79–$129 ste. Extra person $15. Children under age 20 stay free. Lower rates off-season. Parking: Indoor/outdoor, free. Special packages include wedding/anniversary and weekend programs. AE, CB, DC, DISC, EC, ER, JCB, MC, V.

Hotel de Ville

319 W Miller, 65101; tel 573/636-5231 or toll free 800/392-3366; fax 573/636-5260. 1 block S of state capitol. Clean, comfortable rooms. Small but attractive lobby is decorated with potted plants and trees, oil paintings, and brass light fixtures. Easy access to US 50. **Rooms:** 98 rms and stes. CI 2pm/CO noon. Nonsmoking rms avail. **Amenities:** 🛁 ⚴ A/C, satel TV w/movies. **Services:** ✕ 🛁 ⟿ **Facilities:** ⓕ 🛁 ⅋ 1 restaurant (see "Restaurants" below), 1 bar (w/entertainment). Access to full-service gym with steam room and masseur. **Rates:** $47–$58 S; $54–$65 D; $67–$80 ste. Extra person $7. Children under age 12 stay free. Parking: Outdoor, free. Honeymoon package avail. AE, CB, DC, DISC, MC, V.

Ramada Inn

1510 Jefferson St, 65110; tel 573/635-7171 or toll free 800/2-RAMADA; fax 573/635-8006. Jefferson St exit off US 54. Easily accessible to US 54 and adjacent to a movie theater. The very attractive lobby is decorated with hardwood floors, hutches, coffee tables, brass chandeliers, potted plants and trees, and floral arrangements. **Rooms:** 236 rms and stes. CI 3pm/CO 11am. Nonsmoking rms avail. **Amenities:** 🛁 ⚴ 🖵 A/C, satel TV w/movies. Some units w/terraces. **Services:** ✕ 🚐 🛁 ⟿ ⟿ **Facilities:** ⓕ 🛁 🔲 ☐ ⅋ 1 restaurant (see "Restaurants" below), 1 bar (w/entertainment), games rm, playground. **Rates:** $55 S; $60 D; $85–$125 ste. Extra person $5. Children under age 16 stay free. Parking: Outdoor, free. Honeymoon package includes complimentary champagne, full breakfast, and complimentary suite for first anniversary. AE, CB, DC, DISC, EC, ER, JCB, MC, V.

MOTEL

Best Western Inn

1937 Christy Dr, 65101; tel 573/635-4175 or toll free 800/528-1234; fax 573/635-6709. Ellis Blvd exit off US 54 W. Standard chain motel. **Rooms:** 79 rms and stes. CI 2pm/CO noon. Nonsmoking rms avail. **Amenities:** 🛁 ⚴ 🖵 A/C, cable TV w/movies, dataport. Some units w/whirlpools. **Services:** ✕ 🛁 ⟿ **Facilities:** ⓕ 🛁 🔲 ⅋ 1 restaurant, 1 bar (w/entertainment), whirlpool, washer/dryer. **Rates:** $45–$55 S; $54–$59 D; $60–$70 ste. Children under age 12 stay free. Parking: Outdoor, free. AE, CB, DC, DISC, MC, V.

RESTAURANTS 🍴

Bingham's

In Ramada Inn, 1510 Jefferson St; tel 573/635-5388. Jefferson St exit off US 54. **American.** Attractive dining room decorated with etched glass dividers, potted plants, and trees, with a special room reserved for cigar smokers. The chicken scampi thermidor, a boneless chicken breast sautéed with shrimp and served with thermidor sauce, is a nice addition to more common varieties of steaks, pasta, chicken, and seafood. **FYI:** Reservations accepted. Children's menu. **Open:** Breakfast daily 6:30–11am; lunch daily 11am–2pm; dinner daily 5–10pm. **Prices:** Main courses $9–$17. AE, CB, DC, DISC, ER, MC, V. 🔽 ⅋

Cafe de Ville

In Hotel de Ville, 319 W Miller; tel 573/636-5231. 1 block S of state capitol. **New American.** Floral arrangements, potted trees, and ceiling fans all add to this attractive restaurant. Extensive menu includes a variety of gourmet appetizers and salads, as well as entrees of steaks, chicken, lamb, pasta, and seafood. Special selections change nightly, but you can almost always get the grilled salmon with peppercorn sauce and red caviar. **FYI:** Reservations recommended. Piano. Children's menu. **Open:** Mon–Sat 6am–10pm, Sun 6am–3pm. **Prices:** Main courses $10–$22. AE, CB, DC, DISC, MC, V. ⅋

Carnegie's at the Plaza

In Capitol Plaza Hotel, 415 W McCarty; tel 573/635-1234. 2 blocks from state capitol. **Continental.** This upscale restaurant is overflowing with bright floral arrangements; paintings and many mirrors fill the walls. The menu offers a nice selection of appetizers, soups, and salads, and a wide variety of entrees including steak, pheasant, veal, lamb, and seafood. A standout is the herb-crusted rack of lamb with pecan pesto, served on a bed of spinach. **FYI:** Reservations accepted. Children's menu. **Open:** Tues–Sat 5:30–11pm. **Prices:** Main courses $14–$25. AE, CB, DC, DISC, ER, MC, V. ⅋

Das Stein Haus

1436 Southridge Dr; tel 573/634-3869. **French/German.** Lots of German beer mugs predictably figure in the decor of "The Stein House." Predominantly German menu features veal and frogs' legs alongside seafood and items like steak à la Diana flambé, sautéed with fresh mushrooms, garlic, and onions and covered with cognac. **FYI:** Reservations accepted. Additional location: 623 E High (tel 314/634-6011). **Open:** Lunch Mon–Fri 11:30am–1:30pm; dinner daily 5–9:30pm. **Prices:** Main courses $11–$17. AE, MC, V.

Joplin

See also Carthage

Founded in the 1830s, this small city enjoyed economic success with the discovery of lead and zinc deposits nearby. A thriving mining town by the late 1800s, Joplin since has become a cultural and entertainment mecca along I-44. It is graced by nearly a thousand acres of parkland within the city limits and is home to Missouri Southern College. Joplin also serves as the gateway to the southwestern corner of the state. **Information:** Joplin Convention & Visitors Bureau, PO Box 1384, Joplin, 64802-1384 (tel 417/625-4791).

HOTEL

≣≣≣ Holiday Inn
3615 Rangeline Rd, 64804; tel 417/782-1000 or toll free 800/HOLIDAY; fax 417/623-4093. Exit 8B off I-44 W. This attractively landscaped property has a gorgeous atrium with skylights, many plants and trees, and a large brick waterfall. **Rooms:** 264 rms and stes. Executive level. CI 3pm/CO noon. Nonsmoking rms avail. **Amenities:** A/C, satel TV w/movies. Some units w/minibars. **Services:** **Facilities:** 1 restaurant, 2 bars (1 w/entertainment), sauna, steam rm, whirlpool. **Rates:** $75 S or D; $159 ste. Extra person $8. Children under age 12 stay free. Parking: Outdoor, free. Honeymoon packages avail. AE, DC, DISC, MC, V.

MOTELS

≣≣ Best Inns of America
3508 S Rangeline Rd, 64804; tel 417/781-6776 or toll free 800/237-8466. At jct I-44 and US 71. Close to major highways, motel is fine for short stays. **Rooms:** 112 rms and stes. CI open/CO 1pm. Nonsmoking rms avail. **Amenities:** A/C, cable TV w/movies. Some units w/whirlpools. **Services:** **Facilities:** **Rates (CP):** $39–$45 S; $42–$52 D; $150 ste. Extra person $6. Children under age 18 stay free. Parking: Outdoor, free. AE, CB, DC, DISC, MC, V.

≣ Motel 6
3031 S Rangeline Rd, 64601; tel 417/781-6400 or toll free 800/440-6000; fax 417/781-5140. 1 mi N of exit 8B off I-44. Although this motel doesn't have much to offer in the way of landscaping or decor, its basic rooms are clean and fairly comfortable. **Rooms:** 122 rms. CI 2pm/CO noon. Nonsmoking rms avail. **Amenities:** A/C, TV w/movies. **Services:** Restaurant nearby delivers exclusively to motel. **Facilities:** Washer/dryer. **Rates:** $29 S or D. Extra person $6. Children under age 17 stay free. Parking: Outdoor, free. AE, CB, DC, DISC, MC, V.

≣≣ Ramada Inn
3320 Rangeline Rd, 64804; tel 417/781-0500 or toll free 800/272-6232; fax 417/781-9388. I-44 to US 171. Standard property best for overnight guests or weekend visitors. **Rooms:** 171 rms and stes. Executive level. CI open/CO noon. Nonsmoking rms avail. **Amenities:** A/C, cable TV w/movies. Refrigerators in executive-level rooms. **Services:** Car-rental desk. **Facilities:** 1 restaurant, 1 bar (w/entertainment), basketball, sauna, whirlpool, playground. Free passes to fitness center and health spa. **Rates:** Peak (June 5–Sept 5) $58–$64 S; $68–$74 D;

$125 ste. Children under age 18 stay free. Lower rates off-season. Parking: Outdoor, free. AE, CB, DC, DISC, EC, MC, V.

Kansas City

See also Blue Springs, Independence

Founded in 1838 as a fur trading post, this city and its surrounding metropolitan area have grown into the state's second-largest population center. The city hosts a symphony orchestra, professional ballet and theatrical groups, excellent museums, and a wide assortment of nightlife attractions. Yet despite its size and cultural opportunities, Kansas City retains a small-town atmosphere with its large number of parks, gently rolling hills, and tree-lined streets. The nearby Missouri River offers floating casinos, and pari-mutuel betting is available in Leavenworth, Kansas, to the west. **Information:** Greater Kansas City Convention & Visitors Bureau, 1100 Main St, #2550, Kansas City, 64105 (tel 816/221-5242).

PUBLIC TRANSPORTATION
The **Metro** is the public bus system, serving all counties except Johnson County, Kansas. There are 43 routes, most in a north–south direction. Fare is 90¢ for regular buses and $1.10 for express buses. Children under 5 ride free; children 6–11 pay half-fare. Exact change required. Free transfers available. For information call 816/221-0660. The easiest way to travel between downtown, Crown Center, Westport, and Country Club Plaza is by the Trolley. The fare is $3 (exact fare only), which allows you to get on and off the Trolley three times during the day. Children 5 and under ride free. For more information call 816/221-3399.

HOTELS

≣≣≣ Adam's Mark
9103 E 39th St, 64133; tel 816/737-0200 or toll free 800/444-ADAM; fax 816/737-4713. I-70 at Blue Ridge cutoff. This beautiful hotel has a large, comfortable lobby with marble tables, plush furniture, and colorful art hanging from the walls. Located near the football and baseball stadiums, it's a good choice for visiting sports fans. **Rooms:** 374 rms and stes. CI 3pm/CO noon. Nonsmoking rms avail. **Amenities:** A/C, satel TV w/movies, dataport, voice mail. **Services:** Car-rental desk, social director, children's program, babysitting. **Facilities:** 2 restaurants, 2 bars (1 w/entertainment), games rm, spa, sauna, steam rm, whirlpool, washer/dryer. **Rates:** Peak (May–Nov) $79–$129 S; $89–$139 D; $125–$500 ste. Children under age 18 stay free. Lower rates off-season. Parking: Outdoor, free. New Year's package avail. AE, CB, DC, DISC, MC, V.

≣≣≣ Courtyard by Marriott
500 E 105th St, 64131; tel 816/941-3333 or toll free 800/321-2211; fax 816/941-7971. Attractive landscaping with shrubs and flowers and spacious, beautiful lobby with marble-

topped tables make this more appealing than standard hotels. Easy access from interstate. **Rooms:** 149 rms and stes. CI 4pm/CO noon. Nonsmoking rms avail. **Amenities:** 🛅 🍷 A/C, cable TV w/movies, dataport. All units w/terraces. **Services:** 🚐 ⊠ ⊸ Several local restaurants provide room service. **Facilities:** 🛗 🏌 ⌞30⌟ ⅙ 1 restaurant (bkfst only), 1 bar, whirlpool, washer/dryer. **Rates:** $77–$79 S; $87–$89 D; $89–$95 ste. Extra person $10. Children under age 12 stay free. Parking: Outdoor, free. AE, CB, DC, DISC, JCB, MC, V.

≣≣≣≣ Crowne Plaza

4445 Main St, 64111; tel 816/531-3000 or toll free 800/2-CROWNE; fax 816/531-3007. On Country Club Plaza. Convenient and luxurious, this hotel is worth the money for an exceptional vacation in Kansas City. Gold-plated and glass coffee tables, attractive floral drapes, potted trees, flowers, and plants accent the nicely decorated lobby. **Rooms:** 296 rms and stes. Executive level. CI 4pm/CO noon. Nonsmoking rms avail. **Amenities:** 🛅 🍷 🍽 A/C, cable TV w/movies, dataport, voice mail. **Services:** ✗ 🖛 🆅🅿 🚐 ⊠ ⊸ 🐾 **Facilities:** 🛗 🏌 ⌞500⌟ 🖳 ⅙ 1 restaurant, 1 bar, spa, whirlpool. **Rates:** Peak (Sept 10–Dec 20) $109–$129 S; $119–$149 D; $175–$350 ste. Extra person $10. Children under age 18 stay free. Lower rates off-season. Parking: Indoor, free. Honeymoon package avail. AE, CB, DC, DISC, MC, V.

≣≣≣ DoubleTree Kansas City Airport

8801 NW 112th St, 64195; tel 816/891-8900 or toll free 800/525-6322; fax 816/891-8030. Exit 12 off I-29. Very pleasant grounds landscaped with large trees and lovely flowers. Spacious lobby features green plants, marble tiles, and comfortable upholstered sofas and chairs. **Rooms:** 347 rms and stes. CI 3pm/CO noon. Nonsmoking rms avail. **Amenities:** 🛅 🍷 A/C, dataport. **Services:** ✗ 🚐 ⊠ ⊸ Car-rental desk, babysitting. **Facilities:** 🛗 🚲 🎿 📷 🏌 ⌞1000⌟ 🖳 ⅙ 1 restaurant, 1 bar, basketball, volleyball, games rm, spa, sauna, steam rm, whirlpool, washer/dryer. Bike trail. **Rates:** $79–$99 S; $89–$109 D; $160–$350 ste. Extra person $10. Children under age 13 stay free. Parking: Outdoor, free. Packages include weekend, honeymoon, and romance. AE, CB, DC, DISC, MC, V.

≣≣≣ Embassy Suites Plaza Hotel

220 W 43rd St, 64111; tel 816/756-1720 or toll free 800/EMBASSY; fax 816/756-3260. 3 blocks N of Country Club Plaza. Very spacious atrium/lobby decorated with hanging plants and potted trees, large skylights, and gorgeous fountain. **Rooms:** 266 stes. CI 3pm/CO noon. Nonsmoking rms avail. **Amenities:** 🛅 🍷 🍽 A/C, cable TV w/movies, refrig, dataport, voice mail. All units w/terraces, some w/fireplaces. **Services:** ✗ ⊠ ⊸ Babysitting. **Facilities:** 🛗 🏌 ⌞300⌟ ⅙ 1 restaurant (lunch and dinner only), 2 bars (1 w/entertainment), games rm, spa, sauna, steam rm, whirlpool, washer/dryer. **Rates (BB):** Peak (June–Aug/Dec) $99–$159 ste. Extra person $10. Children under age 17 stay free. Lower

rates off-season. Parking: Indoor/outdoor, free. Rates increase for conventions and sporting events. AE, CB, DC, DISC, ER, JCB, MC, V.

≣≣≣ Hampton Inn Airport

11212 N Newark Circle, 64153; tel 816/464-5454 or toll free 800/426-7866; fax 816/464-5416. I-29 and NW 112th St; 1 mi S of KCI Airport. Standard chain property distinguished by attractive lobby with flowers, potted plants, and ceiling fans. **Rooms:** 120 rms. CI 3pm/CO noon. Nonsmoking rms avail. **Amenities:** 🛅 🍷 🍽 A/C, satel TV w/movies, dataport. **Services:** 🚐 ⊠ ⊸ **Facilities:** 🛗 ⌞36⌟ ⅙ Washer/dryer. **Rates (CP):** Peak (May–Sept) $59 S; $65 D. Children under age 18 stay free. Lower rates off-season. Parking: Outdoor, free. Rates increase for FFA Convention. Football packages avail. AE, CB, DC, DISC, MC, V.

≣≣ Historic Suites

612 Central Ave, 64105 (Garment District); tel 816/842-6544 or toll free 800/733-0612; fax 816/842-0656. Downtown Broadway exit off of I-35 and I-70. Average-size hotel tastefully decorated with potted plants and trees. Hallways overlook lovely atrium. **Rooms:** 100 stes. CI 3pm/CO noon. Nonsmoking rms avail. Nicely decorated rooms have plants, chairs, and sofas. **Amenities:** 🛅 🍷 🍽 A/C, cable TV w/movies, refrig, voice mail. Ceiling fans. **Services:** ⊠ ⊸ 🐾 VCRs available on request. Complimentary shuttle to restaurants and shopping areas. **Facilities:** 🛗 🏌 ⌞70⌟ ⅙ Spa, sauna, whirlpool, washer/dryer. Free access to Gold's Gym. **Rates (CP):** $79–$180 ste. Parking: Indoor/outdoor, free. Rates subject to change during conventions and sporting events. Special packages for Chiefs football and Royals baseball games avail. AE, DC, DISC, MC, V.

≣≣ Holiday Inn Express

801 Westport Rd, 64111; tel 816/931-1000 or toll free 800/HOLIDAY; fax 816/561-0447. I-29 S to I-35 S to SW Trafficway to Westport Rd. Larger-than-average rooms in a small but comfortable hotel. Children eat free next door. **Rooms:** 109 rms. CI 2pm/CO noon. Nonsmoking rms avail. **Amenities:** 🛅 🍷 A/C, cable TV w/movies, dataport. **Services:** ✗ 🚐 ⊠ ⊸ **Facilities:** ⌞120⌟ 🖳 ⅙ Guests over age of 21 have access to St Lukes Health Facility, which includes fitness center, swimming pool, and health spa. **Rates (CP):** $79 S or D. Children under age 12 stay free. Parking: Outdoor, free. Corporate rates avail. AE, CB, DC, DISC, MC, V.

≣≣ Hotel Savoy

219 W 9th St, 64105 (Garment District); tel 816/842-3575 or toll free 800/728-6922; fax 816/842-3575. Kansas City's oldest hotel, established in 1888, the Savoy is located in the old garment district of the city. A gorgeous, stained-glass dome lights the lobby and showcases the beautiful paintings displayed on the walls; an art gallery is adjacent. Management is slowly transforming the property into a European-style bed-and-breakfast. **Rooms:** 14 stes. CI 3pm/CO 1pm. No smoking. Furniture in rooms is old, but comfortable and

attractive. **Amenities:** ⬜ ⬜ ⬜ A/C, cable TV w/movies. **Services:** ⬜ ⬜ ⬜ Complimentary liqueur offered. **Facilities:** ⬜ 1 restaurant (*see* "Restaurants" below), 1 bar, washer/dryer. **Rates (BB):** $80–$120 ste. Extra person $20. Parking: Outdoor, free. AE, CB, DC, DISC, MC, V.

⬜⬜⬜⬜ Hyatt Regency Crown Center

2345 McGee St, 64108 (Crown Center); tel 816/421-1234 or toll free 800/233-1234; fax 816/435-4190. Downtown at Hallmark's Crown Center Complex. Luxurious, with beautiful atrium/lobby adorned with various hanging and potted plants and impressive palm trees, as well as plenty of comfortable sofas and chairs. Gorgeous, multi-colored fountain is focal point. **Rooms:** 731 rms and stes. Executive level. CI 3pm/CO noon. Nonsmoking rms avail. **Amenities:** ⬜ ⬜ ⬜ A/C, cable TV w/movies, dataport, voice mail. Some units w/minibars, some w/whirlpools. Every room has big-screen TV. **Services:** ✕ ⬜ ⬜ ⬜ ⬜ ⬜ Babysitting. **Facilities:** ⬜ ⬜ ⬜ ⬜ ⬜ 3 restaurants (*see* "Restaurants" below), 3 bars, sauna, steam rm, whirlpool. **Rates:** $155 S; $180 D; $195–$800 ste. Extra person $25. Children under age 18 stay free. Parking: Indoor, $9/day. Romance package, Royals baseball and Chiefs football games package, Worlds of Fun package avail. AE, CB, DC, DISC, JCB, MC, V.

⬜⬜⬜ Kansas City Airport Marriott Hotel

775 Brasilia Ave, 64153; tel 816/464-2200 or toll free 800/228-9290; fax 816/464-5915. 1 mi NE of airport. Convenient to airport, hotel grounds are attractively landscaped with large trees and gorgeous flowers surrounding a peaceful lake. Lobby is luxuriously furnished with plush chairs and sofas, beautiful carpet, marble tiles, and brass chandelier. **Rooms:** 382 rms and stes. Executive level. CI 3pm/CO noon. Nonsmoking rms avail. **Amenities:** ⬜ ⬜ A/C, dataport, voice mail. **Services:** ✕ ⬜ ⬜ ⬜ ⬜ ⬜ Car-rental desk. **Facilities:** ⬜ ⬜ ⬜ ⬜ ⬜ 1 restaurant, 1 bar, basketball, volleyball, games rm, sauna, steam rm, whirlpool, washer/dryer. **Rates:** $133 S; $143 D; $150–$250 ste. Children under age 18 stay free. Parking: Outdoor, free. Special breakfast package avail. AE, CB, DC, DISC, ER, JCB, MC, V.

⬜⬜⬜ Kansas City Marriott Downtown

200 W 12 St, 64105; tel 816/421-6800 or toll free 800/548-4782; fax 816/855-4418. Jct I-35 and I-70. Perfect for travelers looking for a touch of luxury in their accommodations. Large atrium/lobby with quiet, little waterfall, green plants, lovely trees, and comfortable leather chairs. Easy access to interstate. **Rooms:** 573 rms and stes. Executive level. CI 3pm/CO noon. Nonsmoking rms avail. **Amenities:** ⬜ ⬜ A/C, dataport, voice mail. All units w/minibars. **Services:** ✕ ⬜ ⬜ ⬜ ⬜ ⬜ Masseur. Car rental can be arranged. **Facilities:** ⬜ ⬜ ⬜ ⬜ ⬜ 1 restaurant, 1 bar (w/entertainment), sauna. **Rates:** Peak (May–June/Sept–Nov) $63–$114 S or D; $250–$500 ste. Extra person $20. Children under age 18 stay free. Lower rates off-season.

Parking: Indoor, free. Special packages include breakfast for two, entertainment, Worlds of Fun, and honeymoon. AE, CB, DC, DISC, MC, V.

⬜⬜⬜ Park Place Hotel

1601 N Universal Ave, 64120; tel 816/483-9900 or toll free 800/821-8532; fax 816/231-1418. I-435 and Front St. Clean rooms and friendly service. Easy access to I-435. Bright, spacious public areas. **Rooms:** 328 rms. CI 3pm/CO noon. Nonsmoking rms avail. **Amenities:** ⬜ ⬜ ⬜ A/C. Some units w/terraces. Some rooms have dataports. **Services:** ✕ ⬜ ⬜ ⬜ ⬜ ⬜ **Facilities:** ⬜ ⬜ ⬜ ⬜ ⬜ 1 restaurant, 1 bar (w/entertainment), sauna, steam rm. **Rates:** Peak (June–Aug) $59–$125 S or D. Lower rates off-season. Parking: Outdoor, free. Worlds of Fun and Oceans of Fun packages avail. AE, CB, DC, DISC, MC, V.

⬜⬜⬜ The Plaza Inn

1 E 45th St, 64111; tel 816/753-7400 or toll free 800/525-6321; fax 816/753-0359. On Country Club Plaza. Roomy hotel near restaurants, shops, and entertainment spots. Lobby has plenty of seating, potted plants, and lovely aquarium. **Rooms:** 229 rms and stes. CI 3pm/CO noon. Nonsmoking rms avail. **Amenities:** ⬜ ⬜ A/C, cable TV w/movies, dataport, voice mail. Some units w/terraces. **Services:** ✕ ⬜ ⬜ ⬜ ⬜ Car-rental desk, babysitting. **Facilities:** ⬜ ⬜ ⬜ ⬜ 1 restaurant, 1 bar, games rm, beauty salon. **Rates:** $69–$99 S or D; $109–$175 ste. Children under age 17 stay free. Parking: Indoor/outdoor, free. Casino, shopping, and other packages avail. AE, CB, DC, DISC, JCB, MC, V.

⬜⬜⬜ Radisson Suite Hotel Kansas City

106 W 12th St, 64105; tel 816/221-7000 or toll free 800/333-3333; fax 816/221-3477. At Baltimore; 3 blocks E of I-35. Largely suite hotel, convenient to many restaurants and shops. **Rooms:** 214 rms and stes. CI 3pm/CO noon. Nonsmoking rms avail. **Amenities:** ⬜ ⬜ A/C, cable TV, refrig, dataport. **Services:** ✕ ⬜ ⬜ ⬜ ⬜ **Facilities:** ⬜ ⬜ ⬜ ⬜ 3 restaurants (*see* "Restaurants" below), 1 bar, washer/dryer. Adult guests have complimentary use of nearby Gold's Gym. **Rates (CP):** $85–$125 S; $95–$135 D; $250 ste. Extra person $10. Children under age 12 stay free. Rates may increase during frequent conventions held at hotel. AE, CB, DC, DISC, MC, V.

⬜⬜⬜ Ramada Hotel Airport

7301 NW Tiffany Springs Rd, 64153; tel 816/741-9500 or toll free 800/234-9501; fax 816/741-0655. Exit 10 off I-29. Suitable for all travelers. You'll receive a friendly greeting upon entering the very inviting lobby decorated with potted plants and trees. **Rooms:** 249 rms and stes. CI 3pm/CO noon. Nonsmoking rms avail. **Amenities:** ⬜ ⬜ ⬜ A/C, cable TV w/movies, dataport. Some units w/whirlpools. **Services:** ✕ ⬜ ⬜ ⬜ ⬜ Car-rental desk. Free shuttle to nearby restaurants and shopping. **Facilities:** ⬜ ⬜ ⬜ ⬜ 1 restaurant, 1 bar, basketball, volleyball, games rm, spa, sauna, steam rm, whirlpool, washer/dryer. **Rates:** Peak (May–Sept) $74–$84 S; $79–$89 D; $175–$225 ste. Extra person $10. Children under age 12 stay free. Lower rates off-season. Parking: Outdoor, free. Special packages include bed-and-breakfast and park-and-fly. AARP discounts avail. AE, CB, DC, DISC, JCB, MC, V.

⊟⊟⊟ The Raphael

325 Ward Pkwy, 64112; tel 816/756-3800 or toll free 800/821-5343. On Country Club Plaza. Within walking distance of many shops and restaurants, this hotel is wonderfully decorated with hanging chandeliers, potted plants and trees, marble tile, and sofas and chairs. **Rooms:** 123 rms and stes. CI 1pm/CO 1pm. Nonsmoking rms avail. **Amenities:** 🛅 ♨ ☎ A/C, cable TV, refrig, dataport, voice mail, bathrobes. All units w/minibars. **Services:** ﴾○﴿ ➡ VP ⬜ ↩ Twice-daily maid svce, babysitting. **Facilities:** 1 restaurant (lunch and dinner only), 1 bar (w/entertainment), washer/dryer. For $10, guests have access to nearby fitness center and swimming pool. **Rates (CP):** Peak (Sept 5–Jan 2) $95 S; $115 D; $120–$150 ste. Extra person $20. Children under age 18 stay free. Lower rates off-season. Parking: Indoor/outdoor, free. AE, CB, DC, DISC, EC, JCB, MC, V.

⊟⊟⊟⊟ The Ritz-Carlton

401 Ward Pkwy, 64112; tel 816/756-1500 or toll free 800/241-3333; fax 816/531-1483. On Country Club Plaza. Elegant hotel with marble tiles and fireplace, crystal chandeliers, large paintings, exquisite dark wood accents, and incredible wooden pillars. The place to stay if you're looking for something extra. Near golf, tennis, and jogging facilities. **Rooms:** 373 rms and stes. Executive level. CI 3pm/CO noon. Nonsmoking rms avail. Spacious rooms have marble counters and crystal fixtures. **Amenities:** 🛅 ♨ ☎ A/C, cable TV w/movies, dataport, in-rm safe, bathrobes. All units w/minibars, all w/terraces. **Services:** ﴾○﴿ ➡ VP 🚗 ⬜ ↩ Twice-daily maid svce, car-rental desk, masseur, babysitting. **Facilities:** ℹ ⚽ 600 ⬜ ♿ 2 restaurants (see "Restaurants" below), 2 bars (w/entertainment), spa, sauna, steam rm. **Rates:** $149–$159 S or D; $225–$275 ste. Parking: Indoor, free. AE, CB, DC, DISC, MC, V.

⊟⊟⊟ Sheraton Suites Country Club Plaza

770 W 47th St, 64112; tel 816/934-4400 or toll free 800/227-2416; fax 816/561-7330. On Country Club Plaza. Better than average, within walking distance of more than 180 shops, restaurants, and entertainment spots. Great for weekend visits. **Rooms:** 259 stes. Executive level. CI 3pm/CO noon. Nonsmoking rms avail. **Amenities:** 🛅 ♨ 🖭 ☎ A/C, satel TV w/movies, refrig, dataport. Some units w/terraces. Nintendo games. **Services:** ✕ VP ⬜ ↩ Babysitting. **Facilities:** ℹ ⚽ 100 ♿ 1 restaurant, 1 bar (w/entertainment), whirlpool, washer/dryer. **Rates:** Peak (Mar 8–9/Sept 20–21/Nov 28–Dec 14) $159–$229 ste. Extra person $20. Children under age 18 stay free. Lower rates off-season.

Parking: Indoor, free. Special packages include baseball, Worlds of Fun, Oceans of Fun, honeymoon, and weekends with breakfast. AE, CB, DC, DISC, EC, ER, JCB, MC, V.

⊟⊟⊟ Westin Crown Center

1 Pershing Rd, 64108 (Crown Center); tel 816/474-4400 or toll free 800/228-3000; fax 816/391-4438. Large, comfortable lobby decorated with lovely plants, and atrium with large trees, waterfall, and fountain. **Rooms:** 724 rms and stes. Executive level. CI 3pm/CO noon. Nonsmoking rms avail. **Amenities:** 🛅 ♨ ☎ A/C, TV w/movies, dataport, voice mail. All units w/minibars, all w/terraces, some w/fireplaces, some w/whirlpools. **Services:** ﴾○﴿ ➡ VP ⬜ ↩ ↩ Car-rental desk, masseur, children's program, babysitting. **Facilities:** ℹ ⚽2 ⚽ ⚽ 1000 ⬜ ♿ 3 restaurants (see "Restaurants" below), 3 bars (1 w/entertainment), basketball, spa, sauna, steam rm, whirlpool. Outdoor putting green. **Rates:** $155–$175 S; $180–$200 D; $250–$1,000 ste. Extra person $25. Children under age 18 stay free. Parking: Indoor, $9/day. Honeymoon and anniversary packages avail. AE, CB, DC, DISC, ER, JCB, MC, V.

MOTELS

⊟⊟ Budgetel Inn

8601 Hillcrest Rd, 64138; tel 816/822-7000 or toll free 800/428-3438; fax 816/822-8488. South Kansas City. Small hotel with modest but clean rooms. Good for those on budgets. **Rooms:** 106 rms. CI 1pm/CO noon. Nonsmoking rms avail. **Amenities:** 🛅 ♨ ☎ A/C, satel TV w/movies, dataport, voice mail. **Services:** ⬜ ↩ ↩ Car-rental desk. **Facilities:** 12 ♿ Washer/dryer. **Rates (CP):** Peak (June–Labor Day) $40–$62 S; $47–$62 D. Children under age 18 stay free. Lower rates off-season. Parking: Outdoor, free. AE, CB, DC, DISC, MC, V.

⊟⊟ Days Inn North

2232 Taney St, 64116; tel 816/421-6000 or toll free 800/329-7466; fax 816/421-6675. Exit 6A off I-35. Dependable chain property good for a short visit. **Rooms:** 89 rms and stes. Executive level. CI 2pm/CO noon. Nonsmoking rms avail. **Amenities:** 🛅 A/C, cable TV w/movies. Dataports available on luxury level. **Services:** ⬜ ↩ **Facilities:** ♿ Washer/dryer. **Rates (CP):** Peak (Mem Day–Aug) $45–$55 S; $55–$65 D; $65–$85 ste. Extra person $6. Children under age 13 stay free. Lower rates off-season. Parking: Outdoor, free. AE, CB, DC, DISC, MC, V.

⊟ Super 8 Motel

6900 NW 83rd Terrace, 64152; tel 816/587-0808 or toll free 800/800-8000. Exit 8 off I-29. Basic motel offering low rates but very few extras. **Rooms:** 50 rms and stes. CI 2pm/CO 11am. Nonsmoking rms avail. **Amenities:** 🛅 A/C, cable TV w/movies. **Services:** ↩ ↩ **Facilities:** ♿ **Rates:** Peak (May–Sept/Nov) $40–$45 S; $41–$67 D; $63–$68 ste. Extra person $5. Children under age 12 stay free. Lower rates off-season. Parking: Outdoor, free. Rates increase for conventions and sporting events. AE, DC, DISC, MC, V.

≡≡ Travelodge

1051 N Cambridge Ave, 64120; tel 816/483-7900 or toll free 800/500-7878; fax 816/483-8887. Front St exit off I-435. Easy access to I-435 makes this small but comfortable property a nice, convenient choice for an overnight stay or weekend visit. **Rooms:** 134 rms and stes. CI noon/CO noon. Non-smoking rms avail. **Amenities:** ☎ ⌨ A/C, cable TV w/movies. **Services:** ⬇ ↺ ⬳ **Facilities:** ⬚ ⬛ ᕫ Basketball, whirlpool, washer/dryer. **Rates (CP):** Peak (Mem Day–Aug) $50–$55 S or D; $75 ste. Extra person $5. Children under age 19 stay free. Lower rates off-season. Parking: Outdoor, free. AE, CB, DC, DISC, EC, ER, JCB, MC, V.

INN

≡≡≡ Southmoreland on the Plaza

116 E 46th St, 64112; tel 816/531-7979; fax 816/531-2407. 1½ blocks E of Main St. Bed-and-breakfast located on small, well-shaded, attractively landscaped lot. Great views and peaceful setting. Unsuitable for children under 13. **Rooms:** 12 rms. CI 4:30pm/CO 11am. No smoking. Rooms attractively decorated with Shaker- and Chippendale-style furniture. **Amenities:** ☎ ⌨ A/C, dataport. No TV. Some units w/terraces, some w/fireplaces, some w/whirlpools. **Services:** Wine/sherry served. Great service and friendly staff. **Facilities:** ⬚ ᕫ Guest lounge w/TV. Free access to nearby fitness center with pool and tennis courts. Dining on screened porch or enclosed solarium. **Rates (BB):** $90–$135 S; $100–$145 D. Parking: Outdoor, free. Special corporate rates avail. AE, MC, V.

RESTAURANTS ▯▯

The American Restaurant

In the Crown Center, 200 E 25th St; tel 816/426-1133. Penway exit off I-35 N. **New American.** One of the top places for fine dining in Kansas City, this formal eatery is beautifully decorated with solid oak and satin wood furniture, brass accents, and fan-shaped networks of oak bentwood along the high ceilings. Large, colorful, floral arrangements are placed throughout. The extensive menu features coriander-encrusted rack of lamb with squash linguine and oven-roasted bell peppers, broiled Maine lobster, and Missouri farm-raised ostrich. The seared sea scallops with lemongrass-shiitake broth and jasmine rice is a favorite. **FYI:** Reservations accepted. Piano. Dress code. **Open:** Lunch Mon–Fri 11:15am–1:45pm; dinner Mon–Thurs 6–10pm, Fri–Sat 6–11pm. **Prices:** Main courses $18–$26. AE, CB, DC, MC, V. ♥ VP ᕫ

Annie's Santa Fe

100 Ward Pkwy; tel 816/753-1621. **Southwestern.** On Country Club Plaza. This popular spot on the Plaza serves American versions of Mexican favorites. The famous spicy burritos are made with cubed pork and beef and refried beans, topped with chile verde and melted cheese, and served with Mexican rice. **FYI:** Reservations recommended. Children's menu. Ad-

ditional locations: 5600 E Bannister Rd (tel 966-1400); 11855 W 95th St (tel 492-6121). **Open:** Peak (Thanksgiving–Christmas) Sun–Thurs 11am–10pm, Fri–Sat 11am–11pm. **Prices:** Main courses $5–$9. AE, CB, DC, DISC, MC, V. ▦

Arthur Bryant's

1727 Brooklyn; tel 816/231-1123. 2 blocks S of I-70. **Barbecue.** The clean and simple decor fits this barbecue sandwich joint. Once you try the barbecue sauce, you might want to take a jar home with you. Catering available. **FYI:** Reservations accepted. Beer and wine only. **Open:** Mon–Thurs 10am–9:30pm, Fri–Sat 10am–10pm, Sun 11am–9:30pm. **Prices:** Main courses $6–$14. AE, MC, V. ▦

Benton's Steak and Chop House

In Westin Crown Center, 1 Pershing Rd; tel 816/474-4400. **Steak.** Enjoy a panoramic view of the Crown Center and downtown Kansas City while enjoying a cocktail in the lounge or a meal of charbroiled steak, chops, or fresh seafood. The restaurant features a few original works of the muralist Thomas Hart Benton, a Missouri native. **FYI:** Reservations recommended. Children's menu. **Open:** Mon–Sat 5:30–10pm, Sun 10–2pm, Sun 5–9pm. **Prices:** Main courses $19–$45. AE, CB, DC, DISC, MC, V. ♥ ⛰ ⬛ VP

Blvd Cafe

703 Southwest Blvd; tel 816/842-6984. 2 blocks W of Broadway. **Mediterranean/Spanish.** This hip, funky, and laid-back downtown spot serves an array of Spanish and Middle Eastern delights to a fashionable crowd. Guests enjoy regularly scheduled live jazz performances while sampling a long list of tapas and other hot and cold appetizers and dishes like paella and sumac chicken, which is marinated in olive oil and sumac (a tart, red, Middle Eastern spice). Interesting wine list. **FYI:** Reservations recommended. Jazz. **Open:** Lunch Mon–Fri 11am–2pm; dinner Mon–Thurs 5–10pm, Fri–Sat 5–11pm; brunch Sun 10am–2pm. **Prices:** Main courses $4–$14. DC, MC, V. ▦ ᕫ

Cafe Allegro

1815 W 39th St; tel 816/561-3663. At State Line. **New American.** Casually elegant and cheerful, this restaurant is frequented by a well-to-do, older crowd. The brick walls are hung with large, colorful oil paintings, and an exquisite, intricately etched glass divider separates the bar from the restaurant. Available are items like homemade fresh pasta, veal loin stuffed with wild mushrooms, and Asian tuna tartar. A favorite specialty is thick swordfish steak grilled over pecan and set atop a zesty couscous and enriched by a relish of roast tomato and niçoise olive. The wine list is one of the largest in the city; some 40 wines are available by the glass. **FYI:** Reservations recommended. Dress code. No smoking. **Open:** Lunch Mon–Fri 11:30am–2pm; dinner Mon–Sat 6–10pm. **Prices:** Main courses $16–$22. AE, DC, MC, V. ♥ VP ᕫ

Californos

4124 Pennsylvania (Westport); tel 816/531-7878. 1 block S of Westport Rd. **American.** Upscale yet casual, this popular bistro with pleasant outdoor seating offers innovative West Coast fare. Fare includes grilled tuna, swordfish, crab, steak, and lamb chops. A house specialty is Monterey chicken with a Parmesan crust, artichokes, and green chilies. **FYI:** Reservations accepted. **Open:** Lunch Mon–Sat 11am–3pm, Sun 1–8pm; dinner Mon–Thurs 5–10pm, Fri–Sat 5–11pm. **Prices:** Main courses $8–$20. AE, MC, V. ▦

Fedora Cafe and Bar

210 W 47th St; tel 816/561-6565. **New American.** On Country Club Plaza. A place for celebrating special occasions, this elegant restaurant is also well known for its wide selection of handcrafted beer and single-malt scotches. The dining area is handsomely decorated with stained-glass light fixtures, dark sculpted wood dividers, and colorful paintings and pictures. The menu, which is changed weekly and seasonally in order to take advantage of available fresh vegetables and game, consists of French, Italian, and American dishes, as well as some exotic items. Potato cakes with shallot and mustard sauce is a special favorite. **FYI:** Reservations recommended. Piano. BYO. **Open:** Peak (Thanksgiving–Jan 1) breakfast Mon–Sat 7–10:30am; lunch Mon–Sat 11:30am–4:30pm; dinner Sun–Thurs 4:30–11pm, Fri–Sat 4:30pm–midnight; brunch Sun 9am–4:30pm. **Prices:** Main courses $12–$24. AE, CB, DC, DISC, ER, MC, V. ● ▧ VP &

Figlio

209 W 46th St; tel 816/561-0505. On Country Club Plaza. Across from JC Nichols Memorial Fountain. **Italian.** A fine choice for gourmet, wood-fired pizza and homemade pasta. The simple dining area has neon lights and signs, walls covered with old photographs from Italy, and lovely brass railings. One of the favorite dishes is Gorgonzola-stuffed veal scaloppine, pan-seared and finished with a port wine glaze and shiitake mushrooms. Stromboli and three-cheese ravioli are also offered. **FYI:** Reservations recommended. Accordion. Children's menu. **Open:** Mon–Thurs 11am–10pm, Fri–Sat 11am–11pm, Sun 10:30am–10pm. **Prices:** Main courses $8–$15. AE, DC, DISC, MC, V. ▦ ▧ &

Garozzo's

526 Harrison; tel 816/221-2455. Just E of the River Market. **Italian.** Casual dining spot for moderately priced Italian cuisine. Ceiling fans blow cool air over the dining room, which features lovely photographs of Italian art. The menu highlights more than a dozen pastas. One specialty is the lightly breaded veal sautéed in butter and lemon, with fresh mushrooms, capers, and black olives. Another good bet is the bistecca Montana, beef tenderloin stuffed with lobster, charbroiled, and served with white wine, lemon, butter, fresh mushrooms, and bits of prosciutto. **FYI:** Reservations accepted. Additional location: 12801 E I-40, Independence (tel 737-2400). **Open:** Mon–Thurs 11am–10pm, Fri 11am–11pm, Sat 4–11pm. **Prices:** Main courses $8–$22. AE, DISC, MC, V. ▦ &

Gates & Sons Bar-B-Q

47th and Paseo; tel 816/921-0409. 1½ mi E of Country Club Plaza. **Barbecue.** Doing business since 1945, this barbeque joint ranks as one of the best in the city. An famously ingratiating staff serves up tasty ribs with spicy sauce, sandwiches, sausage, chicken, and mutton. **FYI:** Reservations not accepted. Beer and wine only. Additional locations: Linwood and Main (tel 753-0828); 1211 Brooklyn (tel 483-3880). **Open:** Mon–Sat 10am–2am, Sun 10am–midnight. **Prices:** Main courses $4–$11. No CC. ▦

Golden Ox

1600 Genessee; tel 816/842-2866. Across from Kemper Arena. **Steak.** One of the best steak houses in the city, this dimly lit establishment—decorated everywhere with busts of golden oxen—features beef that is aged and cut on the premises. Prime rib and steak are broiled over a hickory charcoal fire and served with baked potato or french fries, salad, and garlic toast. Some chicken and seafood dishes are also available. **FYI:** Reservations recommended. **Open:** Lunch Mon–Fri 11:30am–2:30pm; dinner Mon–Fri 4:30–10pm, Sat–Sun 4–10pm. **Prices:** Main courses $9–$19. AE, CB, DC, DISC, MC, V. ▦ &

The Grill

In the Ritz-Carlton, 401 Ward Pkwy; tel 816/756-1500. **American.** On Country Club Plaza. Located on top of the hotel, where there is an excellent view of Country Club Plaza. The dining room boasts crystal light fixtures, a marble fireplace, and large reproductions of beautiful oil paintings. The menu features a variety of beef, poultry, and seafood dishes, with items such as Maine lobster, Ozark trout, and Kansas City strip steak. A fine example is basil-marinated shrimp and porcini mushroom linguine, served in an olive oil hollandaise sauce flavored with saffron and garlic. **FYI:** Reservations accepted. Piano. Children's menu. **Open:** Peak (Thanksgiving–Dec) daily 5:30–10:30pm. **Prices:** Main courses $29–$43. AE, DC, DISC, MC, V. ▦ ▦ VP &

Hereford House

20th and Main; tel 816/842-1080. 3 blocks N of Crown Center. **Steak.** Serving prime beef since 1957. Seating includes comfortable upholstered booths and sturdy wooden tables and chairs; Old West scenes decorate the walls. Lunch offers lots of burgers, steaks, sandwiches, chicken, and seafood; dinner brings steak, lobster, shrimp, and fish. A favorite is steak Dijon, a fillet topped with Dijon mustard and melted brown sugar. **FYI:** Reservations recommended. Children's menu. **Open:** Mon–Thurs 11am–10pm, Fri 11am–10pm, Sat 4–10:30pm, Sun 4–9pm. **Prices:** Main courses $11–$24. AE, CB, DC, DISC, MC, V. ▦ ▧ VP &

Houlihan's

4743 Pennsylvania Ave; tel 816/561-3141. **American.** On Country Club Plaza. A comfortable, informal, and fun restaurant, this was the one that launched the national chain. The diverse menu offers items like sandwiches, burgers, stuffed chicken breast, fajitas, quesadillas, and teriyaki steak. **FYI:**

Reservations not accepted. Children's menu. Additional location: 11600 W 95th, Overland Park, KS (tel 913/492-3926). **Open:** Mon–Thurs 11am–11pm, Fri–Sat 11am–midnight, Sun 11am–10pm. **Prices:** Main courses $7–$14. AE, CB, DC, DISC, MC, V. 🎦 🚗 📹

♥ Jasper's

405 W 75th St; tel 816/363-3003. **Continental/Italian.** This Kansas City gem offering fine dining and highly professional service is the destination for many who are celebrating special occasions. The formal, elegant setting is adorned with crystal chandeliers and mirrors imported from Italy. Stemware is exquisite, handcrafted Miners crystal. The menu includes many varieties of pasta, veal, beef, chicken, and seafood. A highlight is conchiglia alla sorrento, fresh scallops in a buttery sherry cream sauce served over angel-hair pasta. **FYI:** Reservations recommended. **Open:** Mon–Thurs 6–10pm, Fri–Sat 6–11pm. **Prices:** Main courses $16–$27. AE, CB, DC, DISC, MC, V. ♥ 🎦

Jennie's

511 Cherry St; tel 816/421-3366. 3 blocks E of River City Market. **Italian.** Open since 1938, this old standby serves Sicilian-style Italian dishes to a diverse crowd. The dining room is decorated with pastel sketches and stained glass windows. Red sauce standouts include lasagna and cheese ravioli; veal Parmigiana is another specialty. **FYI:** Reservations accepted. Children's menu. **Open:** Mon–Thurs 11am–9pm, Fri 11am–10pm, Sat noon–10pm, Sun noon–8pm. **Prices:** Main courses $7–$16. AE, DC, MC, V. 🎦 ♿

Kiki's Bon Ton

1515 Westport Rd (Westport); tel 816/931-9417. 2 blocks E of state line. **Cajun/Creole.** Pictures and models of crabs, shrimp, and alligators decorate this fun, lively, off-beat place to give it a bit of Cajun-bayou ambience. Ceiling fans provide gentle breezes. Creole and Cajun creations include gumbo, alligator sausage, crab cakes, jambalaya, and po-boy sandwiches. A house specialty is the Baton Rouge crawfish, a seasoned plate of tails, tails, and more tails served with crawfish rice cakes. **FYI:** Reservations accepted. Zydeco. Children's menu. **Open:** Mon–Thurs 11am–10pm, Fri–Sat 11am–11pm, Sun 11:30am–8:30pm. **Prices:** Main courses $5–$13. AE, DC, MC, V.

Margarita's

2829 Southwest Blvd; tel 816/931-4849. At jct I-35. **Mexican.** Very popular and very crowded. The lively eatery offers primarily Mexican fare, though burgers are also available. Margarita's Special is the most often ordered dish; it's a flour tortilla stuffed with pork, beef, beans, cheese, and onions, topped with chili con queso, and served with rice. Happy hour daily 3–6pm. **FYI:** Reservations not accepted. **Open:** Sun–Thurs 11am–10pm, Fri–Sat 11am–11:30pm. **Prices:** Main courses $7–$8. AE, DISC, MC, V. 🎦 ♿

Mario's

204 Westport Rd (Westport); tel 816/531-7187. E of Broadway. **Italian.** A great Kansas City bargain for grinders, sandwiches, spaghetti, lasagna, and steak Parmigiana (all served in styrofoam containers). Eat in or take out. **FYI:** Reservations not accepted. No liquor license. **Open:** Mon–Sat 10:30am–7:30pm. **Prices:** Main courses $5–$6. AE, CB, DC, DISC, MC, V. 🎦

Metropolis

303 Westport Rd (Westport); tel 816/753-1550. Entertainment District. **New American/Eclectic.** This sophisticated spot is a big hit with those looking for creative, inspired grill fare. An attractive piece of modern sculpture, showcased against one wall, contributes to the chic, very contemporary decor. Greek, Italian, Vietnamese, and other cuisines show their influences in such dishes as salmon stuffed with chorizo sausage and topped with caviar-and-cheese sauce; tandoori sea bass; and grilled steak. **FYI:** Reservations recommended. **Open:** Lunch Mon–Fri 11:30am–2:30pm; dinner Mon–Thurs 5:30–10pm, Fri–Sat 5:30–11pm. Closed Jan 1–20. **Prices:** Main courses $10–$20. AE, CB, DC, DISC, MC, V.

Milano

In Crown Center, 2450 Grand Ave; tel 816/426-1130. **Italian.** Large columns entwined with beautiful vines stretch to the top of the glass ceiling, providing the dining area and its potted plants and lovely palm trees with warm sunlight. This greenhouse-like space is the setting for northern Italian fare like shellfish risotto, sautéed veal, broiled salmon medallions, and a variety of pasta dishes. The grilled chicken breast with lemon-rosemary vinaigrette, feta cheese, kalamata olives, and sautéed spinach is recommended by the staff. **FYI:** Reservations recommended. Jazz. Children's menu. **Open:** Mon–Thurs 11:30am–10pm, Fri–Sat 11:30am–11pm, Sun noon–9pm. **Prices:** Main courses $8–$17. AE, DC, DISC, MC, V. ♥ 🎦 📹 ♿

The New Majestic Steak House

931 Broadway; tel 816/471-8484. Historic Fitzpatrick Saloon Building. **Steak.** Originally constructed in the 1920s and recently restored to preserve the look of that era, this restaurant will delight with its gorgeous antique furniture, stained-glass windows, antique mirrors, paintings, and photographs carefully placed throughout. Although steaks are the specialty and buffalo is available, lighter fare is offered. **FYI:** Reservations recommended. Jazz. **Open:** Mon–Thurs 11:30am–10pm, Fri 11:30am–11pm, Sat 5–11pm, Sun 4–9pm. **Prices:** Main courses $13–$30. AE, CB, DC, DISC, ER, MC, V. ♥ VP

The Old Spaghetti Factory

304 W 8th St; tel 816/842-1801. 3 blocks E of I-35. **Italian.** The atmosphere is classic Italian. Guests are seated around large, hardwood tables with velvet seats and headboards. Many brass chandeliers hang from the ceiling, helping to illuminate the authentic old trolley car displayed in the center of the room. Besides spaghetti, there's the popular spinach

and cheese ravioli, plus many more traditional dishes. **FYI:** Reservations not accepted. Children's menu. BYO. **Open:** Lunch Mon–Fri 11:30am–2pm; dinner Mon–Thurs 5–9:30pm, Fri 5–11pm, Sat 4:30–11pm, Sun 4–9:30pm. **Prices:** Main courses $6–$10. DISC, MC, V.

Papagallo's

3535 Broadway; tel 816/756-3227. **Italian/Mediterranean/ Vegetarian.** Delight in the delicious creations of renowned chef Ray Katton, whose menu dabbles in a variety of cuisines. A house favorite is the tenderloin, which is sautéed and served with artichoke hearts and pomegranate sauce and a choice of saffron rice or pasta. Rotating exhibits of Italian/ Mediterranean sculptures, paintings, and photographs from local artists enliven and vary the decor. **FYI:** Reservations recommended. Piano/singer. Children's menu. Dress code. **Open:** Mon–Fri 11am–11pm, Sat 5–11pm. **Prices:** Main courses $8–$14. AE, DC, DISC, MC, V.

Peppercorn Duck Club

In the Hyatt Regency Crown Center, 2345 McGee St (Crown Center); tel 816/421-1234. **New American.** This elegant establishment features a beautiful floral decor. Fresh flowers and potted plants grace the common areas and marbled salad bar. Duck is the specialty, though steak and seafood are also available, like lobster and duck fettuccine with sun-dried tomato sauce. Included with the meal is the Ultra Chocolatto Bar, an assortment of cakes, pastries, and fruits. The dress is usually casual, but jackets are required on Friday and Saturday nights. **FYI:** Reservations recommended. Dress code. **Open:** Lunch Mon–Fri 11:30am–2pm; dinner Sun–Thurs 5:30–10pm, Fri–Sat 5:30–10:30pm; brunch Sun 10am–2pm. **Prices:** Main courses $21–$36. AE, CB, DC, DISC, MC, V.

Ponak's

2856 Southwest Blvd; tel 816/753-0775. Near I-35; 6 blocks E of State Line. **Mexican.** Colorful pictures and reproductions adorn the dark paneled walls of this authentic Mexican eatery. Recommended are menudo (a clear broth soup with tripe and hominy), chicken mole, and huevos con chorizo. More than 50 bottled beers and several drafts are offered. **FYI:** Reservations accepted. **Open:** Mon–Thurs 11am–10pm, Fri–Sat 11am–11pm, Sun noon–9pm. **Prices:** Main courses $5–$7. AE, MC, V.

Rozelle Court

In Nelson-Atkins Museum of Art, 4525 Oak; tel 816/751-1279. On Country Club Plaza; 3 blocks E of Main St exit off I-70. **Eclectic.** A lovely and unusual setting for a casual meal. The room lies within a large atrium constructed of sturdy stone pillars and arches, and the trickling of water from the fountain gently resonates throughout the courtyard. Meals are served cafeteria-style; the choices, which change daily, include items like stuffed catfish, roast duck in peanut sauce, stuffed crab, and lasagna. **FYI:** Reservations not accepted. Beer and wine only. No smoking. **Open:** Tues–

Thurs 10am–3pm, Fri 10am–8pm, Sat 10am–3:30pm, Sun 1–3:30pm. **Prices:** Lunch main courses $5–$8. AE, MC, V.

Savoy Grill

In Hotel Savoy, 219 W 9th St (Garment District); tel 816/842-3890. 2 blocks E of Broadway. **American/Seafood.** The decor emphasizes brass and glass—gorgeous brass fixtures hang from the ceilings of six different dining rooms, while beautiful stained glass windows filter much of the light. Guests are seated in booths of dark, engraved wood. The menu specializes in steak and lobster dishes and offers a wide assortment of appetizers. **FYI:** Reservations recommended. Children's menu. **Open:** Mon–Thurs 11am–11pm, Fri–Sat 11am–midnight, Sun 4–10pm. **Prices:** Main courses $13–$29. AE, CB, DC, DISC, MC, V.

Skies

In the Hyatt Regency Crown Center, 2345 McGee St (Crown Center); tel 816/421-1234. **New American.** Located on top of the tallest building in Missouri, this place offers a revolving, panoramic view of Kansas City and beyond. The emphasis is on mesquite-smoked meats and seafood. Perhaps the most intriguing dish is sautéed shellfish in vodka-tomato broth, served with steamed vegetables and angel-hair pasta. **FYI:** Reservations recommended. **Open:** Fri–Sat 6–10:30pm, Sun–Thurs 6–10pm. **Prices:** Main courses $15–$26. AE, CB, DC, DISC, MC, V.

Stephenson's Apple Farm Restaurant

US 40 at Lee's Summit Rd; tel 816/373-5400. **Regional American.** A handsome restaurant with a country motif—evident in the farm-style cooking implements that hang on the walls. Specialities are hickory-smoked beef, pork, and chicken, and the menu also includes many homemade desserts and dessert drinks. Baked chicken with butter and cream is a particular favorite. **FYI:** Reservations recommended. Children's menu. Additional location: 5755 NW Northwood Rd (tel 587-9300). **Open:** Mon–Sat 11:30am–10pm, Sun 10am–9pm. **Prices:** Main courses $13–$25. AE, CB, DC, DISC, MC, V.

★ Strouds

1015 E 85th St; tel 816/333-2132. Off I-435. **American.** This magnet for lovers of pan-fried chicken has been drawing in crowds since 1933. Yellow lace curtains hang over the stained-glass windows of the modest, rustic dining area, a suitable setting for enjoying the simple country cooking. Pork chops, catfish, sandwiches, and homemade cinnamon rolls are some of the other popular items. **FYI:** Reservations not accepted. Piano. Children's menu. Additional location: 5410 NE Oakridge Dr (tel 454-9600). **Open:** Mon–Thurs 4–10pm, Fri 11am–11pm, Sat 2–11pm, Sun 11am–10pm. **Prices:** Main courses $7–$15. AE, CB, DC, DISC, MC, V.

Torre's Pizzaria

4112 Pennsylvania (Westport); tel 816/931-0146. **Italian.** Decorated with interesting, old railroad molds and mirrors hanging on beautiful, dark wooden walls, this pizza parlor also serves spaghetti, ravioli, and sandwiches. **FYI:** Reservations accepted. Children's menu. Additional location: 8310 Wornal (tel 363-1040). **Open:** Mon–Thurs 11am–10pm, Fri–Sat 11am–12:30am, Sun 4–10pm. **Prices:** Main courses $5–$15. AE, DISC, MC, V.

Trader Vic's

In the Westin Crown Center, 1 Pershing Rd (Crown Center); tel 816/391-4444. **Polynesian.** The Polynesian theme is carried out here with large bamboo light fixtures, upholstered, wicker chairs, interesting statues, and a large Polynesian fishing boat hanging from the ceiling. Peachblossom Duck—a favorite specialty—is marinated in five spices and served with chutney and bok choy. **FYI:** Reservations recommended. Children's menu. **Open:** Lunch Mon–Fri 11:30am–2pm; dinner Sun–Thurs 5–9:30pm, Fri–Sat 5–10:30pm. **Prices:** Main courses $14–$29. AE, CB, DC, DISC, ER, MC, V.

Walt Bodine's

In Radisson Suite Hotel Kansas City, 106 W 12th St; tel 816/221-7000. **Steak.** Located in a historic downtown hotel, this steak restaurant boasts handsomely engraved wood pillars and posts, large colorful paintings, and etched glass dividers. One house special is the Kansas City steak au poivre, a 12-oz strip rolled in crushed black peppercorns, grilled, and topped with a brandy cream sauce. Fresh fish, lobster tail, and chicken are also available. **FYI:** Reservations recommended. **Open:** Lunch Mon–Fri 11am–2pm; dinner Mon–Thurs 5–10pm, Fri–Sat 5–11pm, Sun 5–10pm. **Prices:** Main courses $13–$35. AE, CB, DC, DISC, MC, V.

Westport Flea Market & Grill

817 Westport Rd (Westport); tel 816/931-1986. ¼ block E of SW Trafficway. **Burgers.** Neon beer signs and hanging lamps over each table add to the bar-and-grill atmosphere of this restaurant located in the middle of an indoor flea market. The place is well known for its gigantic hamburgers and Cajun chicken, though the menu also offers hot dogs, Italian sausage, and sandwiches. Darts, Foosball, and table shuffleboard add some competitive fun. **FYI:** Reservations recommended. **Open:** Mon–Thurs 11am–11pm, Fri–Sat 11am–11:30pm, Sun 11am–10pm. **Prices:** Main courses $4–$7. No CC.

Winslow's Smokehouse

20 E 5th St; tel 816/471-RIBS. At Walnut. **Barbecue.** A good place to stop for lunch when visiting City Market, this family-owned eatery is well-regarded for its ribs and spicy smoked chicken wings. Barbecue sandwiches are also a hit. The certified black-Angus beef is slow-cooked over green hickory, while the sauce is made with fresh produce along with blackstrap molasses. **FYI:** Reservations not accepted. Blues. Children's menu. **Open:** Peak (May–Sept) Tues–Sat 10am–10pm, Sun 11am–7pm. **Prices:** Main courses $5–$15. AE, CB, DC, DISC, MC, V.

Winstead's

191 Brush Creek; tel 816/753-2244. Just E of Country Club Plaza. **Burgers.** This restaurant has the look and feel of a 1950s diner, and the waitstaff is dressed accordingly. Neon signs, clocks, and lights hang on the walls, and an old-fashioned jukebox is prominently featured. Great burgers, fries, onion rings, and fountain drinks. **FYI:** Reservations not accepted. No liquor license. **Open:** Sun–Thurs 6:30am–midnight, Fri–Sat 6:30am–1am. **Prices:** Main courses $3–$5. No CC.

ATTRACTIONS

Country Club Plaza

47th and Main Sts; tel 816/753-0100. Begun in 1922, the country's first suburban shopping center features Spanish courtyards and stucco buildings with red-tile roofs. Visitors can browse through more than 180 shops and 25 restaurants, all set amongst European sculptures, fountains, and horse-drawn carriages. **Open:** Mon–Wed and Fri–Sat 10am–7pm, Thurs 10am–9pm, Sun noon–5pm. **Free**

Crown Center

2450 Grand Ave; tel 816/274-8444. Spanning 85 acres, this huge, living-and-working environment contains three levels of shops, boutiques, and restaurants, as well as an outdoor ice-skating rink, the American Heartland Theatre, the Coterie Children's Theatre, and Kaleidoscope, a free creative arts workshop for children ages 5–12. Since the complex is owned by the Hallmark Company, Crown Center also houses the Hallmark Visitors Center with displays on the Hallmark Hall of Fame TV series and the production of Hallmark products, and a film about craftspeople at work. Free outdoor concerts in the summer. **Open:** Mon–Wed and Sat 10am–6pm, Thurs–Fri 10am–9pm, Sun noon–5pm. **Free**

Nelson-Atkins Museum of Art

4525 Oak St; tel 816/561-4000. The museum is internationally noted for its extensive art collection, which ranges from 3000 BC to the present. Among the highlights are the collections of Oriental art, including Japanese art and screens, Chinese porcelain, furniture, and sculpture, and pottery figures produced during the Tang dynasty (AD 618–906). In the museum's European collection are works by Degas, Monet, Pissarro, van Gogh, Gauguin, and Paul Klee. American artists represented include Georgia O'Keeffe, Andrew Wyeth, and Willem de Kooning. The sculpture garden boasts bronze pieces by Henry Moore. **Open:** Tues–Sat 10am–5pm, Sun 1–5pm. **$$**

Toy and Miniature Museum of Kansas City

5235 Oak St; tel 816/333-2055. Located in a 1911 mansion, this museum houses an extensive collection of antique toys and exact-to-scale miniatures of houses, rooms, and furniture dating from the 19th century to present. Miniatures are fully functional—scissors can cut, clocks can be wound, and musical instruments can be played. Puppet shows are given the first Saturday of every month. **Open:** Wed–Sat 10am–4pm, Sun 1–4pm. **$**

Liberty Memorial and Museum

100 W 26th St; tel 816/221-1918. Reputed to be the only military museum and archive in the United States devoted to World War I. Its towering Torch of Liberty, a familiar Kansas City landmark, rises 300 feet and contains an observation platform providing a panoramic view of the downtown skyline. The museum displays military clothing, medals and decorations, posters, and other memorabilia. Full-scale trench replica. **Open:** Wed–Sun 9:30am–4:30pm. **Free**

Arabia Steamboat Museum

400 Grand Ave; tel 816/471-4030. The steamboat *Arabia* sank in 1856, and its cargo was preserved in the cold mud of the Missouri River until it was unearthed in 1988. Today, items from the ship's cargo that are on display include 1,000 pieces of china; 4,000 leather boots and shoes; tools and hardware ranging from doorknobs to square nails; jewelry; perfume; and glass bottles of ketchup, pickles, and pie fillings. A short film about the ship's excavation is also shown. **Open:** Mon–Sat 10am–6pm, Sun noon–5pm. **$$$**

Thomas Hart Benton Home

3636 Belleview; tel 816/931-5722. This 2½-story stone house was the home and studio of Kansas City's most famous contemporary artist from 1939 until his death in 1975. On display are many of Benton's personal belongings, a handful of original works, some reproductions, and some prints and lithographs. **Open:** Mon–Sat 10am–4pm, Sun noon–5pm. **$**

John Wornall House Museum

146 W 61st Terrace (Brookside); tel 816/444-1858. This Greek Revival farmhouse was built in 1858, in what was then farmland. Located near the dividing lines of the Civil War, it was the site of hospitals for both the Confederate and Union armies. Today, tours recreate the daily life of a typical prosperous farm family in the years just before the Civil War. Tours include the extensive herb and perennial garden and open-hearth cooking demonstrations. **Open:** Feb–Dec, Tues–Sat 10am–4pm, Sun 1–4pm. **$**

Kansas City Board of Trade

4800 Main, 3rd floor; tel 816/753-7500. Founded in 1856, this is the world's predominant marketplace for wheat and grain sorghum, as well as a trading place for soybeans, corn, and oats. A visitors' gallery on the third floor allows guests to observe futures trading in the pit, with explanations provided. **Open:** Mon–Fri 8:30am–3:15pm. **Free**

Harry S Truman Sports Complex

I-70; tel 816/921-8000 (Royals) or 924-9400 (Chiefs). Major league baseball's Kansas City Royals play at Royals Stadium, and the Kansas City Chiefs football team plays at Arrowhead Stadium, both located in the Complex. Concerts and special events are also held here throughout the year. **$$$$**

Worlds of Fun

4545 Worlds of Fun Ave; tel 816/454-4545. Five themed "continents" featuring 140 rides, shows, and attractions. Major rides include Cyclone Sam's (a roller coaster with special effects and video to simulate a cyclone), the Timber Wolf (a wooden roller coaster with a 95-foot drop), and the Orient Express (a steel-track coaster with two interlocking loops). Also includes 14 kiddie rides. **Open:** Peak (Mem Day–Labor Day) Sun–Fri 10:30am–sunset, Sat 10am–sunset. Reduced hours off-season. Closed Nov–Mar. **$$$$**

Oceans of Fun

4545 Worlds of Fun Ave; tel 816/454-4545. Sixty acres of water rides, pools, and attractions. Children's play area features Captain Kidd's pirate ship, which combines a playground with water slides and water cannons. Castaway Cove (for adults only) features refreshment cabana, whirlpool tubs, and a sun deck. **Open:** Mem Day–Labor Day, Sun–Fri 10:30am–sunset, Sat 10am–sunset. **$$$$**

Kingdom City

See Fulton

Kirksville

Unusual for a town of its relatively small size, Kirksville is the home of two institutions of higher education: Northeast Missouri State University and Kirksville College of Osteopathic Medicine. This northeastern Missouri town is near Thousand Hills State Park, one of the most popular preserves in the state park system. **Information:** Kirksville Area Chamber of Commerce, 304 S Franklin, PO Box 251, Kirksville, 63501 (tel 816/665-3766).

HOTEL 🏨

≣≣ Days Inn

US 63 S, 63501; tel 816/665-8244 or toll free 800/DAYS-INN; fax 816/665-6854. Clean, comfortable lodging at affordable prices. Better lobby than most standard chain hotels, with lush potted plants and trees. **Rooms:** 104 rms and stes. CI 3pm/CO 11am. Nonsmoking rms avail. **Amenities:** 🛆 A/C, cable TV w/movies. Some units w/whirlpools. **Services:** ✕ 🚗 🖾 ⇔ ⇔ **Facilities:** 🛋 📼 👌 2 restaurants, 2 bars, games rm, whirlpool, washer/dryer. Complimentary use of local YMCA. **Rates (BB):** $46–$56 S or D; $95 ste. Extra person $5. Children under age 17 stay free. **Parking:** Outdoor, free. AE, DC, DISC, JCB, MC, V.

MOTEL

≣≣ Best Western Shamrock Inn

MO 6 and US 63 S, 63501; tel 816/665-8352 or toll free 800/528-1234; fax 816/665-0072. Comfortable chain motel with a small lobby. **Rooms:** 45 rms. CI noon/CO 11am.

Nonsmoking rms avail. **Amenities:** 🕾 A/C, cable TV w/movies. **Services:** 🛏 🖐 **Facilities:** 🔥 🛏150 1 restaurant, playground. **Rates:** $48 S; $56 D. Extra person $6. Children under age 13 stay free. Parking: Outdoor, free. AE, CB, DC, DISC, MC, V.

Ladue

RESTAURANTS 🍴

Busch's Grove

9160 Clayton Rd; tel 314/993-0011. **American.** With its many screened cabanas offering ceiling fans and table service, this local institution has been a favorite for al fresco dining for many years. An uncomplicated American menu offers a wide variety of appetizers, salads, burgers, and sandwiches, as well as steaks, chicken, veal, pork, and seafood. Some nights feature prime rib or barbecue. **FYI:** Reservations recommended. Children's menu. **Open:** Tues–Sat 11am–11pm. **Prices:** Main courses $14–$19. AE, DC, MC, V. 🍴 💟 VP &

Schneithorst's Hofamberg Inn

Lindbergh and Clayton Rds; tel 314/993-5600. E on US 40 off I-270, S on Lindbergh Blvd, left on Clayton Rd. **German.** Decorated with old German steins, clocks, and numerous pictures. Enjoy authentic specialties in the dark and cozy dining room. The house specialty is the Bavarian platter, a roast loin of pork and pan-fried bratwurst and knockwurst, served with sweet-and-sour red cabbage. **FYI:** Reservations recommended. Children's menu. **Open:** Mon–Thurs 11am–10pm, Fri–Sat 11am–11pm, Sun 10am–8pm. **Prices:** Main courses $13–$17. AE, CB, DC, DISC, MC, V. 💟 &

Lake Ozark

This resort town owes both its name and existence to a lake that was, for a time, the largest man-made lake in the world. Scenic beauty and a variety of leisure activities make this tiny town a major tourist destination. **Information:** Lake Area Chamber of Commerce, 3502 Bagnell Dam Blvd, PO Box 1570, Lake Ozark, 65049 (tel 573/348-2730).

MOTEL 🏨

≣ ≣ ≣ Holiday Inn

US 54, 65049; tel 573/365-2334 or toll free 800/532-3575; fax 573/365-6887. On the lake. This standard chain motel greets guests with an average size lobby decorated with lush potted trees and floral arrangements. **Rooms:** 213 rms and stes. CI 4pm/CO noon. Nonsmoking rms avail. Some rooms have a view of Lake Ozark. **Amenities:** 🕾 🍷 A/C, satel TV. Some units w/minibars. **Services:** ✗ 🍴 🖐 🛏 Babysitting. Movies available for rent. Free morning newspaper. **Facilities:** 🔥 🏓 🛏600 & 1 restaurant, 2 bars, games rm, sauna, whirlpool, playground, washer/dryer. Rooftop pool

and sundeck. **Rates:** Peak (Mem Day–Labor Day) $88–$130 S; $93–$135 D; $112–$135 ste. Extra person $5. Children under age 20 stay free. Lower rates off-season. Parking: Outdoor, free. Special packages include Heart to Heart, Great Rates, and Golf. AE, CB, DC, DISC, JCB, MC, V.

ATTRACTION 🖼

Lake of the Ozarks State Park

MO 42; tel 573/348-2694. SE of Osage Beach. Missouri's largest state park has 89 miles of shoreline as well as two public swimming beaches and boat launching areas. Hiking trails, a fishing area, and picnic sites. **Open:** Daily sunrise–sunset. **Free**

Lebanon

Known for its wood products and furniture, Lebanon serves as the central commercial hub for the region. The Laclede County seat attracts many visitors due to its location along I-44 and proximity to Bennett Spring State Park. **Information:** Lebanon Area Chamber of Commerce, 321 S Jefferson, Lebanon, 65536 (tel 417/588-3256).

MOTELS 🏨

≣ Bestway Inn

1710 W Elm St, 65536; tel 417/532-3128; fax 417/532-1593. Exit 127 off I-44. Very basic economy motel suitable for a brief stay. **Rooms:** 33 rms. CI open/CO 11am. Nonsmoking rms avail. Room furnishings are dated but clean. **Amenities:** 🕾 A/C, cable TV w/movies. **Services:** 🛏 🖐 **Facilities:** 🛏15 **Rates:** $26 S; $32 D. Extra person $3–$5. Children under age 12 stay free. Parking: Outdoor, free. Special rates for truckers and construction crews. Special packages for family reunions and weddings. AE, DISC, MC, V.

≣ ≣ Super 8 Motel

1831 W Elm St, 65536; tel 417/588-2574 or toll free 800/800-8000; fax 417/588-2580. Exit 127 off I-44. Basic, clean, comfortable budget accommodations. **Rooms:** 83 rms and stes. CI 2pm/CO 11am. Nonsmoking rms avail. **Amenities:** 🕾 A/C, cable TV w/movies, dataport. **Services:** 🛏 **Facilities:** 🔥 & Washer/dryer. **Rates (CP):** $37 S; $44 D; $44 ste. Extra person $3–$5. Children under age 12 stay free. Parking: Outdoor, free. AE, CB, DC, DISC, MC, V.

Macon

Noted for the beautiful maple trees in the area, the town anchors the southern end of Long Branch Lake. That, combined with Thomas Hill Reservoir to the southwest, makes Macon central to one of the most popular water recreation areas of north-central Missouri. **Information:** Macon Area Chamber of Commerce, 116 Bourke St, Macon, 63552 (tel 816/385-2811).

MOTEL

Super 8 Motel
US 63, 63552; tel 816/385-5788 or toll free 800/800-8000; fax 816/385-5788. Basic budget operation close to restaurants and nightlife. **Rooms:** 59 rms and stes. CI 2pm/CO 11am. Nonsmoking rms avail. **Amenities:** A/C, cable TV w/movies. **Services:** **Facilities:** **Rates:** $39 S; $45 D; $72 ste. Extra person $5. Children under age 13 stay free. Parking: Outdoor, free. AE, CB, DC, DISC, MC, V.

Maryland Heights

HOTELS

Best Western Westport Park Hotel
2434 Old Dorsett Rd, 63043; tel 314/291-8700 or toll free 800/528-1234; fax 314/291-2891. Across from airport. The highlight is the games room/atrium off the lobby; it is adorned with lovely plants and large trees and houses the hotel's pool. **Rooms:** 150 rms and stes. Executive level. CI 3pm/CO 11am. Nonsmoking rms avail. **Amenities:** A/C, cable TV w/movies. Some units w/whirlpools. **Services:** X **Facilities:** 1 restaurant, 1 bar (w/entertainment), games rm, sauna, whirlpool. **Rates (CP):** Peak (Mar–Oct) $69–$109 S; $79–$119 D; $150–$175 ste. Extra person $10. Children under age 18 stay free. Lower rates off-season. Parking: Outdoor, free. Honeymoon, weekend, and New Year's Eve packages avail. AE, CB, DC, DISC, MC, V.

DoubleTree Club Hotel
13735 Riverport Dr, 63043; or toll free 800/222-TREE; fax 314/770-0208. At airport. Semi-luxury accommodations near the airport. **Rooms:** 176 rms and stes. CI 3pm/CO 1pm. Nonsmoking rms avail. **Amenities:** A/C, cable TV, dataport, voice mail. **Services:** X Movies and Nintendo video games available for rent. **Facilities:** 1 restaurant (bkfst and dinner only), 1 bar, sauna, whirlpool, washer/dryer. **Rates (CP):** Peak (May–Aug) $99 S; $109 D; $148 ste. Extra person $10. Children under age 18 stay free. Lower rates off-season. Parking: Outdoor, free. Honeymoon and B&B packages avail. AE, DC, DISC, MC, V.

Drury Inn
12220 Dorsett Rd, 63043; tel 314/576-9966 or toll free 800/325-8300; fax 314/576-9966. At jct I-270. An attractive but bare-bones motel; fine for one night. **Rooms:** 130 rms. CI 3pm/CO noon. Nonsmoking rms avail. **Amenities:** A/C, satel TV w/movies. **Services:** **Facilities:**

Rates (CP): Peak (June–Dec) $64–$69 S; $74–$79 D. Extra person $8. Children under age 18 stay free. Lower rates off-season. Parking: Outdoor, free. AE, CB, DC, DISC, MC, V.

Hampton Inn Westport
2454 Dorsett Rd, 63043; tel 314/298-7878 or toll free 800/HAMPTON; fax 314/298-7429. At jct I-270. This cozy, welcoming hotel has a lobby decorated with lovely potted plants and trees and cooled by large ceiling fans. **Rooms:** 124 rms. CI 3pm/CO noon. Nonsmoking rms avail. **Amenities:** A/C, cable TV w/movies. **Services:** Car-rental desk. **Facilities:** **Rates (CP):** $69–$75 S; $67–$73 D. Children under age 16 stay free. Parking: Outdoor, free. AE, CB, DC, DISC, MC, V.

Sheraton Plaza Hotel
900 Westport Plaza, 63146; tel 314/434-5010 or toll free 800/822-3535; fax 314/434-0140. I-270 and Page Ave. Located in a shopping and entertainment complex across from the interstate, this modern high-rise with spacious rooms caters to business types. Its lobby, decorated with potted plants and trees, floral arrangements, and comfortable chairs and sofas, provides a welcome place for guests to relax. **Rooms:** 209 rms and stes. Executive level. CI 3pm/CO 1pm. Nonsmoking rms avail. Rattan furniture and Asian-accented art. **Amenities:** A/C, cable TV w/movies, dataport, voice mail. All units w/terraces. **Services:** X VP Car-rental desk, babysitting. Free morning coffee and newspaper. **Facilities:** 1 restaurant, 1 bar, sauna, whirlpool. Indoor pool with sunning deck. **Rates:** $89–$139 S or D; $175 ste. Children under age 12 stay free. Parking: Indoor/outdoor, free. Weekend discounts and honeymoon package avail. AE, CB, DC, DISC, ER, JCB, MC, V.

Sheraton Westport Inn
191 Westport Plaza, 63146; tel 314/878-1500 or toll free 800/822-3535; fax 314/878-2837. I-270 and Page Ave. Located on the opposite end of the outside mall as the Sheraton Plaza, this resortlike, Alpine-style lodge features lakeside rooms among its accommodations, which are in two buildings—the main structure and a newer tower. The spacious lobby decorated with several brass chandeliers, comfortable chairs and sofas, and many lovely plants. **Rooms:** 300 rms and stes. CI 3pm/CO 1pm. Nonsmoking rms avail. Suites are particularly roomy and feature a living area, wet bar, and two bathroom sinks. **Amenities:** A/C, cable TV w/movies, dataport. Some units w/terraces, some w/fireplaces. **Services:** X VP Car-rental desk. Same-day laundry service. Free morning coffee and newspaper. **Facilities:** 1 restaurant, 1 bar. Complimentary use of fitness center. **Rates:** $125 S or D; $165–$350 ste. Extra person $10. Children under age 18 stay free. Parking: Indoor/outdoor, free. AE, CB, DC, DISC, JCB, MC, V.

MOTEL

≣≣ Budgetel Inn

12330 Dorsett Rd, 63043; tel 314/878-1212 or toll free 800/4-BUDGET; fax 314/878-3409. On I-270. Pleasant little motel with lots of attention to detail. The comfortable and homey lobby is filled with paintings, plants, trees, and floral arrangements. **Rooms:** 145 rms and stes. CI 1pm/CO noon. Nonsmoking rms avail. **Amenities:** 🛏 ♨ 🖥 A/C, satel TV w/movies, dataport. **Services:** 🖎 🛁 🍴 **Facilities:** 🔲 ♿ Washer/dryer. **Rates (CP):** Peak (Mem Day–Sept) $50 S; $57 D; $56–$63 ste. Extra person $7. Children under age 18 stay free. Lower rates off-season. Parking: Outdoor, free. AE, CB, DC, DISC, MC, V.

RESTAURANT 🍴

Caleco's

In Club Riverport, 13729 Riverport Dr; tel 314/298-1515. Earth City exit off I-70. **Italian.** A large aquarium and hanging and potted plants decorate the dining area, while the large bar area features several pool tables. Ample selection of appetizers, soups, and salads. The usual entrees include pastas, sandwiches, steaks, chicken, and seafood. **FYI:** Reservations accepted. Children's menu. **Open:** Mon–Thurs 11am–10pm, Fri 11am–11pm, Sat noon–11pm, Sun 5–10pm. **Prices:** Main courses $8–$14. AE, CB, DC, DISC, MC, V. ♿

Mehlville

See St Louis

Moberly

MOTELS 🏨

≣≣ Ramada Inn

Jct US 24/63, 65270; tel 816/263-6540 or toll free 800/2-RAMADA; fax 816/263-0092. Clean, comfortable, standard lodging. Attractive lobby decorated with potted plants, trees, floral arrangements, and brass chandelier. **Rooms:** 98 rms and stes. CI noon/CO noon. Nonsmoking rms avail. **Amenities:** 🛏 ♨ A/C, satel TV w/movies. **Services:** ✗ 🚗 🖎 🛁 🍴 **Facilities:** 🔲 🍽 ♿ 1 restaurant, 1 bar, whirlpool, washer/dryer. **Rates:** $47 S; $54 D; $90 ste. Extra person $5. Children under age 18 stay free. Parking: Outdoor, free. Corporate rates avail. Bed-and-breakfast package avail. AE, DC, DISC, JCB, MC, V.

≣ Super 8 Motel

300 US 24 E, 65270; tel 816/263-8862 or toll free 800/800-8000; fax 816/263-8862. 2 blocks W of US 63. Budget motel with easy access off US 63 and US 24. **Rooms:** 60 rms. CI 2pm/CO 11am. Nonsmoking rms avail. **Amenities:** 🛏

A/C, cable TV w/movies. **Services:** 🛁 **Facilities:** ♿ **Rates (CP):** Peak (May–Sept) $38 S; $50 D. Extra person $7. Children under age 12 stay free. Lower rates off-season. Parking: Outdoor, free. AE, CB, DC, DISC, MC, V.

Nevada

Headquarters for Confederate guerrillas during the Civil War—which led to the sobriquet "Bushwhackers Capital"—Nevada was burned by Federal troops in 1863. Today its location between the state's western prairie and the southwestern Ozarks makes the city a thriving regional trade center. **Information:** Nevada–Vernon County Chamber of Commerce, 110 S Adams, Nevada, 64772-3163 (tel 417/667-5300).

MOTELS 🏨

≣≣ Comfort Inn

2345 Marvel Dr, 64772; tel 417/667-6777 or toll free 800/221-2222; fax 417/667-6135. Camp Clark exit off US-71. Just average. **Rooms:** 47 rms and stes. CI 2pm/CO 11am. Nonsmoking rms avail. **Amenities:** 🛏 A/C, cable TV w/movies. 1 unit w/whirlpool. **Services:** 🍴 **Facilities:** 🔲 🔲 ♿ Whirlpool. **Rates (CP):** Peak (June–Sept) $42 S; $45–$53 D; $47–$66 ste. Extra person $2. Children under age 13 stay free. Lower rates off-season. Parking: Outdoor, free. AE, CB, DC, DISC, MC, V.

≣≣ Super 8 Motel

2301 E Austin, 64772; tel 417/667-8888 or toll free 800/800-8000; fax 417/667-8883. Camp Clark exit off US 71. A standardized motel that's comfortable and affordable. Located near major highways. **Rooms:** 59 rms. CI noon/CO 11am. Nonsmoking rms avail. **Amenities:** 🛏 A/C, cable TV. **Services:** 🛁 🍴 **Facilities:** ♿ **Rates (CP):** $34–$47 S; $42–$49 D. Extra person $3. Children under age 13 stay free. Parking: Outdoor, free. AE, CB, DC, DISC, MC, V.

ATTRACTION 🏛

Harry S Truman Birthplace State Historic Site

1009 Truman, Lamar; tel 417/682-2279. 20 mi SE of Nevada. Bought by John Anderson Truman for $685 in 1882, the first home of Harry Truman measures a very humble 20-by-28-feet. It has been restored and redecorated with furnishings from the period of the Trumans' occupancy. The grounds also include an outdoor smokehouse and hand-dug well. **Open:** Mon–Sat 10am–4pm, Sun noon–4pm. **Free**

Poplar Bluff

Established in the early 1800s, this community located on a high bluff covered with tulip poplars draws travelers because of its proximity to Lake Wappapello, a large portion of the Mark Twain National Forest, and the Mingo National Wildlife

Refuge. **Information:** Greater Poplar Bluff Area Chamber of Commerce, 1111 W Pine, PO Box 3986, Poplar Bluff, 63901 (tel 573/785-7761).

MOTELS 🏨

🏨🏨🏨 Drury Inn

2220 N Westwood Blvd, 63901; tel 573/686-2451 or toll free 800/325-8300; fax 573/686-2451. US 67 N and US 60 Business. A spotless, contemporary-style motel. Located near several restaurants and a few miles from Mark Twain National Forest. **Rooms:** 78 rms. CI open/CO noon. Nonsmoking rms avail. **Amenities:** 🔔 🛁 A/C, satel TV w/movies. Some king-deluxe rooms have refrigerators and microwaves. **Services:** 🖼️ 🛏️ 📶 **Facilities:** 🏊 🔥 **Rates (CP):** Peak (May–Sept) $47–$52 S; $56–$68 D. Children under age 18 stay free. Lower rates off-season. Parking: Outdoor, free. AE, DC, DISC, MC, V.

🏨🏨🏨 Holiday Inn

2115 N Westwood Blvd, 63901; tel 573/785-7711 or toll free 800/HOLIDAY; fax 573/785-7711. US 67 N and US 60 Business. Well-maintained motel just north of town. Features a spacious courtyard/pool area and large poolside gazebo offering bar and food service. **Rooms:** 143 rms and stes. CI 3pm/CO noon. Nonsmoking rms avail. **Amenities:** 🔔 🛁 A/C, cable TV w/movies. Some units w/whirlpools. Mirrored honeymoon suite with whirlpool. **Services:** 🖼️ 🚐 🖼️ 🛏️ 📶 **Facilities:** 🏊 🎱 🔥 1 restaurant, 1 bar (w/entertainment), whirlpool, washer/dryer. **Rates (BB):** $56 S; $64 D; $151 ste. Children under age 18 stay free. Parking: Outdoor, free. Full breakfast for one person included in rates. AE, DISC, MC, V.

ATTRACTION 🎭

Sam A Baker State Park

MO 143, Patterson; tel 573/856-4411. This park, named for a former Missouri governor, dates to the 1920s and encompasses 5,163 acres of the St François Mountains. Nature center, hiking trails, canoeing, fishing, and swimming on the St François River and Big Creek. **Open:** Daily sunrise–sunset. **Free**

Richmond Heights

LODGE 🏨

🏨🏨🏨 Cheshire Inn and Lodge

6300 Clayton Rd, 63177; tel 314/647-7300 or toll free 800/325-7378; fax 314/647-0442. At I-64/US 40. Located in a mock Tudor–style building, this whimsically conceived hostelry with heavy English decor features several "fantasy suites," each uniquely designed with lots of fun, kitschy touches. **Rooms:** 106 rms and stes. CI 3pm/CO 2pm. Nonsmoking rms avail. The Tree House suite—the most popular one—boasts a waterfall and waterbed. Regular rooms have a reproduction antique hutch/entertainment center and large,

wooden four-poster bed. Some first-floor rooms lead directly to the pool. **Amenities:** 🔔 🛁 A/C, cable TV w/movies, dataport. Some units w/terraces, 1 w/fireplace, some w/whirlpools. **Services:** 🖼️ VP 🖼️ 🛏️ 📶 Free shuttle to downtown areas. **Facilities:** 🏊 🎱 🎱 🔥 1 restaurant, 2 bars (w/entertainment), spa, sauna, whirlpool. Golf, tennis, a baseball field, and a jogging/cycling trail are nearby. **Rates (CP):** $99–$111 S or D; $130–$250 ste. Extra person $6. Children under age 18 stay free. Parking: Indoor/outdoor, free. Wedding and anniversary packages avail. AE, CB, DC, DISC, MC, V.

Ridgedale

See Branson

Rolla

See also Waynesville

This key military transportation site during the Civil War was created during the railroad expansion of the mid-1800s. Today the city is home to one of the University of Missouri's four campuses as well as the army's Fort Leonard Wood training center, and it serves as the headquarters for Mark Twain National Forest. **Information:** Rolla Area Chamber of Commerce, 1301 Kingshighway, PO Box 823, Rolla, 65401 (tel 573/364-3577).

MOTELS 🏨

🏨 Bestway Inn

1631 Martin Springs Dr, 65401; tel 573/341-2158. Exit 184 off I-44. Clean, affordable lodging located near several restaurants. **Rooms:** 20 rms. CI noon/CO 11am. Nonsmoking rms avail. **Amenities:** 🔔 A/C, cable TV w/movies. **Services:** 🛏️ 📶 **Facilities:** 🏊 **Rates:** Peak (June–Sept) $35–$40 S; $40–$45 D. Extra person $4. Children under age 6 stay free. Lower rates off-season. Parking: Outdoor, free. AE, CB, DC, DISC, MC, V.

🏨 Econo Lodge

1417 Martin Springs Dr, 65401; tel 573/341-3130 or toll free 800/553-2666; fax 573/341-2129. Exit 184 off I-44. Clean, cheap rooms suitable for a brief stay. **Rooms:** 60 rms. CI 3pm/CO 11am. Nonsmoking rms avail. **Amenities:** 🔔 🛁 A/C, cable TV w/movies. **Services:** 🚐 🖼️ 🛏️ 📶 **Facilities:** 🏊 **Rates (CP):** Peak (June–Oct) $31–$41 S; $39–$49 D. Extra person $5. Children under age 18 stay free. Lower rates off-season. Parking: Outdoor, free. AE, CB, DC, DISC, MC, V.

🏨 Travelodge

1605 Martin Springs Dr, 65401; tel 573/341-3050 or toll free 800/578-7878; fax 573/341-2772. Exit 184 off I-44. Standard chain accommodations. Well maintained. **Rooms:**

38 rms, stes, and effic. CI 2pm/CO noon. Nonsmoking rms avail. **Amenities:** 📠 🔲 A/C, cable TV w/movies, refrig. **Services:** 🚐 🛎 🎇 **Facilities:** 🔲 🏊 🕹 **Rates (CP):** Peak (June–Oct) $41 S; $48 D; $56 ste; $56 effic. Extra person $5. Children under age 17 stay free. Lower rates off-season. Parking: Outdoor, free. AE, CB, DC, DISC, MC, V.

St Charles

See also Wentzville

Perhaps best known as the site of the 1804 departure of the Lewis and Clark expedition, St Charles marks this event each May with a major festival. The city's most distinctive feature is a historic district featuring Missouri's first capitol building and a number of renovated homes. **Information:** Greater St Charles Convention & Visitors Bureau, 230 S Main, St Charles, 63301 (tel 314/946-7776 or toll free 800/366-2427).

HOTELS 🏨

🏩 **Best Western Noah's Ark**
1500 S 5th St, 63303; tel 314/946-1000 or toll free 800/528-1234; fax 314/723-6670. At jct I-70. A family-friendly motel offering comfortable accommodations. The offbeat yet attractive lobby is decorated with stuffed animals (for the Ark theme) and lovely potted plants and trees. **Rooms:** 100 rms and stes. CI 3pm/CO 11am. Nonsmoking rms avail. **Amenities:** 📠 🔲 A/C, satel TV w/movies, dataport, voice mail. Some units w/whirlpools. **Services:** ✕ 🚐 🖼 🛎 **Facilities:** 🔲 🕹 🏊 🕹 1 restaurant (lunch and dinner only), 1 bar, games rm, sauna, steam rm, whirlpool, beauty salon, washer/dryer. **Rates (CP):** $50–$65 S; $55–$65 D; $115–$175 ste. Extra person $7. Children under age 13 stay free. Parking: Outdoor, free. Casino package avail. AE, CB, DC, DISC, EC, ER, JCB, MC, V.

🏩 **Hampton Inn**
3720 W Clay, 63301; tel 314/947-6800 or toll free 800/HAMPTON; fax 314/947-0020. Exit 225 off I-70 W. Easy access from the interstate makes this clean, comfortable motel fine for an overnight stop. **Rooms:** 119 rms. CI 3pm/CO 11am. Nonsmoking rms avail. **Amenities:** 📠 A/C, satel TV w/movies. **Services:** 🚐 🖼 🛎 **Facilities:** 🔲 🕹 🏊 🕹 **Rates (CP):** Peak (Mem Day–Labor Day) $50–$56 S; $59–$65 D. Children under age 19 stay free. Lower rates off-season. Parking: Outdoor, free. AE, CB, DC, DISC, MC, V.

MOTELS

🏩 **Econo Lodge**
3040 W Clay, 63301; tel 314/946-9992 or toll free 800/553-2666; fax 314/724-7266. Clean, comfortable economy rooms. **Rooms:** 52 rms. CI 11am/CO 11am. Nonsmoking rms avail. **Amenities:** 📠 A/C, cable TV w/movies. Dataports available. **Services:** 🛎 VCRs available for rent. **Facilities:** 🔲

🕹 Washer/dryer. **Rates (CP):** Peak (May–Sept) $50–$66 S; $60–$70 D. Extra person $5. Children under age 18 stay free. Lower rates off-season. Parking: Outdoor, free. AE, DC, DISC, MC, V.

🏩 **Red Roof Inn**
2010 Zumbehl Rd, 63303; tel 314/947-7770 or toll free 800/THE-ROOF; fax 314/947-0268. At I-70. Clean, comfortable economy rooms. **Rooms:** 108 rms. CI 1pm/CO noon. Nonsmoking rms avail. **Amenities:** 📠 A/C, satel TV w/movies. Some rooms have dataports. **Services:** 🖼 🛎 🎇 **Facilities:** 🕹 **Rates:** Peak (Mem Day–Oct) $37–$50 S; $46–$65 D. Extra person $9. Children under age 19 stay free. Lower rates off-season. Parking: Outdoor, free. AE, CB, DC, DISC, MC, V.

St Joseph

The starting point of the famed Pony Express and a major outfitting point for 19th-century wagon trains heading west, this city offers visitors a historical look at the Old West without the dust and danger. The largest city in northwest Missouri, St Joseph has become a major commercial center. Site of Missouri Western State College. **Information:** St Joseph Convention & Visitors Bureau, 109 S 4th, PO Box 445, St Joseph, 64502 (tel 816/233-6688).

HOTELS 🏨

🏩 **Holiday Inn**
102 S 3rd St, 64501 (Downtown); tel 816/279-8000 or toll free 800/824-7402; fax 816/279-8000. Average Holiday Inn located near interstate and suitable for all travelers. **Rooms:** 170 rms and stes. CI 2pm/CO noon. Nonsmoking rms avail. **Amenities:** 📠 🕹 🍴 A/C, cable TV w/movies. **Services:** ✕ 🚐 🖼 🛎 🎇 **Facilities:** 🔲 🏊 🕹 1 restaurant, 1 bar, games rm, sauna, steam rm, whirlpool, washer/dryer. **Rates:** $70 S or D; $70–$125 ste. Parking: Outdoor, free. Honeymoon, riverboat casino, and bed-and-breakfast packages avail. AE, CB, DC, DISC, JCB, MC, V.

🏩 **Ramada Inn**
4016 Frederick, 64506; tel 816/233-6192 or toll free 800/2-RAMADA; fax 816/233-6001. Exit 47 off I-29. Average accommodations. Attractive lobby with potted trees and floral arrangements. **Rooms:** 165 rms and stes. CI 2pm/CO noon. Nonsmoking rms avail. **Amenities:** 📠 🕹 🔲 A/C, cable TV w/movies, dataport. **Services:** ✕ 🖼 🛎 🎇 **Facilities:** 🔲 🏊 🕹 1 restaurant, 1 bar, games rm, whirlpool, washer/dryer. **Rates:** $49–$59 S or D; $85 ste. Children under age 18 stay free. Parking: Outdoor, free. Honeymoon, riverboat casino, and bed-and-breakfast packages avail. AE, CB, DC, DISC, EC, ER, JCB, MC, V.

ATTRACTIONS

Pony Express National Memorial

914 Penn St; tel 816/279-5059 or toll free 800/530-5930. The history of the Pony Express is conveyed in 21 exhibits, many of them interactive. Visitors can view paintings depicting Pony Express riders and trails, pump water from the same well that watered Pony Express horses, and tour a relay station. **Open:** Peak (June–Sept) Mon–Sat 9am–6pm, Sun 1–6pm. Reduced hours off-season. **$**

Patee House Museum

1202 Penn St (Pateetown); tel 816/232-8206. A fine hotel built in 1858 that also served as headquarters for the Pony Express. Today it houses a museum of transportation and communication and exhibits on local history. On view are an old steam locomotive, Walter Cronkite's father's dentist office, and a collection of 40 paintings depicting Old West outlaws and their families. **Open:** Peak (June–Aug) Mon–Sat 10am–5pm, Sun 1–5pm. Reduced hours off-season. **$**

Jesse James Home

12th and Penn Sts (Pateetown); tel 816/232-8206. The four-room house where Jesse James was shot and killed in 1882 is now restored to look as it did when the notorious outlaw and his family lived there. Tourists can see the legendary "bullet hole," as well as several photographs and drawings of James and his family. **Open:** Peak (June–Aug) Mon–Sat 10am–5pm, Sun 1–5pm. Reduced hours off-season. **$**

St Joseph Museum

1100 Charles St; tel 816/232-8471 or toll free 800/530-8866. Housed in a 43-room Gothic mansion built in 1879, exhibits relate Native American history, the westward expansion, and the natural history of the Midwest. Visitors can view beaded moccasins of the Sioux, storage baskets of the Apache, an extensive vertebrate and invertebrate collection, and the flora and fauna of the Midwest. **Open:** Mon–Sat 9am–5pm, Sun 1–5pm. **$**

Albrecht-Kemper Museum of Art

2818 Frederick; tel 816/233-7003. Houses an extensive collection of 18th-, 19th-, and 20th-century American art, including works by Thomas Hart Benton and Wayne Thiebaud. **Open:** Tues–Sat 10am–4pm, Sun 1–4pm. **$**

St Louis

See also Bridgeton, Clayton, Ladue, Maryland Heights, Richmond Heights, St Charles, University City, Woodson Terrace

Situated at the confluence of the Missouri and Mississippi rivers, St Louis began as a French trading post in 1764. Known during pioneer years as the "Gateway to the West" and as the last bastion of eastern culture on the nation's frontier, this city now forms the largest metropolitan area in the state. It offers a variety of cultural attractions and professional sports as well as a flashy nightlife that ranges from blues/jazz bars to riverboat casinos. **Information:** St Louis Convention & Visitors Commission, 10 S Broadway, #1000, St Louis, 63102 (tel 314/421-1023).

PUBLIC TRANSPORTATION

The **Metro Link** is an 18-mile light rail line running from Lambert–St Louis International Airport through downtown to East St Louis. There are 20 stations, including stops at Delmar Blvd, Forest Park, Central West End, Union Station, Busch Stadium, 8th and Pine, St Louis Centre, and Laclede's Landing. Fare is $1.80. For more information, call 314/421-1023. The **Bi-State Transit System** operates city-wide bus service; most bus routes start downtown and then fan out to outlying districts. Bus stops do not identify the destination or route of buses that stop there, so you'll need to know beforehand the route of the bus you want to take. For information on specific routes, call 314/231-2345. Fare for local buses is $1 for adults and 50¢ for children 5 through 12. Express buses cost $1.30 for adults and 65¢ for children. Transfers cost 20¢. Downtown is known as the Free Ride Zone, in which passengers can ride from one point to any other without paying. From May to December, there's the Levee Line, special buses transporting passengers between Union Station and the Gateway Arch. These buses, identifiable because they are painted like paddlewheel steamboats, are free.

HOTELS

Adam's Mark Hotel

4th and Chestnut Sts, 63102 (Riverfront); tel 314/241-7400 or toll free 800/444-ADAM; fax 314/241-6618. Memorial Dr exit off I-70, right on Market St. One of the city's premier hotels, located in the shadow of the Gateway Arch. The three-story atrium—sometimes noisy and busy with visitors strolling about and patrons on their way to or from one of the popular restaurants located here—amazes with the glitz and glamour of its towering marble and wooden pillars, mirrors and brass fixtures, Regency chandeliers, marble floors and tables, and nine-foot-tall bronze horses. With the many business services offered, it is ideal for the corporate traveler. **Rooms:** 910 rms and stes. Executive level. CI 3pm/CO noon. Nonsmoking rms avail. First-class rooms, some facing the Arch, some the Mississippi. **Amenities:** A/C, cable TV, dataport, voice mail. 1 unit w/fireplace. Full-length mirrors. **Services:** Car-rental desk, masseur, babysitting. **Facilities:** 2 restaurants (see "Restaurants" below), 4 bars (3 w/entertainment), racquetball, spa, sauna, steam rm, whirlpool, beauty salon. Indoor and outdoor rooftop pools provide breathtaking vistas. AJ's is one of downtown's most popular nightspots. **Rates:** $155 S; $175 D; $250–$1,200 ste. Children under age 12 stay free. Parking: Indoor, $10/day. Weekend and romance packages avail. AE, CB, DC, DISC, MC, V.

≣≣ Best Western Kirkwood Inn

1200 S Kirkwood Rd, 63122; tel 314/821-3950 or toll free 800/435-4656; fax 314/984-9798. Average property with acceptable accommodations. **Rooms:** 113 rms. CI 3pm/CO noon. Nonsmoking rms avail. **Amenities:** 🛁 🍴 A/C, satel TV w/movies. **Services:** ✕ 🖐 🛏 🐾 Children's program, babysitting. **Facilities:** 🏋 🏊95 🛎 1 restaurant, 1 bar. Free access to nearby YMCA. **Rates:** Peak (June–Aug) $70–$75 S; $75 D. Extra person $5. Children under age 19 stay free. Lower rates off-season. Parking: Outdoor, free. AE, CB, DC, DISC, JCB, MC, V.

≣≣≣ Clarion Regal Riverfront Hotel

200 S 4th St, 63102; tel 314/241-9500 or toll free 800/325-7353; fax 314/241-6171. Near Memorial Dr exit off I-70. Popular, often busy and crowded convention hotel featuring two towers of rooms and a revolving restaurant with an inspiring view of the Arch. Spacious, comfortable lobby has tall windows and floral arrangements and potted plants. **Rooms:** 780 rms and stes. Executive level. CI 4pm/CO noon. Nonsmoking rms avail. Traffic noise can be heard in some rooms. **Amenities:** 🛁 🍴 A/C, cable TV. Some units w/terraces. **Services:** ✕ 🔑 🛏 🖐 🐾 Car-rental desk. Movie rentals available. **Facilities:** 🏋 🍽 🏊3000 🖥 🛎 3 restaurants (*see* "Restaurants" below), 2 bars, games rm, beauty salon, washer/dryer. **Rates:** $115–$137 S; $132–$152 D; $250–$1,000 ste. Extra person $10. Children under age 18 stay free. Parking: Indoor, $9/day. Romance and casino packages avail. AE, CB, DC, DISC, MC, V.

≣≣≣ Courtyard by Marriott

11888 Westline Industrial Dr, 63146; tel 314/997-1200 or toll free 800/321-2211; fax 314/997-4215. Page E exit off I-270. The lobby of this very attractive hotel is decorated with hanging plants and beautiful floral arrangements. Caters to business professionals. **Rooms:** 149 rms and stes. CI 3pm/CO noon. Nonsmoking rms avail. **Amenities:** 🛁 🍴 📺 A/C, cable TV w/movies, dataport. Some units w/terraces. **Services:** 🖐 🐾 Babysitting. **Facilities:** 🏋 🍽 🏊40 🛎 1 restaurant (bkfst only), 1 bar, whirlpool, washer/dryer. **Rates:** $89–$92 S; $99–$102 D; $105 ste. Extra person $10. Children under age 16 stay free. Min stay special events. Parking: Outdoor, free. Weekend bed-and-breakfast package avail. AE, CB, DC, DISC, MC, V.

≣≣≣ Courtyard by Marriott

2340 Market St, 63101 (Downtown); tel 314/241-9111 or toll free 800/321-2211; fax 314/241-8113. Features rooms built around an inner courtyard containing an expanse of green and a terrace. Small but attractive lobby decorated with brass chandeliers, potted plants and trees, and floral arrangements. **Rooms:** 151 rms and stes. CI 4pm/CO noon. Nonsmoking rms avail. Most rooms have king-size beds and sofas. Those on third and fourth floors offer views of downtown and the Arch from balconies. **Amenities:** 🛁 🍴 📺 A/C, cable TV w/movies, dataport. Some units w/terraces. **Services:** 🖐 **Facilities:** 🏋 🍽 🏊25 🛎 1 restaurant (bkfst only), 1 bar,

whirlpool, washer/dryer. **Rates:** Peak (Apr–Oct) $69–$94 S or D; $89–$112 ste. Children under age 18 stay free. Lower rates off-season. Parking: Outdoor, free. AE, CB, DC, DISC, MC, V.

≣≣≣ DoubleTree Mayfair Suites

806 St Charles St, 63101; tel 314/421-2500 or toll free 800/222-TREE; fax 314/421-6254. Built in 1925, this luxury hotel was overhauled in 1990 and is listed on the National Register of Historic Places. The small but elegant lobby features elaborate crystal chandeliers, marble floors, potted plants, and colorful floral arrangements. **Rooms:** 184 rms and stes. Executive level. CI 3pm/CO noon. Nonsmoking rms avail. Spacious, modernized rooms, many with French doors separating the bedroom from the parlor. **Amenities:** 🛁 🍴 A/C, cable TV, dataport. All units w/minibars, some w/fireplaces, some w/whirlpools. **Services:** ✕ 🆅🅿 🛏 🖐 🐾 Car-rental desk, babysitting. **Facilities:** 🍽 🏊130 🛎 1 restaurant (*see* "Restaurants" below), 1 bar. **Rates:** Peak (Apr–May/Oct–Nov) $135 S; $145 D; $135–$145 ste. Extra person $10. Children under age 19 stay free. Lower rates off-season. Parking: Outdoor, $9/day. AE, DC, DISC, JCB, MC, V.

≣≣≣ Drury Inn Gateway Arch

711 N Broadway, 63101 (Downtown); tel 314/231-8100 or toll free 800/325-8300; fax 314/231-8100. Near Convention Center St exit off I-70. Located in a building that once served as the city market, this newer hotel offering a good array of services and fair rates is well suited for business travelers and families. The sleek, comfortable lobby features a crystal chandelier and large marble pillars. **Rooms:** 178 rms and stes. CI 3pm/CO noon. Nonsmoking rms avail. The sound-proofed rooms face either inner atrium or the outside. **Amenities:** 🛁 🍴 A/C, cable TV w/movies, dataport. **Services:** ✕ 🖐 🐾 Car-rental desk, babysitting. **Facilities:** 🏋 🏊80 🛎 1 restaurant, 1 bar, whirlpool. **Rates (CP):** Peak (Apr–Oct) $89–$107 S; $99–$119 D; $99–$119 ste. Extra person $10. Children under age 18 stay free. Lower rates off-season. Parking: Indoor, free. Casino package avail. AE, CB, DC, DISC, MC, V.

≣≣≣ Embassy Suites

901 N 1st St, 63102 (Laclede's Landing); tel 314/241-4200 or toll free 800/241-5151; fax 314/241-6513. Near Convention Center St exit off I-70. Part of national chain offering extra touches and services. Features an eight-story skylight atrium with a courtyard, lovely fountain, and well-tended plants. **Rooms:** 297 stes. CI 4pm/CO noon. Nonsmoking rms avail. Rooms on lowest floors have balconies, but those on higher floors facing the Arch provide better views. **Amenities:** 🛁 🍴 A/C, cable TV w/movies, refrig, dataport, voice mail. Some units w/terraces. Two TVs; Nintendo video games available. **Services:** ✕ 🖐 🐾 Babysitting. **Facilities:** 🏋 🍽 🏊500 🛎 1 restaurant (lunch and dinner only), 2 bars (1 w/entertainment), games rm, sauna, steam rm, whirlpool, washer/dryer. **Rates (BB):** Peak (June–Oct) $125–$145 ste.

Extra person $15. Children under age 13 stay free. Min stay special events. Lower rates off-season. Parking: Outdoor, $6/day. AE, CB, DC, DISC, JCB, MC, V.

≣≣≣ Hampton Inn

2211 Market St, 63101; tel 314/241-3200 or toll free 800/HAMPTON; fax 314/241-3200. Off US 40. Suitable for all travelers, this simple hotel in a tall building greets every guest in its average-size but comfortable lobby with lovely sofas and chairs and large potted plants and trees. **Rooms:** 239 rms and stes. CI 3pm/CO noon. Nonsmoking rms avail. No downtown views, despite height of building. **Amenities:** 🛗 ⓐ A/C, cable TV w/movies, dataport. **Services:** ✕ 🖼 ⟲ ⟳ **Facilities:** ⌂ ⌂ ⌂ ⌂ 🖼 ⌂ ⌂ 1 restaurant (lunch and dinner only), 1 bar, whirlpool, washer/dryer. **Rates (CP):** Peak (Apr–Oct) $79 S; $89 D; $125 ste. Extra person $10. Children under age 18 stay free. Lower rates off-season. Parking: Indoor/outdoor, free. AE, DC, DISC, MC, V.

≣≣≣ Holiday Inn Downtown Riverfront

200 N 4th St, 63102 (Riverfront); tel 314/621-8200 or toll free 800/925-1395; fax 314/621-8073. Near Memorial Dr exit off I-70. Originally built as an apartment complex in the '70s, this downtown property features many extra-large rooms plus a rooftop pool and observation deck. The average-size lobby offers many comfortable chairs and sofas for relaxing. **Rooms:** 456 rms, stes, and effic. Executive level. CI 3pm/CO noon. Nonsmoking rms avail. **Amenities:** 🛗 ⓐ 📺 A/C, satel TV, refrig. Some units w/terraces. **Services:** ✕ ⚷ 🖼 ⟲ ⟳ **Facilities:** ⌂ ⌂ 🖼 ⌂ ⌂ 2 restaurants, 2 bars, games rm, whirlpool, washer/dryer. **Rates:** Peak (May–Aug) $89 S; $99 D; $125–$350 ste; $59–$89 effic. Extra person $10. Children under age 18 stay free. Min stay special events. Lower rates off-season. Parking: Indoor, $7/day. Special packages include Great Rates and Best Breaks. AE, CB, DC, DISC, EC, ER, JCB, MC, V.

≣≣≣ Marriott Pavilion Downtown

1 Broadway, 63102 (Downtown); tel 314/421-1776 or toll free 800/228-9290; fax 314/331-9029. Memorial Dr exit off I-70, right on Market St, 2 blocks to Broadway. Well-suited for all travelers but especially for baseball fans, these two towers (one taller, one shorter) are located beside Busch Stadium, home of the Cardinals. The large, elegant lobby is decorated with verdant plants and floral arrangements, a fountain, marble floors, and large brass chandeliers. **Rooms:** 672 rms and stes. Executive level. CI 4pm/CO noon. Nonsmoking rms avail. Some rooms provide views. **Amenities:** 🛗 ⓐ A/C, satel TV, dataport, voice mail. Some units w/minibars, some w/whirlpools. **Services:** ✕ ⚷ 🆅🅿 🚗 🖼 ⟳ Twice-daily maid svce, car-rental desk, social director, babysitting. Additional movies can be rented. **Facilities:** ⌂ ⌂ 🖼 ⌂ ⌂ 2 restaurants, 1 bar, games rm, spa, sauna, steam rm, whirlpool, washer/dryer. JW Carver's offers elegant dining, while One Broadway sports bar is the place for pregame cocktails. **Rates:** Peak (Mar 17–Thanksgiving) $125 S; $140 D; $250–$750 ste. Extra person $10. Children under age 12 stay free.

Min stay special events. Lower rates off-season. Parking: Indoor, $11/day. Casino package avail. AE, DC, DISC, JCB, MC, V.

≣≣ Ramada Inn at the Arch

333 Washington Ave, 63102 (Downtown); tel 314/621-7900 or toll free 800/2-RAMADA; fax 314/421-6468. Memorial Dr exit off I-70. Comfortable and dependable hotel close to the Arch and the new Rams football stadium and thus perfect for the traveling sports fan. **Rooms:** 182 rms and stes. CI 3pm/CO noon. Nonsmoking rms avail. **Amenities:** 🛗 ⓐ A/C, cable TV w/movies, dataport, voice mail. All units w/terraces. **Services:** ✕ 🖼 ⟲ **Facilities:** ⌂ ⌂ 🖼 ⌂ 🖼 1 restaurant (bkfst and dinner only), 1 bar, games rm, spa, sauna, whirlpool, washer/dryer. **Rates:** Peak (Apr–Oct) $69–$129 S; $79–$129 D; $125–$200 ste. Extra person $10. Children under age 12 stay free. Min stay special events. Lower rates off-season. Parking: Indoor/outdoor, $5/day. AE, CB, DC, DISC, MC, V.

MOTELS

≣ Oak Grove Inn

6602 S Lindbergh Blvd, Mehlville, 63123; tel 314/894-9449 or toll free 800/894-9449; fax 314/894-6859. At jct I-55. Comfortable economy motel. **Rooms:** 97 rms and stes. CI 3pm/CO 11am. Nonsmoking rms avail. One room has king-size bed and whirlpool bathtub. **Amenities:** 🛗 A/C, cable TV w/movies, dataport. Some units w/whirlpools. **Services:** ⟳ Complimentary coffee and juice in lobby. **Facilities:** ⌂ Whirlpool, washer/dryer. **Rates:** Peak (Apr–Sept) $43 S; $47 D; $65 ste. Children under age 13 stay free. Lower rates off-season. Parking: Outdoor, free. AE, DC, DISC, MC, V.

≣ Red Roof Inn

11837 Lackland Rd, 63146; tel 314/991-4900 or toll free 800/THE-ROOF; fax 314/991-0047. Page exit E off I-270. A standard chain motel offering clean, comfortable accommodations with easy access to the interstate. Fine for a brief stay. **Rooms:** 160 rms. CI 2pm/CO noon. Nonsmoking rms avail. **Amenities:** 🛗 A/C, satel TV w/movies. **Services:** 🖼 ⟳ **Facilities:** ⌂ ⌂ Washer/dryer. **Rates (CP):** Peak (Mar–Nov) $41 S; $49 D. Extra person $9. Children under age 18 stay free. Lower rates off-season. Parking: Outdoor, free. AE, CB, DC, DISC, MC, V.

RESTAURANTS 🍴

Agusti's

2300 Edward's Ave (The Hill); tel 314/772-6003. **Italian.** The dining room is dark and cozy. The menu offers several appetizers, pizzas, salads, sandwiches, and pastas. Entrees include steak, veal, chicken, and seafood. A standout dish is beef Agusti: tenderloin in mushroom and wine sauce. **FYI:** Reservations accepted. **Open:** Tues–Thurs 5–10pm, Fri–Sat 5–11pm, Sun 4:30–9pm. **Prices:** Main courses $7–$16. AE, CB, DC, DISC, MC, V. ⌂

Al's Steak House

1200 N 1st St; tel 314/421-6399. 6th St exit off I-70. **Seafood/Steak.** A longtime St Louis favorite, Al's has been a top place to go for business lunches and special occasions since 1926. The old-time Italian restaurant is attractively decorated with oil paintings, brass chandeliers, and statuary. There is no printed menu; the waiter displays a platter of steak, veal, rack of lamb, and seafood and carefully explains the preparations for each dish. **FYI:** Reservations accepted. Children's menu. Jacket required. **Open:** Mon–Sat 5–11pm. **Prices:** Main courses $20–$45. AE, MC, V. VP &

Balban's

405 N Euclid Ave (Central West End); tel 314/361-8085. **New American.** One of the places to be seen in town, this hip, fun, colorfully and cheerfully decorated West End standout offers some of the best New American food around. Chef David Timney works his magic with pasta with morels and mesquite-grilled swordfish with wilted spinach and balsamic vinegar. **FYI:** Reservations recommended. **Open:** Lunch Mon–Fri 11am–3pm, Sat–Sun 10am–3pm; dinner Mon–Thurs 6–10:30pm, Fri–Sat 5:30–11:30pm, Sun 5–10:30pm. **Prices:** Main courses $15–$20. AE, CB, DC, DISC, MC, V. &

Bartolino's

2524 Hampton Ave; tel 314/644-2266. 3 blocks S of I-44. **Italian.** Attractive dining room decorated with marble statues, ceiling fans, and hanging plants provides a pleasant setting for enjoying a variety of salads, pastas, pizzas, sandwiches, and veal, chicken, and steak entrees. The chicken piccata is a favorite. **FYI:** Reservations accepted. No smoking. Additional location: 5914 S Lindberg (tel 487-4945). **Open:** Mon–Thurs 11am–11pm, Fri–Sat 5pm–midnight. **Prices:** Main courses $7–$15. AE, DISC, MC, V.

Cafe de France

410 Olive St (Downtown); tel 314/231-2204. **French.** Crystal chandeliers and light fixtures, lovely oil paintings, and fresh cut flowers on the tables set the scene for elegant, formal dining. Classic French cooking marked by modern touches is evident in elegant preparations of seafood, quail, pheasant, veal, and beef. Poached salmon in red wine sauce is a favorite specialty. Dishes are beautifully presented. **FYI:** Reservations recommended. **Open:** Lunch Mon–Fri 11:30am–2pm; dinner Mon–Thurs 5–10pm, Fri–Sat 5–11:30pm. **Prices:** Main courses $17–$21; prix fixe $25–$28. AE, CB, DC, DISC, MC, V. ● VP &

Caleco's

101 N Broadway; tel 314/421-0708. Memorial Dr exit off I-70; right on Pine, left on Broadway. **American/Italian.** Quirkily decorated with colorful paintings, musical instruments, baseball memorabilia, and numerous plants. Pastas predominate, but you can always get salads, seafood, steaks, pizza, or sandwiches. A special pasta is Caleco's linguine, made with olive oil, red and green peppers, onions, mushrooms, garlic, and Parmesan cheese. **FYI:** Reservations accepted. Children's menu. Additional locations: 14007 Man-

chester (tel 391-0808); 3818 Laclede (tel 534-7878). **Open:** Daily 11am–3am. **Prices:** Main courses $7–$15. DC, DISC, MC, V. &

Casa Gallardo

12380 St Charles Rock Rd, Bridgeton; tel 314/739-5700. At jct I-270. **Mexican.** This charming, cantina/restaurant is bursting with color from its hanging plants, murals, and interesting paintings. The menu offers a wide variety of standard items: flautas, fajitas, chimichangas. **FYI:** Reservations accepted. Children's menu. **Open:** Mon–Thurs 11am–11pm, Fri–Sat 11am–midnight, Sun 10am–10pm. **Prices:** Main courses $6–$12. AE, CB, DC, DISC, MC, V. &

Culpeppers

300 N Euclid Ave (Central West End); tel 314/361-2828. **American.** A simple neighborhood pub/eatery specializing in hot chicken wings. Wings come in varying degrees of spiciness, from mild to infernal. Burgers, sandwiches, and salads are available for anybody not "winging it." **FYI:** Reservations not accepted. Additional locations: 12316 Olive St (tel 469-3888); 312 S Kirkwood Rd (tel 821-7322). **Open:** Mon–Sat 11am–midnight, Sun noon–11pm. **Prices:** Main courses $5–$7. AE, DC, DISC, MC, V.

Dierdorf & Hart's

In Union Station, 18th and Market; tel 314/421-1772. US 40 E off I-70; exit at 20th and Chestnut. **Steak.** Relax in the plush leather booths and soak up the soothing sight of verdant plants, floral arrangements, and trees. Enjoy excellent New York strip, T-bone, and filet mignon, as well as fresh fish and lobster and burgers and sandwiches. Extensive bar and wine list. The restaurant was established by former local pro football stars Dan Dierdorf and Jim Hart. **FYI:** Reservations recommended. Piano. Dress code. Additional location: 734 Westport Plaza, Suite 262 (tel 878-1808). **Open:** Sun–Thurs 11am–10pm, Fri–Sat 11am–11pm. **Prices:** Main courses $13–$37. AE, CB, DC, DISC, MC, V. &

♛ Dominic's

5101 Wilson (The Hill); tel 314/771-1632. **Italian.** Formal and very elegant (and just a bit pretentious), this Hill temple of gourmet Italian dining provides seamless and classy service, a comprehensive wine list, and fantastic food. Scores of paintings, huge crystal chandeliers, and statuary create quite an eyeful. Veal saltimbocca, rack of lamb, chateaubriand, and fresh seafood are a few reasons to splurge. **FYI:** Reservations recommended. Jacket required. **Open:** Mon–Thurs 5–11pm, Fri–Sat 5pm–midnight. **Prices:** Main courses $17–$23. AE, CB, DC, DISC, MC, V. ● VP &

Duff's

392 N Euclid Ave (Central West End); tel 314/361-0522. 1½ mi N of US 40. **Eclectic.** Casual and friendly, the dining area is decorated with ceiling fans, mirrors, and brass light fixtures. The building itself dates to 1907. The seasonally changing, sometimes exotic menu includes entrees like North African chick-pea stew, duck Andre, and chicken Maui. For a

real treat, try the twin tournedos: charbroiled beef served with mushroom ragout and tomato horseradish. **FYI:** Reservations recommended. **Open:** Tues–Thurs 11am–10pm, Fri 11am–midnight, Sat 10am–midnight, Sun 10am–10:30pm. **Prices:** Main courses $9–$16. AE, CB, DC, DISC, MC, V. &

Faust's

In Adam's Mark Hotel, 4th and Chestnut Sts; tel 314/241-7400. Memorial Dr exit off I-70; right on Market, right on 4th St, right on Chestnut. **American/Continental.** This luxurious dining room featuring bronze statues, brass chandeliers, stone columns, and a stone fireplace could be mistaken for part of some European baron's castle. The creative menu changes often to utilize seasonal ingredients. It's hard to go wrong with dishes like roast rack of Sonoma lamb served with a minted balsamic glaze and caviar-mustard sauce, or pheasant seared with rosemary, juniper, and game glaze. **FYI:** Reservations recommended. Jazz/piano. Dress code. **Open:** Lunch Mon–Fri 11:30am–2pm; dinner Sun–Thurs 5:30–10pm, Fri–Sat 5:30–10:30pm; brunch Sun 10:30am–2:30pm. **Prices:** Main courses $16–$34. AE, CB, DC, DISC, MC, V.

Favazza's

5201 Southwest Ave at Marconi (The Hill); tel 314/772-4454. **Italian.** Decorated with stained glass and ceiling fans, this dining room is quite cozy. Reliably prepared if unimaginative Italian fare includes veal piccata, Sicilian steaks, and good pasta. **FYI:** Reservations recommended. **Open:** Mon–Thurs 11am–10pm, Fri 11am–midnight, Sat 5pm–12am. **Prices:** Main courses $11–$15. AE, DC, DISC, MC, V. &

Fourth Street Grill

In Clarion Regal Riverfront Hotel, 200 S 4th St; tel 314/241-9500. Memorial Dr exit off I-70 to Broadway, left to Spruce, left to 4th St, left. **New American.** The large windows offer jaw-dropping views of the Arch. Colorful paintings, potted plants, and trees make the scene inside almost as appealing. Entrees like beef, ribs, chicken, and prawns are slowly roasted in the fruitwood smoker. Breakfast and lunch buffets are available. **FYI:** Reservations accepted. Children's menu. No liquor license. **Open:** Breakfast daily 6:30–11am; lunch daily 11am–2pm; dinner daily 5–10pm. **Prices:** Main courses $9–$13. AE, CB, DC, DISC, MC, V.

Gian-Peppe's

2126 Marconi (The Hill); tel 314/772-3303. **Italian.** Not the most famous Italian restaurant in St Louis, but it does offer delicately prepared veal, seafood, and pasta dishes in an attractive, if small and somewhat stark, room. Service is friendly and efficient. **FYI:** Reservations recommended. Jacket required. **Open:** Peak (Sept–Dec) lunch Mon–Fri 11am–1:30pm; dinner Mon–Sat 5pm–close. **Prices:** Main courses $12–$24. AE, CB, DC, MC, V.

Giovanni's

5201 Shaw (The Hill); tel 314/772-5958. **Italian.** Elegant and romantic, this top trattoria offers some of the best pasta in town, served in a Renaissance-style room marked by large crystal chandeliers, paintings, mirrors, and marble statues. The menu offers a variety of hot and cold appetizers, pastas, and salads. Entrees include seafood, veal, lamb, chicken, and beef dishes. **FYI:** Reservations recommended. Jacket required. Additional location: 14560 Manchester Rd (tel 227-7230). **Open:** Mon–Sat 5–11pm. **Prices:** Main courses $15–$39. AE, DC, DISC, MC, V.

Kemoll's

In Metropolitan Sq, 211 N Broadway; tel 314/421-0555. 2 blocks N of Busch Stadium. **Italian.** Very attractive dining room decorated with paintings, elaborately framed mirrors, and luxurious drapes. The menu features a great selection of gourmet appetizers and salads. The shrimp and artichoke moutarde recipe was once published in *Bon Appétit* magazine. One of the better entrees is the sautéed shrimp with sliced artichokes in a mustard cream sauce. **FYI:** Reservations recommended. Dress code. **Open:** Lunch Mon–Fri 11am–2pm; dinner Mon–Sat 5–10pm. **Prices:** Main courses $15–$30. AE, DC, DISC, MC, V.

Key West

In Union Station, 18th and Market; tel 314/241-2566. US 40 E exit off I-70; 20th and Chestnut exit off US 40 E. **Seafood.** The emphasis is on the sea, both in the decor and the cuisine. Fish nets, large models of fish, and numerous nautical photographs adorn the walls of this combination bar/restaurant. Great Key West specialties include conch fritters, Florida rock shrimp, and shark. There is also a variety of burgers, sandwiches, and hot dogs. **FYI:** Reservations not accepted. **Open:** Mon–Sat 11am–2am, Sun 11am–midnight. **Prices:** Main courses $6–$9. AE, CB, DC, DISC, MC, V.

★ La Sala

513 Olive; tel 314/231-5620. Between Broadway and 6th. **Mexican.** This local favorite for weekday happy hour offers fajitas, fajitas, and more fajitas. The menu at this dark and cozy place is also strong on burritos, enchiladas, and chimichangas. **FYI:** Reservations not accepted. **Open:** Mon–Sat 11am–10pm. **Prices:** Main courses $4–$8. AE, CB, DC, DISC, MC, V. &

Lou Boccardi's

5424 Magnolia (The Hill); tel 314/647-1151. **Italian.** The unpretentious dining room, marked by large murals of old Italy and ceiling fans, is the proper setting for wonderful thin-crust pizza available with a variety of toppings. Also pastas, salads, sandwiches, and entrees of veal, chicken, seafood. **FYI:** Reservations accepted. **Open:** Tues–Thurs 11am–11pm, Fri–Sat 11am–midnight, Sun 2–10pm. **Prices:** Main courses $7–$14. MC, V. &

Mayfair Bar and Grill

In DoubleTree Mayfair Suites, 806 St Charles St; tel 314/421-2500. **American.** Attractive dining area decorated with brass chandeliers, stained-glass windows, and potted plants. The menu has a modest variety of soups and appetizers; entrees include steaks, ribs, seafood, pasta, and Jamaican chicken, a grilled breast served with mango chutney sauce. **FYI:** Reservations accepted. Children's menu. **Open:** Daily 6:30am–11pm. **Prices:** Main courses $10–$17. AE, CB, DC, DISC, MC, V. VP &

Museum Cafe

In St Louis Art Museum, Forest Park, 1 Fine Arts Dr; tel 314/721-5325. **Eclectic.** One of the walls is entirely glass, providing a view of statues, a waterfall, trees, and flowers. Paintings adorn the other walls. Fare consists mainly of salads and sandwiches, but there are a few entrees; one of the more popular is the grilled marinated salmon fillet with orange fennel salsa, capers, and green olives. **FYI:** Reservations accepted. Children's menu. No smoking. **Open:** Tues–Sat 11am–3:30pm, Sun 10am–2pm. **Prices:** Lunch main courses $6–$8. AE, CB, DC, DISC, MC, V. &

Norton's Cafe

808 Geyer; tel 314/436-0828. 7th St exit off I-70. **Cajun/Creole.** With a pub atmosphere, Norton's offers a relaxed and casual ambience in a dining area decorated with stained-glass windows and fast-spinning ceiling fans. Cajun dishes (like blackened shark), sandwiches served with Irish potatoes, steaks, and seafood populate the menu. **FYI:** Reservations accepted. **Open:** Daily 11am–midnight. **Prices:** Main courses $8–$13. AE, CB, DC, DISC, MC, V.

O'Connell's Pub

Kingshighway and Shaw; tel 314/773-6600. US 40 E exit off I-70. **Pub.** This old-fashioned, simple pub is the place to go for some of the best burgers in the city. Hot and cold sandwiches, salads, and appetizers are other options. **FYI:** Reservations not accepted. **Open:** Mon–Sat 11am–midnight, Sun noon–10pm. **Prices:** Main courses $4–$5. AE, DC, DISC, MC, V. &

Ozzie's Restaurant and Sports Bar

645 Westport Plaza; tel 314/434-1000. Page exit off I-270. **American.** Standard sports paraphenalia and plenty of TVs are what you'll find at this popular hangout. Fairly standard fare includes burgers, sandwiches, and entrees like chicken Yucatan (marinated, grilled chicken breast topped with pico de gallo, melted jack cheese and red chimayo sauce). **FYI:** Reservations not accepted. Children's menu. **Open:** Mon–Thurs 11am–11pm, Fri–Sat 11am–midnight, Sun 11am–10pm. **Prices:** Main courses $9–$19. AE, DC, MC, V. &

Patty Long's 9th St Abby

1808 S 9th (Soulard); tel 314/621-9598. 2 blocks S of Soulard Market. **Eclectic.** A renovated church, complete with high ceilings and numerous stained-glass windows. Don't miss the turkey harvest pie: breast of turkey in a rich white wine cream sauce with fresh vegetables, all topped with a flaky pastry. Also on the menu are salads, sandwiches, quiche, fish, chicken, and spinach linguine. **FYI:** Reservations recommended. Children's menu. Additional location: 3536 Washington (tel 534-3663). **Open:** Tues–Fri 11am–2pm, Sun 10am–2pm. **Prices:** Lunch main courses $7–$10. AE, DC, DISC, MC, V. VP &

Premio

Gateway One Building, 701 Market St; tel 314/231-0911. Memorial Dr exit off I-70. **Italian.** This downtown restaurant decorated with lots of potted plants and trees caters to the downtown business crowd. The kitchen features a dozen or so pasta dishes in addition to risottos, fresh seafood, and veal. For a sensory overload, try the gamberi al fornaio: Gulf shrimp, spinach, pine nuts, and feta cheese wrapped in a flaky pastry. **FYI:** Reservations accepted. **Open:** Lunch Mon–Fri 11am–2pm; dinner Mon–Thurs 5–10pm, Fri–Sat 5–11pm. **Prices:** Main courses $8–$21. AE, CB, DC, DISC, MC, V. &

Redel's

310 De Baliviere Ave; tel 314/367-7005. At Pershing. **American.** The truly eclectic decor of this casual, youthful dining room includes colorful pottery and dishes, neon signs, and antique cameras and radios. The staff recommends the Atlantic salmon, chargrilled and served with a caper, basil, and chive sauce. Other choices are the popular pizzas, baby back ribs, chicken, and seafood. **FYI:** Reservations accepted. **Open:** Lunch Mon–Fri 11:30am–2:30pm; dinner Mon–Thurs 5:30–10pm, Fri–Sat 5:30–11:30pm, Sun 5–9:30pm. **Prices:** Main courses $7–$15. AE, MC, V. &

Restaurant

In the De Menil Mansion, 3352 De Menil Place (Soulard); tel 314/771-5829. At Cherokee. **American.** Located in an old, beautifully restored house with a rustic flavor and elegant garden dining amid trees and shrubbery. Light fare (salads and sandwiches) is available at lunch, while Cornish game hen, prime rib, and fresh fish are a few highlights of the dinner menu. Many desserts. **FYI:** Reservations recommended. **Open:** Tues–Sat 11:30am–2pm. Closed Jan. **Prices:** Lunch main courses $6–$9. AE, MC, V. ■

Rigazzi's

4945 Daggett Ave (The Hill); tel 314/772-4900. Off I-44. **Italian.** This informal, family-style Italian is very popular for its lunch buffets and dinner pasta specials—not to mention its famous 32-oz "fishbowls" of beer. Standard Italian fare is complemented by sandwiches, burgers, steak, and seafood. One special dish is chicken Mediterranean—two boneless breasts of chicken prepared in a tomato-basil sauce with red wine and green and black olives, and topped with melted Provolone. **FYI:** Reservations recommended. **Open:** Mon–Sat 10am–11:30pm. **Prices:** Main courses $5–$10. AE, MC, V.

Ruth's Chris Steak House

101 S 11th St; tel 314/241-7711. At Walnut, 3 blocks W of Busch Stadium. **Steak.** The St Louis outpost of the chain of steakhouses with the funny name and top-quality steaks. This one is distinguished by potted plants and framed sketches on the walls. Besides steak, diners can choose from lamb, veal, chicken, and seafood dishes. **FYI:** Reservations recommended. **Open:** Daily 5pm–close. **Prices:** Main courses $19–$28. AE, CB, DC, DISC, MC, V. VP &

ⓢ Silk Road

510 N Euclid Ave (Central West End); tel 314/367-9370. **Chinese.** Pleasant, cheerful Chinese restaurant providing very good value and very good food with its all-you-can-eat lunch and dinner buffets. **FYI:** Reservations accepted. **Open:** Sun–Thurs 11:30am–10pm, Fri–Sat 11:30am–11pm. **Prices:** Main courses $5–$15. AE, DC, DISC, MC, V. &

Sunshine Inn

8½ Euclid Ave (Central West End); tel 314/367-1413. **Vegetarian.** A beautiful stained-glass sign greets every guest, while colorful prints hang on the walls to give the dining area a casual, welcoming atmosphere. The entrees are primarily vegetarian, but chicken and seafood are available. Good to try are the grilled vegetables, seasoned and lightly steamed on a charbroiler and served with teriyaki sauce and the grain of the day. **FYI:** Reservations accepted. No smoking. **Open:** Tues–Sat 11:30am–10pm, Sun 10am–2:30pm, Sun 5–9pm. **Prices:** Main courses $8–$11. AE, DC, DISC, MC, V. &

♥ Tony's

410 Market St; tel 314/231-7007. Pine St exit off I-70, right then left on Broadway, left on Market St. **Italian.** Agreement is near unanimous that Tony's is the finest restaurant in St Louis. Great attention to detail—in the elegant setting, with its marble pillars, statues, and oil paintings, in the exquisite cuisine, and in the top-flight service—is the reason why. Lobster, thick veal chops and aged steaks, game, made-to-order pastas, and seafood flown in daily are all available. **FYI:** Reservations recommended. Jacket required. **Open:** Mon–Thurs 5–11pm, Fri–Sat 5–11:30pm. **Prices:** Main courses $19–$29. DC, DISC, MC, V. ◉ VP &

Top of the Riverfront

In Regal Riverfront Hotel, 200 S 4th St; tel 314/241-9500. Memorial Dr exit off I-70, right on Market, left on Broadway, left on Spruce, left on 4th. **New American.** The dining room revolves to offer every guest spectacular views of the Arch, the Mississippi River, Busch Stadium, and downtown. And if you're not too busy watching the show, enjoy the St Louis pepper steak served with a cognac mustard sauce, or enjoy any of the other gourmet chicken, buffalo, duck, or beef entrees. **FYI:** Reservations recommended. **Open:** Tues–Sun 5–10pm, Sun 9am–2pm. **Prices:** Main courses $13–$24. AE, CB, DC, DISC, MC, V. ◢ &

Yen Ching

1012 S Brentwood Blvd; tel 314/721-7507. At Clayton. **Chinese.** A better Chinese restaurant with a restrained decor of hanging Chinese lanterns, mirrors, and some paintings. The menu offers a variety of appetizers and soups, a comprehensive list of standard Szechuan dishes, and Ming's beef specialty: tenderloin beef, wood ears, and Chinese vegetables, sautéed and garnished with fried rice sticks. **FYI:** Reservations accepted. **Open:** Lunch Mon–Fri 11:30am–2pm; dinner Mon–Thurs 5–9:30pm, Fri–Sat 5–10:30pm, Sun 4:30–9pm. **Prices:** Main courses $7–$13. AE, DC, MC, V.

Zia's

5256 Wilson (The Hill); tel 314/776-0020. **Italian.** Dependable and inexpensive, this traditionally decorated family-style restaurant is dark and cozy, and often quite noisy. One tantalizing specialty is the pesce asparogi: baked orange roughy fillet topped with fresh asparagus, mushrooms, and cheese. **FYI:** Reservations not accepted. **Open:** Peak (June–Aug) Mon–Thurs 11am–10pm, Fri–Sat 11am–11pm. **Prices:** Main courses $9–$15. AE, DC, DISC, MC, V.

ATTRACTIONS 🏛

TOP ATTRACTIONS

Gateway Arch, Jefferson National Expansion Memorial

11 N 4th St; tel 314/425-4465. America's tallest monument commemorates the westward expansion of pioneers in the 1800s. (Visitors may ride a tram to the top of the 650-foot stainless steel arch, but the wait can be up to three hours in summer and on weekends.) Under the arch, the **Museum of Westward Expansion** traces the journey of Lewis and Clark and Tucker Theater shows a 35-minute documentary film, *Monument to the Dream.* **Open:** Peak (Mem Day–Labor Day) daily 8am–10pm. Reduced hours off-season. **Free**

St Louis Union Station

1820 Market St (Downtown); tel 314/421-6655. At one time the busiest passenger-rail terminal in the United States, it once served more than 100,000 passengers daily. The restored 100-year-old terminal now contains a hotel, 80 specialty shops, more than 12 restaurants, a 10-screen theater, and even a small lake. Memories Theater provides historical films on Union Station and the building of railroads in the United States. **Open:** Mon–Thurs 10am–9pm, Fri–Sat 10am–10pm, Sun 11am–7pm. **Free**

Anheuser-Busch Brewery Tours

13th and Lynch; tel 314/577-2153. This brewery is the company's largest facility and is also where Anheuser-Busch began. Its 100 acres contain old brick buildings—some very ornate, with turreted tops and detailed facades—and streets lined with shade trees. The oldest building dates from 1868; the brew house was built in 1892. The guided tour begins with the brewing process; visitors view the huge vats, follow the fermentation process, watch the packaging lines in action, and see the famous Clydesdale horses in their stables. The tour culminates with complimentary samples of beer, including Busch, Budweiser, and Michelob. **Open:** Mon–Sat 9am–5pm. **Free**

MUSEUMS

St Louis Art Museum

Forest Park; tel 314/721-0067. Housed in an American Renaissance–style building originally constructed for the 1904 World's Fair. The museum's pre-Columbian and German Expressionist collections are considered among the best in the world. Other galleries feature Islamic and ancient art, an Asian collection, an Egyptian collection which includes a mummy, and art from Africa, Oceania, and the Americas. There are also displays of Chinese, European, and American decorative arts, including furniture, vases, ceramics, silver, and armor. **Open:** Tues 1:30–8:30pm, Wed–Sun 10am–5pm. **Free**

St Louis Science Center

5050 Oakland Ave; tel 314/289-4444 or toll free 800/456-7572. Interactive learning exhibits include life-size moving dinosaurs, a laser show, an earthquake center where participants experience "tremors," and a live stage show featuring an "alien xenologist" from another galaxy. The Discovery Room (for ages 4 to 10) allows children to dress up in Native American costumes and explore a Missouri cave. **Open:** Sun–Thurs 9:30am–5pm, Fri–Sat 9:30am–9pm. **Free**

St Louis History Museum

Jefferson Memorial Building, Forest Park; tel 314/361-1424. The museum traces important events in the history of the city, the state of Missouri, and the American West. It also houses memorabilia from the people who played indispensable roles in St Louis's development, including Charles Lindbergh, Daniel Boone, and Lewis and Clark. **Open:** Tues–Sun 9:30am–4:45pm. **Free**

Museum of Transportation

3015 Barrett Station Rd; tel 314/965-7998. Exhibits covering 150 years of transportation history include 65 locomotives, the Stanley Steamer and Model T, and one of two existing Chrysler turbine cars. **Open:** Daily 9am–5pm. **$$**

National Bowling Hall of Fame

8th and Walnut; tel 314/231-6340. The history of bowling, from its origins in medieval Europe through the present, is illustrated here. An eight-lane bowling alley in the basement has four automated lanes and four lanes operated by pin setters. The museum also houses the American Bowling Congress and Women's International Hall of Fame. **Open:** Peak (June–Aug) Mon–Sat 9am–7pm, Sun noon–7pm. Reduced hours off-season. **$**

Magic House

516 S Kirkwood Rd, Kirkwood; tel 314/822-8900. 1 mi N of St Louis. Maintains a collection of interactive exhibits that encourage kids to challenge themselves and use all of their senses. There's an electrostatically charged ball that makes hair stand on end, a human-sized maze, a three-story spiraling slide, and a variety of computers. In addition, children can test their reaction times, identify smells, watch their pupils change size, and test for color blindness. **Open:** Peak (Mem Day–Labor Day) Tues–Thurs 9:30am–5:30pm, Fri 9:30am–9pm, Sat 9:30am–5:30pm, Sun 11:30am–5:30pm. Reduced hours off-season. **$**

The Dog Museum

1721 S Mason Rd; tel 314/821-3647. A large collection of art, artifacts, and literature dedicated to man's best friend. In addition to a permanent collection, special exhibits change three to four times a year. On Sundays, pedigreed dogs are on display with their owners. Displays, lectures, research library. **Open:** Tues–Sat 9am–5pm, Sun noon–5pm. **$**

HISTORIC BUILDINGS

Old Courthouse

11 N 4th St; tel 314/425-4468. Built in Greek Revival style with a 150-foot dome, the courthouse is best known as the site of the 1857 Dred Scott trial, in which a slave sued for freedom and lost. On the ground floor is a museum dedicated to the history of St Louis; on the second floor are restored courtrooms; and on the fourth floor is an observation area around the rotunda. **Open:** Daily 8am–4:30pm. **Free**

St Louis Cathedral

4431 Lindell Blvd; tel 314/533-2824. Begun in 1907 and incorporating Byzantine and Romanesque architecture, the church contains the largest collection of mosaics in the world, some 145 million pieces of stone and glass covering 83,000 square feet of ceilings, domes, arches, and wall panels. **Open:** Daily 6am–6pm. **Free**

Cupples House

3673 W Pine Blvd; tel 314/658-3025. Located on the campus of St Louis University, this was the home of Samuel Cupples, a millionaire who made his fortune as a wood merchant. The Romanesque Revival–style mansion (circa 1889) is constructed of pink Missouri granite and Colorado sandstone, and contains 42 rooms and 20 fireplaces. In the basement, in what was formerly a bowling alley, is the McNamee Gallery, which features modern paintings. **Open:** Tues–Fri noon–4pm, Sun 2–4pm. **$**

Scott Joplin House

2658A Delmar Blvd; tel 314/533-1003. The musician and composer popularly known as the "King of Ragtime" lived in this modest four-family antebellum home from 1900 to 1903. In 1902, "The Entertainer" was published and became popular, but it was not until 1973 that it became his most famous piece when it was used as the theme song for the movie *The Sting*. In 1976, the building was listed on the National Register of Historic Places, and a few years later was granted the status of National Historic Landmark. Twenty-minute tours include Joplin's second-floor flat and conclude with a player piano equipped with Joplin's tunes. **Open:** Mon–Sat 10am–4pm, Sun noon–5pm. **$**

Chatillon-De Menil Mansion

3352 De Menil Place (Soulard); tel 314/771-5828. The 1848 four-room farmhouse was later expanded to 14 rooms and renovated in the Greek Revival style. It now contains period furnishings and two oil paintings by famed Missouri artist George Caleb Bingham. Tours given continuously throughout the day. **Open:** Feb–Dec, Wed–Sat 10am–4pm. **$$**

Campbell House Museum

1508 Locust St; tel 314/421-0325. With the exception of a few items, most of the original furnishings are present in this 1851 residence. Guided tours given throughout the day with an optional 27-minute video on the elegant Victorian homestead. **Open:** Tues–Sat 10am–4pm, Sun noon–5pm. Closed Jan–Feb. **$**

Eugene Field House and Toy Museum

634 S Broadway; tel 314/421-4689. The boyhood home of children's poet Eugene Field, who wrote "Little Boy Blue." The 1845 house is the oldest standing residence in downtown St Louis and has been restored to its early Victorian origins. The antique toy and doll collection spans more than 300 years. **Open:** Mar–Dec, Wed–Sat 10am–4pm, Sun noon–4pm. Open by appointment Jan–Feb. **$**

Grant's Farm

10501 Gravois Rd; tel 314/843-1700. Ulysses S Grant built a log cabin here in 1856, several years before he became the 18th president. Now a part of the 281-acre Busch estate (of Anheuser-Busch fame), the farm is open to the public, along with a game preserve, beer garden, antique carriage collection, and a small zoo. Two-hour miniature train tours must be reserved in advance. **Open:** June–Sept, call for schedule. **Free**

PARKS AND GARDENS

Missouri Botanical Garden

4344 Shaw; tel 314/577-5100. The 79-acre botanical garden was first opened to the public in 1859, making it one of the oldest in the country. It is home to two rose gardens with more than 6,000 roses, an iris garden, and an azalea/rhododendron garden. The 14-acre Japanese Garden contains a lake with carp, a teahouse, and traditional bridges. The Climatron greenhouse is the world's first geodesic-domed greenhouse and contains landscaped tropical vegetation that includes orchids. Tram ride, home gardening center, restaurant. **Open:** Peak (Mem Day–Labor Day) daily 9am–8pm. Reduced hours off-season. **$**

St Louis Zoological Park

Forest Park; tel 314/781-0900. Spanning 83 acres in Forest Park, the zoo is home to 2,800 animals, including apes, lions, tigers, jaguars, birds, penguins, and reptiles. The Bird Cage dates from the 1904 World's Fair, where it served as the Smithsonian Institution's walk-through bird-exhibit. Living World is an educational center designed to teach visitors about the balance of nature. It houses 150 animals chosen for their diversity, from bats and sponges to tarantulas and microscopic creatures. **Open:** Daily 9am–5pm. **Free**

Laumeier Sculpture Park

12580 Rott Road, Sunset Hills; tel 314/821-1209. 12 mi SW of downtown. A 96-acre exhibition of freestanding contemporary sculpture in a rolling, partly wooded setting. Centered in the park, the Laumeier Museum mounts exhibits by contemporary artists year-round. Hands-on workshops for children, hiking trails, self-guided tours, and picnic sites are available; on summer evenings, the park hosts drama, music, and dance performances. **Open:** Daily 8am–sunset. **Free**

OTHER ATTRACTIONS

Six Flags Over Mid-America

Allenton Rd, Eureka; tel 314/938-5300. 30 mi SW of St Louis, off I-44. Amusement rides, arcade games, entertainment, and food are all featured at this theme park. Among its many attractions are a dolphin show, the Screaming Eagle roller coaster (reputedly one of the longest, tallest, and fastest in the world), the NINJA roller coaster with a 360° loop, and an old-fashioned carousel. The park is divided into six sections, each representing one of the six countries that have flown their flags over the Midwest through the centuries. **Open:** Peak (June–Aug) Sun–Thurs 10am–9pm, Fri 10am–11pm, Sat 10am–10pm. Reduced hours off-season. **$$$$**

Busch Memorial Stadium

100 Stadium Plaza; tel 314/421-FAME or 421-3060 (tickets). Located in the heart of downtown, the stadium is home to the St Louis Cardinals baseball team. A highlight of the stadium is the **St Louis Cardinals Hall of Fame,** located between gates 5 and 6 on Walnut St. It contains a large collection of St Louis baseball memorabilia, including more than 1,000 items relating to the legendary St Louis player Stan Musial. On game evenings the museum is open only to ticket holders. Tours of Busch Stadium, include visits to the press box, the umpire's corridor, the dugout, and portions of the field; Tickets are available from the gift shop, located next to the Hall of Fame. **$$$**

Dental Health Theatre

727 N 1st St, Suite 103; tel 314/241-7391. Visitors learn about oral health and hygiene in a theater featuring 16 three-foot-high teeth, movies, and a marionette show. Exhibits include hands-on dental equipment and an antique dentist's office. Call for show times. **Open:** June–Aug, Mon–Fri 9am–4pm; Sept–May, Mon–Fri 8am–3pm. **Free**

Bob Kramer Marionnettes

4143 Laclede Ave (Central West End); tel 314/531-3313. Guests learn the history and craft of marionette making—from idea and sketch to puppet and performance—in a one-hour demonstration. Call for reservations. **$$$**

St Louis–Lambert Int'l Airport

HOTELS 🛄

▐▐▐ Henry VIII Hotel

4690 N Lindbergh, Bridgeton, 63044; tel 314/731-3040 or toll free 800/325-1588; fax 314/731-4210. Exit 235B off US 67. Easy access from the interstate and airport make this large hotel with a mock Tudor facade and other period touches convenient for those awaiting flights or resting from the road. Gleaming lobby has marble walls and pillars, large crystal chandeliers, and comfortable furniture. **Rooms:** 385 rms and stes. CI 3pm/CO noon. Nonsmoking rms avail. Honeymoon packages avail. **Amenities:** 🛆 🕹 A/C, cable TV, refrig. Some units w/terraces, some w/fireplaces, some w/whirlpools. **Services:** ✗ �car 🖥 🛎 🍷 **Facilities:** 🎱 🏋 🛁 🏊 & 2 restaurants, 2 bars (1 w/entertainment), games rm, sauna, whirlpool, washer/dryer. Irish pub. **Rates:** $108 S; $118 D; $128–$150 ste. Extra person $10. Children under age 17 stay free. Parking: Outdoor, free. Honeymoon packages avail. AE, CB, DC, DISC, MC, V.

▐▐▐ Holiday Inn Airport Oakland Park

4505 Woodson Rd, Woodson Terrace, 63134; tel 314/427-4700 or toll free 800/426-4700; fax 314/427-6086. Exit 236 off I-70. Not your average chain hotel, this one has European character and homelike coziness. Numerous original paintings adorn the walls of the small but very attractive lobby, which also featues leather sofas and chairs, flowers, and a crystal chandelier. **Rooms:** 155 rms and stes. CI 3pm/CO 1pm. Nonsmoking rms avail. **Amenities:** 🛆 🕹 A/C, cable TV, dataport, voice mail. 1 unit w/whirlpool. **Services:** ✗ 🚗 🖥 🍷 Car-rental desk. Free shuttle provided for immediate vicinity. Movie rentals available. **Facilities:** 🎱 🏋 🛁 & 1 restaurant, 1 bar, games rm, sauna, whirlpool, washer/dryer. **Rates:** $84–$94 S; $89–$99 D; $150–$159 ste. Extra person $5. Children under age 19 stay free. Parking: Outdoor, free. Senior discounts, B&B and honeymoon packages avail. AE, DC, DISC, JCB, MC, V.

▐▐▐ Holiday Inn Airport West

I-270 at St Charles Rock Rd, Bridgeton, 63044; tel 314/291-5100 or toll free 800/HOLIDAY; fax 314/291-3546. I-270 N exit off I-70, St Charles Rock Rd exit off I-270 N. Recently renovated hotel with comfortable rooms and a lovely pool housed in a large atrium along with a miniature golf course and horseshoe pit. **Rooms:** 249 rms and stes. CI 3pm/CO noon. Nonsmoking rms avail. **Amenities:** 🛆 🕹 🖥 A/C, cable TV w/movies, dataport. **Services:** ✗ 🚗 🖥 🍷 Babysitting. **Facilities:** 🎱 🏋 🛁 & 1 restaurant, 1 bar (w/entertainment), basketball, volleyball, games rm, sauna, whirlpool, washer/dryer. **Rates:** Peak (June 15–Aug) $79–$99 S; $84–$104 D; $150 ste. Extra person $5. Children

under age 16 stay free. Lower rates off-season. Parking: Outdoor, free. Special packages include the Great Rates and Bed & Breakfast. AE, CB, DC, DISC, EC, ER, JCB, MC, V.

▐▐▐ Radisson Hotel St Louis Airport

11228 Lone Eagle Dr, Bridgeton, 63044; tel 314/291-6700 or toll free 800/333-3333; fax 314/770-1205. At jct I-70 and Lindberg. Guests are greeted by a large atrium lobby decorated with a waterfall and beautiful fountain, lots of plants and trees, and lovely floral arrangements. **Rooms:** 353 rms and stes. CI 3pm/CO noon. Nonsmoking rms avail. **Amenities:** 🛆 🕹 A/C, dataport. Some units w/terraces. **Services:** ✗ 🚗 🖥 🍷 **Facilities:** 🎱 🏋 🛁 & 2 restaurants, 2 bars, games rm, whirlpool. **Rates:** $109–$124 S; $109–$129 S or D; $379 ste. Extra person $10. Children under age 17 stay free. Parking: Outdoor, free. Romantic Adventure package avail. AE, CB, DC, DISC, JCB, MC, V.

▐▐▐ Renaissance St Louis Hotel

9801 Natural Bridge Rd, St Louis, 63134; tel 314/429-1100 or toll free 800/468-3571; fax 314/429-3625. At I-70. This 12-story luxury hotel has a sleek black exterior highlighted by a fountain with silver, cylindrically shaped sculptures that lend a modernistic look. The spacious lobby, which includes a restaurant and lounge, is decorated with fountains, potted trees and plants, and plenty of comfortable upholstered chairs. Located only five minutes from Lambert Airport. **Rooms:** 394 rms and stes. Executive level. CI 4pm/CO 1pm. Nonsmoking rms avail. Rooms feature contemporary muted decor and very comfortable chairs. **Amenities:** 🛆 🕹 🖥 A/C, satel TV w/movies, voice mail. All units w/minibars, some w/whirlpools. **Services:** ✗ 🖥 VP 🚗 🛁 🍷 Masseur, babysitting. **Facilities:** 🎱 🏋 🛁 🖥 & 1 restaurant (see "Restaurants" below), 1 bar, spa, sauna, whirlpool. **Rates:** $79–$122 S; $89–$132 D; $160–$550 ste. Extra person $15. Children under age 12 stay free. Parking: Outdoor, $3/day. Casino packages avail. AE, CB, DC, DISC, EC, MC, V.

▐▐▐ St Louis Airport Hilton

10330 Natural Bridge Rd, Woodson Terrace, 63134; tel 314/426-5500 or toll free 800/345-5500. Exit 236 off I-70. This welcoming hotel directly across from the airport has a gracious, relaxing atmosphere. The large, attractive lobby is decorated in earth tones and has colorful floral arrangements throughout. Car rental agency next door. **Rooms:** 220 rms and stes. Executive level. CI 4pm/CO 1pm. Nonsmoking rms avail. Rooms have contemporary styling and blond wood furniture. **Amenities:** 🛆 🕹 🖥 A/C, cable TV w/movies, dataport, voice mail. Some units w/whirlpools. Some suites have wet bars and pool tables. **Services:** 🍽 🖥 VP 🚗 🛁 🍷 Masseur, babysitting. Hotel shuttle links guests to Metro Link light rail system. **Facilities:** 🎱 🏋 🛁 🖥 & 1 restaurant, 1 bar (w/entertainment), volleyball, games rm, sauna, whirlpool, washer/dryer. **Rates:** Peak (Mar–Nov 15) $98–$133 S; $108–$143 D; $175 ste. Children under age 18 stay free.

Lower rates off-season. Parking: Outdoor, free. Weekend, romantic, and shopper's packages avail. AE, CB, DC, DISC, EC, ER, JCB, MC, V.

MOTELS

Days Inn
4545 Woodson Rd, Woodson Terrace, 63134; tel 314/423-6770 or toll free 800/DAYS-INN; fax 314/423-6770. Typical chain motel with dependable service. **Rooms:** 202 rms. CI 3pm/CO noon. Nonsmoking rms avail. **Amenities:** A/C, cable TV w/movies. **Services:** **Facilities:** **Rates (CP):** Peak (May–Sept 15) $55–$65 S or D. Extra person $7. Children under age 18 stay free. Lower rates off-season. Parking: Outdoor, free. Sleep and Fly packages avail. AE, DC, DISC, MC, V.

Motel 6
4576 Woodson Rd, Woodson Terrace, 63134; tel 314/427-1313 or toll free 800/440-6000; fax 314/427-0826. Exit 236 off I-70. A basic economy motel near the airport providing clean, comfortable rooms. **Rooms:** 106 rms. CI noon/CO noon. Nonsmoking rms avail. **Amenities:** A/C, cable TV w/movies. **Services:** Free local phone calls. **Facilities:** **Rates:** Peak (June–Sept) $36 S; $42 D. Extra person $6. Children under age 18 stay free. Lower rates off-season. Parking: Outdoor, free. AE, CB, DC, DISC, MC, V.

Red Roof Inn
3470 Hollenberg Dr, Bridgeton, 63044; tel 314/291-3350 or toll free 800/THE-ROOF; fax 314/291-5603. At jct I-270 and St Charles Rock Rd. Nothing special, but okay for a brief stay. **Rooms:** 108 rms. CI noon/CO noon. Nonsmoking rms avail. **Amenities:** A/C, satel TV w/movies. **Services:** **Facilities:** **Rates:** Peak (May–Oct) $46 S; $56 D. Extra person $10. Children under age 19 stay free. Lower rates off-season. Parking: Outdoor, free. AE, CB, DC, DISC, MC, V.

RESTAURANTS

Faraday's
In Renaissance St Louis Hotel, 9801 Natural Bridge Rd, St Louis; tel 314/429-1100. At I-70. **American.** Nice setting includes a fountain in the middle of the dining room complete with goldfish. A good variety of appetizers and soups are offered along with steak, chicken, veal, and a fresh daily seafood selection. **FYI:** Reservations recommended. Children's menu. **Open:** Mon–Fri 6:30am–11pm, Sat–Sun 7am–11pm. **Prices:** Main courses $14–$15. AE, CB, DC, DISC, MC, V. **VP**

Grone Cafeteria
4409 Woodson Rd, Woodson Terrace; tel 314/423-7880. ¼ mi S of I-70. **American/Cafeteria.** Comfortable country ambience. Weekly menu relies on staples such as chicken potpie, beef Stroganoff, and chicken fried steak. Delicious homemade pies and cakes. **FYI:** Reservations accepted. Children's menu. No liquor license. **Open:** Sun–Fri 11am–8pm. **Prices:** Main courses $4–$7. No CC.

Sedalia

Called the "Queen City of the Prairies," Sedalia was a successful railroad town during the 1800s. Currently it plays host to the Missouri State Fair each August. Every June, the city hosts the Scott Joplin Ragtime Festival in honor of its best-known native son. **Information:** Sedalia Area Chamber of Commerce & Convention & Visitors Bureau, 113 E 4th St, Sedalia, 65301-4499 (tel 816/826-2222).

HOTEL

Ramada Inn
3501 W Broadway, 65301; tel 816/826-8400 or toll free 800/2-RAMADA; fax 816/826-1230. 1 mi W of US 65. Affordable rooms exhibiting excellent housekeeping standards. **Rooms:** 124 rms. CI 3pm/CO noon. Nonsmoking rms avail. **Amenities:** A/C, cable TV w/movies. All units w/terraces. **Services:** **Facilities:** 1 restaurant, 1 bar. **Rates:** Peak (Aug) $50 S; $55 D. Extra person $6. Children under age 19 stay free. Lower rates off-season. Parking: Outdoor, free. AE, CB, DC, DISC, MC, V.

MOTELS

State Fair Motor Inn Best Western
32nd and US 65 S, 65301; tel 816/826-6100 or toll free 800/528-1234; fax 816/827-3850. Standard chain motel offering clean rooms. Average-size lobby with comfortable furniture. **Rooms:** 119 rms. CI 3pm/CO noon. Nonsmoking rms avail. **Amenities:** A/C, cable TV. 1 unit w/minibar. **Services:** **Facilities:** 1 restaurant, 1 bar, games rm, sauna, whirlpool, washer/dryer. **Rates:** Peak (Aug 15–30) $44–$49 S; $49–$54 D. Extra person $5. Children under age 16 stay free. Lower rates off-season. Parking: Outdoor, free. AE, CB, DC, DISC, MC, V.

Super 8 Motel
3402 W Broadway, 65301; tel 816/827-5890 or toll free 800/800-8000; fax 816/827-5890. Basic budget accommodations located off US 65. **Rooms:** 83 rms. CI 2pm/CO 11am. Nonsmoking rms avail. **Amenities:** A/C, cable TV w/movies. **Services:** **Facilities:** **Rates (CP):** $40 S; $47 D. Extra person $3. Children under age 13 stay free. Parking: Outdoor, free. AE, CB, DC, DISC, MC, V.

RESTAURANTS

Around the Fireside
1975 W Broadway Blvd; tel 816/826-9743. ¼ mi W of US 65. **American.** Hanging plants, stained-glass windows, and colorful pictures of flowers adorn the dining area. A modest selection of appetizers accompanies entrees that include

seafood, chicken, and ham dishes. The chicken Damien (boneless breast of chicken smothered with mushrooms, cheese, and cream sauce) may not be lean cuisine, but it's worth the splurge. **FYI:** Reservations accepted. Children's menu. **Open:** Lunch Mon–Fri 11am–2pm; dinner Mon–Fri 5–10:30pm, Sat 4–10:30pm. **Prices:** Main courses $8–$32. AE, CB, DC, DISC, MC, V. &

McGraths
2901 W Broadway; tel 816/826-9902. On US 50. **American.** Rustic country atmosphere, with walls featuring photographs, animal skins, and large feathers. Chicken, steak, large selection of fresh seafood. **FYI:** Reservations not accepted. Children's menu. **Open:** Lunch Mon–Fri 11:30am–2pm; dinner Mon–Thurs 4:30–10pm, Fri–Sat 4:30–10:30pm. **Prices:** Main courses $7–$18. AE, DISC, MC, V. &

Sikeston

Established by John Sikes in 1860, this town's gingerbread mansions and cotton gins give travelers a taste of the Old South. Cotton remains a major crop in this economic hub of southeast Missouri. **Information:** Sikeston Area Chamber of Commerce, #1 Industrial Dr, Sikeston, 63801 (tel 573/471-2498).

HOTEL

≡≡ Best Western Coach House Inn & Suites
220 S Interstate Dr, 63801; tel 573/471-9700 or toll free 800/528-1234. Near US 62; accessible from exit 67 off I-55. Built seven years ago as a retirement home, this hotel has been remodeled into an all-suite property. Located in a relaxing country setting, the ambience is very residential—a few permanent residents from the retirement home still live here. A baby grand piano and a winding staircase distinguish the spacious lobby. **Rooms:** 50 stes. CI open/CO noon. Nonsmoking rms avail. **Amenities:** A/C, cable TV. A few units have refrigerators. **Services:** Facilities: 1 restaurant, games rm, washer/dryer. Pool table. **Rates (CP):** $45–$77 ste. Extra person $9. Children under age 18 stay free. Parking: Outdoor, free. AE, CB, DC, DISC, MC, V.

MOTELS

≡≡≡ Drury Inn Sikeston
2602 E Malone St, 63801; tel 573/471-4100 or toll free 800/325-8300. Exit 67 off I-55, W on US 62. Exceptionally nice and relatively new four-story motel with an atrium lobby, lush plants, ample seating, and a large breakfast area. **Rooms:** 80 rms and stes. CI 3pm/CO noon. Nonsmoking rms avail. Quality furnishings, including armoires to hold TVs. **Amenities:** A/C, cable TV w/movies, dataport. King-deluxe suites have microwaves and refrigerators. **Services:** Small pets only—and they must be attended or

caged. **Facilities:** Whirlpool. **Rates (CP):** Peak (Apr–Dec) $52–$65 S; $59–$67 D; $65–$72 ste. Children under age 18 stay free. Lower rates off-season. Parking: Outdoor, free. AE, CB, DC, DISC, MC, V.

≡≡ Hampton Inn
1330 S Main St, 63801; tel 573/471-3930 or toll free 800/HAMPTON; fax 573/471-8838. Exit 66B off I-55, 3 mi W on US 60. Located south of town with a comfortable lobby and ample sitting area. Best suited for the business traveler on a budget. **Rooms:** 127 rms. CI noon/CO noon. Nonsmoking rms avail. Rooms have armoires for closet space. **Amenities:** A/C, cable TV, dataport. VCRs and refrigerators in some rooms. **Services:** Babysitting. **Facilities:** Indoor pool is poorly maintained and needs remodeling. **Rates (CP):** $47–$52 S; $56–$61 D. Children under age 18 stay free. Parking: Outdoor, free. AE, CB, DC, DISC, MC, V.

≡≡ Holiday Inn Express Sikeston
2602 Rear E Malone, 63801; tel 573/471-8660 or toll free 800/HOLIDAY. Exit 67 off I-55. This 1970s-era hotel was completely renovated and reopened in 1994. A good budget choice. **Rooms:** 67 rms. CI 3pm/CO noon. Nonsmoking rms avail. **Amenities:** A/C, cable TV w/movies, dataport. **Services:** Facilities: **Rates (CP):** Peak (Apr–Dec) $39–$50 S; $46–$57 D. Children under age 18 stay free. Lower rates off-season. Parking: Outdoor, free. Rates vary by floor. AE, CB, DC, DISC, MC, V.

RESTAURANT

★ Lambert's Cafe
2515 E Malone; tel 573/471-4261. 1 block W of exit 67 off I-55. **American.** A Missouri institution for more than 50 years. Lambert's has been featured on television several times. It's known as the home of the "thrown rolls," since the red suspender–clad waiters will throw you a roll to enjoy with your chicken, pork, or beef plate, which comes complete with your choice of more than 15 vegetables options. The decor is festive, rustic, and patriotic, with state flags hanging from the ceiling. **FYI:** Reservations not accepted. Piano. Children's menu. No liquor license. No smoking. Additional location: MO 65, Ozark (tel 417/581-7655). **Open:** Daily 10:30am–9pm. **Prices:** Main courses $7–$15. No CC. &

Springfield

The third-largest city in Missouri and the northeastern gateway to the Ozarks, Springfield was founded prior to 1850. Visitors today find a diverse city offering historic homes, cultural events, and a wide range of outdoor activities. Several institutions of higher education make their home in Springfield, including Southwest Missouri State University. **Information:** Springfield Convention & Visitors Bureau, 3315 E Battlefield Rd, Springfield, 65804-4048 (tel 417/881-5300 or toll free 800/678-8767).

HOTELS

Holiday Inn University Plaza

333 John Q Hammons Pkwy, 65806; tel 417/864-7333 or toll free 800/HOLIDAY; fax 417/831-5893. Exit 80A off I-44. This hotel, which claims to be the largest convention center in the state, features a spacious atrium/lobby with skylights, a waterfall, trees, and plants. Beautiful and peaceful. Good for business or pleasure. **Rooms:** 271 rms and stes. Executive level. CI 2pm/CO noon. Nonsmoking rms avail. **Amenities:** A/C, cable TV w/movies. Refrigerators available in suites. **Services:** Babysitting. **Facilities:** 1 restaurant, 1 bar, basketball, games rm, sauna, steam rm, whirlpool, beauty salon, washer/dryer. **Rates:** $89 S or D; $112 ste. Extra person $10. Parking: Outdoor, free. June–Labor Day, children under 12 stay and eat free. AE, CB, DC, DISC, MC, V.

Markham Inn of the Ozarks

2820 N Glenstone Ave, 65803; tel 417/866-3581 or toll free 800/2-RAMADA; fax 417/865-5378. Exit 80A off I-44. Recently renovated, standard accommodations. Golf course nearby. **Rooms:** 131 rms. CI 2pm/CO noon. Nonsmoking rms avail. **Amenities:** A/C, cable TV w/movies. **Services:** **Facilities:** 1 restaurant, 1 bar (w/entertainment). **Rates:** Peak (June–Oct) $60–$75 S or D. Extra person $5. Children under age 11 stay free. Lower rates off-season. Parking: Outdoor, free. AE, CB, DC, DISC, EC, JCB, MC, V.

Park Inn International

1772 S Glenstone Ave, 65804; tel 417/882-1113 or toll free 800/749-7275; fax 417/882-8869. I-44 to Sunshine exit off US 65 S, W 2 mi. Located at an intersection of two major local business routes, this hotel is convenient and dependable. **Rooms:** 120 rms and stes. CI 3pm/CO 11am. Nonsmoking rms avail. Modestly decorated rooms. **Amenities:** A/C, cable TV. Some units w/whirlpools. **Services:** **Facilities:** 1 restaurant (lunch and dinner only), 1 bar, whirlpool. **Rates (CP):** Peak (Mar–Oct) $38–$48 S; $40–$50 D; $85 ste. Extra person $4. Children under age 16 stay free. Lower rates off-season. Parking: Outdoor, free. AE, CB, DC, DISC, EC, JCB, MC, V.

Quality Inn North

3050 N Kentwood, 65803; tel 417/833-3108 or toll free 800/955-1833; fax 417/833-0477. I-44 and N Glenstone. Wonderfully landscaped property with inviting rooms and a tastefully decorated lobby. Easy access to interstate. **Rooms:** 197 rms and stes. CI 3pm/CO noon. Nonsmoking rms avail. **Amenities:** A/C, cable TV w/movies, voice mail. Some units w/whirlpools. Refrigerators available in suites; coffee and hair dryers available in corporate rooms. **Services:** Babysitting. **Facilities:** 1 restaurant, 2 bars (1 w/entertainment), games rm, sauna, whirlpool. **Rates**

(CP): Peak (Apr–Oct) $57–$69 S or D; $185 ste. Extra person $5. Children under age 18 stay free. Lower rates off-season. Parking: Outdoor, free. AE, DC, DISC, MC, V.

Residence Inn Battlefield Mall

1550 E Raynell Place, 65804; tel 417/883-7300 or toll free 800/331-3131; fax 417/883-5779. Off US 65. Apartmentlike accommodations, a well-shaded courtyard, and outdoor cooking facilities make this a home-away-from-home. Located across the street from a large shopping mall. **Rooms:** 80 effic. CI 3pm/CO noon. Nonsmoking rms avail. Some rooms offer separate upstairs bedrooms; some have Murphy beds. **Amenities:** A/C, satel TV w/movies, refrig. Some units w/terraces, some w/fireplaces. **Services:** Children's program, babysitting. Complimentary beer, wine, cocktails, and appetizers Mon–Thurs. **Facilities:** Basketball, volleyball, racquetball, whirlpool, washer/dryer. Free access to nearby fitness and health spa. **Rates (CP):** Peak (May–Oct) $69–$139 effic. Lower rates off-season. Parking: Outdoor, free. AE, CB, DC, DISC, EC, JCB, MC, V.

Rodeway Inn

2610 N Glenstone Ave, 65803; tel 417/866-6671; fax 417/866-6088. Exit 804 off I-44. Basic property recommended for short stays. **Rooms:** 224 rms and stes. CI 4pm/CO noon. Nonsmoking rms avail. **Amenities:** A/C, cable TV w/movies. Some units w/terraces. Rooms for seniors available featuring extra-large digital clocks, phones with large buttons, and commode rails. **Services:** **Facilities:** 1 restaurant (lunch and dinner only), 1 bar, games rm, playground, washer/dryer. **Rates:** Peak (Mar–Apr/June–Aug) $39–$47 S; $41–$49 D; $65 ste. Extra person $6. Children under age 18 stay free. Lower rates off-season. Parking: Outdoor, free. AE, DISC, EC, MC, V.

Sheraton Hawthorn Park Hotel

2431 Glenstone Ave, 65803; tel 417/831-3131 or toll free 800/223-0092, 800/492-5041 in MO; fax 417/831-9786. Exit 80A off I-44, ½ mi S on Glenstone. Tastefully decorated hotel with spacious atrium on lower level. **Rooms:** 203 rms. Executive level. CI 3pm/CO 11am. Nonsmoking rms avail. **Amenities:** A/C, cable TV w/movies, dataport, voice mail. Bathrooms have TVs. **Services:** Babysitting. Complimentary cocktails, appetizers, continental breakfast, and turndown service on club level. **Facilities:** 1 restaurant, 2 bars, games rm, sauna, whirlpool, washer/dryer. **Rates:** $89–$99 S or D. Children under age 18 stay free. Parking: Outdoor, free. AE, CB, DC, DISC, JCB, MC, V.

MOTELS

Best Inns of America

2355 N Glenstone Ave, 65803; tel 417/866-6776 or toll free 800/BEST-INN; fax 417/866-6776. Exit 80A off I-44. This average motel is a great bargain for all travelers. **Rooms:** 132 rms. CI open/CO 1pm. Nonsmoking rms avail. Basic, but clean accommodations. **Amenities:** A/C, cable TV w/movies. 1 unit w/whirlpool. **Services:** 🖼 🖨 **Facilities:** 🖼 🛏 🛆 **Rates (CP):** $39 S; $42 D. Extra person $6. Children under age 18 stay free. Parking: Outdoor, free. AE, DC, DISC, MC, V.

🔳🔳 Best Western Coach House Inn
2535 N Glenstone Ave, 65803; tel 417/862-0701 or toll free 800/528-1234; fax 417/862-5713. Exit 80A off I-44 W or E. Near several restaurants. Okay for short stays. **Rooms:** 130 rms and stes. CI 1pm/CO noon. Nonsmoking rms avail. **Amenities:** 🛋 A/C, cable TV w/movies, dataport. Some units w/terraces. Some rooms have refrigerators; hair dryers available for rent. **Services:** 🖼 🖨 🖱 VCRs available for rent. **Facilities:** 🖼 🛏 🛆 Playground. **Rates (CP):** Peak (May–Oct) $50–$55 S or D; $65 ste. Extra person $5. Children under age 16 stay free. Lower rates off-season. Parking: Outdoor, free. AE, DC, DISC, MC, V.

🔳🔳 Econo Lodge
2611 N Glenstone Ave, 65803; tel 417/864-3565 or toll free 800/424-4777; fax 417/865-0567. Reliable accommodations for short stays. **Rooms:** 122 rms. CI 3pm/CO 11am. Nonsmoking rms avail. **Amenities:** 🛋 A/C, cable TV w/movies, dataport. **Services:** 🖼 🖨 **Facilities:** 🖼 🛆 Washer/dryer. **Rates (CP):** $42–$46 S; $45–$50 D. Extra person $5. Children under age 18 stay free. Parking: Outdoor, free. AE, CB, DC, DISC, MC, V.

🔳🔳🔳 Holiday Inn North I-44
2720 N Glenstone Ave, 65803; tel 417/865-8600 or toll free 800/HOLIDAY; fax 417/862-9415. Exit 80A off I-44. Relaxing establishment with attractive atrium decorated with small plants and trees. Golf and volleyball available nearby for priority club members. **Rooms:** 188 rms and stes. Executive level. CI 6pm/CO noon. Nonsmoking rms avail. **Amenities:** 🛋 ⚱ A/C, cable TV w/movies. Some units w/whirlpools. Suites have refrigerators. **Services:** ✕ 🚐 🖼 🖨 Twice-daily maid svce. VCRs available for rent. **Facilities:** 🖼 🏐 🛆 🛆 1 restaurant, 1 bar, sauna, steam rm, whirlpool, playground. **Rates:** $89 S or D; $96–$200 ste. Extra person $10. Children under age 12 stay free. Parking: Outdoor, free. Honeymoon package avail. AE, CB, DC, DISC, JCB, MC, V.

🔳 Super 8 Motel
3022 N Kentwood Ave, 65803; tel 417/833-9218 or toll free 800/800-8000; fax 417/833-9218. Exit 80B off I-44. Standardized, no-frills budget rooms. **Rooms:** 50 rms and stes. CI 3pm/CO 11am. Nonsmoking rms avail. **Amenities:** 🛋 A/C, cable TV w/movies. **Services:** 🖨 🖱 **Facilities:** 🛆 **Rates:** Peak (June–Aug) $33–$42 S; $35–$46 D; $40–$50 ste. Extra person $5. Children under age 12 stay free. Lower rates off-season. Parking: Outdoor, free. AE, CB, DC, DISC, JCB, MC, V.

INNS

🔳🔳🔳 The Mansion at Elfindale Inn
1701 S Fort, 65807; tel 417/831-5400 or toll free 800/443-0237. E 1 mi off US 60 and Battlefield, N ¾ mi to S Fort. 13 acres. This lovely stone mansion doubles as a quaint bed-and-breakfast. Built in the late 1800s, it's beautifully decorated with many antiques. Unsuitable for children under 12. **Rooms:** 13 stes. CI 3pm/CO 11am. Elaborate antique furnishings and 14-foot ceilings. Because of the cost of the furnishings, evidence of cigarette or alcohol use in the rooms results in a $75 charge. **Amenities:** 🛋 ⚱ A/C. No TV. 1 unit w/terrace. **Services:** ✕ **Facilities:** 🖼 🛆 Guest lounge w/TV. **Rates (BB):** $70–$125 ste. Extra person $10–$15. Parking: Outdoor, free. Special rates for business, clergy, and senior citizens. AE, DISC, MC, V.

🔳🔳🔳 Walnut Street Inn
900 E Walnut St, 65806; tel 417/864-6346 or toll free 800/593-6346; fax 417/864-6184. A bed-and-breakfast located in a quiet, secluded section of town, this makes for an extra-special visit to Springfield. The house, more than 100 years old, features Queen Anne Corinthian architecture and a cozy guest lounge with several antiques, including a piano from 1860. **Rooms:** 14 rms, stes. CI 5pm/CO 11am. All rooms are individually decorated with antiques. **Amenities:** 🛋 ⚱ A/C, cable TV, refrig, bathrobes. Some units w/terraces, some w/fireplaces, some w/whirlpools. Some rooms have coffeemakers and hair dryers. **Services:** ✕ 🖨 Babysitting, afternoon tea served. **Facilities:** 🛆 1 restaurant (bkfst only), guest lounge. **Rates (BB):** $85–$135 S or D; $135 ste. Extra person $20. Parking: Outdoor, free. Honeymoon, anniversary, birthday, Civil War, and hot air balloon packages avail. AE, CB, DC, DISC, MC, V.

RESTAURANTS 🍴

Country Kitchen
2415 N Glenstone Ave; tel 417/862-0195. ¼ mi S of exit 80A off I-44. **American.** Pleasant and comfortable establishment featuring a glass atrium and lots of plants. The menu offers a modest variety of breakfast, lunch, and dinner items. One specialty is a tender breast of chicken served with onions, baby red potatoes, broccoli, fresh tomatoes, and tangy herbs. **FYI:** Reservations not accepted. Children's menu. Beer and wine only. Additional location: 3405 E Battlefield (tel 887-4545). **Open:** Daily 24 hrs. **Prices:** Main courses $5–$9. AE, DISC, MC, V. 🚗 🍴 🛆

Hemingway's Blue Water Cafe
In the Bass Pro Shop, 1935 S Campbell; tel 417/887-3388. At Sunshine. **Seafood.** An attractive choice for family or casual dining, this restaurant features a scenic indoor waterfall with live fish and a large atrium playfully adorned with stuffed animals and cooled by large ceiling fans. Seafood is the main draw here, but pasta, beef, poultry, veal, and lamb dishes are also prepared. A good bet is the red snapper

Hemingway, a poached fillet laced with sauce normande and garnished with mushrooms, seafood, and hollandaise. **FYI:** Reservations recommended. Children's menu. No smoking. **Open:** Mon–Sat 7am–10pm, Sun 9am–5pm. **Prices:** Main courses $8–$15. AE, DISC, MC, V. 🖼️ &

Old Country Buffet
In Glen Isle Center, 1536 S Glenstone Ave; tel 417/883-9713. 4 mi from Glenstone exit off I-44. **American.** Minimally decorated restaurant featuring an all-you-can-eat, country-style buffet of soups, salads, fresh fruits, meats, and vegetables. **FYI:** Reservations not accepted. Children's menu. No liquor license. **Open:** Peak (May–Sept) Sun–Thurs 11am–9pm, Fri–Sat 11am–10pm. **Prices:** Prix fixe $8. MC, V. 🖼️ &

The Olive Garden
3105 S Glenstone Ave; tel 417/886-3188. S on US 65, W on Battlefield Rd. **Italian.** Chain Italian offering a wide variety of dishes. One specialty is shrimp primavera, made with red and green peppers, mushrooms, sautéed onions, and a zesty tomato sauce and served over angel-hair pasta. **FYI:** Reservations not accepted. Children's menu. **Open:** Sun–Thurs 11am–10pm, Fri–Sat 11am–11pm. **Prices:** Main courses $7–$13. AE, CB, DC, DISC, ER, MC, V. 🖼️ &

Shady Inn
524 W Sunshine St; tel 417/862-0369. At Campbell. **American.** Dark, fairly large room with English-style decor and candles set in kerosene lamps on the tables. The menu consists primarily of steaks, prime rib, and seafood but offers some chicken dishes as well. One house specialty is the steak Neptune, an 8-oz filet mignon or prime rib crowned with crabmeat dressing, asparagus spears, and cheese sauce. **FYI:** Reservations recommended. Piano. **Open:** Lunch Mon–Sat 11am–2:30pm; dinner Mon–Thurs 4:30–10pm, Fri–Sat 4:30–11pm. **Prices:** Main courses $8–$40. AE, MC, V. &

Trotter's Bar-B-Q
1155 E Battlefield; tel 417/883-0366. At National. **Barbecue.** The tasty ribs and other barbecue items served here are smoked in a hickory wood pit. Attractive brick interior has high ceilings and many plants and trees. **FYI:** Reservations not accepted. Children's menu. Beer and wine only. No smoking. Additional location: 635 N Glenstone (tel 865-4485). **Open:** Sun–Thurs 11am–9pm, Fri–Sat 11am–10pm. **Prices:** Main courses $7–$10. AE, CB, DC, DISC, MC, V. 🖼️ &

ATTRACTIONS 🏛️

Springfield Art Museum
1111 E Brookside Dr; tel 417/866-2716. Started in 1928 with the purchase of two Mary Butler seascapes, this museum now houses 5,000 objects in its permanent collection. Highlights include pre-Columbian artifacts, Renaissance etchings, and a large collection of paintings by important American artists. **Open:** Tues–Wed and Fri–Sat 9am–5pm, Thurs 9am–8pm, Sun 1–5pm. **Free**

Dickerson Park Zoo
3043 N Fort; tel 417/833-1570. Animals of the African Plains (a herd of elephants, among them) and species native to Missouri are among the creatures featured in naturalistic settings. Animal rides, playground, picnic area, and gift shop. **Open:** Peak (mid-Apr–mid-Oct) daily 9am–6pm. Reduced hours off-season. **$$**

Crystal Cave
Exit 80B off I-44; tel 417/833-9599. Living cave with a variety of spelethons in unusual shapes. Cave is a constant 59°F. Guided tours available. **Open:** Daily 9am–1:30pm. **$$**

Sullivan

Southwest of St Louis via I-44, Sullivan is home to Meramec State Park and serves as a good canoe access point for the Meramec River. **Information:** Sullivan Area Chamber of Commerce, #2 Springfield, PO Box 536, Sullivan, 63080 (tel 573/468-3314).

MOTELS 🏨

▤▤ Ramada Inn
309 N Service Rd, 63080; tel 573/468-4172 or toll free 800/2-RAMADA; fax 573/468-5367. Exit 225 off I-44. Features an attractive if small lobby decorated with plants and potted trees. **Rooms:** 80 rms. CI noon/CO noon. Nonsmoking rms avail. **Amenities:** 🎛️ 🅰️ A/C, satel TV w/movies. **Services:** ⚌ 🍴 Movies are available for rent. **Facilities:** 🏀 🎱 & 1 restaurant, 1 bar, basketball, volleyball, games rm, lawn games, washer/dryer. **Rates:** Peak (May–Aug) $60 S; $72 D. Extra person $6. Children under age 18 stay free. Lower rates off-season. Parking: Outdoor, free. AE, CB, DC, DISC, MC, V.

▤ Super 8 Motel
601 N Service Rd, 63080; tel 573/468-8076 or toll free 800/800-8000; fax 573/468-8076. Exit 225 or 226 off I-44. Dependable no-frills motel rooms. **Rooms:** 60 rms and stes. CI 2pm/CO 11am. Nonsmoking rms avail. **Amenities:** 🎛️ A/C, cable TV w/movies. Some units w/whirlpools. **Services:** ⚌ 🍴 **Facilities:** & Washer/dryer. **Rates (CP):** $37 S; $44 D; $61 ste. Extra person $5. Children under age 12 stay free. Parking: Outdoor, free. AE, DC, DISC, MC, V.

University City

A western suburb of St Louis, this separate city is well known for its "loop"—four blocks filled with specialty shops, art galleries, and interesting eateries. One section is a historic district listed on the National Register of Historic Places. **Information:** University City Chamber of Commerce, 7233 Delmar Blvd, University City, 63130 (tel 314/725-6545).

RESTAURANTS

Blueberry Hill
6504 Delmar Blvd (University City Loop); tel 314/727-0880. Between Big Bend and Skinker. **American/Pub.** Pub-style atmosphere in a setting of antique jukeboxes, authentic photographs from the 1950s, pinball machines, and stuffed animals. Go for the widely praised burgers and the famous jukebox offering more than 2,000 selections. **FYI:** Reservations recommended. Blues/reggae/rock. **Open:** Mon–Sat 11am–1:30am, Sun 11am–midnight. **Prices:** Main courses $3–$8. AE, CB, DC, DISC, MC, V. &

Brandt's Market & Cafe
6525 Delmar Blvd (University City Loop); tel 314/727-3663. **Cafe/International.** This cafe is partner to a gourmet retail specialty food store; outdoor tables are available. People-watch as others shop at the adjacent market, or simply enjoy tasty and simple dishes such as the house specialty: fettuccine topped with fresh diced tomatoes, toasted pine nuts, garlic, fresh basil pesto, and grated Parmesan. **FYI:** Reservations accepted. Folk/jazz. No smoking. **Open:** Mon–Thurs 11am–midnight, Fri 11am–1am, Sat 9:30am–1am, Sun 9:30am–midnight. **Prices:** Main courses $8–$14. AE, DC, DISC, MC, V.

La Patisserie
6269 Delmar Blvd; tel 314/725-4902. Delmar Loop. **Vegetarian.** Small, quaint dining area decorated with artwork by local and national artists. The menu consists of a variety of salads and sandwiches. Entrees include quiche, shrimp, chicken, and pizza. **FYI:** Reservations accepted. Poetry readings. BYO. No smoking. **Open:** Mon–Thurs 7:30am–3:30pm, Fri–Sat 7:30am–11:30pm, Sun 8am–7pm. **Prices:** Main courses $3–$9. AE, DC, MC, V. &

Painted Plates
6235 Delmar Blvd; tel 314/725-6565. Delmar Loop Area. **New American.** This modestly decorated dining room has the feel of a street-side cafe. The menu features several exotic appetizers and salads such as pheasant ravioli. Entrees include pork, lamb, beef, chicken, and fish. A good bet is the pecan-encrusted walleye pike served with purée of baked sweet potatoes and sautéed snow peas. **FYI:** Reservations recommended. No smoking. **Open:** Tues–Thurs 5:30–11pm, Fri–Sat 5:30pm–midnight, Sun 5:30–11pm. **Prices:** Main courses $10–$12. AE, DC, MC, V. &

Riddles Penultimate Cafe and Wine Bar
6307 Delmar Blvd (University City Loop); tel 314/725-6985. **New American.** The dark and cozy dining room features a large mural and several paintings and photographs from local artists. Try the spicy smoked shrimp rémoulade dinner: jumbo spicy smoked shrimp served ice cold with Riddles' rémoulade (a zippy Creole mustard sauce). A special menu of seasonal cuisine changes daily. **FYI:** Reservations recommended. Blues. **Open:** Tues–Thurs 5–11pm, Fri–Sat 5pm–midnight, Sun 5–10pm. **Prices:** Main courses $4–$18. AE, CB, DC, MC, V. &

Royal Chinese Barbecue
8406 Olive Blvd; tel 314/991-1888. Olive E exit off I-170. **Barbecue/Chinese.** The emphasis here is on grilled, roasted, and barbecued entrees, but there are standard Chinese items as well. A sculptured wildlife fountain and Chinese murals provide the backdrop. **FYI:** Reservations accepted. Beer and wine only. **Open:** Mon–Thurs 11am–9:30pm, Fri 11am–10:30pm, Sat 10am–10:30pm, Sun 10am–9:30pm. **Prices:** Main courses $5–$12. MC, V. &

Waynesville

Accessible by I-44, this mid-state city is both the Pulaski County seat and the entrance to Fort Leonard Wood, a massive military training center. **Information:** Waynesville–St Robert Area Chamber of Commerce, PO Box 6, Waynesville, 65583-0006 (tel 573/336-5121).

MOTELS

Days Inn
US 28 and I-44, 65583; tel 573/336-5556 or toll free 800/DAYS-INN; fax 573/336-3918. Exit 163 off US 28 and I-44. Nice, affordable lodging with convenient interstate access. **Rooms:** 35 rms. CI 2pm/CO 11am. Nonsmoking rms avail. **Amenities:** A/C, cable TV w/movies, refrig. All rooms have microwaves and 25″ TVs. Dataports available upon request. **Services:** **Facilities:** & Washer/dryer. **Rates (CP):** Peak (May–Oct) $40–$45 S; $50–$55 D. Extra person $5. Children under age 12 stay free. Lower rates off-season. Parking: Outdoor, free. AE, CB, DC, DISC, MC, V.

Super 8 Motel
US 28, 65583; tel 573/336-3036 or toll free 800/800-8000; fax 573/336-3036. Basic budget motel suitable for a brief stay. **Rooms:** 49 rms. CI 2pm/CO 11am. Nonsmoking rms avail. **Amenities:** A/C, cable TV w/movies. Some rooms have microwaves and refrigerators. **Services:** **Facilities:** Washer/dryer. **Rates:** $37 S; $44 D. Extra person $5. Children under age 12 stay free. Parking: Outdoor, free. AE, DC, DISC, MC, V.

Wentzville

Wentzville straddles I-70 on the western border of the St Louis metro communities. Cuivre River State Park and August A Busch Wildlife Area offer many natural sights and outdoor activities. **Information:** Wentzville Chamber of Commerce, 9 W Allen, PO Box 11, Wentzville, 63385 (tel 314/327-6914).

HOTEL 🏨

≡≡≡ Holiday Inn

900 Corporate Pkwy, 63385; tel 314/327-7001 or toll free 800/HOLIDAY; fax 314/327-7019. Exit 212 off I-70. Attractive lobby boasts elegant mirrors, a marble floor, and potted plants. **Rooms:** 138 rms and stes. Executive level. CI 3pm/CO 1pm. Nonsmoking rms avail. **Amenities:** 🛏 👗 A/C, satel TV w/movies, dataport. **Services:** ✗ ⊶ 🚗 ⊿ ⊲ 🐾 Babysitting. **Facilities:** 🏋 ⌷350⌷ ♿ 1 restaurant, 1 bar. **Rates:** $64–$74 S or D; $125 ste. Children under age 19 stay free. Parking: Outdoor, free. B&B and other packages avail. AE, CB, DC, DISC, JCB, MC, V.

Weston

Founded in 1837, this pretty river town lies north of Kansas City along the Missouri River. Attractions include fruit orchards, antiques stores, an interesting tobacco market, and more than 100 preserved buildings and homes built prior to the Civil War.

RESTAURANT 🍴

America Bowman Restaurant

526 Welt; tel 816/640-5235. One block E of City Hall. **American.** The building, once a brewery, was constructed in 1842, and the ambience of the restaurant that occupies it today is reminiscent of a 19th-century Irish pub. Large kerosene lamps are placed on the tables, and old-fashioned cooking utensils hang on the walls. Only five entrees are available, ranging from shrimp and beef to chicken and ham. Desserts are a specialty. **FYI:** Reservations recommended. **Open:** Lunch Tues–Sun 11:30am–3pm; dinner Fri–Sat 7:30pm. **Prices:** Main courses $13–$17. DISC, MC, V. 🏛

ATTRACTIONS 🏛

Weston Historical Museum

601 Main St; tel 816/386-2977. Founded in 1960, exhibits feature displays depicting life in Platte County and Weston from prehistoric days through World War II. Exhibits range from a diorama of native Hopewellian culture to historical artifacts covering slavery, the Civil War, pioneer supplies, and World War I items. **Open:** Mid-Mar–mid-Dec, Tues–Sat 1–4pm, Sun 1:30–5pm. **Free**

Pirtle's Weston Winery

502 Spring St; tel 816-640-5728. The cellars of this 13-acre vineyard are located in an 1867 church, where locally grown grapes are crushed, fermented, and bottled. Wine-tasting is offered in an upstairs room of the old church. **Open:** Peak (mid-Mar–Dec) Mon–Sat 10am–6pm, Sun noon–6pm. Reduced hours off-season. **Free**

Woodson Terrace

See St Louis–Lambert Int'l Airport

Native America

John Steinbeck never set foot in Oklahoma, but the dry, flat, desolate image the author described in *The Grapes of Wrath* defined this state for decades. Never mind that it was never an *accurate* description (only a handful of the state's western-most counties experienced the Dust Bowl of the 1920s and 1930s). Steinbeck's fiction made the reality of Oklahoma's quiet, unspoiled beauty all but irrelevant. On the other end of the spectrum, the 1955 Rodgers and Hammerstein movie musical *Oklahoma!* introduced Technicolor visions of singing cowhands and "corn as high as an elephant's eye" as the popular conception of the state.

It took the tragedy of April 19, 1995, to dislodge the fictional Oklahoma from the American psyche. The bombing of the Alfred P Murrah Building in downtown Oklahoma City focused all eyes on a state many couldn't locate on a map (it's the pan-shaped one in the middle of the United States). Quickly it became apparent Oklahoma was more than prairies and wind. The state's response to what would become known as the most deadly terrorist bombing on US soil underscored the independent but friendly nature of Oklahomans—always cited by travelers as one of the state's greatest assets.

Oklahoma remains that rare untrammeled place where crowds are limited to the snow cone line at the state fair. Though a state only since 1907, its history is ancient and colorful, encompassing Civil War battlegrounds, remnants of Native American cities, prehistoric dinosaur tracks, the original Black Wall Street, and the birthplace of Will Rogers, as well as icons of the Old West—from the Santa Fe Trail to the Comanche warrior Geronimo.

Yet Oklahoma is also the New West at its best: home to some of the best Native American artists and musicians, as well as cowpokes who still throw a rope for a living.

Natural scenery here is subtle; those looking for 14,000-foot mountains or crashing waves might not appreciate Oklahoma's

STATE STATS

CAPITAL
Oklahoma City

AREA
69,903 square miles

BORDERS
New Mexico, Colorado, Kansas, Missouri, Arkansas, Texas

POPULATION
3,277,700 (1995)

ENTERED UNION
November 16, 1907
(46th state)

NICKNAME
Sooner State

STATE FLOWER
Mistletoe

STATE BIRD
Scissortailed flycatcher

FAMOUS NATIVES
Ralph Ellison, Woody Guthrie, Mickey Mantle, Tony Randall, Will Rogers, Jim Thorpe

rolling hills or placid rivers. That said, travelers can find a little bit of every other kind of scenery—situated as the state is at North America's ecological and geographical crossroads. Within its borders are local versions of the high plains of Colorado, the swamps of Louisiana, the tallgrass prairies of eastern Kansas, the clear lakes of Minnesota, the hills and dales of Missouri, the forests of Arkansas, the mountains of Tennessee, and, yes, the arid flatlands of West Texas.

Oklahoma is a land-locked state, but a traveler need never know it: vast lakes create miles upon miles of pristine shoreline and sandy beaches. Tourism is still more a pleasant notion than a reality here. But in a time of overcrowding and overdevelopment at so many US destinations, it can be refreshing to come upon a place where a bed-and-breakfast inn is often the fanciest address in town, where pastures still separate one community from the next, and a traveler looking for solitude can readily find it.

A Brief History

Oklahoma's First People

The area's earliest inhabitants were nomadic big-game hunters who arrived more than 11,000 years ago. (Archeologists know this from carbon-dating spear points the hunters left behind in skeletons of woolly mammoths.) Next on the scene were people who survived by foraging and hunting locally. It is believed that about 2,000 years ago, Oklahoma's foragers became farmers—raising corn, pumpkins, squash, and beans. Nine hundred years later, they yielded to the ancestors of the Caddoan Mound Builders, whose distinctive earthen mounds can still be seen near Spiro in northeastern Le Flore County.

By the time the first Europeans arrived in Oklahoma in 1541, the area was home to native tribes whose economies combined farming, hunting, gathering, and commerce. These people lived in towns of grass lodges or teepees (during their annual buffalo hunts). They made pottery and fry bread, farmed and hunted buffalo, and designed intricate body

tattoos. Now known as the Wichita and Affiliated Tribes, their descendants still live near Anadarko—making the Wichita Oklahoma's oldest historical community. The Wichita thrived for centuries in western Oklahoma without serious competition. But by the 18th century they were coexisting, albeit not very happily, with the Plains Apache, Comanche, and Osage—all of whom, like the Wichita, call Oklahoma home today.

Indian Territory Days By 1837, what would become Oklahoma was known as Indian Territory, home to five ancient Indian nations transplanted from the East: the Creeks, Chickasaws, Cherokees, Seminoles, and Choctaws. They were known as the Five Civilized Tribes because of their sophisticated systems of government and education, and their European-style dress. Yet their ability to assimilate did not deter the US government from forcing the Cherokee to sell their eastern lands (for $5 million) and walk to their new home.

On that wrenching journey —what has become known as the Trail of Tears—more than 2,000 Cherokee died from starvation, sickness, and cold. (The Choctaw, Seminole, Creek, and Chickasaw experienced similar woes on their forced walks to Oklahoma.)

In a matter of years, however, the Five Civilized Tribes carved civilization out of the wilds of Indian Territory: The Choctaw Nation penned the first constitution to be written here, the Creeks ran large herds of cattle and hogs, the Choctaws built large plantations (some of which still stand in southeastern Oklahoma), and the Cherokee operated not only the area's first newspaper (the *Cherokee Advocate*) but also sawmills and cotton gins. Indeed the educational system the Cherokees founded was so formidable it earned the moniker, "the Harvard of the West."

Indians, Cowboys & Outlaws By the end of the Civil War in 1865, some 50,000 Native Americans called Indian Territory home. That number remained constant until 1900, when the number of

---

Fun Facts

• Oklahoma has more shoreline than the Atlantic and Gulf Coasts combined.

• Oklahoma is home to 65 tribes, 37 tribal council houses, and more than 250,000 Native Americans—more than any other state.

• Oklahoma is Pond Country, boasting more ponds than any other state but Texas—and more square miles of ponds than any state in the Union.

• Filmmakers scouting locations for the Hollywood version of *Oklahoma!* failed to find what they were looking for in the movie's namesake. The final location? Arizona and its miles of flat cornfields.

• Oklahoma is known as the Sooner State because it was settled by those who got there "sooner" during the Oklahoma land rush of 1889.

coal miners, cowboys, tenant farmers, and merchants swelled to more than 100,000. Outnumbered, the tribes saw their power ebb and their homelands become increasingly populated by the likes of the Dalton Brothers, the bandit queen Belle Starr, and the Younger Gang. Indian Territory was so rife with desperadoes at one point it was nicknamed Robber's Roost and in 1871, tribal leaders actually turned to the United States for help in fighting crime.

The Great Oklahoma Land Run   The increasing number of non–Native Americans in the territory combined with dwindling free land in the West created great pressure on politicians in Washington to open for settlement a strip of land in Oklahoma known as the Unassigned Lands (so called because it belonged to no tribe). In 1889, Congress did just that. On April 22, tens of thousands of people lined up waiting for a gun shot to signal the opening of the land to settlement. By nightfall of that day, 10,000 people has settled Oklahoma City. The land run effectively started a process that no one would be able to stop: the opening of native lands to settlement.

Statehood   Few states are younger than Oklahoma. But by statehood in 1907, Oklahoma (the name means "land of the red man" in the Choctaw language) had been home to Native American tribes for centuries. The merging of Oklahoma Territory in the west and Indian Territory to the east to form the 46th state was celebrated in Guthrie (the territorial capitol of Oklahoma Territory) on November 16, 1907, with a mock wedding between a man in cowboy garb and a woman dressed as an Indian maiden. The symbolism was clear; an era was over.

The new state's economy took off as fast as the land runners had done decades before. By 1919, the Cushing-Drumright field in north-central Oklahoma produced nearly one-fifth of all the oil marketed in

DRIVING DISTANCES

Oklahoma City
84 mi SE of Enid
98 mi NE of Lawton
115 mi SW of Tulsa
204 mi N of Dallas, TX
225 mi NW of Beavers Bend
327 mi SE of Boise City

Tulsa
115 mi NE of Oklahoma City
124 mi E of Enid
212 mi NE of Lawton
236 mi NW of Beavers Bend
340 mi SW of St Louis, MO
394 mi E of Boise City

Lawton
115 mi SW of Oklahoma City
149 mi SW of Enid
200 mi E of Amarillo, TX
212 mi SW of Tulsa
245 mi NW of Beavers Bend
355 mi SE of Boise City

the United States. The 1920s saw Oklahoma produce over $3 billion worth of oil and natural gas—roughly one-fourth of all the money earned from American oil and gas during the Roaring Twenties. Much of Oklahoma's architectural legacy—from the Marland Mansion in Ponca City to Villa Philbrook (now the home of the Philbrook Museum of Art) in Tulsa—was built at this time.

The Dust Bowl Years   Drought and the Great Depression in the 1930s sent many from western Oklahoma looking for a better life in California. Though their counterparts in the Great Plains of Kansas and Texas also moved West, it was the Okies who came to personify this exodus. Meanwhile in eastern Oklahoma, changes in federal land policy pushed almost as many tenant farmers off the land; these Oklahomans—many of them Yankees—quietly packed up and returned East.

Oklahomans learned from the Dust Bowl. The decades that followed saw shelter belts (long rows of trees) planted against the wind and rivers damned to fill lakes and make irrigation possible; having seen how fickle Mother Nature could be, Oklahomans opted to hedge future bets.

By the 1950s, oil and agriculture reigned supreme in Oklahoma, but its heart belonged to an Indian cowboy with a lopsided grin who the world knew as Will Rogers. Rogers' down-home witticisms brought both him—and his home state—friends around the world; when he died with aviator Wiley Post in 1935 in a plane crash over Point Barrow, Alaska, the world mourned with Oklahoma.

Modern-Day Oklahoma   Most Oklahomans remain just a generation off the land or the rig (the last big oil bust was only a decade ago). State leaders have worked hard to diversify Oklahoma's economy but for a state built on speculators and optimists, dreams of gushers and living off the land die hard. (As one popular bumper sticker half-jokes, "God, grant us one more oil boom and we promise this time not to piss it away.")

The 1990s have seen a reversal of Steinbeck's Okie migration as people increasingly look to Oklahoma as a place where one can safely raise a family, retire, or reap the benefits of a simple life. Land is plentiful and cheap—the same powerful combination that in 1889 brought thousands from around the world knocking at her door.

A Closer Look

GEOGRAPHY

Four hundred million years ago, Oklahoma was at the bottom of a flat, shallow sea broken only by an occasional point of land. The skeletons and shells of the prehistoric creatures that lived in these warm waters eventually settled to the bottom of the sea, forming deposits of dolomite and limestone (some are still visible today along I-35 as it passes through the Arbuckle Mountains north of Ardmore). A series of volcanoes and earthquakes eventually pushed parts

AVG TEMPS (°F) & INCHES OF RAINFALL		
	Oklahoma City	Boise City
Jan	36/0.2	36/0.9
Feb	37/2.6	37/0.0
Mar	53/3.4	47/1.4
Apr	59/3.4	54/1.5
May	67/2.7	65/3.7
June	80/1.7	79/1.6
July	80/2.2	78/2.5
Aug	80/1.8	77/2.7
Sept	71/2.2	69/0.4
Oct	63/1.9	57/0.8
Nov	50/5.7	43/0.4
Dec	43/1.6	39/0.9

of that flat sea floor toward the sky, creating in one fell swoop the Kiamichi Mountains of southeastern Oklahoma, the Wichita Mountains in the southwest, and the Arbuckles to the south. As the mountains rose, adjacent land dropped, forming large basins. In Oklahoma, they became the Anadarko Basin in the west and the Arkoma Basin in the east. Over millions of years, these great depressions filled with water and marine life and were sporadically covered by sand and silt that ran off the mountains. Today these ancient swamps and marshlands—some buried far beneath the surface—fuel some of the world's richest reserves of natural gas and oil (black crude has been found in 66 of Oklahoma's 77 counties).

The lifting, tilting, cracking, and eroding that made Oklahoma one of the most oil-rich states in the union also formed the state's distinct regions. The arid, flat strip of land in far northwestern Oklahoma is now called **the Panhandle** but it was once known as No Man's Land, because the lack of water and the threat of Native American attacks made it no place for a man (or woman) to be. Prone to blizzards in the

winter and flash flooding in the summer, the area is so remote—jutting out due west from the rest of the state—that part of it is actually in a different time zone.

Because the state's two main interstates cross in **central Oklahoma,** this is the landscape most people conjure up when thinking of the state; it is also the most nondescript: low plains, pasture, cedar trees, and the occasional lazy river—filled with water tinged blood red by Oklahoma's infamous red dirt. One of the last remnants of the great tallgrass prairie that once blanketed middle America to Canada resides in **northeastern Oklahoma.** Ever since the Nature Conservancy bought up some of the biggest ranches in the Osage to create the Tallgrass Prairie Preserve, the wildflowers and bison herds that call the prairie home have been the hottest ticket in the region, engendering a steady stream of filmmakers, photographers, journalists, and out-of-state visitors.

The scenic Ouachita mountain chain in **southeastern Oklahoma** is a western extension of the Appalachian Mountains. Sugar Loaf Mountain, near Poteau, towers 2,100 feet above the valley floor and was an important landmark for Native Americans and European explorers in early times. **South-central Oklahoma** is home to Lake Texoma (Oklahoma's second-largest lake at 88,000 acres) and Lake Murray, two of the 1,800 lakes built in Oklahoma since the late 1930s. Though both bodies of water draw hordes of visitors during the summer, the area's main attraction remains Turner Falls in the heart of the Arbuckle Mountains; Honey Creek plunges 77 feet at this point before entering the Washita River.

The original homeland of the Southern Plains Indians, **southwestern Oklahoma** is filled with places sacred to the Kiowa, Apache, and Comanche. The region is dominated by the Wichita Mountains, a chain of granite boulders and peaks that rise spectacularly above miles of surrounding plains.

CLIMATE

Will Rogers, Oklahoma's favorite son, once said if you don't like the weather in Oklahoma just wait a minute and it's bound to change. Situated in the heart of tornado alley, Oklahoma can sometimes seem like the place where all the country's weather converges. On any given day, it may be snowing in the Panhandle, sweltering in Little Dixie in the southeast, and threatening drought in the southwest.

The state's best climatic features are an unusual amount of sunny days, only rare deep freezes, and months of warm days and cool nights. The cost of such bounty, however, is August highs that give new meaning to the words "dog days of summer" and winds so steady and strong Oklahoma is one of the best sailing venues in Middle America.

WHAT TO PACK

With such fickle weather, packing light in Oklahoma can be difficult. While a heavy coat and gloves may only be needed December through February, a cotton sweater and jeans come in handy most of the year. Then again, football fans have been known to wear shorts and shirtsleeves one Saturday afternoon only to drag out the mittens the next.

Such erratic weather combined with Oklahoman's penchant for cowboy boots has produced a mode of dress that is deliberately casual. A denim skirt (or blazer and jeans) is accepted garb for all but the fanciest restaurants or destinations, and most travelers will find shorts and swimsuits by far the preferred summer choices (sweatsuits take over in fall and winter).

TOURIST INFORMATION

The **Oklahoma Tourism and Recreation Department** publishes an annual 100-plus-page *Vacation Guide*, which lists points of interest, lodging, and restaurants in most Oklahoma communities, as well as an annual Calendar of Events. Both are available free from Oklahoma Tourism and Recreation, Travel and Tourism Division, 2401 N Lincoln Blvd, 505 Will Rogers Building, Oklahoma City 73105 (tel toll free 800/652-6552 or 405/521-2409). The State of Oklahoma maintains a Web page (http://oklaosf. state.ok.us) with general information about the state.

HUNTING AND FISHING REGULATIONS

Licenses for both hunting and fishing are required for anyone older than 16. Both are available from the Department of Wildlife Conservation, 1801 N Lincoln, Oklahoma City 73105 (tel 405/521-3851).

DRIVING RULES AND REGULATIONS

Oklahoma requires the driver and all front-seat passengers to wear seatbelts. Children four years old and younger—or who weigh less than 60 pounds—must be in a child restraint seat. Children four and five years of age must wear seatbelts. Unless posted, a right turn is permitted on red after coming to a complete stop. Speed limits are 25 to 35 mph in most towns and cities, 15 mph in school zones. On highways, the prudent driver watches speed signs closely—speeds can vary from 55 mph on two-lane roads to 75 mph on the interstates.

RENTING A CAR

It wasn't too long ago that the only rental car offices were at the two major airports: Will Rogers International Airport in Oklahoma City and Tulsa International Airport in Tulsa. Rental car offerings now extend to some of the smaller cities, but rarely will more than one company be found in these markets. A word of advice: Before you rent, know whether or not your credit card or personal automobile insurance extends coverage to rental cars. Using existing insurance can cut the bill by 25 percent.

Major rental car companies with offices in Oklahoma include:

- **Alamo** (Oklahoma City, Tulsa; tel toll-free 800/327-9633)
- **Avis** (Enid, Lawton, Norman, Oklahoma City, Tulsa; 800/331-1212)
- **Budget** (Lawton, Oklahoma City, Tulsa; 800/527-0700)
- **Dollar** (Oklahoma City, Tulsa) 800/800-4000
- **Enterprise** (Duncan, Edmond, Enid, Lawton, Norman, Oklahoma City, Stillwater, Tulsa; 800/325-8007)
- **Hertz** (Lawton, Oklahoma City, Ponca City, Stillwater, Tulsa; 800/654-3131)
- **National** (Oklahoma City, Tulsa; 800/227-7368)
- **Thrifty** (Muskogee, Oklahoma City, Tulsa; 800/367-2277)

ESSENTIALS

Area Code: Oklahoma has two area codes. The vast majority of Oklahoma—all points west of I-35 as well as much of the southeastern part of the state—falls into the **405** calling area. A bite-size portion of northeastern Oklahoma—including Tulsa—that extends to the Kansas, Missouri, and Arkansas borders, the town of Pawnee to the west, and the city of McAlester to the south comprise the **918** calling area.

Emergencies: For police, an ambulance, or the fire department in most cities and towns, dial **911.** In smaller communities and rural areas, dial 0 for the operator and he or she will connect you to whatever emergency service is needed. Cellular phone users can dial *55.

Liquor Laws: Alcoholic beverages may be purchased by anyone 21 years of age or older, with proof of age, but where and when one can purchase alcoholic beverages depends on the county you happen to be in. Though alcohol can be sold in package stores in all of Oklahoma's 77 counties, only 37 counties have liquor by the drink and only 3.2 beer is sold in grocery stores. Those that have liquor by the drink operate under restrictions unique to each county. The Oklahoma Alcoholic Beverage Laws Enforcement Commission (tel 405/521-3484) can answer any questions you may have.

Road Info: Call the Oklahoma State Police at 405/425-2385; for turnpike tolls and access information call 405/425-3600.

Smoking: Most public buildings are smoke-free but, like restaurants, the majority have a designated smoking section. Outside the big cities, avid nonsmokers should be aware that smoking is commonplace at many small-town diners and cafes.

Taxes: Oklahoma has a 4.5% state sales tax and a 2% hotel tax. Local sales taxes run 1% to 4% (the average is 3%), and most counties tack on an additional 0.5% to 1%. Oklahoma City has no car rental tax, but in Tulsa it's 10%.

Time Zone: Oklahoma is on Central standard time from the last Sunday of October until the first Sunday in April (otherwise it is on daylight saving time). The one exception: the town of Kenton in the westernmost tip of the Panhandle is on Mountain standard time.

Best of the State

WHAT TO SEE AND DO

Below is a general overview of some of the top sights and attractions in Oklahoma. To find out more detailed information, look under "Attractions" for individual cities in the listings portion of this book.

State & National Parks Buffalo herds still run free at the **Wichita Mountains National Wildlife Refuge,** and travelers are welcome to observe the refuge's annual roundup and sale (helicopters and four-wheel-drive vehicles herd the big animals into an elaborate corral). The refuge is a favorite with rock climbers, hikers, and campers but access is limited; call ahead for permit information.

The pine-laden mountains and hills that surround **Beavers Bend State Park** and **Broken Bow Lake** are so wild and remote most Oklahomans haven't ever seen them. Texas license plates are most frequently seen, and their growing numbers have fueled a building spurt that includes a small touring train, cabins, horseback riding, and canoe rentals. The **Tallgrass Prairie Preserve** is a one-of-a-kind experience that recalls a time when all of central America was undulating fields of grass. Interpretive trails, eagles, fields of wildflowers, and buffalo herds are just bonuses.

Family Favorites Oil tycoon Frank Phillips built himself a rural playground outside Bartlesville that he called **Woolaroc.** Phillips filled the lodge with Native American blankets and conversation pieces, and the acreage with hundreds of exotic animals (including a petting barn). The lodge, grounds, and art museum combine to deliver an experience that never disappoints—no matter one's age. In keeping with Phillips' wishes, children always enter free. Plan to spend a full day.

The **Jasmine Moran Children's Museum** in Seminole and **Leonardo's Warehouse** in Enid are new hands-on museums that have received rave reviews not only from children but also parents and teachers; in 1996, Leonardo's opened a sprawling outdoor wonderland.

Oklahoma inspired one of the most successful musicals ever to hit not only Broadway but the Silver Screen. Each summer the professional troupe known as Discoveryland (tel 918/245-6552) stages *Oklahoma!* in a rustic outdoor amphitheater 5 miles west of Sand Springs (a suburb of Tulsa) on OK 97. The evening starts with an optional barbecue dinner at 5:30pm, followed by a pre-show (clogging, the Territorial Dancers) at 7:30pm and the musical at 8pm.

Gardens & Zoos   The **Myriad Gardens** in downtown Oklahoma City is built around a distinctive tube-shaped greenhouse that houses exotic tropical flora; outside, visitors can see trees and plants native to Oklahoma. The formal gardens at the **Philbrook Museum of Art** in Tulsa are even more spectacular when one realizes they were created in large part using plants and trees native to Oklahoma. At the Gilcrease Museum in Tulsa, visitors can see a small version of a traditional Victorian garden (as well as a good example of a native stone house).

A special ⅛-cent city sales passed in 1990 has made the **Oklahoma City Zoo** one of the wealthiest zoos in the country; thus far, the zoo has also met—or exceeded—expectations. Its Great Escape, which places silverback gorillas, orangutans, and chimps in naturalistic settings, opened to applause in 1994; it was followed by Island Life, which houses Galapagos turtles and mynah birds found on the islands of Madagascar and Indonesia. The OKC Zoo has one of the most successful breeding programs in the country, which translates into many exotic babies—a particular favorite with kids.

Historical Sites   On any given weekend at the **Pawnee Bill Museum and Ranch** outside Pawnee, workshop attendees can learn how to churn butter, make a cowboy breakfast, do Kiowa beadworking, or groom a horse. For those who prefer spectator history, the Oklahoma Historical Society (tel 405/521-2491) also stages a variety of historical re-enactments—from Civil War battles to lawn socials to mountain men rendezvous—throughout the year.

It is said that Oklahoma is the cradle of **Route 66.** Cyrus Avery, the man who pushed the highway through Congress, was from Tulsa, and he fought hard to see that America's Main Street passed through his home state. Oklahoma lays claim to more drivable miles of the Mother Road than any other state. Must-see stops on the route include the totem poles of Foyil, the blue whale of Catoosa, Arrowwood Trading Post near Claremore, the round barn in Arcadia, the new Route 66 Museum in Clinton (another is being built in nearby Elk City), and Lucille's near Hydro.

Though it may be years before a spade of dirt is turned on the official federal memorial to the victims of the April 1995 Oklahoma City bombing, the site of the **Alfred P Murrah building,** between Robinson and Harvey between 4th and 5th in downtown Oklahoma City, almost immediately became a place to which people make pilgrimages. No matter how many times historical society staffers strip the outer fence that surrounds the site of flowers and wreaths and T-shirts and messages, within a matter of days—sometimes hours—they are back. They vary with the season and the messenger but they resound one common note: "We will not forget."

Museums   Both the **Philbrook Museum of Art** and the **Gilcrease Museum** in Tulsa have collections of Native American art and artifacts to rival any in the world; the Gilcrease also has an astounding assembly of western art (the Philbrook is also strong in Italian and African works). On the other side of the state, the **National Cowboy Hall of Fame and Western Heritage Center** in Oklahoma City is second to none as a place to see both the great names in western art—both painters and sculptors—as well as its best modern practitioners. Each year in early June, the Hall, which is in the midst of a massive expansion project, hosts the Prix de West Invitational Exhibition (entries vie for the Prix de West, the Oscar in western art); the Prix de West winner becomes a part of the Hall's permanent collection.

Native American Sites   Native American heritage is definitely prominent in Oklahoma—from its name to its flag to the state's license plates. It is literally possible to find a powwow somewhere every weekend of the summer. Anadarko is the home of the Kiowa; Tahlequah of the Cherokee. Determining which place a traveler would prefer requires a traveler know something about how the tribes differ: The Kiowa lived in teepees, wore buckskin, and did intricate beadwork. The Cherokee wore calico dresses, lived in Georgian-style homes, and made baskets. Indeed the differences to be found are as varied as the tribes themselves. The 37 federally recognized Indian nations that reside in Oklahoma have historic landmarks throughout the state—old tribal capitols, mission schools, dance grounds—but it is important travelers realize the tribes are also modern functioning nations that in some instances issue their own license plates, maintain their own police forces, and are as comfortable in Washington as Muskogee.

In the case of the Cherokee (the nation's largest Indian nation), the tribe stages the **Trail of Tears Drama** each summer in its own outdoor amphitheater and mans a living history village (both south of Tahlequah).

Shopping   No self-respecting town or city in Oklahoma lacks an antique mall, a relatively recent phenomenon not to be confused with antique stores or flea markets. Antique malls are sort of an antique-lovers' cooperative, where those with more stuff than they can justify keeping rent booths or rooms in which to display their antiques or collectibles and sell them to those who have less (or who simply want more). Quality, hours, and inventory vary widely— sometimes at the same mall. More traditional antique districts can be along Cherry Street in Tulsa and along NW Western Street in Oklahoma City.

The Native American art at **Oklahoma Indian Art Gallery** in southwest Oklahoma City and the **Kachina Gallery** in Bessie draw collectors and buyers from around the world; **Choctaw Indian Trading Post** in Oklahoma City, **Mohawk Lodge** on Route 66, and **Lyon's Indian Store** in Tulsa do the same for Native American artifacts and crafts.

EVENTS AND FESTIVALS

- **Twelve Miles of Hell,** Fort Sill, Lawton. Rugged off-road bicycle race. Mid-February. Call 405/355-1808.
- **World Championship Hog Calling Competition,** Weatherford. Hog callers from all over the country, plus pork barbecue, greased pig contest, Hog Call Ball. Late February. Call 405/772-3301.
- **Cowboy Poetry Gathering,** National Cowboy Hall of Fame, Oklahoma City. The best Western bards show off their skills. April. Call 405/478-2250.
- **Cimarron Territory Celebration & Cow Chip Throw,** Beaver. April. Celebration of homesteader days, when pioneers used cow chips for fuel. Call 405/625-4726.
- **Ben Johnson Pro Celebrity Rodeo,** Lazy E Arena, Guthrie. Mid-May. Top-flight rodeo with national competitors. Call 405/234-3393.

- **Red Earth Native American Cultural Festival,** Oklahoma City. Early June. Arts and crafts, traditional music, storytelling, dance performances, and ethnic food. Call 405/427-5228.
- **Wild West Festival,** Pawnee Bill Ranch, Pawnee. Early June. Trick riders, historical reenactments, parade, arts and crafts, mansion tours. Call 918/762-2513.
- **Will Rogers Days,** Claremore. Craft show, chili cookoff, music, PRCA Stampede rodeo. Early June. Call 918/341-2818.
- **OK Mozart International Festival,** Bartlesville. Early to mid-June. Orchestral and ensemble concerts, art exhibits, outdoor markets, and more. Call 918/336-9900.
- **Aerospace America,** Will Rogers International Airport, Oklahoma City. July. Aerobatic feats, military jet demonstrations, antique and classic aircraft displays. Call 405/236-5000.
- **Powwow of Champions,** State fairgrounds, Tulsa. Over 700 Native American dancers, plus an indoor arts and crafts festival. August. Call 918/836-1523.
- **Jazz Celebration on Greenwood,** Tulsa. Mid-August. National and local jazz artists perform on three downtown stages. Ethnic food, gospel jubilee. Call 918/586-0706.
- **American Indian Exposition,** Fairgrounds, Anadarko. Mid-August. Traditional Native American food, crafts, and World Championship dance contests. Call 405/247-6651.
- **Dusk 'til Dawn Blues Festival,** Down Home Blues Club, Rentiesville. Two nights of blues (and some gospel). Labor Day weekend. Call 918/473-2411.
- **Cherokee National Holiday,** Tahlequah. Early September. Powwow, rodeo, parade, sporting tournaments, and other events honoring the signing of the first Cherokee Constitution in September 1839. Call 918/456-0671.
- **Festival of the Horse,** Oklahoma City. Mid-October. Thoroughbred racing, rodeo, World Championship Morgan Horse Show, National Children's Cowboy Festival, and more. Call 405/842-4141.
- **Cowboy Chuck Wagon Gathering,** National Cowboy Hall of Fame, Oklahoma City. Late October. Authentic chuckwagons gather on the grounds of the museum, to offer authentic food and entertainment. Call 405/468-6403.
- **Territorial Christmas Celebration,** Guthrie.

Thanksgiving through December. Strolling carolers, candlelight home tours, and Victorian-style street decorations. Call 405/282-1947.

SPECTATOR SPORTS

Baseball Professional baseball in Oklahoma is limited to the AAA **Oklahoma City 89ers** (tel 405/946-8989) and the AA **Tulsa Drillers** (tel 918/744-5901). The 89ers (the 1992 American Association national champions) get a new home in 1998 in downtown Oklahoma City's historic Bricktown. Season runs from April through the end of August.

With an earlier season (February to May) and two college baseball teams that make frequent appearances at both the regional and national level, it's little wonder the **Oklahoma State University Cowboys** (tel 405/744-5745) and the **University of Oklahoma Sooners** (tel 405/325-2424) compete with the pros for Oklahoma hearts.

Basketball The 1990–1991 season was the first for the **Oklahoma City Cavalry** (the state's only professional basketball team). The Cavs (tel 405/297-3000) endeared themselves to fans by becoming the 1994–1995 Southern Division champs of the Continental Basketball Association.

In 1995 the **Oklahoma State Cowboys** (tel 405/744-5745) went to the NCAA Final Four, and the **University of Oklahoma** Sooners (tel 405/325-2424) consistently produce national-caliber basketball teams.

Football College football in Oklahoma has been likened to a religion but it is more like an obsession. Little boys grow up dreaming of executing the wishbone on Owen Field, like youngsters elsewhere pine for a chance in the NFL. This despite a spate of lackluster seasons by not only the perennially disappointing **Oklahoma State Cowboys** but also the famed University of Oklahoma Sooners.

Records aside, few activities are more quintessentially Oklahoma than a tailgate party in the parking lot of Lewis Stadium or Owen Field, followed by an afternoon of watching the Sooners or the Cowboys lumber up and down their respective fields. Winning is just a plus. Tickets run $20 to $70 for the Cowboys (tel 405/744-5745) and $25 to $30 for the Sooners (tel 405/325-2424).

Horse Racing Horse racing in Oklahoma was thrust into the big leagues in the late 1980s with the opening of **Remington Park** in Oklahoma City (tel 405/424-9000). The track is known for its fine dining, luxury penthouse suites, clever special events, and $300,000 Remington Park Derby in March. Racing is held in February, March, and April, from mid-May through mid-July, and from early September to the first weekend of December (though at press time the track was negotiating for an expanded season). In eastern Oklahoma, racing fans patronize **Blue Ribbon Downs** (tel 918/775-7771) in Sallisaw (the state's first pari-mutuel racetrack), where along with quarter horses and thoroughbreds one can also watch appaloosas and paint horses race.

Ice Hockey It is rare that Oklahoma gets cold enough to freeze over even a pond but this lack of outdoor ice has not cooled Okie passions for indoor ice hockey. Late October through early April, the **Tulsa Drillers** (tel 918/744-5901) and the **Oklahoma City Blazers** (tel 405/235-7825) draw sell-out crowds in their respective venues (the Blazers are the 1996 Central Hockey League champions).

Polo Polo has been a staple pastime in Oklahoma since the 1920s; even cowboy humorist Will Rogers was a big fan and a player. The horses and players train year-round (and don't mind people stopping by to watch), but polo season itself opens in April, breaks for the heat of late July and August, then resumes in September. Games (both collegiate and professional) are usually played Tuesday and Thursday evenings and Saturday afternoons at the **Broad Acres Polo Fields** (tel 405/364-7035) southwest of Norman on OK 9.

Rodeo Spring through fall, small-town outdoor rodeos, like powwows, happen with regularity. But world-class rodeo and horse competitions are almost as common. Guthrie's **Lazy E Arena** (tel 800/234-3393) hosts Bullnanza in February, the Timed Event Championship in March, the US Team Roping Championships in October, and the National Finals Steer Roping in November. Oklahoma City is home to World Championship Barrel Racing, the International Finals Rodeo, the National Reining Horse Futurity, and the World Championship Quarter Horse Show. Tulsa frequently hosts the Longhorn World Championship Rodeo.

Roller Hockey When ice hockey became such a hot ticket in Oklahoma City no one was certain whether the appeal was the ice or the hockey, but a few businessmen soon put their money on the latter and introduced professional roller hockey to town. The **Oklahoma Coyotes** (tel 405/236-4695) don't draw the crowds that regularly encircle the ice, but they do provide affordable hockey from the end of May through mid-August.

Soccer Both Oklahoma State University in Stillwater and the University of Oklahoma in Norman now sport women's soccer teams, and smaller private universities like Oklahoma City University in Oklahoma City and the University of Tulsa in Tulsa have had nationally ranked NAII teams in their respective divisions for years. Both Tulsa and Oklahoma City also field semi-pro teams—the **Tulsa Roughnecks** (tel 918/258-1881) and the **Oklahoma City Heat** (tel 405/773-1700).

ACTIVITIES A TO Z

Ballooning Oklahoma winds can make ballooning an iffy activity at best, but so long as passengers understand that a ride depends on wind velocity and direction, **Balloonport of Oklahoma** (tel 405/794-4668) will take them up. For $250 per couple, passengers get an hour-long aerial tour of the state's capital city. A normal ride will cover eight to ten miles, and the balloon will hover at about 1,000 feet. (Passengers must be between the ages of 12 and 70.)

Bicycling Bicycle rentals are few and far between (try the state-owned resort parks and tourist-savvy towns like Guthrie), and bicycle paths are even more rare. Cyclists who don't mind sharing the road with automobiles will fare fine; others may well be disappointed. Though some lakes, parks, and university towns have bike trails, they rarely connect downtown with the local park or a hotel with local sights. Thankfully Oklahoma is a small, uncrowded state so there's usually plenty of room on the roads for all.

Bird Watching Acres of ponds, lakes, and wetlands make Oklahoma a popular stopover for any of a number of migrating birds, but the biggest success story in recent years has been the return of the American bald eagle. Some 1,500 eagles winter in Oklahoma, and eagle sightings are now so common the **Oklahoma Department of Wildlife Conservation** (tel 405/521-4616) publishes a "Bald Eagle Viewing" brochure. Eagle-viewing bus tours have become a winter favorite at both Keystone Lake outside Tulsa and at the Wichita Mountains National Wildlife Refuge.

Camping With 55 state parks, Oklahoma has camping terrain to suit the most esoteric tastes: mesas, salt plains, prairie (short grass and tall grass), mountains, lakeside, islands. Sites are both primitive —or come with all the amenities (read: RV friendly). Permits are needed only at the **Wichita Mountains National Wildlife Refuge** north of Lawton (tel 405/429-3222) and a few other preserves or refuges, but camping is so popular in Oklahoma it is best to call ahead to ensure a spot to your liking on holidays or sunny summer weekends.

Canoeing The Illinois River in northeastern Oklahoma is a Class II River, and a full 70 miles of it is protected as a Wild and Scenic River (one of only six such designated rivers in the state). The most popular portions of the river for floaters are the 8 miles between Round Hollow State Park and Comb's Bridge and the 12-plus miles from Pea Vine to No Head Hollow. Six public access areas for canoeists are strewn along OK 10.

Nearly a dozen canoe liveries line the river; they can arrange trips as short as four hours and as long as four days. Most provide canoes, life vests, and paddles, as well as access to ice, snacks, showers, and free or cheap camping. Canoeing is also popular on the Mountain Fork River in Broken Bow State Park in southeastern Oklahoma. For a list of regulations, canoe liveries, safety tips, and river conditions, call the **Scenic River Commission** (toll free 800/299-3251).

Dude Ranches Oklahoma's cowboy and Native American heritage makes dude, or guest, ranches a natural. At **Coyote Hills** (tel 405/497-3931) in western Oklahoma, city slickers overnight in five teepees or a 20-room bunkhouse, have access to mountain bikes, a stable of more than 20 horses, and a hot tub for relaxing after all that activity. Coyote Hills is known for its wildlife and its extracurricular activities: two annual powwows, Native American concerts, cowboy poetry gatherings, and theatrical events. A social barn houses a library, a 200-seat theater, and a trading post.

At **Island Guest Ranch** (tel 405/753-4574) near Enid, the allure is staying at a 3,000-acre ranch that sits in the middle of the red waters of the Cimarron River. Horseback riding, trolley rides, powwows, square dancing, and horseshoes join a thrice-a-year overnight wagon train as the big draws. **Deer Run Guest Lodge** (tel 405/924-4402) near Durant offers riding lessons, trail rides, volleyball, croquet, hayrides, campfire sing-alongs, hunting, and fishing in

20 well-stocked ponds.

Fishing Fishing enthusiasts willing to travel can find just about any kind of fresh water fish they desire in Oklahoma: Lake Murray in the south is famous for its guide-led striper outings, the chilly Mountain Fork River in the southeast is full of brown and rainbow trout, and most any other body of water—whether large or small—is likely to be full of catfish or bass.

Fly-fishing workshops are held weekends on the Mountain Fork River in January, February, March, and April at **Beavers Bend State Park** (tel 800/654-8240); year-round, two miles of the Lower Mountain Fork River (south of the park dam) are reserved for fishermen using artificial flies and unbarbed hooks. All fish, however, must be released.

Golf Oklahoma has its share of both public and private golf courses by big-name designers. It also gets its share of the pro-golf limelight: Tulsa's Southern Hills Country Club regularly hosts the PGA Championships (it also routinely makes *Golf Digest* and *Golf* magazines' lists of the top private courses in the nation). In addition, nine state parks have golf courses tucked amid their hiking trails, cabins, and swimming pools. **Arrowhead State Park** (tel 918/339-2769) in east-central Oklahoma has an 18-hole, par 72 course with a putting green, driving range, and bent grass greens; the 18 holes at **Cedar Creek Golf Course** (tel 405/494-6300) at Beavers Bend State Park are arguably the prettiest in the state. **Lake Murray Golf Course** (tel 405/223-6613) and **Lake Texoma Golf Course** (tel 405/564-3333) on Oklahoma's southern border cater to golfers who like to play year-round.

Hiking What Oklahoma lacks in urban trail systems, it makes up for in its fifty-plus state parks—most of which feature extensive systems of marked hiking and nature trails. (For details on trail lengths and difficulty, check with individual park offices.) The Oklahoma Nature Conservancy (tel 918/585-1117) controls some 14 preserves in Oklahoma, some of which offer hiking trails (these trails are rarely marked). Among them: Black Mesa Nature Preserve in the Panhandle, E C Springer Prairie Preserve in north-central Oklahoma, Tallgrass Prairie Preserve north of Pawhuska, Katy Railroad Trail (a 5.2-mile jogging, bicycling, and walking trail that links Tulsa to Sand Springs), Redbud Valley Nature Preserve, and Little River Nature Preserve in southeastern Oklahoma.

Horseback Riding The Oklahoma Department of Tourism and Recreation operates stables at several state parks. One of the best interpretive trail rides in the state now operates out of Roman Nose State Park, where stable manager Mark Farris, himself a cavalry re-enactor, regularly leads a three-hour prairie ride that includes a campfire steak dinner. The stable (tel 405/623-4354) stocks mustangs and quarter horses, and corrals are provided to those with their own horses for a $3 a day fee.

Mountain Biking Trails are plentiful but bike rentals are not, so it's best to bring your own bike if possible. The state's most technical trails are found on Army land west of **Lake Elmer Thomas Recreation Area** in the Wichita Mountains (tel 405/429-3222), the stage for the annual Twelve Miles of Hell off-road race. In the pine-laden and mountainous **Ouachita National Forest** (tel 918/581-6510) in southeastern Oklahoma, only the Ouachita Trail is off limits. The **Oklahoma Corps of Engineers** (tel 918/669-7396) allows mountain biking on the 12-mile Eagle View Hiking Trail around Kaw Lake near Ponca City, the 18-mile Will Rogers Centennial Trail near Lake Oologah, and the 60-mile Jean-Pierre Chouteau Trail that follows the Verdigris River from Tulsa to Fort Gibson. The **Oklahoma Tourism and Recreation Department** (tel 800/652-6552) publishes a free map to biking trails throughout the state.

Rock Climbing At its best, rock climbing in Oklahoma is challenging, varied, and relatively crowd free. Climbers can pick from soaring granite boulders in the Wichita Mountains or tricky canyon walls in places like Tulsa's Cleveland Park or Red Rock Canyon in southwestern Oklahoma. If traveling without guide and gear, it is best to climb with one of the university organizations like **Outdoor Adventure** at Oklahoma State University in Stillwater (tel 405/744-5510).

Sailing Consistent, strong winds (with occasional gusts) have made Oklahoma one of the premier regatta sites in the country; in season, one can find a race somewhere in the state most any weekend. Lake Hefner in Oklahoma City, Lake Arcadia outside Edmond, and Grand Lake in the northeastern corner of the state are well-known sailing strongholds. One caveat: sailboat rentals are all but unheard of in Oklahoma—so bring your own boat.

The one exception to the above rule is a summer sailing program offered by Oklahoma City's Community on the Water, a nonprofit organization that promotes sailing by teaching both children and adults the mechanics of the sport. For $75 to $85, a student gets a week of half-day sailing lessons on Lake Hefner (one of the country's premier lakes for racing). Classes range from beginning sailing to racing for youngsters with a course on navigation thrown in for good measure. A course perk: students have free access to OCCW sailboats for after-class sailing.

Scuba Diving Believe it or not, landlocked Oklahoma is home to a thriving scuba diving population. **Gene's Aqua Pro Shop** (tel 918/487-5221) on Lake Tenkiller is the granddaddy of Okie dive shops, and rightly so—Lake Tenkiller traditionally offers the best visibility of the state's three diving lakes as well as the most diving options: island diving and night diving, as well as lessons and equipment rental. In southeastern Oklahoma, **Broken Bow Scuba Service** (tel 405/584-9149) in Broken Bow (about ten miles south of Broken Bow Lake) maintains a full-service dive shop six days a week (and Sundays in summer). On the west shore of Lake Murray just north of the Texas-Oklahoma border, **The Great Escape Dive Center** (tel 405/223-6494) in Overbrook offers lessons and maintains a year-round full-service dive shop.

Tennis Free public and university tennis courts abound in Oklahoma but to find out where the tournaments are any given weekend call the **Oklahoma City Tennis Center** (tel 405/946-2739). At **Shangri-La** (tel 800/331-4060) on Grand Lake in far northeastern Oklahoma, golf and tennis packages pair travelers with top-notch pros (in the case of tennis, one who helped Arnold Schwarzenegger perfect his swing).

Tours Tours in Oklahoma are as eclectic as the state's history and personality. For $2,000, **Whirlwind Tours** of Norman (tel 405/329-2308) offers a two-week, fifteen-night tornado-chasing tour. In tornado season, tour operator Marty Feely leads tourists all over his home state as well as other portions of tornado alley—Texas, Kansas, Nebraska —chasing storms. But remember: There are no guarantees. A tornado isn't a static mountain or beach; it's a moving act of nature. The weekly Oklahoma travel show, *Discover Oklahoma,* has spun off a series of monthly bus tours in which TV camera crews record participants' visits to off-the-beaten-path sites—from small-town festivals to bed-and-

breakfast inns. Most **Discover Oklahoma Kincaid Travel Tours** (tel 800/998-1903) are day trips (a few include an overnight stay); trip price for one runs about $75 per day ($179 for overnights), and reservations are necessary.

Train Excursions The **Hugo Heritage Railroad and Frisco Museum** (tel 405/326-6630) in the pine-laden southeastern tip of Oklahoma operates a restored Harvey House restaurant and excursion train on Saturdays April through November. The train boards at 2pm for a 2 ½-hour roundtrip (destination is dictated by what rails are open); train tickets, which include light refreshments, are $15 for adults, $10 for children. (Charters are available year round; the museum is also open on Sunday afternoons in season.)

SELECTED PARKS & RECREATION AREAS

- **Chickasaw National Recreation Area,** PO Box 201, Sulphur 73086 (tel 405/622-3165)
- **Alabaster Caverns State Park,** Box 32, Freedom 73842 (tel 405/621-3381)
- **Beavers Bend State Resort Park,** PO Box 10, Broken Bow 74728 (tel 405/494-6301)
- **Black Mesa State Park,** HCR-1 Box 8, Kenton 73946 (tel 405/426-2222)
- **Fountainhead State Park,** HC 60 Box 1340, Checotah 74426 (tel 918/689-5311)
- **Lake Murray State Resort Park,** 3310 S Lake Murray Drive #1, Ardmore 73401 (tel 405/223-4044)
- **Lake Texoma State Resort Park,** PO Box 279, Kingston 73439 (tel 405/564-2566)
- **Little Sahara State Park,** Box 132, Waynoka 73860 (tel 405/824-1471)
- **Osage Hills State Park,** HC-73 Box 84, Pawhuska 74056 (tel 918/336-5635)
- **Quartz Mountain State Resort Park,** Box 35, Lone Wolf 73655 (tel 405/563-2520)
- **Robbers Cave State Park,** PO Box 9, Wilburton 74578 (tel 918/465-2565)
- **Roman Nose State Resort Park,** Rte 1, Watonga 73772 (tel 405/623-4215)
- **Tenkiller State Park,** HCR-68 Box 1095, Vian 74962 (tel 918/489-5643)
- **Western Hills State Resort Park,** Rte 1 Box 198-3, Hulbert 74441 (tel 918/772-2046)

Driving the State

Start	Bartlesville
Finish	Guthrie
Distance	Approximately 250 miles
Time	3 days
Highlights	Rolling prairie grasslands and buffalo herds; art museums devoted to cowboys, Native Americans, and frontier life; Native American art and crafts; Will Rogers' birthplace and memorial; historic Route 66; a beautifully preserved 19th-century downtown

This driving tour of northeast and central Oklahoma brings to life four key emblems of the state's history and development: the legacy of the cowboy; the rich heritage of Native Americans; the oil industry; and the spirit of America on the move, as dramatized by the land rush of 1889 and the Dust Bowl exodus of the 1930s.

The tour begins in Bartlesville, home of Frank Phillips and his Phillips Petroleum Company, then heads west to the Tallgrass Prairie Preserve. It is followed by a loop tour that takes in Hominy with its dozens of murals, and Oologah and Claremore, respectively the birthplace and final resting spot of Will Rogers. Then it's onward to Tulsa, which boasts a fine collection of art deco buildings as well as a couple of world-class museums. From there the tour follows historic Route 66, a nostalgic romp down memory lane, before bringing us to Oklahoma City, the state capital. The tour terminates in Guthrie, one of Oklahoma's most attractive historic towns.

For additional information on lodgings, dining, and attractions in the region covered by the tour, refer to specific cities in the listings portion of this chapter.

US 60 and US 75 provide easy access to:

1. **Bartlesville,** which owes its fortunes to oil. Founded as a trading station in the late 1800s, it quickly became a sprawling oil boom town after Frank Phillips and his brothers struck black gold and founded their Phillips Petroleum Company, which still has its headquarters here and plays a major role in the town's prosperity. In the center of the small downtown is a striking example of Bartlesville's wealthy past, the 19-story **Price Tower** at 6th St and Dewey Ave. An office and apartment complex designed by Frank Lloyd Wright (who called it "the tree that escaped the crowded forest") in 1956 for a

pipeline construction firm, it earned a place on the National Register of Historic Places a mere 18 years later. The **Bartlesville Museum,** housed on the ground floor of the building, is devoted to architecture and offers a permanent exhibition highlighting local works by Edward Buehler Delk, Wes Peters, Bruce Goff, and others, in addition to Wright.

The other main attraction in town is the **Frank Phillips Home,** 1107 S Cherokee, a Greek Revival mansion built in 1909 by Frank and Jane Phillips. Decorated with the Phillipses' original furnishings and personal items, the home is like a step back into the 1920s and '30s, when the oilman and his wife wined and dined luminaries from around the world.

From Bartlesville, take OK 123 south 11 miles, passing a large refuge for wild horses managed by the US Department of Interior, to:

2. **Woolaroc,** which began in the 1920s as the ranch retreat of oil millionaire Frank Phillips. Will Rogers, Harry Truman, and Herbert Hoover were just some of the big names entertained here. Now open to the public, it is one of Oklahoma's best attractions, yet surprisingly it is relatively unknown. Encompassing 3,600 acres, this wildlife preserve is home to more than 700 free-ranging animals and birds, including a 170-strong bison herd, deer, elk, longhorn cattle, wild turkeys, emus, llamas, and ostriches. Most of these you encounter during the two-mile drive beginning at the front gate; others are elusive and may be glimpsed only from April through mid-October when the five-mile gravel North Road Loop is open. But the highlight of the place is the eclectic **Woolaroc Museum** and its breathtaking collection of Western art and artifacts, South American archeological finds (Phillips was an enthusiastic amateur archeologist), sculpture, and American Indian art. Next to the museum is the **Frank Phillips Lodge,** a rustic yet grand log home built in 1927 overlooking a lake. Its walls are covered with trophies of all the animals that roamed the grounds of the ranch. Across from the museum is the **National Y-Indian Guide Center and Native American Heritage Center,** where performances and programs illuminate the culture of America's first inhabitants. Surrounding these buildings is refined nature at its best, with beautifully choreographed pines, boulders, streams, lawns, ponds, and a 1½-mile nature trail through the "Enchanted Canyon."

Take a right out of Woolaroc and continue south

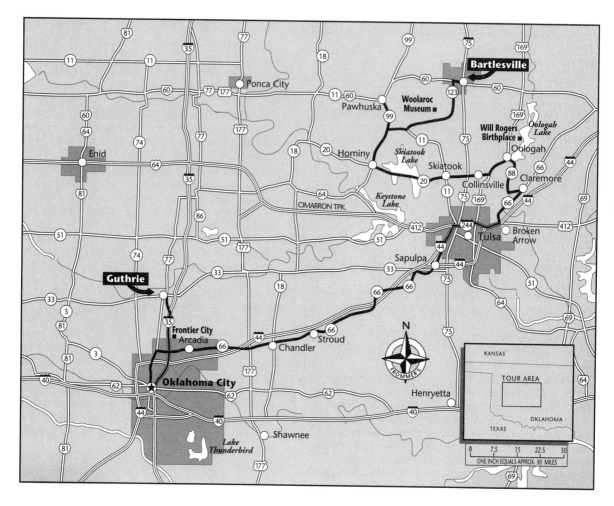

on OK 123 for 7 miles, turning right where it dead-ends at OK 11, and head west. This is ostrich and emu country, where several farms raise the exotic animals along this two-lane stretch of highway. After 11 miles you'll come to the junction of OK 11 and OK 99. If the grounds of Woolaroc whetted your appetite for nature, turn right and take OK 11 north 6 miles to:

3. **Pawhuska,** the capital of the Osage Nation, America's wealthiest Native American tribe, due to their retention of oil and mineral rights for their lands. The small **Osage Tribal Museum,** 819 Grandview, was established in 1939 as the nation's first tribal museum. It displays changing art exhibitions, as well as Osage artifacts.

Pawhuska is also gateway to the **Tallgrass Prairie Preserve,** reached by taking Osage Ave north from Main St and following the signs approximately 17 miles to preserve headquarters. Whereas Woolaroc is essentially a wealthy entrepreneur's garden,

the prairie preserve is nature in the raw, the way it looked before humans tried to tame it by ploughing fields and planting trees. Managed by the Nature Conservancy, the 30,000-acre preserve is home to hundreds of bison and cattle, whose grazing plays an important role in maintaining the prairie ecosystem. To protect the prairies and animals (and you from them), visitors are requested to stay on the Tallgrass Prairie Preserve Dr, which covers approximately 50 miles on gravel road. There are also two self-guided nature trails.

But if by the time you reach the junction of OK 11 and OK 99 your appetite for nature has been satisfied by Woolaroc, take a left and go south 14 miles (or, from Pawhuska, south on OK 99 for 20 miles) to:

4. **Hominy,** population 2,500. Due to the efforts of Cha' Tullis, a Northern Blackfoot jeweler and artist, Hominy is fast becoming known as the "city of murals." Tullis began the outdoor murals, based on

Native American themes, in 1990 and has now completed more than 45, mostly on buildings on Main St and OK 99 and OK 20. Stop by his gallery, **Cha' Tullis Designs** at 108 W Main St in Hominy, to pick up a pamphlet describing several murals and their locations.

From Hominy head east on OK 20 past the Skiatook lake system for 33 miles until it takes you to the downtown of:

5. **Collinsville,** founded in 1899 as a stop on the Santa Fe railway and now home of several antiques stores. Most noticeable is **Tut Uncommon Treasures,** located on the corner of Main and 11th Sts, a brightly painted brick building within which lies an antiques mall housing more than 30 dealers selling furniture, books, dolls, jewelry, kitchenware, quilts, pottery, and more.

Follow OK 20 to the east end of town, and then take four-lane US 169 north 8 miles to:

6. **Oologah.** Stay on US 169 through town and follow the signs directing you to the **Will Rogers Birthplace.** This simple white clapboard home on Dog Iron Ranch was once located on the Verdigris River, but now overlooks Oologah Lake. The home was built room by room by Rogers's father, with the oldest two rooms made of hand-hewn logs.

Approximately 12 miles away, on OK 88 going south from Oologah, is:

7. **Claremore,** where you'll find the **Will Rogers Memorial** to your right at 1720 W Will Rogers Blvd. Originally purchased by Rogers for his retirement home, the 20-acre grounds became his final resting place after his death in a plane crash in Alaska in 1935. The memorial and museum is an impressive tribute to one of America's great humorists.

Another fascinating stop is the **JM Davis Gun Museum,** 333 N Lynn Riggs Blvd, home to some 20,000 guns and gun-related items, as well as swords, knives, John Rogers's statuary, and 1,200 beer steins.

Lynn Riggs Boulevard is actually OK 66, a busy four-lane that will take you 12 miles south to I-44 west and then I-244 to downtown:

8. **Tulsa,** Oklahoma's second-largest city. Like Bartlesville, it owes its development to the discovery of oil, with more than 1,200 oil and oil-related companies located in the area. Tulsa's downtown boasts a number of art deco buildings built during the oil boom of the 1920s and '30s; a walking tour map identifying 25 historic and art deco buildings in the downtown area is available at the Tulsa Convention & Visitors Bureau, 616 S Boston Ave. The **Philbrook Museum of Art,** 2727 S Rockford Rd, south of downtown just off Peoria Ave at 27th Place, houses Italian Renaissance paintings and sculpture; 19th- and 20th-century American and European paintings; and African and Asian collections, including Chinese decorative arts and Japanese screens.

Tulsa's other well-known museum is the **Gilcrease Museum,** 1400 Gilcrease Museum Rd, just north of downtown, which boasts one of the finest and most comprehensive collections of art of the American West. It documents the discovery and settlement of North America, with an emphasis on the Old West and Native Americans.

Heading west from Tulsa on OK 66 brings you within minutes to the suburb:

Sapulpa, where you'll find the:

9. **Frankoma Pottery** factory outlet and gift shop, 2400 Frankoma Rd, to the right. Begun in 1933 with a small kiln, a butter churn for mixing clay, and a fruit jar for grinding glazes, the company today sells dozens of different patterns, including those with Native American, Southwest, and country farmhouse themes.

Continue west on OK 66 through the attractive, historic brick buildings of downtown Sapulpa to the outskirts of town. Now, 66 resembles any other four-lane highway, but just west of Sapulpa look for a narrow, nondescript road leading to the right and crossing an old iron-and-brick bridge. This is a very rare, original stretch of the old historic **Route 66,** which officially opened in 1926 as a 2,400-mile highway linking Chicago with Santa Monica. Passing through eight states and three time zones, it was the mother of all roads, America's main street traveled by families, dreamers, drifters, and the destitute. During the Dust Bowl of the 1930s it carried countless "Okies" to the west in search of a better life, and during the '50s and '60s it was the epitome of family vacations and the freedom of the open road, with its motor courts, diners, gas stations, and cheap attractions. More of the old route exists here than in any other state, with over 400 driveable miles of it. Keep your eyes open for ghosts of the past—abandoned motor courts, rusty gas pumps, dilapidated buildings, and overgrown roadside parks.

If you're looking for a place to rest on Route 66, the **Stroud House,** 110 E 2nd St in Stroud (tel 800/259-2978) is an expensive bed-and-breakfast that offers one suite and three rooms, all with private bath, in a 1900 Victorian built by the town's founder. The budget-priced **Lincoln Motel,** 740 E 1st St in Chandler (tel 405/258-0200), is a classic Route 66 motel built in 1939. It consists of 10 little wooden duplexes separated by parking spaces, with metal gliders on the front lawn.

Thirteen miles west of Stroud on Route 66 is:

10. **Chandler,** boasting a small historic downtown and vintage gas stations (now serving other purposes). Stop by the **Lincoln County Museum of Pioneer History,** 719 Manvel, which documents local lore in a 1880 stone building through clothing, household items, a stage coach, and other items from the past.

    After driving 4 miles west of Chandler turn right and go another 2 miles until you reach:

11. **Read Ranch,** which offers guided trail rides, pony rides for youngsters, hay wagon rides, a petting zoo, and a snack bar. Call 405/258-2999 for more information.

    Another 22 miles west on Route 66, passing perpetual yard sales and fields of red dirt, you'll find yourself in:

12. **Arcadia,** home to one of Route 66's most distinctive landmarks, the **Old Round Barn.** Constructed in 1898 and painted a brilliant red, it measures 60 feet in diameter and 43 feet to the peak of its dome. Inside are photographs and a souvenir shop. Just across the way is **The Old Store,** an old-fashioned full-line grocery, meat market, and deli located in a stone, early-1900s former drug store.

    From Arcadia, it's only 6 miles before Route 66 joins I-35 south to:

13. **Oklahoma City,** state capital and Oklahoma's largest city. It was born in a single afternoon, when the Great Land Run of 1889 brought thousands of land claims around a solitary railroad station. In 1910 Oklahoma City became the state capital; in 1928 it discovered it was sitting on a gold mine—a vast deposit of oil. These days there are oil wells even on the grounds of the Capitol.

    Oklahoma City's best-known museum is undoubtedly the **National Cowboy Hall of Fame,** 1700 NE 63rd St, just north of I-44 at the Martin Luther King exit. This magnificent collection of Western art and historic artifacts enlightens visitors with a visual lesson in the history of the Old West.

Masters such as Frederic Remington, Charles M Russell, and William R Leigh are represented. Other highlights include New Mexico artist Wilson Hurley's five triptychs comprising the world's largest Western landscape; the **Rodeo Hall of Fame;** and the **Western Performers Hall of Fame,** which pays tribute to John Wayne, Gary Cooper, Roy Rogers and Dale Evans, Gene Autry, and others. Every summer the Prix de West Invitational Exhibition and Sale showcases the talents of more than 70 of the nation's top contemporary Western artists.

Other Oklahoma City attractions include the **Myriad Botanical Gardens,** located downtown at Reno and Robinson Sts, which features a unique tropical conservatory called the Crystal Bridge, a translucent cylinder of acrylic and steel stretching 224 feet over a sunken lake; and **Stockyard City,** Agnew and Exchange Sts, a National Register Historic District founded in 1910 and popular now for its restaurants and Western-related shops selling saddles, cowboy boots, and Western wear. It's located next to the **Oklahoma National Stockyards,** which claims to be the largest cattle and livestock market in the world, with public auctions held all day Monday and Tuesday. Children will enjoy **Frontier City,** a Western theme park whose roller coasters, Ferris wheel, and other thrill rides are set against a colorful backdrop of log cabins, stockade fences, wagon trains, and Wild West storefronts. It's located in northeast Oklahoma on I-35.

You'll be hard put to find anyone who thinks Oklahoma City is the state's most attractive city, but head north on I-35 about 16 miles and you'll find what could be a top contender:

14. **Guthrie.** Like Oklahoma City, Guthrie was born in a day during the land rush and even served as the state's first capital from 1907 to 1910. And that's about where the city has stayed, with 400 blocks of more than 2,000 historic structures now on the National Register of Historic Places. There are more than a half-dozen antiques shops and malls throughout the brick buildings of downtown, along with specialty shops, restaurants, and the **Frontier Drug Store,** 214 W Oklahoma St—a re-creation of a turn-of-the-century pharmacy with wooden fixtures, antique wall cabinets, artifacts and memorabilia, and a working soda fountain.

Should you decide to spend the night in Guthrie, the **Harrison House,** 124 W Harrison (tel 405/282-1000), is a moderately priced hotel located in the midst of the wonderful downtown area. It occupies two historic brick buildings and is decorated with turn-of-the-century antiques.

Oklahoma Listings

Altus

Located on the plains of southwest Oklahoma, this city is home to the Altus Air Force Base. The downtown district is popular with collectors of fine art, crafts, and antiques. Nearby state parks offer seasonal hunting, fishing, and other recreational activities. **Information:** Altus Chamber of Commerce, PO Box 518, Altus, 73522 (tel 405/482-0210).

MOTEL 🏨

≣ ≣ ≣ Best Western Altus

2804 N Main, 73521; tel 405/482-9300 or toll free 800/528-1234; fax 405/482-2245. On US 283. A comfortable, well-maintained lodging close to the air force base. **Rooms:** 100 rms and stes. CI 2pm/CO noon. Nonsmoking rms avail. **Amenities:** 🏨 🔥 📺 A/C, satel TV w/movies. Microwaves and mini-refrigerators in some rooms; many rooms have dataports. **Services:** ✕ 🖨 🛎 🐾 Pets $5/night. **Facilities:** 🏋 🛣 ♿ 1 restaurant, 1 bar, sauna, whirlpool, washer/dryer. **Rates (CP):** Peak (May–Sept) $54 S or D; $60 ste. Extra person $6. Children under age 12 stay free. Lower rates off-season. Parking: Outdoor, free. AE, CB, DC, DISC, MC, V.

RESTAURANT 🍴

Polynesian Garden

1700 Falcon St; tel 405/482-2831. **Chinese.** A miniature rock garden and lovely Asian/Polynesian decorations set the mood at this unique and fun place. Chow mein, sweet-and-sour chicken and beef, and seafood dishes share the menu with more unusual offerings such as Mandarin flower steak kew, beef cube steak marinated in barbecue sauce and served over crispy broccoli. **FYI:** Reservations accepted. Children's menu. **Open:** Mon–Thurs 11am–10pm, Fri–Sat 11am–10:30pm, Sun noon–10pm. **Prices:** Main courses $4–$31. MC, V.

ATTRACTIONS 🏛

Quartz Mountain Resort Park

OK 44A, Lone Wolf; tel 405/563-2238. 25 mi N of Altus. Once the sacred grounds of the Kiowa and Camanache, this state park's rugged beauty features wildflowers, caves, and wildlife. Activities and facilities include indoor and outdoor swimming pools, tennis courts, an 18-hole golf course, hiking, paddle boats, fishing, and a nature center. Supervised recreational programs, including nature talks and "eagle watch," are also available. **Open:** Daily 24 hours. **Free**

Museum of the Western Prairie

1100 Memorial Dr; tel 405/482-1044. The story of the determined settlers of southwest Oklahoma is told through artifacts and photographs. The exhibits include a working wind mill and a reconstructed hall dugout (a home built into the side of a hill). **Open:** Tues–Fri 9am–5pm, Sat–Sun 2–5pm. **Free**

Alva

A quiet community, Alva is within easy reach of the Great Salt Plains Lake and Wildlife Refuge and both Alabaster Caverns and Little Sahara state parks. Alva is the Woods County seat and home to Northwestern Oklahoma State University. **Information:** Alva Area Chamber of Commerce, 410 College, Alva, 73717 (tel 405/327-1647).

MOTEL 🏨

≣ Wharton's Vista Motel

1330 W Oklahoma Blvd, 73717; tel 405/327-3232 or toll free 800/322-1821; fax 405/327-1236. On US 64 W. Simple hotel is a good choice for travelers on a budget. **Rooms:** 20 rms and stes. CI open/CO 11am. Dark wood paneling in rooms. **Amenities:** 🏨 A/C, cable TV. Ceiling fans. **Services:** 🚐 🛎 🐾 **Facilities:** ♿ **Rates:** $20–$25 S; $26–$29 D; $26 ste. Extra person $3. Children under age 10 stay free. Parking: Outdoor, free. AE, DC, DISC, MC, V.

ATTRACTION 🏛

Cherokee Strip Museum

901 14th St; tel 405/327-2030. The 40 rooms of this museum contain a pioneer drugstore, a prisoner of war room, a kitchen, a country store, and a gun room. Outbuildings open for touring include an agricultural building, implement yard,

and a one-room schoolhouse. Tours available by appointment. **Open:** Peak (June–Aug) Tues–Sun 2–5pm. Reduced hours off-season. **Free**

Anadarko

Sometimes referred to as the "Indian Capital of the Nation," this town hosts many Native American cultural events throughout the year. Fort Cobb State Park to the west offers camping and seasonal water sports. **Information:** Anadarko Chamber of Commerce, 514 W Kentucky, PO Box 366, Anadarko, 73005-0366 (tel 405/247-6651).

MOTEL

Inn of the Southwest
1602 E Central, 73005; tel 405/247-2538; fax 405/247-5047. On US 62 E. Located at the edge of town, this extremely basic motel is geared for budget travelers. **Rooms:** 50 rms and stes. CI 2pm/CO 11am. Nonsmoking rms avail. **Amenities:** A/C, cable TV. **Facilities:** Rates: $34 S; $40 D; $46 ste. Extra person $4. Children under age 12 stay free. Parking: Outdoor, free. AE, MC, V.

ATTRACTIONS

Indian City USA
OK 8; tel 405/247-5661 or toll-free 800/433-5661. Outdoor museum features authentic replicas of seven villages of the Plains Indians: Wichita, Pueblo, Caddo, Apache, Kiowa, Pawnee, and Navajo. Guided tours include the Indian City Museum and Native American dance ceremonies. Campground, swimming, handicraft shop. **Open:** Peak (June–Aug) daily 9am–6pm. Reduced hours off-season. **$$$**

National Hall of Fame for Famous American Indians
115 US 62 E; tel 405/247-5555. This 10-acre garden is home to 39 bronze statues of well-known Native Americans such as Sequoyah, Sitting Bull, Oceola, Sacajawea, Tohausan, and Geronimo. **Open:** Mon–Sat 9am–5pm, Sun 1–5pm. **Free**

Ardmore

Brick sidewalks and period lighting help heighten the atmosphere of this Carter County seat in southern Oklahoma. Museums, antiques stores, festivals, and a rodeo win visitors' attention. **Information:** Ardmore Chamber of Commerce, 410 W Main, PO Box 1585, Ardmore, 73402 (tel 405/223-7765).

MOTELS

Days Inn of Ardmore
2432 Veterans Blvd, 73401; tel 405/223-7976 or toll free 800/325-2525; fax 405/223-7976. Exit 33 off OK 142. Very clean hotel within 10 miles of Lake Murray and within 30 miles of Turner Falls. **Rooms:** 65 rms. CI 2pm/CO 11am. Nonsmoking rms avail. **Amenities:** A/C, cable TV. **Services:** Facilities: Washer/dryer. **Rates (CP):** $39–$45 S; $45 D. Extra person $6. Children under age 12 stay free. Parking: Outdoor, free. AE, CB, DC, DISC, MC, V.

Guest Inn
2519 W OK 142, 73401; tel 405/223-1234 or toll free 800/460-4064; fax 405/223-1234. Near I-35. Average motel with a restaurant in the same parking lot. **Rooms:** 126 rms and stes. CI 3pm/CO noon. Nonsmoking rms avail. Many rooms in need of remodeling. **Amenities:** A/C, cable TV. **Services:** VCR and movie rentals available at front desk for a charge. Small pets only. **Facilities:** Washer/dryer. **Rates:** $32–$36 S; $33–$38 D; $65 ste. Extra person $3. Children under age 12 stay free. Parking: Outdoor, free. Special rates for AARP members. AE, CB, DC, DISC, MC, V.

Holiday Inn
2705 Holiday Dr, 73401; tel 405/223-7130 or toll free 800/HOLIDAY; fax 405/223-7130. Exit 31A off I-35. Pleasant, standard motel. Close to restaurants, about 30 minutes from Arbuckle Wilderness and Turner Falls, with easy access to I-35. Great for families traveling with small children. **Rooms:** 171 rms and stes. CI 2pm/CO noon. Nonsmoking rms avail. **Amenities:** A/C, cable TV w/movies, dataport. 1 unit w/whirlpool. **Services:** Denny's restaurant attached to hotel offers room service. **Facilities:** 1 restaurant, 1 bar (w/entertainment), playground, washer/dryer. **Rates:** Peak (May–Aug) $59 S or D; $95–$150 ste. Children under age 12 stay free. Lower rates off-season. Parking: Outdoor, free. AE, CB, DC, DISC, MC, V.

RESORT

Lake Murray Country Inn
3310 S Lake Murray Dr, 73401; tel 405/223-6600 or toll free 800/654-8240; fax 405/223-6154. 3 mi E of exit 24 off I-35. 6,500 acres. Lake Murray has 115 miles of shoreline, and this rustic lodge offers a multitude of outdoor activities. Make reservations six months in advance, because the place is always packed. **Rooms:** 52 rms and stes; 83 cottages/villas. CI 3pm/CO noon. Nonsmoking rms avail. Lodge rooms are small and plain, some with lake view. Other accommodations range from villas to cottages to family cabins with full kitchens. **Amenities:** A/C, TV. 1 unit w/minibar, 1 w/terrace, some w/fireplaces. Villas have microwaves and mini-refrigerators. Cottages have two-burner stoves, small refrigerators, and sink. **Services:** Social director, children's program. Pets may stay in cabins, but are not allowed in lodge. VCRs and movie rentals available at front desk. **Facilities:** 1 restaurant, 1 bar, 1 beach (lake shore), basketball, volleyball, games rm, lawn games, playground, washer/dryer. Tucker Tower Nature Center offers exhibits and a great view. Marina and watersport charges may not be billed to your room. **Rates:** Peak (May–Aug) $58 S; $63 D; $150 ste; $48–$225

cottage/villa. Extra person $10. Children under age 18 stay free. Min stay peak. Lower rates off-season. Parking: Outdoor, free. Minimum stay summer weekends. AE, CB, DC, DISC, MC, V.

ATTRACTIONS

Eliza Cruce Hall Doll Museum
320 E St NW; tel 405/223-8290. Displays of more than 300 antique dolls, including wooden "Court Dolls" which belonged to Marie Antoinette. **Open:** Mon–Thurs 10am–8:30pm, Fri–Sat 10am–4pm. **Free**

Lake Murray Resort State Park
Exit 24 off I-35; tel 405/223-4044. The 12,496-acre park features 5,728-acre Lake Murray, a swimming beach, a marina, two golf courses, and hiking and equestrian trails, as well as camping, cottages, and a resort lodge. **Open:** Daily sunrise–sunset. **Free**

Bartlesville

Bartlesville combines the atmosphere of a small town with all the advantages of a large city. In addition to a historic district containing 48 structures built during the 1900–1920 oil boom, Bartlesville is home of the world-renowned OK Mozart Festival held every June. **Information:** Bartlesville Area Chamber of Commerce, 201 SW Keeler, PO Box 2366, Bartlesville, 74005 (tel 918/336-8708).

HOTELS

Holiday Inn
1410 SE Washington Blvd, 74006; tel 918/333-8320 or toll free 800/HOLIDAY; fax 918/333-8979. Just N of jct US 60/75. Conveniently located near Washington Park Mall, this motel has a lovely pool area with a quiet and serene atmosphere. **Rooms:** 105 rms and stes. CI 2pm/CO noon. Nonsmoking rms avail. Average rooms. **Amenities:** A/C, cable TV. **Services:** Car-rental desk. **Facilities:** 1 restaurant, 1 bar (w/entertainment), games rm, sauna, washer/dryer. **Rates:** $46 S; $52 D; $65–$70 ste. Extra person $6. Children under age 18 stay free. Parking: Outdoor, free. AE, CB, DC, DISC, JCB, MC, V.

Hotel Phillips
821 Johnstone, 74003; tel 918/336-5600 or toll free 800/331-0706; fax 918/336-0350. 3 mi from jct US 75/60. A nice change from the standardized chain property, this attractive hotel is run by Marriott but possesses a unique, personal charm. **Rooms:** 164 rms, stes, and effic. CI 3pm/CO noon. **Amenities:** A/C, cable TV. Some units w/minibars, 1 w/whirlpool. **Services:** Social director, babysitting. **Facilities:** 1 restaurant (bkfst and dinner only; see "Restaurants" below), 1 bar (w/entertainment). Free passes to Phillips Recreation Center available on weekdays. **Rates:** $65–$75 S or D; $75–$125 ste; $65 effic.

Extra person $10. Children under age 16 stay free. Parking: Outdoor, free. Weekend packages avail. AE, CB, DC, DISC, MC, V.

RESTAURANTS

Garfield's Restaurant and Pub
3650 Washington Park Mall; tel 918/333-7020. **Eclectic.** Perfect for families, this simple eatery has a bright, cheery decor and friendly service. **FYI:** Reservations not accepted. Children's menu. Additional locations: 5840 S Memorial Dr, Tulsa (tel 662-5777); 14002 E 21st, Tulsa (tel 234-9266). **Open:** Daily 11am–10pm. **Prices:** Main courses $5–$7. AE, CB, DC, DISC, MC, V.

Villa Italia
In Hotel Phillips, 821 Johnstone; tel 918/336-5600. **Italian/Steak.** This small restaurant offers daily pasta and seafood specials in a casual, romantic atmosphere. **FYI:** Reservations recommended. Children's menu. No smoking. **Open:** Peak (June) breakfast Mon–Fri 6:30–10am, Sat–Sun 7–11am; dinner Mon–Thurs 5–10pm, Fri–Sun 5–11pm. **Prices:** Main courses $8–$19. AE, DC, DISC, MC, V.

ATTRACTIONS

Price Tower
6th and Dewey Sts; tel 918/335-2468. A 19-story glass and copper skyscraper (circa 1956) designed by Frank Lloyd Wright for construction magnate H C Price. The design is based on a diamond module of 30- and 60-degree triangles. Guided tours. **Free**

Frank Phillips Home Site
1107 Cherokee Ave; tel 918/336-2491. Built for oil baron Frank Phillips in 1908, this 26-room Greek Revival mansion is richly decorated with imported woods, marble, and damask wall coverings. There are even his-and-hers bathrooms, which include a barber chair for the husband and gold fixtures for the wife. **Open:** Wed–Sat 10am–5pm, Sun 1–5pm. **Free**

La Quinta Foster Mansion
2201 Silver Lake Rd; tel 918/336-6943. Built by pioneer oil man H V Foster and designed by noted American architect Edward Delk, the 1932 Spanish-style mansion consists of 32 rooms with 14 baths and 7 fireplaces. Visitors can examine the stained-glass windows, a fountain and gardens, bell towers, and a formal dining room, among other features. **Open:** Thurs 10:30am–noon and by appointment. **Free**

Woolaroc Museum
OK 123; tel 918/336-0307. Located 14 mi SW of Bartlesville, this museum houses Native American artifacts and Western art, including paintings by Frederic Remington and Charles M Russell. A wildlife preserve covers 3,500 acres and features a herd of buffalo as well as longhorn cattle, elk, and deer. Also on the premises are Frank Phillips Lodge home (circa

1927) and the Native American Heritage Center. **Open:** Peak (Mem Day–Labor Day) daily 10am–8pm. Reduced hours off-season. **$$**

Osage Hills State Park
US 60, Pawhuska; tel 918/336-5635. 20 mi SW of Bartlesville. Once an Osage Indian settlement, the densely wooded, 1,000-acre park now serves visitors as a camping and recreational facility. It features an 18-acre lake with boating and fishing, swimming pool, picnic facilities, and playgrounds. **Open:** Daily sunrise–sunset. **Free**

Broken Bow

Surrounded by the piney woods of southeast Oklahoma, this old lumber town is near two state parks and a national forest. Broken Bow Lake to the north is popular for scuba diving. The nearby community of Idabel abuts the Ouachita National Forest. **Information:** Broken Bow Chamber of Commerce, 214 Martin Luther King Dr, Broken Bow, 74728 (tel 405/584-3393).

ATTRACTIONS

Gardner Mansion and Museum
US 70; tel 405/584-6588. Located 6 mi E of Broken Bow. Patrons can tour the 1884 home of Jefferson Gardner, chief of the Choctaw in 1894–96, which features steamboat Gothic architecture, hand carvings, and prehistoric tribal artifacts. Also on the grounds is a 2,000-year-old giant cypress tree which served as a landmark for prehistoric Native Americans and later as a backdrop to the Trail of Tears. **Open:** Peak (June–Aug) Mon–Sat 8am–6pm, Sun 1–6pm. Reduced hours off-season. **$**

Magnolia Mansion-Spaulding/Olive House
601 SE Adams St, Idabel; tel 405/286-3200. 10 mi SW of Broken Bow. Restored colonial mansion (circa 1910) listed on the National Register of Historic Places. Historic rooms furnished with pieces from the turn of the century. Guided tours available. **Open:** Call for schedule. **Free**

Beavers Bend and Hochatown State Parks
US 259; tel 405/494-6300. The Beavers Bend main entrance is 7 mi N of Broken Bow on US 259; Hochatown is four miles further north. The parks are adjacent to Broken Bow Lake and together encompass 3,482 acres. Activities at the park include hiking (24-mile trail), boating, waterskiing, trout fishing, swimming, tennis, miniature golf, and two golf courses. **Open:** Daily sunrise–sunset. **Free**

Claremore

The Rogers County seat and southern gateway to Oologah Lake, Claremore is best known as the hometown of cowboy actor and philosopher Will Rogers. The town honors its celebrated native son with Will Rogers Days in early Novem-

ber. **Information:** Claremore Area Chamber of Commerce, 419 W Will Rogers Blvd, Claremore, 74017-6820 (tel 918/341-2818).

MOTELS

Best Western Will Rogers Motor Inn
940 S Lynn Riggs, 74017; tel 918/341-4410 or toll free 800/644-WILL; fax 918/341-6045. Close to restaurants, shopping, and the highway. Standard, nothing fancy. **Rooms:** 52 rms and stes. CI 2pm/CO noon. Nonsmoking rms avail. **Amenities:** A/C, cable TV, refrig. 1 unit w/whirlpool. Dataports in some rooms; mini-refrigerators in most rooms. **Services:** **Facilities:** 1 restaurant, 1 bar (w/entertainment), steam rm, beauty salon, washer/dryer. **Rates:** $48 S; $51 D; $61–$89 ste. Extra person $5. Children under age 12 stay free. Parking: Outdoor, free. AE, CB, DC, DISC, MC, V.

Claremore Motor Inn
1709 N Lynn Riggs, 74017; tel 918/342-4545 or toll free 800/828-4540; fax 918/341-3983. On OK 66. This family-owned and -operated motel is fine for a clean room and friendly service. **Rooms:** 29 rms. CI open/CO 11am. Non-smoking rms avail. Dated decor. Larger rooms are available above the office. **Amenities:** A/C. **Services:** Car-rental desk. **Facilities:** The "meeting room" is a large room with a Murphy bed and a long glass table. **Rates:** $33 S; $43 D. Extra person $3. Children under age 10 stay free. Parking: Outdoor, free. AE, CB, DC, DISC, MC, V.

RESTAURANT

Hammett House
1616 W Will Rogers Blvd; tel 918/341-7333. Next to Will Rogers Memorial. **American/Eclectic.** Featuring daily lunch specials and nightly ethnic dining. Dinner menu is available at all hours. Well known for pies. **FYI:** Reservations not accepted. Children's menu. Beer and wine only. **Open:** Tues–Sun 11am–9pm. **Prices:** Main courses $4–$17. AE, CB, DC, DISC, MC, V.

ATTRACTIONS

Will Rogers Birthplace
2 mi E of US 169, Oologah; tel 918/275-4201. 10 mi NW of Claremore. In 1879, when Oklahoma still was part of the Cherokee Nation, the performing cowboy was born here to a Cherokee senator-judge and his wife. The ranch where the Rogers family ran 10,000 head of Texas Longhorn cattle is now open for tours, and a video describing the life of Will Rogers is shown in the barn. **Open:** Daily sunrise–sunset. **Free**

Will Rogers Museum
1720 W Will Rogers Blvd; tel 918/341-0719 or toll free 800/324-9455. The grounds of the museum include the tomb of the cowboy, humorist, and down-home philosopher. The

museum houses eight galleries of art and artifacts depicting his life and career. Movies and interactive exhibits are also offered. **Open:** Daily 8am–5pm. **Free**

Clinton

Settled around the turn of the century on the banks of the Washita River, Clinton hit the travel big time when Route 66 came through town in 1926. Nearby Foss Lake, the largest lake in western Oklahoma, is the winter home for numerous bald eagles and geese. **Information:** Clinton Chamber of Commerce, 400 Gary Blvd, PO Box 1595, Clinton, 73601 (tel 405/323-2222 or toll free 800/759-1397).

MOTELS

⋿⋿ Comfort Inn
2247 Gary Blvd, 73601; tel 405/323-6840 or toll free 800/228-5150; fax 405/323-4067. Exit 65 off I-40. Average lodgings approximately three blocks from the Route 66 Museum. **Rooms:** 80 rms. CI 11am/CO 11am. Nonsmoking rms avail. King rooms have sofas. Furniture in some rooms needs repair. **Amenities:** A/C, cable TV. **Services:** Car-rental desk. **Facilities:** 1 restaurant. **Rates (CP):** Peak (May–Oct) $38–$47 S; $52 D. Extra person $5. Children under age 18 stay free. Lower rates off-season. Parking: Outdoor, free. AE, CB, DC, DISC, MC, V.

⋿⋿ Super 8 Motel
1120 S 10th St, 73601; tel 405/323-4979 or toll free 800/800-8000. Exit 65A off I-40. This relatively new budget motel has easy interstate access. **Rooms:** 26 rms. CI open/CO 11am. Nonsmoking rms avail. Very clean. Some rooms are unusually large; all rooms have extra sinks, towel racks, mirrors, and plugs in bedroom area. **Amenities:** A/C, cable TV. **Services:** **Facilities:** **Rates (CP):** $34 S; $44 D. Extra person $3. Children under age 12 stay free. Parking: Outdoor, free. AE, CB, DC, DISC, MC, V.

Davis

ATTRACTIONS

Cedarvale Botanic Garden
US 77 S; tel 405/369-3224. On the banks of Honey Creek, the gardens include many varieties of tropical plants, wildflowers, and unusual geological formations. A waterfowl yard, rose garden, nature trails, and art studio are also featured. **Open:** Peak (May–Sept) daily 11am–9pm. Reduced hours off-season. Closed Nov–Mar. **$**

Arbuckle Wilderness
Exit 51 off I-35; tel 405/369-3383. A 400-acre, drive-through, exotic animal theme park. An eight-mile scenic drive allows visitors to see more than 2,000 free-roaming animals up-close. Visitors may feed the animals from their cars with food bought on the premises. Petting zoo, camel rides, and hayrides. **Open:** Daily 8am–dusk. **$$$$**

Chickasaw National Recreation Area
US 177, Sulphur; tel 405/622-3165. 10 mi E of Davis. Water in all forms—springs, streams, and lakes—is the main attraction here, with activities ranging from swimming, waterskiing, and boating, to fishing for largemouth bass and white crappie. Programs include nature walks, history talks, and seasonal programs led by rangers. **Open:** Daily 24 hours. **Free**

Turner Falls Park
US 77; tel 405/369-2917. The oldest park in Oklahoma has been a popular recreation area since 1898. The 720-acre grounds include a 77-foot waterfall, wagon-wheel cave, castles, beaches, hiking, picnicking facilities, natural springs, and fishing. **Open:** Daily 24 hours. **$$**

Duncan

Duncan has grown from an outpost on the Chisholm Trail to a leading support location for the energy industry. The Old Military Trail, an 1852 army route, traverses the town, and four nearby lakes are known for trophy-size bass. **Information:** Duncan Chamber of Commerce & Industry, 911 Walnut, PO Box 699, Duncan, 73534-0699 (tel 405/255-3644).

HOTEL

⋿⋿ The Lodge of Duncan
2535 US 81 N, 73533; tel 405/252-0810; fax 405/255-6591. US 81 exit off I-44. Average accommodations with good housekeeping standards. Near many dining options, shopping areas, and a hospital. **Rooms:** 69 rms, stes, and effic. CI open/CO noon. Nonsmoking rms avail. **Amenities:** A/C, cable TV. **Services:** Car-rental desk. **Facilities:** 1 restaurant, 1 bar, washer/dryer. **Rates:** $39–$44 S or D; $60 ste; $60 effic. Extra person $5. Children under age 18 stay free. Parking: Outdoor, free. AE, CB, DC, DISC, MC, V.

MOTEL

⋿ Heritage Inn
1515 US 81, 73533; tel 405/252-5612; fax 405/252-5620. US 81 exit off I-44. Very clean, basic motel located right on the highway. **Rooms:** 37 rms. CI 11am/CO 11am. Nonsmoking rms avail. **Amenities:** A/C, cable TV. **Rates:** $25–$27 S; $29 D. Extra person $2. Children under age 8 stay free. Parking: Outdoor, free. AE, CB, DC, DISC, MC, V.

Elk City

Elk City serves as the healthcare center for the western Oklahoma/eastern Texas Panhandle region. Home to one of the world's tallest oil drilling rigs, this city is a popular rest stop along I-40 in Beckham County. The nearby Washita National Wildlife Refuge attracts large numbers of migratory birds. **Information:** Elk City Chamber of Commerce, 1016 Airport Blvd, PO Box 972, Elk City, 73648 (tel 405/225-0207).

HOTELS

HoJo Inn
2604 E OK 66, 73644; tel 405/225-2241 or toll free 800/I-GO-HOJO; fax 405/225-2246. Exit 41 off I-40. Easy access to I-40 and restaurants make this standard, budget hotel very convenient. **Rooms:** 60 rms. CI noon/CO noon. Nonsmoking rms avail. Basic accommodations. Rooms were under construction upstairs. **Amenities:** A/C, cable TV. **Services:** Pets $4. Complimentary use of Sega video games for children. **Rates (CP):** $28–$29 S; $34–$37 D. Extra person $6. Children under age 17 stay free. Parking: Outdoor, free. AE, CB, DC, DISC, MC, V.

Holiday Inn
I-40 and OK 6, 73648; tel 405/225-6637 or toll free 800/HOLIDAY; fax 405/225-6637. Exit 38 off I-40. A Holidome property with an impressive recreational facility. **Rooms:** 151 rms and stes. CI 2pm/CO noon. Nonsmoking rms avail. King rooms have sofas. Some rooms have views of Holidome. **Amenities:** A/C, satel TV. 1 unit w/whirlpool. Hair dryers available. **Services:** Complimentary coffee and newspapers placed outside each room every morning. **Facilities:** 1 restaurant, 1 bar, volleyball, games rm, steam rm, whirlpool, washer/dryer. Holidome has a creek, shuffleboard, miniature golf, and separate pool room with outdoor sun deck. **Rates:** $59 S or D; $85 ste. Extra person $6. Children under age 18 stay free. Parking: Outdoor, free. AE, CB, DC, DISC, JCB, MC, V.

MOTELS

Best Western Elk City Inn
2015 W 3rd St, 73648; tel 405/225-2331 or toll free 800/528-1234. Exit 41 off I-40 W; exit 32 off I-40 E. Basic accommodations near restaurants, interstate, and major highways. **Rooms:** 81 rms. CI open/CO 11am. Nonsmoking rms avail. Some rooms notably better than others, so ask to switch rooms if you're not satisfied. Some rooms specifically designated for pets. **Amenities:** A/C, cable TV. **Services:** **Facilities:** Rates (BB): $32–$35 S; $38–$42 D. Extra person $3. Children under age 12 stay free. Parking: Outdoor, free. AE, CB, DC, DISC, MC, V.

Quality Inn
102 B J Hughes Access Rd, 73648; tel 405/225-8140 or toll free 800/228-5150; fax 405/225-8233. Exit 38 off I-40. Standard chain motel with easy interstate access. **Rooms:** 50 rms. CI open/CO 11am. Nonsmoking rms avail. **Amenities:** A/C, cable TV. Executive rooms have coffeemakers, clock radios, and dataports. **Services:** Linens changed daily upon request. **Facilities:** Games rm, whirlpool,

washer/dryer. **Rates (CP):** $30–$36 S; $33–$42 D. Extra person $4. Children under age 18 stay free. Parking: Outdoor, free. Discounts for senior citizens and military. AE, DC, DISC, JCB, MC, V.

ATTRACTION

Anadarko Basin Museum of Natural History
107 E 3rd St; tel 405/243-0437. Located in historic old Casa Grande Hotel. On display are western Oklahoma fossils, and gas and oil exhibits. Adjacent to the museum is one of the tallest oil rigs in the world, the 179-foot Parker Drilling Rig #114. **Open:** Daily 10am–3pm. $

El Reno

Founded in the early 1870s as a cavalry outpost during the Cheyenne Indian uprising, El Reno now is a satellite community northwest of Oklahoma City. Each May the townspeople band together to create the world's largest hamburger, some 500 pounds. Red Rock Canyon State Park is west of town. **Information:** El Reno Chamber of Commerce, 206 N Bickford, PO Box 67, El Reno, 73036 (tel 405/262-1188).

MOTEL

Days Inn
2700 S Country Club Rd, 73036; tel 405/262-8720 or toll free 800/DAYS-INN; fax 405/262-1473. Exit 123 off I-40. No frills, but clean. Convenient to interstate. **Rooms:** 52 rms. CI open/CO 11am. Nonsmoking rms avail. **Amenities:** A/C, cable TV. **Services:** **Facilities:** Rates (CP): Peak (Apr–Nov) $48 S or D. Extra person $4. Children under age 12 stay free. Lower rates off-season. Parking: Outdoor, free. AE, CB, DC, DISC, MC, V.

ATTRACTIONS

Fort Reno
OK 66; tel 405/262-5291. 5 mi W, 2 mi N on OK 66. Exhibits items from the calvary outpost, which was built in 1875 to protect settlers from the Cheyenne uprising. General Custer's head scout, Ben Clark, is buried at the cemetery, as well as soldiers from the Indian wars, World War I, Korean War, and German POWs from World War II. Today the fort is an agricultural research center. **Open:** Daily 8am–4:30pm. **Free**

Canadian County Historical Museum
300 S Grand St; tel 405/262-5121. Visitors can explore the area's pioneer past with historical memorabilia and original buildings, including an Indian jail, Red Cross canteen, General Sheridan's headquarters, and the 1892 Hotel El Reno (where rooms once rented for 50 cents a night). The Rock Island railroad depot, built in 1906, now houses a museum featuring a buffalo head and a Mastodon tusk found 14 miles west of the town. **Open:** Wed–Sat 10am–5pm, Sun 1:30–5pm. **Free**

Enid

The fourth-largest rodeo in the country brightens up this town in northwest Oklahoma's old Cherokee Strip every September. Enid is home to Vance Air Force Base and Phillips University. **Information:** Enid Convention & Visitors Bureau, 210 Kenwood Blvd, PO Box 907, Enid, 73702-0907 (tel 405/237-2494 or toll free 800/299-2494).

MOTEL 🏨

🇪🇪🇪 Holiday Inn

2901 S Van Buren, 73703; tel 405/237-6000 or toll free 800/HOLIDAY. On US 81 S. Comfortable motel was undergoing major exterior and room renovations. Convenient to Cherokee Convention Center. **Rooms:** 100 rms and stes. CI 3pm/CO noon. Nonsmoking rms avail. Older rooms have smaller shower but larger vanity area. South wing rooms have interior corridor accessibility. **Amenities:** 🛁 🛆 A/C, cable TV, dataport. **Services:** ✗ 🖾 🖵 ⬔ Car-rental desk. Small pets only (and they may not be left unattended). **Facilities:** 🖃 🛏 🛆 1 restaurant, 1 bar, washer/dryer. **Rates:** $46 S; $52 D; $55–$61 ste. Extra person $6. Children under age 19 stay free. Parking: Outdoor, free. AE, CB, DC, DISC, JCB, MC, V.

RESTAURANT 🍽

Best of the Orient

518 S Van Buren; tel 405/234-2737. On US 81. **Chinese/Thai.** A plainly decorated restaurant offering a huge (over 60 items), eclectic selection of dishes from the Far East. A limited American menu is also available. **FYI:** Reservations accepted. Children's menu. No liquor license. **Open:** Lunch daily 11am–2pm; dinner daily 5–9pm. **Prices:** Main courses $5–$9. AE, MC, V. 🖭

Guthrie

This turn-of-the-century town bills itself as "30 minutes and 100 years north of Oklahoma City." Its urban district (400 blocks) is the largest listed on the National Historic Register, and replicas of old-time trolleys transport folks around town. **Information:** Guthrie Convention & Visitors Bureau, PO Box 995, Guthrie, 73044 (tel 405/282-1947 or toll free 800/299-1889).

HOTEL 🏨

🇪🇪 Best Western Territorial Inn

2323 Territorial Trail, 73044; tel 405/282-8831 or toll free 800/528-1234; fax 405/282-8831. Exit 157 off I-35. Less than 10 miles from the Lazy E Arena, this standard motel is a perfect stop for rodeo fans. Not much more than a typical Best Western. **Rooms:** 84 rms. CI 4pm/CO 11am. Nonsmoking rms avail. **Amenities:** 🛁 A/C, satel TV. **Services:** ✗ 🖾 🖵

Facilities: 🖃 🛐 🛆 1 restaurant, 1 bar. **Rates:** $43–$51 S or D. Extra person $3. Parking: Outdoor, free. Senior discounts avail. AE, DC, DISC, MC, V.

INN

🇪🇪🇪 Harrison House Inn

124 W Harrison, 73044; tel 405/282-1000 or toll free 800/375-1001; fax 405/282-4304. Exit 153 off I-35 S; exit 157 off I-35 N. Charming and unique Victorian inn set within three historic buildings. Hallways decorated with period clothing, sewing machines, and other antiques. **Rooms:** 31 rms and stes. CI 3pm/CO 11am. No smoking. Rooms honor such people as Will Rogers, Tom Mix, and O Henry; each is individually decorated with handmade quilts, old-fashioned telephones, and antique furniture. Baths are very modern. **Amenities:** 🛁 🛆 A/C. No TV. **Services:** ✗ 🖵 ⬔ Cats allowed but must be kept in cages. **Facilities:** 🛐 🛆 1 restaurant, guest lounge w/TV. **Rates (CP):** $67–$87 D; $107 ste. Extra person $10. Children under age 12 stay free. Parking: Outdoor, free. AE, CB, DC, DISC, MC, V.

RESTAURANTS 🍽

Blue Belle Saloon & Restaurant

224 W Harrison; tel 405/282-6660. At 2nd St. **American.** First opened as a saloon in 1889, it retains some of the decor from its earlier days, including old photos and an antique piano. Waitresses wear saloon dresses, and the mock gunfights held every Saturday afternoon offer some excitement. A limited menu includes chili, sandwiches, burgers, steak, and seafood. **FYI:** Reservations accepted. Karaoke/piano. **Open:** Tues–Sat 11am–2am, Sun noon–6pm. **Prices:** Main courses $4–$16. AE, CB, DC, DISC, MC, V. 🖭 ♥

Miss Carolyn's Territorial House

224 N Division; tel 405/282-6733. At Noble St. **American.** Historic pictures of Guthrie cover the walls of this otherwise plain, casual restaurant serving breakfast throughout the day. Sandwiches, burgers, steaks, ribs, seafood, and chicken are on hand as well. Homemade cream and fruit pies. **FYI:** Reservations not accepted. Children's menu. No liquor license. **Open:** Daily 6am–10pm. **Prices:** Main courses $3–$11. AE, CB, DC, DISC, MC, V. 🖭 🛆

ATTRACTION 🏛

Oklahoma Territorial Museum

402 E Oklahoma; tel 405/282-1889. Displays artifacts and exhibits relating to all phases of life in the Oklahoma Territory, beginning with the Oklahoma Land Run in 1889. Complex includes the Carnegie Library, built in 1902–1903, which is the location of the inaugurations of the last territorial governor and the first state governor. **Open:** Tues–Fri 9am–5pm, Sat 10am–4pm, Sun 1–4pm. **Free**

Henryetta

See also Okmulgee

Located halfway between the Oklahoma-Arkansas border and Oklahoma City, Henryetta anchors the southeast corner of Oklahoma's "Green Country," a major recreation region. Lake Eufaula to the east is the largest lake in the state and is known for its numerous sandy beaches. **Information:** Henryetta Chamber of Commerce, 115 S 4th, Henryetta, 74437-5272 (tel 918/652-3331).

MOTEL

◼◼ HoJo Inn

US 75 and Trudgeon St, 74430; tel 918/652-4448 or toll free 800/I-GO-HOJO. Basic accommodations at a rock-bottom price. **Rooms:** 38 rms. CI open/CO noon. Nonsmoking rms avail. **Amenities:** A/C, cable TV. **Services:** Small pets allowed with $25 security deposit. **Facilities:** Playground. **Rates (CP):** $36 S; $41 D. Extra person $5. Children under age 18 stay free. Parking: Outdoor, free. AARP discounts avail. AE, CB, DC, DISC, MC, V.

Hugo

A thriving railroad hub in its early years, Hugo is now better known as Circus City, USA, the winter home of the Carson & Barnes and Kelly-Miller Brothers circuses. Hunting, fishing, and other recreational activities await visitors at area lakes, streams, and state parks. **Information:** Hugo Chamber of Commerce, 200 S Broadway, Hugo, 74743-4626 (tel 405/326-7511).

ATTRACTIONS

Hugo Heritage Railroad

300 W Jackson; tel 405/326-6630. Passengers ride two restored 1940 coach trains with refreshments and air conditioning. In the depot, the Frisco Museum displays the history of Hugo since its founding at the turn of the century. Patrons view a typical Oklahoma still, railroad artifacts, a miniature circus, and a barber shop. **Open:** Apr–mid-Nov, Tues–Sat 10am–4pm. $$$$

Mount Olivet Cemetery

800 E Trice St; tel 405/326-9263. Located in "Circus City, USA," the cemetery features unusual monuments to the town's deceased circus performers, trainers, owners, and workers. Visitors may see the grave of famous bull rider Freckles Brown and the *Eight Seconds* movie autobiography of Lane Frost. **Open:** Daily 8am–6pm. **Free**

Lawton

See also Duncan

Home of the beautiful Wichita Mountains and gateway to Fort Sill Military Reservation, Lawton is rich in frontier lore and Native American history. The Wichita Mountains Wildlife Refuge and Lake Lawtonka create one of the most scenic recreation areas in the state. This Comanche County seat is home to Cameron University. **Information:** Lawton Chamber of Commerce & Industry, 607 SW C Ave, PO Box 1376, Lawton, 73502 (405/355-3541 or toll free 800/872-4540).

HOTEL

◼◼◼ Howard Johnson Hotel

1125 E Gore Blvd, 73507; tel 405/353-0200 or toll free 800/359-0020; fax 405/353-6801. Gore exit off I-44. Pleasant hotel popular with business travelers, featuring a large outdoor pool in a beautiful courtyard with a gazebo and walking path. Near downtown, Fort Sill Army Post, Cameron University, and airport. **Rooms:** 144 rms and stes. CI 2pm/CO noon. Nonsmoking rms avail. **Amenities:** A/C, cable TV, dataport. Some units w/whirlpools. Rooms have extra sink with mirror and outlets. King rooms have mini-refrigerator/microwave. **Services:** Car-rental desk, babysitting. Pets $25. **Facilities:** 1 restaurant, 2 bars, sauna. **Rates:** $44–$59 S or D; $110–$140 ste. Extra person $5. Children under age 18 stay free. Parking: Outdoor, free. AE, CB, DC, DISC, ER, JCB, MC, V.

MOTELS

◼ Best Western Sandpiper Inn

2202 US 277 N/US 281 N, 73507; tel 405/353-0310 or toll free 800/749-0310; fax 405/357-7388. Exit 40A off I-44. Fine for overnight or budget traveling, but in need of slight repairs. Easy highway and interstate access. **Rooms:** 124 rms. CI noon/CO noon. Nonsmoking rms avail. **Amenities:** A/C, cable TV. Some rooms have mini-refrigerators, and some have dataports. **Services:** Car-rental desk. Pets $6. **Facilities:** 1 restaurant, 1 bar. **Rates:** $36 S; $40 D. Extra person $2. Children under age 18 stay free. Parking: Outdoor, free. AE, CB, DC, DISC, MC, V.

◼◼ Holiday Inn

3134 Cache Rd, 73507; tel 405/353-1682 or toll free 800/HOLIDAY; fax 405/353-2872. On US 62. Located on the main road in Lawton, near Cameron University, this Holiday Inn offers standard services and amenities. **Rooms:** 173 rms and stes. CI 2pm/CO noon. Nonsmoking rms avail. **Amenities:** A/C, cable TV w/movies, dataport. 1 unit w/whirlpool. Stocked mini-refrigerators in half the rooms. **Services:** Car-rental desk. **Facilities:** 1 restaurant, 1 bar, washer/dryer. Free access to nearby health club. **Rates:** $52 S or D; $175 ste. Extra person $5. Children under age 18 stay free. Parking: Outdoor, free. AE, CB, DC, DISC, JCB, MC, V.

🛏🍴 Ramada Inn

601 N 2nd St, 73507; tel 405/355-7155 or toll free 800/2-RAMADA; fax 405/353-6162. 2nd St exit off I-44. Adjacent to the Great Plains Museum and within miles of Fort Sill, the airport, and Cameron University, this standard Ramada has a deck overlooking a beautiful courtyard. **Rooms:** 98 rms and stes. CI noon/CO noon. Nonsmoking rms avail. Rooms have extra counter space outside bathroom with additional outlets. **Amenities:** 🛁🗄📺 A/C, cable TV. **Services:** ✕🖨🍴🌐 Car-rental desk. VCR and movie rentals at front desk. Pet fee $10. **Facilities:** 🏋🛗🏃 1 restaurant, 1 bar. **Rates:** $44 S; $50 D; $80 ste. Extra person $6. Children under age 18 stay free. Parking: Outdoor, free. AE, CB, DC, DISC, JCB, MC, V.

RESTAURANTS 🍴

Bianco's Italian Restaurant

113 N 2nd St; tel 405/353-9543. 2nd St exit off I-44. **Italian.** A small, family-operated trattoria, serving customers since 1952. Family and celebrity photos line the walls; red-and-white checkered tablecloths complete the idyllic picture. Available are Italian favorites like lasagna, veal parmigiana, spaghetti, and pizzas, as well as sandwiches and some non-Italian options. **FYI:** Reservations accepted. Children's menu. **Open:** Mon–Thurs 11am–9:30pm, Fri–Sat 11am–10:30pm. **Prices:** Main courses $5–$12. MC, V. 🖼

Calico County

5203 Cache Rd; tel 405/353-7976. On US 62. **American.** Bring your appetite to this casual restaurant with a country decor of quilt squares, rolling pins, flour sacks, and old ad posters. Home-style cooking features large portions of chicken-fried steak, meat loaf, pot roast, and chicken potpie. Also lots of vegetables, soups, salads, and burgers. **FYI:** Reservations accepted. Children's menu. **Open:** Sun–Thurs 11am–9pm, Fri–Sat 11am–10pm. **Prices:** Main courses $4–$9. AE, DISC, MC, V. 🖼

Martin's

2107 NW Cache Rd; tel 405/353-5286. On US 62. **Seafood/Steak.** An upscale restaurant decorated with subtle blue and mauve tones and attractive paintings. The dining room comes complete with a player piano and a dark, comfortable bar. The dinner menu offers a variety of steaks and seafood, as well as specialty entrees like veal Oscar, filet mignon, and roast Long Island duck. **FYI:** Reservations recommended. Piano. Children's menu. Dress code. **Open:** Lunch Mon–Fri 11am–2pm; dinner Tues–Sat 5:30–10:30pm. **Prices:** Main courses $10–$40. AE, CB, DC, DISC, MC, V. ⬤

ATTRACTIONS 🏛

Museum of the Great Plains

601 Ferris Ave; tel 405/581-3460. The history, archeology, and anthropology of the Great Plains are detailed from prehistoric settlements through the early 1900s. Special attractions include an outdoor prairie dog village, a recreation of an 1840s fortified trading post, and a 19th-century train depot and main street. Living history interpretive programs Wednesday through Sunday. **Open:** Mon–Fri 8am–5pm, Sat 10am–6pm, Sun 1–6pm. **$**

Wichita Mountains Wildlife Refuge

OK 49; tel 405/429-3222. 12 mi W on US 62, then 3 mi N of Cache on OK 115. The 59,060-acre refuge contains a roaming herd of 480 buffaloes, long-horn cattle, prairie dogs, elk, and deer. Visitors boat, fish, and swim in the park's 12 man-made lakes. A visitors center offers natural wildlife exhibits and a slide program. **Open:** Daily sunrise–sunset. **Free**

McAlester

In 1870, James J McAlester opened a tent store where the California Trail and the Texas Road met. His namesake city now has Eufaula Lake on its northern limits. An unusual attraction is the Oklahoma State Penitentiary Outlaw Rodeo, located entirely behind prison walls. **Information:** McAlester Chamber of Commerce, 17 E Carl Albert Pkwy, PO Box 759, McAlester, 74502-0759 (tel 918/423-2550).

HOTEL 🏨

🛏🛏🛏 Holiday Inn

1500 George Nigh Expwy, 74502; tel 918/423-7766 or toll free 800/HOLIDAY; fax 918/426-0068. On US 69 bypass S. With its Holidome sports and recreation complex, this Holiday Inn was designed for vacationing families. **Rooms:** 161 rms and stes. CI open/CO noon. Nonsmoking rms avail. **Amenities:** 🛁🗄📺 A/C, satel TV w/movies, dataport. Some units w/whirlpools. **Services:** ✕🚐🖨🍴🌐 Car-rental desk, babysitting. **Facilities:** 🏋🏊🛗🏃 1 restaurant, 1 bar, games rm, spa, sauna, whirlpool, washer/dryer. Golf course and driving range nearby. **Rates:** $45 S; $48–$49 D; $89–$178 ste. Extra person $5. Children under age 18 stay free. Parking: Outdoor, free. AE, CB, DC, DISC, JCB, MC, V.

MOTELS 🏨

🛏🛏 Comfort Inn

1215 George Nigh Expwy, 74502; tel 918/426-0115 or toll free 800/221-2222; fax 918/426-3634. On US 69 bypass. This spotlessly clean budget motel offers a convenient location and comfortable rooms. **Rooms:** 61 rms and stes. CI noon/CO noon. Nonsmoking rms avail. **Amenities:** 🛁 A/C, cable TV. **Services:** 🚐🖨🍴🌐 **Facilities:** 🏋🏃 1 restaurant. **Rates:** $38 S; $44 D; $75 ste. Extra person $5. Children under age 18 stay free. Parking: Outdoor, free. AE, CB, DC, DISC, EC, ER, JCB, MC, V.

Super 8 Motel
2400 S Main, 74501; tel 918/426-5400 or toll free 800/800-8000. No-frills property with an RV park in the rear. **Rooms:** 32 rms. CI 11am/CO 11am. Nonsmoking rms avail. Decor is dated and worn. **Amenities:** A/C, cable TV. **Services:** Car-rental desk. **Facilities:** 1 restaurant, 1 bar, basketball, volleyball, lawn games, playground, washer/dryer. **Rates:** $33 S; $41 D. Extra person $4. Children under age 4 stay free. Parking: Outdoor, free. AE, CB, DC, DISC, MC, V.

RESTAURANTS

Fish & Filet
1415 George Nigh Expwy; tel 918/426-1467. **Seafood/Steak.** Six separate dining rooms—and a banquet room to boot. The catfish is recommended. **FYI:** Reservations not accepted. Children's menu. No liquor license. **Open:** Mon–Thurs 11am–9pm, Sat 11am–10pm. **Prices:** Main courses $7–$26. AE, MC, V.

Giacomo's Italian Cuisine
US 69 and Comanche; tel 918/423-2662. **Italian/Steak.** This family-owned and -operated restaurant has been around for over 35 years and employs four generations of Giacomo's. Three separate dining areas decorated with a few plants and framed photos of famous sights in Italy give this restaurant a familiar yet cozy and comfortable feel. Steaks, chicken, shrimp, lamb fries, and veal are offered in either traditional American or Italian preparations. Entrees come with salad, bread, a meat and cheese platter, and spaghetti and meatballs. **FYI:** Reservations recommended. Children's menu. Beer and wine only. **Open:** Tues–Sat 11:30am–9:30pm. **Prices:** Main courses $8–$19. DISC, MC, V.

Kettle Restaurant
600 S US 69 Bypass; tel 918/423-4151. **American.** Traditional diner food in a casual environment. A good choice for families. **FYI:** Reservations not accepted. Children's menu. No liquor license. **Open:** Daily 24 hrs. **Prices:** Main courses $3–$9. AE, DC, DISC, MC, V.

Trolley's
21 E Monroe St; tel 918/423-2446. **Seafood/Steak.** The main house was built in 1886 and restored in 1980. Decorated around a theme of old movie theaters, the dining room is fun and interesting. Cajun dishes are available in addition to steak and seafood. The bar is housed in a 1908 streetcar attached to the side of the building. **FYI:** Reservations accepted. Children's menu. **Open:** Mon–Sat 5–10pm. **Prices:** Main courses $7–$22. AE, DISC, MC, V.

ATTRACTION

JT Puterbaugh House and Ardenium
5th and Adams Sts; tel 918/423-1555. Group of four homes owned by one of the founding fathers of the town's coal industry. On display are a costume gallery, Native American artifacts, two libraries (including one containing the history of local families), historical furnishings, paintings, wood carvings, and rock and azalea gardens. **Open:** Call for schedule. **Free**

Miami

Situated between the Neosha and Spring rivers that form the headwaters of Grand Lake O' the Cherokees, Miami is a convenient stop for travelers on I-44. This Ottawa County seat provides easy access to four area state parks and a water sports wonderland. **Information:** Miami Chamber of Commerce, 111 N Main, PO Box 760, Miami, 74355-0760 (tel 918/542-4481).

MOTEL

Best Western Continental Motor Inn
2225 E Steve Owens Blvd, 74354; tel 918/542-6681 or toll free 800/528-1234; fax 918/542-3777. On OK 10. A basic motel located off Will Rogers Turnpike. **Rooms:** 82 rms and stes. CI noon/CO noon. Nonsmoking rms avail. **Amenities:** A/C, cable TV, refrig. **Services:** Twice-daily maid svce. **Facilities:** 1 restaurant, 1 bar. Restaurant next door caters to large groups. **Rates:** $44–$48 S; $49–$52 D; $89 ste. Extra person $5. Children under age 12 stay free. Parking: Outdoor, free. AE, CB, DC, DISC, MC, V.

Muskogee

See also Tahlequah

Established in the Fort Gibson Lake region, Muskogee is rich in Native American culture and history. A thriving commercial center on the banks of the Arkansas River, the city celebrates its heritage with the Grand Moccasin Festival every April. **Information:** Greater Muskogee Area Chamber of Commerce, 425 Boston, PO Box 797, Muskogee, 74402-0797 (tel 918/682-2401).

HOTEL

Ramada Inn
800 S 32nd St, 74401; tel 918/682-4341 or toll free 800/2-RAMADA; fax 918/682-7400. On US 69 S. One of the nicest properties in town, this Ramada offers quality accommodations. Suitable for all travelers. **Rooms:** 135 rms and stes. CI 2pm/CO noon. Nonsmoking rms avail. Rooms decorated in tasteful Southwestern motif with cool green and mauve color scheme. Some have views of recreation/pool area. **Amenities:**

A/C, satel TV. **Services:** ✕ ▨ ⊷ ⊸ **Facilities:** ⌂ ▣ ⅄ 1 restaurant, 1 bar, games rm, sauna, whirlpool, washer/ dryer. The only heated pool in town with beautiful glass wall and weight machines on upper level. **Rates:** $50–$55 S; $48– $53 D; $95–$125 ste. Extra person $5. Children under age 18 stay free. Parking: Outdoor, free. AE, DC, DISC, MC, V.

MOTELS

≡≡ Best Western Trade Winds Inn

534 S 32nd St, 74401; tel 918/683-2951 or toll free 800/ 528-1234; fax 918/683-2951. On US 69. This no-frills motel with good highway access is a great budget choice. **Rooms:** 110 rms. CI 11am/CO noon. Nonsmoking rms avail. Some rooms face pool. Fourteen rooms are newer and have interior access. **Amenities:** ⌂ A/C, cable TV, dataport. Some rooms have clocks and coffeemakers. **Services:** ✕ ▨ ⊷ ⊸ Only small pets allowed. **Facilities:** ⌂ ▣ 1 restaurant, 1 bar (w/entertainment), washer/dryer. **Rates:** Peak (May–Sept) $39–$43 S; $47 D. Extra person $4. Children under age 12 stay free. Lower rates off-season. Parking: Outdoor, free. AE, CB, DC, DISC, MC, V.

≡≡ Days Inn

900 S 32nd St, 74401; tel 918/683-3911 or toll free 800/ DAYS-INN; fax 918/683-5744. On US 69. Much higher quality than the typical Days Inn. **Rooms:** 43 rms. CI noon/ CO 11am. Nonsmoking rms avail. Two rooms have sleeper/ sofas. **Amenities:** ⌂ ▣ A/C, cable TV. Some rooms have microwaves and mini-refrigerators; some have recliners. **Services:** ⊷ ⊸ Car-rental desk. Pets $5. **Facilities:** ⌂ ▣ ⅄ **Rates (CP):** $38 S; $43 D. Extra person $5. Children under age 12 stay free. Parking: Outdoor, free. AE, CB, DC, DISC, MC, V.

RESTAURANTS ▦

Kettle Restaurant

323 S 32nd St; tel 918/682-6611. On US 69 S. **American.** Simple restaurant with tables and booths. Traditional breakfast, lunch, and dinner items are all available at any time. You can watch TV in one area that's great for casual lunches. **FYI:** Reservations accepted. Children's menu. No liquor license. **Open:** Daily 24 hrs. **Prices:** Main courses $3–$8. AE, CB, DC, DISC, MC, V. ▦ ▣ ⅄

★ Little Italy Restaurant

2432 N 32nd; tel 918/687-5699. On US 69. **Italian.** Quaint and cozy, this is one of Muskogee's nicer and more popular restaurants. A tasteful green and burgundy decor is complemented by impressionist art prints, dim lighting, and ceiling fans. Standard Italian fare offers lots of pasta with various sauces. The tortellini alla Little Italy, made with chicken, prosciutto, diced mushrooms, peas, and a cognac cream sauce, is a specialty. **FYI:** Reservations not accepted. **Open:** Lunch Tues–Fri 11am–2pm, Sun 11am–2pm; dinner Tues– Thurs 5–9pm, Fri–Sat 5–10pm, Sun 5–9pm. **Prices:** Main courses $7–$14. AE, MC, V. ♥ ⅄

Szechuan Chinese Restaurant

In Curt's Center, 2218 E Shawnee; tel 918/683-1552. On US 62 (Shawnee Bypass). **Chinese.** Decor includes lamps, wall hangings, and a gold dragon archway. The standard menu lists more than 60 items; General Tso's chicken, pepper steak, and moo goo gai pan are the most popular choices. Buffet. **FYI:** Reservations accepted. Beer and wine only. **Open:** Lunch Mon–Fri 11am–3pm, Sat 11:30am–3pm, Sun noon– 3pm; dinner Mon–Sat 5–9pm. **Prices:** Main courses $5–$8. MC, V.

ATTRACTIONS ▥

The Five Civilized Tribes Museum

Agency Hill on Honor Heights Dr; tel 918/683-1701. Presents the history, art, and culture of the Cherokee, Choctaw, Creek, Chickasaw, and Seminole peoples, who were once known as the Five Civilized Tribes. Exhibits display jewelry, books, costumes, crafts, photographs, sculpture, and wood carvings, among other items. **Open:** Mon–Sat 10am–5pm, Sun 1–5pm. $

USS *Batfish*–War Memorial Park

Port of Muskogee; tel 918/682-6294. During World War II, the *Batfish* sank three submarines and 11 other vessels, earning nine battle stars in the process. Today, her torpedo room, decks, and engine room are all open to visitors, who can also view a special war memorial to the more than 3,500 submarine sailors lost during the war. **Open:** Peak (Mar 15– Oct 15) Mon–Sat 9am–5pm, Sun noon–5pm. Reduced hours off-season. $

Norman

Called "Festive City," Norman is known for its many celebrations and special events. Home to the University of Oklahoma, this major suburb of Oklahoma City includes the Little River State Park and Lake Thunderbird within its boundaries. **Information:** Norman Chamber of Commerce, 115 E Gray, PO Box 982, Norman, 73070 (tel 405/321-7260).

HOTELS ▥

≡≡≡ Holiday Inn

1000 N Interstate Dr, 73072; tel 405/364-2882 or toll free 800/HOLIDAY; fax 405/321-5264. Robinson St exit off I-35. Comfortable hotel with easy access to I-35 and area restaurants. **Rooms:** 149 rms and stes. CI 3pm/CO noon. Nonsmoking rms avail. Third- and fourth-floor rooms are newly remodeled and notably nicer than other rooms. **Amenities:** ⌂ ⊛ ▣ ▤ A/C, cable TV, dataport. **Services:** ✕ ▨ ⊷ **Facilities:** ⌂ ▦ ▣ ⅄ 1 restaurant, 1 bar, games rm, whirlpool, washer/dryer. Sliding roof covers indoor pool. **Rates:** $70 S or D; $80–$135 ste. Extra person $10. Children under age 18 stay free. Parking: Outdoor, free. AE, CB, DC, DISC, MC, V.

▤ Ramada Inn

1200 SW 24th Ave, 73072; tel 405/321-0110 or toll free 800/2-RAMADA; fax 405/360-5629. Exit 108B off I-35. Very basic, with easy access to I-35. **Rooms:** 150 rms and stes. CI 1pm/CO noon. Nonsmoking rms avail. **Amenities:** ▨ A/C, cable TV, dataport. Some rooms have coffeemakers. **Services:** ✕ ▨ ⌂ ⌁ Only small pets allowed. **Facilities:** ⛨ ▣ ⅙ 1 restaurant (see "Restaurants" below), 1 bar (w/entertainment). **Rates:** $46 S; $48 D; $75–$105 ste. Extra person $6. Children under age 10 stay free. Parking: Outdoor, free. AE, DC, DISC, MC, V.

▤ ▤ ▤ Residence Inn By Marriott

2681 Jefferson St, 73072; tel 405/366-0900 or toll free 800/331-3131; fax 405/360-6552. Pleasant property offering apartmentlike accommodations in a quiet area. **Rooms:** 126 stes and effic. CI 3pm/CO noon. Nonsmoking rms avail. **Amenities:** ▨ ⌂ ▣ A/C, cable TV w/movies, refrig. All units w/terraces, some w/fireplaces. **Services:** ▨ ⌂ ⌁ Masseur. VCRs and movie rentals available. Complimentary beverages and snacks Mon–Thurs evenings. Free cookouts Thurs nights in summer. **Facilities:** ⛨ ▧ ▣ ⅙ Basketball, volleyball, whirlpool, playground, washer/dryer. Free access to YMCA facilities. Sports court offers basketball, tennis, and other sports. **Rates (CP):** Peak (Mar–Sept) $89–$109 ste; $89–$109 effic. Children under age 18 stay free. Lower rates off-season. Parking: Outdoor, free. AE, CB, DC, DISC, JCB, MC, V.

MOTELS

▤ ▤ ▤ Guest Inn

2543 W Main St, 73069; tel 405/360-1234 or toll free 800/460-4619; fax 405/360-1234. Downtown exit off I-35. Recently remodeled, with access to I-35 and area restaurants. **Rooms:** 110 rms. CI 7am/CO noon. Nonsmoking rms avail. **Amenities:** ▨ ⌂ A/C, satel TV. Some units w/terraces. Rooms facing pool have small patio with plastic chairs. **Services:** ▧ ▨ ⌂ ⌁ Small pets only. Denny's restaurant next door provides 24-hour room service. **Facilities:** ⛨ ▣ ⅙ Washer/dryer. **Rates:** $40 S; $50–$60 D. Extra person $4. Children under age 17 stay free. Parking: Outdoor, free. AE, CB, DC, DISC, MC, V.

▤ ▤ The Stratford House Inn

225 N Interstate Dr, 73069; tel 405/329-7194; fax 405/329-7194 ext 123. Exit 109 off I-35. Simple hotel convenient to I-35 and area restaurants. **Rooms:** 40 rms. CI noon/CO 11am. Nonsmoking rms avail. Two of four walls in rooms are brick. Bathrooms are very nice, and tubs in every unit have bubble jets. **Amenities:** ▨ A/C, cable TV. All units w/whirlpools. **Services:** ⌂ ⌁ **Facilities:** ⅙ **Rates (CP):** $35–$41 S; $48 D. Extra person $3. Children under age 12 stay free. Parking: Outdoor, free. AE, CB, DC, DISC, MC, V.

▤ Thunderbird Lodge

1430 24th Ave SW, 73072; tel 405/329-6990 or toll free 800/432-2473; fax 405/360-4072. Exit 108B off I-35, right on 24th Ave. Standard, no-frills motel with nice landscaping. **Rooms:** 97 rms, stes, and effic. CI 1pm/CO 11am. Nonsmoking rms avail. Carpet is old and worn, but bathrooms are very nice. **Amenities:** ▨ A/C, satel TV. Dishes for suites available for extra charge. **Services:** ▨ ⌁ Books available in lobby. **Facilities:** ⛨ ⅙ Washer/dryer. **Rates:** $37 S or D; $44 ste; $39 effic. Extra person $3. Children under age 10 stay free. Parking: Outdoor, free. AE, CB, DC, DISC, MC, V.

RESTAURANTS ⑪

Arthur's

In Ramada Inn, 1200 SW 24th Ave; tel 405/321-0110. Exit 108B (Lindsey St) off I-35. **American.** A small restaurant offering casual dining in a room where the light from antique-style street lamps reflects off an attractive glass wall. Fare consists of sandwiches and five kinds of steaks. **FYI:** Reservations accepted. **Open:** Breakfast Mon–Sun 6–11am; lunch Mon–Sun 11am–1:30pm; dinner Tues–Sat 5–9pm. **Prices:** Main courses $6–$16. AE, MC, V. ⅙

Border Crossing Restaurante Y Cantina

606 W Main St; tel 405/364-7617. Main St/Downtown exit off I-35. **Southwestern.** Norman's oldest Mexican restaurant seems like a small place, but it actually houses four separate cozy dining areas and two bars. The restaurant is dimly lit at night, so take special care to note the Native American and Mexican artwork covering the walls. Smoked chicken flautas and the green chile special are popular; original house specialties include smoked shrimp and crab enchiladas. **FYI:** Reservations not accepted. Children's menu. **Open:** Mon–Thurs 11:30am–10pm, Fri–Sat 11:30am–11pm, Sun 5–10pm. **Prices:** Main courses $5–$9. AE, MC, V. ▦ ⅙

★ Indian Hills Inn

6221 N Interstate Rd; tel 405/364-7577. **Seafood/Steak.** The large, noisy room of this very popular restaurant has a dining hall atmosphere. The steaks, considered among the best in town, come prepared 10 different ways. Also seafood, chicken, and pork dishes. **FYI:** Reservations accepted. Children's menu. **Open:** Mon–Sat 5–10pm, Sun 5–9pm. **Prices:** Main courses $7–$26. AE, MC, V. ⅙

★ Interurban Restaurant

115 W Main St; tel 405/364-7942. Main St/Downtown exit off I-35. **Eclectic.** This microbrewery housed in the old Norman Train Depot (and retaining its brick walls and archways) is a fun place to go with family or friends. Five different beers are brewed on premises; eats include salads, burgers, pasta, and Mexican dishes, but the house specialty is wood-fired brick-oven pizza. The restaurant's famous Honey Blonde Ale and Honey Blonde muffins are served with many meals. **FYI:** Reservations not accepted. Children's menu. Additional locations: 50 Penn Place, Oklahoma City (tel 840-1911); 1301 E Danforth, Edmond (tel 348-2792). **Open:** Sun–Thurs 11am–10pm, Fri–Sat 11–11pm. **Prices:** Main courses $6–$15. AE, CB, DC, DISC, MC, V. ▦ ⅙

Legends

1313 W Lindsey; tel 405/329-8888. Lindsey exit off I-35. **Continental.** This award-winning restaurant is furnished with pieces from the Huskings Hotel, Oklahoma City's first state capitol building. Its dimly lit interior features local artists' works hanging on the walls; window seating, overlooking the patio, is considered an honor. Be sure to save room for the delicious homemade desserts. **FYI:** Reservations not accepted. Children's menu. **Open:** Mon–Sat 11am–11pm, Sun 10am–10pm. **Prices:** Main courses $6–$19. AE, CB, DC, DISC, MC, V. 🖤 &

Luciano's

1816 W Lindsey; tel 405/366-1800. Lindsey exit off I-35. **Italian/Steak.** A fairly quiet restaurant with separate rooms for smokers and nonsmokers that makes a good choice for casual or romantic dining. Local artist's bright, semi-abstract works adorn the walls. House specialties include salmon Wellington and veal scaloppine. **FYI:** Reservations accepted. **Open:** Mon–Thurs 5–10pm, Fri–Sat 5–10:30pm, Sun 5–9pm. **Prices:** Main courses $8–$17. AE, CB, DC, DISC, MC, V. &

Tulio's Mexican Restaurant

In Robinson Crossing Shopping Center, 1350 N Interstate Dr; tel 405/364-6700. Robinson St exit off I-35. **Mexican/Tex-Mex.** A cheerful, colorful, and casual restaurant that offers both traditional Mexican specialties and Tex-Mex favorites. The dining area is decorated with flags, piñatas, colored rugs and blankets, and huge strings of dried peppers. House specialties include the fajitas al carbón, menudo, and the huevos rancheros, but for a taste of the Mexican exotic, the barbacoa (steamed, shredded beef tongue) is recommended. **FYI:** Reservations accepted. Children's menu. **Open:** Sun–Thurs 10:30am–10:30pm, Fri–Sat 11am–midnight. **Prices:** Main courses $5–$17. AE, DC, DISC, MC, V. 📷 &

ATTRACTIONS 🏛

University of Oklahoma Museum of Art

Fred Jones Art Center, 410 W Boyd; tel 405/325-3272. The center includes changing exhibitions of contemporary student and local artists' work. The permanent collection contains an international selection of African, Oriental, and European paintings, sculptures, and artifacts. **Open:** Tues–Wed and Fri 10am–4:30pm, Fri 10am–9pm. **Free**

Oklahoma Museum of Natural History

1335 Asp Ave; tel 405/325-4712. The collection, numbering over 5 million items, includes a 10,000-year-old mammoth skeleton, bird and mammal fossils, Spiro Mounds artifacts, and Greek and Roman antiquities. Films, lectures, and special events on topics such as Native Americans and dinosaurs are given. **Open:** Tues–Fri 10am–5pm, Sat–Sun 2–5pm. **Free**

Oklahoma City

See also Norman, Shawnee

Established by settlers in the Great Land Rush of 1889, Oklahoma City grew from a collection of tents into the state's capital and largest city. Centrally located in the state and surrounded by a crescent of suburban communities, this metro area supports a philharmonic orchestra, resident ballet company, theater, and fine museums. Oklahoma City is the site of the Red Earth Festival in June, the country's largest celebration of Native American culture. **Information:** Oklahoma City Convention & Visitors Bureau, 123 Park Ave, Oklahoma City, 73102-9028 (tel 405/297-8912 or toll free 800/225-5652).

PUBLIC TRANSPORTATION

The **Metro Transit (MT)** offers citywide bus service along 24 local routes, and 4 commuter routes. The standard fare is $1, 50¢ for seniors and disabled passengers. Children under five ride free. Exact change required. For information call 405/235-7433.

HOTELS 🏨

🏢🏢 Best Western Santa Fe Inn

6101 N Santa Fe, 73118 (Nichols Hills); tel 405/848-1919 or toll free 800/369-7223; fax 405/840-1581. 63rd St exit off I-44, I-235/US 77. Respectable hotel with large corporate clientele, located about 10 minutes from nearby racetrack and close to attractions. **Rooms:** 96 rms and stes. CI 3pm/CO 11am. Nonsmoking rms avail. Rooms are clean but decor is a little garish with bright floral spreads, purple carpet, and Spanish-style art. Even-numbered rooms larger than odd-numbered rooms. **Amenities:** 🛁 📶 A/C, cable TV. Some units w/terraces, 1 w/whirlpool. Executive king rooms have mini-refrigerator and microwave. **Services:** ✕ 🖨 🛎 **Facilities:** 🖼 🏊 & 1 restaurant, 1 bar, whirlpool. **Rates (BB):** $56 S; $63 D; $65–$125 ste. Extra person $7. Children under age 12 stay free. Parking: Outdoor, free. AE, CB, DC, DISC, MC, V.

🏢🏢🏢 Clarion Hotel & Conference Center

4345 N Lincoln, 73105; tel 405/528-2741 or toll free 800/741-2741; fax 405/525-8185. Lincoln Blvd exit off I-44 or I-235. Quality hotel with spacious hallways, mini-lobby on each floor, and furnishings originally ordered for the Jim and Tammy Faye Bakker Hotel. Good rates for services provided. Located near racetrack and National Cowboy Hall of Fame. **Rooms:** 311 rms and stes. Executive level. CI 3pm/CO noon. Nonsmoking rms avail. **Amenities:** 🛁 📶 A/C, cable TV w/movies, dataport, bathrobes. **Services:** ✕ 🍽 🛎 🧺 Car-rental desk, babysitting. Pets allowed if under 15 lbs. Complimentary beverages and hors d'oeuvres offered, and complimentary papers delivered Mon–Fri. **Facilities:** 🖼 📷 🏋 🎱 💻 & 1 restaurant (see "Restaurants" below), 1 bar, racquetball. **Rates (CP):** $92 S; $102 D; $175–$225 ste. Extra person $10. Children under age 18 stay free. Parking: Outdoor, free. AE, CB, DC, DISC, MC, V.

≡≡≡ Courtyard by Marriott
4301 Highline Blvd, 73108; tel 405/946-6500 or toll free 800/321-2211; fax 405/946-7638. Meridian Exit off I-40. Convenient to I-40, the Will Rogers World Airport, and many local restaurants. **Rooms:** 149 rms and stes. CI 3:30pm/CO 1pm. Nonsmoking rms avail. Nicely furnished rooms. **Amenities:** A/C, satel TV w/movies, dataport, voice mail. All units w/terraces. Balconies have seating. **Services:** **Facilities:** 1 restaurant (bkfst only), 1 bar, whirlpool, washer/dryer. Small gazebo and courtyard with plenty of seating and raised sunbathing deck. **Rates:** Peak (May–Aug) $81 S; $91 D; $99–$109 ste. Extra person $10. Children under age 18 stay free. Lower rates off-season. Parking: Outdoor, free. AE, DC, DISC, MC, V.

≡≡≡ Embassy Suites
1815 S Meridian Ave, 73108; tel 405/682-6000 or toll free 800/362-2779; fax 405/682-9835. About 1 mi S of I-40. A few miles from Celebration Station with go-carts, miniature golf, and games, this property is a good fit for families or anyone interested in above-average accommodations. Pleasant atrium with fountain. **Rooms:** 236 stes. CI 2pm/CO noon. Nonsmoking rms avail. Living room sports Southwestern decor. Extra sink/cabinet space in bedroom. **Amenities:** A/C, satel TV w/movies, refrig, voice mail. Some units w/terraces. TVs in bedrooms and living area. Dataports available. **Services:** Babysitting. Security patrol at night. **Facilities:** 2 restaurants, 1 bar, spa, sauna, whirlpool, washer/dryer. **Rates (BB):** $135 ste. Extra person $10. Children under age 12 stay free. Parking: Outdoor, free. AE, CB, DC, DISC, JCB, MC, V.

≡≡≡ Fifth Season Hotel
6200 N Robinson, 73118; tel 405/843-5558 or toll free 800/682-0049, 800/522-9458 in OK; fax 405/840-8410. Just S of Broadway Extension. Remington Park Racetrack, the Cowboy Hall of Fame, the zoo, and other attractions are minutes away from this better-than-average hotel. Accessible to major interstates. **Rooms:** 202 rms and stes. CI 2pm/CO noon. Nonsmoking rms avail. Large rooms, but some need new carpeting. **Amenities:** A/C, cable TV. Some units w/whirlpools. **Services:** Social director. Complimentary cocktails 5–7pm each evening. **Facilities:** 1 restaurant, 1 bar, games rm, sauna, whirlpool, washer/dryer. Pleasant restaurant with atrium seating near lovely fountain. **Rates (BB):** $79 S; $89 D; $65–$95 ste. Extra person $10. Children under age 12 stay free. Parking: Outdoor, free. AE, CB, DC, DISC, MC, V.

≡≡ Hampton Inn I-40 Airport
1905 S Meridian Ave, 73108; tel 405/682-2080 or toll free 800/HAMPTON; fax 405/682-3662. About 1 mi S of I-40. Standard chain hotel offering acceptable accommodations.

Rooms: 156 rms and stes. CI 2pm/CO noon. Nonsmoking rms avail. **Amenities:** A/C, cable TV, dataport. **Services:** Car-rental desk. **Facilities:** Access to nearby weight room with pass from front desk. **Rates (CP):** Peak (May–Oct) $63 S; $73 D; $97 ste. Extra person $10. Children under age 12 stay free. Lower rates off-season. Parking: Outdoor, free. AE, CB, DC, DISC, MC, V.

≡≡≡ Hilton Inn Northwest
2945 NW Expwy, 73112; tel 405/848-4811 or toll free 800/848-4811; fax 405/842-4328. At May Ave. The only Hilton in Oklahoma, this property has recently completed a $6 million renovation. Close to the Baptist Medical Center. Good value. **Rooms:** 212 rms and stes. Executive level. CI 3pm/CO noon. Nonsmoking rms avail. **Amenities:** A/C, cable TV w/movies, dataport, voice mail. 1 unit w/whirlpool. Robes, irons, and ironing boards available in honors floor rooms. **Services:** Babysitting. **Facilities:** 1 restaurant, 1 bar (w/entertainment), whirlpool. Very large pool and 14-seat hot tub. **Rates:** Peak (Mar–Sept) $89–$129 S; $99–$139 D; $175–$299 ste. Extra person $10. Children under age 18 stay free. Lower rates off-season. Parking: Outdoor, free. AE, CB, DC, DISC, MC, V.

≡≡≡ Meridian Plaza Hotel
2101 S Meridian Ave, 73108; tel 405/685-4000 or toll free 800/622-7666; fax 405/685-0574. Just S of jct I-40 and Meridian. Pleasant hotel with fun dome including pool, pool tables, and video games. Perfect for families with young children. Easy access to I-40, the Will Rogers World Airport, and local restaurants. **Rooms:** 245 rms and stes. CI 3pm/CO noon. Nonsmoking rms avail. **Amenities:** A/C, cable TV w/movies, dataport. Some units w/whirlpools. Suites have dry bar. **Services:** Happy hour 4–7pm with free hors d'oeuvres. **Facilities:** 1 restaurant, 1 bar, games rm, spa, steam rm, whirlpool. **Rates:** $57 S; $63 D; $75 ste. Extra person $6. Parking: Outdoor, free. Weekend rate $48/night single or double. AE, DC, DISC, MC, V.

≡≡≡ Oklahoma City Marriott
3233 NW Expwy, 73112; tel 405/842-6633 or toll free 800/228-9290; fax 405/840-5338. Pleasant property with small lobby overlooking courtyard pool area, located across from Baptist Medical Center. **Rooms:** 354 rms and stes. Executive level. CI 3pm/CO noon. Nonsmoking rms avail. **Amenities:** A/C, satel TV w/movies, dataport, voice mail. Some units w/terraces, 1 w/whirlpool. All rooms have irons and ironing boards. **Services:** Babysitting can be arranged with 48 hours notice. Delta and American Airlines have desks in lobby. **Facilities:** 2 restaurants (see "Restaurants" below), 1 bar (w/entertainment), spa, sauna, whirlpool, washer/dryer. Large pool surrounded by trees for privacy, with men's and women's lockers. **Rates:** $129 S; $139 D; $175–$350 ste. Extra person $10. Children under age 17 stay free. Parking: Outdoor, free. AE, CB, DC, DISC, ER, JCB, MC, V.

≣≣≣ **Residence Inn by Marriott**
4361 W Reno, 73107; tel 405/942-4500 or toll free 800/
331-3131; fax 405/942-7777. 5 mi N of Will Rogers World
Airport. Comfortable, apartmentlike accommodations near
I-44 and accessible from I-35. Good choice for business
travelers. **Rooms:** 135 stes and effic. CI 3pm/CO noon.
Nonsmoking rms avail. Accommodations vary from studio
apartments to two-bedroom units. **Amenities:** 🛁 🕹 🎬 A/C,
satel TV, refrig. Some units w/terraces, some w/fireplaces.
All rooms have kitchens. **Services:** 🚐 📠 🧺 🐕 Babysitting.
Children's program one day per week. **Facilities:** 🏋 🍸1 ⛳35
🏊 Basketball, volleyball, whirlpool, washer/dryer. On-site
sport court available for badminton, basketball, tennis, etc.
Also access to All-American Fitness Center. **Rates (CP):** $96–
$116 ste; $96–$116 effic. Children under age 18 stay free.
Parking: Outdoor, free. AE, CB, DC, DISC, ER, JCB, MC, V.

≣≣≣≣ **The Waterford Hotel**
6300 Waterford Blvd, 73118 (Nichols Hills); tel 405/
848-4782 or toll free 800/992-2009; fax 405/848-7810. This
luxury hotel employs a full-time florist to keep the beautiful
public areas bright with floral arrangements. Located in a
quiet suburban area 20 minutes from the Will Rogers Airport. **Rooms:** 197 rms and stes. Executive level. CI 3pm/CO
noon. Nonsmoking rms avail. Separate mirrored sitting area
with vanity outside bathrooms. **Amenities:** 🛁 🕹 🎬 A/C, cable
TV w/movies, dataport. Some units w/terraces, 1
w/whirlpool. **Services:** ✕ 🚐 🆅🅿 🚐 📠 🧺 Masseur, babysitting. **Facilities:** 🏋 🍴 ⛳300 🏊 2 restaurants (see "Restaurants"
below), 1 bar (w/entertainment), spa, sauna, steam rm,
whirlpool. Poolside meal and cocktail service available. **Rates:**
$118 S or D; $145 ste. Extra person $10. Children under age
18 stay free. Parking: Outdoor, free. AE, CB, DC, DISC, MC,
V.

MOTELS

≣≣ **Best Western Inn at Hensley's**
I-40 and Country Club Rd, El Reno, 73036; tel 405/
262-6490 or toll free 800/528-1234; fax 405/262-7642. Exit
123 off I-40. Basic motel located along the interstate with
reasonable rooms and prices. **Rooms:** 60 rms. CI 11am/CO
11am. Nonsmoking rms avail. **Amenities:** 🛁 A/C, satel TV.
Services: 🧺 🐕 Only small pets allowed. **Facilities:** 🏋 ⛳30 🏊
1 restaurant, washer/dryer. **Rates (BB):** Peak (Apr–Sept) $43
S; $48 D. Extra person $4. Children under age 12 stay free.
Lower rates off-season. Parking: Outdoor, free. AE, CB, DC,
DISC, MC, V.

≣≣≣ **Best Western Saddleback Inn**
4300 SW 3rd St, 73108; tel 405/947-7000 or toll free 800/
228-3903; fax 405/948-7636. Near jct I-40 and Meridian.
Conveniently located near I-40, within 10 minutes of major
attractions. Cozy lobby with small fountains. **Rooms:** 220 rms
and stes. CI 1pm/CO noon. Nonsmoking rms avail. Small
rooms. **Amenities:** 🛁 🕹 🎬 A/C, satel TV, dataport. **Services:**
✕ 🚐 📠 🧺 🐕 Car-rental desk. Complimentary USA Today.

In summer, barbecue at pool on Tuesday for $8. **Facilities:**
🏋 🍴 ⛳300 🏊 1 restaurant, 1 bar, sauna, whirlpool, washer/
dryer. Spacious pool area with plenty of outdoor seating.
Rates (CP): $58 S; $65 D; $68–$75 ste. Extra person $7.
Children under age 18 stay free. Parking: Outdoor, free. AE,
CB, DC, DISC, MC, V.

≣≣ **Carlyle Motel**
3600 NW 39th Expwy, 73112; tel 405/946-3355 or toll free
800/299-3355. At Park Lane. Clean, basic motel with rooms
grouped by threes in small, separate buildings. The Will
Rogers public park is behind the building, and Lake Heffner
and the state fairgrounds are a short distance away. **Rooms:**
22 rms. CI open/CO noon. Nonsmoking rms avail.
Amenities: 🛁 A/C, cable TV. **Services:** 🧺 🐕 Only small
pets allowed. **Facilities:** 🏋 **Rates:** $28–$30 S; $36–$38 D.
Children under age 14 stay free. Parking: Outdoor, free. AE,
DISC, MC, V.

≣≣ **Comfort Inn**
4017 NW 39th Expwy, 73112; tel 405/947-0038 or toll free
800/628-5011; fax 405/946-7450. On OK 66, 1 mi W of exit
123B off I-44. Very basic but dependable motel located 15
minutes from Will Rogers World Airport, Remington Racetrack, and Whitewater Amusement Park. Adequate for families traveling on a budget. **Rooms:** 111 rms, stes, and effic. CI
1pm/CO noon. Nonsmoking rms avail. Bathrooms are clean
but in need of small repairs (stains on tubs, cracks in ceiling).
Amenities: 🛁 🎬 A/C, cable TV w/movies. King suites have
small refrigerators and microwaves; dataports available in
some rooms. **Services:** 📠 🧺 🐕 Movies/VCRs rented at
front desk. **Facilities:** 🏋 ⛳70 🏊 Washer/dryer. **Rates (CP):**
$46–$52 S or D; $54–$61 ste; $61 effic. Extra person $6.
Children under age 18 stay free. Parking: Outdoor, free. AE,
CB, DC, DISC, EC, MC, V.

≣≣ **Days Inn Northwest**
2801 NW 39th Expwy, 73112; tel 405/946-0741 or toll free
800/992-3297; fax 405/942-0181. May exit off I-44. Newly
remodeled in 1993, this hotel is great for families because of
its large pool and proximity to Frontier City and the Wet 'n
Wild water park. **Rooms:** 192 rms and stes. CI 4pm/CO
11am. Nonsmoking rms avail. **Amenities:** 🛁 A/C, cable TV,
dataport. **Services:** ✕ 🚐 📠 🧺 🐕 **Facilities:** 🏋 ⛳450 🏊 1
restaurant, 1 bar, washer/dryer. **Rates:** Peak (Mar–Aug)
$39–$45 S; $55–$65 D; $75–$89 ste. Extra person $6.
Lower rates off-season. Parking: Outdoor, free. AE, CB, DC,
DISC, MC, V.

≣ **Holiday Inn North**
12001 NE Expwy, 73131; tel 405/478-0400 or toll free 800/
HOLIDAY; fax 405/478-2774. 122nd St exit off I-35 N;
Heffner exit off I-35 S. This very basic motel has some
renovations planned, and needs them. Located next to Frontier City theme park, it's suited for families with small
children. Easy access to I-35 and I-44. **Rooms:** 210 rms. CI
3pm/CO noon. Nonsmoking rms avail. King rooms have sofa

beds. **Amenities:** 🛏 ⚘ A/C, satel TV w/movies, dataport. **Services:** ✗ ⊠ ⊰ ⊲ **Facilities:** 🔗 200 ⚿ 1 restaurant, 1 bar, basketball, volleyball, games rm, sauna, whirlpool, playground, washer/dryer. **Rates:** Peak (Mem Day–Aug) $65 S or D. Children under age 18 stay free. Lower rates off-season. Parking: Outdoor, free. AE, DC, DISC, MC, V.

🏨🏨 Holiday Inn Northwest

3535 NW 39th Expwy, 73112; tel 405/947-2351 or toll free 800/HOLIDAY; fax 405/948-7752. Exit 123B off I-44. Average family motel with rooms in need of remodeling, but in a great location—near National Cowboy Hall of Fame, Remington Racetrack, and zoo. **Rooms:** 243 rms and stes. CI 2pm/CO noon. Nonsmoking rms avail. Connecting rooms only available with double units. **Amenities:** 🛏 ⚘ A/C, satel TV w/movies, dataport. **Services:** ✗ 🚐 ⊠ ⊰ ⊲ No cats allowed—dogs only. **Facilities:** 🔗 450 ⚿ 1 restaurant, 1 bar, games rm, washer/dryer. Large pool and game room. Access to nearby All American Fitness Center. **Rates:** $51–$53 S; $58–$60 D; $95 ste. Extra person $7. Children under age 18 stay free. Parking: Outdoor, free. AE, CB, DC, DISC, JCB, MC, V.

🏨🏨 La Quinta Inn South

8315 I-35 S, 73149; tel 405/631-8661 or toll free 800/531-5900; fax 405/631-1892. Exit 121A off I-35 S. Southwestern-styled chain motel. Close to Will Rogers Airport. **Rooms:** 122 rms and stes. CI 2pm/CO noon. Nonsmoking rms avail. **Amenities:** 🛏 ⚘ A/C, satel TV w/movies. **Services:** ⊠ ⊰ ⊲ **Facilities:** 🔗 30 ⚿ **Rates (CP):** $53–$60 S; $61–$68 D; $70 ste. Extra person $5. Children under age 18 stay free. Parking: Outdoor, free. Special rates for AARP members. AE, CB, DC, DISC, MC, V.

🏨🏨 Ramada Inn Airport South

6800 I-35 S, 73149; tel 405/631-3321 or toll free 800/2-RAMADA; fax 405/631-3489. Exit 122A off I-35. This motel at the South Crossroads Mall is great for families. A Discovery Zone is across the street, and many restaurants and entertainment opportunities are nearby. **Rooms:** 120 rms. CI 1pm/CO noon. Nonsmoking rms avail. Some rooms have interior access. Mini-suites available. **Amenities:** 🛏 ⚘ A/C, satel TV w/movies. Hairdryer on request. **Services:** ✗ 🚐 ⊠ ⊰ ⊲ Pets 20 lbs and under allowed. 24-hour maid service available. **Facilities:** 🔗 170 ⚿ 1 restaurant, 1 bar. **Rates:** $48 S; $52–$59 D. Extra person $5. Children under age 17 stay free. Parking: Outdoor, free. AE, CB, DC, DISC, JCB, MC, V.

🏨🏨🏨 Richmond Suites

1600 NW Expwy, 73118; tel 405/840-1440 or toll free 800/843-1440; fax 405/843-4272. All-suite hotel located near racetrack, Cowboy Hall of Fame, and zoo. **Rooms:** 51 stes. CI 2:30pm/CO noon. Nonsmoking rms avail. Rooms are spacious; poolside suites have tiled breakfast areas. **Amenities:** 🛏 ⚘ 📺 A/C, cable TV, refrig, dataport. Some units w/terraces, some w/fireplaces. **Services:** ✗ 🚐 ⊠ ⊰ ⊲ Social

director. Pet deposit $50. **Facilities:** 🔗 35 ⚿ 1 restaurant (lunch and dinner only), 1 bar (w/entertainment). Shade trees surround nice pool area. **Rates (CP):** $88–$150 ste. Extra person $10. Children under age 17 stay free. Parking: Outdoor, free. AE, DC, DISC, MC, V.

🏨 Travelers Inn

504 S Meridian Ave, 73108; tel 405/942-8294 or toll free 800/633-8300; fax 405/947-3529. Just N of jct I-40. No-frills property located near Celebration Station (games/mini-golf) and Will Rogers World Airport. **Rooms:** 136 rms and stes. CI 2pm/CO 11am. Nonsmoking rms avail. **Amenities:** 🛏 A/C, satel TV. **Services:** ⊠ ⊰ **Facilities:** 🔗 ⚿ Washer/dryer. **Rates:** $31 S; $38 D; $44–$51 ste. Extra person $4. Children under age 11 stay free. Parking: Outdoor, free. AE, CB, DC, DISC, MC, V.

RESTAURANTS 🍴

Ann's Chicken Fry House

4106 NW 39th St; tel 405/943-8915. On OK 66. **Regional American.** Designed in the style of the 1950s and '60s, this diner has it all: rock 'n' roll, Elvis and Marilyn posters, authentic postcards, prints, license plates, and other memorabilia. An original, pink, fin-tailed car is parked at the entrance. Menu includes steaks, barbecue, burgers, sandwiches, salads, and whips, malts, and Coke floats. **FYI:** Reservations not accepted. Children's menu. No liquor license. **Open:** Mon–Sat 11am–9pm. **Prices:** Main courses $3–$8. No CC. 👥 ⚿

Applewood's

4301 SW 3rd St; tel 405/947-8484. 1 block E of Meridian. **Regional American/Steak.** A large restaurant appropriate for casual dining or special meals, with several tastefully decorated dining rooms. Upholstered rolling chairs provide comfortable seating at the tables or at the large bar. Specialties includes apple fritters, homemade rolls, individual pot roast, and baked pork chops. There is a limited dietetic selection on the menu with low-fat, low-sodium items. The lunch menu includes sandwiches, burgers, and steaks. **FYI:** Reservations not accepted. Children's menu. **Open:** Lunch Mon–Thurs 11am–2pm, Sun 11am–3pm; dinner Mon–Thurs 5–10pm, Fri 5–11pm, Sat 4–11pm, Sun 4:30–10pm. **Prices:** Main courses $9–$18. AE, CB, DC, DISC, MC, V. ⚿

★ Cattlemen's Cafe

1309 S Agnew; tel 405/236-0416. Agnew exit off I-40. **Steak.** The oldest restaurant in the state, this fun and historic place is worth a visit. When it originally opened its doors in 1910, it served ranchers, cowboys, and cattle haulers; today, it is filled with every type of customer imaginable. Walls are covered with sketches of famous cowboys and actors like John Wayne and Gene Autry. The restaurant boasts that its prime, aged steaks are the best around. Also available are lamb fries, fried catfish and shrimp, homemade rolls. **FYI:** Reservations not accepted. Children's menu. **Open:** Sun–Thurs 6am–10pm, Fri–Sat 6am–midnight. **Prices:** Main courses $7–$18. AE, CB, DC, DISC, MC, V. 🖼️ &

Charlie Newton's

1025 NW 70th St; tel 405/840-0115. E of Western St. **American/Steak.** Created from three separate houses, Charlie Newton's offers several separate cozy and quiet dining areas. Dark wooden furniture, green walls, and artwork with an equestrian motif add charm and style. Salads, pasta, fish, chicken, pork, and steaks are available (the chicken-fried New York strip steak is quite tasty). Meals include delicious rolls (served with apple butter) and dessert. **FYI:** Reservations recommended. **Open:** Mon–Thurs 5–9pm, Fri–Sat 5–10pm. **Prices:** Main courses $9–$23. AE, MC, V.

Chinatown Restaurant

6315 N Meridian; tel 405/722-3331. At 63rd St. **Chinese.** A simple Cantonese eatery decorated with Chinese-style lamps, tassels, and artwork representing "good health," "long life," and other happy wishes. Family-size dinners and lunch specials make this a great place for families with children. **FYI:** Reservations accepted. Children's menu. No liquor license. **Open:** Lunch Tues–Fri 11am–2pm, Sat 11am–5pm, Sun 11am–5pm; dinner Tues–Thurs 5–9:30pm, Fri 5–10pm, Sat 5–10pm, Sun 5–9:30pm. **Prices:** Main courses $5–$30. MC, V. 🖼️

Chinatown Restaurant

937 SW 59th St; tel 405/634-0271. **Chinese.** A relatively new establishment with standard Chinese restaurant decor but country music playing in the background. All the usual menu favorites are available. **FYI:** Reservations accepted. Children's menu. Beer and wine only. **Open:** Mon–Thurs 11am–9pm, Fri–Sat 11am–9pm, Sun noon–9pm. **Prices:** Main courses $3–$8. No CC.

Eagle's Nest

In United Founders Tower, 5900 Mosteller Dr; tel 405/840-5655. **Continental.** This rotating restaurant on the 20th floor of the United Founders Tower offers a full view of Oklahoma City and is a great choice for a special occasion. The wide-ranging menu features seafood fra diavlo (shrimp, scallops, and angel-hair pasta in a spicy marinara sauce)—recommended for those who relish spicy dishes—and filet mignon au poivre. Special menu offered for Jazz in the Round on Wednesday nights. **FYI:** Reservations recommended. Big band/jazz/rock. Dress code. **Open:** Lunch Sun–Fri 11am–2pm; dinner Mon–Thurs 6–10pm, Fri–Sat 6pm–midnight, Sun 6–9pm; brunch Sun 11am–2pm. **Prices:** Main courses $15–$24. AE, CB, DC, DISC, MC, V. 💜 🏔️

Eddy's Steak House

4227 N Meridian; tel 405/787-2944. **Seafood/Steak.** Great for either casual or special dining. Six separate dining rooms offer comfortable seating surrounded by silk flowers and plants. The restaurant has been serving 11 steak entrees and 5 seafood entrees for over 28 years, but there are other items

as well—lamb loin chops, ribs, and chicken. All entrees are served with Eddy's signature Lebanese hors d'oeuvres. **FYI:** Reservations recommended. Children's menu. **Open:** Mon–Sat 5–10:30pm. **Prices:** Main courses $10–$19. AE, CB, DC, DISC, MC, V. &

The Governor's Club

In Clarion Hotel & Conference Center, 4345 N Lincoln Blvd; tel 405/528-2741. Near I-235 exit off I-35. **Seafood/Steak.** An open kitchen provides an opportunity to view the chefs at work at this nicely furnished bistro. The small menu offers eight main entrees, the most popular being filet mignon and surf-and-turf. Hot apple pie in brandy butter is a specialty dessert. **FYI:** Reservations recommended. **Open:** Breakfast daily 6:30–11am; lunch Mon–Sat 11am–2pm; dinner daily 5–10pm; brunch Sun 11am–3pm. **Prices:** Main courses $12–$17. AE, CB, DC, DISC, MC, V. &

The Horny Toad Saloon and Restaurant

6714 N Western (Nichols Hills); tel 405/848-3070. Just off Broadway Extension. **Regional American/Eclectic.** A newer restaurant with a Western theme, as evidenced by framed original Western movie posters and story magazines plus a pair of John Wayne's chaps. Menu includes salads, chicken dishes, burgers, steaks, and seafood. The chicken tequila Santa Fe and deep-fried cheesecake are popular. **FYI:** Reservations not accepted. Children's menu. **Open:** Mon–Thurs 11am–midnight, Fri–Sat 11am–2am, Sun 5–11pm. **Prices:** Main courses $6–$17. AE, MC, V. 🖼️ &

Hunan Chinese Restaurant

In Casady Square, 9211 N Penn Place (The Village); tel 405/843-6233. I-35 to Britain Rd to Penn Place. **Chinese.** Pleasant Szechuan/Hunan restaurant with a central fountain and flower arrangements housed in oriental pots and vases. Cleopatra Chicken and Four Seasons Delight are menu favorites. **FYI:** Reservations recommended. Beer and wine only. Additional locations: 203 Hal Muldrow Dr, Norman (tel 360-0394); 1500 SW 74th St (tel 685-5288). **Open:** Daily 11am–10pm. **Prices:** Main courses $6–$20. AE, MC, V. &

JW's Steakhouse

In Oklahoma City Marriott, 3233 NW Expwy; tel 405/842-6633. **Seafood/Steak.** Named after its designer, J Willard Marriott Sr, this cozy, comfortable restaurant is perfect for business meals or a quiet, casual dinner. Cowboy-and-Indian artwork hangs from the walls. Steaks, filet mignon, and prime rib are the recommended specialties. Also available are chops, chicken, seafood, and a few salads. **FYI:** Reservations recommended. **Open:** Mon–Thurs 6–10pm, Fri–Sat 6–11pm. **Prices:** Main courses $14–$28. AE, CB, DC, DISC, MC, V. 🆅🅿 &

Laredo's Mexican Restaurant

936 NW 63rd St; tel 405/840-9772. W of Western St. **Mexican.** A great place for family dining, this Peruvian-owned restaurant featuring Mexican music and decor offers a unique approach to the usual Mexican eatery. The menu

includes eight lunch specials, plus salads, traditional dishes, and combination dinners. Fajitas are a favorite. Children under 13 eat for $2.50. **FYI:** Reservations not accepted. Children's menu. **Open:** Mon–Thurs 11am–10pm, Fri–Sun 11am–11pm. **Prices:** Main courses $6–$9. AE, CB, DC, DISC, MC, V.

Mamasita's
1121 NW 63rd St (Nichols Hills); tel 405/848-0541. W of Western. **Tex-Mex.** TVs, radio music, and fans hum over the booths and tables at this festive Tex-Mex eatery featuring splashy orange and pink decor. The only tequila bar in the city, it offers guests 27 brands from which to choose. Kids eat for 99¢. **FYI:** Reservations accepted. Rock. Children's menu. **Open:** Sun–Thurs 11am–10pm, Fri–Sat 11am–11pm. **Prices:** Main courses $5–$16. AE, CB, DC, DISC, MC, V.

Rita's Del Rio Cafe
5708 N May; tel 405/842-8185. Just N of NW Expwy. **Southwestern/Tex-Mex.** A casual sports bar and restaurant with lots of windows, plants, several TVs, a pool table, and video games. Menu includes burgers, salads, sandwiches, and Tex-Mex platters. **FYI:** Reservations accepted. Blues/jazz/rock. Children's menu. **Open:** Mon–Thurs 11am–11pm, Fri–Sat 11am–12:30am, Sun 11am–11:30pm. **Prices:** Main courses $5–$13. AE, MC, V.

Split-T
5701 N Western Ave; tel 405/848-2919. Western exit from I-44. **Burgers.** Split-T's first owner was an Oklahoma University football fan, and he named his restaurant after the team's wishbone offense formation. A very plain dining room, with some sports jerseys and photos on the walls, is the setting for charbroiled hamburgers, frankfurters, steaks, and chicken. Smoking allowed only in the upstairs bar. **FYI:** Reservations not accepted. Dancing/rock. **Open:** Mon–Sat 11am–10pm. **Prices:** Main courses $3–$12. AE, DC, DISC, MC, V.

Texanna Red's
4600 W Reno; tel 405/947-8665. ½ mi N of I-40 at Meridian. **Tex-Mex.** Decorated in Old West style, complete with 1940s and '50s movie posters, wagon wheels, and horse yokes, this is your basic Tex-Mex joint. The menu includes steaks, burgers, salads, along with fajitas and other typical fare. A lunch buffet and nightly specials are available Mon–Fri. The upstairs bar offers a limited menu along with pool tables and longer hours. **FYI:** Reservations not accepted. Children's menu. **Open:** Mon–Thurs 11am–10:30pm, Fri–Sat 11am–11pm, Sun 11:30am–10pm. **Prices:** Main courses $5–$16. AE, CB, DC, DISC, MC, V.

The Waterford Dining Room
In the Waterford Hotel, 6300 Waterford Blvd; tel 405/848-4782. **Seafood/Steak.** This dimly lit restaurant, furnished in dark colors and decorated with sketches on the walls, offers a limited menu of steaks, salmon, chicken, and ostrich and an extensive wine list. Semiformal attire encour-

aged. **FYI:** Reservations recommended. Blues/dancing/jazz. **Open:** Mon–Thurs 6–10pm, Fri–Sat 6–10pm. **Prices:** Main courses $15–$26. AE, CB, DC, DISC, MC, V.

ATTRACTIONS

Oklahoma State Capitol
NE 23rd St and Lincoln Blvd; tel 405/521-3356. The Roman Corinthian–style building features an oil well. Though it no longer pumps oil, the well serves as a monument to the state's great oil boom and its major source of wealth. On the grounds is the State Museum of History, featuring Native American artifacts. Daily tours on the hour. **Open:** Daily 8am–7pm. **Free**

Oklahoma Heritage Center
201 NW 14th St; tel 405/235-4458. The 1917 home of Judge RA Hefner, former mayor (1939–47) and state supreme court justice (1927–32). The first two floors have been restored and feature German, Early American, Italian, English, and French antique furniture, the highlight being a 1780 Louis XVI table. The third floor houses the Oklahoma Hall of Fame Galleries honoring distinguished Oklahomans since its induction in 1928. Also on the grounds are a memorial garden and chapel. **Open:** Mon–Sat 9am–5pm, Sun 1–5pm. **$**

Harn Homestead and 1889er Museum
313 NE 16th St; tel 405/235-4058. Built on land claimed during the Great Land Run of 1889, the pre-statehood farmhouse (circa 1904) is furnished with period pieces by the families of the 1889er Society. The stone and cedar barn contains antique farm implements. Also located on the grounds are the 1890 Shepherd House, an 1897 one-room school, and a 1900 working farm. **Open:** Tues–Sat 10am–4pm. **$**

Overholser Mansion
405 NW 15th St; tel 405/528-8485. Built in 1901 by Henry Overholser, one of the city's founders. The three-story Châteauesque mansion features Brussels lace curtains, English carpets, stained-glass windows, and period furnishings. Tours conducted on the hour. **Open:** Tues–Fri 10am–4pm, Sat–Sun 2–4pm. **Free**

Oklahoma City Art Museum on the Fairgrounds
3113 Pershing Blvd; tel 405/946-4477. Founded in 1936, the museum features a permanent collection of more than 3,000 works which include 13th- through 20th-century American and European paintings, prints, drawings, and sculptures. Changing exhibitions display the art of private collections and museums from around the world. Films, lectures, and educational displays accompany exhibits. **Open:** Tues–Sat 10am–5pm, Sun 1–5pm. **$$**

The 45th Infantry Division Museum
2145 NE 36th St; tel 405/424-5313. The only state-operated museum dedicated to military history displays objects and equipment relevant to the history of Oklahoma's citizen-

soldiers. More than 200 Bill Mauldin World War II cartoons depicting soldier life through "Willie and Joe," two typical GI characters, are on display. (The cartoons earned the artist a Pulitzer Prize.) Other exhibits include rare military weapons, vehicles, and aircraft. Special events held on Memorial Day and Veterans Day. **Open:** Tues–Fri 9am–4:15pm, Sat 10am–5pm, Sun 1–5pm. **Free**

National Cowboy Hall of Fame

1700 NE 63rd St; tel 405/478-2250. A monument to the men and women who pioneered the 17 western states. Visitors tour a typical Old West town, where each building is filled with 19th-century artifacts; the Rodeo Hall of Fame, where cowboys and cowgirls are immortalized in portraits and displays of their trophies, saddles, and lassoes; the Western Performers Hall of Fame, honoring the personalities who contributed to the Western film genre; and a 1,200-seat theater. Annual special events include the Chuck Wagon Gathering, the Cowboy Poetry Gathering, and the Bolo Ball. **Open:** Peak (Mem Day–Labor Day) daily 8:30am–6pm. Reduced hours off-season. **$$$**

Enterprise Square, USA

2501 E Memorial Rd; tel 405/425-5030. Entertainment complex with a multimedia show introducing visitors to the world of economics and the American free enterprise system. The 2½-hour tour includes interactive exhibits and singing dollar bills. **Open:** Mon–Sat 9am–5pm, Sun 1–4pm. **$$**

Oklahoma City Zoological Park

2101 NE 50th St; tel 405/424-3344. One of the oldest zoos in the Southwest. More than 2,500 animals are exhibited on 110 landscaped acres. Visitors can view gorillas, orangutans, and chimpanzees in a tropical forest setting, watch dolphin and sea lion shows, pet tame animals in the children's zoo, and ride a sky safari spanning the zoo grounds. A covered tram takes visitors on a narrated tour. **Open:** Peak (Apr–Sept) daily 9am–6pm. Reduced hours off-season. **$$**

Frontier City Theme Park

11501 NE Expwy; tel 405/478-2140. Offering more than 50 rides and live shows. Among the major thrill rides are the Time Warp (a 360° gigantic swing that resembles a clock), Jesse James' Treasure Mountain (where mine cars zigzag through the dark tunnels, culminating in a face-to-face encounter with the outlaw himself), and the Silver Bullet (a steel-track looping roller coaster featuring a 78-foot drop). Kiddie rides, special events, and summer concerts also offered. **Open:** Apr 13–Oct 27. Call for schedule. **$$$$**

White Water Bay

3908 W Reno; tel 405/948-7921. Water park featuring more than 30 water rides, slides, pools, and activities, including the 65-foot "free-fall" Acapulco Cliff Dive. The Kids Kove is a play area for children under eight, with kid-safe activities and soft-play characters such as an alligator and flamingo. The

Bay Club for teens is held on Tuesday nights and features music, dances, and contests. **Open:** May 11–Sept 8. Call for schedule. **$$$$**

Remington Park

1 Remington Place; tel 405/424-9000 or toll free 800/456-9000. Thoroughbred horse racing is held at this state-of-the-art, pari-mutuel track from fall to spring. Quarter horses, appaloosas, and paints run late-May through mid-July. Clubhouse; dining. **Open:** Call for schedule. **$$**

Okmulgee

See also Henryetta

An original Creek Council House, built by the Muscogee (Creek) Indians in 1878, is at the center of the town square and establishes this town's Native American personality. Dripping Springs and Okmulgee state parks offer seasonal recreation nearby. **Information:** Okmulgee Chamber of Commerce, 112 N Morton, PO Box 609, Okmulgee, 74447-0609 (tel 918/756-6172).

HOTEL 🏨

≣≣≣ Best Western

3499 N Wood Dr, 74447; tel 918/756-9200 or toll free 800/552-9201; fax 918/756-9200. On US 75. Standard chain accommodations. **Rooms:** 51 rms and stes. CI 3pm/CO 11am. Nonsmoking rms avail. All rooms have microwaves. **Amenities:** 🜇 A/C, cable TV, refrig. All units w/whirlpools. **Services:** 🖐 🤚 A continental breakfast is served on Sunday, when the restaurant is closed. Small pets allowed. **Facilities:** 🛝 ⎣75⎦ ⅙ 1 restaurant, 1 bar. **Rates:** $36–$52 D; $60–$75 ste. Extra person $5. Children under age 18 stay free. Parking: Outdoor, free. AE, CB, DC, DISC, ER, MC, V.

ATTRACTION 🏛

Creek Council House Museum

106 W 6th St; tel 918/756-2324. The original council house was constructed in 1878 by the Muscogee Creek tribe after their forced removal from tribal lands in Georgia and Alabama. Today, the house contains archives on the tribe's history, government, religion, and artists. Docent-guided tours available by arrangement. **Open:** Tues–Sat 10am–4:30pm. **Free**

Pauls Valley

South of Oklahoma City just off I-35, this charming community of brick streets and restored historic homes is the seat of Garvin County and a pleasant stop for picnics or relaxation. **Information:** Pauls Valley Chamber of Commerce, 112 E Paul, PO Box 638, Pauls Valley, 73075 (tel 405/238-6491).

MOTEL

≡≡ Days Inn
I-35 and OK 19 W, 73075; tel 405/238-7548 or toll free 800/325-2525. Newly remodeled, basic accommodations located about 30 minutes from Arbuckle Wilderness Area, an exotic animal theme park; great for traveling families. **Rooms:** 54 rms. CI noon/CO noon. Nonsmoking rms avail. **Amenities:** A/C, cable TV. **Services:** **Facilities:** **Rates (CP):** Peak (July–Sept) $36 S; $46 D. Extra person $5. Children under age 14 stay free. Lower rates off-season. Parking: Outdoor, free. AE, CB, DC, DISC, MC, V.

Perry

See also Stillwater

Founded in 1893 during the famous Cherokee Strip land rush, this community is the seat of Nobles County in north-central Oklahoma. Minutes away, Lake Carl Blackwell and Sooner Reservoir offer outdoor recreation. **Information:** Perry Chamber of Commerce, 300 6th St, PO Box 426, Perry, 73077 (tel 405/336-4684).

MOTELS

≡≡ Best Western Cherokee Strip Motel
I-35 and US 77, 73077; tel 405/336-2218 or toll free 800/528-1234; fax 405/336-9753. Exit 185 off I-35. Average motel. **Rooms:** 89 rms. CI 6am/CO noon. Nonsmoking rms avail. **Amenities:** A/C, satel TV. Some rooms have ceiling fans. **Services:** **Facilities:** 1 restaurant, 1 bar. **Rates:** $45 S; $51 D. Extra person $6. Children under age 12 stay free. Parking: Outdoor, free. Discounts offered for school groups. AE, CB, DC, DISC, MC, V.

≡ Dan-D-Motel
515 Fir St, 73077; tel 405/336-4463. On US 64, 2½ mi E of I-35. Hotel has outdated furnishings, but is clean and neat. Good choice for travelers on a budget. Century Park, a public park, is only a few blocks away. **Rooms:** 26 rms. CI noon/CO 11am. Nonsmoking rms avail. **Amenities:** A/C, cable TV. **Services:** **Facilities:** **Rates:** $18 S; $24 D. Extra person $2. Parking: Outdoor, free. AE, MC, V.

ATTRACTION

Cherokee Strip Museum
2617 Fir St; tel 405/336-2405. A complex of re-created and restored buildings depicting the history of pioneer life in the area. A one-room schoolhouse from 1895 features living history programs during the school year. Other exhibits include an antique dentist's office, a general store, and a barn with early farm machinery. On display are Native American artifacts from the settlement of the Cherokee Outlet. **Open:** Tues–Fri 9am–5pm, Sat–Sun 2–5pm. **Free**

Ponca City

Ponca City was settled in 1893 during the great rush into open land known as the Cherokee Strip land run. There are a number of historic sites and buildings, and Lake Ponca and Kaw Lake provide hunting, fishing, and water recreation. **Information:** Ponca City Convention & Visitors Bureau, 420 E Grand, PO Box 1109, Ponca City, 74601 (fax 405/765-2798).

HOTELS

≡ Days Inn
1415 E Bradley, 74604; tel 405/767-1406 or toll free 800/749-1406; fax 405/762-9589. At N 14th St. Average, no-frills motel in need of minor renovations, such as new carpeting. Near restaurants and only a couple of miles from downtown. **Rooms:** 59 rms. CI 1pm/CO 11am. Nonsmoking rms avail. King suites have sofa or recliner. **Amenities:** A/C, cable TV. 1 unit w/whirlpool. Some rooms have dataports. **Services:** **Facilities:** **Rates (CP):** $34 S; $36 D. Extra person $3. Children under age 12 stay free. Parking: Outdoor, free. AE, CB, DC, DISC, MC, V.

≡≡≡ Marland Estate Conference Center Hotel
901 Monument Rd, 74601; tel 405/767-0422 or toll free 800/532-7559; fax 405/762-8182. Ponca City exit off I-35, US 60 to US 77 N to Lake Rd, follow signs. Located on Marland Mansion Estate, hotel actually connects to mansion itself. In a quiet, secluded area, with easy access to major highways. **Rooms:** 35 rms and stes. CI 3pm/CO noon. Nonsmoking rms avail. Simple rooms. Gatehouse cottage has full kitchen. **Amenities:** A/C, cable TV. **Services:** Car-rental desk, babysitting. **Facilities:** **Rates (CP):** $40 S; $45 D; $89–$125 ste. Extra person $5. Children under age 12 stay free. Parking: Outdoor, free. Gatehouse cottage $125/day. AE, MC, V.

MOTEL

≡≡≡ Holiday Inn Ponca City
2215 N 14th St, 74601; tel 405/462-8311 or toll free 800/HOLIDAY; fax 405/765-0014. On US 77 N. Standard, clean motel just a few miles north of downtown, near many restaurants. **Rooms:** 139 rms and stes. CI noon/CO noon. Nonsmoking rms avail. King rooms have sofas. **Amenities:** A/C, dataport, voice mail. **Services:** Babysitting. **Facilities:** 1 restaurant, 1 bar. **Rates:** $52 S or D; $89 ste. Extra person $5. Children under age 18 stay free. Parking: Outdoor, free. AE, CB, DC, DISC, JCB, MC, V.

ATTRACTIONS

Marland Mansion and Estate
901 Monument Rd; tel 405/767-0420. The 1920s home of E W Marland, 10th governor of the state and oil baron. The 55-room mansion was modeled after an Italian Renaissance estate, featuring elaborate artwork and hand-painted ceilings.

Visitors tour exhibits pertaining to Oklahoma history and the oil boom. **Open:** Peak (June–Sept) daily 10am-4pm. Reduced hours off-season. **$$**

Pioneer Woman Museum
701 Monument Rd; tel 405/765-6108. Erected in 1930 at a cost of $300,000, this 30-foot bronze statue of a typical pioneer woman weighs 12,000 pounds. The nearby museum houses relics and mementos relating to the Oklahoma pioneer woman. **Open:** Tues–Sat 9am–5pm, Sun 1–5pm. **$**

Sallisaw

This Sequoyah County seat is a convenient stop for travelers on I-40. Best known as the opening locale for John Steinbeck's novel, *The Grapes of Wrath*, Sallisaw also is home to Bushy Creek and Sallisaw State Parks. **Information:** Sallisaw Chamber of Commerce, 111 N Elm, PO Box 251, Sallisaw, 74955 (tel 918/775-2558).

MOTELS 🏨

⬛⬛ Best Western Blue Ribbon Motor Inn
706 S Kerr Blvd, 74955; tel 918/775-6294 or toll free 800/554-9532; fax 918/775-6294. On US 59 S, exit 308 off I-40. Close to Blue Ribbon Downs Racetrack, with good highway/interstate access. **Rooms:** 81 rms and stes. CI open/CO 11am. Nonsmoking rms avail. Suites are one large room or two smaller, connecting rooms. **Amenities:** 🛁 A/C, cable TV. **Services:** ✕ 🛎 🍽 Linens changed daily on request. **Facilities:** 🏋 🏌 🏊 ⛴ 1 restaurant, whirlpool, washer/dryer. **Rates (BB):** $39 S; $45 D; $55–$120 ste. Extra person $5. Children under age 12 stay free. Parking: Outdoor, free. AE, CB, DC, DISC, MC, V.

⬛ Ramada Limited
1300 E Cherokee, 74955; tel 918/775-7791 or toll free 800/2-RAMADA; fax 918/775-7795. On US 64; exit 311 off I-40. No-frills motel located within miles of Blue Ribbon Downs Racetrack and close to many restaurants. **Rooms:** 49 rms. CI 2pm/CO noon. Nonsmoking rms avail. **Amenities:** 🛁 🍸 A/C, cable TV. **Services:** 🚐 🛎 🍽 **Facilities:** ⛴ ⛸ **Rates (CP):** $40 S; $44 D. Extra person $4. Children under age 19 stay free. Parking: Outdoor, free. AARP discounts avail. AE, CB, DC, DISC, EC, MC, V.

ATTRACTIONS 📷

Sequoyah's Home Site
OK 101; tel 918/775-2413. The inventor of the Cherokee alphabet is remembered through the preservation of the log cabin he built in 1829. Interpretive exhibits feature Cherokee culture and history, examples of Sequoyah's alphabet, and a life-size statue of the artist and inventor. **Open:** Tues–Fri 9am–5pm, Sat–Sun 2–5pm. **Free**

Sequoyah National Wildlife Refuge
Vian; tel 918/773-5251. 15 mi W of Sallisaw. Lying at the junction of the Canadian and Arkansas rivers, this 28,000-acre refuge provides habitat for waterfowl and other migratory birds. A photo blind, hiking trails, and observation towers are available. Activities include fishing, hunting, boating, and pecan picking. **Open:** Daily sunrise–sunset. **Free**

Blue Ribbon Downs
3700 W Cherokee; tel 918/775-7771. Clubhouse offers a climate-controlled atmosphere where wagerers and onlookers dine in comfort while watching American quarter horse and thoroughbred racing. **Open:** Call for schedule. **$**

Shawnee

Established in 1894, this community accesses the Shawnee Indian Reservation to the west and celebrates its Native American heritage with outdoor festivals in the fall. **Information:** Greater Shawnee Area Chamber of Commerce, 131 N Bell, PO Box 1613, Shawnee, 74802-1613 (tel 405/273-6092).

HOTEL 🏨

⬛⬛ Econo Lodge
5107 N Harrison, 74801; tel 405/275-6720 or toll free 800/553-2666. Exit 186 off I-40. Budget hotel with simple accommodations. Easy access to interstate and close to mall and restaurants. **Rooms:** 53 rms. CI open/CO 11am. Nonsmoking rms avail. **Amenities:** 🛁 A/C, cable TV. Room for guests with disabilities under construction. **Services:** 🚐 🛎 Car-rental desk. Guests can request daily linen service. **Rates:** $37 S; $45 D. Extra person $4. Children under age 18 stay free. Parking: Outdoor, free. AE, CB, DC, DISC, ER, JCB, MC, V.

MOTELS

⬛⬛ Best Western Cinderella Motor Inn
623 Kickapoo Spur, 74801; tel 405/273-7010 or toll free 800/420-5111. Exit 185 off I-40. Standard chain property with an exceptionally large indoor pool, located within miles of the Expo Center, the mall, and historic downtown. **Rooms:** 92 rms and stes. CI 4pm/CO noon. Nonsmoking rms avail. Rooms are somewhat crowded, but have table and two chairs. Rooms with king-size bed or two double beds have larger upholstered chair with ottoman. Half the rooms have interior access. **Amenities:** 🛁 🍸 A/C, cable TV. **Services:** ✕ 🚐 🛎 🍽 Free transportation to Shawnee airport provided, but not to Oklahoma City. **Facilities:** ⛴ ⛸ 1 restaurant, 1 bar, whirlpool, washer/dryer. **Rates:** $52 S; $65 D; $60–$90 ste. Children under age 18 stay free. Parking: Outdoor, free. AE, CB, DC, DISC, MC, V.

≡≡≡ Holiday Inn

4900 N Harrison, 74801; tel 405/275-4404 or toll free 800/HOLIDAY; fax 405/275-4998. Exit 186 off I-40. Very nice property located along the interstate, close to the mall and many restaurants. Good for a brief or extended stay. **Rooms:** 106 rms and stes. CI noon/CO noon. Nonsmoking rms avail. Bathrooms larger than average. Some rooms face recreational area; half the rooms have interior access. **Amenities:** 📺 ⚲ A/C, cable TV, dataport. Mini-refrigerators available. **Services:** ✗ ⬛ 🖭 ⬭ Car-rental desk. **Facilities:** 🛁 1000 ⬧ 1 restaurant, 1 bar (w/entertainment), games rm, washer/dryer. **Rates:** $55 S; $60 D; $125 ste. Extra person $5. Children under age 18 stay free. Parking: Outdoor, free. AE, CB, DC, DISC, JCB, MC, V.

≡ Super 8 Motel

4900 N Harrison, 74802; tel 405/275-0089 or toll free 800/800-8000. Exit 186 off I-40. Just a basic budget motel, though this Super 8 has very large rooms. Convenient to local mall with dining and shopping. **Rooms:** 36 rms. CI 2pm/CO 11am. Nonsmoking rms avail. **Amenities:** 📺 A/C, cable TV. **Services:** ⬛ ⬭ 🖭 $20 pet deposit is usually waived. **Facilities:** ⬧ **Rates:** $35 S; $43 D. Extra person $3. Children under age 12 stay free. Parking: Outdoor, free. AE, CB, DC, DISC, MC, V.

ATTRACTIONS 🏛

Santa Fe Depot Museum

614 E Main St; tel 405/275-8412. Designed by architect Joseph Schuetter using the Romanesque Revival style of the late 1800s, this passenger station is filled with quirky and charming details. The two-foot thick walls are made of local Bedford rock, ceilings are made from boxcar siding, and the floors were originally cement cinders held together by railroad ties and rails. Visitors may tour the former Ladies Waiting Room (featuring pioneer household items), the Main Waiting Room (featuring a pump organ, doctor's corner, and antique dolls), and the Jim Crow Waiting Room used by blacks in the days of segregation. **Open:** Tues–Fri 10am–4pm, Sat–Sun 2–4pm. **Free**

Mabee-Gerrer Museum of Art

1900 W McArthur; tel 405/878-5300. Extensive collection dating from ancient times to the present. Artifacts from around the world are on display, including Native American relics. Among the highlights are European paintings from 1300 and two Egyptian mummies. **Open:** Tues–Sun 1–4pm. Free

Stillwater

See also Perry

Stillwater was established in the 1880s and was the first settlement in Oklahoma Territory to be called a town. This city is the seat of Payne County and home to Oklahoma State University. **Information:** Stillwater Convention & Visitors Bureau, 409 S Main, PO Box 1687, Stillwater, 74076-1687 (tel 405/372-0765).

HOTEL

≡≡ Best Western

600 E McElroy, 74075; tel 405/377-7010 or toll free 800/528-1234; fax 405/743-1686. On US 177, 1 mi N of OK 51. Standard chain property near a movie theater and the Industrial Park. **Rooms:** 122 rms and stes. CI 2pm/CO noon. Nonsmoking rms avail. Corner rooms are smaller than others. **Amenities:** 📺 ⚲ 🖬 A/C, cable TV w/movies. Some units w/terraces. **Services:** ✗ 🚐 ⬛ ⬭ 🖭 Car-rental desk. **Facilities:** 🛁 🏓 400 ⬧ 1 restaurant (bkfst only), 1 bar, games rm, spa, sauna, whirlpool, washer/dryer. Table tennis and billiards tables in pool area. **Rates:** $47 S; $52 D; $91 ste. Extra person $5. Children under age 12 stay free. Parking: Outdoor, free. AE, CB, DC, DISC, MC, V.

MOTELS

≡≡ Days Inn

5010 W 6th St, 74075; tel 405/743-2570 or toll free 800/DAYS-INN; fax 405/743-3904. On OK 51. Average Days Inn, located at the edge of town, offering clean, dependable accommodations at standard rates. **Rooms:** 74 rms. CI 2pm/CO 11am. Nonsmoking rms avail. **Amenities:** 📺 A/C, cable TV. **Services:** ⬭ 🖭 Small pets accepted with $20 deposit. Movie rentals available at front desk. **Facilities:** 🛁 ⬧ **Rates (CP):** Peak (late Nov–Dec) $32–$38 S; $42 D. Children under age 12 stay free. Lower rates off-season. Parking: Outdoor, free. AE, CB, DC, DISC, MC, V.

≡≡≡ Holiday Inn

2515 W 6th St, 74075; tel 405/372-0800 or toll free 800/HOLIDAY; fax 405/377-8212. On OK 51. This Holidome property has plans for a complete exterior renovation and work on the Holidome. Near restaurants. **Rooms:** 141 rms and stes. CI 3pm/CO noon. Nonsmoking rms avail. Rooms with interior and exterior access. **Amenities:** 📺 ⚲ 🍽 A/C, cable TV. 1 unit w/whirlpool. Dataports available in some rooms. **Services:** ✗ 🚐 ⬛ ⬭ 🖭 **Facilities:** 🛁 300 ⬧ 1 restaurant, 1 bar, games rm, sauna, whirlpool, washer/dryer. Pool area has mini-golf, billiards, and weight room. Restaurant offers deli buffet—no ordering off menu. **Rates:** $46–$48 S; $53–$55 D; $62–$125 ste. Extra person $7. Children under age 18 stay free. Parking: Outdoor, free. AE, CB, DC, DISC, MC, V.

RESTAURANTS 🍴

Bobo's Mexican Restaurant

5020 W 6th St; tel 405/372-9353. On OK 51. **Mexican/Southwestern.** A large restaurant with several separate dining areas laid out in bright colors and festive decorations. Long á la carte menu has something for everyone. **FYI:** Reservations accepted. Children's menu. **Open:** Sun–Wed

10:30am–10pm, Thurs 10:30am–11pm, Fri–Sat 10:30am–midnight. **Prices:** Main courses $7–$14. AE, CB, DC, DISC, MC, V. 🖼 &

★ Eskimo Joe's

501 W Elm; tel 405/372-8896. I-35 to OK 51 E, left on Duck St. **American.** A fun two-level restaurant offering casual dining and a standard menu. A perfect place for families and groups of friends, this local favorite has been in business for over 20 years. Walls are covered with old soft drink and cigarette signs, and there are several bars and a nice gift shop. **FYI:** Reservations not accepted. Country music/rock. Children's menu. **Open:** Mon–Sat 11am–10pm, Sun 11am–9pm. **Prices:** Main courses $4–$11. AE, CB, DC, DISC, MC, V. 🖼 &

Stillwater Bay

623 ½ S Husband St; tel 405/743-2780. I-35 to OK 51 E to Husband St, right. **Seafood/Steak.** An upscale restaurant located on the second floor of the Meff building, where window seating provides a limited view of downtown Stillwater. Steaks, orange roughy and other seafood, chicken, sandwiches, pasta. **FYI:** Reservations accepted. Children's menu. **Open:** Mon–Thurs 11am–10pm, Fri–Sat 11am–11pm, Sun 11am–9pm. **Prices:** Main courses $6–$30. AE, DC, DISC, MC, V.

ATTRACTION 🖼

Gardiner Art Gallery

Corner of Morrill and Knoblock Sts; tel 405/744-6016. Located on the OSU campus. The gallery rotates the work of local and national artists and houses a permanent collection of various media. In addition to its exhibitions, the old Georgian-style dormitory provides studio space for artists. **Open:** Sept–May Mon–Fri 8am–5pm, Sun 1–5pm. **Free**

Tahlequah

The end of the Cherokee's "Trail of Tears," Tahlequah became the capital of the Cherokee Nation in 1841 and still functions in that capacity. The Illinois River to the east is one of the best known canoeing spots in the state. **Information:** Tahlequah Area Chamber of Commerce Tourism Council, 123 E Delaware St, Tahlequah, 74464-2817 (tel 918/456-3742).

MOTEL 🖼

🛏 Tahlequah Motor Lodge

2501 S Muskogee Ave, 74464; tel 918/456-2350; fax 918/456-4580. On OK 82. Plain but acceptable lodgings near the hub of town, convenient to shopping and dining. **Rooms:** 53 rms. CI 2pm/CO 11am. Nonsmoking rms avail. **Amenities:** 🛁 A/C, cable TV. **Services:** 🍴 🐾 Pet deposit $25. Daily linen service on request. **Facilities:** 🏛 🏊 & 1 restaurant. **Rates:** Peak (May–Sept) $40 S; $44 D. Extra person $3.

Children under age 12 stay free. Lower rates off-season. Parking: Outdoor, free. Extra people in rooms are charged in winter. AE, CB, DC, DISC, MC, V.

RESTAURANT 🍴

Jasper's Restaurant

2600 S Muskogee Ave; tel 918/456-0100. On US 62. **Seafood/Steak.** New and popular, with window seating, ceiling fans, plants and trees everywhere, and a fireplace. There's even a family-size table under a gazebo. Menu ranges from sandwiches and burgers to steaks, lobster, and shrimp. Specialties include steak tournedos Oscar and filet mignon. **FYI:** Reservations recommended. Karaoke/piano. Children's menu. Additional location: 1702 W Okmulgee, Muskogee (tel 682-7867). **Open:** Mon–Sat 11am–10pm. **Prices:** Main courses $4–$20. AE, CB, DC, DISC, MC, V. 🖼

ATTRACTION 🖼

Cherokee Heritage Center

Off Willis Rd; tel 918/456-6007 or toll free 800/850-0348. Ancient village re-creating the lifestyle of the Cherokee during the 16th century. Guided tours relate Cherokee history and customs as visitors see villagers going about daily work of preparing food, making arrowheads, shaping baskets, and sometimes performing stomp dances. The Cherokee National Museum uses multimedia displays, artifacts, and artwork to present Cherokee history from their arrival in North America to the present day. **$$$**

Tulsa

See also Claremore

The second-largest city in Oklahoma, Tulsa is known for its beautiful parks, numerous museums and art galleries, and other cultural attractions. A walking tour map directs visitors to numerous buildings designed in the art deco style during the city's oil baron heydays of the 1920s and '30s. The Arkansas River flows through town, and a number of parks are located on its banks. Horse racing, Wild West celebrations, and professional sports keep things lively. Both Tulsa University and Oral Roberts University are located here. **Information:** Tulsa Convention & Visitors Bureau, 616 S Boston, #100, Tulsa, 74119-1298 (tel 918/585-1201).

PUBLIC TRANSPORTATION

The **Tulsa Transit** operates citywide bus service. Standard fare for local routes is 75¢, for express routes $1; for seniors and disabled persons, fare is 35¢ for the local, 50¢ for the express. Children under 5 ride free. Transfers cost 5¢. Call 918/582-2100 for information.

HOTELS 🏨

≣≣≣≣ Adam's Mark Tulsa at Williams Center

100 E 2nd St, 74103 (Downtown); tel 918/582-9000 or toll free 800/444-ADAM; fax 918/560-2263. A very business-oriented hotel located in the heart of downtown. Guests are greeted by an indoor fountain in the lower lobby, where lovely modern art covers the walls. Escalators transport guests to the second-level lobby. **Rooms:** 462 rms and stes. Executive level. CI 3pm/CO noon. Nonsmoking rms avail. **Amenities:** 🛏 👤 A/C, satel TV w/movies, refrig, dataport, voice mail. All units w/minibars, all w/terraces, some w/whirlpools. Premier-level rooms have phones and TVs in the bath. **Services:** 🍽 ▥ 🚗 🖨 ↩ Masseur, babysitting. **Facilities:** ⌂ ⛳ 1250 🖥 ♿ 1 restaurant, 2 bars (1 w/entertainment), spa, whirlpool. **Rates:** $120 S; $132 D; $275–$950 ste. Children under age 18 stay free. Weekend B&B package avail. AE, CB, DC, DISC, MC, V.

≣≣≣ DoubleTree Hotel at Warren Place

6110 S Yale Ave, 74136; tel 918/495-1000 or toll free 800/222-TREE; fax 918/495-1944. 1 mi S of I-44. Well-appointed and -landscaped property; good for an extended, luxurious visit. **Rooms:** 371 rms and stes. Executive level. CI 3pm/CO noon. Nonsmoking rms avail. **Amenities:** 🛏👤▥ A/C, cable TV, dataport. Some units w/terraces, some w/whirlpools. Bathrooms have a TV audio channel. **Services:** 🍽 ▥ 🚗 🖨 ↩ Babysitting. **Facilities:** ⌂ 🏊 900 🖥♿ 2 restaurants (see "Restaurants" below), 1 bar (w/entertainment), sauna, steam rm, whirlpool. A half-mile walking path is shaded with beautiful towering trees and lined with lovely flowers. Award-winning restaurant. **Rates:** Peak (Feb–Oct) $99 S or D; $125–$350 ste. Extra person $15. Children under age 18 stay free. Lower rates off-season. Parking: Indoor/outdoor, free. Special weekend rates avail. AE, CB, DC, DISC, MC, V.

≣≣≣ Embassy Suites Hotel

3332 S 79th E Ave, 74145; tel 918/622-4000 or toll free 800/362-2779; fax 918/665-2347. Attractive, featuring a beautiful atrium lobby with a wonderful fountain. **Rooms:** 240 stes. CI 3pm/CO 1pm. Nonsmoking rms avail. Bathrooms are unusually large. **Amenities:** 🛏👤▥ A/C, cable TV w/movies, refrig, voice mail. All units w/terraces. **Services:** 🍽 🚗 🖨 ↩ **Facilities:** ⌂ ⛳ 250 ♿ 1 restaurant (lunch and dinner only; see "Restaurants" below), 1 bar (w/entertainment), sauna, steam rm, whirlpool, washer/dryer. **Rates (BB):** $109 ste. Extra person $10. Children under age 12 stay free. Parking: Outdoor, free. AE, CB, DC, DISC, EC, ER, JCB, MC, V.

≣≣ Holiday Inn (Holidome Tulsa Central)

8181 E Skelly Dr, 74129; tel 918/663-4541 or toll free 800/HOLIDAY; fax 918/665-7109. 31st and Memorial exit off I-44. Very basic. **Rooms:** 211 rms and stes. CI 3pm/CO noon. Nonsmoking rms avail. At the time of inspection, the hallways were dim and in need of remodeling. **Amenities:** 🛏

👤 A/C, cable TV. **Services:** 🍽 🚗 🖨 ↩ 🐕 Car-rental desk. **Facilities:** ⌂ ⛳ 600 ♿ 1 restaurant, 1 bar (w/entertainment), games rm, spa, sauna, steam rm, whirlpool, beauty salon, washer/dryer. **Rates:** Peak (Feb–Nov) $64 S or D; $70–$130 ste. Extra person $5. Children under age 18 stay free. Lower rates off-season. Parking: Outdoor, free. AE, CB, DC, DISC, MC, V.

≣≣≣ Lexington Hotel Suites

8525 E 41st St, 74145; tel 918/627-0030 or toll free 800/927-8483; fax 918/627-0587. At Memorial St. Attractive and clean with lots of storage space, this hotel is designed for an extended visit. **Rooms:** 162 stes and effic. CI 3pm/CO noon. Nonsmoking rms avail. All rooms have a furnished mini-kitchen. **Amenities:** 🛏👤▥ A/C, satel TV w/movies, refrig, dataport. **Services:** 🚗 🖨 ↩ **Facilities:** ⌂ 150 ♿ Washer/dryer. Guests receive a free pass to Bally's Health Club (two miles away). Complimentary shuttle to Woodland Hills Mall. **Rates (CP):** Peak (Mar–Oct) $59–$89 ste; $59–$89 effic. Extra person $7. Children under age 16 stay free. Lower rates off-season. Parking: Outdoor, free. AE, CB, DC, DISC, ER, JCB, MC, V.

≣≣≣ Marriott Hotel

10918 E 41st St, 74146; tel 918/627-5000 or toll free 800/228-9290; fax 918/627-9572. 41st St exit off US 169. Opened in 1993, this hotel offers above-average, comfortable accommodations to its largely business customers. **Rooms:** 336 rms. Executive level. CI 4pm/CO 1pm. Nonsmoking rms avail. **Amenities:** 🛏 👤 A/C, satel TV w/movies, dataport, voice mail. **Services:** 🍽 🗝 🚗 🖨 ↩ 🐕 **Facilities:** ⌂ ⛳ 1390 🖥 ♿ 1 restaurant (see "Restaurants" below), 1 bar (w/entertainment), basketball, games rm, spa, sauna, steam rm, whirlpool, washer/dryer. **Rates:** $95–$110 S or D. Children under age 18 stay free. Parking: Outdoor, free. AE, CB, DC, DISC, ER, JCB, MC, V.

≣≣≣ Radisson Inn Tulsa Airport

2201 N 77th E Ave, 74115; tel 918/835-9911 or toll free 800/333-3333; fax 918/838-2452. Off OK 11. Located on airport property, this business hotel offers great meeting facilities. **Rooms:** 172 rms and stes. CI 3pm/CO noon. Nonsmoking rms avail. **Amenities:** 🛏 👤 A/C, cable TV, dataport. **Services:** 🍽 🚗 🖨 ↩ Car-rental desk, babysitting. **Facilities:** ⌂ ⛳ 400 ♿ 2 restaurants, 1 bar, sauna. Pizza Hut on site. **Rates:** $76–$85 S; $86–$95 D; $100 ste. Extra person $10. Children under age 18 stay free. Parking: Outdoor, free. Weekend B&B package avail. AE, CB, DC, DISC, MC, V.

≣≣≣ Ramada Hotel Tulsa

5000 E Skelly Dr, 74135; tel 918/622-7000 or toll free 800/685-8240; fax 918/664-9353. Yale exit off I-44. Comfortable accommodations near Lafortune Park, Tulsa Promenade Shopping Center, and Expo Square and within walking distance of an 18-hole golf course. Large meeting rooms make this a popular convention site. **Rooms:** 318 rms and stes. CI 3pm/CO noon. Nonsmoking rms avail. **Amenities:** 🛅 A/C, satel TV w/movies. Some units w/terraces, some w/whirlpools. Some rooms have dataports. **Services:** ✗ 🚐 🖂 🖵 🛎 Car-rental desk. Courtesy van. **Facilities:** 🛅 🛢 📦500 1 restaurant, 2 bars (w/entertainment), games rm, beauty salon, washer/dryer. **Rates:** $60–$70 S; $65–$75 D; $125–$250 ste. Extra person $6. Children under age 18 stay free. Parking: Outdoor, free. B&B package avail. AE, DC, DISC, MC, V.

🌊🇺🇸 Tulsa Marriott Southern Hills

1902 E 71st St S, 74136; tel 918/493-7000 or toll free 800/ 493-7000; fax 918/481-7147. 2 mi E of 71st St exit off US 75. Since it became a Marriott in 1994, this hotel has had a complete $5.5 million renovation. Well-kept public areas include a beautiful pool and sundeck. **Rooms:** 372 rms and stes. Executive level. CI 3pm/CO noon. Nonsmoking rms avail. **Amenities:** 🛅 🛢 🍽 A/C, satel TV w/movies. **Services:** ✗ 🖀 🔑 ⒱🅿 🚐 🖂 🖵 🛎 Car-rental desk, social director, masseur, babysitting. $50 deposit for small pets. **Facilities:** 🛅 🛢 📦1200 🖥 🛢 2 restaurants, 2 bars, spa, sauna, whirlpool. Guests may use the health club facilities at the nearby Jewish Community Center free of charge. **Rates:** Peak (Apr–Sept) $79–$89 S or D; $125–$350 ste. Children under age 12 stay free. Lower rates off-season. Parking: Outdoor, free. AE, CB, DC, DISC, ER, JCB, MC, V.

MOTELS

🌊🌊 Best Western Trade Winds Central Inn

3141 E Skelly Dr, 74105; tel 918/749-5561 or toll free 800/ 528-1234; fax 918/749-6312. Harvard St exit off I-44. Rooms are clean, comfortable, and functional—but not very pretty. **Rooms:** 167 rms and stes. CI 2pm/CO noon. Nonsmoking rms avail. **Amenities:** 🛅 A/C, satel TV w/movies. Some units w/terraces, 1 w/whirlpool. **Services:** ✗ 🚐 🖂 🖵 🛎 Small pets only. **Facilities:** 🛅 📦225 🛢 1 restaurant, 1 bar (w/entertainment). **Rates:** $57 S; $63 D; $66–$88 ste. Extra person $4. Children under age 12 stay free. Parking: Outdoor, free. AE, CB, DC, DISC, JCB, MC, V.

🌊🌊 Comfort Inn

4717 S Yale Ave, 74135; tel 918/622-6776 or toll free 800/ 235-8937; fax 918/622-1809. Yale exit off I-244 or I-44. Basic motel located seven blocks from the Tulsa Promenade Shopping Center and three blocks from Lafortune Park. **Rooms:** 109 rms, stes, and effic. CI 11am/CO 1pm. Nonsmoking rms avail. **Amenities:** 🛅 A/C, cable TV. Some units w/whirlpools. **Services:** 🖵 🛎 **Facilities:** 🛅 🛢 **Rates (CP):** $38 S; $45 D; $110 ste; $95 effic. Extra person $5. Children under age 18 stay free. Parking: Outdoor, free. AE, CB, DC, DISC, EC, ER, JCB, MC, V.

🌊🌊 Days Inn

5525 W Skelly Dr, 74107; tel 918/446-1561 or toll free 800/ DAYS-INN; fax 918/446-1943. 49th St exit off I-44. A basic, no-frills motel with access to I-44. **Rooms:** 77 rms and stes. CI 6am/CO 11am. Nonsmoking rms avail. **Amenities:** 🛅

A/C, cable TV. **Services:** 🚐 🖂 🖵 🛎 Pet fee is $4. **Facilities:** 🛅 📦75 1 restaurant, 1 bar, washer/dryer. **Rates (CP):** $34–$50 S; $50–$60 D; $50–$54 ste. Extra person $4. Children under age 12 stay free. Parking: Outdoor, free. AE, CB, DC, DISC, MC, V.

🌊 Econo Lodge Airport

11620 E Skelly Dr, 74128; tel 918/437-9200 or toll free 800/ 424-4777; fax 918/437-2935. Exit 235 off I-44. Attactive motel, but bad soundproofing is a definite minus. **Rooms:** 120 rms and stes. CI open/CO 11am. Nonsmoking rms avail. **Amenities:** 🛅 A/C, cable TV. **Services:** 🚐 🖵 The front desk staff lacks security savvy, so be aware. **Facilities:** 🛅2 📦500 🛢 1 restaurant, 1 bar, whirlpool. **Rates (CP):** Peak (Apr–Sept) $36–$49 S; $45–$65 D; $75 ste. Children under age 18 stay free. Lower rates off-season. Parking: Outdoor, free. AE, DC, DISC, JCB, MC, V.

🌊🌊🌊 Holiday Inn Express

3131 E 51st, 74105; tel 918/743-9811 or toll free 800/ HOLIDAY; fax 918/743-6499. Harvard exit off I-44. Spotlessly maintained and comfortable. **Rooms:** 117 rms and stes. CI 3pm/CO noon. Nonsmoking rms avail. **Amenities:** 🛅 🛢 A/C, cable TV. Some units w/terraces. Water and air filters in each room. **Services:** 🖂 🖵 Car-rental desk. Complimentary beer and wine, pizza, sausages, cheese, and other snacks served every evening. **Facilities:** 🛅 📦 📦125 🛢 Sauna, washer/ dryer. **Rates (CP):** $62 S; $67 D; $75–$150 ste. Extra person $5. Children under age 18 stay free. Parking: Outdoor, free. AE, CB, DC, DISC, ER, JCB, MC, V.

🌊 La Quinta Inn Airport

35 N Sheridan Rd, 74115; tel 918/836-3931 or toll free 800/ 531-5900; fax 918/836-5428. Sheridan exit off I-244. Average property with rooms in need of an upgrade. Good access to I-244 and all major highways. **Rooms:** 101 rms and stes. CI noon/CO noon. Nonsmoking rms avail. Dated furnishings, worn carpets. **Amenities:** 🛅 🛢 A/C, cable TV w/movies. **Services:** 🚐 🖂 🖵 🛎 Babysitting. **Facilities:** 🛅 📦20 🛢 **Rates (CP):** $52–$62 S; $60–$70 D; $63–$75 ste. Extra person $7. Children under age 18 stay free. Parking: Outdoor, free. AE, CB, DC, DISC, MC, V.

🌊🌊 Quality Inn Airport

222 N Garnett Rd, 74116; tel 918/438-0780 or toll free 800/ 228-5151; fax 918/438-0780. Garnett exit off I-244. Basic motel for frugal business travelers. Near the airport but far enough to avoid the noise. **Rooms:** 118 rms and stes. CI 3pm/CO 11am. Nonsmoking rms avail. **Amenities:** 🛅 A/C, cable TV, dataport. 1 unit w/whirlpool. Many rooms have recliners. **Services:** ✗ 🚐 🖂 🖵 🛎 Car-rental desk. Small pets allowed in smoking rooms only. **Facilities:** 🛅 📦250 🛢 1 restaurant, 1 bar (w/entertainment). **Rates:** $40–$55 S; $44–$59 D; $85 ste. Extra person $4. Children under age 18 stay free. Parking: Outdoor, free. AE, CB, DC, DISC, ER, JCB, MC, V.

Residence Inn by Marriott

8181 E 41st St, 74145; tel 918/664-7241 or toll free 800/331-3131; fax 918/622-0314. Memorial exit off Broken Arrow Expwy. Quality, apartment-style accommodations at standard rates. **Rooms:** 135 stes and effic. CI 2pm/CO noon. Nonsmoking rms avail. **Amenities:** A/C, cable TV, refrig. All units w/terraces, some w/fireplaces. **Services:** Car-rental desk, babysitting. Linens changed every other day unless otherwise requested. **Facilities:** Basketball, whirlpool, washer/dryer. Guests receive free passes to Bally's Health Club. Free barbecues on Wednesday nights during summer; theme dinners during winter. **Rates (CP):** $95–$115 ste; $95–$115 effic. Children under age 18 stay free. Parking: Outdoor, free. AE, CB, DC, DISC, JCB, MC, V.

Super 8 Motel

11525 E Skelly Dr, 74128; tel 918/438-7700 or toll free 800/800-8000; fax 918/438-7700. 11th St exit off I-44 or US 169. This basic hotel needs repairs and remodeling but still offers a cheap, minimally comfortable place to stay for those who are just passing through. **Rooms:** 115 rms and stes. CI 7am/CO noon. Nonsmoking rms avail. Bathrooms need maintenance. **Amenities:** A/C, cable TV. Some units w/whirlpools. **Services:** **Facilities:** **Rates:** $31–$35 S; $37–$39 D; $50–$65 ste. Extra person $4. Children under age 12 stay free. Parking: Outdoor, free. AE, DC, DISC, MC, V.

RESTAURANTS

Atlantic Sea Grill

In Eton Square Shopping Center, 8321-A E 61st St; tel 918/252-7966. 1 mi N of Woodland Hills Mall. **Continental/Seafood.** This grill offers the freshest seafood prepared a number of ways. Also available are veal, steak, and pasta. **FYI:** Reservations recommended. Dress code. **Open:** Lunch Mon–Fri 11:30am–2:30pm; dinner Sun–Thurs 5:30–10pm, Fri–Sat 5:30–11pm. **Prices:** Main courses $8–$20. AE, CB, DC, DISC, MC, V.

Bamboo Garden

In Highland Plaza Shopping Center, 3966 Hudson; tel 918/622-6227. **Chinese/Vietnamese.** Ordinary decor but great Vietnamese and Chinese food. Daily lunch buffet. **FYI:** Reservations not accepted. Beer and wine only. **Open:** Lunch Mon–Sat 11am–3pm; dinner Mon–Sat 5–9pm. **Prices:** Main courses $5–$9. AE, CB, DC, MC, V.

Bangkok Restaurant

3313 E 32nd Place; tel 918/743-9669. 1½ mi N of Harvard exit off I-44. **Chinese/Thai.** Thai-owned restaurant offering a very popular weekday noon buffet. Menu is varied, and individual dishes can be prepared with your tastes in mind. **FYI:** Reservations not accepted. Beer and wine only. **Open:** Mon–Sat 11am–9pm. **Prices:** Main courses $6–$8. AE, CB, DC, MC, V.

Beechwood's

In Marriott Hotel, 10918 E 41st St; tel 918/627-5000. Off US 169. **American/Steak.** Walls of windows bring in lots of light and nourish the greenery that thrives inside. Quality steaks and pasta dishes are mainstays of the menu. **FYI:** Reservations recommended. Children's menu. **Open:** Breakfast Mon–Fri 6–10:30am; lunch Mon–Fri 10:30am–2pm; dinner Mon–Fri 5–10pm, Sat–Sun 7–10pm; brunch Sun 11am–2pm. **Prices:** Main courses $7–$16. AE, CB, DC, DISC, ER, MC, V.

Blue Corn Cafe

In Harvard Park, 8218 Harvard; tel 918/494-3878. Off I-44. **Southwestern.** This relatively new restaurant offers a variety of specialty sandwiches and burgers. Favorites include black bean and goat cheese dip, blue-corn fried chicken salad, and blue-corn stacked enchiladas. The Southwestern atmosphere is casual and fun. **FYI:** Reservations not accepted. Children's menu. **Open:** Tues–Thurs 10am–11pm, Fri–Sat 10am–midnight, Sun 10am–11pm. **Prices:** Main courses $4–$13. AE, CB, DC, DISC, MC, V.

Bodean Seafood Restaurant

3323 E 51st St; tel 918/743-3861. Harvard exit off I-44. **Seafood.** More than casual but not quite formal, this restaurant, featuring paintings by local artists, flies in fresh seafood daily from around the world. Specialties include trout amandine, white fish Argentine, and gulf shrimp scampi. **FYI:** Reservations recommended. **Open:** Lunch Mon–Fri 11am–2:30pm; dinner Mon–Fri 5–10:30pm, Sat 5–10:30pm, Sun 5–9pm. **Prices:** Main courses $10–$29. AE, CB, DC, DISC, MC, V.

Casa Bonita

In Alameda Shopping Center, 2120 S Sheridan; tel 918/836-6464. At 21st St. **Mexican.** With its 30-foot waterfall in the Acapulco Room, an erupting volcano, and the almost claustrophobia-inducing Cave Room, this huge establishment is a local attraction in itself. It easily caters to large groups with its many separate dining areas. Plenty of entertainment is provided by strolling musicians, puppet shows, and the games room. With all this, how can the food be anything but an afterthought? **FYI:** Reservations not accepted. Children's menu. Beer and wine only. **Open:** Sun–Thurs 11am–9:30pm, Fri–Sat 11am–10pm. **Prices:** Main courses $6–$18. AE, CB, DC, DISC, MC, V.

Cattleman's Steakhouse

In Embassy Suites Hotel, 3332 S 79th E Ave; tel 918/622-4000. **Steak.** Quality cuts of aged beef. Seating is available in the dining room or in the hotel's atrium. **FYI:** Reservations recommended. Dancing/rock. Children's menu. **Open:** Sun–Thurs 11am–10pm, Fri–Sat 11am–11pm. **Prices:** Main courses $9–$17. AE, CB, DC, DISC, ER, MC, V.

CJ's Restaurant

2124 S Garnett; tel 918/437-9334. **American.** Casual restaurant adorned with sports memorabilia. The menu includes steak, catfish, and homemade pies and cobblers. **FYI:** Reservations not accepted. Children's menu. No liquor license. **Open:** Mon–Fri 11am–8pm. **Prices:** Main courses $4–$7. No CC. 📇

Denver Grill

112 S Denver (Downtown); tel 918/582-3790. **American.** This smoky, old-style joint decorated with celebrity portraits offers bar seating and a casual, friendly atmosphere. **FYI:** Reservations not accepted. No liquor license. **Open:** Mon–Fri 6am–8pm, Sat–Sun 8am–4pm. **Prices:** Main courses $4–$9. No CC.

Frank's Country Inn

9058 E 27th St; tel 918/622-9803. ½ block N of Memorial exit off I-44. **American.** Features an all-you-can-eat buffet of smoked and fried meats and country-style vegetables. Bring a healthy appetite. **FYI:** Reservations not accepted. Children's menu. **Open:** Daily 11am–9pm. **Prices:** Main courses $5–$7. AE, DC, DISC, MC, V. 📇 &

Ichiban Teriyaki Japanese Restaurant

In All-State Center Mall, 7982 E 41st St; tel 918/664-2933. At Memorial St. **Japanese.** Authentic decor and soft Japanese music match the simple menu. **FYI:** Reservations not accepted. Beer and wine only. **Open:** Lunch Mon–Fri 11:30am–2pm; dinner Tues–Sat 5:30–9pm. **Prices:** Main courses $7–$15. AE, MC, V. &

Interurban

717 S Houston (Downtown); tel 918/585-3134. Between 7th and 11th Sts. **Eclectic.** A spacious and attractive room, decorated with dark wood but featuring lots of windows and greenery to make things bright and lighthearted. Fare includes excellent hamburgers, some Mexican dishes, salads. Expect a large business crowd at lunch. **FYI:** Reservations not accepted. Children's menu. **Open:** Sun–Thurs 11am–10pm, Fri–Sat 11am–midnight. **Prices:** Main courses $4–$13. AE, DC, DISC, MC, V. 📇 &

Joe Vigg's Italian Eatery

3030 S Harvard; tel 918/747-6200. Off I-44 at 31st St. **Italian.** Joe Vigg's genuine brick ovens produce irresistible pizzas. Those who lean toward unusual toppings might want to try the Cascia Gourmet, a pie with sun-dried tomatoes, artichoke hearts, mushrooms, and Gouda cheese. The menu also includes a variety of classic Italian dishes. **FYI:** Reservations accepted. Children's menu. Additional location: 6902 S Lewis (tel 493-1818). **Open:** Peak (Apr–Oct) Sun–Thurs 11am–9pm, Fri 11am–10pm, Sat 4–10pm. **Prices:** Main courses $4–$7. AE, DC, DISC, MC, V. &

Julio Tumatoe's Mexicali Border Cafe

In Summit Square Shopping Center, 7104 S Sheridan; tel 918/481-1114. 1½ mi W of US 169. **Mexican.** Mexican movie posters add a little cinematic flavor to the festive dining room. Traditional favorites are served along with some more unusual dishes such as Pechugas Popeye, chicken stuffed with spinach and cream cheese topped with mushrooms. Tuesday and Wednesday are "fajita nights." **FYI:** Reservations accepted. Children's menu. Additional location: 14 W Brady (tel 582-3383). **Open:** Mon–Thurs 11am–10pm, Fri–Sat 11am–11pm, Sun 11am–10pm. **Prices:** Main courses $6–$12. AE, CB, DC, MC, V. 📇 &

Knotty Pine Barbeque

3301 W 5th; tel 918/584-0171. 3 mi W of downtown. **Barbecue.** Everything you would expect from a Southern barbecue joint: noisy dining room, old posters, and ample servings of ribs, chicken, and sides. **FYI:** Reservations not accepted. Beer and wine only. Additional location: 71st and Lynn Lane, Broken Arrow (tel 258-1544). **Open:** Sun–Mon 11am–10pm, Wed–Thurs 11am–10pm, Fri–Sat 11am–11:30pm. **Prices:** Main courses $4–$9. AE, DC, DISC, MC, V.

Mondo's Ristoranté Italiano

6000 S Lewis Ave; tel 918/749-2233. Off I-44. **Italian.** Italian owned and operated, this casual, reasonably priced restaurant provides the expected: classic Italian cuisine and lots of garlic bread. Chicken and veal marsala are very popular, as is the cannoli. **FYI:** Reservations accepted. Children's menu. Additional location: 6746 S Memorial Dr (tel 254-7778). **Open:** Peak (June–Aug) Mon–Thurs 11:30am–10pm, Fri–Sat 11:30am–11pm, Sun 11:30am–10pm. **Prices:** Main courses $7–$20. AE, CB, DC, DISC, MC, V. &

Paddy's Irish Pub & Restaurant

In Paddington Square Shopping Center, 8056 S Memorial; tel 918/250-3626. Exit 81st off US 169. **Irish/Steak.** Paddy's is casual and relaxed with dim lighting, lots of charm, and solid pub fare. The bar is always busy at night. **FYI:** Reservations accepted. Children's menu. **Open:** Mon–Thurs 11:30am–10pm, Fri–Sat 11:30am–11pm. **Prices:** Main courses $4–$13. AE, CB, DC, DISC, MC, V. &

Peppers

6175 E 61st St; tel 918/494-0592. ½ mi E of St Francis Hospital. **Eclectic.** Set up for families, this establishment provides a small game room for kids' pre-meal entertainment so parents can enjoy their meals. Casual, contemporary atmosphere. **FYI:** Reservations not accepted. Children's menu. Additional locations: 1950 Utica Sq (tel 749-2163); 1331 W Will Rogers Blvd, Claremore (tel 342-0592). **Open:** Sun–Thurs 11am–11pm, Fri–Sat 11am–2am. **Prices:** Main courses $6–$16. AE, CB, DC, DISC, MC, V. 📇

Ricardo's

In Highland Plaza, 5629 E 41st; tel 918/622-2668. Off S Kelly Dr. **Tex-Mex.** The multi-level dining room provides comfortable booths and a fun family atmosphere. Often crowded because of the good food and reasonable prices, this is a solid choice for casual or family dining. Standard Tex-Mex fare: enchiladas, tacos, burritos, various combination platters. **FYI:** Reservations not accepted. Children's menu. **Open:** Lunch Mon–Fri 11am–2pm, Sat 11am–10pm; dinner Mon–Thurs 5–9:30pm, Fri 5–10pm. **Prices:** Main courses $5–$8. AE, DISC, MC, V. 📷

Rosie's Rib Joint
8125 E 49th St; tel 918/663-2610. **Seafood/Steak.** This accommodating spot offers a 40-item salad bar and smoked ribs, steaks, and seafood. It's all good, fast, and comfortable. **FYI:** Reservations accepted. Children's menu. **Open:** Lunch Mon–Fri 11am–2pm; dinner Sun 5–9pm, Mon–Sat 5–10pm. **Prices:** Main courses $10–$17. AE, CB, DC, DISC, MC, V. 📷 ᵴ

♀ Warren Duck Club
In DoubleTree Hotel at Warren Place, 6110 S Yale Ave; tel 918/495-1000. Off I-44. **American.** This elegant, award-winning restaurant features a sophisticated menu and an extensive wine list. Rotisserie duck, Cajun-style tenderloin, and seafood are all well prepared. Experienced, multilingual staff. **FYI:** Reservations recommended. Jacket required. **Open:** Lunch Mon–Fri 11am–2pm; dinner Mon–Sat 6–11pm. **Prices:** Main courses $18–$40. AE, CB, DC, DISC, MC, V. ● VP ᵴ

ATTRACTIONS 🏛

Philbrook Museum of Art
2727 S Rockford Rd; tel 918/749-7941. The museum is housed in the Italian Renaissance–style Villa Philbrook, built in 1927 by oilman Waite Phillips and his wife Genevieve. The permanent collections include Italian Renaissance paintings and sculpture, 19th- and 20th-century European and American paintings, Native American baskets and pottery, and African and Asian collections. Situated on 23 acres of gardens and grounds which are accessible to visitors. **Open:** Tues–Wed and Fri–Sat 10am–5pm, Thurs 10am–8pm, Sun 1–5pm. **$**

Gilcrease Museum
1400 Gilcrease Museum Rd; tel 918/596-2700. A large collection of American art, artifacts, and documents, largely relating to the settlement of the West and the Native American peoples. The 440-acre grounds are landscaped with historic theme gardens, an extensive rock collection, and a wildflower meadow. Tours available daily at 2pm. **Open:** Peak (Mem Day–Labor Day) Mon–Wed and Fri–Sat 9am–5pm, Thurs 9am–8pm, Sun 1–5pm. Reduced hours off-season. **$**

The Fenster Museum of Jewish Art
1223 E 17 Place (Maple Ridge); tel 918/582-3732. The largest collection of Jewish art in the Southwest spans 4,000 years of Jewish history and heritage. Exhibits range from oil lamps from the time of the exodus from Egypt, to a sampler cross-stitch by Jewish Canadian pioneer women, to paintings by contemporary Israeli artists. Docent guided tours available with two weeks notice. **Open:** Sun–Thurs 10am–4pm. **Free**

Harwelden Mansion
2210 S Main St; tel 918/584-3333. The four-story, 30-room Tudor-gothic mansion was built in 1923 and was formerly the home of oil baron and philanthropist Earl Palmer Harwell. Today it is an opulent reminder of Oklahoma's oil wealth and serves as home to the Arts and Humanities Counsel of Tulsa. **Open:** Mon–Fri 9am–5pm. **Free**

Oxley Nature Center
Mohawk Park; tel 918/832-8112. Winding paths through the 800-acre tract feature hands-on exhibits of native flora and fauna. The visitors' center displays interesting birds from the area, poisonous snakes, and a beehive behind a see-through panel. **Open:** Daily 8am–5pm. **Free**

Tulsa Zoological Park
5701 E 36th St N; tel 918/596-2400. A 2,800-acre zoo with natural woodlands that is one of the largest city parks in the country. It features more than 800 animals from 250 species, a children's petting zoo, and a miniature steam train. The Robert J LaFortune North American Living Museum comprises four buildings featuring audiovisual displays, live animals, graphics, and artifacts. Sea Lion feedings daily at 2pm. **Open:** Peak (May–Aug) daily 10am–6pm. Reduced hours off-season. **$$**

Discoveryland!
W 41st St; tel 918/245-OKLA. Located 10 mi W of downtown Tulsa. The 2,000-seat outdoor theater features performances of Rodgers and Hammerstein's *Oklahoma!* Visitors may also watch Native American dancers and walk through a Native American village featuring teepees and lodges dating from the early 19th century. Wagon rides offered through wooded trails. **Open:** June 13–Aug 17, Mon–Sat 5:30–11:30pm. **$$$$**

Big Splash Family Water Park
4707 E 21st St; tel 918/749-7385. This 12-acre water park features a speed slide, wave pool, kiddie pool, water roller coaster, arcade, and concession stand. **Open:** Mem Day–Labor Day, Mon and Wed 10am–6pm, Tues and Thurs 10am–10pm, Fri–Sat 10am–8pm, Sun noon–8pm. **$$$$**

Bell's Amusement Park
3900 E 21st St; tel 918/744-1991. In operation since 1951, the park features a wooden roller coaster. Other traditional rides include a log flume ride and sky ride. Two 18-hole miniature golf courses, arcade. **Open:** Peak (June–Aug) daily, call for schedule. **$$$$**

Weatherford

See also Clinton

Located west of Oklahoma City on I-40 and originally on historic Route 66, this thriving commercial center is home to Southwestern State University and lies close to Crowder Lake State Park to the south. **Information:** Weatherford Area

Chamber of Commerce, 522 W Rainey, PO Box 729, Weatherford, 73096-0729 (tel 405/772-7744 or toll free 800/725-7744).

MOTELS 🖼

☷☷ Best Western Mark Motor Hotel

525 E Main St, 73096; tel 405/772-3325 or toll free 800/528-1234; fax 405/772-8950. Exit 82 off I-40. Motel has small but pleasant lobby area and is close to restaurants and shops. Fine for overnight. **Rooms:** 59 rms. CI 1pm/CO noon. Nonsmoking rms avail. Comfortable rooms have cactus plants. **Amenities:** 🛁 🕭 🖵 A/C, cable TV. All rooms have mini-refrigerators and coffee. Rooms at back of motel have extra amenities, such as irons, ironing boards, and makeup mirrors. Some rooms have dataports. **Services:** ✕ 🖳 🛏 🖑 **Facilities:** 🖵 1 restaurant. **Rates:** Peak (Mar–Oct) $39–$45 S; $42–$49 D. Extra person $3. Children under age 12 stay free. Lower rates off-season. Parking: Outdoor, free. AE, CB, DC, DISC, MC, V.

☷☷ Days Inn

1019 E Main St, 73096; tel 405/772-5592 or toll free 800/DAYS-INN; fax 405/774-2551. Exit 82 off I-40. Standard motel across from an antique mall, close to many restaurants and about a mile from the airport. **Rooms:** 59 rms, stes, and effic. CI noon/CO 11am. Nonsmoking rms avail. **Amenities:** 🛁 A/C, cable TV. **Services:** 🛏 🖑 **Facilities:** 🖵 🕭 **Rates (CP):** $43 S; $50 D; $55–$75 ste; $65 effic. Extra person $5. Children under age 17 stay free. Parking: Outdoor, free. AE, CB, DC, DISC, MC, V.

ATTRACTIONS 🏛

Gen TP Stafford Museum

3000 Logan Rd; tel 405/772-6143. Astronaut Stafford displays his collection of space memorabilia, including aircraft and space models, several space suits, a Titan second-stage rocket engine, and a seat from *Gemini IX*. A 15-minute presentation is given on the general's career. **Open:** Daily 8am–5pm. **Free**

Roman Nose Resort Park

Watonga; tel 405/623-7281 or toll free 800/654-8240. 30 mi NE of Weatherford. Located in a canyon filled with streams and lakes, the park was once a favored retreat of the Cheyenne. Today's visitors can partake in fishing, boating, swimming, golf, and many other recreational activities. A theme resort park, where visitors gather at a teepee encampment for traditional foods and dancing, highlights the Cheyenne and Plains Indian heritage of the area. **Open:** Daily sunrise–sunset. **Free**

Woodward

A commercial center in northwestern Oklahoma's ranchland, this town hosts the Annual Woodward Elks Rodeo in July,

considered the toughest in the state. Walking tour brochures lead visitors through the Main Street historic area. Boiling Springs State Park and Fort Supply Lake are nearby. **Information:** Woodward Chamber of Commerce, 1006 Oklahoma Ave, PO Box 1026, Woodward, 73802 (tel 405/256-7411).

MOTEL 🖼

☷☷ Wayfarer Inn

2901 Williams Ave, 73801; tel 405/256-5553 or toll free 800/832-3273; fax 405/256-5553. On US 270/183. Small, simple property on Woodward's main street, with convenient access to local attractions and many restaurants. **Rooms:** 92 rms and stes. CI noon/CO noon. Nonsmoking rms avail. **Amenities:** 🛁 A/C, cable TV, dataport. Coffeemakers on request. **Services:** 🚐 🖳 🛏 🖑 Movie and VCR rentals available in lobby. Small pets may stay in rooms; large pets may board in hotel's kennel free of charge. **Facilities:** 🖵 🖵 🕭 1 bar, playground, washer/dryer. **Rates (CP):** $32–$43 S; $38 D; $60 ste. Extra person $3. Children under age 12 stay free. Parking: Outdoor, free. 10% AARP discount avail. AE, CB, DC, DISC, MC, V.

RESTAURANTS 🍴

Marie's Villa

3611 Williams Ave; tel 405/256-7907. On US 270/183. **Barbecue/Tex-Mex.** A very casual restaurant with ceiling fans and Indian posters on the walls. Specialties include fajitas, combination platters, chili rellenos, and even steak, shrimp, chicken, ribs, and barbecue plates and baskets. All-you-can-eat barbecue is $10 for adults, $4 for children. **FYI:** Reservations accepted. Children's menu. **Open:** Mon–Sat 11am–9pm. **Prices:** Main courses $5–$26. AE, MC, V. 🖼 🕭

Rib Ranch

2424 Williams Ave; tel 405/256-6081. On US 183/270. **Barbecue.** In business for over 20 years, this casual eatery housed in a log cabin–style building is great for family dining. Sandwiches, ribs, and chicken are served in large portions. "Tenderfoot" selections offer lighter portions for the less hungry. **FYI:** Reservations not accepted. Children's menu. Beer and wine only. **Open:** Lunch Tues–Fri 11am–2pm, Sat 11am–5pm, Sun 11am–5pm; dinner Tues–Fri 5–9pm, Sat 5–9pm, Sun 5–7pm. **Prices:** Main courses $4–$10. DISC, MC, V. 🖼

ATTRACTIONS 🏛

Plains Indians and Pioneer Museum

2009 Williams Ave; tel 405/256-6136. Changing and permanent displays depict Native American culture and early settler life on the Plains. Art gallery; historic Bank of Fargo; original Fort Supply trader's shop; agricultural center; and Native American artifacts and clothing. **Open:** Tues–Sat 10am–5pm, Sun 1–4pm. **Free**

Boiling Springs State Park
OK 34C; tel 405/256-7664. 6 mi E on OK 34C. Featuring cold springs that "boil up" through the white sand of the North Canadian River at 200 gallons per minute. The 820-acre park comprises the last stand of big timber in western Oklahoma and is known for its views. Seven-acre lake for fishing, swimming pool, hiking, picnic area, 18-hole golf course with driving range and putting greens. **Open:** Daily sunrise–sunset. **Free**

TEXAS

An American Epic

STATE STATS

CAPITAL

Austin

AREA

267,339 square miles

BORDERS

New Mexico, Mexico,
Louisiana, Arkansas,
Oklahoma, the Gulf of Mexico

POPULATION

17,059,805 (1990)

ENTERED UNION

December 29, 1845
(28th state)

NICKNAME

Lone Star State

STATE FLOWER

Bluebonnet

STATE BIRD

Mockingbird

FAMOUS NATIVES

Carol Burnett,
Dwight D Eisenhower,
Janis Joplin, Barbara Jordan,
Katherine Anne Porter,
Lyndon Baines Johnson

An unbridled American phenomenon, Texas seems to demand superlatives: "most," "only," "greatest," "best," or "meanest," "toughest," "ugliest," and "orneriest." It doesn't matter so much what you say about the state or even whether it's accurate, as long as you turn up the volume. JR Ewing of TV's *Dallas* may have been too bad to be true but, in keeping with the Lone Star myth, he never did anything halfway.

Texas's history, especially its stint as an independent country, helps explain the state's larger-than-life reputation. As resident author James Michener observed, the tale of Texas is an epic with a roller coaster plot, encompassing the end of an empire, the birth of a republic, and the rapid rise and fall of liquid fortunes. It would be hard for even Hollywood to improve on some of the particulars. The choice of Austin as state capital, for example, was conceived during a buffalo hunt by a man whose middle name was Bonaparte.

And then, of course, there's the fact that the state really is BIG: upstart Alaska may have filched the "largest" title in 1959, but Texas still reigns supreme over the continental United States. If you could drive directly from north to south, you'd put 801 miles on your odometer, and it's another 773-mile stretch from east to west. Although the state doesn't really measure its ranches in RIs (Rhode Islands) as some residents wryly claim, West Texas's Brewster County alone is larger than the state of Connecticut.

Which suggests that such a vast place might be home to some diversity. From mirrored skyscrapers and dry gulches, the state offers almost every landscape and urban setting you can think of. You'll need to travel some distance to find the dramatic climatic and geographic differences between, say, the steamy Gulf Coast and desertlike West Texas, but you don't have to go very far to notice the unique character of the cities.

From Austin, a liberal college town, it's only 80 miles to San Antonio, economically driven by the military. Dallas, a banking and insurance center, is far more status-conscious than Fort Worth, its freewheeling next-door neighbor.

If it's impossible to expect consistency here, there are nevertheless a few statewide constants—one of them being flamboyance. Who but a good ol' local boy like Lyndon Baines Johnson would show off an appendix scar to reporters when he was president? Nor is this bent towards attention-getting restricted by gender. A white leather–clad Ann Richards straddled a motorcycle for a *Texas Monthly* cover while she was governor. Texas chauvinism is a trait you can depend on, too. After all, this is the place that inspired the song, "When I Die, Let Me Go to Texas."

But the flip side of an over-weening love for their home turf is that locals want you to adore it, too. Friendliness may be the one Texas quality that's not been exaggerated in the telling. Along with a capacity for being welcoming, Texans also have a facility for laughing at themselves. So if you're up for excess and not overly finicky about formality, you're bound to have a hearty good time.

Fun Facts

• Texas has changed its capital 15 times, and has flown the flags of France, Spain, Mexico, the Republic of Texas, the Confederacy, and the United States.

• The King Ranch, the biggest ranch in America, covers an area larger than the state of Rhode Island.

• Ninety percent of the world's helium is produced in Amarillo, Texas.

• According to the articles annexing Texas to the United States, the Lone Star State has the right to subdivide into five smaller states.

• Washateria, the world's first laundromat, opened in Fort Worth in 1934.

A Brief History

The Accidental Tourist Archeological evidence shows that Paleo-Indians inhabited the vast expanse now called Texas some 10,000 to 13,000 years ago. When the Europeans arrived in the 1500s, they found tribes ranging from nomadic groups to complex agricultural societies. The first written reports of the territory came from Spaniard Cabeza de Vaca, who was shipwrecked off the coast of Galveston in 1528. If de Vaca's descriptions of his reluctant hosts—among them the cannibalistic Karankawa Indians—didn't encourage further exploration of the area, the rumors he brought back of the seven golden cities of Cíbola helped pique the conquistadors' interest in the lands to the north of Mexico.

On a Mission Sporadic forays by Francisco Vasquez de Coronado into the territory notwithstanding, the Spanish only began to evince real enthusiasm for Texas when the French started moving in. They established two east Texas missions near Fort St Louis, a Gulf Coast settlement founded by the French explorer La Salle and abandoned in 1688. The state derives its name from the first of these, San Francisco de los Tejas. The Tejas ("friends") Indians were anxious to trade with the Spanish and didn't mind being converted to Christianity as the price. But the cost turned out to be much higher: the Tejas Indians soon perished from a variety of imported European diseases.

The Spanish Franciscans subsequently moved west, establishing five missions in the San Antonio area from 1718 to 1731—including the one that later came to be called the Alamo. These peaceful settlements were continually raided, however, by the Apaches and Comanches, who were also battling each other. And until 1762, when France ceded the Louisana territory in return for Spain's help in the Seven Years' War, the French continued to be a hostile presence.

Land for Free By 1824, the many missions established in the territory had been secularized. With the incentive of converting the native populations eliminated and the Apaches and Comanches still roaming freely, the Spanish found it was next to impossible to persuade their countrymen to move there. So although it was rightly suspicious of Anglo-American designs on the land, when Missouri-born empresario (land agent) Moses Austin arrived in San Antonio in 1820, the Spanish government reluctantly agreed to allow him to settle some 300 Anglo-American families in the region.

Austin died before he could see his plan carried out and Spain lost its hold on Mexico in 1821, when the country won its war of independence, but Moses's son, Stephen, convinced the new Mexican government to honor the terms of the original agreement. Between 1824 and 1828 Stephen Austin brought 300 colonists to San Felipe and was granted permission to settle another 900. By 1830, there were some 15,000 settlers, with Anglo Texans outnumbering Mexican Texans by about four to one. At this point, the Mexicans prohibited all further US immigration to the territory. When, in 1835, General Antonio López de Santa Anna abolished Mexico's democratic 1824 constitution, Tejanos (Hispanic Texans) and Anglos alike balked at his dictatorship and a cry rose up for a separate republic.

Remember the Alamo The first two battles for Texas independence fell to the rebels; in the second, fought December 1835, Mexican General Martín Perfecto de Cós surrendered San Antonio to the settlers. But it was the return engagement, that glorious doomed fight against the odds, that forever captured the American imagination. From February 23 through March 6, 1836, some 180 volunteers—among them Davy Crockett and Jim Bowie—serving under the command of William Travis died trying to defend San Antonio's Alamo fortress against a vastly greater number of Santa Anna's men. One month later, the memory of their martyrdom was used to exhort Sam Houston's troops on to victory at the Battle of San Jacinto, thus securing Texas's freedom.

From Nationhood to Secession The independent Republic of Texas's lone star flag flew from 1836 to 1845. During these years, Mexicans as well as Native Americans continued to raid the debt-ridden new nation; the Texas Rangers were created to help protect the frontier. The republic's first president, war hero Sam Houston, saw joining the United States as the solution to these various problems. On December 29, 1845, he was gratified to witness the induction of Texas as the 28th state.

But by 1859, the populace had opted to join the Confederacy. They drove the pro-Union Houston, a two-term US senator and the current governor, out of office. Texas formally seceded in 1861 and spent most of the Civil War supplying cloth and ammunition to the rest of the Confederacy. Although Texas went through a difficult Reconstruction, no battles

DRIVING DISTANCES

Dallas–Fort Worth

195 miles W of Shreveport, LA
202 miles NE of Austin
204 miles SE of Oklahoma City, OK
242 miles NW of Houston
281 miles NE of San Antonio
323 miles SW of Little Rock, AR
363 miles SE of Amarillo
639 miles NE of El Paso

Houston

50 miles NW of Galveston
160 miles SE of Austin
199 miles NE of San Antonio
207 miles NE of Corpus Christi
242 miles SE of Dallas–Fort Worth
357 miles NE of Brownsville
608 miles SE of Amarillo
753 miles SE of El Paso

El Paso

165 SW of Carlsbad, NM
199 miles SW of Roswell, NM
344 miles SW of Lubbock
415 miles SW of Amarillo
566 miles NW of San Antonio
592 miles NW of Austin
639 miles SW of Dallas–Fort Worth
753 miles NW of Houston

had been fought on native soil, so the state suffered less than did many others on the losing side.

Cotton remained Texas's dominant industry after the war, but cattle was soon running a close second; huge drives north to Kansas and Missouri became common. In the 1870s, ranching was revolutionized by the introduction of barbed wire. John W Gates made a fortune selling the new fencing, which allowed for vast improvements in cattle breeding.

Oiled Again Texas entered the 20th century with a boom when oil was discovered at Spindletop, three miles from Beaumont, in 1901. The site produced over three million barrels in its first year of operation. Barbed wire king Gates was one of the first to cash in on the liquid wealth; his Texas Company eventually became Texaco. The discovery of other gushers led to the formation of hundreds of companies and an economy afloat on a sea of oil.

The introduction of air-conditioning in the first half of the century made Texas's sultry summers bearable, while the airplane shortened the state's vast distances and large-scale irrigation projects ended the problems of drought. During World War II, shipbuilding and aircraft manufacturing grew in importance and petroleum companies expanded as fuel demands increased. At the end of the Second World War, Texas was for the first time more urban than rural. By 1970, three Texas cities—Houston, Dallas, and San Antonio—were among the ten largest in the United States. But when the nation turned its eyes to the state it was not because of the boom but because President John F Kennedy was assassinated in Dallas in November, 1963, and Texan Lyndon B Johnson acceded to his office.

After the Fall The crash of oil prices in the 1980s has forced the state to focus more and more on the accomplishments of pioneers like Texas Instruments' Jack Kilby, who developed the first microchip in 1959. Along with the high-tech sector, the service industries, especially tourism, are getting increasing attention. More and more, Texas has begun to bank on such above-ground natural resources as its natives' friendliness and their penchant for having fun.

A Closer Look

GEOGRAPHY

Visitors to Texas can take their pick of terrain: the largest state in the continental United States encompasses forests, swamps, beaches, plains, mountains, and deserts in an arresting array of geographical zones.

East Texas, at the westernmost reaches of the southern Appalachian woodlands, shares lush pine forests with neighboring Louisiana. A unique group of ecosystems converge in **Big Thicket National Preserve,** one of the region's most impressive sights. The trees begin to thin as you head west towards the prairieland; many of those that remained were cleared to make way for a massive urban metroplex. **Dallas,** a former trading post, is now the most expensive city in Texas, but remembers its roots with a weekly rodeo. One-time ranching center **Fort Worth** may still be called a "cowtown," but it is as sophisticated as its larger neighbor.

To the south, the **Gulf Coast** sweeps down from Beaumont, site of the first major oil strike in Texas, to the Rio Grande Valley and the Mexican border at Brownsville. Such coastal cities as Galveston and Corpus Christi draw outdoor enthusiasts, but those seeking unspoiled beaches head for the **Padre Island National Seashore.** The entire area is dominated by **Houston,** Texas's largest—and, some say, most energetic—city. Once driven by oil, Houston's economy has relied on high-tech industry and banking since the 1980s bust.

The forests of East Texas and scrubby brushland of West Texas are separated in central Texas by the Balcones Escarpment, an extended fault zone. Running along the limestone-based escarpment, the rolling **Hill Country** is dotted with small Germanic towns; in spring, it hosts a profusion of wildflowers.

AVG HIGH/LOW TEMPS (°F)		
	Dallas–Fort Worth	Houston
Jan	56/36	62/46
Feb	60/39	66/50
Mar	67/45	71/54
Apr	75/55	78/61
May	83/63	85/67
June	91/72	90/74
July	95/75	92/75
Aug	95/75	93/75
Sept	88/67	89/71
Oct	79/57	82/63
Nov	66/44	71/53
Dec	58/38	64/47

At the northeastern edge of the region lies **Austin,** Texas's lake-laced capital and a lively university town. Visitors head south to **San Antonio** to see the Alamo and stay to enjoy the city's Hispanic flavor and its appealing River Walk.

The southern tip of America's Great Plains spills into Texas's famed **Panhandle.** Termed the Llano Estacado ("staked plains") by the Spanish, who drove stakes into the featureless land as guideposts, this flat prairie is home to the cattle ranches and oil derricks that often represent Texas in the popular imagination. **Lubbock,** birthplace of rocker Buddy Holly, is an agricultural center with a western flair. **Amarillo,** the Panhandle's largest and northernmost town, is a major cattle-shipping center. Twenty miles to the southeast, the stunning **Palo Duro Canyon** exposes strata from four major geological periods.

West Texas, encompassing more than 30 mountain ranges (including the Rockies and Guadalupes) as well as part of the Chihahauan Desert, covers a starkly beautiful, classic southwestern landscape. The Rio Grande separates **El Paso,** the largest city on the US–Mexican border, from the spread of Juarez, but the two effectively function as one sun-baked, multicultural megalopolis. Almost 300 miles to the southeast, the river curves to create the southern boundary of Big Bend National Park, a vast expanse of haunting beauty believed by the Apaches to be a repository for rocks left over from the world's creation.

CLIMATE

Forget the water-starved images of Texas you've seen in countless cowboy flicks. There are dry patches in the southern Rio Grande section, but the only region that lives up to the screen stereotype is West Texas: the area between Big Bend and El Paso gets only 9 to 12 inches of rain a year—most of it in summer and fall—and often sees temperatures above 100°F in summer.

Except for the Panhandle, which can get blustery in winter, the rest of the state is fairly warm, but not nearly as dry as West Texas. East Texas and the Gulf Coast region are particularly humid and wet; the area around Houston gets up to 52 inches of rain a year. Spring is the drippiest season here, with fall running a close second.

In between the two extremes, south-central Texas is generally temperate, though visitors to San Antonio and Austin will find both cities pretty steamy in summer. Nearby Hill Country, slightly higher and thus cooler, makes for a good escape at that time of year. Avoid autumn in this area if you don't want to get wet. "Winter Texans"—seasonal refugees from colder climes—tend to head even farther south to the Rio Grande Valley to warm their bones.

March to May is tornado season, but most of the twisters are confined to the "Tornado Alley" of the North Texas plains. Hurricanes tend to blow into the eastern gulf area in August and September; some also turn up in June, July, and October. Fortunately, these storms don't tend to hit Texas as hard as they do some other states.

WHAT TO PACK

The weather and terrain vary widely in this huge state. Remember that temperatures can drop dramatically at night in the desert and that air conditioning is likely to be going full blast in humid cities such as Houston, so you'll want to bring a light sweater or jacket even in summer.

Because Texas is so casual, jeans and T-shirts will probably be the most frequently worn items in your suitcase. The big cities, especially Dallas, boast some of the country's toniest restaurants and hotels, so by all means throw in some fancy duds, but keep comfort your primary packing goal.

Sunscreen, sunglasses, a hat, and sturdy shoes are essential if you're going to be trekking around the desert, and broken-in footwear is crucial for sightseeing everywhere. Bring along a bathing suit, too; even if it's not the season for outdoor swimming, most hotels and motels have heated pools.

TOURIST INFORMATION

The **Texas Department of Transportation** operates 12 travel information centers that can help you chart your trip through the state and provide printed travel resources. Open daily from 8am to 5pm (except major holidays), the centers are located in: Amarillo on I-40 (from Oklahoma and New Mexico); Anthony on I-10 (from New Mexico); Austin (Capitol Complex); Denison on US 75/69 (from Oklahoma); Gainesville on US 77/I-35 (from Oklahoma);

Langtry on US 90, Loop 25; Laredo on I-35 (from Mexico); Orange on I-10 (from Louisiana); Texarkana on I-30 (from Arkansas); Valley at the junction of US 77 and US 83 in Harlingen; Waskom on I-20 (from Louisiana); and Wichita Falls on I-44, US 277/281 (from Oklahoma).

You can also phone the **Department of Transportation** at 800/452-9292 to ask specific questions or to receive the comprehensive *Texas State Travel Guide*, which includes a listing of the state's individual convention and visitors bureaus, regional and state hotel associations, and camping and wildlife associations. The Department of Transportation also maintains a Web page (with the Department of Commerce) at (http://traveltex.com) with general information about the state.

DRIVING RULES AND REGULATIONS

The minimum age for drivers in Texas is 16 with an approved driver's education course, 18 without. Drivers of all motor vehicles must be able to produce proof of liability insurance. Front-seat occupants in cars and light trucks (pickups, panels, vans, etc) are required to wear seat belts, and children under age 2 must be secured in a federally approved child safety seat; those between 2 and 4 can either ride in such a seat or use a standard safety belt. Safety helmets are required for both motorcycle drivers and passengers.

Call the Texas Department of Transportation (tel 800/452-9292) to check current road conditions.

RENTING A CAR

You'll find representatives of all the major car rental firms in Texas. Minimum rental ages range from 21 to 25 years; some companies have an additional charge for drivers between 21 and 24. Although most companies don't allow their cars to be driven into Mexico, some offer special insurance for that purpose.

- **Alamo** (tel 800/327-9633)
- **Avis** (tel 800/331-1212)
- **Budget** (tel 800/527-0700)
- **Dollar** (tel 800/421-6868 or 800/800-4000)
- **General** (tel 800/327-7607)
- **Hertz** (tel 800/654-3131)
- **National** (tel 800/328-4567 or 800/227-7368)
- **Thrifty** (tel 800/367-2277)

ESSENTIALS

Area code: Texas has nine different area codes. **Northeast:** The area code for Dallas is 214, that for the rest of the region is 903. **Central Gulf Coast:** For Houston the code is 713; other areas, including Galveston, use 409. **South Gulf Coast/Central:** The code for this area, which includes Corpus Christie and extends inland to Austin, is 512. **Rio Grande Valley/Central:** Code 210 covers this part of Texas, which includes Brownsville, Laredo, and San Antonio. **North Central:** This section, encompassing Fort Worth, Waco, and Witchita Falls, uses the 817 code. **Panhandle:** Amarillo and Lubbock are the two major cities in the 806 code region. **West Texas:** Code 915 covers the largest stretch of the state, from Abiline in the northeast to El Paso in the west.

Emergencies: Under urgent circumstances only, call 911 to reach the police, fire department, or an ambulance.

Liquor Laws: The legal drinking age in Texas is 21. Underage drinkers can imbibe if they stay within sight of their legal age spouses or parents—but they must be prepared to show proof of the relationship. Open containers are prohibited in public and in vehicles. Liquor cannot be served before noon on Sunday except at brunches.

Taxes: The state sales tax is 6 ¼%. Cities or counties can add up to 2% more taxes to your purchases. The hotel occupancy tax varies, but can run as high as 6%. The car rental tax is 10% for one to 30 days, decreasing with the length of the rental.

Time Zones: Most of Texas is in the central time zone, two hours ahead of the West Coast and one hour behind the East Coast; the El Paso area, however, observes mountain time, one hour ahead of the West Coast and two hours behind the East.

Best of the State

WHAT TO SEE AND DO

Below is a general overview of some of the top sights and attractions in Texas. To find out more detailed information, look under "Attractions" for individual cities in the listings portion of this book.

Big Bend National Park One of nature's great dramas unfolds in the 800,000-acre arena of Big Bend National Park in southwest Texas. Eerie volcanic rock formations, the Rio Grande, and eroded canyons provide a stunning geological backdrop, while the cactus-studded **Chihuahuan Desert** and cool **Chisos Mountains** create a vivid stage set for an animal cast of thousands, from coyotes and javelinas to bighorn sheep and white-tail deer. Hundreds of miles of hiking trails criss-cross the park, including the **Lost Mine Peak Trail,** which takes visitors back to the days when prospectors flocked here for the rich cinnabar (mercury) deposits. For sheer beauty, Big Bend easily ranks among the top national parks, but it's far less crowded than its better-known peers.

Other Natural Wonders Among the Texas sites that the nation, state, and various municipalities have deemed worthy of protection, **Big Thicket National Preserve** in the northeast is a highly unusual meeting ground for swamp, forest, plains, and desert. Its diversity of plant and animal life are unique to this ecologically aberrant wilderness. To the south, on a peninsula jutting into the Gulf of Mexico near Rockport, **Aransas National Wildlife Refuge** provides a safe winter haven for the endangered whooping crane. Other rare species, including the brown pelican, peregrine falcon, and bald eagle, share their marshy turf. Paralleling the Texas coast between Port Isabel and Corpus Christi, **Padre Island National Seashore** sets aside 66 unspoiled miles of Padre Island (at 113 miles one of the longest coast-barrier islands in the world). Its rolling sand dunes are little changed from the days when the Karankawa Indians roamed these shores.

The part of south-central Texas dubbed Hill Country is one of the most scenic regions in the state, especially in early spring when wildflowers daub it with every pigment in nature's palette. The area's year-round attractions include **Enchanted Rock State Park** (18 miles north of Fredericksburg), a 640-acre pink granite dome which draws thousands of hikers. The creaking noises that emanate from it at night—likely caused by the cooling of the rock's outer surface—led the area's Native Americans to believe the rock was inhabited by evil spirits. The limestone base underpinning Hill Country renders the water that rises up in natural pools such as Austin's **Barton Springs** remarkably clear. At this urban recreational hub, some 32 million gallons from the Edwards Aquifer bubble to the ground's surface each day, maintaining a constant temperature of approximately 68°F. The limestone also acts as a filter for the area's six **Highland Lakes,** a sparkling 150-mile long chain formed by a series of dams. It is responsible, too, for such subterranean treasures as **Natural Bridge Caverns,** 12 miles west of New Braunfels. Named for the 60-foot limestone arch spanning its entryway, this cave system features more than a mile of huge rooms and passages filled with stunning, multihued formations.

In the western high plains, **Palo Duro Canyon State Park** (27 miles south of Amarillo) displays the plunging canyons and soaring spires that the Red River carved into the flat expanse more than 200 million years ago. The formations' variegated colors enhance the startling effect. The park also marks the site of Texas's last great battle with the Comanches in 1874. At an outdoor amphitheater backed by a 600-foot cliff, the historical drama *Texas* is presented from late June to August.

Manmade Wonders Rather than cement over San Antonio's constantly flooding central waterway, architect Robert Hugman designed the **River Walk** to control it. His cobblestoned walks and romantic arched bridges of the late 1930s now vie with high-rise hotels and glitzy riverside restaurants for visitors' attention. More recently, Disney teamed up with the National Aeronatics and Space Administration (NASA) to create the dazzling **Space Center Houston,** the new visitor facility for the NASA-Johnson Space Center. The $70 million complex features retired spacecraft like Skylab, as well as the latest in interactive flight simulations and shuttle mockups.

Historic Sites Texans tend to assume you know everything about their state's past. And indeed when you're in San Antonio, it's impossible *not* to remember the Alamo. The historic complex that marks the site of Texas's heroic but failed battle for independence from Mexico sits smack in the heart of downtown. More difficult to recall is the fact that the Alamo was just the first of five Franciscan missions

established along the San Antonio River. The other four now comprise **San Antonio Missions National Historic Park,** accessible by a 5½-mile trail that extends to the city's south side. To see where Sam Houston exhorted his troops on to final victory in the fight for freedom from Mexican rule, you'll have to head 21 miles east of Houston to the **San Jacinto Battle Historical Park.** The **State Capitol** in Austin is not the original built for the short-lived Texas Republic, but this 1888 structure, second only to the US Capitol in size, is very impressive, especially since its recent refurbishing and annex addition.

In this century, tragic history was made at the Texas School Book Depository in Dallas on November 22, 1963; the **Sixth Floor** exhibit hall details that day's fatal shooting of President John F Kennedy from the building. The life of the man who assumed his office is the focus of the **Lyndon B Johnson State and National Historical Parks at LBJ Ranch.** This local hero's Hill Country spread is a lovely spot in which to absorb some pioneer history.

Some Texas neighborhoods have acquired cachet with age, while others have been lovingly preserved or resurrected. In Fort Worth's once-rowdy cattle trading center and meatpacker's mecca—now the **Stockyard Historic District**—modern western-wear outlets sit cheek-by-jowl with turn-of-the-century wooden sidewalks and shopfronts. Galveston's historic districts date back to the late 1800s, when the city was the largest and most prosperous in Texas. **The Strand,** modeled after the London street of that name, was once the ''Wall Street of the Southwest,'' while the cream of Galveston society resided in the **East End Historic District.** San Antonio's **King William Historic District,** where nouveau riche German merchants competed by building ever grander mansions, has recently been restored to its late-19th-century glory.

A number of mid-1800s European settlements seem set in amber in Hill Country: Dude ranches help maintain the frontier atmosphere of **Bandera,** one of the nation's oldest Polish communities, while **New Braunfels** and **Fredericksburg,** two offshoots of a single German immigration society, celebrate their Teutonic roots with frequent *wurstfests.* Just outside Dallas, Victoriana thrives in Waxahachie, which boasts 20% of the Texas buildings listed on the National Register of Historic Places. East Texas's **Jefferson,** once a major steamboat port, hearkens back to the old south with its many antebellum mansions.

Museums High culture is most prominently represented in Houston. For art lovers, the highlights include the **Museum of Fine Arts,** whose huge acquisitions span the ages and include pieces from such master as Monet, Matisse, and Van Gogh; the **Menil Collection,** where tribal art and modernism mingle in a building designed by the co-creator of Paris's Pompidou Center; and the **Rothko Chapel,** a meditation center hung with 14 panels by the minimalist master. In Fort Worth, the **Kimball Art Museum,** housed in architect Louis Kahn's last building, has a fine collection of early-20th-century European paintings. The Remingtons and Russells in that city's **Amon Carter Museum** appeal to aficionados of Western art, who also also flock to the **Cowboy Artists of America Museum** in Hill Country's Kerrville. You don't have to be religious to appreciate **Dallas's Biblical Arts Center:** Every 30 minutes the world's largest oil painting, *The Miracle at Pentecost* is the subject of a dramatic sound-and-light-show not unworthy of Cecil B DeMille.

History buffs should enjoy the **Panhandle-Plains Historical Museum,** south of Amarillo, the oldest (1933) and largest state museum. Some two million artifacts, from fossils to fashions, illuminate every aspect of the West Texas's past. The **Admiral Nimitz Museum State Historical Park** in Fredericksburg explores the career of the World War II naval hero; outside, the **History Walk of the Pacific War,** containing three acres of large WWII relics, abuts the **Japanese Garden of Peace.** Austin's **LBJ Library and Museum,** overlooking the University of Texas campus, traces the 36th President's long career in Washington. Exhibits include Johnson's collection of political cartoons, which he relished even when he was their target.

Family Favorites Even the children's attractions in this state must be described with superlatives. Trust Texas to have built the largest **Sea World** on Earth; the popular marine theme park covers 250 water-filled acres in San Antonio. The city also hosts **Fiesta Texas,** where the food booths, rides, and live entertainment all have a state motif. Houston offers two major amusement centers: families can buy a combination ticket to **Six Flags Astroworld,** home to the largest wooden roller coaster anywhere, and splashy **Waterworld,** right across the road. Wetness also reigns supreme at New Braunfels's **Schlitterbahn,** which features an uphill water coaster among its many aquatic delights.

EVENTS AND FESTIVALS

DALLAS–FORT WORTH AND EAST TEXAS

- **Cotton Bowl Football Game and Parade,** Dallas. January 1. Call 214/634-7525 (parade), 638-2695 (game).
- **Southwestern Exposition Stock Show and Rodeo,** Fort Worth. One of the largest in the United States. Two weeks in late January/early February. Call 817/877-2400.
- **Texas Fiddlers Contest & Reunion,** Athens. Fiddlers from all around the country converge. Last Friday in May. Call 903/675-2325.
- **Chisolm Trail Roundup,** Fort Worth. Cowboy parade, square dancing, barbecue. second or third weekend in June. Call 817/625-7005.
- **National Championship Pow-Wow,** Grand Prairie. American Indian dancing competitions, craft shows, food booths. First weekend after Labor Day. Call 214/647-2331.
- **Texas State Fair,** Dallas. Largest state fair in the country. Late September to mid-October. Call 214/565-9931.
- **Texas Rose Festival,** Tyler. The state's rose capital flowers with shows, parades, garden tours, and the Rose Queen coronation. Mid-October. Call 903/597-3130.

HOUSTON AND SOUTHEAST TEXAS

- **Mardi Gras,** Galveston. State's largest such celebration. Masked balls, coronations, parades, Cajun and Creole cook-offs. Ten days, peaking weekend before Ash Wednesday. Call 409/763-4311.
- **Houston Livestock Show & Rodeo,** Houston Astrodome. World's largest event of its kind. Mid-February. Call 713/791-9000.
- **Charro Days,** Brownsville. Celebration of the Mexican cowboy: rodeos, bullfights, mariachis, cookoffs. Four days in late February. Call 210/542-4341.
- **Buccaneer Days,** Corpus Christi. Spanish landing celebrated with sailing regattas, parades, coronation ball, rodeo. Ten days in late April/early May. Call 512/882-3242.
- **Juneteenth Festival,** Houston. Blues, gospel, and other musicfests celebrate the day slavery was abolished in Texas. Weekend nearest June 19th. Call 713/520-3290.

AUSTIN, SAN ANTONIO, AND CENTRAL TEXAS

- **South by Southwest (SXSW) Music and Media

Conference, Austin. Hundreds of concerts at more than two dozen city venues plus famous keynote speakers from the music industry. Four days in mid-March. Call 512/467-7979.

- **Texas Hill Country Wine and Food Festival,** Austin. Cooking demonstrations, food and wine tastings, celebrity chefs. First week in April. Call 512/329-0770.
- **Fiesta San Antonio,** San Antonio. Huge celebration of city's Hispanic heritage with costume balls, royal court, and more. Third week in April. Call 210/227-5191.
- **Cinco de Mayo,** San Antonio and other cities with Hispanic populations. Mexican celebration of victory over France, with food, music, and dance. Weekend closest to May 5. Call 210/299-8600 (San Antonio).
- **Wurstfest,** New Braunfels. State's largest German festival. First full week of November. Call 210/625-9167 or 800/221-4369.

THE PANHANDLE AND WEST TEXAS

- **Southwestern Livestock Show and Rodeo,** El Paso. Since 1929, the largest livestock exposition in West Texas. Nine days starting the first week in February. Call 915/932-1401.
- **Shakespeare Festival,** Odessa. Held at a replica of the Bard's Globe Theatre. Every weekend from February to April. Call 915/332-1586.
- **Tri-State Fair,** Amarillo. New Mexicans and Oklahomans join Texans in a week-long farm fest, rodeo, and carnival. Mid-September. Call 806/376-7767.
- **South Plains Fair,** Lubbock. Second only to the Dallas State Fair in size. Late September to early October. Call 806/763-2833.
- **International Championship Chili Cook-offs,** Terlingua (just west of Big Bend National Park). First Saturday in November. Call 806/352-8783 or 903/874-5601.

SPECTATOR SPORTS

Baseball The **Houston Astros** of the National League play at the Astrodome (tel 713/799-9555), while the American League Texas Rangers can be seen at Arlington Stadium (tel 817/273-5100) in the Dallas–Fort Worth area.

Basketball The 1994 and 1995 NBA world champion **Houston Rockets** play at The Summit (tel 713/627-3865). Their close competitors, the **San Antonio Spurs,** hoop it up at HemisFair Arena (tel 210/554-7773). The less renowned **Dallas Mavericks** play at Reunion Arena (tel 214/939-2800).

College Football It wouldn't be Thanksgiving in Texas without the annual contest between the **University of Texas** and **Texas A&M,** the state's premier college football teams. UT's home games are played in the Austin campus's huge Texas Memorial Stadium (tel 512/477-6060); the town of College Station hosts Kyle Field (tel 409/845-2311), which the Aggies call home.

Pro Football The **Dallas Cowboys**—as well-known for their cheerleaders as for their regular Super Bowl contender status—huddle at Texas Stadium (tel 214/373-8000). The **Houston Oilers** butt heads at the Astrodome (tel 713/797-1000 or 713/629-3700).

Horse Racing The biggest horse-racing action in Texas now takes place at **Retama Park** (tel 210/651-7000), which opened in northeast San Antonio in 1995. The thoroughbreds compete in spring and summer, the quarter horses run in fall, and races from all over the country are simulcast year-round.

Rodeo You can catch this classic gathering of such wild west events as calf roping, steer wrestling, and bull riding in practically every sizable Texas city at some time or other, but only in Mesquite, just outside Dallas, is the rodeo a regular weekly occurrence (April to September); contact the Mesquite Arena (tel 214/222-BULL) for details. During the summer, you can also depend on finding a rodeo in the Hill Country town of Bandera (tel 800/364-3833). The festive Latin version of the sport, called *charreada,* is widespread in south Texas, especially near the Mexican border. For up-to-date information on rodeo events all around the state, get hold of the monthly *Rodeo Times.* You can write away for a subscription (2823 Hillcrest, San Antonio 78201) or pick up a free copy at many local western-wear stores.

ACTIVITIES A TO Z

Bicycling The state of Texas takes cycling so seriously that it has a Bicycle Coordinator on the payroll. Call 512/416-3125 to obtain information— including maps—on urban bicycling paths or state park trails for bikes in the areas you're interested in visiting.

Bird Watching Aficionados of the feathered can

find more types of birds in Texas than in any other state—three-quarters of all US species are represented here. On the Gulf Coast you can observe the rare whooping crane at the **Aransas National Wildlife Refuge,** and **Galveston Island State Park** is especially popular for viewing pelicans, egrets, terns, herons, and other shorebirds. The only place in America to see such tropical species as the white fronted dove, chachalaca, and green jay is the Rio Grande Valley. Besides arranging birding trips, the Travis Audubon Society in Austin (tel 512/926-8751) can tell you whether rare golden-cheeked warblers and black capped vireos have flown into town.

Boating & Sailing   A number of Texas's myriad lakes have marinas that rent motorboats and sailboats. The sparkling chain of Highland Lakes stretching some 150 miles northwest of Austin is a great hub for this type of recreation in central Texas. East Texas options for fun on the water include Sam Rayburn Lake in the Angelina National Forest and the atmospheric Caddo Lake, which extends into Louisiana. The *Texas State Travel Guide* (see "Tourist Information," above) includes a comprehensive list of the state's lakes and sketches their available facilities.

Camping   You're sure to find someplace desireable to park your sleeping bag, tent, or RV in Texas: Counting all the federal, state, and private land set aside for this purpose, there are more than 200 campgrounds in the state. The free *Texas Public Campgrounds* details the facilities and visit limits of all the national, state, and municipal parks that offer sleepover options. For a copy of this brochure and the Official Highway Travel Map to which it is handily keyed, write Texas Public Campgrounds, PO Box 5064, Austin 78763. To secure a spot in one of the state parks, call the Texas Parks and Wildlife Department's centralized reservation number, 512/389-8900.

Fishing   More than 5,175 miles of fresh water, including creeks, rivers, and lakes, provide places to hook such native game fish as black bass, crappie, bluegill, and catfish. Many Texas lakes and rivers have also been stocked in recent years with outsiders like Florida bass, walleye, and rainbow trout. Deepsea fishing in the Gulf of Mexico is extremely popular as well. Along the gulf's 624 miles of shore and additional tidal bays, you're likely to come across redfish, wahoo, bonito, tuna, marlin, red snapper, and black drum. For information about seasons and laws, write to the Texas Parks & Wildlife Department, 4200 Smith School Rd, Austin 78744. You can also get answers to your fishing questions by calling 512/389-4800 or 800/792-1112.

Golf   You might expect the state that produced such pros as Ben Hogan, Tom Kite, and Ben Crenshaw to be a good golf destination, and Texas doesn't disappoint. Not only does mild weather allow year-round play in a number of places—including Houston, San Antonio, and Austin—but a large percentage of the greens are public. To find out where to tee off in the state (there are almost 500 courses), a good sourcebook is *Golf Courses in Texas,* available on newsstands. You can call for a copy at 713/623-4613 or write to the publisher at 5 Briar Dale, Houston 77027.

Hiking   Thousands of miles of trails wind their way through every type of terrain imaginable in Texas. The national and state park offices can provide you with detailed descriptions and maps. Another good source of statewide trail information is the Public Lands Division of the Texas Parks and Wildlife (tel 512/389-4439). Those interested in hiking the section of the 140-mile Lone Star Trail that traverses Sam Houston National Forest can contact the Forest Supervisor, 701 N 1st St, Lufkin 75901 (tel 409/639-8501).

Horseback Riding   Riding opportunities abound in this former domain of the cowboy, even in major cities. Several state parks feature riding trails and rentals. Most outfitters are prepared for every level of expertise, and many have hayrides for those who don't want to actually mount an animal. Equine enthusiasts should consider a stay on one of the many dude ranches around the town of Bandera; it's a great way to get in lots of riding time, and the surrounding landscape is superb.

Hunting   Hunting is a long-standing tradition in Texas. White-tailed deer tend to be the target in central Texas, while enthusiasts take their best shot at mule deer and pronghorns in West Texas. Several ranches, including the **YO** near Kerrville, stock exotic game animals for year-round hunting (it should be noted that some of these ranches help maintain species that are extinct in their native lands).

SELECTED PARKS & RECREATION AREAS

• **Big Bend National Park**, Big Bend National Park 79834 (tel 915/477-2251)

• **Guadalupe Mountains National Park**, HC 60, Box 400, Salt Flat 79847 (tel 915/828-3251)

• **Bastrop State Park**, TX 21, Bastrop 78602 (tel 512/321-2101)

• **Bentsen–Rio Grande Valley State Park**, PO Box 988, Mission 78572 (tel 512/585-1107)

• **Brazos Bend State Park**, 21901 FM 762, Needville 77461 (tel 409/553-5101)

• **Choke Canyon State Park**, Box 2, Calliham 78007 (tel 512/786-3868)

• **Davis Mountains State Park**, PO Box 1458, Fort Davis 79734 (tel 915/426-3337)

• **Dinosaur Valley State Park**, Park Rd 59, Glen Rose 76043 (tel 817/897-4588)

• **Eisenhower State Park**, Park Rd 20, Denison 75020 (tel 903/465-1956)

• **Enchanted Rock State Natural Area**, Rte 4, Box 170, Fredericksburg 78624 (tel 512/247-3903)

• **Falcon State Park**, PO Box 2, Falcon Heights 78545 (tel 210/848-5327)

• **Galveston Island State Park**, Rte 1, Box 156-A, Galveston 77554 (tel 409/737-1222)

• **Garner State Park**, Concan 78838 (tel 512/232-6132)

• **Goose Island State Recreation Area**, Star Rte 1, Box 105, Rockport 78382 (tel 512/729-2858)

• **Guadalupe River State Park**, HC 54, Box 2087, Bulverde 78163 (tel 512/438-2656)

• **Huntsville State Park**, Park Rd 40, Huntsville 77340 (tel 409/295-5644)

• **Inks Lake State Park**, Park Rd 4, Buchanan Dam 78609 (tel 512/793-2223)

• **McKinney Falls State Park**, 7102 Scenic Loop Rd, Austin 78744 (tel 512/243-1643)

• **Marin Dies Jr State Park**, Park Rd 48, Jasper 75951 (tel 409/384-5231)

• **Mustang Island State Park**, PO Box 326, Port Aransas 78373 (tel 512/749-5246)

• **Palo Duro Canyon State Park**, Rte 2, Box 285, Canyon 79015 (tel 806/488-2227)

• **Tyler State Park**, Park Rd 16, Tyler 75710 (tel 903/597-5338)

River Sports   White-water rafting, tubing, kayaking, and canoeing are big on 22 miles of the Guadalupe River between Canyon Dam (north of San Antonio) and New Braunfels. Don't bother bringing your own equipment—more than 40 outfitters line the river's banks along this stretch (even coolers are available) and most won't allow you to launch from their property if you don't rent from them. For current information about river conditions, call 210/964-3342.

Spelunking   Underlying the Edwards Plateau, which comprises much of the central portion of Texas, is a huge slab of limestone. And where there is limestone, there are caves. If you're looking for dark places to poke around when you visit the state, contact the National Speleological Society at 205/852-1300. They can tell you where the organization's chapters—called grottoes—are located in Texas.

Wildflower Watching   More than 5,000 types of wildflowers grow around Texas. Bluebonnets (the official flower), buttercups, and Indian paintcups are particularly prevalent, but you'll find everything from bougainvillea in the tropical Rio Grande Valley to ocotillo blossoms in the western desert. Recently dedicated by originator Lady Bird Johnson, the new facility of the National Wildflower Research Center in Austin (tel 512/929-3600) is a wonderful resource for finding out what's blooming where and when. You might also write away to PO Box 5064, Austin 78763 for a free *Wildflowers of Texas* folder.

Driving the State

Start	Barton Springs, Austin
Finish	LBJ National Historical Park, Johnson City
Distance	175 miles
Time	1–3 days
Highlights	Texas's best artesian springs; an authentic western ranch and exotic wildlife preserve; natural caverns; the awe-inspiring Enchanted Rock

The Hill Country extends west to tiny Mountain Home, known for its colorful outpost, the YO Ranch; north to Enchanted Rock; south to the outskirts of San Antonio; and east to Austin, which is where this tour begins. The Hill Country is not only the geographic heart of Texas but also, many would argue, the spiritual one as well. Nowhere else in Texas can travelers experience such a rich potpourri of cultures, topographies, and diverse attractions; a visit can recharge the soul in a day or a weekend (though you may want to stay even longer).

For additional information on lodgings, dining, and attractions in the region covered by the tour, refer to specific cities in the listings portion of this chapter.

From downtown Austin, take Barton Springs Dr west to Zilker Park, where you will find:

1. **Barton Springs,** 2201 Barton Springs Dr (tel 512/476-9044). The Balcones Fault is an eons-old crack in the earth that bisects central Texas and separates the coastal lowland from the Rocky Mountains upland. The escarpment reaches a height of 300 feet between Austin and New Braunfels, where it turns into an extended range of wooded hills. A unique product of the Balcones Fault is the group of large artesian springs that have risen for millions of years from the fault's limestone strata. Most notable among them is Barton Springs, located on Barton Creek about a half-mile from its junction with the Colorado River. Approximately 32 million gallons of water from the Edwards Aquifer bubble to the surface of this 68°F natural swimming pool, which is set amid the picnic areas, soccer fields, and other recreations of 400-acre **Zilker Park.**

Returning downtown and taking I-35 south to San Marcos you can experience another watery creation of the Balcones Fault:

2. **Aquarena Springs Resort,** 1 Aquarena Springs Dr (tel 512/396-8900 or 800/999-9767). San Marcos's **Spring Lake** is far more commercialized than Barton Springs—in fact, it's surrounded by Aquarena Springs Resort, a theme park. But for travelers with children, this park is definitely the ticket. The attractions here include glass-bottom boat tours, an Alpine Sky Ride, Submarine Theatre, and a bird show—not to mention Ralph the Swimming Pig, a genuine ham who draws the cheers of visitors by taking a dive into the spring daily. Nearby, a second theme park, **Wonder World,** offers an introduction to another Hill Country signature: caves and caverns. Wonder Cave, which can be toured daily, was formed during the earthquake that created the Balcones Fault.

If you plan to stay overnight in San Marcos, you might consider the Crystal River Inn (tel 512/396-3739) is a reasonably priced, stylish seven-room country inn.

Returning to I-35, drive south to New Braunfels and head downtown to the:

3. **Sophienburg Museum,** 401 W Coll at Academy (tel 210/629-1572). The Hill Country is an ethnic melting pot dotted by small towns that retain the architecture and character of their original European settlers: Czechs, Poles, Scandinavians, and—in the case of Fredericksburg and New Braunfels—Germans. New Braunfels is a merry town with its German bakeries, cafes, and annual **October Wurstfest,** but at the **Sophienburg Museum,** visitors learn that this happiness was bought at a dear price to the town's early settlers. Built on the hilltop site of the log cabin of Prince Carl—New Braunfels' first seat of government—the museum chronicles the tribulations of the Germans who followed the prince here in 1845, only to fall victim to the sickness and disease that would kill as many as

---

Take a Break

If any single restaurant sums up the eclectic charms of Austin, it's **Threadgill's,** 6416 N Lamar (tel 512/451-5440). This legendary home-style restaurant offers the best chicken-fried steak in central Texas, but it doesn't stop there. Threadgill's is equally renowned for its hip vegetable dishes, which make this inexpensive restaurant a place where the unrepentant meat lover and committed vegetarian can break bread together. Be sure to try the vegetable jambalaya—it's especially tasty.

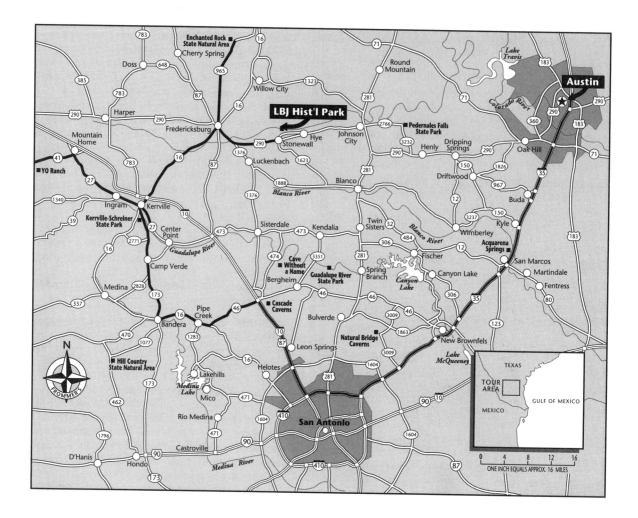

3,000 within the colony's first two years of existence. The museum features an extensive collection of memorabilia and a knowledgeable staff.

For another historical attraction, take TX 46 south, turning left on Garden and then right on Comal to the **Ferdinand Lindheimer Home and Museum,** 489 Comal. Lindheimer, a former German revolutionary who led some of the first colonists to New Braunfels, built and lived in a meticulously restored German *fachwerk* (log-and-stone cabin) home.

From New Braunfels, follow I-35 south to its junction with I-10 northwest of San Antonio. Take I-10 north to the Cascades Caverns Rd exit. (For a more scenic route, take TX 46 from New Braunfels.)

4. **Cascade Caverns,** Cascade Caverns Rd (tel 210/ 755-8080). Celebrated for its 90-foot interior waterfall that flows from an underground stream,

Cascade Caverns is a water-formed cave that is about 98 percent active— the stalactite and stalagmite formations grow at the rate of about an inch per century. The half-mile guided tour of the cave takes about 45 minutes (rubber-souled shoes are recommended), and picnic facilities, a swimming pool,and a snack bar are open to visitors.

After touring Cascade Caverns, take Farm Rd 474 east to Kruetzberg Rd, which runs into another spelunker's delight, **Cave Without a Name** (tel 210/537-4212). This is not as well known as Cascade Caverns (as you might have guessed from the unassuming moniker), but it is one of Texas's largest caves, with many limestone formations and an underground river.

Take TX 46 west to downtown Bandera and the:

5. **Old Bandera Courthouse and Jail,** 12th and Cypress Bandera. For a taste of Bandera's authentic Wild West days, visit the complex where justice was

meted out in the late 19th and early 20th centuries. While the 1868 courthouse is a simple converted storefront, the jail, built in 1891, is a sturdy and elaborate limestone fortress—it had to be, to discourage jailbreaks. Bandera's downtown area boasts a number of other 19th-century buildings, including a bank, a general store, and a blacksmith shop. At 7th and Cypress, **St Stanislaus Catholic Church** marks the site of the second-oldest Polish Catholic Church in the United States. Round out your stop in Bandera at the **Frontier Times Museum,** 506 13th St (tel 210/796-3864), which contains an eclectic collection of more than 40,000 items, including antique firearms, Native American artifacts, and empty liquor bottles from Judge Roy Bean's saloon.

Go north on TX 173 to:

6. **Kerrville.** Over the past several years Kerrville, as well as Ingram, a smaller town six miles west on TX 39, has earned a reputation as a thriving arts community. In May, Kerrville is alive with folk art and music festivals, and in January, the town hosts the **World Mohair Extravaganza,** which features a goat-shearing competition and a mohair fashion show. The **Cowboy Artists of America Museum,**1550 Bandera Hwy (TX 173) (tel 210/896-2553) is home to the sculptures and paintings of about 30 living artists of the Western American Realism school. The exhibit provides a rugged glimpse at cowboy life, interpreted through the eyes of some of the nation's foremost Western artists. The Mexican-flavored museum building is as much an attraction as the artwork inside. The ceiling is a rare treat; it features 18 boveda brick domes, remarkable in that they are suspended without supporting forms or wiring. The **Hill Country Museum,** also in Kerrville, is housed in the 100-year-old, cut-limestone mansion of Charles Schreiner, the savvy developer and sheep farmer who helped raise the town to prominence in the late 19th century. The elegantly restored house-turned-museum contains a wide assortment of Hill Country memorabilia, much of it centered on the Schreiner family and its many noteworthy accomplishments. Charles Schreiner's grandson, for example, was instrumental in bringing the endangered Texas longhorn back from near-extinction. (The Schreiner family also created the famed YO Ranch, the next stop on this tour.)

Ingram is home to the **Hill Country Arts Foundation,** which stages outdoor theater performances on most summer evenings at Point Theatre, located along the banks of the Guadalupe River. Take the Ingram Loop to "Old Ingram," where a variety of arts and crafts shops are located. Where the Ingram

Loop meets TX 39, you will see a large, elaborate mural on the walls of the TJ Moore Lumberyard warehouse depicting the history of Kerr County.

Before heading to your next stop, you should also make a side trip to **Stonehenge II,** a reproduction of the mysterious stone complex in England, located along Farm Rd 1340, about two miles north of its junction with TX 39. Rest assured that this Stonehenge was produced by area residents, not Druids or extraterrestrials. The otherworldly ambience is enhanced by replicas of two of the Easter Island stone faces, which watch stoically over the site.

Take a Break

Because a trek across the Hill Country can work up a hearty appetite, you may well find yourself in the mood for an all-you-can-eat buffet. **Annamarie's Alpine Lodge Restaurant,** 1001 Junction Hwy (tel 210/257-8282) in Kerrville offers a great one. The buffet—available for lunch and dinner most days—features rotating cuisines. On Thursdays you can sample schnitzel, sauerbraten, red cabbage, and other German fare; other nights showcase prime rib, seafood, and brisket.

Return to TX 27 and drive north to Mountain Home, then head about 8 miles west on TX 41 to:

7. **The YO Ranch** (tel 210/640-3222). Since 1880 the Charles Schreiner family has owned and managed this legendary 40,000-acre ranch, where visitors can meet working cowboys, see original Western artifacts, and tour the ranch's headquarters. The Schreiners pioneered the ranching of exotic wildlife, now a growing Texas industry. The YO maintains one of the country's largest collections of natural-roaming exotic animals, including a number of rare or endangered species. Zebra, ostrich, wildebeest, black buck antelope, and giraffe are among the 56 species that roam free on the ranch grounds. Visitors are encouraged to embark on photo safaris. Twice-daily ranch tours are $24 for adults and half-price for children; the tours last about two hours and include lunch or dinner.

Take I-10 east to TX 16, following it north to:

8. **Fredericksburg's Main Street.** The first thing you'll notice about Main Street in Fredericksburg is how wide it is, a reminder of the time when it was a prosperous city's major thoroughfare for stagecoach traffic. Today this German-American community of 7,000 is once again thriving, with thou-

sands of day-trippers and bed-and-breakfast enthusiasts pouring in each weekend to sample the city's charms. Main Street is a shopper's delight; in the string of storefronts you can find a variety of German and Western antiques and collectibles—not to mention a mean jar of peach preserves.

Two notable museums are also located on Main Street. At 340 E Main, the **Admiral Nimitz Museum** (tel 210/997-4379) is housed in the restored Nimitz Steamboat Hotel, whose guests over the years have ranged from Robert E Lee to Jesse James. At 309 W Main, the **Pioneer Memorial Museum** (tel 210/997-2835) is a complex of three well-preserved mid-19th-century homes and a mercantile store that sheds light on the lives of the German farmers, craftspeople, and merchants who settled Fredericksburg. Of particular interest is the Weber family "Sunday house." Sunday houses were tiny, one-room cabins built by farmers and ranchers who lived in the countryside during the week but came to town on the weekends in order to purchase supplies, visit with neighbors, and attend church.

Nearby is the **Vereins Kirche (Society's Church),** a reproduction of the first public building erected in Fredericksburg (1846). The German coffee mill–style church also served as a school and meeting hall.

Should you decide to spend the night in Fredericksburg, you have a wide range of choices. The town has more than 75 bed-and-breakfasts—or, more accurately, *gastehauses* (unattended guest houses where the morning meal is in the home's refrigerator when guests arrive). **Settlers Crossing** (tel 210/997-5612) is a gastehaus complex featuring German log cabins in a picturesque setting of mesquite trees, rolling countryside, and deer that aren't afraid to peer into your bedroom window.

Take a Break

About 10 miles north of Fredericksburg on US 87, the **Hill Top Cafe** (tel 210/997-8922) is one of the Hill Country's most popular restaurants—and not only because of the food. The proprietor, a country-and-western musician and ersatz member of the band Asleep at the Wheel, often steps behind the piano to entertain his visitors. The cooks, meanwhile, do their part preparing a variety of tasty Greek and Cajun dishes, including a perfectly seasoned crawfish étoufée.

From Fredericksburg, travel about 18 miles north on Ranch Rd 965 to:

9. Enchanted Rock (tel 915/247-3903). The most striking natural wonder of the Hill Country, Enchanted Rock is the second-largest granite structure in the United States (exceeded in size only by Georgia's Stone Mountain). A 70-acre pink batholith rising nearly 2,000 feet above sea level, Enchanted Rock is part of Native American legend. The Comanches are said to have journeyed to Enchanted Rock annually to hold sacred rites, and other tribes believed it was haunted. Some mid-19th-century white visitors were killed by Indians as they attempted to gain a glimpse of the structure.

The site was officially opened to tourists in the 1920s, and today the rock is the centerpiece of **Enchanted Rock State Natural Area,** a 1,643-acre park. The grounds feature 60 primitive campsites as well as shade and picnic areas and hiking trails. The climb to the top of the rock is about one mile. It's worth it just for the spectacular view of unspoiled countryside; also, the entrance to **Enchanted Rock Cave,** one of the world's largest granite caves, is near the rock's summit.

Returning south to US 290, you may want to take a couple of detours before your next stop. About 15 miles north of Fredericksburg on TX 16, the **Oberhellmann Vineyards** (tel 210/685-3297) is one of a small number of Hill Country wineries. The vineyard, which is nestled in the side of Bell Mountain, offers tours and wines for sampling on Saturdays.

Driving east from Fredericksburg on US 290, you might also head down Ranch Rd 1376 to **Luckenbach.** There's not much to the town, made famous by the classic Waylon Jennings song—just a general store, a barbecue stand, and a post office. But it's a nice place to enjoy a Shiner Bock longneck and watch a lazy game of dominoes on the storefront porch. Chili cook-off T-shirts and other souvenirs are for sale in the general store.

Take US 290 to Stonewall and the:

10. LBJ National Historical Site/LBJ State Historical Park, Park Rd 1 (tel 210/644-2252). Lyndon Baines Johnson, the 36th President of the United States and one of Texas's truly larger-than-life figures, grew up along the Hill Country's Pedernales River—the "Purd-nallis," as area natives call it. At the park, a cooperative effort of the National Park Service and the Texas Parks and Wildlife Department, visitors can tour the former **LBJ Ranch,** including the ranch house, Johnson's birthplace, and his burial site. Driving west on US 290 in Johnson City you can also visit LBJ's boyhood home, where he lived from age 5 to 18.

Continue west on US 290 to return to Austin.

Driving the State

Start	Laguna Atacosa National Wildlife Refuge
Finish	Matamoros, Mexico
Distance	60 miles
Time	6–8 hours
Highlights	Texas's most beautiful white-sand beaches; a preserve for 300 species of waterfowl and other birds; a world-class zoo; shopping in a Mexican border city

South Padre Island is Texas's premier beach destination. Although its status as a spring break mecca may evoke images of over-the-top revelry, for most of the year South Padre is a place for families. It is also a great jumping-off point for a driving tour of the Texas coast and the Rio Grande Valley (which, technically speaking, is really a broad delta, not a valley). The climate in the area is subtropical—in the continental United States only the tip of Florida lies farther south—and a drive from the eastern Rio Grande Valley to the coast will take you through a unique mix of plant life, from oaks and mesquites to banana trees and palms.

Should you choose to spend a day at the beach and a second day seeing the sights, try one of South Padre's many condominiums (there are about three times as many condos as motels on the island). One of the most luxurious is the **Bridgepoint** (tel 800/221-1402), the tallest structure on the island with great views of the Gulf of Mexico and Laguna Madre. The Bridgepoint, like many condos, requires a minimum two-night stay. Among hotels, the **Sheraton Fiesta** (tel 800/672-4747) boasts two sizable swimming pools. For travelers on a budget, the **Palms Resort Motel** offers good accommodations at a moderate price (tel 800/221-5218).

For additional information on lodging, dining, and attractions in the region covered by the tour, refer to specific cities in the listings portion of the chapter.

The tour begins in **Harlingen,** which as the home of Valley International Airport is the jumping-off point for most visits to the area. If you're driving into the region, take I-77 south or I-83 east into Harlingen. I-83 merges south with I-77 in Harlingen. From the highway, take Loop 499 north to Boxwood and Raintree, location of the Harlingen Industrial Air Park, near Valley International Airport. Here you will find the first stop, the:

1. **Rio Grande Valley Historical Museum Complex** (tel 210/430-8500). The museum offers an over-

view of the cultural and natural history of the Lower Rio Grande Valley, the 100-mile-long delta stretching from Brownsville west to Falcon Lake. But this museum complex is more than a repository for photographs and artifacts; three of the Valley's historical buildings have actually been picked up and brought to the site. The **Paso Real Stagecoach Inn** is a restored 19th-century inn that charged visitors 35¢ a night for room and board. Harlingen's first **hospital,** built in 1923, now serves as a medical museum. The third building, the **Lon C Hill Home,** was built in 1905 by Harlingen's founder, who brought irrigation to the Valley.

Just across from the airport, at 320 Iwo Jima Blvd, you can also visit Harlingen's other main attraction, the **Texas Iwo Jima War Memorial** (tel 210/423-6006). This is the original model that was used to cast the famed bronze monument standing in Arlington National Cemetery. In this version, 32-foot-tall soldiers erect a 78-foot-high American flag. Corporal Harlon H Block, the man immortalized placing the flag in the ground, was a Valley resident later killed in the fighting at Iwo Jima. The memorial is on the campus of **Marine Military Academy,** a private prep school where you may happen upon a uniformed parade or precision drill during your visit. A small World War II museum and gift shop are also at the site.

Return to Loop 499, take Farm Rd 106 east until it dead-ends, then drive north on Buena Vista Rd (which is unmarked) about two miles to the headquarters of:

2. **Laguna Atacosa National Wildlife Refuge** (tel 210/748-3607). Stretching across 45,000 acres on the Laguna Madre, this coastline sanctuary is the largest wildlife preserve in the Rio Grande Valley. It is also a birdwatcher's paradise: the refuge is located along the **Great Central Flyway,** the migration path for more than 300 species of waterfowl and other birds that travel from Canada to the Gulf and back each year. Tour roads and walking paths provide great opportunities for ornithology and photography.

Take Buena Vista Rd to TX 100 and head east to Port Isabel, home of:

3. **The *Lady Bea*,** TX 100 near the Queen Isabella Causeway. A monument to the local shrimping industry, the *Lady Bea* is dry-docked next to Port Isabel's library. Peer through windows in the hull to

277

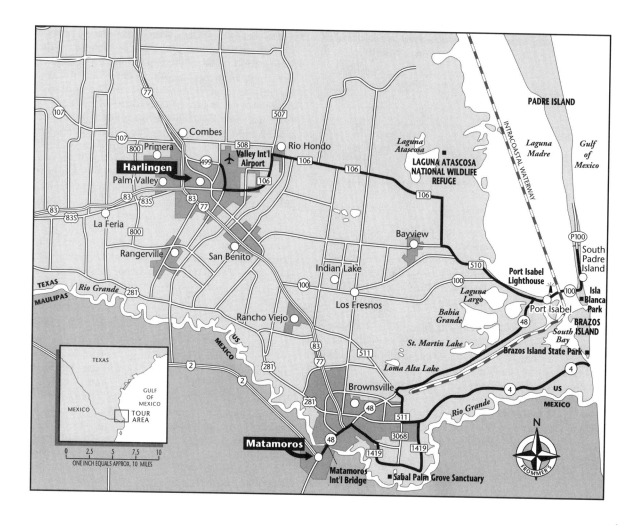

see the captain's quarters, engine room, and other innards of this 45-foot vessel. Nearby a statue of the pirate Jean Lafitte stands watch. To see Port Isabel's current shrimp fleet in action, visit Port Isabel's docks, located just south of the Queen Isabella Causeway. Although you can't buy shrimp directly from the boats, the day's catch is available in area markets.

Take a Break

The best restaurant in the area is **Port Isabel's Yacht Club,** 700 Yturria (tel 210/943-1301), which has been dishing up fresh seafood for residents and tourists since 1926. Talk about fine dining in a casual setting: visitors can walk in wearing shorts and a T-shirt, then choose from a wine list that offers more than 150 selections.

Take TX 100 east to:

4. **Port Isabel Lighthouse,** TX 100 and Tarvana (tel 210/943-1172.) Sitting at the mainland end of Queen Isabella Causeway, Texas's longest bridge and the link to South Padre Island, the lighthouse offers a bird's-eye view of the island, the Gulf, and Laguna Madre (the bay that separates the island from the mainland.) Built in 1853, the lighthouse functioned as a beacon on the Texas coast for more than a half-century, surviving occupation by both sides during the Civil War, as well as a number of hurricanes. The climb up 70 winding steps to the top of the lighthouse isn't easy, but the view is worth the effort. As you gaze out, you will likely be struck by the region's relative lack of commercial development. Directly across Laguna Madre is the town of South Padre, but for miles north and south are unpopulated state-preserved beaches.

After descending from the lighthouse, take

Queen Isabella Causeway to South Padre Island, where you will be greeted by the statue of Padre Jose Nicolas Balli, the first American-born Spaniard ordained by the Catholic Church in North America and the man who settled the island in 1804. Turn right on Padre Blvd at the statue, passing restaurants, bars, and condos to get to the southern end of the island and the site of South Padre's most popular beach:

5. **Isla Blanca Park** (tel 210/761-5493). Also known as Cameron County Park, this park covers the island's southern tip. The park offers shaded picnic tables, grills, shower and changing areas, a fishing jetty, and well-kept beaches. Nearby the **Sea Ranch** marina offers dolphin-watching cruises and deep-sea fishing on the Gulf and Laguna Madre.

Also at the park is the **University of Texas–Pan American Coastal Studies Laboratory** (tel 210/761-2644), which has 12 tanks showcasing sea horses, stingrays, bighead sea robins, Kemp's ridley sea turtles, and other aquatic species.

While walking the South Padre shoreline look for elaborate **sand castles** in front of the Holiday Inn Beach Resort, courtesy of the Sons of the Beach (SOBs) (tel 210/761-5943). On most summer weekends, the SOBs can be spotted building incredibly complex sand creations, complete with spiraling staircases and daring arches.

Take Padre Blvd north to Palm St, turn left, and take a right onto Laguna Blvd, heading north to:

6. **South Padre Island Aquarium,** 2305 Laguna Blvd (tel 210/761-6406). Located at Louie's Backyard, the aquarium is a 40-foot diameter tank with portholes for viewing the eclectic sea life—which includes sharks—within. And here's a fun twist for the adventuresome: for an additional $10, the Louie's folks will actually put you in a shark cage and let you swim in the tank with the fishes. (Give them another sawbuck and they'll even videotape it for you.)

7. **The Sea Turtle,** 5805 Gulf Blvd (tel 210/761-2544.) Diminutive, 90-something Ila Loetscher is the "Turtle Lady," and she has gained the status of legend on South Padre Island through her tireless efforts to rehabilitate endangered sea turtles. Loetscher's staff—and a few costumed turtles—put on an adorably cheesy (and information-rich) show each Tuesday and Saturday to raise money for their cause.

Take the Causeway back to Port Isabel, then follow TX 48 south to Farm Rd 511, taking that south to TX 4. Go east to Boca Chica, the main beach on:

8. **Brazos Island State Park.** South Padre's throngs of

---

visitors and variety of commercial attractions may have you longing for a change of pace. If so, there's no starker one than Brazos Island. At least twice since the Civil War Texans have attempted to develop Brazos Island, only to have their settlements crushed by hurricanes. Today the island is an undeveloped state park where you can camp, swim, fish, or stretch out on the largely uninhabited beach. Driving along the several miles of empty beach is permitted, although you shouldn't try it unless you have a four-wheel-drive vehicle.

Drive TX 4 west to Farm Rd 1419. Turn left and follow the winding road about 7 miles to the entrance to:

9. **Sabal Palm Grove Sanctuary,** near the intersection of Farm Rd 1419 and Farm Rd 3068 (tel 210/541-8034). This Audubon Society preserve covers 172 acres along the Rio Grande, including 32 acres of stately sabal palms, which are native to Texas. Driving through the sanctuary you may also spot unusual animals, such as ocelots or jaguarundis, as well as a variety of birds.

Continue on Farm Rd 1419 northwest to Brownsville, where it becomes Southmost Rd. Turn left at International Blvd and follow to:

10. **Fort Brown,** May St and International Blvd. In a move that hastened the start of the Mexican-American War, President Polk sent General Zachary Taylor to build this border post in 1846. At the time, Brownsville was disputed territory (today it is the most populous city in the Rio Grande Valley). The dispute exploded when the Mexican Army laid seige to the fort shortly after its erection. Two of the war's important battles were fought in Brownsville, both before Polk officially declared war on May 13, 1846. More than 120 Americans and 1,300 Mexicans lost their lives at the battles of Palo Alto and Resaca de la Palma. A marker near the intersection of Farm Rds 1847 and 511, just north of town, commemorates the battles. Fort Brown was finally closed in 1948, but many of its buildings, including

the fort's headquarters, hospital, and morgue, are intact. The complex is located on the grounds of the University of Texas at Brownsville, and the public is permitted to tour the campus free of charge. To identify the historic buildings pick up a map and brochure at the Brownsville Convention and Visitors Bureau, 650 Farm Rd 802 (tel 800/626-2639).

Another downtown attraction is the:

11. **Gladys Porter Zoo,** Ringgold and Sixth (tel 210/546-2177). This scenic contemporary zoo is among the nation's most widely praised. Virtually all animals live in open exhibits that are separated from one another only by natural flowing waterways—there are no cages. In some areas the visitor is given the illusion that predator and prey are actually living together. The 31-acre zoo is divided into geographic zones, with 1,800 animal species representing the continents of Asia, Africa, Australia, and North and South America.

From the zoo, take Ringgold east to International Blvd, then head south to Gateway International Bridge. Although you can drive across the border, most visitors prefer to park on the US side, walk across, and then hop aboard one of the many cabs and mini-vans for hire in Mexico's largest border city:

12. **Matamoros.** Shopping and dining are the prime attractions here for tourists. Stop by the Mexican tourism office, located just past the border crossing, to get a map and ask questions.

Take a Break

Although it's called the **Drive In,** this is *not* a drive-in restaurant. In fact, it's one of the classiest dining establishments in Matamoros. Located at Sixth and Hildalgo, about a mile from the international bridge, the Drive In offers a mixture of continental and Mexican cuisine in a red-plush, crystal chandelier atmosphere. An added attraction is the aviary filled with tropical birds.

There's shopping—and bargaining—to be done throughout this city of more than a half-million. One of the most well-known stores is **Barbara de Matamoros,** 37 Avenida Alvaro Obregron, where you'll find a high caliber of jewelry and ceramic goods and a boutique with clothing designed by the owner, as well as colorful papier-mâché birds and animals and other original creations. **Mercado Juarez,** Matamoros and Ninth, is an open-air market with many small shops. The quality of goods here varies wildly, so inspect your potential purchases carefully. And remember to *bargain.* Not bargaining at Mercado Juarez is like walking onto a used car lot and agreeing to pay the sticker price.

Take TX 48 to I-77 and head north to return to Harlingen.

Texas Listings

Abilene

This Chisholm Trail city was founded in 1881 as a stock shipping station on the Texas and Pacific Railroad. Abilene now boasts numerous museums and cultural events, but its Old West beginnings resurface during the Western Heritage Classic celebration in May. **Information:** Abilene Convention & Visitors Bureau, PO Box 2281, 1101 N 1st, Abilene, 79604 (tel 915/676-2556).

RESTAURANT

★ **Oxford Street Restaurant**
W Frontage Rd; tel 915/695-1770. Corner of S 14th and Winter Pkwy. **American.** Located near the college, this restaurant has standard steakhouse decor with lots of wood and a dark atmosphere. It offers the usual grilled fare and a full salad bar. **FYI:** Reservations accepted. Children's menu. **Open:** Sun–Thurs 11am–10pm, Fri–Sat 11am–11:30pm. **Prices:** Main courses $7–$16. AE, CB, DC, DISC, MC, V. ♥ ♣ &

ATTRACTIONS

Museums of Abilene
102 Cypress St; tel 915/673-4587. Located in the Grace Hotel (now known as the Grace Cultural Center and listed in the National Register of Historic Places), this Mission-style building from 1909 houses three museums devoted to art, history, and children. The art museum features a wide range of temporary and permanent exhibits focusing on American folk art, sculpture, contemporary art, Western art, and photography. The historical museum's re-created rooms offer a glimpse of Abilene in its formative years of the early 1900s. At the children's museum, the Whisper Tube, KIDD-TV station, gravity well, Tot Spot, and "Fingerpaint" computer are some of the exhibits introducing art, science, technology, and other subjects to children. **Open:** Tues–Sat 10am–5pm, Thurs 10am–8:30pm. Closed some hols. $

Abilene Zoological Gardens
TX 36 at Loop 322; tel 915/676-6085. The 13-acre complex is home to more than 500 species of birds, mammals, reptiles, amphibians, and invertebrates from Southwest Texas and the plains of Africa. The Discovery Center compares both regions through exhibits and multimedia presentations, large aquariums, an aviary, and the Terrestrial Trail, which features lemurs, mongooses, and ringtails. The Texas Plains exhibit has bison, sandhill cranes, and black-tailed jackrabbits, while the African Veldt display showcases zebras, gnus, and giraffes. The herpetarium houses more than 75 species of reptiles and amphibians that live on both continents. Appointments for special guided tours should be arranged in advance. **Open:** Daily 9am–5pm. $

Dyess Linear Air Park
Dyess Air Force Base; tel 915/696-2196. A collection of aircraft representing the history of the Air Force. Home to 30 aircraft from World War II, the Korean War, and the Vietnam War; one plane from Operation Desert Storm on display. Visitors must stop at the main gate entrance to Dyess and pick up a temporary vehicle pass. (Note: park may be temporarily closed to the public during military exercises.) Reservations must be prearranged for the extensive base tours to flight lines. **Open:** Daily sunrise–sunset. **Free**

Pioneer City-County Museum
610 E 3rd, Sweetwater; tel 915/235-8547. Exhibits illustrate local and regional history. Of special interest are the Montgomery Arrow Head Collection, which holds over 800 arrow heads; an early General Electric stove, circa 1916; a 1926 fire engine used in Sweetwater up until the 1950s; and a collection of antique toys and books. Tours available. **Open:** Tues–Sat 1–5pm. **Free**

Fort Phantom Hill Ruins
FM 600; tel 915/677-1309. Established in 1851 to protect frontier settlements from local tribes, the post was eventually abandoned in 1854—some historians argue that many desertions were due to boredom and loneliness. The fort burned shortly after, and now its chimneys, foundations, store commissary, guardhouse, and powder magazine are all that remain. **Open:** Daily sunrise–sunset. $

Abilene State Park
150 Park Rd 32; tel 915/572-3204. This 621-acre parkland runs along Cedar Creek near Lake Abilene and offers picnic sites, trailer facilities, shelters, swimming pool, rest rooms and showers, fishing, and hiking. A large grove of some 4,000

native pecan trees, once a campground for the Comanche tribe, is now a favorite spot for picnicking. **Open:** Daily 8am–10pm.

Addison

See Dallas

Alpine

See also Big Bend National Park, Fort Stockton

Founded in the early 1880s as a railroad water stop, Alpine now serves as the commercial center for a vast ranching area. It is home to Sul Ross State University and the jumping-off point for exploring Big Bend National Park. **Information:** Alpine Chamber of Commerce, 106 N 3rd St, Alpine, 79830 (tel 915/837-2326).

ATTRACTIONS

Davis Mountains State Park
TX 118, Park Road 3, Fort Davis; tel 915/426-3337. The 2,677-acre park is located in the rolling foothills of the Davis Mountains, the most extensive mountain range in Texas. Located between the desert plains grasslands of lower elevations and the woodlands of the intermediate elevation, it has the flora and fauna of both areas. One of the most popular places in the park is Skyline Drive, a scenic road that winds its way up to overlooks at 6,000 feet. From here you can see Mount Livermore, at 8,382 feet the second-highest peak in the state. A hilly, 4½-mile hiking trail connects the park with Fort Davis National Historic Site. A wildlife watering station affords bird-watching opportunities. Camping, picnicking, dining room, trailer facilities (37 RV sites), rest rooms, nature study. **Open:** Peak (Mar–Aug) Sun–Thur 8am–8pm, Fri–Sat 8am–9pm. Reduced hours off-season. **$$**

Fort Davis National Historic Site
TX 118 and TX 17, Fort Davis; tel 915/426-3224. Fort Davis played an important role in the defense of West Texas in the second half of the 19th century. From 1854 to 1891, troops based at the post guarded immigrants, freighters, and stagecoaches on the San Antonio–El Paso road and contended with the Comanche and Apache tribes who fought to maintain control of the area. The fort remains one of the best preserved of those in the Southwest—half of the more than 50 original structures have been saved. There are audio programs, a slide show, and self-guided tours of the grounds and several buildings. During summer, park rangers and volunteers dressed as soldiers, officers' wives, or servants are stationed at some of the buildings to provide information. **Open:** Peak (Mem Day–Labor Day) daily 8am–6pm. **$**

Museum of the Big Bend
Sul Ross State University; tel 915/837-8143. Located on the campus of Sul Ross State University, this museum showcases the history of the Big Bend region by focusing on the four groups that shaped it: Native American, Spanish, Mexican, and Anglo-American. There are panels, dioramas, artifacts, and paintings, as well as displays of a stagecoach, buggies, a reconstructed general store, and a blacksmith's shop. **Open:** Tues–Sat 9am–5pm, Sun 1–5pm. **Free**

Woodward Ranch
TX 118 (16 mi S of Alpine); tel 915/364-2271. This is the source of famed Texas agates (such as red plume, pom-pom, and a multitude of other types), colorful jasper, labradorite feldspar, calcite, precious opal, and other minerals. This 4,000-acre site offers collecting opportunities; 50 cents per gram is charged. Guide service is offered for a fee. Campground, RV park; store. **Open:** Daily 8am–6pm. **$**

Amarillo

See also Hereford

Up until the late 1880s, this part of the Texas Panhandle, also referred to as the *Llano Estacado*, or staked plains, looked almost as empty as when Coronado explored it in 1541. Then came the railroads, and by the time Amarillo was incorporated in 1892, it was both a thriving crossroads of railroad commerce and the Potter County seat. The "Grand Canyon of Texas"—the Palo Duro Canyon—lies just south of town. **Information:** Amarillo Chamber of Commerce, 1000 S Polk St, PO Box 9480, Amarillo, 79105-9480 (tel 806/373-7800).

HOTELS

Ambassador Hotel
3100 W I-40, 79102; tel 806/358-6161 or toll free 800/537-8483; fax 806/358-9869. Georgia exit off I-40. Luxury hotel featuring a lush atrium indoor courtyard with glass elevators. **Rooms:** 265 rms and stes. CI 3pm/CO 11am. Nonsmoking rms avail. **Amenities:** A/C, cable TV w/movies. **Services:** Sega Genesis video games available. **Facilities:** 1 restaurant, 1 bar, games rm, sauna, whirlpool. **Rates (CP):** Peak (Apr–Aug) $102 ste. Lower rates off-season. Parking: Outdoor, free. AE, DISC, MC, V.

Best Western Amarillo Inn
1610 Coulter Dr, 79106; tel 806/358-7861 or toll free 800/528-1234; fax 806/352-7287. 3 mi N of I-40. Modern exterior and decor, attractive blue lobby. Near suburban shopping areas. **Rooms:** 103 rms. CI 3pm/CO 11am. Nonsmoking rms avail. **Amenities:** A/C, cable TV w/movies, dataport. **Services:** Facilities: 1 restaurant, sauna. Small pool area. **Rates (CP):** Peak (May–Aug)

$65 S; $73 D. Children under age 12 stay free. Lower rates off-season. Parking: Outdoor, free. AE, CB, DC, DISC, ER, JCB, MC, V.

▤▤▤ Holiday Inn

1911 I-40 at Ross, 79102; tel 806/372-8741 or toll free 800/465-4329; fax 806/372-2913. At jct I-27. Small but well-appointed hotel located a block from the International Quarterhorse Association Headquarters and Museum. Pool area has attractive sun terrace. **Rooms:** 248 rms and stes. CI 3pm/CO 11am. Nonsmoking rms avail. **Amenities:** 🛅 🐾 A/C, cable TV w/movies, voice mail. All units w/terraces. **Services:** ✗ 🚐 🗺 🕹 **Facilities:** 🖼 🛎 ᵴ 1 restaurant, 1 bar, games rm, sauna, whirlpool. **Rates (CP):** $79 S; $89 D; $200 ste. Extra person $10. Children under age 1 stay free. Parking: Outdoor, free. AE, CB, DC, DISC, JCB, MC, V.

▤▤▤ Radisson Inn

7909 I-40 E, 79104; tel 806/373-3303 or toll free 800/333-3333; fax 806/373-3353. At jct Loop 335. With its convenient location next to the airport, this full-service hotel serves many business travelers and conventions. The elegant lobby features exquisite tile floors, fountains, chandeliers, and plenty of sunlight. **Rooms:** 208 rms and stes. CI 3pm/CO noon. Nonsmoking rms avail. Well-appointed rooms. **Amenities:** 🛅 A/C, cable TV w/movies. Some units w/whirlpools. **Services:** ✗ 🚐 🗺 🕹 **Facilities:** 🖼 ▢500 ᵴ 1 restaurant (*see* "Restaurants" below), 2 bars, games rm, whirlpool. **Rates: Rates (CP):** $69 S; $79 D; $189–$239 ste. Extra person $10. Children under age 17 stay free. Parking: Outdoor, free. AE, CB, DC, DISC, EC, ER, JCB, MC, V.

▤▤▤ Westar Suites

6800 I-40 W, 79110; tel 806/358-7943 or toll free 800/255-1765; fax 806/358-8475. ½ mi W of Bell. All-suite, business-oriented hotel ideal for extended stays. Accommodations are tastefully appointed and exceptionally nice. **Rooms:** 126 stes. CI 3pm/CO noon. Nonsmoking rms avail. **Amenities:** 🛅 🐾 🎬 A/C, cable TV, refrig. All units w/terraces. **Services:** ✗ 🗺 🕹 **Facilities:** 🖼 ▢40 Washer/dryer. **Rates (CP):** $57 ste. Children under age 18 stay free. Parking: Outdoor, free. AE, CB, DC, DISC, MC, V.

MOTELS

▤▤ Big Texan Inn

7703 I-40 E, 79120; tel 806/372-5000 or toll free 800/657-7177. ¼ mi E of Loop 335. Budget motel near the airport with rooms featuring Wild West decor and huge murals. **Rooms:** 54 rms and stes. CI 1pm/CO noon. Non-smoking rms avail. **Amenities:** 🛅 A/C, cable TV w/movies. **Services:** 🕹 🗺 **Facilities:** 🖼 1 restaurant (lunch and dinner only; *see* "Restaurants" below). **Rates (CP):** Peak (May–July) $41 S; $50 D; $85–$95 ste. Extra person $5. Children under age 12 stay free. Lower rates off-season. Parking: Outdoor, free. AE, DC, DISC, MC, V.

▤▤ Econo Lodge of Amarillo

1803 Lakeside Dr, 79111; tel 806/335-1561 or toll free 800/847-6556; fax 806/335-1808. At jct Loop 335 and I-40. Standard budget lodging located on the far west side of town. **Rooms:** 99 rms, stes, and effic. CI open/CO noon. Nonsmoking rms avail. **Amenities:** 🛅 🐾 A/C, cable TV w/movies. Most rooms have coffeemakers. Twelve suites/efficiencies have refrigerators, microwaves, stove tops, and coffeemakers. **Services:** 🚐 🕹 **Facilities:** 🖼 1 restaurant. **Rates (CP):** $37–$52 S; $42–$57 D; $53 ste; $53 effic. Extra person $5. Children under age 18 stay free. Parking: Outdoor, free. AE, CB, DC, DISC, MC, V.

▤▤ La Quinta Motor Inn Airport

1708 I-40 E, 79103; tel 806/373-7486 or toll free 800/531-5900; fax 806/372-4100. At jct I-27. Located near the International Quarterhorse Headquarters and Museum. Trademark Southwestern facade and decor, but rooms have stark appearance. **Rooms:** 130 rms and stes. CI open/CO noon. Nonsmoking rms avail. **Amenities:** 🛅 🐾 A/C, cable TV w/movies. **Services:** 🚐 🕹 🗺 **Facilities:** 🖼 **Rates (CP):** Peak (May–Sept 5) $71 S; $81 D; $96 ste. Extra person $6. Children under age 17 stay free. Lower rates off-season. Parking: Outdoor, free. AE, DISC, MC, V.

RESTAURANTS 🍴

Beef Rigger Steakhouse
4000 I-40, westbound Western St exit; tel 806/355-9901. **Seafood/Steak.** Classic steak house with a very dark interior. **FYI:** Reservations accepted. **Open:** Mon–Thurs 5–10pm, Fri–Sat 5–11pm, Sun 4–9pm. **Prices:** Main courses $8–$15. AE, DC, DISC, MC, V. ⬤

♥★ Big Texan Steak Ranch
7701 I-40 E; tel 806/372-6000. ¼ mi E of Loop 335. **Steak.** This restaurant occupies 2½ stories, its Old West facade surrounding a huge dining area. Its reputation was made on its monstrous 72-oz steak, which diners get for free if they can eat it in less than an hour. Those proving capable of the feat get their name added to a list of only 2,000 other guests. (If you can't finish it, the steak costs a whopping $50.) **FYI:** Reservations accepted. Children's menu. **Open:** Daily 9:30am–10pm. **Prices:** Main courses $5–$50. AE, DC, DISC, MC, V. 🖼 📷

Calico County
2410 Paramount Blvd; tel 806/358-7664. 3 blocks S of I-40. **Burgers/Southwestern.** Hearty repasts are the trademark of this cafe. Chicken-fried steaks and sandwiches are two of the favorite menu choices. A nice place for families with children. **FYI:** Reservations accepted. Children's menu. No smoking. **Open:** Daily 7am–10pm. **Prices:** Main courses $4–$8. AE, DISC, MC, V. 📷

Copperfield's
2511 Paramount; tel 806/353-6112. 3 blocks S of I-40. **Burgers/Pizza.** A pizza joint with a huge games room. **FYI:**

Reservations accepted. Children's menu. No smoking. **Open:** Sun–Thurs 11am–10pm, Fri–Sat 10am–midnight. **Prices:** Main courses $5–$10. AE, DC, DISC, MC, V. 📽

The Steakery
In Radisson Inn, 7909 I-40 E; tel 806/373-3303. At jet Loop 335. **American.** The small dining room features a modern decor with lots of dark wood. The professional waitstaff serves standard American pub fare such as salads, sandwiches, burgers, and steaks. Full salad bar. **FYI:** Reservations accepted. Beer and wine only. **Open:** Breakfast daily 6am–2pm; dinner daily 5–10pm. **Prices:** Main courses $5–$12. AE, CB, DC, DISC, MC, V. 📽

ATTRACTIONS 📷

Palo Duro Canyon State Park
TX 217 and Park Rd 5, Canyon; tel 806/373-7800. Some of the most dramatic scenery on the relatively flat High Plains of Texas are the canyon gorges of Palo Duro Canyon—sometimes cited as Texas's scaled-down version of the Grand Canyon. Within the 16,402-acre park is perhaps the most spectacular portion of the canyon. In addition to observing the unique formations, visitors can see the multihued clays and rocks of the canyon walls change colors with the position of the sun. Park wildlife includes mule deer and aoudad sheep, and more than 200 species of birds. An interpretive center houses exhibits on the area's geology, history, and wildlife. There are miles of both hiking and equestrian trails, many to scenic overlooks. Six campgrounds offer 53 multiuse campsites, 20 trailer sites with hookups, and 43 tent sites. The Sad Monkey, a miniature railroad, offers 2-mile journeys through the canyon. A 1,742-seat outdoor amphitheater—whose backdrop is a 600-foot cliff—hosts summer performances of *TEXAS*, a musical drama of Texas history. **Open:** Daily sunrise–sunset. $$

Lake Meredith National Recreation Area
419 E Broadway, Fritch; tel 806/857-3151. Located on the High Plains of the Texas Panhandle, the lake is surrounded by white limestone caprock, scenic buttes, pinnacles, and red-brown, wind-eroded coves. Eight primary and several secondary recreation areas edge the lake, offering facilities ranging from off-road vehicle trails to picnic and camping areas, shelters, rest rooms, boat ramps and docks, and marina service. Waterskiing, fishing, and swimming are popular activities. **Open:** Daily 24 hours. **Free**

Buffalo Lake National Wildlife Refuge
12 mi S via US 60, Umbarger; tel 806/499-3382. This 7,677-acre waterfowl refuge is a winter haven for approximately one million ducks and 80,000 geese, though the lake itself holds very little water. The refuge offers an interpretive walking trail and a 4½-mile auto trail. Picnicking, bird-watching, and camping are popular activities. **Open:** Daily 8am–6pm. **$**

Alibates Flint Quarries National Monument
419 E Broadway, Fritch; tel 806/857-3151. Mined from about 10,000 BC to perhaps as late as the 1800s, these quarries yielded multicolored flint, highly prized by ancient man for its use as tools, weapons, and even currency. The quarries consist of a large number of small pits scattered along the edge of the bluffs above the Canadian River. Adjacent to them are the ruins of villages built by miners over the years. The site is still under development by the National Park Service, so entry is by ranger-guided tours (1½ miles) only. The trail is demanding at various points and is recommended only for those in good physical condition. **Open:** Mem Day–Labor Day. **Free**

Panhandle-Plains Historical Museum
2401 4th Ave, Canyon; tel 806/656-2244. Located on the campus of West Texas State University in a 1933 art deco building, the museum explores the cultural, natural, and economic history of northwestern Texas. Among the Old West exhibits are a chuck wagon, an extensive gun collection, prehistoric fossils, an examination of prehistoric Native American cultures, and a wildlife display. The Don Harrington Petroleum Wing illustrates geological processes and tells the story of oil exploration. Other highlights include a Southwestern art gallery; a decorative arts collection; and the T-Anchor Ranch headquarters from 1877, one of the Panhandle's oldest buildings. Research library on premises. **Open:** Mon–Sat 9am–5pm, Sun 1–6pm. **Free**

Amarillo Art Center
2200 S Van Buren; tel 806/371-5050. Located on the Amarillo College campus, this three-building complex, designed by Edward Stone (whose work includes the Kennedy Center in Washington, DC), is devoted to the fine arts, music, and drama. It houses a permanent collection of paintings and sculpture that includes pieces by Georgia O'Keeffe, Fritz Scholder, Franz Kline, Elaine de Kooning, and numerous others. A theater and outdoor amphitheater present performances. Seminars are also offered at the center. **Open:** Tues–Fri 10–5, Sat–Sun 1–5. **Free**

Don Harrington Discovery Center
1200 Streit Dr (Amarillo Medical Center Complex); tel 806/355-9547. Located in Medical Center Park, the center offers a variety of hands-on exhibits, an aquarium, and a planetarium which presents star shows, astronomy programs, and 360-degree films with special visual effects. Displays geared towards children explore the worlds of architecture, music, and the physical sciences. Gift shop. **Open:** Tues–Sat 10–5, Sun 1–5 **$**

American Quarter Horse Heritage Center and Museum
2601 I-40 E; tel 806/376-5181. The world of the American quarter horse, illustrated through hands-on interactive exhibits, unique artifacts, dramatic video displays, live demonstrations, and artwork. Displays include a scale-model horse, an actual equine skeleton, and a vintage chuck wagon. Orienta-

tion show in the 70-seat theater. Research library and archives open by appointment. **Open:** Peak (May–Labor Day) Mon–Sat 9am–5pm, Sun noon–5pm. Reduced hours off-season. **$$**

Harrington House
1600 S Polk; tel 806/374-5490. Exquisite rugs, 18th-century parquet floors, fine French and English furniture, porcelain, crystal, silver, and paintings on display in a 1914 neoclassical mansion. Guided tours available. **Open:** Apr–Dec, Tues–Thur 10–12:30. **Free**

Livestock Auction at Western Stockyards
S Manhattan at E 3rd; tel 806/373-7464. Amarillo is the headquarters for an immense ranch and cattle feed-lot area. At this site, livestock are processed and brought to the precise weight and grade requirements of meat packers. More than 600,000 cattle are sold at the auction ring every year. Auctions take place every Tuesday beginning at 9am. **Open:** Every Tuesday; times vary. **Free**

Arlington

Although both originally prospered as railroad towns on the stretch of prairie between Dallas and Fort Worth, Arlington and its neighbor Grand Prairie now form a solid entertainment strip along I-30. Either is a good base for exploring the entire region. **Information:** Arlington Convention & Visitors Bureau, 1250 E Copeland Rd, #650, Arlington, 76011 (tel 817/265-7721 or toll free 800/433-5374).

HOTELS 🏨

▆▆▆ Arlington Hilton
2401 East Lamar Blvd, 76006; tel 817/640-3322 or toll free 800/445-8667; fax 817/652-0243. Near TX 360. Tucked away in a peaceful, wooded setting overlooking Six Flags amusement park and the Arlington entertainment district, this comfortable hotel caters to many families and other tourists. **Rooms:** 310 rms and stes. CI 3pm/CO noon. Nonsmoking rms avail. Bright and airy decor. **Amenities:** 🛎 🕹 A/C, cable TV w/movies. **Services:** ✕ 🚐 🖼 🛅 🕭 Car-rental desk, babysitting. **Facilities:** 🔥 🍹 🏊 ☐ 👤 1 restaurant, 2 bars (1 w/entertainment), games rm, sauna, whirlpool, washer/dryer. **Rates:** Peak (June–Aug) $94–$125 S; $99–$145 D; $125–$375 ste. Extra person $10. Children under age 17 stay free. Lower rates off-season. Parking: Outdoor, free. AE, CB, DC, DISC, MC, V.

▆▆▆ Arlington Marriott
1500 Convention Center Dr, 76011; tel 817/261-8200 or toll free 800/442-7275. Near Capeland Rd and I-30, adjacent to Arlington Stadium. This large convention hotel is located adjacent to Arlington Stadium within 5 minutes of Six Flags amusement park. Business travelers and families both stay here. **Rooms:** 310 rms and stes. Executive level. CI 3pm/CO noon. Nonsmoking rms avail. **Amenities:** 🛎 🕹 🍹 A/C, satel

TV w/movies, dataport. **Services:** ✕ 🔑 🖼 🛅 Car-rental desk. **Facilities:** 🔥 🍹 🏊 ☐ 👤 1 restaurant, 3 bars, whirlpool, washer/dryer. American and Delta airline ticket offices are on site, as is Pizza Hut. **Rates:** Peak (May–Aug) $55–$134 S or D; $175–$500 ste. Extra person $10. Children under age 6 stay free. Lower rates off-season. Parking: Outdoor, free. AE, CB, DC, DISC, ER, JCB, MC, V.

▆▆▆ Radisson Suite Hotel Arlington
700 Avenue H E, 76011; tel 817/640-0440 or toll free 800/333-3333; fax 817/649-2480. Near jct I-30 and TX 360. Centrally located hotel with a contemporary design including a sleek, arching canopy and a bright multistory atrium. **Rooms:** 202 rms and stes. Executive level. CI 3pm/CO noon. Nonsmoking rms avail. **Amenities:** 🛎 🕹 A/C, satel TV w/movies, refrig. **Services:** ✕ 🖼 🛅 Complimentary morning newspapers and evening cocktails. **Facilities:** 🔥 🍹 👤 1 restaurant (lunch and dinner only), 2 bars, games rm, sauna, steam rm, whirlpool. **Rates (BB):** Peak (May–Aug) $84–$104 S or D; $94–$124 ste. Extra person $10. Children under age 17 stay free. Lower rates off-season. Parking: Outdoor, free. Romantic Adventure and many other packages avail. AE, CB, DC, DISC, MC, V.

MOTELS

▆▆▆ Ballpark Inn
903 N Collins, 76011; tel 817/261-3621. On TX 157, between Division and Randel Mill. Convenient to nearby attractions. Reserves a majority of its rooms for its corporate accounts. **Rooms:** 186 rms and stes. CI 3pm/CO noon. Nonsmoking rms avail. **Amenities:** 🛎 🕹 A/C, satel TV w/movies, voice mail. Some units w/terraces. Dataports and coffeemakers in some rooms. **Services:** ✕ 🖼 🛅 **Facilities:** 🔥 🍹 🏊 👤 1 restaurant, 1 bar (w/entertainment), games rm, washer/dryer. **Rates:** Peak (Apr–Sept) $64–$119 S; $69–$119 D; $89–$94 ste. Extra person $5. Children under age 17 stay free. Lower rates off-season. Parking: Outdoor, free. AE, CB, DC, DISC, MC, V.

▆▆▆ Best Western Great Southwest Inn
3501 E Division St, 76011; tel 817/640-7722 or toll free 800/346-BEST; fax 817/640-9043. E of TX 360. Catering to families and weekend travelers, this average property is very close to downtown, the Arlington Stadium, and Six Flags amusement park. **Rooms:** 122 rms. CI 4pm/CO noon. Nonsmoking rms avail. **Amenities:** 🛎 🕹 🍹 A/C, satel TV. **Services:** 🚐 🖼 🛅 **Facilities:** 🔥 🍹 👤 1 restaurant, whirlpool, playground, washer/dryer. **Rates:** Peak (May–Aug) $56–$82 S or D. Extra person $4. Children under age 12 stay free. Lower rates off-season. Parking: Outdoor, free. AE, CB, DC, DISC, ER, JCB, MC, V.

▆▆ Comfort Inn
1601 E Division St, 76011; tel 817/261-2300 or toll free 800/472-9258; fax 817/861-8679. Between Ballpark Way and Collins Ave. With its games room and its location near Six Flags, Wet 'n' Wild, and the Arlington Stadium, this

makes a good budget option for vacationing families. **Rooms:** 156 rms and stes. CI 3pm/CO noon. Nonsmoking rms avail. **Amenities:** 🛁 🗄 A/C, cable TV. **Services:** 🚗 📠 🛎 Complimentary morning copy of *USA Today*. **Facilities:** 🏊 🖥 & Games rm, washer/dryer. **Rates (CP):** Peak (May–Aug) $59–$109 S; $69–$129 D; $139 ste. Extra person $5. Children under age 12 stay free. Lower rates off-season. Parking: Outdoor, free. Group, corporate, senior, and government discounts avail. AE, CB, DC, DISC, ER, MC, V.

📧📧 Hampton Inn

121 I-20 E, 76018; tel 817/467-3535 or toll free 800/426-7866. W of TX 360. Clean and well-managed budget motel, close to Six Flags. **Rooms:** 142 rms. CI 3pm/CO noon. Nonsmoking rms avail. **Amenities:** 🛁 🗄 A/C, satel TV w/movies, dataport. **Services:** 📠 🛎 Car-rental desk. **Facilities:** 🏊 & Washer/dryer. **Rates (CP):** $65–$75 S or D. Extra person $10. Children under age 18 stay free. Parking: Outdoor, free. AE, CB, DC, MC, V.

📧 Oasis Motel

818 W Division St, 76012; tel 817/274-1616. Basic budget accommodations. Acceptable for overnight. **Rooms:** 30 rms. CI open/CO noon. Nonsmoking rms avail. Rooms are comfortable and clean, but unadorned. **Amenities:** 🛁 🗄 A/C, cable TV. **Services:** 🛎 **Facilities:** 🏊 Washer/dryer. **Rates:** Peak (June–Aug) $40–$45 S or D. Extra person $4. Children under age 18 stay free. Lower rates off-season. Parking: Outdoor, free. AE, CB, DC, DISC, MC, V.

📧📧📧 Ramada Inn Arlington

700 E Lamar Blvd, 76011; tel 817/265-7711 or toll free 800/228-2828; fax 817/861-9633. Near TX 157 Collins. Standard, dependable, affordable. **Rooms:** 180 rms and stes. CI 3pm/CO noon. Nonsmoking rms avail. **Amenities:** 🛁 🗄 📻 A/C, satel TV w/movies, refrig, dataport. Some units w/terraces. **Services:** ✕ 📠 🛎 ⚲ Car-rental desk. **Facilities:** 🏊 🖥 📇 & 1 restaurant, 1 bar, washer/dryer. **Rates:** Peak (June–Aug) $37–$58 S; $45–$68 D; $82–$126 ste. Extra person $8. Children under age 18 stay free. Lower rates off-season. Parking: Outdoor, free. AE, CB, DC, DISC, EC, ER, JCB, MC, V.

RESTAURANTS 🍴

♣ Cacharel

2221 E Lamar Blvd; tel 817/640-9981. Near jct I-30 and TX 360. **New American/French.** Its ninth-floor windows afford fabulous views of the Arlington entertainment district, and in summer Cacharel is a great place to see the nightly fireworks displays put on by the Six Flags theme park across the freeway. Hardwood floors, soft colors, plants, and a brick kitchen lend a very cozy French bistro atmosphere. The prix-fixe menu changes daily but almost always includes that trendy bird, ostrich, along with seafood, chicken, and lamb. **FYI:** Reservations recommended. Jacket required. No smok-

ing. **Open:** Lunch Mon–Fri 11:30am–2:30pm; dinner Mon–Sat 6–11pm. **Prices:** Prix fixe $33. AE, CB, DC, DISC, MC, V. ♥ 🖼 &

Country Kitchen

1409 N Collins St; tel 817/261-5663. S of I-30. **Eclectic.** A good 24-hour restaurant offering something for everyone with its wide variety of down-home menu items. Reasonable prices and a fun atmosphere make this a great place to take the kids. **FYI:** Reservations not accepted. Children's menu. Beer and wine only. **Open:** Daily 24 hrs. **Prices:** Main courses $3–$11. AE, CB, DC, DISC, MC, V. 📷 🍴 &

Marsala

1618 TX 360 N, Grand Prairie; tel 972/988-1101. At Ave K. **French/Italian.** A great place for a romantic evening, the posh, richly decorated dining room features a red rose on every table. Cuisine is a well-prepared amalgamation of Italian and French dishes. Service is professional, if a tad stuffy. **FYI:** Reservations recommended. Dress code. **Open:** Lunch Mon–Sat 11:30am–2pm; dinner Mon–Sat 5:30–10:30pm. **Prices:** Main courses $10–$22. AE, CB, DC, DISC, MC, V. ♥

ATTRACTIONS 🏛

Six Flags Over Texas

2201 Road to Six Flags; tel 817/640-8900. Fun and fantasy on 200 acres of lavish and exotic landscapes and thrilling rides. The renowned theme park offers breathtaking rides like the Texas Giant, a massive wooden roller coaster that climbs 143 feet in the sky and reaches a top speed of 62 mph; the Texas Chute-Out, a 17-story parachute drop; the Texas Cliff Hanger, whose gondolas drop like falling elevators; the huge Shock Wave double-loop roller coaster; the Flashback, a roller coaster ride that drops from a 125-foot tower and careens through three loops at speeds of 55 mph; white-water boating on the Roaring Rapids attraction. Yet not everything in the park is devoted to wild, thrill-a-minute rides. For those who prefer something a little slower, there is an elegant, restored mid-1920s carousel, the Silver Star, which boasts some 66 wooden horses. Looney Tunes Land offers "soft play" fun, especially for younger kids. Musical review, puppet theater, and Batman stunt show. Fright Nights at Halloween (three weekends in October) feature haunted houses plus special shows; "Holiday in the Park" features Christmas musicals, ice show, and Bugs Bunny holiday show. Food, beverages, and souvenirs available. Admission tickets are all-inclusive. **Open:** Peak (Mem Day–Labor Day) 10am–10pm. Reduced hours off-season. Closed Jan–Feb. $$$$

Wet 'n' Wild

1800 E Lamar; tel 817/640-8000. This expansive water-oriented theme park features 10 separate entertainment areas, including rides such as the Black Hole, a futuristic ride through 500 twisting feet of completely enclosed black tubes accompanied by spaceship sound effects, and the Kamikaze slide that plunges down a 300-foot water speedway from a height of 60 feet. Ocean-sized waves are generated in Surf Lagoon, and visitors can experience the Raging Rapids through waterfalls, rain tunnel, and whirlpools. Other notable attractions include a bubble machine and a water trolley. All-inclusive admission ticket. Picnicking at the park. **Open:** Daily mid-May–mid-Aug 10am–9pm. Weekends only mid-Aug– mid-Sept 10am–6pm. Times may vary. Call ahead. **$$$$**

Arlington Historical Park

621 W Arkansas; tel 817/460-4001. A collection of historical buildings ranging from the 19th to early 20th centuries. Displays include two mid-19th-century log cabins, a one-room schoolhouse, and a way station for the Interurban Trolley that served Dallas and Fort Worth from 1902 until 1936. **Open:** June–September. By appointment. **$**

The Palace of Wax and Ripley's Believe It or Not

601 E Safari Pkwy, Grand Prairie; tel 972/263-2391. The new building which houses a collection of the unusual, the bizarre, and the unbelievable is itself quite intriguing. An "Arabian fantasy," it features huge onion domes, minarets, and exotic detailing. Artifacts from around the world are displayed at the Ripley's museum, such as the overgrown ruins of a mystic temple, shrunken heads, and arts and weapons from primitive peoples. Visitors can experience an earthquake or a Texas tornado, or explore the ocean floor in the undersea world of Atlantis.

Wax figures in a variety of settings can be found at the wax museum. Theme areas include Hollywood, historical figures, horror, fantasy, and religion. Visitors can also watch the resident sculptor at work. **Open:** Peak (Mem Day–Labor Day) 10am–9pm. Reduced hours off-season. **$$$**

Athens

See also Palestine, Tyler

Founded in 1850, the town was named for Athens, Greece because the founders believed it would become the cultural center of the area. Now it is known for its production of black-eyed peas; a jamboree is held every July to celebrate the legume. **Information:** Athens Chamber of Commerce, 1206 S Palestine, PO Box 2600, Athens, 75751 (tel 903/675-5181).

MOTEL 🏨

📛📛 Spanish Trace Inn

716 E Tyler St, 75751; tel 903/675-5173 or toll free 800/488-5173; fax 903/677-1529. On TX 31 E. One of the few choices in Athens, this clean, little motel is located right along the highway. **Rooms:** 80 rms and stes. CI 2pm/CO noon. Nonsmoking rms avail. All king rooms have loveseat. **Amenities:** 🛏 A/C, cable TV. **Services:** ✕ 🖼 🧺 🐕 **Facilities:** 👥 🛒 👤 1 restaurant, 1 bar. Guests have free access to nearby fitness center. **Rates:** $44 S; $40 D; $72 ste.

Extra person $6. Children under age 18 stay free. Parking: Outdoor, free. Rates are always higher on first weekend of every month. AE, CB, DC, DISC, MC, V.

ATTRACTION 🏛

Pioneer Village

912 W Park, Corsicana; tel 903/872-1468. A collection of restored and authentically furnished houses and buildings from the mid-1800s. Included are frontier homes, stores, doctor's office, slaves' quarters, barn, blacksmith's shop, covered wagon, stagecoach, and trading post. **Open:** Mon–Sat 9am–5pm, Sun 1–5pm. **$**

Austin

See also Georgetown, San Marcos

Selected in 1839 as the site for a new capital city for the Republic of Texas and eventually renamed in honor of Stephen F Austin, this enjoyable destination combines country-style living with big-city amenities. Set against the Balcones escarpment that defines the Texas Hill Country, Austin is home to the University of Texas at Austin as well as several other major institutions of higher education. The city is also home to a thriving live music scene, and each year hosts the South by Southwest Conference, a huge event promoting up-and-coming musicians. Lake Austin, an impoundment of the Colorado River, offers scenic walks and water recreation in the heart of town. **Information:** Austin Convention & Visitors Bureau, 201 E 2nd St, Austin, 78701 (tel 512/474-5171).

PUBLIC TRANSPORTATION

The **Capital Metropolitan Transportation Authority** includes more than 50 bus lines. Regular adult one-way fare on Metro routes is 50¢; express service from various Park & Ride lots costs $1. Four 'Dillo routes—Downtown Austin, the Capitol Complex, the University of Texas campus, and the Convention Center—are free. Exact change required; free transfers are good for three hours. Call 512/474-1200 (TDD 385-5872) for information. With the exception of Special Transit Service and Public Event shuttles, seniors and persons with disabilities may ride all fixed bus routes for free with a Capital Metro ID card; these cards are available for a $3 charge from Passport Express, 1107 Rio Grande, or from Capital Metro's administration office, 2910 W 5th St. Children under 5 ride free.

HOTELS 🏨

📛📛📛 Austin Marriott at Capitol

701 E 11th St, 78701; tel 512/478-1111 or toll free 800/228-9290; fax 512/478-3700. 11th St/12th St exit off I-35. Elegant capitol area hotel. **Rooms:** 375 rms and stes. Executive level. CI 2pm/CO noon. Nonsmoking rms avail. Some of the rooms with large windows offer great views of the city.

Amenities: A/C, satel TV w/movies, refrig, dataport, voice mail, bathrobes. Some units w/minibars, some w/terraces, some w/whirlpools. **Services:** Twice-daily maid svce, social director. **Facilities:** 1 restaurant, 1 bar (w/entertainment), racquetball, sauna, steam rm, whirlpool. **Rates (CP):** Peak (Apr–Sept) $79–$89 S; $89–$99 D; $99–$110 ste. Extra person $10. Min stay special events. Lower rates off-season. MAP rates avail. Parking: Indoor/outdoor, free. AE, DC, DISC, MC, V.

Austin North Hilton and Towers
6000 Middle Fiskville Rd, 78752; tel 512/451-5757 or toll free 800/445-8667. Exit 238B off I-35. A posh high-rise hotel with an all-marble lobby and elegant grounds. **Rooms:** 300 rms and stes. Executive level. CI 2pm/CO noon. Nonsmoking rms avail. All rooms have two TVs and a refrigerator. **Amenities:** A/C, satel TV w/movies, refrig, dataport, voice mail, bathrobes. Some units w/minibars, some w/terraces. **Services:** Twice-daily maid svce, social director. **Facilities:** 1 restaurant, 1 bar (w/entertainment), racquetball, sauna, whirlpool. **Rates (CP):** Peak (Apr–Sept) $134–$144 S or D; $195–$250 ste. Extra person $5. Min stay peak. Lower rates off-season. MAP rates avail. Parking: Indoor/outdoor, free. AE, DC, DISC, MC, V.

Best Western Austin
7928 Gessner Dr, 78753 (Downtown); tel 512/339-7311 or toll free 800/528-1234. US 183 exit off I-35, right on Gessner Dr. Standard chain hotel with dependable and affordable accommodations, and a comfortable lobby. **Rooms:** 150 rms. CI 2pm/CO noon. Nonsmoking rms avail. Rooms are average in size but have fairly new furnishings. **Amenities:** A/C, cable TV. Some units w/terraces. **Services:** **Facilities:** Rates (CP): $49 S; $59 D. Extra person $7. Min stay wknds. Parking: Outdoor, free. AE, DC, DISC, MC, V.

Country Inn
5656 N I-35, 78751; tel 512/452-1177. Exit 238A off I-35S. An economy motel with friendly service and large, tasteful rooms—a pleasant surprise. Located near the interstate and the airport. **Rooms:** 100 rms. CI 2pm/CO noon. Nonsmoking rms avail. **Amenities:** A/C, cable TV. Some units w/terraces. Free morning coffee and newspapers. **Services:** **Facilities:** Rates (CP): $57 S; $63 D. Extra person $7. Min stay wknds. Parking: Outdoor, free. AE, DISC, MC, V.

DoubleTree Hotel Austin
6505 N I-35, 78752; tel 512/454-3737. An exceptional, elegant hotel that is a great choice for corporate travel, meetings, and banquets but is also suitable for tourists. **Rooms:** 240 rms and stes. Executive level. CI 3pm/CO noon. Nonsmoking rms avail. The large rooms have attractive paisley print decor. **Amenities:** A/C, cable TV. Some units w/terraces. **Services:** Social director.

Facilities: Rates (CP): $180 S or D; $258–$343 ste. Extra person $5. Min stay peak. Parking: Outdoor, free. AE, DC, DISC, MC, V.

Driskill Hotel
604 Brazos St, 78701; tel 512/474-5911. 3rd-8th Sts exit off I-35 S, right on 6th St. Since 1886, politicians, lawmen, and celebrities have stayed at this classy, posh hostelry. Great for history buffs or anyone who loves elegant historical ambience; the hotel even offers guided tours. **Rooms:** 100 rms and stes. Executive level. CI 3pm/CO noon. Nonsmoking rms avail. Somewhat shabby hallways lead to large guest rooms with beautiful, antique-style furnishings. **Amenities:** A/C, cable TV. Some units w/terraces. **Services:** Social director. **Facilities:** 1 restaurant, 1 bar (w/entertainment), whirlpool. **Rates (CP):** Peak (Feb–Aug) $125–$185 S or D. Extra person $7. Min stay peak. Lower rates off-season. Parking: Outdoor, free. AE, DISC, MC, V.

Embassy Suites Airport North
5901 I-35 N, 78723; tel 512/454-8004 or toll free 800/362-2779; fax 512/454-9047. 51st St exit off I-35. Upscale hotel featuring a glass atrium lobby with elaborate aquariums. Staff here aims to pamper guests. **Rooms:** 175 stes. Executive level. CI 3pm/CO noon. Nonsmoking rms avail. **Amenities:** A/C, cable TV w/movies, refrig, dataport, voice mail, bathrobes. Some units w/minibars, some w/terraces. **Services:** Twice-daily maid svce, social director, masseur. **Facilities:** 1 restaurant, 1 bar (w/entertainment), racquetball, sauna, whirlpool. Amazing recessed-floor restaurant and bar with beautiful marble architecture. **Rates (CP):** $89–$100 ste. Extra person $10. Min stay peak. Parking: Indoor/outdoor, free. AE, DC, DISC, MC, V.

Four Seasons Hotel Austin
98 San Jacinto Blvd, 78701; tel 512/478-4500 or toll free 800/332-3442; fax 512/478-3117. 1st and Holly Sts exit off I-35. Upscale, posh, and exceptionally luxurious. Dramatic, classical decor dominates the glamorous lobby. Exceptional service. **Rooms:** 292 rms and stes. Executive level. CI 3pm/CO noon. Nonsmoking rms avail. Elegant guest rooms have Southwestern touches: Native American patterned bedspreads, leatherette headboards, light-wood furnishings. **Amenities:** A/C, cable TV w/movies, refrig, dataport. Some units w/terraces. Ironing boards and irons in all rooms. **Services:** Social director. Special room service menu for pets. **Facilities:** 1 restaurant, 1 bar (w/entertainment). The patio of the hotel cafe is a very popular spot for bat watching. **Rates (CP):** Peak (Mar–Oct) $210 S; $255 D; $255–$1,400 ste. Min stay peak. Lower rates off-season. Parking: Indoor, $7–$12/day. AE, DC, DISC, MC, V.

Guest Quarters Suite Hotel
303 W 15th St, 78701; tel 512/478-7000 or toll free 800/424-2900; fax 512/478-5103. 15th St exit off I-35. Excep-

tionally nice all-suite hotel suited for extended stays. Very popular with lobbyists, who descend on Austin when the state legislature is in session. **Rooms:** 150 stes. Executive level. CI 3pm/CO noon. Nonsmoking rms avail. Suites are spacious, with a large dining area and a work desk. Separate kitchen area is furnished with full-size appliances. **Amenities:** 🛅 🕹 📠 🍴 A/C, satel TV w/movies, refrig, dataport. Some units w/terraces. Complimentary morning newspaper. **Services:** 🚐 🦾 Social director. **Facilities:** 🛋 👾 🚤 💻 ♿ Sauna, whirlpool. **Rates (CP):** Peak (Mar–Aug) $129 ste. Extra person $5. Min stay peak. Lower rates off-season. Parking: Outdoor, free. AE, DC, DISC, MC, V.

🏨🏨🏨 Hampton Inn Austin North

7619 I-35 N, 78752; tel 512/452-3300 or toll free 800/ 366-1800. US 18B exit off I-35 N. Upscale hotel offering dependable accommodations and friendly service. Standout lobby with attractive colonial-style furnishings. **Rooms:** 125 rms and stes. Executive level. CI 2pm/CO noon. Nonsmoking rms avail. Large rooms with pretty cherrywood furnishings. **Amenities:** 🛅 🍴 A/C, satel TV w/movies, refrig. Some units w/terraces. **Services:** 🚐 🖼 Social director. **Facilities:** 🛋 📦 💻 ♿ Whirlpool. **Rates (CP):** Peak (Apr–Sept) $59 S; $69 D; $75–$80 ste. Extra person $5. Min stay peak. Lower rates off-season. Parking: Outdoor, free. AE, DISC, MC, V.

UNRATED Holiday Inn Austin Airport

6911 N I-35, 78752; tel 512/459-4251 or toll free 800/ 465-4329. Attractive, comfortable accommodations. **Rooms:** 200 rms and stes. Executive level. CI 2pm/CO noon. Non-smoking rms avail. Comfortable rooms with reclining chairs. **Amenities:** 🛅 A/C, satel TV w/movies. Some units w/ter-races. **Services:** ✗ 🔑 🆅🅿 🚐 🖼 Twice-daily maid svce, social director. **Facilities:** 🛋 📦 ♿ 1 restaurant, 1 bar (w/enter-tainment). Guests may use nearby gym for a $5 fee. **Rates (CP):** Peak (Apr–Aug) $59 S; $69 D; $75–$80 ste. Extra person $10. Children under age 5 stay free. Min stay peak. Lower rates off-season. MAP rates avail. Parking: Outdoor, free. AE, DC, DISC, MC, V.

🏨🏨🏨 Hyatt Regency Austin

208 Barton Springs Rd, 78704; tel 512/477-1234 or toll free 800/233-1234; fax 512/480-2069. Riverside exit off I-35 S. A top-of-the-line luxury hotel located on beautiful Town Lake in the heart of the business, shopping, and financial district. Popular with business travelers, who can relax or take meetings in the elegant lobby. **Rooms:** 250 rms and stes. Executive level. CI 2pm/CO noon. Nonsmoking rms avail. Well-designed rooms have floor-to-ceiling windows, beautiful dark-wood armoires. **Amenities:** 🛅 🕹 📠 🍴 A/C, satel TV w/movies, refrig, dataport, voice mail, bathrobes. Some units w/minibars, some w/terraces. **Services:** ✗ 🔑 🆅🅿 🚐 🖼 🦾 Twice-daily maid svce, social director. **Facilities:** 🛋 👾 🚤 250 💻 ♿ 1 restaurant (see "Restaurants" below), 1 bar (w/enter-tainment), whirlpool. **Rates (CP):** Peak (May–Sept) $99–$136 S; $99–$160 D; $250 ste. Extra person $5. Children under

age 10 stay free. Min stay peak. Lower rates off-season. MAP rates avail. Parking: Indoor/outdoor, $3/day. AE, DC, DISC, MC, V.

🏨🏨🏨 Lakeway Inn, A Conference Center

101 Lakeway Dr, 78734; tel 512/261-6600. 2½ mi from exit 252B off I-35. Large business hotel with well-appointed rooms. Public areas are large and luxurious. **Rooms:** 125 rms. CI 3pm/CO noon. Nonsmoking rms avail. **Amenities:** 🛅 🍴 A/C, cable TV. Some units w/terraces. **Services:** ✗ 🚐 🦾 Social director, babysitting. **Facilities:** 🛋 🚴 △ 🏊 ⛳36 🚤 🛥 375 ♿ Volleyball, whirlpool. Indoor tennis facilities. **Rates (CP):** $200–$240 S or D. Extra person $5. Min stay special events. Parking: Indoor/outdoor, free. AE, DISC, MC, V.

🏨🏨🏨 Omni Austin at Southpark

4140 Governor's Row, 78744; tel 512/448-2222 or toll free 800/822-4200; fax 512/442-8028. Ben White exit off I-35. This posh hotel specializes in pampering its guests. Relax in its luxurious lobby with beautiful glass ceilings and tile floors and enjoy the plush bar and restaurant. Ideal for an extended weekend getaway. **Rooms:** 350 rms and stes. Executive level. CI 2pm/CO noon. Nonsmoking rms avail. **Amenities:** 🛅 🕹 📠 🍴 A/C, satel TV w/movies, refrig, dataport, voice mail, bathrobes. Some units w/minibars, some w/terraces. **Services:** ✗ 🆅🅿 🚐 🖼 🦾 Twice-daily maid svce, social director. **Facilities:** 🛋 👾 300 💻 ♿ 1 restaurant, 1 bar (w/entertainment), sauna, steam rm, whirlpool. **Rates (CP):** $119 S or D; $350 ste. Extra person $10. Min stay peak. MAP rates avail. Parking: Indoor/outdoor, $3/day. AE, DISC, MC, V.

🏨🏨🏨🏨 Omni Austin Hotel

700 San Jacinto Blvd, 78701; tel 512/476-3700 or toll free 800/843-6664; fax 512/320-5882. 8th St exit off I-35 S. Very upscale, modern, and posh. The huge atrium lobby sets the tone for the rest of this giant hotel (which shares the sleek Austin Center with tony boutiques and offices): marble floors, glass walls, glass elevators, beautiful fountains, large aquariums, trees, and other greenery. Ideal for business travelers, but also appropriate for splurging couples. Expen-sive, but worth it. **Rooms:** 300 rms and stes. Executive level. CI 2pm/CO 1pm. Nonsmoking rms avail. Rooms are notably large and feature polished parquet floors, antique-style fur-nishings, and armoires. **Amenities:** 🛅 🕹 📠 🍴 A/C, satel TV w/movies, refrig, dataport, VCR, voice mail, in-rm safe, bathrobes. Some units w/minibars, some w/terraces, some w/whirlpools. Two TVs in each room. **Services:** ✗ 🔑 🆅🅿 🚐 🖼 🦾 Twice-daily maid svce, social director. **Facilities:** 🛋 300 💻 ♿ 1 restaurant, 1 bar (w/entertainment), whirlpool, beauty salon. Offices and rooms are available for business needs. Great view from rooftop pool and sundeck. **Rates (CP):** $135 S; $155 D; $180 ste. Extra person $8. Min stay peak. MAP rates avail. Parking: Indoor/outdoor, $3/day. AE, DC, DISC, MC, V.

≣≣≣ Radisson Hotel on Town Lake

111 E 1st St, 78701; tel 512/478-9611 or toll free 800/333-3333. 3rd-8th Sts exit off I-35 S. This elegant, downtown luxury hotel is a great choice for business travelers. The posh lobby is beautifully tiled. Friendly service. **Rooms:** 275 rms and stes. Executive level. CI 2pm/CO noon. Nonsmoking rms avail. The rooms are notably large, with a separate office area and comfortable living area. **Amenities:** 🛅 🍴 🅿️ 🎧 A/C, satel TV w/movies, refrig, dataport, voice mail, bathrobes. Some units w/minibars, some w/terraces. **Services:** ✕ 📠 🆅🅿️ 🚐 ⛵ 🐾 Twice-daily maid svce, social director, babysitting. **Facilities:** 🏊 🏋️ 🅿️275 🖥️ & 1 restaurant, 1 bar (w/entertainment), whirlpool. **Rates (CP):** $79–$150 S or D; $135–$150 ste. Extra person $10. Min stay peak. MAP rates avail. Parking: Indoor/outdoor, free. AE, DC, DISC, MC, V.

≣≣≣ Ramada Inn Airport

5660 N I-35, 78751; tel 512/458-2340 or toll free 800/726-2321. Caters to air travelers waiting for arriving or connecting flights. Exhausted travelers will appreciate the opportunity to relax in the beautiful lobby or take refuge in the comfortable, clean rooms. **Rooms:** 239 rms and stes. Executive level. CI 2pm/CO noon. Nonsmoking rms avail. **Amenities:** 🛅 🍴 🅿️ 🎧 A/C, cable TV w/movies, refrig. Some units w/minibars, some w/terraces. **Services:** ✕ 🚐 ⛵ 🐾 Social director. **Facilities:** 🏊 🅿️300 🖥️ & 1 restaurant, 1 bar (w/entertainment), whirlpool. **Rates (CP):** Peak (Apr–Oct) $59 S; $69 D; $75–$80 ste. Extra person $5. Min stay wknds. Lower rates off-season. MAP rates avail. Parking: Indoor/outdoor, free. AE, DISC, MC, V.

≣≣≣ Red Lion Inn

6121 N I-35, 78752; tel 512/323-5466. Exit 238B off I-35. Although rather expensive for the area, the Red Lion is recommended for the personal attention provided guests. **Rooms:** 205 rms and stes. Executive level. CI 2pm/CO noon. Nonsmoking rms avail. **Amenities:** 🛅 🍴 🅿️ 🎧 A/C, satel TV w/movies, refrig, dataport, voice mail, bathrobes. Some units w/minibars, some w/terraces. **Services:** ✕ 🆅🅿️ 🚐 ⛵ 🐾 Twice-daily maid svce, social director, babysitting. **Facilities:** 🏊 🏋️ 🅿️275 🖥️ & 1 restaurant, 1 bar (w/entertainment), racquetball, sauna, steam rm, whirlpool, washer/dryer. **Rates (CP):** $89 S; $92 D; $100–$130 ste. Extra person $10. Min stay peak. MAP rates avail. Parking: Indoor, free. AE, DC, DISC, MC, V.

≣≣ Red Roof Inn

8210 N I-35, 78753; tel 512/835-2200 or toll free 800/325-2525; fax 512/339-9043. Exit 241 off I-35. Fine for a respite from the road. Comfortable lobby, dependable service. **Rooms:** 135 rms. CI 2pm/CO noon. Nonsmoking rms avail. **Amenities:** 🛅 A/C, cable TV w/movies. Some units w/terraces. **Services:** 🚐 🐾 **Facilities:** 🏊 🅿️30 & **Rates (CP):** $49 S; $59 D. Extra person $5. Min stay peak. Parking: Outdoor, free. AE, DISC, MC, V.

≣≣≣ Renaissance Austin Hotel

9721 Arboretum Blvd, 78759; tel 512/343-2626. US 183 exit off I-35 to Loop 360. Exceptionally elegant hotel with multi-story atrium and indoor public areas boasting numerous trees. Open courtyard is a wonderful place to unwind. Attentive service provided. **Rooms:** 250 rms and stes. Executive level. CI 2pm/CO noon. Nonsmoking rms avail. Rooms are well decorated in expensive, colonial-style furniture; all face the atrium. **Amenities:** 🛅 🍴 🅿️ 🎧 A/C, satel TV w/movies, refrig, dataport, voice mail, bathrobes. Some units w/minibars, some w/terraces. **Services:** ✕ 🆅🅿️ 🚐 ⛵ 🐾 Twice-daily maid svce, social director, babysitting. **Facilities:** 🏊 🏋️ 🅿️250 🖥️ & 1 restaurant, 1 bar (w/entertainment), sauna, steam rm, whirlpool, washer/dryer. **Rates (CP):** $89 S; $99 D; $100–$130 ste. Extra person $10. Children under age 5 stay free. Min stay peak. MAP rates avail. Parking: Indoor/outdoor, free. AE, DISC, MC, V.

≣≣≣ Sheraton Austin Hotel

500 N I-35 at 6th St, 78701; tel 512/480-8181 or toll free 800/325-3535. An upscale hotel located on Austin's main entertainment strip. Alert, efficient service. **Rooms:** 250 rms and stes. Executive level. CI 2pm/CO 1pm. Nonsmoking rms avail. **Amenities:** 🛅 🎧 A/C, satel TV, refrig. **Services:** 📠 🆅🅿️ ⛵ Twice-daily maid svce, social director. **Facilities:** 🏊 🅿️175 🖥️ & 1 restaurant, 1 bar (w/entertainment), whirlpool. **Rates (CP):** Peak (Apr–Oct) $154 S or D; $249 ste. Extra person $10. Min stay peak. Lower rates off-season. Parking: Outdoor, free. AE, DC, DISC, MC, V.

MOTELS

≣≣ Best Western Chariot Inn

7300 North IH-35, 78752; tel 512/452-9371 or toll free 800/528-1234. Exit 240 A on I-35S. A nice corporate motel offering standard accommodations at dependable prices. **Rooms:** 185 rms. CI 2pm/CO noon. Nonsmoking rms avail. **Amenities:** 🛅 A/C, cable TV, voice mail. Some units w/terraces. **Services:** 🚐 🐾 Twice-daily maid svce. **Facilities:** 🏊 🅿️50 & **Rates (CP):** $49 S; $52 D. Extra person $5. Min stay wknds. Parking: Outdoor, free. AE, DC, DISC, MC, V.

≣≣ La Quinta Inn Motor Inn Capitol

300 E 11th St, 78701; tel 512/476-1166 or toll free 800/531-5900. 11th St/12th St exit off I-35. Standard accommodations, lively, friendly staff. **Rooms:** 175 rms. CI 2pm/CO noon. Nonsmoking rms avail. Cozy, attractive rooms with Southwestern decor. **Amenities:** 🛅 A/C, cable TV. Some units w/terraces. Complimentary morning newspaper and evening snack. **Services:** 🚐 Social director. **Facilities:** 🏊 🅿️25 & **Rates (CP):** Peak (Apr–Aug) $59 S; $69 D. Extra person $5. Min stay peak. Lower rates off-season. Parking: Outdoor, free. AE, DC, DISC, MC, V.

RESORT

⚏⚏⚏⚏ Barton Creek Conference Resort
8212 Barton Club Dr, 78735; tel 512/329-4000. Exit 183 off I-35. 10 acres. Luxury hotel with very ornate decor. Caters to large conventions. **Rooms:** 200 rms and stes. Executive level. CI 2pm/CO noon. Nonsmoking rms avail. **Amenities:** 🛗 🗝 🖥 📞 A/C, satel TV w/movies, refrig, dataport, bathrobes. Some units w/minibars, some w/terraces. **Services:** ✗ 🆅🅿 🚐 🖼 ⬳ Twice-daily maid svce, social director. **Facilities:** 🛂 🚴 ⛳🔟₈ 🎾 🏊 🏐 🛅 375 ⅙ 1 restaurant, 1 bar (w/entertainment), lawn games, racquetball, sauna, steam rm, whirlpool, washer/dryer. **Rates (CP):** $89 S; $99 D; $125–$130 ste. Extra person $10. Min stay wknds. MAP rates avail. Parking: Outdoor, free. AE, DC, DISC, MC, V.

RESTAURANTS 🍴

Basil's
10th and Lamar (Downtown); tel 512/477-5576. Off I-35. **Italian.** Fine northern Italian cuisine served in a lovely romantic setting of lace curtains and swirling ceiling fans. Specialty fish dishes include pesce Anjelica, sautéed with artichokes and crab in a mustard cream sauce. Pasta primavera features a heap of fresh vegetables prepared al dente. **FYI:** Reservations accepted. Children's menu. Dress code. **Open:** Sun–Thurs 6–10pm, Fri–Sat 6–10:30pm. **Prices:** Main courses $9–$17. AE, MC, V. 🅥 🆅🅿

Cafe Serranos
1111 Red River (Downtown); tel 512/322-9080. **Mexican.** Fun and festive atmosphere, fabulous fajitas. The family-oriented Mexican has a colorful decor and reliable food at reasonable prices. **FYI:** Reservations not accepted. Children's menu. Beer and wine only. **Open:** Sun–Fri 11am–10pm, Sat 11am–11pm. **Prices:** Main courses $6–$9. No CC. 🏧 🅥 🆅🅿 ⅙

Carmelo's
504 E 5th St (Downtown); tel 512/477-7497. **American/Italian.** This family-oriented restaurant features standard Italian entrees and appealing pasta in large portions. **FYI:** Reservations not accepted. **Open:** Lunch Mon–Fri 11:30am–2:30pm; dinner Sun–Thurs 5–10:30pm, Fri–Sat 5–11pm. **Prices:** Main courses $9–$16. AE, DISC, MC, V. 🅥 🆅🅿

Chinatown
3407 Greystone; tel 512/343-9307. Take Loop 1 S to far W exit, stay on Service Rd for 2 blocks. **Chinese.** This standard Chinese offers all the familiar fare, with lemon chicken and egg drop soup especially noteworthy. **FYI:** Reservations not accepted. Beer and wine only. **Open:** Mon–Sat 11:30am–10pm. **Prices:** AE, MC, V. 🅥 ⅙

★ City Grill
401 Sabine; tel 512/479-0817. **Barbecue/Burgers.** Fine burgers (particularly the bacon cheeseburger) and barbecue.

FYI: Reservations not accepted. Children's menu. Beer and wine only. **Open:** Sun–Thurs 5–10pm, Fri–Sat 5–10:30pm. **Prices:** Main courses $4–$9. AE, DC, MC, V. 🅥 ⅙

Fonda San Miguel
2330 W North Loop (Downtown); tel 512/459-4121. **Mexican.** Inspired Mexican regional cuisine served in a lovely, spacious dining room that is an upscale version of a Mexican cantina. The menu might include Veracruz-style ceviche or Yucatán-influenced pork in banana leaves; more familiar northern Mexican fare (like incredible enchiladas) is always available. **FYI:** Reservations accepted. Children's menu. Beer and wine only. **Open:** Daily 11am–11:30pm. **Prices:** Main courses $6–$10. No CC. 🏧 🅥 ⅙

Foothills Grill
In Hyatt Regency Austin, 208 Barton Springs; tel 512/477-1234. **American.** This romantic spot offers a terrific view of Town Lake and the downtown Austin skyline. House specialties are steak and beef and chicken fajitas. **FYI:** Reservations accepted. Singer. Children's menu. **Open:** Sun 11am–2:30pm, Tues–Thurs 6–10pm, Fri–Sat 6–11pm. **Prices:** Main courses $7–$11. AE, MC, V. ♥ 🅥 🆅🅿 ⅙

$ Green Mesquite Barbecue
1400 Barton Springs Rd; tel 512/479-0485. Off I-35 N. **Barbecue.** This rustic setting is the place for authentic slow-roasted barbecue; the sweet, smoky wood of the mesquite tree, native to Texas, is used in the fire. The ribs are addictive. **FYI:** Reservations not accepted. **Open:** Daily 11am–11pm. **Prices:** Main courses $5–$8. AE, MC, V.

Gunther's Restaurant
11606 I-35 N; tel 512/834-0474. **German.** Folksy decor, authentic German cuisine. Specialties are bratwurst and braunschweiger. **FYI:** Reservations not accepted. Folk music. Beer and wine only. **Open:** Daily 10:30am–10pm. **Prices:** Main courses $6–$8. No CC. 🍴 🅥 ⅙

Mexico Tipico
1707 E 6th (Downtown); tel 512/472-3222. 8 blocks E of I-35. **Mexican.** Surprisingly attractive, this popular eatery on the 6th Street strip offers huge margaritas and authentic renditions of Mexican specialties. Caldo, a hearty beef and vegetable soup, and rojas con queso, a dip of ham, poblano peppers, onions, and cheese served with hot tortillas, make tasty appetizers. Flame-roasted chicken, chimichangas, and chile rellenos are some of the main dishes. Lovely flower-filled patio. **FYI:** Reservations not accepted. Children's menu. **Open:** Daily 11am–10pm. **Prices:** Main courses $7–$13. AE, MC, V. 🏧 🅥 ⅙

$ Threadgill's
6416 N Lamar Blvd; tel 512/451-5440. **International.** Bustling, very casual family-style eatery offering an array of down-home favorites, from a huge chicken fried steak to a great T-bone and baked potato. Cheap daily blue-plate specials; great vegetable side dishes. The adjoining club featured legendary jam sessions in the 1960s; blues/rock icon Janis

Joplin showed up regularly. **FYI:** Reservations not accepted. Children's menu. No liquor license. **Open:** Daily 9am–10:30pm. **Prices:** Main courses $4–$16. AE, MC, V.

West Lynn Cafe

1110 W Lynn St; tel 512/482-0950. Off I-35 N. **International.** This small cafe has a folksy country decor and an extensive menu for breakfast, lunch, and dinner; the filling ranch omelette fits the bill any time of day. **FYI:** Reservations not accepted. Children's menu. No liquor license. **Open:** Daily 8:30am–10:30pm. **Prices:** Main courses $6–$10. AE, MC, V.

ATTRACTIONS

Emma Long Metropolitan Park

1706 City Park Rd; tel 512/346-1831. More than 1,000 acres of woodland and a mile of shore along Lake Austin make Emma Long Park—named for the first woman to sit on Austin's city council—an appealing metropolitan space. Water activities are centered around two boat ramps and a fishing dock; there's also a protected swimming area, with lifeguards on duty during the summer weekends. Camping permits are available. A hike through the stands of oak, ash, and juniper to an elevation of 1,000 feet offers a great view of the city. **Open:** Daily 7am–10pm. **$$**

MUSEUMS

Mexic-Arte Museum

419 Congress Ave (Downtown); tel 512/480-9373. The first organization in Austin to promote multicultural contemporary art when it was formed in 1983, this museum is now the largest art space in the city, with 24,000 square feet of exhibition space. A small permanent collection of 20th-century Mexican art, including an array of masks from the state of Guerrero, is supplemented by visiting shows, including some from Mexico, such as a major retrospective of the work of muralist Diego Rivera. The museum also programs performing arts events each weekend. **Open:** Mon–Sat 10am–6pm. **Free**

Laguna Gloria Art Museum

3809 W 35 St; tel 512/458-8191. This intimate art museum sits on 28 palm- and pecan-shaded acres overlooking Lake Austin; they're believed by some to be part of a claim staked out for retirement by Stephen F Austin, who didn't live to enjoy the view. The lovely Mediterranean-style villa that houses the exhibits was built in 1916 by Austin newspaper publisher Hal Sevier and his wife, Clara Driscoll, best known for her successful crusade to save the Alamo from commercial development. Dedicated to 20th-century American art, the gallery hosts 7 to 10 shows a year; they might feature the works of Austin and central Texas artists, or contemporary Mexican photographers. **Open:** Tues–Sat 10am–5pm, Sun 1–5pm. **$**

Umlauf Sculpture Garden and Museum

605 Robert E Lee Rd; tel 512/445-5582. An art instructor at the University of Texas for 40 years, Charles Umlauf donated his home, studio, and more than 250 pieces of artwork to the city, which maintains the native garden where much of the sculpture is displayed. Umlauf, whose pieces reside in such galleries as the Smithsonian Institution and New York's Metropolitan Museum, worked in many media and styles. **Open:** Peak (June–Aug) Thurs and Sat–Sun 1–4:30pm, Fri 10am–4:30pm, Sat 10am–4:30pm. Reduced hours off-season. **$**

Lyndon Baines Johnson Library and Museum

2313 Red River; tel 512/482-5137, ext 221. Set on a hilltop commanding an impressive view of the University of Texas, the library contains some 40-million documents relating to the colorful 36th president, along with gifts, memorabilia, and other historical objects. Johnson himself kept an office here from 1971, when the building was dedicated, until his death in 1973. Photos trace his long political career, starting with his early successes as a state representative and continuing through the Kennedy assassination and the Civil Rights movement; LBJ's success in enacting social programs is depicted in an Alfred Leslie painting of the Great Society. Museum store. **Open:** Daily 9am–5pm. **Free**

George Washington Carver Museum

1165 Angelina St; tel 512/472-4809. The many contributions of Austin's African American community are highlighted at this museum, the first one in Texas to be devoted to black history. Rotating exhibits of contemporary artwork share the space with photographs, videos, oral histories, and other artifacts from the community's past. Cultural events are often held here, too. The museum's collection is housed in the city's first public-library building, opened in 1926 and moved to this site in 1933; the newer George Washington Carver Branch of the public library is next door. **Open:** Tues–Thurs 10am–6pm, Fri–Sat noon–5pm. **Free**

Texas Memorial Museum

2400 Trinity, University of Texas at Austin; tel 512/471-1604. This art deco–style museum is dedicated to the study and interpretation of the natural and social sciences, with an emphasis on Texas, the Southwest, and Latin America. The fields of geology, paleontology, zoology, botany, ecology, anthropology, and history are covered. Highlights include displays of minerals and fossils, a reconstructed mosasaur, an antique firearms collection, life-size dioramas of Texas wildlife, Native American artifacts, and pre-Colombian pottery. The building is fronted by a university landmark, a sculpture of plunging mustangs by A Phimister Proctor. Museum gift shop. **Open:** Mon–Fri 9am–5pm, Sat 10am–5pm, Sun 1–5pm. **Free**

Elisabet Ney Museum

304 E 44th St; tel 512/458-2255. Strong-willed and eccentric, German-born sculptor Elisabet Ney nevertheless charmed Austin society in the late 19th century; when she

died, her admirers turned her Hyde Park studio into a museum. In the former loft and working area—part Greek temple, part medieval battlement—visitors can view plaster replicas of many of her pieces. Ney had created busts of Schopenhauer, Garibaldi, and Bismarck, as well as Texas heroes such as Stephen F Austin and Sam Houston. **Open:** Wed–Sat 10am–5pm, Sun noon–5pm. **Free**

The Neill-Cochran Museum House

2310 San Gabriel St; tel 512/478-2335. Abner Cook, the architect-contractor responsible for the governor's mansion and many of Austin's other gracious Greek Revival mansions, built this home in 1855. It bears his trademark portico with six Doric columns and a balustrade designed with crossed sheaves of wheat. Almost all of its doors, windows, shutters, and hinges are original. Antique furnishings and historic documents are exhibited inside. **Open:** Wed–Sun 2–5pm. **$**

O Henry Museum

409 E 5th St; tel 512/472-1903. When William Sidney Porter—better known as O Henry—lived in Austin (1884–1898), he published a popular satirical newspaper called the *Rolling Stone*. He also held down an odd string of jobs, including a stint as a teller at the First National Bank of Austin, where he was later accused of embezzling funds. It was while he was serving time for this crime that he wrote 13 short stories that established his literary reputation. The modest Victorian cottage in which O Henry lived with his wife and daughter from 1893 to 1895 contains the family's bedroom furniture, silverware, china, and other period furniture. **Open:** Wed–Sun noon–5pm. **Free**

OTHER ATTRACTIONS

State Capitol Complex

112 E 11th St; tel 512/463-0063. The Texas Capitol is the largest state capitol building in the country—it is even taller than the nation's Capitol. This magnificent Renaissance Revival structure is built of pink granite and features impressive wainscoting of oak, pine, cherry, cedar, walnut, and mahogany. It covers 3 acres of ground with 8½ acres of floor space. Tours available. **Open:** Mon–Fri 8:30am–4:30pm, Sat–Sun 9:30–4:30. **Free**

The Governor's Mansion

1010 Colorado St; tel 512/463-5518. Although it's one of the oldest (1856) buildings in the city, this opulent house is far from a museum piece—state law requires that the governor live here whenever he or she is in Austin. Elegant rooms and antique furnishings can be viewed. Among the many historical artifacts on display are a desk belonging to Stephen F Austin and portraits of Davy Crockett and Sam Houston. Only a limited number of people are allowed to tour the mansion during the few hours it's open to the public, so visitors should arrive as close to opening time as possible. **Open:** Tours every 20 min Mon–Fri 10–11:40am (Mar–May 9:30–11:40am). **Free**

French Legation Museum

802 San Marcos St; tel 512/472-8180. The oldest residence still standing in Austin was built in 1841 for Comte Alphonse Dubois de Saligny, France's representative to the fledgling Republic of Texas. Although his home was very extravagant for the then-primitive capital, the flamboyant de Saligny didn't stay around to enjoy it very long. The house is a unique example of fine French Colonial–style architecture outside Louisiana; in back is a re-creation of a Creole kitchen. **Open:** Tues–Sun 1–5pm. **$**

City of Austin Nature Preserves

301 Nature Center Dr; tel 512/327-5437. Austin boasts a diverse group of natural habitats in its city-run nature preserves. At Blunn Creek, 40 acres of upland woods and meadows are traversed by a spring-fed creek; one of the two lookout areas is made of compacted volcanic ash. The 500-acre Forest Ridge affords impressive views of surrounding Hill Country and Bull Creek waterfalls. Spelunkers can enjoy Karst, which is honeycombed with limestone caves and sinkholes. Mayfield Park directly abuts the Barrow Brook Cove of Lake Austin; peacocks and hens roam freely around lily ponds and trails cross over bridges in oak and juniper woods. Visitors to the rock-walled ramada at the Zilker Preserve, with its meadows, streams, and cliff, can look out over downtown Austin. All the preserves offer natural surface trails; no rest rooms. **Open:** Daily, dawn to dusk. **Free**

Barton Springs Pool

2201 Barton Springs Rd (Zilker Park); tel 512/476-9044. Each day, approximately 32 million gallons of water from the underground Edwards Aquifer bubble to the surface here. At one time, this force powered several Austin mills. Although the original limestone bottom remains, concrete was added to the banks to form uniform sides to what is now a swimming pool of about 1,000 feet by 125 feet. Maintaining a constant 68°F temperature, the amazingly clear water is bracing in summer and warming in winter when many hearty souls brave the cold for a dip. Lifeguards are on duty for most of the day, and a large bathhouse operated by the Parks and Recreation Department offers changing facilities. **Open:** Tues–Wed 5am–10pm, Fri–Sun 5am–10pm, Mon and Thur 5am– 7:30. **Free**

Zilker Park

2201 Barton Springs Rd; tel 512/476-9044. This 347-acre park is Austin's favorite public playground. Its centerpiece is Barton Springs, but visitors also flock to the **Zilker Botanical Garden,** the **Austin Nature Preserves,** and the **Umlauf Sculpture Garden and Museum.** In addition to its athletic fields (eight for soccer, two for softball, and one for rugby), the park also contains a nine-hole disc (Frisbee) golf course. The Zilker Eagle Train, a narrow-gauge, light-rail miniature train, starts out near Barton Springs and winds around the park, passing Barton Creek and Town Lake. **Open:** Daily 5am–10pm. **Free**

Zilker Botanical Gardens

2220 Barton Springs Rd; tel 512/477-8672. A variety of gardens occupy this 60-acre space, including a Xeriscape garden (which showcases the seven principles of Xeriscape design and features native and low–water-use plants), cactus and succulent garden, rose garden, azalea garden (with green brook and shaded patio), and an Oriental garden. The latter, which founder Isamu Taniguchi intended as "a symbol of universal peace," features waterfalls, water lily ponds, and handmade oriental lanterns, complete with an authentic teahouse. The cherry trees bloom mid-March through April; the water lilies bloom mid-June through October. Among the other attractions are a butterfly garden and trail filled with local flowers and plants attracting numerous species of Texas butterflies; herb and fragrance garden; reconstructed pioneer settlement, with 19th-century log cabin and blacksmith's shop; and tours of 100-million-year-old dinosaur tracks recently discovered on the grounds. Shows, research programs. **Open:** Daily 7:30am–8pm. **Free**

Wild Basin Wilderness Preserve

805 N Capital of Texas Hwy; tel 512/327-7622. Scenic Hill Country wilderness west of the city. The 227-acre preserve is home to two endangered bird species: golden-cheeked warbler and black-capped vireo. The grounds include four miles of hiking trails and a special trail for the handicapped. Moon watching and stargazing tours are sponsored twice a month. **Open:** Daily sunrise–sunset. **$**

Lake Bastrop

PO Box 546; tel 512/321-3307. A 906-acre lake set amid low hills and the "lost pines". Two recreational areas, on the north and south rims, with fishing, swimming, boating, and waterskiing. Picnic sites available. **Open:** Daily 24 hours. **$**

Bastrop State Park

1 mi E of intersection of TX 21/71, Bastrop; tel 512/321-2101. Located in the "lost pines," this 3,550-acre park has quiet, rolling lands and plenty of pine trees. Recreational activities include camping, picnicking, fishing, hiking, swimming, and golf (nine-hole course). Trailer sites and cabins available. **Open:** Daily sunrise–sundown. **$**

Harry Ransom Humanities Research Center

W 21st St; tel 512/471-8944. The special collections here contain approximately one million rare books, 36 million manuscripts, 5 million photographs, and more than 100,000 works of art. Most of this wealth is stashed away for scholars' use, but permanent and rotating exhibits of the holdings are held in two buildings: the Harry Ransom Center and the Leeds Gallery of the Flawn Academic Center. A Gutenberg Bible—one of only five complete copies in the United States—is on permanent display on the first floor of the former. Also on display: costumes from the movie *Gone with the Wind*, the original manuscript of Arthur Miller's *Death of a Salesman*, and letters written by novelist Isaac Bashevis Singer. **Open:** Mon–Fri 9am–5pm. **Free**

National Wildflower Research Center

4801 La Crosse Ave; tel 512/292-4200. Founded by Lady Bird Johnson in 1982, the 42-acre center is dedicated to the study and preservation of native plants. A variety of display gardens, shade pavilions, and greenhouses, along with a wildflower meadow. Gift shop on the premises. **Open:** Tues–Sun 9am–5:30pm. **$$**

Bastrop Opera House

711 Spring St, Bastrop; tel 512/321-6283. Built in 1889, this was the scene for many touring theater spectacles of the time, as well as a community theater and social hall. Reopened in 1984, it now presents plays and shows on a regular basis, mostly on weekends. Recent productions have included *Frankenstein, Don't Tell Mother,* and *Billy the Kid.* **Open:** Tues–Sat 9am–5pm. **$$$**

Austin & Texas Central Railroad Hill Country Flyer Steam Train

Capital Metro Park & Ride in Cedar Park; tel 512/477-8468. The Austin Steam Train Association restored five historic coaches and a 1916 locomotive that can be boarded for a 33-mile excursion from Cedar Park, northwest of Austin. The train crosses the South San Gabriel River and travels past scenic Hill Country vistas; at the end of the line, the town of Burnet, an Old West gunfight is staged. **Open:** Mar–Dec, Sat and Sun, call for schedule. **$$$$**

Fall Creek Vineyards

1111 Guadalupe St; tel 512/476-4477. A 65-acre vineyard whose wines have been praised by critics around the country. Here you can sample the full range of award winners, including carnelians, Rieslings, and zinfandels. Tours available. **Open:** Tours Mon–Fri 11am–3pm, Sat noon–5pm. Open Sun noon–4pm Mar–Nov for tastings and sales only. **Free**

Celis Brewery

2431 Forbes Dr; tel 512/835-0884. Established in 1991 by distinguished Belgian brewer Pierre Celis, the brewery produces five styles of beer using traditional Belgian recipes that date back to 1483. The building's history dates to the turn of the century; the brewery features three copper kettles that were hand-hammered in Belgium during the 1930s. Tours are conducted Tues–Sat and are followed by a sampling. **Open:** Tues–Sat 2–4pm. **Free**

Bandera

Calling itself "The Cowboy Capital of the World," this Hill Country town succeeds in retaining its frontier look and heritage. Known for its many dude ranches, Bandera gives visitors a taste of Texas-style cowboy and ranch life. **Information:** Bandera Convention & Visitors Bureau, 1808 TX 16 S, PO Box 171, Bandera, 78003-0171 (tel 210/796-3045 or toll free 800/364-3833).

MOTEL

≡≡ Econo Lodge Bandera
1900 TX 16 S, 78003; tel 210/796-3093 or toll free 800/553-2666. TX 16 exit off I-410. A very agreeable and clean budget motel. **Rooms:** 100 rms. CI open/CO noon. Non-smoking rms avail. **Amenities:** A/C, cable TV. **Facilities:** Whirlpool. **Rates:** $39 S; $42 D. Extra person $10. Parking: Outdoor, free. AE, DC, DISC, MC, V.

RESORTS

≡≡ Dixie Dude Ranch
Ranch Rd 1077, PO Box 548, 78003; tel 210/796-7771. Serving patrons since 1937, this working ranch allows guests to participate in its day-today operations plus enjoy cookouts and a variety of Western-style entertainment. A great escape for city slickers and country folk alike. **Rooms:** 100 rms and stes. CI open/CO 1pm. Nonsmoking rms avail. **Amenities:** A/C, satel TV w/movies, refrig, dataport, bathrobes. Some units w/minibars, some w/terraces, some w/fireplaces. **Services:** Twice-daily maid svce, social director, children's program, babysitting. **Facilities:** Steam rm, beauty salon, playground, washer/dryer. **Rates (BB):** $79 S; $89 D; $100–$110 ste. Children under age 5 stay free. Min stay wknds. MAP rates avail. Parking: Outdoor, free. AE, DC, DISC, MC, V.

≡≡≡ Lost Valley Resort Ranch
TX 165, PO Box 2170, 78003; tel 210/796-3299. TX 16 exit off I-410. 10 acres. Located in the beautiful Texas country-side, this ranch really lives up to its name—it's very secluded and quiet. **Rooms:** 75 rms, stes, and effic. CI open/CO noon. Nonsmoking rms avail. Luxurious rooms with rustic decor. **Amenities:** A/C, satel TV w/movies, refrig, VCR, bathrobes. Some units w/minibars, some w/terraces. **Services:** Twice-daily maid svce, social director, children's program, babysitting. Social functions include country music shows, games, and barbecues. **Facilities:** 1 restaurant, 1 bar (w/entertainment), sauna, steam rm, whirlpool. **Rates (CP):** $79–$82 S; $82–$89 D; $99–$120 ste; $59 effic. Min stay wknds. MAP rates avail. Parking: Outdoor, free. AE, DC, DISC, MC, V.

≡≡ Twin Elm Ranch
Farm Rd (TX 470), PO Box 117, 78003; tel 210/796-3628. Off TX 16. Guests at this scenic and fully functioning dude ranch can choose to rope cattle and ride horses or just relax and enjoy the scenery. **Rooms:** 100 rms and stes. CI open/CO noon. Nonsmoking rms avail. Exceptionally large rooms give the feel of a small, cozy apartment. **Amenities:** A/C, cable TV, dataport. Some units w/minibars, some w/terraces. **Services:** Social director, children's program. Great country breakfast served every morning. **Facilities:** Whirlpool, beauty salon, playground.

Rates (BB): $85 S; $95 D; $100–$110 ste. Extra person $5. Min stay wknds. MAP rates avail. Parking: Outdoor, free. AE, DC, DISC, MC, V.

ATTRACTIONS

Cascade Caverns
226 Cascade Caverns Rd, Boerne; tel 210/755-8080. Caverns contain a 100-foot waterfall (dramatically heightened by lighting effects) and also feature unique translucent formations and crystal pools laced with profuse cave growth. The active caverns extend 140 feet below ground. The tours last 45 minutes; constant 68°F temperature in the caverns. The site also offers picnic grounds, RV camping (with 30–50 amp service), swimming pool, recreational area, snack bar, and gift shop. **Open:** Peak (June–Aug) daily 9am–6pm. Reduced hours off-season. **$$$**

Hill Country State Natural Area
Ranch Rd 1077; tel 210/796-4413. A scenic mosaic of rocky hills, flowing springs, oak groves, grasslands, and canyons—all the representative features of the Texas Hill Country. The pristine 5,400-acre site has 34 miles of multipurpose trails and is popular for hiking, backpacking, primitive camping, all-terrain bicycling, and equestrian use. There are 4 designated camping areas with fire pits as well as 10 individual walk-in tent sites. **Open:** Peak (Mar–Oct) Thurs–Mon 8am–10pm. Reduced hours off-season. **$**

Frontier Times Museum
506 13th St; tel 210/796-3864. A tribute to eclecticism. Everything from Native American artifacts, Old West relics, centuries-old Chinese temple bells, and Buffalo Bill Wild West Show posters to a shrunken head from South America, a baby incubator, and a two-headed goat are on display. Approximately 40,000 objects exhibited. **Open:** Mon–Sat 10am–4:30pm, Sun 1–4:30pm. **$**

Beaumont

See also Orange, Port Arthur

Chartered in 1838, Beaumont hit the national headlines in 1901 when black gold was discovered at nearby Spindletop, marking the beginning of the famous Texas oil boom. Lumber, agriculture, and its location on the Neches River also helped this small city prosper. Now an important port slightly inland from the Gulf of Mexico, Beaumont joins with neighboring Port Arthur and Orange to form the "Golden Triangle." **Information:** Beaumont Convention & Visitors Bureau, 801 Main St, #100, PO Box 3827, Beaumont, 77704-3827 (tel 409/880-3749 or toll free 800/392-4401).

HOTEL

≡≡ Beaumont Hilton
2355 I-10 S, 77705; tel 409/842-3600 or toll free 800/445-8667; fax 409/842-1355. N of US 287. A conference

and convention center catering to business travelers seeking attractive and comfortable lodgings. The hotel and grounds are kept in immaculate condition. **Rooms:** 290 rms. CI 3pm/ CO noon. Nonsmoking rms avail. **Amenities:** 📷 🕭 A/C, cable TV w/movies. Some units w/minibars, some w/whirlpools. Microwaves and refrigerators available. **Services:** ✗ 🚐 🖎 **Facilities:** 🛠️ 🛶 📦 🕭 1 restaurant, 1 bar, spa, whirlpool. **Rates:** $109–$119 S or D. Extra person $10. Children under age 18 stay free. Parking: Outdoor, free. AE, CB, DC, DISC, MC, V.

MOTELS

🏨🏨 Best Western Beaumont Inn
2155 N 11th St, 77703; tel 409/898-8150 or toll free 800/ 528-1234; fax 409/898-0078. At jct I-10. An above-average Best Western surrounded by a lovely wooded area. Near a local shopping mall and downtown Beaumont. **Rooms:** 152 rms. CI 4pm/CO noon. Nonsmoking rms avail. **Amenities:** 📷 🕭 A/C, cable TV. **Services:** 🛎️ **Facilities:** 🛠️ 🕭 Washer/dryer. **Rates (CP):** $41–$49 S or D. Extra person $6. Children under age 18 stay free. Parking: Outdoor, free. AE, DISC, MC, V.

🏨 Econo Lodge
1155 I-10 S, 77701; tel 409/835-5913 or toll free 800/ 424-4777. S of jct I-10/US 287 at College St. Fairly comfortable but bare-bones motel catering to those on a tight budget. **Rooms:** 80 rms. CI 4pm/CO noon. Nonsmoking rms avail. **Amenities:** 📷 🕭 A/C, cable TV. Some units w/whirlpools. **Services:** 🖎 🛎️ 🍷 **Facilities:** 🛠️ 🕭 Whirlpool, washer/dryer. **Rates:** $35–$56 S or D. Extra person $5. Children under age 18 stay free. Parking: Outdoor, free. AE, CB, DC, DISC, MC, V.

🏨🏨 La Quinta Motor Inn
220 I-10 N, 77702; tel 409/838-9991 or toll free 800/ 531-5900; fax 409/832-1266. S of jct US 287. Adjacent to major highways. Acceptable rooms. **Rooms:** 122 rms. CI 3pm/CO noon. Nonsmoking rms avail. **Amenities:** 📷 🕭 A/C, cable TV. **Services:** 🖎 🛎️ **Facilities:** 🛠️ 📦 🕭 **Rates (CP):** $52–$67 S or D. Extra person $7. Children under age 18 stay free. Parking: Outdoor, free. AE, CB, DC, DISC, MC, V.

RESTAURANTS 🍴

Chula Vista
1135 N 11th St; tel 409/898-8855. Just S of I-10. **Tex-Mex.** Located near the downtown bar scene, this fun, upbeat place serves great Mexican food. Bright, tropical setting features a central fountain and cooling ceiling fans. **FYI:** Reservations accepted. Children's menu. **Open:** Sun–Thurs 11am–10pm, Fri–Sat 11am–11pm. **Prices:** Main courses $4–$10. AE, CB, DC, DISC, MC, V. 🕭

David's Upstairs
In Gaylynn Theater Building, 745 N 11th St; tel 409/ 898-0214. Between Harrison and North. **Continental.** Locat-

ed near downtown, this restaurant places a strong emphasis on healthy cuisine. The vegetable burger, chicken dishes, sandwiches, and steaks—all prepared with a light touch— make great choices for lunch. **FYI:** Reservations accepted. Dress code. **Open:** Lunch Mon–Fri 11am–2pm; dinner Mon– Thurs 5–9:30pm, Fri–Sat 5–10:30pm. **Prices:** Main courses $4–$10. AE, CB, DC, DISC, MC, V. 🕭

Green Beanery
2121 McFaddin at 6th; tel 409/833-5913. **Continental.** Located alongside several shops in an old house, this homey restaurant has a deck at the entrance, a fireplace in the dining room, and colorful flowers on each table. The menu includes pizza, snapper, veal, pork loin, and lamb chops. **FYI:** Reservations accepted. Dress code. Beer and wine only. **Open:** Lunch Tues–Fri 11am–2pm, Sat 11:30am–2pm; dinner Wed–Thurs 6–9pm, Fri–Sat 6–10pm. **Prices:** Main courses $6–$19. AE, MC, V. 🍷

Patrizi's Restaurant
2050 I-10 S; tel 409/842-5151. Near US 90. **Italian.** Large and popular multi-level restaurant with small-town atmosphere but an elegant, contemporary decor. Steak, seafood, and pasta predominate; pies are delicious. The lunch buffet offers good value. **FYI:** Reservations accepted. Country music/folk/jazz. Children's menu. **Open:** Mon–Thurs 11am– 10pm, Fri 11am–11pm, Sat 5–11pm, Sun 11am–9pm. **Prices:** Main courses $8–$27. AE, CB, DC, DISC, MC, V. 🕭

Sartin's Seafood
6725 Eastex Frwy; tel 409/892-6771. Near Lucas St. **Seafood.** Casual cafeteria-style restaurant serving large portions of very good seafood. **FYI:** Reservations not accepted. Children's menu. Beer and wine only. **Open:** Daily 11am–10pm. **Prices:** Main courses $9–$17. No CC. 📷 🕭

ATTRACTIONS 🏛️

Big Thicket National Preserve
3785 Milam; tel 409/839-2689. One of the country's most biologically diverse wilderness areas, encompassing close to 86,000 acres of dense woods, swamps, savannahs, and streams. This vast area is home to five standard North American environs: Eastern and Appalachian forests, Southeastern swamps, Midwestern prairies, and Southwestern desert. Accordingly, one will find a variety of plants and animals that are rarely found in the same surroundings; Eastern bluebirds coexist with road runners, while lush bogs abut sandhills adorned with cactus and yucca. There are four river corridors and eight land tracts ranging in size from the 550-acre Loblolly Unit to the 25,000-acre Lance Rosier Unit. Deer, coyote, raccoons, otters, bobcats, and armadillos are among the many animals that inhabit the area; over 300 bird species. Recreational opportunities include hiking (eight trails) and canoeing (rentals available); also RV sites and camping (nearest units include Beech Creek, Turkey Creek, and Big Sandy Creek). **Open:** Mon–Sat 9:30am–5:30pm, Sun 9:30am–5pm. **Free**

Art Museum of Southeast Texas

500 Main St; tel 409/832-3432. The focus of the permanent and traveling exhibits is Texas artists. Paintings, sculpture, and mixed media works are featured; there is also a sculpture garden. The museum hosts films, lectures, art classes, and musical performances. **Open:** Mon–Sat 9am–5pm, Sun noon–5pm. **Free**

Edison Plaza Museum

350 Pine St; tel 409/839-3089. Extensive collection of Thomas Edison artifacts, housed in the historic Travis St Substation, the first building to distribute electric power in East Texas. Exhibits focus on Edison's inventions and the advancements that have been made on them. Of special interest are the "Banner Front" Standard Model A cylinder phonograph, circa 1901; copper from the world's first underground electric light and power distribution system laid in New York City in 1882; the incandescent light bulb; the telephone; and the "carry and sell" miniature mimeograph manufactured circa 1880. The section of the museum devoted to the future of energy sources has displays on coal and solar energy, lasers, holograms, and the superconductor. Guided tours by appointment. Museum gift shop. **Open:** Mon–Fri 8am–noon and 12:30–4:30pm. **Free**

Texas Energy Museum

600 Main St; tel 409/833-5100. The collection preserves and interprets the history and development of energy and petroleum industry in Texas. State-of-the-art exhibits featuring cinematic robots, working props (one of which is a gushing oil well), and realistic backgrounds describe petroleum geology, the paleontologic formation of oil and gas, the history of oil production since 1901, current drilling techniques, and petroleum refining. Permanent and changing exhibits. Guided tours (by request) and educational programs designed for all age levels. **Open:** Tues–Sat 9am–5pm, Sun 1–5pm. **$**

John Jay French Museum

2995 French Rd; tel 409/898-3269. This 1845 Greek Revival house was originally a trading post. The city's first two-story dwelling, it now exhibits period furnishings, clothing, and pioneer household utensils. **Open:** Tues–Sat 10am–4pm. **$**

Gladys City—Spindletop Boomtown

University Dr on Lamar University; tel 409/880-8896. Beaumont came of age in 1901 with the world's first great oil gusher at Spindletop. Here is a re-creation of the typical oil boom towns that emerged in the area at that time, with clapboard buildings, wooden oil derricks, post office, livery stable, surveyor's office, saloon, and blacksmith's shop. **Open:** Tues–Sun 1–5pm. **$**

The McFadden-Ward House

1906 McFaddin; tel 409/832-2134. This beaux-arts colonial mansion and carriage house built in 1906 houses a decorative arts collection, furniture, silver, porcelain, Oriental rugs, and sculpture. Also features restored servants' quarters, exhibits on transportation at the turn-of-the-century, and the original

full-size gynasium upstairs. Listed on the National Register of Historic Places. Guided tours available. **Open:** Mon–Sat 10am–11:30pm 1–3pm, Sun 1–3pm **$**

Big Bend National Park

For lodgings and dining, see Alpine, Fort Stockton

The 802,541-acre park is characterized by the majesty of its vastness, its spectacular canyons, and its stark, beautiful stretches of empty desert. There are three main divisions to the park: the river, the desert, and the mountains. The name Big Bend refers to the great U-turn the Rio Grande makes in this region; the river defines the park's southern boundary for 118 miles and cuts a swath through its colossal canyons. The park lies in the northern third of the Chihuahuan Desert, abutting the Chisos Mountains—a green island in a desert sea. It is home to more than a thousand different plants, including rare species that grow only here. Animals such as the coyote, ringtail, javelina, and roadrunner are some of the many indigenous animals roaming the park. In the lush mountains grow junipers, small oak trees, and pinyon. The park is also archaeologically significant: the bones of the pterodatcyl, the largest flying creature ever known, were discovered here.

Activities at the park include hiking (350 miles of trails), boating (permit required), camping, horseback riding, and bird-watching (the park furnishes habitat for many Mexican birds found nowhere else in the United States). Recommended hiking trips include the Santa Elena Canyon, a massive box-like gorge carved through limestone cliffs, and the Lost Mine Trail. There are no equipment rentals for river rafting in the park. There are 62 camping sites at Chisos Basin, and 99 at Rio Grande Village. Lodge and trailer sites within the park, and numerous lodgings nearby. For more information contact the superintendent, Big Bend National Park, TX 79834 (tel 915/477-2251).

Big Spring

See also Midland

Established in 1849 on the Santa Fe Trail and named for a nearby natural spring, Big Spring became a booming railroad center with the arrival of the Texas & Pacific Railroad in 1881. Cotton and oil are the town's economic base today, and the spring can be seen in a local city park. **Information:** Big Spring Convention & Visitors Bureau, 215 W 3rd St, PO Box 1391, Big Spring, 79721-1391 (tel 915/263-7641).

MOTEL

≡≡ Best Western Mid-Continent Inn

I-20 at US 87, 79720; tel 915/267-1601 or toll free 800/528-1234; fax 915/267-6916. On N side of I-20 access road.

Slightly worn budget motel with blue decor and a small lobby. **Rooms:** 153 rms and stes. CI noon/CO noon. Nonsmoking rms avail. **Amenities:** 🛏 🗜 🍴 A/C, cable TV w/movies. **Services:** ✗ ⤢ 🔊 **Facilities:** 🛗 🚹 1 restaurant, 1 bar. **Rates (CP):** $38 S; $44 D; $70–$120 ste. Extra person $6. Children under age 12 stay free. Parking: Outdoor, free. AE, CB, DC, DISC, JCB, MC, V.

RESTAURANT 🍴

★ Big John's Feed Lot
802 W 3rd; tel 915/263-3178. 2 blocks W of US 87. **Barbecue.** This small, lunchtime barbecue joint has very limited seating and fills up fast, so it's best to come early. **FYI:** Reservations not accepted. Beer and wine only. **Open:** Mon–Fri 11am–3pm. **Prices:** AE, DISC, MC, V. 👥

ATTRACTIONS 🏛

Big Spring State Park
Box 1064; tel 915/263-4931. The 382-acre park covers what is locally known as "Scenic Mountain," a 200-foot-high limestone-capped mesa overlooking the city, and features picnic sites, jogging and nature trails, playground, dance pavilion, and prairie-dog town. A 3-mile scenic drive overlooks the city and a ⅓-mile nature trail provides a glimpse of native animals. An interpretive center includes displays of Native American artifacts, assorted fossils found in the area, and mounted local wildlife. **Open:** Peak (Mar–Aug) daily 8am–10pm. Reduced hours off-season. **$**

Heritage Museum
510 S Scurry; tel 915/267-8255. The region's history is illustrated through pioneer and Native American artifacts, art exhibits, and displays of local history and early West Texas. Houses an impressively large collection of Texas Longhorn steer horns, and also boasts a number of rare phonographs: late-1800s to 1920s models made by Edison, Victor, Columbia, and others. **Open:** Mon–Fri 9am–5pm, Sat 10am–5pm **$**

Potton House
Gregg St at 2nd; tel 915/263-0511. This restored Victorian home of the Potton family, built around 1901, is listed in the National Register of Historic Places and features turn-of-the-century furnishings. **Open:** Tues–Sat 1–5pm. **$**

Bonham

ATTRACTIONS 🏛

Sam Rayburn House
US 82; tel 903/583-5558. The home of Sam Rayburn, who served as Speaker of the House for 17 years, longer than any other Speaker in US history. All the furnishings in the house belonged to the Rayburn family. A 13-minute video about the man is presented prior to the tour. Groups need advance reservations. **Open:** Tues–Fri 10am–5pm, Sat 1–5pm, Sun 2–5pm. **Free**

Sam Rayburn Library
W Sam Rayburn Dr at Elphis; tel 903/583-2455. The library preserves the books, records, and mementos accumulated by the legendary Speaker of the House over his career. There is also a replica of his US Capitol office, from the pattern on the tile floor to the barrel-vaulted ceiling. Over the desk is a crystal chandelier, more than a century old, which hung in both the White House and Capitol. Other items include gavels used on historic occasions, and a 2,500-year-old Grecian urn given by the Athens Palace Guard in appreciation for American economic aid. Also included in the collection is a set of the *Congressional Record* dating from the first meeting in 1789 to the present. **Open:** Mon–Fri 9am–5pm, Sat 1–5pm, Sun 2–5pm. **Free**

Fort Inglish Museum and Park
W Sam Rayburn Dr at Chinner St; tel 903/583-4811. The site features a replica of a log blockhouse and stockade built by Bailey Inglish in 1837, as well as an array of homesteads that became the town of Bonham. Three restored log cabins; pioneer furnishings and artifacts. **Open:** April–August Tues–Sat 10–4, Sun 12–4. **Free**

Bonham State Recreation Area
Rte 1, Box 337; tel 903/583-5022. A 65-acre lake surrounded by red cedars and hardwoods is one of the highlights of this 261-acre park. Recreational options include swimming, fishing, picnic sites, campsites (fee charged), and playgrounds. **Open:** Daily 8am–5pm. **$$**

Brazosport

Actually made up of nine small cities and towns, Brazosport surrounds the mouth of the Brazos River in south Brazoria County. Known for inexpensive recreation, this community's biggest visitor attraction is saltwater fishing and the gulf coast beach at Surfside. **Information:** Brazosport Area Chamber of Commerce, 420 W TX 332, Brazosport, 77531 (tel 409/265-2505).

MOTELS 🏨

🔳🔳 Best Western Lake Jackson Inn
915 TX 332, Lake Jackson, 77566; tel 409/297-3031 or toll free 800/528-1234; fax 409/297-9875. Offering decent rooms about 10 minutes from the Gulf, this is a good budget option. **Rooms:** 100 rms. CI 4pm/CO noon. Nonsmoking rms avail. **Amenities:** 🛏 🗜 A/C, cable TV. **Services:** 🖨 ⤢ 🔊 **Facilities:** 🛗 🏊 🚹 1 bar (w/entertainment). **Rates (CP):** $45–$55 S or D. Extra person $5. Children under age 12 stay free. Parking: Outdoor, free. AE, CB, DC, DISC, JCB, MC, V.

≣ Motel 6
1000 TX 332, Clute, 77531; tel 409/265-4764; fax 409/265-4758. At TX 228. A little bit away from the middle of the action, this is a good, frugal choice for a Gulf vacation. **Rooms:** 122 rms. CI open/CO noon. Nonsmoking rms avail. **Amenities:** 🛁 🐾 A/C, cable TV. **Services:** 🍽 🛎 **Facilities:** 🛗 🦽 Washer/dryer. **Rates:** $27–$31 S or D. Extra person $4. Children under age 17 stay free. Parking: Outdoor, free. AE, CB, DC, DISC, MC, V.

ATTRACTIONS

Brazoria National Wildlife Refuge
1212 N Velasco, Angleton; tel 409/849-6062. The 100-year-old Country Boy Mine descends 1,000 feet underground. Visitors may gold pan in Eureka Creek and explore the mining exhibit and the five-story 75-year-old mill. Guided tours interpret the daily life and routine of a miner. **Open:** Peak (Nov–May) 1st and 3rd weekend 8am–5pm. Reduced hours off-season. **Free**

Brazosport Museum of Natural Science
400 College Dr, Lake Jackson; tel 409/265-7831. The museum boasts one of the largest shell collections on the gulf coast, as well as a nature center which houses displays on plants and wildlife, a ¾-mile nature trail, and a planetarium (part of the Brazosport Center for the Arts and Sciences; shows periodically open to the public). There are also sections devoted to regional Native American artifacts, jade and ivory carvings, rocks, fossils, and minerals, and "touch tables" for children. Saturday programs on natural science topics and lapidary classes offered; reference library. Guided tours available. **Open:** Tues–Sat 10am–5pm, Sun 2–5pm. **Free**

Brenham

Founded in 1844, this agricultural community is undergoing major restoration and becoming a center for antiques. Brenham is known statewide as the home of both Blue Bell ice cream and Blinn College, the first county-owned public junior college in Texas. **Information:** Brenham/Washington County Convention and Visitors Bureau, 314 S Austin, Austin, 77833 (tel 409/836-3695).

ATTRACTIONS

Monastery Miniature Horses
Monastery of St Clare, TX 105; tel 409/836-9652. This monastery supports itself financially by raising, showing, and selling these miniature horses. Approximately 60 horses are displayed, and visitors can pet them. Ceramics studio and gift shop also on the premises. **Open:** Daily 2–4pm. **$$**

Giddings-Wilkin House
805 Crockett; tel 409/830-0807. This antebellum house (1843) is the oldest in Brenham, and now serves as home to the Heritage Society of Washington County, which has its offices here. Group tours available by appointment. **Open:** Mar–Nov, Fri 10am–3pm, Sat 11am–2pm. **Free**

Blue Bell Tours
FM Loop 577; tel 409/830-2197 or toll free 800/327-8135. This ice cream plant has been in operation since 1911. Visitors to the Little Creamery are treated to a short film and then allowed to watch all the steps in the ice cream–making process. The tour ends with a Texas-size dip of ice cream. A store sells company items and other gifts. Tours are offered weekdays, and it is recommended that visitors call in advance to inquire about times. **Open:** Mon–Fri. **$**

Brownsville

See also Harlingen, Port Isabel, South Padre Island

This lively border town was founded in 1846 as a fort along the Rio Grande River, an act that sparked the Mexican War. Today, Brownsville joins with Matamoros on the Mexican side of the border in providing a bicultural experience for visitors. Nearby is South Padre Island, whose wide, sandy beaches make it a popular vacation spot. **Information:** Brownsville Convention & Visitors Bureau, 650 FM 802, Brownsville, 78521 (tel 210/546-3721 or toll free 800/626-2639).

HOTEL 🏨

≣≣≣ Sheraton Inn Plaza Royale
3777 N Expwy, 78520; tel 210/350-9191 or toll free 800/325-3535. McAllen Rd exit off US 77/83. This very luxurious hotel has elegant marble floors and exquisite masonry. Worth the money. **Rooms:** 300 rms and stes. Executive level. CI 2pm/CO noon. Nonsmoking rms avail. **Amenities:** 🛁 A/C, satel TV w/movies. Some units w/terraces. **Services:** ✕ 🔑 VP 🛎 Twice-daily maid svce, social director. **Facilities:** 🛗 🏊 🖥 🦽 1 restaurant, 1 bar (w/entertainment), sauna, whirlpool. **Rates (CP):** $69–$79 S; $79–$85 D; $86–$90 ste. Extra person $10. Min stay wknds. MAP rates avail. Parking: Outdoor, free. AE, DC, DISC, MC, V.

MOTELS

≣≣ Days Inn
715 Frontage Rd, 78520; tel 210/541-2201 or toll free 800/325-2525. Price Rd exit off US 77/US 83. Surprisingly clean with relatively new furnishings and Mexican decor. **Rooms:** 175 rms. CI 2pm/CO noon. Nonsmoking rms avail. **Amenities:** 🛁 A/C, cable TV. Some units w/terraces. Complimentary morning newspaper. **Services:** 🚗 Social director. **Facilities:** 🛗 🏊 🖥 🦽 **Rates (CP):** $59–$69 S; $69–$70 D. Extra person $5. Min stay wknds. Parking: Outdoor, free. AE, DC, DISC, MC, V.

≣≣≣ La Quinta Motor Inn
55 San Perl Blvd, 78520; tel 210/546-0381 or toll free 800/531-5900. Boca Chica exit off US 77/US 83. A standard La

Quinta, complete with the chain's trademark Southwestern decor. Very popular for its dependable rooms and attentive service. **Rooms:** 120 rms. CI 2pm/CO noon. Nonsmoking rms avail. **Amenities:** ⛶ ▣ A/C, satel TV. Some units w/terraces. **Services:** ⛟ **Facilities:** ⛶ ⛗ ♿ **Rates (CP):** $59 S; $69 D. Extra person $5. Min stay peak. Parking: Outdoor, free. AE, DC, DISC, MC, V.

▤▤▤ Plaza Square Motel

2255 Central Blvd, 78520; tel 210/546-5104. Ruben Towes exit off US 77/83. This lovely, upscale motel with historical ambience in the center of town is convenient for vacationing couples or families. **Rooms:** 175 rms. Executive level. CI 2pm/CO noon. Nonsmoking rms avail. Spacious rooms are decorated with antique furnishings. **Amenities:** ⛶ A/C, cable TV. Some units w/terraces. **Services:** ⛟ Social director. **Facilities:** ⛶ ⛗ ♿ Washer/dryer. **Rates (CP):** $65–$72 S; $72–$79 D. Extra person $7. Parking: Outdoor, free. AE, DC, DISC, MC, V.

RESORT

▤▤▤ Rancho Viejo Resort and Country Club

1 Rancho Viejo Dr, Rancho Viejo, 78575; tel 210/350-4000 or toll free 800/531-7400. Rancho Viejo exit off US 77. 9 acres. Located between Brownsville and the beaches at South Padre Island, this luxurious resort and country club, with Spanish-style adobe facade and red-tile roof, makes an ideal spot for a romantic vacation. Guests may choose from a variety of activities, from shopping in nearby Mexico to spending the day at the beaches. **Rooms:** 275 rms and stes. Executive level. CI open/CO noon. Nonsmoking rms avail. Apartmentlike accommodations are luxuriously furnished and feature beautiful armoires and a dining table. **Amenities:** ⛶ ⛗ ▣ ⛾ A/C, satel TV w/movies, refrig, VCR, voice mail, bathrobes. Some units w/minibars, some w/terraces, some w/whirlpools. **Services:** ⛾ ⛗ ⛶ ⛾ ⛾ Twice-daily maid svce, social director, masseur, babysitting. **Facilities:** ⛶ ▶18 ⛾ ⛾1 ⛾ ⛾ ⛗ 🖳 ♿ 1 restaurant, 1 bar (w/entertainment), games rm, racquetball, sauna, steam rm, whirlpool, beauty salon. The 6,000-sq-ft swimming pool is surrounded by towering palm trees and waterfalls. Two championship golf courses and the John Jacobs' Golf School are also on site. **Rates (CP):** $89–$99 S; $99–$110 D; $115–$130 ste. Extra person $5. MAP rates avail. Parking: Indoor/outdoor, free. AE, DC, DISC, MC, V.

RESTAURANTS ⛾

ⓢ Lotus Inn

905 N Expwy; tel 210/542-5715. **Chinese.** Beautiful flowers and lovely paintings set the tone of the attractive dining room. Beef with broccoli is a favorite of the fine selection of affordable Asian dishes. Good food at affordable prices. **FYI:** Reservations accepted. Dress code. Beer and wine only. **Open:** Daily 11:30am–10pm. **Prices:** Main courses $5–$11. AE, DISC, MC, V. ⛾

Maria's Better Mexican Food

1124 Central; tel 210/542-9819. **Mexican/Tex-Mex.** A family-style restaurant serving refreshingly authentic Tex-Mex/ Mexican dishes. The house specialty is beef fajitas. **FYI:** Reservations not accepted. Children's menu. **Open:** Daily 8am–10pm. **Prices:** Main courses $4–$8. No CC. ⛾ ⛾ ♿

ATTRACTIONS 🏛

Sabal Palm Grove Sanctuary

FM 1419; tel 210/541-8034. These 172 acres provide a kind of time-capsule glimpse at how the Rio Grande landscape looked before it became heavily developed. The sanctuary protects the last remaining sabal palm grove in the Delta— the tallest palm rises to a height of almost 50 feet—and encompasses coastal dunes, wetlands, Texas ebony, anacua, brasil, manzanita, Barbados cherry, and a host of other protected vegetation. The site is also a popular bird-watching spot. Half-mile nature trail and a visitors center. **Open:** Daily 8am–5pm. **$**

Gladys Porter Zoo

500 Ringgold St; tel 210/546-2177. This elaborate zoo is considered to be one of the best in the country. Over 1,500 mammals, birds, reptiles, invertebrates, and fish (many of them endangered species) are housed in a 31-acre preserve that is divided along four major geographic areas: Tropical America, Indo-Australia, Asia, and Africa. Moats, streams, rocks, and caves, set up to resemble various natural habitats, separate the animals from each other and from humans; there are no bars or cages. Some of the many exotic animals which are featured include the jaguarundi, oryx, rare African and Asian deer, spectacled bears, baboons, crocodiles, Siberian tigers, elephants, and giraffes. The site also boasts a herpetarium, aquatic wing, children's zoo and nursery, bear grottoes, and a free-flight aviary. There are half-hour narrated train tours on Sunday afternoons between 1:30 and 3:30pm. Strollers and wheelchairs available for rent. Gift shop, snack bars, and restaurants. **Open:** Daily 9am–5pm. **$$$**

Palo Alto Battlefield National Historic Site

Jct FM 1847 and FM 511; tel 210/541-2785. The site of the artillery duel on May 8, 1846 between Zachary Taylor's forces and those of Mexican General Mariano Arista, which started the Mexican War. Historical markers provide details. **Open:** Mon–Fri 8am–5pm. **Free**

Historic Brownsville Museum

641 E Madison St; tel 210/548-1313. Located in an old Southern Pacific depot, a Spanish Colonial Revival structure which is listed in the National Register of Historic Places. The museum houses a variety of exhibits interpreting the heritage of Brownsville and the region. These include a refurbished 1870 narrow-gauge wood-burning Baldwin railroad locomotive; artifacts from early Brownsville; and rooms dedicated to the Mexican-American War, the Civil War, the Mexican

Border Campaign, and the impact of the Mexican Revolutions upon the region. Museum gift shop. **Open:** Mon–Sat 10am–4:30pm, Sun 2–5pm. **$**

Stillman House Museum
1305 E Washington; tel 210/542-3929. The residence of Charles Stillman, founder of Brownsville. This house, circa 1850, contains Stillman's possessions and memorabilia, original furnishings, mementos of early Brownsville, heirlooms, books, and photographs. The oldest item is a 1790 grandfather clock. The house is listed in the National Register of Historic Places. **Open:** Mon–Fri 10–noon and 2–5, Sun 3–5. Schedule may vary. Call ahead. **$**

Brownwood

A cattle and agricultural community founded in the 1850s, Brownwood prospered with the arrival of the Santa Fe Railroad in 1885. This city entertains itself with the annual Rattlesnake Roundup held in mid-March. **Information:** Brown County Chamber of Commerce, 521 E Baker, PO Box 880, Brownwood, 76804 (tel 915/646-9535).

ATTRACTION 📷

Douglas MacArthur Academy of Freedom
Austin Ave at Coggin; tel 915/643-7830. Located on the campus of Howard Payne University, the academy is devoted to interpreting the pursuit of freedom throughout Western civilization. Five large halls represent different eras throughout history: the Mediterranean Room is flanked by replicas of Egyptian tomb statues; Magna Carta Hall contains a replica of an English castle room; Philadelphia's Independence Hall has a re-created meeting room; a three-story mural depicts man's relationship to God. Personal memorabilia of Gen Douglas MacArthur is also on display. Tours available. **Open:** Tours conducted Sun–Fri at 1:30, 2:30, and 3:30pm; Sat at 10 and 11am and at 1:30, 2:30, and 3:30pm. Closed school vacations. **Free**

Bryan

See also College Station

Bounded by the Navasota River on the east and the Brazos River on the west, this town was founded in 1855 and thrived when the Houston & Texas Central Railroad arrived in 1866. Sister city to College Station to the south and separated only by their respective city limit signs, Bryan serves as the Brazos County seat. **Information:** Bryan/College Station Convention & Visitors Bureau, 715 University Dr E, College Station, 77840-1804 (tel 409/260-9898 or toll free 800/777-8292).

RESTAURANT 🍴

The Texan
3204 S College; tel 409/822-3588. **Seafood/Steak.** The exterior is somewhat run-down, but lots of wood accents provide an attractive interior, and the food is of high quality. **FYI:** Reservations recommended. **Open:** Wed–Sat 5–11pm. **Prices:** Main courses $15–$25. AE, CB, DC, DISC, MC, V. ❤

ATTRACTIONS 📷

Brazos Valley Museum of Natural History
3232 Briarcrest Dr; tel 409/776-2195. Exhibits illustrate the natural history of the region. An interactive science and nature room has live animals; there are also archaeological displays. Small nature trail on the grounds; environmental education programs offered. **Open:** Peak (June–Aug) Mon–Fri 8am–5pm, Sat 10am–5pm. Reduced hours off-season. **$**

Messina Hof Wine Cellars
4545 Old Reliance Rd; tel 409/778-9463. Guided tours of the winery and complimentary tastings. Wine can be purchased at the visitors center. The grape stomp in mid-April is one of the numerous special events held here. **Open:** Mon–Fri 1–2:30pm, Sat 11am–12:30pm and 2:30–4pm, Sun 12:30–2:30pm. **Free**

Burnet

Established as Fort Croghan in 1849, the settlement that sprang up was originally called Hamilton Creek. Renamed in 1852, Burnet has been designated by the Texas Legislature as the "Bluebonnet Capital of Texas." The city honors this title every year in April with the Bluebonnet Festival and also by serving as a stop on the Highland Lakes Bluebonnet Trails. **Information:** Burnet Chamber of Commerce, 705 Buchanan Dr, PO Drawer M, Burnet, 78611 (tel 512/756-4297).

HOTEL 🏨

HoJo Inn by Howard Johnson
Buchanan Dr, 78611; tel 512/756-4747 or toll free 800/531-5900. On TX 29 W. A better-than-average budget hotel with higher-than-average prices. **Rooms:** 275 rms and stes. Executive level. CI 2pm/CO noon. Nonsmoking rms avail. **Amenities:** 🛏 A/C, cable TV. Some units w/terraces. **Services:** ✗ Social director. **Facilities:** 🔏 200 🔥 1 restaurant, 1 bar (w/entertainment). **Rates (CP):** Peak (Apr–Aug) $59–$65 S; $65–$69 D; $70–$79 ste. Extra person $10. Lower rates off-season. MAP rates avail. Parking: Outdoor, free. AE, DC, DISC, MC, V.

ATTRACTIONS 📷

Longhorn Caverns
Park Road #4; tel 512/756-6976. This Registered Natural Landmark, located 6 miles southwest of Burnet in the heart of the scenic Highland Lakes, offers two miles of limestone

caves, many of which are named for their unique formations; among them are Frozen Waterfall, Crystal City, and Hall of Gems. The historical significance of these caves is not limited to geology. Cavemen are believed to have lived here, and the caverns were used as a Confederate stronghold and manufacturing base for gunpowder during the Civil War. They are also rumored to have been a hideout for many desperadoes, including the legendary Texas outlaw, Sam Bass. Temperature is a constant 64°F. On the property are a nature trail (½ mile) and hiking trail (1½ miles), gift shop, and snack bar. **Open:** Daily 9am–5pm. **$$**

Fort Croghan Museum
703 Buchanan Dr; tel 512/756-8281. This fort, built in 1849, was part of a line of forts extending from Fort Worth to Uvalde that the US government established to protect frontier settlements from local tribes. It was abandoned in 1853, and none of the buildings remain. The museum houses over 1,200 items pertaining to early central Texas history; old musical instruments such as a "pump" organ and a square grand piano; farming equipment, including horse-drawn farm machinery; a human-drawn fire engine; domestic artifacts; early telephone equipment; six restored 19th-century buildings, including a blacksmith's shop, powder house, store, and three cabins. On Fort Croghan Day, the second Saturday in October, there are demonstrations of butter-churning, molasses-making, sheep-shearing, and bread-making. Tours available; gift shop. **Open:** Apr–Oct, Thurs–Sat 10am–5pm, Sun 1–5pm. **Free**

Childress

MOTEL 🏨
📶📶 Econo Lodge Chateau Inn
1612 E Northwest (US 287), 79201; tel 817/937-3695 or toll free 800/424-4777. A satisfactory motel in the center of town, near a number of recreational opportunities. **Rooms:** 28 rms. CI 4pm/CO noon. Nonsmoking rms avail. **Amenities:** 🛁 ⌕ A/C, cable TV w/movies. **Services:** ⌂ **Facilities:** 🔁 ᕇ 1 restaurant (lunch and dinner only). **Rates (BB):** $48–$50 S or D. Extra person $3. Children under age 18 stay free. Parking: Outdoor, free. AE, CB, DC, DISC, MC, V.

ATTRACTION 🏛
Childress County Heritage Museum
210 3rd St NW; tel 817/937-2261. Located in the old post office, this museum chronicles local and regional history. It also houses exhibits on industry (cattle, cotton, railroad), local Native American artifacts, photographs, maps, and furnished period rooms. **Open:** Mon–Fri 9am–5pm. **Free**

Cleburne

ATTRACTION 🏛
Layland Museum
201 N Caddo; tel 817/645-0940. Housed in the 1905 Carnegie Library Building, the museum exhibits the objects of W J Layland, a local plumber who was also an avid collector. Its focus is on preserving regional culture. Holdings include almost 1,500 historic photographs; over 500 volumes in the non-circulating research library; material relating to the history of the Santa Fe Railroad in Cleburne, housed in a caboose; a display on Native American history; a 12-foot mammoth tusk; and a gun collection dating from the 1750s. Other museum artifacts deal with home life in Texas, especially Cleburne and Johnson County. Off-site structures include the Doty-Fullerton House (circa 1869) and the Lowell Smith Sr History Center. Special programs and group tours available by appointment; caboose tours available on request. **Open:** Mon–Fri 9am–5pm, Sat 9am–1pm. **Free**

Clute

See Brazosport

College Station

See also Bryan

College Station was named for a stop on the Houston & Texas Railroad and is home to the state's first institution of higher education, Texas A&M University, founded in 1876. The university was placed on the prairie south of Bryan to distance students from Bryan's saloons. **Information:** Bryan/College Station Convention & Visitors Bureau, 715 University Dr E, College Station, 77840-1804 (tel 409/260-9898 or toll free 800/777-8292).

HOTEL 🏨
UNRATED Ramada Inn Aggieland
1502 Texas Ave S, 77840; tel 409/693-6891 or toll free 800/228-2828; fax 409/693-9891. 1 block E of campus. A high-quality hotel with extensive services and an elegant red decor. Located near Texas A&M, on restaurant row. **Rooms:** 168 rms and stes. CI 2pm/CO noon. Nonsmoking rms avail. **Amenities:** 🛁 ⌕ A/C, cable TV. **Services:** ✕ 🚗 ⌂ **Facilities:** 🔁 [675] ᕇ 1 restaurant, 1 bar (w/entertainment), whirlpool, washer/dryer. **Rates (CP):** $55 S or D. Children under age 18 stay free. Parking: Outdoor, free. AE, CB, DC, MC, V.

MOTEL

UNRATED **Best Western at Chimney Hill**
901 University Dr E, 77803; tel 409/260-9150 or toll free 800/528-1234; fax 409/846-0467. Near campus and major highway. Standard decor. **Rooms:** 100 rms and stes. CI 3pm/CO noon. Nonsmoking rms avail. **Amenities:** 🛏 A/C, cable TV. **Services:** ✕ 🚐 🖼 🎣 ⟳ **Facilities:** 🛋 🔥 1 restaurant. **Rates (CP):** $49–$54 S; $78 D. Extra person $5. Children under age 13 stay free. Parking: Outdoor, free. Rates higher on football weekends. AE, CB, DC, DISC, MC, V.

RESTAURANT 🍽

★ **Cenare**
404 University Dr E; tel 409/696-7311. **Italian.** Located near the Texas A&M campus, this traditional Italian restaurant with red checkered tablecloths offers standard Italian fare. Veal marsala, manicotti, lasagna, cannelloni, and tossed pastas are available along with grilled shrimp and beef tenderloin. All entrees come with house salad or homemade soup. Attentive, professional service. **FYI:** Reservations recommended. **Open:** Mon–Sat 11am–11pm, Sun 11am–10pm. **Prices:** Main courses $7–$15. AE, CB, DC, DISC, MC, V. ⟳ 👪 🔥

Corpus Christi

See also Kingsville, Port Aransas

Founded in 1839 as a trading post and named for the bay it overlooks, this deep-water port city offers an appealing gulf front filled with beaches, marinas, museums, fountains, and promenades. Corpus Christi is near both Mustang Island and North Padre Island National Seashore. **Information:** Greater Corpus Christi Business Alliance, 1201 N Shoreline Blvd, PO Box 640, Corpus Christi, 78403 (tel 512/881-1888).

HOTELS 🏨

𝄫 𝄫 **Bayfront Inn**
601 Shoreline Blvd, 78401; tel 512/883-7271. Shoreline exit off I-37 S. A privately owned beachfront motel with friendly owners and nice facilities, although the service is rather limited. Fine for budget-minded beachgoers. **Rooms:** 135 rms. CI 3pm/CO noon. **Amenities:** 🛏 A/C, cable TV, dataport. Some units w/terraces. Two rooms have refrigerators. **Services:** ⟳ **Facilities:** 🛋 🔥 1 beach (bay), lifeguard. **Rates (CP):** Peak (Apr–Sept) $59 S; $69 D. Extra person $10. Min stay peak. Lower rates off-season. Parking: Outdoor, free. AE, MC, V.

𝄫 𝄫 **Best Western Sandy Shores Beach Hotel**
3200 Surfside Blvd, 78403; tel 512/883-7456 or toll free 800/528-1234. Exit 181 off I-37 S. Located in Aquarium Village and near the Bayfront Convention Center, this highrise hotel offering standard rooms towers over the beach.

Rooms: 275 rms and stes. CI 2pm/CO noon. Nonsmoking rms avail. All the rooms have been recently redecorated; some have beautiful views over the bay. **Amenities:** 🛏 🔥 🍳 A/C, cable TV. Some units w/terraces. Some rooms have dataports, and maintenance will install one if needed. **Services:** ✕ 🆅🅿 🚐 🖼 ⟳ Social director. **Facilities:** 🛋 🎳 🔢 🖥 🔥 1 restaurant, 1 bar (w/entertainment), 1 beach (bay), lifeguard, washer/dryer. Kite History Museum located on site. **Rates (CP):** $60 S; $65 D; $70–$75 ste. Extra person $10. Parking: Outdoor, free. AE, DISC, MC, V.

𝄫 𝄫 𝄫 **Corpus Christi Marriott Bayfront**
900 N Shoreline Blvd, 78401; tel 512/887-1600 or toll free 800/228-9290; fax 512/887-6715. Off I-37S at MM 0. Located on the bay, this elegant hotel is a great place to spend a weekend or an entire week. Beautiful accommodations and luxurious facilities may entice you to stay even longer. **Rooms:** 350 rms and stes. Executive level. CI 2pm/CO noon. Nonsmoking rms avail. **Amenities:** 🛏 🔥 🍳 A/C, satel TV w/movies, refrig, bathrobes. Some units w/minibars, some w/terraces. Some rooms have recliner chairs and refrigerators. **Services:** ✕ 🆅🅿 🚐 🖼 ⟳ Twice-daily maid svce, social director, masseur. **Facilities:** 🛋 🏊 ⛵ 🎳 🔢 🖥 🔥 1 restaurant, 1 bar (w/entertainment), 1 beach (bay), lifeguard, board surfing, sauna, steam rm, whirlpool. **Rates (CP):** $98 S; $100 D; $109–$115 ste. Extra person $10. Min stay peak. MAP rates avail. Parking: Indoor/outdoor, $3/day. AE, DISC, MC, V.

𝄫 𝄫 𝄫 **Embassy Suites**
4337 S Padre Island Dr, 78411; tel 512/853-7899 or toll free 800/362-2779. Weber exit off TX 358. Located on the island near the beach, this tastefully appointed hotel is private and secluded. Great service and many extras. **Rooms:** 300 stes. Executive level. CI 2pm/CO noon. Nonsmoking rms avail. All rooms have microwaves. **Amenities:** 🛏 🔥 🍳 A/C, cable TV, refrig, dataport, voice mail, bathrobes. Some units w/minibars, some w/terraces. **Services:** ✕ 🆅🅿 🚐 🖼 Twice-daily maid svce, social director. Complimentary snacks and drinks offered every evening. **Facilities:** 🛋 🔢 🖥 🔥 1 restaurant, 1 bar (w/entertainment), beauty salon, washer/dryer. **Rates (CP):** $69–$79 ste. Extra person $10. Min stay peak. MAP rates avail. Parking: Outdoor, free. AE, DISC, MC, V.

𝄫 𝄫 𝄫 **Holiday Inn Airport**
5549 Leopard St, 78408; tel 512/289-5100 or toll free 800/465-4329. Off TX 358. Basic family-oriented hotel with attractive, modern decor. **Rooms:** 250 rms and stes. Executive level. CI 2pm/CO noon. Nonsmoking rms avail. **Amenities:** 🛏 🔥 🍳 A/C, cable TV, dataport, bathrobes. Some units w/minibars, some w/terraces. **Services:** ✕ 🆅🅿 🚐 🖼 Twice-daily maid svce, social director. **Facilities:** 🛋 🎳 🔢 🔥 1 restaurant, 1 bar (w/entertainment), day-care ctr, washer/dryer. **Rates (CP):** $69 S; $79 D; $89–$110 ste. Extra person $10. Children under age 5 stay free. Min stay peak. MAP rates avail. Parking: Outdoor, free. AE, DISC, MC, V.

Ramada Inn Bayfront

601 N Water St, 78401; tel 512/882-8100. Off I-37 S. Clean and dependable, and comparatively inexpensive for beachfront accommodations. Good for families. **Rooms:** 200 rms. CI 3pm/CO noon. Nonsmoking rms avail. **Amenities:** A/C, cable TV. Some units w/terraces. **Services:** Social director. Refrigerators available for $10/day. **Facilities:** 1 beach (bay), lifeguard. **Rates (CP):** Peak (Mar–Apr) $55 S; $65 D. Extra person $7. Min stay peak. Lower rates off-season. Parking: Outdoor, free. AE, DISC, MC, V.

Sheraton Corpus Christi Bayfront Hotel

707 N Shoreline Dr, 78401; tel 512/882-1700 or toll free 800/325-3535; fax 512/882-3113. Off I-37 S at MM 0. Stay right on the beach in this luxurious vacation hotel. **Rooms:** 250 rms and stes. Executive level. CI 3pm/CO noon. Nonsmoking rms avail. The roomy suites are ideal for families. **Amenities:** A/C, satel TV w/movies, refrig, bathrobes. Some units w/minibars, some w/terraces. **Services:** Twice-daily maid svce, social director. **Facilities:** 1 beach (cove/inlet), lifeguard, snorkeling, squash, sauna, whirlpool, playground, washer/dryer. **Rates (CP):** Peak (Apr–Sept) $79 S; $89 D; $95–$110 ste. Extra person $5. Min stay. Lower rates off-season. MAP rates avail. Parking: Outdoor, free. AE, DC, DISC, MC, V.

MOTELS

Island House

15340 Leward Dr, 78418; tel 512/949-8166. Padre Island split off TX 358, left on Whitecap, left on Windward. This basic hotel is a good choice for those seeking a frugal beach vacation. Convenient and economical, it offers few extras but does have standard accommodations and friendly service. **Rooms:** 75 rms. CI open/CO noon. Nonsmoking rms avail. **Amenities:** A/C, cable TV. **Facilities:** **Rates (CP):** $49 S; $55 D. Extra person $10. Min stay peak. Parking: Outdoor, free. AE, MC, V.

Val-U Inn Corpus Christi

5224 I-37 El Paso Navigation, 78407; tel 512/883-2951. Navigation exit off I-37. Very plain but comfortable motel. **Rooms:** 100 rms. CI 2pm/CO noon. Nonsmoking rms avail. **Amenities:** A/C, cable TV. Some rooms have hair dryers. **Facilities:** **Rates (CP):** $42 S; $52 D. Extra person $10. Parking: Outdoor, free. AE, MC, V.

RESORT

Holiday Inn Corpus Christi Gulf Beach

15202 Windward Dr, 78418; tel 512/949-8041 or toll free 800/465-4329; fax 512/949-9139. TX 358 exit off I-37 to Park Rd exit. 7 acres. An elegant hotel on the beach and only 20 minutes from downtown. Great for getting away without being too secluded. **Rooms:** 239 rms and stes. Executive level. CI 2pm/CO noon. Nonsmoking rms avail. **Amenities:** A/C, satel TV w/movies, refrig, dataport, bath-robes. Some units w/terraces. **Services:** Twice-daily maid svce, social director. Planned activities available daily. **Facilities:** 1 restaurant, 1 bar (w/entertainment), 1 beach (bay), lifeguard, board surfing, racquetball, sauna, whirlpool, playground, washer/dryer. **Rates (CP):** $69 S; $79 D; $89–$115 ste. Extra person $10. Children under age 5 stay free. Min stay peak. Lower rates off-season. MAP rates avail. Parking: Outdoor, free. AE, DC, DISC, MC, V.

RESTAURANTS

★ Elmo's City Diner and Oyster Bar

622 N Water (Downtown); tel 512/993-4588. **Eclectic.** A basic diner offering "good eats"—all the usual favorites like burgers and fries. The notable selection of seafood includes some great oysters. **FYI:** Reservations not accepted. Singer. Children's menu. **Open:** Daily 10:30am–11pm. **Prices:** Main courses $6–$10. AE, DISC, MC, V.

Elmo's Staple St Seafood Grille & Oyster Bar

5253 S Staples; tel 512/992-3474. Near beach. **Regional American/International.** Upscale dining near the beach. Specializes in grilled shrimp. **FYI:** Reservations accepted. Singer. Children's menu. Dress code. **Open:** Daily 11:30am–11:30pm. **Prices:** Main courses $7–$16. AE, DISC, MC, V.

★ Landry's Seafood

Peoples Street T-Head; tel 512/882-6666. **Seafood.** Located right on the river in a large riverboat, this restaurant's atmosphere is somehow elegant yet fun. Diners can sit indoors or outside. The Shrimp Basic is the house specialty. **FYI:** Reservations not accepted. Country music. Children's menu. Beer and wine only. **Open:** Sun–Thurs 11am–10:15pm, Fri–Sat 11am–11:15pm. Closed Mar–Nov. **Prices:** Main courses $7–$11. AE, DC, DISC, MC, V.

The Lighthouse Restaurant and Oyster Bar

Lawrence Street T-Head; tel 512/883-3982. Near beach. **International/Seafood.** Located right on the bay, this restaurant is the perfect way to start a romantic evening or a long walk on the beach. Seafood and steak are specialties. **FYI:** Reservations accepted. Blues. Dress code. **Open:** Daily 11am–10pm. **Prices:** Main courses $8–$16. AE, DISC, MC, V.

ATTRACTIONS

Padre Island National Seashore

9405 S Padre Island Dr; tel 512/949-8068. This 113-mile-long peninsula with an average width of 3 miles makes up one of the longest stretches of undeveloped ocean beach in the United States. Almost entirely uninhabited, this long sweep of sand—with high dunes (rising to 45 feet in places), grasslands, tidal flats teeming with shore life, and warm offshore waters—is a popular spot for campers (fully equipped camping grounds available), fishermen, waterskiers, and sailors. The spine of the peninsula has been made into a nature reserve for some 350 species of birds, including herons, killdeer, meadowlarks, and sandhill cranes. Other animals inhabiting the island include coyotes, black-tailed jackrabbits, lizards, and rattlesnakes. The park is connected to Corpus Christi by the John F Kennedy Causeway and to Port Isabel by the South Padre Causeway. Malaquite Beach Campground is a site for tent and recreational vehicle camping; primitive camping allowed at designated sites along Laguna Madre and all along the gulf beach except in the Malaquite Beach area. The latter offers 55 miles of beach open to four-wheel-driving. **Open:** Daily 24 hours. $$

Art Museum of South Texas
1902 N Shoreline; tel 512/884-3844. Rotating schedule of exhibits of prints, paintings, sculpture, photography, and folk art, set in a stark-white, cast-concrete museum designed by renowned architect Philip Johnson. Several exhibitions each year celebrate Latin American artists; regional artists are frequently displayed. Film series, lectures, literary readings, and concerts are among the special programs offered. **Open:** Tues–Sat 10am–5pm, Sun 1–5pm. $

World of Discovery
1900 N Chaparral; tel 512/883-2862. Collections, exhibits, and activities cover history, natural history, and art, with an emphasis on the region of South Texas. The museum features anthropological exhibits depicting the area's blend of Spanish, Mexican, and Native American heritages; natural history and science collections of shells, fish birds, and fossils indigenous to the gulf coast; photographic collection (over 300,000 images); and fine arts. Of special interest is the wide-ranging World of Discovery, an extensive collection which focuses on Columbus and the discovery of the New World. One of its exhibits, "Seeds of Change," originally presented at the Smithsonian Institution and now on permanent display here, tells the story of the New World's discovery and its impact. The Columbus Fleet features authentic replicas of the Pinta and Santa María (built by the government of Spain to commemorate the Columbus Quincentenary) which can be toured. Also at the museum are hands-on children's exhibits such as "Reptiles of South Texas," featuring a live alligator; "Shipwreck!," the story of a 1554 Spanish shipwreck; "DinoScape," which explores the world of dinosaurs; and "Hurricane/Weather Station," which centers around a computer that gives weather information. Educational programs, library. Tours available. **Open:** Daily 10am–5pm. $$$

Museum of Oriental Cultures
418 Peoples St, Ste 200; tel 512/883-1303. The history and culture of the Orient expressed through art, architecture, artifacts, and the decorative arts. Scale models of famous pagodas, shrines, and temples. Buddhist art (including a bronze Buddha from 1766), sculpture, furniture, paintings, pottery, kimonos, bronzeware, masks, and a collection of handcrafted Hakata dolls. The museum has a library and gift shop, and offers films and floral art studies. **Open:** Mon–Sat 10am–4pm. $

Texas State Aquarium
2710 N Shoreline Blvd; tel 512/881-1200. Close-up views of the wonders of the Gulf of Mexico in a wide variety of marine habitats. Highlights include an artificial reef community created by the massive leg of an offshore oil rig; the color and beauty of the Flower Gardens Coral Reef; and a 132,000-gallon deep-water exhibit where visitors can talk to the diver. The Sea Star Discovery Pool allows visitors to touch a variety of sea creatures. A glass-enclosed tunnel provides a 180° view of the fish. More than 250 gulf species are represented here. Gift shop on the premises. **Open:** Mon–Sat 9am–5pm, Sun 10am–5pm. $$$

USS *Lexington*
2914 N Shoreline Blvd; tel 512/888-4873. This vintage wartime aircraft carrier, one of the most decorated carriers in naval history—the ship was sunk four times, but always returned to action—is now a floating naval museum. Visitors can take self-guided tours of the 910-foot ship. Museum displays explore the history of the USS *Lexington*, from its origins as a gunboat in the American Revolution through its three succeeding incarnations. Films on naval aviation shown. **Open:** Daily 9am–5pm. $$$

Fulton Mansion State Historical Park
317 Fulton Beach Rd, Fulton; tel 512/729-0386. Extravagant home, built in 1874, overlooking Aransas Bay. Highlights include the ornate trimwork and furnishings, as well as the technological conveniences of the period, such as modern plumbing and a gas lighting system. "Christmas at the Mansion" is a two-day event held in December during which a traditional 1880s Christmas is celebrated; "All Hallow Even" is a two-day event held in October. Guided tours available. **Open:** Wed–Sun 9am–4pm. $$

Goose Island State Park
12 mi N off SR 35, Rockport; tel 512/729-2858. Located on the Lamar Peninsula, between Copano and St Charles Bays, the 307-acre park encompasses live oak and redbay woodlands, meadowlands, and coastal prairies. Goose Island itself consists of salt flats, grasslands, and salt marshes. This is a popular spot for viewing a wide variety of waterfowl, such as Louisiana herons, killdeer, sandpipers, and blue-winged teals. This is also the site of "Big Tree," an immense live oak (certified as the largest in Texas) estimated to be over 1,000 years old. Facilities include a fishing pier, a fish-cleaning table, boat ramp, picnic sites, rest rooms, showers, open shelters, tent sites, and children's play area. **Open:** Daily 8am–5pm. $

Dallas

See also Arlington, Denton, Fort Worth, Greenville, Irving, McKinney

From its beginnings as a trading post along the Trinity River in 1840, Dallas has blossomed into a cosmopolitan city that today is considered by many to be the cultural center of Texas. Opera, symphony, museums, and theatrical companies as well as several entertainment districts keep the activity level high. Dallas has diversified its economy, founded on business and finance, and become the third-largest fashion market and film production area in the nation. Dallas is home to both Southern Methodist University and the University of Texas at Dallas. **Information:** Dallas Convention & Visitors Bureau, 1201 Elm St, #2000, Dallas, 75270 (tel 214/746-6677).

PUBLIC TRANSPORTATION

The **Dallas Area Rapid Transit (DART)** operates citywide bus service. Stops are indicated by yellow signs. Regular fare is $1, express fares $2. Seniors and persons with disabilities ride both the express and local lines for 50¢ each way. Exact change required. For information call 214/979-1111.

HOTELS 📠

▤▤▤▤ The Adolphus

1321 Commerce St, 75202 (Financial District); tel 214/742-8200 or toll free 800/221-9083; fax 214/651-3561. Near the Arts Center. This modern 19-story hotel was tacked onto a smaller grand hotel built by beer baron Adolphus Busch in 1912. Highlights include the handsome original beaux arts facade, spacious motorcourt entrance, and ornate lobby and lounge featuring a two-story skylight, carved wood and Flemish tapestries, and numerous antiques—including a bronze Dore Gueridon table and an 1893 Steinway grand piano. **Rooms:** 435 rms and stes. CI 3pm/CO 1pm. Nonsmoking rms avail. Larger-than-usual rooms, with 10-foot ceilings; each has a sitting area for three or four guests. Furniture is mostly of Queen Anne and Chippendale styles (some pieces needing buffing up), but decor is generally unremarkable. Some rooms on inner courtyard are gloomy. City views available from limited number of rooms on higher floors and from penthouse suite with large terrace. All guestroom windows are sealed. Separate shower stalls. **Amenities:** 📺 ⚗ 🍸 A/C, cable TV w/movies, dataport, voice mail, bathrobes. All units w/minibars. Tie racks and fax machines in some rooms. **Services:** 🍽 🔑 📼 🚐 📬 ➴ Twice-daily maid svce, car-rental desk, babysitting. 24-hour concierge. Town car for complimentary drop-offs in downtown area. Room service from French Room menu, with meals served course by course. Afternoon tea accompanied by pianist. **Facilities:** 🍽 🚃 ⚑ 3 restaurants (see "Restaurants" below), 3 bars (1 w/entertainment), day-care ctr. Attractive Bistro with espresso bar for breakfast and lunch; outstanding dining room. **Rates:** $180–$220 S or D; $295 ste. Extra person $20. Children under age 12 stay free. Parking: Indoor, $20/day. Rates vary by floor and size, with best values being the "superiors." AE, CB, DC, DISC, MC, V.

▤▤▤ Best Western Windsor Suites Hotel

2363 Stemmons Trail, 75220; tel 214/350-2300 or toll free 800/528-1234. Accessible from I-35 and Northwest Hwy. Newer property designed for multinight stays. Posh, soothing atmosphere. In a good location for access to northwest Dallas. **Rooms:** 96 stes. CI 3pm/CO noon. Nonsmoking rms avail. **Amenities:** 📺 ⚗ A/C, satel TV, refrig, dataport. Microwave. **Services:** 🚐 📬 ➴ Babysitting. **Facilities:** 🍽 🏋 [65] ⚗ Whirlpool, washer/dryer. **Rates (CP):** $85–$169 ste. Children under age 18 stay free. Parking: Outdoor, free. AE, CB, DC, DISC, MC, V.

▤▤▤ Bristol Suites Hotel

7800 Alpha Rd, 75240; tel 972/233-7600 or toll free 800/922-9222; fax 972/701-8618. Near Jct I-635 and Coit Rd. Elegant facility with a luxurious 10-story atrium and public areas done in dark colors and rich, beautiful wood. In a very good location near the junction of major interstates. **Rooms:** 295 stes. CI 3pm/CO 1pm. Nonsmoking rms avail. **Amenities:** 📺 ⚗ 🖥 🍸 A/C, cable TV w/movies, refrig, dataport, voice mail. All units w/minibars. Microwave. **Services:** ✕ 🔑 🚐 📬 ➴ 🔔 Twice-daily maid svce, car-rental desk. Transportation provided to local malls. **Facilities:** 🍽 🏋 🏋 [400] 🖥 ⚗ 1 restaurant, 1 bar, volleyball, whirlpool, washer/dryer. **Rates (BB):** $99–$170 ste. Extra person $10. Children under age 18 stay free. Parking: Outdoor, free. AE, CB, DC, DISC, MC, V.

▤▤ Clarion Hotel Dallas

1241 W Mockingbird Lane, 75247; tel 214/630-7000 or toll free 800/442-7547; fax 214/638-6943. Visitors are welcomed into a small atrium lobby and restaurant area, and although the architecture is somewhat bland, the interior is quite nice and relaxing. **Rooms:** 364 rms and stes. Executive level. CI 3pm/CO 1pm. Nonsmoking rms avail. **Amenities:** 📺 ⚗ A/C, cable TV w/movies, dataport, voice mail. Some units w/terraces. In-room Nintendo video games available. **Services:** ✕ 🚐 📬 ➴ **Facilities:** 🍽 🏋 [1100] ⚗ 1 restaurant, 1 bar, games rm, washer/dryer. **Rates:** $109–$139 S; $119–$149 D; $150–$450 ste. Extra person $10. Children under age 16 stay free. Parking: Indoor/outdoor, free. Government discounts avail. AE, CB, DC, DISC, MC, V.

▤▤▤ Courtyard by Marriott–LBJ at Josey

2930 Forest Lane, 75229; tel 972/620-8000 or toll free 800/321-2211; fax 972/620-9267. Near I-35 and I-635. Small, cozy, friendly hotel in quiet, shaded area away from interstate. Very safe and secluded. **Rooms:** 146 rms and stes. CI 3pm/CO 1pm. Nonsmoking rms avail. **Amenities:** 📺 ⚗ A/C, cable TV w/movies, dataport, voice mail. All units w/terraces. Instant hot water for coffee or tea in all rooms. **Services:** 📬 ➴ Babysitting. **Facilities:** 🍽 🏋 [40] ⚗ 1 restaurant (bkfst only), 1 bar, whirlpool, washer/dryer. **Rates:** $75–$85 S or D; $89–$99 ste. Extra person $10. Children under age 16 stay free. Parking: Outdoor, free. AE, CB, DC, DISC, MC, V.

▤▤▤▤ The Crescent Court Hotel

400 Crescent Court, 75201; tel 214/871-3200 or toll free 800/654-6541; fax 214/871-3272. Large, elegant hotel with magnificent European atmosphere and exquisite landscaping. Huge lobby has top-quality furnishings. Caters to busi-

ness travelers and celebrities. Shopping complex adjacent to hotel. **Rooms:** 216 rms and stes. Executive level. CI 3pm/CO 1pm. Nonsmoking rms avail. Large, nicely furnished rooms with automatic lighting when door is opened. **Amenities:** 🛎 🕭 🍷 A/C, cable TV, dataport. All units w/terraces, 1 w/fireplace, 1 w/whirlpool. **Services:** 🍽 🔑 VP 🚐 🖼 🛎 💁 Twice-daily maid svce, masseur, babysitting. Guests leave shoes outside their rooms for complimentary shoe shine. Transportation to shopping and airport can be arranged. Down-to-earth, friendly staff offers exceptional, personal service. **Facilities:** 🛋 ⚐ 🔌 💻 ♿ 2 restaurants, 1 bar (w/entertainment), spa, sauna, steam rm, whirlpool, beauty salon. **Rates:** $245–$340 S; $275–$370 D; $450–$1,350 ste. Parking: Indoor, $5–$10/day. AE, CB, DC, DISC, JCB, MC, V.

☰☰☰ The Dallas Grand Hotel
1914 Commerce St, 75201 (Downtown); tel 214/747-7000 or toll free 800/421-0011; fax 214/742-1337. Near Harwood. A large, arc-shaped budget hotel east of downtown, the Grand is very spacious and uncrowded. **Rooms:** 710 rms and stes. CI 3pm/CO noon. Nonsmoking rms avail. **Amenities:** 🛎 ⚐ A/C, cable TV w/movies, voice mail. **Services:** ✕ 🔑 VP 🚐 🖼 💁 Twice-daily maid svce, babysitting. **Facilities:** ⚐ 🔌 ♿ 2 restaurants, 1 bar, whirlpool, washer/dryer. **Rates:** $110–$120 S; $120–$130 D; $175–$400 ste. Extra person $10. Children under age 18 stay free. Parking: Indoor, $3–$9.50/day. AE, CB, DC, DISC, MC, V.

☰☰☰ Dallas Marriott Quorum
14901 Dallas Pkwy, 75240 (Addison); tel 972/661-2800 or toll free 800/228-9290; fax 972/991-1376. Dallas N Tollway near Beltline. Hotel was undergoing full renovation. Has professional, rather sterile atmosphere and efficient if unpersonable staff. A golf and athletic club is located nearby. **Rooms:** 548 rms and stes. Executive level. CI 3pm/CO 1pm. Nonsmoking rms avail. Concierge-level rooms feature innovative, moveable desk/workplace area with adjustable light fixture. **Amenities:** 🛎 ⚐ A/C, cable TV w/movies, dataport, voice mail. Concierge-level rooms have irons, and ironing boards. **Services:** ✕ 🔑 🚐 🖼 💁 Car-rental desk, babysitting. Auto rental arrangement available. **Facilities:** 🛋 🏊 ⚐ 🔌 💻 ♿ 2 restaurants, 1 bar, basketball, sauna, whirlpool, washer/dryer. **Rates:** $129–$139 S or D; $350–$500 ste. Children under age 17 stay free. Parking: Indoor/outdoor, free. Special packages for honeymoons, weekends, and military guests. AE, CB, DC, DISC, MC, V.

UNRATED Dallas Radisson Park Central Hotel
7750 LBJ Fwy at Coit Rd, 75251; tel 972/233-4421 or toll free 800/487-PARK; fax 972/233-3679. I-635 at Coit near US 75. This quite comfortable, medium-size hotel was undergoing major renovations that should result in more amenities and improved accommodations. Jogging trail, tennis courts, and golf course nearby. **Rooms:** 449 rms and stes. CI 3pm/CO noon. Nonsmoking rms avail. **Amenities:** 🛎 ⚐ 📺 🍷 A/C, cable TV w/movies. **Services:** ✕ 🚐 🖼 💁 Babysitting.

Transportation provided within five-mile radius. American Airlines ticket office in lobby. **Facilities:** 🛋 🏊 ⚐ 275 💻 ♿ 1 restaurant, 2 bars, whirlpool, washer/dryer. Health and fitness club nearby. **Rates (BB):** $89 S; $109–$119 D; $209 ste. Extra person $10. Children under age 18 stay free. Parking: Indoor/outdoor, free. AE, CB, DC, DISC, JCB, MC, V.

☰☰☰ DoubleTree Hotel at Campbell Centre
8250 North Central Expressway, 75206; tel 214/691-8700 or toll free 800/222-TREE; fax 214/706-0187. Easily accessible from US 75 and from all points in the metroplex, including shopping malls, nightlife, airports, downtown, and North Dallas. Very elegant lobby has two pianos, and the conference center is enclosed in glass and overlooks the pretty Dallas skyline. For business or pleasure. **Rooms:** 302 rms and stes. Executive level. CI 3pm/CO noon. Nonsmoking rms avail. Corner rooms are circular with full windows affording terrific views of the city. **Amenities:** 🛎 ⚐ A/C, cable TV w/movies, dataport. Refrigerators on request. **Services:** ✕ 🔑 🖼 💁 Babysitting. Two chocolate chip cookies in rooms. Movies supplied on request. Pet deposit $100. Child care arranged for nominal fee. **Facilities:** 🏊 ⚐ 500 ♿ 1 restaurant, 1 bar (w/entertainment), basketball, whirlpool, beauty salon. **Rates:** $114–$144 S; $124–$154 D; $225–$500 ste. Extra person $10. Children under age 18 stay free. Parking: Indoor/outdoor, free. Small increase in rates in summer. Rates depend on availability. AE, CB, DC, DISC, MC, V.

☰☰☰ DoubleTree Hotel at Lincoln Centre
5410 LBJ Freeway, 75240; tel 972/934-8400 or toll free 800/222-TREE; fax 972/701-5105. I-635 and Dallas N Tollway, near Galleria. Contemporary hotel in sleek office building complex with small pond and reflecting pool. Elegant, relaxing atmosphere. **Rooms:** 500 rms and stes. Executive level. CI 4pm/CO noon. Nonsmoking rms avail. Rooms feature vanity area and desk with game table. **Amenities:** 🛎 ⚐ A/C, cable TV w/movies. Some units w/whirlpools. **Services:** ✕ 🔑 VP 🚐 🖼 💁 Twice-daily maid svce, babysitting. Shuttle provided to Galleria mall. ATM, Federal Express, flower shop, copy center, and travel agency. **Facilities:** 🛋 🏊 ⚐ 800 💻 ♿ 3 restaurants, 2 bars (1 w/entertainment), whirlpool, washer/dryer. Access to Lincoln City Club health and fitness facilities for small fee. **Rates:** $160–$180 S; $170–$190 D; $250–$850 ste. Extra person $10. Children under age 18 stay free. Parking: Indoor/outdoor, free. AE, CB, DC, DISC, MC, V.

☰☰☰ Embassy Suites Dallas Market Center
2727 Stemmons Freeway, 75207; tel 214/630-5332 or toll free 800/EMBASSY. Conveniently located 5 minutes from downtown and 15 minutes from DFW, this friendly hotel offering personal service features a nine-story atrium with a fountain. **Rooms:** 244 stes. CI 3pm/CO noon. Nonsmoking rms avail. Executive, two-bedroom, king, and double units available. Some sofabeds. **Amenities:** 🛎 ⚐ 📺 🍷 A/C, satel TV w/movies, refrig, dataport, voice mail. All units w/terraces.

Microwave. **Services:** ✗ ⌨ ⌂ Babysitting. Transportation provided within three-mile radius of hotel. Electronic information center. **Facilities:** ⌂ ⌨ 🔲300 ♿ 1 restaurant (lunch and dinner only), 1 bar, games rm, sauna, steam rm, whirlpool, washer/dryer. **Rates (BB):** $112–$149 ste. Extra person $10. Children under age 12 stay free. Parking: Outdoor, free. AE, CB, DC, DISC, JCB, MC, V.

≣≣≣ Embassy Suites Hotel

13131 N Central Expwy, 75243; tel 972/234-3300 or toll free 800/362-2779; fax 972/437-4247. NW corner of jct I-635/US 75. Located near the convergence of several interstates, this bright pink hotel catches every traveler's attention with its unusual color and architecture. Fortunately, the interior is much more peaceful, with a large sunlit atrium and well-kept public areas. **Rooms:** 279 stes. CI 3pm/CO noon. Nonsmoking rms avail. **Amenities:** 📺 ♨ 🔲 🍴 A/C, cable TV w/movies, refrig, dataport, voice mail. **Services:** ✗ ⌨ ⌂ **Facilities:** ⌂ ⌨ 🔲600 🖥 ♿ 1 restaurant, 1 bar, sauna, whirlpool, washer/dryer. **Rates (BB):** $129–$144 ste. Extra person $15. Children under age 12 stay free. Parking: Outdoor, free. AE, CB, DC, DISC, JCB, MC, V.

≣≣≣ Fairmont

1717 N Akard St, 75201 (Downtown); tel 214/720-2020 or toll free 800/527-4727; fax 214/720-5269. S of Woodall Rogers Fwy. An upscale, very modern complex with a marble-floored lobby and two large towers. Specializes in conventions. Easy access to downtown locations. **Rooms:** 600 rms and stes. CI 3pm/CO 1pm. Nonsmoking rms avail. **Amenities:** 📺 ♨ 🍴 A/C, cable TV w/movies, dataport, voice mail. Some units w/minibars. **Services:** ⍾ ⌨ VP ⌂ ⌂ Twice-daily maid svce, social director, babysitting. Multilingual staff. Quiktix (instant airline ticket delivery service) available. On-staff florist. **Facilities:** ⌂ 🔲2000 🖥 ♿ 3 restaurants (see "Restaurants" below), 3 bars (2 w/entertainment), games rm. The Pyramid Room offers exquisite dining. Jewelry and clothing stores. **Rates:** $189–$215 S or D; $325–$650 ste. Extra person $25. Children under age 18 stay free. Parking: Indoor, $12/day. AE, CB, DC, DISC, ER, JCB, MC, V.

≣≣≣ The Grand Kempinski Dallas

15201 Dallas Pkwy, 75248 (Addison); tel 972/386-6000 or toll free 800/426-3135; fax 972/404-1848. Dallas N Tollway, near Beltline Rd. A fashionable convention hotel with a European atmosphere, this is one of the few North American locations for the German-based Kempinski hotel chain. A very spacious atrium allows light to flood the marble floors in the elegant lobby. Jogging trail and golf course nearby. **Rooms:** 529 rms and stes. Executive level. CI 3pm/CO noon. Nonsmoking rms avail. **Amenities:** 📺 ♨ 🍴 A/C, satel TV w/movies, dataport, voice mail. Some units w/minibars, some w/terraces, some w/whirlpools. **Services:** ⍾ ⌨ VP 🚗 ⌂ ⌂ Car-rental desk, masseur, babysitting. Transportation within a limited area provided. **Facilities:** ⌂ 🏊 🏀 ⌨ 🔲3000 🖥 ♿ 3 restaurants, 3 bars (2 w/entertainment), basketball, racquetball, sauna, steam rm, whirlpool, beauty salon. On-

site pastry shop and several other shops near lobby. **Rates:** $175–$195 S; $195–$215 D; $350–$1,500 ste. Extra person $20. Children under age 17 stay free. Parking: Indoor/outdoor, free. AE, CB, DC, DISC, MC, V.

≣≣≣ Harvey Hotel Addison

14315 Midway Rd, 75244 (Addison); tel 972/980-8877 or toll free 800/922-9222; fax 972/788-2758. Near I-635, between Beltline and Spring Valley. A sprawling business and convention hotel with a wide range of services and amenities. Beautiful sunlit atrium/lobby. **Rooms:** 429 rms and stes. CI 3pm/CO noon. Nonsmoking rms avail. **Amenities:** 📺 ♨ A/C, cable TV w/movies, voice mail. 1 unit w/whirlpool. **Services:** ✗ ⌂ ⌂ 🚐 Car-rental desk. Complimentary *USA Today*. Van service to nearby shopping centers. Delta and American Airlines ticketing offices on premises. **Facilities:** ⌂ ⌨ 🔲1000 🖥 ♿ 2 restaurants, 1 bar, whirlpool, washer/dryer. **Rates:** $99–$129 S or D; $125–$275 ste. Children under age 18 stay free. Parking: Indoor/outdoor, free. Parking: Outdoor, free. AE, CB, DC, DISC, MC, V.

≣≣≣ The Harvey Hotel Downtown Dallas

400 N Olive St, 75201 (Downtown); tel 214/922-8000 or toll free 800/922-9222; fax 214/922-0308. Between Live Oak and Pearl Sts. Beautiful hotel with sunlit lobby connected to many downtown buildings through underground pedestrian system and skywalks. Conference areas on two floors make this a great place for business travel or corporate conventions. **Rooms:** 502 rms and stes. CI 3pm/CO 1pm. Nonsmoking rms avail. **Amenities:** 📺 ♨ A/C, cable TV w/movies, dataport. **Services:** ✗ ⌨ VP 🚗 ⌂ ⌂ 🚐 Babysitting. **Facilities:** ⌨ 🔲1400 🖥 ♿ 1 restaurant, 1 bar, spa, washer/dryer. **Rates:** $79–$149 S or D; $149–$249 ste. Extra person $10. Children under age 18 stay free. Parking: Indoor, $8–$10/day. AE, CB, DC, DISC, EC, JCB, MC, V.

≣≣≣ Holiday Inn Aristocrat

1933 Main St, 75201 (Downtown); tel 214/741-7700 or toll free 800/231-4235; fax 214/939-3639. Between Harwood and Ervay. Built in 1925 by Conrad Hilton, this was the first property to bear the Hilton name. Today, the Holiday Inn is a nationally registered landmark with elegant architecture and decor. Lobby and lounge areas are cozy and charming. Connected to downtown pedestrian system. **Rooms:** 172 rms and stes. CI 3pm/CO noon. Nonsmoking rms avail. Each room is individually decorated with antique furniture. **Amenities:** 📺 ♨ A/C, cable TV w/movies, refrig, dataport, voice mail. All units w/minibars. **Services:** ✗ 🚐 ⌂ ⌂ Complimentary coffee in club room daily. **Facilities:** ⌨ 🔲232 ♿ 1 restaurant, 1 bar. Free access to Texas Club health and fitness center. **Rates:** $99–$160 S or D; $120–$160 ste. Extra person $10. Children under age 18 stay free. Parking: Indoor, $3/day. AE, CB, DC, DISC, ER, JCB, MC, V.

≣≣≣ Holiday Inn North

2645 LBJ Fwy, 75234; tel 972/243-3363 or toll free 800/ HOLIDAY. Near I-35. Well-equipped hotel with a spacious, plant-filled lobby. **Rooms:** 375 rms and stes. CI 3pm/CO 1pm. Nonsmoking rms avail. **Amenities:** 🔒🐶🖥️🍽️A/C, cable TV w/movies, dataport. Some units w/terraces. **Services:** ✕ 🚐🌳🍴 **Facilities:** 🏋️🎱🖼️ 500 🖥️♿ 3 restaurants, 2 bars, whirlpool, washer/dryer. Pizza Hut in lobby. Gabriel's nightclub is a high-energy hot spot. **Rates:** $129–$159 S or D; $199 ste. Extra person $10. Children under age 19 stay free. Parking: Outdoor, free. AE, CB, DC, DISC, ER, MC, V.

≣≣≣ Hyatt Regency Dallas at Reunion

300 Reunion Blvd, 75207 (Downtown/West End); tel 214/651-1234 or toll free 800/233-1234; fax 214/742-8126. This very sleek and modern hotel is best known for being featured in the opening sequence of the popular 1980s TV show *Dallas*. Located near Reunions Arena and the Dallas Convention Center. Amtrak and Union Station are a short walk through a tunnel. An 18-story atrium lobby features an exquisite water garden, sculptures, artwork, and plants. **Rooms:** 939 rms and stes. Executive level. CI 6pm/CO noon. No smoking. Country ambience includes wood furniture reminiscent of rustic lodge, accented with plush chairs. **Amenities:** 🔒🐶🖥️🍽️A/C, cable TV w/movies, dataport, voice mail. All units w/minibars. Rooms for guests with disabilities have raised toilet seats, roll-in showers, lights with touch activation, telephones with large numbers, climate control with levers, closed-captioned TV decoder, and signs in braille. **Services:** ✕🗝️VP🚐🌳🍴Babysitting. Complimentary shoe shine. Electronic information center. **Facilities:** 🏋️🎱🎱🖼️ 3000 🖥️♿ 3 restaurants (*see* "Restaurants" below), 2 bars (1 w/entertainment), basketball, spa, sauna, steam rm, whirlpool, playground, washer/dryer. Rotating restaurant and lounge on top floor have spectacular views of city. Swimming pool has lift for guests with disabilities to access water. **Rates:** $175–$200 S; $200–$250 D; $250–$3,000 ste. Children under age 12 stay free. Parking: Indoor/outdoor, $6–$12/day. Business rates avail. AE, CB, DC, DISC, EC, ER, JCB, MC, V.

UNRATED Le Méridien Dallas

650 N Pearl St, 75201 (Downtown); tel 214/979-9000 or toll free 800/543-4300; fax 214/953-1931. Between Bryan and San Jacinto Sts. Located in the Plaza of the America's Office, a shopping complex, this hotel is connected to other office buildings by the downtown pedestrian system, a skywalk and tunnel. Deep Ellum, the Arts District, and the West End are nearby. Known for catering to business travelers and conventions. Extensive renovations were under way due to new management. **Rooms:** 392 rms, stes, and effic. Executive level. CI 3pm/CO noon. Nonsmoking rms avail. Rooms on west side have great view of unique architecture of downtown office buildings. Most rooms have large windows, nice vanity areas, and cushioned bed benches. Club President rooms are spacious and have plants. **Amenities:** 🔒🐶 A/C, cable TV w/movies, voice mail. Some units w/minibars, some w/terraces. **Services:** ✕🗝️VP🌳🍴Twice-daily maid svce, car-rental desk, masseur, babysitting. Staff is fluent in Spanish and French. Hotel also has medical staff. 24-hour security. **Facilities:** 🏋️2 🖼️ 1000 🖥️♿ 1 restaurant, 1 bar, basketball, racquetball, spa, sauna, steam rm, whirlpool, beauty salon, day-care ctr. Top floor, reserved for special functions, has stage, dance area, built-in bars, and view of downtown. Ice rink and various shops in 15-story atrium. Plaza has comprehensive fitness center with aerobic classes for guests. **Rates:** Peak (Jan–June/Sept–Oct) $128–$150 S; $130–$160 D; $125–$1000 ste; $325 effic. Extra person $20. Children under age 12 stay free. Lower rates off-season. Parking: Indoor, $7–$10/day. Rates vary with availability. AE, CB, DC, DISC, MC, V.

≣≣≣≣ The Mansion on Turtle Creek

2821 Turtle Creek Blvd, 75219 (Oaklawn/Turtle Creek); tel 214/559-2100 or toll free 800/527-5432; fax 214/528-4187. 5 minutes from the Financial and Arts District. The flagship of the classy Rosewood Hotel group—cherished by an elite clientele for its pampering privacy—this small, luxurious hotel is fashioned around a former cotton baron's manor house. A nine-floor annex in matching pink lends a touch of Beverly Hills to this quiet, unremarkable corner of Dallas, seven minutes from downtown. The lobby, a 32-foot-high rotunda adorned with travertine marble, boasts an exceptional array of artworks, antiques, and floral extravaganzas. **Rooms:** 141 rms and stes. CI 3pm/CO 2pm. Nonsmoking rms avail. Rooms (measuring 440 sq ft) and suites are in the annex, each exquisitely furnished with top-of-the-line fixtures, refined decor, and ceiling moldings. Most rooms have French windows opening to tiny Romeo-and-Juliet balconies (many with parking lot views), but a few rooms open directly to the pool terrace. TV armoires double as desk (too small for spreading out) in most rooms, but the tradeoff is space for an armchair with ottoman and reading lamp. **Amenities:** 🔒🐶🍽️A/C, cable TV w/movies, dataport, bathrobes. Some units w/terraces. Two-line phones. Wet bars and butler pantries in sumptuous suites. **Services:** 🍴🗝️VP🚐🌳🍴🔔Twice-daily maid svce, babysitting. Staff-to-guest ratio is two to one. Concierge and small business center available around the clock. Courtesy car within five-mile radius. In-room meals served course by course on Bauscher Weiden china. **Facilities:** 🏋️🖼️ 300 🖥️♿ 1 restaurant (*see* "Restaurants" below), 1 bar (w/entertainment), sauna, steam rm, whirlpool, beauty salon. Attractive roofdeck pool with pergola-shaded tables and poolside service (but the serenity is sometimes disturbed by planes heading for nearby Love Field). Light-filled conservatory, The Promenade, for breakfast and lunch. Outstanding main dining room. **Rates:** $245–$340 S; $285–$380 D; $495–$1380 ste. Extra person $40. Children under age 18 stay free. Min stay special events. Parking: Indoor/outdoor, $10/day. AE, CB, DC, DISC, ER, JCB, MC, V.

≣≣≣ Melrose Hotel

3015 Oak Lawn Ave, 75219 (Oak Lawn); tel 214/521-5151 or toll free 800/MELROSE; fax 214/521-9306. Near Cedar Springs. Located in an upscale area, this historic establishment, opened in 1924 and recently renovated, offers elegant accommodations with distinctive furnishings. **Rooms:** 182 rms and stes. Executive level. CI 3pm/CO noon. Nonsmoking rms avail. **Amenities:** 🔆 A/C, cable TV w/movies, dataport. Some units w/minibars. Most rooms have ceiling fans. **Services:** ✕ 🞂 VP 🚗 ⛱ 🍷 Babysitting. VCRs on request. Free transportation provided to Love Field Int'l Airport, but fee charged for trips to Dallas/Ft Worth. **Facilities:** 🔳₁₈₀ 💻 ᕕ 1 restaurant, 1 bar (w/entertainment). Centrum Health Club is nearby. Library Bar provides quaint, cozy lounging with English pub ambience. **Rates:** Peak (Sept–June) $150–$195 S or D; $250–$300 ste. Extra person $10. Children under age 12 stay free. Lower rates off-season. Parking: Outdoor, free. AE, CB, DC, DISC, EC, JCB, MC, V.

≣ ≣ ≣ Omni Richardson Hotel

701 E Campbell Rd, Richardson, 75081; tel 972/231-9600 or toll free 800/THE-OMNI; fax 972/907-2578. On US 75 at Campbell. Catering to businesses, (specifically, the local telecommunications companies) this very nice hotel offers an elegant lobby with soft, contemporary colors. Located near Southfork Ranch (featured in TV's *Dallas*). **Rooms:** 342 rms and stes. Executive level. CI 3pm/CO noon. Nonsmoking rms avail. **Amenities:** 🔆 A/C, cable TV w/movies, dataport. 1 unit w/whirlpool. **Services:** ✕ 🞂 🚗 ⛱ 🍷 Twice-daily maid svce, car-rental desk, masseur, babysitting. **Facilities:** 🔳 🏋 🍷 ₉₀₀ ᕕ 2 restaurants, 2 bars, spa, sauna, whirlpool. **Rates:** $159–$199 S; $169–$209 D; $249–$809 ste. Children under age 18 stay free. Parking: Outdoor, free. AE, CB, DC, DISC, JCB, MC, V.

≣ ≣ Quality Hotel Market Center

2015 N Market Center Blvd, 75207; tel 214/741-7481 or toll free 800/421-2555; fax 214/747-6191. Market Center exit off I-35. Average-size hotel located near downtown. Standard accommodations at standard prices. Fine for overnight stay or weekend visit. **Rooms:** 255 rms and stes. CI 3pm/CO noon. Nonsmoking rms avail. **Amenities:** 🔆 A/C, dataport. Some units w/terraces. **Services:** ⛱ 🍷 Babysitting. Complimentary coffee and danish, or a $3 breakfast option. **Facilities:** 🔳 🍷 ₂₀₀ ᕕ 1 restaurant, games rm, washer/dryer. Food court. **Rates (CP):** $65–$85 S; $75–$95 D; $125 ste. Extra person $10. Children under age 18 stay free. Parking: Outdoor, free. AE, CB, DC, DISC, EC, ER, JCB, MC, V.

≣ ≣ ≣ Radisson Hotel

6060 N Central Expwy, 75206; tel 214/750-6060 or toll free 800/333-3333; fax 214/750-5959. On US 75, N of Mockingbird. Catering primarily to business travelers, this very accommodating hotel provides comfortable rooms and friendly service while being just minutes from downtown, the Greenville entertainment area, and SMU. **Rooms:** 288 rms. CI 3pm/CO noon. Nonsmoking rms avail. **Amenities:** 🔆 A/C, cable TV w/movies. **Services:** ✕ ⛱ 🍷 **Facilities:** 🔳 🍷 ₁₀₀ ᕕ 1 restaurant, 1 bar, whirlpool. **Rates:** $104–$124 S; $114–

$134 D. Extra person $10. Children under age 18 stay free. Parking: Indoor/outdoor, free. AE, CB, DC, DISC, ER, MC, V.

≣ ≣ ≣ Radisson Hotel and Suites

2330 W Northwest Hwy, 75220; tel 214/351-4477 or toll free 800/333-3333; fax 214/351-4499. E of I-35. Conveniently located hotel featuring poolside suites. Near Love Field, Texas Stadium, downtown, and "restaurant row." **Rooms:** 198 rms and stes. Executive level. CI 3pm/CO noon. Nonsmoking rms avail. **Amenities:** 🔆 A/C, satel TV w/movies, dataport, voice mail. **Services:** ✕ 🚗 ⛱ 🍷 🛎 Babysitting. **Facilities:** 🔳 🍷 ₆₅₀ ᕕ 1 restaurant, 1 bar, whirlpool, washer/dryer. **Rates:** $109–$149 S or D; $129–$169 ste. Extra person $10. Children under age 18 stay free. Parking: Outdoor, free. AE, CB, DC, DISC, MC, V.

≣ ≣ Ramada Hotel

1011 S Akard, 75215 (Downtown); tel 214/421-1083 or toll free 800/527-7606; fax 214/428-6827. S of I-30 near Convention Center. Unadorned hotel catering to business conventions. **Rooms:** 238 rms and stes. CI 3pm/CO noon. Nonsmoking rms avail. **Amenities:** 🔆 A/C, cable TV w/movies. All units w/terraces. Some rooms have coffeemakers. **Services:** ✕ 🚗 ⛱ 🍷 🛎 Babysitting. Free transportation provided to Love Field Int'l Airport, but fee charged for trip to Dallas/Fort Worth. **Facilities:** 🔳 🍷 ₃₀₀ 💻 ᕕ 1 restaurant, 1 bar, games rm, whirlpool, washer/dryer. **Rates:** $89–$119 S; $125–$135 D; $375–$425 ste. Extra person $10. Children under age 12 stay free. Parking: Indoor/outdoor, free. AE, CB, DC, DISC, ER, MC, V.

≣ ≣ ≣ Renaissance Dallas Hotel

2222 Stemmons Fwy, 75207; tel 214/631-2222 or toll free 800/468-3591; fax 214/634-9319. I-35 and Wyclif. This elegant, elliptical high-rise building with a stunning rooftop pool and observation deck is home to the world's longest continuous chandelier. A very ornate and beautiful lobby also houses several interesting aquariums. **Rooms:** 540 rms and stes. Executive level. CI 3pm/CO noon. Nonsmoking rms avail. **Amenities:** 🔆 A/C, cable TV w/movies, dataport. All units w/minibars, 1 w/whirlpool. Some rooms have refrigerators. **Services:** 🍴 🞂 VP 🚗 ⛱ 🍷 🛎 Car-rental desk, babysitting. Guests can call hotel's "guest request line" for any special needs or problems. **Facilities:** 🔳 🍷 ₄₀₀ 💻 ᕕ 2 restaurants (see "Restaurants" below), 1 bar (w/entertainment), spa, sauna, steam rm, whirlpool. **Rates:** Peak (Sept–Feb) $159–$179 S; $179–$199 D; $219–$239 ste. Extra person $20. Children under age 18 stay free. Lower rates off-season. Parking: Outdoor, free. AE, CB, DC, DISC, ER, JCB, MC, V.

≣ ≣ ≣ Sheraton Park Central Hotel

12720 Merit Dr, 75251; tel 972/385-3000 or toll free 800/325-3535; fax 972/991-4557. I-635 and US 25. The posh executive level makes this perfect for business travelers and/or corporate meetings. Large, elegant atrium/lobby. Jogging trail across the street. **Rooms:** 545 rms and stes. Executive level. CI 3pm/CO noon. Nonsmoking rms avail. Room decor is bright and airy. **Amenities:** 🛎 🍸 📺 🍷 A/C, cable TV w/movies, dataport, voice mail. Most rooms have Nintendo game system, and trouser rack. **Services:** 🍽 🗝 VP 🚐 🧺 🛎 Masseur, babysitting. Transportation provided within five-mile radius. **Facilities:** 🏊 🛳 2000 🖥 ♿ 3 restaurants, 3 bars (2 w/entertainment), spa, sauna, steam rm, whirlpool, washer/dryer. Health club across the street. Top-floor restaurant considered among the most romantic fine dining establishments in Dallas. **Rates:** $135–$155 S or D; $300–$900 ste. Extra person $20. Children under age 16 stay free. Parking: Indoor/outdoor, free. AE, CB, DC, DISC, EC, ER, JCB, MC, V.

🏨🏨🏨 The Stoneleigh Hotel

2927 Maple Ave, 75201 (Turtle Creek); tel 214/871-7111 or toll free 800/255-9299. Near Cedar Springs. A historic hotel built in 1924, this establishment has been continually operated longer than any other hotel in Dallas. It offers a romantic ambience in a posh and beautiful area of Dallas. Though it lacks in facilities and services, it's cozy and elegant. A home-away-from-home for many show business celebrities. **Rooms:** 132 rms and stes. Executive level. CI 3pm/CO noon. Nonsmoking rms avail. Exceptionally large rooms offer great views of downtown. **Amenities:** 🛎 🍸 A/C, cable TV w/movies, dataport, voice mail. 1 unit w/whirlpool. **Services:** 🍽 🗝 VP 🚐 🧺 🛎 Masseur, babysitting. Complimentary newspapers, turndown service with chocolates, shuttle service. **Facilities:** 🏊 400 ♿ 1 restaurant, 1 bar. Health and sporting facilities across the street. **Rates:** $160–$190 S or D; $220–$350 ste. Extra person $10. Children under age 18 stay free. Parking: Indoor/outdoor, free. AE, CB, DC, DISC, MC, V.

🏨🏨 Travelodge Hotel

4500 Harry Hines Blvd, 75219; tel 214/522-6650 or toll free 800/578-7878; fax 214/526-0049. Off I-35. Although the exterior is very dated, the interior is adequate and rates are affordable. Near Market Center, hospitals, and I-35. **Rooms:** 212 rms and stes. CI noon/CO noon. Nonsmoking rms avail. **Amenities:** 🛎 🍸 📺 A/C, cable TV w/movies. **Services:** ✗ 🚐 🧺 🛎 Shuttle service provided within seven-mile radius. **Facilities:** 🏊 60 ♿ 1 restaurant (bkfst and dinner only), 1 bar, games rm. **Rates:** $58–$70 S or D; $85 ste. Children under age 17 stay free. Parking: Outdoor, free. AE, CB, DC, DISC, MC, V.

🏨🏨🏨 The Westin Hotel Galleria Dallas

13340 Dallas Pkwy, 75240; tel 972/934-9494 or toll free 800/228-3000; fax 972/450-2979. I-635 and Dallas N Tollway. Located in one of the most prestigious areas of Dallas, near the Galleria Mall and its more than 200 shops, food court, and ice skating rink. **Rooms:** 431 rms and stes. Executive level. CI 3pm/CO 1pm. Nonsmoking rms avail. **Amenities:** 🛎 🍸 📺 🍷 A/C, cable TV w/movies, dataport, voice mail. All units w/minibars, some w/terraces, 1 w/whirlpool. **Services:** 🍽 🗝 VP 🧺 🛎 🦽 Car-rental desk, children's program, babysitting. Discounts available at some Galleria stores. **Facilities:** 🏊 🏋 🛳 1500 🖥 ♿ 3 restaurants, 3 bars, playground. Access to health and fitness facilities. Huntington's restaurant offers fine dining with specialties such as seasonal game and ostrich. **Rates:** $144–$192 S or D; $350–$1,250 ste. Extra person $25. Children under age 18 stay free. Parking: Indoor/outdoor, free. AE, CB, DC, DISC, ER, JCB, MC, V.

🏨🏨🏨🏨 Wyndham Anatole Hotel

2201 Stemmons Fwy, 75207; tel 214/748-1200 or toll free 800/WYNDHAM; fax 214/761-7520. One of the largest hotels in Texas, sitting on 45 acres and including a 7-acre park. The hotel itself is more than a half-mile long and features two 12-story atriums and a 27-story tower; decor contains Far East accents. The concierge will lead tour of the extensive collection of art in the lobby. Very large meeting facilities attract business guests. **Rooms:** 1,620 rms and stes. Executive level. CI 4pm/CO noon. Nonsmoking rms avail. Luxurious furnishings. **Amenities:** 🛎 🍸 📺 🍷 A/C, cable TV w/movies, refrig, voice mail, in-rm safe, bathrobes. All units w/minibars. **Services:** 🍽 🗝 VP 🚐 🧺 🛎 Car-rental desk, masseur, children's program, babysitting. **Facilities:** 🏊 🏋 🛳6 🛳 10000 🖥 ♿ 6 restaurants, 6 bars (2 w/entertainment), basketball, games rm, racquetball, squash, spa, sauna, steam rm, whirlpool, beauty salon. **Rates:** $149–$189 S or D; $250–$625 ste. Children under age 18 stay free. Parking: Indoor/outdoor, free. Rates vary with availability. AE, CB, DC, DISC, MC, V.

MOTELS

🏨🏨 Best Western Market Center

2023 Market Center Blvd, 75207; tel 214/741-9000 or toll free 800/275-7419; fax 214/741-6100. Market Center exit off I-35. Standard Best Western catering to business travelers but adequate for any frugal traveler. **Rooms:** 97 rms. CI noon/CO noon. Nonsmoking rms avail. **Amenities:** 🛎 🍸 📺 A/C, satel TV, dataport. Some units w/terraces. **Services:** ✗ 🚐 🧺 🛎 Babysitting. **Facilities:** 🏊 🛳 50 ♿ 1 restaurant (lunch and dinner only), 1 bar (w/entertainment), washer/dryer. **Rates (CP):** $67–$77 S; $77–$87 D. Extra person $10. Children under age 18 stay free. Parking: Outdoor, free. Weekend rate $49. AE, CB, DC, DISC, MC, V.

🏨🏨🏨 Best Western Preston Suites Hotel

6104 LBJ Fwy, 75240; tel 972/458-2626 or toll free 800/524-7038; fax 972/385-8331. I-635 and Preston Rd. This facility is a converted condo/apartment complex, and the suite and cottage-style lodging has retained a homelike atmosphere. Small, cozy lobby with sitting room and fireplace. Great for extended stays. **Rooms:** 85 stes. CI 3pm/CO noon. Nonsmoking rms avail. One-, two- and three-bedrooms available with kitchen and living area. **Amenities:** 🛎 🍸 📺 A/C, cable TV, refrig, dataport. All units w/terraces. Dishwashers, microwaves, and electric ranges available. **Services:** 🛎 Babysitting. Special events include poolside cookouts twice weekly in summer. Small, friendly staff. **Facilities:** 🏊 🎱 🖥 ⅃ Whirlpool, washer/dryer. **Rates (BB):** $80–$135 ste. Children under age 12 stay free. Parking: Outdoor, free. AE, CB, DC, DISC, MC, V.

≣≣ Classic Motor Inn
9229 Carpenter Fwy, 75247; tel 214/631-6633 or toll free 800/662-7437; fax 214/631-6616. TX 114 near Regal Row. A convenient interstate motel with a unique twist—"antique" rooms with waterbeds. **Rooms:** 135 rms. CI 1pm/CO noon. Nonsmoking rms avail. **Amenities:** 🏠 ♨ A/C, satel TV w/movies, dataport, VCR. **Services:** 🚐 🛏 ⅃ Car-rental desk, babysitting. Shuttle to market and conventions. **Facilities:** 🏊 🏀 🍴 ⅃ Sauna, washer/dryer. Pool area features adjacent indoor sitting area. **Rates (CP):** $39–$65 S or D. Extra person $5. Children under age 12 stay free. Parking: Outdoor, free. AE, CB, DC, DISC, MC, V.

≣≣ Comfort Inn
3536 W Kingsley Rd, 75041; tel 214/340-3501 or toll free 800/221-2222. Near I-635. Convenient to local parks, shopping and dining opportunities, this motel offers standard, comfortable accommodations for frugal travelers. **Rooms:** 103 rms and stes. CI open/CO noon. Nonsmoking rms avail. **Amenities:** 🏠 ♨ A/C, satel TV w/movies, dataport, voice mail. Some units w/whirlpools. **Services:** ⅃ **Facilities:** 🏊 🏀 ⅃ Sauna, whirlpool, washer/dryer. **Rates (CP):** $50–$65 S; $54–$65 D; $110 ste. Extra person $4. Children under age 18 stay free. Parking: Outdoor, free. AE, CB, DC, DISC, ER, JCB, MC, V.

≣≣ Days Inn Texas Stadium
2200 E Airport Fwy, 75062; tel 972/438-6666 or toll free 800/325-2525. On TX 183. Located directly across from Texas Stadium, this place is booked during the fall football season. **Rooms:** 178 rms and stes. CI 1pm/CO noon. Nonsmoking rms avail. **Amenities:** 🏠 ♨ A/C, satel TV, dataport. **Services:** ⅃ 🛏 **Facilities:** 🏊 ⅃ Washer/dryer. **Rates:** $40–$68 S; $46–$68 D; $85–$95 ste. Extra person $6. Children under age 17 stay free. Parking: Outdoor, free. AE, CB, DC, DISC, MC, V.

≣≣ Hawthorn Suites Hotel
7900 Brookriver Dr, 75247; tel 214/688-1010 or toll free 800/527-1133; fax 214/638-5215. S of Mockingbird Lane, near I-35. A growing and increasingly favored chain of suite hotels, great for extended stays. Located in a quiet and secluded section of town within minutes of I-35. **Rooms:** 100 stes. CI 3pm/CO noon. Nonsmoking rms avail. **Amenities:** 🏠 ♨ 📺 🍴 A/C, satel TV w/movies, refrig, dataport, voice mail. All units w/terraces, all w/fireplaces. Murphy beds. **Services:** 🚐 🛏 ⅃ 🖐 Car-rental desk. **Facilities:** 🏊 🏈 🍴 ⅃ Basketball, washer/dryer. Arrangement with local fitness club allows guests to use services and facilities. **Rates (BB):** $114–$144 ste. Children under age 18 stay free. Parking: Outdoor, free. AE, CB, DC, DISC, MC, V.

≣≣ Holiday Inn Express
4103 Belt Line Rd, 75244 (Addison); tel 972/991-8888 or toll free 800/465-4329; fax 972/991-3609. W of Dallas N Tollway. Located just outside of Dallas, this comfortable, reliable motel provides typical accommodations with no surprises. **Rooms:** 115 rms. CI 3pm/CO noon. Nonsmoking rms avail. **Amenities:** 🏠 ♨ 📺 A/C, cable TV, dataport. **Services:** 🛏 ⅃ **Facilities:** 🏊 🍴 ⅃ Washer/dryer. **Rates (CP):** $59–$65 S; $64–$70 D. Extra person $5. Children under age 17 stay free. Parking: Outdoor, free. AE, CB, DC, DISC, JCB, MC, V.

≣ La Quinta Inn Central
4440 N Central Expwy, 75206; tel 214/821-4220 or toll free 800/531-5900; fax 214/821-7685. Standard budget chain motel close to State Fair Park. **Rooms:** 101 rms and stes. CI open/CO noon. Nonsmoking rms avail. Large C-unit rooms with couches and chairs are good for families. Suites with three beds also available. **Amenities:** 🏠 ♨ A/C, cable TV w/movies. **Services:** 🛏 ⅃ 🖐 Babysitting. **Facilities:** 🏊 🍴 ⅃ **Rates (CP):** $58–$74 D; $74–$95 ste. Extra person $8. Children under age 18 stay free. Parking: Outdoor, free. Rates vary according to number of people in each room. Slight increase in rates during State Fair, occasional conventions, and football season. AE, CB, DC, DISC, EC, JCB, MC, V.

UNRATED La Quinta Inn Northpark
10001 N Central Expwy (US 75), 75231; tel 214/361-8200 or toll free 800/531-5900; fax 214/691-0482. Attractive property with Southwestern-style architecture and decor was undergoing renovations. Convenient to US-75 and I-635, as well as shopping and entertainment areas. **Rooms:** 129 rms and stes. CI open/CO noon. Nonsmoking rms avail. **Amenities:** 🏠 ♨ A/C, cable TV w/movies. **Services:** 🛏 ⅃ 🖐 Free transportation to nearby medical facilities. Pets allowed in smoking rooms only; must weigh under 30 lbs. **Facilities:** 🏊 🍴 ⅃ Washer/dryer. **Rates (CP):** $71–$87 S; $59–$75 D; $92–$108 ste. Extra person $8. Children under age 18 stay free. Parking: Outdoor, free. AE, CB, DC, DISC, MC, V.

≣≣ Lexington Hotel Suites
4150 Independence Dr, 75237; tel 972/298-7014 or toll free 800/53-SUITE; fax 972/709-1680. Off Camp Wisdom Rd. Near I-20 and Redbird Mall, this attractive hotel is convenient and cozy. Great for leisure travelers looking for something extra. Friendly staff. **Rooms:** 108 stes. CI 3pm/CO noon. Nonsmoking rms avail. **Amenities:** 🏠 ♨ 📺 A/C, cable TV w/movies, refrig. Nintendo video games. **Services:** 🛏 ⅃ Transportation and free pass provided to President's Health club. Cookouts held every Wednesday night during summer. **Facilities:** 🏊 ⅃ Whirlpool, washer/dryer. **Rates (CP):** $140–$149 ste. Children under age 12 stay free. Parking: Outdoor, free. AE, CB, DC, DISC, JCB, MC, V.

≣≣ Motel 6 North LBJ
2753 Forest Lane, 75234; tel 972/620-2828 or toll free 800/440-6000; fax 972/620-9061. Between Josey and Denton.

Standard chain property offering average budget accommodations. **Rooms:** 100 rms. CI noon/CO noon. Nonsmoking rms avail. **Amenities:** 🔌 💧 A/C, satel TV, dataport. **Services:** 🍴 🛎 **Facilities:** 🏊 ♿ Washer/dryer. **Rates:** $30–$42 S or D. Children under age 17 stay free. Parking: Outdoor, free. AE, CB, DC, DISC, MC, V.

UNRATED **Ramada Park Cities Inn**

6101 Hillcrest Ave, 75205 (Park Cities); tel 214/521-0330 or toll free 800/2-RAMADA; fax 214/521-0336. Was undergoing renovations. Located in one of the nicest areas of Dallas. Away from the main highways, but close to all major areas and SMU. **Rooms:** 53 rms. CI 2pm/CO noon. Nonsmoking rms avail. **Amenities:** 🔌 💧 A/C, satel TV, in-rm safe. Microwaves, refrigerators, and hairdryers available on request. **Services:** 🛎 🍴 Twice-daily maid svce. Fax service available. **Facilities:** 🏋 🏊 Washer/dryer. Use of SMU swimming pool. **Rates (CP):** $58 S or D. Extra person $8. Children under age 12 stay free. Parking: Outdoor, free. AE, CB, DISC, JCB, MC, V.

INN

🔶🔶🔶🔶 **Hotel St Germain**

2516 Maple Ave, 75201; tel 214/871-2516 or toll free 800/683-2516; fax 214/871-0740. Near Cedar Springs Rd, across from the Crescent. This gem of an inn is located in an old house near downtown. With its highly acclaimed restaurant, not only is it a great place to spend the weekend, it is ideal for special occasions like wedding receptions, teas, luncheons, and dinner parties. Very attentive staff. Unsuitable for children under 18. **Rooms:.** CI 4pm/CO noon. Nonsmoking rms avail. 7 stes (all w/private bath). Individually decorated with 19th-century French motif featuring feather beds with lavish canopies, cherry sleigh beds, and chaise lounges. **Amenities:** 🔌 💧 🍷 A/C, cable TV, CD/tape player, bathrobes. Some units w/terraces, all w/fireplaces, some w/whirlpools. **Services:** ✗ ⌲ VP 🛎 Twice-daily maid svce, wine/sherry served. A full-time butler will take care of most any need. **Facilities:** 1 restaurant (bkfst and dinner only), 1 bar, guest lounge. **Rates (BB):** $225–$600 ste. AE, MC, V.

RESTAURANTS 🍴

★ **Adelmo's Ristorante**

4537 Cole Ave (Knox-Henderson); tel 214/559-0325. Near Knox St. **Mediterranean.** Very cozy and friendly place possessing much charm and romantic appeal. Mediterranean cuisine includes veal and steak entrees; delicious homemade bread. **FYI:** Reservations recommended. Dress code. **Open:** Lunch Mon–Fri 11:30am–2pm; dinner Mon–Sat 6–10:30pm. **Prices:** Main courses $12–$23. AE, CB, DC, DISC, MC, V. ♥

Alfredo's Trattoria

5404 Lemmon Ave; tel 214/526-3331. Between Inwood Rd and Dallas N Tollway. **Italian.** This local restaurant serves typical Italian fare in a light and airy setting. Large helpings

of pasta in many varieties are the specialty. Children eat for half-price. Staff is very courteous and friendly. **FYI:** Reservations accepted. Dress code. **Open:** Lunch Mon–Fri 11am–2pm; dinner Mon–Thurs 5–10:30pm, Fri–Sat 5–11pm, Sun 5–9:30pm. **Prices:** Main courses $9–$22. AE, CB, DC, DISC, MC, V.

Allen Street Bar & Grill

2900 McKinney Ave; tel 214/871-0256. **American.** With its large, horseshoe-shaped bar and *Cheers*-like ambience, this pub/eatery offering standard fare caters to a neighborhood crowd despite its location in a popular tourist area. **FYI:** Reservations accepted. **Open:** Mon–Thurs 11am–11pm, Fri–Sat 11am–midnight, Sun 11am–10pm. **Prices:** Main courses $7–$10. AE, DC, DISC, MC, V. 🍴 ♿

Antares

In Hyatt Regency Dallas at Reunion, 300 Reunion Blvd (Downtown); tel 214/651-1234. At jct I-35. **New American.** The Hyatt's fine dining restaurant, located at the top of Reunion Tower, revolves every hour to provide some great views of Dallas. When not gawking at the skyline, patrons dine on interesting New American preparations of beef, chicken, and seafood. A romantic setting for couples. **FYI:** Reservations recommended. Piano. Jacket required. **Open: Prices:** Main courses $15–$30. AE, CB, DC, DISC, MC, V. ♥ 🏔 VP ♿

Ⓢ **Arcodaro Bar**

2520 Cedar Springs Rd (Turtle Creek); tel 214/871-1924. Near Maple Ave. **Italian.** A companion bar and restaurant to Pomodoro (see listing below), this relatively quiet spot (although it can get noisy during the Thursday complimentary happy hour buffet) done in marble and wood serves pizza and sandwiches. The owner has a very expensive Grappa collection. **FYI:** Reservations accepted. Dress code. **Open:** Daily 11am–midnight. **Prices:** Main courses $5–$12. AE, DC, MC, V. VP

★ **Aw Shucks**

3601 Greenville Ave; tel 214/821-9449. S of Mockingbird. **Seafood.** Popular with locals and SMU students, this noisy and fast-paced eatery has outdoor tables on a very active section of Greenville Ave, making it a prime people-watching spot. Shrimp cocktail is a specialty of the house, and there are very good crab legs, crawfish, and gumbo. **FYI:** Reservations not accepted. Beer and wine only. **Open:** Peak (Feb–Oct) Mon–Thurs 11am–11pm, Fri–Sat 11am–11:45pm, Sun 11:30am–10pm. **Prices:** Main courses $5–$8. AE, DC, DISC, MC, V.

Baby Doe's Matchless Mine

3305 Harry Hines Blvd (Oak Lawn); tel 214/871-7310. **Steak.** An abandoned mineshaft leads from the restaurant down to a bar and dance area at this rustic, Western steak and rib joint. The dining room sits atop a hill, with a great view. Don't miss their famous beer cheese soup. **FYI:** Reservations accepted. Children's menu. Dress code. **Open:** Lunch Mon–

Fri 11am–3pm; dinner Mon–Thurs 5–11pm, Fri 5pm–midnight, Sat 4:30pm–midnight, Sun 5–10pm; brunch Sun 9:30am–3pm. **Prices:** Main courses $11–$25. AE, CB, DC, DISC, MC, V. 🏔️ VP

Bay Tree
In Renaissance Dallas Hotel, 2222 Stemmons Fwy; tel 972/631-2222. At I-35 and Wyclif. **Seafood/Steak.** Soft, discrete colors and Southwestern decor lend a relaxing ambience to this upscale restaurant offering pricey steak and seafood entrees. **FYI:** Reservations recommended. Children's menu. **Open:** Tues–Sat 6–10pm. **Prices:** Main courses $19–$35. AE, CB, DC, DISC, ER, MC, V. VP ♿

Benavides
1804 Fort Worth Ave (Oak Cliff); tel 214/742-6911. Between Westmoreland and Hampton. **Tex-Mex.** This well-established, family-run restaurant serves some of the best Tex-Mex dishes in town. You're unlikely to find more authentic cuisine or friendlier service. Try the fajitas with a companion. Great for inexpensive family outings. **FYI:** Reservations accepted. **Open:** Mon–Thurs 11am–2:30pm, Fri–Sat 11am–10:30pm. **Prices:** Main courses $4–$11. AE, DISC, MC, V. 👪♿

Big Al's Smokehouse Barbeque
3125 Inwood Rd at Cedar Springs; tel 214/350-2649. **Barbecue.** Down-home barbecue joint offering great, inexpensive eats in an informal setting. Order at the counter and sit down and enjoy barbecue lunch specials (perfect for families) or one of the regular steak or chicken dishes offered. **FYI:** Reservations not accepted. Children's menu. Beer and wine only. **Open:** Mon–Sat 11am–8pm. **Prices:** Main courses $4–$9. AE. 👪

The Blind Lemon
2805 Main St (Deep Ellum); tel 214/939-0010. E of Downtown. **Eclectic.** Located in the middle of Deep Ellum, this bar and dancing complex (including Club Clearview and the Art Bar) serving French- and Italian-accented food is a great place to cut loose and have fun. Its 10 bar stations are always packed with a young crowd. The Art Bar offers respite from the noise and reverie of the Blind Lemon and Club Clearview. **FYI:** Reservations accepted. Blues/country music/rock. **Open:** Thurs–Sat 6pm–midnight. **Prices:** Main courses $7–$13. AE, DC, DISC, MC, V.

The Butcher Shop
808 Munger Ave (West End); tel 214/720-1032. At Market. **Steak.** A casual steakhouse with a woodsy decor and a rustic appeal. The hickory charcoal pit in the middle of the restaurant is where the chef prepares your choice of cut—whether filet mignon, ribeye, T-bone, top sirloin, or Kansas City strip—before your eyes. Chicken and fish dishes also offered. **FYI:** Reservations accepted. **Open:** Sun–Thurs 5–10pm, Fri 5–10:30pm, Sat 5–11pm. **Prices:** Main courses $17–$26. AE, CB, DC, DISC, MC, V. 🍴♿

★ **Cafe Madrid**
4501 Travis St (Knox-Henderson); tel 214/528-1731. **Spanish.** Located in an upscale section of Dallas, this very casual and busy place is one of the very few restaurants in the area that specializes in authentic Spanish cuisine. They serve tapas; paella is the house specialty. **FYI:** Reservations not accepted. Beer and wine only. **Open:** Mon–Thurs 5–11:30pm, Fri–Sat 5pm–12:30am. **Prices:** Main courses $8–$20. MC, V.

♟ **Cafe Pacific**
24 Highland Park Village (Highland Park); tel 214/526-1170. Near Douglas St entrance. **Seafood.** A posh seafood restaurant appealing to an upscale clientele. The classy interior features black and white floors, brass and wood accents, and an airy atmosphere. Specialties include fresh grilled salmon, shrimp, scallops, swordfish, and lobster. Friendly and professional service. **FYI:** Reservations recommended. Dress code. **Open:** Lunch Mon–Fri 11:30am–2pm, Sat 11:30am–2:30pm; dinner Mon–Thurs 6–10pm, Fri 6–11pm, Sat 5:30–11pm. **Prices:** Main courses $12–$24. AE, CB, DC, DISC, MC, V. VP

Cafe Society
In Travis Walk, 4514 Travis St (Knox-Henderson); tel 214/528-6543. S of Knox St. **Coffeehouse/Eclectic.** An upscale coffeehouse with a laid-back atmosphere serving great vegetarian and seafood dishes. It also doubles as a bookshop. **FYI:** Reservations accepted. Guitar. Beer and wine only. **Open:** Tues–Thurs 10am–11pm, Fri–Sat 10am–midnight, Sun 10am–10pm. **Prices:** Main courses $5–$10. AE, MC, V. ♿

Calluaud's Bistro
5405 W Lovers Lane (University Park); tel 214/352-1997. Between Inwood Rd and Dallas N Tollway. **French.** Inconspicuously located in a strip mall, this attractive bistro features beautiful tapestries, lovely flowers, and antique furniture. Some specialties include Dover sole, rack of lamb, and grilled chicken breast with provençal herbs. **FYI:** Reservations accepted. **Open:** Lunch Mon–Fri 11am–2pm; dinner Mon–Thurs 5:30–11pm, Fri–Sat 5:30pm–midnight. **Prices:** Main courses $12–$25. AE, CB, DC, DISC, MC, V. ♥ VP

Cerveceria—The Big Mex Cafe
1800 N Market St (West End Historical District); tel 214/969-0310. Near jct Ross and Market Sts. **Tex-Mex.** Located in the heart of the West End, this fun, colorful, multi-leveled Tex-Mex restaurant lends Southwestern decor and bright colors to the neighborhood. A very friendly and lively waitstaff also helps to make it welcoming for families. **FYI:** Reservations accepted. Country music/jazz/reggae/rock. Children's menu. **Open:** Sun–Thurs 11am–10pm, Fri–Sat 11am–midnight. **Prices:** Main courses $3–$25. AE, CB, DC, DISC, MC, V. 🍴👪

Chamberlain's Prime Chop House
In Town Hall Sq, 5330 Belt Line Rd, Dallas (Addison); tel 972/934-CHOP. Just E of Dallas N Tollway. **Seafood/Steak.** Well-known chef and Dallas native Richard Chamberlain

presents this straightforward steak-and-chop house. Decor in the spacious dining room is not particularly distinctive, but it is well chosen and tasteful. Staff is professional and personable. **FYI:** Reservations recommended. Children's menu. Dress code. **Open:** Mon–Thurs 5:30–10:30pm, Fri–Sat 5:30–11pm. **Prices:** Main courses $14–$25. AE, CB, DC, DISC, MC, V. **VP** &

Chez Gérard
4444 McKinney Avenue (Knox-Henderson); tel 214/522-6865. At Knox. **French.** A quaint French bistro serving simple, traditional fare, located in an old house with a covered patio. Seating may be a bit cramped, but the food is well-executed. **FYI:** Reservations recommended. Dress code. **Open:** Lunch Mon–Fri 11:30am–2pm; dinner Mon–Sat 6–10:30pm. **Prices:** Main courses $15–$23. AE, DC, DISC, MC, V. ♥

City Java
2639 Elm St (Deep Ellum); tel 214/742-5282. **Coffeehouse.** A small storefront coffeehouse that looks and feels the part. It is laid-back and casual, with cigarette smoke rising from the ground floor to the upstairs loft. Excellent sandwiches, salads, and pizzas. Desserts, like cheesecake, pies, and chocolate-covered coffee beans, are a specialty. **FYI:** Reservations not accepted. No liquor license. **Open:** Tues–Thurs 7am–midnight, Fri 7am–2am, Sat noon–2am, Sun noon–6pm. **Prices:** Main courses $3–$8. No CC.

Dakota's
600 N Akard St (Downtown); tel 214/740-4001. At San Jacinto. **New American.** A very unique, design award-winning restaurant located below ground—the above-ground entrance is simply a canopied elevator. The elegant interior is marked by Italian marble, an incredible bar area, and a floor of Brazilian wood. The Sun Room features a waterfall that begins at street level and cascades down a rocky, verdant landscape into a small pool, while outdoor seating offers views of the downtown skyscrapers. The kitchen turns out many mesquite-grilled items and seafood dishes; specialties include homemade pasta, blackened red snapper, mesquite-grilled steak, and game dishes. **FYI:** Reservations recommended. Piano. Dress code. **Open:** Lunch Mon–Fri 11am–2:30pm; dinner Mon–Thurs 5–10pm, Fri–Sat 5–10:30pm, Sun 5:30–9pm. **Prices:** Main courses $10–$20. AE, CB, DC, DISC, MC, V. ⛴ ♥ **VP** &

♣ Dallas Palm Restaurant
701 Ross Ave (West End Historical District); tel 214/698-0470. At Market St. **Seafood/Steak.** Part of a chain located in major US cities, this friendly, busy steak-and-seafood establishment features beautiful wooden floors and elegant dining areas. Walls are filled with autographed portraits of famous visitors. **FYI:** Reservations accepted. Dress code. **Open:** Mon–Fri 11:30am–10:15pm, Sat 5:30–10:30pm, Sun 5:30–9:30pm. **Prices:** Main courses $12–$26. AE, CB, DC, MC, V. **VP** &

Dick's Last Resort
1701 N Market St (West End Historical District); tel 214/747-0001. Jct I-35 and Woodall Rogers Fwy; NW corner of Downtown Loop. **Eclectic.** Facing downtown skyscrapers, this fun, lively, and loud establishment is designed and operated for partygoers. Steaks, ribs, and burgers provide sustenance for revelers. **FYI:** Reservations accepted. Blues/jazz/rock/gospel. **Open:** Sun–Thurs 11am–midnight, Fri–Sat 11am–2am. **Prices:** Main courses $9–$17. AE, CB, DC, DISC, MC, V. ⛴ &

♥ Enigma
In 150 Chateau Plaza, 2515 McKinney Ave at Fairmont; tel 214/953-1111. **Eclectic.** A small, cozy, and largely undiscovered gem. The owner, a London millionaire, has created a museumlike setting with sculpture, over 800 pieces of colorful, custom-designed china, and a dining table that by itself qualifies as a work of art. The diverse, game-rich menu includes ostrich, emu, quail, pheasant, duck, wild boar, venison, and buffalo, as well as more familiar items like steak, seafood, and pasta. (Note: If you want pepper, ask for the six-foot pepper mill.) **FYI:** Reservations accepted. Harp. Dress code. **Open:** Mon–Sat 5:30–11pm. **Prices:** Main courses $12–$45. AE, CB, DC, DISC, MC, V. ♥ **VP** &

Fog City Diner
2401 McKinney; tel 214/220-2401. Near Pearl Expwy and the Crescent. **New American.** Very popular and trendy, this eatery (partially owned by Cowboys quarterback Troy Aikman) offers superb diner atmosphere. The classic look includes a reflective metal exterior and counter and booth seating inside. **FYI:** Reservations recommended. **Open:** Sun–Wed 11:30am–11pm, Thurs–Sat 11:30am–midnight. **Prices:** Main courses $10–$16. AE, CB, DC, DISC, MC, V. &

♥ The French Room
In the Adolphus, 1321 Commerce St (Downtown); tel 214/742-8200. **Neo-classic.** Surely one of the most gracious settings in the country, this jewel-box chateau adjoining a wood-paneled, antique-filled bar/lounge dazzles with its tall windows splashing light on marble floors and potted ferns reaching for cherubs on hand-painted ceilings. Service, by waiters in spiffy white jackets, is attentive but unobtrusive, the elegance of Versailles softened by the bonhomie of Texas. Some of the fine dishes include roasted yellowfin tuna au poivre with green pepper sauce; Colorado rack of lamb with seasonal vegetables in a roasted garlic and rosemary sauce; and warm apple tart tatin with Chambord chocolate ice cream and fruit coulis. **FYI:** Reservations recommended. Jacket required. **Open:** Mon–Sat 6–10:30pm. **Prices:** Main courses $29–$45. AE, CB, DC, DISC, MC, V. ♥ **VP** &

★ Gloria's
600 W Davis St (Oak Cliff); tel 214/948-3672. W of Zangs Blvd, near I-35. **Latin American.** This little storefront eatery has developed a strong reputation in Dallas for its excellent Latin American cuisine. Dishes like Salvadoran fried yucca or tamales wrapped in banana leaves make for deliciously differ-

ent lunch or dinner fare. **FYI:** Reservations not accepted. Children's menu. Additional location: 4140 Lemmon Ave #102 (tel 521-7576). **Open:** Mon–Fri 11am–10pm, Sat–Sun 10am–10pm. **Prices:** Main courses $4–$11. AE, CB, DC, DISC, MC, V.

Hofstetter's

In Plaza at Bachman Creek, 3840 W Northwest Hwy, Suite 400; tel 214/358-7660. Between Marsh-Lemmon and Midway. **Continental.** Owned and operated by a friendly Austrian couple, the comfortable and very spacious dining area overlooks a lovely stream running into Bachman Lake; outdoor seating offers fabulous views. Decor is contemporary but service is old-fashioned and friendly. Seafood dishes, Austrian and German specialties. **FYI:** Reservations accepted. Children's menu. Beer and wine only. **Open:** Lunch Mon–Sat 11am–2:30pm; dinner Mon–Thurs 5–10pm, Fri–Sat 5–10:30pm. **Prices:** Main courses $11–$17. AE, DC, MC, V. 🍴 &

★ **Humperdink's Bar & Grill**

6050 Greenville Ave; tel 214/368-6597. Near Caruth Haven. **Eclectic.** This loud sports bar offers many TVs, pool tables, and electronic trivia games, as well as food (burgers, sandwiches, salads, and more) that is surprisingly good. **FYI:** Reservations accepted. Children's menu. Additional locations: 1601 N Central Expwy, Plano (tel 690-4867); 4021 Beltline Rd (tel 934-2612). **Open:** Daily 11am–2am. **Prices:** Main courses $6–$15. AE, CB, DC, DISC, MC, V. &

Indian Palace Restaurant & Bar

In Preston Valley Shopping Center, 12817 Preston Rd, Suite 105; tel 972/392-0190. I-635 at Forest Lane. **Indian.** This intimate and cozy restaurant operated by a friendly couple serves some of the best tandoori in Dallas. Extensive array of breads, vegetarian dishes, and northern Indian dishes. **FYI:** Reservations recommended. Children's menu. Dress code. **Open:** Lunch Mon–Fri 11:30am–2:30pm, Sat–Sun noon–3pm; dinner Sun–Thurs 5:30–10pm, Fri–Sat 5:30–11pm. **Prices:** Main courses $9–$19. AE, CB, DC, DISC, MC, V. ♥ &

Juniper

2917 Fairmont St (Oak Lawn); tel 214/855-0700. Near Cedar Springs Rd. **French.** A quaint, elegant restaurant located in a 92-year-old converted house. The inside is decorated with white walls and forest green accents, and outdoor dining is offered on a converted residential street. The menu, which features different entrees, soufflés, and desserts each night, includes duck, shrimp, and rack of lamb. Escargots and crab cakes are favorite appetizers. **FYI:** Reservations accepted. Dress code. **Open:** Tues–Thurs 6–10:30pm, Fri–Sat 6–11pm. **Prices:** Main courses $15–$24. AE, CB, DC, DISC, MC, V. ♥ 🍴 VP

★ **Kathleen's Art Cafe**

4424 Lovers Lane, University Park; tel 214/691-2355. Lovers Lane exit off I-75. **New American/Eclectic.** Dubbed the

"quintessential art bistro," this very popular, small neighborhood bar, restaurant, and bakery doubles as an art gallery. Seafood, pizza, down-home desserts, great late-night snacks, and a fine weekend brunch sustain the loyal clientele. **FYI:** Reservations recommended. **Open:** Breakfast Mon–Fri 7–11am; lunch Mon–Fri 11am–3pm; dinner Sun–Thurs 5:30–11pm, Fri–Sat 5:30pm–1am; brunch Sat–Sun 8am–3pm. **Prices:** Main courses $9–$17. MC, V. 🎬

L'Ancestral

In Travis Walk, 4514 Travis (Knox-Henderson); tel 214/528-1081. Knox exit off US 75. **French.** Located in an upscale section of Dallas, this elegant French bistro has a decor highlighted by exquisite oil paintings and delicate lace curtains. Excellent classic French fare includes several seafood dishes, as well as chicken, veal, lamb chops, and filet mignon. Steak tartare is a standout. Impressive service. **FYI:** Reservations recommended. Dress code. **Open:** Lunch Mon–Sat 11:30am–2pm; dinner Mon–Thurs 6–10pm, Fri–Sat 6–11pm. **Prices:** Main courses $13–$20; prix fixe $23. AE, CB, DC, DISC, MC, V. &

♣ **The Mansion on Turtle Creek**

2821 Turtle Creek Blvd (Oak Lawn/Turtle Creek); tel 214/559-2100. 5 minutes from the financial and arts districts. **New American/Southwestern.** Guests enter this gem of a restaurant, located in the Mediterranean Renaissance–style Sheppard King Mansion (1925), via a two-story interior courtyard outfitted with 19th-century Spanish cathedral doors, stained glass, and carved ceilings. The pace-setting Southwestern cuisine is created by star chef Deal Fearing, who makes frequent circuits of the tables where guests rave about his tortilla soup, jalapeño Caesar salad with shrimp diablo tamale, farfalle pasta with roast tomato–basil sauce and broiled mozzarella toast, and—Freaing's signature dish—the wondrous warm lobster taco with yellow tomato salsa. Exemplary service is polished, polite, and professional. **FYI:** Reservations recommended. Piano. Children's menu. **Open:** Lunch Mon–Fri noon–2:30pm; dinner Sun–Thurs 6–10:30pm, Fri–Sat 6–11pm; brunch Sat noon–2:30pm, Sun 11am–2:30pm. **Prices:** Main courses $28–$45. AE, CB, DC, DISC, ER, MC, V. ♥ VP &

Mario's Chiquita

In Travis Walk, 4514 Travis St, Suite 105 (Knox-Henderson); tel 214/521-0721. Near Knox St. **Mexican.** Upscale yet unpretentious, this Tex-Mex restaurant has an extremely friendly staff and a soothing, pleasant atmosphere. The Mexican decor and the open and airy building decorated in spring colors accent the wonderfully tantalizing food. Traditional beef and chicken dishes, as well as creative fare involving pork and seafood, are offered; specialties include tacos al carbón, chile rellenos, and mole poblano. **FYI:** Reservations accepted. Children's menu. **Open:** Sun–Thurs 11:30am–9pm, Fri–Sat 11:30am–10pm. **Prices:** Main courses $5–$11. AE, CB, DC, DISC, MC, V. &

★ Mia's

4322 Lemmon Ave; tel 214/526-1020. Near Dallas N Tollway. **Tex-Mex.** Very popular family-owned and -operated Mexican restaurant that has attracted a loyal following. If you're seeking an informal, unpretentious setting, a taste of Tex-Mex cuisine, and a friendly place to take the family for an affordable and entertaining evening, this is the place for you. Specialties include bean-and-bacon soup, queso fameado with chorizo, chicken burritos, chimichangas, and chiles rellenos. **FYI:** Reservations not accepted. Children's menu. Beer and wine only. **Open:** Mon–Sat 11am–10pm. **Prices:** Main courses $5–$10. MC, V. 👥 ♿

Moctezuma

2847 N Henderson; tel 214/827-1114. E of US 75. **Seafood/Tex-Mex.** Housed in an adobe-style building with a wide, open interior, this health-oriented restaurant (whose motto is "eating well is the best revenge") uses only fresh produce, hormone- and chemical-free beef, canola oil for frying and olive oil for sautéeing, and minimal amounts of butter in sauces. **FYI:** Reservations accepted. Salsa. **Open:** Peak (late Apr–mid-Sept) Sun–Wed 11am–11pm, Thurs–Fri 11am–midnight, Sat 11am–3am. **Prices:** Main courses $8–$15. AE, DC, MC, V. 🍴 ♿

Monica Aca Y Alla

2915 Main St (Deep Ellum); tel 214/748-7140. E of US 75 near downtown. **Eclectic/Tex-Mex.** Located in Deep Ellum, one of Dallas's top nightspots, this establishment has a wonderfully dramatic atmosphere created by the contrast of red walls, large golden serpents, and black ceilings. Lunch menus are set at $5. **FYI:** Reservations accepted. Salsa. **Open:** Lunch Mon–Fri 11am–2pm; dinner Tues–Thurs 5–10pm, Sat 5–11pm, Sun 8pm–midnight, Fri 5–11pm. **Prices:** Main courses $7–$15. AE, DC, DISC, MC, V. VP ♿

Natura Cafe

2909 McKinney Ave; tel 214/855-5483. At jct Allen St. **Health/Spa.** Minimalist, earthy decor goes well with the organic and health-conscious food provided here. Meals are served with a detailed nutrition guide; staff is knowledgeable and friendly. **FYI:** Reservations accepted. Children's menu. **Open:** Mon–Fri 11am–11pm, Sat–Sun 9am–11pm. **Prices:** Main courses $8–$17. AE, CB, DC, DISC, MC, V. 🍴 📷 VP ♿

Newport's Seafood

In the brewery, 703 McKinney Ave, Ste 101 (West End Historical District); tel 214/954-0220. Near I-35. **Seafood.** Located in an old brewery dating back to the 1800s, this spacious and elegant restaurant with old wooden floors and lots of historical ambience is a great place to enjoy fresh seafood—trout, tuna, salmon, snapper, crab, shrimp, lobster, swordfish. The well that the brewery once used to make its beer in now sits in the middle of the restaurant and separates the dining room from the attractive bar area. **FYI:** Reservations recommended. Dress code. **Open:** Lunch Mon–Fri 11:30am–2:30pm; dinner Mon–Thurs 5:30–10:30pm, Fri–Sat 5:30–11pm, Sun 5:30–10pm. **Prices:** Main courses $13–$16. AE, CB, DC, DISC, MC, V. ♥ 🍴 ♿

♟ Old Warsaw

2610 Maple (Oak Lawn); tel 214/528-0032. Between Cedar Springs and McKinney Aves. **French.** Established in 1948, this elegant restaurant offers sophisticated dining in a setting that features romantic candle lighting, wooden walls, intricate model ships, gorgeous chandeliers, and oriental accents to create a unique ambience. The menu includes chicken, duck, veal, and lots of rich desserts. The wine room, which can be used for private dining, connects to a posh full-service bar. **FYI:** Reservations recommended. Piano/violin. Jacket required. **Open:** Daily 5:30–10:30pm. **Prices:** Main courses $21–$48. AE, CB, DC, DISC, MC, V. ♥ VP

Patrizio

Preston and Mockingbird (Highland Park); tel 214/526-1170. **Italian.** This popular Italian restaurant located in posh Highland Park Village is a great place to spend the afternoon people-watching. Classic dishes such as ravioli, lasagne, fettucine Alfredo, and manicotti are available, as are several vegetarian dishes. Lively and friendly staff. **FYI:** Reservations accepted. Additional location: Preston Park Village, Plano (tel 964-2200). **Open:** Tues–Thurs 11:30am–11pm, Fri–Sat 11:30am–midnight, Sun 11:30am–10:30pm. **Prices:** Main courses $7–$9. AE, CB, DC, DISC, MC, V. 🍴 VP ♿

Pierre's by the Lake

3430 Shorecrest Dr; tel 214/358-2379. Between Lemmon Ave and Denton Dr. **Seafood/Steak.** Overlooking Bachman Lake on the north side of Love Field, this elegant restaurant sits in the middle of Dallas but nevertheless maintains a very peaceful setting. Plush red carpet, French Impressionist prints, fireplace, and piano contribute to a setting compatible with the continental classics served, including chateaubriand and rack of lamb. Variety of seafood, too. **FYI:** Reservations recommended. Piano. Dress code. **Open:** Mon–Thurs 10am–10pm, Fri 10am–11pm, Sat 5–11pm. **Prices:** Main courses $9–$12. AE, CB, DC, DISC, MC, V. 🍴 📷 🏞 VP ♿

Ⓢ Pomodoro

2520 Cedar Springs Rd (Turtle Creek); tel 214/871-1924. Near Maple Ave. **Italian.** Located in posh Turtle Creek, this popular upscale restaurant attracts a very diverse clientele, including many celebrities. While it can be noisy, the food is worth the trip. Menu consists of northern Italian cuisine, including pasta, risotto, and frittate dishes. It features specialties such as bresaola with pine nuts, orange and raisins; swordfish carpaccio with tomato-basic vinaigrette; and osso buco. The lasagne primavera is the vegetarian specialty. **FYI:** Reservations recommended. Dress code. **Open:** Lunch Mon–Fri 11:30am–2pm; dinner Mon–Thurs 6–10pm, Fri–Sat 6–11pm. **Prices:** Main courses $6–$13. AE, DC, MC, V. 🍴 VP

The Pyramid

In the Fairmont, 1717 N Akard St (Downtown); tel 214/720-2020. S of Woodall Rogers Fwy. **New American.** One of the most highly rated and elegant restaurants in Dallas has been going strong for more than 20 years now. Fresh flowers add warmth to the trademark pyramid motif. Good bets among the distinctive contemporary American dishes are Dover sole and rack of lamb. **FYI:** Reservations recommended. Jazz/piano. Children's menu. Jacket required. **Open:** Lunch Mon–Fri 11:30am–2pm; dinner Sun–Sat 6–10:30pm; brunch Sun 10:30am–2pm. **Prices:** Main courses $19–$42; prix fixe $24–$41. AE, CB, DC, DISC, MC, V. 💟 VP &

Queen of Sheba

3527 McKinney Ave at Lemmon; tel 214/521-0491. **Ethiopian.** This small eatery bedecked in bamboo features private dining huts (which can be reserved) that are great for couples. Spicy Ethiopian specialties are served with spiced tea and Ethiopian honey wine; Italian dinners are available for the less adventurous. Be sure to take part in the traditional handwashing ceremony. Children eat for half-price. **FYI:** Reservations accepted. Dress code. **Open:** Daily 11am–11pm. **Prices:** Main courses $4–$12; prix fixe $30. AE, CB, DC, DISC, MC, V. 💟 &

The Riviera

7709 Inwood Rd; tel 214/351-0094. S of Lovers Lane. **Mediterranean.** A highly regarded, upscale restaurant featuring the talents of local favorite chefs David Holben and Michael Winsein. Beautiful decorations and gorgeous floral arrangements set the scene for fettucine with smoked chicken and wild mushrooms, rack of lamb, and duck breast with orange brandy. Service is warm and attentive. **FYI:** Reservations recommended. Dress code. **Open:** Mon–Sat 6:30–10pm. **Prices:** Main courses $26–$30. AE, CB, DC, MC, V. 💟 VP &

♣ Royal Tokyo

7525 Greenville Ave; tel 214/368-3304. Near Meadow Rd. **Japanese.** In operation since 1972, this top-quality Japanese steakhouse with kimono-clad waitresses offers a variety of seating arrangements: private gazebo areas, traditional floor tables, a sushi bar, regular steakhouse seating, and "boat dinners" for entire families. Dine in privacy or sit at the large, tepanyaki tables, where you can watch the chefs prepare the wonderful food. Tea rooms offer piano bar and karaoke. **FYI:** Reservations accepted. **Open:** Lunch Mon–Fri 11:30am–2pm, Sat 11:30am–2:30pm; dinner Sun–Mon 5:30–10:30pm, Tues–Thurs 5:30–11pm, Fri–Sat 5:30–11:30pm; brunch Sun 11:30am–2:30pm. **Prices:** Main courses $15–$40; prix fixe $45–$60. AE, CB, DC, DISC, MC, V. 💟

S&D Oyster Company

2701 McKinney Ave at Boll St; tel 214/823-6350. **Seafood.** The building that houses this classy restaurant dates from 1891. Its architecture, along with the featured jazz bands, will make you feel like you're in the middle of New Orleans. Wonderful oysters, shrimp, and other Gulf seafood is pre-

sented by the thoroughly professional, formally attired waitstaff. **FYI:** Reservations not accepted. Children's menu. Beer and wine only. **Open:** Mon–Thurs 11am–10pm, Fri–Sat 11am–11pm. **Prices:** Main courses $3–$13. MC, V. ■

Sfuzzi

2504 McKinney Ave (State-Thomas); tel 214/871-2606. Near Fairmount. **Italian.** A fun, trendy, and upbeat restaurant with a colorful decor reminiscent of Roman ruins. This is the original Sfuzzi of what is now a nationwide chain. Italian fare focuses on creative pizzas and pastas. **FYI:** Reservations recommended. Dress code. Additional locations: 15101 Addison at Belt Line, Addison (tel 960-2606); 2405 Preston at Park, Plano (tel 964-0700). **Open:** Lunch Mon–Sat 11am–4pm, Sun 3–5pm; dinner Mon–Wed 4–10pm, Thurs–Sat 4–11pm, Sun 3–10pm; brunch Sun 11am–3pm. **Prices:** Main courses $10–$16. AE, CB, DC, DISC, MC, V. 🍴 VP &

Sinbad's Palace

9220 Skillman St, Ste 227; tel 214/340-4445. Near I-63S. **Middle Eastern.** Straight from the tale of Aladdin, this restaurant features a Khalil Gibran quote and a life-size Sinbad and friend on a magic carpet. Sinbad's menu offers Greek and Lebanese dishes and a variety of kabobs. Don't miss the excellent bread. **FYI:** Reservations accepted. Children's menu. **Open:** Lunch daily 11am–3pm; dinner Sun–Thurs 5–10pm, Fri–Sat 5–11pm. **Prices:** Main courses $8–$17. AE, DC, MC, V. 🚻 &

Sipango

4513 Travis St (Knox-Henderson); tel 214/522-2411. S of Knox. **New American.** Trendy, popular, and expensive, and located in the fashionable Knox-Henderson area. Dishes include seafood, pasta, and chicken. It's often crowded, so expect a wait. **FYI:** Reservations recommended. Dress code. **Open:** Lunch Mon–Fri 11:30am–2:30pm; dinner Mon–Thurs 5:30–10:30pm, Fri–Sat 5:30–11:30pm, Sun 5–10:30pm. **Prices:** Main courses $12–$20. AE, CB, DC, DISC, MC, V. VP &

Sonny Bryan's

2202 Inwood Rd; tel 214/357-7120. Near Harry Hines, off I-35. **Barbecue.** Nonchalant atmosphere and great barbecue brings many repeat customers. Eat outside in the large open parking lot or get your food to go; there's no seating available. **FYI:** Reservations not accepted. Beer and wine only. Additional locations: 302 N Market (tel 744-1610); 4701 Frankford (tel 447-0102). **Open:** Mon–Fri 10am–4pm, Sat 10am–3pm, Sun 11am–2pm. **Prices:** Main courses $4–$10. No CC. &

The Spaghetti Warehouse

1815 N Market St (West End Historical District); tel 214/651-8475. NW Corner of downtown loop. **Italian.** A fun and festive spot in the West End designed for families with children—balloons, neon lighting, arcade games, and other kid diversions abound. The staff is very friendly and the well-priced Italian fare is bound to please young palates. **FYI:**

Reservations accepted. Children's menu. **Open:** Sun–Thurs 11am–10pm, Fri–Sat 11am–12am. **Prices:** Main courses $5–$9. AE, CB, DC, DISC, MC, V. 🖼️ ♿

♣ Star Canyon
In the Centrum, 3102 Oak Lawn (Oak Lawn); tel 214/520-7827. Between Cedar Springs and Lennon. **New Texas.** Very friendly and fashionable upscale restaurant featuring what innovative chef Stephan Pyles terms New Texas cuisine, incorporating Southwestern, Southern, Texas, and Latin influences. Large steaks and fresh seafood are prepared in new ways; the popular barbecue shrimp enchilada is a fine way to sample his talent. And the Heaven and Hell cake, a combination of devil's food and angel food cakes, truly does seem out of this world. **FYI:** Reservations recommended. Dress code. **Open:** Lunch Mon–Fri 11:30am–2pm; dinner Mon–Thurs 6–10:30pm, Fri–Sat 6–11pm, Sun 6–10pm. **Prices:** Main courses $15–$29. AE, CB, DC, DISC, MC, V. 🅥🅟 ♿

Terilli's Restaurant & Bar
2815 Lower Greenville Ave; tel 214/827-3993. S of Monticello. **Italian.** A casual Italian restaurant in the heart of lively Lower Greenville. Outdoor seating affords great people watching. Excellent lasagna and ravioli are the highlights of the menu. **FYI:** Reservations accepted. Jazz. **Open:** Sun–Thurs 11:30am–2am, Fri–Sat 11:30am–1:30am. **Prices:** Main courses $6–$14. AE, CB, DC, MC, V. 🍰

Thai Soon
2018 Greenville Ave; tel 214/821-7666. **Thai.** Located on a busy stretch of Greenville Ave, this small, modestly decorated restaurant serves authentic Thai cuisine to a devoted clientele. Fresh seafood and vegetarian dishes are specialties. Service is pleasant and helpful. **FYI:** Reservations accepted. Beer and wine only. **Open:** Lunch Mon–Fri 11am–3pm; dinner Mon–Thurs 5–10pm, Fri 5pm–midnight, Sat 11am–midnight, Sun noon–10pm. **Prices:** Main courses $7–$14. AE, DC, DISC, MC, V. 🍰 ♿

Tolbert's Texas Chili Parlor
In One Dallas Center, 350 N St Paul; tel 214/953-1353. At Bryan St. **Tex-Mex.** One of the state's most celebrated chili parlors, this Tex-Mex has been around for years. A fun, casual atmosphere and affordable prices make it easy for families to enjoy "donkey tails" (hot-dog tortillas) and chile con carne. **FYI:** Reservations accepted. Children's menu. **Open:** Mon–Fri 11am–7pm. **Prices:** Main courses $6–$8. AE, CB, DC, DISC, MC, V. 🖼️ ♿

ATTRACTIONS 🏛️

Dallas Museum of Art
1717 N Harwood St; tel 214/922-1200. This most recent (1984) of the large Texas museums houses pre-Columbian art, works by great European masters (Cézanne, Gauguin, Monet, Pissarro, van Gogh), modern American painting (notably Jackson Pollock), and rich collections of African art;

a giant sculpture by Claes Oldenburg, *Stake Hitch,* is also here. The building was designed by Edward Larrabee Barnes and features lovely gardens with waterfalls, shaded groves, and an uninterrupted view of the Dallas skyline. **Open:** Tues, Wed, and Fri 11am–4pm, Thurs 11am–9pm, Sat–Sun 11am–5pm. **Free**

The Sixth Floor Museum
Elm and Houston Sts (West End Historic District); tel 214/653-6659. Located on the sixth floor of the Dallas County Administration Building, formerly the Texas School Book Depository Building, this is the site from which Lee Harvey Oswald assassinated President Kennedy. A 9,000-square-foot exhibit, pertinently titled "The Sixth Floor," features films, 400 photographs, artifacts, and interpretive displays on the cultural context of John F Kennedy's death. The window area from which Oswald fired the fatal shots has been re-created as it was that day, but it's protected behind a wall of glass. Visitors can look out through immediately adjacent windows with almost the same view of the motorcade route and Dealy Plaza. Museum shop. **Open:** Daily 9am–6pm. **$$$**

Dallas Museum of Natural History
3535 Grand Ave; tel 214/421-3466. Neoclassical building houses this museum of Southwest and Texas natural history. More than 50 replicas of natural habitats plus rich zoological and botanical collections, including a 90-million-year-old fossil fish and a 32-foot reconstructed mosasaur. **Open:** Daily 10am–5pm. **$**

Reunion Tower
300 Reunion Blvd; tel 214/651-1234. This 50-story tower, capped with a geodesic dome where computer-operated lights dance at night, is one of the new symbols of Dallas. Observation deck at the top; also restaurant and revolving lounge. The tower is linked to the Hyatt Regency Hotel, the Union railway station, and the Reunion Arena. **Open:** Mon–Fri 9am–10pm, Sat–Sun 10am–midnight. **$**

Dallas Arboretum
8525 Garland Rd; tel 214/327-8263. These 66 acres of beautiful gardens are located on the eastern shore of White Rock Lake, just minutes from downtown. The headquarters are in the Camp Estate, designed by Texas's most famous residential architect, John Staub, and completed in 1938. Also on the grounds is historic DeGolyer House, a magnificent Spanish Colonial-style mansion. More than 2,000 variations of azaleas are on display in the 5½-acre Jonsson Color Garden; the 1-acre Palmer Fern Dell holds more than 30 species of ferns. Wildflower trail and 11-mile path around the lake. Tours available. **Open:** Peak (Mar–Oct) daily 10am–6pm. Reduced hours off-season. **$$$**

Dallas World Aquarium
1801 N Griffin St; tel 214/720-1801. One of the most modern and complete aquariums in the Southwest, with 350

species of fish, reptiles, and amphibians. The aquarium is home to indigenous species as well as tropical and exotic ones. **Open:** Daily 10am–5pm. **$**

Morton H Meyerson Symphony Center

2301 Flora St, Ste 100; tel 214/670-3600. The only concert hall designed by I M Pei, this shoebox-shaped limestone building with striking glass curves, soaring lobbies, and unusually high ceilings was built at a cost of $106 million and inaugurated in 1989. Home of the Dallas Symphony, the 2,066-seat hall is acoustically impressive: a huge canopy of wood and onyx above the stage moves up and down to adjust the sound to the performances. Guided tours available. **Open:** Mon, Wed, Fri, Sat 1pm. **Free**

Dallas Theater Center

3636 Turtle Creek Blvd; tel 214/526-8857. The center, designed by Frank Lloyd Wright, hosts major productions during its seven-month season, ranging from Shakespeare to contemporary theatrical works. **$$$$**

Southfork Ranch

3700 Hogge Rd; tel 972/442-7800. The Texas ranch became internationally famous as the location for the long-running CBS TV series *Dallas*. It operates today as both a tourist attraction and event/conference facility. Guests can tour the infamous Ewing Mansion, explore the ranch grounds on a guided tram tour, and visit the *Dallas* museum, which contains memorabilia from the show. Other facilities include an expanded visitors center, the Lincolns and Longhorns Western Wear Store, and the Front Porch Cafe. **Open:** Daily 9am–5pm. **$$$**

The Science Place

1318 2nd Ave; tel 214/428-5555. Permanent and changing state-of-the-art, hands-on exhibits explore the world of science. Visitors can bend a giant arm in the medical exhibits and see the action of the muscles inside, slide down an endoscope, sing into an oscilloscope, play with electrical current, or lift a thousand pounds with one hand. Some of the recent traveling exhibits have featured rare documents from Einstein's experiments and robot dinosaurs. Planetarium with daily shows; IMAX theater. **Open:** Daily 9:30am–5:30pm. **$$$**

Texas Commerce Tower

2200 Ross Ave; tel 214/922-2300. One of the most distinguished and compelling buildings in Dallas. Designed by Richard Keating, of Skidmore, Owings & Merrill, this 55-story skyscraper of glass and granite is crowned by a great arch. A vast Osky window (75 feet high, 27 feet wide) slices out the center of the 41st through 49th floors. **Open:** Mon–Thurs 9am–4pm, Fri 9am–5pm. **Free**

Biblical Arts Center

7500 Park Lane (North Dallas); tel 214/691-4661. A 124- by 20-foot painting of the miracle of Pentecost, a 30-minute sound-and-light show, and a replica of Christ's tomb are of special interest. **Open:** Tues–Sat 10am–5pm. Sun 1–5pm. **Free**

Farmers Produce Market

1010 S Pearl (Downtown); tel 214/939-2808. Located in the southeast corner of downtown Dallas, this collection of stands offers a large variety of seasonal fresh fruits, vegetables, flowers, and plants from the surrounding area. Special events, educational classes on food-related, agricultural, and gardening topics, as well as cooking classes, are held throughout the year. **Open:** Daily 7am–6pm. **Free**

Dallas–Fort Worth Int'l Airport

See also Dallas, Fort Worth, Irving

HOTELS 🏨

≣≣≣ Dallas/Fort Worth Airport Marriott

8440 Freeport Pkwy, Irving, 75063; tel 972/929-8801 or toll free 800/228-9290; fax 972/929-6599. At TX 114. A lovely indoor/outdoor pool is the outstanding feature of this tropical themed Marriott offering dependable accommodations. **Rooms:** 498 rms and stes. Executive level. CI 3pm/CO 1pm. Nonsmoking rms avail. Corporate discounts, B&B and honeymoon packages avail. **Amenities:** 🛆 🗌 🍽 A/C, cable TV w/movies, dataport, voice mail. Some units w/terraces. **Services:** ✕ ☞ 🚗 🖳 🗑 Car-rental desk, babysitting. **Facilities:** ⛳ 🏋 [1200] 🖳 ᾥ 2 restaurants, 2 bars, games rm, spa, sauna, whirlpool, washer/dryer. Golf and tennis are close by. **Rates:** $144–$149 S or D; $250–$400 ste. Children under age 18 stay free. Parking: Outdoor, free. Corporate discounts, B&B and honeymoon packages avail. AE, CB, DC, DISC, EC, JCB, MC, V.

≣≣≣ DFW Hilton Executive Conference Center

1800 TX 26 E, Grapevine, 76051; tel 817/481-8444 or toll free 800/645-1018; fax 817/481-3160. Bethel Rd exit from TX 121 or I-635. Situated on the very outskirts of the metropolitan area, this resortlike Hilton is located in a tranquil, peaceful setting. Extensive grounds include a stocked lake. Variety of entertainment facilities. **Rooms:** 395 rms and stes. Executive level. CI 3pm/CO noon. Nonsmoking rms avail. **Amenities:** 🛆 🗌 🍽 A/C, satel TV w/movies, dataport. All units w/minibars. **Services:** ✕ ☞ �P 🚗 🖳 🗑 Car-rental desk, masseur, children's program, babysitting. **Facilities:** ⛳ 🏊 🏋 🛶 🏋 [500] 🖳 ᾥ 3 restaurants, 2 bars, racquetball, steam rm, whirlpool. 2,600-sq-ft fitness center. **Rates:** Peak (Sept–June) $139–$169 S; $154–$184 D; $275–$1,000 ste. Extra person $15. Children under age 18 stay free. Lower rates off-season. Parking: Outdoor, free. AE, CB, DC, DISC, MC, V.

☲☲☲ DoubleTree Guest Suites

4650 W Airport Fwy, Irving, 75062; tel 972/790-0093 or toll free 800/222-8733; fax 972/790-4768. TX 183 at Valley View. You can't miss this uniquely designed, bright pinkish hotel near the south entrance to DFW Airport. Guests can relax in a beautiful atrium featuring a tropical stream and verdant plant life and a pool stocked with colorful Japanese koi fish. **Rooms:** 308 stes. CI 3pm/CO noon. Nonsmoking rms avail. **Amenities:** 🛅 🐾 ▣ 🍴 A/C, cable TV w/movies, refrig, dataport, voice mail. Some units w/minibars, some w/terraces. Microwave. **Services:** ✗ 🚐 ⊠ 🗘 **Facilities:** 🗗 🔯 500 ₺ 2 restaurants, 1 bar, sauna, whirlpool, washer/dryer. **Rates:** $159–$189 ste. Extra person $10. Children under age 18 stay free. Parking: Outdoor, free. AE, CB, DC, DISC, MC, V.

☲☲☲ The Harvey Hotel DFW Airport

4545 W John Carpenter Fwy, Irving, 75063; tel 972/929-4500 or toll free 800/922-9222; fax 972/929-0733. On TX 114 at Esters Blvd. One of the largest hotels in Irving. Suitable for all types of travelers. **Rooms:** 506 rms and stes. Executive level. CI 3pm/CO 1pm. Nonsmoking rms avail. **Amenities:** 🛅 🐾 A/C, cable TV w/movies, dataport, voice mail. 1 unit w/whirlpool. Half the rooms offer extra amenities, so be sure to ask. **Services:** ✗ 🗝 🚐 ⊠ 🗘 🖘 Car-rental desk. **Facilities:** 🗗 🔯 1600 🖥 ₺ 2 restaurants, 1 bar, spa, whirlpool, washer/dryer. ATM on site. Scoops Diner is an affable 1950s-style eatery good for burgers and ice cream. Golf and tennis nearby. **Rates:** $129–$134 S; $144–$149 D; $149–$164 ste. Parking: Outdoor, free. AE, CB, DC, DISC, MC, V.

☲☲☲ Holiday Inn DFW Airport South

4440 W Airport Fwy, Irving, 75062; tel 972/399-1010 or toll free 800/HOLIDAY; fax 972/790-8545. Holidome with many amenities and services. Located midway between Dallas and Fort Worth. **Rooms:** 409 rms and stes. Executive level. CI 2pm/CO noon. Nonsmoking rms avail. Rooms slightly larger than average. King-size beds available. Many rooms have couches. **Amenities:** 🛅 🐾 A/C, satel TV w/movies, dataport, voice mail. Some units w/terraces. **Services:** ✗ 🗝 🚐 ⊠ 🗘 Twice-daily maid svce, car-rental desk, children's program, babysitting. **Facilities:** 🗗 🔯 600 ₺ 2 restaurants, 1 bar, games rm, spa, sauna, whirlpool, playground, washer/dryer. Holidome has miniature golf course, delicatessen, and Pizza Hut. Tennis and track facilities under contract with Irving Fitness. **Rates:** $129 D; $150–$350 ste. Children under age 19 stay free. Parking: Outdoor, free. AE, CB, DC, DISC, EC, ER, JCB, MC, V.

☲☲☲ Hyatt Regency DFW Airport

International Pkwy, PO Box 619014, Dallas, 75261; tel 972/453-1234 or toll free 800/233-1234; fax 972/456-8668. This facility claims to be the world's largest airport hotel. Connected to the airport tram service, it comprises two large towers and offers 1,500 free parking spaces. Major interstates are easily accessible. **Rooms:** 1,400 rms and stes. Executive level. CI 3pm/CO noon. Nonsmoking rms avail. **Amenities:** 🛅 🐾 🍴 A/C, satel TV w/movies, voice mail. Some units w/minibars, some w/terraces, 1 w/fireplace, 1 w/whirlpool. Rooms offer devices for the deaf and hard-of-hearing. Video check-out. Fax machines and coffeemakers available upon request. For the most in-room amenities and services, ask for Gold Passport and Business plans. **Services:** ✗ 🗝 VP 🚐 ⊠ 🗘 Car-rental desk, masseur. **Facilities:** 🗗 ►18 🔯 🖥 🤾 3000 🖥 ₺ 4 restaurants, 3 bars (1 w/entertainment), basketball, volleyball, racquetball, spa, sauna, steam rm, whirlpool, beauty salon. American and Delta airline ticket offices, retail stores on site. Bear Creek Golf and Racquet Club offers many sport facilities on its beautifully landscaped, 335-acre grounds. **Rates:** $145–$155 S or D; $275–$1,200 ste. Children under age 18 stay free. Parking: Indoor/outdoor, free. AE, CB, DC, DISC, EC, MC, V.

MOTELS

☲☲ La Quinta Inn DFW Airport East

4105 W Airport Fwy, Irving, 75062; tel 972/252-6546 or toll free 800/531-5900; fax 972/570-4225. TX 183 at Esters Rd. Located very near Las Colinas shopping and dining options, this standardized motel offers basic rooms and facilities. **Rooms:** 166 rms. CI open/CO noon. Nonsmoking rms avail. **Amenities:** 🛅 🐾 A/C, satel TV w/movies, dataport. **Services:** 🚐 ⊠ 🗘 🖘 **Facilities:** 🗗 ₺ **Rates (CP):** $58–$75 S or D. Extra person $10. Children under age 18 stay free. Parking: Outdoor, free. AE, CB, DC, DISC, JCB, MC, V.

☲☲ Ramada Inn DFW Airport South

4110 W Airport Fwy, Irving, 75062; tel 972/399-2005 or toll free 800/228-2828; fax 972/986-7620. On TX 183, near Esters. A well-priced option for the budget-conscious. **Rooms:** 138 rms. CI open/CO 1pm. Nonsmoking rms avail. **Amenities:** 🛅 🐾 ▣ A/C, cable TV w/movies. **Services:** 🚐 ⊠ 🗘 **Facilities:** 🗗 ₺ 1 bar, whirlpool, washer/dryer. **Rates (CP):** $64–$86 S or D. Extra person $8. Children under age 17 stay free. Parking: Outdoor, free. AE, CB, DC, DISC, JCB, MC, V.

☲☲☲ Westar Suites/Irving (DFW Airport South)

3950 W Airport Fwy, Irving, 75062; tel 972/790-1950 or toll free 800/255-1755; fax 972/790-4750. Between Esters and Beltline. This cozy, all-suite property features a lobby designed like a contemporary ski lodge, complete with a huge fireplace. **Rooms:** 126 stes. CI 3pm/CO noon. Nonsmoking rms avail. **Amenities:** 🛅 🐾 ▣ A/C, cable TV w/movies, refrig, dataport. Microwave. **Services:** 🚐 ⊠ 🗘 Complimentary newspapers. **Facilities:** 🗗 50 ₺ Whirlpool, washer/dryer. Free use of local health club's facilities. **Rates (CP):** Peak (Mar–Sept) $71–$79 ste. Extra person $5. Children under age 18 stay free. Lower rates off-season. Parking: Outdoor, free. AE, CB, DC, DISC, MC, V.

Dayton

RESTAURANT ⑪

Frank's Cafe
603 E US 90; tel 409/258-2598. E of TX 146. **American.** Small-town diner that is a great place to stop for friendly service and good food. The building may need some repairs, but the food is just right. Fresh homemade pies are recommended. **FYI:** Reservations not accepted. Beer and wine only. **Open:** Wed–Sun 8am–10pm. **Prices:** Main courses $3–$12. MC, V.

Del Rio

See also Eagle Pass

Discovered and named by Spanish explorers in the early 1600s, the first real settlement of the city came after the Civil War, when ranchers discovered natural springs here and used them for irrigation. The general area has more than 400 archeological sites, including aboriginal cave paintings. **Information:** Del Rio Chamber of Commerce, 1915 Ave F, Del Rio, 78840 (tel 210/775-3551).

HOTEL 🏨

≣≣≣ Ramada Inn
2101 Ave F, 78840; tel 210/775-1511 or toll free 800/325-4747. Off US 90. Centrally located high-rise hotel. **Rooms:** 240 rms and stes. Executive level. CI 2pm/CO noon. Nonsmoking rms avail. **Amenities:** 🛏 ⓐ 🖪 ⌐ A/C, cable TV, refrig, dataport. Some units w/terraces. **Services:** ✕ ⓋⓅ 🚐 🛄 Social director. **Facilities:** 🏋 📷 ⑤ 1 restaurant, 1 bar (w/entertainment), whirlpool. **Rates (CP):** Peak (Apr–Aug) $59–$69 S; $69–$72 D; $72–$89 ste. Extra person $5. Min stay peak. Lower rates off-season. MAP rates avail. Parking: Indoor/outdoor, free. AE, DC, DISC, MC, V.

RESTAURANT ⑪

★ Memo's
804 E Losoya; tel 210/775-8104. **Italian/Mexican.** This nice little restaurant serves both traditional American and Italian favorites at moderate prices. **FYI:** Reservations not accepted. Beer and wine only. **Open:** Lunch Mon–Sat 11am–2pm; dinner daily 6–10pm. **Prices:** Main courses $6–$9. No CC. ⑥

ATTRACTIONS 🏛

Amistad National Recreation Area
TX 90 W; tel 210/775-7491. Swimming beaches, marinas, boat ramps, and free campgrounds administered by National Park Service on the US side of the huge international Amistad Reservoir. Information, maps, brochures, and directions to Panther Cave can be obtained from the headquarters. **Open:** Daily sunrise–sunset. **Free**

Alamo Village Movie Location
Shahan Ranches, RR 674, Bracketville; tel 210/563-2580. This Western family-recreation center was built around the movie set for John Wayne's *The Alamo*, filmed in 1959. The set was one of the largest and most complete ever constructed in the United States; it took 5,000 men two years to build. The Alamo replica, built by adobe craftsmen from Mexico, overlooks a complete frontier village of the 1800s. The set includes a cantina-restaurant, trading post, Indian store, authentic stage depot, old-time jail, bank, saddle shop, and other typical Old West structures. Country-western shows staged during summer months. The set is still used for movies, television, and commercials. Food available. **Open:** Peak (Mem Day–Labor Day) daily 9am–6pm. Reduced hours off-season. **$$$**

Whitehead Memorial Museum
1308 S Main St; tel 210/774-7568. Dedicated to the heritage of the Southwest, the museum's exhibits are spread throughout several buildings which are historically significant in themselves. The main building is the Perry Store, a trading post built in 1870; also included in the complex is a log cabin, a barn house, the Hal Patton Labor Office from 1905, and an old caboose. Other highlights are displays on the history of Seminole Scouts and African American Texans; artifacts from early settlers and Native Americans; original farming and transportation equipment; and a replica of the Jersey Lilly Saloon run by the famed Judge Roy Bean ("The Law West of the Pecos"). **Open:** Tues–Sat 9am–4:30pm, Sun 1–5pm. **$**

Val Verde Winery
100 Qualia; tel 210/775-9714. This family-owned and -operated winery, founded in 1883, is among the oldest in Texas. The 20-minute tours include a complimentary tasting. Eight different wines are produced here and can be purchased on site. **Open:** Mon–Sat 9am–5pm. **Free**

Amistad Tours
US 90 W; tel 210/774-3484. Boat tours (lasting approximately four hours) of Amistad Lake and the Pecos and Rio Grande rivers. Some of the highlights of the tour are the dam, high bridges, and Native American pictures on the canyon walls. **Open:** Call ahead to arrange tour. **$$$$**

Denison

See also Bonham, Sherman

Originally a stop on the Butterfield Stage Line in the 1850s, Denison was established as a railhead in 1872. Dwight D Eisenhower was born here in 1890. Lake Texoma and the Hagerman National Wildlife Refuge are nearby. **Information:** Denison Area Chamber of Commerce, 313 W Woodard, PO Box 325, Denison, 75020 (tel 903/465-1551).

MOTEL

≡≡≡ Ramada Inn

1600 S Denison Ave, 75020; tel 903/465-6800 or toll free 800/2-RAMADA; fax 903/465-6800. At jct US 69/75. Near Lake Texoma and the birthplace of President Eisenhower. **Rooms:** 100 rms. CI 3pm/CO noon. Nonsmoking rms avail. **Amenities:** A/C, cable TV w/movies. **Services:** Fax and copy services available. **Facilities:** 1 restaurant, 1 bar. Access to local fitness center. **Rates:** $40–$70 S or D. Extra person $8. Children under age 18 stay free. Parking: Outdoor, free. AE, CB, DC, DISC, MC, V.

ATTRACTIONS

Lake Texoma

TX 91; tel 903/465-4990. This huge reservoir spreads over 89,000 acres of Texas and Oklahoma; the 580 miles of shoreline includes scenic coves and inlets. There are 57 campgrounds, scores of trailer parks, over 100 picnic areas, more than 100 shelter buildings, and over 80 boat ramps. Marinas and luxury resorts are situated on both the Texas and Oklahoma shores. Visitors can enjoy fishing as well as hiking on the Cross Timbers trail, which follows the shoreline for 14 miles. **Open:** Daily 24 hours. **Free**

Grayson County Frontier Village

Loy Lake Park; tel 210/463-2487. The spirit of the frontier comes alive at this site, a collection of 13 restored and furnished buildings dating from 1840 to 1900. They include a log cabin and log schoolhouse, homes (including the Greek Revival–style Bullock-Bass House) and businesses, and a jail lockup. The Frontier Village Museum exhibits household utensils, antique crystal and enamelware, pioneer clothing, tools, and farm machinery. Crafts and gift shop. **Open:** May–Oct, Wed–Sat 10am–5pm, Sun 2–5pm. **Free**

Denton

Established in 1857, Denton is the home to the University of North Texas as well as Texas Woman's University, the nation's largest university for women. Denton is bracketed by Lake Lewisville and Lake Ray Roberts. **Information:** Denton Convention & Visitors Bureau, PO Drawer P, Denton, 76202 (tel 817/382-7895).

HOTEL

≡≡≡ Radisson Hotel Denton

2211 I-35 N, 76205; tel 817/565-8499 or toll free 800/333-3333; fax 817/387-4729. Convention-oriented hotel, attractive and well maintained. Offers great view of Denton. **Rooms:** 150 rms and stes. CI 3pm/CO noon. Nonsmoking rms avail. **Amenities:** A/C, cable TV w/movies, dataport. **Services:** Car-rental desk. **Facilities:** 18 2 restaurants, 1 bar (w/entertainment). Eagle Point Golf Club on premises. **Rates:** $79–$99 S or D;

$169–$369 ste. Extra person $10. Children under age 18 stay free. Parking: Outdoor, free. AE, CB, DC, DISC, ER, JCB, MC, V.

MOTELS

≡≡ The Denton Inn

820 I-35 S, 76201; tel 817/387-0591. Near Fort Worth Dr. A unique find, this otherwise standard roadside motel sets itself apart with its themed "Fantasy Suites": Caesar's Court, Arabian Nights, the Pink Cadillac, and the Geisha Garden. A great budget option for a fun getaway weekend in Denton. **Rooms:** 85 rms and stes. CI open/CO noon. Nonsmoking rms avail. **Amenities:** A/C, cable TV w/movies. Some units w/whirlpools. **Services:** **Facilities:** 1 restaurant (lunch and dinner only), washer/dryer. **Rates (CP):** $40–$55 S; $45–$55 D; $149–$199 ste. Extra person $5. Children under age 16 stay free. Parking: Outdoor, free. AE, CB, DC, DISC, MC, V.

≡≡≡ Holiday Inn

1500 Dallas Dr, 76205; tel 817/387-3511 or toll free 800/HOLIDAY; fax 817/387-7917. At I-35. Standard, affordable accommodations easily accessible from nearby Dallas and Fort Worth. Near dining and shopping. **Rooms:** 144 rms and stes. CI 2pm/CO noon. Nonsmoking rms avail. **Amenities:** A/C, satel TV w/movies. **Services:** **Facilities:** 1 restaurant, 1 bar, washer/dryer. **Rates:** $67–$82 S or D; $95–$125 ste. Extra person $5. Children under age 18 stay free. Parking: Outdoor, free. AE, CB, DC, DISC, MC, V.

≡≡ La Quinta Inn

700 Fort Worth Dr, 76201; tel 817/387-5840 or toll free 800/531-5900; fax 817/387-2493. Near I-35. This standard La Quinta offers a comfortable overnight stay in suburban surroundings. **Rooms:** 99 rms and stes. CI 3pm/CO noon. Nonsmoking rms avail. **Amenities:** A/C, cable TV. Some dataports are available. **Services:** **Facilities:** Washer/dryer. **Rates (CP):** $51–$58 S; $59–$66 D; $61–$72 ste. Extra person $8. Children under age 18 stay free. Parking: Outdoor, free. AE, CB, DC, DISC, MC, V.

RESTAURANTS

Clark's Outpost Restaurant & Club

101 US 377 at Gene Autry Dr, Tioga; tel 817/437-2414. **Barbecue.** Very casual, often crowded cafe and barbecue pit serving authentic Texas barbecue. Great for a quick lunch. **FYI:** Reservations accepted. **Open:** Mon–Thurs 11am–9pm, Fri–Sat 11am–9:30pm, Sun 11am–8:30pm. **Prices:** Main courses $4–$16. AE, DC, DISC, MC, V.

The Homestead

401 S Locust; tel 817/566-3240. Near McKinney. **French.** An old, yellow Victorian home is the setting for this friendly restaurant near downtown Denton. Lunch menu features home-style food such as hearty soups and baked chicken with lima beans, while dinner might include various crepes, ribeye,

and red snapper. **FYI:** Reservations accepted. No liquor license. No smoking. **Open:** Lunch Mon–Sat 7am–2:30pm, Sun 8:30am–2pm; dinner Fri 6–9pm. **Prices:** Main courses $6–$13. AE, DISC, MC, V. &

⑤ **Mercado Juarez Cafe**
419 S Elm; tel 817/380-0755. Between McKinney and Prairie. **Tex-Mex.** Friendly and upbeat setting featuring large piñatas hanging from the ceiling, sombreros, and other Latin accents. A nice spot for families. **FYI:** Reservations accepted. Children's menu. **Open:** Sun–Thurs 11am–9pm, Fri–Sat 11am–10pm. **Prices:** Main courses $4–$10. AE, CB, DC, DISC, MC, V. 👥 &

ATTRACTION 🏛

Denton County Historical Museum
1896 Courthouse-on-the-Square, 110 W Hickory; tel 817/565-8697. Located in an 1896 historic courthouse (called "the most picturesque pile of rocks in North Texas"), the museum depicts Denton County history through a collection that includes lifestyle displays of a century ago, featuring a country kitchen, Victorian parlor, music room, farm tools, antique textiles, and folk art; also antique guns, dolls, and Native American pottery. Rotating displays examine Texas and local history; seasonal and thematic exhibits as well. Guided tours available. **Open:** Mon–Fri 10:30am–4:30pm, Sat 1–4:30pm. **Free**

Eagle Pass

See also Del Rio

MOTEL 🏨

🏨🏨 **La Quinta Motor Inn**
2525 Main St, 78852; tel 210/773-7000 or toll free 800/531-5900; fax 210/773-8852. On US 57 W. Attractive motel with Southwestern designs and architecture. Suitable for all types of travelers. **Rooms:** 175 rms and stes. CI 2pm/CO noon. Nonsmoking rms avail. **Amenities:** 🏨 A/C, satel TV w/movies. Some units w/terraces. Complimentary morning newspaper. **Facilities:** 🏋 🏊 & **Rates (CP):** $52–$57 S; $57–$60 D; $65–$75 ste. Extra person $10. Min stay wknds. Parking: Outdoor, free. AE, DC, DISC, MC, V.

El Paso

This is the westernmost city in Texas and the largest city on the US-Mexican border. Originally a Spanish mission built in the 1600s, El Paso is now a major manufacturing and mining center and home to the US Army's Fort Bliss. Professional ballet and theatrical companies as well as a symphony orchestra provide cultural excitement. The Tigua Indian Reservation is the only one of its kind within a major Texas city.

Home to a branch of the University of Texas. **Information:** El Paso Convention & Visitors Bureau, #1 Civic Center Plaza, El Paso, 79901 (tel 915/534-0696).

PUBLIC TRANSPORTATION
The **Sun Metro** operates citywide bus service along 47 routes. Standard fare is 85¢; transfers are 10¢. Fare for seniors and disabled passengers is 20¢, for students 40¢. Children under 6 ride free. Exact change or tokens required. The **Sun Metro Trolley** operates two routes; one goes to the international bridges and the other services the downtown area. Fare is 25¢, 10¢ for seniors and persons with disabilties. Call 915/533-3333 for information.

HOTELS 🏨

🏨🏨🏨 **El Paso Airport Hilton**
2027 Airway Blvd, 79925; tel 915/778-4241 or toll free 800/445-8667; fax 915/772-6871. Airway exit off I-10. Full-service luxury hotel featuring Southwestern decor in elegant pink hues. Large staff provides friendly, efficient service. **Rooms:** 272 rms and stes. Executive level. CI 2pm/CO noon. Nonsmoking rms avail. Headboards have shelves and drawers. Bathrooms are extremely attractive. **Amenities:** 🏨 🛁 A/C, cable TV. Some units w/minibars, some w/terraces, some w/whirlpools. **Services:** ✗ 🍽 🚐 🗄 🛎 **Facilities:** 🏋 🍴 🏊 & 2 restaurants, 1 bar, sauna, whirlpool, washer/dryer. Yogurt store and gourmet coffee bar in lobby. **Rates (BB):** $59–$101 S or D; $99–$111 ste. Children under age 17 stay free. Parking: Outdoor, free. AE, CB, DC, DISC, MC, V.

🏨🏨🏨 **El Paso Marriott**
1600 Airway Blvd, 79925; tel 915/779-3300 or toll free 800/228-9290; fax 915/779-4591. 3 blocks S of airport. A full-service hotel catering to many business travelers. **Rooms:** 296 rms and stes. Executive level. CI 4pm/CO 1pm. Nonsmoking rms avail. Tastefully decorated with quality furnishings. Suites start as one room for $225; then one or two rooms can be connected to it for an additional $75 each. **Amenities:** 🏨 🛁 📺 🍷 A/C, cable TV w/movies. **Services:** ✗ 🚐 🛎 **Facilities:** 🏋 🍴 🏊 & 2 restaurants (see "Restaurants" below), 1 bar, games rm, sauna, steam rm, whirlpool, playground, washer/dryer. **Rates (CP):** $99–$114 S or D; $225–$375 ste. Parking: Outdoor, free. AE, CB, DC, DISC, JCB, MC, V.

🏨🏨🏨 **Embassy Suites**
6100 Gateway E, 79905; tel 915/779-6222 or toll free 800/362-2779; fax 915/779-8846. This beautiful all-suite hotel features an atrium with fountains and lush plants and trees and a popcorn machine. **Rooms:** 185 stes. CI 3pm/CO 1pm. Nonsmoking rms avail. **Amenities:** 🏨 🛁 📺 A/C, cable TV w/movies, voice mail. **Services:** ✗ 🚐 🗄 🛎 Sega Genesis video games available. Complimentary evening cocktails and snacks served in atrium. **Facilities:** 🏋 🍴 🏊 & 1 restaurant, whirlpool, washer/dryer. **Rates (BB):** $79–$109 ste. Extra person $10. Parking: Outdoor, free. AE, DC, DISC, MC, V.

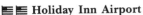

Holiday Inn Airport
6655 Gateway W, 79925; tel 915/778-6411 or toll free 800/ 882-6411; fax 915/778-6517. 2 mi W of airport on I-10. A small Holiday Inn with a lounge area in the lobby. Near the airport and interstate. **Rooms:** 203 rms and stes. CI 2pm/CO 1pm. Nonsmoking rms avail. Rooms have an older decor, but the floor-to-ceiling windows provide a light, airy atmosphere. **Amenities:** ▢ A/C, cable TV. **Services:** ✕ ▢ ▢ ▢ **Facilities:** ▢ ▢ ▢ ▢ 1 restaurant, 1 bar, whirlpool. **Rates (CP):** $64–$79 S or D; $76–$81 ste. Children under age 18 stay free. Parking: Outdoor, free. AE, CB, DC, DISC, JCB, MC, V.

UNRATED Holiday Inn Park Place
325 N Kansas St, 79901; tel 915/533-8241 or toll free 800/ 465-4329; fax 915/544-9979. At Main St. Located in the center of downtown El Paso, this older full-service hotel offers historic ambience. Many amenities and services focus on business travelers. **Rooms:** 119 rms and stes. CI 2pm/CO noon. Nonsmoking rms avail. **Amenities:** ▢ ▢ ▢ A/C, cable TV w/movies. Some units w/terraces. **Services:** ✕ ▢ VP ▢ ▢ ▢ ▢ **Facilities:** ▢ ▢ ▢ 2 restaurants, 1 bar. Very large pool deck. **Rates (CP):** $54–$56 S or D; $75 ste. Extra person $10. Children under age 12 stay free. Parking: Indoor, free. AE, CB, DC, DISC, JCB, MC, V.

International Hotel
113 W Missouri St, 79901; tel 915/544-3300 or toll free 800/668-3466; fax 915/544-9990. Near public library. This unique, historic, downtown business hotel is elegantly decorated with lots of gold. **Rooms:** 210 rms and stes. Executive level. CI open/CO noon. Nonsmoking rms avail. Rooms are spacious but need some refurbishing. **Amenities:** ▢ ▢ A/C, cable TV w/movies. Some units w/terraces. **Services:** ✕ ▢ VP ▢ ▢ ▢ ▢ **Facilities:** ▢ ▢ ▢ 1 restaurant, 1 bar, games rm. Huge ballroom across from bar with fabulous view of city is great for parties and weddings. Pool on third-floor roof. **Rates (CP):** $40 S or D; $85 ste. Extra person $5. Children under age 17 stay free. AP and MAP rates avail. Parking: Indoor, free. Secured, 24-hour parking available. AE, DC, DISC, MC, V.

Radisson Suite Inn
1770 Airway Blvd, 79925; tel 915/772-3333; fax 915/ 779-3323. Airway exit off I-10. Located near the airport and many restaurants, this luxurious all-suite property features extremely spacious guestrooms and attractive Southwestern decor. **Rooms:** 151 stes. CI open/CO noon. Nonsmoking rms avail. **Amenities:** ▢ ▢ A/C, cable TV w/movies. **Services:** ✕ ▢ ▢ ▢ **Facilities:** ▢ ▢ ▢ 1 restaurant, whirlpool. **Rates (BB):** $55–$115 ste. Parking: Outdoor, free. AE, CB, DC, DISC, MC, V.

Westar Suites
8250 Gateway E, 79907; tel 915/591-9600 or toll free 800/ 255-1755; fax 915/591-3263. On I-10 E. An all-suite hotel located near Cielo Vista Mall and International Bridge. **Rooms:** 126 stes. CI 2pm/CO noon. Nonsmoking rms avail.

Amenities: ▢ ▢ A/C, cable TV w/movies. **Services:** ✕ ▢ ▢ ▢ **Facilities:** ▢ ▢ ▢ Whirlpool, washer/dryer. Affiliated with Golds Gym. **Rates (CP):** $77 ste. Children under age 18 stay free. Parking: Outdoor, free. AE, CB, DC, DISC, MC, V.

MOTELS

Best Western Airport Inn
7144 Gateway E, 79915; tel 915/779-7700 or toll free 800/ 528-1234. Basic accommodations located near Cielo Vista Mall and many restaurants and night clubs. **Rooms:** 179 rms and stes. CI 2pm/CO noon. Nonsmoking rms avail. **Amenities:** ▢ ▢ A/C, cable TV w/movies. Some units w/minibars. **Services:** ✕ ▢ ▢ ▢ **Facilities:** ▢ 1 restaurant. **Rates (CP):** $59 S; $63 D; $68 ste. Extra person $5. Children under age 16 stay free. Parking: Outdoor, free. AE, CB, DC, DISC, MC, V.

Days Inn El Paso
9125 Gateway Dr, 79925; tel 915/593-8400 or toll free 800/ 329-7466; fax 915/599-1268. On I-10. This standard chain motel is near the Tony Lama Factory and International Bridge. Amenities and services are business oriented. Mall nearby. **Rooms:** 105 rms. CI open/CO noon. Nonsmoking rms avail. **Amenities:** ▢ ▢ A/C, cable TV w/movies. **Services:** ▢ ▢ ▢ ▢ **Facilities:** ▢ ▢ ▢ Whirlpool. **Rates (CP):** $48–$65 S; $54–$70 D; $70–$80 ste. Extra person $8. Children under age 18 stay free. Parking: Outdoor, free. AE, CB, DC, DISC, JCB, MC, V.

Howard Johnson Lodge
8887 Gateway W, 79925; tel 915/591-9471 or toll free 800/ 446-4656; fax 915/591-5602. A budget, family motel with comfortable, clean rooms located next to Cielo Vista Mall. **Rooms:** 140 rms. CI 2pm/CO noon. Nonsmoking rms avail. **Amenities:** ▢ A/C, cable TV w/movies. **Services:** ▢ ▢ ▢ ▢ ▢ For multiple-night stays with pets, rooms must be cleaned daily. **Facilities:** ▢ ▢ ▢ 1 restaurant, 1 bar, washer/dryer. **Rates (CP):** $57–$66 S or D. Extra person $5. Children under age 18 stay free. Parking: Outdoor, free. AE, CB, DC, DISC, MC, V.

La Quinta Motor Inn Lomaland
11033 Gateway Blvd W, 79935; tel 915/591-2244 or toll free 800/531-5900; fax 915/592-9300. 2 blocks W of Yarborough on I-10. Located near the interstate and many restaurants, this standard La Quinta features an attractive Southwestern decor with stucco walls and desert hues. **Rooms:** 138 rms and stes. CI open/CO noon. Nonsmoking rms avail. **Amenities:** ▢ A/C, cable TV w/movies. **Services:** ▢ ▢ ▢ **Facilities:** ▢ ▢ ▢ Whirlpool. **Rates (CP):** $55 S; $63 D; $69–$77 ste. Extra person $5. Children under age 18 stay free. Parking: Outdoor, free. AE, CB, DC, DISC, MC, V.

Quality Inn
6201 Gateway, 79925; tel 915/778-6611 or toll free 800/ 228-5151; fax 915/779-2270. On I-10. Standard chain motel with well-manicured grounds and acceptable accommoda-

tions. **Rooms:** 307 rms and stes. CI open/CO 2pm. Non-smoking rms avail. **Amenities:** 🛗 🛁 A/C, cable TV w/movies, VCR. **Services:** ✗ 🖥 🖼 🍽 🛎 VCRs, movie rentals available in gift shop. **Facilities:** 🏊 🔢 ♿ 1 restaurant. **Rates:** $46 S; $51 D; $72–$95 ste. Parking: Outdoor, free. AE, CB, DC, DISC, JCB, MC, V.

RESTAURANTS 🍴

Chatfeld

In El Paso Marriott, 1600 Airway Blvd; tel 915/779-3300. **American.** An upscale restaurant with a small, well-lit dining room and a highly competent waitstaff. The menu centers around nightly specials. You can try such delectable appetizers as escargot and smoked salmon, then move on to pecan-encrusted salmon, lamb chops, and filet mignon. Look for creative pasta specials, too. **FYI:** Reservations accepted. **Open:** Daily 5:30–10pm. **Prices:** Main courses $10–$15. AE, CB, DC, DISC, MC, V. 📼

Gabriel's Cafe

1270 Giles; tel 915/858-3839. McRae exit on I-10. **Mexican.** A helpful staff and lively atmosphere distinguish this Mexican eatery, which serves traditional fare like chile rellenos and burritos. It has two well-lit dining areas. **FYI:** Reservations accepted. **Open:** Sun–Thurs 7am–9pm, Fri–Sat 7am–10pm. **Prices:** Main courses $5–$8. AE, DISC, MC, V. 📼

★ Griggs

9007 Montana; tel 915/598-3451. Across from Cielo Vista Golf Course. **Mexican.** This establishment has been serving quality Mexican fare since 1967. Its subdued Southwestern decor and relatively laid-back atmosphere make it a nice change of pace from more typically loud and garish Mexican eateries. **FYI:** Reservations accepted. Additional location: 5800 Doniphan (tel 584-0451). **Open:** Daily 11am–9pm. **Prices:** Main courses $7–$13. AE, DC, DISC, MC, V. 🖥 📼

⑤ ★ Gunther's Edelweiss

11055 Gateway W; tel 915/592-1084. Near Yarborough Ave. **German/Seafood.** Owned and operated by an Austrian family, this restaurant serves fine yet affordable traditional German dishes such as bratwurst, spaetzle, and knockwurst. A live oompah band plays on Friday and Saturday. **FYI:** Reservations accepted. Children's menu. **Open:** Lunch Mon–Sat 11am–3pm; dinner Mon–Sat 5–9pm. **Prices:** Main courses $7–$13. AE, DISC, MC, V. ❤ 📼

Hudson's Grill

1770 Lee Trevino; tel 915/595-2769. At Montwood. **Burgers.** Reminiscent of a 1950s diner, with a jukebox serving as the focal point of the dining area. The menu offers a variety of burgers and sandwiches. There is also seating at the bar. **FYI:** Reservations not accepted. **Open:** Sun–Thurs 11am–midnight, Fri–Sat 11am–1am. **Prices:** Main courses $5–$7. AE, DISC, MC, V. 📼

★ Julio's Cafe Corona

8050 Gateway E; tel 915/591-7676. 1 block S of Yarborough. **Mexican.** This family-owned restaurant with small, well-lit dining areas has been serving reliable Mexican fare since 1944. **FYI:** Reservations not accepted. Dress code. **Open:** Mon–Sat 11am–10pm, Sun 8am–8pm. **Prices:** Main courses $5–$15. AE, CB, DC, DISC, MC, V. 📼

ATTRACTIONS 🏛

Tigua Indian Reservation and Pueblo

122 S Old Pueblo Rd; tel 915/859-7913. This is the oldest community in Texas, established in 1681 by refugees from a bloody Indian uprising that expelled Spanish and Christian Indians from what is now New Mexico. Spanish missionaries and loyal Tiguia Indians settled here at El Paso del Norte and built Isleta Mission. The mission church is still the religious focal point of the Tigua Indian community. Today, the extensive adobe complex, reconstructed in the traditional style, offers a visitors program and arts and crafts center. There is a kiva, or council chamber, dance area, and bread ovens. The arts and crafts center, the only part of the reservation open to the public, has workshops on jewelry, weaving, and pottery. A museum and a restaurant featuring Tigua specialties are on the grounds. **Open:** Mon–Fri 8am–5pm. **Free**

Chamizal National Memorial

800 S San Marcial; tel 915/532-7273. This site commemorates the amicable settlement of a longstanding border dispute between Texas and Mexico. There is a visitors center, plus exhibits and films (in English and Spanish) on Chamizal and border history. **Open:** Daily 8am–5pm. **Free**

Hueco Tanks State Historical Park

6900 Hueco Tanks Rd; tel 915/857-1135. Named for the natural rock basins, or huecos, that have furnished supplies of trapped rain water to dwellers and travelers in this arid region for millennia. Drawings from prehistoric settlers and the more recent Mescalero Apaches adorn the rocks. Other attractions include an old ranch house and the relocated ruins of an overland stage station. Rock climbing, hiking, and camping (20 campsites) are popular here. Picnic areas available. **Open:** Daily 8am–sunset. **$**

El Paso Museum of Art

1211 Montana Ave; tel 915/541-4040. The highlight of this museum is the Kress Collection of European paintings from 1300 to 1800, featuring works by Van Dyke, Canaletto, Lippi, Di Pietro, Murillo, and others. There are also a number of American paintings, including a Gilbert Stuart portrait of George Washington and Frederic Remington's *Sign of Friendship*. Exhibits of classical and contemporary Mexican and Southwestern art are shown. Films, lectures, and workshops offered. **Open:** Tues–Wed and Fri–Sat 9am–5pm, Thurs 9am–9pm, Sun 1am–5pm. **Free**

Wilderness Park Museum
4301 TransMountain Rd; tel 915/755-4332. Natural and Native American history in the El Paso region is explored through life-size dioramas, artifacts, and a mile-long nature trail that winds past reconstructions of a pueblo ruin and pithouse. A series of murals illustrates the ways in which humans have coexisted with the environment in the Southwest throughout history. **Open:** Tues–Sun 9am–4:45pm. **Free**

Magoffin Home State Historic Site
1120 Magoffin Ave; tel 915/533-5147. Built in 1875, this 19-room territorial-style adobe structure was designed by and constructed for Joseph Magoffin, an El Paso pioneer, politician, and businessman. Noted for its unique architecture, the house is furnished with original family artifacts ranging from a one-of-a-kind suite of 1884 New Orleans World's Fair bedroom furniture to numerous works of art. Guided tours offered. **Open:** Wed–Sun 9am–4pm. **$**

El Paso Zoo
4011 E Paisano; tel 915/544-1928. This 10-acre zoo exhibits birds, reptiles, fish, and mammals in appropriate environments. Renowned for its exotic reptiles (including alligators) and colorful primate collections. One indoor exhibit contrasts the animal communities of the Central American rain forest with those of the Chihuahuan Desert. Another exhibit allows visitors to see the behavior of nocturnal animals, by virtue of red lighting which simulates the nighttime environment. **Open:** Daily 9:30am–4pm. **$**

Fort Davis

See Alpine

Fort Worth

See also Arlington, Irving; for airport lodgings see Dallas-Fort Worth Int'l Airport

Established in 1849 as a frontier military outpost overlooking the Trinity River, Fort Worth later was nicknamed "Cowtown" because of its position as a major railhead for shipping cattle. Cultural attractions include a refurbished stockyards area, the world's largest honky-tonk, and three of the finest art museums in the country. City-owned Lake Worth offers recreation northwest of town. **Information:** Fort Worth Convention & Visitors Bureau, 415 Throckmorton St, Fort Worth, 76102 (tel 817/336-8791 or toll free 800/433-5747).

PUBLIC TRANSPORTATION
The **Fort Worth Transportation Authority (FWTA)** operates 33 main bus routes citywide (the bus is also known as the T). Standard fare is 80¢; seniors and persons with disabilities pay 40¢. Children ages 6–18 pay 40¢; children under 5 ride free. Tokens or exact change required. Call 817/871-6200 for information.

HOTELS

Green Oaks Inn & Conference Center
6901 West Fwy, 76116; tel 817/738-7311 or toll free 800/433-2174, 800/772-2341 in TX. At jct TX 183 and I-30. With its resort atmosphere, this facility draws vacationers and conventioneers. Close to Carswell AFB, the zoo, and Texas Christian University. **Rooms:** 284 rms and stes. CI 3pm/CO noon. Nonsmoking rms avail. **Amenities:** A/C, cable TV w/movies. Some units w/terraces. **Services:** Twice-daily maid svce. **Facilities:** 1 restaurant, 1 bar (w/entertainment), spa, sauna, whirlpool. **Rates:** Peak (Oct) $79–$109 S or D. Extra person $10. Children under age 12 stay free. Lower rates off-season. Parking: Outdoor, free. AE, CB, DC, DISC, JCB, MC, V.

Radisson Plaza Hotel
815 Main St, 76102 (Downtown); tel 817/870-2100 or toll free 800/333-3333. At 8th St. Claiming to be the largest hotel in town, this convention-oriented business hotel featuring an attractive rooftop pool and a multilingual staff consists of two towers connected by a skywalk. John F Kennedy stayed here the night before his assassination. **Rooms:** 517 rms and stes. Executive level. CI 2pm/CO noon. Nonsmoking rms avail. **Amenities:** A/C, satel TV w/movies, voice mail. 1 unit w/whirlpool. Plaza level offers turndown service, bathrobes, newspapers, evening hors d'oeuvres, and breakfast. Dataports also available. **Services:** Twice-daily maid svce, car-rental desk, babysitting. Fax machines and computers can be provided. **Facilities:** 2 restaurants, 2 bars, spa, beauty salon. Video store. **Rates:** $138–$158 S; $148–$168 D; $225–$1,200 ste. Extra person $10. Children under age 17 stay free. Parking: Indoor, $6/day. AE, CB, DC, DISC, JCB, MC, V.

Ramada Hotel Fort Worth
1701 Commerce St, 76102 (Downtown); tel 817/335-7000 or toll free 800/228-2828; fax 817/335-3333. N of I-30. A reasonably priced lodging providing free covered parking—a rarity for downtown. **Rooms:** 430 rms and stes. Executive level. CI 3pm/CO noon. Nonsmoking rms avail. **Amenities:** A/C, cable TV w/movies, dataport, voice mail. All units w/terraces. **Services:** Car-rental desk, babysitting. **Facilities:** 1 restaurant, 2 bars, whirlpool. YMCA facilities available to guests. **Rates:** Peak (Mar–Sept) $89–$109 S; $99–$119 D; $175–$300 ste. Extra person $10. Children under age 18 stay free. Lower rates off-season. Parking: Indoor/outdoor, free. AE, CB, DC, DISC, JCB, MC, V.

Stockyards Hotel
109 E Exchange Ave, PO Box 4558, 76106 (Stockyards); tel 817/625-6427 or toll free 800/423-8471; fax 817/624-2571. 1 block E of Main St. A grand wooden staircase leads from

the lobby to the guest rooms at this unique, Old West–inspired hotel housed in a 1907 building. Located in the stockyards section of Fort Worth, 10 minutes from downtown and I-35. **Rooms:** 52 rms and stes. CI 3pm/CO noon. Nonsmoking rms avail. **Amenities:** ☎ ⚿ A/C, TV, voice mail. 1 unit w/minibar, 1 w/fireplace, 1 w/whirlpool. **Services:** ✕ 🆅🅿 ⌐ 🕪 **Facilities:** 🛏150 1 restaurant (*see* "Restaurants" below), 1 bar. **Rates:** $85–$120 S or D; $140–$350 ste. Extra person $15. Children under age 18 stay free. Parking: Outdoor, $5/day. AE, CB, DC, DISC, MC, V.

≡≡≡≡ Worthington

200 Main St, 76102 (Downtown); tel 817/870-1000 or toll free 800/433-5677; fax 817/338-9176. At 2nd St. Across from Sundance Square stands one of the most luxurious hotels in Fort Worth. Guests are welcomed into a huge, posh, multilevel lobby. **Rooms:** 504 rms and stes. Executive level. CI 3pm/CO noon. Nonsmoking rms avail. **Amenities:** ☎ ⚿ A/C, cable TV w/movies, dataport. All units w/minibars, some w/terraces. **Services:** ⦿ 🔑 🆅🅿 🚐 🖼 ⌐ Twice-daily maid svce, masseur, babysitting. **Facilities:** 🛏 🟦 🎱 🍴 1000 💻 ⚿ 3 restaurants, 1 bar, spa, sauna, whirlpool. Well-regarded Reflections restaurant offers fine dining in elegant surroundings. **Rates:** $140–$205 S or D; $300–$850 ste. Extra person $15. Children under age 18 stay free. Parking: Indoor, $6–$9/day. AE, CB, DC, DISC, MC, V.

MOTELS

≡≡ Best Western West Branch Inn

7301 W Fwy, 76116; tel 817/244-7444 or toll free 800/528-1234; fax 817/244-7902. Off I-30. A great budget choice, near Ridgeman Mall, Carswell AFB, and downtown. **Rooms:** 118 rms. CI 4pm/CO noon. Nonsmoking rms avail. **Amenities:** ☎ ⚿ A/C, cable TV. **Services:** 🖼 ⌐ **Facilities:** 🛏 ⚿ 1 bar, washer/dryer. **Rates (CP):** $39–$50 S or D. Extra person $5. Children under age 12 stay free. Parking: Outdoor, free. AE, CB, DC, DISC, MC, V.

≡≡≡ Courtyard by Marriott

3150 Riverfront Dr, 76107; tel 817/335-1300 or toll free 800/321-2211; fax 817/336-6926. Near University Dr and I-30. Located in a nice wooded area across the road from the Trinity River, this better-than-average chain property is near TCU and convenient to downtown. Good for those who don't want to stay in the hustle and bustle of downtown. **Rooms:** 130 rms. CI 3pm/CO noon. Nonsmoking rms avail. **Amenities:** ☎ ⚿ A/C, cable TV w/movies, dataport. **Services:** 🖼 ⌐ **Facilities:** 🛏 🎱 130 ⚿ 1 restaurant (bkfst only), washer/dryer. **Rates:** $85–$115 S or D. Extra person $10. Children under age 18 stay free. Parking: Outdoor, free. AE, CB, DC, DISC, MC, V.

≡≡ Days Inn

4213 S Fwy, 76115; tel 817/923-1987 or toll free 800/325-2525; fax 817/923-8692. Exit 46B off I-35. Basic chain property near shopping mall, Texas Christian University, and downtown. **Rooms:** 60 rms and stes. CI 2pm/CO noon.

Nonsmoking rms avail. **Amenities:** ☎ ⚿ A/C, cable TV w/movies. **Services:** ⌐ 🕪 **Facilities:** 🛏 ⚿ **Rates:** Peak (May–Aug) $45–$50 S; $60–$65 D; $75–$85 ste. Extra person $10. Children under age 12 stay free. Lower rates off-season. Parking: Outdoor, free. AE, CB, DC, DISC, JCB, MC, V.

≡≡ HoJo Inn

4201 S Fwy, 76115; tel 817/923-8281 or toll free 800/446-4656; fax 817/926-8756. An economical motel that is great for families. Convenient to I-35. **Rooms:** 98 rms. CI open/CO noon. Nonsmoking rms avail. **Amenities:** ☎ ⚿ A/C, cable TV w/movies. **Services:** ✕ 🚐 🖼 ⌐ **Facilities:** 🛏 ⚿ 1 restaurant. **Rates:** $40–$60 S or D. Extra person $8. Children under age 18 stay free. Parking: Outdoor, free. AE, CB, DC, DISC, MC, V.

≡≡ La Quinta Motor Inn Northeast

7920 Bedford-Euless Rd, 76180; tel 817/485-2750 or toll free 800/531-5900; fax 817/656-8977. Off TX 183. Dependable motel with Southwestern accents, convenient to TX 183 and I-820 in the suburbs of northeast Fort Worth. **Rooms:** 100 rms and stes. CI 3pm/CO noon. Nonsmoking rms avail. **Amenities:** ☎ ⚿ A/C, cable TV w/movies. **Services:** 🖼 ⌐ 🕪 **Facilities:** 🛏 ⚿ **Rates (CP):** $55–$62 S; $60–$67 D; $75–$85 ste. Extra person $7. Children under age 18 stay free. Parking: Outdoor, free. AE, CB, DC, DISC, MC, V.

≡ Motel 6 North

3271 I-35 W, 76106; tel 817/625-4359; fax 817/625-8256. Cheap, clean, reliable accommodations minutes away from the airports. **Rooms:** 106 rms. CI open/CO noon. Nonsmoking rms avail. **Amenities:** ☎ ⚿ A/C, cable TV. **Services:** 🚐 ⌐ 🕪 **Facilities:** 🛏 **Rates:** $28–$40 S or D. Extra person $6. Children under age 17 stay free. Parking: Outdoor, free. AE, DC, DISC, MC, V.

≡≡≡ Residence Inn by Marriott

1701 S University Dr, 76107; tel 817/870-1011 or toll free 800/331-3131; fax 817/877-5500. S of I-30. Located in a busy section of town near Trinity River Park and TCU, this motel's contemporary, apartment-style accommodations are secluded from the city scene by a nice wooded area. **Rooms:** 120 stes. CI 3pm/CO noon. Nonsmoking rms avail. Suites have fully equipped kitchens. **Amenities:** ☎ ⚿ 🖭 A/C, cable TV, refrig. Some units w/terraces, some w/fireplaces. **Services:** 🖼 ⌐ 🕪 Grocery services available. Shuttle service to various locations. **Facilities:** 🛏 🟦 🎱 30 ⚿ Basketball, whirlpool, washer/dryer. Health club privileges available. **Rates (CP):** $99–$129 ste. Parking: Outdoor, free. AE, DC, DISC, JCB, MC, V.

≡≡ Royal Western Suites

8401 W I-30, 76116; tel 817/560-0060; fax 817/244-3047. Near Las Vegas Trail. Near I-820, Carswell AFB, Ridgeman Mall, and downtown, this property doesn't look like much from the outside, but the inside is clean and cozy. **Rooms:** 112 stes. CI 3pm/CO noon. Nonsmoking rms avail. Basic, comfortable rooms—but nothing more. **Amenities:** ☎ ⚿ 🖭

A/C, cable TV, refrig. Some units w/terraces. Suites have full kitchenettes and microwaves. **Services:** 🖨 Fax and copy services available. **Facilities:** 🔲 Washer/dryer. **Rates (CP):** $80–$140 ste. Children under age 16 stay free. Parking: Outdoor, free. AE, CB, DC, DISC, MC, V.

▄▄ ▄▄ Sandpiper Airport Inn
4000 N Main St, 76106; tel 817/625-5531. S of Blue Mound near Meacham Airport. In a building that was formerly an airplane hangar, this rather unique motel at Meacham Field offers individualized hospitality to its guests—many of whom are airplane pilots and owners and students in flight training. **Rooms:** 81 rms and stes. CI 2pm/CO noon. Nonsmoking rms avail. **Amenities:** 🎗 👗 A/C, satel TV, voice mail. Some units w/terraces, some w/whirlpools. **Services:** 🖨 Big-screen TVs in lounge areas. **Facilities:** 🔲 🕭 Whirlpool, washer/dryer. Beautifully tiled pool. **Rates:** $45–$55 S or D; $80–$300 ste. Extra person $5. Children under age 18 stay free. Parking: Outdoor, free. AE, DC, DISC, MC, V.

RESTAURANTS 🍴

Angelo's Barbecue
2533 White Settlement Rd; tel 817-332-0357. Between Hendersen and University, near downtown. **Barbecue.** A Western theme pervades this downhome barbecue joint. Spicy and tangy, this is authentic, Texas-style barbecue, and the numerous awards displayed on the wall attest to its quality. **FYI:** Reservations not accepted. Beer and wine only. **Open:** Mon–Sat 11am–10pm. **Prices:** Main courses $7–$12. No CC. 🕭

The Balcony of Ridglea
In Ridglea Village Shopping Center, 6100 Camp Bowie; tel 817/731-3719. S of I-30. **Continental.** French motifs dominate this elegant, fairly small restaurant. Located on the second floor of a shopping center, it features a glassed-in balcony, comfortable seating, chandeliers, and a nice piano at the entrance. Continental classics include rack of lamb and chateaubriand. **FYI:** Reservations recommended. Piano. Dress code. **Open:** Lunch Mon–Fri 11:30am–2pm; dinner Mon–Thurs 6–10pm, Fri–Sat 6–10:30pm. **Prices:** Main courses $11–$22. AE, CB, DC, DISC, MC, V. ♥ ▲ 🕭

Bella Italia West
5139 Camp Bowle; tel 817/738-1700. W of University. **Italian.** Elegant restaurant great for family dining. Extensive Italian menu has something for everyone. Professional and friendly waitstaff. **FYI:** Reservations recommended. Dress code. **Open:** Lunch Mon–Fri 11:30am–2pm; dinner Mon–Sat 6pm–close. **Prices:** Main courses $8–$21. AE, CB, DC, DISC, MC, V. 🕭

Booger Red's Restaurant & Saloon
In Stockyards Hotel, 109 E Exchange Ave; tel 817/625-6427. 1 block E of Main St. **Steak.** Booger Red's was built in 1907, but the atmosphere is more Old West than turn-of-the-century. The bar stools are replicas of saddles; a large bison

trophy adorns the wall, and an old player piano sits to one side. Even the ceiling fans are authentic, all connected by a large belt and turned by a single motor. The specialty is steak. **FYI:** Reservations accepted. Country music. Children's menu. **Open:** Sun–Wed 6:30am–9pm, Thurs 6:30am–10pm, Fri–Sat 6:30am–11pm. **Prices:** Main courses $5–$15. AE, CB, DC, DISC, MC, V. 🍴 VP

Cattlemen's Steak House
2458 N Main; tel 817/624-3945. Near Exchange at Stockyards. **Steak.** Suave, posh, and romantic, this authentic steak house in the old stockyards is very well known in the Dallas/Fort Worth area—it's been around since 1947 and may well have perfected the steak. **FYI:** Reservations accepted. Children's menu. **Open:** Mon–Thurs 11am–10:30pm, Fri–Sat 11am–11pm, Sun 4–10pm. **Prices:** Main courses $10–$26. AE, DC, DISC, MC, V.

City Park Cafe
2418 Forest Park; tel 817/921-4567. N of Berry and S of I-30. **Eclectic.** This friendly neighborhood restaurant is great for a quick, delicious lunch. Try one of the tasty sandwiches with a fresh green salad, or the hearty and appealing chef's salad. **FYI:** Reservations accepted. Dress code. **Open:** Lunch Mon–Fri 11am–2:30pm; dinner Mon–Fri 5:15–9:30pm, Fri–Sat 5–11pm, Sun 5–9pm; brunch Sat–Sun 11am–3pm. **Prices:** Main courses $9–$14. AE, CB, DC, DISC, MC, V. 🕭

Edelweiss
3801-A Southwest Blvd; tel 817/738-5934. At jct US 377, TX 183 and TX 580. **German.** A loud establishment with a gregarious clientele and staff, this is a great place for revelry and fun, where sing-alongs are held regularly (lyrics to popular German beer-drinking songs are printed on the menu), weekday happy hours draw crowds, and the traditional German fare is tasty and filling. **FYI:** Reservations accepted. Folk. Children's menu. **Open:** Tues–Thurs 5–10:30pm, Fri–Sat 5–11pm. **Prices:** Main courses $9–$16. AE, CB, DC, DISC, MC, V. 🕭

Hubba Hubba's Great American Diner
8320 TX 580 W; tel 817/560-2930. Near Las Vegas Trail. **Diner.** Blaring music from a large jukebox, nostalgic decor, and the celebration of the American automobile establish the appropriate 1950s atmosphere at this traditional American diner. A fun place for families, where the kids will find something to like on the menu of diner favorites and standard Tex-Mex fare. **FYI:** Reservations not accepted. Children's menu. No liquor license. **Open:** Mon–Thurs 11am–10pm, Fri 11am–11pm, Sat 9am–11pm, Sun 9am–10pm. **Prices:** Main courses $6–$14. AE, DC, DISC, MC, V. 👥 🕭

Hunan Restaurant
4500 Bellaire Dr S; tel 817/737-7285. At Hulen Blvd. **Chinese.** A fairly elegant Chinese restaurant offering an extensive menu and big portions. **FYI:** Reservations not

accepted. Children's menu. **Open:** Mon–Thurs 11am–10pm, Fri–Sat 11am–11pm, Sun 11:30am–10pm. **Prices:** Main courses $7–$18. AE, CB, DC, DISC, MC, V.

★ **Joe T Garcia's**
2201 N Commerce St; tel 817/626-4356. Near Main St and Stockyards. **Mexican.** Behind the small unpretentious entrance, you'd never know there's an outdoor patio seating 300 people amid fountains, a swimming pool, and a miniature park. Seating is also available in a small, indoor dining room. Choose between two entrees at dinner: beef or chicken fajitas, or a family-style enchilada dinner. For lunch, the chicken flautas are the specialty. Celebrities have taken to hanging out here, but the service remains casual and friendly. **FYI:** Reservations accepted. Children's menu. **Open:** Lunch Mon–Thurs 11am–2:30pm; dinner Mon–Thurs 5–10pm, Fri–Sat 11am–11pm, Sun 11am–10pm. **Prices:** Main courses $3–$10. No CC.

Juanita's
In Sundance Square, 115 W 2nd St; tel 817/335-1777. **Tex-Mex.** A popular, festive Tex-Mex restaurant situated amid the downtown nightlife spots. Fajitas and other favorites, plus specialities like quail braised in tequila. **FYI:** Reservations accepted. **Open:** Mon–Thurs 11am–midnight, Fri 11am–1am, Sat noon–1am, Sun noon–midnight. **Prices:** Main courses $2–$12. AE, CB, DC, DISC, MC, V.

★ **Kincaid's**
4901 Camp Bowie Blvd; tel 817/732-2881. At Eldridge, near Hulen Blvd. **Burgers.** Recognized for serving some the best burgers in Fort Worth, this well-known family-owned and -operated restaurant/grocery store has been serving quality food since 1946. Picnic seating in front of the restaurant is nice for lunch or early dinner. The grocery shelves serve as tables for the large lunch crowd. Very unique, it's worth a visit. **FYI:** Reservations not accepted. Children's menu. No liquor license. No smoking. **Open:** Mon–Sat 11am–6pm. **Prices:** Main courses $2–$5. No CC.

Mac's House
4255 Camp Bowie; tel 817/377-3744. W of University. **Continental.** This formal restaurant with warm service offers a wide-ranging menu that includes great steaks, quail, roasted hen, salmon, swordfish, shrimp, scrod, and pasta. **FYI:** Reservations recommended. Dress code. **Open:** Mon–Thurs 5:30–10pm, Fri–Sat 5:30–11pm. **Prices:** Main courses $15–$25. AE, CB, DC, DISC, MC, V.

Maharaja
6308 Hulen Bend Blvd; tel 817/263-7156. **Indian.** Plain and simple Indian eatery with well-prepared food and an ample lunch buffet. Friendly service. **FYI:** Reservations accepted. **Open:** Lunch Mon–Fri 11am–2pm, Sat–Sun 11:30am–2:30pm; dinner Sun–Thurs 5:30–10pm, Fri–Sat 5:30–11pm. **Prices:** Main courses $6–$12. AE, CB, DC, DISC, MC, V.

Michael's
3413 W 7th St; tel 817/877-3413. W of University. **Regional American.** Unique floral arrangements and modern art decorate this contemporary restaurant with hardwood floors and black tables. A very suave, professional staff serves specialties such as pistachio-encrusted salmon, pan-seared tenderloin, and charbroiled lamb chops. **FYI:** Reservations accepted. Dress code. **Open:** Lunch Mon–Fri 11am–2:30pm; dinner Mon–Wed 5:30–10pm, Thurs–Sat 5:30–11pm. **Prices:** Main courses $12–$25. AE, DC, DISC, MC, V.

Ol' South Pancake House
1507 S University Dr; tel 817/336-0311. S of I-30. **American.** With its numerous arcade games and gumball/toy machines, this 24-hour fun house is every kid's dream. It's also good for a late-night snack. Delicious sugar-loaded treats are specialties, and breakfast can be ordered at any time. **FYI:** Reservations accepted. No liquor license. **Open:** Daily 24 hrs. **Prices:** Main courses $3–$8. MC, V.

Ristorante La Piazza
3431 W 7th St; tel 817/334-0000. W of University. **Italian.** This trendy, elegant trattoria may err a bit on the side of stuffiness, but the wonderful service and fine food more than compensate. A good bet is the veal parmigiana or the creamy fettucine Alfredo. **FYI:** Reservations recommended. Dress code. **Open:** Lunch Mon–Fri 11:30am–2:30pm; dinner Mon–Thurs 5:30–10pm, Fri–Sat 5:30–11pm. **Prices:** Main courses $14–$26. AE, CB, DC, DISC, MC, V.

Saint Emilion
3617 W 7th St; tel 817/737-2781. W of University Dr. **French.** Very charming restaurant resembling a modest but elegant French country home. The wooden roof beams are exposed on the interior, drawing the eye skyward. The simple menu includes items like Australian rack of lamb, roast duck, beef tenderloin, Dover sole in lemon butter, and pasta. **FYI:** Reservations accepted. Dress code. **Open:** Mon–Sat 6–10pm. **Prices:** Main courses $7–$20. AE, CB, DC, DISC, MC, V.

Sardine's
3410 Camp Bowie Blvd; tel 817/332-9937. Between Montgomery and University. **Italian.** Fairly intimate despite its size, this casual Italian restaurant with family photos on one wall attracts a diverse crowd, who come for delicious Italian fare. Waitstaff is young and professional. **FYI:** Reservations accepted. Jazz. **Open:** Mon–Thurs 5–11:30pm, Fri–Sat 5pm–12:30am, Sun 3–11:30pm. **Prices:** Main courses $9–$17. AE, CB, DC, MC, V.

Star Cafe
111 W Exchange (Stockyards); tel 817/624-8701. W of Main St. **Steak.** One of the few places in the Dallas/Fort Worth area that serves prime steak, this tourist favorite located in the stockyards has two separate dining areas and a unique, old-fashioned bar downstairs reserved for parties. Besides steak, burgers, sandwiches, and other options are available.

FYI: Reservations accepted. **Open:** Mon–Fri 11am–9:30pm, Sat 11am–10:30pm. **Prices:** Main courses $5–$20. AE, MC, V.

Szechuan

5712 Locke Ave at Camp Bowie Blvd; tel 817/738-7300. Just S of I-30. **Chinese.** Casual and contemporary, this attractive establishment adorned with sculptures and vases prepares delicious Szechuan chicken, Peking duck, sweet-and-sour shrimp, and many other specialties. **FYI:** Reservations accepted. Additional location: 4750 Bryant Irvin at I-20 (tel 346-6111). **Open:** Sun–Thurs 11am–10pm, Fri–Sat 11am–11pm. **Prices:** Main courses $8–$23. AE, DISC, MC, V. ♿

ATTRACTIONS

Amon Carter Museum

3501 Camp Bowie Blvd (Cultural District); tel 817/738-1933. The collection, housed in a Philip Johnson–designed, international-style building, features outstanding works of 19th- and early 20th-century American art (paintings, sculpture, and prints), as well as an impressive collection of American photographs. Highlights include sculpture and paintings from Frederic Remington and Charles M Russell (two galleries are devoted to their work); paintings by Martin Johnson Head (*Thunderstorm Over Narragansett Bay*), Georgia O'Keeffe (*Ranchos Church–Taos, New Mexico*), Childe Hassam (*Flags on the Waldorf*), and William Merritt Chase (*Idle Hours*); also prints from Edward Hopper, Martin Lewis, and Thomas Hart Benton. The research library holds over 30,000 volumes and an extensive microfilm collection of 19th-century American newspapers, periodicals, and important rare publications. Special programs such as film series, gallery talks, and children's workshops are offered. Bookstore; guided museum tours available. **Open:** Sept–mid-June, Tues–Sat 10am–5pm, Sun noon–5pm. **Free**

Modern Art Museum of Fort Worth

1309 Montgomery St (Cultural District); tel 817/738-9215. Established in 1892, this is among the oldest art museums in Texas. The permanent collection contains works by modern and contemporary masters, notably Picasso, Kandinsky, Still, Rothko, Judd, Marden, Dine, Rauschenberg, Oldenburg, Lichtenstein, Warhol, Hodgkin, Avery, Scully, and Motherwell. Program offerings include lectures, gallery talks, children's workshops, inter-museum loans, educational programs, and guided tours.

The Modern at Sundance Square is the museum annex, located on the ground floor of the historic Sanger Building downtown. The 5,760-square-foot space hosts selections from the Modern's permanent collection and small-scale traveling exhibitions. Museum shop. **Open:** Tues–Fri 10am–5pm, Sat 11am–5pm, Sun noon–5pm. **Free**

Kimbell Art Museum

3333 Camp Bowie Blvd; tel 817/332-8451. Housed in an acclaimed modern building designed by renowned architect Louis I Kahn, the collection ranges in period from antiquity to the 20th century. Among its most famous holdings are Giovanni Bellini's *Christ in Benediction*, Caravaggio's *The Cheaters*, Goya's *Matador Pedro Romero*, Rembrandt's *Portrait of a Young Jew*, and Picasso's *Man with a Pipe*. Masterworks from Fra Angelico, El Greco, La Tour, Velázquez, Houdon, David, Delacroix, Cézanne, Mondrian, and Matisse also featured. The museum also holds a substantial collection of Asian art, as well as a group of Mesoamerican and African pieces and Mediterranean antiquities. Past exhibits have dealt with Mayan art, the era of Japanese Buddhist sculpture, and paintings from Spain's golden age, in addition to important retrospectives dedicated to Poussin, Ludovico, Matisse, and Carracci, to name a few. Lectures, symposia, and workshops, as well as a Sunday family hour and a summer family film festival, are offered. The museum bookstore carries slides, postcards, posters, art-related videotapes, puzzles, T-shirts, and reproductions, as well as books. Restaurant; guided museum tours available. **Open:** Tues–Thurs 10am–5pm, Fri noon–8pm, Sat 10am–5pm, Sun noon–5pm. **Free**

Fort Worth Museum of Science and History

1501 Montgomery St (Culture District); tel 817/732-1631. Nine galleries present hands-on exhibits dealing with the human body, rocks and fossils, medicine, dinosaurs, and computers. Visitors can dig for dinosaur bones beside a stream in an outdoor area, view a 20-foot Tenontosaurus, and test their computer skills. The Noble Planetarium offers astronomy programs, and the 80-foot domed Omni Theater uses advanced 70-millimeter and multi-image projection and sound systems to present films on science and nature. More than 600 classes and workshops offered year-round. Museum store; cafe. **Open:** Mon 9am–5pm, Tues–Thurs 9am–8pm, Fri–Sat 9am–9pm, Sun noon–8pm. **$$**

Sid Richardson Collection of Western Art

309 Main St; tel 817/332-6554. This one-room gallery holds a collection of Western art assembled by the late oil tycoon Sid Richardson. The two most famous artists of this 19th-century romantic movement—Frederic Remington and Charles M Russell—are represented by some 50 paintings. **Open:** Tues–Wed 10am–5pm, Thurs–Fri 10am–8pm, Sat 11am–8pm, Sun 1–5pm. **Free**

Thistle Hill

1509 Pennsylvania Ave; tel 817/336-1212. Built in 1903 and remodeled in 1910, this mansion is one of the few remaining examples of Georgian Revival architecture in the Southwest, and is listed in the National Register of Historic Places. The house was built as a wedding present from cattle baron W T Waggoner to his daughter. Original interior features of interest are the 14-foot-wide oak staircase, solid granite pillars, oak-paneled halls, massive foyer, Oriental rugs, and elegant dining room. Guided tours describe the architectural highlights, as well as family anecdotes and local history. **Open:** Mon–Fri 10am–3pm, Sun 1–4pm. **$$**

Log Cabin Village

2100 Log Cabin Village Lane; tel 817/926-5881. This living history museum, a 2½-acre site, is comprised of seven authentic log homes from the late 1800s furnished with period antiques and implements. Historical interpreters demonstrate pioneer crafts daily, including spinning, weaving, and candle-making. There is also a working grist mill. **Open:** Tues–Fri 9am–5pm, Sat 10am–5pm, Sun 1–5pm. **$**

Will Rogers Memorial Center

3400 W Lancaster St; tel 817/871-8150. Dedicated to the famous cinema cowboy and humorist, this vast exhibition center includes the Memorial Coliseum and the Will Rogers Auditorium. A mounted statue of Rogers graces the entrance of the center. Site of large concerts, rodeos, auto shows, and other Fort Worth events, as well as several major Fort Worth museums (see Amon Carter Museum, Kimbell Art Museum, Museum of Science and History). **Open:** Grounds, 8am–5pm. Call for events schedule. **Free**

Botanic Gardens

3200 Botanic Garden Dr; tel 817/871-7686. A showcase of 150,000 plants representing 2,500 species, displayed in both formal and natural settings. A 10,000-square-foot glass conservatory is planted with more than 2,500 tropical plants native to Central and South America. Small waterfalls, ponds, and pathways heighten the verisimilitude of the site. An enchanting Japanese garden features an authentic tea house. **Open:** Daily sunrise–sundown. Japanese garden open Tues–Sun 10am–4pm. Conservatory open Mon–Fri 10am–9pm, Sat–Sun 10am–4pm. **$**

Casa Mañana

3101 Lancaster; tel 817/332-2272. Texas's most famous theater-in-the-round, housed in a geodesic dome. Broadway hits, concerts, and modern theater works are presented. **$$$$**

La Buena Vida Vineyards

8917 W Jacksboro Hwy; tel 817/481-9463. Tastings and winery tours are available by appointment. Visitors center and gift shop on the property. **Open:** Mon–Sat 10am–5pm, Sun noon–5pm. **Free**

Fredericksburg

See also Kerrville

Settled by German immigrants in 1846, this charming Gillespie County seat located in central Texas Hill Country is known for its large number of historic buildings and antique shops. In August, Fredericksburg hosts the state's oldest county fair, started in 1888. Johnson City, some 30 miles east, is the birthplace and ancestral territory of former President Lyndon B Johnson. **Information:** Fredericksburg Convention & Visitors Bureau, 106 N Adams, Fredericksburg, 78624 (tel 210/997-6523).

MOTELS 🏨

▤▤ Ad Dietzel Motel

US 290 at US 87, 78624; tel 210/997-3330. A quaint little motel with German country decor, owned by a local German family. Friendly, helpful staff. **Rooms:** 75 rms. CI open/CO noon. Nonsmoking rms avail. **Amenities:** 🛁 A/C, cable TV. Continental breakfast features authentic German pastries. **Facilities:** 🛋 ⅙ **Rates (CP):** $59–$60 S; $60–$61 D. Extra person $10. Parking: Outdoor, free. AE, MC, V.

▤▤ Best Western Sunday House Inn

501 E Main, 78624; tel 210/997-4333 or toll free 800/528-1234. Off US 290. Located among the beautiful scenic hills, this facility's large rooms and friendly staff make it a good choice for a weekend visit with the family. **Rooms:** 100 rms. CI 2pm/CO noon. Nonsmoking rms avail. Colorful, newer furnishings. **Amenities:** 🛁 A/C, cable TV w/movies. Some units w/terraces. Continental breakfast on Sunday is exceptionally elaborate. **Services:** ⬱ **Facilities:** 🛋 🏊 ⅙ Whirlpool. **Rates (CP):** Peak (May–Oct) $49–$52 S; $52–$56 D. Extra person $5. Min stay wknds. Lower rates off-season. Parking: Outdoor, free. AE, DC, DISC, MC, V.

▤▤ Comfort Inn

908 S Adams St, 78624; tel 210/997-9811 or toll free 800/221-2222. Off US 290. A dependable, newish motel with Southwestern decor throughout and interesting Native American pottery in the lobby. **Rooms:** 200 rms. CI 2pm/CO noon. Nonsmoking rms avail. Rooms are large and cheerful, with white oak furnishings and nice carpeting. **Amenities:** 🛁 A/C, satel TV w/movies. Some units w/terraces. **Services:** ✕ 🛒 **Facilities:** 🛋 🏊 ⅙ **Rates (CP):** $49–$52 S; $52–$57 D. Extra person $5. Parking: Outdoor, free. AE, DC, DISC, MC, V.

RESTAURANTS 🍽

Ⓢ Altdorf Burgarten & Restaurant

301 Main; tel 210/997-7774. In town center. **German.** A historic German restaurant with folksy Bavarian decor and authentic German music playing in the background. There is a large selection of authentic German dishes. Try the "kraut 'n' wieners." **FYI:** Reservations not accepted. Folk music. Beer and wine only. No smoking. **Open:** Daily 11am–10pm. **Prices:** Main courses $6–$12. AE, DISC, MC, V. ▮ ♥ ⅙

Freideim's Bavarian Inn

905 Main; tel 210/997-6300. In town center. **German.** A family-style eatery decorated like a country tavern, featuring beer steins and other German knicknacks. Available are a wonderful selection of German beers and traditional offerings such as sausages and spaetzle. **FYI:** Reservations accepted. Children's menu. Beer and wine only. **Open:** Daily 11am–10:30pm. **Prices:** Main courses $5–$11. AE, DISC, MC, V. ⅙

★ Hill Top Cafe

US 87; tel 210/997-8922. **American.** This cafe catering to families offers basic American fare plus some Tex-Mex items.

FYI: Reservations not accepted. Children's menu. Beer and wine only. **Open:** Daily 10:30am–11:30pm. **Prices:** Main courses $5–$9. AE, DISC, MC, V. ▼

ATTRACTIONS 📷

Enchanted Rock State Natural Park

RR 965; tel 210/247-3903. This 640-acre, 500-foot-high pink granite dome is a Registered Natural Landmark. The creaking noises which emanate from it at night—likely caused by the cooling of the rock's outer surface—led the area's original Native American tribes to believe the rock was inhabited by evil spirits. A 4-mile loop trail winds through the 1,643-acre park; one trail leads to the top of the dome. Rock climbing and rappelling allowed; picnicking; primitive camping in designated areas. **Open:** Daily sunrise–sundown. **$$**

Lyndon B Johnson National Historical Park

100 E 10th St, Johnson City; tel 210/868-7128. The park is divided into two separate districts, 14 miles apart. The **Johnson City District,** located in Johnson City, includes tours of the boyhood home of President Lyndon B Johnson. Furnishings include Johnson family household items and period furniture. One block west is an old ranch complex called Johnson Settlement, owned by the President's grandfather and great-uncle from 1867 to 1872. It includes an original 1856 dog-run cabin, barn, and other buildings, as well as a visitors center, which shows movies and displays exhibits on the life of LBJ. It is from the visitors center that bus tours depart for the **LBJ Ranch District,** located 14 miles west of Johnson City (this is the only way to view the ranch). The 1½-hour tour includes the school LBJ attended at age 4, a reconstruction of his birthplace, the exterior of his Texas White House, the ranch itself (still in operation), and the Johnson family cemetery where he is buried. **Open:** Daily 9am–5pm. **$**

Bell Mountain Vineyards and Winery

TX 16; tel 210/685-3295. The winery produces an array of wines, including chardonnay, Johannisberg Riesling, gewürztraminer, fumé blanc, semillon, cabernet sauvignon, and pinot noir. Public tour and tasting on Saturday only. Picnic area on the grounds; winery store. **Open:** Mar–Dec, Sat, call for hours. **Free**

Oberhellmann Vineyards

TX 16; tel 210/685-3297. Located near Bell Mountain, this winery produces chardonnays, Rieslings, and pinot noir. Tours and complimentary tastings available. **Open:** Tours conducted Sat 11am, 1pm, and 3pm. **Free**

Gainesville

MOTEL 🏨

≡≡ Best Western Southwinds

2103 N I-35, 76240; tel 817/665-7737 or toll free 800/731-1501; fax 817/668-2651. N of US 82. A standard chain motel with dependable, affordable accommodations. **Rooms:** 35 rms. CI 4pm/CO 11am. Nonsmoking rms avail. **Amenities:** 🅱 ⚬ A/C, cable TV. **Services:** ⌂ 🖘 **Facilities:** 🔧 ⚬ **Rates (CP):** $35–$46 S or D. Extra person $4. Children under age 12 stay free. Parking: Outdoor, free. AE, CB, DC, DISC, JCB, MC, V.

Galveston

The largest city in Texas prior to a devastating hurricane in 1900, this barrier island/city 60 miles south of Houston is undergoing a revival. An array of restored buildings and landmarks recall its glory days in the 19th century, and more than 32 miles of beaches offer recreational opportunities. **Information:** Galveston Island Convention & Visitors Bureau, 2106 Seawall Blvd, Galveston, 77550 (tel 409/763-4311).

HOTELS 🏨

≡ Flagship Hotel Over the Water

2501 Seawall Blvd, 77550; tel 409/762-9000. This large, somewhat worn hotel sits on a pier in the Gulf. The views are the primary reason to stay here. **Rooms:** 150 rms. CI 3pm/CO noon. Nonsmoking rms avail. **Amenities:** 🅱 ⚬ A/C, cable TV. All units w/terraces. **Services:** 🖘 🍽 **Facilities:** 🔧 ⚬ 1 restaurant (bkfst only), washer/dryer. **Rates:** $50–$100 S or D. Extra person $10. Children under age 12 stay free. Parking: Outdoor, free. AE, CB, DC, DISC, MC, V.

≡≡ Holiday Inn on the Beach

5002 Seawall Blvd, 77551; tel 409/740-3581 or toll free 800/465-4329. Near 50th St. A large oceanfront property, with all rooms facing the Gulf. A great place for families wanting proximity to the beach. **Rooms:** 180 rms and stes. CI 4pm/CO noon. Nonsmoking rms avail. Rooms are large, clean, and comfortable. **Amenities:** 🅱 ⚬ A/C, cable TV. All units w/terraces. **Services:** ✕ ⌂ 🖘 **Facilities:** 🔧 🏋 🐾 ⚬ 1 restaurant, 1 bar (w/entertainment), sauna, whirlpool, washer/dryer. **Rates:** Peak (June–Aug) $55–$124 S or D; $395 ste. Extra person $5. Children under age 18 stay free. Lower rates off-season. Parking: Outdoor, free. AE, CB, DC, DISC, JCB, MC, V.

≡≡≡ Hotel Galvez

2024 Seawall Blvd, 77550; tel 409/765-7721 or toll free 800/392-4285. At 21st St. With its circular drive, large courtyard, and rows of palm trees, this mammoth cream-colored hotel with red Spanish-style roof looks like a grand, tropical estate.

Great for couples and special occasions, this hotel combines old-world luxury with spectacular views of the Gulf. **Rooms:** 228 rms and stes. CI 3pm/CO noon. Nonsmoking rms avail. **Amenities:** 🏧 🐧 A/C, cable TV w/movies. Some units w/terraces. **Services:** ✗ 🆅🅿 🛆 🖵 Babysitting. Afternoon snacks, cocktails, and cordials available in the veranda restaurant. **Facilities:** 🗗 🛏300 🕭 1 restaurant, 1 bar (w/entertainment). Pool has a "swim-up" bar. Guests have membership privileges at the Galveston Country Club. **Rates:** $105–$135 S or D; $175–$350 ste. Extra person $10. Children under age 18 stay free. Parking: Indoor/outdoor, free. AE, CB, DC, DISC, MC, V.

🏨🏨🏨 San Luis Resort & Conference Center

5222 Seawall Blvd, 77551; tel 409/744-1500 or toll free 800/445-0090; fax 409/744-8452. E of 61st St. A large hotel with great facilities, overlooking the Gulf and located in the center of Galveston. The adjoining multimillion dollar conference center and a convenient location near the Moody Center make this a perfect stop for the business traveler or conventioneer. **Rooms:** 244 rms and stes. Executive level. CI 3pm/CO noon. Nonsmoking rms avail. **Amenities:** 🏧 🐧 🖭 🗐 A/C, cable TV w/movies. All units w/terraces. **Services:** ✗ 🛆 🖵 **Facilities:** 🗗 🏊 🔱 🛏1000 🕭 1 restaurant, 1 bar, whirlpool, washer/dryer. **Rates:** $90–$149 S; $100–$159 D; $129–$300 ste. Extra person $10. Children under age 12 stay free. Parking: Outdoor, free. AE, CB, DC, MC, V.

🏨🏨🏨🏨 The Tremont House

2300 Ship's Mechanic Row, 77550 (Strand Historical District); tel 409/763-0300 or toll free 800/874-2300; fax 409/480-8201. Between 23rd and 24th Sts. An elegant hotel with European ambience. The visitor's first impression is of a luxurious four-story atrium and live palm trees in the lobby. The Tremont is located in the Strand Historical District with many specialty shops nearby. Great for a romantic getaway. **Rooms:** 117 rms and stes. CI 3pm/CO noon. Nonsmoking rms avail. Rooms are decorated in period furniture. The living area has hardwood floors, and the bathrooms are covered in Italian tile. High ceilings and floor-to-ceiling windows give rooms an open, airy feel. **Amenities:** 🏧 🐧 🖭 🗐 A/C, cable TV w/movies, bathrobes. Some units w/terraces. **Services:** ✗ 🖛 🆅🅿 🛆 🖵 Guests have membership privileges at the Galveston Country Club. **Facilities:** 🛏350 🕭 6 restaurants, 1 bar. Rooftop terrace has a spectacular view. **Rates:** $130–$175 S or D; $250–$350 ste. Extra person $15. Children under age 18 stay free. Parking: Indoor/outdoor, $6/day. AE, CB, DC, DISC, MC, V.

MOTELS

🏨🏨 Casa Del Mar

6102 Seawall Blvd, 77551; tel 409/740-2431 or toll free 800/392-1205. At 61st St. The chief attraction at this all-suite motel is the spectacular view of the Gulf. The building consists of two wings, and all rooms face the beach. **Rooms:** 180 stes. CI 3pm/CO noon. Nonsmoking rms avail. All the rooms have balconies, fully furnished kitchens, and sofa-sleepers. **Amenities:** 🏧 🐧 🖭 A/C, cable TV w/movies, refrig, voice mail. All units w/terraces. **Services:** 🖵 **Facilities:** 🖼 Washer/dryer. **Rates:** Peak (Mar 10–Aug 31) $59–$124 ste. Extra person $5. Children under age 12 stay free. Min stay special events. Lower rates off-season. Parking: Indoor/outdoor, free. AE, CB, DC, DISC, MC, V.

🏨🏨 The Commodore on the Beach

3618 Seawall Blvd, PO Box N, Galveston Island, 77552; tel 409/763-2375 or toll free 800/231-9921; fax 409/763-2379. At 37th St. With the atmosphere of a small country inn, this family-owned motel offers clean, comfortable accommodations and friendly service. Built in a large arc, so that most of the rooms face the ocean. **Rooms:** 90 rms. CI 3pm/CO noon. Nonsmoking rms avail. Rooms have brick walls and a nautical motif and feature tasteful art. **Amenities:** 🏧 🐧 A/C, cable TV. All units w/terraces. **Services:** 🛆 🖵 Complimentary morning newspaper and coffee or tea available in lobby. **Facilities:** 🗗 🕭 Coffee shop located on the premises. **Rates (CP):** Peak (June–Labor Day) $55–$99 S or D. Extra person $6. Children under age 12 stay free. Min stay wknds. Lower rates off-season. Parking: Outdoor, free. Special rates avail for Mardi Gras and the Dickens festival. AE, CB, DC, DISC, MC, V.

🏨 Hilltop Motel

8828 Seawall Blvd, 77551; tel 409/744-4423. At 88th St. A simple motel with comfortable, clean accommodations and a great view of the Gulf. **Rooms:** 40 rms. CI 3pm/CO 11am. Nonsmoking rms avail. **Amenities:** 🏧 🐧 A/C, cable TV. **Services:** 🖵 🖵 **Facilities:** 🗗 🕭 1 restaurant. **Rates:** $35–$55 S or D. Extra person $5. Children under age 12 stay free. Parking: Outdoor, free. AE, CB, DC, DISC, MC, V.

🏨🏨 La Quinta Inn Galveston

1402 Seawall Blvd, 78550; tel 409/763-1224 or toll free 800/531-5900; fax 409/765-8663. At 14th St. These simple, dependable accommodations would be a great option for the vacationing family or couple on a budget. **Rooms:** 117 rms. CI 3pm/CO 11am. Nonsmoking rms avail. Some rooms have Gulf views. **Amenities:** 🏧 🐧 A/C, satel TV w/movies. **Services:** 🛆 🖵 🖵 **Facilities:** 🗗 🛏30 🕭 **Rates (CP):** $49–$99 S; $56–$99 D. Extra person $7–$10. Children under age 18 stay free. Parking: Outdoor, free. AE, CB, DC, DISC, MC, V.

🏨🏨🏨 The Victorian Condo Hotel

6300 Seawall Blvd, 77551; tel 409/740-3555 or toll free 800/231-6363; fax 409/744-3801. Near 61st St. These spacious condominium units feature exquisite Victorian architecture, comfortable quarters, and great views of the coast. Perfect for families and couples on vacation, it is very near many recreational facilities. **Rooms:** 200 stes. CI 4pm/CO noon. Nonsmoking rms avail. **Amenities:** 🏧 🐧 🖭 A/C, cable TV w/movies, refrig, in-rm safe. All units w/terraces. **Services:** ✗ 🛆 🖵 Grocery shopping service available; picnic lunches can be arranged. **Facilities:** 🗗 🏐3 🛏150 🕭 Basketball, whirlpool, playground, washer/dryer. Barbecue/picnic area. **Rates:** Peak (May–Sept) $149–$199 ste. Lower rates off-season. Parking: Outdoor, free. AE, CB, DC, DISC, MC, V.

RESTAURANTS 🍴

Benno's on the Beach
1200 Seawall; tel 409/762-5950. At 12th. **Seafood.** A very casual beachfront restaurant. A miniature lighthouse in front guides guests to outdoor seating overlooking the beach. Seafood selections include crab, shrimp, oyster loaf, gumbo, snapper, and flounder. **FYI:** Reservations not accepted. Beer and wine only. **Open:** Sun–Thurs 11am–10pm, Fri–Sat 11am–11pm. **Prices:** Main courses $3–$11. AE, DISC, MC, V. 🏞 &

Casey's Seafood Cafe
38th and Beach; tel 409/762-9625. **Seafood.** Casual seafood restaurant operated by the locally well-known Guido family. Extensive menu. **FYI:** Reservations not accepted. Children's menu. Beer and wine only. **Open:** Sun–Thurs 11am–8:30pm, Fri 11am–9:30pm. **Prices:** Main courses $5–$16. AE, CB, DC, DISC, MC, V. &

Clary's
8509 Teichman; tel 409/740-0771. Just off I-45. **Seafood.** All types of fresh seafood are offered in this homey, cream-colored, tastefully decorated restaurant. Its glass garden room overlooks the bayou. Desserts—especially the cheesecake—are very good. **FYI:** Reservations accepted. **Open:** Lunch Tues–Fri 11:30am–2:30pm; dinner Tues–Fri 5:30–10pm, Sat 5–10pm, Sun noon–9pm. **Prices:** Main courses $13–$20. AE, CB, DC, DISC, MC, V. &

Gaido's of Galveston
3828 Seawall Blvd; tel 409/762-9625. At 38th. **Seafood.** Overlooking the beach, this elegant, old-time establishment is a step above other beachfront restaurants. The Gulf seafood is very good. Great for a family dinner. **FYI:** Reservations not accepted. Children's menu. Dress code. **Open:** Peak (June–Aug) Sun–Thurs 11:45am–9:30pm, Fri–Sat 11:45am–10:30pm. **Prices:** Main courses $11–$17. AE, DISC, MC, V. 🏞 &

The Wentletrap
In T Jeff League Building, 1871 the Strand at Tremont (Strand Historical District); tel 409/765-5545. Between 23rd and 24th. **Continental.** Located in the center of the Strand tourist district, this elegant, formal establishment features a three-story atrium that provides a bright, open atmosphere. An enormous, beautiful staircase leads down from the entrance and shops to the dining area. Enjoy expertly prepared seafood, lamb, beef, veal, and chicken. Large buffet. **FYI:** Reservations accepted. Piano. Dress code. **Open:** Lunch daily 11:30am–2:30pm; dinner daily 6–10pm. **Prices:** Main courses $15–$30. AE, CB, DC, DISC, MC, V. 🆅🅿 &

ATTRACTIONS 🏛

Galveston County Historical Museum
2219 Market St; tel 409/766-2340. Scenes from Galveston's past come alive at this museum, situated in a 1919 bank building that boasts an impressive interior. Of special interest are exhibits on the works of Nicholas Clayton, architect of numerous Galveston landmarks, Gulf coast lighthouse and lightships. Audio-visual presentation on the 1900 hurricane, as well as a wide range of displays on the city's history. **Open:** Mon–Sat 10am–4pm, Sun noon–4pm. **Free**

Lone Star Flight Museum
2002 Terminal Dr; tel 281/480-7722. The golden age of aviation is recalled by the presence of more than 34 vintage aircraft, from a meticulously restored B-177 Flying Fortress and "razorback" P-47 Thunderbolt, to a P-38 Lightning, a Spitfire, and other bombers, trainers, and wartime "executive" aircraft, all in flying condition. The Conoco Hall of Power showcases historic engines, photos, air combat memorabilia, and wartime vehicles. **Open:** Daily 10am–5pm. $$$

The Moody Mansion and Museum
2628 Broadway Dr; tel 409/762-7668. This 1892 mansion, the former home and center of the business empire of Texas entrepreneur W L Moody Jr from 1900 to 1954, exemplifies transitional Victorian architecture. The opulent structure has a steel frame, with red brick, Texas limestone, and terra cotta tile; the interior boasts stained glass, custom-designed carved woods, fancy plaster and tile work, and stencils in 42 rooms covering 28,000 square feet. The collection includes antiques, silver, photographs, and other works of art. Tours available; gift shop and restaurant. **Open:** Tues–Sat 10am–4pm, Sun 1–4:30pm. $$$

The Great Storm
Pier 21; tel 409/763-8808. The 1900 hurricane that struck Galveston was a turning point in the city's history—the storm is still listed as one of the worst natural disasters in American history—killing over 6,000 people and eviscerating whole sections along the Gulf. The Pier 21 Theater presents a panoramic, multi-image documentary that re-creates this tumultuous event, and narrates the city's efforts to rebuild itself and safeguard against future hurricanes. Shows begin on the hour and last about 30 minutes. **Open:** Sun–Thurs 11am–6pm, Fri–Sat 11am–8pm. $$

Texas Seaport Museum
Pier 21; tel 409/763-1877. A museum which chronicles the Galveston seaport and marine technology in the nineteenth century, located on the restored *Elissa*, a square-rigged, 400-ton barkentine built in Scotland in 1877. Among the displays housed aboard this National Historic Landmark are a series of walk-through exhibits evoking 19th-century port business, including a bank, union hall, and boarding house for sailors; an interactive scale model of the port; a computer database containing the names of more than 130,000 immigrants who entered the United States through Galveston, accompanied

by exhibits on the immigrant experience; and exhibits on the physics of sailing. Multimedia presentations about the *Elissa* and maritime legends; self-guided tours of the ship's deck hold and officers' quarters. **Open:** Daily 10am–5pm. **$$**

Mardi Gras Museum

2211 Strand, 3rd Floor; tel 409/763-1133. This museum celebrates Galveston's carnival tradition, which dates to 1867. Three galleries of colorful exhibits showcase a collection of historic costumes, elaborate masks, crowns and scepters, and other Galveston Mardi Gras memorabilia. **Open:** Wed–Sun noon–6pm. **$**

Galveston Island State Park

13 Mile Rd; tel 409/737-1222. Spanning Galveston Island from gulf to bay, the 1,935-acre park boasts salt marshes, bayous, tidal flats, coastal dunes, and a 1½-mile beach on the gulf side. Activities include fishing, swimming, hiking (4 miles of nature trails), and bird-watching. There are campsites with hookups, screened shelters, picnic sites, rest rooms, and showers. The Mary Moody Northern Amphitheater presents outdoor musicals nightly from early June through late August. **Open:** Daily sunrise–sundown. **$$$**

Moody Gardens

1 Hope Blvd; tel 409/744-4673 or toll free 800/582-4673. A multifaceted 142-acre project put forth by the Moody Foundation. The 10-story glass Rainforest Pyramid allows visitors to experience the rain forests of Asia, Africa, and the Americas. A Japanese garden, more than 2,000 species of plants, animals, tropical fish, and butterflies, and an acre of natural wonders; a waterfall, cliffs, caverns, and a Mayan colonnade can be found here. Palm Beach, Texas's only white sand beach, offers freshwater swimming lagoons, whirlpools, volleyball, and paddleboats. Seaside Safari offers guided tours introducing a variety of animals and crystal and mineral displays in a garden setting. IMAX theater, several restaurants, gift shop. **Open:** Peak (Mar–Oct) daily 10am–9pm. Reduced hours off-season. **$$$$**

1859 Ashton Villa

2328 Broadway; tel 409/762-3933. Museum featuring antebellum and Victorian items and furnishings, located in a restored Italianate mansion from 1859. The house was the social center of the city through the end of the 19th century, and an emblem of a period during which Galveston was a thriving seaport city. The museum features antiques, original artwork, and heirlooms from the family of James Moreau Brown, the original builder and owner of the mansion. The ornate dining room, palatial Gold Room, and elegant family quarters represent Gilded Age opulence. Tours include an audio-visual presentation on the 1900 hurricane and the construction of the city's sea wall. The villa is listed in the National Register of Historic Places. **Open:** Mon–Sat 10am–4pm, Sun noon–4pm. **$$**

The Grand 1894 Opera House

2020 Postoffice St; tel 409/765-1894 or toll free 800/821-1894. A historic theater (designated the official Opera House of the State of Texas by the 73rd legislature) where distinguished artists such as Sarah Bernhardt, Paderewski, and Anna Pavlova performed, and where popular music, dance, and theater presentations continue to be showcased. Recently, musicals such as *Crazy for You* and *Gigi* have been presented here. Other notables who have appeared here during the theater's history include John Philip Sousa, the Marx Brothers, George Burns and Gracie Allen, Sarah Vaughan, Ray Charles, and Lionel Hampton. The restored theater features double-curved balconies, and there is no seat farther than 70 feet from the stage, which was once the largest in the state. Open for self-guided tours. **Open:** Contact box office for info on self–guided tours. **$**

Georgetown

Georgetown was established in 1848 as a farming community and became a staging area for cattle drives north on the Chisholm Trail. Located a short drive north of Austin, the city is known for its Victorian courthouse and downtown. **Information:** Georgetown Chamber of Commerce, 100 Stadium Dr, PO Box 346, Georgetown, 78627-0346 (tel 512/930-3535).

HOTEL

Ramada Inn Georgetown

333 N I-35, 78628; tel 512/869-2541 or toll free 800/726-2321. Located in a lovely, scenic location near the river, it's perfect for guests who would rather enjoy the Texas frontier in style and comfort. **Rooms:** 240 rms and stes. Executive level. CI 2pm/CO noon. Nonsmoking rms avail. **Amenities:** A/C, cable TV. Some units w/terraces. **Services:** Social director. **Facilities:** 1 restaurant, 1 bar (w/entertainment), whirlpool. **Rates (CP):** Peak (Apr–July) $59–$65 S; $65–$69 D; $70–$79 ste. Extra person $5. Min stay peak. Lower rates off-season. MAP rates avail. Parking: Outdoor, free. AE, DC, DISC, MC, V.

ATTRACTION

Inner Space Cavern

4200 I-35 S; tel 512/863-5545. Unique formations of stalactites and stalagmites, enhanced by light-and-sound shows, can be viewed at this cave, over 80,000 years in the making (relatively young, by Texas cavern standards). Remains of prehistoric mastadons, dire wolves, and other Ice Age animals are also featured. The 1¼-hour tour begins with a ride on a unique cable car down into the cavern; average temperature is 72°F. Gift shop on premises. **Open:** Mem Day–Labor Day, daily 9am–6pm. Reduced hours off-season. **$$$**

Goliad

For lodgings, see Victoria

ATTRACTIONS 🖼

Goliad State Historical Park
US 183; tel 512/645-3405. This 178-acre park commemorates the Texans slain at the Battle of Goliad and is home to the restored Mission Nuestra Senora del Espiritu Santo de Zuniga, generally called Mission Espiritu Santo. This mission was established in 1749 to convert local tribes. Park headquarters offer multimedia presentations and hold displays of colonial and Aranama artifacts. A nature trail winds through a wide range of indigenous flora, such as yucca, prickly pear cactus, bluewood, and blackbrush acacia, and another trail meanders along the San Antonio River. Camping areas, RV hookups available. **Open:** Daily 8am–5pm. **$**

Presidio La Bahia
TX 183; tel 512/645-3752. Established in 1749 to protect Mission Espiritu Santo de Zuniga, this was one of the more important forts on the Spanish frontiers, and is perhaps the finest known example of a complete Spanish presidio, fully restored. Its chapel is still in regular use for religious services. It was here that Col James Fannin's men, during the 1836 Texas Revolution, were imprisoned and massacred, an infamous event in Texas history. A museum houses memorabilia of the Texas Revolution as well as artifacts indicating nine levels of civilization at the site. A living history program recreates various events in the fort's history. **Open:** Daily 9am–4:45pm. **$**

Granbury

A growing tourist town on the shores of Lake Granbury, this Hood County seat has restored its courthouse square to its original 19th-century appearance. The nearby lake offers water recreation and camping. **Information:** Lake Granbury Area Chamber of Commerce, 208 N Crockett St, PO Box 277, Granbury, 76048 (tel 817/573-1622).

MOTEL 🏨

≣≣ Best Western Classic Inn
1209 N Plaza Dr (US 377 Bypass), 76048; tel 817/573-8874 or toll free 800/528-1234; fax 817/573-8874. Near jct US 377 Business. Standard, no-nonsense motel offering only the basics: central location, dependable rooms, and friendly service. **Rooms:** 42 rms. CI 4pm/CO noon. Nonsmoking rms avail. **Amenities:** 🛁 ⚬ 🍴 A/C, cable TV w/movies, refrig. **Services:** 🛏 ⌂ 🦽 **Facilities:** 🚗🅿️ 🏋️ 🕹 1 bar. **Rates (CP):** $39–$66 S or D. Extra person $5. Children under age 12 stay free. Parking: Outdoor, free. AE, CB, DC, DISC, ER, JCB, MC, V.

LODGE

≣≣≣ The Lodge of Granbury
400 E Pearl, 76048; tel 817/573-2606 or toll free 800/551-6388; fax 817/573-7662. On US 377 Business. This lakeside lodge has so many recreational opportunities, you may think you're staying at a resort. Though it caters to businesses and corporate conferences, this is a great place for families. **Rooms:** 51 stes. CI 3pm/CO noon. Nonsmoking rms avail. **Amenities:** 🛁 ⚬ 📺 A/C, cable TV w/movies, refrig. Some units w/terraces, some w/fireplaces. **Services:** ✕ 🛏 ⌂ 🦽 **Facilities:** 🚗🅿️ 🏊 🍴🍷 🏋️ 🏊100 ♿ 1 restaurant, 1 bar (w/entertainment), volleyball, whirlpool. Boat slips for private docking, tropical cabana bar. The *Brazos Belle* riverboat is available for parties and receptions. **Rates (CP):** $89–$149 ste. Extra person $10. Children under age 18 stay free. Parking: Outdoor, free. AE, CB, DC, DISC, MC, V.

RESTAURANTS 🍴

Cuckoo's Nest Restaurant
110 Pearl; tel 817/573-9722. In town square. **Eclectic.** Housed in an old stone building in the historic town square, this quaint small-town diner is decorated with old town memorabilia and various knickknacks. Specialties are steaks and burgers. **FYI:** Reservations accepted. Children's menu. **Open:** Tues–Sun 11:30am–9pm. **Prices:** Main courses $6–$14. AE, CB, DC, DISC, MC, V.

The Nutt House
E Bridge and Crockett; tel 817/573-9362. **American.** Located in the historic town square. Great for family dining, the restaurant offers a home-style buffet, delicious pies and cobblers, and many vegetable dishes. **FYI:** Reservations accepted. Children's menu. No liquor license. No smoking. **Open:** Lunch Tues–Fri 11:30am–2pm, Sat–Sun 11:30am–3pm; dinner Fri–Sat 6–8pm. **Prices:** Main courses $6–$8. AE, CB, DC, DISC, MC, V. ♿

Grand Prairie

See Arlington

Grapevine

See Dallas–Fort Worth Int'l Airport

Greenville

Located northeast of the Dallas metroplex on I-30, this thriving community of business and manufacturing was once known as the "Cotton Capital of Texas." Lake Tawakoni, south of town, offers complete recreational facilities.

Information: Greenville Chamber of Commerce, 2713 Stonewall, PO Box 1055, Greenville, 75403-1055 (tel 903/455-1510).

MOTEL

≣≣ Best Western Inn and Suites

1216 I-30 W, 75401; tel 903/454-1792 or toll free 800/795-2300; fax 903/454-1792. Exit 94B off I-30. Clean, basic, well-maintained motel. **Rooms:** 99 rms and stes. CI noon/CO noon. Nonsmoking rms avail. King rooms have recliners. **Amenities:** A/C, cable TV. King rooms have mini-refrigerators. Microwaves available for extra charge. **Services:** **Facilities:** 1 restaurant, 1 bar, washer/dryer. **Rates:** $40 S; $45 D; $57 ste. Extra person $4. Children under age 12 stay free. Parking: Outdoor, free. Military, senior, and trucker discounts avail. AE, CB, DC, DISC, MC, V.

RESTAURANT

The Spare Rib

7818 Wesley; tel 903/455-0219. On TX 34 S. **Barbecue.** A family-operated business for more than 45 years. The walls of this very casual dining room (which is not air conditioned) are covered with artwork depicting African-American religious and country life as well as famous figures like Martin Luther King, Jr. Customers can see the huge smokers where the beef, pork, chicken, and turkey are slow-cooked. **FYI:** Reservations not accepted. No liquor license. **Open:** Tues–Sat 11am–7:30pm, Sun–Mon 11am–5pm. **Prices:** Main courses $2–$5. AE, DISC, MC, V.

Guadalupe Mountains National Park

For lodgings and dining, see El Paso, Van Horn

Over 86,000 acres of rugged, remote wilderness encompassing the plains of the Chihuahuan Desert and the Guadalupe Mountains, including 8,749-foot Guadalupe Peak, the highest elevation point in Texas. Over 100 miles from El Paso, the Guadalupe Mountains stand like an island in the desert. The most prominent feature of the 86,416-acre park is El Capitan, a sheer, 1,000-foot, whitish-colored cliff. Here also is one of the world's most extensive and significant fossil reefs, dating from the Permian period, between 230 and 280 million years ago.

Other features of the park are its deep canyons and rare mixture of plant and animal life. **McKittrick Canyon** has been described as "the most beautiful spot in Texas." Forests of ponderosa pines mingle with aspens, maples, mountain junipers, and madronas. Abundant deer and elk graze upland meadows. The barren outer mountain slopes belie a wooded, game-rich interior of great scenic beauty. Most access to the

park's rugged interior is by hiking and backpack camping along 80 miles of marked trails. The National Park Service advises that only experienced, well-equipped backpackers should enter the primitive back country for extended stays. The park's visitors center offers rest rooms, drinking water, brochures, books, trail guides, exhibits, and maps; a slide show focuses on the park wilderness. A self-guided, two-mile hike to Smith and Manzanita Springs can be made at any time. Permits are required for overnight trips and camping is allowed in designated areas only. No overnight facilities in the park. For more information, contact Superintendent, Guadalupe Mountains National Park, HC60, Box 400, Salt Flat, 79847 (tel 915/828-3251).

Harlingen

This south Texas community, chartered in 1903, serves as a major agricultural center for the Rio Grande Valley region. Flaming bougainvillea and palm trees mark the landscape in this subtropical climate. The Laguna Atascosa National Wildlife Refuge provides a safe haven for waterfowl and other birds migrating between Canada and the Gulf. **Information:** Harlingen Area Chamber of Commerce, 311 E Tyler, PO Box 189, Harlingen, 78551 (tel 210/423-5440).

HOTEL

≣≣ Sun Valley Motor Hotel

1900 S 77 Sunshine Strip, 78550; tel 210/423-7222. Ed Carey Dr exit off US 77 S. Clean and attractive lodgings in the center of town offering guests the kind of personal attention not generally available at chain properties. **Rooms:** 75 rms. CI open/CO noon. Nonsmoking rms avail. Rooms are large and clean but furnishings are a little worn. **Amenities:** A/C, cable TV, refrig. **Facilities:** **Rates (CP):** $49–$52 S; $52–$55 D. Extra person $5. Parking: Outdoor, free. AE, DC, DISC, MC, V.

MOTEL

≣≣ Hudson House Motel

500 Ed Carey Dr, 78550; tel 210/428-8911. Off US 77S. An independently owned motel on the outskirts of town that is extremely affordable and clean. **Rooms:** 65 rms. CI open/CO noon. Nonsmoking rms avail. **Amenities:** A/C, cable TV. **Facilities:** **Rates:** $39 S; $49 D. Extra person $10. Parking: Outdoor, free. AE, MC, V.

Henderson

HOTEL

≣≣ Best Western Inn

1500 US 259 S, 75652; tel 903/657-9561 or toll free 800/528-1234; fax 903/657-9183. US 259 exit off I-20. Provides a decent place to spend the night, but not much more. **Rooms:** 80 rms. CI 4pm/CO noon. Nonsmoking rms avail. **Amenities:** 🛎 A/C, cable TV. **Services:** 🐾 Kennels located on property. **Facilities:** 🏊 🍴175 ♿ 1 restaurant (bkfst only). **Rates:** $44 S; $48 D. Extra person $5. Children under age 18 stay free. Parking: Outdoor, free. AE, CB, DC, DISC, JCB, MC, V.

Hereford

Named for the cattle breed—some three million cattle move through its feedlots annually—this Panhandle town is surrounded by some of the richest agricultural land in the state. Southwest of Amarillo via US 60, Hereford is the Deaf Smith County seat. **Information:** Deaf Smith County Chamber of Commerce, 701 N Main, PO Box 192, Hereford, 79045 (tel 806/364-3333).

MOTEL 🏨

🚻🚻 **Best Western Red Carpet Inn**
830 W 1st St, 79045; tel 806/364-0540 or toll free 800/433-7234; fax 806/364-0540. Located at the junction of US 60 and US 385, south of town. Though somewhat worn, this budget hotel offers probably the best accommodations in Hereford. **Rooms:** 90 rms, stes, and effic. CI 2pm/CO noon. Nonsmoking rms avail. Rooms are spacious and clean. **Amenities:** 🛎 A/C, cable TV w/movies. **Services:** 🐾 **Facilities:** 🏊 **Rates:** $40–$44 S; $46 D. Extra person $4. Children under age 12 stay free. Parking: Outdoor, free. AE, CB, DC, DISC, MC, V.

ATTRACTIONS 🏛

Deaf Smith County Historical Museum
400 Sampson St; tel 806/364-4338. Exhibits depict pioneer life in this region in the early 1900s and include a chapel, a general store, a schoolroom, and a unique hand-carved three-ring circus. A Santa Fe caboose is on exhibition in the rear yard, as well as a genuine Aermotor windmill, a reconstructed dugout, and early-day farm implements. Built in 1909, the building is listed in the National Register of Historic Places. **Open:** Mon–Sat 10am–5pm. **Free**

National Cowgirl Hall of Fame
515 Avenue B; tel 806/364-5252. The 6,000-square-foot museum houses exhibits honoring the pioneer spirit of Western women and great women of rodeo. Cowgirl memorabilia such as saddles, tack, trophies, historical and modern photos, paintings, and sculpture. The center sponsors the nation's largest all-girl rodeo in late summer. Rotating exhibits of Western art; research library. **Open:** Mon–Fri 9am–5pm. **$**

Hillsboro

See Waco

Houston

The seat of Harris County, Houston is the largest city in Texas and the fourth-largest in population in the country. The city was founded as a real estate venture in 1836 and named for Gen Sam Houston, the leader of Texas's successful fight for independence from Mexico that same year. Fully recovered from a recession in the 1980s, Houston is home to a major branch of America's space program, as well as internationally known universities, museums, ballet company, and symphony that make it a culturally diverse city. A 50-mile-long ship channel links this inland city with the Gulf of Mexico, making it the third-largest seaport in the United States. **Information:** Greater Houston Convention & Visitors Bureau, 801 Congress Ave, Houston, 77002 (tel 713/227-3100).

PUBLIC TRANSPORTATION

The **Metropolitan Transportation Authority (MTA)** operates citywide bus service. Stops are indicated by red, white, or blue signs. Standard fare for the local is $1; the express costs $1.50. Senior and disabled riders pay 40¢; children under 4 ride free. The **Texas Special Red, White, and Blue** is a route that services the downtown area only. Fare is 25¢. Call 713/635-4000 for more information.

HOTELS 🏨

🚻🚻🚻 **Adam's Mark**
2900 Briarpark Dr at Westheimer, 77042; tel 713/978-7400 or toll free 800/444-ADAM; fax 713/735-2727. Near Beltway 8. Extravagant, large hotel in a predominantly residential area. The main feature is the 10-story atrium, on the ground level of which are shops and restaurants. The spacious lobby is often bustling with business types and conventioneers. **Rooms:** 604 rms and stes. Executive level. CI 3pm/CO noon. Nonsmoking rms avail. **Amenities:** 🛎 🗄 📷 A/C, cable TV w/movies. Some units w/minibars, some w/terraces, 1 w/whirlpool. **Services:** 🍽 🛎 🚐 🧺 🐾 Car-rental desk, babysitting. Language interpreters are available. **Facilities:** 🏊 🎾 🍴4500 💻 ♿ 1 restaurant, 2 bars (1 w/entertainment), games rm, spa, sauna, whirlpool, beauty salon, day-care ctr. **Rates:** $125–$175 S or D; $195 ste. Extra person $15. Children under age 18 stay free. Parking: Indoor/outdoor, free. AE, CB, DC, DISC, MC, V.

🚻🚻🚻 **DoubleTree Guest Suites Houston**
5353 Westheimer Rd, 77056 (Galleria); tel 713/961-9000 or toll free 800/222-TREE. Near Sage. Posh high-rise offering plush accommodations. Near major interstates and Galleria Mall. **Rooms:** 335 stes. CI 3pm/CO noon. Nonsmoking rms avail. **Amenities:** 🛎 🗄 📷 A/C, cable TV w/movies, refrig,

dataport, voice mail. Some units w/terraces. **Services:** [○] [VP] [⊠] [↵] [◁] Car-rental desk. Free tea and coffee offered daily. **Facilities:** [↗] [⛳] [200] [♿] 1 restaurant, 1 bar, whirlpool, washer/dryer. Convenience store on site. **Rates:** $189–$289 ste. Extra person $10. Children under age 18 stay free. Parking: Indoor/outdoor, $8/day. AE, CB, DC, DISC, MC, V.

≣≣≣ DoubleTree Houston at Allen Center

400 Dallas St, 77002 (Downtown); tel 713/759-0202 or toll free 800/222-TREE; fax 713/759-1166. At Bagby, near I-45. A very business-oriented hotel with access to an underground pedestrian system that connects to most area office buildings. Staff is very accommodating. **Rooms:** 341 rms and stes. CI 3pm/CO noon. Nonsmoking rms avail. **Amenities:** [📺] [⚷] A/C, cable TV w/movies. **Services:** [○] [VP] [🚐] [⊠] [↵] [◁] Babysitting. Freshly baked chocolate chip cookies available on arrival. **Facilities:** [⛳] [250] [♿] 2 restaurants, 1 bar (w/entertainment). **Rates:** $139–$159 S; $159–$179 D; $225–$675 ste. Extra person $20. Children under age 18 stay free. Parking: Indoor, $11/day. AE, CB, DC, DISC, MC, V.

≣≣ Drury Inn Houston Galleria

1615 W Loop St, 77027; tel 713/963-0700 or toll free 800/325-8300. E side of I-610, S of I-10. A large atrium lobby gives the entrance an elegant, fresh atmosphere. Near the Galleria Mall. **Rooms:** 134 rms. CI 3pm/CO noon. Nonsmoking rms avail. **Amenities:** [📺] [⚷] A/C, cable TV w/movies. **Services:** [⊠] [↵] Complimentary evening cocktails Mon–Thurs. **Facilities:** [⛳] [45] [♿] Whirlpool. **Rates (CP):** $68–$88 S or D. Extra person $10. Children under age 18 stay free. Parking: Outdoor, free. AE, CB, DC, DISC, MC, V.

≣≣≣≣≣ Four Seasons Hotel Houston Center

1300 Lamar St, 77010 (Downtown); tel 713/650-1300 or toll free 800/332-3442; fax 713/650-8169. Across from Houston Center, near Convention Center. Twenty floors of stylish, efficient, soothing luxury. Spacious, marble-clad lobby with low coffered ceiling displays original art, including collection of bronze statuettes of baseball and hockey players. Grand, skylit atrium/staircase to restaurants and meeting rooms. **Rooms:** 399 rms and stes. CI 3pm/CO 1pm. Nonsmoking rms avail. Rooms are designed for traveling executives, with just about everything where it should be—full size desk/dresser with telephone and proper chair, armchairs in bay window. Cabana-style Poolside Rooms feature sliding glass doors opening directly to pool terrace; Four Seasons Rooms have separate parlors. **Amenities:** [📺] [⚷] [🍷] A/C, cable TV w/movies, dataport, voice mail, bathrobes. All units w/minibars, some w/whirlpools. Elevated, air-conditioned walkway to Houston Center indoor shopping mart. **Services:** [○] [🍴] [VP] [⊠] [↵] [◁] Twice-daily maid svce, car-rental desk, children's program, babysitting. 24-hour concierge. Town car for complimentary transfers to downtown locations. Poolside room service. **Facilities:** [⛳] [⛳] [800] [♿] 3 restaurants (see "Restaurants" below), 2 bars (1 w/entertainment), sauna, whirlpool, beauty salon. Two bright, airy dining rooms on

third floor with floor-to-ceiling windows. Terrace lap pool with pergolas and ferns, palm and lime trees. Fitness center and indoor whirlpool open 24 hours (attended 6am–11pm). Guest privileges at local athletic club (reached via air-conditioned walkway). **Rates:** $190–$220 S; $220–$250 D; $240–$1,175 ste. Extra person $25. Children under age 18 stay free. Parking: Indoor, $14/day. Outstanding weekend city cultural packages (opera, ballet, theater). AE, CB, DC, ER, JCB, MC, V.

≣≣≣ Harvey Suites Houston Medical Center

6800 Main St, 77030 (Texas Medical Center); tel 713/528-7744 or toll free 800/922-9222; fax 713/528-6983. Near Holcombe. A good option for longer stays. Elegant decor; friendly, attentive staff. **Rooms:** 294 rms and stes. Executive level. CI 3pm/CO 1pm. Nonsmoking rms avail. **Amenities:** [📺] [⚷] [📺] [🍷] A/C, satel TV w/movies, dataport, voice mail, in-rm safe. **Services:** [✕] [🍴] [🚐] [⊠] [↵] Twice-daily maid svce, car-rental desk, masseur. Free shuttle to medical center, Astrodome, and Galleria shopping. Personal grocery service and multilingual guest services. **Facilities:** [⛳] [🏊] [⛳] [75] [♿] 1 restaurant, 1 bar, washer/dryer. Travel agency. **Rates:** $85–$200 S or D; $85–$200 ste. Children under age 19 stay free. Parking: Outdoor, free. Medical rates avail. AE, CB, DC, DISC, MC, V.

≣ Heaven on Earth Plaza Hotel

801 Calhoun St, 77002 (Downtown); tel 713/659-2222. At Louisiana, near I-45. A dormitory-style, high-rise hotel attracting many long-term guests, it's a little old and in need of renovation but nevertheless clean and comfortable. A decent budget option. **Rooms:** 325 rms. CI 2pm/CO noon. Nonsmoking rms avail. **Amenities:** [📺] [⚷] A/C, TV w/movies. **Services:** [↵] **Facilities:** [⛳] [⛳] Washer/dryer. **Rates:** $46–$52 S or D. Extra person $5. Children under age 12 stay free. Parking: Indoor, free. MC, V.

≣≣ Holiday Inn

7611 Katy Fwy, 77024; tel 713/688-2221 or toll free 800/HOLIDAY; fax 713/680-0147. Silber exit off I-10, near I-610 loop. A gate surrounds this very secure property near the junction of two major interstates. Easy access to downtown and Galleria shopping mall. **Rooms:** 250 rms and stes. CI 6pm/CO 1pm. Nonsmoking rms avail. **Amenities:** [📺] [⚷] A/C, cable TV. **Services:** [✕] [⊠] [↵] **Facilities:** [⛳] [300] [♿] 1 restaurant, 1 bar, washer/dryer. **Rates:** $65–$75 S or D; $110–$150 ste. Extra person $10. Children under age 19 stay free. Parking: Outdoor, free. AE, CB, DC, DISC, JCB, MC, V.

≣≣ Holiday Inn Astrodome

8111 Kirby Dr, 77054; tel 713/790-1900 or toll free 800/HOLIDAY. Near Old Spanish Trail. Located on the north side of the Astrodome. Major changes were being planned that should result in improved services in the future. **Rooms:** 235 rms and stes. Executive level. CI 3pm/CO noon. Nonsmoking rms avail. **Amenities:** [📺] [⚷] A/C, cable TV w/movies, dataport. **Services:** ✗ 🚐 🖼 ↵ Babysitting. **Facilities:** 🏋 🏌 🏊400 ♿ 2 restaurants, 1 bar, whirlpool. **Rates:** Peak (June–Aug) $79–$109 S or D; $225–$295 ste. Extra person $10. Children under age 19 stay free. Lower rates off-season. Parking: Outdoor, free. AE, CB, DC, DISC, JCB, MC, V.

🏨🏨🏨 Holiday Inn Medical Center

6701 S Main St, 77030; tel 713/797-1110 or toll free 800/ HOLIDAY. At Holcombe, near Texas Medical Center. Features spacious guest rooms and ample parking—it sits atop a parking garage. **Rooms:** 296 rms and stes. CI 1pm/CO 1pm. Nonsmoking rms avail. **Amenities:** 🏧 🍺 A/C, cable TV, dataport. **Services:** ✗ 🖼 ↵ Babysitting. Breakfast buffet offered. Complimentary shuttle to the medical center. **Facilities:** 🏋 🏊700 ♿ 1 restaurant, 1 bar, washer/dryer. **Rates:** $85–$95 S or D; $135–$200 ste. Extra person $5. Children under age 19 stay free. Parking: Indoor/outdoor, free. AE, CB, DC, DISC, ER, JCB, MC, V.

🏨🏨🏨 Houston Airport Marriott

18700 John F Kennedy Blvd, 77032 (Houston Intercontinental Airport); tel 281/443-2310 or toll free 800/228-9290; fax 281/443-5271. Between terminals B and C. Located in the middle of the airport is this long, tall cylindrical structure housing guest rooms, shops, and restaurants. **Rooms:** 566 rms and stes. Executive level. CI 3pm/CO 1pm. Nonsmoking rms avail. **Amenities:** 🏧 🍺 🍴 A/C, cable TV w/movies, dataport, voice mail. Some units w/terraces. "On-command" video with over 50 movie selections. **Services:** ✗ 🛎 VP 🚐 🖼 ↵ 🛏 Car-rental desk, babysitting. Complimentary newspaper and coffee and shoeshine. Safe deposit boxes available. **Facilities:** 🏋 🏌 🏊2000 💻 ♿ 2 restaurants, 1 bar, spa, sauna, whirlpool, beauty salon, washer/dryer. Hydrotherapy pool. **Rates:** $75–$130 S or D; $275–$350 ste. Children under age 18 stay free. Parking: Indoor/outdoor, $10–$15/day. AE, CB, DC, DISC, MC, V.

🏨🏨🏨 The Houstonian Hotel

111 N Post Oak Lane, 77024 (Galleria); tel 713/680-3805 or toll free 800/231-2759; fax 713/686-3701. N of Woodway near I-610 W loop. Located on 18 wooded acres, this relaxing and comfortable facility sits in a very quiet, almost rural setting. It looks like a large, country lodge; the lobby features a huge stone fireplace, hardwood floors, and animal figurines and statuary. **Rooms:** 291 rms and stes. Executive level. CI 4pm/CO noon. Nonsmoking rms avail. **Amenities:** 🏧 🍺 🍴 A/C, cable TV w/movies, dataport, bathrobes. All units w/minibars, 1 w/whirlpool. **Services:** ✗ 🛎 VP 🚐 🖼 ↵ Twice-daily maid svce, car-rental desk, social director, masseur, children's program, babysitting. **Facilities:** 🏋 🏌 🏓5 🏊450 💻 ♿ 4 restaurants, 2 bars, basketball, volleyball, racquetball, squash, spa, sauna, whirlpool, beauty salon, playground. Indoor rock-climbing wall; running track with pacing lights; Olympic-size pool. **Rates:** $154–$184 S or D; $225–$950 ste. Children under age 18 stay free. Parking: Indoor, free. AE, CB, DC, DISC, JCB, MC, V.

🏨🏨🏨 Houston Marriott Westside

13210 Katy Fwy, 77079; tel 281/558-8338 or toll free 800/ 228-9290; fax 281/558-4028. On I-10 at Eldridge Rd. Unique urban oasis located on beautiful, green grounds next to a lake. A trickling stream flows lazily through the lobby, which is filled with lots of plants and small pools inhabited with turtles and tropical fish. You'll have a hard time believing you're in the center of Houston. **Rooms:** 400 rms and stes. Executive level. CI 4pm/CO noon. Nonsmoking rms avail. **Amenities:** 🏧 🍺 🍴 A/C, cable TV w/movies, dataport, voice mail. 1 unit w/whirlpool. **Services:** ✗ 🛎 VP 🚐 🖼 ↵ Twice-daily maid svce, car-rental desk, babysitting. Shoeshines available. **Facilities:** 🏋 🏌 🏊2 🏓 🏊1500 ♿ 1 restaurant, 2 bars (1 w/entertainment), whirlpool. Nearby Bear Creek provides extensive recreational opportunities. **Rates:** $140–$150 S or D; $199–$499 ste. Children under age 18 stay free. Parking: Indoor/outdoor, free. AE, CB, DC, DISC, JCB, MC, V.

🏨🏨🏨 Houston Plaza Hilton

6633 Travis St, 77030; tel 713/524-6633 or toll free 800/ HILTONS; fax 713/529-6806. Located right in the middle of the Texas Medical Center and close to Rice University, this comfortable hotel faces a residential district. **Rooms:** 185 rms. Executive level. CI 3pm/CO 1pm. Nonsmoking rms avail. **Amenities:** 🏧 🍺 A/C, cable TV w/movies. All units w/minibars. **Services:** ✗ 🚐 🖼 ↵ 🛏 Babysitting. Aerobic classes and swimming lessons offered. **Facilities:** 🏋 🏌 🏓 🏊210 💻 ♿ 1 restaurant, 1 bar (w/entertainment), spa, sauna, whirlpool. Health club arrangements are available to guests; the roof provides a nice sundeck, pool, and jogging path. **Rates:** $115–$165 ste. Extra person $15. Children under age 17 stay free. Parking: Indoor, $7/day. AE, CB, DC, DISC, JCB, MC, V.

🏨🏨🏨 Houston West Hilton Inn

12401 Katy Fwy, 77079; tel 713/496-9090 or toll free 800/ HILTONS; fax 713/496-5623. Near Dairy Ashford Rd. Located in Houston's energy corridor near Beltway 8, this Hilton offers comfortable and dependable accommodations to business travelers and others. **Rooms:** 174 rms and stes. CI 3pm/CO 1pm. Nonsmoking rms avail. **Amenities:** 🏧 🍺 A/C, cable TV w/movies, dataport. All units w/minibars. **Services:** ✗ 🖼 ↵ **Facilities:** 🏋 🏓 🏊120 ♿ 1 restaurant, 1 bar. **Rates:** $102–$142 S or D; $195 ste. Extra person $10. Children under age 17 stay free. Parking: Outdoor, free. AE, CB, DC, DISC, JCB, MC, V.

🏨🏨🏨 Hyatt Regency Houston

1200 Louisiana St, 77002 (Downtown); tel 713/654-1234 or toll free 800/233-1234; fax 713/951-0934. Between Dallas and Polk Sts. A dramatic, 30-story atrium is the central feature of this contemporary downtown hotel connected to the underground pedestrian system. Attention to detail and a high level of service are Hyatt hallmarks. **Rooms:** 959 rms and stes. Executive level. CI 3pm/CO noon. Nonsmoking rms avail. **Amenities:** 🏧 🍺 🍴 A/C, cable TV w/movies, dataport, voice mail. All units w/minibars. **Services:** ✗ 🔌 VP 🚐 🛄 🛎️ 🛋️ Twice-daily maid svce, car-rental desk, babysitting. **Facilities:** 🏋️ 🛫 5000 🖥️ & 3 restaurants, 2 bars (w/entertainment), beauty salon. The hotel has an arrangement with the local YMCA. Houston's only revolving restaurant is here. **Rates:** $130–$190 S or D; $350–$650 ste. Children under age 18 stay free. Parking: Indoor, $6.50–$11/day. AE, CB, DC, DISC, JCB, MC, V.

▤▤▤ JW Marriott Hotel Houston

5150 Westheimer Rd, 77056 (Galleria); tel 713/961-1500 or toll free 800/228-9290; fax 713/961-5045. Just W of I-610 W Loop Fwy. The attractive brick building stands amidst trees in a green, grassy lot near the Galleria shopping complex. Soft lighting, wood paneling, fresh flowers, and tasteful furnishings make for an inviting lobby area. **Rooms:** 503 rms and stes. Executive level. CI 4pm/CO noon. Nonsmoking rms avail. **Amenities:** 🛁 🌡️ 🍷 A/C, satel TV w/movies, voice mail. **Services:** ✗ 🔌 VP 🛄 🛋️ 🛎️ Masseur, babysitting. Newspapers and coffee are offered in the lobby every weeknight. **Facilities:** 🏋️ 🛫 1200 & 1 restaurant, 1 bar, basketball, games rm, racquetball, sauna, steam rm, whirlpool, beauty salon. American and Delta airlines have ticket offices on-site. **Rates:** Peak (Sept–May) $149–$159 S or D; $175–$600 ste. Extra person $10. Children under age 18 stay free. Lower rates off-season. Parking: Indoor/outdoor, $6/day. AE, CB, DC, DISC, JCB, MC, V.

▤▤▤▤ Lancaster Hotel

701 Texas Ave, 77002 (Theater District); tel 713/228-9500 or toll free 800/231-0336; fax 713/223-4528. At Louisiana. Dwarfed by nearby skyscrapers, this charming, little hotel with real personality is housed in a historic building in the middle of the theater district. Outstanding, friendly service and attention to detail distinguish this property from most others. Antiques, original paintings, and fresh flowers add grace and beauty. **Rooms:** 93 rms and stes. CI 3pm/CO 1pm. Nonsmoking rms avail. **Amenities:** 🛁 🌡️ 🍷 A/C, cable TV w/movies, dataport, VCR, CD/tape player, bathrobes. Some units w/minibars. Two-line speaker phones, dedicated fax line available. **Services:** 🍽️ 🔌 VP 🛄 🛋️ Twice-daily maid svce, babysitting. **Facilities:** 40 & 1 restaurant, 1 bar. Arrangement with Texas club provides guests with health and fitness facilities. **Rates:** $98–$230 S or D; $335–$865 ste. Children under age 18 stay free. Parking: Indoor, $12/day. AE, CB, DC, DISC, MC, V.

▤▤▤ Omni Houston Hotel

Four Riverway, 77056; tel 713/871-8181 or toll free 800/THE-OMNI; fax 713/871-0719. Built in the 1980s as a Four Seasons hotel (the old corporate logo still graces the elevators), this white, curvaceous 12-story structure rises above lawns, red slab sculptures, fountains, cascades, and a gazebo with a flock of black swans. It's an urban oasis surrounded by sleek, contemporary high-rise offices. The elegant, roomy two-story lobby sports lots of original art and the spacious, airy Palm Court with its potted plants and panoramic windows overlooking the garden. **Rooms:** 381 rms and stes. CI 3pm/CO 1pm. Nonsmoking rms avail. Spacious, efficient rooms are done in soothing hues and feature full-size desk and armoire housing the TV; most offer separate sitting area for three guests. Rooms overlooking entrance and driveway can be noisy despite soundproofed windows. **Amenities:** 🛁 🌡️ 🍷 A/C, cable TV w/movies, dataport, voice mail, bathrobes. All units w/minibars, 1 w/terrace, 1 w/fireplace. Two-line phone. Basket of snacks on sideboard. **Services:** 🍽️ 🔌 VP 🛄 🛋️ 🛎️ Twice-daily maid svce, masseur, babysitting. Overnight laundry is delivered on the dot next morning. 24-hour concierge—though not 100% dependable (service in general can vary from polished to inept). Complimentary limousine to nearby Post Oak/Galleria shops and offices. Afternoon tea served in Palm Court. **Facilities:** 🏋️ 🍷4 🛫 600 🖥️ & 3 restaurants (see "Restaurants" below), 2 bars (w/entertainment), sauna, whirlpool. Lap pool with underwater music plus smaller pool; bar/snack service at both. Token business center. Attractive dining rooms; convivial and comfy Black Swan Pub with darts, pool table. **Rates:** Peak (Aug 21–Dec 31) $200 S; $226 D; $375–$475 ste. Extra person $30. Children under age 18 stay free. Min stay special events. Lower rates off-season. Parking: Indoor, $11/day. Rates vary with floor and view. AE, CB, DC, DISC, EC, JCB, MC, V.

▤▤▤ Renaissance Houston Hotel

6 Greenway Plaza E, 77046 (Greenway Plaza); tel 713/629-1200 or toll free 800/HOTELS-1; fax 713/629-4706. Buffalo Speedway/Edloe St exit off US 59. Located in the center of Greenway Plaza, this large convention-friendly hotel is connected to the Summit Arena via an underground walkway. Convenient to downtown, the Galleria Mall, and the Astrodome. **Rooms:** 389 rms and stes. Executive level. CI 1pm/CO 11am. Nonsmoking rms avail. **Amenities:** 🛁 🌡️ 🍷 A/C, cable TV w/movies, dataport. Some units w/whirlpools. **Services:** 🍽️ VP 🛄 🛋️ 🛎️ Twice-daily maid svce, car-rental desk, babysitting. Courtesy shuttle within 5-mile radius. Complimentary shoeshine. **Facilities:** 🏋️ 🎾 🏊10 🛫 600 🖥️ & 2 restaurants, 2 bars (1 w/entertainment), racquetball, spa, steam rm, whirlpool, beauty salon. Hotel is connected to a mini-mall with food court, movie theaters, ATMs, post office, and florist. **Rates:** $119–$159 S or D; $300–$750 ste. Children under age 18 stay free. Parking: Indoor, $10/day. AE, CB, DC, DISC, EC, JCB, MC, V.

▤▤▤▤ The Ritz-Carlton Houston

1919 Briar Oaks Lane, 77027; tel 713/840-7600 or toll free 800/241-3333; fax 713/840-0616. Near River Oaks and Post Oak Park; inside Loop 610. Sleek 12-story tower in a district of sleek high-rises, located near Texas Medical Center and Galleria and Saks Pavilion shopping malls. Lobby and lounge are trimmed with oak and decorated with original art and antiques. **Rooms:** 232 rms and stes. Executive level. CI 3pm/CO noon. Nonsmoking rms avail. Spacious (approximately 500 sq ft) and efficient rooms feature sitting area with two armchairs and circular coffee table; Queen Anne furnishings;

botanical and hunting prints; freestanding marble-topped desk; and marble-clad bathrooms. Four balconies overlook roofdeck swimming pool. **Amenities:** 🔒 🛁 🖥 A/C, cable TV w/movies, dataport, in-rm safe, bathrobes. All units w/minibars, some w/terraces, some w/whirlpools. Armoire incorporates TV and bar/snacks set-up. Two-line phone. **Services:** 🍽 🗝 VP 🚐 🛍 🛎 🕊 Twice-daily maid svce, car-rental desk, children's program, babysitting. Snappy concierge service; complimentary limousine to nearby offices and Galleria shopping mall. Afternoon tea in lounge. **Facilities:** 🏋 🏊 🈸700 🛁 2 restaurants (see "Restaurants" below), 2 bars (1 w/entertainment). Attractive pool and fitness center (open 6am–9pm). Poolside meal service. **Rates:** Peak (Sept 16–May 27) $175–$255 S or D; $260–$395 ste. Extra person $30. Children under age 18 stay free. Lower rates off-season. Parking: Indoor, $13.50/day. Weekend rates beginning at $99 double are a downright bargain for this caliber of service and luxury. AE, CB, DC, DISC, ER, JCB, MC, V.

≡≡≡ Sheraton Astrodome Hotel
8686 Kirby Dr, 77054; tel 713/748-3221 or toll free 800/627-6461; fax 713/795-8420. At jct I-610. A large hotel in a great location near the Astrodome, AstroWorld, Rice University, and the University of Texas Medical Center. Caters to families as well as to businesspeople and conventioneers. **Rooms:** 669 rms and stes. Executive level. CI 3pm/CO noon. Nonsmoking rms avail. **Amenities:** 🔒 🛁 🖥 A/C, cable TV w/movies, dataport, voice mail. Some units w/terraces. **Services:** ✕ 🗝 🛍 🛎 🕊 Car-rental desk, babysitting. **Facilities:** 🏋 🏊 🈸4500 🖥 1 restaurant, 2 bars (1 w/entertainment), sauna, whirlpool, beauty salon. **Rates:** $90–$150 S; $105–$165 D; $270–$370 ste. Extra person $15. Children under age 17 stay free. Parking: Outdoor, free. AE, CB, DC, DISC, ER, JCB, MC, V.

≡≡≡ Sheraton Crown Hotel & Conference Center
15700 John F Kennedy Blvd, 77032 (Airport); tel 281/442-5100 or toll free 800/444-2217; fax 281/987-9130. Between Beltway 8 and Greens Rd. A large, modern hotel on airport property, catering primarily to corporate flyers. **Rooms:** 418 rms and stes. Executive level. CI 3pm/CO noon. Nonsmoking rms avail. **Amenities:** 🔒 🛁 🖥 A/C, cable TV w/movies, voice mail. Some units w/terraces. **Services:** ✕ 🗝 VP 🚐 🛍 🛎 Car-rental desk, babysitting. **Facilities:** 🏋 🏊 🈸1000 🛁 1 restaurant, 2 bars, whirlpool, washer/dryer. On-site travel agency. Putting green. **Rates:** $120–$140 S; $130–$150 D; $150–$350 ste. Extra person $10. Children under age 17 stay free. Parking: Outdoor, free. AE, CB, DC, DISC, EC, ER, JCB, MC, V.

≡≡ Travelodge Hotel Houston Greenway Plaza
2828 Southwest Fwy, 77098 (Greenway Plaza); tel 713/526-4571 or toll free 800/578-7878; fax 713/526-8709. Kirby exit off US 59. An clean, inexpensive option near US 59 offering easy access to Greenway Plaza, the Summit, and downtown. **Rooms:** 205 rms and stes. Executive level. CI 3pm/CO noon. Nonsmoking rms avail. **Amenities:** 🔒 🛁 🖥 🖥 A/C, cable TV w/movies, voice mail. **Services:** ✕ 🛍 🛎 **Facilities:** 🏋 🏊 🈸180 🛁 1 restaurant, 1 bar. **Rates:** Peak (June–Aug) $59–$69 S or D; $79–$159 ste. Children under age 17 stay free. Lower rates off-season. Parking: Outdoor, free. AE, CB, DC, DISC, JCB, MC, V.

≡≡≡ Westchase Hilton
9999 Westheimer, 77042; tel 713/974-1000 or toll free 800/445-8667; fax 713/974-6866. Near Gessner. Very professional, businesslike hotel with multilingual staff. Sunlit lobby and lounge areas are very inviting. **Rooms:** 300 rms and stes. Executive level. CI 3pm/CO 1pm. Nonsmoking rms avail. **Amenities:** 🔒 🛁 🖥 🖥 A/C, satel TV w/movies, dataport. All units w/minibars. Towers and concierge levels provide unique amenities such as video phones, electric massage chairs, and cocktail bars. **Services:** 🍽 🗝 🛍 🛎 Twice-daily maid svce, masseur, babysitting. Complimentary newspapers, shoeshine. **Facilities:** 🏋 🏊 🈸700 🖥 🛁 1 restaurant, 2 bars, sauna, whirlpool, beauty salon. **Rates:** $129–$184 S or D; $144–$174 ste. Extra person $15. Children under age 17 stay free. Parking: Outdoor, free. AE, CB, DC, DISC, JCB, MC, V.

≡≡≡ Westin Galleria
5060 W Alabama, 77056 (Galleria); tel 713/960-8100 or toll free 800/228-3000; fax 713/960-6553. Between Sage and S Post Oak. Connected to both the Galleria Mall (with its ice skating rink, bank, medical facilities, art galleries, and over 300 other stores) and the Westin Oaks (see below), this sleek property receives much corporate/convention business and offers many services and dining and entertainment options. **Rooms:** 485 rms and stes. Executive level. CI 3pm/CO 1pm. Nonsmoking rms avail. **Amenities:** 🔒 🛁 🖥 A/C, cable TV w/movies, voice mail. All units w/minibars, all w/terraces, some w/whirlpools. Trouser rack, iron and ironing board in each room. **Services:** 🍽 🗝 VP 🚐 🛍 🛎 🕊 Twice-daily maid svce, car-rental desk, children's program, babysitting. AT&T language translation line available. Items and services of Westin Oaks can be used and charges transferred. **Facilities:** 🏋 🎾 🏊 🈸 🈸2000 🖥 🛁 3 restaurants, 2 bars (1 w/entertainment). **Rates:** Peak (Sept–Mar) $165–$210 S or D; $210–$1,200 ste. Extra person $30. Children under age 18 stay free. Lower rates off-season. Parking: Indoor, free. AE, CB, DC, DISC, JCB, MC, V.

≡≡≡ The Westin Oaks
5011 Westheimer Rd, 77056 (Galleria); tel 713/960-8100 or toll free 800/228-3000; fax 713/960-6553. At Post Oaks. Linked with the Westin Galleria and the Galleria Mall, this property caters primarily to families and tourists. Services and facilities at both hotels are available to guests, and any charges can be transferred. **Rooms:** 406 rms and stes. CI 3pm/CO 1pm. Nonsmoking rms avail. **Amenities:** 🔒 🛁 🖥 A/C, cable TV w/movies, voice mail. All units w/minibars, all w/terraces, some w/whirlpools. Trouser rack, iron and ironing board available in each room. **Services:** 🍽 🗝 VP 🚐 🛍

⚲ ⚲ Twice-daily maid svce, car-rental desk, children's program, babysitting. AT&T language translation line available. **Facilities:** ⚲ ⚲ ⚲ ⚲ 2000 ⚲ ⚲ 3 restaurants, 2 bars (1 w/entertainment). **Rates:** Peak (Sept–Mar) $165–$210 S or D; $210–$1,200 ste. Extra person $30. Children under age 18 stay free. Lower rates off-season. Parking: Indoor, free. AE, CB, DC, DISC, JCB, MC, V.

Wyndham Greenspoint Hotel

12400 Greenspoint Dr, 77060 (Greenspoint); tel 281/875-2222 or toll free 800/WYNDHAM, 800/822-4200 in the US, 800/631-4200 in Canada; fax 281/875-1652. At jct I-45 and Sam Houston Pkwy. A very contemporary twist on old Gothic architecture, this hotel offers unique surroundings and structural beauty. Relax in the beautiful, two-story atrium/lobby or spend time shopping in the nearby Galleria Mall. A popular convention site. **Rooms:** 472 rms and stes. Executive level. CI 3pm/CO noon. Nonsmoking rms avail. **Amenities:** ⚲ ⚲ ⚲ A/C, cable TV w/movies. **Services:** ✗ ⚲ ⚲ ⚲ ⚲ Babysitting. **Facilities:** ⚲ ⚲ ⚲ 3000 ⚲ 2 restaurants, 2 bars (1 w/entertainment), basketball, racquetball, sauna, whirlpool. Aerobics facility, sundeck, florist, gift shop. Greenspoint Club is adjacent to the property. **Rates:** $125–$169 S or D; $135–$179 ste. Extra person $10. Children under age 12 stay free. Parking: Indoor/outdoor, free. AE, CB, DC, DISC, ER, JCB, MC, V.

The Wyndham Warwick

5701 S Main St, 77251; tel 713/526-1991 or toll free 800/822-4200 in the US, 800/631-4200 in Canada; fax 713/639-4545. Near Hermann St. Originally built in 1926, this elegant European-style hotel located in the museum district features authentic 18th-century antique furnishings and tapestries—some actually acquired from the estate of Napoleon Bonaparte's sister. This place is great for Houston visitors who want a little something extra from their lodgings. **Rooms:** 308 rms and stes. CI 3pm/CO noon. Nonsmoking rms avail. **Amenities:** ⚲ ⚲ ⚲ ⚲ A/C, cable TV w/movies, dataport. All units w/terraces. **Services:** ✗ ⚲ VP ⚲ ⚲ ⚲ **Facilities:** ⚲ ⚲ 600 ⚲ 2 restaurants, 1 bar (w/entertainment), spa, sauna, beauty salon. **Rates:** $115–$155 S or D; $175–$195 ste. Extra person $10. Children under age 12 stay free. Parking: Indoor, $6.50/day. AE, CB, DC, DISC, EC, ER, JCB, MC, V.

MOTELS

Allen Park Inn

2121 Allen Pkwy, 77019; tel 713/521-9321 or toll free 800/231-6310; fax 713/521-9321. Taft between I-45 and Mantrose. It's hard to imagine you're in downtown when staying at this pleasant motel with beautiful landscaping and a pool area surrounded by palm trees, all within the lovely, secluded Bayou Park area. **Rooms:** 242 rms and stes. CI 3pm/CO noon. Nonsmoking rms avail. **Amenities:** ⚲ ⚲ ⚲ A/C, cable TV w/movies, dataport, in-rm safe, bathrobes. Some units w/terraces. **Services:** ⚲ ⚲ ⚲ **Facilities:** ⚲ ⚲ 150 ⚲ 2

restaurants, 1 bar, sauna, whirlpool, beauty salon. **Rates:** $88–$110 S or D; $135–$250 ste. Extra person $8. Children under age 10 stay free. Parking: Outdoor, free. AE, CB, DC, DISC, MC, V.

Best Western Greenspoint Plaza Inn

11211 N Fwy, 77037 (Greenspoint); tel 281/447-6311 or toll free 800/528-1234; fax 281/447-3719. Near Sam Houston Pkwy. Quite attractive, with a large guest area and lobby. **Rooms:** 141 rms. CI 3pm/CO noon. Nonsmoking rms avail. **Amenities:** ⚲ ⚲ A/C, cable TV w/movies, refrig, dataport. **Services:** ✗ ⚲ ⚲ **Facilities:** ⚲ 400 ⚲ 1 restaurant, 1 bar (w/entertainment), washer/dryer. **Rates:** $85–$120 S or D. Extra person $5. Children under age 18 stay free. Parking: Outdoor, free. AE, DISC, MC, V.

Days Inn Galleria

9041 Westheimer Rd, 77063; tel 713/783-1400. Between Fondren and Gessner. Set back from the road, this comfortable, newish motel is nestled among lush foliage. Convenient to the cities of Piney Point, Bunker's Hill, and Hunter's Creek. **Rooms:** 90 rms. CI 3pm/CO noon. Nonsmoking rms avail. **Amenities:** ⚲ ⚲ A/C, cable TV w/movies, dataport. Some units w/whirlpools. **Services:** ⚲ ⚲ **Facilities:** ⚲ ⚲ 25 ⚲ Washer/dryer. **Rates (CP):** $51–$56 S or D. Extra person $5. Children under age 12 stay free. Parking: Outdoor, free. AE, DC, DISC, JCB, MC, V.

Days Inn Wayside

2200 S Wayside Dr, 77023; tel 713/928-2800 or toll free 800/DAYS-INN; fax 713/928-3473. At I-45, near Hobby. Although a bit dated, this motel is very "broken-in" and comfortable. Great for travelers on a budget. Downtown universities, the port of Houston, the Convention Center, Hobby Airport, and AstroWorld are all within a five-mile radius. **Rooms:** 100 rms. CI 4pm/CO noon. Nonsmoking rms avail. **Amenities:** ⚲ ⚲ A/C, cable TV. **Services:** ⚲ ⚲ **Facilities:** ⚲ ⚲ **Rates (CP):** $34–$47 S or D. Extra person $5. Children under age 12 stay free. Parking: Outdoor, free. AE, CB, DC, DISC, JCB, MC, V.

Galleria Inn

4723 W Alabama, 77027 (Galleria); tel 713/621-2797. E of I-610 W Loop. A budget motel with a very nice courtyard and larger-than-average rooms. **Rooms:** 53 rms. CI noon/CO noon. Nonsmoking rms avail. **Amenities:** ⚲ ⚲ A/C, cable TV w/movies. **Services:** ⚲ ⚲ **Facilities:** ⚲ Washer/dryer. **Rates:** $65–$84 S or D. Extra person $10. Children under age 12 stay free. Parking: Outdoor, free. AE, CB, DC, DISC, MC, V.

The Grant Motor Inn

8200 South Main, 77025; tel 713/668-8000 or toll free 800/255-8904. Near Kirby. This independent motel with conscientious management and an attentive staff boasts a nicely landscaped courtyard and pool surrounded by palm trees. **Rooms:** 64 rms. CI 1pm/CO 1pm. Nonsmoking rms avail. **Amenities:** ⚲ ⚲ A/C, cable TV w/movies. All units w/terraces. VCRs and movies available. **Services:** 🛎 **Facilities:** 🏋 ఉ Whirlpool, playground, washer/dryer. **Rates (CP):** Peak (June–Aug) $31–$48 S or D. Extra person $4. Lower rates off-season. **Parking:** Outdoor, free. AE, CB, DC, DISC, MC, V.

≣≣ La Quinta Inn Greenway Plaza
4015 Southwest Fwy, 77027; tel 713/623-4750 or toll free 800/531-5900; fax 713/963-0599. Wesleyan exit off US 59. Standard, affordable accommodations located near the I-610 loop and other major interstates. **Rooms:** 131 rms. CI 6pm/CO noon. Nonsmoking rms avail. **Amenities:** 📺 ☕ A/C, cable TV w/movies. **Services:** 🛄 🛎 **Facilities:** 🏋 🍴₃₅ ఉ Washer/dryer. **Rates (CP):** $61–$78 S or D. Extra person $8. Children under age 18 stay free. **Parking:** Outdoor, free. AE, CB, DC, DISC, MC, V.

≣≣≣ Lexington Hotel Suites
16410 I-45 N, 77090; tel 281/821-1000 or toll free 800/53-SUITE; fax 281/821-1420. Between N Vista and W Richey. This all-suite motel located in the extreme north of Houston has a distinctive, rustic lobby designed like a hunting/ski lodge, complete with a huge, welcoming fireplace. Friendly staff. **Rooms:** 247 stes. CI 3pm/CO noon. Nonsmoking rms avail. **Amenities:** 📺 ☕ 🖭 A/C, cable TV, refrig. Nintendo video games available. **Services:** 🛄 🛎 **Facilities:** 🏋 ఉ Washer/dryer. **Rates:** $69–$109 ste. Children under age 12 stay free. **Parking:** Outdoor, free. AE, CB, DC, DISC, JCB, MC, V.

≣≣ Motel 6
9638 Plainfield Rd, 77036; tel 713/778-0008; fax 713/771-2248. At jct US 59. Near major interstates, the beltway, shopping malls, and dining opportunities, this standard Motel 6 is adequate for short stays. **Rooms:** 205 rms. CI open/CO noon. Nonsmoking rms avail. **Amenities:** 📺 ☕ A/C, cable TV. **Services:** 🛎 🛷 **Facilities:** 🏋 ఉ Washer/dryer. **Rates:** $32–$38 S or D. Extra person $6. Children under age 17 stay free. **Parking:** Outdoor, free. AE, DC, DISC, MC, V.

≣≣≣ Quality Inn Intercontinental Airport
6115 Will Clayton Pkwy, 77205; tel 281/446-9131 or toll free 800/221-2222; fax 281/446-2251. W of US 59 Eastex Fwy. Located among the trees in a forest that surrounds the airport, this motel is both quiet and convenient. **Rooms:** 172 rms. CI 4pm/CO 11am. Nonsmoking rms avail. **Amenities:** 📺 ☕ A/C, cable TV w/movies, dataport. **Services:** ✗ 🚐 🛄 🛎 Car-rental desk. **Facilities:** 🏋 🏊₁ 🍴₁₅₀ ఉ 1 restaurant, 1 bar (w/entertainment). On-site travel agency and gift/snack shop. **Rates:** $59–$75 S or D. Extra person $7. Children under age 18 stay free. **Parking:** Outdoor, free. AE, CB, DC, DISC, ER, JCB, MC, V.

≣≣ Rodeway Inn Hobby Airport
1505 College Ave, 77587; tel 713/946-5900 or toll free 800/424-4777. E of I-45. With great access to the airport, the Astrodome, universities, and the medical center, this motel is perfect for the overnight guest or airport patron. **Rooms:**

124 rms. CI 3pm/CO noon. Nonsmoking rms avail. **Amenities:** 📺 ☕ A/C, cable TV. **Services:** 🛎 🛷 **Facilities:** 🏋 ఉ **Rates:** $44–$56 S or D. Extra person $6. Children under age 18 stay free. **Parking:** Outdoor, free. AE, CB, DC, DISC, JCB, MC, V.

≣≣ Rodeway Inn Memorial Park
5820 Katy Fwy, 77007 (Memorial Park); tel 713/869-9211 or toll free 800/424-4777. At Washington. Located across from the park, these well-priced, dependable standard accommodations are good for the tourist on a budget. **Rooms:** 107 rms. CI 4pm/CO noon. Nonsmoking rms avail. **Amenities:** 📺 ☕ 🖭 A/C, cable TV. **Services:** 🛎 **Facilities:** 🏋 ఉ 1 restaurant, washer/dryer. **Rates (CP):** $46–$55 S or D. Extra person $6. Children under age 18 stay free. **Parking:** Outdoor, free. AE, DC, DISC, JCB, MC, V.

INN

≣≣≣ Sara's Bed and Breakfast Inn
941 Heights Blvd, 77008 (Heights); tel 713/868-1130 or toll free 800/593-1130; fax 713/868-1160. Between 9th and 10th Sts near I-10. A traditional B&B in a spotlessly maintained Victorian home. Located in a pretty, quaint neighborhood, the inn is perfect for that romantic getaway. Unsuitable for children under 12. **Rooms:** 14 rms (all w/shared bath). CI 3pm/CO noon. Nonsmoking rms avail. **Amenities:** 📺 ☕ A/C, cable TV, VCR. **Services:** 🛄 🛎 **Rates (CP):** $55–$95 S. Extra person $10. **Parking:** Outdoor, free. AE, CB, DC, DISC, JCB, MC, V.

RESTAURANTS 🍴

♣ Américas
1800 Post Oak Blvd (Galleria); tel 713/961-1492. Near San Felipe. **Seafood/South American.** Named Restaurant of the Year for 1993 by *Esquire* magazine, Américas is fun, unique, and imaginative in both cuisine and decor. The setting is a cartoonish version of a South American rain forest, with a stairway to the second floor designed like a rickety, wooden bridge spanning a deep ravine. Bright colors and wooden artwork mingle along the walls. The most popular menu items are grilled poultry and seafood in a variety of tasty sauces. **FYI:** Reservations recommended. Dress code. **Open:** Mon–Thurs 11am–10pm, Fri 11am–11pm, Sat 5–11pm. **Prices:** Main courses $12–$24. AE, CB, DC, DISC, MC, V. 🈴 ᵛᴾ ఉ

Anthony's
4007 Westheimer; tel 713/961-0552. Between Weslayan and I-610 W Loop Fwy. **Continental/French.** Dark colors, wood floors, lots of stained-glass fixtures, and reproductions of Greek and Roman sculptures characterize the beautiful interior of this very elegant and trendy restaurant. Sit in the wine storage room or in the main dining area where a large glass window offers a view of the cooks. Fine European-accented American cuisine is presented by a highly professional staff. **FYI:** Reservations recommended. Jacket required. **Open:** Lunch Mon–Fri 11:30am–2pm, Sun 11:30am–2pm; dinner

Mon 5:30–10pm, Tues–Thurs 5:30–11pm, Fri–Sat 5:30–11:30pm. **Prices:** Main courses $14–$28. AE, CB, DC, DISC, MC, V. 🅥🅿 &

Armando's

2300 Westheimer; tel 713/521-9757. Near Kirby. **Italian/Mexican.** This secluded restaurant, with its minimalist, contemporary design, and well-prepared Mexican and Italian fare, is quite a hidden treasure. Patio seating available behind a vine-covered wall. **FYI:** Reservations accepted. **Open:** Lunch Mon–Fri 11am–2pm; dinner Thurs–Sat 5:30–11pm, Sun–Wed 5:30–10pm. **Prices:** Main courses $7–$16. AE, CB, DC, MC, V. 🍴 🅥🅿 &

Ashland House Tea Room & Restaurant

1801 Ashland Rd (Heights); tel 713/863-7613. Between 18th and 20th, near I-610 N Loop Fwy. **Eclectic.** The menu at this elegant restaurant changes daily, but the beautiful Victorian building that houses it hasn't changed in years. (It's listed in the National Register of Historic Places.) Lace curtains and breezy ceiling fans create a casual, homey atmosphere. Great home-style meals, and alcohol-free environment is a plus for families with children. **FYI:** Reservations accepted. No liquor license. **Open:** Mon–Sat 11am–3pm. **Prices:** Main courses $5–$7. AE, DISC, MC, V. &

Atchafalaya River Cafe

14904 I-45 N Fwy; tel 281/821-1567. At Airtex. **Cajun/Seafood.** Part of a large chain of seafood restaurants, this place offers enormous portions of gumbo, blackened redfish, shrimp, and other favorites. There's something for everyone, and lots of it. **FYI:** Reservations accepted. Additional locations: 2504 North Loop W (tel 683-8880); 8507 Gulf Fwy (tel 943-9999). **Open:** Sun–Thurs 11am–10pm, Fri–Sat 11am–11pm. **Prices:** Main courses $8–$22. AE, CB, DC, DISC, MC, V. &

Brennan's

3300 Smith St; tel 713/522-9711. At Stuart near Spur 527 terminus. **Creole.** This spacious, elegant restaurant may have one of the loveliest patios in Houston, but it's the delicious Creole cuisine that you are most likely to remember. This is true New Orleans–style dining, with specialties such as shrimp rémoulade, veal cutlet Tchoupitoulas, and sautéed redfish with crabmeat. Special treats are the oyster specialties and turtle soup. Save room for the excellent bread pudding. **FYI:** Reservations recommended. Jazz. Jacket required. **Open:** Lunch Mon–Fri 11:30am–2pm; dinner Mon–Sun 5:30–10pm; brunch Sat 11am–1:30pm, Sun 10am–1:30pm. **Prices:** Main courses $16–$31. AE, CB, DC, DISC, MC, V. 🅥🅿 &

Cadillac Bar

1802 Shepherd Dr at Katy Fwy; tel 713/862-2020. **Tex-Mex.** The waitstaff's black-tie attire may seem a bit incongruous in these very informal surroundings—but then, anything goes at this very popular Texas dive. Graffiti on the walls is hardly discouraged by the owners—in fact, it is permitted. The food

is great, with cabrito (roasted baby goat) and frog legs among the favorites. Very swift and attentive service. **FYI:** Reservations not accepted. **Open:** Mon–Thurs 11am–11pm, Fri 11am–midnight, Sat noon–midnight, Sun noon–10pm. **Prices:** Main courses $5–$12. AE, CB, DC, DISC, MC, V.

Cafe Annie

1728 Post Oak Blvd (Galleria); tel 713/840-1111. Near San Felipe. **Southwestern.** Cutting-edge cuisine is the draw at this upscale, elegant restaurant—a favorite among those in the know. The contemporary design features beautiful tile floors and a lovely mural. Always interesting Southwestern creations include such items as grilled sea scallops with roasted tomato sauce and garlic cream, cinnamon roasted pheasant with green-chili vinaigrette, and rabbit in red jalapeño sauce. Professional waitstaff is very friendly and attentive. **FYI:** Reservations recommended. Jacket required. **Open:** Lunch Mon–Fri 11:30am–2pm; dinner Mon–Thurs 6:30–10pm, Fri 6:30–10:30pm, Sat 6–10:30pm. **Prices:** Main courses $19–$35. AE, CB, DC, DISC, ER, MC, V. 🅥🅿 &

$ ★ Cafe Express

1800 Post Oak Blvd (Galleria); tel 713/963-9222. Near San Felipe. **Eclectic.** A self-serve restaurant with a trendy decor and very modern ambience. Decorated in bright colors with tropical accents such as a fountain and lush tropical plants. An eclectic menu includes fruits and vegetables, grilled items, and sandwiches. Cappuccino, espresso, or Italian sorbet for finishers. **FYI:** Reservations not accepted. Additional locations: 3200 Kirby (tel 522-3994); 1422 W Gray (tel 522-3100). **Open:** Sun–Thurs 11am–11pm, Fri–Sat 11am–midnight. **Prices:** Main courses $5–$8. AE, CB, DC, DISC, MC, V. 🅿 &

$ The Cafe on the Green

In Omni Houston Hotel, Four Riverway; tel 713/871-8181. **American/Continental.** Relaxed coffee shop style in an upscale setting, with panoramic windows overlooking lavish gardens and pool. Lively at lunchtime, the restaurant offers some of the best values in town. There is a wide selection of salads and sandwiches, but many diners are drawn to the pastas—prepared by the pasta chef right before your eyes—available for just $9.95. Pleasant service. **FYI:** Reservations recommended. Children's menu. **Open:** Daily 6am–11pm. **Prices:** Main courses $6–$12. AE, CB, DC, DISC, MC, V. 🅥🅿 &

★ Captain Benny's Seafood & Oyster Bar

8018 Katy Fwy; tel 713/683-1042. Near Antoine. **Seafood.** This loud and crowded oyster bar is a great place to go for delicious Houston seafood and for experiencing a bit of the city's nightlife as well. **FYI:** Reservations not accepted. Beer and wine only. Additional locations: 8506 S Main (tel 666-5469); 4715 Westheimer (tel 877-1028). **Open:** Mon–Sat 11am–11:45pm. **Prices:** Main courses $4–$9. No CC.

Charley's 517
517 Louisiana (Downtown); tel 713/224-4438. Between Prairie and Texas. **Regional American.** Elegant and cozy restaurant located in the downtown theater district, great for pretheater dining and socializing. The very professional service, formal atmosphere, great food, and extensive wine list can really add something special to an evening out. Game and seafood are specialties. **FYI:** Reservations recommended. Jacket required. **Open:** Lunch Mon–Fri 11:30am–2pm; dinner Mon–Wed 5:30–10pm, Thurs–Sat 5:30–11pm. **Prices:** Main courses $18–$36; prix fixe $34–$62. AE, CB, DC, MC, V. ⓥ ♿

Churrascos
9788 Bissonnet; tel 713/541-2100. Near jct US 59 and Beltway 8. **South American.** Located in far southwest Houston is this lively, informal place for great South American fare. The dish that is the restaurant's namesake consists of butterflied beef tenderloin in a garlicky sauce. Empanadas, plantains, and other traditional foods are served as well. **FYI:** Reservations accepted. Dress code. Additional location: 2055 Westheimer at Shepherd (tel 527-8300). **Open:** Lunch Mon–Fri 11:30am–2pm; dinner Mon–Thurs 5:30–10pm, Fri–Sat 5–10:30pm. **Prices:** Main courses $12–$22. AE, CB, DC, DISC, MC, V. ♿

County Line Barbecue
13850 Cutten Rd; tel 281/537-2454. 1 mi N of FM 1960. **Barbecue.** Lodge-type restaurant secluded on a large wooded estate in far north Houston. The western theme starts at the entrance to the kitchen, which is designed like the back of an old stagecoach wagon, and continues in the waiting room, with its rustic chairs covered in cowhide and light fixtures designed like cacti. Smoked prime rib and chicken and brisket are the popular items. Come with a big appetite; an all-you-can-eat buffet is $14 ($6 for kids). **FYI:** Reservations accepted. Children's menu. Beer and wine only. **Open:** Lunch Wed–Fri 11:30am–2pm, Sat noon–3:30pm, Sun 11:30am–3:30pm; dinner Tues–Thurs 5:30–9pm, Fri 5–10pm, Sat 3:30–10pm, Sun 3:30–9pm. **Prices:** Main courses $4–$13. AE, CB, DC, MC, V. ♿

Damian's Cucina Italiana
3011 Smith St; tel 713/522-0439. Near downtown and jct Elgin. **Italian.** Light and refreshing atmosphere and formal, professional service make this a pleasant setting for fine Italian dining. Food highlights are the large antipasti selection and the veal and seafood dishes. Recommended desserts include tiramisù, cannoli, chocolate tarte, and tartufo. **FYI:** Reservations recommended. Dress code. No smoking. **Open:** Lunch Mon–Fri 11am–2pm; dinner Mon–Thurs 5:30–10pm, Fri 5:30–11:30pm, Sat 5–11:30pm. **Prices:** Main courses $11–$25. AE, CB, DC, MC, V. ⓥ ♿

♥ **DeVille**
In Four Seasons Hotel Houston Center, 1300 Lamar St (Downtown); tel 713/650-1300. **Regional American/Italian.** Cool and contemporary furnishings set off by floor-to-ceiling windows and widely spaced tables contribute to an air of quiet, unhurried elegance. Begin with the likes of Italian toasted lentil soup, or jícama and radicchio cigars with tomatoes and cucumbers and roasted pepper vinaigrette. Move on to herb grilled whole snapper on lemon-scented basmati rice, or five-pepper crusted venison loin on roast fennel risotto, served with summer fruit chutney and port sauce. Unusually interesting selection of house wines by the glass. (Note: The adjoining Terrace Cafe is ideal for lighter, faster, less expensive fare in a quiet, uncrowded setting.) **FYI:** Reservations recommended. Children's menu. **Open:** Lunch Mon–Sat 11am–2pm; dinner daily 6–10:30pm; brunch Sun 10:30am–2pm. **Prices:** Main courses $19–$27. AE, CB, DC, ER, MC, V. ⓥ ♿

Dong Ting
611 Stuart St; tel 713/527-0005. Between Smith and Louisiana. **Chinese.** This huge restaurant offers a large selection of traditional dishes and some unique clay-baked specialties. The lamb dumplings are a knockout. For outdoor dining, it's hard to beat the beautiful courtyard. **FYI:** Reservations accepted. Dress code. **Open:** Lunch Mon–Fri 11am–2pm; dinner Sat–Sun 5–11pm, Mon–Fri 5:30–10:30pm. **Prices:** Main courses $8–$12. AE, CB, DC, DISC, MC, V. 🍴 ⓥ ♿

Goode Company Texas Barbecue
5109 Kirby Dr; tel 713/522-2530. S of US 59 SW Fwy. **Barbecue.** Buffalo trophies, snake skins, and stuffed armadillos adorn this very popular cowboy barbecue pit—a prime destination for those who love great, authentic barbecue. Ribs, brisket, sausage, chicken, and terrific jalapeño bread are all available. **FYI:** Reservations not accepted. Beer and wine only. Additional location: 8911 Katy Fwy (tel 464-1901). **Open:** Daily 11am–10pm. **Prices:** Main courses $4–$8. AE, CB, DC, DISC, MC, V. 🍴

♥ **The Great Caruso**
In Carillon Shopping Center, 10001 Westheimer; tel 713/780-4900. E of Beltway 8. **American/Continental.** The elaborate setting—chandeliers, ornate balcony facades, opera memorabilia, a grand Italian marble staircase, and fine European antiques—and the singing waitstaff make dining here a theatrical, romantic affair. The delicious menu includes steak, veal, and prime rib, and seafood such as lobster, squid, swordfish, and octopus. Light operetta and Broadway performances are staged nightly. **FYI:** Reservations accepted. Cabaret/jazz. Dress code. **Open:** Tues–Sun 6–10pm. **Prices:** Main courses $13–$23. AE, CB, DC, DISC, MC, V. ♥ ⓥ ♿

★ **The Grill and Bar**
In the Ritz-Carlton Houston, 1919 Briar Oaks Lane; tel 713/840-7600. Near Post Oaks Park and River Oaks; inside Loop 610. **American/Continental.** Clubby and pubby, with lots of wood paneling and hunting prints. The two dining rooms are separated by a bar and small dance floor. Dry-aged meats are complemented by innovative regional touches like wild dove quesadilla with mushrooms and ancho chili; house

pecanwood-smoked salmon with potato cake; lump crab meat and ricotta cheese raviolis; sautéed seabass with oven-roasted tomatoes and lemon-cactus sauce; veal tenderloin au poivre with morel mushrooms and truffle-shallot butter; and fruit empanadas (guava, papaya, mango) with chocolate rum sauce. **FYI:** Reservations recommended. Dancing/combo. Children's menu. **Open:** Daily 6–11pm. **Prices:** Main courses $17–$27. AE, CB, DC, DISC, ER, MC, V. 🆅🅿 ♿

Hard Rock Cafe

2801 Kirby; tel 713/520-1134. Between Alabama and Westheimer. **Eclectic.** Like all the other Hard Rocks scattered throughout the world, this one is loud and crowded with the standard rock-and-roll memorabilia. The wait for burgers or souvenir T-shirts is about the same. **FYI:** Reservations accepted. Children's menu. **Open:** Mon–Thurs 11am–midnight, Fri–Sat 11am–1am, Sun 11am–11:30pm. **Prices:** Main courses $6–$14. AE, DC, MC, V. ♿

The Hobbit Hole Cafe

1715 S Shepherd; tel 713/528-3418. Near San Felipe. **Eclectic.** Inspired by JRR Tolkien's fantastical novel, this unique health food restaurant is great for kids or any fan of *The Hobbit*. Sandwiches are named after characters from the book, and a variety of vegetarian dishes are offered. Wooded outdoor seating is available. **FYI:** Reservations accepted. Beer and wine only. No smoking. **Open:** Mon–Thurs 11am–10pm, Fri–Sat 11am–11pm, Sun 11:30am–9pm. **Prices:** Main courses $5–$10. AE, CB, DC, DISC, MC, V. ♿

The Hofbrau

1803 Shepherd; tel 713/869-7074. Near I-610 N Loop Fwy. **Steak.** A casual Texas-style restaurant and bar with a roadhouse dive atmosphere. Great steaks (like the T-bone topped with grilled onions), chicken dishes, and burgers are served. **FYI:** Reservations not accepted. **Open:** Mon–Tues 11am–10pm, Wed–Fri 11am–10:30pm, Sat 5:30–10:30pm, Sun 11am–10pm. **Prices:** Main courses $5–$15. MC, V.

India's Restaurant

5704 Richmond; tel 713/266-0131. Near Chimney Rock. **Indian.** The stark interior belies the rich, complex flavors of the food, considered by some to be the best Indian in Houston. A very extensive and inexpensive lunch buffet offers good value. Tandoori bread is a favorite. **FYI:** Reservations accepted. Dress code. Beer and wine only. **Open:** Lunch daily 11am–2:30pm; dinner Sun–Thurs 5:30–10pm, Fri–Sat 5:30–10:30pm. **Prices:** Main courses $9–$14. AE, CB, DC, DISC, MC, V. ♿

Kim Son

2001 Jefferson (Downtown); tel 713/222-2461. At Chartres, near US 59. **Vietnamese.** With close to 100 menu options, this highly regarded Vietnamese restaurant demonstrates that more can be better. Great spring rolls, crab dishes, and other delicacies are served in a lovely, contemporary setting. Look for the exotic fish pool and fountain at the entrance. **FYI:** Reservations accepted. Children's menu. Additional location:

8200 Wilcrest (tel 498-7841). **Open:** Daily 10:30am–11pm. **Prices:** Main courses $4–$11. AE, CB, DC, DISC, MC, V. 👥 ♿

La Mora Cucina Toscana

912 Lovett; tel 713/522-7412. At Montrose near Westheimer. **Italian.** Situated atop a beautiful wooded lot is this restaurant serving wonderful Tuscan cuisine. The atrium dining room with fireplace is lovely, and there is also a garden area. Menu features excellent antipasti, tagliatelle in cream sauce and other pastas, quail with polenta, grilled meats, and daily fish specials. Excellent Italian wine list. **FYI:** Reservations recommended. Dress code. **Open:** Lunch Mon–Fri 11am–2pm; dinner Mon–Thurs 6–10pm, Fri–Sat 5:30–11pm. **Prices:** Main courses $13–$21. AE, CB, DC, DISC, MC, V. 🆅🅿

La Réserve

In Omni Houston Hotel, Four Riverway (Galleria); tel 713/871-8177. Near Woodway. **French.** One of Houston's best restaurants serves wonderful haute cuisine in a dining room decorated with tasteful yet unique furnishings, elaborate floral arrangements, and many plants and trees. Caviar pie is a luxurious specialty, and ostrich and wild game are available. Ask about the grand menu, which offers the best specialties and includes wine. **FYI:** Reservations accepted. Piano. Dress code. **Open:** Mon–Thurs 6:30–10pm, Fri–Sat 6–10:30pm. **Prices:** Main courses $19–$37; prix fixe $50–$70. AE, CB, DC, DISC, ER, MC, V. ♥ 🆅🅿 ♿

🏆 La Tour l'Argent

2011 Ella Blvd; tel 713/864-9864. Between 20th and 21st Sts. **French.** Housed in a 1920s log cabin overlooking the bayou, this unique place offers rustic and romantic hunting lodge atmosphere. Guests can stroll down the walking paths to the gazebo and the trickling stream, and dine beneath the exotic hunting trophies lining the walls. Two fireplaces and a huge tigerskin rug contribute to the cozy, singular ambience. Menu specialties are pheasant, duck, and seafood. **FYI:** Reservations recommended. Jacket required. **Open:** Lunch Mon–Fri 11:30am–2pm; dinner Mon–Wed 6–10pm, Thurs–Sat 6–11pm. **Prices:** Main courses $18–$26. AE, CB, DC, DISC, MC, V. ♥ 🏔 🆅🅿 ♿

Maxim's

In Greenway Plaza, 3735 Richmond (Greenway Plaza); tel 713/877-8899. Between Weslayan and Edloe, near US 59 SW Fwy. **Continental/French.** Very popular and very professional, this heavyweight located near the Summit features plush seating and carpeting, a beautiful pastoral painting behind the bar, statuary, and soft classical music to create a romantic setting for enjoying the high-priced fare. Seafood, lamb, and veal selections are superb. Extensive wine list. **FYI:** Reservations recommended. Jacket required. **Open:** Mon–Fri 11:30am–10:30pm, Sat 5:30–11pm. **Prices:** Main courses $16–$26. AE, CB, DC, DISC, MC, V. 🆅🅿 ♿

Ninfa's

2704 Navigation; tel 713/228-1175. E of downtown near York. **Tex-Mex.** This family-owned chain serves excellent Tex-Mex cuisine in a casual setting. Tacos al carbón are a good bet. **FYI:** Reservations accepted. Additional locations: 3601 Kirby (tel 520-0203); 6154 Westheimer (tel 781-2740). **Open:** Daily 11am–10pm. **Prices:** Main courses $6–$19. AE, CB, DC, DISC, MC, V. &

Nino's

2817 S Dallas; tel 713/522-5120. Between Yale and Montrose. **Italian.** A great place for a fun evening with friends or family, this upbeat, semi-casual two-story restaurant offers an excellent, large antipasti bar, good seafood, and a fine veal chop. Young and friendly waitstaff. **FYI:** Reservations recommended. Dress code. **Open:** Lunch Mon–Fri 11am–2:30pm; dinner Mon–Thurs 5:30–10pm, Fri–Sat 5:30–11pm. **Prices:** Main courses $8–$18. AE, CB, DC, MC, V. &

Nippon

4464 Montrose Blvd; tel 713/523-3939. Near US 59 SW Fwy. **Japanese.** Casual Japanese restaurant with attactive decor of black tables and dark colors with gold accents. Many items are available, but sushi is the real specialty. Waitstaff dresses in traditional clothing. **FYI:** Reservations accepted. Children's menu. **Open:** Lunch daily 11:30am–2:30pm; dinner daily 5–10:30pm. **Prices:** Main courses $8–$23. AE, CB, DC, DISC, MC, V. &

Old San Francisco

8611 Westheimer Rd; tel 713/783-5990. 2½ mi W of Galleria. **Seafood/Steak.** This huge dining room takes its decor straight from an Old West saloon, with dueling pianos for entertainment and a woman swinging over the bar. A fun atmosphere for enjoying tasty steak and seafood. **FYI:** Reservations recommended. Piano. Children's menu. Dress code. **Open:** Dinner Mon–Sat 4–11pm, Sun noon–10pm. **Prices:** Main courses $11–$31. AE, CB, DC, DISC, MC, V. 🍽 VP &

Otto's Barbecue

5502 Memorial Dr; tel 713/864-2573. Between Wescott and Shepherd. **Barbecue.** Though it's a bit difficult to locate (just enter through the adjoining burger place), this barbecue restaurant—serving customers since 1950—is definitely worth the trouble. The beef barbecue is considered some of the best in the city. Good for a quick lunch. **FYI:** Reservations not accepted. No liquor license. **Open:** Mon–Sat 11am–9pm. **Prices:** Main courses $12–$22. AE, DISC, MC, V. 🍴 &

Outback Steakhouse

13240 NW Fwy; tel 713/460-5639. On US 290 near Holister. **Steak.** Part of a large chain of restaurants featuring an Australian outback motif; good for casual family dining. Good steaks, coconut shrimp, and a variety of chicken and seafood dishes are offered. **FYI:** Reservations not accepted. Children's menu. Additional locations: 10001 Westheimer (tel 978-6283); 5710 FM 1960 W (tel 580-4329). **Open:** Mon–Fri 4–11:30pm, Sat–Sun 3–11:30pm. **Prices:** Main courses $9–$18. AE, CB, DC, DISC, MC, V. &

Pappas Seafood House

6894 Southwest Fwy; tel 713/784-4729. On US 59 near Savoy and Regency Sq. **Seafood.** This very busy, casual seafood restaurant lets you choose your fish or shellfish blackened, broiled, or fried. Healthy menu items are available. Gumbo and Greek salad are house favorites. **FYI:** Reservations not accepted. Children's menu. Additional locations: 12010 I-10 E (tel 453-3265); 3001 S Shepherd (tel 522-4595). **Open:** Sun–Thurs 11am–10pm, Fri–Sat 11am–11pm. **Prices:** Main courses $10–$35. AE, MC, V. &

River Oaks Grill

2630 Westheimer Rd at Kirby (River Oaks); tel 713/520-1738. **Eclectic.** Located in the exclusive River Oaks neighborhood. Formal, clublike, and somewhat stuffy, the restaurant features a posh interior with dark colors and rich woods. Specialties include grilled salmon, ribeye steak, fresh Maine lobster, and excellent cheesecakes. **FYI:** Reservations recommended. Jacket required. **Open:** Lunch Mon–Fri 11am–2:30pm; dinner Mon–Sat 6–10:30pm. **Prices:** Main courses $14–$29. AE, CB, DC, DISC, MC, V. VP &

Rotisserie for Beef and Bird

2200 Wilcrest Dr; tel 713/977-9524. 3 blocks N of Westheimer, near Beltway 8. **Continental.** Owned by well-known Houston chef Joe Mannke, this serene restaurant located in a residential area is predictably elegant and upscale, yet unpretentious. A rotisserie and an open hearth face one of the dining areas. Great beef and venison, roast duckling, and other items, cooked to perfection. **FYI:** Reservations recommended. Jacket required. **Open:** Lunch Mon–Fri 11:30am–2pm; dinner Mon–Sat 6–10pm. **Prices:** Main courses $18–$29. AE, CB, DC, DISC, MC, V. VP &

Ruth's Chris Steak House

6213 Richmond Ave; tel 713/789-2333. Near Greenridge. **Steak.** Very popular (especially among corporate lunchers) and very pricey, this two-level steakhouse and its counterparts nationwide are well known for their giant steaks prepared in sizzling butter. Decor is upscale and elegant, with rich wood paneling and cradles of winebins scattered throughout. **FYI:** Reservations accepted. Dress code. **Open:** Daily 5–11pm. **Prices:** Main courses $18–$29. AE, CB, DC, DISC, MC, V. VP &

Sammy's Lebanese Restaurant

5825 Richmond; tel 713/780-0065. Near Fountainview; accessible from US 59. **Lebanese.** This very friendly, homey, and casual restaurant offers great inexpensive Middle Eastern food. Very popular for its appetizer platters, Sammy's offers a large seafood selection plus lamb, beef, chicken, and vegetarian dishes. The freshly squeezed apple and carrot juice drink is recommended. **FYI:** Reservations accepted.

Beer and wine only. **Open:** Mon–Fri 11am–10:30pm, Sat 11am–11pm, Sun noon–10pm. **Prices:** Main courses $9–$15. AE, CB, DC, DISC, MC, V.

Spanish Village
4720 Almeda; tel 713/523-2861. S of US59, near downtown. **Tex-Mex.** While this Tex-Mex establishment is in need of some repair and is located in a somewhat rundown neighborhood south of downtown, it does possess a certain charm. Christmas lights strung throughout help create a festive atmosphere. And the food—especially the stuffed chili—and margaritas are great. **FYI:** Reservations accepted. **Open:** Tues–Thurs 11am–9:30pm. **Prices:** Main courses $4–$10. AE, MC, V.

Thai Pepper
2120 Post Oak Blvd (Galleria); tel 713/963-0341. Near San Felipe. **Thai.** Contemporary decor includes light colors, Asian vases, and tile floors. Standard Thai fare makes up for in taste what it lacks in originality. **FYI:** Reservations accepted. Dress code. Additional location: 2049 Alabama (tel 520-8225). **Open:** Lunch Mon–Fri 11:30am–2:30pm; dinner Mon–Thurs 5–10:30pm, Fri–Sat 5–11pm. **Prices:** Main courses $9–$15. AE, CB, DC, DISC, MC, V.

Tony Mandola's Blue Oyster Bar
8105 Gulf Fwy; tel 713/640-1042. Between Belfort and Broadway about 2 mi S of I-610 S Loop Fwy. **Seafood.** Oysters and snapper head an extensive menu at this casual, often crowded seafood place. **FYI:** Reservations not accepted. Beer and wine only. **Open:** Mon–Thurs 11am–10pm, Fri–Sat 11am–11pm, Sun noon–9pm. **Prices:** Main courses $4–$12. AE, CB, DC, DISC, MC, V.

Treebeard's
In Baker-Travis Bldg, 315 Travis (Downtown); tel 713/225-2160. Between Congress and Preston. **Cajun/Creole.** A casual downtown cafeteria-style restaurant located in the historic Baker-Travis building. Vines adorn the entrance and enhance an outdoor seating area. Mainly caters to the downtown lunch crowd. An inexpensive menu concentrates on Louisiana-style cuisine. **FYI:** Reservations accepted. Children's menu. Dress code. Beer and wine only. **Open:** Lunch Mon–Fri 11am–2pm; dinner Fri 5–9pm. **Prices:** Main courses $5–$15. AE, CB, DC, DISC, MC, V.

Van Loc Restaurant
3010 Milam St; tel 713/528-6441. Near Elgin; accessible off US 59 or I-45. **Vietnamese.** Casual Vietnamese restaurant offering a very good, wide selection of creative entrees and appetizers. **FYI:** Reservations not accepted. Beer and wine only. Additional location: 825 Travis St (tel 236-0548). **Open:** Sun–Thurs 9am–11pm, Fri–Sat 9am–midnight. **Prices:** Main courses $4–$15. AE, MC, V.

Vargo's
2401 Fondren; tel 713/782-3888. N of Westheimer. **Continental.** This well-established restaurant is very popular in the Houston area. The large, secluded, eight-acre lot includes beautiful trees, a gorgeous lake, and a lovely gazebo. Huge windows provide excellent views of the grounds, and peacocks and swans roam the property. Enjoy specialties such as prime rib, snapper amandine, and filet mignon. **FYI:** Reservations recommended. Piano. Jacket required. **Open:** Lunch Mon–Fri 11am–2pm; dinner Mon–Thurs 5:30–10:30pm, Fri–Sat 5–11pm; brunch Sun 11am–2:30pm. **Prices:** Main courses $12–$24. AE, CB, DC, DISC, MC, V.

Willie's Grill & Ice House
17492 Northwest Fwy; tel 713/937-0456. US 290 near Beltway 8. **Burgers.** Not the seediest of dives, but a dive nonetheless. Casual and loud, with empty beer bottles doubling as salt and pepper shakers and empty beer boxes decorating the common area. Discarded ties hang from the rafters, and dollar bills decorate the walls and ceilings. But this place is well known for its beer and burgers. **FYI:** Reservations not accepted. **Open:** Mon–Thurs 11am–10pm, Fri–Sat 11am–11pm, Sun 11am–9pm. **Prices:** Main courses $4–$9. AE, DISC, MC, V.

ATTRACTIONS

MUSEUMS

Museum of Fine Arts, Houston
1001 Bissonnet; tel 713/639-7300. A mixture of neoclassical and modern architecture (the interior of one of its modern wings, designed by Mies van der Rohe, has an unusual theme of broken concrete shafts), this museum houses an impressive collection of European art from throughout the ages, as well as works by renowned American painters (particularly Frederic Remington), Native American pottery, and pre-Columbian art. Some of the works on display are Fra Angelico's *Temptation of St Anthony, Virgin and Child* by Rogier van der Weyden, *Water Lilies* by Claude Monet, *Woman in a Purple Coat* by Henri Matisse, and van Gogh's *The Rocks.* Major exhibitions of world cultures are also presented; shows on African royal art, the ancient Americas, and the rediscovery of Pompeii are recent examples. The Lillie and Hugh Roy Cullen Sculpture Garden, created by distinguished sculptor Isamu Noguchi, measures 43,560 square feet and provides a setting for major 19th- and 20th-century sculpture, including works by Henri Matisse, Alberto Giacometti, Marino Marini, Auguste Rodin, Ellsworth Kelly, Louise Bourgeois, and Frank Stella. The Glassell School of Art, established in 1927, is nationally known for its training in the fine arts; it also offers a wide variety of programs and classes for adults and children, as well as one- and two-year residencies. Reference library; guided tours available. **Open:** Tues–Sat 10am–5pm, Thurs 10am–9pm, Sun 12:15–6pm. $

The Menil Collection
1515 Sul Ross; tel 713/525-9400. The personal collection of Dominique de Menil, which drew large crowds when it was exhibited a few years ago at the Petit Palais in Paris, is now housed here. This is among the world's most highly regarded

private museums, comprising more than 15,000 works of art spanning over 5,000 years of history. Etruscan and Anatolian sculpture; medieval paintings; works from native cultures around the world, including masks, effigies, carvings, and cast-metal objects; works of avant-garde painters such as Picasso, Pollock, Leger, Rauschenberg, and Warhol, and surrealists like de Chirico and Magritte. The 9,300-square-foot Cy Twombly Gallery features a permanent collection of the artist's works. The unique, light-filled modern building was designed by Renzo Piano, architect of many distinguished buildings, including Paris's famous Centre Pompidou. Bookstore in the museum **Open:** Wed–Sun 11am–7pm. **Free**

Contemporary Arts Museum
5216 Montrose Blvd; tel 713/526-3129. This unique, silvered-aluminum parallelogram presents movies and temporary exhibitions of modern art and industrial design. Focuses on post-1945 American art. **Open:** Tues–Wed 10am–5pm, Thurs 10am–9pm, Fri–Sat 10am–5pm, Sun noon–5pm. **$**

Rothko Chapel
3900 Yupon St; tel 713/524-9839. This octagonal chapel in an out-of-the-way district was designed by Philip Johnson in austere, reinforced concrete. It houses 14 dark, brooding paintings created by Mark Rothko in 1965 and 1966. Barnett Newman's *Broken Obelisk,* a sculpture dedicated to Martin Luther King Jr, sits in a reflection pool in front of the chapel. A fine setting for meditation and contemplation. **Open:** Daily 10am–6pm. **Free**

Houston Museum of Natural Science
1 Hermann Circle Dr; tel 713/639-IMAX. From the diplodocus to the space rocket and from oil wells to artificial earthquakes, this is one of the biggest and most impressive natural science museums in the country. Special highlights are the Hall of Medical Science, with its giant models of the human body, and the Burke Baker Planetarium, where visitors can follow the paths of comets and the motion of the planets across the star-studded dome. **Open:** Mon–Sat 9am–6pm, Sun 11am–6pm. **$**

Bayou Bend
1 Westcott St; tel 713/639-7750. Beautiful collection of American furniture from the 17th through 19th centuries housed in 28 rooms of the vast Renaissance-style home of Ima Hogg, daughter of a former governor of Texas. Under the auspices of the Museum of Fine Arts; the collection can be viewed Tues–Sat by appointment. **Open:** Tues–Fri 10am–2:45pm, Sat 10am–5pm, Sun 1–5pm. **$$$**

The Children's Museum of Houston
1500 Binz; tel 713/522-1138. Designed by award-winning architect Robert Venturi, the building is supported by giant caricatures of smiling children. Hands-on exhibits geared toward children age 14 and under cover the areas of science, history, culture, and the arts. At the KID-TV studio, children can watch themselves perform on TV or experiment with TV production. At the Technikids gallery, children can build their own toy race car then compete on a timed race track that drops eight feet from the upper level. The New Perspectives gallery contains a Mexican village and a Chinese market town. In all, there are thirteen permanent and changing exhibition areas, plus a resource center for parents, child care workers, and educators, a 164-seat auditorium, and a retail shop. **Open:** Tues–Sat 9am–5pm, Sun noon–5pm. **$$**

OTHER ATTRACTIONS

Sam Houston Historical Park
1100 Bagby; tel 713/655-1912. Located in the modern downtown area are eight of the city's oldest structures. Restored and furnished in 19th-century fashion, these buildings reflect a range of styles and uses, and are open for guided tours. The Kellum-Noble House from 1847 is the oldest surviving brick house in the city; the Nichols-Rice-Cherry House from around 1850 reflects the Greek Revival style; the mid-Victorian Pillot House from 1868 features significant innovations of the period, including its kitchen, believed to have been the first attached kitchen in the city. An 1891 church, along with a log cabin (circa 1823), an 1870s cottage, and a turn-of-the-century Victorian-style bandstand are other highlights of the area. Also situated in the park is the **Heritage Museum,** which features permanent exhibits covering many facets of Texas history, as well as a complete country store. The complex also includes a gift shop and a tearoom. **Open:** Mon–Sat 10am–4pm, Sun 1–5pm. **$$**

Space Center Houston
1601 NASA Rd 1; tel 281/244-2100. Hands-on exhibits tell the story of manned space flight. Visitors can land the shuttle or retrieve a satellite through computer simulations, touch a moon rock or try on space helmets. There are behind-the-scenes tram tours of NASA's Johnson Space Center which include visits to Mission Control, the Weightless Environment Training Facility, and other areas of JSC. Actual Mercury, Gemini, and Apollo spacecraft can be viewed; a film on being an astronaut is shown on a screen 80 feet wide and almost 5 stories high. Current information about space flight and training activities is provided through special monitors and presentations. JSC scientists, engineers, and astronauts visit the facility daily to share their experiences and answer questions. Food available. **Open:** Mon–Fri 10am–5pm, Sat–Sun 10am–7pm. **$$$$**

Houston Zoological Gardens
1513 N MacGregor; tel 713/523-5888. This 50-acre zoo features a gorilla habitat, rare albino reptiles, cat facility, huge aquarium, and vampire bats which eat lunch every day at 2:30pm. The tropical bird house resembles an Asian jungle and is home to more than 200 exotic birds flying freely through this rain-forest environment. The Brown Education Center allows visitors to interact with the animals. **Open:** Daily 10am–6pm. **$**

Rice University

6100 S Main St; tel 713/527-4929. This 31,000-student university is greatly renowned for its science and engineering faculties (it's been referred to as the "Harvard of the South"). Founded in 1912, the university boasts dozens of neoclassical and Mediterranean-style buildings, including Lovett Hall and the Sewall Art Gallery, as well as the ultramodern and original Herring Hall by architect Cesar Pelli. Rice Stadium seats 70,000. **Free**

Downtown Houston Tunnel System

(Downtown); tel 713/840-9255. The oldest and one of the largest indoor pedestrian tunnel/skywalk systems in the country—55 contiguous buildings spread out over 60 blocks—helps workers and visitors avoid the brunt of the downtown traffic, as well as the city's notoriously hot and humid climate. The tunnel runs under most of the area's major buildings (some as old as 1910), and its decor changes with each building. Restaurants and shops dot the underground landscape. Guided tours available. **Open:** Mon–Fri 7am–7pm. **$$**

Six Flags AstroWorld

9001 Kirby Dr; tel 713/799-1234. Huge 75-acre amusement park with more than 100 attractions, including the giant "Texas Cyclone" roller coaster. Shows and concerts are also presented. **Open:** Peak (Mem Day–Labor Day) daily 10am–10pm. Reduced hours off-season. Closed Dec–Feb. **$$$$**

Six Flags WaterWorld

9001 Kirby Dr; tel 713/799-1234. Very popular aquatic amusement park adjoining AstroWorld. Highlights include an enormous pool with artificial waves for surfers; giant slides; and a lagoon swimming pool with waterfalls. **Open:** Peak (May–Aug) 10am–6pm. Reduced hours off-season. **$$$$**

The Orange Show

2401 Munger St (East End); tel 713/926-6368. A unique urban folk-art park built by Jeff McKissack, an ex-postman who spent 25 years assembling a collection of found objects and mundane daily artifacts in order to, as he himself stated, "encourage people to eat oranges, drink oranges, and be highly amused." The structure is a labyrinth of outdoor and indoor passages, stairs, and platforms, amid unique whirligigs, wrought-iron gewgaws, colored folk antiques, junk, and rudimentary art embellished with memorable mottoes and parables ("Oranges for Energy," "Love me, orange, please love me," "Be alert"). McKissack died in 1980, but a group of artists and city officials formed the Orange Show Foundation to preserve the complex, which is also used as an educational and cultural community center to host children's theater, poetry workshops, art shows, and musical performances. The foundation sponsors programs such as Eyeopeners, which documents and conducts public tours of Texas art environments, and the Brown Lectures at the Orange Show, in which nationally-regarded scholars and artists discuss art and artists. **Open:** Peak (Mem Day–Labor Day) Wed–Fri 9am–1pm, Sat–Sun noon–5pm. Reduced hours off-season. **$**

Jesse H Jones Hall for the Performing Arts

615 Louisiana St; tel 713/227-3974. Home of the Houston Symphony Orchestra. In the past, performers here have included James Taylor, Neil Sedaka, Hildegard Behrens, and Midori. **$$$$**

Wortham Theater Center

510 Preston Blvd; tel 713/853-8000. Opened in 1987, this is the home of the Houston Grand Opera, which performs from September to March, as well as the Houston Ballet, the major permanent dance company in the Southwest. **$**

Nina Vance Alley Theatre

615 Texas Ave; tel 713/228-8421. This futurist structure, comprising two auditoriums divided by a party wall, is one of Houston's most innovative buildings. Designed by Ulrich Fransen, it has the appearance of a 21st-century fortress. Recent productions have included *Julius Caesar, Antony and Cleopatra, Angels in America,* and *Jekyll and Hyde.* **$$$$**

Society for the Performing Arts

615 Louisiana St; tel 713/227-5134 or toll free 800/828-2787. The largest non-profit organization of its kind in the Southwest, the SPA sponsors artists and productions from all areas of the performing arts. Past events have featured such distinguished artists as Itzhak Perlman, Arthur Rubenstein, Vladimir Horowitz, and Leontyne Price. Educational programs, master classes, and lectures are also included in its regular season schedule. **Open:** Contact for performance schedules. **$$$$**

Anheuser-Busch Brewery Tours

I-10 E at I-610 Loop; tel 713/670-1695. Guided hour-long tour of the brewery offers a live demonstration of the brewing process and explains the history of one of the world's most prominent beer producers. Complimentary samplings in the Hospitality Room; gift shop. **Open:** Mon–Sat 9am–4pm. **Free**

Astrodome USA

8400 Kirby Dr; tel 713/799-9544. Among the highest-domed stadiums in the world, with 76,000 seats; the plastic roof rises 18 stories. Home of the Astros baseball and Oilers football teams, the stadium is used not only for sports events but also for concerts, exhibitions, and political meetings. This impressive structure is one of the most visited in Texas. Guided tours available. **Open:** Tours conducted daily 11am, 1pm, and 3pm. **$$**

George Ranch Historical Park

10215 FM 762, Richmond; tel 281/545-9212. This 470-acre "working ranch" features a number of restored historic buildings (which can be toured) as well as demonstrations and historical reconstructions provided by costumed guides and craftsmen. Visitors can have Victorian-style tea on the porch of an 1890s mansion, or sit around the campfire with cowboys during a roundup, and watch crafts demonstrations such as the making of lye soap or old-fashioned rope twisting. Picnic areas provided. **Open:** Apr–Dec, Sat–Sun 9am–6pm. **$$**

Huntsville

Originally an 1830s Indian trading post, Huntsville is home to Sam Houston State University and a major destination for antique lovers. The Walker County seat is the final resting place of General Sam Houston, the first president of the Republic of Texas. **Information:** Huntsville-Wasker County Chamber of Commerce, 1327 11th Ave, PO Box 538, Huntsville, 77342-0538 (tel 409/295-8113 or toll free 800/289-0389).

HOTEL

≣≣ University Hotel
Ave H at 16th St, 77341; tel 409/291-2151. On Sam Houston University campus. Reasonably comfortable despite its dormitory atmosphere. On the Sam Houston State University campus. **Rooms:** 95 rms. CI 3pm/CO noon. Nonsmoking rms avail. **Amenities:** A/C, cable TV, refrig. **Services:** Facilities: 1 restaurant (bkfst only). Use of College Health Center for $2 fee. **Rates:** $35–$40 S or D. Extra person $3. Children under age 18 stay free. Parking: Outdoor, free. AE, CB, DC, MC, V.

MOTELS

≣≣ Econo Lodge
1501 I-45 N, 77340; tel 409/295-6401 or toll free 800/424-4777. Exit 116 off I-45. This standard roadside motel is a reliable budget choice for Sam Houston Historical Park visitors. Located minutes from downtown Huntsville and universities. **Rooms:** 57 rms. CI 4pm/CO noon. Nonsmoking rms avail. **Amenities:** A/C, cable TV. **Services:** Facilities: **Rates (CP):** $35–$49 S or D. Extra person $6. Children under age 18 stay free. Parking: Outdoor, free. AE, CB, DC, DISC, MC, V.

≣≣≣ Sam Houston Inn
3296 I-45 S, 77340; tel 409/295-9151 or toll free 800/395-9151. Near 22nd St; exit 114 off I-45. A cozy motel with lodgelike ambience situated among the trees lining this stretch of I-45, near Sam Houston Historical Park. The fireplace is the focal point of the quaint lobby. Friendly, service-oriented staff. **Rooms:** 76 rms. CI 2pm/CO noon. Nonsmoking rms avail. **Amenities:** A/C, cable TV. **Services:** **Facilities:** Sauna. **Rates (CP):** $42–$64 S or D. Extra person $6. Children under age 17 stay free. Parking: Outdoor, free. AE, CB, DC, DISC, MC, V.

RESTAURANT

The Junction
2641 11th St; tel 409/291-2183. E of I-45. **Seafood/Steak.** This restored, grand country manor house, an excellent choice for special dining, presides over a large wooded lot. The rustic interior boasts skylights over the dining area and many antiques. Prime rib, catfish, lobster, and shrimp highlight the menu; there's also a salad bar. **FYI:** Reservations accepted. Children's menu. **Open:** Sun–Thurs 10am–10pm, Fri–Sat 10am–11pm. **Prices:** Main courses $5–$14. AE, CB, DC, DISC, MC, V.

ATTRACTIONS

Sam Houston Memorial Museum
19th St and Ave N; tel 409/294-1832. Sam Houston led the fight for Texas's independence and then served as President of the Republic of Texas, United States Senator, and Governor. This museum, located on the grounds of Sam Houston State University, is dedicated to preserving his memory and his era. The museum complex is built on a portion of the former Houston farm and features the Woodland Home, built in 1848 and occupied by him during much of the time he spent in the Senate. The kitchen is a replica of the original. The Steamboat House, built in the 1850s, is where Houston spent his last years. The Exhibit Hall contains artifacts and displays on 19th-century life, including the "Touch of Texas," the museum's hands-on discovery center. The Memorial Museum building houses the permanent exhibits, including an extensive collection of Houston artifacts and memorabilia—his leopard-skin vest and the saddle captured from General Santa Anna at the battle of San Jacinto are popular exhibits. The Education Center offers a video presentation, as well as a reading room and multipurpose classroom; museum store on premises. **Open:** Tues–Sun 9am–4:30pm. **Free**

Texas Prison Museum
1113 12th St; tel 409/295-2155. Chronicles the past and present of the Texas prison system. Highlights include an authentic 9-by-6-foot prison cell which visitors can experience; Bonnie and Clyde's rifles; "Old Sparky," the Texas electric chair; prison-made weapons confiscated from inmates; musical and artistic contributions of inmates; relics of the Carrasco prison siege in 1974; Texas prison rodeo; and an exhibit on inmate education. Guided tours by appointment. **Open:** Tues–Fri noon–5pm, Sat 9am–5pm, Sun noon–5pm. **$**

Irving

See also Arlington, Dallas–Ft Worth Int'l Airport

What is now a suburb west of Dallas began as a railroad switching town in 1903. One of the fastest-growing small cities in the Dallas area, it is home to Texas Stadium and the Dallas Cowboys, and a good mid-territory base for touring Dallas and Fort Worth. **Information:** Irving Convention & Visitors Bureau, 3333 N MacArthur Blvd, #200, Irving, 75062 (tel 214/252-7476 or toll free 800/2-IRVING).

HOTELS

Omni Mandalay Hotel at Las Colinas
221 E Las Colinas Blvd, 75039 (Las Colinas); tel 972/556-0800 or toll free 800/THE-OMNI; fax 972/869-9053. Near O'Connor and TX 114. Aimed primarily at business travelers but certainly suitable for vacationers, this facility situated along the Mandalay Canal in Las Colinas is serviced by numerous water taxis for transportation to local shopping and dining outlets and office complexes. The marble lobby is richly decorated with tropical foliage. **Rooms:** 410 rms and stes. CI 3pm/CO noon. Nonsmoking rms avail. **Amenities:** A/C, cable TV w/movies, dataport, voice mail, bathrobes. Some units w/terraces, 1 w/fireplace, 1 w/whirlpool. **Services:** Twice-daily maid svce, car-rental desk, social director, masseur, children's program, babysitting. **Facilities:** 2 restaurants, 2 bars (1 w/entertainment), spa, sauna, steam rm, whirlpool, playground. **Rates:** $99–$190 S or D; $160–$500 ste. Extra person $20. Children under age 18 stay free. Parking: Indoor/outdoor, free. AE, CB, DC, DISC, EC, ER, JCB, MC, V.

Wyndham Garden Hotel
110 W Carpenter Fwy, 75039 (Las Colinas); tel 972/650-1600 or toll free 800/WYNDHAM; fax 972/541-0501. On TX 114, near O'Connor. This small, inconspicuous property with a residential atmosphere is a hidden treasure of comfort. The lush garden area is the hotel's focal point. Popular with business guests. **Rooms:** 168 rms and stes. CI 3pm/CO noon. Nonsmoking rms avail. **Amenities:** A/C, cable TV w/movies, voice mail. Some units w/terraces. **Services:** Car-rental desk, babysitting. **Facilities:** 1 restaurant, 1 bar, sauna, whirlpool. American Airlines desk on site. Access to local health and fitness facilities can be arranged. **Rates (BB):** $119 S; $129 D; $200 ste. Extra person $10. Parking: Outdoor, free. AE, CB, DC, DISC, MC, V.

RESORT

Four Seasons Resort and Club Dallas
4150 N MacArthur Blvd, 75038 (Las Colinas); tel 972/717-2441 or toll free 800/545-4000; fax 972/717-2486. N of jct Northgate Rd. 400 acres. The exterior of the resort's building is rather imposing, but the interior decor is elegant, light, comfortable, and casual. Service is warm and very professional. Great for an extended visit to the Irving area. **Rooms:** 365 rms and stes; 50 cottages/villas. CI 3pm/CO 1pm. Nonsmoking rms avail. Villa suites overlook the golf course or pool; tower rooms have great views, too.

Amenities: A/C, cable TV w/movies, refrig, dataport, voice mail, bathrooms. All units w/minibars, all w/terraces, 1 w/fireplace, some w/whirlpools. **Services:** Twice-daily maid svce, car-rental desk, social director, masseur, children's program, babysitting. One-hour pants pressing; shoeshine. Nutrition and make-up services. City tours and transportation within a limited area provided. Afternoon tea features a boutique fashion show. **Facilities:** 4 restaurants, 4 bars (1 w/entertainment), basketball, volleyball, racquetball, squash, spa, sauna, steam rm, whirlpool, beauty salon, day-care ctr. Tournament golf course is home to the GTE Byron Nelson Classic. **Rates:** $220–$270 S or D; $450–$1,050 ste; $280–$1,150 cottage/villa. Parking: Outdoor, free. AE, CB, DC, DISC, MC, V.

ATTRACTION

The Mustangs of Las Colinas
5205 N O'Connor Blvd; tel 972/869-9047. This bronze sculpture (created by renowned wildlife artist Robert Glen) of nine mustangs that appear to be splashing through a stream of water is thought to be one of the world's largest equestrian sculptures. Each horse is 1½ times life-size and weighs between 2,000 and 3,000 pounds. **Open:** Tues–Sat 10am–6pm **Free**

Jasper

MOTELS

Holiday Inn Express
2100 N Wheeler, 75951; tel 409/384-8600 or toll free 800/HOLIDAY. On US 96, N of US 190. This very new hotel is located near area parks, lakes, and forests. Accommodations are clean, quiet, and comfortable. **Rooms:** 57 rms. CI 3pm/CO noon. Nonsmoking rms avail. **Amenities:** A/C, cable TV. **Services:** **Facilities:** Washer/dryer. **Rates (CP):** $40–$60 S or D. Extra person $4. Children under age 18 stay free. Parking: Outdoor, free. AE, CB, DC, DISC, JCB, MC, V.

Ramada Inn Jasper
259 E Gibson, 75951; tel 409/384-9021 or toll free 800/2-RAMADA. On US 190, W of TX 96. Located in a wooded location, this motel is a reasonably priced getaway for couples. **Rooms:** 100 rms. CI 3pm/CO noon. Nonsmoking rms avail. **Amenities:** A/C, cable TV w/movies. **Services:** **Facilities:** 1 restaurant, 1 bar (w/entertainment), washer/dryer. **Rates:** Peak (Mar–Aug) $54–$75 S or D. Extra person $4. Children under age 17 stay free. Min stay special events. Lower rates off-season. Parking: Outdoor, free. AE, CB, DC, DISC, JCB, MC, V.

Jefferson

See also Marshall

Once an important inland port founded in 1830, the town's economy collapsed when the waters of the bayou became impassable to steamboats. Now a living museum of early Texana, Jefferson's historical district contains many restored homes built during the town's boom days in addition to numerous shops. **Information:** Marion County Chamber of Commerce, 116 W Austin, Jefferson, 75657 (tel 903/665-2672).

HOTEL

The Excelsior House

211 W Austin, 75657; tel 903/665-2513. US 59 N exit off I-20. Built in the 1850s by a riverboat captain, this historic landmark filled with Victorian antiques has been beautifully restored. Its courtyard and ballroom are exquisite. Famous guests have included Ulysses Grant, Oscar Wilde, and Lyndon Johnson. Historic documents and articles on display in lobby. **Rooms:** 13 rms and stes. CI 2:30pm/CO noon. No smoking. Rooms individually decorated in period furniture, such as claw-foot tubs and fainting couches. **Amenities:** A/C, TV. No phone. Some units w/terraces. **Services:** Guided tours of building and grounds available. Great Southern-style breakfasts. **Facilities:** Rates: $55–$70 S or D; $80–$90 ste. Extra person $10. Children under age 2 stay free. Parking: Outdoor, free. No CC.

MOTEL

Best Western Inn of Jefferson

400 S Walcott, 75657; tel 903/665-3983 or toll free 800/528-1234; fax 903/665-3983. On US 59. A clean, comfortable motel with accommodations suitable for those just passing through town. **Rooms:** 65 rms, stes, and effic. CI 3pm/CO noon. Nonsmoking rms avail. Many are mini-suites with a sitting area partitioned off from the bedroom. Only one room is accessible for guests with disabilities. **Amenities:** A/C, cable TV. Some units w/whirlpools. **Services:** Small pets only. **Facilities:** Sauna, whirlpool. **Rates:** Peak (May–Aug) $46–$52 S; $50–$56 D; $74–$84 ste; $58 effic. Extra person $8. Children under age 16 stay free. Lower rates off-season. Parking: Outdoor, free. AE, CB, DC, DISC, ER, MC, V.

INN

Pride House

409 Broadway, 75657; tel 903/665-2675 or toll free 800/894-3526. 3 blocks E of jct US 59 and TX 49. 2 acres. Built in 1880 as Texas's first bed-and-breakfast. **Rooms:** 10 rms and stes. CI 3pm/CO 11am. No smoking. Rooms are available in the Main House or Servant's Quarters. The bathrooms are old-fashioned and minimal; armoires serve as closets. Only

one room is accessible to guests with disabilities. **Amenities:** A/C. No phone or TV. 1 unit w/terrace, some w/fireplaces. TV and phone available on request. **Services:** Babysitting, afternoon tea served. **Facilities:** Guest lounge. **Rates (BB):** $65–$100 S; $100 ste. Extra person $15. Children under age 2 stay free. Min stay wknds. Parking: Outdoor, free. MC, V.

RESTAURANT

Stillwater Inn

203 E Broadway at Owens; tel 903/665-8415. 1 block E of jct US 59/TX 49. **American/French.** Housed in a beautiful, antique-filled Victorian house with high ceilings and wood floors. Grilled game, other meats, and seafood are specialties. Sunday brunch—a special treat—is served only on the last Sunday of the month. **FYI:** Reservations recommended. Dress code. **Open:** Tues–Thurs 6–8:30pm, Fri–Sun 6–10pm. **Prices:** Main courses $13–$25. AE, MC, V.

ATTRACTIONS

Jefferson Historical Museum

223 W Austin St; tel 903/665-2775. Located in the 1890 Federal Building. Four floors of artifacts, documents, and antiques illustrate the heritage of the region. Mementos of pioneer days, early steamboat commerce, and antebellum society. Highlights include the gun collection and Native American items. **Open:** Daily 9am–5pm. $

The House of the Seasons

409 S Alley; tel 903/665-1218. Built in 1872, during the heyday of Jefferson, then the largest inland port in Texas, the house is a cross between Greek Revival and Victorian styles of architecture. Original artwork, stained glass windows, and the impressive frescoes adorning the dome are special features of the house. The reconstructed carriage house has been turned into three suites, each decorated with antiques and period furnishings. Tours available. **Open:** Daily 10am–5pm. $$

Atalanta

200 W Austin St; tel 903/665-2513. Built in 1890, this was the private railroad car of financier Jay Gould. The luxurious interior of the restored car features four staterooms, lounge, dining room, kitchen, butler's pantry, and bathroom. Tours available. **Open:** Daily 9am–noon and 2:45–4:15pm. $

Surrey Ride Tour

200 W Austin St; tel 903/665-2857. Horse-drawn carriage tour of the city's historic district and riverside area. **Open:** Daily 10am–5pm. $$

Kerrville

See also Bandera, Fredericksburg

A booming tourist town on the banks of the beautiful Guadalupe River, Kerrville's scenic beauty draws artists, retirees, and travelers. Kerrville is known for its pleasant climate and healthy air, and it offers numerous galleries, craft shops, antique stores, and summer camps. **Information:** Kerrville Convention & Visitors Bureau, 1700 Sidney Baker, #200, Kerrville, 78028 (tel 210/792-3535).

HOTELS

Hillcrest Inn
1508 Sidney Baker, 78028; tel 210/896-7400. Exit 508 off I-10, S 1¼ mi. This large and elegant older hotel has been kept in mint condition. Its rooms are extremely spacious and appointed with upscale furnishings. **Rooms:** 150 rms and stes. Executive level. CI 2pm/CO noon. Nonsmoking rms avail. **Amenities:** A/C, satel TV w/movies. Some units w/minibars, some w/terraces. **Services:** Social director. VCRs rented at front desk. Very courteous staff. **Facilities:** 1 restaurant, 1 bar (w/entertainment). **Rates (CP):** $57–$63 S; $63–$67 D; $70–$80 ste. Extra person $10. Min stay special events. Parking: Outdoor, free. AE, DISC, MC, V.

Ramada Hill Country Inn
2127 Sidney Baker, 78028; tel 210/896-1511. Exit 508 off I-10. Situated in beautiful Hill Country, this hotel has the ambience of a quaint, old-fashioned inn and offers a spectacular view of the rolling hills. **Rooms:** 175 rms and stes. CI 2pm/CO noon. Nonsmoking rms avail. Antique furnishings. **Amenities:** A/C, cable TV w/movies. Some units w/minibars, some w/terraces. **Services:** Twice-daily maid svce. **Facilities:** Whirlpool. **Rates (CP):** Peak (Apr–Sept) $59–$69 S; $70–$79 D; $100–$125 ste. Extra person $10. Min stay wknds. Lower rates off-season. MAP rates avail. Parking: Outdoor, free. AE, DISC, MC, V.

Riverhill Country Club
100 Riverhill Club Lane, 78028; tel 210/896-1400. Convenient to I-10 and TX 16. Deluxe accommodations in a secluded setting on the edge of a hill. Spectacular view of Hill Country. **Rooms:** 200 rms and stes. Executive level. CI 2pm/CO noon. Nonsmoking rms avail. Rooms are spacious with posh furnishings. **Amenities:** A/C, cable TV w/movies. Some units w/minibars, some w/terraces. **Services:** VP **Facilities:** 1 restaurant, 1 bar (w/entertainment), whirlpool. Sports facilities, restaurant, and bar are near the river. **Rates (CP):** $79–$89 S; $89–$99 D; $100–$130 ste. Extra person $5. Min stay wknds. MAP rates avail. Parking: Outdoor, free. AE, DC, DISC, MC, V.

YO Ranch Holiday Inn
2033 Sidney Baker St, 78028; tel 210/257-4440 or toll free 800/445-8667. Exit 508 off I-10. The beautiful lobby in this large, deluxe hotel is reminiscent of an exclusive hunting lodge with its large stone fireplace, plush leather chairs, antiques, and intricate oriental rugs. **Rooms:** 350 rms and stes. Executive level. CI 2pm/CO noon. Nonsmoking rms avail. Rooms are spacious, with thick carpeting and cherry furniture. **Amenities:** A/C, cable TV w/movies, refrig, dataport, voice mail, bathrobes. Some units w/mini-bars, some w/terraces. **Services:** VP Twice-daily maid svce, social director. **Facilities:** 1 restaurant, 1 bar (w/entertainment), games rm, whirlpool, beauty salon. **Rates (CP):** $79–$89 S; $89–$99 D; $100–$125 ste. Extra person $5. Min stay peak. MAP rates avail. Parking: Indoor/outdoor, free. AE, DC, DISC, MC, V.

MOTEL

Sands Motel
1145 Junction Hwy, 78028; tel 210/896-5000. Exit 505 off I-10. Older economy motel with clean, basic rooms and somewhat dated furnishings. **Rooms:** 75 rms and stes. CI 2pm/CO noon. Nonsmoking rms avail. **Amenities:** A/C, cable TV w/movies, bathrobes. Some units w/terraces. **Facilities:** **Rates (CP):** $49–$55 S; $55–$59 D; $60–$70 ste. Extra person $5. Min stay wknds. Parking: Outdoor, free. AE, DISC, MC, V.

RESORT

Inn of the Hills River Resort
1001 Junction Hwy, 78028; tel 210/895-5000. Exit 505 off I-10. 9 acres. This luxurious resort provides a variety of activities for guests and a staff willing and able to meet guests' needs. **Rooms:** 250 rms and stes. Executive level. CI 2pm/CO noon. Nonsmoking rms avail. **Amenities:** A/C, cable TV w/movies, refrig, dataport, bathrobes. Some units w/minibars, some w/terraces. **Services:** Twice-daily maid svce, social director. **Facilities:** 1 restaurant (see "Restaurants" below), 1 bar (w/entertainment), whirlpool. **Rates (CP):** $79–$85 S; $85–$90 D; $95–$130 ste. Extra person $5. Min stay peak. MAP rates avail. Parking: Indoor/outdoor, free. AE, DC, DISC, MC, V.

RESTAURANT

Annemarie's
In the Inn of the Hills River Resort, 1001 Jct Hwy; tel 210/257-8282. **American.** A romantic restaurant serving quality American food, such as an excellent roast beef and potatoes. Great for both casual dining and special occasions. **FYI:** Reservations not accepted. Beer and wine only. No smoking. **Open:** Mon–Sat 6am–10pm, Sun 6am–9pm. **Prices:** Main courses $6–$11. AE, DISC, MC, V.

ATTRACTIONS

Cowboy Artists of America Museum
1550 Bandera Hwy; tel 210/896-2553. A celebration of art relating to cowboys and the West, established by the Cowboy Artists of America, an organization of 27 active artists from the school of Western American Realism. Works by Joe Beeler, James Boren, Robert Duncan, Melvin Warren, and others. There are special exhibitions as well as workshops by artists in residence; also a library, auditorium, and museum store. **Open:** Mon–Sat 9am–5pm, Sun 1–5pm. $

Kerrville Camera Safari

TX 16, exit 508 off I-10; tel 210/792-3600. An opportunity to view hundreds of exotic animals from around the world from the safety of your car. Zebra, scimitar-horned oryx, axis deer, kudu, antelope, gemsbok, and ostrich are among the many animals that can be viewed from the 4½ miles of road here on the drive-through Wilson-Haley Ranch, in the center of the Texas Hill Country. On the premises is a 9-acre lake, as well as a waterfall, picnic area, petting area, observation point, and gift shop. **Open:** Daily 9am–sunset. **$$$**

Killeen

See also Temple

Killeen was founded in the 1880s and developed as an agricultural trading and railroad center. When the US Army established Fort Hood on the city's west side during World War II, the town's primary focus became the military, and it has remained that way ever since. Nearby Belton Lake and Stillhouse Hollow Lake provide recreation. **Information:** Killeen Convention & Visitors Bureau, One Santa Fe Plaza, PO Box 548, Killeen, 76540-0548 (tel 817/526-9551 or toll free 800/869-8265).

HOTEL

Plaza Hotel

1721 Central Texas Expwy, 76541; tel 817/634-1555; fax 817/634-1555. On US 190 between Young and Trimmer. Primarily catering to visitors to Fort Hood, this large, six-story hotel sports a fairly plush lobby. Good for business trips or conventions. **Rooms:** 148 rms. CI 3pm/CO 1pm. Nonsmoking rms avail. **Amenities:** A/C, cable TV w/movies. Some units w/whirlpools. **Services:** **Facilities:** 1 restaurant, 1 bar, whirlpool. **Rates:** $48–$82 S; $58–$92 D. Extra person $10. Children under age 16 stay free. Parking: Outdoor, free. AE, CB, DC, DISC, MC, V.

MOTELS

Hallmark Motor Inn

4500 E Central Texas Expwy, 76543; tel 817/634-1313. On US 190, E of TX 195. Standard motel for vacationers on a budget. **Rooms:** 100 rms and stes. CI 3pm/CO 11am. Nonsmoking rms avail. **Amenities:** A/C, cable TV, refrig. **Services:** **Facilities:** Washer/dryer. **Rates:** $49–$65 S or D; $52 ste. Extra person $5. Children under age 12 stay free. Parking: Outdoor, free. AE, CB, DC, DISC, MC, V.

La Quinta Motor Inn

1112 Fort Hood St, 76541; tel 817/526-8331 or toll free 800/531-5900; fax 817/526-0394. At jct US 190. This standard, three-story La Quinta offers a prime location near the entrance to Fort Hood. Reliable budget accommodations. **Rooms:** 105 rms. CI 3pm/CO noon. Nonsmoking rms

avail. **Amenities:** A/C, cable TV. **Services:** **Facilities:** 35 **Rates (CP):** $52–$60 S or D. Extra person $7. Children under age 18 stay free. Parking: Outdoor, free. AE, CB, DC, DISC, MC, V.

Kingsville

This ranching community was established in 1904 as a railhead for the St Louis, Brownsville, and Mexico railroad. The city is filled with parks and is surrounded by the famous King Ranch, the largest ranch in the continental United States. It is also home to Texas A&I University and a US Naval Air Station. **Information:** Kingsville Chamber of Commerce, 635 E King St, PO Box 1030, Kingsville, 78363 (tel 512/592-6438).

HOTEL

HoJo Inn

105 US 77 S Bypass, 78363; tel 512/592-6471 or toll free 800/446-4656. Near jct TX 141. Surprisingly nice accommodations. **Rooms:** 150 rms and stes. Executive level. CI 2pm/CO noon. Nonsmoking rms avail. **Amenities:** A/C, cable TV w/movies. Some units w/terraces. **Services:** Social director. **Facilities:** 300 1 restaurant, 1 bar (w/entertainment). **Rates (CP):** Peak (Apr–Sept) $59–$69 S; $69–$79 D; $80–$95 ste. Extra person $7. Min stay wknds. Lower rates off-season. MAP rates avail. Parking: Indoor/outdoor, free. AE, DC, DISC, MC, V.

MOTEL

Best Western Kingsville Inn

2402 E King Ave, 78363; tel 512/595-5656 or toll free 800/528-1234. Off US 77 S. This relatively new facility seems very eager to please. Service and accommodations are fresh, and the prices are competitive. **Rooms:** 100 rms and stes. CI 2pm/CO noon. Nonsmoking rms avail. **Amenities:** A/C, satel TV w/movies. Some units w/terraces. **Facilities:** 25 **Rates (CP):** $42–$45 S; $45–$47 D; $49–$52 ste. Extra person $5. Children under age 5 stay free. Min stay special events. Parking: Outdoor, free. DC, DISC, MC, V.

ATTRACTIONS

King Ranch

TX 141; tel 512/592-8055. This National Historic Landmark is recognized as the birthplace of the American ranching industry. Founded by Captain Richard King in 1853, King Ranch developed the Santa Gertrudis and King Ranch Santa Cruz breeds of cattle and produced the first registered American quarter horse. The ranch now sprawls across 825,000 acres of South Texas land, an area larger than the state of Rhode Island, and is home to 60,000 cattle and 300 quarter horses. A diversity of wildlife can be found here: many tropical and migratory bird species, white-tailed deer, javelinas, and coyotes are common sights. The King Ranch Museum displays photographs, vintage cars, and a collection of saddles from around the world. A few tours are available: the standard 1¾-hour tour visits the cattle operations site—the auction arena, stud barns, and the area where the cattle are vaccinated, tagged, and branded—as well as the wildlife area; a longer, more comprehensive tour of the ranch can be arranged and designed around a specific interest, such as the wildlife, cattle and horse operations, or farming. These usually last 4–5 hours. Wildlife and bird-watching retreats are also offered. Saddle shop on the premises. **Open:** Mon–Sat noon–4pm, Sun 1–5pm. **$$$**

John E Conner Museum

821 W Santa Gertrudis Ave; tel 512/595-2819. Located at Texas A&I University, this museum chronicles the history of the region. The Hall of South Texas History has exhibits relating to Native American, Spanish, Mexican, and pioneer Texan cultures, including displays of ranching and agriculture equipment, railroads, and land promotion. The Kleberg Hall of Natural History features the flora and fauna of South Texas in natural habitats. Changing exhibits monthly and lectures during the school year; gift shop. **Open:** Mon–Sat 9am–5pm. **Free**

La Grange

ATTRACTION 🏛

Monument Hill and Kreische Brewery State Historical Parks

414 TX Loop 92; tel 409/968-5658. These parks are located on a high bluff overlooking the Colorado River and La Grange. The Monument Hill site is the final resting place for the Texas heroes killed on the Dawson and Mier expeditions. The monument is a 48-foot marker of stone, bronze, and polychrome. Facilities include a visitors center, playground, and large picnic area with fire grills and rest rooms.

The Kreische Brewery site contains the ruins of one of Texas's first commercial breweries, built in the early 1870s, and the residence of H L Kreische, constructed around 1855. An interpretive trail begins at the headquarters and winds through both sites, and leads to a scenic bluff overlook trail. Guided tours available; gift shop. **Open:** Daily 8am–5pm. **$**

Lake Jackson

See Brazosport

La Porte

ATTRACTIONS 🏛

San Jacinto Monument and Museum of History

3800 Park Rd; tel 281/479-2421. A 570-foot obelisk (believed to be one of the world's tallest masonry monuments) marks the site of the 1836 battle, in which Texan revolutionaries won independence from Mexico by defeating Santa Anna's army. Visitors can go up to the top of the obelisk and look out over the gulf coast and Houston. At the monument's base is a museum which chronicles regional history, from Native American civilizations through the Civil War period. A half-hour multimedia documentary depicts the battle and the Texas Revolution. **Open:** Daily 9am–6pm. **$$**

Battleship *Texas*

3527 Battleground Rd; tel 281/479-2411. Commissioned in 1914, the USS *Texas* is the last of the "Dreadnoughts" and the only surviving US naval vessel to have seen service in both world wars. Visitors can tour the ship. **Open:** Daily 10am–5pm. **$$**

Laredo

One of the oldest cities in Texas, Laredo was settled as a Spanish land grant in 1755. Its location along the Rio Grande helps make it one of the nation's largest inland ports. Along with Nuevo Laredo, its sister city across the border in Mexico, Laredo offers great shopping opportunities. Lake Casa Blanca, east of town, boasts outstanding bass fishing. **Information:** Laredo Convention & Visitors Bureau, PO Box 579, Laredo, 78040 (tel 210/712-1230 or toll free 800/361-3360).

HOTELS 🏨

≣≣≣ Holiday Inn Civic Center

800 Garden St at I-35, 78040; tel 210/727-5800 or toll free 800/465-4329; fax 210/727-0278. International Airport exit off I-35. An unusually attractive Holiday Inn offering easy access to the interstate, the international airport, and the gateway to Mexico. Great for business travelers because of its proximity to the Civic Center. **Rooms:** 200 rms and stes. Executive level. CI 2pm/CO noon. Nonsmoking rms avail. The surprisingly spacious rooms were renovated in 1994. **Amenities:** 🛁 🔥 🖭 🖫 A/C, cable TV w/movies, refrig, bathrobes. Some units w/minibars, some w/terraces. **Services:** ✗ ➡ VP 🚗 ⟨🖐 Twice-daily maid svce, social director. **Facilities:** 🔁 🖫 ⌷300⌷ 🖵 ⅙ 1 restaurant, 1 bar (w/entertainment), whirlpool. **Rates (CP):** $52–$59 S; $59–$65 D; $75–$85 ste. Extra person $10. Children under age 10 stay free. Min stay special events. MAP rates avail. Parking: Outdoor, free. AE, DC, DISC, MC, V.

🏳 Holiday Inn Rio Grande

1 S Main Ave, 78040; tel 210/722-2411. Scott and Washington exit off I-35 S. Although this Holiday Inn is nothing special and its facilities are a little worn, it's okay for a short stay or a cheap vacation. **Rooms:** 75 rms. CI open/CO noon. Nonsmoking rms avail. **Amenities:** 🛁 A/C, cable TV. **Facilities:** 🕎 ⅙ **Rates:** $40–$42 S; $42–$45 D. Extra person $5. Parking: Outdoor, free. MC, V.

MOTEL

🏳 Loma Alta Motel

391 San Bernardo Ave, 78041; tel 210/726-1628. San Bernardo exit off I-35 S. This single-level motel with attached units has a very "low budget" atmosphere. **Rooms:** 70 rms. CI 2pm/CO noon. Nonsmoking rms avail. Limited furnishings. **Amenities:** 🛁 A/C, cable TV. **Facilities:** 🕎 ⅙ **Rates:** $42–$45 S or D. Extra person $5. Parking: Outdoor, free. AE, DC, DISC, MC, V.

RESTAURANT 🍴

Unicorn Restaurant

3810 San Bernardo; tel 210/727-4663. San Bernado exit off I-35. **Regional American.** This family-oriented restaurant serves all-American favorites along with some great Tex-Mex choices. Comfortable atmosphere and satisfying food. **FYI:** Reservations not accepted. Children's menu. No liquor license. **Open: Prices:** Main courses $4–$8. No CC. 🖼 ⅙

ATTRACTION 🏛

Republic of the Rio Grande Museum

1003 Zaragoza St; tel 210/727-3480. Located in the building that served as the capitol for the short-lived Republic of the Rio Grande (1839–1841). Displays of guns, saddles, and household goods of frontier homes from that period. **Open:** Tues–Sun 9am–4pm. **Free**

Longview

See also Marshall

Settled in the early 1800s, the Gregg County seat—and center of a growing industrial area—is surrounded by numerous lakes. Longview hosts the annual Great Texas Balloon Race in August. **Information:** Longview Convention & Visitors Bureau, 410 N Center, PO Box 472, Longview, 75606 (tel 903/753-3281).

MOTELS 🏨

🏳🏳 Comfort Inn

203 N Spur 63, 75601; tel 903/757-7031 or toll free 800/221-2222; fax 903/757-7031. At jct US 80. Centrally located motel offering clean, average rooms. **Rooms:** 64 rms. CI noon/CO noon. Nonsmoking rms avail. Some rooms have loveseats. **Amenities:** 🛁 A/C, cable TV. Some rooms have mini-refrigerator and microwave. **Services:** 🛄 🖨 Car-rental desk. **Facilities:** 🕎 ⅙ 1 bar (w/entertainment). **Rates (BB):** $45 S; $55 D. Extra person $5. Children under age 18 stay free. Parking: Outdoor, free. AE, CB, DC, DISC, EC, ER, JCB, MC, V.

🏳🏳🏳 Holiday Inn Longview

3119 Estes Pkwy at I-20, 75602; tel 903/758-0700 or toll free 800/HOLIDAY; fax 903/758-8705. The only full-service property in Longview, this Holidome motel has easy access to the interstate. Holidome area has fountain and recreational facilities. **Rooms:** 193 rms and stes. CI 3pm/CO 1pm. Nonsmoking rms avail. **Amenities:** 🛁 🖨 A/C, cable TV, dataport. 1 unit w/whirlpool. **Services:** ✗ 🚗 🛄 🖨 ↔ **Facilities:** 🕎 [500] ⅙ 1 restaurant, 1 bar, games rm, whirlpool, washer/dryer. **Rates:** $69–$100 S or D; $150 ste. Extra person $7. Children under age 18 stay free. Parking: Outdoor, free. AE, CB, DC, DISC, MC, V.

🏳🏳 Longview Inn

605 Access Rd, 75602; tel 903/753-0350 or toll free 800/933-1139; fax 903/753-0350. Exit 595 off I-20. Basic property located right along the interstate, near many restaurants. **Rooms:** 120 rms and effic. CI 7am/CO 1pm. Nonsmoking rms avail. **Amenities:** 🛁 A/C, cable TV. 1 unit w/whirlpool. **Services:** 🚗 🛄 🖨 ↔ Pet deposit $10. **Facilities:** 🕎 [225] Washer/dryer. **Rates (CP):** $42 S; $45 D; $42 effic. Extra person $4. Children under age 16 stay free. Parking: Outdoor, free. AE, CB, DC, DISC, MC, V.

🏳🏳 Stratford House Inn

3100 Estes Pkwy, 75602; tel 903/758-4322; fax 903/758-4322. Estes Pkwy exit off I-20. This nice, little motel is only a few miles from downtown Longview. A good choice if you want to stay out of the city without losing convenience. **Rooms:** 40 rms. CI 11am/CO 11am. Nonsmoking rms avail. Rooms have brick walls on two sides. **Amenities:** 🛁 🖐 🖨 A/C, cable TV w/movies, refrig, dataport, VCR. All units w/whirlpools. Ironing boards available in all rooms. **Services:** 🚗 🛄 🖨 ↔ Movies rented at front desk. **Facilities:** 🕎 ⅙ Whirlpool. **Rates (CP):** $47 S; $51–$65 D. Extra person $4. Children under age 12 stay free. Parking: Outdoor, free. Weekend rates are higher. AE, DC, DISC, MC, V.

RESTAURANTS 🍴

Bodacious Bar-B-Q

904 6th; tel 903/753-2714. Just N of US 80 E. **Barbecue.** This very casual, self-serve barbecue joint is decorated with art depicting the life of the cowboy. Actual saddles, hats, and riding equipment can be found scattered about; old Coca-Cola and Wonder Bread signs hang over booths and tables. Sandwiches, barbecue, and vegetable plates provide quick, tasty meals. **FYI:** Reservations accepted. Beer and wine only. Additional locations: 1402 W Marshall (tel 236-3215); 1300 NW Loop 281 (tel 759-3914). **Open:** Mon–Sat 10am–9pm, Sun 11am–8pm. **Prices:** Main courses $3–$8. AE, MC, V. 🖼

★ Johnny Cace's Seafood & Steak House
1501 E Marshall (US 80 E); tel 903/753-7691. **Seafood/ Steak.** When Johnny Cace opened his restaurant in 1949, it could accommodate only 37 guests. Today, it holds 450 and is usually filled to capacity. The more casual dining areas are decorated with posters of Louisiana life; the more formal area boasts crystal chandeliers and decorative fine china. Special dishes are rock lobster tail, catfish Lafayette, crawfish etoufée, and filet mignon. **FYI:** Reservations not accepted. Piano. Children's menu. Additional location: 7011 S Broadway, Tyler (tel 581-0744). **Open:** Sun–Mon 3–10pm, Tues–Thurs 11am–10pm, Fri–Sat 11am–11pm. **Prices:** Main courses $8–$26. AE, CB, DC, DISC, MC, V. 🖼🕹&

Oxford Street Restaurant
421 N Spur 63; tel 903/758-9130. ½ mi N of jct US 80. **Eclectic.** A subtle decor featuring dark furniture, dim lighting, old photos and posters of cricket, tennis, and polo games, and shelves filled with books and china give this restaurant its cozy, casual, and private ambience. It is a great place for intimate dining. Good bets on the menu are pineapple chicken, blackened prime rib sandwich, and stuffed flounder. **FYI:** Reservations recommended. Children's menu. Additional location: 3300 Troup Hwy, Tyler (tel 593-2655). **Open:** Lunch Mon–Fri 11am–2pm, Sun 11am–9pm; dinner Mon–Thurs 5–10pm, Fri–Sat 5–10:30pm, Sun 11am–9pm. **Prices:** Main courses $5–$18. AE, CB, DC, DISC, MC, V. &

ATTRACTION 🖻

Gregg County Historical Museum
214 N Fredonia St; tel 903/753-5840. Exhibits that illustrate the heritage of the region are housed in a historical 1910 bank building. Replicas of early rooms include a banker's office, parlor, kitchen, and interior of a log cabin. Also memorabilia from a local bank robbery in 1894. Museum gift shop. **Open:** Tues–Sat 10am–4pm. **$**

Lubbock

See also Plainview

Perhaps best known as the hometown of famed rocker Buddy Holly, Lubbock also offers interesting museums, historical parks, and two wineries. This Panhandle city is home to Texas Tech University and Reese Air Force Base. **Information:** Lubbock Chamber of Commerce, 1120 14th St, PO Box 561, Lubbock, 79408 (tel 806/763-4666).

HOTELS 🏨

≣≣≣ Barcelona Courts
5215 S Loop 289 at Slide Road, 79424; tel 806/794-5353 or toll free 800/222-1122. This full-service, extremely secure hotel has a beautiful interior atrium with trickling fountains, wood furniture, structural accents, and many vibrant plants.

Located near South Plains Mall and its numerous entertainment, shopping, and dining options. **Rooms:** 161 stes. CI 3pm/CO noon. Nonsmoking rms avail. **Amenities:** 🔒 A/C, cable TV w/movies. Some units w/terraces. **Services:** 🚐 🖂 🖵 **Facilities:** 🖟 🔲150 & Sauna, steam rm. **Rates (BB):** $83 ste. Children under age 18 stay free. Parking: Outdoor, free. AE, DC, DISC, MC, V.

≣≣≣ Holiday Inn Civic Center
801 Ave Q, 79401; tel 806/763-1200 or toll free 800/465-4329; fax 806/763-2656. Located next to the Lubbock Civic Center across the street from a statue of legendary rocker Buddy Holly, this hotel is great for business travelers. Near a number of restaurants. **Rooms:** 291 rms and stes. Executive level. CI 2pm/CO noon. Nonsmoking rms avail. **Amenities:** 🔒 🕹 A/C, cable TV w/movies. Some units w/terraces, some w/whirlpools. **Services:** ✕ 🚐 🖂 🖵 🖘 Car-rental desk. The bellhops will drive guests anywhere within a two-mile radius. **Facilities:** 🖟 🏋 🔲1200 & 1 restaurant, 1 bar, games rm, steam rm, whirlpool, washer/dryer. **Rates:** $69–$74 S; $84 ste. Extra person $10. Children under age 16 stay free. Parking: Outdoor, free. Bed-and-breakfast package avail. AE, DC, DISC, MC, V.

≣≣≣ Lubbock Inn
3901 19th St, 79410; tel 806/792-5181 or toll free 800/545-8226; fax 806/792-1319. Next to St Mary's Hospital. Very good value offering better-than-average accommodations and a convenient location near several major hospitals and many restaurants. **Rooms:** 146 rms, stes, and effic. CI open/CO noon. Nonsmoking rms avail. Rooms are quite nice, but not well lit. **Amenities:** 🔒 🕹 A/C, cable TV w/movies. **Services:** ✕ 🚐 🖂 🖵 **Facilities:** 🖟 🔲100 & 1 restaurant. **Rates:** $50 S; $58 D; $90 ste; $50–$58 effic. Extra person $6. Children under age 13 stay free. Parking: Outdoor, free. AE, CB, DC, DISC, MC, V.

MOTELS

≣ Country Inn
4105 19th St, 79410; tel 806/795-5271. 2 blocks S of St Mary's Hospital. Budget motel catering primarily to visitors at nearby hospitals. Rather worn on the outside, it has typical chain property decor on the inside. Also suitable for families. **Rooms:** 75 rms. CI open/CO noon. Nonsmoking rms avail. **Amenities:** 🔒 🕹 A/C, cable TV w/movies. **Services:** 🖵 **Facilities:** 🖟 **Rates (CP):** $40 S; $50 D. Extra person $4. Children under age 18 stay free. Parking: Outdoor, free. AE, MC, V.

≣≣ The Gateway Inn Motel
1401 TX 16 S, PO Box 1299, Graham, 76450; tel 817/549-0222; fax 817/549-4301. S of US 380 and TX 61/67. Located in the heart of Hill Country, this basic motel can serve as a base for outdoor activities such as hunting, fishing, boating, hiking, and camping. **Rooms:** 78 rms. CI 3pm/CO noon. Nonsmoking rms avail. **Amenities:** 🔒 🕹 🖵 A/C, cable TV. **Services:** ✕ 🚐 🖂 🖵 Supper club memberships are

available. **Facilities:** 🛅 🕭 1 restaurant, whirlpool, washer/dryer. **Rates:** $32–$39 S or D. Extra person $4. Children under age 18 stay free. Parking: Outdoor, free. AE, CB, DC, DISC, MC, V.

☰☰ La Quinta Motor Inn
601 Ave Q, 79401 (Downtown); tel 806/792-0065 or toll free 800/531-5900; fax 806/792-0178. Located right next to the Lubbock Convention Center, this is a solid option for business travelers. Southwestern decor. Restaurants nearby. **Rooms:** 137 rms. CI noon/CO 1pm. Nonsmoking rms avail. **Amenities:** 🛅 🕭 A/C, cable TV w/movies. **Services:** 🖃 🖾 🗘 **Facilities:** 🛅 🕭 1 restaurant. **Rates (CP):** $62–$72 S; $62–$67 D. Extra person $10. Children under age 18 stay free. Parking: Outdoor, free. AE, CB, DC, DISC, MC, V.

RESTAURANTS 🍴

★ Brittany
In South Plains Mall, 6002 Slide Rd; tel 806/795-5533. **Burgers.** The pleasant wooden-accented decor has a fireplace in the center of the dining area and bright red booths and chairs. Here's the fun part, though—diners call in their orders from a phone at the table. Outstanding hickory-flavored sauce accompanies many of the barbecue specialties. **FYI:** Reservations not accepted. Children's menu. No liquor license. **Open:** Mon–Sat 11am–9pm, Sun 12:30–6pm. **Prices:** Main courses $4–$8. AE, DISC, MC, V. 🖾 🖾

Chez Suzette
In Quaker Square Shopping Center, 4423 50th St; tel 806/795-6796. **French.** Candle-lit tables and an attentive waitstaff make this a fine spot for a romantic meal. Traditional French and Italian dishes. Chateaubriand is a specialty. **FYI:** Reservations recommended. Children's menu. **Open:** Mon–Thurs 5:30–10pm, Fri–Sat 5:30–10:30pm. **Prices:** Main courses $8–$15. AE, DC, MC, V. ♥ 🕭

♣★ The Depot
19th and Ave G; tel 806/747-1646. 5 blocks N of Convention Center. **Seafood/Steak.** Formerly a train station, it is now one of Lubbock's finest restaurants, offering elegant dining and plenty of historic ambience—as well as a beer garden. Prime rib and stuffed potatoes are especially good, and there's also a salad bar. **FYI:** Reservations accepted. **Open:** Lunch Mon–Fri 11:30am–3pm, Sun 11:30am–2pm; dinner Mon–Sat 5–10pm, Sun 5–9pm. **Prices:** Main courses $9–$42. AE, CB, DC, DISC, MC, V. ♥ 🖾 🕭

Gardski's Restaurant
2009 Broadway; tel 806/744-2391. 1 mi E of Texas Tech University. **Southwestern/Steak.** Located in an old, restored two-story home, this restaurant is known for outstanding food—including aged steaks and delicious gourmet hamburgers—and terrific atmosphere. **FYI:** Reservations accepted. Additional location: 6251 Slide Rd (tel 793-0373). **Open:** Sun–Thurs 7am–11pm, Fri–Sat 7am–midnight. **Prices:** Main courses $5–$9. AE, DC, DISC, MC, V. 🖾 🖾

Harrigan's
In Memphis Place Mall, 3801 50th; tel 806/792-4648. At Quaker. **Southwestern/Steak.** Outstanding prime rib is served by an excellent waitstaff. The comfortable dining area features antiques, rich wood accents, and low lighting. **FYI:** Reservations accepted. Children's menu. **Open:** Lunch Mon–Fri 11am–2pm, Sun 10:30am–2pm; dinner Mon–Fri 5–10pm, Sat 11am–11pm, Sun 5–11pm. **Prices:** Main courses $8–$15. AE, DC, MC, V.

Lone Star Oyster Bar
34th and Flint; tel 806/796-0101. **Seafood.** A boisterous, casual bar with TVs and music and nautical decorations like fish nets and seafaring paintings on the walls. Seafood is the specialty. **FYI:** Reservations not accepted. Additional location: 5116-C 58th (tel 797-3773). **Open:** Mon–Sat 4pm–2am. **Prices:** Main courses $6–$12. AE, MC, V. 🖾

Mesquite's BBQ & Steaks
2419 Broadway; tel 806/763-1159. 1 block E of Texas Tech University. **Barbecue.** Built around a tree, the unique dining room with a cheerful air is a favorite with college students at Texas Tech, located next door. **FYI:** Reservations not accepted. **Open:** Sun–Thurs 7am–10pm, Fri–Sat 7am–11pm. **Prices:** Main courses $5–$10. AE, DC, DISC, MC, V. 🖾

Santa Fe Station
4th and Ave Q; tel 806/763-6114. S of Convention Center. **Mexican.** Conveniently located in the convention center area, this festive restaurant features an adobe facade and Mexican-style decor. Mexican and American traditional fare. **FYI:** Reservations accepted. Additional location: 5501 Slide Rd (tel 796-3999). **Open:** Sun–Thurs 11am–10am, Fri–Sat 11am–10:30am. **Prices:** Main courses $5–$11. AE, DC, DISC, MC, V. 🖾

ATTRACTIONS 🏛

Museum of Texas Tech University
4th and Indiana Aves; tel 806/742-2442. The collection of over 1½ million objects focuses on the natural and cultural history of the Southwest. Recent exhibits on the art of sculptor Nicolai Fechin, contemporary Native American prints, and the science of wind are examples of the range of subjects treated by the museum. The Ranching Heritage Center (see below) provides both indoor and outdoor exhibits on the history of Texas ranching. The Lubbock Lake Landmark is an archeological site which contains a complete cultural record of the 12,000-year-old Clovis period. The Moody Planetarium offers public shows and specially designed school programs about physics and astronomy. Guided tours available. **Open:** Tues–Sat 10am–5pm, Thurs 10am–8:30pm, Sun 1–5pm. **Free**

Ranching Heritage Center
4th and Indiana Ave; tel 806/742-2498. Part of the Museum of Texas Tech University, this 12-acre exhibit tells the story of Panhandle ranching with 33 relocated authentic structures.

There are restored and furnished bunkhouses, barns, dug-outs, windmills, a school, and ranch homes, from the 19th and 20th centuries. Self-guiding trails through the site; docents in period attire provide information. **Open:** Tues–Sat 10am–5pm, Sun 1am–5pm. **Free**

Lubbock Fine Arts Center

2600 Ave P; tel 806/767-2686. An alternative art space presenting contemporary artworks (sculpture, photography, painting) and cultural programs. Hosts 8 to 12 exhibitions per year. **Open:** Tues–Fri 9am–5pm, Sat 10am–4pm. **Free**

Buddy Holly Statue and Walk of Fame

8th and Avenue Q; tel 806/747-5232 or toll free 800/692-4035. Impressively large bronze statue is a lasting tribute to Lubbock's most famous son, one of the pioneers of American rock and roll. Bronze plaques along the Walk of Fame honor additional West Texas natives who have made significant contributions in the entertainment industry, such as Mac Davis, Waylon Jennings, and Jimmy Dean. **Free**

Llano Estacado Winery

FM 1585; tel 806/745-2258. This award-winning winery, founded in 1976, produces a wide range of wines, including chardonnay, sauvignon blanc, merlot, chenin blanc, and Johannisberg Riesling, to name a few. The winery offers tours and tastings. Gift shop sells wines as well as wine-serving paraphernalia. **Open:** Mon–Sat 10am–5pm, Sun noon–5pm. **Free**

Pheasant Ridge Winery

FM 1729; tel 806/746-6033. An estate vineyard covering 47 acres, devoted solely to vinifera varieties such as cabernet sauvignon, merlot, and sauvignon blanc. This boutique winery offers tours and tastings. **Open:** By appointment only, on the second Saturday of each month. **Free**

Lufkin

See also Nacogdoches

Located between the Davy Crockett and Angelina National Forests, this timber town is close to the Sam Rayburn Reservoir east of town. **Information:** Lufkin Visitor & Convention Bureau, 1615 S Chestnut, PO Box 1606, Lufkin, 75901 (tel 409/634-6305).

MOTEL

≡≡ La Quinta Motor Inn

2119 S 1st St, 75901; tel 409/634-3351 or toll free 800/531-5900; fax 409/634-9475. Clean, comfortable, and close to restaurants, with easy highway access. **Rooms:** 106 rms. CI open/CO noon. Nonsmoking rms avail. **Amenities:** A/C, cable TV w/movies, dataport. **Services:** **Facilities:** **Rates (CP):** $50 S; $56–$71 D. Extra person $6. Children under age 18 stay free. Parking: Outdoor, free. AE, CB, DC, DISC, MC, V.

RESTAURANTS

The Cattle Company of Texas

2115 S 1st St; tel 409/632-6969. On US 59. **American.** This dining room, which is heated in the winter by a large fireplace, has a very casual ambience. Old West decor is complemented with antiques like an old gasoline pump and a Coke machine. The menu offers salads, sandwiches, burgers, ribs, steaks, seafood, and more. The TCC strip and grilled red snapper are highly recommended. **FYI:** Reservations not accepted. Children's menu. **Open:** Sun–Thurs 6am–10pm, Fri–Sat 6am–11pm. **Prices:** Main courses $5–$17. AE, DC, DISC, MC, V.

Lemke's Wurst Haus German Restaurant

4105 Ted Trout Dr; tel 409/875-2205. 1½ mi W of town on TX 94. **German.** When Felton Lemke turned his carpet shop into a German restaurant, he aimed for authenticity in decor and cuisine. The quaint building itself has a peaked roof and a bright blue, red, and yellow paint job, while the backyard, a beer garden, features picnic tables covered by a grapevine roof, a gazebo, and a children's playground. The interior is decorated with empty bottles of the 200-plus beers that are served. As far as food, there are sausage dinners, sauerbraten, seafood, and American favorites like chicken-fried steak and ribeye. **FYI:** Reservations accepted. Dancing. Children's menu. **Open:** Mon–Thurs 3–9:30pm, Fri–Sat 3–11pm. **Prices:** Main courses $5–$24. AE, CB, DC, DISC, MC, V.

ATTRACTIONS

Museum of East Texas

503 N 2nd St; tel 409/639-4434. Located in a 1905 Episcopal church, the museum houses changing exhibits dealing with art, science, and history, as well as the heritage of the region. A permanent gallery features East Texas artists. **Open:** Tues–Fri 10am–5pm, Sat–Sun 1–5pm. **Free**

Texas Forestry Museum

1905 Atkinson Dr; tel 409/632-9535. Located in the heart of the East Texas Piney Woods, this museum offers a look at the history of logging in Texas and the development of one of Texas's oldest industries, wood products. Exhibits include a full-sized logging locomotive and loader, forest lookout tower, blacksmith's shop, and other relics from logging's early years. Orientation video; tours by appointment. **Open:** Mon–Sat 10am–5pm, Sun 1–5pm. **Free**

Marshall

See also Jefferson, Longview

Founded in 1839 and named for former Supreme Court Justice John Marshall, this county seat in northeast Texas offers several historic sites plus access to cypress-studded Caddo Lake, a huge expanse of 26,800 acres that has a primeval aura. **Information:** Marshall Convention & Visitors Bureau, 213 W Austin St, PO Box 520, Marshall, 75671 (tel 903/935-7868).

HOTEL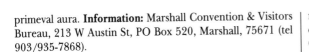

≡≡ Ramada Inn
5301 E End Blvd S, 75670; tel 903/938-9261 or toll free 800/2-RAMADA; fax 903/935-1868. Exit 617 off I-20. A good choice for business travelers, with dependable services and easy access to the interstate. **Rooms:** 102 rms and stes. CI open/CO noon. Nonsmoking rms avail. Very nice rooms. **Amenities:** 🛍 ♨ A/C, cable TV. Guests anticipating a long stay can request a mini-refrigerator. **Services:** ✗ ⊠ ⇦ ⇨ Car-rental desk. **Facilities:** ⚐ 📶 ♿ 1 restaurant, 1 bar, washer/dryer. **Rates:** $54 S; $53 D; $150–$200 ste. Extra person $5. Children under age 18 stay free. Parking: Outdoor, free. AE, CB, DC, DISC, EC, JCB, MC, V.

MOTEL

≡≡ Best Western Marshall
5555 E End Blvd S, 75670; tel 903/935-1941 or toll free 800/528-1234; fax 903/938-0071. Exit 617 off I-20, on US 59. Average Best Western with acceptable accommodations and easy interstate access. **Rooms:** 100 rms. CI noon/CO noon. Nonsmoking rms avail. **Amenities:** 🛍 ♨ 🍴 A/C, cable TV. Microwave available. **Services:** ✗ ⊠ ⇦ ⇨ **Facilities:** ⚐ 📶 ♿ 1 restaurant, 1 bar. **Rates:** Peak (Nov–Dec) $44 S; $48–$65 D. Extra person $4. Children under age 16 stay free. Lower rates off-season. Parking: Outdoor, free. AE, CB, DC, DISC, JCB, MC, V.

ATTRACTIONS 🏛

Michelson Museum of Art
215 N Bolivar; tel 903/935-9480. A collection of more than 1,000 paintings, drawings, and prints by French Impressionist Leo Michelson. Traveling exhibits are hosted as well. Guided tours available. **Open:** Tues–Fri noon–5pm, Sat–Sun 1–4pm. $

Harrison County Historical Society Museum
Peter Whetstone Square; tel 903/938-2680. Located in a restored former county courthouse, with exhibits depicting the history of Marshall and Harrison County; also Native American artifacts and pioneer and Civil War displays. **Open:** Tues–Sat 9am–5pm. $

Starr Family Home
407 W Travis St; tel 903/935-3044. This early 1870s mansion, built in the transitional Italianate–style, was the home of the Starrs, a Texas family prominent in politics and the business world. Better known as Maplecroft, the house features impressive period furnishings and decorative art objects, as well as singular construction materials. Tours available. During the Christmas season, the interior is deco-

rated in a Victorian motif, and the mansion hosts live entertainment, candlelight dinners, and candlelight tours. **Open:** Fri–Sat and Mon 10am–4pm, Sun 1–5pm. $

Caddo Lake State Park
FM 2198, Karnack; tel 903/679-3351. The 480-acre park is located beside 26,000-acre Caddo Lake, whose dense forests, Spanish moss, and lush aquatic growth exude a primeval aura. Camping areas, trailer sites, and cabins are available, and popular activities include fishing, swimming, boating (rentals available), and hiking. Interpretive center on the grounds. **Open:** Daily sunrise–sunset. $

McAllen

See also Harlingen

Incorporated in 1911 and dotted with palms, this Rio Grande Valley town thrives on agriculture and "snowbirds"—winter travelers from up north fleeing cold weather. The nearby town of Reynosa, Mexico, is a shopper's delight. **Information:** McAllen Chamber of Commerce, 10 N Broadway, PO Box 790, McAllen, 78505 (tel 210/682-2871).

HOTELS 🏨

≡≡≡ DoubleTree Club Hotel Casa De Palmas
101 N Main St, 78501; tel 210/631-1101. Business US 83 to N Main St. One of the more upscale hotels in McAllen, this DoubleTree is in excellent condition. Most suitable for business travelers. **Rooms:** 165 rms. Executive level. CI 3pm/CO noon. Nonsmoking rms avail. **Amenities:** 🛍 ♨ 🍴 A/C, cable TV w/movies, dataport. Some units w/terraces. **Services:** 🆅🅿 **Facilities:** ⚐ 📶 ♿ **Rates (CP):** $65 S; $75 D. Extra person $10. Min stay peak. MAP rates avail. Parking: Outdoor, free. AE, DISC, MC, V.

≡≡≡ Embassy Suites Hotel
1800 S 2nd St, 78503; tel 210/686-3000 or toll free 800/362-2779. 2nd St exit off US 83. All rooms open to the beautiful atrium lobby of this circular building. Luxurious and peaceful, the hotel is decorated with many plants and a fish motif. Although suitable for all travelers, the Embassy caters mainly to a business clientele. **Rooms:** 175 stes. Executive level. CI 2pm/CO noon. Nonsmoking rms avail. Rooms on the seventh and eighth floors have dataports. **Amenities:** 🛍 ♨ 📺 🍴 A/C, satel TV w/movies, refrig. Some units w/minibars, some w/terraces. **Services:** ✗ 🚐 ⊠ ⇨ Twice-daily maid svce, social director. **Facilities:** ⚐ 🏋 📶 🍽 ♿ 1 restaurant, 1 bar (w/entertainment), sauna, whirlpool, washer/dryer. **Rates (CP):** $80–$90 ste. Extra person $10. Min stay peak. MAP rates avail. Parking: Outdoor, free. AE, DISC, MC, V.

≡≡ Holiday Inn Civic Center
200 US 83, 78501; tel 210/686-2471 or toll free 800/465-4329. Take 2nd and 10th Sts exit off US 83. Two-story

Holiday Inn offering better-than-average mid-range chain accommodations. **Rooms:** 210 rms and stes. Executive level. CI 2pm/CO noon. Nonsmoking rms avail. **Amenities:** 🛅 🐾 🖭 🍴 A/C, cable TV, dataport. Some units w/terraces. **Services:** ✕ 🕿 📼 🚐 🖂 Twice-daily maid svce, social director. **Facilities:** 🖼 🖵 200 💻 🚻 1 restaurant, whirlpool. Indoor pool has a tropical atmosphere, with many lush plants. **Rates (CP):** $59 S; $69 D; $75–$89 ste. Extra person $10. Children under age 5 stay free. Min stay peak. MAP rates avail. Parking: Outdoor, free. AE, DC, DISC, MC, V.

🏨🏨🏨 McAllen Airport Hilton Inn

2721 S 10th St, 78503; tel 210/687-1161 or toll free 800/445-8667. 2nd and 10th Sts exit off US 83. Upscale hotel most suitable for airport patrons waiting on arriving or connecting flights. **Rooms:** 350 rms and stes. Executive level. CI 2pm/CO noon. Nonsmoking rms avail. **Amenities:** 🛅 🐾 A/C, cable TV, dataport. Some units w/terraces. VCRs, CD/tape players, refrigerators, and hair dryers are all available upon request. **Services:** ✕ 📼 🚐 🖂 Social director. **Facilities:** 🖼 🖵 300 💻 🚻 1 restaurant, 1 bar (w/entertainment), steam rm. **Rates (CP):** $69 S; $79 D; $110–$120 ste. Extra person $10. Min stay peak. MAP rates avail. Parking: Outdoor, free. AE, DC, DISC, MC, V.

MOTELS

🏨🏨🏨 Imperial Motor Inn

601 S 10th St, 78501; tel 210/686-0281. Take 10th St N exit off US 83. Part of a small, family-owned chain, the Imperial offers most of the advantages of—and more personal service than— "the big guys." Suitable for any traveler. **Rooms:** 150 rms. CI 3pm/CO noon. Nonsmoking rms avail. **Amenities:** 🛅 A/C, cable TV, dataport. Some units w/terraces. **Facilities:** 🖼 🖵 30 🚻 **Rates (CP):** $49 S; $55 D. Extra person $10. Min stay peak. Parking: Outdoor, free. AE, DISC, MC, V.

🏨🏨 La Quinta Motor Inn

1100 S 10th St, 78501; tel 210/687-1101 or toll free 800/531-5900; fax 210/687-9265. 10th St exit off US 83 W. Basic La Quinta with the standard Southwestern design and decor. Clean and comfortable. **Rooms:** 100 rms. CI 2pm/CO noon. Nonsmoking rms avail. **Amenities:** 🛅 🐾 A/C, cable TV. Some units w/terraces. **Services:** 🚐 🖂 Dataports available upon request. **Facilities:** 🖼 20 🚻 **Rates (CP):** $59 S; $69 D. Extra person $10. Min stay peak. Lower rates off-season. Parking: Outdoor, free. AE, DISC, MC, V.

RESORT

🏨🏨🏨 Fairway Resort

2105 S 10th St, 78503; tel 210/682-2445; fax 210/686-0935. 2nd St/10th St exit off US 83. Although it's a bit aged now, this classic, spacious resort remains elegant, spacious, and well maintained. Located in a wonderfully scenic part of the city amid tropical gardens. **Rooms:** 130 rms and stes. Executive level. CI 2pm/CO noon. Nonsmoking rms avail. Rooms were recently remodeled. **Amenities:** 🛅 🖭 🍴 A/C, cable TV

w/movies. Some units w/terraces. Some rooms have refrigerators. **Services:** 📼 🚐 🖂 Social director. **Facilities:** 🖼 ▶18 🖵 150 🚻 1 restaurant. **Rates (CP):** $69 S; $79 D; $80–$95 ste. Extra person $10. Min stay peak. MAP rates avail. Parking: Outdoor, free. AE, DC, DISC, MC, V.

RESTAURANT 🍴

Ianelli

321 S Main; tel 210/631-0666. **International/Italian.** Good portions, affordable prices, and an adequate children's menu make this Italian restaurant suitable for families. Shrimp and pasta is the specialty. **FYI:** Reservations accepted. Children's menu. Dress code. **Open:** Daily 11:30am–11pm. **Prices:** Main courses $7–$13. AE, DC, DISC, MC, V. 👪 💟 🚻

ATTRACTIONS 🏛

Santa Ana National Wildlife Refuge

Rt 2, Box 202A; tel 210/787-3079. About 2,000 acres of thick, brushy growth—prevalent throughout the Rio Grande Valley before agricultural development—preserves and protects abundant wildlife and plant varieties. There are over 370 bird species, such as the red-billed pigeon, rose-throated becard, and green jay. The mix of temperate, tropical, coastal, and desert environs is home to many species found nowhere else in the United States. Interpretive wildlife tram rides operate from November through April. There is a 7-mile wildlife road for cars on days when the tram isn't operating. Walk-through access any time during daylight. Three self-guided nature walks; one is wheelchair accessible. Visitors center offers exhibits on the region's flora and fauna. **Open:** Visitors Center daily 9am–4:30pm. Road open Mon–Fri 9am–4:30pm. Schedule may vary. Call ahead. **$**

McAllen International Museum

1900 Nolana; tel 210/682-1564. Accredited by the American Association of Museums. Strengths of the permanent collection are Mexican folk art, 20th-century American and European prints, and the Caton Collection of 16th to 19th-century European oil paintings, as well as exhibits on geology, archaeology, and natural history. There are about 15 short-term exhibits annually. Educational classes and programs; children's activities; also cinema and gift shop. **Open:** Tues–Sat 9am–5pm, Sun 1–5pm. **$**

McKinney

Founded in 1848, McKinney is an agricultural community located north of Dallas on US 75. Lavon Lake, to the southeast of this Collin County seat, provides camping and good fishing. **Information:** McKinney Chamber of Commerce, 1801 W Louisiana St, PO Box 621, McKinney, 75070-0621 (tel 972/542-0163).

MOTELS

≡≡ Comfort Inn
2104 N Central Expwy, 75070; tel 972/548-8888 or toll free 800/221-2222. On US 75, N of US 380. Newish, standard motel on a large lot in quiet, secluded environs on the north side of McKinney. Homey rooms. **Rooms:** 82 rms. CI 3pm/CO noon. Nonsmoking rms avail. **Amenities:** A/C, cable TV w/movies. **Services:** **Facilities:** Washer/dryer. **Rates (CP):** $52–$80 S or D. Extra person $4. Children under age 18 stay free. Parking: Outdoor, free. AE, CB, DC, DISC, MC, V.

≡≡ Holiday Inn
1300 N Central Expwy, 75069; tel 972/542-9471 or toll free 800/465-4329. On US 75, near White Ave. Offers a reasonably priced one-night stay. **Rooms:** 100 rms. CI 1pm/CO noon. Nonsmoking rms avail. **Amenities:** A/C, cable TV, dataport. **Services:** **Facilities:** 1 restaurant, 1 bar. Fitness facilities can be arranged. **Rates:** $54–$80 S or D. Extra person $6. Children under age 19 stay free. Parking: Outdoor, free. AE, CB, DC, DISC, JCB, MC, V.

ATTRACTION

Bolin Wildlife Exhibit
1028 N McDonald St; tel 972/542-2639. An array of mounted animal trophies from around the world, complemented by an audio presentation. Other displays include Mobil Oil Company memorabilia centered around turn-of-the-century storefront; a 1913 Model T and a 1928 Model A truck and roadster; and exhibits on pioneer life and early transportation. **Open:** Mon–Fri 9am–noon and 1–4pm. **Free**

Midland

See also Big Spring, Odessa

Named for its location midway between the Dallas–Fort Worth metroplex and El Paso, what was once an agricultural town grew into a city of culture following the discovery of oil in 1923. Visitors find numerous parks, vintage airplanes, several outstanding museums, and a busy venue for opera, ballet, and theater. **Information:** Midland Convention & Visitors Bureau, PO Box 1890, Midland, 79702 (tel 915/683-3381 or toll free 800/624-6435).

HOTEL

≡≡≡ Holiday Inn
4300 W Mull, 79703; tel 915/697-3181 or toll free 800/465-4329; fax 915/694-7754. On Business US 20. Located on restaurant row, near numerous business offices; attracts business travelers. **Rooms:** 267 rms and stes. CI 2pm/CO noon. Nonsmoking rms avail. Pleasing floral decor. **Amenities:** A/C, cable TV w/movies. **Services:** **Facilities:** 1 restaurant, 1 bar, games rm, washer/dryer. **Rates (CP):** $63–$67 D; $89–$99 ste. Children under age 12 stay free. Parking: Outdoor, free. AE, CB, DC, DISC, MC, V.

MOTELS

≡≡ Hampton Inn Midland
3904 W Wall St, 79703; tel 915/694-7774 or toll free 800/426-7866; fax 915/694-0134. On Business US 20. Standard accommodations. Restaurants nearby. **Rooms:** 110 rms. CI open/CO noon. Nonsmoking rms avail. **Amenities:** A/C, cable TV w/movies. 1 unit w/whirlpool. **Services:** Car-rental desk. **Facilities:** Sauna, steam rm, whirlpool. **Rates (CP):** $45–$51 D. Children under age 18 stay free. Parking: Outdoor, free. AE, CB, DC, DISC, MC, V.

≡≡≡ La Quinta Inn
4130 W Wall St, 79703; tel 915/697-9900 or toll free 800/531-5900; fax 915/689-0617. Located on restaurant row, this typical La Quinta (Southwestern design) offers comfortable rooms that benefit from excellent housekeeping standards. **Rooms:** 146 rms and stes. CI open/CO noon. Nonsmoking rms avail. **Amenities:** A/C, cable TV w/movies. **Services:** **Facilities:** **Rates (CP):** $39 S; $39–$58 S or D; $61 ste. Children under age 18 stay free. Parking: Outdoor, free. AE, CB, DC, DISC, MC, V.

≡≡ Plaza Inn
4108 N Big Spring St, 79705; tel 915/686-8733 or toll free 800/365-3222; fax 915/685-0530. E edge of Midland Airport. Ordinary motel located near the airport. **Rooms:** 113 rms. CI open/CO 1pm. Nonsmoking rms avail. **Amenities:** A/C, cable TV w/movies. **Services:** **Facilities:** **Rates (CP):** $55 S or D. Children under age 18 stay free. Parking: Outdoor, free. AE, CB, DC, DISC, MC, V.

≡≡≡ Ramada Inn Midland Airport
100 S Airport Plaza Dr, 79711; tel 915/561-8000 or toll free 800/272-6232. On airport property. Standard chain property fine for business travelers. **Rooms:** 98 rms and stes. CI 10am/CO noon. Nonsmoking rms avail. **Amenities:** A/C, cable TV w/movies. **Services:** **Facilities:** 1 restaurant, 1 bar. **Rates (CP):** $51–$58 S or D; $51–$58 ste. Extra person $10. Children under age 18 stay free. Parking: Outdoor, free. AE, DC, DISC, MC, V.

RESTAURANT

Harry's Bar & Grill
In Best Western, 3100 W Wall; tel 915/699-4144. 1 mi E of Business US 20. **American.** Wooden tables and chairs give this place real bar ambience; it serves traditional grilled foods at affordable prices. **FYI:** Reservations not accepted. **Open:** Daily 5–11pm. **Prices:** Main courses $5–$11. AE, DISC, MC, V.

ATTRACTIONS

Permian Basin Petroleum Museum

1500 I-20 W; tel 915/683-4403. A unique museum whose focus is the history of the oil industry. There are historic photos of early boom-town activities; paintings, models, and hardware related to well-drilling; three-dimensional models of oil strata; geological audiovisual shows and information on the process of oil formation; actual oil-well cores from deep underground; and antique drilling rigs. Other highlights include thousand-year-old reed mats and woven fiber articles from the area's prehistoric population; also historical paintings. One hands-on exhibit enables visitors to step back 230 million years and walk 30 feet "under water" in a Permian Age sea; another simulates a wild well blowout. **Open:** Mon–Sat 9am–5pm, Sun 2–5pm. **$$**

Confederate Air Force and American Airpower Heritage Museum

9600 Wright Dr; tel 915/563-1000. Former World War II service pilots founded this museum with the aim of acquiring, restoring, and preserving in flying condition the military aircraft of the war. The extensive collection includes planes from the United States, Britain, Germany, and Japan, with approximately 20 of the more than 140 aircraft on display at any one time. Some of the classics that can be viewed are the P-40 Warhawk, P-38 Lightning, P-47 Thunderbolt, P-51 Mustang, F4F Wildcat, F6F Hellcat, B-17 Flying Fortress, C-47 Skytrain, F4U Corsair, British Supermarine Spitfires, German Heinkel HE-111, Junkers JU-52, and the Messerschmitt. A 30-minute documentary on the Ghost Squadron is shown daily. The museum presents a flying demonstration and WWII aviation re-enactment in October; there are WW II and contemporary aircraft displays at the Wings N Things festival during Armed Services weekend in May. Research library; guided tours available. **Open:** Mon–Fri 9am–5pm, Sun 12–5pm. **$$**

Museum of the Southwest

1705 W Missouri Ave (Historic District); tel 915/683-2882. Dedicated to the preservation and interpretation of Southwestern art and culture. Part of the museum is housed in the historic Turner Mansion (listed in the National Register of Historic Places), and the entire complex takes up a city block. Exhibits feature Southwestern paintings, sculpture, ceramics, and archaeological artifacts. The permanent collection includes works by Karl Bodmer, Frederic Remington, Doug Hyde, John Woodhouse Audubon, Fritz Scholder, T C Cannon, and Allan Houser. The Marian Blakemore Planetarium offers astronomy programs. Special classes and events for children and adults; summer lawn concerts. **Open:** Tues–Sat 10am–5pm, Sun 2–5pm. **Free**

Monahans

ATTRACTION

Monahans Sandhills State Park

Exit 86 off I-20; tel 915/943-2092. The 4,000 acres of wind-sculptured sand dunes resemble the landscape of the Sahara Desert. The park has a 600-acre equestrian area, modern museum and interpretive center, gift shop, and picnicking and camping areas. One popular sport here is sandsurfing; disk rentals available. **Open:** Daily 8am–10pm. **$**

Mount Pleasant

Surrounding mineral springs made this town a popular health spa in the early 1900s, but the area's economy now centers on farming, ranching, and industry. Numerous lakes nearby offer excellent fishing. **Information:** Mount Pleasant–Titus County Chamber of Commerce, 1604 N Jefferson, PO Box 1237, Mount Pleasant, 75456-1237 (tel 903/572-8567).

MOTEL

≡≡≡ Holiday Inn

2402 Ferguson Rd, 75455; tel 903/572-6611 or toll free 800/HOLIDAY; fax 903/572-6640. Exit 160 off I-30. Attractive motel with simple rooms and small private fishing lake, many picnic tables, and walking path. **Rooms:** 102 rms and stes. CI 1pm/CO 1pm. Nonsmoking rms avail. Loveseats in some king rooms; mini-suites available. **Amenities:** A/C, cable TV, dataport. Some units w/whirlpools. **Services:** Pet fee $10. VCRs and movies for rent at front desk. **Facilities:** 1 restaurant, 1 bar, whirlpool, washer/dryer. **Rates:** $45 S or D; $85–$200 ste. Extra person $4. Children under age 19 stay free. Parking: Outdoor, free. AE, CB, DC, DISC, JCB, MC, V.

Nacogdoches

See also Lufkin

Dubbed "the oldest town in Texas," Nacogdoches started as a Spanish mission that was initially abandoned in 1773. It became a permanent settlement in 1779 when Antonio Gil Ybarbo returned and built a stone house known today as the Old Stone Fort. The town, a regional trade center in East Texas, is home to Stephen F Austin State University as well as some of the state's most historic landmarks. **Information:** Nacogdoches Convention & Visitors Bureau, 5131 North St, Nacogdoches, 75963 (tel 409/564-7351).

HOTEL

≡≡≡ Holiday Inn

3400 South St, 75961; tel 409/569-8100 or toll free 800/HOLIDAY; fax 409/569-0332. On US 59. Standard accommodations and services. Restaurants nearby. **Rooms:** 126 rms and stes. CI 2pm/CO noon. Nonsmoking rms avail. Nicer rooms located in new wing. Some king rooms have sofas. Some rooms face pool. Mini-suite is a good value. **Amenities:** 🛁 ⓠ A/C, cable TV. Some units w/whirlpools. **Services:** ✕ 🖥 ⌇ **Facilities:** 🛋 🛍 300 ♿ 1 restaurant (bkfst and dinner only), 1 bar, volleyball, whirlpool, washer/dryer. Sports court was being built that will offer basketball and volleyball. Free access to nearby fitness center. **Rates:** $55 S; $61–$69 D; $150 ste. Extra person $6. Children under age 18 stay free. Parking: Outdoor, free. AE, CB, DC, DISC, JCB, MC, V.

MOTEL

🚮 Continental Inn
2728 North St, 75961; tel 409/564-3726. On US 59 Business. Average economy motel with no-frills accommodations. Next door to Chinese restaurant. Close to Stephen F Austin State University. **Rooms:** 80 rms and stes. CI 9am/CO 11am. Nonsmoking rms avail. Some rooms need repairs, but others are all right, so be sure to ask. **Amenities:** 🛁 A/C, cable TV. Some rooms have microwave/mini-refrigerator. **Services:** ⌇ **Facilities:** 🛋 **Rates:** $30–$36 S or D; $42 ste. Extra person $6. Children under age 12 stay free. Parking: Outdoor, free. AE, DC, DISC, MC, V.

RESTAURANTS 🍴

The Californian Restaurant and Oyster Bar
342 N University Dr; tel 409/560-1987. Off Loop 224. **Seafood/Steak.** A great choice for quiet, upscale dining in a subdued, tastefully decorated room. The menu includes fish, shrimp, oysters, lobster, prime rib, and veal. Lunch is a more casual affair, served in a separate room with large windows and a huge tropical mural. The food is lighter too, with sandwiches, salads, and smaller dishes from the dinner menu. **FYI:** Reservations recommended. Big band. Children's menu. **Open:** Sun–Thurs 11am–9:30pm, Fri–Sat 11am–10:30pm. **Prices:** Main courses $8–$30. AE, CB, DC, DISC, MC, V. ♥ 🖼♿

La Hacienda
1411 North St; tel 409/564-6450. On US 59 Business. **Southwestern.** Spacious restaurant in a 1913 family home houses six dining rooms, some with fireplaces, all with light from large windows. The large upstairs bar stays open late. Southwestern-inspired fare includes seafood, barbecue, and salads. Full dining is available on the lighted patio. **FYI:** Reservations accepted. Children's menu. **Open:** Sun–Thurs 11am–midnight, Fri–Sat 11am–1am. **Prices:** Main courses $6–$14. AE, CB, DC, DISC, MC, V. 🖼♿

ATTRACTIONS 🏛

Sterne-Hoya Museum
211 S Lanana St; tel 409/560-5426. This house carries much historical significance for the state. It was built around 1830 by pioneer merchant Nicholas Adolphus Sterne, a conspira-

tor in the ill-fated Fredonian Rebellion in 1826 and a founder of the Texas Republic. Sam Houston was baptized a Catholic here, and Thomas J Rusk, the first US senator from Texas, was a frequent guest; Davy Crockett also spent a fortnight here, in 1836. Chief Bowles of the Cherokee nation signed a peace treaty here. The front rooms and the upstairs are original parts of Sterne's house. One parlor has been furnished and restored to reflect the early Texas period of the Sternes, and the other to echo the Victorian times of the late-19th-century owner Joseph von der Hoya. The house is also the site for the city library, which includes the Jewel Norwood Tilford Children's Collection and the Texana Collection. **Open:** Mon–Sat 9–11:30am and 2–4:30pm. **Free**

Stone Fort Museum
Stephen F Austin State University; tel 409/468-2408. Located on the campus of Stephen F Austin State University, this museum is housed in a 1936 replica of the stone house built around 1780 by Don Antonio Gil Y'Barbo, the founder of present-day Nacogdoches. The original fort was the headquarters for four unsuccessful attempts to establish the Republic of Texas. Exhibits interpret the history of East Texas and Nacogdoches prior to 1900, with an emphasis on the Spanish and Mexican periods extending from 1690 to 1836, when Texas revolutionaries won independence from the Mexican government. Other points of interest are the Native American artifacts, gun and coin collections, and period rooms. Guided tours available by reservation only. Gift shop on the premises. **Open:** Tues–Sat 9am–5pm, Sun 1–5pm. **Free**

Millard's Crossing
6020 North St; tel 409/564-6631. The spirit of pioneer life is evoked in this complex of historical East Texas homes and assorted buildings, one of the earliest settlements in Texas. The 37-acre tract comprises a broad sample of restored 19th-century East Texas architecture, dating from 1830 through 1900. The 1837 Millard-Lee house has an extensive collection of early Texas documents and maps, as well as turn-of-the-century furnishings; an 1830 log house contains antique toys and patchwork quilts; the 1843 chapel is still available for weddings. An 1830 corn storehouse, 1840 home with period furnishings, 1895 home, and 1900 parsonage are also of interest. Tours available. **Open:** Mon–Sat 9am–4pm, Sun 1–4pm. **$$**

Needville

ATTRACTION 🏛

Brazos Bend State Park
FM 762; tel 409/553-5101 or toll free 800/792-1112. The 4,897-acre park is home to an abundant and diverse wildlife population, including white-tailed deer, coyotes, Russian boar, migratory waterfowl, and alligators. Most of the park is in the Brazos River floodplains, but there are also areas of flat

upland coastal prairie, as well as marshes, sloughs, bayous, and oxbow lakes. The live-oak woodlands are draped with wild grape vines and Spanish moss, and the creeks and riverbanks are lined with sycamore, cottonwood, and black willow. There are campsites and picnicking areas; 9 miles of hiking and bicycling trails, 12 miles of unsurfaced hiking trails; fishing opportunities; and an observation tower. Visitors center offers slide-show programs; guided nature walks conducted every weekend. The George Observatory conducts astronomy programs every Saturday. Dining hall; gift shop. **Open:** Mon–Thurs 8am–10pm, Fri–Sun 7am–10pm. **$$**

New Braunfels

Settled by German immigrants in 1845, this resort community along the Comal and Guadalupe Rivers celebrates its heritage with the November Wurstfest, the largest sausage festival in the nation. Downtown is a thriving center for antiques, and the local rivers offer some of the wildest water fun in the state. **Information:** New Braunfels Convention & Visitors Bureau, 390 S Seguin, PO Box 311417, New Braunfels, 78130 (tel 210/625-2385 or toll free 800/572-2626).

MOTEL 🏨

≣≣ Hill Country Motor Inn
210 US 81 at I-35, 78130; tel 210/625-7373; fax 210/629-2713. Exit 187 off I-35. Near Hill Country and the river, this adequate motel has the advantage of a scenic location. **Rooms:** 175 rms. CI 2pm/CO noon. Nonsmoking rms avail. **Amenities:** 🛏 A/C, cable TV w/movies. Some units w/terraces. **Facilities:** 🛋 ⅙ **Rates (CP):** Peak (Mem Day–Labor Day) $79 S; $89 D. Extra person $10. Min stay peak. Lower rates off-season. Parking: Outdoor, free. AE, MC, V.

RESORT

≣≣ New Braunfels Resorts
405 S Sequin, 78130; tel 210/629-5924. McQueeny exit off I-35. 10 acres. Although less luxurious than most resorts, the New Braunfels is relatively well priced and has an attractive location right on the river. **Rooms:** 85 rms. Executive level. CI 3pm/CO noon. No smoking. Nonsmoking rms avail. **Amenities:** 🛏 🍴 🗜 A/C, cable TV, refrig. **Services:** 🗺 Social director. **Facilities:** 🛋 ⅙ **Rates (CP):** Peak (May 15–Sept 15) $69 S; $79 D. Extra person $10. Lower rates off-season. Parking: Outdoor, free. DISC, MC, V.

RESTAURANTS 🍴

Krause's Cafe
148 S Castell; tel 210/625-7581. **German.** Bavarian-styled diner serving up substantial German fare and blue-plate specials. The oldest restaurant in town. **FYI:** Reservations not accepted. Folk. Beer and wine only. **Open:** Mon–Thurs 6:30am–8:30pm, Fri–Sat 6:30am–9pm. **Prices:** Main courses $5–$8. No CC. 🍴 💟

New Braunfels Smokehouse
TX 81 at TX 46; tel 210/625-2416. **Barbecue.** An informal German barbecue restaurant with dining available outside at picnic tables and benches. Smoked meats and sausages, German potato salad, strudel. **FYI:** Reservations not accepted. Beer and wine only. **Open:** Daily 7:30am–9pm. **Prices:** Main courses $5–$9. AE, DC, MC, V. 👥 💟 ⅙

ATTRACTIONS 🏛

Landa Park
Landa St; tel 210/608-2160. This 196-acre scenic park is centered around the spring-fed Comal River (Comal Springs are the largest springs in the state), which visitors can enjoy through the tube chute. Also popular are the 18-hole golf course, the arboretum walking tour featuring over 96 species of trees, and the 1½-million gallon, spring-fed swimming pool. A miniature train ride winds through the park. Nature programs, picnic facilities, and boat rentals also available. **Open:** Daily 8am–midnight. **Free**

Schlitterbahn
400 N Liberty; tel 210/625-2351. Schlitterbahn is German for "slippery road," and that's what visitors will find at this 65-acre water park, which boasts 17 waterslides (including some descending from a German-style castle tower), tube chutes, swimming lagoon, sand beach, bumper boats, giant hot tub, and children's water play areas. **Open:** Peak (Mem Day–Labor Day) daily 10am–8pm. Reduced hours off-season. **$$$$**

Natural Bridge Caverns
I-35; tel 210/651-6101. This US Natural Landmark is located 12 miles west of New Braunfels. Named for the 60-foot-high limestone bridge that spans its entrance, this cavern is among Texas's largest. There are over 10,000 different formations inside these living caverns, whose vast subterranean rooms and corridors stretch more than a mile. (The constant drip of water means that many formations, begun more than 140 million years ago, are still growing and changing.) The many highlights include the Castle of the White Giants, a chamber filled with immense formations of white calcite; The Bomb-Burst, which resembles the mushroom cloud of an atomic blast; the nearby 50-foot Watchtower, the tallest formation in the caverns; the Chandelier, marked by delicate folds and vibrant colors; the part of the cave which runs alongside Emerald Lake; the majestic views offered at Inspiration Point; and the 152-foot man-made bridge spanning Purgatory Creek. Temperature is a constant 70°F. Interpretive center; also picnic area, snack bar, and gift shop. Guided tours. **Open:** Daily 9am–4pm; Mem Day–Labor Day 9am–6pm. **$$$**

Odessa

See also Midland

Created as a stopover on the Texas & Pacific Railroad in the early 1880s, this city located on the barren plain of west Texas has become known as the petroleum service capital of the Permian Basin. Along with Midland, her sister city to the northwest, Odessa has become a center for recreation and culture. The area's wind currents attract sailplane enthusiasts. **Information:** Odessa Convention & Visitors Bureau, 700 N Grant, PO Box 3626, Odessa, 79760-3626 (tel 915/333-7871).

HOTEL

UNRATED Odessa Raddison
5200 E University, 79761; tel 915/368-5885 or toll free 800/333-3333; fax 915/362-8958. On Loop 328, 1 mi N of Business US 20. This hotel is primarily concerned with its business clientele, but is also suitable for families. Great value; convenient to I-20 and airport. **Rooms:** 190 rms and stes. CI 3pm/CO noon. Nonsmoking rms avail. **Amenities:** A/C, cable TV w/movies. Some units w/whirlpools. **Services:** Facilities: 1 restaurant (*see* "Restaurants" below), 2 bars. Exceptional dining in hotel restaurant. **Rates:** $55 S or D; $175–$250 ste. Extra person $10. Children under age 12 stay free. Parking: Outdoor, free. AE, CB, DC, DISC, MC, V.

MOTELS

La Quinta Motor Inn
5001 East Business I-20, 79761; tel 915/333-2820 or toll free 800/531-5900; fax 915/333-4208. 1 block W of Loop 328. Standard chain property with the Southwestern look of its counterparts and 1970s ambience in guestrooms. **Rooms:** 122 rms and stes. CI open/CO noon. Nonsmoking rms avail. **Amenities:** A/C, cable TV w/movies. **Services:** **Facilities:** Washer/dryer. **Rates (CP):** $53 S; $58 D; $61 ste. Extra person $10. Children under age 18 stay free. Parking: Outdoor, free. AE, CB, DC, DISC, MC, V.

Odessa Motor Inn
2021 E Second, 79761; tel 915/332-7341. On Business I-70. Budget motel offering standard chain decor. Convenient to restaurants and business areas. **Rooms:** 61 rms. CI open/CO noon. Nonsmoking rms avail. **Amenities:** A/C, cable TV w/movies. **Services:** **Facilities:** 1 restaurant. **Rates (CP):** $21–$23 S; $24–$27 D. Extra person $3. Children under age 18 stay free. Parking: Outdoor, free. AE, DC, DISC, MC, V.

RESTAURANTS

★ The Barn Door and Pecos Depot
2140 N Grant (Andrews Hwy); tel 915/337-4142. 2 mi N of I-20. **Steak.** From the outside, this restaurant looks like an authentic barn. Inside, the country kitchen decor has a country-style menu to match. House favorites include chicken-fried steak and steak specialties. Dining and catering facilities are available for groups in its large dining area. **FYI:** Reservations not accepted. Children's menu. No liquor license. **Open:** Lunch Mon–Fri 11am–2pm; dinner Mon–Thurs 5–9:30pm, Fri–Sat 5–10pm. **Prices:** Main courses $7–$20. AE, DISC, MC, V.

$ Legends
In Odessa Raddison, 5200 E University; tel 915/368-5885. 1 mi N of Business I-20 on Loop 328. **Eclectic.** The kitchen turns out unusual creations such as strawberry soup but also serves traditional fare as well as an outstanding gourmet lunch buffet for only $5.95. **FYI:** Reservations not accepted. Children's menu. Beer and wine only. **Open:** Breakfast Mon–Fri 6:30am–2pm, Sat–Sun 7am–2pm; dinner Mon–Fri 5–10pm, Sat–Sun 5–10pm. **Prices:** Main courses $4–$12. AE, MC, V.

ATTRACTIONS

Presidential Museum
622 N Lee Ave; tel 915/332-7123. Unique museum devoted solely to the US presidency and its history. On display are presidential medals; campaign buttons and posters, as well as the coin-like campaign medalettes popular as give-away tokens during much of the 19th century; a collection of dolls wearing the hairstyles and inaugural gowns of every first lady. The John Ben Shepperd Jr Library of the Presidents contains 3,500 volumes on subjects relating to presidents and the office of the presidency. Traveling exhibits featured; also guided tours and educational programs. **Open:** Tues–Sat 10am–5pm. **Free**

Water Wonderland
10113 US 80 E; tel 915/563-2200. For relief from the desert heat, this 18-acre, water-theme recreational park offers water slides, water tobogganing, swimming and diving pools, Mountain Rapids tube ride, wave pool, sandy beach, and playgrounds. Picnic sites available. **Open:** May–Labor Day Mon–Wed and Fri–Sun noon–7pm, Thurs noon–9pm. **$$$**

Orange

Named for a landmark of orange trees flanking the banks of the Sabine cited by early French and Spanish boatmen, this city, the easternmost in Texas, became the county seat in 1836. Today's Orange is a major deepwater port with several interesting historic sites. **Information:** Orange Convention & Visitors Bureau, 1012 Green Ave, Orange, 77630-5620 (tel 409/883-3538).

MOTELS

≣≣ Best Western Inn of Orange
2630 I-10, PO Box 1839, 77630; tel 409/883-6616 or toll free 800/528-1234; fax 409/883-3427. W of TX 87. Located near many recreational opportunities. Standard motel rooms. **Rooms:** 60 rms. CI 4pm/CO noon. Nonsmoking rms avail. **Amenities:** A/C, cable TV. **Services:** **Facilities:** **Rates (CP):** $42–$63 S or D. Extra person $5. Children under age 18 stay free. Parking: Outdoor, free. AE, CB, DC, DISC, ER, MC, V.

≣≣ Ramada Inn of Orange
2610 I-10, 77630; tel 409/883-0231 or toll free 800/228-2828; fax 409/883-8839. Between TX 87 and TX 62. Overlooking the interstate with great views of the forest, this standard Ramada is great for overnight guests and highway travelers. Rooms are clean, comfortable and dependable but are nothing fancy. It is only a few miles from the Louisiana border. **Rooms:** 125 rms. CI 3pm/CO noon. Nonsmoking rms avail. **Amenities:** A/C, cable TV w/movies. 1 unit w/minibar, 1 w/whirlpool. **Services:** **Facilities:** 1 restaurant, 1 bar (w/entertainment). **Rates:** $55–$125 S or D. Extra person $5. Children under age 18 stay free. Parking: Outdoor, free. AE, CB, DC, DISC, ER, MC, V.

Ozona

A welcome watering hole on I-10 in west Texas, Ozona is the largest unincorporated municipality in the nation and the only town in Crockett County. One of the nation's major wool-producing areas, Ozona is also thought to have the most millionaires per capita in the nation. **Information:** Ozona Chamber of Commerce, 1110 Ave E, PO Box 1135, Ozona, 76943 (tel 915/392-3737).

MOTELS

≣≣ Comfort Inn
1307 Ave A, 76943; tel 915/392-3791 or toll free 800/221-2222; fax 915/392-5277. Exit 365 off I-10. Highway motel with a stucco exterior and well-appointed rooms. **Rooms:** 50 rms. CI 1pm/CO 11am. Nonsmoking rms avail. Contemporary furnishings and bed coverings. **Amenities:** A/C, cable TV w/movies. **Services:** **Facilities:** Washer/dryer. **Rates (CP):** $51 S; $59 D. Children under age 18 stay free. Parking: Outdoor, free. AE, DC, DISC, MC, V.

≣ Daystop
820 Loop 466 W, 76943; tel 915/392-2631; fax 915/392-2633. 1 mi N of I-10. Small, budget motel offering comfortable, clean rooms near the interstate. **Rooms:** 24 rms. CI 2pm/CO 11am. Nonsmoking rms avail. **Amenities:** A/C, cable TV w/movies. **Services:** Pets allowed only in smoking rooms. **Facilities:** Washer/dryer. **Rates:** $52–$54 S or D. Children under age 18 stay free. Parking: Outdoor, free. AE, DC, DISC, MC, V.

Palestine

One of the crazier laws passed in the early days of the Texas Legislature required that county seats be located within three miles of the county's central point. Thus did Palestine came into civic being in 1846 in Anderson County. Nearby lakes and a wildlife management area offer birding, hunting, and fishing opportunities. **Information:** Palestine Chamber of Commerce, 502 N Queen St, PO Box 1177, Palestine, 75802-1177 (tel 903/729-6066 or toll free 800/659-3484).

MOTEL

≣≣ Best Western Palestine Inn
1601 W Palestine Ave, 75801; tel 903/723-4655 or toll free 800/523-0121; fax 903/723-2519. On US 79 S. Average, but well maintained, close to restaurants, with good access to highway. Within 10 miles of the State Railroad Park. **Rooms:** 66 rms. CI 2pm/CO 1pm. Nonsmoking rms avail. **Amenities:** A/C, cable TV. **Services:** Free transportation to Palestine Airport; fee charged for transportation to Tyler Airport. **Facilities:** 1 restaurant. **Rates:** $38 S; $44 D. Extra person $3. Children under age 12 stay free. Parking: Outdoor, free. AE, CB, DC, DISC, JCB, MC, V.

ATTRACTION

Fairfield Lake State Park
FM 488, FM 1124, and Park Road 64, Fairfield; tel 903/389-4514. This 1,460-acre park adjacent to Lake Fairfield offers camping, rest rooms with showers, swimming beach, boat ramp, fishing pier, and fish-cleaning shelter, plus a 4½-mile hiking trail. **Open:** Daily 6am–10pm. $$

Paris

Major fires in 1877 and 1916 destroyed much of this town's historic heart, so downtown now reflects the architecture of the 1920s. Following the lead of its famous French namesake, Paris hosts an annual Bastille Day Celebration every July. **Information:** Paris Visitor & Convention Office, 1651 Clarksville St, Paris, 75460-6036 (tel 903/784-2501 or toll free 800/PARIS-TX).

MOTEL

≣≣≣ Holiday Inn Paris
3560 Northeast Loop 286, 75460; tel 903/785-5545 or toll free 800/HOLIDAY; fax 903/785-9510. TX 19/24 exit off I-30. The only Paris lodging with a restaurant and lounge, this motel is very convenient for business travelers. Close to downtown and civic center. **Rooms:** 124 rms. CI 3pm/CO

noon. Nonsmoking rms avail. Rooms are decorated in tasteful, soft colors. King deluxe room has sitting area. **Amenities:** 📺 🛁 A/C, satel TV w/movies. **Services:** ✕ 🚐 🖼 🛎 ⚬ **Facilities:** 🛗 200 ⚬ 1 restaurant, 1 bar, whirlpool, washer/dryer. **Rates:** $60 S or D. Extra person $6. Children under age 19 stay free. Parking: Outdoor, free. AE, CB, DC, DISC, MC, V.

Pecos

This commercial center for ranching, farming, and oil production was established in 1881, during which time it was notorious as one of the most lawless frontier towns. Pecos, which claims to be the site of the first rodeo (1883), hosts the West of the Pecos Rodeo in early July. **Information:** Pecos Chamber of Commerce, 111 S Cedar, PO Box 27, Pecos, 79772-0027 (tel 915/445-2406).

HOTEL 🏨

☰☰☰ Holiday Inn
4002 S Cedar, 79772; tel 915/445-5404 or toll free 800/465-4329; fax 915/445-2484. Exit 42 off I-20. Close to I-20 and convenient for those wanting to be near the business district. Gold and red decor throughout lobby and hallways. Excellent entertainment and dining opportunities nearby. **Rooms:** 91 rms. CI open/CO 1pm. Nonsmoking rms avail. **Amenities:** 📺 🛁 A/C, cable TV w/movies. **Services:** ✕ 🚐 🖼 ⚬ 🛎 **Facilities:** 🛗 75 ⚬ 1 restaurant, 1 bar. **Rates (CP):** $56 S; $61 D. Children under age 18 stay free. Parking: Outdoor, free. AE, CB, DC, DISC, MC, V.

Plainview

Named for the expansive and unobstructed view of the plains that characterize this part of the Texas Panhandle, Plainview was founded as an agricultural center in 1887. Today it is known as a major antique market and home of Wayland Baptist University. **Information:** Plainview Chamber of Commerce, 710 W 5th St, Plainview, 79072-6234 (tel 806/296-7431).

MOTEL 🏨

☰☰ Best Western Conestoga
600 I-27 N, 79072; tel 806/293-9454 or toll free 800/528-1234; fax 806/293-9454. At jct I-70. Near downtown Plainview, this convenient motel is about an hour from Palo Duro Canyon. Average decor. **Rooms:** 82 rms and stes. CI open/CO noon. Nonsmoking rms avail. **Amenities:** 📺 🛁 A/C, cable TV w/movies. **Services:** ✕ ⚬ 🛎 **Facilities:** ⚬ **Rates (CP):** $44–$55 D; $90 ste. Extra person $7. Children under age 13 stay free. Parking: Outdoor, free. AE, DISC, MC, V.

ATTRACTION 💼

Llano Estacado Museum
1900 W 7th St; tel 806/296-4735. Exhibits illustrate the history and geology of the "Staked Plain" or Llano Estacado, the southernmost region of the Great Plains. Included are Native American artifacts, early photos of the region, blacksmithing items, and re-created rooms of the pioneer era. **Open:** Mon–Fri 9am–5pm, Sat–Sun 1–5pm. **Free**

Port Aransas

Located on the northern end of Mustang Island, this small fishing port is popular for its easy access to saltwater sport fishing. Port Aransas also draws retirees year-round, and thousands of college students during spring break, to bask in the sun. **Information:** Port Aransas Convention & Visitors Bureau, 421 W Cotter, PO Box 356, Port Aransas, 78373 (tel 512/749-5919 or toll free 800/452-6278).

MOTEL 🏨

☰ Driftwood Motel
300 W Ave G, 78373; tel 512/749-6427. TX 361 N exit off TX 358, left on Ave G. A very basic roadside motel in need of some refurbishing. Acceptable for an overnight stay, but offers very little for its relatively high rates. **Rooms:** 100 rms. CI 2pm/CO noon. Nonsmoking rms avail. Room furniture is older and mismatched. **Amenities:** 📺 A/C, cable TV. Some units w/terraces. **Facilities:** 🛗 ⚬ Whirlpool. **Rates:** $45–$49 S; $49–$55 D. Extra person $10. Parking: Outdoor, free. AE, DC, DISC, MC, V.

RESORT

☰☰☰ Channel View Condominiums
631 Channel View Dr, 78373; tel 512/749-6649. Off TX 361. 3 acres. These elegant condominiums are located just down the street from the beach and make for a romantic getaway destination or great vacation with the kids. Gates add security and elegance to the rustic wood shingle exterior. **Rooms:** 75 stes and effic; 80 cottages/villas. Executive level. CI open/CO 2pm. Nonsmoking rms avail. Luxurious rooms have colorful, modern decor with glass tables and wicker furniture. **Amenities:** 📺 🛁 📻 🍴 A/C, satel TV w/movies, refrig, VCR, voice mail. Some units w/minibars, some w/terraces. **Services:** 🛎 **Facilities:** 🛗 🍴 ⚬ Playground, washer/dryer. **Rates:** Peak (May–Sept) $125–$145 ste; $145–$156 effic; $145–$156 cottage/villa. Children under age 5 stay free. Min stay wknds. Lower rates off-season. Parking: Indoor/outdoor, free. Rates are based on length of stay. AE, DISC, MC, V.

RESTAURANTS ▯

Crazy Cajun Seafood Restaurant

Alister St Sq; tel 512/749-5069. **Cajun/Seafood/Steak.** Upscale family restaurant with lovely seaside decor. Steak and lobster. **FYI:** Reservations accepted. Children's menu. Dress code. **Open:** Daily 11am–11pm. **Prices:** Main courses $8–$16. AE, DC, MC, V. ▯ ▯ ▯

Seafood and Spaghetti Works

710 Alister at Ave G; tel 512/749-5069. **Italian/Seafood.** Housed in a geodesic dome, this family-style eatery offers ample balcony seating for diners hungry for the likes of pasta primavera and grilled salmon and shrimp. **FYI:** Reservations accepted. Children's menu. Dress code. Beer and wine only. **Open:** Dinner daily 5–10pm; brunch Sun 8:30am–1pm. **Prices:** Main courses $9–$16. AE, DC, DISC, MC, V. ▯ ▯ ▯

ATTRACTION ▯

Mustang Island State Park

14 mi S of Port Aransas on Texas 361; tel 512/749-5246. This park offers 3,474 acres of sand dunes, troughs, grassy flats, marshes, and tidal flats. Jackrabbits, armadillos, coyotes, and a variety of waterfowl are protected here. The gulf side of the park is set off from the island's interior by dunes (some rise as high as 35 feet), and features 5 miles of beach frontage offering seaside camping, surfing, fishing, and swimming. Facilities include multiuse campsites with hookups, picnic arbors, rest rooms, showers, a nature trail, and a fish-cleaning station. **Open:** Daily 8am–10pm. **$$**

Port Arthur

Situated near the Gulf on Sabine Lake and self-labeled the "Energy City," Port Arthur contains the world's largest refinery complex. Settled in 1840, this primarily industrial city offers an ever-increasing number of sites of interest, including nearby Sea Rim State Park. **Information:** Port Arthur Convention & Visitors Bureau, 3401 Cultural Center Dr, Port Arthur, 77642 (tel 409/985-7822).

MOTEL ▯

▤ ▤ ▤ Ramada Inn

3801 TX 73, 77642; tel 409/962-9858 or toll free 800/2-RAMADA; fax 409/962-3685. Conveniently located near many local attractions, this is a dependable place to stay while visiting Port Arthur, Orange, and Beaumont. Lobby is very plush with an elegant staircase and a beautiful grandfather clock. A great place for families, too. **Rooms:** 125 rms. CI 4pm/CO noon. Nonsmoking rms avail. **Amenities:** ▯ ▯ A/C, cable TV. **Services:** ✕ ▯ ▯ ▯ Babysitting. **Facilities:** ▯ ▯ ▯ ▯ ▯ 1 restaurant, 1 bar (w/entertainment), whirlpool, washer/dryer. Hotel has a nice, covered patio neat the pool

for relaxing afternoons. **Rates:** $58–$76 S or D. Extra person $8. Children under age 18 stay free. Parking: Outdoor, free. AE, CB, DC, DISC, JCB, MC, V.

RESTAURANT ▯

★ Esther's Seafood and Oyster Bar

7237 Rainbow Lane; tel 409/962-6288. TX 87, at foot of Rainbow Bridge over the Neches River. **Cajun/Seafood.** Located in a swampy, bayou section of Port Arthur, the building (brought in by barge from Louisiana) rests on stilts at the foot of Rainbow Bridge, one of the highest bridges in the South. The restaurant itself is a local favorite for Louisiana/Cajun ambience and cuisine. **FYI:** Reservations accepted. Children's menu. Beer and wine only. **Open:** Sun–Thurs 11am–9pm, Fri 11am–10pm, Sat 5–10pm. **Prices:** Main courses $7–$22. AE, DISC, MC, V.

ATTRACTIONS ▯

Museum of the Gulf Coast

701 4th St; tel 409/982-7000. The history of the Gulf coast, from prehistoric times to the present, is illustrated through artifacts, photographs, fossils, and memorabilia. Relics from the Battle of Sabine Pass and an Edison Talking Machine are of special interest. The Southeast Musical Heritage Exhibit documents the region's musical and sports heritage, focusing on figures such as Janis Joplin, Edgar and Johnny Winter, Bum Phillips, and Jimmy Johnson. Artworks by Port Arthur native Robert Rauschenberg featured; also decorative arts collection. **Open:** Mon–Sat 9am–5pm, Sun 1–5pm. **$$**

Pompeiian Villa

1953 Lakeshore Dr; tel 409/983-5977. Built in 1900 by barbed-wire tycoon Isaac Ellwood, this house is modeled after an AD 79 Pompeiian villa and is listed on the National Register of Historic Places. The pink stucco structure boasts a courtyard with a fountain in the middle and is furnished with art from the 18th through 20th centuries. **Open:** Mon–Fri 9am–4pm. **$**

Port Isabel

See also Brownsville, South Padre Island

Established in the 1840s as a supply post for US forces during the Mexican War, Port Isabel is now a small fishing community. Anchoring the mainland end of the Queen Isabella Causeway, this town serves as the gateway to South Padre Island. **Information:** Port Isabel Chamber of Commerce, 213 Yturria St, Port Isabel, 78578 (tel 210/943-2262).

HOTEL ▯

▤ ▤ ▤ Yacht Club Hotel

700 Yturria St, 78578; tel 210/943-1301. Off TX 100. An upscale hotel with a posh, nautical atmosphere and decor, this independently owned hotel is great for all types of guests.

Staffers will go out of their way to accommodate any need. **Rooms:** 250 rms and stes. Executive level. CI 2pm/CO noon. Nonsmoking rms avail. **Amenities:** 🛎 A/C, satel TV w/movies, refrig. Some units w/minibars, some w/terraces. **Services:** VP 🚐 🖂 ➰ Twice-daily maid svce, social director. **Facilities:** 🔧 🏊 ⛳ 150 🚹 1 restaurant (see "Restaurants" below), 1 bar (w/entertainment), whirlpool. Grounds are especially well kept and beautiful. **Rates (CP):** Peak (Apr–Sept) $69–$79 S; $79–$89 D; $99–$140 ste. Extra person $10. Min stay special events. Lower rates off-season. MAP rates avail. Parking: Indoor/outdoor, free. AE, DC, DISC, MC, V.

RESTAURANT 🍴

The Yacht Club
700 Yturria; tel 210/943-1301. 2 blocks N of TX 100. **Seafood/Steak.** True to its name, this restaurant has a very clublike atmosphere (built in 1926, it once did serve as a yacht club). The thoroughly nautical decor makes patrons feel that they're dining in the interior of a very posh yacht. Popular dishes include flounder, red snapper, and prime rib. **FYI:** Reservations accepted. Singer. Dress code. **Open:** Thurs–Tues 6–9:30pm. **Prices:** Main courses $6–$11. AE, DISC, MC, V. 🏞 💟 🚹

Port Lavaca

See Victoria

Rancho Viejo

See Brownsville

Richardson

See Dallas

Rusk

ATTRACTION 📷

Rusk State Park
3 mi W of Rusk on US 84; tel 903/683-5126. These 100 acres of mixed pine and hardwood forest around the Rusk terminal of Texas State Railroad offer group shelter, bathhouse, tennis courts, picnic facilities, and primitive and hookup camping. Antique steam engines power vintage coaches on the 25½-mile trip to Palestine through dense East Texas forestland. The railroad is in operation weekends from March

through May; then daily except Tuesday and Wednesday through mid-August; weekends through October. Fees for train rides. **Open:** Daily 8am–10pm. **$**

Salado

See Temple

San Angelo

Like many west Texas towns, San Angelo developed around a reliable source of water. Today the Concho River still flows through town, giving a park like atmosphere to the city and courthouse square. The downtown historic district contains many antique shops along its boardwalk. The city is home to San Angelo State University and has five lakes nearby for recreation. **Information:** Convention & Visitors Bureau, 500 Rio Concho Dr, San Angelo, 76903 (tel 915/653-1206 or toll free 800/375-1206).

HOTEL 🏨

UNRATED Holiday Inn Convention Center
441 Rio Concho Dr, 76903; tel 915/658-2828. This hotel has been newly redecorated with an attractive floral peach and green decor. **Rooms:** 148 rms and stes. Executive level. CI 3pm/CO noon. Nonsmoking rms avail. **Amenities:** 🛎 ☕ 📺 A/C, satel TV w/movies, voice mail. Some units w/whirlpools. **Services:** ✗ 🚐 🖂 ➰ Social director. A bus stops at hotel and takes guests to a mall (about 15 minutes away). **Facilities:** 🔧 250 🚹 1 restaurant, 1 bar, whirlpool, washer/dryer. **Rates:** $62 S or D; $75 ste. Extra person $8. Children under age 18 stay free. Parking: Outdoor, free. AE, CB, DC, DISC, JCB, MC, V.

MOTELS

≋≋ El Patio Motor Inn
1901 W Beauregard, 76901; tel 915/655-5711 or toll free 800/677-2735; fax 915/653-2717. 2 mi W of Concho River. Basic motel containing larger-than-average rooms facing an interior courtyard and attractive pool area. Convenient to San Angelo State University. **Rooms:** 100 rms. CI open/CO noon. Nonsmoking rms avail. **Amenities:** 🛎 A/C, cable TV. **Services:** ➰ ➰ **Facilities:** 🔧 100 1 restaurant (dinner only). **Rates (CP):** $23–$32 S. Children under age 18 stay free. Parking: Outdoor, free. AE, CB, DC, DISC, MC, V.

≋≋ Inn of the Conchos
2021 N Bryant, 76903; tel 915/658-2811 or toll free 800/621-6041. ½ mi E of Concho River. A motel with a welcoming exterior and a pleasant Southwestern decor inside. **Rooms:** 126 rms and stes. Executive level. CI 2pm/CO noon. Nonsmoking rms avail. Rooms are spacious. **Amenities:** 🛎 A/C, cable TV, voice mail. **Services:** ✗ 🖂 ➰ ➰ **Facilities:** 🔧 250 🚹 1 restaurant (bkfst and lunch only). **Rates:** $37–$43

S or D; $85–$125 ste. Extra person $6. Children under age 12 stay free. Parking: Outdoor, free. AE, CB, DC, DISC, MC, V.

RESTAURANTS

Dun Bar East

1728 Pilliam; tel 915/655-8780. Off US 67. **American.** Great for families, this restaurant features an attractive Southwestern decor and inexpensive dining. **FYI:** Reservations accepted. Children's menu. Jacket required. Beer and wine only. **Open:** Daily 6am–9:30pm. **Prices:** Main courses $5–$11. AE, CB, DC, DISC, MC, V.

Mejor Que Nada

1911 S Bryant; tel 915/655-3553. **Mexican/Southwestern.** Lively hacienda atmosphere and the Mexican music playing in the background makes this a popular hangout. **FYI:** Reservations accepted. **Open:** Mon–Fri 10:30am–9pm, Sat–Sun 10:30am–10:30pm. **Prices:** Main courses $6–$8. AE, DISC, MC, V.

ATTRACTION

Fort Concho National Historic Landmark

213 E Ave D; tel 915/657-4441. From 1867 through 1889, this fort served as a pivot post on the frontier line, and its troops were useful in protecting stagecoaches and wagon trains, exploring and mapping new territory, and escorting the US mail. Troops also occasionally clashed with local tribes. Many of the original buildings have been restored (including barracks, officers' quarters, commissary, and headquarters), and the site continues to hold events through the year. The 20-acre fort is also home to several museums: the **San Angelo Museum of Fine Arts** has changing exhibits of historic and contemporary works of art, along with a gift shop; the **EH Danner Museum of Telephony** features various models of telephones, from Alexander Graham Bell's Gallows Frame phone (only five ever built) to wooden phones and push-button phones of the 1880s to present versions; the **Robert Wood Johnson Museum of Frontier Medicine** boasts instruments, medicines, surgical kits, and other items from a typical 19th-century frontier hospital. **Open:** Tues–Sat 10am–5pm, Sun 1–5pm. $

San Antonio

See also Bandera, New Braunfels

Founded in 1718 with the construction of a Spanish mission later known as the Alamo, this large city at the southern end of the Hill Country offers visitors an almost endless list of activities. The Alamo survives, along with four sister missions and several other 18th-century Spanish sites. Other popular attractions include the River Walk and the city's noted museums, historic districts, and theme parks. Although strongly Hispanic in flavor, San Antonio was also strongly influenced by heavy German immigration during the 19th century. Major events include Fiesta San Antonio in April, the Texas Folklife Festival in August, and Fiesta de las Luminaries in early December. **Information:** San Antonio Convention & Visitors Bureau, PO Box 2277, San Antonio, 78298 (tel 210/270-8700).

PUBLIC TRANSPORTATION

The **VIA Metropolitan Transit Service** runs 90 bus routes. The cost is 40¢ for regular routes, 75¢ to $1 for express buses. The number 7/40 route, the Cultural Route, stops at many popular tourist attractions. Call 210/227-2020 for information. VIA also offers four convenient downtown streetcar routes covering the most popular tourist stops. These replicas of turn-of-the-century trolleys cost 25¢. A $2 Day-Tripper pass, good for an entire day of travel on all VIA transportation except express buses, can be purchased at VIA's downtown Information Center.

HOTELS

Best Western Crockett Hotel

320 Bonham St, 78205 (Downtown); tel 210/225-6500 or toll free 800/292-1050. A fine location near many historic sites and a bright central atrium area are highlights of this hotel built in 1900. **Rooms:** 250 rms and stes. Executive level. CI 2pm/CO noon. Nonsmoking rms avail. **Amenities:** A/C, satel TV w/movies, dataport, bathrobes. Some units w/minibars, some w/terraces. **Services:** Twice-daily maid svce, social director. **Facilities:** 1 restaurant (bkfst only), 1 bar (w/entertainment), sauna, steam rm, whirlpool, beauty salon, washer/dryer. **Rates (CP):** $95–$120 S or D; $150–$400 ste. Extra person $10. Children under age 10 stay free. MAP rates avail. Parking: Indoor/outdoor, $2/day. AE, DISC, MC, V.

Courtyard by Marriott

600 S Santa Rosa, 78216; tel 210/229-9449 or toll free 800/321-2211. Durango exit off I-35. A chain hotel for business travelers, convenient to downtown attractions. Clean and comfortable, with a very friendly staff. **Rooms:** 175 rms and stes. Executive level. CI 2pm/CO noon. No smoking. **Amenities:** A/C, satel TV w/movies, refrig, dataport, VCR, bathrobes. Some units w/minibars, some w/terraces, some w/whirlpools. **Services:** Twice-daily maid svce, social director. **Facilities:** 1 restaurant, 1 bar (w/entertainment), racquetball, sauna, whirlpool. **Rates (CP):** $89–$99 S or D; $109–$139 ste. Extra person $7. Children under age 5 stay free. MAP rates avail. Parking: Indoor/outdoor, $3/day. AE, DC, DISC, MC, V.

Embassy Suites Northwest

7750 Briaridge, 78230; tel 210/340-5421 or toll free 800/362-2779. Off US 281. Upscale hotel with sunlit atrium area and many amenities. Plush without being flashy. Located near the airport. **Rooms:** 217 stes. Executive level. CI 2pm/CO noon. Nonsmoking rms avail. **Amenities:** A/C, satel

TV w/movies, refrig, dataport, VCR, CD/tape player, voice mail, in-rm safe, bathrobes. Some units w/minibars, some w/terraces, some w/fireplaces, some w/whirlpools. **Services:** ✗ 🚐 ◁⑦ Car-rental desk, social director, masseur. Complimentary evening cocktail hour. **Facilities:** 🛋 🍴 🔟75 💻 ⚕ 1 restaurant, 1 bar (w/entertainment), steam rm, whirlpool, beauty salon. **Rates (CP):** $99–$109 ste. Extra person $20. Parking: Outdoor, free. AE, DISC, MC, V.

🏃🏃🏃 Executive Guesthouse Hotel
12828 US 281 N, 78216; tel 210/494-7600 or toll free 800/362-8700. 1 mi N of airport. Business traveler–oriented hotel located north of downtown, about a mile from the airport. **Rooms:** 105 rms and stes. Executive level. CI 2pm/CO noon. Nonsmoking rms avail. **Amenities:** 📻 ⚕ ⚡ 🍴A/C, cable TV w/movies, voice mail, bathrobes. Some units w/minibars, some w/terraces, some w/whirlpools. **Services:** 🚐 ◁⑦ **Facilities:** 🛋 🍴 🔟35 ⚕ 1 restaurant, 1 bar (w/entertainment), sauna, whirlpool. **Rates (CP):** Peak (Mar–Sept) $89–$99 S or D. Extra person $10. Children under age 10 stay free. Lower rates off-season. Parking: Outdoor, free. AE, DISC, MC, V.

🏃🏃🏃🏃 Fairmount Hotel
401 S Alamo St, 78205 (Downtown); tel 210/224-8800 or toll free 800/642-3363. Commerce St exit off I-37. Built in 1865, this elegant, historic boutique hotel across the street from HemisFair Park is housed in a restored Victorian building located a few miles from the Alamo. Intimate and luxurious, it provides the kind of personal service you might expect from a small inn. Great ambience and style in a great location. **Rooms:** 215 rms, stes. Executive level. CI 2pm/CO noon. No smoking. Rooms are outstandingly decorated with rich wood furniture, plants, original art. Balconies overlook the city or a small central courtyard. Luxurious bathrooms are done in Italian marble and brass. **Amenities:** 📻 ⚕ ⚡ 🍴A/C, cable TV w/movies, refrig, VCR, voice mail, in-rm safe, bathrobes. Some units w/minibars, some w/terraces, some w/fireplaces, some w/whirlpools. **Services:** ✗ ➡ VP 🚐 ◸ ◁⑦ Twice-daily maid svce, social director. Film library available. **Facilities:** 🛋 🍴 🔟250 💻 ⚕ 1 restaurant (*see* "Restaurants" below), 1 bar (w/entertainment), sauna, whirlpool, beauty salon. Complimentary use of nearby health club and pool. **Rates:** Peak (Apr–Sept) $155–$425 S or D; $185–$425 ste. Extra person $10. Children under age 7 stay free. Lower rates off-season. Parking: Indoor/outdoor, free. AE, DC, DISC, MC, V.

🏃🏃🏃 Hawthorn Suites Hotel
4041 Bluemel Rd, 78240; tel 210/561-9660 or toll free 800/527-1133. Off I-10. All-suite property designed for extended stays. Pleasantly decorated. **Rooms:** 50 stes. Executive level. CI 3pm/CO 11am. Nonsmoking rms avail. **Amenities:** 📻 ⚕ ⚡ 🍴A/C, cable TV w/movies, refrig, VCR, bathrobes. Some units w/minibars, some w/terraces, some w/fireplaces. **Services:** 🚐 ◸ ◁⑦ Car-rental desk, social director. Compli-

mentary evening refreshments. **Facilities:** 🛋 🔟25 ⚕ **Rates (CP):** $138–$168 ste. Extra person $5. Parking: Outdoor, free. AE, DC, DISC, ER, MC, V.

🏃🏃🏃 Hilton Palacio del Rio
200 S Alamo St, 78205 (Downtown); tel 210/222-1400 or toll free 800/445-8667. A true "palace of the river," this pricey, upscale hotel is located downtown on the River Walk, near all the attractions and restaurants. The lobby impresses with its polished parquet floors, grand piano, and deluxe leather couches. **Rooms:** 275 rms and stes. Executive level. CI 3pm/CO 1pm. Nonsmoking rms avail. Tower rooms are more elegant than dated standard rooms. Balconies provide spectacular views of downtown or the river. **Amenities:** 📻 ⚕ ⚡ 🍴 A/C, satel TV w/movies, refrig, dataport, VCR, voice mail, bathrobes. Some units w/minibars, some w/terraces, some w/fireplaces, some w/whirlpools. **Services:** ✗ ➡ VP 🚐 ◸ ◁⑦ ◁⑦ Twice-daily maid svce, car-rental desk, social director. **Facilities:** 🛋 🍴 🔟350 💻 ⚕ 1 restaurant, 1 bar (w/entertainment), sauna, steam rm, whirlpool, beauty salon. Airline and car rental desks. Stetson's restaurant offers great views and refined regional American fare, while fun Durty Nelly's Irish Pub has sing-alongs. **Rates (CP):** Peak (Mar–Sept) $160–$233 S or D; $375–$550 ste. Extra person $10. Children under age 7 stay free. Lower rates off-season. AP and MAP rates avail. Parking: Indoor/outdoor, free. AE, DISC, MC, V.

🏃🏃 Holiday Inn Express Sea World
7043 Culebra Rd, 78238; tel 210/521-1485 or toll free 800/465-4329. Off Loop I-410. Located off the main loop near military bases and several restaurants. **Rooms:** 50 rms and stes. CI 2pm/CO noon. Nonsmoking rms avail. Comfortable, brightly colored rooms have tasteful paisley print furniture, carpet, and drapes. **Amenities:** 📻 ⚕ A/C, cable TV, voice mail. Some units w/terraces. **Services:** 🚐 **Facilities:** 🛋 🔟20 ⚕ **Rates (CP):** $52–$60 S; $60–$65 D; $70–$85 ste. Extra person $5. Children under age 5 stay free. Min stay peak. Lower rates off-season. Parking: Outdoor, free. AE, DC, DISC, MC, V.

🏃🏃🏃 Howard Johnson Riverwalk Plaza Hotel
100 Villita St, 78205; tel 210/226-2271 or toll free 800/554-4678. This large, older hotel features accommodations that overlook the beautiful downtown River Walk area. **Rooms:** 210 rms and stes. CI 2pm/CO 11am. Nonsmoking rms avail. Rooms have older furnishings with new carpet and bedspreads. **Amenities:** 📻 ⚡ A/C, cable TV w/movies. Some units w/terraces. **Facilities:** 🛋 ⚕ **Rates (CP):** Peak (Feb–Oct) $89–$105 S; $105–$110 D; $120 ste. Extra person $5. Min stay peak. Lower rates off-season. Parking: Outdoor, free. AE, DC, DISC, MC, V.

🏃🏃🏃🏃 Hyatt Regency
123 Losoya St, 78205 (Downtown); tel 210/222-1234. Located downtown on River Walk and near the Alamo, this bustling social/business hub is all glass and steel and light. An extension of the river runs right through the bright atrium

lobby. If you want all the conveniences and you want to be in the center of the action, this is the hotel for you. **Rooms:** 300 rms, stes, and effic. Executive level. CI 2pm/CO 1pm. Nonsmoking rms avail. Very attractive, Santa Fe–styled guest rooms, many overlooking the atrium area facing the river. **Amenities:** 🅱 🛁 🎙 🍷 A/C, satel TV w/movies, refrig, dataport, VCR, CD/tape player, voice mail, in-rm safe, bathrobes. Some units w/minibars, some w/terraces, some w/fireplaces, some w/whirlpools. **Services:** ✗ 🗝 VP 🚐 🖐 ⛱ 🖐 Car-rental desk, babysitting. **Facilities:** 🏋 🍴 1000 🏊 1 restaurant, 1 bar, racquetball, whirlpool. Dixieland jazz at the Landing nightclub. **Rates (CP):** $135–$239 S or D; $260–$715 ste. Extra person $10. Children under age 10 stay free. AP and MAP rates avail. Parking: Indoor/outdoor, $5/day. AE, DC, DISC, MC, V.

≡≡≡ La Mansion Del Rio
112 College St, 78205 (Downtown); tel 210/225-2581 or toll free 800/292-7300. Commerce St exit off I-37. Converted from a 19th-century seminary, this elegant, Spanish hacienda–style downtown hotel features Mediterranean arches, wrought-iron balconies, and an interior courtyard. Antiques abound. Excellent service. **Rooms:** 240 rms and stes. Executive level. CI 2pm/CO noon. Nonsmoking rms avail. Large, apartment-style rooms with rough-hewn beamed ceilings and brick walls. Some rooms overlook River Walk, some the inner courtyard. **Amenities:** 🅱 🛁 🎙 🍷 A/C, cable TV w/movies, refrig, VCR, CD/tape player, voice mail, in-rm safe, bathrobes. Some units w/minibars, some w/terraces, some w/fireplaces, some w/whirlpools. **Services:** ✗ 🗝 VP 🚐 🖐 🖐 Social director, masseur, children's program, babysitting. **Facilities:** 🏋 300 🏊 1 bar (w/entertainment), sauna, whirlpool, beauty salon. Courtyard around lovely garden and pool. Las Canarias serves fine American regional cuisine and affords a splendid river view; cocktails are served in adjoining courtyard garden. **Rates:** $210–$280 S or D; $375–$760 ste. Extra person $10. Parking: Indoor/outdoor, $2/day. AE, DISC, MC, V.

≡≡≡ La Quinta Convention Center
1001 E Commerce St, 78205; tel 210/222-9181 or toll free 800/531-5900. E Commerce St exit off I-37 N. Better-than-average chain accommodations with Southwestern motif. (Be careful while driving in this area, since this a heavily trafficked area with one-way streets.) **Rooms:** 110 rms and stes. Executive level. CI 2pm/CO 1pm. Nonsmoking rms avail. Rooms were recently renovated. **Amenities:** 🅱 🛁 🎙 🍷 A/C, cable TV w/movies, refrig, dataport. Some units w/minibars, some w/terraces. Very nice toiletries package. **Services:** 🖐 Social director, babysitting. **Facilities:** 🏋 100 🏊 **Rates (CP):** Peak (Feb–Sept) $59–$69 S; $79–$89 D; $95–$125 ste. Extra person $10. Children under age 5 stay free. Lower rates off-season. Parking: Indoor/outdoor, free. AE, DC, DISC, MC, V.

≡≡≡ Marriott Rivercenter
101 Bowie St, 78205 (Downtown); tel 210/223-1000 or toll free 800/648-4462. A recent entry on the hotel scene is this 38-story, twin tower structure with a slick, contemporary look. Connected to the River Walk and River Center Mall. **Rooms:** 310 rms and stes. Executive level. CI 2pm/CO noon. No smoking. **Amenities:** 🅱 🛁 🎙 🍷 A/C, satel TV w/movies, refrig, dataport, VCR, CD/tape player, in-rm safe, bathrobes. Some units w/minibars, some w/terraces. **Services:** ✗ 🗝 VP ⛱ 🖐 Twice-daily maid svce, car-rental desk, social director. **Facilities:** 🏋 350 🏊 1 restaurant, 1 bar (w/entertainment), sauna, whirlpool. Large indoor/outdoor pool. Very well-equipped fitness center. **Rates (CP):** $150–$200 S; $174–$209 D; $275–$950 ste. Extra person $10. MAP rates avail. Parking: Indoor/outdoor, $3/day. AE, DC, DISC, MC, V.

≡≡≡ Menger Hotel
204 Alamo Plaza, 78205; tel 210/223-4361. The first major hotel in San Antonio (built in 1862), the historic Menger occupies a prime location next to the Alamo and covers an entire corner block. The building, all marble with wrought-iron railings and awnings, contains a lush tropical garden area, a rotunda decorated with 19th-century art, and phone booths that date from 1910 (and the phones work, too). **Rooms:** 239 rms and stes. Executive level. CI 2pm/CO noon. Nonsmoking rms avail. Comfortable rooms appointed with beautiful cherry furnishings; those overlooking tropical garden have more character. Separate dressing areas. **Amenities:** 🅱 🛁 🎙 🍷 A/C, cable TV w/movies, refrig, dataport, bathrobes. Some units w/terraces, some w/fireplaces. Stocked refrigerators. Two TVs. **Services:** ✗ 🗝 VP 🖐 Twice-daily maid svce, social director. **Facilities:** 🏋 🍴 300 🖥 🏊 1 restaurant, 1 bar (w/entertainment), whirlpool, beauty salon. **Rates (CP):** Peak (Feb–Oct) $112–$132 S or D; $182–$364 ste. Extra person $10. Children under age 5 stay free. Lower rates off-season. MAP rates avail. Parking: Indoor, free. AE, DC, DISC, MC, V.

≡≡≡ Omni San Antonio
9821 Colonnade Blvd, 78230; tel 210/691-8888 or toll free 800/460-8881. On I-10 access road. This luxury, polished granite high-rise towers over the neighboring commercial establishments. The exquisite lobby is filled with marble floors, countertops, and tile, and an airy, tropical ambience is created by the glass walls and many lush plants. **Rooms:** 326 rms and stes. Executive level. CI 2pm/CO noon. Nonsmoking rms avail. Rooms are nicely decorated in deep reds and blues and feature thick, plush carpets. Porcelain tubs and countertops. **Amenities:** 🅱 🛁 🎙 🍷 A/C, cable TV w/movies, refrig, dataport, bathrobes. Some units w/minibars, some w/terraces. **Services:** ✗ 🗝 VP 🚐 ⛱ 🖐 Twice-daily maid svce, social director. **Facilities:** 🏋 🍴 250 🏊 1 restaurant, 1 bar (w/entertainment), whirlpool, beauty salon. Clublike lobby lounge with plush leather chairs and nightly piano music. La Camellia, the softly lit fine dining restaurant, serves innovative seafood. Impressive Sunday brunch on 19th floor, which

affords great views of Hill Country. **Rates (CP):** Peak (Feb–July) $82–$160 S or D. Extra person $10. Children under age 5 stay free. Min stay peak. Lower rates off-season. MAP rates avail. Parking: Indoor/outdoor, $2–$4/day. AE, DC, DISC, MC, V.

Plaza San Antonio
555 S Alamo St, 78205; tel 210/229-1000 or toll free 800/421-1172. Durango St exit off I-10. Located in a quiet area of downtown, across from HemisFair Park and near the historic "missionaries trail" and buildings and missions that date from the 1700s. The gracious hotel, which includes four 19th-century buildings (used for conference centers and the health club), is set on six acres of gorgeous gardens; pheasants stroll the grounds. Offers a good deal of luxury and personal service for the money. **Rooms:** 250 rms and stes. Executive level. CI 2pm/CO noon. Nonsmoking rms avail. Spacious, elegant rooms have modern conveniences yet are individually decorated with antique-style furnishings. Separate dressing and living areas. **Amenities:** A/C, cable TV w/movies, refrig, dataport, VCR, bathrobes. Some units w/minibars, some w/terraces. **Services:** Twice-daily maid svce, social director. **Facilities:** 1 restaurant (see "Restaurants" below), 1 bar (w/entertainment), whirlpool, beauty salon. The Anaqua Grill offers fine eclectic cuisine in a garden setting. **Rates (CP):** Peak (Mar–Oct) $179–$185 S; $199–$205 D; $250–$400 ste. Extra person $10. Children under age 5 stay free. Min stay peak and wknds. Lower rates off-season. MAP rates avail. Parking: Indoor, $5/day. AE, DISC, MC, V.

Ramada Emily Morgan Hotel
705 E Houston, 78205 (Downtown); tel 210/225-8486 or toll free 800/824-6674. This mammoth, historic hotel situated across from Alamo Plaza is named for a heroine of the Mexican-American War. The stunning 1926 Gothic Revival building was one of the first skyscrapers in the West. An excellent value downtown. **Rooms:** 250 rms and stes. Executive level. CI 2pm/CO noon. Nonsmoking rms avail. Bright, modern rooms. **Amenities:** A/C, cable TV w/movies, refrig, bathrobes. Some units w/minibars, some w/terraces, some w/fireplaces, some w/whirlpools. **Services:** Social director, babysitting. Highly attentive service. **Facilities:** 1 restaurant, sauna, whirlpool, beauty salon, washer/dryer. **Rates (CP):** Peak (Mar–Sept) $94–$149 S or D; $139–$225 ste. Extra person $10. Children under age 10 stay free. Lower rates off-season. Parking: Indoor/outdoor, $7/day. AE, DC, DISC, MC, V.

Ramada Inn Airport
1111 Northeast Loop 410, 78209; tel 210/828-9031 or toll free 800/426-2321. On I-410 access road. Located about 20 minutes from downtown, this recently remodeled hotel with an urban atmosphere offers spacious guestrooms. **Rooms:** 230 rms and stes. Executive level. CI 2pm/CO noon. Nonsmoking rms avail. Rooms are tastefully appointed with upscale cherry furniture and Southwestern colors.

Amenities: A/C, refrig, dataport. Some units w/minibars, some w/terraces. **Services:** Social director, babysitting. **Facilities:** 1 restaurant, 1 bar (w/entertainment). **Rates (CP):** Peak (Apr–Oct) $49–$59 S; $59–$62 D; $75–$110 ste. Extra person $5. Children under age 5 stay free. Lower rates off-season. Parking: Indoor/outdoor, free. AE, DISC, MC, V.

Red Lion
37 Northeast Loop 410, 78216; tel 210/366-2424 or toll free 800/535-1980. Located down the street from the airport and within the I-410 Loop business district, this Mediterranean-styled hotel features Moorish arches and stone fountains. An open, airy courtyard area with an attractive pool area is the hotel's focal point. **Rooms:** 175 rms and stes. Executive level. CI 2pm/CO 2pm. No smoking. Wood-beamed ceilings, colorful art in attractive guest rooms. **Amenities:** A/C, cable TV w/movies, dataport, voice mail, bathrobes. Some units w/minibars, some w/terraces. **Services:** Twice-daily maid svce, social director, children's program, babysitting. Free van service provided to local malls. **Facilities:** 1 restaurant, 1 bar (w/entertainment), sauna, steam rm, whirlpool, washer/dryer. Cascabel restaurant is known for innovative Southwestern cuisine. **Rates (CP):** Peak (Apr–Sept) $159–$169 S; $169–$175 D; $179–$199 ste. Extra person $10. Children under age 17 stay free. Lower rates off-season. MAP rates avail. Parking: Outdoor, free. AE, DC, DISC, MC, V.

UNRATED St Anthony Hotel
200 E Travis St, 78205 (Downtown); tel 210/227-4392 or toll free 800/338-1338. Not the premier address it was when it opened in 1909, this hotel across from Travis Park does manage to retain some of its old elegance—especially evident in the gleaming marble lobby. Popular with conventioneers. **Rooms:** 275 rms and stes. Executive level. CI 2pm/CO noon. Nonsmoking rms avail. **Amenities:** A/C, satel TV w/movies, dataport, bathrobes. Some units w/minibars, some w/terraces. **Services:** Twice-daily maid svce, social director. Excellent service. **Facilities:** 1 restaurant, 1 bar (w/entertainment), sauna, whirlpool, beauty salon, washer/dryer. Rooftop pool enclosed by chain-link fence. **Rates (CP):** Peak (Feb–Oct) $95–$145 S or D; $200–$300 ste. Extra person $10. Lower rates off-season. MAP rates avail. Parking: Indoor/outdoor, $3/day. AE, DISC, MC, V.

San Antonio Riverwalk Marriott
711 E River Walk, 78205; tel 210/224-4555 or toll free 800/228-9290; fax 210/224-2754. Commerce exit off I-37 E, left on Alamo, left on Machet. Located right on the river, this very urban hotel with large, luxurious rooms is positioned amidst downtown attractions, directly across from the Convention Center. **Rooms:** 350 rms and stes. Executive level. CI 2pm/CO noon. Nonsmoking rms avail. Rooms have separate areas for dressing, dining, and sleeping; suites also have an office area with desk. **Amenities:** A/C, cable TV

w/movies, refrig, voice mail, in-rm safe, bathrobes. Some units w/minibars, some w/terraces. All rooms have two TVs, some have wet bars and stocked refrigerators. **Services:** ✗ 📞 VP 🧺 🚲 🛎️ Twice-daily maid svce, social director, children's program, babysitting. VCRs available for rent. **Facilities:** 🅵 🖥️ ⛳ 375 💻 🔌 ♿ 1 restaurant, 1 bar (w/entertainment), whirlpool, beauty salon. River-level bar. **Rates (CP):** Peak (Apr–Sept) $164–$199 S; $184–$225 D; $225–$495 ste. Extra person $10. Min stay peak. Lower rates off-season. MAP rates avail. Parking: Indoor/outdoor, $3/day. AE, DC, DISC, MC, V.

🏨🏨🏨 Sheraton Gunther

205 E Houston St, 78205 (Downtown); tel 210/227-3241 or toll free 800/535-1980. This historic hotel, built in 1909, recently completed some much-needed renovations. Crystal chandeliers, marble halls, and potted palms are indicative of its posh style. The location is ideal for visiting tourists. **Rooms:** 200 rms and stes. Executive level. CI 3pm/CO noon. Nonsmoking rms avail. Rooms feature armoires. Hallways are somewhat dark and shadowy. **Amenities:** 📺 🍸 🔌 ⛄ A/C, satel TV w/movies, refrig, dataport, bathrobes. Some units w/minibars, some w/terraces, some w/fireplaces, some w/whirlpools. **Services:** ✗ 📞 VP 🧺 🚲 🛎️ Twice-daily maid svce, social director, masseur. **Facilities:** 🅵 ⛳ 🎾 300 💻 ♿ 1 restaurant, 1 bar (w/entertainment), sauna, whirlpool, beauty salon, washer/dryer. **Rates (CP):** Peak (Apr–Oct) $89–$135 S; $115–$135 D; $155–$700 ste. Extra person $10. Children under age 7 stay free. Lower rates off-season. MAP rates avail. Parking: Indoor/outdoor, $3/day. AE, DC, DISC, ER, MC, V.

🏨🏨 Travelodge Suites

4934 Northwest Loop 410, 78229; tel 210/680-3351 or toll free 800/267-3605. Comfortable suite accommodations located in a heavily trafficked area convenient to shopping and SeaWorld, less than 30 minutes from downtown. **Rooms:** 100 stes. Executive level. CI 2pm/CO noon. Nonsmoking rms avail. Rooms have older furniture and could use new carpeting. **Amenities:** 📺 🍸 🔌 A/C, cable TV w/movies, refrig. Some units w/minibars, some w/terraces. **Services:** 🚐 🛎️ Social director. Transportation available to downtown, Sea World, and Fiesta Texas theme park. Cookouts Wednesday evenings. **Facilities:** 🅵 25 ♿ **Rates (CP):** $59–$99 ste. Extra person $5. Children under age 5 stay free. Parking: Outdoor, free. AE, DC, DISC, MC, V.

MOTELS

🏨🏨 Alamo Travelodge

405 Broadway, 78205 (Downtown); tel 210/222-9401. Basic economy motel near the zoo and museums. Closeby entertainment and dining options are plentiful. **Rooms:** 45 rms and stes. CI 2pm/CO noon. Nonsmoking rms avail. **Amenities:** 📺 🍸 A/C, cable TV. Some units w/terraces.

Services: 🛎️ **Facilities:** 🅵 15 ♿ **Rates (CP):** $110 S or D. Extra person $5. Children under age 5 stay free. Parking: Outdoor, free. AE, DISC, MC, V.

🏨🏨🏨 Clarion Suites

13101 East Loop 1604 N, 78233; tel 210/655-9491. Conveniently located near Sea World and Fiesta Texas theme park, this all-suite property offers attractive accommodations with good housekeeping standards. **Rooms:** 102 stes. CI open/CO 2pm. Nonsmoking rms avail. Suites have stove, sink, dining table, and chairs. **Amenities:** 📺 🍸 🔌 ⛄ A/C, cable TV, refrig. Some units w/minibars, some w/terraces. All suites have ironing boards; some offer dataports. **Services:** 🧺 Babysitting. **Facilities:** 🅵 ♿ Whirlpool. **Rates (CP):** $79–$99 ste. Extra person $5. Children under age 3 stay free. Parking: Outdoor, free. AE, DC, DISC, MC, V.

🏨🏨🏨 Comfort Inn Airport

2635 Northeast Loop 410, 78217; tel 210/653-9110 or toll free 800/329-7466. Near airport. This economical lodging offers clean, comfortable accommodations to air travelers. A good value. **Rooms:** 60 rms. CI 2pm/CO noon. Nonsmoking rms avail. New furnishings. **Amenities:** 📺 A/C, cable TV, VCR. Some units w/terraces. **Services:** Babysitting. **Facilities:** 🅵 20 ♿ Whirlpool, washer/dryer. **Rates (CP):** Peak (Feb–Oct) $55–$60 S or D. Extra person $5. Lower rates off-season. Parking: Outdoor, free. AE, DC, DISC, MC, V.

🏨🏨 Days Inn Northeast

3443 N Pan Am Expwy, 78219; tel 210/225-4521 or toll free 800/329-7466. Off I-410. Located in a nice, quiet area central to the main highways. Fine for an overnight stay. **Rooms:** 60 rms and stes. CI 2pm/CO noon. Nonsmoking rms avail. **Amenities:** 📺 🍸 A/C, cable TV. Some units w/terraces. **Facilities:** 🅵 20 ♿ Sauna, whirlpool, washer/dryer. **Rates (CP):** $78–$85 S or D. Extra person $5. Parking: Outdoor, free. AE, DC, DISC, MC, V.

🏨🏨 La Quinta Airport East

333 NE Loop I-410, 78216; tel 210/828-0781 or toll free 800/531-5900. Standard chain motel with dependable rooms. **Rooms:** 40 rms and stes. CI 2pm/CO noon. Nonsmoking rms avail. **Amenities:** 📺 🍸 A/C, cable TV, voice mail. Some units w/terraces. **Services:** 🚐 **Facilities:** 🅵 15 ♿ **Rates (CP):** Peak (Feb–Sept) $69–$89 S or D; $85 ste. Extra person $10. Children under age 18 stay free. Lower rates off-season. Parking: Outdoor, free. AE, CB, DC, DISC, MC, V.

🏨 Motel 6 East

138 NW White Rd, 78219; tel 210/333-1850. Off I-35N. Economy motel with clean, no-frills rooms. **Rooms:** 75 rms. CI 2pm/CO noon. Nonsmoking rms avail. **Amenities:** 📺 A/C, cable TV. Some units w/terraces. **Services:** 🛎️ **Facilities:** 🅵 ♿ Whirlpool. **Rates (CP):** Peak (Feb–Sept) $49–$55 S; $56–$60 D. Extra person $5. Lower rates off-season. Parking: Outdoor, free. AE, DISC, MC, V.

▤▤▤ Quality Inn & Suites
3817 I-35 N, 78219; tel 210/224-3030. Newish motel with a
well-appointed lobby. **Rooms:** 100 rms and stes. CI 2pm/CO
noon. Nonsmoking rms avail. Nicely decorated Southwestern-styled rooms with large dresser and mirror. **Amenities:** ▥
A/C, cable TV. Some units w/terraces. Large-screen TV.
Facilities: ▥ ▤ ▤ Beautiful landscaping, colorful chairs in
pool area. **Rates (CP):** $49–$59 S; $59–$65 D; $69–$79 ste.
Extra person $6. Parking: Outdoor, free. AE, DISC, MC, V.

▤ Rodeway Inn Downtown
900 N Main Ave, 78204; tel 210/223-2951 or toll free 800/
228-2000. Exit 157A off I-35. Basic economy motel with
standard appointments. **Rooms:** 145 rms. CI 2pm/CO noon.
Nonsmoking rms avail. **Amenities:** ▥ ▤ A/C, cable TV. Some
units w/terraces. **Facilities:** ▥ ▤ **Rates (CP):** $39–$49 S;
$49–$59 D. Extra person $5. Parking: Outdoor, free. AE,
DISC, MC, V.

RESORT

▤▤▤▤ Hyatt Regency Hill Country Resort
9800 Hyatt Resort Dr, 78251; tel 210/647-1234 or toll free
800/233-1234. 39 acres. Resting in the beautiful countryside
about 25 minutes outside of downtown, this Hyatt Regency is
the ultimate in serenity and peace. A modest, four-story,
limestone building houses the guest accommodations and
provides a luxurious and comfortable stay. The standout
among the superb recreation facilities is 950-foot-long
Ramblin' River, a lushly landscaped water park. **Rooms:** 230
rms, stes. Executive level. CI 2pm/CO noon. No smoking.
Nonsmoking rms avail. Rooms are elegant, though not ornate, and have a bright, airy ambience. Many have french
doors opening onto a porch. **Amenities:** ▥ ▤ ▤ ▤ A/C, satel
TV w/movies, refrig, dataport, VCR, CD/tape player, voice
mail, in-rm safe, bathrobes. Some units w/minibars, some
w/terraces, some w/fireplaces, some w/whirlpools. **Services:**
✕ ▤ ▥ ▤ ▤ ▤ Twice-daily maid svce, social director,
masseur, children's program, babysitting. **Facilities:** ▥ ▸18
▤ ▤2 ▤ ▤ ▤ ▤ 1 restaurant, 1 bar, racquetball, spa,
sauna, steam rm, whirlpool, beauty salon. The championship
golf course is one of the most spectacular in the area. **Rates
(CP):** $240–$315 S or D; $425–$2,000 ste. Extra person $10.
Children under age 10 stay free. AP and MAP rates avail.
Parking: Outdoor, free. AE, DISC, MC, V.

RESTAURANTS ▥

Adelante
21 Brees, off Austin Hwy (Alamo Heights); tel 210/
882-7681. **Tex-Mex.** Very friendly service and extremely
fresh food make this a particularly fine choice for a simple
Mexican meal. The house specialty is the wide variety of
tamales. Both table and counter service are available. **FYI:**
Reservations not accepted. Children's menu. **Open:** Daily
9am–10pm. **Prices:** Main courses $5–$10. AE, DISC, MC, V.
▥ ▤ ▤

Alamo Cafe
9714 San Pedro; tel 210/341-4526. Near US 281. **Ameri-
can/Mexican.** An especially interesting stop for Old West
history buffs: The rustic decor and old-fashioned interior are
reminiscent of the original Alamo of lore. The predominantly
Mexican fare is very good. **FYI:** Reservations not accepted.
Children's menu. Beer and wine only. Additional location:
10060 I-10 W (tel 691-8827). **Open:** Daily 11am–11:30pm.
Prices: Main courses $5–$9. AE, DC, DISC, MC, V. ▥ ▤

Anaqua Grill
In the Plaza San Antonio, 555 S Alamo St (Downtown); tel
210/229-1000. **International.** This classy restaurant overlooks the hotel's beautifully landscaped courtyard. Diners can
choose from an intriguing variety of dishes from many
cuisines, including Spanish tapas, oak-smoked beef, Moroc-
can lamb, and scallops with black bean sauce. **FYI:** Reservations accepted. Children's menu. Jacket required. **Open:**
Mon–Sat 8am–10pm, Sun 11am–7pm. **Prices:** Main courses
$8–$16. AE, DC, DISC, MC, V. ▥ ▤ ▤

★ The Barn Door
8400 N New Braunfels (Central); tel 210/824-0116. Near
Loop I-410. **American/Steak.** The old-fashioned decor of
this down-home steak house—in operation for over 40
years—includes checkered tablecloths and wooden chairs.
Huge T-bones and various sizes of fillets, prepared either
charcoal or mesquite grilled, are the attraction. **FYI:** Reservations not accepted. Children's menu. Beer and wine only.
Additional locations: 8327 Marbach Rd (tel 673-0090); 1455
SW Military Dr (tel 977-1050). **Open:** Lunch Mon–Sat
11am–2pm; dinner Mon–Thurs 5–10pm, Fri–Sat 5–
10:30pm. **Prices:** Main courses $6–$11. AE, DISC, MC, V.
▥ ▤

The Bayou's
River Walk off N Presa (Downtown); tel 210/223-6403.
Cajun/Seafood. This simple, lively riverside restaurant,
where diners can sit inside or outdoors on the patio, offers an
oyster bar plus Cajun preparations of red snapper, shrimp,
crab claws, and other seafood. **FYI:** Reservations accepted.
Dress code. Beer and wine only. **Open:** Sun–Thurs 11:30am–
11pm, Fri–Sat 11:30am–midnight. **Prices:** Main courses $8–
$13. AE, MC, V. ▥ ▤

Biga and Locust St Bakery
206 E Locust St; tel 210/225-0722. Off McCullough Ave.
New American. Converted from the downstairs of a 100-
year-old San Antonio mansion, this romantic yet not overly
formal restaurant offers a special night out. The regularly
changing New American menu offers many spicy and some
exotic choices, with possibilities like seared foie gras on a
Stilton tart and oak-roasted antelope or pheasant. Wonderful
peasant breads come from the attached bakery. Extensive
wine and beer selection. **FYI:** Reservations not accepted.
Children's menu. Beer and wine only. **Open:** Lunch Tues–Fri
11am–2pm; dinner Mon–Thurs 6–10:30pm, Fri–Sat 5:30–
11pm. **Prices:** Main courses $2–$8. MC, V. ▥ ▤

Boudro's

421 E Commerce St (Downtown); tel 210/224-8484. Between Hyatt and Mariott. **New American.** Set in a turn-of-the-century limestone building, this River Walk restaurant has earned its fine reputation with expertly prepared dishes made from fresh local ingredients. Originally a New Orleans–style restaurant, Boudro's still retains Cajun specialties like the blackened prime rib, blackened redfish, and coconut-battered shrimp. But the majority of the menu is devoted to nouvelle options like an herb-smoked salmon taco appetizer and skewered shrimp and scallops with mango sauce and tomatillo cream. **FYI:** Reservations accepted. Blues. Children's menu. Dress code. Beer and wine only. **Open:** Daily 10:30am–11:30pm. **Prices:** Main courses $8–$16. AE, DC, DISC, MC, V. &

★ Cappy's

5011 Broadway (Downtown); tel 210/828-9669. Off loop 410 W. **American.** Cappy Lawton owns several restaurants in the San Antonio area; this is his oldest one. A casual place equally suitable for families or business lunches, it offers American cuisine with a southwestern flair. Specialties include Santa Fe chicken and Cajun blackened redfish. **FYI:** Reservations accepted. Children's menu. Jacket required. **Open:** Daily 11am–10pm. **Prices:** Main courses $7–$11. AE, DISC, MC, V. 📷 💟 &

Casa Rio

430 E Commerce St on River Walk (Downtown); tel 210/225-6718. **Mexican.** Upscale restaurant serving traditional Mexican fare. The outdoor tables along the River Walk offer a romantic setting for an evening meal. **FYI:** Reservations accepted. Children's menu. Dress code. Beer and wine only. **Open:** Daily 11am–11pm. **Prices:** Main courses $6–$11. AE, DC, DISC, MC, V. 🏔 &

Chez Ardid

1919 San Pedro Ave; tel 210/732-3203. Near downtown. **French.** This beautifully restored 1902 home is the setting for expertly prepared classical French fare. Of all the appealing dining rooms, the Versailles Room is the one that retains the most original detail—parquet floors, carved oak mantel, tin ceiling. The chef uses the freshest regional ingredients in his dishes, which include fillet of Texas lamb in puff pastry, terrine of Muscovy duck, and many fish and shellfish selections. Be sure to ask about the French desserts, some of which are not on the menu. **FYI:** Reservations accepted. Dress code. **Open:** Mon–Sat 6–10pm. **Prices:** Main courses $8–$16. AE, CB, DC, DISC, MC, V. 💟 💟 &

Chili's Grill & Bar

4983 NW Loop 410 (Mid-City); tel 210/522-1210. **Regional American/Burgers.** Mexican tiles and road signs from all over the country add a friendly note to the room. Eclectic offerings include burgers (turkey or beef), large salads, and many sandwiches. Beef and chicken fajitas are the featured items. **FYI:** Reservations not accepted. Additional location: 9938 San Pedro (tel 522-1210). **Open:** Daily 11:30am–11:30pm. **Prices:** Main courses $7–$11. AE, MC, V. &

Chinatown Cafe

Broadway and Nacogdoches; tel 210/822-3522. Off Loop 410. **Chinese.** A family-owned Chinese restaurant with a traditional menu and a buffet. A specialty is shrimp fried rice. **FYI:** Reservations not accepted. Beer and wine only. No smoking. **Open:** Daily 11:30am–10pm. **Prices:** Main courses $5–$9. AE, DISC, MC, V. 📷 💟 &

College St Grill

203 College; tel 210/227-1830. Near downtown. **Tex-Mex.** Casual, reliable Tex-Mex eatery displaying basic cafe-style decor with some hints of Mexico. **FYI:** Reservations not accepted. Children's menu. Beer and wine only. **Open:** Daily 9am–10:30pm. **Prices:** Main courses $5–$8. AE, DISC, MC, V. 📷 &

Crumpet's

In Cambridge Place, 5800 Broadway (Alamo Heights); tel 210/821-5454. **Eclectic.** Pleasant atmosphere and decor. Eclectic cuisine offers veal and fresh seafood, plus many European pastries. **FYI:** Reservations accepted. Children's menu. Dress code. Beer and wine only. No smoking. **Open:** Daily 11am–10pm. **Prices:** Main courses $6–$11. AE, DISC, MC, V. 🌣 💟 &

★ Earl Abel's

4200 Broadway (Downtown); tel 210/822-3358. **American.** Earl Abel's granddaughter now runs this well-liked, dependable eatery, which first opened in 1940. The place for many for late-night meals and snacks, offering fried chicken, steak, salads, mashed potatoes, biscuits and gravy, country-style vegetables, and delicious pies. **FYI:** Reservations accepted. Children's menu. Dress code. Beer and wine only. **Open:** Daily 9am–10pm. **Prices:** Main courses $7–$11. AE, DC, DISC, MC, V. 📷 💟 &

Edelweiss

4400 Rittiman Rd; tel 210/829-5552. Near I-35. **German.** One of the few German restaurants still left in San Antonio. The limited menu features authentic, carefully prepared dishes like jagerschnitzel and German-style potatoes. Don't miss the strudel. **FYI:** Reservations not accepted. Beer and wine only. No smoking. **Open:** Lunch Wed–Sat 11am–3pm; dinner Wed–Sat 4–9pm. **Prices:** Main courses $6–$10. No CC. 📷 &

El Mirador

722 St Marys St (Downtown); tel 210/225-9444. **Mexican.** Quality Mexican in an informal setting. Expect a wait, especially at lunch, for a table on the outdoor patio. Breakfast is the time for huge plates of scrambled eggs with a spicy dried beef called machacado, while the enchilada platters are a great lunch deal. Garlicky shrimp diablo is a fine dinner choice. The Xochitl and Azteca, two tasty broth soups made with chicken and various vegetables, have a large following.

FYI: Reservations accepted. Mariachi. Children's menu. **Open:** Mon–Sat 11:30am–11:30pm, Sun 11:30am–9pm. **Prices:** Main courses $5–$11. AE, DISC, V. ♥ ⛴ ♿

★ E-Z's Restaurant

5720 Bandera Rd; tel 210/681-2222. Off Loop 410. **Burgers.** The 1950s-style decor has a black-and-white checkered tile floor and lots of shiny chrome and bright plastic. The uncomplicated food is consistently good and features items like grilled burgers, caesar salads, and broiled chicken, but pizza is the specialty. **FYI:** Reservations not accepted. No liquor license. Additional location: 734 W Bitters (tel 490-6666). **Open:** Daily 11:30am–10pm. **Prices:** Main courses $3–$6. AE, MC, V. ♿

♥ The Grey Moss Inn

Scenic Loop Rd, between TX 16 and I-10; tel 210/695-8301. **American/Steak.** Located in a castle that was moved to Texas from England in the 1920s, this unique place makes for a romantic dinner. Filet mignon is the house specialty. **FYI:** Reservations recommended. Dress code. **Open:** Daily 11:30am–10:30pm. **Prices:** Main courses $12–$20. AE, DC, DISC, MC, V. ♥ VP ♿

Hunan River Garden

506 River Walk (Downtown); tel 210/222-0808. Along the San Antonio River. **Chinese.** A very elegant restaurant right on the River Walk. Authentic Chinese art and design create an attractive space. Diners can sit by the large windows to watch the goings-on along the River Walk or encamp near the aquatic gardens and waterfall. The house specialty is the Mandarin steak strips. **FYI:** Reservations accepted. Children's menu. Dress code. Beer and wine only. **Open:** Daily 11am–10pm. **Prices:** Main courses $7–$13. AE, DC, DISC, MC, V. 🏔 ▼ ♿

La Calesa

2103 Hildebrand St (Downtown); tel 210/822-4475. Near Broadway. **Mexican.** La Calesa offers fun, fun, and more fun in its festive dining area. Authentic Mexican dishes include rajas poblanos (chile strips in cheese and cream), and pollo escabeche (chicken in a cumin-flavored sauce). This is the real thing. **FYI:** Reservations not accepted. Children's menu. Beer and wine only. **Open:** Daily 11am–11pm. **Prices:** Main courses $5–$10. AE, DISC, MC, V. ♥ ♿

La Fogata

2427 Vance Jackson Rd (Northwest); tel 210/340-1337. Off Loop 410. **Mexican.** This sprawling restaurant is not the place for a quick dinner; in fact, it's an entire evening, albeit a highly entertaining one. Live birds sing as busy waiters rush around the crowded tables. Cuisine includes familiar favorites plus authentic dishes like frijoles barrachos (a bowlful of flavorful Mexican beans) and chile poblano al carbon (pepper stuffed with chicken and cheese and charcoal flamed). Dishes can be small, so be prepared to order more than usual. **FYI:** Reservations not accepted. Mariachi. Children's menu. Beer and wine only. Additional location: 932 North Star Mall (tel

342-3603). **Open:** Mon–Sat 11am–midnight, Sun noon–10pm. **Prices:** Main courses $6–$13. AE, DISC, MC, V. ♥ ⛴ ♿

L'Etoile

6106 Broadway at Albany (Alamo Heights); tel 210/826-4551. **French.** Tucked away in a small shopping complex, this upscale yet casual French bistro may surprise you with its moderate prices. Diners can be seated in the Mediterranean-style enclosed patio or the intimate upstairs dining room with skylight. The focus of the daily menu is seafood, particularly lobster (plucked fresh from the lobster tank) prepared a variety of ways—flamed with cognac, baked, poached, etc. A good wine list list offers several affordable selections. **FYI:** Reservations accepted. Blues. Children's menu. Jacket required. **Open:** Daily 11am–10pm. **Prices:** Main courses $10–$16. AE, DC, DISC, MC, V. ♥ VP ♿

★ Liberty Bar

328 E Josephine (Downtown); tel 210/227-1187. Near US 281 and Broadway. **New American.** This 1876 building close to St Mary's Strip slants to the left just like the Leaning Tower of Pisa. The menu changes daily, but always popular are the mixed vegetable salad and the many homemade dessert cobblers. A house specialty is grilled muenster cheese sandwich served on the Bar's fresh-baked bread. **FYI:** Reservations not accepted. **Open:** Daily 9am–11:30pm. **Prices:** Main courses $4–$11. AE, DISC, MC, V. ■ ♿

Little Rhein Steak House

231 S Alamo Plaza (Downtown); tel 210/225-2111. **American.** With its Old West ambience and close proximity to the Alamo, this elegant steakhouse will fascinate history buffs. The 1847 building—the oldest two-story structure in the city—abuts the river. Inside the main dining rooms are numerous antiques and replicas, and a miniature train runs its route overhead. Beef is the specialty, and house favorites are the T-bone and any of the specially prepared porterhouse steaks. Wine selections are suggested for each entree. **FYI:** Reservations accepted. Children's menu. Dress code. Beer and wine only. **Open:** Daily 11:30am–10:30pm. **Prices:** Main courses $19–$30. AE, DC, DISC, MC, V. ■ 👪 ♿

Luna Notte

6402 N New Braunfels St (Downtown); tel 210/822-4242. Near I-35 and Fort Sam Houston. **International.** One of the places to be seen in San Antonio. The fashionable art deco/modern decor is done in stark grays and black, with steel rafters and doors and black tables. Local art adorns the walls. A popular pasta dish, cappelini Napoletana, has large Roman tomatoes, extra virgin olive oil, basil, and garlic served over angel hair pasta with chicken or shrimp. Other dishes include duck salad with arugula, spinach, roasted pears, pine nuts, and gorgonzola, and pork tenderloin with sun-dried cherries. The martini menu lists 15 different versions of the cocktail; the specialty drink, bellini, is frozen and delicious. **FYI:**

Reservations not accepted. Children's menu. Beer and wine only. **Open:** Daily 11am–10pm. **Prices:** Main courses $8–$16. AE, DISC, MC, V. ▦ ♿

Nona's Homemade Pasta

2809 N St Mary's (Downtown); tel 210/736-9896. **Italian.** Located in a small wooden building is this modest, red-checked-tablecloth Italian with a special twist: belly dancing. The owner, an aficionada of the art, performs on weekends. Homemade pasta includes a special three-meat lasagna; pizza, too. **FYI:** Reservations accepted. Jazz/reggae/singer. Beer and wine only. **Open:** Daily 11am–10pm. **Prices:** Main courses $6–$12. AE, DISC, MC, V. ▦ ♿

★ Paesano's Italian Restaurant

1715 McCullough Ave (Downtown); tel 210/226-9541. Near historic Alamo. **Italian.** This traditional Italian, famous for its shrimp Paesano and its veal dishes, always seems to pack them in. Be sure to check the board at the entrance for the freshest and most flavorful dishes. Seafood is flown in fresh daily. Excellent, inexpensive lunch specials available Tues–Fri. **FYI:** Reservations accepted. Children's menu. Dress code. **Open:** Daily 11am–11pm. **Prices:** Main courses $7–$11. AE, DC, DISC, MC, V. ▨ ♿

★ Polo's

In the Fairmount Hotel, 401 S Alamo (River area); tel 210/224-8800. **International.** A lovely setting for a special dinner, Polo's has produced some of the most talented chefs in the area in past years. The open wood-burning pizza oven turns out imaginative pizzas and delicious sourdough rolls. Entrees, many of which reveal Mexican/Southwestern influences, might include salmon with dill sauce or smoked shrimp with Asiago cheese and chile sauce. **FYI:** Reservations accepted. Children's menu. Dress code. **Open:** Daily 10am–10pm. **Prices:** Main courses $6–$10. AE, DC, MC, V. ▆ ♿

Rio Rio Cantina

421 E Commerce St; tel 210/226-8462. On River Walk. **Mexican.** Joe Cosniac's Paesano's was so successful he opened a second restaurant. This one is an upscale Mexican cantina serving good food in large portions. In nice weather, the outdoor tables on the River Walk are a great place to pass a few hours. Chimichangas are a specialty. **FYI:** Reservations accepted. Karaoke. Dress code. **Open:** Sun–Thurs 11am–10pm, Fri–Sat 11am–11:30pm. **Prices:** Main courses $9–$13. AE, DISC, MC, V. ▰ ♿

Rosario's

1014 S Alamo (Downtown); tel 210/223-1806. Near Alamo Plaza. **Mexican/Tex-Mex.** Stylish and hip, this dimly lit hot spot really comes alive on weekend nights when a live tropical band performs. Authentic fare includes starters like hearty black bean soup and delicious poblano pepper strips with melted cheese. Chicken and corn enchiladas are topped with white cheese, sour cream, and tomatillo sauce. The fiesta platter offers a tasty feast. Also fine are the shrimp in spicy hot garlic sauce. **FYI:** Reservations accepted. Children's

menu. Beer and wine only. **Open:** Breakfast daily 8–11am; lunch daily 11am–2pm; dinner daily 2:30–10pm. **Prices:** Main courses $4–$9. AE, MC, V. ▦ ♿

★ Tomatillo's y Cantina

3210 Broadway (Downtown); tel 210/824-3005. **Mexican.** The rustic Mexican decor includes large wooden tables providing plenty of room to line up glasses of the renowned fruity margaritas (choose from four varieties). Beef fajitas and other simple fare. **FYI:** Reservations not accepted. Children's menu. **Open:** Daily 11am–11pm. **Prices:** Main courses $6–$9. AE, DISC, MC, V. ♿

Vienna Weinstrube

1006 Holbrook; tel 210/650-0097. **German.** Folksy Bavarian-themed eatery serving good bratwurst and German ale. Fun and festive atmosphere. **FYI:** Reservations accepted. Folk. Dress code. Beer and wine only. No smoking. **Open:** Lunch Mon–Sat 11am–3:30pm; dinner Mon–Sat 4–10pm. **Prices:** Main courses $7–$10. No CC. ▦ ▨ ♿

★ Zuni Grill

511 River Walk; tel 210/227-0864. **Eclectic.** The cutting-edge contemporary decor of this local favorite, which displays an artful use of color and interesting drawings and paintings on textured walls, goes well with the chic Southwestern menu. Enjoy the unique prickly pear margarita before digging into pecan-crusted chicken salad on mixed greens or the more substantial peppered pork chops with whipped sweet potatoes. The low-cal menu is very good, offering favorites such as cucumber pitas. **FYI:** Reservations accepted. Dress code. No smoking. **Open:** Mon–Sun 11:30am–10:30pm. **Prices:** Main courses $9–$17. AE, DC, DISC, MC, V. ▨ ♿

ATTRACTIONS ▥

MISSIONS

The Alamo

300 Alamo Plaza; tel 210/225-1391. Sitting in the heart of downtown San Antonio, the Alamo is the most visited site in Texas, the silhouette of its graceful mission church an instantly recognizable symbol of the state. It was here that 188 Texas volunteers defied Gen Santa Anna (with his much larger Mexican army), for 13 days in March 1836. Although all the men were killed—among them pioneers Davy Crockett and Jim Bowie—their death became a rallying cry for Sam Houston, who defeated the Mexican army at the Battle of San Jacinto one month later and secured Texas's independence. The Alamo was originally founded on a nearby site in 1718 as the Mission San Antonio de Valero. The complex was secularized by the end of the 18th century and leased out to a Spanish cavalry unit; by the time the famous battle took place, it had been abandoned.

Little remains of the original mission today; only the Long Barrack (formerly the convento, or living quarters for the missionaries) and the mission church are still here. The former houses a museum detailing the history of Texas in general and the battle in particular; the latter includes artifacts of the Alamo fighters, along with an information desk and small gift shop. A larger museum and gift shop are at the back of the complex; there's also a peaceful garden and an excellent research library on the grounds. **Open:** Mon–Sat 9am–5:30pm, Sun 10am–5:30pm. **Free**

San Antonio Missions National Historical Park
2202 Roosevelt Ave; tel 210/229-5701. The Alamo was the first of five missions established by the Franciscans along the San Antonio River to Christianize the native population. The four missions that now fall under the aegis of the National Parks Department are still active parishes, run in cooperation with the Archdiocese of San Antonio.

The missions were complex communities, not merely churches, and the Parks Department has assigned each of the four an interpretive theme to educate visitors about the roles they played in early San Antonio society. Signs direct visitors from the Alamo to the 5½-mile mission trail that begins at Mission Concepción and winds its way south through the city streets at Mission Espada. **Free**

Mission San José
6539 San José Dr; tel 210/229-4770. Established in 1720, this was the largest, best-known, and most beautiful of the Texas missions. Designed to give visitors a complete picture of life in a mission community—right down to the granary, mill, and Indian pueblo. Popular mariachi masses are held here every Sunday at noon (guests should come early to get a seat), and pageants and plays are staged at an outdoor arena. **Open:** Daily 8am–5pm; during daylight saving time, 9am–6pm. **Free**

Mission Concepción
807 Mission Rd; tel 210/229-5732. Built in 1731, this is the oldest unrestored Texas mission, and it looks much as it did 200 years ago. Although some may think of religious sites as somber and austere, the traces of color on the facade and restored wall paintings inside show how cheerful this one was in its day. **Open:** Daily 8am–4:30pm. **Free**

Mission San Juan Capistrano
9102 Graf; tel 210/229-5734. Moved from an earlier site in East Texas to its present location in 1731, this mission does not have the grandeur of the missions to the north—the larger church intended for it was never completed—but the original simple chapel and the wilder setting give it a peaceful, spiritual aura. A short ⅓-mile interpretive trail, with a number of overlook platforms, winds through the woods to the banks of the old river channel. **Open:** Daily 8am–5pm; during daylight saving time, 9am–6pm. **Free**

Mission San Francisco de la Espada
10040 Espada Rd; tel 210/627-2021. The southernmost mission in the San Antonio chain, this also has an ancient, isolated feel, although the beautifully-kept church shows just how vital it still is to the local community. Of special interest is the Espada Aqueduct, part of the mission's original acequia

(irrigation ditch) system, about one mile to the north of the mission; dating from 1740, it's one of the oldest Spanish aqueducts in the United States. **Open:** Daily 8am–5pm; during daylight saving time, 9am–6pm. **Free**

HISTORICAL ATTRACTIONS

San Fernando Cathedral
115 Main Plaza; tel 210/227-1297. Construction of a church on this site, overlooking what was once the town's central plaza, was begun in 1738 by San Antonio's original Canary Island settlers and completed in 1749. Part of the early structure of this historic cathedral sanctuary and parish church was incorporated into the magnificent Gothic Revival–style cathedral built in 1868. General Santa Anna raised the flag of "no quarter" from the cathedral's roof during the siege of the Alamo in 1836. Of special interest are the baptismal font, believed to be a gift of Charles III, a pipe organ from 1884, and the burial grounds of the heroes of the Alamo. Services still held here. **Open:** Daily 6am–6pm. **Free**

Spanish Governor's Palace
105 Plaza De Armas; tel 210/224-0601. The Commandancia, now known as the Spanish Governor's Palace, was originally intended to house the commander of the Presidio de San Antonio de Bejar, which was built in the early 18th century to protect the Mission San Antonio de Valero. In 1722, when Villa de San Fernando (San Antonio) was made the capital of the Spanish Province of Texas, the residence became the seat of Texas government. In later years, after 1822, the building was used for some unexpected purposes that belied its prestigious origins: it served as a second-hand clothing store, a tailor's shop, a barroom, a restaurant, and a schoolhouse. In 1931 the palace was restored and reopened, and can now be toured. The adobe-walled building is typical of colonial Spain with its carved doors, low-beamed ceilings, grape arbor, and mosaic-tiled patio. Other period details and furnishings heighten the historical ambience of the structure. **Open:** Mon–Sat 9am–5pm, Sun 10am–5pm. **$**

La Villita
418 Villita St (Downtown); tel 210/207-8610. La Villita, Spanish for "little town," is the original settlement of Old San Antonio. Located on the east bank of the San Antonio River, it was developed in the mid- to late-19th century as a settlement adjacent to Mission San Antonio de Valero (The Alamo). Today, this single square block in the heart of the city's downtown is an active arts and crafts community that also boasts shops and restaurants. It is set against a backdrop of landscaped grounds and historic buildings which reflect the influences of the Spanish, Mexican, German, French, American, and native Texan peoples who settled here. Architectural styles range from simple adobe structures to early Victorian and natural cut limestone buildings. Many annual events celebrate the past here, including Fiesta, which com-

memorates Texas's independence from Mexico. The village is a National Registered Historic District. Self-guided walking tours. **Open:** Daily 7am–10pm. **Free**

Yturri-Edmunds Historic Site

257 Yellowstone at Mission Trail; tel 210/534-8237. Exhibits on this site span more than 150 years of the city's architecture. Acquired in 1824 by Spanish native Manuel Yturri-Castillo, this property formerly belonged to Mission Concepción and included a gristmill that may have been built as early as 1720, and also one of the mission's irrigation ditches. A six-room adobe house, one of the few that still exists in San Antonio, was constructed between 1840 and 1860. Also here are an 1881 carriage house from the King William Historic District and an 1855 block-and-rubble house that was originally located downtown. Tours available. **$**

José Antonio Navarro State Historical Park

228 S Laredo St; tel 210/226-4801. A key player in the transition of Texas from Spanish territory to American statehood, José Antonio Navarro was a Mexican mayor of San Antonio in 1821, a signer of the 1836 declaration of Texas's independence, and the only native Texan to take part in the convention that ratified the annexation of Texas to the United States in 1845. His former living quarters, built around 1850, are an interesting amalgam of the architectural fashions of his time: a restored office, house, and separate kitchen, constructed of adobe and limestone, blend elements from Mexican, French, German, and pioneer styles. Guided tours and demonstrations available. **Open:** Wed–Sun 10am–4pm. **$**

Steves Homestead

509 King William St (King William Historic District); tel 210/225-5924. Located in the King William Historic District on the banks of the San Antonio River, this Victoria-era mansion was built in 1876 by lumber magnate Edward Steves. Constructed of ashlar limestone with a Second Empire–style mansard roof and iron cresting, the house features elaborate wood trim and decorative floral and stenciled artwork on walls and ceilings, as well as original furnishings. The natural and formal landscape includes laurel gardens, cypress, pecan, magnolia, palm, black walnut, and anaqua trees. Antique carriges are on display in the carriage house, while the gardener's quarters now serve as the visitors center. **Open:** Daily 10am–4:15pm. **$**

MUSEUMS

San Antonio Museum of Art

200 W Jones Ave; tel 210/829-7262. A number of the castle-like buildings of the 1904 Lone Star Brewery were gutted, connected, and transformed into a visually exciting exhibition space in 1981. The spare, and in some sections, skylit interior of the structures contrasts strikingly with the more intricately detailed brick exterior; the multiwindowed cross-walk between the two buildings affords fine views of down-

town. The Latin American folk art collection is extensive, and the other collection boasts pieces ranging from early Egyptian, Greek, and Asian to 19th- and 20th-century American. Works by Hans Hofmann, William Merritt Chase, and Ernest Lawson, among others; also early Texas furniture on display. **Open:** Mon 10am–5pm, Tues 10am–9pm, Wed–Sat 10am–5pm, Sun noon–5pm. **$$**

The Institute of Texan Cultures

801 Bowie St; tel 210/558-2300. Located at the University of Texas at San Antonio. Twenty-eight different cultures are represented in a variety of exhibits depicting where they came from and what they did, their food and clothing, their music and festivals. Multimedia show four times daily in the Dome Theater. Volunteer docents frequently put on puppet shows. **Open:** Tues–Sun 9am–5pm. **Free**

Mexican Cultural Institute

600 HemisFair Park; tel 210/227-0123. Sponsored by the Mexican Ministry of Foreign Affairs, the institute hosts changing displays of art and artifacts relating to Mexican history and culture, from pre-Colombian to contemporary. Latin American film series, conferences, performances, contests, and workshops—on language, literature, and folklore as well as art—are also held here. **Open:** Tues–Sun 9:30am–5:30pm, Sat–Sun 11am–5pm. **Free**

Hertzberg Circus Collection and Museum

210 Market St; tel 210/207-7810. Pink elephants posted on the sides of the front steps are an apt symbol of the spirit of this museum. Displays chosen from the massive collection of "circusana" that Harry Hertzberg bequeathed to the San Antonio Public Library (of which this is a branch) include Tom Thumb's carriage, a flea circus, photographs of Buffalo Bill's Wild West show, and pictures of sideshow performers. **Open:** Mon–Sat 10am–5pm. **$**

Lone Star Buckhorn Museums

600 Lone Star Blvd; tel 210/270-9469. Huge stuffed animals, mounted fish, and Lone Star memorabilia located on the grounds of an active brewery. In addition to the Hall of Horns (antlers and horns from the four corners of the world), Hall of Feathers (birds from around the world), Hall of Fins (fish from around the world), and the Texas History Wax Museum, there's an office that was once occupied by the short-story writer O Henry, as well as an international collection of hundreds of beer bottles, including, of course, Lone Star Beer bottles from the brand's beginning to the present day. Lake and picnic grounds on the premises. Free beer or soft drink included in the price of admission. **Open:** Daily 9:30am–5pm. **$$**

OTHER ATTRACTIONS

Tower of the Americas

HemisFair Park; tel 210/207-8615. Completed in 1968, this served as the theme structure of the HemisFair, Texas's world's fair held that year. Located in the 15-acre HemisFair Park, the tower rises 750 feet to the top of its antenna; from the observation level of 579 feet, the tower offers extraordinary views of San Antonio which can be enjoyed inside or outside (the observation deck is encircled by an outdoor walkway). A revolving restaurant located at the observation level. Eight panels inside the observation area feature photographs highlighting major sites visible from the tower. The observation level and rest rooms are fully accessible to the handicapped. **Open:** Daily 8am–11pm. **$**

Natural Bridge Wildlife Ranch
26515 Natural Bridge Caverns Rd; tel 210/438-7400. Over 200 acres of scenic Texas Hill Country ranchland is the site for this drive-through safari (on 3½ miles of paved road). Against a landscape marked by hills and live oak, elm, Spanish oak, and cedar trees is an eclectic array of animals from around the world, including many endangered species, such as the scimitar-horned oryx from northern Africa, the addax antelope, the dama gazelle, and the aoudad sheep, as well as elk, blackbuk antelope, fallow deer, llamas, cougars, gemsbok oryx, bison, zebras, ostrich, and giraffes. Visitors are provided with animal feed and are encouraged to feed the exotic animals through the windows of their vehicles. There is also a special walking area that allows access to petting enclosures featuring species such as reticulated giraffes, bennett wallabies, white-tailed deer, and a variety of unusual birds. The visitors center includes a gift shop and a snack bar. **Open:** Peak (June–Aug) daily 9am–6:30pm. Reduced hours off-season. **$$$**

Japanese Tea Garden
3800 N St Mary's St; tel 210/734-0816. Beautiful flower arrangements, miniature bridges, and lotus ponds make this one of the more popular sections of Brackenridge Park. **Open:** Daily 8am–sunset. **Free**

San Antonio Zoo
3903 N St Mary's; tel 210/734-7183. Located in Brackenridge Park, this zoo hosts one of North America's largest animal collections. It houses over 3,000 animals of 700 species, and is renowned for captive breeding—it is one of the only zoos that exhibit the endangered whooping crane, and it was one of the first zoos to hatch and rear flamingos; it also produced the first white rhino to be born in the United States and the first penguin in Texas. Exhibit areas reproduce habitats from around the world—the Amazon, Africa's Rift Valley Track, and the Australian Walkabout—as well as Texas. Impressive botanical collection of both native and exotic species. The children's zoo features a Tropical Tour (which includes a boat ride that visits miniature exhibits of animals from many countries), as well as a playground, desert building, arena for lectures, Everglades displays with alligators and water birds, and education center with a rain forest exhibit. Fresh- and saltwater aquariums; sea lion demonstrations are another highlight. **Open:** Daily 9:30am–sunset. **$$$**

Blue Star Arts Complex
1400 S Alamo; tel 210/227-6960. Located at the edge of the King William neighborhood, this huge former warehouse hosts a collection of working studios and galleries, along with a performance space for the Jump-Start theater company; the 11,000-square-foot Contemporary Art Museum is its anchor. The style of work varies from gallery to gallery—visitors can see everything from Latin American folk art to feminist photography. **Open:** Wed–Sun noon–6pm. **Free**

Majestic Theatre
230 E Houston St; tel 210/226-3333. Everyone from Jack Benny to Mae West played this opulent vaudeville and film palace, designed in baroque Moorish and Spanish Revival style by John Eberson in 1929 and impressively restored in 1989. One of the last "atmospheric" theaters to be built—the stock market crashed four months after it opened and no one could afford such elaborate showplaces again—it's also one of few such theaters remaining in the country, and was recently designated a National Historic Landmark. It is now used as a performing arts space. One of its outstanding features is the overhead dome, with its simulated stars and clouds. The theater is not generally open to the public during the day, but visitors may be able to join a group guided tour. **$$$$**

Fiesta Texas
17000 I-10 W; tel 210/697-5050. Since South Texas is a bit too large to explore in a single afternoon, this $100 million theme park is a good way to get a taste of the attractions of the state. A vast variety of food booths share the 200-acre amusement arena with rides, games, and crafts demonstrations galore. Dramatic 100-foot cliffs surround the park, which is set in an abandoned limestone quarry on the north end of town.

The attractions are organized around four themes: Mexican fiesta, German village, country and western, and vintage rock and roll (Buddy Holly was from Texas). There's also a water park (bring a bathing suit) and the newest feature, a simulated seaside boardwalk with a Ferris wheel, roller-skating rink, and nine-hole miniature-golf course. Park highlights include the **Rattler,** one of the highest and fastest wooden roller coasters in the world; the **Gully Washer,** a river rapids ride; and, for the less daring, a variety of professionally presented performances that range from mariachis to oompah bands. Laser-light show each evening at closing. **Open:** Peak (Mem Day–Labor Day) Sun–Thurs 10am–9pm, Fri–Sat 10am–10pm. Reduced hours off-season. Closed Dec–Feb. **$$$$**

Spoetzl Brewery
603 E Brewery St, Shiner; tel 512/594-3383. Founded in 1909 by Bavarian-born Kosmos Spoetzl. One of the few remaining breweries whose product is made, bought, and consumed entirely in Texas. Tour of the brewery and complimentary tasting. Gift shop/museum. **Open:** Mon–Fri 11am and 1:30pm. **Free**

Alamodome

100 Montana St; tel 210/207-3652. This state-of-the-art arena has the world's largest retractable seating system, and its roof encompasses nine acres. Home of the professional basketball team, the Spurs, it also holds major concerts and events; Paul McCartney, the Eagles, and Elton John have all performed at this 70,000-plus-capacity area. Tours, lasting 45 minutes, are available. **Open:** Tues–Sat 10am, 1pm, 3pm. **$$$$**

San Marcos

The pristine, spring-fed waters of the San Marcos River still draw visitors, much as they did the early Anglo settlers in 1846. San Marcos has capitalized on this by creating river walks and parks and recreational attractions along the river banks. The city is also home to Southwest Texas State University. **Information:** Convention & Visitors Bureau, 202 CM Allen Pkwy, PO Box 2310, San Marcos, 78666 (tel 512/396-2495 or toll free 800/782-7653 ext 177).

MOTEL 🗂

≣≣ Days Inn San Marcos

1005 I-35 N, 78666; tel 512/353-5050 or toll free 800/325-2525. Off I-35 access road. Quite new motel in a great location right off the interstate and near popular attractions. **Rooms:** 150 rms. CI 2pm/CO noon. Nonsmoking rms avail. Functional rooms have bright, colorful decor; some have desk. **Amenities:** 🛁 A/C, cable TV w/movies. Some units w/terraces. **Facilities:** 🛗 ⅙ Whirlpool. **Rates (CP):** $42–$49 S; $49–$52 D. Extra person $5. Min stay peak. Parking: Outdoor, free. AE, DISC, MC, V.

INN

≣≣≣ Aquarena Springs Inn

1 Aquarena Springs Dr, 78666; tel 512/245-7595. A popular tourist attraction, this antique-filled historic hotel occupies a beautiful setting near the springs and water park. The landscaping is magnificent. **Rooms:** 24 rms and stes. CI 2pm/CO noon. Nonsmoking rms avail. (all w/private bath). Rooms are extremely spacious and individually furnished with antiques. **Amenities:** 🛁 ⚬ 📺 🕾 A/C, cable TV w/movies, refrig. Some units w/minibars, some w/terraces. **Services:** ⇦ Social director, children's program. **Facilities:** 🛗 ⅙ 1 restaurant, whirlpool. **Rates (CP):** Peak (Mar–Oct) $59–$69 S; $89 ste; $79 effic; $99 cottage/villa. Extra person $5. Children under age 3 stay free. Min stay peak. Lower rates off-season. Higher rates for special events/hols. Parking: Outdoor, free. AE, DISC, MC, V.

ATTRACTIONS 🖼

Aquarena Springs Resort

Tel 512/245-7575 or toll free 800/999-9767. Located on Spring Lake, at the headwaters of the San Marcos River, this sprawling resort complex features a historic inn, golf course, two restaurants, and parks. The lake's clear spring water stays at a relatively constant temperature of between 68°F and 72°F. Numerous attractions are offered, including underwater shows; glass-bottomed-boat rides; Ralph, the swimming pig; the birds of paradise show; alpine sky ride; 220-foot Sky Spiral Tower providing panoramic views; and Texana Village, a re-created frontier town. **Open:** Daily, hours vary. **$$$$**

Wonder World

1000 Prospect St; tel 512/392-3760. Back when prehistoric oceans covered central Texas, an enormous earthquake rocked the area, creating a huge underground cave; this is part of the 1,800-mile-long Balcones Fault line that divides Texas into its two most prominent geographical regions. The tour of the well-lit Wonder Cave (the temperature is a constant 71°F) affords visitors an illuminating glimpse into Texas's geological history—prehistoric fossils, mammoth keystones, and a subterranean view of the meeting point of two gigantic land masses. An elevator ride travels from deep inside the cave to the top of the observation tower, 110 feet up, which offers inspiring vistas of the scenic Hill Country as well as the drop-off point of the fault line. Other highlights include a train ride through the wildlife petting park, the Anti-Gravity House, where water flows uphill and everything is topsy-turvy, and a pottery studio. Guided tours, gift shop. **Open:** Mar–Oct, daily 8am–8pm. **$$$$**

Shamrock

RESTAURANT 🍴

★ Mitchell's Family Restaurant

I-40 and US 83; tel 806/256-3424. Exit 164 off I-40. **American/Burgers.** A family diner with a standard breakfast and burger menu. The spacious dining rooms sports a country motif. **FYI:** Reservations not accepted. No liquor license. **Open:** Daily 6am–9:30pm. **Prices:** Main courses $3–$8. AE, DC, DISC, MC, V. 🖭

Sherman

See also Bonham, Denison

Located immediately south of the Oklahoma border at the intersection of US 75 and US 82, this business community was founded as a stagecoach stop in 1846. Visitors can enjoy a historical driving tour, art galleries and shops in vintage buildings, and Lake Texoma (15 miles northwest). **Information:** Sherman Convention & Visitors Bureau, 400 N Crockett, #1, PO Box 1029, Sherman, 75091-1029 (tel 903/893-1184).

HOTEL

⌸⌸⌸ Sheraton Inn

3605 US 75 S, 75090; tel 903/868-0555 or toll free 800/325-3535 in the US, 800/268-9393 in Canada. Nice, spacious hotel equidistant from Lake Texama, the Dallas/Fort Worth metro area, and the Oklahoma border. Located on the south side of Sherman next to several corporate facilities, it caters to conventions and business travelers. **Rooms:** 150 rms. CI 2pm/CO noon. Nonsmoking rms avail. **Amenities:** 🛅 👁 ⬜ A/C, cable TV w/movies. **Services:** ✗ ⬜ ⬜ **Facilities:** ⬜ ⬜ ⬜ 👤 1 restaurant, 1 bar (w/entertainment), whirlpool. **Rates:** $60–$75 S or D. Extra person $10. Children under age 18 stay free. Parking: Outdoor, free. AE, CB, DC, DISC, MC, V.

MOTELS

⌸⌸ Best Western Grayson House

2105 Texoma Pkwy, 75090; tel 903/892-2161 or toll free 800/528-1234; fax 903/893-3045. On TX 93, S of US 82. Located near Lake Texoma, this average property offers many opportunities for recreation. A standard motel with dependable accommodations, it is perfect for travelers on a budget. **Rooms:** 145 rms. CI 3pm/CO noon. Nonsmoking rms avail. **Amenities:** 🛅 👁 ⬜ A/C, cable TV. **Services:** 🍴 ⬜ ⬜ **Facilities:** ⬜ 👤 1 bar, whirlpool, washer/dryer. **Rates:** $45–$68 S or D. Extra person $8. Children under age 12 stay free. Parking: Outdoor, free. AE, CB, DC, DISC, MC, V.

⌸ Inn of Sherman

1831 Texoma Pkwy, 75090; tel 903/892-0433 or toll free 800/255-1011; fax 903/893-8199. On TX 93, near US 82. A great option for short stays, this motel is good for average accommodations at an affordable price. Located near the interstates, it is also very convenient. **Rooms:** 85 rms. CI 4pm/CO noon. Nonsmoking rms avail. **Amenities:** 🛅 👁 ⬜ A/C, cable TV w/movies, refrig. **Services:** 🍴 ⬜ **Facilities:** ⬜ 👤 1 bar, washer/dryer. **Rates (CP):** $30–$35 S; $35–$45 D. Extra person $5. Children under age 17 stay free. Parking: Outdoor, free. AE, CB, DC, DISC, MC, V.

ATTRACTION

Hagerman National Wildlife Refuge

On Refuge Rd off FM 1417; tel 903/786-2826. Approximately 3,000 acres of water and marsh and 8,000 acres of uplands provide food and shelter for many birds and animals. Canada geese are the predominant waterfowl inhabiting the refuge; other geese include white-fronted geese, snow geese, and the smaller Ross's geese. During the southward migration period, ducks such as mallard, pintail, and teal arrive here. Pelicans, quail, doves, and white-tailed deer are among the many other animals that can be observed. Sight-seeing, nature study, bird-watching, and photography are popular activities. Self-guided auto tour route; hiking; fishing; boating

(permitted from April through September only). The visitors center has information, interpretive exhibits, and rest room facilities. **Open:** Mon–Fri 7:30am–4pm. **Free**

Sonora

MOTEL

⌸⌸ Devil's River Inn

103 Golf Course Rd, 76950; tel 915/387-3516; fax 915/387-2854. Budget, family-oriented motel located on north side of Sonora. A steak house shares the parking lot. **Rooms:** 112 rms. CI 3pm/CO 11am. Nonsmoking rms avail. **Amenities:** 🛅 A/C, cable TV. **Services:** 🍴 ⬜ **Facilities:** ⬜ 👤 1 restaurant. **Rates (CP):** $32–$40 S; $40–$47 D. Extra person $6. Parking: Outdoor, free. AE.

ATTRACTION

Caverns of Sonora

Exit 392 off I-10; tel 915/387-6507. Glittering, crystal-like stalagmites, stalactites, and helictites in this incredibly beautiful and unusual cave. Millions of years in the making, the delicate formations are still active and continually changing. The 1½-mile tour trail zigzags through translucent and phosphorescent formations, enormous rooms (the Hall of White Giants, Devils Pit, and the Palace of Angels are highlights), and a small "lake." The temperature is a constant 70°F. Picnic grounds, 48-unit RV hook-ups, shower facilities, and camping; also a gift shop and snack bar. **Open:** Peak (Mar–Sept) daily 8am–6pm. **$$$$**

South Padre Island

See also Brownsville, Port Isabel

The southern tip of this long barrier island is now a bustling resort area with hotels, eateries, and numerous entertainment venues. Connected to the mainland via the Queen Isabella Causeway, South Padre offers excellent sport fishing and exceptional beaches. **Information:** South Padre Island Convention & Visitors Bureau, 600 Padre Blvd, South Padre Island, 78597 (tel 210/761-6433 or toll free 800/343-2368).

MOTEL

⌸⌸ Best Western Fiesta Isles

5701 Padre Blvd, 78597; tel 210/761-4913 or toll free 800/528-1234. Small but functional rooms. Located off Main St, on the beach. **Rooms:** 100 rms and stes. CI open/CO noon. Nonsmoking rms avail. **Amenities:** 🛅 A/C, cable TV w/movies. Some units w/terraces. **Facilities:** ⬜ ⬜ 👤 1 beach (ocean), lifeguard, whirlpool. **Rates (CP):** Peak (Sept–Mar) $55–$60 S; $60–$65 D; $70–$79 ste. Extra person $10. Children under age 5 stay free. Min stay peak. Lower rates off-season. Parking: Outdoor, free. AE, DISC, MC, V.

RESORTS

≣≣≣ Holiday Inn Beach Resort

100 Padre Blvd, 78597; tel 210/761-5401 or toll free 800/465-4329. 6 acres. Recently overhauled beachfront property offering daily coordinated activities for guests and children. **Rooms:** 250 rms and stes. Executive level. CI 2pm/CO noon. Nonsmoking rms avail. Upscale rooms have plush carpeting and newer furnishings. Suites have large dining table with four chairs. **Amenities:** 🛏 🔓 📺 🍽 A/C, cable TV w/movies, refrig, voice mail. Some units w/minibars, some w/terraces. Suites have two TVs. **Services:** ⍾ VP ⌷ ⇦ Social director. Twice-daily maid service on request. **Facilities:** 🛢 ⛰ 🛶 🏄 🍹 🏊 🍴 🎱 💻 ♿ 1 restaurant, 1 bar (w/entertainment), 1 beach (ocean), lifeguard, volleyball, board surfing, snorkeling, whirlpool, playground. The Padre Cantina restaurant offers great Tex-Mex fare; a poolside bar serves cocktails and refreshments. Many water sports available on site, such as parasailing and wave runners. **Rates (CP):** $59–$69 S; $69–$79 D; $89–$99 ste. Extra person $10. Children under age 5 stay free. Min stay peak. MAP rates avail. Parking: Indoor/outdoor, free. AE, DC, DISC, MC, V.

≣≣≣ Radisson Resort South Padre Island

500 Padre Blvd, 78597; tel 210/761-6511 or toll free 800/333-3333. 7 acres. A sprawling luxury resort offering endless amenities and upscale accommodations. **Rooms:** 250 rms and stes. Executive level. CI open/CO 2pm. Nonsmoking rms avail. Rooms are spacious and feature large beds and spectacular views of the white sandy beaches. **Amenities:** 🛏 🔓 📺 🍽 A/C, cable TV w/movies, refrig, bathrobes. Some units w/minibars, some w/terraces, some w/whirlpools. **Services:** ✕ 🔑 VP ⇦ Twice-daily maid svce, social director. **Facilities:** 🛢 🚲 ⛰ 🛶 🏄 🎿 📺 🛝 🍹 275 ♿ 1 restaurant, 1 bar (w/entertainment), 1 beach (ocean), lifeguard, volleyball, board surfing, snorkeling, whirlpool. **Rates (CP):** Peak (Mar–Sept) $59–$69 S; $69–$79 D; $85–$110 ste. Extra person $10. Children under age 3 stay free. Min stay peak. Lower rates off-season. MAP rates avail. Parking: Indoor/outdoor, free. AE, DC, DISC, MC, V.

≣≣≣ Sheraton South Padre Island Beach Resort

310 Padre Blvd, 78597; tel 210/761-6551 or toll free 800/325-3535. Located right on the white sand beach, this posh hotel featuring magnificent views of the Gulf of Mexico offers something for everyone—not least of all the spectacular pool with cascading waterfall and swim-up bar. Off-season rates are a good value. **Rooms:** 239 rms and stes. Executive level. CI 2pm/CO 11am. Nonsmoking rms avail. **Amenities:** 🛏 🔓 📺 🍽 A/C, cable TV w/movies, refrig, dataport, bathrobes. Some units w/minibars, some w/terraces, some w/whirlpools. **Services:** ✕ 🔑 VP Social director. Parasailing, jet skiing, and sunset and dolphin cruises available at the beach. **Facilities:** 🛢 ⛰ 🛝 100 ♿ 1 restaurant, 1 bar (w/entertainment), 1 beach (ocean, cove/inlet), lifeguard. **Rates (CP):** Peak (Sept–Feb) $59–$69 S; $69–$79 D; $89–

$100 ste. Extra person $10. Children under age 5 stay free. Min stay peak. Lower rates off-season. MAP rates avail. Parking: Indoor/outdoor, free. AE, DISC, MC, V.

RESTAURANTS 🍴

Bahia Mar Resort-Hotel Restaurant

6300 Padre Blvd; tel 210/761-1343. **American.** Select from Indian, Mexican, Asian, and American cuisines at this upscale hotel restaurant. Daily specials. **FYI:** Reservations not accepted. Children's menu. **Open:** Daily 11am–10pm. **Prices:** Main courses $4–$13. AE, DISC, MC, V. 💟 ♿

Black Beards

103 E Saturn; tel 210/761-2962. **Seafood.** A carefully coordinated pirate theme is the main feature here. Known for a wide variety of alcoholic specialty drinks as well as seafood and steakburgers; the menu specialty is "sword" fish. **FYI:** Reservations accepted. Blues. Children's menu. Dress code. **Open:** Mon–Sat 11:30am–11:30pm. **Prices:** Main courses $7–$11. AE, DISC, MC, V. 🍽 💟 ♿

Grill Room at the Pantry

708 Padre Blvd in Franke Plaza; tel 210/761-9331. **Barbecue/Burgers.** An informal grill providing lovely outdoor seating in addition to tables in its relaxed, casual dining room. The kitchen turns out a variety of burgers, grilled quail and other game, and delicious seafood. **FYI:** Reservations not accepted. Children's menu. Dress code. Beer and wine only. **Open:** Daily 11:30am–10pm. **Prices:** Main courses $3–$7. No CC. 🍽 ♿

★ Scampi's

206 W Aries at Laguna; tel 210/761-1755. Cross bridge from Port Isabel, left onto Padre Blvd to Aries, left. **Seafood.** This upscale seafood restaurant with bayside dining has excellent food available at moderate to expensive prices. Besides shrimp scampi, diners can order oysters Rockefeller, fresh local fish, and pasta. **FYI:** Reservations accepted. Children's menu. Dress code. Beer and wine only. **Open:** Daily 11:30am–11:30pm. **Prices:** Main courses $9–$13. AE, MC, V. 💟 ♿

Sergio's by the Bay

In Bermuda Night Club, 205 W Palm; tel 210/761-4308. **Regional American.** Enjoy great food at Sergio's and maybe one or two of the tasty margaritas before stepping over to the nightclub for dancing. A great combination for fun. **FYI:** Reservations accepted. Singer. Dress code. **Open:** Daily noon–11:30pm. **Prices:** Main courses $9–$17. AE, DC, MC, V. 🍽 ♿

Stephenville

This small town in north-central Texas was settled in 1850 and is of interest to tourists primarily for its collection of vintage homes. **Information:** Stephenville Chamber of Commerce, 187 W Washington St, PO Box 306, Stephenville, 76401 (tel 817/965-5313 or 965-5323).

MOTEL

Holiday Inn
2865 W Washington, 76401; tel 817/968-5256 or toll free 800/HOLIDAY; fax 817/968-4255. A standard Holiday Inn, this average property is great for an overnight stay or weekend visit. Also perfect for vacationers on a budget. This motel can cater to business meetings. **Rooms:** 100 rms. CI 3pm/CO noon. Nonsmoking rms avail. **Amenities:** A/C, cable TV. **Services:** **Facilities:** 1 restaurant, 1 bar, whirlpool. **Rates:** $50–$52 S or D. Extra person $5. Children under age 19 stay free. Parking: Outdoor, free. AE, CB, DC, DISC, JCB, MC, V.

Temple

A railroad town established in 1880, Temple is also the Wildflower Capital of Texas—March and April are the prime months for viewing. Lake Belton, nine miles northwest, offers excellent outdoor recreation year-round. **Information:** Temple Chamber of Commerce, 2 N 5th St, PO Box 158, Temple, 76503-0158 (tel 817/773-2105).

MOTELS

Best Western Inn at Scott & White
2625 S 31st St, 76504; tel 817/778-5511 or toll free 800/749-0318. N of US 190 and TX 363. This Best Western property is adjacent to the Scott & White Medical Clinic. It primarily caters to patrons and businesspeople of the clinic, but is still a great place for tourists. The lobby is elegant with plush carpeting and beautiful furniture. **Rooms:** 127 rms and stes. CI 3pm/CO noon. Nonsmoking rms avail. **Amenities:** A/C, cable TV. Some units w/terraces. **Services:** **Facilities:** 2 restaurants, 1 bar. **Rates:** $49–$70 S or D; $55–$125 ste. Extra person $8. Children under age 17 stay free. Parking: Outdoor, free. AE, CB, DC, DISC, JCB, MC, V.

Econo Lodge
1001 N General Bruce Dr, 76504; tel 817/771-1688 or toll free 800/424-4777. A well-maintained property that is great for families and overnight guests. Close to the downtown area, this location offers access to local shopping, restaurants, and entertainment. Great for travelers on a budget. **Rooms:** 55 rms. CI 4pm/CO noon. Nonsmoking rms avail. **Amenities:** A/C, cable TV w/movies. **Services:** **Facilities:** Washer/dryer. **Rates:** $32–$40 S; $38–$50 D. Extra person $5. Children under age 18 stay free. Parking: Outdoor, free. AE, CB, DC, DISC, ER, MC, V.

Stagecoach Inn
1 Main St, Salado, 76571; tel 817/947-5111 or toll free 800/732-8994; fax 817/947-5111. At jct I-35, S of Royal St. Offering many recreational opportunities on-site, this motel is perfect for families. Located in a beautiful, peaceful, wooded area and possessing a historic, Old West ambience, it is quiet and secluded. Originally founded in the early 1860s and reopened in 1945, this motel offers nice accommodations and great service. **Rooms:** 82 rms and stes. CI 3pm/CO 1pm. Nonsmoking rms avail. **Amenities:** A/C, cable TV. Some units w/terraces. **Services:** Babysitting. **Facilities:** 2 restaurants, 1 bar (w/entertainment), volleyball, lawn games, whirlpool, washer/dryer. A golf course is located adjacent to the property. **Rates:** $42–$52 S; $49–$59 D; $75 ste. Extra person $3. Children under age 12 stay free. Parking: Outdoor, free. AE, CB, DC, DISC, MC, V.

RESTAURANT

Bluebonnet Cafe
705 S 24th St; tel 817/773-6654. S of Adams, near I-35. **Cafe.** A small, very casual cafe offering everything from steaks and chicken to sandwiches and Mexican fare. Good for healthy, family dining. **FYI:** Reservations not accepted. Children's menu. No liquor license. No smoking. **Open:** Tues–Sun 6am–8:30pm. **Prices:** Main courses $3–$12. No CC.

ATTRACTION

Railroad and Pioneer Museum
710 Jack Baskin; tel 817/778-6873. Housed in a restored, vintage depot, exhibits devoted to pioneer farm, ranch, and home articles, hand tools, and clothing, as well as the early days of railroading in Texas. Early railroad station equipment and furniture, including a working telegraph for train orders. Retired steam engine and other railroad equipment; large collection of railroad timetables and passes, photographs, and papers from around the world. **Open:** Tues–Fri 1–4pm, Sat 10am–4pm. $

Texarkana

Straddling the Texas-Arkansas border in the northeastern corner of the state and just a short drive from both Oklahoma and Louisiana, Texarkana actually is two different cities that share a common name. Capitalizing on its unique four-state site, this city hosts the annual Four States Fair and Rodeo in early October. **Information:** Texarkana Chamber of Commerce, 819 State Line Ave, PO Box 1468, Texarkana, 75504-1468 (tel 903/792-7191).

HOTEL 📠

☰☰☰ Four Points Hotel Texarkana

5301 N Stateline, 75503; tel 903/792-3222 or toll free 800/325-3535; fax 903/793-3930. Exit 223B off I-30. Very convenient to downtown and the fairgrounds, this full-service hotel caters primarily to business travelers. **Rooms:** 145 rms and stes. Executive level. CI 3pm/CO noon. Nonsmoking rms avail. King rooms have sleeper/sofas. **Amenities:** 📺 ☕ 🖥 A/C, cable TV, dataport. **Services:** ✕ ➡ 🚗 🖼 🗂 🧹 Secretarial services available. Pets $25. **Facilities:** 🔲 500 🔲 ᕆ 1 restaurant, 1 bar (w/entertainment), whirlpool. **Rates:** $75–$95 S or D; $140–$210 ste. Extra person $10. Children under age 18 stay free. Parking: Outdoor, free. AE, DC, DISC, MC, V.

MOTELS

☰ Comfort Inn

5105 Stateline Ave, 75501; tel 903/792-6688 or toll free 800/228-5150; fax 903/792-6688. Exit 223A off I-30. Close to I-35 and right across the street from Texarkana, AR, this chain motel offers very basic rooms and services. **Rooms:** 79 rms. CI noon/CO noon. Nonsmoking rms avail. King rooms have love seats. **Amenities:** 📺 A/C, cable TV. Some units w/whirlpools. **Services:** 🖼 🗂 🧹 Pets $6. **Facilities:** 🔲 ᕆ 1 bar, washer/dryer. **Rates (CP):** $39 S; $45 D. Extra person $6. Children under age 18 stay free. Parking: Outdoor, free. AE, DC, DISC, JCB, MC, V.

☰☰ La Quinta Motor Inn

5201 Stateline Ave, 75503; tel 903/794-1900 or toll free 800/531-5900; fax 903/792-5506. Exit 223A off I-30. Located on the main road in Texarkana, this standard La Quinta is near shopping, dining, and the fairgrounds. Accommodations are simple and dependable. **Rooms:** 130 rms and stes. CI 3pm/CO noon. Nonsmoking rms avail. **Amenities:** 📺 ☕ A/C, cable TV w/movies. King rooms have dataports. **Services:** 🚗 🖼 🗂 🧹 **Facilities:** 🔲 35 ᕆ Free access to nearby health club. **Rates (CP):** $56–$64 S or D; $67–$81 ste. Extra person $8. Children under age 18 stay free. Parking: Outdoor, free. AE, CB, DC, DISC, MC, V.

ATTRACTIONS 📠

Texarkana Historical Museum

219 State Line Ave; tel 903/793-4831. The museum is housed in the city's first brick structure, dating from 1879 and listed in the National Register of Historic Places. Holdings include archaeological findings, pioneer items, early medical instruments, and farm tools, as well as Native American artifacts; also a period parlor, kitchen, and office. Exhibits illustrate the region's development and the history of its industries. **Open:** Tues–Sat 10am–4pm. $

Perot Theatre

221 Main St; tel 903/792-8681 or toll free 800/333-0927. This Italian Renaissance–style theater, opened in 1924 (originally the Saenger Theatre), was restored through the efforts of H Ross Perot and is now a major performing arts center. Major symphony orchestras, pop and country music luminaries, Broadway shows, ballet, and other dance performances are featured. The season lasts from September through May.

The newly restored Regional Arts Center is housed in what was originally a United States District Courthouse. The 1909 building is now a grand hall with a 26-foot-high ceiling. Touring art exhibitions, classes, lectures, workshops, film series, and performances are held here. **Free**

Three Rivers

ATTRACTION 📠

Choke Canyon State Park

Off I-37, Calliham; tel 512/786-3868. The park offers opportunities for fishing and boating on the 26,000-acre Choke Canyon Reservoir. Camping, picnic sites, and rest rooms on the grounds. The town site of Old Calliham, within the park, provides campsites and screened shelters, seven-lane boat ramp, rock jetty, fishing pier, swimming area, and fish-cleaning stations. **Open:** Mon–Thurs 8am–5pm, Fri–Sat 8am–10pm, Sun 8am–5pm. $$

Tioga

See Denton

Tyler

Tyler was named after John Tyler, the 10th president of the United States. The town's climate and soil condition have made it a popular site for commercial rose production. The annual East Texas Fair and Texas Rose Festival are held in September and October, respectively. **Information:** Tyler Convention & Visitors Bureau, 407 N Broadway, PO Box 390, Tyler, 75710 (tel 903/592-1661).

HOTEL 📠

☰☰☰ Sheraton Hotel

5701 S Broadway, 75703; tel 903/561-5800 or toll free 800/325-3535; fax 903/561-9916. On US 69S, 1¾ mi S of Loop 323. One of the nicest hotels in Tyler, conveniently located near shopping areas, business district, and numerous restaurants. Recommended for business travelers, but suitable for anyone wanting quality accommodations. **Rooms:** 185 rms and stes. Executive level. CI 3pm/CO noon. Nonsmoking rms avail. Some rooms face pool. **Amenities:** 📺 ☕ 🖥 A/C, cable TV w/movies. Some units w/terraces. **Services:** ✕ ➡ 🚗 🖼 🗂 Car-rental desk. Complimentary *USA Today*. **Facilities:** 🔲 600 ᕆ 1 restaurant, 1 bar (w/entertainment), whirlpool. Sun deck near pool. Free access to fitness center across the street. **Rates:** $89 S; $99 D; $135 ste. Extra person $10. Children under age 17 stay free. Parking: Outdoor, free. AE, CB, DC, DISC, MC, V.

MOTELS

≣≣ Best Western Inn and Suites
2828 N Northwest Loop 323, 75702; tel 903/595-2681 or toll free 800/528-1234; fax 903/592-5672. US 271 exit off I-20. Close to the rose gardens, the convention center, and many restaurants, it's suitable for short stays. **Rooms:** 90 rms, stes, and effic. CI 2pm/CO noon. Nonsmoking rms avail. **Amenities:** A/C, cable TV, refrig. Some units w/whirlpools. Microwaves available in suites. **Services:** Car-rental desk. Complimentary drinks and hors d'oeuvres Mon–Thurs 5:30–7:30pm. **Facilities:** Washer/dryer. **Rates (CP):** $45 S; $52 D; $53–$85 ste; $70–$90 effic. Extra person $5. Children under age 12 stay free. Parking: Outdoor, free. AE, CB, DC, DISC, MC, V.

≣ Days Inn
3300 Mineola Hwy, 75702; tel 903/595-2451 or toll free 800/DAYS-INN; fax 903/595-2261. On US 69 N. Standard chain hotel close to rose gardens, fairgrounds, and airport. **Rooms:** 187 rms, stes, and effic. CI noon/CO noon. Nonsmoking rms avail. Most rooms are in need of minor refurbishing. **Amenities:** A/C, satel TV. Some units w/whirlpools. A few rooms have dataports. **Services:** VCRs and movies rented at front desk. **Facilities:** 1 restaurant, 1 bar, games rm, whirlpool, beauty salon, washer/dryer. **Rates:** $36–$42 S; $41–$47 D; $75–$90 ste; $36 effic. Extra person $6. Children under age 17 stay free. Parking: Outdoor, free. AE, CB, DC, DISC, ER, JCB, MC, V.

≣≣≣ Holiday Inn Tyler
3310 Troup Hwy, 75701; tel 903/593-3600 or toll free 800/HOLIDAY; fax 903/533-9571. US 271 exit off I-20. Less than 5 miles from zoo and rose gardens, it's a good bet for families. **Rooms:** 160 rms and stes. CI 3pm/CO noon. Nonsmoking rms avail. King rooms have sleeper/sofas. **Amenities:** A/C, cable TV w/movies, dataport. **Services:** Car-rental desk, babysitting. Complimentary drinks and hors d'oeuvres Mon–Thurs 5–7pm. **Facilities:** 1 restaurant, 1 bar, washer/dryer. **Rates:** $69 S or D; $145 ste. Extra person $5. Children under age 18 stay free. Parking: Outdoor, free. AE, CB, DC, DISC, JCB, MC, V.

≣≣ La Quinta Motor Inn
1601 W Southwest Loop 323, 75701; tel 903/561-2223 or toll free 800/531-5900; fax 903/581-5708. US 271 exit off I-20. Dependable accommodations and services near the airport and all local attractions. **Rooms:** 130 rms. CI noon/CO noon. Nonsmoking rms avail. Mini-suites available. **Amenities:** A/C, cable TV. King-plus rooms have

dataports. **Services:** **Facilities:** **Rates (CP):** $55 S; $65 D. Extra person $10. Children under age 18 stay free. Parking: Outdoor, free. AE, CB, DC, DISC, MC, V.

≣≣ Super 8
2616 N Northwest Loop 323, 75703; tel 903/593-8361 or toll free 800/800-8000; fax 903/593-8756. US 271 exit off I-20. A family-friendly budget motel. There aren't a lot of amenties here, but the location is very convenient and the rooms are adequate. **Rooms:** 125 rms and stes. CI noon/CO noon. Nonsmoking rms avail. Single rooms have love seats. **Amenities:** A/C, cable TV. Microwave and mini-refrigerator in some rooms. **Services:** Car-rental desk. Pets $10. **Facilities:** 1 restaurant, 1 bar (w/entertainment). **Rates:** Peak (May–Sept) $43 S; $56 D; $55–$75 ste. Extra person $5. Children under age 18 stay free. Lower rates off-season. Parking: Outdoor, free. AE, CB, DC, DISC, ER, JCB, MC, V.

RESTAURANTS

The Black-Eyed Pea
In Tyler Town Center, 322 E Southeast Loop 323; tel 903/581-0242. At Broadway. **American.** A large painting of Tyler attractions is featured on one wall of the dining room of this comfortable, relaxed restaurant. The country-style menu includes favorites like chicken-fried steak, pot roast, meatloaf, catfish fillets, sandwiches, burgers, and vegetable sides. Friendly and competent service. **FYI:** Reservations not accepted. Children's menu. **Open:** Sun–Thurs 11am–10pm, Fri–Sat 11am–10:30pm. **Prices:** Main courses $5–$11. AE, CB, DC, DISC, MC, V.

Cace's Seafood
7011 S Broadway; tel 903/581-0744. On US 69 S. **Seafood.** Part of a chain of New Orleans–style seafood restaurants, good for casual family dining. The large menu offers oysters, shrimp, lobster tail, blackened orange roughy, stuffed flounder, and crawfish etoufée, and alternatives such as steak and chicken. **FYI:** Reservations not accepted. Children's menu. Additional location: 1501 E Marshall, Longview (tel 753-7691). **Open:** Mon 4–10pm, Tues–Thurs 11am–10pm, Fri–Sat 11am–10:30pm, Sun 11am–9pm. **Prices:** Main courses $7–$28. AE, CB, DC, DISC, MC, V.

Oxford Street Restaurant
3300 Troup Hwy; tel 903/593-2655. **Eclectic.** This cozy, dimly-lit restaurant offers several separate areas for secluded dining, and is great for business lunches or family dining. Framed artwork, books, and china are on display near the dark wood booths and tables. The menu offers prime rib and steaks, chicken, seafood, salads, pastas, and sandwiches. Santa Fe chicken, grilled salmon, blackened red snapper, and the blackened chicken sandwich are all recommended. **FYI:** Reservations accepted. Children's menu. Additional location: 421 N Spur 63, Longview (tel 758-9130). **Open:** Lunch

Mon–Fri 11am–2pm, Sun 11am–9pm; dinner Mon–Thurs 5–10pm, Fri–Sat 5–10:30pm, Sun 11am–9pm. **Prices:** Main courses $5–$18. AE, CB, DC, DISC, MC, V. ♿

Potpourri House

In Off Broadway Shopping Ctr, 2301 S Broadway; tel 903/592-4171. On US 69 S. **Eclectic/Tea Room.** The pleasant dining area is decorated with soft mauve tones and impressionist prints; colored light filters through stained-glass windows. The menu offers salads and specialty sandwiches, like one stuffed with cream cheese, avocados, bacon, and tomatoes. Gourmet desserts include deep-dish hot apple pie and fudge cheesecake. **FYI:** Reservations accepted. No liquor license. **Open:** Daily 11am–3pm. **Prices:** Lunch main courses $6–$8. AE, MC, V.

Sweet Sue's Restaurant

3350 S Southwest Loop 323; tel 903/581-5464. Off US 271. **American.** Casual country restaurant offering daily lunch and dinner buffets at reasonable prices. Menu includes chicken, burgers, sandwiches, seafood, and a few healthy dishes. **FYI:** Reservations not accepted. Children's menu. No liquor license. **Open:** Mon–Sat 6am–8:30pm, Sun 6am–3pm. **Prices:** Main courses $2–$8. AE, DISC, MC, V. 🖼♿

ATTRACTIONS 🏛

Goodman Museum

624 N Broadway; tel 903/531-1286. Housed in a stately, 1859 colonial mansion, the museum exhibits antebellum artifacts, 18th-century dental and medical tools, period furniture, and early photographs of Tyler and Smith County. **Open:** Peak (Mar–Nov) Wed–Sun 1–5pm. Reduced hours off-season. **Free**

Municipal Rose Garden

1900 W Front St; tel 903/531-1212. The 22-acre garden is one of the nation's largest rose showcases, with 38,000 rose bushes representing nearly 500 varieties, set among fountains, ponds, gazebos, and tall pines. The peak season lasts from May through November. Museum offers educational exhibits on the rose-growing industry and also displays former Rose Festival memorabilia, including the dresses of festival queens. **Open:** Peak (mid-Mar–mid-Nov) Mon–Fri 9am–5pm, Sat 9am–5pm, Sun 1–5pm. Reduced hours off-season. **Free**

Caldwell Zoo

2203 Martin Luther King Blvd; tel 903/593-0121. Elephant and giraffe houses, a monkey island, birds, bears, alligators, herpetarium, and aquarium, petting zoo, native Texas exhibit, and even a cow (milking hours posted) are featured at this 35-acre zoo. A collection of ducks from around the world and flamingos are of special interest. There is a nature trail that has six sensory activity stations. Snack bar and picnic area. **Open:** Daily 9:30am–4:30pm. **Free**

Tyler State Park

FM 14; tel 903/597-5338. This 985-acre park, situated in the Piney Woods, features a lake and steep hillsides and offers fishing, boating, camping, and hiking (2½ miles of trails). Deer, squirrels, raccoons, opossums, and numerous species of birds inhabit the park. Campsites and shelters accommodate eight people each (picnic table, grill, and water at each site). Amphitheater on lake shore. **Open:** Daily 8am–10pm. **$$**

University Park

See Dallas

Uvalde

This ranching and market town in south Texas is a great stop on the way to or from the Frio River–Lost Maples area of the Hill Country. Uvalde entertains with a museum and a vintage opera house, and is also becoming known as a fine spot for antiques shopping. **Information:** Uvalde Chamber of Commerce and Convention & Visitors Bureau, 300 E Main, PO Box 706, Uvalde, 78802-0706 (tel 210/278-3361 or 278-4115).

MOTEL 🏨

🖫🖫 **Best Western Continental Inn**

701 E Main St, 78801; tel 210/278-5671 or toll free 800/528-1234. Off US 90. A pleasant chain motel with modern Santa Fe decor and affordable rooms. **Rooms:** 75 rms and stes. CI 2pm/CO noon. Nonsmoking rms avail. **Amenities:** 📺 A/C, cable TV. Some units w/terraces. **Facilities:** 🖼 🏊 ♿ **Rates (CP):** $42–$45 S; $45–$47 D; $59–$62 ste. Extra person $5. Parking: Outdoor, free. DC, DISC, MC, V.

ATTRACTION 🏛

Garner State Park

US 83 and Park Rd 29, Concan; tel 210/212-6132. Located on the Frio River, in an exceptionally scenic Hill Country area, this 1,420-acre site is popular for swimming, canoeing, and fishing. Facilities include stone-and-timber cabins; a camping area for tents and trailers; screened shelters; rest rooms with showers; a grocery store; a snack bar and restaurant in summer season; pedal boats; and a miniature golf course. **Open:** Peak (Mem Day–Labor Day) daily 8am–midnight. Reduced hours off-season. **Free**

Van Horn

Located 100 miles east of El Paso, Van Horn originated as a way station for stagecoaches, wagon trains, and the railroad, and it still fills that role for travelers heading west via I-10.

Two museums and good hunting terrain make the stop worthwhile. **Information:** Van Horn Convention & Visitors Bureau, 1801 W Broadway, PO Box 488, Van Horn, 79855 (tel 915/283-2682).

MOTEL

≡≡ Best Western Inn of Van Horn

1705 W Broadway, 79855; tel 915/283-2410 or toll free 800/367-7589. ¼ mi N of I-10. This family-style motel has a rustic ranch-house atmosphere both inside and out. Two restaurants are located next door. **Rooms:** 58 rms and stes. CI open/CO noon. Nonsmoking rms avail. **Amenities:** � A/C, cable TV w/movies. **Services:** 🔼 🞐 **Facilities:** 🔒 & Washer/dryer. Pool is very large with surprisingly attractive grounds. **Rates (CP):** $37–$40 S; $41–$45 D; $65 ste. Children under age 18 stay free. Parking: Outdoor, free. AE, CB, DC, DISC, MC, V.

Vernon

This upper Panhandle town was incorporated in 1880 and named for George Washington's home in Virginia. The WT Waggoner Ranch, one of the largest in the state, has its headquarters here. **Information:** Vernon Chamber of Commerce, PO Box 1538, Vernon, 76385 (tel 817/552-2564 or 552-0568).

MOTEL

≡≡ Best Western Village Inn

1615 Expressway, 76384; tel 817/552-5417 or toll free 800/528-1234; fax 817/552-5417. On US 283 at jct US 287. Located in the middle of town, this budget property is convenient to local shops and restaurants. **Rooms:** 47 rms. CI 3pm/CO noon. Nonsmoking rms avail. **Amenities:** � A/C, cable TV w/movies. **Services:** 🔼 🞐 **Facilities:** 🔒 & Washer/dryer. **Rates:** $41–$50 S or D. Extra person $4. Children under age 12 stay free. Parking: Outdoor, free. AE, CB, DC, DISC, MC, V.

RESTAURANT

Canton Cafe

287 E Wilbarger St; tel 817/552-9702. On Business US 287 near town center. **Cafe.** This friendly, casual roadside cafe has a homey atmosphere and solid, simple fare. Ideal for a quick sandwich or burger while traveling. **FYI:** Reservations not accepted. No liquor license. **Open:** Sun–Thurs 11am–9pm, Fri–Sat 11am–10pm. **Prices:** Main courses $3–$10. AE, CB, DC, DISC, MC, V. &

Victoria

Settled in 1824 and the third town in Texas to receive a charter, this small city southwest of Houston has two interesting museums and more than 90 structures listed on the National Register of Historic Places. **Information:** Victoria Convention & Visitors Bureau, 700 Main Center, #101, PO Box 2465, Victoria, 77902-2465 (tel 512/573-5277 or toll free 800/926-5774).

HOTELS

≡≡≡ Holiday Inn

2705 E Houston Hwy, 77901; tel 512/575-0251 or toll free 800/465-4329. Standard chain property with well-kept grounds; located right off an access road. Highly professional staff. **Rooms:** 325 rms and stes. Executive level. CI 2pm/CO 11am. Nonsmoking rms avail. Spacious suites. **Amenities:** � 🞐 A/C, satel TV w/movies, refrig, voice mail, bathrobes. Some units w/minibars, some w/terraces. **Services:** ✕ 🆅🅿 🞐 Social director. **Facilities:** 🔒 🏊 ⬜ & 1 restaurant, 1 bar (w/entertainment), whirlpool. **Rates (CP):** $69–$79 S; $79–$85 D; $85–$95 ste. Extra person $10. Children under age 10 stay free. Min stay special events. MAP rates avail. Parking: Outdoor, free. AE, DC, DISC, MC, V.

UNRATED Ramada Inn

3001 E Houston Hwy, 77901; tel 512/578-2723 or toll free 800/426-2321. Off US 59. Standard accommodations. Well maintained. **Rooms:** 240 rms and stes. Executive level. CI 2pm/CO noon. Nonsmoking rms avail. **Amenities:** � 🞐 A/C, cable TV w/movies, refrig. Some units w/minibars, some w/terraces. **Services:** ✕ Social director. **Facilities:** 🔒 🏊 & 1 restaurant, 1 bar (w/entertainment). **Rates (CP):** $65–$72 S; $72–$75 D; $81–$89 ste. Extra person $5. Min stay wknds. MAP rates avail. Parking: Indoor/outdoor, free. DC, DISC, MC, V.

MOTELS

≡ The Corral

3502 Houston Hwy, 76624; tel 512/576-1277. Off US 59. Older, single-level motel OK for overnight stays. **Rooms:** 65 rms. CI open/CO noon. Nonsmoking rms avail. Small rooms with older furnishings and limited counter space. **Amenities:** � A/C, cable TV. Some units w/terraces. **Facilities:** 🔒 & **Rates:** $39–$42 S; $42–$45 D. Extra person $5. Parking: Outdoor, free. AE, MC, V.

≡≡ Days Inn

2100 N Bypass 35, Port Lavaca, 77979; tel 512/552-4511 or toll free 800/325-2525. Off US 87. A newer motel in a nice, quiet area of town. Dependable accommodations, standard rates. **Rooms:** 150 rms and stes. CI 2pm/CO noon. Nonsmoking rms avail. Rooms have attractive ash furniture with colorful Southwestern-style bedspreads, curtains, and carpet. **Amenities:** � 🞐 A/C, cable TV. Some units w/terraces. Some rooms have refrigerators; some have hair dryers. **Services:** 🔼 **Facilities:** 🔒 🏊 & **Rates (CP):** $49–$51 S; $51–$55 D; $72–$78 ste. Extra person $5. Min stay peak. Parking: Outdoor, free. AE, DC, DISC, MC, V.

La Quinta Motor Inn

7603 N Navarro St, 77904; tel 512/572-3585 or toll free 800/531-5900. Off US 77. Southwestern decor featuring Mexican tile and ceramic pieces. Manicured grounds. **Rooms:** 145 rms and stes. Executive level. CI 2pm/CO noon. Nonsmoking rms avail. **Amenities:** 🐴 🕭 A/C, cable TV w/movies, voice mail. Some units w/minibars, some w/terraces. **Services:** 🕭 Social director. **Facilities:** 🕭 🞉 🖵 🕭 **Rates (CP):** $59–$62 S; $62–$69 D; $72–$79 ste. Extra person $10. Min stay special events. Parking: Outdoor, free. AE, DC, DISC, MC, V.

Waco

A thriving city in the heart of the Brazos River Valley, Waco began as a fort established by Texas Rangers in 1837. The soft drink Dr Pepper was born here in 1885. Today it boasts Baylor University and several sites of interest to travelers. **Information:** Waco Convention & Visitors Bureau, 100 Washington Ave, PO Box 2570, Waco, 76702 (tel 817/750-5810 or toll free 800/321-9226).

HOTELS 🏨

Holiday Inn Waco

1001 Lake Brazos Dr, 76704; tel 817/753-0261 or toll free 800/HOLIDAY; fax 817/753-0227. At jct I-35. With a great view of the Brazos River, this four-story hotel offers a nice, comfortable place to spend the evening or the weekend. **Rooms:** 172 rms. CI 4pm/CO noon. Nonsmoking rms avail. **Amenities:** 🐴 🕭 A/C, satel TV w/movies. Some units w/terraces. **Services:** ✗ 🕭 🞉 **Facilities:** 🕭 🞉 1 restaurant, 1 bar, washer/dryer. **Rates:** $58–$75 S or D. Extra person $6. Children under age 19 stay free. Parking: Outdoor, free. Higher rates for Baylor football weekends. AE, CB, DC, DISC, MC, V.

Waco Hilton Inn

113 S University Park, 76701; tel 817/754-8484 or toll free 800/234-5244; fax 817/752-2214. At Franklin Dr. Located in a convenient spot near Baylor University and downtown, this attractive, 11-story hotel overlooks the Brazos River and offers some beautiful views. Adjacent to the convention center, this Hilton caters primarily to business travelers. **Rooms:** 199 rms. CI 3pm/CO noon. Nonsmoking rms avail. **Amenities:** 🐴 🕭 A/C, cable TV. **Services:** ✗ 🕭 🞉 **Facilities:** 🕭 🞉 🞉 🞉 🕭 1 restaurant, 1 bar, whirlpool. **Rates:** $69–$79 S or D. Extra person $10. Children under age 18 stay free. Parking: Indoor/outdoor, free. AE, CB, DC, DISC, MC, V.

MOTELS

Best Western Old Main Lodge

I-35 at Baylor University, PO Box 174, 76706; tel 817/753-0316 or toll free 800/299-WACO; fax 817/753-3811. A nice motel near Baylor University. Only a few minutes from downtown. **Rooms:** 84 rms. CI 4pm/CO noon. Nonsmoking rms avail. **Amenities:** 🐴 🕭 A/C, cable TV w/movies. **Services:** 🕭 🞉 **Facilities:** 🕭 🕭 Washer/dryer. **Rates:** $50–$66 S or D. Extra person $6. Children under age 18 stay free. Parking: Outdoor, free. AE, CB, DC, DISC, MC, V.

La Quinta Motor Inn

1110 S 9th St, 76706; tel 817/752-9741 or toll free 800/531-5900; fax 817/757-1600. At jct I-35. Affordable, dependable chain motel situated on a well-maintained lot of grass and trees along the interstate. **Rooms:** 102 rms. CI 3pm/CO noon. Nonsmoking rms avail. **Amenities:** 🐴 🕭 A/C, cable TV w/movies. **Services:** 🕭 🞉 **Facilities:** 🕭 🞉 🕭 **Rates (CP):** $57–$78 S or D. Extra person $7. Children under age 18 stay free. Parking: Outdoor, free. AE, CB, DC, DISC, MC, V.

Lexington Inn

115 Jack Kultgen, 76706; tel 817/754-1266 or toll free 800/537-8483; fax 817/755-8612. The stone exterior and cozy dark wood interior of this little motel lend it the look of a quaint country lodge. Great for extended stays. **Rooms:** 113 rms. CI 3pm/CO noon. Nonsmoking rms avail. **Amenities:** 🐴 🕭 🞉 A/C, satel TV w/movies, refrig. Nintendo video games available. **Services:** 🕭 🞉 Social hour every Tuesday and Thursday evening; cookouts every Wednesday. **Facilities:** 🕭 🞉 🕭 Whirlpool, washer/dryer. Guests have access to a local fitness facility. **Rates (CP):** $52–$59 S; $59–$66 D. Extra person $7. Children under age 16 stay free. Parking: Outdoor, free. AE, CB, DC, DISC, MC, V.

Quality Inn

801 S 4th St, 76706; tel 817/757-2000 or toll free 800/ASK-WACO; fax 817/757-1110. At jct I-35. In a central location to Baylor University, downtown, and the Brazos River, this standard chain motel provides adequate lodging. The two-story atrium, filled with lush greenery, offers a nice area in which to relax. **Rooms:** 150 rms. CI 3pm/CO noon. Nonsmoking rms avail. Some rooms available with water and air purification systems. **Amenities:** 🐴 🕭 🞉 A/C, cable TV w/movies. Refrigerators and microwaves are available. **Services:** 🞉 🕭 🞉 **Facilities:** 🕭 🞉 🞉 🖵 🕭 1 restaurant, 1 bar, whirlpool, washer/dryer. **Rates (CP):** $59–$71 S or D. Extra person $6. Children under age 17 stay free. Parking: Outdoor, free. AE, CB, DC, DISC, MC, V.

Ramada Inn

I-35 and TX 22, PO Box 1205, Hillsboro, 76645; tel 817/582-3493 or toll free 800/2-RAMADA; fax 817/582-2755. A pleasant enough place to stop for the night, this interstate motel has clean, comfortable rooms. **Rooms:** 94 rms. CI 4pm/CO noon. Nonsmoking rms avail. **Amenities:** 🐴 🕭 A/C, cable TV w/movies. **Services:** 🕭 🞉 🞉 **Facilities:** 🕭 🞉 🕭 1 restaurant. **Rates:** $50–$65 S or D. Extra person $8. Children under age 18 stay free. Parking: Outdoor, free. AE, CB, DC, DISC, JCB, MC, V.

⊞ Riverplace Inn
101 N I-35, 76704; tel 817/752-8222 or toll free 800/792-3267. At Lake Brazos Dr. Average budget lodging located on the north bank of the Brazos River. **Rooms:** 160 rms. CI 4pm/CO noon. Nonsmoking rms avail. **Amenities:** 🗄️ 🛁 A/C, cable TV. **Services:** 🍽️ **Facilities:** 🛗 🏊 🍴250 ♿ Washer/dryer. **Rates (CP):** $35–$55 S or D. Extra person $5. Children under age 12 stay free. Parking: Outdoor, free. AE, CB, DC, DISC, MC, V.

RESTAURANTS 🍴

El Conquistador
4531 W Waco Dr; tel 817/772-4596. At 45th St near Valley Mills. **Eclectic.** Informal restaurant with a comfortable interior. An eclectic menu includes Tex-Mex fare, beef, chicken, and seafood. **FYI:** Reservations accepted. **Open:** Lunch Mon–Fri 11am–2pm; dinner Mon–Fri 5–10pm, Sat 11am–10pm. **Prices:** Main courses $3–$10. AE, DISC, MC, V. ♿

★ Elite Cafe
2132 S Valley Mills at I-35; tel 817/754-4941. **Eclectic.** You can usually find a large contingent of regulars here at any given time. The ambience is small-town and homey, and the fajitas, marinated chicken, and steak are good and inexpensive. **FYI:** Reservations accepted. Children's menu. Beer and wine only. **Open:** Sun–Thurs 10:30–10pm, Fri–Sat 10:30–11pm. **Prices:** Main courses $5–$14. AE, CB, DC, DISC, MC, V. ♿

★ George's
1525 Circle Rd at Speight; tel 817/753-1421. W of I-35. **Regional American.** It looks like a real dive, but the rustic and informal atmosphere and quality down-home food mean George's is often packed with locals. The best of its country cooking includes country-fried steak, fried chicken, and cheeseburger baskets. **FYI:** Reservations not accepted. Children's menu. Beer and wine only. **Open:** Mon–Sat 6:30am–11pm. **Prices:** Main courses $3–$11. DISC, MC, V.

Lone Star Tavern Steakhouse
4713 US 84 E/Bellmead Dr; tel 817/799-0027. **Steak.** Good-quality steaks are served here amid informal, rustic surroundings. Friendly waitstaff. **FYI:** Reservations accepted. Children's menu. Beer and wine only. **Open:** Mon–Thurs 11am–9:30pm, Fri 11am–10pm, Sat 4–10pm. **Prices:** Main courses $6–$16. AE, DC, DISC, MC, V.

Nick's
4508 W Waco Dr; tel 817/772-7790. At 45th St near Valley Mills. **Greek.** Owned by the same family for more than 30 years. Specializes in Greek cuisine (a rarity in this part of Texas), including much steak and seafood. **FYI:** Reservations accepted. Children's menu. **Open:** Lunch Mon–Fri 11am–2:30pm; dinner Fri–Sat 5–9:30pm. Closed Dec 24–Jan 2. **Prices:** Main courses $7–$15. AE, CB, DC, DISC, MC, V. ♿

ATTRACTIONS

Strecker Museum
S 4th St, Baylor University; tel 817/755-1110. Founded in 1856, this museum has been in continuous operation since then. Its collection ranges from Native American artifacts to geological, biological, and anthropological displays. The **Governor Bill and Vara Daniel Historic Village,** a 13-acre site located along the banks of the Brazos River, adjacent to the museum, is a complex of more than 20 wood-frame buildings which represent a Texas farming community of the 1890s. It includes a cotton gin, blacksmith's shop, livery stable, hotel, saloon, church, school, and farmers' homes; an open-air museum illustrates Texas's agricultural heritage. Live reptiles, a reconstructed 1835 log cabin, and an interpretation of the human development of central Texas are other exhibits featured. Special events, workshops; guided tours available. **Open:** Tues–Fri 9am–noon and 1:30–4pm, Sat 10am–4pm, Sun 2–5pm. **Free**

Armstrong Browning Library
700 Speight Ave; tel 817/755-3566. Located at Baylor University, the library holds the world's largest collection of materials relating to Robert Browning and his poetry, including letters and manuscripts written by, or to, Browning; all of the editions of his poetry; secondary works and materials; his poetry set to music; and portraits and memorabilia. The library also serves as a research center on 19th-century literature and culture and features book and manuscript collections from Elizabeth Barrett Browning, John Ruskin, Charles Dickens, Matthew Arnold, and Ralph Waldo Emerson, as well as other research materials. One of the highlights of the library is the Foyer of Meditation, a sanctuary for students and visitors; the room, which culminates in a 23-carat gold-leaf dome, is marked by marble columns, a 2-ton handcrafted chandelier, and cathedral windows. Group tours and lectures available, but should be arranged well in advance. Special tours available upon request. **Open:** Mon–Fri 9am–noon and 2–4pm, Sat 9am–noon. **Free**

Texas Ranger Hall of Fame and Museum
I-35; tel 817/750-8631. Displays commemorate the heritage of the Texas Rangers, past and present. Twenty-six are honored here. A 20-minute multimedia slide presentation on the history of the Texas Rangers is shown. The Moody Texas Ranger Memorial Library contains over 1,400 volumes as well as a microfilm bank of Ranger service records from 1847 to the present. The museum exhibits arms, photographs, displays of Sam Houston and Native Americans, and artifacts relating to Texas in frontier times. Camping and picnic sites available. **Open:** Daily 9am–5pm. **$$**

Wichita Falls

See also Vernon

Established as a railroad town in 1882, this small but thriving city is a good place to circle the wagons for the night when traveling across northern Texas. In addition to several museums, Wichita Falls sports a symphony orchestra, ballet company, community theater, and 38 parks. **Information:** Wichita Falls Board of Commerce & Industry, 900 8th St, #218, PO Box 1860, Wichita Falls, 76307 (tel 817/723-2741).

HOTEL

▄▄▄ Sheraton Wichita Falls Hotel
100 Central Fwy, 76301; tel 817/761-6000 or toll free 800/325-3535. On I-44, S of US 287. Large facility with pleasant rooms; on a wooded lot with a creek running nearby. Popular for conventions. **Rooms:** 175 rms and stes. Executive level. CI 3pm/CO noon. Nonsmoking rms avail. **Amenities:** A/C, cable TV w/movies. **Services:** **Facilities:** 1 restaurant, 1 bar, whirlpool. **Rates:** $68–$74 S or D; $125–$225 ste. Extra person $10. Children under age 18 stay free. Parking: Outdoor, free. AE, CB, DC, DISC, MC, V.

MOTELS

▄▄ Days Inn Airport
1211 Central Expwy, 76305; tel 817/723-5541 or toll free 800/329-7466. I-44 at Maurine St. Two-story budget option located along the interstate. **Rooms:** 100 rms and stes. CI 4pm/CO noon. Nonsmoking rms avail. **Amenities:** A/C, cable TV. **Services:** Facilities: Washer/dryer. **Rates (CP):** $42–$78 S or D; $90–$120 ste. Extra person $6. Children under age 18 stay free. Parking: Outdoor, free. AE, CB, DC, DISC, JCB, MC, V.

▄▄▄ Holiday Inn
401 Broad St, 76301; tel 817/766-6000 or toll free 800/HOLIDAY; fax 817/766-5942. At 5th St near I-44 and US 287. Situated adjacent to the convention center, this property receives many corporate guests, but its Holidome entertainment center makes it also suitable for families. **Rooms:** 248 rms and stes. CI 3pm/CO noon. Nonsmoking rms avail. **Amenities:** A/C, cable TV w/movies, dataport. Nintendo video games available. **Services:** **Facilities:** 1 restaurant, 1 bar, games rm, sauna, whirlpool, washer/dryer. **Rates:** $62–$92 S or D. Extra person $10. Children under age 19 stay free. Parking: Outdoor, free. AE, CB, DC, DISC, MC, V.

▄▄ La Quinta Motor Inn
1128 Central Fwy N, 76305; tel 817/322-6971 or toll free 800/531-5900; fax 817/723-2573. Pleasant, family-oriented motel located along the interstate north of downtown. **Rooms:** 140 rms. CI 3pm/CO noon. Nonsmoking rms avail. **Amenities:** A/C, cable TV. **Services:** **Facilities:** Washer/dryer. **Rates (CP):** $53–$66 S or D. Extra person $8. Children under age 18 stay free. Parking: Outdoor, free. AE, CB, DC, DISC, MC, V.

RESTAURANTS

Hacienda Hernandez
1105 Broadway; tel 817/767-5932. **Tex-Mex.** Delicious, "no-frills" Tex-Mex fare is heaped on a large buffet table in this festive and friendly Mexican eatery. **FYI:** Reservations accepted. Children's menu. No smoking. **Open:** Lunch Mon–Fri 11am–2pm; dinner Mon–Thurs 4:30–8:30pm, Fri–Sat 4:30–9pm. **Prices:** Main courses $5–$10. AE, CB, DC, DISC, MC, V.

★ McBride Land & Cattle Co
501 Scott; tel 817/692-2462. At 5th St, 6 blocks E of I-44. **Steak.** Homey, Western–style restaurant with a dark interior, large fireplace, and rustic ambience. Steak, chicken, frogs' legs. **FYI:** Reservations not accepted. Children's menu. No smoking. **Open:** Lunch Mon–Fri 11am–1:30pm; dinner Sun–Sat 5–10pm. **Prices:** Main courses $6–$16. AE, CB, DISC, MC, V.

ATTRACTIONS

Wichita Falls Museum and Art Center
2 Eureka Circle; tel 817/692-0923. Permanent display of science, art, and history exhibits. The collection has more than 350 prints, including *The Boston Massacre* by Paul Revere. Also here is the first map of America actually made in America. Planetarium shows held on weekends (shows change monthly). **Open:** Tues–Sun 10am–5pm. **$**

Lake Arrowhead State Park
15 mi SE via US 281 and FM 1954; tel 817/528-2211. Lake Arrowhead comprises 16,000 acres of what used to be an oilfield. In fact, oil derricks still stand in the middle of the lake. The park itself covers 524 acres and offers fishing (the derricks are supposedly where some of the best fishing in the lake can be found), boating, swimming, waterskiing, hiking, picnicking, and camping. **Open:** Daily 8am–5pm. **$**

Index

Listings are arranged alphabetically, followed by a code indicating the type of establishment, and then by city, state, and page number. The codes for type of establishment are defined as follows: (H) = Hotel, (M) = Motel, (I) = Inn, (L) = Lodge, (RE) = Resort, (R) = Restaurant, (RS) = Refreshment Stop, (A) = Attraction.

A

Abigail's Restaurant (R), Wichita, KS 93

Abilene State Park (A), Abilene, TX 281

Abilene Zoological Gardens (A), Abilene, TX 281

Acadian Village (A), Lafayette, LA 125

A Cajun Man's Swamp Cruise (A), Houma, LA 122

Acme Oyster House (R), New Orleans, LA 138

Adam's Mark (H), Kansas City, MO 183; Houston, TX 339

Adam's Mark Hotel (H), St Louis, MO 198

Adam's Mark Tulsa at Williams Center (H), Tulsa, OK 255

Ad Dietzel Motel (M), Fredericksburg, TX 332

Adelante (R), San Antonio, TX 379

Adelmo's Ristorante (R), Dallas, TX 313

Adolphus, The (H), Dallas, TX 306

Agusti's (R), St Louis, MO 200

Airport Hilton & Conference Center (H), Wichita, KS 91

Alamo, The (A), San Antonio, TX 382

Alamo Cafe (R), San Antonio, TX 379

Alamodome (A), San Antonio, TX 386

Alamo Travelodge (M), San Antonio, TX 378

Alamo Village Movie Location (A), Del Rio, TX 322

Albrecht-Kemper Museum of Art (A), St Joseph, MO 198

Alexander's Steak House (R), Columbia, MO 177

Alfredo's Trattoria (R), Dallas, TX 313

Alibates Flint Quarries National Monument (A), Amarillo, TX 284

Allendale Resort and Sharp's Resort (RE), Branson, MO 170

Allen Park Inn (M), Houston, TX 344

Allen Street Bar & Grill (R), Dallas, TX 313

Alouette's (R), Little Rock, AR 45

Also Ran Gallery (A), Norton, KS 85

Al's Steak House (R), St Louis, MO 201

Altdorf Burgarten & Restaurant (R), Fredericksburg, TX 332

Amarillo Art Center (A), Amarillo, TX 284

Ambassador Hotel (H), Amarillo, TX 282

Amelia Earhart Birthplace (A), Atchison, KS 69

America Bowman Restaurant (R), Weston, MO 214

American Quarter Horse Heritage Center and Museum (A), Amarillo, TX 284

American Restaurant, The (R), Kansas City, MO 187

American Rose Center (A), Shreveport, LA 152

Américas (R), Houston, TX 345

Amerisuites (M), Little Rock, AR 44

Amigos (R), Lawrence, KS 80

Amistad National Recreation Area (A), Del Rio, TX 322

Amistad Tours (A), Del Rio, TX 322

Amon Carter Museum (A), Fort Worth, TX 331

Anacapri (R), New Orleans, LA 138

Anadarko Basin Museum of Natural History (A), Elk City, OK 237

Anaqua Grill (R), San Antonio, TX 379

Anderson House Inn, The (I), Heber Springs, AR 39

Andrea's (R), Metairie, LA 126

Angelle's (R), Lafayette, LA 124

Angelo's Barbecue (R), Fort Worth, TX 329

Anheuser-Busch Brewery Tours (A), St Louis, MO 204; Houston, TX 352

Annemarie's (R), Kerrville, TX 356

Annie's Santa Fe (R), Topeka, KS 90; Kansas City, MO 187

Ann's Chicken Fry House (R), Oklahoma City, OK 247

Antares (R), Dallas, TX 313

Anthony Miller's Chateau Briand Restaurant (R), Wichita, KS 93

Anthony's (R), Houston, TX 345

Antoine's (R), New Orleans, LA 138

Applebee's Neighborhood Grill & Bar (R), Kansas City, KS 78

Appletree Inn (H), Coffeyville, KS 70; Independence, KS 76

Applewood's (R), Oklahoma City, OK 247

AQ Chicken House (R), Fayetteville, AR 36; Springdale, AR 53

Aquarena Springs Inn (I), San Marcos, TX 386

Aquarena Springs Resort (A), San Marcos, TX 386

Aquarium of the Americas (A), New Orleans, LA 149

Arabia Steamboat Museum (A), Kansas City, MO 192

Arbuckle Wilderness (A), Davis, OK 236

Arcodaro Bar (R), Dallas, TX 313

Arkansas Air Museum (A), Fayetteville, AR 37

Arkansas Arts Center (A), Little Rock, AR 46

Arkansas Excelsior (H), Little Rock, AR 43

Arkansas Museum of Science and History (A), Little Rock, AR 46

Arkansas Oil and Brine Museum (A), El Dorado, AR 32

Arkansas Strip Land Rush Museum (A), Arkansas City, KS 69

Arkansas Territorial Restoration (A), Little Rock, AR 46

Arlington Hilton (H), Arlington, TX 285

Arlington Historical Park (A), Arlington, TX 287

Arlington Marriott (H), Arlington, TX 285

Arlington Resort Hotel & Spa (RE), Hot Springs National Park, AR 41

Armando's (R), Houston, TX 346

Armstrong Browning Library (A), Waco, TX 395

Arnaud's (R), New Orleans, LA 138

Around the Fireside (R), Sedalia, MO 208

Arthur Bryant's (R), Kansas City, MO 187

Arthur's (R), Norman, OK 243

Art Museum of Southeast Texas (A), Beaumont, TX 297

Art Museum of South Texas (A), Corpus Christi, TX 305

Ashland House Tea Room & Restaurant (R), Houston, TX 346

Astrodome USA (A), Houston, TX 352

Astro Motel (M), Dodge City, KS 71

Atalanta (A), Jefferson, TX 355

Atchafalaya River Cafe (R), Houston, TX 346

Atchison Motor Inn (M), Atchison, KS 69

Atchison Rail Museum (A), Atchison, KS 69

Atlantic Sea Grill (R), Tulsa, OK 257
Audubon Park (A), New Orleans, LA 148
Audubon Zoological Gardens (A), New Orleans, LA 148
Augie's Seafood Restaurant (R), Metairie, LA 126
Austin & Texas Central Railroad Hill Country Flyer Steam Train (A), Austin, TX 294
Austin Marriott at Capitol (H), Austin, TX 287
Austin North Hilton and Towers (H), Austin, TX 288
Avanelle Motor Lodge (M), Hot Springs National Park, AR 41
Avenue Plaza Hotel (H), New Orleans, LA 130
Aw Shucks (R), Dallas, TX 313

B

Baby Doe's Matchless Mine (R), Dallas, TX 313
Bacco (R), New Orleans, LA 138
Bahia Mar Resort-Hotel Restaurant (R), South Padre Island, TX 388
Bailey's (R), New Orleans, LA 138
Balban's (R), St Louis, MO 201
Balcony of Ridglea, The (R), Fort Worth, TX 329
Baldknobbers Motor Inn (M), Branson, MO 168
Ballpark Inn (M), Arlington, TX 285
Bamboo Garden (R), Tulsa, OK 257
Bangkok Restaurant (R), Tulsa, OK 257
Barcelona Courts (H), Lubbock, TX 360
Barn Door, The (R), San Antonio, TX 379
Barn Door and Pecos Depot, The (R), Odessa, TX 369
Barnwell Memorial Gardens and Art Center (A), Shreveport, LA 151
Bartolino's (R), St Louis, MO 201
Barton County Historical Museum and Village (A), Great Bend, KS 74
Barton Creek Conference Resort (RE), Austin, TX 291
Barton Springs Pool (A), Austin, TX 293
Basil's (R), Austin, TX 291
Bastrop Opera House (A), Austin, TX 294
Bastrop State Park (A), Austin, TX 294
Battleship *Texas* (A), La Porte, TX 358
Bavarian Inn (M), Eureka Springs, AR 32
Bayfront Inn (H), Corpus Christi, TX 303
Bayona (R), New Orleans, LA 139
Bayou Bend (A), Houston, TX 351
Bayou Folk Museum/Kate Chopin Home (A), Natchitoches, LA 129
Bayou's, The (R), San Antonio, TX 379
Bay Tree (R), Dallas, TX 314
Beaumont Hilton (H), Beaumont, TX 295
Beauregard-Keyes House (A), New Orleans, LA 147
Beaver Lake State Park (A), Rogers, AR 52
Beavers Bend and Hochatown State Parks (A), Broken Bow, OK 235
Beechwood's (R), Tulsa, OK 257
Beef Rigger Steakhouse (R), Amarillo, TX 283

Beijing Restaurant (R), Salina, KS 88
Bella Italia West (R), Fort Worth, TX 329
Belle of Hot Springs Riverboat (A), Hot Springs National Park, AR 42
Bell Mountain Vineyards and Winery (A), Fredericksburg, TX 333
Bell's Amusement Park (A), Tulsa, OK 259
Benavides (R), Dallas, TX 314
Benno's on the Beach (R), Galveston, TX 335
Benton's Steak and Chop House (R), Kansas City, MO 187
Best Inns of America (M), Joplin, MO 183; Springfield, MO 210
Best of the Orient (R), Enid, OK 238
Bestway Inn (M), Lebanon, MO 193; Rolla, MO 196
Best Western (H), Liberal, KS 81; Okmulgee, OK 250; Stillwater, OK 253
Best Western (M), Natchitoches, LA 129; New Iberia, LA 129
Best Western Airline Motor Inn (M), Bossier City, LA 119
Best Western Airport Inn (M), El Paso, TX 325
Best Western Altus (M), Altus, OK 232
Best Western Amarillo Inn (H), Amarillo, TX 282
Best Western Angus Inn (M), Great Bend, KS 74
Best Western at Chimney Hill (M), College Station, TX 303
Best Western Austin (H), Austin, TX 288
Best Western Beaumont Inn (M), Beaumont, TX 296
Best Western Blue Ribbon Motor Inn (M), Sallisaw, OK 252
Best Western Carriage Inn (M), Mountain Home, AR 47
Best Western Chariot Inn (M), Austin, TX 290
Best Western Château Louisianne (H), Baton Rouge, LA 116
Best Western Château Suite Hotel of Shreveport (H), Shreveport, LA 150
Best Western Cherokee Strip Motel (M), Perry, OK 251
Best Western Cinderella Motor Inn (M), Shawnee, OK 252
Best Western Civic Center (M), Monroe, LA 127
Best Western Classic Inn (M), Granbury, TX 337
Best Western Coach House Inn (M), Springfield, MO 211
Best Western Coach House Inn & Suites (H), Sikeston, MO 209
Best Western Coachman's Inn (M), Magnolia, AR 47
Best Western Columbia Inn (M), Columbia, MO 176
Best Western Conestoga (M), Plainview, TX 371
Best Western Continental Inn (M), Arkadelphia, AR 28; Manhattan, KS 83; Uvalde, TX 392
Best Western Continental Motor Inn (M), Miami, OK 241

Best Western Copa Motel (M), Medicine Lodge, KS 84
Best Western Cotton Inn (M), Blytheville, AR 30
Best Western Crockett Hotel (H), San Antonio, TX 374
Best Western Crown Motel (M), Colby, KS 71
Best Western Elk City Inn (M), Elk City, OK 237
Best Western Eureka Inn (M), Eureka Springs, AR 32
Best Western Fiesta Isles (M), South Padre Island, TX 387
Best Western Fort Scott Inn (M), Fort Scott, KS 73
Best Western Governor's Inn (M), Little Rock, AR 44
Best Western Grayson House (M), Sherman, TX 387
Best Western Great Southwest Inn (M), Arlington, TX 285
Best Western Greenspoint Plaza Inn (M), Houston, TX 344
Best Western Hallmark Inn (H), Wichita, KS 92
Best Western Hallmark Inn (M), Lawrence, KS 79; Ottawa, KS 86; Overland Park, KS 87
Best Western Hallmark Motor Inn (H), Arkansas City, KS 69
Best Western Hotel Acadiana (H), Lafayette, LA 123
Best Western Hotel Clemens (H), Hannibal, MO 178
Best Western Inn (H), Henderson, TX 338
Best Western Inn (M), Benton, AR 30; Russellville, AR 52; Abilene, KS 68; Kansas City, MO 78; Jefferson City, MO 182
Best Western Inn and Suites (M), Greenville, TX 338; Tyler, TX 391
Best Western Inn at Hensley's (M), Oklahoma City, OK 246
Best Western Inn at Scott & White (M), Temple, TX 389
Best Western Inn of Bourbon St (H), New Orleans, LA 131
Best Western Inn of Hope (M), Hope, AR 40
Best Western Inn of Jefferson (M), Jefferson, TX 355
Best Western Inn of Orange (M), Orange, TX 370
Best Western Inn of the Ozarks (M), Eureka Springs, AR 32
Best Western Inn of Van Horn (M), Van Horn, TX 393
Best Western J-Hawk Motel (M), Greensburg, KS 74
Best Western Kings Inn of Conway (M), Conway, AR 31
Best Western Kings Row Inn (M), Fort Smith, AR 37; Texarkana, AR 53
Best Western Kingsville Inn (M), Kingsville, TX 357
Best Western Kirkwood Inn (H), St Louis, MO 199

Best Western Lake Jackson Inn (M), Brazosport, TX 298

Best Western Landmark Hotel (H), Metairie, LA 126

Best Western Limetree Inn (M), Mena, AR 47

Best Western Market Center (M), Dallas, TX 311

Best Western Mark Motor Hotel (M), Weatherford, OK 260

Best Western Marshall (M), Marshall, TX 363

Best Western Mid-Continent Inn (M), Big Spring, TX 297

Best Western Motel (M), Iola, KS 77

Best Western Music Capital Inn (H), Branson, MO 167

Best Western Noah's Ark (H), St Charles, MO 197

Best Western Northpark Inn (M), Covington, LA 120

Best Western of Alexandria (H), Alexandria, LA 115

Best Western of Harrison (M), Harrison, AR 38

Best Western Old Main Lodge (M), Waco, TX 394

Best Western Palestine Inn (M), Palestine, TX 370

Best Western Pines (H), Pine Bluff, AR 50

Best Western Prairie Inn (H), Independence, KS 76

Best Western Preston Suites Hotel (M), Dallas, TX 311

Best Western Red Carpet Inn (M), Hereford, TX 339

Best Western Red Coach Inn (M), El Dorado, KS 72; Newton, KS 85

Best Western Saddleback Inn (M), Oklahoma City, OK 246

Best Western Sandpiper Inn (M), Lawton, OK 239

Best Western Sandy Shores Beach Hotel (H), Corpus Christi, TX 303

Best Western Santa Fe Inn (H), Oklahoma City, OK 244

Best Western Scenic Motor Inn (M), Batesville, AR 29

Best Western Shamrock Inn (M), Kirksville, MO 192

Best Western Southwinds (M), Gainesville, TX 333

Best Western Sunday House Inn (M), Fredericksburg, TX 332

Best Western Surf Motel (M), Marysville, KS 83

Best Western Territorial Inn (H), Guthrie, OK 238

Best Western Trade Winds Central Inn (M), Tulsa, OK 256

Best Western Trade Winds Inn (M), Muskogee, OK 242

Best Western Village Inn (M), Vernon, TX 393

Best Western West Branch Inn (M), Fort Worth, TX 328

Best Western Westport Park Hotel (H), Maryland Heights, MO 194

Best Western Wheat Lands Motor Inn (M), Garden City, KS 73

Best Western Will Rogers Motor Inn (M), Claremore, OK 235

Best Western Windsor Suites Hotel (H), Dallas, TX 306

Bethany Lutheran Church (A), Lindsborg, KS 82

Bianco's Italian Restaurant (R), Lawton, OK 240

Biblical Arts Center (A), Dallas, TX 320

Biga and Locust St Bakery (R), San Antonio, TX 379

Big Al's Smokehouse Barbeque (R), Dallas, TX 314

Big Bend National Park, TX 297

Big Cedar Lodge (RE), Branson, MO 170

Big John's Feed Lot (R), Big Spring, TX 298

Big Splash Family Water Park (A), Tulsa, OK 259

Big Spring State Park (A), Big Spring, TX 298

Big Texan Inn (M), Amarillo, TX 283

Big Texan Steak Ranch (R), Amarillo, TX 283

Big Thicket National Preserve (A), Beaumont, TX 296

Bingham's (R), Jefferson City, MO 182

Bingham-Waggoner Estate (A), Independence, MO 181

Black Angus Steak Ranch (R), Great Bend, KS 74

Black Beards (R), South Padre Island, TX 388

Black-Eyed Pea, The (R), Tyler, TX 391

Blaine Kern's Mardi Gras World (A), New Orleans, LA 146

Blind Lemon, The (R), Dallas, TX 314

Blue Belle Saloon & Restaurant (R), Guthrie, OK 238

Blue Bell Tours (A), Brenham, TX 299

Blueberry Hill (R), University City, MO 213

Bluebonnet Cafe (R), Temple, TX 389

Blue Corn Cafe (R), Tulsa, OK 257

Blue Ribbon Downs (A), Sallisaw, OK 252

Blue Star Arts Complex (A), San Antonio, TX 385

Blvd Cafe (R), Kansas City, MO 187

Bobby Vinton Blue Velvet Theatre (A), Branson, MO 171

Bob Kramer Marionnettes (A), St Louis, MO 206

Bobo's Mexican Restaurant (R), Stillwater, OK 253

Bodacious Bar-B-Q (R), Longview, TX 359

Bodean Seafood Restaurant (R), Tulsa, OK 257

Bofinger (R), Clayton, MO 175

Boiling Springs State Park (A), Woodward, OK 261

Bolin Wildlife Exhibit (A), McKinney, TX 365

Bombay Bicycle Club Restaurant & Bar (R), Wichita, KS 93

Bonham State Recreation Area (A), Bonham, TX 298

Bon Ton Cafe (R), New Orleans, LA 139

Booger Red's Restaurant & Saloon (R), Fort Worth, TX 329

Boone Tavern (R), Columbia, MO 177

Boot Hill Museum (A), Dodge City, KS 72

Border Crossing Restaurante Y Cantina (R), Norman, OK 243

Botanica, The Wichita Gardens (A), Wichita, KS 95

Botanic Gardens (A), Fort Worth, TX 332

Boudro's (R), San Antonio, TX 380

Bowen's (R), Arkadelphia, AR 29

Bozo's (R), Metairie, LA 126

Bradford Inn (I), Branson, MO 170

Branberry's (R), Baton Rouge, LA 117

Branding Iron (R), Liberal, KS 81

Brandt's Market & Cafe (R), University City, MO 213

Branson Cafe (R), Branson, MO 170

Branson Towers Hotel (H), Branson, MO 167

Brazoria National Wildlife Refuge (A), Brazosport, TX 299

Brazos Bend State Park (A), Needville, TX 367

Brazosport Museum of Natural Science (A), Brazosport, TX 299

Brazos Valley Museum of Natural History (A), Bryan, TX 301

Brennan's (R), New Orleans, LA 139; Houston, TX 346

Brigtsen's (R), New Orleans, LA 139

Bristol Suites Hotel (H), Dallas, TX 306

Brit Spaugh Park and Zoo (A), Great Bend, KS 74

Brittany (R), Lubbock, TX 361

Brooks Motel (M), Norton, KS 85

Broussard's (R), New Orleans, LA 139

Brownell Memorial Park and Carillon Tower (A), Morgan City, LA 128

Brown Mansion, The (A), Coffeyville, KS 70

Bruning's Seafood on the Lake (R), New Orleans, LA 139

Bruno's Little Italy (R), Little Rock, AR 45

Brunswick Hotel Restaurant (R), Lindsborg, KS 82

BT Bones (R), Branson, MO 170

Buckingham's Restaurant and Oasis (R), Branson, MO 170

Buckler's Deli and Pizza (R), Hermann, MO 180

Buddy Holly Statue and Walk of Fame (A), Lubbock, TX 362

Budgetel Inn (H), Baton Rouge, LA 116

Budgetel Inn (M), Fort Smith, AR 37; Kansas City, MO 186; Maryland Heights, MO 195

Budget Host (H), Garden City, KS 73

Budget Host (M), Slidell, LA 152; Columbia, MO 176; Fulton, MO 178

Budget Host Vagabond II (M), Salina, KS 88

Buffalo Lake National Wildlife Refuge (A), Amarillo, TX 284

Buffalo National River (A), Harrison, AR 39

Buffalo Roam Steak House (R), Mankato, KS 83

Bull Shoals State Park (A), Bull Shoals, AR 31

Busch Memorial Stadium (A), St Louis, MO 206

Busch's Grove (R), Ladue, MO 193

Butcher Shop, The (R), Dallas, TX 314

C

Cabildo (A), New Orleans, LA 147

Cace's Seafood (R), Tyler, TX 391

Cacharel (R), Arlington, TX 286

Caddo Lake State Park (A), Marshall, TX 363

Cadillac Bar (R), Houston, TX 346

Cafe Allegro (R), Kansas City, MO 187

Cafe Annie (R), Houston, TX 346

Cafe Chicago Sports Bar and Grill (R), Wichita, KS 94

Cafe de France (R), St Louis, MO 201

Cafe de Ville (R), Jefferson City, MO 182

Cafe du Monde (RS), New Orleans, LA 146

Cafe Express (R), Houston, TX 346

Cafe Lagniappe Too (R), New Iberia, LA 130

Cafe Madrid (R), Dallas, TX 314

Cafe Margaux (R), Lake Charles, LA 125

Cafe Maspero (R), New Orleans, LA 139

Cafe Napoli (R), Clayton, MO 175

Cafe on the Green, The (R), Houston, TX 346

Cafe Pacific (R), Dallas, TX 314

Cafe Pontalba (R), New Orleans, LA 139

Cafe Saint Moritz (R), Little Rock, AR 45

Cafe Sbisa (R), New Orleans, LA 139

Cafe Serranos (R), Austin, TX 291

Cafe Society (R), Dallas, TX 314

Cafe Vermilionville (R), Lafayette, LA 124

Cajun Tours of Terrebonne (A), Houma, LA 122

Cajun Tours Swamp Tour (A), Houma, LA 122

Caldwell Zoo (A), Tyler, TX 392

Caleco's (R), Maryland Heights, MO 195; St Louis, MO 201

Calico County (R), Lawton, OK 240; Amarillo, TX 283

Calico County Restaurant (R), Fort Smith, AR 38

Californian Restaurant and Oyster Bar, The (R), Nacogdoches, TX 367

Californos (R), Kansas City, MO 187

Calluaud's Bistro (R), Dallas, TX 314

Camelot Hotel (H), Little Rock, AR 44

Campbell House Museum (A), St Louis, MO 206

Canadian County Historical Museum (A), El Reno, OK 237

Candicci's (R), Clayton, MO 175

Cane Creek State Park (A), Pine Bluff, AR 51

Canton Cafe (R), Vernon, TX 393

Capitol Plaza Hotel (H), Jefferson City, MO 181

Cappy's (R), San Antonio, TX 380

Captain Benny's Seafood & Oyster Bar (R), Houston, TX 346

Cardwell's (R), Clayton, MO 175

Caribbean Room (R), New Orleans, LA 140

Carlyle Motel (M), Oklahoma City, OK 246

Carmelo's (R), Austin, TX 291

Carnegie Center for the Arts (A), Dodge City, KS 72

Carnegie's at the Plaza (R), Jefferson City, MO 182

Carolyn's Ozark Swiss Inn (M), Eureka Springs, AR 33

Carry Nation Home (A), Medicine Lodge, KS 84

Casa Bonita (R), Tulsa, OK 257

Casa Del Mar (M), Galveston, TX 334

Casa Gallardo (R), St Louis, MO 201

Casa Garcia (R), Metairie, LA 127

Casa Mañana (A), Fort Worth, TX 332

Casa Rio (R), San Antonio, TX 380

Cascade Caverns (A), Bandera, TX 295

Cascades Inn (H), Branson, MO 167

Casey's Seafood Cafe (R), Galveston, TX 335

Cassinelli 1700 (R), North Little Rock, AR 50

Castle Tea Room (R), Lawrence, KS 80

Catfish Cove (R), Fort Smith, AR 38

Cattle Company of Texas, The (R), Lufkin, TX 362

Cattleman's Steakhouse (R), Texarkana, AR 54; Tulsa, OK 257

Cattlemen's Cafe (R), Oklahoma City, OK 247

Cattlemen's Steak House (R), Fort Worth, TX 329

Caverns of Sonora (A), Sonora, TX 387

Cedar Crest–Residence of the Governor of Kansas (A), Topeka, KS 91

Cedar Street (R), Cape Girardeau, MO 173

Cedarvale Botanic Garden (A), Davis, OK 236

Celis Brewery (A), Austin, TX 294

Cenare (R), College Station, TX 303

Cerveceria—The Big Mex Cafe (R), Dallas, TX 314

Chamberlain's Prime Chop House (R), Dallas, TX 314

Chamizal National Memorial (A), El Paso, TX 326

Channel View Condominiums (RE), Port Aransas, TX 371

Chaplin Nature Center (A), Arkansas City, KS 69

Charley's 517 (R), Houston, TX 347

Charlie Newton's (R), Oklahoma City, OK 248

Chastains Bull Shoals Resort (RE), Bull Shoals, AR 31

Château Charles Hotel & Conference Center (M), Lake Charles, LA 125

Château Motor Hotel (H), New Orleans, LA 131

Château Sonesta Hotel (H), New Orleans, LA 131

Chatfeld (R), El Paso, TX 326

Chatillon-De Menil Mansion (A), St Louis, MO 206

Chelsea Bar and Grill (R), Wichita, KS 94

Cherokee Heritage Center (A), Tahlequah, OK 254

Cherokee Strip Museum (A), Alva, OK 232; Perry, OK 251

Cheshire Inn and Lodge (L), Richmond Heights, MO 196

Chez Ardid (R), San Antonio, TX 380

Chez Gérard (R), Dallas, TX 315

Chez Suzette (R), Lubbock, TX 361

Chickasaw National Recreation Area (A), Davis, OK 236

Children's Museum of Houston, The (A), Houston, TX 351

Children's Museum of Kansas City (A), Kansas City, MO 196

Childress County Heritage Museum (A), Childress, TX 302

Chili's Grill & Bar (R), San Antonio, TX 380

China Town (R), Conway, AR 32

Chinatown (R), Austin, TX 291

Chinatown Cafe (R), San Antonio, TX 380

Chinatown Restaurant (R), Oklahoma City, OK 248

Choke Canyon State Park (A), Three Rivers, TX 390

Chretien Point Plantation (A), Lafayette, LA 125

Christian's (R), New Orleans, LA 140

Chubby's Bar-B-Q (R), Junction City, KS 77

Chula Vista (R), Beaumont, TX 296

Churrascos (R), Houston, TX 347

City Grill (R), Austin, TX 291

City Java (R), Dallas, TX 315

City of Austin Nature Preserves (A), Austin, TX 293

City Park (A), New Orleans, LA 149

City Park Cafe (R), Fort Worth, TX 329

CJ's Restaurant (R), Tulsa, OK 258

Claremore Motor Inn (M), Claremore, OK 235

Clarion Hotel & Conference Center (H), Oklahoma City, OK 244

Clarion Hotel Dallas (H), Dallas, TX 306

Clarion Inn (M), Fayetteville, AR 36

Clarion Regal Riverfront Hotel (H), St Louis, MO 199

Clarion Suites (M), San Antonio, TX 378

Clark's Outpost Restaurant & Club (R), Denton, TX 323

Clary's (R), Galveston, TX 335

Classic Motor Inn (M), Dallas, TX 312

Clinton's (RS), Independence, MO 181

Clinton State Park (A), Lawrence, KS 80

Clubhouse Inn (H), Wichita, KS 92

Coffee Pot Restaurant, The (R), New Orleans, LA 140

College St Grill (R), San Antonio, TX 380

Colonial Mansion Inn (M), Eureka Springs, AR 33

Colonial Steakhouse (R), Oakley, KS 85

Combat Air Museum (A), Topeka, KS 91

Comfort Inn (H), Russellville, AR 52; Searcy, AR 52; Springdale, AR 53; Atchison, KS 69; Hays, KS 75; Wichita, KS 92; Baton Rouge, LA 116; Lafayette, LA 123

Comfort Inn (M), Conway, AR 31; El Dorado, AR 32; Eureka Springs, AR 33; Hutchinson, KS 76; Ruston, LA 150; Columbia, MO 176; Nevada, MO 195; Clinton, OK 236; McAlester, OK 240; Oklahoma City, OK 246; Tulsa, OK 256; Arlington, TX 285; Dallas, TX 312; Fredericksburg, TX 332; Longview, TX 359; McKinney, TX 365; Ozona, TX 370; Texarkana, TX 390

Comfort Inn Airport (M), San Antonio, TX 378

Comfort Inn of Blytheville (M), Blytheville, AR 30

Comfort Suites (H), Wichita, KS 92

Commander's Palace (R), New Orleans, LA 140

Commodore on the Beach, The (M), Galveston, TX 334

Confederate Air Force and American Airpower Heritage Museum (A), Midland, TX 366

Confederate Museum (A), New Orleans, LA 146

Contemporary Arts Center (A), New Orleans, LA 146

Contemporary Arts Museum (A), Houston, TX 351

Continental Inn (M), Nacogdoches, TX 367

Copeland's (R), New Orleans, LA 140

Copperfield's (R), Amarillo, TX 283

Corpus Christi Marriott Bayfront (H), Corpus Christi, TX 303

Corral, The (M), Victoria, TX 393

Cossatot River State Park (A), Mena, AR 47

Country Club Plaza (A), Kansas City, MO 191

Country Inn (H), Austin, TX 288

Country Inn (H), Lubbock, TX 360

Country Kitchen (R), Junction City, KS 78; Springfield, MO 211; Arlington, TX 286

County Line Barbecue (R), Houston, TX 347

Courthouse Exchange, The (R), Independence, MO 180

Court of Two Sisters (R), New Orleans, LA 140

Courtyard by Marriott (H), Little Rock, AR 44; Overland Park, KS 86; Kansas City, MO 183; St Louis, MO 199; Oklahoma City, OK 245; San Antonio, TX 374

Courtyard by Marriott (M), Baton Rouge, LA 117; Fort Worth, TX 328

Courtyard by Marriott–LBJ at Josey (H), Dallas, TX 306

Cowboy Artists of America Museum (A), Kerrville, TX 356

Cowboy Cafe (R), Branson, MO 170

Coy's (R), Hot Springs National Park, AR 42

Coy's Place (R), Fayetteville, AR 36

Crater of Diamonds State Park (A), Arkadelphia, AR 29

Crazy Cajun Seafood Restaurant (R), Port Aransas, TX 372

Crazy Johnnie's Steak House (R), Metairie, LA 127

Creek Council House Museum (A), Okmulgee, OK 250

Crescent City Brewhouse (R), New Orleans, LA 140

Crescent Court Hotel, The (H), Dallas, TX 306

Cristy Lane Theatre (A), Branson, MO 172

Crossroads Motel (M), Iola, KS 77

Crowley's Ridge State Park (A), Jonesboro, AR 43

Crown Center (A), Kansas City, MO 191

Crowne Plaza, The (H), Branson, MO 168

Crowne Plaza (H), Kansas City, MO 184

Crown Sterling Suites (H), Baton Rouge, LA 116

Crozier's Restaurant Francais (R), Metairie, LA 127

Crumpet's (R), San Antonio, TX 380

Crumpet Tea Room (R), Rogers, AR 51

Crystal Cave (A), Springfield, MO 212

Cuckoo's Nest Restaurant (R), Granbury, TX 337

Culpeppers (R), St Louis, MO 201

Cupples House (A), St Louis, MO 205

Custer House (A), Junction City, KS 78

Cytec Louisiana Wildlife and Fisheries Museum (A), Kenner, LA 123

D

Daisy Mae's Cafe (R), Arkansas City, KS 69

Daisy State Park (A), Arkadelphia, AR 29

Dajonel's (R), Baton Rouge, LA 117

Dakota's (R), Dallas, TX 315

Dallas Arboretum (A), Dallas, TX 319

Dallas/Fort Worth Airport Marriott (H), Dallas–Fort Worth Int'l Airport, TX 320

Dallas Grand Hotel, The (H), Dallas, TX 307

Dallas Marriott Quorum (H), Dallas, TX 307

Dallas Museum of Art (A), Dallas, TX 319

Dallas Museum of Natural History (A), Dallas, TX 319

Dallas Palm Restaurant (R), Dallas, TX 315

Dallas Radisson Park Central Hotel (H), Dallas, TX 307

Dallas Theater Center (A), Dallas, TX 320

Dallas World Aquarium (A), Dallas, TX 319

Dalton Defenders Museum (A), Coffeyville, KS 70

Dalton Gang Hideout (A), Liberal, KS 81

Damian's Cucina Italiana (R), Houston, TX 347

Dan-D-Motel (M), Perry, OK 251

Danny's Restaurant (R), Hiawatha, KS 75

Das Stein Haus (R), Jefferson City, MO 182

Dauphine Orleans Hotel (H), New Orleans, LA 131

Dave's Cajun Kitchen (R), Houma, LA 121

David's Upstairs (R), Beaumont, TX 296

Davis Mountains State Park (A), Alpine, TX 282

Days Inn (H), Rogers, AR 51; Kirksville, MO 192; Ponca City, OK 251

Days Inn (M), Benton, AR 30; Blytheville, AR 30; Fayetteville, AR 36; Hope, AR 40; Newport, AR 49; Hays, KS 75; Manhattan, KS 83; Bossier City, LA 119; Hammond, LA 121; Jennings, LA 122; Monroe, LA 128; Ruston, LA 150; Shreveport, LA 151; Columbia, MO 176; St Louis–Lambert Int'l Airport, MO 208; Waynesville, MO 213; El Reno, OK 237; Muskogee, OK 242; Pauls Valley, OK 251; Stillwater, OK 253; Tulsa, OK 256; Weatherford, OK 260; Brownsville, TX 299; Fort Worth, TX 328; Tyler, TX 391; Victoria, TX 393

Days Inn Airport (M), Wichita Falls, TX 396

Days Inn Country Inn (M), Wichita, KS 93

Days Inn El Paso (M), El Paso, TX 325

Days Inn Galleria (M), Houston, TX 344

Days Inn Lawrence (M), Lawrence, KS 80

Days Inn Newton (M), Newton, KS 85

Days Inn North (M), Kansas City, MO 186

Days Inn Northeast (M), San Antonio, TX 378

Days Inn Northwest (M), Oklahoma City, OK 246

Days Inn of Ardmore (M), Ardmore, OK 233

Days Inn San Marcos (M), San Marcos, TX 386

Days Inn South (M), Little Rock, AR 44

Days Inn Texas Stadium (M), Dallas, TX 312

Days Inn Tudor Wichita (M), Wichita, KS 93

Days Inn Wayside (M), Houston, TX 344

Daystop (M), Ozona, TX 370

Deaf Smith County Historical Museum (A), Hereford, TX 339

DeGray Lake Resort State Park (A), Arkadelphia, AR 29

Delmonico Restaurant (R), New Orleans, LA 140

Dental Health Theatre (A), St Louis, MO 206

Denton County Historical Museum (A), Denton, TX 324

Denton Inn, The (M), Denton, TX 323

Denver Grill (R), Tulsa, OK 258

Depot, The (R), Lubbock, TX 361

Destrehan Manor (A), Kenner, LA 123

DeVille (R), Houston, TX 347

Devil's Den State Park (A), Fayetteville, AR 37

Devil's Pool (R), Branson, MO 171

Devil's River Inn (M), Sonora, TX 387

Devitos (R), Eureka Springs, AR 35

DFW Hilton Executive Conference Center (H), Dallas–Fort Worth Int'l Airport, TX 320

Diamond Motel (M), Abilene, KS 68

Dickerson Park Zoo (A), Springfield, MO 212

Dick's Last Resort (R), Dallas, TX 315
Dierdorf & Hart's (R), St Louis, MO 201
Dillon Nature Center (A), Hutchinson, KS 76
Dipiazza's (R), New Orleans, LA 140
Discoveryland! (A), Tulsa, OK 259
Dixie Dude Ranch (RE), Bandera, TX 295
Dodge City, Ford & Bucklin Railroad Company (A), Dodge City, KS 72
Dog Museum, The (A), St Louis, MO 205
Dogwood Inn (M), Eureka Springs, AR 33
Dogwood Lodge (L), Bull Shoals, AR 31
Dogwood Motel (M), Mountain View, AR 49
Dominic's (R), St Louis, MO 201
Dong Ting (R), Houston, TX 347
Don Harrington Discovery Center (A), Amarillo, TX 284
Don's Seafood (R), Lafayette, LA 124
Don's Seafood & Steak House (R), Hammond, LA 121; Shreveport, LA 151
Dooky Chase (R), New Orleans, LA 141
Dorothy's House (A), Liberal, KS 81
DoubleTree Club Hotel (H), Maryland Heights, MO 194
DoubleTree Club Hotel Casa De Palmas (H), McAllen, TX 363
DoubleTree Guest Suites (H), Dallas–Fort Worth Int'l Airport, TX 321
DoubleTree Guest Suites Houston (H), Houston, TX 339
DoubleTree Hotel at Campbell Centre (H), Dallas, TX 307
DoubleTree Hotel at Lincoln Centre (H), Dallas, TX 307
DoubleTree Hotel at Warren Place (H), Tulsa, OK 255
DoubleTree Hotel Austin (H), Austin, TX 288
DoubleTree Houston at Allen Center (H), Houston, TX 340
DoubleTree Kansas City Airport (H), Kansas City, MO 184
DoubleTree Mayfair Suites (H), St Louis, MO 199
Douglas MacArthur Academy of Freedom (A), Brownwood, TX 301
Downtown Houston Tunnel System (A), Houston, TX 352
Driftwood Motel (M), Port Aransas, TX 371
Driskill Hotel (H), Austin, TX 288
Drury Inn (H), Maryland Heights, MO 194
Drury Inn (M), Columbia, MO 177; Poplar Bluff, MO 196
Drury Inn Gateway Arch (H), St Louis, MO 199
Drury Inn Houston Galleria (H), Houston, TX 340
Drury Inn Sikeston (M), Sikeston, MO 209
Drury Pennel House (R), Atchison, KS 69
Drusilla's (R), Baton Rouge, LA 117
Duff's (R), St Louis, MO 201
Dun Bar East (R), San Angelo, TX 374
Dyche Museum of Natural History (A), Lawrence, KS 80

Dyess Linear Air Park (A), Abilene, TX 281

E

Eagle's Nest (R), Oklahoma City, OK 248
Earl Abel's (R), San Antonio, TX 380
East Mountain Lodge (M), Eureka Springs, AR 33
Econo Lodge (H), Junction City, KS 77; Ottawa, KS 86; Shawnee, OK 252
Econo Lodge (M), Benton, AR 30; Hot Springs National Park, AR 41; Slidell, LA 152; Carthage, MO 173; Hannibal, MO 178; Rolla, MO 196; Springfield, MO 211; St Charles, MO 197; Beaumont, TX 296; Huntsville, TX 353; Temple, TX 389
Econo Lodge Airport (M), Tulsa, OK 256
Econo Lodge Bandera (M), Bandera, TX 295
Econo Lodge Chateau Inn (M), Childress, TX 302
Econo Lodge of Amarillo (M), Amarillo, TX 283
Eddy's Steak House (R), Oklahoma City, OK 248
Edelweiss (R), Fort Worth, TX 329; San Antonio, TX 380
Edison Plaza Museum (A), Beaumont, TX 297
Edwardian Inn (I), Helena, AR 40
1850 House (A), New Orleans, LA 147
1859 Ashton Villa (A), Galveston, TX 336
1859 Jail, Marshal's Home and Museum (A), Independence, MO 181
1876 Inn (M), Eureka Springs, AR 34
Eisenhower Presidential Library (A), Abilene, TX 68
El Conquistador (R), Waco, TX 395
Eldridge Hotel (H), Lawrence, KS 79
Elisabet Ney Museum (A), Austin, TX 292
Elite Cafe (R), Waco, TX 395
Eliza Cruce Hall Doll Museum (A), Ardmore, OK 234
El Mirador (R), San Antonio, TX 380
Elmo's City Diner and Oyster Bar (R), Corpus Christi, TX 304
Elmo's Staple St Seafood Grille & Oyster Bar (R), Corpus Christi, TX 304
El Paso Airport Hilton (H), El Paso, TX 324
El Paso Marriott (H), El Paso, TX 324
El Paso Museum of Art (A), El Paso, TX 326
El Paso Zoo (A), El Paso, TX 327
El Patio Motor Inn (M), San Angelo, TX 373
Embassy Suites (H), St Louis, MO 199; Oklahoma City, OK 245; Corpus Christi, TX 303; El Paso, TX 324
Embassy Suites Airport North (H), Austin, TX 288
Embassy Suites Dallas Market Center (H), Dallas, TX 307
Embassy Suites Hotel (H), Overland Park, KS 86; Tulsa, OK 255; Dallas, TX 308; McAllen, TX 363
Embassy Suites Northwest (H), San Antonio, TX 374

Embassy Suites Plaza Hotel (H), Kansas City, MO 184
Emeril's (R), New Orleans, LA 141
Emma Long Metropolitan Park (A), Austin, TX 292
Emporia Zoo (A), Emporia, KS 72
Emy-Lou Biedenharn Foundation (A), Monroe, LA 128
Enchanted Rock State Natural Park (A), Fredericksburg, TX 333
Enigma (R), Dallas, TX 315
Enola Prudhomme's Cajun Cafe (R), Lafayette, LA 124
Enterprise Square, USA (A), Oklahoma City, OK 250
Ernst's Cafe (R), New Orleans, LA 141
Eskimo Joe's (R), Stillwater, OK 254
Esther's Seafood and Oyster Bar (R), Port Arthur, TX 372
Eugene Field House and Toy Museum (A), St Louis, MO 206
Eureka Matterhorn Towers (M), Eureka Springs, AR 33
Eureka Springs and North Arkansas Railway (A), Eureka Springs, AR 35
Eureka Springs Gardens (A), Eureka Springs, AR 36
Everett's (R), Columbia, MO 177
Excelsior House, The (H), Jefferson, TX 355
Executive Guesthouse Hotel (H), San Antonio, TX 375
Executive Inn (M), Springdale, AR 53
Expressway Inn (M), Branson, MO 169
E-Z's Restaurant (R), San Antonio, TX 381

F

Fairfield Inn (M), Overland Park, KS 87
Fairfield Lake State Park (A), Palestine, TX 370
Fairmont (H), Dallas, TX 308
Fairmont Hotel (H), New Orleans, LA 131
Fairmount Hotel (H), San Antonio, TX 375
Fairway Resort (RE), McAllen, TX 364
Fall Creek Vineyards (A), Austin, TX 294
Faraday's (R), St Louis–Lambert Int'l Airport, MO 208
Farmers Produce Market (A), Dallas, TX 320
Fatted Calf, The (R), Clayton, MO 175
Faust's (R), St Louis, MO 202
Favazza's (R), St Louis, MO 202
Fayetteville Hilton (H), Fayetteville, AR 36
Fedora Cafe and Bar (R), Kansas City, MO 188
Felix's (R), New Orleans, LA 141
Fellow-Reeve Museum of History and Science (A), Wichita, KS 94
Fenster Museum of Jewish Art, The (A), Tulsa, OK 259
Fiesta Texas (A), San Antonio, TX 385
Fifth Season (H), Fort Smith, AR 37
Fifth Season Hotel (H), Oklahoma City, OK 245
Figlio (R), Kansas City, MO 188

Finnup Park/Lee Richardson Zoo (A), Garden City, KS 73
First National Black Historical Museum (A), Wichita, KS 94
Fish & Filet (R), McAlester, OK 241
Fish Net Family Restaurant (R), Arkadelphia, AR 29
Five Civilized Tribes Museum, The (A), Muskogee, OK 242
Flagship Hotel Over the Water (H), Galveston, TX 333
Fog City Diner (R), Dallas, TX 315
Fonda San Miguel (R), Austin, TX 291
Foothills Grill (R), Austin, TX 291
Fort Concho National Historic Landmark (A), San Angelo, TX 374
Fort Croghan Museum (A), Burnet, TX 302
Fort Davis National Historic Site (A), Alpine, TX 282
Fort Hays State Historic Site (A), Hays, KS 75
Fort Inglish Museum and Park (A), Bonham, TX 298
Fort Jesup State Commemorative Area (A), Many, LA 126
Fort Larned National Historic Site (A), Larned, KS 79
Fort Phantom Hill Ruins (A), Abilene, TX 281
Fort Reno (A), El Reno, OK 237
Fort Scott National Historic Site (A), Fort Scott, KS 73
Fort Smith National Cemetery (A), Fort Smith, AR 38
Fort Smith National Historic Site (A), Fort Smith, AR 38
Fort Smith Trolley Museum (A), Fort Smith, AR 38
Fort Worth Museum of Science and History (A), Fort Worth, TX 331
45th Infantry Division Museum, The (A), Oklahoma City, OK 249
Fossil Station Museum (A), Russell, KS 88
Four Points Hotel Texarkana (H), Texarkana, TX 390
Four Seasons Hotel Austin (H), Austin, TX 288
Four Seasons Hotel Houston Center (H), Houston, TX 340
Four Seasons Resort and Club Dallas (RE), Irving, TX 354
Fourth Street Grill (R), St Louis, MO 202
Frank Phillips Home Site (A), Bartlesville, OK 234
Frank's Cafe (R), Dayton, TX 322
Frank's Country Inn (R), Tulsa, OK 258
Fred's Fish House (R), Mountain Home, AR 48
Freideim's Bavarian Inn (R), Fredericksburg, TX 332
French Legation Museum (A), Austin, TX 293
Frenchmen, The (I), New Orleans, LA 137
French Quarter Courtyard (H), New Orleans, LA 131
French Quarter Walking Tours (A), New Orleans, LA 149

French Room, The (R), Dallas, TX 315
Frontier Army Museum (A), Leavenworth, KS 81
Frontier City (A), Hays, KS 75
Frontier City Theme Park (A), Oklahoma City, OK 250
Frontier Times Museum (A), Bandera, TX 295
Front Page Cafe, The (R), Jonesboro, AR 43
Fulton Mansion State Historical Park (A), Corpus Christi, TX 305

G

Gables Room (R), Clayton, MO 175
Gabrielle (R), New Orleans, LA 141
Gabriel's Cafe (R), El Paso, TX 326
Gage Park (A), Topeka, KS 91
Gaido's of Galveston (R), Galveston, TX 335
Galatoire's (R), New Orleans, LA 141
Galleria Inn (M), Houston, TX 344
Gallier House Museum (A), New Orleans, LA 147
Galveston County Historical Museum (A), Galveston, TX 335
Galveston Island State Park (A), Galveston, TX 336
G&E Courtyard Grill (R), New Orleans, LA 141
Gardiner Art Gallery (A), Stillwater, OK 254
Gardner Mansion and Museum (A), Broken Bow, OK 235
Gardski's Restaurant (R), Lubbock, TX 361
Garfield's Restaurant and Pub (R), Bartlesville, OK 234
Garner State Park (A), Uvalde, TX 392
Garozzo's (R), Kansas City, MO 188
Gates & Sons Bar-B-Q (R), Kansas City, MO 188
Gates BBQ (R), Kansas City, KS 78
Gateway Arch, Jefferson National Expansion Memorial (A), St Louis, MO 204
Gateway Inn Motel, The (M), Lubbock, TX 360
Gator Swamp Tours (A), Slidell, LA 152
Gautreau's (R), New Orleans, LA 141
Gazebo Inn (R), Branson, MO 168
Gen TP Stafford Museum (A), Weatherford, OK 260
George Ranch Historical Park (A), Houston, TX 352
George's (R), Waco, TX 395
George Washington Carver Museum (A), Austin, TX 292
German Haus Motel and B&B (M), Hermann, MO 179
Giacomo's Italian Cuisine (R), McAlester, OK 241
Gian-Peppe's (R), St Louis, MO 202
Giddings-Wilkin House (A), Brenham, TX 299
Gilcrease Museum (A), Tulsa, OK 259
Giorgio's (R), Manhattan, KS 83
Giorgio's Italian Restaurant (R), Salina, KS 89
Giovanni's (R), St Louis, MO 202

Gladys City—Spindletop Boomtown (A), Beaumont, TX 297
Gladys Porter Zoo (A), Brownsville, TX 300
Glen Campbell Goodtime Theatre (A), Branson, MO 171
Glenn's Cafe (R), Columbia, MO 177
Global Wildlife Center (A), Covington, LA 120
Gloria's (R), Dallas, TX 315
Golden Ox (R), Kansas City, MO 188
Goliad State Historical Park (A), Goliad, TX 337
Goode Company Texas Barbecue (R), Houston, TX 347
Goodland Super 8 (M), Goodland, KS 74
Goodman Museum (A), Tyler, TX 392
Goodnow House State Historic Site (A), Manhattan, KS 83
Good Shepherd Inn (M), Branson, MO 169
Goose Island State Park (A), Corpus Christi, TX 305
Governor's Club, The (R), Oklahoma City, OK 248
Governor's Mansion, The (A), Austin, TX 293
Graffiti's (R), Little Rock, AR 45
Grand Kempinski Dallas, The (H), Dallas, TX 308
Grand 1894 Opera House, The (A), Galveston, TX 336
Grand Palace, The (A), Branson, MO 171
Grant Motor Inn, The (M), Houston, TX 344
Grant's Farm (A), St Louis, MO 206
Grayson County Frontier Village (A), Denison, TX 323
Great Caruso, The (R), Houston, TX 347
Greater Baton Rouge Zoo (A), Baton Rouge, LA 119
Great Passion Play, The (A), Eureka Springs, AR 35
Great Storm, The (A), Galveston, TX 335
Green Acres Restaurant & Lounge (R), Abilene, KS 68
Green Beanery (R), Beaumont, TX 296
Greenery Family Restaurant (R), Iola, KS 77
Green Mesquite Barbecue (R), Austin, TX 291
Green Oaks Inn & Conference Center (H), Fort Worth, TX 327
Gregg County Historical Museum (A), Longview, TX 360
Grenoble House (I), New Orleans, LA 137
Grey Moss Inn, The (R), San Antonio, TX 381
Griggs (R), El Paso, TX 326
Grill, The (R), Kansas City, MO 188
Grill and Bar, The (R), Houston, TX 347
Grill Room, The (R), New Orleans, LA 141
Grill Room at the Pantry (R), South Padre Island, TX 388
Grinter House Museum (A), Kansas City, KS 79
Grone Cafeteria (R), St Louis–Lambert Int'l Airport, MO 208

Guesthouse Inn (H), Little Rock, AR 44
Guest Inn (M), Ardmore, OK 233; Norman, OK 243
Guest Quarters Suite Hotel (H), Austin, TX 288
Gumbo Shop (R), New Orleans, LA 142
Gunther's Edelweiss (R), El Paso, TX 326
Gunther's Restaurant (R), Austin, TX 291

H

Hacienda Hernandez (R), Wichita Falls, TX 396
Haden House (R), Columbia, MO 177
Hagerman National Wildlife Refuge (A), Sherman, TX 387
Hallmark Motor Inn (M), Killeen, TX 357
Hamilton House (R), Hot Springs National Park, AR 42
Hamilton Inn Resort (M), Hot Springs National Park, AR 41
Hammett House (R), Claremore, OK 235
Hampson Museum State Park (A), Blytheville, AR 31
Hampton Inn (H), Overland Park, KS 86; St Charles, MO 197; St Louis, MO 200
Hampton Inn (M), North Little Rock, AR 50; Searcy, AR 52; Hays, KS 75; Sikeston, MO 209; Arlington, TX 286
Hampton Inn Airport (H), Kansas City, MO 184
Hampton Inn Austin North (H), Austin, TX 289
Hampton Inn College (H), Baton Rouge, LA 116
Hampton Inn I-40 Airport (H), Oklahoma City, OK 245
Hampton Inn Little Rock I-30 (M), Little Rock, AR 44
Hampton Inn Midland (M), Midland, TX 365
Hampton Inn Westport (H), Maryland Heights, MO 194
Happy Hollow Motel (M), Hot Springs National Park, AR 41
Hard Rock Cafe (R), Houston, TX 348
Harn Homestead and 1889er Museum (A), Oklahoma City, OK 249
Harrigan's (R), Lubbock, TX 361
Harrington House (A), Amarillo, TX 285
Harrison County Historical Society Museum (A), Marshall, TX 363
Harrison House Inn (I), Guthrie, OK 238
Harry Ransom Humanities Research Center (A), Austin, TX 294
Harry's Bar & Grill (R), Midland, TX 365
Harry S Truman Birthplace State Historic Site (A), Nevada, MO 195
Harry S Truman Library and Museum (A), Independence, MO 181
Harry S Truman National Historic Site (A), Independence, MO 181
Harry S Truman Sports Complex (A), Kansas City, MO 192
Hartland Coach House Inn, The (M), Eureka Springs, AR 33
Hartland Victorian Village Inn (M), Eureka Springs, AR 33
Harvest Inn (M), Junction City, KS 77

Harvey Hotel (H), Wichita, KS 92
Harvey Hotel Addison (H), Dallas, TX 308
Harvey Hotel DFW Airport, The (H), Dallas–Fort Worth Int'l Airport, TX 321
Harvey Hotel Downtown Dallas, The (H), Dallas, TX 308
Harvey Suites Houston Medical Center (H), Houston, TX 340
Harwelden Mansion (A), Tulsa, OK 259
Hawthorn Suites Hotel (H), San Antonio, TX 375
Hawthorn Suites Hotel (M), Dallas, TX 312
Heartland Park Topeka (A), Topeka, KS 91
Heartstone Inn & Cottages (I), Eureka Springs, AR 34
Heaven on Earth Plaza Hotel (H), Houston, TX 340
Hemingway's Blue Water Cafe (R), Springfield, MO 211
Henry VIII Hotel (H), St Louis–Lambert Int'l Airport, MO 207
Hereford House (R), Kansas City, MO 188
Heritage House (I), Topeka, KS 90
Heritage House (R), Topeka, KS 90
Heritage Inn (M), Duncan, OK 236
Heritage Museum (A), Big Spring, TX 298
Hertzberg Circus Collection and Museum (A), San Antonio, TX 384
High Plains Pioneer Museum (A), Goodland, KS 74
Hill Country Motor Inn (M), New Braunfels, TX 368
Hill Country State Natural Area (A), Bandera, TX 295
Hillcrest Inn (H), Kerrville, TX 356
Hill Top Cafe (R), Fredericksburg, TX 332
Hilltop Motel (M), Galveston, TX 334
Hilton Hotel Daniele (H), Clayton, MO 174
Hilton Inn Northwest (H), Oklahoma City, OK 245
Hilton Palacio del Rio (H), San Antonio, TX 375
Historic Brownsville Museum (A), Brownsville, TX 300
Historic French Market Inn, The (H), New Orleans, LA 132
Historic New Orleans Collection, The (A), New Orleans, LA 146
Historic Suites (H), Kansas City, MO 184
Historic Trolley Tours (A), Fort Scott, KS 73
Historic Ward-Meade Park (A), Topeka, KS 91
Hobbit Hole Cafe, The (R), Houston, TX 348
Hodges Gardens (A), Many, LA 126
Hofbrau, The (R), Houston, TX 348
Hofstetter's (R), Dallas, TX 316
HoJo Inn (H), Elk City, OK 237; Kingsville, TX 357
HoJo Inn (M), Henryetta, OK 239; Fort Worth, TX 328

HoJo Inn by Howard Johnson (H), Burnet, TX 301
Holiday Inn (H), Arkadelphia, AR 28; Blytheville, AR 30; North Little Rock, AR 49; Russellville, AR 52; Texarkana, AR 53; Goodland, KS 73; Lawrence, KS 79; Covington, LA 120; Lake Charles, LA 125; Cape Girardeau, MO 173; Clayton, MO 174; Columbia, MO 176; Hannibal, MO 178; Joplin, MO 183; St Joseph, MO 197; Wentzville, MO 214; Bartlesville, OK 234; Elk City, OK 237; McAlester, OK 240; Norman, OK 242; Amarillo, TX 283; Houston, TX 340; Midland, TX 365; Nacogdoches, TX 366; Pecos, TX 371; Victoria, TX 393
Holiday Inn (M), Conway, AR 32; Harrison, AR 39; Hope, AR 40; Mountain Home, AR 48; Great Bend, KS 74; Alexandria, LA 115; Jennings, LA 122; Ruston, LA 150; Lake Ozark, MO 193; Poplar Bluff, MO 196; Ardmore, OK 233; Enid, OK 238; Lawton, OK 239; Shawnee, OK 253; Stillwater, OK 253; Denton, TX 323; McKinney, TX 365; Mount Pleasant, TX 366; Stephenville, TX 389; Wichita Falls, TX 396
Holiday Inn Airport (H), Corpus Christi, TX 303; El Paso, TX 325
Holiday Inn Airport (M), Little Rock, AR 44
Holiday Inn Airport Holidome (H), Kenner, LA 122
Holiday Inn Airport Oakland Park (H), St Louis–Lambert Int'l Airport, MO 207
Holiday Inn Airport West (H), St Louis–Lambert Int'l Airport, MO 207
Holiday Inn Aristocrat (H), Dallas, TX 308
Holiday Inn Astrodome (H), Houston, TX 340
Holiday Inn Austin Airport (H), Austin, TX 289
Holiday Inn Beach Resort (RE), South Padre Island, TX 388
Holiday Inn Central Holidome (H), Lafayette, LA 123
Holiday Inn Château Lemoyne (H), New Orleans, LA 132
Holiday Inn City Centre (H), Topeka, KS 89
Holiday Inn Civic Center (H), Laredo, TX 358; Lubbock, TX 360; McAllen, TX 363
Holiday Inn Convention Center (H), San Angelo, TX 373
Holiday Inn Corpus Christi Gulf Beach (RE), Corpus Christi, TX 304
Holiday Inn Crowne Plaza (H), New Orleans, LA 132
Holiday Inn DFW Airport South (H), Dallas–Fort Worth Int'l Airport, TX 321
Holiday Inn Downtown Riverfront (H), Shreveport, LA 151; St Louis, MO 200

Holiday Inn Downtown Superdome (H), New Orleans, LA 132

Holiday Inn Executive Center (H), Columbia, MO 176

Holiday Inn Express (H), Fayetteville, AR 36; Overland Park, KS 86; Kansas City, MO 184

Holiday Inn Express (M), Eureka Springs, AR 33; Heber Springs, AR 39; Little Rock, AR 44; Pittsburg, KS 87; West Monroe, LA 152; Tulsa, OK 256; Dallas, TX 312; Jasper, TX 354

Holiday Inn Express Sea World (H), San Antonio, TX 375

Holiday Inn Express Sikeston (M), Sikeston, MO 209

Holiday Inn Fort Smith Civic Center (M), Fort Smith, AR 37

Holiday Inn/Holidome (H), Emporia, KS 72; Manhattan, KS 82

Holiday Inn (Holidome Tulsa Central) (H), Tulsa, OK 255

Holiday Inn I-10 (H), Metairie, LA 126

Holiday Inn Longview (M), Longview, TX 359

Holiday Inn Medical Center (H), Houston, TX 341

Holiday Inn New Iberia/Avery Island (M), New Iberia, LA 129

Holiday Inn North (H), Dallas, TX 308

Holiday Inn North (M), Oklahoma City, OK 246

Holiday Inn North I-44 (M), Springfield, MO 211

Holiday Inn Northwest (M), Oklahoma City, OK 247

Holiday Inn Northwest Arkansas (H), Springdale, AR 53

Holiday Inn on the Beach (H), Galveston, TX 333

Holiday Inn Paris (M), Paris, TX 370

Holiday Inn Park Place (H), El Paso, TX 325

Holiday Inn Pine Bluff Convention Center (H), Pine Bluff, AR 50

Holiday Inn Ponca City (M), Ponca City, OK 251

Holiday Inn Rio Grande (H), Laredo, TX 359

Holiday Inn South (H), Baton Rouge, LA 116

Holiday Inn Topeka West (H), Topeka, KS 89

Holiday Inn Tyler (M), Tyler, TX 391

Holiday Inn University Plaza (H), Springfield, MO 210

Holiday Inn Waco (H), Waco, TX 394

Holiday Inn Wichita Airport (H), Wichita, KS 92

Holiday Park (M), Chanute, KS 70

Homestead, The (R), Denton, TX 323

Home Suite Home (H), Branson, MO 168

Honey Island Swamp Tours (A), Slidell, LA 152

Honeysuckle Inn (M), Branson, MO 169

Honfleur Restaurant (R), New Orleans, LA 142

Horny Toad Saloon and Restaurant, The (R), Oklahoma City, OK 248

Hotel de la Poste (H), New Orleans, LA 132

Hotel de Ville (H), Jefferson City, MO 182

Hotel Galvez (H), Galveston, TX 333

Hotel Inter-Continental (H), New Orleans, LA 132

Hotel Maison de Ville (H), New Orleans, LA 132

Hotel Phillips (H), Bartlesville, OK 234

Hotel Provincial (H), New Orleans, LA 133

Hotel Ste Helene (H), New Orleans, LA 133

Hotel St Germain (I), Dallas, TX 313

Hotel St Marie (H), New Orleans, LA 133

Hotel St Pierre (H), New Orleans, LA 133

Hotel Savoy (H), Kansas City, MO 184

Hotel Villa Convento (H), New Orleans, LA 133

Hot Springs Park Hilton (H), Hot Springs National Park, AR 40

Houlihan's (R), Kansas City, MO 188

Houmas House Plantation and Gardens (A), Baton Rouge, LA 119

House of the Seasons, The (A), Jefferson, TX 355

Houston Airport Marriott (H), Houston, TX 341

Houstonian Hotel, The (H), Houston, TX 341

Houston Marriott Westside (H), Houston, TX 341

Houston Museum of Natural Science (A), Houston, TX 351

Houston Plaza Hilton (H), Houston, TX 341

Houston West Hilton Inn (H), Houston, TX 341

Houston Zoological Gardens (A), Houston, TX 351

Howard Johnson (M), Monroe, LA 128

Howard Johnson Hotel (H), Lawton, OK 239

Howard Johnson Lodge (M), El Paso, TX 325

Howard Johnson Plaza Suite Hotel (M), Baton Rouge, LA 117

Howard Johnson Riverwalk Plaza Hotel (H), San Antonio, TX 375

Hubba Hubba's Great American Diner (R), Fort Worth, TX 329

Hudson House Motel (M), Harlingen, TX 338

Hudson's Grill (R), El Paso, TX 326

Hueco Tanks State Historical Park (A), El Paso, TX 326

Hugo Heritage Railroad (A), Hugo, OK 239

Humperdink's Bar & Grill (R), Dallas, TX 316

Hunan Chinese Restaurant (R), Oklahoma City, OK 248

Hunan Restaurant (R), Fort Worth, TX 329

Hunan River Garden (R), San Antonio, TX 381

Huron Indian Burial Ground (A), Kansas City, KS 79

Hyatt Regency (H), San Antonio, TX 375

Hyatt Regency Austin (H), Austin, TX 289

Hyatt Regency Crown Center (H), Kansas City, MO 185

Hyatt Regency Dallas at Reunion (H), Dallas, TX 309

Hyatt Regency DFW Airport (H), Dallas–Fort Worth Int'l Airport, TX 321

Hyatt Regency Hill Country Resort (RE), San Antonio, TX 379

Hyatt Regency Houston (H), Houston, TX 341

Hyatt Regency New Orleans (H), New Orleans, LA 133

Hylander Steak and Ribs (R), Eureka Springs, AR 35

I

Ianelli (R), McAllen, TX 364

Ichiban Teriyaki Japanese Restaurant (R), Tulsa, OK 258

Impastato's Restaurant (R), Metairie, LA 127

Imperial Calcasieu Museum (A), Lake Charles, LA 125

Imperial Motor Inn (M), McAllen, TX 364

Independence Museum (A), Independence, KS 77

Indian City USA (A), Anadarko, OK 233

Indian Hills Inn (R), Norman, OK 243

Indian Palace Restaurant & Bar (R), Dallas, TX 316

India's Restaurant (R), Houston, TX 348

Inn at Mountain View, The (M), Mountain View, AR 49

Inn at Tallgrass, The (H), Wichita, KS 92

Inner Space Cavern (A), Georgetown, TX 336

Inn of Pine Bluff, The (M), Pine Bluff, AR 50

Inn of Sherman (M), Sherman, TX 387

Inn of the Conchos (M), San Angelo, TX 373

Inn of the Hills River Resort (RE), Kerrville, TX 356

Inn of the Southwest (M), Anadarko, OK 233

Institute of Texan Cultures, The (A), San Antonio, TX 384

International Hotel (H), El Paso, TX 325

Interurban (R), Tulsa, OK 258

Interurban Restaurant (R), Norman, OK 243

Irene's Cuisine (R), New Orleans, LA 142

Island House (M), Corpus Christi, TX 304

Isle of Capri Casino & Hotel (H), Bossier City, LA 119

J

Jack's Gourmet Restaurant (R), Columbia, MO 177

Jackson Barracks (A), New Orleans, LA 148

Jacksonport State Park (A), Newport, AR 49

Japanese Tea Garden (A), San Antonio, TX 385

Jasper's (R), Kansas City, MO 189
Jasper's Restaurant (R), Tahlequah, OK 254
Jean Lafitte National Historical Park and Preserve (A), New Orleans, LA 148
Jean Lafitte Swamp Tour (A), New Orleans, LA 149
Jefferson Historical Museum (A), Jefferson, TX 355
Jennie's (R), Kansas City, MO 189
Jesse H Jones Hall for the Performing Arts (A), Houston, TX 352
Jesse James Home (A), St Joseph, MO 198
Jimmie's Diner (R), Wichita, KS 94
Joe T Garcia's (R), Fort Worth, TX 330
Joe Vigg's Italian Eatery (R), Tulsa, OK 258
John E Conner Museum (A), Kingsville, TX 358
John James Audubon (A), New Orleans, LA 149
John Jay French Museum (A), Beaumont, TX 297
Johnny Cace's Seafood & Steak House (R), Longview, TX 360
John Q's (R), Fort Smith, AR 38
John Wornall House Museum (A), Kansas City, MO 192
Jonesboro Best Western (M), Jonesboro, AR 42
José Antonio Navarro State Historical Park (A), San Antonio, TX 384
Josephine's (R), Little Rock, AR 45
Josephine Tussaud Wax Museum (A), Hot Springs National Park, AR 42
Joy Motel (M), Eureka Springs, AR 34
JT Puterbaugh House and Ardenium (A), McAlester, OK 241
Juanita's (R), Fort Worth, TX 330
Juanita's Mexican Cafe & Cantina (R), Little Rock, AR 45
Juban's (R), Baton Rouge, LA 117
Julio's Cafe Corona (R), El Paso, TX 326
Julio Tumatoe's Mexicali Border Cafe (R), Tulsa, OK 258
Jumper's Fiesta (R), Fort Smith, AR 38
Junction, The (R), Huntsville, TX 353
Juniper (R), Dallas, TX 316
JW Marriott Hotel Houston (H), Houston, TX 342
JW's Steakhouse (R), Oklahoma City, OK 248

K

Kabby's Sports Edition & Grille (R), New Orleans, LA 142
Kansas Aviation Museum (A), Wichita, KS 94
Kansas City Airport Marriott Hotel (H), Kansas City, MO 185
Kansas City Board of Trade (A), Kansas City, MO 192
Kansas City Marriott Downtown (H), Kansas City, MO 185
Kansas Cosmosphere and Space Center (A), Hutchinson, KS 76
Kansas Museum of History (A), Topeka, KS 91
Kansas State Capitol (A), Topeka, KS 91

Kathleen's Art Cafe (R), Dallas, TX 316
Katy Station (R), Columbia, MO 177
Kaw Mission Museum (A), Emporia, KS 72
Kearby's Restaurant (R), Manhattan, KS 83
Kemoll's (R), St Louis, MO 202
Kent Plantation House (A), Alexandria, LA 115
Kerrville Camera Safari (A), Kerrville, TX 357
Kettle Restaurant (R), McAlester, OK 241; Muskogee, OK 242
Key West (R), St Louis, MO 202
Kiki's Bon Ton (R), Kansas City, MO 189
Kimbell Art Museum (A), Fort Worth, TX 331
Kim Son (R), Houston, TX 348
Kincaid's (R), Fort Worth, TX 330
King Ranch (A), Kingsville, TX 357
Kirby House (R), Abilene, KS 68
Kliebert's Turtle and Alligator Farm (A), Hammond, LA 121
Knotty Pine Barbeque (R), Tulsa, OK 258
Koester House Museum (A), Marysville, KS 84
Konriko/Conrad Rice Mill (A), New Iberia, LA 130
Konstverk Gallery (A), Lindsborg, KS 82
Krause's Cafe (R), New Braunfels, TX 368

L

La Buena Vida Vineyards (A), Fort Worth, TX 332
La Calesa (R), San Antonio, TX 381
Lafayette Hilton and Towers (H), Lafayette, LA 124
Lafayette Museum (A), Lafayette, LA 125
Lafitte Guest House (I), New Orleans, LA 137
La Flambeau (R), Topeka, KS 90
La Fogata (R), San Antonio, TX 381
Laguna Gloria Art Museum (A), Austin, TX 292
La Hacienda (R), Salina, KS 89; Nacogdoches, TX 367
Lake Arrowhead State Park (A), Wichita Falls, TX 396
Lake Bastrop (A), Austin, TX 294
Lake Catherine State Park (A), Hot Springs National Park, AR 42
Lake Frierson State Park (A), Jonesboro, AR 43
Lake Meredith National Recreation Area (A), Amarillo, TX 284
Lake Murray Country Inn (RE), Ardmore, OK 233
Lake Murray Resort State Park (A), Ardmore, OK 234
Lake of the Ozarks State Park (A), Lake Ozark, MO 193
Lake Queen (A), Branson, MO 172
Lakeside Inn (M), Hot Springs National Park, AR 41
Lakeside Speedway (A), Kansas City, KS 79
Lake Texoma (A), Denison, TX 323
Lakeway Inn, A Conference Center (H), Austin, TX 289

La Madeleine (R), New Orleans, LA 142
La Mansion Del Rio (H), San Antonio, TX 376
Lambert's Cafe (R), Sikeston, MO 209
La Mediterranée (R), Overland Park, KS 87
La Mora Cucina Toscana (R), Houston, TX 348
Lancaster Hotel (H), Houston, TX 342
L'Ancestral (R), Dallas, TX 316
Landa Park (A), New Braunfels, TX 368
Landing, The (R), Natchitoches, LA 129
Landmark Hotel French Quarter (H), New Orleans, LA 133
Land-O-Nod Victorian Inn (M), Eureka Springs, AR 34
Landry's Seafood (R), Corpus Christi, TX 304
Lane's Bar-B-Q (R), Topeka, KS 90
La Patisserie (R), University City, MO 213
La Place d'Evangeline (R), St Martinville, LA 150
La Provence (R), Slidell, LA 152
La Quinta (M), Bossier City, LA 119
La Quinta Airport East (M), San Antonio, TX 378
La Quinta Convention Center (H), San Antonio, TX 376
La Quinta Foster Mansion (A), Bartlesville, OK 234
La Quinta Inn (M), Baton Rouge, LA 117; Denton, TX 323; Midland, TX 365
La Quinta Inn Airport (M), Tulsa, OK 256
La Quinta Inn Central (M), Dallas, TX 312
La Quinta Inn DFW Airport East (M), Dallas–Fort Worth Int'l Airport, TX 321
La Quinta Inn Fair Park (M), Little Rock, AR 45
La Quinta Inn Galveston (M), Galveston, TX 334
La Quinta Inn Greenway Plaza (M), Houston, TX 345
La Quinta Inn Motor Inn Capitol (M), Austin, TX 290
La Quinta Inn Northpark (M), Dallas, TX 312
La Quinta Inn South (M), Oklahoma City, OK 247
La Quinta Motor Inn (H), Wichita, KS 92
La Quinta Motor Inn (M), Beaumont, TX 296; Brownsville, TX 299; Eagle Pass, TX 324; Killeen, TX 357; Lubbock, TX 361; Lufkin, TX 362; McAllen, TX 364; Odessa, TX 369; Texarkana, TX 390; Tyler, TX 391; Victoria, TX 394; Waco, TX 394; Wichita Falls, TX 396
La Quinta Motor Inn Airport (M), Amarillo, TX 283
La Quinta Motor Inn Lomaland (M), El Paso, TX 325
La Quinta Motor Inn Northeast (M), Fort Worth, TX 328
Laredo's Mexican Restaurant (R), Oklahoma City, OK 248
La Réserve (R), Houston, TX 348

La Riviera (R), Metairie, LA 127
La Sala (R), St Louis, MO 202
La Tour l'Argent (R), Houston, TX 348
Latter-Day Saints Mormon Visitor Center (A), Independence, MO 181
Laumeier Sculpture Park (A), St Louis, MO 206
La Villita (A), San Antonio, TX 383
Layland Museum (A), Cleburne, TX 302
Le Bistro (R), New Orleans, LA 142
Legends (R), Norman, OK 244; Odessa, TX 369
Le Méridien Dallas (H), Dallas, TX 309
Le Meridien Hotel (H), New Orleans, LA 134
Lemke's Wurst Haus German Restaurant (R), Lufkin, TX 362
Le Pavillon Hotel (H), New Orleans, LA 134
Le Richelieu Motor Hotel (H), New Orleans, LA 134
L'Etoile (R), San Antonio, TX 381
Lexington Hotel Suites (H), Tulsa, OK 255
Lexington Hotel Suites (M), Dallas, TX 312; Houston, TX 345
Lexington Inn (M), Waco, TX 394
Liberal Inn (H), Liberal, KS 81
Liberty Bar (R), San Antonio, TX 381
Liberty Memorial and Museum (A), Kansas City, MO 192
Lighthouse Inn (H), Branson, MO 168
Lighthouse Restaurant and Oyster Bar, The (R), Corpus Christi, TX 304
Lil Cajun Swamp Tours (A), New Orleans, LA 149
Little House on the Prairie (A), Independence, KS 77
Little Italy Restaurant (R), Muskogee, OK 242
Little Rhein Steak House (R), San Antonio, TX 381
Little Rock Hilton Inn (M), Little Rock, AR 45
Little Rock Zoo (A), Little Rock, AR 46
Live Oak Gardens (A), New Iberia, LA 130
Livestock Auction at Western Stockyards (A), Amarillo, TX 285
Llano Estacado Museum (A), Plainview, TX 371
Llano Estacado Winery (A), Lubbock, TX 362
Lodge of Duncan, The (H), Duncan, OK 236
Lodge of Granbury, The (L), Granbury, TX 337
Lodge of the Ozarks (H), Branson, MO 168
Log Cabin Village (A), Fort Worth, TX 332
Loma Alta Motel (M), Laredo, TX 359
Lone Star Buckhorn Museums (A), San Antonio, TX 384
Lone Star Flight Museum (A), Galveston, TX 335
Lone Star Oyster Bar (R), Lubbock, TX 361
Lone Star Steakhouse (R), Branson, MO 171

Lone Star Tavern Steakhouse (R), Waco, TX 395
Longhorn Caverns (A), Burnet, TX 301
Longue Vue House and Gardens (A), New Orleans, LA 148
Longview Inn (M), Longview, TX 359
Los Bandidos (R), Columbia, MO 177
Lost Spur Guest Ranch (L), Harrison, AR 39
Lost Valley Resort Ranch (RE), Bandera, TX 295
Lotus Inn (R), Brownsville, TX 300
Lou Boccardi's (R), St Louis, MO 202
Louisiana Children's Museum (A), New Orleans, LA 147
Louisiana Purchase Gardens and Zoo (A), Monroe, LA 128
Louisiana's Old State Capitol, Center for Political and Governmental History (A), Baton Rouge, LA 118
Louisiana State Capitol (A), Baton Rouge, LA 118
Louisiana State Exhibit Museum (A), Shreveport, LA 151
Louisiana State University (A), Baton Rouge, LA 118
Louisiana Superdome (A), New Orleans, LA 147
Louisiana Toy and Train Museum (A), Kenner, LA 123
Louis XVI (R), New Orleans, LA 142
LSU Rural Life Museum (A), Baton Rouge, LA 119
Lubbock Fine Arts Center (A), Lubbock, TX 362
Lubbock Inn (H), Lubbock, TX 360
Luciano's (R), Norman, OK 244
Lucky Chang's (R), New Orleans, LA 142
Lujan's Waterworks (R), Emporia, KS 72
Luna Notte (R), San Antonio, TX 381
Lyndon Baines Johnson Library and Museum (A), Austin, TX 292
Lyndon B Johnson National Historical Park (A), Fredericksburg, TX 333

M

Mabee-Gerrer Museum of Art (A), Shawnee, OK 253
Mac's House (R), Fort Worth, TX 330
Madame Wu's Hunan Chinese Restaurant (R), Russellville, AR 52
Maggio's (R), Baton Rouge, LA 118
Magic House (A), St Louis, MO 205
Magnolia Cafe (R), Baton Rouge, LA 118
Magnolia Inn (M), Branson, MO 169
Magnolia Mansion-Spaulding/Olive House (A), Broken Bow, OK 235
Magnolia Mound Plantation (A), Baton Rouge, LA 119
Magoffin Home State Historic Site (A), El Paso, TX 327
Maharaja (R), Fort Worth, TX 330
Mainliner Inn (M), Beloit, KS 70
Maison Dupuy (H), New Orleans, LA 134
Maison Esplanade Guest House (I), New Orleans, LA 137
Maison Lacour (R), Baton Rouge, LA 118
Majestic Theatre (A), San Antonio, TX 385
Mamacita's (R), Baton Rouge, LA 118

Mama Rosa's (R), New Orleans, LA 142
Mamasita's (R), Oklahoma City, OK 249
Mandarin House (R), Columbia, MO 178
Manhattan's Sunset Zoo (A), Manhattan, KS 83
Mansion at Elfindale Inn, The (I), Springfield, MO 211
Mansion on Turtle Creek, The (H), Dallas, TX 309
Mansion on Turtle Creek, The (R), Dallas, TX 316
Mardi Gras Museum (A), Galveston, TX 336
Margarete Motel (M), Hot Springs National Park, AR 41
Margarita's (R), Kansas City, MO 189
Maria's Better Mexican Food (R), Brownsville, TX 300
Marie's Villa (R), Woodward, OK 260
Mario's (R), Kansas City, MO 189
Mario's Chiquita (R), Dallas, TX 316
Market Street Bed & Breakfast (I), Hermann, MO 180
Markham Inn of the Ozarks (H), Springfield, MO 210
Mark Twain Boyhood Home and Museum (A), Hannibal, MO 179
Mark Twain Cave and Village (A), Hannibal, MO 179
Mark Twain Dinette and Family Restaurant (R), Hannibal, MO 179
Mark Twain Riverboat (A), Hannibal, MO 179
Marland Estate Conference Center Hotel (H), Ponca City, OK 251
Marland Mansion and Estate (A), Ponca City, OK 251
Marriott Hotel (H), New Orleans, LA 134; Tulsa, OK 255
Marriott Pavilion Downtown (H), St Louis, MO 200
Marriott Rivercenter (H), San Antonio, TX 376
Marriott's Residence Inn (H), Baton Rouge, LA 116
Marsala (R), Arlington, TX 286
Martin's (R), Lawton, OK 240
Masur Museum (A), Monroe, LA 128
Maximo's Italian Grill (R), New Orleans, LA 143
Maxim's (R), Houston, TX 348
Maxwell Wildlife Refuge (A), McPherson, KS 84
Mayfair Bar and Grill (R), St Louis, MO 203
McAllen Airport Hilton Inn (H), McAllen, TX 364
McAllen International Museum (A), McAllen, TX 364
McBride Land & Cattle Co (R), Wichita Falls, TX 396
McFadden-Ward House, The (A), Beaumont, TX 297
McGraths (R), Sedalia, MO 209
McPherson County Old Mill Museum (A), Lindsborg, KS 82
Medicine Lodge Stockade Museum (A), Medicine Lodge, KS 84
Mejor Que Nada (R), San Angelo, TX 374

Melrose Hotel (H), Dallas, TX 309
Melrose Plantation (A), Natchitoches, LA 129
Mel Tillis Theater (A), Branson, MO 171
Memo's (R), Del Rio, TX 322
Menger Hotel (H), San Antonio, TX 376
Menil Collection, The (A), Houston, TX 350
Mercado Juarez Cafe (R), Denton, TX 324
Merci Beaucoup (R), Natchitoches, LA 129
Meridian Plaza Hotel (H), Oklahoma City, OK 245
Mesquite's BBQ & Steaks (R), Lubbock, TX 361
Messina Hof Wine Cellars (A), Bryan, TX 301
Metropolis (R), Kansas City, MO 189
Mexican Cultural Institute (A), San Antonio, TX 384
Mexic-Arte Museum (A), Austin, TX 292
Mexico Tipico (R), Austin, TX 291
Mia's (R), Dallas, TX 317
Michael's (R), Fort Worth, TX 330
Michelson Museum of Art (A), Marshall, TX 363
Mickey Gilley Theatre (A), Branson, MO 171
Mid America Inn (M), Salina, KS 88
Mike Anderson's Seafood (R), Baton Rouge, LA 118; New Orleans, LA 143
Mike's on the Avenue (R), New Orleans, LA 143
Milano (R), Kansas City, MO 189
Miles Musical Museum (A), Eureka Springs, AR 35
Milford Lake (A), Junction City, KS 78
Millard's Crossing (A), Nacogdoches, TX 367
Millwood State Park (A), Texarkana, AR 54
Miss Brandi's Restaurant (R), Houma, LA 121
Miss Carolyn's Territorial House (R), Guthrie, OK 238
Mission Concepción (A), San Antonio, TX 383
Mission San Francisco de la Espada (A), San Antonio, TX 383
Mission San José (A), San Antonio, TX 383
Mission San Juan Capistrano (A), San Antonio, TX 383
Missouri Botanical Garden (A), St Louis, MO 206
Missouri Territory Restaurant & Lodge (R), Hannibal, MO 179
Mitchell's Family Restaurant (R), Shamrock, TX 386
Moctezuma (R), Dallas, TX 317
Modern Art Museum of Fort Worth (A), Fort Worth, TX 331
Molly's at the Market (R), New Orleans, LA 143
Molly's Irish Pub (RS), New Orleans, LA 146
Monahans Sandhills State Park (A), Monahans, TX 366

Monastery Miniature Horses (A), Brenham, TX 299
Mondo's Ristoranté Italiano (R), Tulsa, OK 258
Monica Aca Y Alla (R), Dallas, TX 317
Monjuni's Italian Cafe (R), Bossier City, LA 120
Monsieur Patou (R), Shreveport, LA 151
Monteleone Hotel (H), New Orleans, LA 134
Monument Hill and Kreische Brewery State Historical Parks (A), La Grange, TX 358
Moody Gardens (A), Galveston, TX 336
Moody Mansion and Museum, The (A), Galveston, TX 335
Morton H Meyerson Symphony Center (A), Dallas, TX 320
Motel 6 (M), Little Rock, AR 45; Joplin, MO 183; St Louis–Lambert Int'l Airport, MO 208; Brazosport, TX 299; Houston, TX 345
Motel 6 East (M), San Antonio, TX 378
Motel 6 North (M), Fort Worth, TX 328
Motel 6 North LBJ (M), Dallas, TX 312
Motel 6 West (M), Topeka, KS 90
Mother's (R), New Orleans, LA 143
Mountain Village 1890 and Bull Shoals Cavern (A), Bull Shoals, AR 31
Mount Olivet Cemetery (A), Hugo, OK 239
Mr B's Bistro and Bar (R), New Orleans, LA 143
Mrs Miller's Chicken & Steak House (R), Hot Springs National Park, AR 42
Mulate's (R), Baton Rouge, LA 118
Mulvane Art Museum (A), Topeka, KS 91
Municipal Rose Garden (A), Tyler, TX 392
Musée Conti Wax Museum (A), New Orleans, LA 147
Museum Cafe (R), St Louis, MO 203
Museum of Anthropology (A), Lawrence, KS 80
Museum of Automobiles, The (A), Morrilton, AR 47
Museum of East Texas (A), Lufkin, TX 362
Museum of Fine Arts, Houston (A), Houston, TX 350
Museum of Oriental Cultures (A), Corpus Christi, TX 305
Museum of Texas Tech University (A), Lubbock, TX 361
Museum of the Big Bend (A), Alpine, TX 282
Museum of the Great Plains (A), Lawton, OK 240
Museum of the Gulf Coast (A), Port Arthur, TX 372
Museum of the Southwest (A), Midland, TX 366
Museum of the Western Prairie (A), Altus, OK 232
Museum of Transportation (A), St Louis, MO 205
Museums of Abilene (A), Abilene, TX 281
Music Mountain Jamboree (A), Hot Springs National Park, AR 42

Mustang Island State Park (A), Port Aransas, TX 372
Mustangs of Las Colinas, The (A), Irving, TX 354
Mutton Hollow Entertainment Park and Village (A), Branson, MO 172

N

Nantucket Cove (R), Clayton, MO 175
Napoleon House (R), New Orleans, LA 143
Natchitoches National Fish Hatchery and Aquarium (A), Natchitoches, LA 129
National Agricultural Center & Hall of Fame (A), Kansas City, KS 78
National Bowling Hall of Fame (A), St Louis, MO 205
National Cowboy Hall of Fame (A), Oklahoma City, OK 250
National Cowgirl Hall of Fame (A), Hereford, TX 339
National Frontier Trails Center (A), Independence, MO 181
National Hall of Fame for Famous American Indians (A), Anadarko, OK 233
National Park Aquarium (A), Hot Springs National Park, AR 42
National Wildflower Research Center (A), Austin, TX 294
Natura Cafe (R), Dallas, TX 317
Natural Bridge Caverns (A), New Braunfels, TX 368
Natural Bridge Wildlife Ranch (A), San Antonio, TX 385
NCAA Hall of Champions (A), Overland Park, KS 87
Neill-Cochran Museum House, The (A), Austin, TX 293
Nelson-Atkins Museum of Art (A), Kansas City, MO 191
New Braunfels Resorts (RE), New Braunfels, TX 368
New Braunfels Smokehouse (R), New Braunfels, TX 368
New Majestic Steak House, The (R), Kansas City, MO 189
New Orleans Airport Hilton (H), Kenner, LA 122
New Orleans Guest House (I), New Orleans, LA 138
New Orleans Hilton Riverside Hotel (H), New Orleans, LA 134
New Orleans Historic Voodoo Museum (A), New Orleans, LA 146
New Orleans Museum of Art (A), New Orleans, LA 146
New Orleans Pharmacy Museum (A), New Orleans, LA 147
Newport's Seafood (R), Dallas, TX 317
Nick's (R), Waco, TX 395
Nina Vance Alley Theatre (A), Houston, TX 352
Ninfa's (R), Houston, TX 349
Nino's (R), Houston, TX 349
Nippon (R), Houston, TX 349
Nola (R), New Orleans, LA 143
Nona's Homemade Pasta (R), San Antonio, TX 382

Northeast Louisiana University (A), Monroe, LA 128
Norton's Cafe (R), St Louis, MO 203
Nutt House, The (R), Granbury, TX 337

O

Oak Alley Plantation (A), Houma, LA 121
Oak Grove Inn (M), St Louis, MO 200
Oaklawn Manor (A), New Iberia, LA 130
Oak Tree Inn (I), Heber Springs, AR 39
Oasis Motel (M), Arlington, TX 286
Oberhellmann Vineyards (A), Fredericksburg, TX 333
Oceans of Fun (A), Kansas City, MO 192
O'Connell's Pub (R), St Louis, MO 203
Odessa Motor Inn (M), Odessa, TX 369
Odessa Raddison (H), Odessa, TX 369
O Henry Museum (A), Austin, TX 293
Oil Patch Museum (A), Russell, KS 88
Oklahoma City Art Museum on the Fairgrounds (A), Oklahoma City, OK 249
Oklahoma City Marriott (H), Oklahoma City, OK 245
Oklahoma City Zoological Park (A), Oklahoma City, OK 250
Oklahoma Heritage Center (A), Oklahoma City, OK 249
Oklahoma Museum of Natural History (A), Norman, OK 244
Oklahoma State Capitol (A), Oklahoma City, OK 249
Oklahoma Territorial Museum (A), Guthrie, OK 238
Old Abilene Town and Western Museum (A), Abilene, KS 68
Old Country Buffet (R), Springfield, MO 212
Old Courthouse (A), St Louis, MO 205
Old Cowtown Museum (A), Wichita, KS 94
Old Davidsonville State Park (A), Pocahontas, AR 51
Olde N'Awlins Cookery (R), New Orleans, LA 143
Old Fort Bissell Museum (A), Norton, KS 85
Old Fort Museum (A), Fort Smith, AR 38
Old Post Office Restaurant, The (R), Fayetteville, AR 36
Old San Francisco (R), Houston, TX 349
Old Shawnee Town (A), Overland Park, KS 87
Old Spaghetti Factory, The (R), Kansas City, MO 189
Old State House (A), Little Rock, AR 46
Old Ursuline Convent (A), New Orleans, LA 148
Old US Mint (A), New Orleans, LA 147
Old Warsaw (R), Dallas, TX 317
Olive Garden, The (R), Springfield, MO 212
Olive Tree, The (R), Wichita, KS 94
Olivier House (H), New Orleans, LA 135
Ol' South Pancake House (R), Fort Worth, TX 330
Omni Austin at Southpark (H), Austin, TX 289
Omni Austin Hotel (H), Austin, TX 289

Omni Houston Hotel (H), Houston, TX 342
Omni Mandalay Hotel at Las Colinas (H), Irving, TX 354
Omni Richardson Hotel (H), Dallas, TX 310
Omni Royal Orleans (H), New Orleans, LA 135
Omni San Antonio (H), San Antonio, TX 376
Omnisphere and Science Center (A), Wichita, KS 95
Orange Show, The (A), Houston, TX 352
Osage Hills State Park (A), Bartlesville, OK 235
Otto's Barbecue (R), Houston, TX 349
Outback Steakhouse (R), Houston, TX 349
Overholser Mansion (A), Oklahoma City, OK 249
Overland Park Marriott Hotel (H), Overland Park, KS 86
Oxford Street Restaurant (R), Abilene, TX 281; Longview, TX 360; Tyler, TX 391
Oxley Nature Center (A), Tulsa, OK 259
Ozarka Lodge (M), Eureka Springs, AR 34
Ozark Folk Center (A), Mountain View, AR 49
Ozark Folk Center Lodge (M), Mountain View, AR 49
Ozark Regal Hotel (M), Branson, MO 169
Ozark Valley Inn (M), Branson, MO 169
Ozzie's Restaurant and Sports Bar (R), St Louis, MO 203

P

Paddy's Irish Pub & Restaurant (R), Tulsa, OK 258
Padre Island National Seashore (A), Corpus Christi, TX 304
Paesano's Italian Restaurant (R), San Antonio, TX 382
Painted Plates (R), University City, MO 213
Palace Cafe (R), New Orleans, LA 144; Opelousas, LA 150
Palace of Wax and Ripley's Believe It or Not, The (A), Arlington, TX 287
Palo Alto Battlefield National Historic Site (A), Brownsville, TX 300
Palo Duro Canyon State Park (A), Amarillo, TX 284
Panhandle-Plains Historical Museum (A), Amarillo, TX 284
Papagallo's (R), Kansas City, MO 190
Pappas Seafood House (R), Houston, TX 349
Paradise Grill (R), Branson, MO 171
Park Inn International (H), Springfield, MO 210
Park Inn of Jonesboro (M), Jonesboro, AR 43
Park Place Hotel (H), Kansas City, MO 185
Parkview Guest House (H), New Orleans, LA 135
Pascal's Manale (R), New Orleans, LA 144

Pasta Factory, The (R), Columbia, MO 178
Patee House Museum (A), St Joseph, MO 198
Patrizio (R), Dallas, TX 317
Patrizi's Restaurant (R), Beaumont, TX 296
Patty Kerr Bed and Breakfast (I), Hermann, MO 180
Patty Long's 9th St Abby (R), St Louis, MO 203
Peach Tree Inn (M), Branson, MO 169
Peking Duck House (R), Metairie, LA 127
Peppercorn Duck Club (R), Kansas City, MO 190
Peppers (R), Tulsa, OK 258
Père Antoine Restaurant (R), New Orleans, LA 144
Permian Basin Petroleum Museum (A), Midland, TX 366
Perot Theatre (A), Texarkana, TX 390
Petit Jean State Park (A), Morrilton, AR 47
Petunia's (R), New Orleans, LA 144
Pheasant Ridge Winery (A), Lubbock, TX 362
Philbrook Museum of Art (A), Tulsa, OK 259
Pierre's by the Lake (R), Dallas, TX 317
Pine Mountain Jamboree (A), Eureka Springs, AR 35
Pine Top Lodge (L), Eureka Springs, AR 34
Pioneer City-County Museum (A), Abilene, TX 281
Pioneer Log Cabin (A), Manhattan, KS 83
Pioneer Village (A), Athens, TX 287
Pioneer Woman Museum (A), Ponca City, OK 252
Pirtle's Weston Winery (A), Weston, MO 214
Pitot House Museum (A), New Orleans, LA 148
PJ Holbrook's Olde Victorian Inn (I), New Orleans, LA 138
Place, The (R), Baton Rouge, LA 118
Place D'Aremes Hotel (H), New Orleans, LA 135
Plains Indians and Pioneer Museum (A), Woodward, OK 260
Plaza Hotel (H), Killeen, TX 357
Plaza Inn, The (H), Kansas City, MO 185
Plaza Inn (M), Midland, TX 365
Plaza San Antonio (H), San Antonio, TX 377
Plaza Square Motel (M), Brownsville, TX 300
Polo's (R), San Antonio, TX 382
Polynesian Garden (R), Altus, OK 232
Polynesian Princess (A), Branson, MO 172
Pomodoro (R), Dallas, TX 317
Pompeiian Villa (A), Port Arthur, TX 372
Ponak's (R), Kansas City, MO 190
Pontchartrain Hotel (H), New Orleans, LA 135
Pony Express Barn-Museum (A), Marysville, KS 84
Pony Express National Memorial (A), St Joseph, MO 198

Poor Boy's Riverside Inn (R), Lafayette, LA 124
Port of Call (R), New Orleans, LA 144
Post Family Vineyards & Winery (A), Altus, AR 28
Potbelly's Restaurant (R), Wichita, KS 94
Potpourri House (R), Tyler, TX 392
Potton House (A), Big Spring, TX 298
Poverty Point State Commemorative Area (A), Epps, LA 120
Prairie Museum of Art and History (A), Colby, KS 71
Praline Connection (R), New Orleans, LA 144
Pratt County Historical Museum (A), Pratt, KS 88
Pratt Super 8 (M), Pratt, KS 88
Prejean's (R), Lafayette, LA 124
Premio (R), St Louis, MO 203
Presbytere (A), New Orleans, LA 147
Preservation Hall (A), New Orleans, LA 149
Presidential Museum (A), Odessa, TX 369
Presidio La Bahia (A), Goliad, TX 337
Price Tower (A), Bartlesville, OK 234
Pride House (I), Jefferson, TX 355
Prime Thyme (R), Hutchinson, KS 76
Prince Conti Hotel (H), New Orleans, LA 135
Pump Boys and Dinettes Dinner Theatre (A), Branson, MO 171
Purple Cow (R), Little Rock, AR 46
Pyramid, The (R), Dallas, TX 318

Q

Quality Hotel Market Center (H), Dallas, TX 310
Quality Inn (M), Arkadelphia, AR 28; Hope, AR 40; Hot Springs National Park, AR 41; Houma, LA 121; Lafayette, LA 124; Elk City, OK 237; El Paso, TX 325; Waco, TX 394
Quality Inn Airport (M), Tulsa, OK 256
Quality Inn & Suites (M), San Antonio, TX 379
Quality Inn Intercontinental Airport (M), Houston, TX 345
Quality Inn North (H), Springfield, MO 210
Quality Inn Sherwood Forest (M), Baton Rouge, LA 117
Quarter Scene, The (R), New Orleans, LA 144
Quartz Mountain Resort Park (A), Altus, OK 232
Queene Anne Mansion (A), Eureka Springs, AR 35
Queen of Sheba (R), Dallas, TX 318
Queen Wilhelmina State Park (A), Mena, AR 47
Quivira National Wildlife Refuge (A), Stafford, KS 89

R

Radio Cafe (R), Branson, MO 171
Radisson (H), Overland Park, KS 86
Radisson Hotel (H), New Orleans, LA 135; Clayton, MO 174; Dallas, TX 310

Radisson Hotel and Suites (H), Dallas, TX 310
Radisson Hotel Denton (H), Denton, TX 323
Radisson Hotel on Town Lake (H), Austin, TX 290
Radisson Hotel St Louis Airport (H), St Louis–Lambert Int'l Airport, MO 207
Radisson Inn (H), Amarillo, TX 283
Radisson Inn Tulsa Airport (H), Tulsa, OK 255
Radisson Plaza Hotel (H), Fort Worth, TX 327
Radisson Resort South Padre Island (RE), South Padre Island, TX 388
Radisson Suite Hotel Arlington (H), Arlington, TX 285
Radisson Suite Hotel Kansas City (H), Kansas City, MO 185
Radisson Suite Inn (H), El Paso, TX 325
Railroad and Pioneer Museum (A), Temple, TX 389
Raintree Restaurant (R), Mountain Home, AR 48
Ralph & Kacoo's (R), Bossier City, LA 120; Metairie, LA 127; New Orleans, LA 144
Ramada Airport Inn (H), Wichita, KS 92
Ramada Emily Morgan Hotel (H), San Antonio, TX 377
Ramada Hill Country Inn (H), Kerrville, TX 356
Ramada Hotel (H), Dallas, TX 310
Ramada Hotel Airport (H), Kansas City, MO 185
Ramada Hotel Fort Worth (H), Fort Worth, TX 327
Ramada Hotel Tulsa (H), Tulsa, OK 255
Ramada Inn (H), Fayetteville, AR 36; North Little Rock, AR 50; Colby, KS 71; Hutchinson, KS 76; Leavenworth, KS 80; Manhattan, KS 82; Columbia, MO 176; Jefferson City, MO 182; Sedalia, MO 208; St Joseph, MO 197; Muskogee, OK 241; Norman, OK 243; Del Rio, TX 322; Marshall, TX 363; Victoria, TX 393
Ramada Inn (M), Mountain Home, AR 48; Alexandria, LA 115; Bossier City, LA 120; Slidell, LA 152; Blue Springs, MO 167; Joplin, MO 183; Moberly, MO 195; Sullivan, MO 212; Lawton, OK 240; Denison, TX 323; Port Arthur, TX 372; Waco, TX 394
Ramada Inn Aggieland (H), College Station, TX 302
Ramada Inn Airport (H), Austin, TX 290; San Antonio, TX 377
Ramada Inn Airport South (M), Oklahoma City, OK 247
Ramada Inn & Tower (H), Topeka, KS 90
Ramada Inn Arlington (M), Arlington, TX 286
Ramada Inn at the Arch (H), St Louis, MO 200
Ramada Inn Bayfront (H), Corpus Christi, TX 304

Ramada Inn DFW Airport South (M), Dallas–Fort Worth Int'l Airport, TX 321
Ramada Inn Georgetown (H), Georgetown, TX 336
Ramada Inn Jasper (M), Jasper, TX 354
Ramada Inn Midland Airport (M), Midland, TX 365
Ramada Inn of Batesville (H), Batesville, AR 29
Ramada Inn of Orange (M), Orange, TX 370
Ramada Inn of Rogers (H), Rogers, AR 51
Ramada Inn Towers (H), Hot Springs National Park, AR 41
Ramada Limited (M), Sallisaw, OK 252
Ramada Park Cities Inn (M), Dallas, TX 313
Ramada St Charles (H), New Orleans, LA 136
Ranching Heritage Center (A), Lubbock, TX 361
Rancho Viejo Resort and Country Club (RE), Brownsville, TX 300
Randol's (R), Shreveport, LA 151
Randol's Seafood Restaurant and Cajun Dance Hall (R), Lafayette, LA 124
Raphael, The (H), Kansas City, MO 186
Red Bud Valley Resort (RE), Eureka Springs, AR 35
Red Coach Inn (M), McPherson, KS 84
Redel's (R), St Louis, MO 203
Red Lantern (R), New Orleans, LA 144
Red Lion (H), San Antonio, TX 377
Red Lion Inn (H), Austin, TX 290
Red Roof Inn (H), Austin, TX 290
Red Roof Inn (M), Little Rock, AR 45; Baton Rouge, LA 117; Shreveport, LA 151; West Monroe, LA 153; Columbia, MO 177; Independence, MO 180; St Charles, MO 197; St Louis, MO 200; St Louis–Lambert Int'l Airport, MO 208
Regas Grill (R), Little Rock, AR 46
Remington Park (A), Oklahoma City, OK 250
Renaissance Austin Hotel (H), Austin, TX 290
Renaissance Dallas Hotel (H), Dallas, TX 310
Renaissance Houston Hotel (H), Houston, TX 342
Renaissance St Louis Hotel (H), St Louis–Lambert Int'l Airport, MO 207
Republic of the Rio Grande Museum (A), Laredo, TX 359
Residence Inn Battlefield Mall (H), Springfield, MO 210
Residence Inn by Marriott (H), Wichita, KS 93
Residence Inn By Marriott (H), Norman, OK 243
Residence Inn by Marriott (H), Oklahoma City, OK 246
Residence Inn by Marriott (M), Tulsa, OK 257; Fort Worth, TX 328
Restaurant (R), Eureka Springs, AR 35; Mountain View, AR 49; Clayton, MO 175; St Louis, MO 203

Reunion Tower (A), Dallas, TX 319
Rheinland Restaurant, The (R), Independence, MO 180
Rib Ranch (R), Woodward, OK 260
Rib Room (R), New Orleans, LA 144
Ricardo's (R), Tulsa, OK 258
Rice University (A), Houston, TX 352
Richmond Suites (M), Oklahoma City, OK 247
Riddles Penultimate Cafe and Wine Bar (R), University City, MO 213
Ride The Ducks (A), Branson, MO 172
Rigazzi's (R), St Louis, MO 203
Rio Rio Cantina (R), San Antonio, TX 382
Ristorante Carmelo (R), New Orleans, LA 145
Ristorante La Piazza (R), Fort Worth, TX 330
Rita's Del Rio Cafe (R), Oklahoma City, OK 249
Rita's Olde French Quarter Restaurant (R), New Orleans, LA 145
Ritz-Carlton, The (H), Clayton, MO 174; Kansas City, MO 186
Ritz-Carlton Houston, The (H), Houston, TX 342
River City USA (A), Kansas City, KS 79
Riverfront Hilton Inn (M), North Little Rock, AR 50
Riverhill Country Club (H), Kerrville, TX 356
River Oaks Grill (R), Houston, TX 349
Riverplace Inn (M), Waco, TX 395
Riverside Park and Zoo (A), Independence, KS 77
Riverview Inn (H), Kansas City, KS 78
Riviera, The (R), Dallas, TX 318
Rockcliffe Mansion (A), Hannibal, MO 179
Rodeway Inn (H), Springfield, MO 210
Rodeway Inn (M), Alexandria, LA 115
Rodeway Inn Downtown (M), San Antonio, TX 379
Rodeway Inn Hobby Airport (M), Houston, TX 345
Rodeway Inn Memorial Park (M), Houston, TX 345
Roman Nose Resort Park (A), Weatherford, OK 260
Rosalie House (A), Eureka Springs, AR 35
Rosario's (R), San Antonio, TX 382
Rosebud Inn (H), Branson, MO 168
Rosie's Rib Joint (R), Tulsa, OK 259
Rothko Chapel (A), Houston, TX 351
Rotisserie for Beef and Bird (R), Houston, TX 349
Royal Cafe (R), New Orleans, LA 145
Royal Chinese Barbecue (R), University City, MO 213
Royal Sonesta (H), New Orleans, LA 136
Royal Tokyo (R), Dallas, TX 318
Royal Western Suites (M), Fort Worth, TX 328
Rozelle Court (R), Kansas City, MO 190
Rue Royal Inn (H), New Orleans, LA 136
Rusk State Park (A), Rusk, TX 373

Ruth's Chris Steak House (R), Lafayette, LA 124; New Orleans, LA 145; St Louis, MO 204; Houston, TX 349
RW Norton Art Gallery (A), Shreveport, LA 151
Ryan's Steak Buffet & Bakery (R), Wichita, KS 94

S

Sabal Palm Grove Sanctuary (A), Brownsville, TX 300
St Ann's Cafe & Deli (R), New Orleans, LA 145
St Anthony Hotel (H), San Antonio, TX 377
St Charles Inn (H), New Orleans, LA 136
Saint Emilion (R), Fort Worth, TX 330
St Joseph Museum (A), St Joseph, MO 198
St Louis (H), New Orleans, LA 136
St Louis Airport Hilton (H), St Louis–Lambert Int'l Airport, MO 207
St Louis Art Museum (A), St Louis, MO 205
Saint Louis Bread Company (R), Clayton, MO 175
St Louis Cathedral (A), New Orleans, LA 148; St Louis, MO 205
St Louis History Museum (A), St Louis, MO 205
St Louis Science Center (A), St Louis, MO 205
St Louis Union Station (A), St Louis, MO 204
St Louis Zoological Park (A), St Louis, MO 206
St Mary's Catholic Church (A), Altus, AR 28
Salina Art Center (A), Salina, KS 89
Salina Holiday Inn Holidome (H), Salina, KS 88
Sam A Baker State Park (A), Poplar Bluff, MO 196
Sam Houston Historical Park (A), Houston, TX 351
Sam Houston Inn (M), Huntsville, TX 353
Sam Houston Memorial Museum (A), Huntsville, TX 353
Sammy's Lebanese Restaurant (R), Houston, TX 349
Sam Rayburn House (A), Bonham, TX 298
Sam Rayburn Library (A), Bonham, TX 298
San Antonio Missions National Historical Park (A), San Antonio, TX 383
San Antonio Museum of Art (A), San Antonio, TX 384
San Antonio Riverwalk Marriott (H), San Antonio, TX 377
San Antonio Zoo (A), San Antonio, TX 385
S&D Oyster Company (R), Dallas, TX 318
Sandpiper Airport Inn (M), Fort Worth, TX 329
Sands Motel (M), Kerrville, TX 356
San Fernando Cathedral (A), San Antonio, TX 383

San Francisco Plantation (A), Kenner, LA 123
San Jacinto Monument and Museum of History (A), La Porte, TX 358
San Luis Resort & Conference Center (H), Galveston, TX 334
Santa Ana National Wildlife Refuge (A), McAllen, TX 364
Santa Fe (R), New Orleans, LA 145
Santa Fe Depot Museum (A), Shawnee, OK 253
Santa Fe Station (R), Lubbock, TX 361
Santa Fe Trail Center (A), Larned, KS 79
Sara's Bed and Breakfast Inn (I), Houston, TX 345
Sardine's (R), Fort Worth, TX 330
Sartin's Seafood (R), Beaumont, TX 296
Saunders Memorial Museum (A), Eureka Springs, AR 35
Savoy Grill (R), Kansas City, MO 190
Scampi's (R), South Padre Island, TX 388
Schlitterbahn (A), New Braunfels, TX 368
Schmidt Natural History Museum (A), Emporia, KS 72
Schneithorst's Hofamberg Inn (R), Ladue, MO 193
Science Place, The (A), Dallas, TX 320
Scotch and Sirloin (R), Wichita, KS 94
Scottish Inn's Colonial Motel (M), Jonesboro, AR 43
Scott Joplin House (A), St Louis, MO 205
Scott Valley Resort & Guest Ranch (RE), Mountain Home, AR 48
Seafood and Spaghetti Works (R), Port Aransas, TX 372
Sebastians (R), New Orleans, LA 145
Sedgwick County Zoo (A), Wichita, KS 95
Sequoyah National Wildlife Refuge (A), Sallisaw, OK 252
Sequoyah's Home Site (A), Sallisaw, OK 252
Sergio's by the Bay (R), South Padre Island, TX 388
Settle Inn (M), Branson, MO 169
Seven Gables Inn (H), Clayton, MO 174
76 Music Hall (A), Branson, MO 172
Sfuzzi (R), Dallas, TX 318
Shadows-on-the-Teche Plantation (A), New Iberia, LA 130
Shady Inn (R), Springfield, MO 212
Shepherd of the Hills (A), Branson, MO 172
Sheraton Astrodome Hotel (H), Houston, TX 343
Sheraton Austin Hotel (H), Austin, TX 290
Sheraton Corpus Christi Bayfront Hotel (H), Corpus Christi, TX 304
Sheraton Crown Hotel & Conference Center (H), Houston, TX 343
Sheraton Gunther (H), San Antonio, TX 378
Sheraton Hawthorn Park Hotel (H), Springfield, MO 210
Sheraton Hotel (H), Tyler, TX 390
Sheraton Inn (H), Sherman, TX 387
Sheraton Inn Fort Smith (M), Fort Smith, AR 37

Sheraton Inn Plaza Royale (H), Brownsville, TX 299

Sheraton North (H), Metairie, LA 126

Sheraton Park Central Hotel (H), Dallas, TX 310

Sheraton Plaza Hotel (H), Maryland Heights, MO 194

Sheraton South Padre Island Beach Resort (RE), South Padre Island, TX 388

Sheraton Suites Country Club Plaza (H), Kansas City, MO 186

Sheraton Westport Inn (H), Maryland Heights, MO 194

Sheraton Wichita Falls Hotel (H), Wichita Falls, TX 396

Shoji Tabuchi (A), Branson, MO 171

Shoney's Inn (M), Texarkana, AR 53; Independence, MO 180

Shoney's Inn of Baton Rouge (M), Baton Rouge, LA 117

Showboat *Branson Belle* (A), Branson, MO 172

Sid Richardson Collection of Western Art (A), Fort Worth, TX 331

Silk Road (R), St Louis, MO 204

Silver Dollar City (A), Branson, MO 172

Silver Leaf Lodge (L), Mountain Home, AR 48

Sinbad's Palace (R), Dallas, TX 318

Sipango (R), Dallas, TX 318

Sir Loin's Inn (R), North Little Rock, AR 50

Sirloin Stockade (R), Coffeyville, KS 70; Hutchinson, KS 76

Six Flags AstroWorld (A), Houston, TX 352

Six Flags Over Mid-America (A), St Louis, MO 206

Six Flags Over Texas (A), Arlington, TX 286

Six Flags WaterWorld (A), Houston, TX 352

1620 Restaurant (R), Little Rock, AR 45

Sixth Floor Museum, The (A), Dallas, TX 319

Skies (R), Kansas City, MO 190

Skyview Restaurant, The (R), Leavenworth, KS 81

Smoky Hill Museum (A), Salina, KS 89

Snow Bluff Ski and Fun Area (A), Branson, MO 172

Society for the Performing Arts (A), Houston, TX 352

Soniat House (H), New Orleans, LA 136

Sonny Bryan's (R), Dallas, TX 318

Southdown Plantation House, The Terrebonne Museum (A), Houma, LA 121

South Dragon (R), Overland Park, KS 87

Southern Oaks Inn (H), Branson, MO 168

Southfork Ranch (A), Dallas, TX 320

Southmoreland on the Plaza (I), Kansas City, MO 187

Space Center Houston (A), Houston, TX 351

Spaghetti Warehouse, The (R), Dallas, TX 318

Spanish Governor's Palace (A), San Antonio, TX 383

Spanish Trace Inn (M), Athens, TX 287

Spanish Village (R), Houston, TX 350

Spare Rib, The (R), Greenville, TX 338

Spencer Museum of Art (A), Lawrence, KS 80

Split-T (R), Oklahoma City, OK 249

Spoetzl Brewery (A), San Antonio, TX 385

Springfield Art Museum (A), Springfield, MO 212

Stagecoach Inn (M), Temple, TX 389

Star Cafe (R), Fort Worth, TX 330

Star Canyon (R), Dallas, TX 319

Star of India (R), Little Rock, AR 46

Starr Family Home (A), Marshall, TX 363

State Capitol (A), Little Rock, AR 46

State Capitol Complex (A), Austin, TX 293

State Fair Motor Inn Best Western (M), Sedalia, MO 208

Steak and Ale (R), Topeka, KS 90

Steakery, The (R), Amarillo, TX 284

Steamboat *Natchez* (A), New Orleans, LA 149

Stephenson's Apple Farm Restaurant (R), Kansas City, MO 190

Sterne-Hoya Museum (A), Nacogdoches, TX 367

Steves Homestead (A), San Antonio, TX 384

Stillman House Museum (A), Brownsville, TX 301

Stillwater Bay (R), Stillwater, OK 254

Stillwater Inn (R), Jefferson, TX 355

Stockyards Hotel (H), Fort Worth, TX 327

Stone Fort Museum (A), Nacogdoches, TX 367

Stone Hill Winery (A), Branson, MO 172

Stoneleigh Hotel, The (H), Dallas, TX 311

Stonewall West Motor Inn (M), Branson, MO 169

Storyland (A), New Orleans, LA 149

Stratford House Inn, The (M), Norman, OK 243

Stratford House Inn (M), Longview, TX 359

Strecker Museum (A), Waco, TX 395

Strouds (R), Kansas City, MO 190

Summit Lake Resort (RE), Hot Springs National Park, AR 42

Sunshine Inn (R), St Louis, MO 204

Sun Valley Motor Hotel (H), Harlingen, TX 338

Super 8 (M), Mountain Home, AR 48; North Little Rock, AR 50; Coffeyville, KS 70; Colby, KS 71; Concordia, KS 71; Dodge City, KS 71; Lawrence, KS 80; Leavenworth, KS 81; Marysville, KS 84; Tyler, TX 391

Super 8 Lodge (H), Shreveport, LA 151

Super 8 Motel (M), Harrison, AR 39; Jonesboro, AR 43; Manhattan, KS 83; Wichita, KS 93; West Monroe, LA 153; Cameron, MO 173; Cassville, MO 174; Fulton, MO 178; Harrisonville, MO 179; Independence, MO 180; Kansas City, MO 186; Lebanon, MO 193; Macon, MO 194; Moberly, MO 195; Nevada, MO 195; Sedalia, MO 208; Springfield, MO 211; Sullivan, MO 212; Waynesville, MO 213; Clinton, OK 236; McAlester, OK 241; Shawnee, OK 253; Tulsa, OK 257

Surrey Ride Tour (A), Jefferson, TX 355

Swamp Gardens (A), Morgan City, LA 128

Swedish Country Inn (I), Lindsborg, KS 82

Swedish Crown Restaurant, The (R), Lindsborg, KS 82

Sweet Sue's Restaurant (R), Tyler, TX 392

Swiss Village Inn (M), Eureka Springs, AR 34

Szechuan (R), Fort Worth, TX 331

Szechuan Chinese Restaurant (R), Muskogee, OK 242

T

Tahlequah Motor Lodge (M), Tahlequah, OK 254

Tale of the Trout (R), Rogers, AR 51

Taliano's Restaurant (R), Fort Smith, AR 38

Tall Pines Motor Inn (M), Eureka Springs, AR 34

Tapas (R), Little Rock, AR 46

Teal Point Resort (RE), Mountain Home, AR 48

Terilli's Restaurant & Bar (R), Dallas, TX 319

Terrace, The (R), Little Rock, AR 46

Texan, The (R), Bryan, TX 301

Texanna Red's (R), Oklahoma City, OK 249

Texarkana Historical Museum (A), Texarkana, TX 390

Texas Commerce Tower (A), Dallas, TX 320

Texas Energy Museum (A), Beaumont, TX 297

Texas Forestry Museum (A), Lufkin, TX 362

Texas Memorial Museum (A), Austin, TX 292

Texas Prison Museum (A), Huntsville, TX 353

Texas Ranger Hall of Fame and Museum (A), Waco, TX 395

Texas Seaport Museum (A), Galveston, TX 335

Texas State Aquarium (A), Corpus Christi, TX 305

Thai Pepper (R), Houston, TX 350

Thai Soon (R), Dallas, TX 319

Thistle Hill (A), Fort Worth, TX 331

Thomas Hart Benton Home (A), Kansas City, MO 192

Thorncrown Chapel (A), Eureka Springs, AR 35
Threadgill's (R), Austin, TX 291
Thunderbird Lodge (M), Norman, OK 243
Tigua Indian Reservation and Pueblo (A), El Paso, TX 326
Tolbert's Texas Chili Parlor (R), Dallas, TX 319
Tomatillo's y Cantina (R), San Antonio, TX 382
Tommassi Restaurant (R), Hutchinson, KS 76
Tony Mandola's Blue Oyster Bar (R), Houston, TX 350
Tony Moran's Old Absinthe House (A), New Orleans, LA 147
Tony's (R), St Louis, MO 204
Topeka Plaza Inn (M), Topeka, KS 90
Topeka Zoological Park (A), Topeka, KS 91
Top of the Dome (R), New Orleans, LA 145
Top of the Riverfront (R), St Louis, MO 204
Torre's Pizzaria (R), Kansas City, MO 190
Tower of the Americas (A), San Antonio, TX 384
Town & Country Kitchen (R), Norton, KS 85
Toy and Miniature Museum of Kansas City (A), Kansas City, MO 191
Trader Vic's (R), Kansas City, MO 191
Travelers Inn (M), Eureka Springs, AR 34; Oklahoma City, OK 247
Travelodge (M), Hannibal, MO 179; Kansas City, MO 187; Rolla, MO 196
Travelodge Hotel (H), Dallas, TX 311
Travelodge Hotel Houston Greenway Plaza (H), Houston, TX 343
Travelodge Suites (H), San Antonio, TX 378
Treebeard's (R), Houston, TX 350
Tremont House, The (H), Galveston, TX 334
Trolley's (R), McAlester, OK 241
Trotter's Bar-B-Q (R), Springfield, MO 212
Tujague's (R), New Orleans, LA 145
Tulio's Mexican Restaurant (R), Norman, OK 244
Tulsa Marriott Southern Hills (H), Tulsa, OK 256
Tulsa Zoological Park (A), Tulsa, OK 259
Tunk's Cypress Inn (R), Alexandria, LA 115
Turner Falls Park (A), Davis, OK 236
Twin Elm Ranch (RE), Bandera, TX 295
Tyler State Park (A), Tyler, TX 392

U

Umlauf Sculpture Garden and Museum (A), Austin, TX 292
Unicorn Restaurant (R), Laredo, TX 359
US Cavalry Museum (A), Junction City, KS 78
US Center Motel (M), Smith Center, KS 89
University Hotel (H), Huntsville, TX 353

University of Oklahoma Museum of Art (A), Norman, OK 244
Upperline (R), New Orleans, LA 145
USS Batfish–War Memorial Park (A), Muskogee, OK 242
USS Kidd and Nautical Center (A), Baton Rouge, LA 119
USS Lexington (A), Corpus Christi, TX 305

V

Vagabond Family Restaurant (R), Hays, KS 75
Vaile Mansion (A), Independence, MO 181
Valentino's Ristorante (R), Topeka, KS 90
Val-U Inn Corpus Christi (M), Corpus Christi, TX 304
Val Verde Winery (A), Del Rio, TX 322
Van Loc Restaurant (R), Houston, TX 350
Vargo's (R), Houston, TX 350
Veranda Restaurant, The (R), New Orleans, LA 146
Vermilionville (A), Lafayette, LA 125
Versailles (R), New Orleans, LA 146
Victorian Condo Hotel, The (M), Galveston, TX 334
Victorian Inn (M), Cape Girardeau, MO 173
Victorian Sampler Restaurant (R), Eureka Springs, AR 35
Vienna Weinstrube (R), San Antonio, TX 382
Viking Motel (M), Lindsborg, KS 82
Villa, The (R), Little Rock, AR 46
Villa Italia (R), Bartlesville, OK 234
Villa Marre (A), Little Rock, AR 46
Vintage 1847 Restaurant (R), Hermann, MO 180

W

Waco Hilton Inn (H), Waco, TX 394
Walnut Street Inn (I), Springfield, MO 211
Walt Bodine's (R), Kansas City, MO 191
War Eagle Cavern (A), Rogers, AR 51
War Eagle Mill (A), Rogers, AR 51
Warehouse No 1 Restaurant (R), Monroe, LA 128
Warren Duck Club (R), Tulsa, OK 259
Washington Artillery Park (A), New Orleans, LA 148
Waterford Dining Room, The (R), Oklahoma City, OK 249
Waterford Hotel, The (H), Oklahoma City, OK 246
Water Town (A), Shreveport, LA 152
Water Wonderland (A), Odessa, TX 369
Wayfarer Inn (M), Woodward, OK 260
Weidman's Old Fort Brew Pub (R), Fort Smith, AR 38
Welk Resort Center and Champagne Theatre (A), Branson, MO 171
Wentletrap, The (R), Galveston, TX 335
Westar Suites (H), Amarillo, TX 283; El Paso, TX 325

Westar Suites/Irving (DFW Airport South) (M), Dallas–Fort Worth Int'l Airport, TX 321
Westchase Hilton (H), Houston, TX 343
Westin Canal Place (H), New Orleans, LA 137
Westin Crown Center (H), Kansas City, MO 186
Westin Galleria (H), Houston, TX 343
Westin Hotel Galleria Dallas, The (H), Dallas, TX 311
Westin Oaks, The (H), Houston, TX 343
West Lynn Cafe (R), Austin, TX 292
Weston Historical Museum (A), Weston, MO 214
Westport Flea Market & Grill (R), Kansas City, MO 191
Wet 'n' Wild (A), Arlington, TX 286
Wharton's Vista Motel (M), Alva, OK 232
White Haven Motor Lodge (M), Overland Park, KS 87
Whitehead Memorial Museum (A), Del Rio, TX 322
White Water Bay (A), Oklahoma City, OK 250
White Water Park (A), Branson, MO 172
Wichita Art Museum (A), Wichita, KS 94
Wichita Falls Museum and Art Center (A), Wichita Falls, TX 396
Wichita Marriott Hotel (H), Wichita, KS 93
Wichita Mountains Wildlife Refuge (A), Lawton, OK 240
Wichita Suites (H), Wichita, KS 93
Wiederkehr Wine Cellars, Inc (A), Altus, AR 28
Wild Basin Wilderness Preserve (A), Austin, TX 294
Wilderness Park Museum (A), El Paso, TX 327
Willie's Grill & Ice House (R), Houston, TX 350
Will Rogers Birthplace (A), Claremore, OK 235
Will Rogers Memorial Center (A), Fort Worth, TX 332
Will Rogers Museum (A), Claremore, OK 235
Wilson Inn (M), Jonesboro, AR 43
Windsor Court Hotel (H), New Orleans, LA 137
Winslow's Smokehouse (R), Kansas City, MO 191
Winstead's (R), Kansas City, MO 191
Woldenberg River Park (A), New Orleans, LA 149
Wolf House Museum (A), Manhattan, KS 83
Wonder World (A), San Marcos, TX 386
Woodward Ranch (A), Alpine, TX 282
Woolaroc Museum (A), Bartlesville, OK 234
World of Discovery (A), Corpus Christi, TX 305
Worlds of Fun (A), Kansas City, MO 192
World Trade Center of New Orleans (A), New Orleans, LA 149
Wortham Theater Center (A), Houston, TX 352
Worthington (H), Fort Worth, TX 328

Wyndham Anatole Hotel (H), Dallas, TX 311

Wyndham Garden Hotel (H), Irving, TX 354

Wyndham Greenspoint Hotel (H), Houston, TX 344

Wyndham Warwick, The (H), Houston, TX 344

Y

Yacht Club, The (R), Port Isabel, TX 373

Yacht Club Hotel (H), Port Isabel, TX 372

Yen Ching (R), St Louis, MO 204

YO Ranch Holiday Inn (H), Kerrville, TX 356

Yturri-Edmunds Historic Site (A), San Antonio, TX 384

Z

Zam's Swamp Tours (A), Houma, LA 122

Zia's (R), St Louis, MO 204

Zilker Botanical Gardens (A), Austin, TX 294

Zilker Park (A), Austin, TX 293

Terms and Conditions
- Offer includes 10% discount off all time and mileage charges on Cruise America or Cruise Canada vehicles only.
- Offer not available in conjunction with other discount offers or promotional rates.
- Excludes rental charges, deposits, sales tax, amd fuels.
- Normal rental conditions and customer qualification procedures apply.
- Members must reserve through Central Reservations only, at least one week in advance of pick up and mention membership affiliation at time of reservation.

  For reservations, call: 1-800-327-7799 US and Canada
- By acceptance and use of this offer, member agrees to the above conditions.
- Offer expires December 31, 1997.

Save 10%   Save 10%

Offer expires December 31, 1997.

Savings are subject to certain restrictions and availability.
Valid for flights on most airlines.

Minimum Ticket Price	Save
$200.00	$25.00
$250.00	$50.00
$350.00	$75.00
$450.00	$100.00

Terms and Conditions
1. Advance reservations required.
2. Coupon must be presented at check-in.
3. Coupon cannot be combined with any other special offers, discounted rates.
4. Subject to availability.
5. Valid through December 31, 1997.
6. No photo copies allowed.

For reservations, call 1-800-578-7878 or your travel agent and ask for the 5CPN discount.

All reservations must be made by calling our toll free reservation system, Superline. Any reservation requiring a guarantee must be guaranteed with the corporate V.I.P. identification number and the individual traveler's major credit card. If a guaranteed reservation is made and subsequently neither used nor cancelled, the corporate traveler will be billed for the one night's room charge plus tax.

expires December 31, 1997

Redeemable at participating Dollar® locations only.

This coupon entitles you to a one class upgrade from a compact or economy car to the next higher car group at no extra charge. Simply make a reservation for a compact or economy class car, then present this coupon to any Dollar rental agent when you arrive. You'll receive an upgrade to the next car class at no additional charge. Upgrade subject to vehicle availability. Renter must meet Dollar age, driver and credit requirements. This coupon must be surrendered at time of rental and may not be used in conjunction with any other offer and has no cash value. **EXPIRES 12/15/97.**

For worldwide reservations, call your travel agent or 800-800-4000

DOLLAR MAKES SENSE.™

Mention code "afbg2" when you place your first order and receive 15% OFF

Offer expires December 31, 1997

PO Box 5485-AF2, Santa Barbara, CA 93150

Magellan's ◑

10% OFF

DAYS INN®
Follow the Sun™

- Available at participating properties.
- This coupon cannot be combined with any other special discount offer.
- Limit one coupon per room, per stay. Expires December 31, 1997.
- Not valid during blackout periods or special events.
- Void where prohibited.
- No reproductions accepted.

1-800-DAYS INN

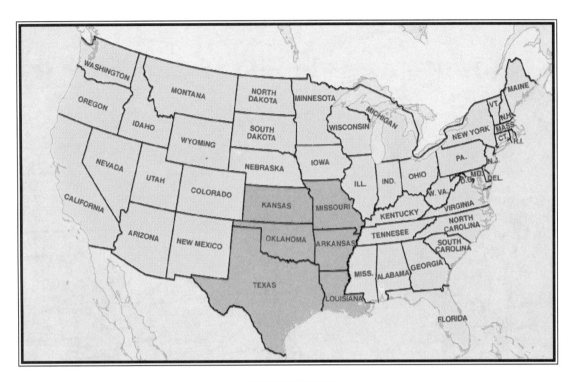

CONTENTS

Interstate Highway Map of the United States ——————— M-2

Kansas ——————————————————————————— M-4

Missouri ——————————————————————————— M-5

Arkansas and Louisiana ——————————————————— M-6

Western Texas / Big Bend National Park ————————————— M-7

Southern Texas / San Antonio and Vicinity ————————————— M-8

Northern Texas and Oklahoma ————————————————— M-10

Dallas / Fort Worth and Vicinity ————————————————— M-12

Houston and Vicinity ——————————————————————— M-14

Central Dallas / Central Fort Worth / Central Houston ——————— M-16

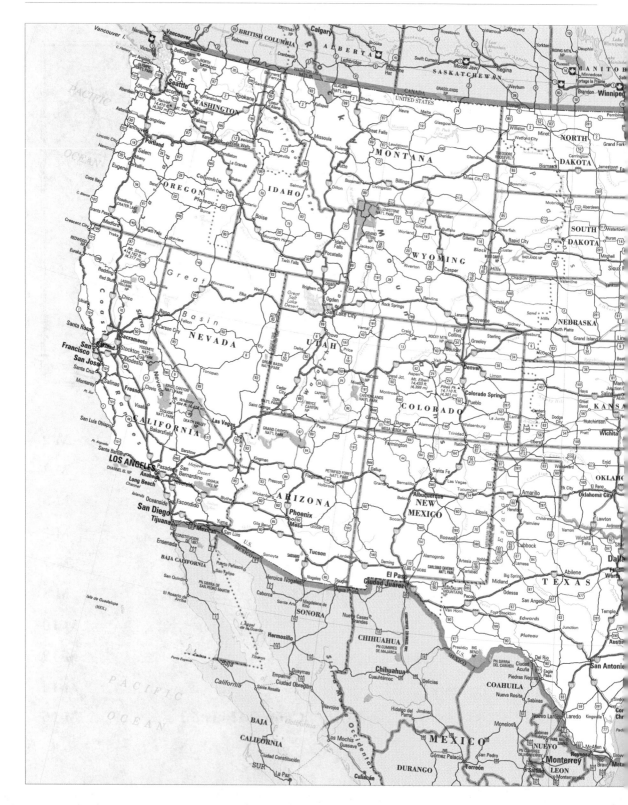

STATE & CITY MAP LEGEND
(SEE MAPS ON FOLLOWING PAGES)

ROAD CLASSIFICATIONS

Limited Access Highways
Toll Roads and Interchanges
National Parkways
Primary Roads
Secondary Roads
Connecting Roads

95 Interstate
76 76 U.S.
160 160 State
Mileage Between Dots
Selected Scenic Roads

SPECIAL FEATURES

National Capital
State Capital
Point Of Interest
Recreation Area
Airports
Ferries

UNITED STATES

LEGEND

Limited Access Highways
Toll Highways
National Parkways
Primary Roads
Other Roads
National Parks
National Capital
State / Provincial Capital
Time Zone Boundary
Ferries

ROUTE MARKERS

Interstate
U.S.
State / Provincial
Trans Canada
Mexico Federal

SCALE 1:7,850,000
ALBERS EQUAL AREA PROJECTION

0   200 Mi.
0   200 Km.

© HAMMOND INCORPORATED, Maplewood, N.J. CC•A

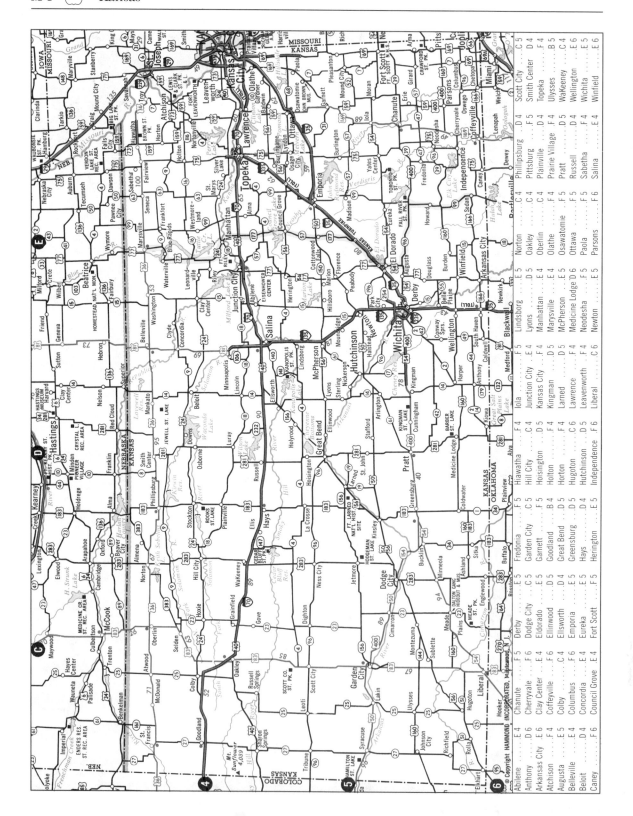

Abilene	E 4	Chanute	F 5	Derby	F 5	Phillipsburg	C 5
Anthony	D 6	Cherryvale	F 6	Dodge City	D 5	Pittsburg	F 5
Arkansas City	E 6	Clay Center	E 4	Eldorado	E 4	Plainville	C 4
Atchison	F 3	Coffeyville	F 6	Ellinwood	D 5	Prairie Village	F 4
Augusta	E 5	Colby	C 4	Ellsworth	D 4	Pratt	D 5
Belleville	E 4	Columbus	F 6	Emporia	E 4	Russell	D 4
Beloit	D 4	Concordia	D 4	Eureka	E 5	Sabetha	F 3
Caney	F 6	Council Grove	E 4	Fort Scott	F 5	Salina	E 4
Scott City	C 5					
Smith Center	D 4					
Topeka	D 4					
Ulysses	B 5					
WaKeeney	C 4					
Wellington	E 6					
Wichita	E 5					
Winfield	E 6					

Fredonia	F 5	Hiawatha	F 5	Lindsborg	F 5	Norton	E 5
Garden City	C 5	Hill City	C 5	Lyons	E 4	Oakley	D 5
Garnett	F 5	Hoisington	F 5	Manhattan	E 4	Oberlin	E 4
Goodland	D 5	Holton	B 4	Marysville	D 5	Olathe	F 5
Great Bend	D 4	Horton	F 4	McPherson	E 5	Osawatomie	F 5
Greensburg	E 5	Hugoton	D 5	Medicine Lodge	D 6	Ottawa	F 4
Hays	E 4	Hutchinson	D 4	Neodesha	F 5	Paola	F 4
Herington	E 5	Independence	F 6	Newton	E 5	Parsons	E 5

© Copyright HAMMOND INCORPORATED, Maplewood, N.J.

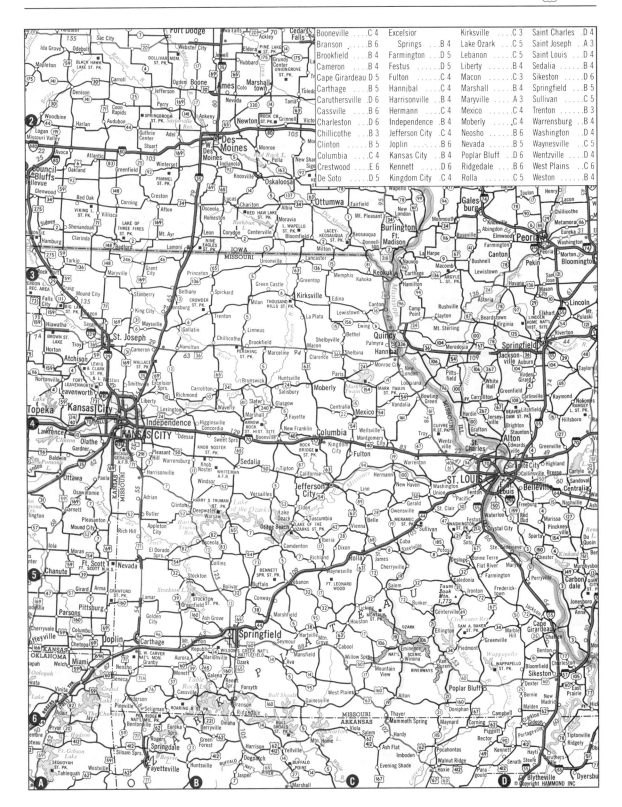

Booneville ....C 4	Excelsior	Kirksville ....C 3	Saint Charles .D 4
Branson ......B 6	Springs ..B 4	Lake Ozark ...C 5	Saint Joseph ..A 3
Brookfield ....B 4	Farmington ..D 5	Lebanon ....C 5	Saint Louis ...D 4
Cameron .....B 4	Festus ......D 5	Liberty .....B 4	Sedalia .....B 4
Cape Girardeau D 5	Fulton ......C 4	Macon ......C 3	Sikeston ....D 6
Carthage .....B 5	Hannibal ....C 4	Marshall ....B 4	Springfield ...B 5
Caruthersville .D 6	Harrisonville ..B 4	Maryville ....A 3	Sullivan ....C 5
Cassville ....B 6	Hermann ....C 4	Mexico .....C 4	Trenton .....B 3
Charleston ...D 6	Independence .B 4	Moberly ....C 4	Warrensburg ..B 4
Chillicothe ...B 3	Jefferson City .C 4	Neosho .....B 6	Washington ..D 4
Clinton ......B 5	Joplin ......B 5	Nevada .....B 5	Waynesville ..C 5
Columbia ....C 4	Kansas City ..B 4	Poplar Bluff ..D 6	Wentzville ...D 4
Crestwood ...E 6	Kennett .....D 6	Ridgedale ...B 6	West Plains ..C 6
De Soto .....D 5	Kingdom City .C 4	Rolla ......C 5	Weston .....B 4

ARKANSAS

Altus .... A 2
Arkadelphia ...... A 3
Ashdown .... A 3
Batesville .... B 2
Benton .... A 3
Blytheville .... C 2
Bull Shoals ...... B 1
Camden .... A 3
Conway .... B 2
El Dorado .... A 3
Eureka Springs ... A 1
Fayetteville ...... A 2
Forrest City ...... B 2
Fort Smith .... A 2
Harrison .... A 1
Heber Springs .... B 2
Helena .... B 3
Hope .... A 3
Hot Springs Nat'l Pk. .. A 3
Jacksonville ...... B 2
Jonesboro .... B 2
Little Rock .... B 2
Magnolia .... A 3
Malvern .... A 3
Mena .... A 2
Mountain Home ... B 1
Mountain View .... B 2
Newport .... B 2
North Little Rock .. B 2
Paragould .... B 2
Pine Bluff .... B 3
Pocahontas .... B 1
Rogers .... A 1
Russellville ...... A 2
Searcy .... B 2
Springdale .... A 1
Stuttgart .... B 3
Texarkana .... A 3
Van Buren .... A 2
Warren .... B 3
West Helena ...... B 3
West Memphis .... C 2

LOUISIANA

Abbeville .... B 5
Alexandria .... A 5
Bastrop .... B 4
Baton Rouge ..... B 5
Bogalusa .... C 5
Bossier City ..... A 4
Covington .... C 5
Crowley .... A 5
De Ridder .... A 5
Denham Springs .. B 5
Donaldsonville ... B 5
Epps .... B 4
Eunice .... B 5
Franklin .... B 5
Gretna .... C 5
Hammond .... B 5
Houma .... B 6
Jennings .... A 5
Kenner .... C 5
Lacombe .... C 5
Lafayette .... B 5
Lake Charles ..... A 5
Mansfield .... A 4
Many .... A 4
Metairie .... C 5
Minden .... A 4
Monroe .... B 4
Morgan City ...... B 6
Natchitoches ..... A 4
New Iberia .... B 5
New Orleans ..... C 5
Opelousas .... B 5
Pineville .... A 5
Plaquemine ...... B 5
Rayne .... B 5
Ruston .... A 4
Saint Martinville . B 5
Shreveport .... A 4
Slidell .... C 5
Sulphur .... A 5
Tallulah .... B 4
Thibodaux .... B 6
Ville Platte ...... A 4
West Monroe ..... B 4
Westwego .... C 5
Winnfield .... A 4

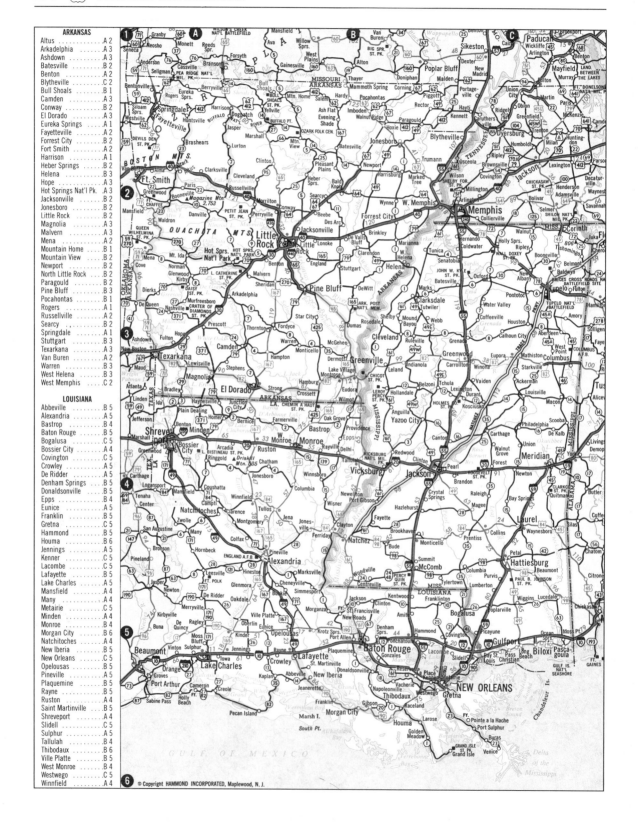

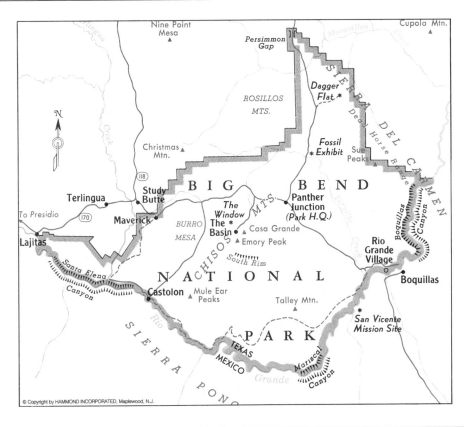

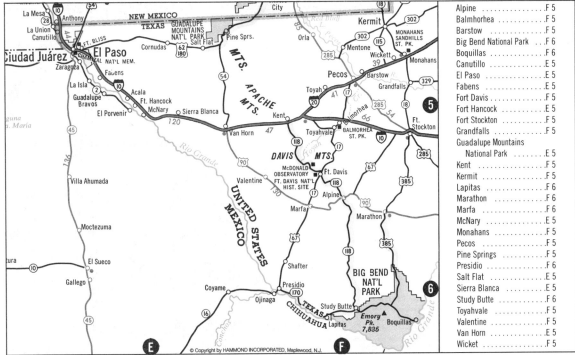

Alpine ....F 5
Balmhorhea ....F 5
Barstow ....F 5
Big Bend National Park ...F 6
Boquillas ....F 6
Canutillo ....E 5
El Paso ....E 5
Fabens ....E 5
Fort Davis ....F 5
Fort Hancock ....E 5
Fort Stockton ....F 5
Grandfalls ....F 5
Guadalupe Mountains
   National Park ....E 5
Kent ....F 5
Kermit ....F 5
Lapitas ....F 6
Marathon ....F 6
Marfa ....F 6
McNary ....E 5
Monahans ....F 5
Pecos ....F 5
Pine Springs ....F 5
Presidio ....F 6
Salt Flat ....E 5
Sierra Blanca ....E 5
Study Butte ....F 6
Toyahvale ....F 5
Valentine ....F 5
Van Horn ....E 5
Wicket ....F 5

Abilene ......C 1	Eagle Pass ....B 4	Marlin ....D 2
Alamo ......C 6	Eastland .....C 1	Marshall ....F 1
Alice ....D 5	Edinburg ....D 6	Mathis ....D 4
Alvin ....E 3	Edna ....D 4	McAllen ....C 6
Andrews ....A 1	El Campo ....E 4	McCamey ....A 2
Angleton ...E 4	Elgin .....D 3	McKinney ....D 1
Anson ......B 1	Ennis ......D 1	Mercedes ....D 6
Aransas Pass .D 5	Falfurrias ....C 5	Mexia ....D 2
Arlington ...D 1	Fannett ....F 3	Midland ....A 2
Athens .....E 1	Fort Stockton ..A 2	Mineola ....E 1
Atlanta .....F 1	Fort Worth ..D 1	Mineral Wells ..D 1
Austin .....D 3	Fredericksburg C 3	Mission ....C 6
Azle ....D 1	Freeport .....E 4	Monahans ....A 2
Ballinger ...B 2	Freer ......C 5	Mount Pleasant ..E 1
Bandera ....C 3	Galveston ....F 4	Nacogdoches ...F 2
Bastrop ....D 3	Gatesville ....D 2	Navasota ....E 3
Bay City ...E 4	Georgetown ..D 3	Nederland .....F 3
Baytown ....E 3	Giddings ....D 3	Needville ......E 3
Beaumont ..F 3	Gilmer .....E 1	New Braunfels ..C 3
Beeville ....D 4	Gladewater ..E 1	Odessa ....A 2
Belton ......D 2	Goliad .....D 4	Orange ....F 3
Benbrook ...D 6	Gonzales ....D 3	Ozona ....B 2
Big Spring ..B 1	Graham .....C 1	Palacios ....E 4
Bishop .....D 5	Granbury ....D 1	Palestine ......E 2
Brady ......C 2	Greenville ....E 1	Pasadena ......E 3
Brazosport ..E 4	Groves .....F 3	Pharr ....D 6
Breckinridge .C 1	Hallettsville ..D 3	Pittsburg ......E 1
Brenham ....E 3	Hamilton ....D 2	Plano ....D 1
Bridgeport ..D 1	Hamlin .....C 1	Pleasanton ....C 4
Brownsville ..D 6	Harlingen ....D 6	Port Aransas ..D 5
Brownwood ..C 2	Haskell .....C 1	Port Arthur ...F 3
Bryan ......E 3	Hearne .....D 2	Port Isabel ....D 6
Burnet ......C 2	Hebbronville ..C 5	
Cameron ....D 2	Henderson ....E 1	
Carrizo Springs B 4	Highlands ....E 3	
Carthage ....F 1	Hillsboro ....D 2	
Center ......F 2	Hitchcock ....E 4	
Cisco ....C 1	Honda .....C 4	
Cleburne ...D 1	Houston .....E 3	
Cleveland ...E 3	Huntsville ....E 2	
Clute ....E 4	Hurst ......E 6	
Coleman ....C 2	Irving ......D 1	
College	Jacksboro ....C 1	
Station ....E 3	Jacksonville ..E 2	
Colorado City .B 1	Jasper ......F 2	
Columbus ...D 3	Jefferson ....F 1	
Comanche ..C 2	Karnes City ..D 4	
Commerce ..E 1	Kaufman ....D 1	
Conroe .....E 3	Kenedy .....D 4	
Copperas	Kermit .....A 2	
Cove .....D 2	Kerrville .....C 3	
Corpus Christi D 5	Kilgore .....E 1	
Corsicana ...E 1	Killeen .....D 2	
Cotulla .....C 4	Kingsville ....D 5	
Crane ....A 2	La Grange ....D 3	
Crockett ....E 2	La Marque ...E 3	
Crystal City ..B 4	Lake Jackson .E 4	
Cuero ......D 4	Lamesa .....A 1	
Daingerfield ..F 1	Lampasas ....C 2	
Dallas ......D 1	Laredo .....C 5	
Dayton .....F 3	League City ..E 3	
Decatur .....D 1	Lewisville ....D 1	
Del Rio .....B 3	Liberty .....F 3	
Denton .....D 1	Llano ......C 2	
Devine .....C 4	Lockhart ....D 3	
Diboll ......F 2	Longview ....E 1	
Donna ......D 6	Lufkin .....F 2	
Eagle Lake ..E 3	Luling .....D 3	

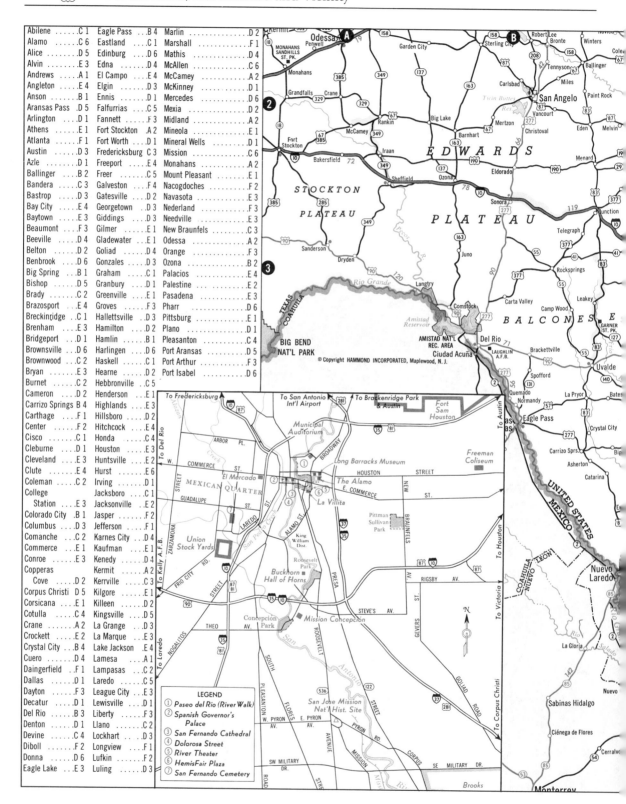

© Copyright HAMMOND INCORPORATED, Maplewood, N. J.

LEGEND
1. Paseo del Rio (River Walk)
2. Spanish Governor's Palace
3. San Fernando Cathedral
4. Dolorosa Street
5. River Theater
6. HemisFair Plaza
7. San Fernando Cemetery

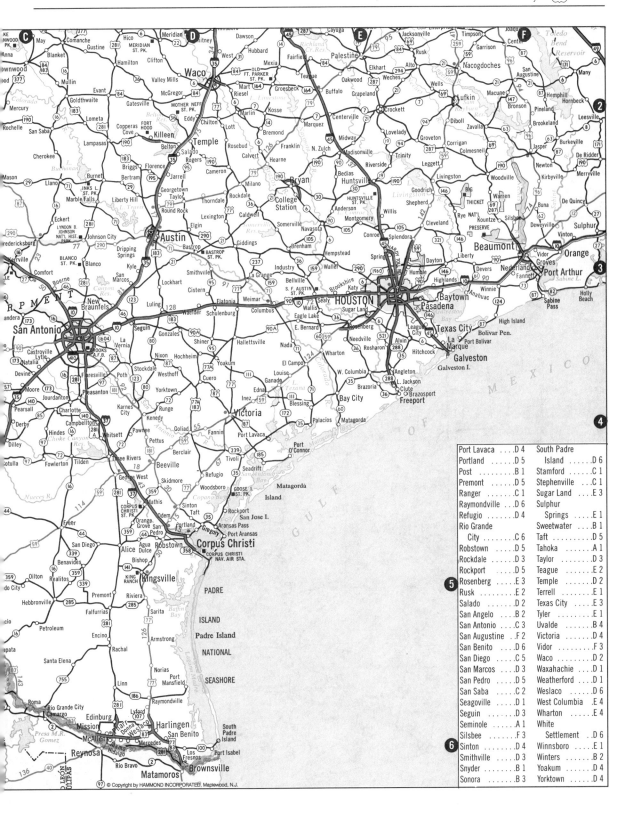

Port Lavaca	....D 4	South Padre	
Portland	......D 5	Island	......D 6
Post	.......B 1	Stamford	......C 1
Premont	.....D 5	Stephenville	..C 1
Ranger	.......C 1	Sugar Land	....E 3
Raymondville	.D 6	Sulphur	
Refugio	.......D 4	Springs	.....E 1
Rio Grande		Sweetwater	....B 1
City	.......C 6	Taft	.......D 5
Robstown	.....D 5	Tahoka	......A 1
Rockdale	.....D 3	Taylor	........D 3
Rockport	.....D 5	Teague	.......E 2
Rosenberg	....E 3	Temple	.......D 2
Rusk	.........E 2	Terrell	........E 1
Salado	.......D 2	Texas City	....E 3
San Angelo	...B 2	Tyler	.........E 1
San Antonio	..C 3	Uvalde	.......B 4
San Augustine	..F 2	Victoria	......D 4
San Benito	...D 6	Vidor	.........F 3
San Diego	.....C 5	Waco	.........D 2
San Marcos	...D 3	Waxahachie	...D 1
San Pedro	.....D 5	Weatherford	...D 1
San Saba	.....C 2	Weslaco	......D 6
Seagoville	....D 1	West Columbia	.E 4
Seguin	.......D 3	Wharton	......E 4
Seminole	.....A 1	White	
Silsbee	.......F 3	Settlement	..D 6
Sinton	.......D 4	Winnsboro	....E 1
Smithville	....D 3	Winters	......B 2
Snyder	.......B 1	Yoakum	.......D 4
Sonora	.......B 3	Yorktown	.....D 4

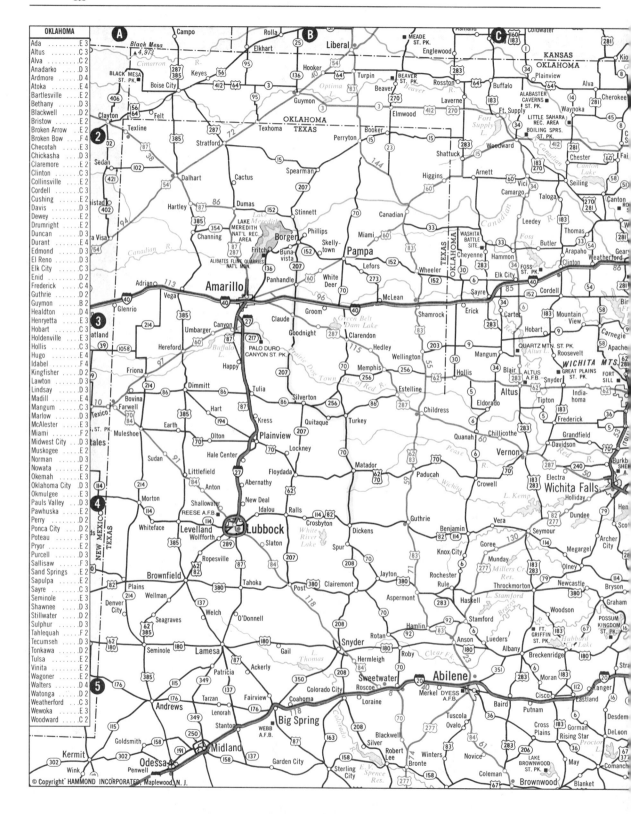

OKLAHOMA

Ada . . . . E 3
Altus . . . . C 3
Alva . . . . C 2
Anadarko . . . . . . D 3
Ardmore . . . . . . D 4
Atoka . . . . E 4
Bartlesville . . . . . E 2
Bethany . . . . D 3
Blackwell . . . . . . D 2
Bristow . . . . E 2
Broken Arrow . . . . E 2
Broken Bow . . . . . F 4
Checotah . . . . . . E 3
Chickasha . . . . . . D 3
Claremore . . . . . . E 2
Clinton . . . . C 3
Collinsville . . . . . E 2
Cordell . . . . C 3
Cushing . . . . E 2
Davis . . . . D 3
Dewey . . . . E 2
Drumright . . . . . . E 2
Duncan . . . . D 3
Durant . . . . E 4
Edmond . . . . D 3
El Reno . . . . D 3
Elk City . . . . C 3
Enid . . . . D 2
Frederick . . . . . . C 4
Guthrie . . . . D 2
Guymon . . . . B 2
Healdton . . . . . . D 4
Henryetta . . . . . . E 3
Hobart . . . . C 3
Holdenville . . . . . E 3
Hollis . . . . C 3
Hugo . . . . E 4
Idabel . . . . F 4
Kingfisher . . . . . . D 2
Lawton . . . . D 3
Lindsay . . . . D 3
Madill . . . . E 4
Mangum . . . . C 3
Marlow . . . . D 3
McAlester . . . . . . E 3
Miami . . . . F 2
Midwest City . . . . D 3
Muskogee . . . . . . E 3
Norman . . . . D 3
Nowata . . . . E 2
Okemah . . . . E 3
Oklahoma City . . . D 3
Okmulgee . . . . . . E 3
Pauls Valley . . . . . D 3
Pawhuska . . . . . . D 2
Perry . . . . D 2
Ponca City . . . . . D 2
Poteau . . . . F 3
Pryor . . . . E 2
Purcell . . . . D 3
Sallisaw . . . . F 3
Sand Springs . . . . E 2
Sapulpa . . . . E 2
Sayre . . . . C 3
Seminole . . . . . . E 3
Shawnee . . . . D 3
Stillwater . . . . . . D 2
Sulphur . . . . D 3
Tahlequah . . . . . . F 2
Tecumseh . . . . . . D 3
Tonkawa . . . . D 2
Tulsa . . . . E 2
Vinita . . . . E 2
Wagoner . . . . E 2
Walters . . . . D 4
Watonga . . . . D 2
Weatherford . . . . . C 3
Wewoka . . . . E 3
Woodward . . . . . . C 2

© Copyright HAMMOND INCORPORATED, Maplewood, N. J.

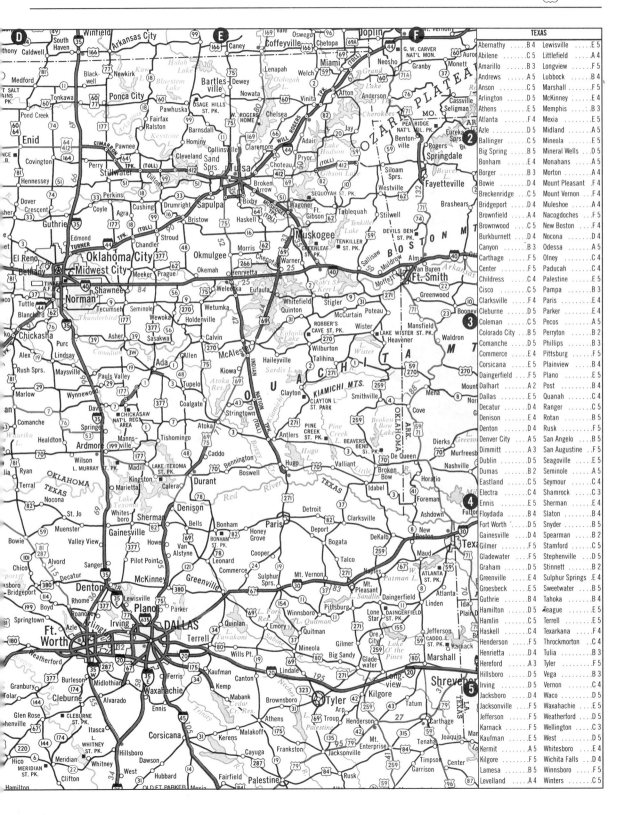

TEXAS	
Abernathy ......B 4	Lewisville .....E 5
Abilene ....C 5	Littlefield ....A 4
Amarillo ......B 3	Longview .....F 5
Andrews ......A 5	Lubbock ......B 4
Anson ....C 5	Marshall ......F 5
Arlington .....D 5	McKinney .....E 4
Athens ....E 5	Memphis .....B 3
Atlanta ....F 4	Mexia ....E 5
Azle ....D 5	Midland ......A 5
Ballinger .....C 5	Mineola ......E 5
Big Spring ....B 5	Mineral Wells ..D 5
Bonham ......E 4	Monahans .....A 5
Borger ....B 3	Morton ....A 4
Bowie ....E 4	Mount Pleasant .F 4
Breckenridge ..C 5	Mount Vernon ..F 4
Bridgeport ....D 4	Muleshoe .....A 4
Brownfield ....A 4	Nacogdoches ...F 5
Brownwood ....C 5	New Boston ....F 4
Burkburnett ...D 4	Nocona ....D 4
Canyon ....B 3	Odessa ....A 5
Carthage .....F 5	Olney ....C 4
Center ....E 5	Paducah ......C 4
Childress .....C 4	Palestine .....E 5
Cisco ....C 5	Pampa ....B 3
Clarksville ....F 4	Paris ....E 4
Cleburne .....D 5	Parker ....E 4
Coleman ......C 5	Pecos ....A 5
Colorado City ..B 5	Perryton ......B 2
Comanche .....D 5	Phillips ......B 3
Commerce .....E 4	Pittsburg .....F 5
Corsicana .....E 5	Plainview .....B 4
Daingerfield ...F 5	Plano ....E 5
Dalhart ....A 2	Post ....B 4
Dallas ....D 5	Quanah ....C 4
Decatur ......D 4	Ranger ....C 5
Denison ......E 4	Rotan ....B 5
Denton ....D 4	Rusk ....F 5
Denver City ...A 5	San Angelo ....B 5
Dimmitt ......A 3	San Augustine ..F 5
Dublin ....D 5	Seagoville ....E 5
Dumas ....B 2	Seminole .....A 5
Eastland ......C 5	Seymour ......C 4
Electra ....C 4	Shamrock .....C 3
Ennis ....E 5	Sherman ......E 4
Floydada .....B 4	Slaton ....B 4
Fort Worth ....D 5	Snyder ....B 5
Gainesville ...D 4	Spearman .....B 2
Gilmer ....F 5	Stamford .....C 5
Gladewater ....F 5	Stephenville ...D 5
Graham ......D 5	Stinnett ......B 2
Greenville ....E 4	Sulphur Springs .E 4
Groesbeck ....E 5	Sweetwater ....B 5
Guthrie ......B 4	Tahoka ....B 4
Hamilton .....D 5	Teague ....E 5
Hamlin ....C 5	Terrell ....E 5
Haskell ......C 4	Texarkana .....F 4
Henderson ....F 5	Throckmorton ..C 4
Henrietta .....D 4	Tulia ....B 3
Hereford .....A 3	Tyler ....F 5
Hillsboro .....D 5	Vega ....B 3
Irving ....D 5	Vernon ....C 4
Jacksboro .....D 4	Waco ....D 5
Jacksonville ...F 5	Waxahachie ...D 5
Jefferson .....F 5	Weatherford ...D 5
Karnack ......F 5	Wellington ....C 3
Kaufman ......E 5	West ....D 5
Kermit ....A 5	Whitesboro ....E 4
Kilgore ....F 5	Wichita Falls ..D 4
Lamesa ......B 5	Winnsboro ....F 5
Levelland .....A 4	Winters ......C 5

Addison .....E 2	Dallas ....E 3	Haslet ....B 2	Mansfield .....C 4	Sachse ....F 2
Arlington .....C 4	Dalworthington	Hebron ....D 2	Mesquite .....F 3	Saginaw .....B 3
Avondale .....A 2	Gardens ...C 4	Hicks ....A 2	Murphy ....F 2	Saint Paul .....F 2
Azle ....A 2	De Soto .....D 4	Highland Park ..E 3	Newark ....A 2	Sand Branch ...F 4
Balch Springs ..F 3	Dido ....A 2	Hurst ....C 3	North Richland	Sanson Park
Bedford ......C 3	Duncanville ...D 4	Hutchins .....E 4	Hills ....B 3	Village .....A 3
Benbrook......A 4	Edgecliff ......B 4	India ....F 4	Oakgrove .....B 4	Seagoville .....F 4
Bisbee ....C 4	Euliss ....C 3	Irving ....D 3	Pantego .....C 3	Southlake .....C 2
Blue Mound ...B 3	Everman .....B 4	Jonesville .....F 3	Pecan Grove ...F 2	Sunnyvale .....F 3
Briar ....A 2	Farmers	Keller ....B 2	Plano ....E 2	Trinity Park .....F 1
Buckingham ..E 2	Branch ...D 2	Kennedale .....B 4	Pleasant Valley .F 2	University Park .E 3
Burleson .....B 4	Ferris ....E 4	Kleberg .....F 4	Red Oak .....E 4	Walnut Springs .F 4
Carrollton .....D 2	Flower Mound ..C 2	Lakeside .....A 3	Rendon ....B 4	Watauga .....B 3
Cedar Hill .....D 4	Forest Hill .....B 4	Lakeview .....A 2	Retta ....B 4	Watsonville .....C 4
Center Point ...A 2	Fort Worth ...B 3	Lake Worth	Rhome ....A 2	Webb ....C 4
Cockrell Hill ...D 3	Garland ....F 2	Village .....A 3	Richardson .....E 2	Westover Hills ..A 3
Colleyville .....C 2	Glenn Heights ..D 4	Lancaster .....E 4	Richland Hills ..B 3	Wheatland .....A 4
Combine .....F 4	Grand Prairie ..D 3	Lawson ....F 3	River Oaks .....A 3	White Settlement A 3
Coppell ......C 2	Grapevine .....C 2	Lewisville .....D 2	Roanoke .....B 2	Wilmer ....E 4
Crowley ......B 4	Haltom City ...B 3	Liberty Grove ...F 2	Rowlett ....F 2	Wylie ....F 2

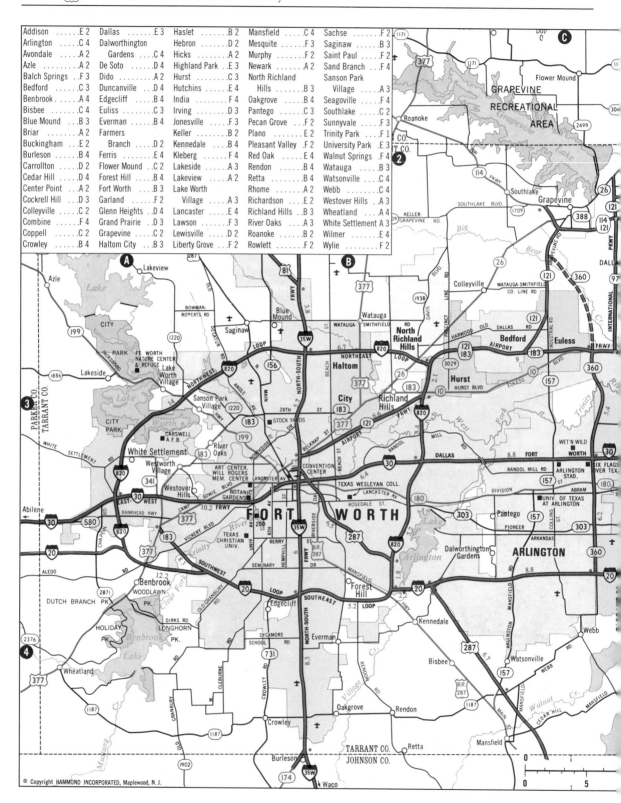

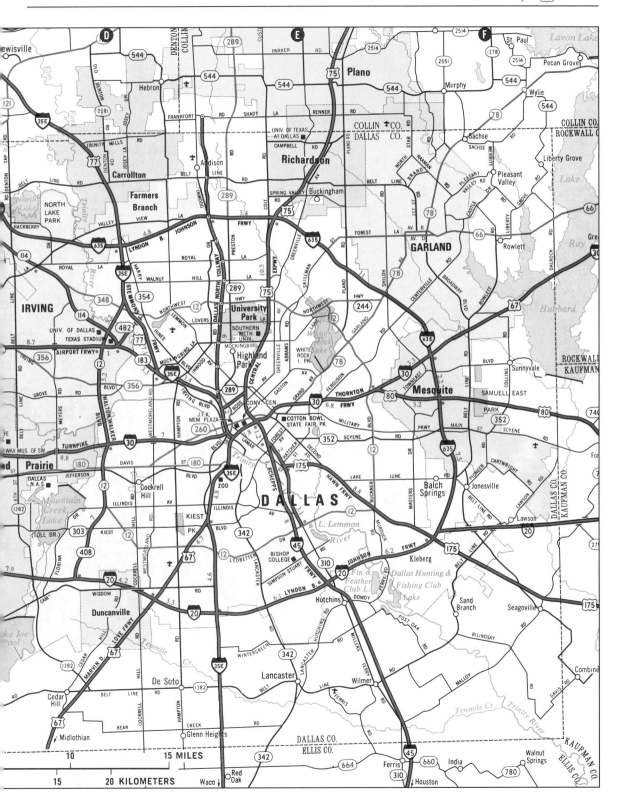

Addicks ......B 2	Channelview ...E 2	Galena Park ....D 2	Kohrville ......B 1	Richmond .....A 3
Aldine ....C 1	Clear Lake City .E 3	Genoa ....E 3	La Porte ......F 3	Rosenberg ....A 4
Alief ....B 3	Clear Lake	Hedwig Village ..C 2	Lomax ....F 3	Satsuma .....B 1
Almeda ......C 3	Shores ......F 4	Highlands ....E 2	Lynchburg ....E 2	Seabrook .....F 4
Bammel .....C 1	Clodine ......B 3	Hillshire Village .C 2	Magnolia	Sheldon .....E 2
Barrett .....F 2	Cloverleaf ....E 2	Houmont Park ..E 2	Gardens .....E 1	Shoreacres ...F 3
Bayside Terrace .F 3	Coady ....F 2	Houston ......D 2	McNair ......F 2	South Houston .D 3
Baytown .....F 2	Crabb ....A 4	Humble ......D 1	Missouri City ...B 3	Southside Place .D 3
Beaumont Place .E 2	Crosby ......E 1	Hunters Creek	Morgans Point .F 3	Spring Valley ...C 2
Bellaire .....C 3	Deer Park ....E 3	Village ......C 2	Nassau Bay ...E 4	Stafford .....B 3
Brookside Village D 3	Dewalt ......B 4	Jacinto City ...D 2	North Houston ..C 1	Sugar Land ...B 3
Bunker Hill	El Lago .....F 3	Jersey Village ..B 2	Pasadena ....E 3	Taylor Lake Vill. .F 3
Village .....B 2	Fauna ....E 2	Katy ....A 2	Pearland .....D 3	Webster .....E 4
Cedar Bayou ..F 2	Four Corners ..B 3	Kemah ....F 4	Pine Grove ...D 1	West University
Champions ....C 1	Four Corners ..F 2	Kinwood .....D 1	Piney Point Vill. .C 2	Place ......C 3

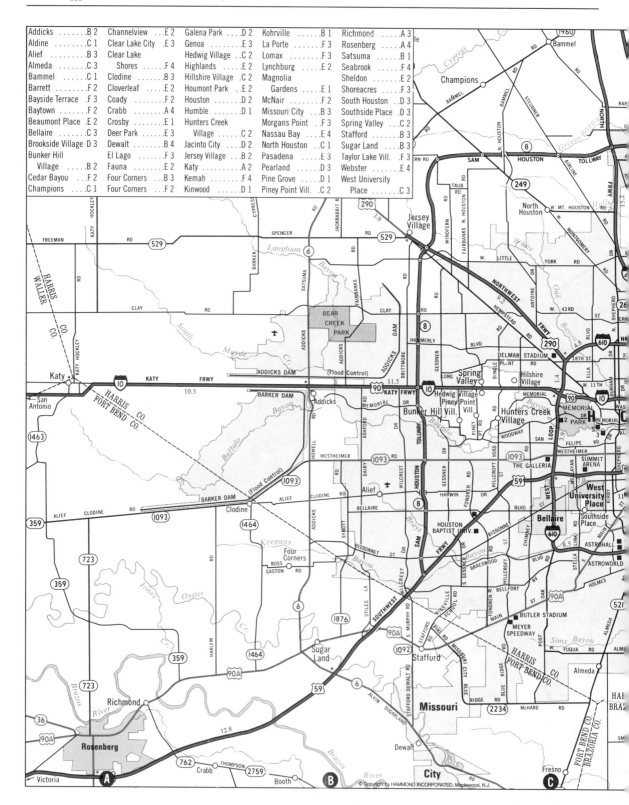

© Copyright by HAMMOND INCORPORATED, Maplewood, N.J.

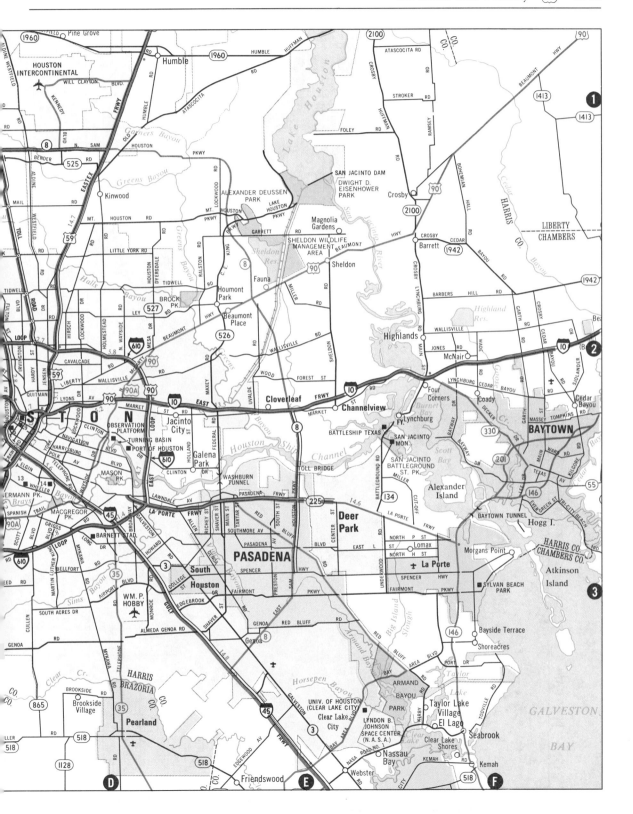

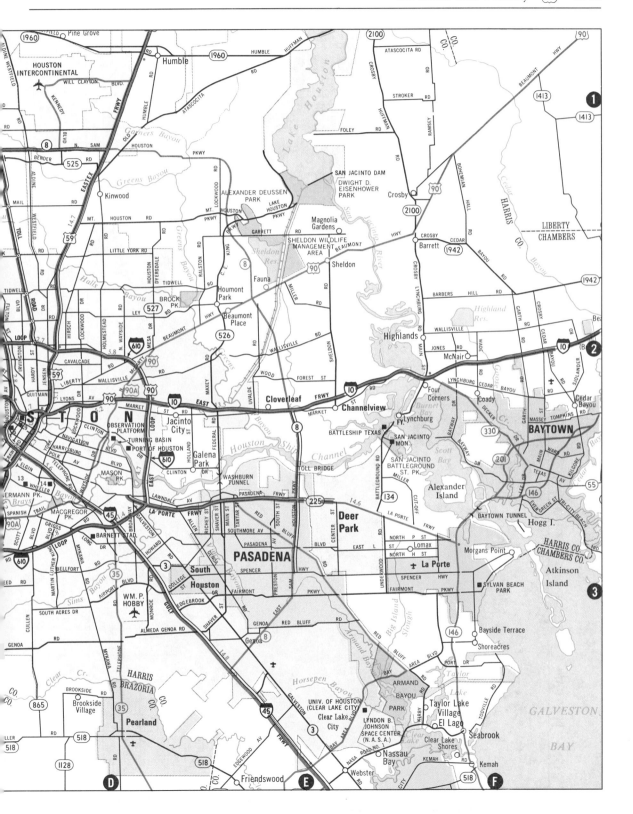

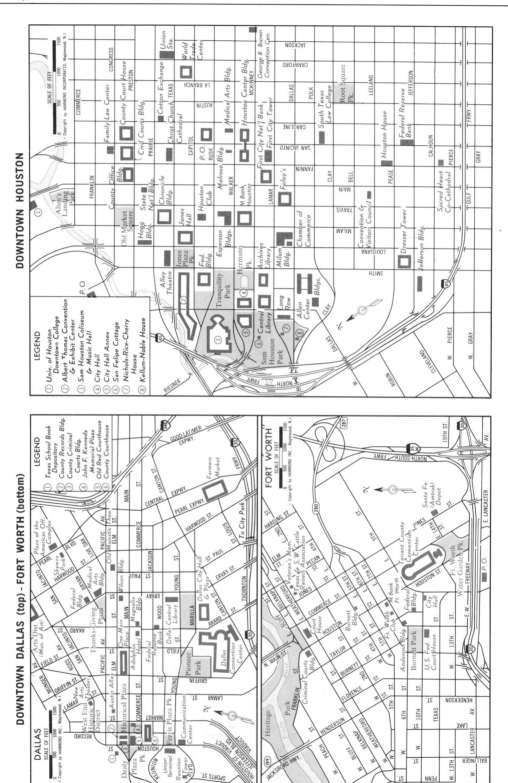

DOWNTOWN HOUSTON

SCALE OF FEET
0 500 1000 1500
Copyright by HAMMOND INCORPORATED, Maplewood, N.J.

LEGEND
① Univ. of Houston Downtown College
② Albert Thomas Convention & Exhibit Center
③ Sam Houston Coliseum & Music Hall
④ City Hall
⑤ City Hall Annex
⑥ San Felipe Cottage
⑦ Nichols-Rice-Cherry House
⑧ Kellum-Noble House

DOWNTOWN DALLAS (top) - FORT WORTH (bottom)

DALLAS
SCALE OF FEET
500 1000 1500
Copyright by HAMMOND INC., Maplewood, N.J.

LEGEND
① Texas School Book Depository
② County Records Bldg.
③ County Criminal Courts Bldg.
④ John F. Kennedy Memorial Plaza
⑤ Old Red Courthouse
⑥ County Courthouse

FORT WORTH
SCALE OF FEET
0 500 1000 1500
Copyright by HAMMOND INC., Maplewood, N.J.